CONTEMPORARY CANADIAN BUSINESS LAW

PRINCIPLES AND CASES

CONTEMPORARY CANADIAN BUSINESS LAW

PRINCIPLES AND CASES

**JOHN A. WILLES, B.A.,
M.B.A., LL.M.**

Barrister-At-Law, Associate Professor in
Industrial Relations and Business Law,
Queen's University

McGRAW-HILL RYERSON LIMITED

Toronto   Montréal   New York   St.
Louis   San Francisco   Auckland   Bogotá
Guatemala   Hamburg   Johannesburg
Lisbon   London   Madrid   Mexico   New
Delhi   Panama   Paris   San Juan   Sao
Paulo   Singapore   Sydney   Tokyo

**CONTEMPORARY CANADIAN
BUSINESS LAW:**
Principles and Cases

ISBN 0-07-548027-1

2 3 4 5 6 7 8 9 0   D   0 9 8 7 6 5 4 3 2

Printed and bound in Canada

Care has been taken to trace ownership of
copyright material contained in this text. The
publishers will gladly take any information
that will enable them to rectify any reference
or credit in subsequent editions.

Canadian Cataloguing in Publication Data

Willes, John A.
Contemporary Canadian business law

Includes index.
ISBN 0-07-548027-1

1. Commercial law—Canada. I. Title.

KE919.W54   346.71'07   C81-094149-X

TABLE OF CONTENTS

ACKNOWLEDGEMENTS:

ALL ENGLAND LAW REPORTS material reproduced by permission of Butterworths Legal Medical and Scientific Publishers, London, England.

Canada Law Book Ltd., Law Publishers, 240 Edward St., Aurora, Ontario for **DOMINION LAW REPORTS.**

ENGLISH REPORTS, Stevens & Sons Ltd., London, William Green & Sons, Edinburgh.

Maritime Law Book Ltd. publishers of the **ALBERTA REPORTS,** the **ATLANTIC PROVINCE REPORTS,** the **MANITOBA REPORTS (2d),** the **NATIONAL REPORTER,** the **NEW BRUNSWICK REPORTS (2d),** the **NEWFOUNDLAND & PRINCE EDWARD ISLAND REPORTS,** the **NOVA SCOTIA REPORTS (2d),** and the **SASKATCHEWAN REPORTS.**

SUPREME COURT REPORTS material reproduced by permission of the Minister of Supply and Services Canada.

The Law Society of Upper Canada for **ONTARIO LAW REPORTS** and **ONTARIO WEEKLY NOTES, ONTARIO REPORTS** and **ONTARIO WEEKLY REPORTER.**

LAW REPORTS and **WEEKLY LAW REPORTER** material reproduced by permission of The Incorporated Council of Law Reporting for England and Wales.

WESTERN WEEKLY REPORTS, MARITIME PROVINCES REPORTS, CANADIAN BANKRUPTCY REPORTS (New Series) material reproduced by permission of the Carswell Company Ltd.

PREFACE

The purpose of *Contemporary Canadian Business Law* is to provide an exposition of some of the major areas of the law that affect organizations which carry on business in Canada. The principles upon which the laws are based are examined in their historical, economic, and social context in an effort to provide the reader with an understanding of their general nature and application.

The development of legal principles and concepts is emphasized, and while a general outline of the current law is provided, the limits imposed by the wide range of subject matter permit only the most elementary and superficial treatment of what are often highly specialized and complex areas of law. For this reason, the function of the text is to provide a general outline of basic legal principles and concepts of the law to assist the reader in the recognition of potential legal problems, rather than provide legal advice. The text is in no way intended to be used as a substitute for the advice of legal counsel, nor should it be used in such a fashion.

To facilitate a general understanding of so broad an area of law, the text is divided into eight parts. In each part, the particular laws associated with the topic heading are developed, first in their historical setting, then on a contemporary basis. The outline begins with an introduction to the law and the legal system, in order to establish the general nature of law and the system by which it is administered. Part II deals with the law of torts, which is one of the oldest areas of the law. Following tort law, the law of contract is examined in considerable detail. Emphasis is placed upon this topic because it represents the foundation of so many business transactions and activities. Part IV, which follows contract law, examines some of the different legal forms which a business entity might assume. This, in turn, is followed by a series of chapters which set out the special legal principles and laws which affect a number of different business activities. Real Property law constitutes Part VI, and this is followed by a section which examines the various devices used to secure debt, and the problems of the insolvent debtor. The last part of the text deals with a brief outline of the law relating to industrial and intellectual property in the form of patent, trade mark, and copyright law.

Each chapter within each section is organized to introduce the subject matter, trace its historical development, and examine some of the general legal concepts or principles associated with that particular area of the law. Brief passages from leading judgements are included in the text of each chapter to illustrate judicial thinking. At the end of the text material in each chapter, a summary, and a dozen or more self-testing or class discussion questions review the content. This is followed by several judicial decisions, chosen to illustrate the application of the law in particular circumstances. At the end of the chapter, hypothetical cases are presented to permit the reader to analyze legal problems, and determine the applicable law.

As a matter of style, the masculine pronoun is used throughout the text to describe persons in general. Until such time as a suitable pronoun is developed to denote both the male and female singular gender, decisions such as this must invariably be made by authors to render the text readable. Also, apart from the use of names and facts in cases based upon reported judicial decisions, the names of persons and corporations in the fictional discussion cases were chosen on a random basis, and any similarity to the names of living persons or existing corporations is unintentional and purely co-incidental.

For the preparation of the manuscript I am indebted to many: The staff of the Queen's University Law Library for their assistance in answering my many requests for information, and their remarkable ability to produce ancient 13th century English statutes and 15th century law reports instantly upon request; Bruce Menchions, William McQuarrie, and William Moore, who assisted me with my research, and who spent many hours in the law library collecting material, tracking down obscure cases, and checking footnotes for accuracy; Rose Marie Baird, and Gail LeSarge, who willingly translated my handwriting into legible copy; my son John, and Brian Gooding, both Queen's University Commerce students, for their comments and suggestions from the student point of view; Professor Henry J. Kaluza of the University of Western Ontario for his careful examination of the draft manuscript, and for his constructive comments from an instructor's point of view; Charles Finley, an old friend, and some of his colleagues at the law firm of Fraser & Beatty, Toronto, Ontario, for their constructive comments on the content of the manuscript, and my wife Fran, who not only devoted long hours to the preparation of the final manuscript, but managed to remain enthusiastic about the book throughout the entire process.

The manuscript was prepared using the Queen's University Q'TEXT word processing program. In this regard, I would like to express my appreciation for the advice of my colleague, Professor John C. Wiginton, and for the assistance of Bob Stevens, Bruce Pond, and the entire Q'TEXT support staff at the Queen's University Computing Centre.

On the publishing end, special thanks must go to Mrs. Mary McCooye for her meticulous care in the editing of the manuscript, and to the entire staff at McGraw-Hill Ryerson for their assistance in the preparation of the book for publication.

ABBREVIATIONS USED FOR LAW REPORTS

A.C. (App. Cas.)	Law Reports Appeal Cases	(U.K.)
All E.R. (All E.Rep.)	All England Reports	(U.K.)
B.&C.	Barnewall & Cresswell Reports	(U.K.)
B.&S.	Best and Smith Reports	(U.K.)
Black.W. (Bl.W.)	William Blackstone Reports	(U.K.)
C.B.R.	Canadian Bankruptcy Reports	
C.P.	Law Reports Common Pleas	(U.K.)
C.P.D.	Law Reports Common Pleas Division	(U.K.)
Ch.	Law Reports Chancery	(U.K.)
Ch. App.	Law Reports Chancery Appeal	(U.K.)
Ch.D.	Law Reports Chancery Division	(U.K.)
Co. Rep.	Coke Reports	(U.K.)
D.L.R.	Dominion Law Reports	
E.R.	English Reports (a reprint series)	(U.K.)
Ex. C.R.	Exchequer Court Reports	
Exch.	Law Reports Exchequer	(U.K.)
F.	Federal Reporter	(U.S.A.)
Godb.	Godbolt Reports	(U.K.)
Hare	Hare Reports	(U.K.)
H.L. Cas.	Clark's House of Lords Cases	(U.K.)
H.&C.	Hurlstone & Coltman Reports	(U.K.)
Ill. App.	Illinois Appellate Court Reports	(U.S.A.)
J.&H.	Johnson & Hemming Reports	(U.K.)
K.B.	Law Reports King's Bench	(U.K.)
L.R. Exch.	Law Reports Exchequer Court	(U.K.)
L.R.C.P.	Law Reports Common Pleas	(U.K.)
L.R.H.L.	Law Reports House of Lords	(U.K.)
M.P.R.	Maritime Provinces Reports	
Mod.	Modern Reports	(U.K.)
My.&Cr.	Mylne & Craig Reports	(U.K.)
N.S.R.	Nova Scotia Reports	
N.Y.	New York Reports	(U.S.A.)
N.E.	North Eastern Reporter	(U.S.A.)
O.L.R.	Ontario Law Reports	
O.R.	Ontario Reports	
O.W.N.	Ontario Weekly Notes	
P. (Pac.)	Pacific Reporter	(U.S.A.)
Popham (Pop.)	Popham Reports	(U.K.)
Q.B.	Law Reports Queen's Bench	(U.K.)
Q.B.D.	Law Reports Queen's Bench Division	(U.K.)

S.C.R.	Supreme Court Reports	
Sty.	Style Reports	(U.K.)
W.L.R.	Weekly Law Reports	(U.K.)
W.W.R.	Western Weekly Reports	
Y.B.	Year Book	(U.K.)

TABLE OF CASES

TABLE OF STATUTES

PART I

Introduction

CHAPTER 1

The Law and the Legal System

THE NATURE OF LAW

The law holds a special fascination for most people. This is perhaps partly due to the fact that the law has become so all-pervasive that we are constantly reminded of its presence, but it cannot be the only reason. It is also of interest because it reflects the society in which we live. It determines the rights and freedoms of the individual, and the extent to which these privileges may be enjoyed. The law, at any given point in time, represents the values and concerns of the people in the jurisdiction from which it arose, and to examine the historical development of the laws of a society is much like an examination of the society itself, for the two are inextricably intertwined. In effect, the law touches so many facets of human endeavour that it would be difficult to imagine how a modern society might exist without it. It has become, in fact, the very essence of society, and this, in itself, is reason enough to justify the study of its principles and application.

The word "law" has been applied to so many rules, principles, and statements that it is probably incapable of exact definition. Legal philosophers have agonized over the meaning of the term, and wrestled with its sources and nature since the earliest of times. Part of the difficulty in reaching a precise definition is the nature of law itself, because it is very much a concept rather than an object or thing which has clearly defined limits or parameters. Simple definitions, however, may be attempted, bearing in mind that the definition may not be precise or all-encompassing.

Irwin Dorfman, a prominent lawyer, explained the term very simply in a speech to the Canadian Bar Association in 1975. He defined the law as "merely a set of rules that enable people to live together and respect each other's rights."[1] This definition encompasses much of the law that affects interpersonal relationships, and in particular, the common law (which is simply the recorded judgements of the courts). Modern society has prompted others to offer definitions of the law, each in an attempt to explain the nature and purpose of the law as succinctly and precisely as possible. Salmond, for example, described the law as the "body of principles, recognized and applied by the state in the administration of justice."[2]

Oliver Wendell Holmes, the distinguished American jurist, once described the law as "a statement of circumstances in which the public force will be brought to bear through the Courts,"[3] and Blackstone, in his famous *Commentaries on the Law of England*, defined the law as "a rule of civil conduct, prescribed by the supreme power in a state, commanding what is right, and prohibiting what is wrong."[4]

Each of these definitions implies that something will happen if an individual does not obey the rules. In Irwin Dorfman's definition of the law, he mentions respect for the "rights" of others. To understand the operation or application of the law then, it is necessary to know what constitutes a "right," and to distinguish this right from that which constitutes a privilege. When we say we have the "right" to do something, we are saying, in essence, that we may do this particular act with impunity, or with the force of the State behind us. Because rights are closely associated with duties, our right to do an act usually imposes a duty on others not to interfere with our actions. What the law does is to set out our rights and duties in order that everyone will know what they are, and to whom they apply. In a similar fashion, the law sets out actions which are not rights and duties, but privileges.

Privileges are actions which may be taken by an individual under specific circumstances, and which may be withdrawn or curtailed by the State. Rights enjoyed by individuals often become privileges as a result of social pressure or public policy. Occasionally, rights may also become privileges out of a desire on the part of the legislators to increase the flow of funds to the public coffers through license fees. Statutes relating to the ownership and operation of automobiles are examples of laws of this nature.

[1]Statement by Irwin Dorfman, President, Canadian Bar Association at the annual meeting of the association, August 1975, at Halifax, Nova Scotia.

[2]Williams, G., *Salmond on Jurisprudence*, 11th ed. (Sweet & Maxwell Ltd., 1954: London), p. 41.

[3]Corley, R.N., and Black, R.L., *The Legal Environment of Business*, 2nd ed. (McGraw-Hill Book Company, 1968: New York), p. 4.

[4]Lewis, W.D., *Blackstone's Commentaries on the Law of England* (Rees, Welsh & Company, 1897: Philadelphia), Book 1, s. 2, para. 44.

THE ROLE OF LAW

The law represents a means of social control, and a law in its most basic form is simply an obligatory rule of conduct.[5] The law, in contrast to a single law, consists of the body of rules of conduct laid down by a sovereign or governing body to control the actions of individuals in its jurisdiction, and which are normally enforced by sanctions. The law develops to meet the needs of the people in a free society, and changes with their changing needs. For this reason, the law tends to respond to the demands of a free society, rather than shape its nature. Laws, however, may arise in other ways as well.

Laws established and enforced by legislators which are not in response to the demands of the majority may be introduced to shape or re-direct society in ways that legislators perceive as desirable. Laws of this type represent a form of social engineering which frequently restricts individual rights and freedom, and which very often transfers individual rights and powers to the governing body. Laws of this nature represent a growing proportion of Canadian law, but this form of legislation is not a recent phenomenon.

Laws which legislatures have attempted to impose on society to alter the behaviour of the majority normally prove to be ineffective unless enforced by oppressive penalties or complete government control of the activity.

Compulsory automobile insurance legislation in a number of provinces in Canada represent examples of legislation of the latter kind. They tend to be of a confiscatory nature in the sense that the government, by decree, transfers the right to engage in the activity to itself and to virtually exclude all private sector insurers. Provinces with this type of legislation have decided that as a matter of public policy the government should engage in the activity for the public good, and without interference or competition from the private sector. In a free society, the only way that a governing body may implement such a policy is through laws that establish an insurance system which, in a variety of ways, excludes all others from engaging in the activity.

The desirability of such legislation which impinges on the freedom of the individual, and which alters the rights and behaviour patterns of those living in the jurisdiction has been the subject of much debate amongst legal philosophers for centuries. The basis of much of this debate is rooted in political philosophy rather than in the law as such. It does, however, illustrate how the law may be used to implement public policies which may not represent the particular desires or wishes of the people, but rather the desires of those in a position of political power at a given point in time.

While social control very broadly represents the role of law in a society, the law itself may be sub-divided into a number of functions which are essentially sub-sets of its principal role. Laws must, first of all, be the vehicle by which disputes between individuals are settled. Some of the earliest laws were simply procedural rules which outlined the manner in which parties would deal with each other in the settlement of their dispute by combat. The sole purpose of these laws was to ensure some degree of fairness in the combat, and a minimum of disruption in the lives of others not directly involved in the dispute. In this sense, the law served a second function: it established rules of conduct for individuals living in close association with

---

[5]Osborn, P.G., *The Concise Law Dictionary*, 4th ed. (Sweet & Maxwell Ltd., 1954: London), p. 194.

others. Such rules direct the energies of individuals in an orderly fashion and minimize conflict between persons engaged in similar activities, or in activities which have the potential for conflict. In the distant past these were rules that determined which hunter was entitled to the game where more than one party was responsible for bringing the animal down. A classic example of a modern application of this type of law would be the "rules of the road" under the various Highway Traffic Acts. These rules dictate where and how a motor vehicle may be driven in order to facilitate the orderly flow of traffic, and to minimize the risk of accident or injury to those who drive motor vehicles.

The third major function of the law is to provide protection for individuals in a society. Self-preservation is of paramount importance to any person, and the law represents a response to this desire or need. Individuals in the earliest societies realized they were dependent upon one another for much of their security, and some of the first laws related to the protection of individuals from intentional or careless assaults by others. These laws soon expanded to include the protection of possessions as well, and established the concepts of individual freedom and property rights. The development of these laws can best be understood by an examination of law in its historical context.

THE DEVELOPMENT OF LAW

The origins of some of our most basic laws and principles are lost in antiquity. Records of early civilizations make reference to a great many laws similar to those that stand today on our statute books, or in our common law as the laws of the land. Even then, the early writings no doubt

simply recorded what had then been long-standing rules or customs.

By using logic and an understanding of human nature one may speculate how the law evolved in early times.

The earliest laws were handed down by word of mouth from generation to generation long before the first words were recorded on parchment or on stone. These early laws, or rules of behaviour, probably had their origins as rules of conduct established to maintain an orderly family life in the families of early man. Later on, they were perhaps expanded to govern conduct between families in a tribe as families began living in close proximity to one another.

Anthropologists have determined a variety of dates that might be considered the dawn of early civilization, but most will agree that as early as 12 000 years ago man had reached the state where he had domesticated some animals, and was engaged in some rudimentary forms of agriculture. Before that time, however, early man was very much a nomad, subsisting on wild foods and animals, with no fixed abode unless it was a cave or some other rough shelter. Yet, even at this stage, some of the more basic rules of behaviour were no doubt established by the eldest (who were usually the biggest and strongest) members of a family to maintain internal harmony and to train the youngest in the art of survival. While these rules of behaviour, backed by the sanction of corporal punishment, possessed many of the attributes of law, their casual nature and lack of uniformity would exclude them from a modern definition. They were, however, the forerunners of many early laws when they became uniform in nature and penalty.

In this primitive stage, some of the early rules of behaviour governing interfamily relationships nevertheless did emerge. The early families were generally patriarchal, and over time, a number of families who were more or less related would often form a loosely knit tribe that followed game herds on their migrations. The mere existence of a number of families living in close proximity to one another increased the potential for conflict, and disputes between families presumably did occur. Rules governing intrafamily behaviour often did not work when applied to conflicts between families over hunting territory, the possession of captured game, or the question of who should occupy a particular cave. These disputes were normally settled by brute force, or where injury was done to a member of a family, by vengeance. The use of force, while an effective means of settling disputes was nevertheless disruptive, and subject to no rules of combat, for none existed. No societal pressures were present to curb this type of interference with the normal routine of living due to the nomadic nature of the people; there was a complete absence of a social order except within the family during this period of history.

In all probability the early hunters soon discovered some animals were much easier to capture than others, and by way of a gradual selection process the hunter undoubtedly identified those animals that could be obtained to provide a convenient source of food and clothing. This change from a hunter to a hunter-herdsman had the effect of limiting the range of the family to a particular area, and increased the tendency for a family to treat a given grazing area as their own territory.

During this period the family was the basic unit, and family rules were the only guides for behaviour. The limited range of the hunter-herdsman, however, had the effect of increasing contact between families living in the general area as herds of animals strayed from place to place unrestrained by fences. As a result of this greater interfamily contact, customs or specific behaviour patterns were gradually established out of a desire to avoid conflict. These customs or behavioural patterns, nevertheless, were not laws, and no clear rules existed to settle disputes. When a dispute did arise, usually over property, the mode of settlement was one of vengeance, and involved entire families.

In the latter part of this pastoral period of development some behavioural rules did emerge, first within the loosely knit tribes, and later, between tribes, as the contact between the groups increased. Within large family groups or tribes, the development of early religions (with their taboos) introduced behavioural rules backed by sanctions. These sanctions took the form of approval or disapproval and banishment, and added a new dimension to the customs and general behavioural pattern that had been established with respect to interfamily activities. In spite of the sanctions attached to these religious rules, they were not laws as such except in a very elementary sense. Disputes between individuals remained matters to be settled by vengeance.

The second phase of what might be described as the early agricultural stage of development occurred with the establishment of more permanent residences by families and the introduction of farming. Attendant with the occupation of a particular area and the recognition of its value for crops, was the desire to protect the land from intruders. Here, the emergence of rudimentary property rights represented a departure from the previous pastoral form of living, and with it came the need to establish rules of behaviour that would permit the family to devote its time to agricultural pursuits rather than fighting.

The possession of land tended to be on a family basis, and possession was maintained by force. Interfamily disputes, however, increasingly became the subject of discussion in loosely knit tribes, and the procedural recommendations of the tribal elders to the disputing parties gradually produced customs or behavioural rules designed to minimize disputes and their inherent disruption of tribal life. Disputes, however, when they did arise, were settled by vengeance rather than discussion, although this period of history saw the emergence of what might be loosely termed rules of combat. There were still no laws as such, since the tribal elders did not constitute a government, nor did they normally possess the power to impose their will on the individual or family.

The possession of land by families and the need to protect it from others fostered the construction of individual family residences close to one another in tribal villages. The relatively permanent nature of this form of living brought with it advantages other than protection. Village life permitted specialization by some members of a family or tribe in activities not directly related to agriculture. Such early activities as rudimentary metallurgy, and the production of goods by some individuals for use by others appeared soon after villages were established.

The concentration of families in a relatively small area, however, was not without its disadvantages. Disruptive behaviour in a village affected a far greater number of individuals than it would in an isolated family setting, and the need to curb activities of this nature took on a new importance. During this period, early attempts to control disruptive behaviour took the form of the selection of individuals, usually family elders (or the strongest members of the community), to hear disputes and recommend non-disruptive, or at least controlled methods of settlement; the disputants were required to accept their decision as the binding resolution of the conflict. Initially, this group decided each dispute on its merits, but gradually some consistency emerged as similar disputes were decided on the basis of the previous decisions. At this point, rules of behaviour for the entire community began to take on meaning. In the beginning, these decisions were imposed by the community if they were considered just and equitable, but as the decision-makers assumed more responsibility for the orderly operation of the affairs of the village, so too, did they acquire the power to impose their decisions on disputants. With the establishment of a governing body, or a sovereign with the power to impose a decision on an individual in the interests of the community good, the law, as an instrument of social control, took form.

This did not happen in any significant way until the village form of living gave way to the establishment of the city and the city state. The city arose with the development of trade and the production of goods and services by individuals for others. This was first in the form of barter, and later by way of some medium of exchange. In any event, the concentration of activity in a relatively small area gave the individual an identification with the community, and a desire to act in a concerted way in the solution of common problems. The answer was usually to form some sort of organization or government to deal with these matters and to direct the efforts of the community as a whole. The formation of these formal bodies, with the authority to decide how individuals in the community should conduct themselves in their dealings with others, and with the power to enforce their decisions, created the first state-legislated laws.

Needless to say, these laws developed gradually over a relatively long period of time, and at different rates amongst different peoples. The earliest known written laws were undoubtedly accepted as the officially sanctioned rules of behaviour long before they were formally recorded. In some cases, when a tribe or race reached the stage of the city state and became rich and weak from "easy living" it would then be plundered by less civilized tribes. The invaders would then adopt the new city life and much of its form of organization. The laws of the city state, necessary for order and tranquility, would often be adopted as well by the invaders, and as a tribe or a race they would move directly from a relatively lawless behavioural system directed by custom, to a society governed by law. In other cases, the law was imposed upon less-developed tribes or races by the armies of the city states. The expansion of the Roman Empire was a notable example of a state which spread the rule of law over much of Western Europe and the Middle East, and which established the first legal institutions.

THE RISE OF THE COURTS AND THE RULE OF LAW

The law, without some system of determining its application, or imposing its sanctions, has little more than a persuasive effect on human behaviour. The rise of the city state brought with it the establishment of the mechanism for its enforcement. The inhabitants of large communities (and later, the city states) were quick to realize that disputes between individuals would increase as the population's density increased. At first, these communities established tribunals, or other bodies officially authorized to hear disputes, which, with the aid of the society, could force restitution, or undertake the vengeance; however, the tribunals lacked sufficient power to compel the use of their system. Eventually, by the process of requiring certain formalities which must be undertaken before vengeance, and by providing the inducement of monetary compensation as a remedy, the state ultimately became powerful enough to force everyone to use the tribunal or court. At this stage, vengeance, because of its negative effect on the community, became, itself, a crime.[6]

Of particular importance in the development of the courts was the nature of their decisions. For the most part, the law relating to relationships between individuals, and the rights and responsibilities of one to another was gradually established in the form of consistent decisions first by tribunals, and later by the courts. As a result, the judgements of the courts preceded the law. The correctness of these early decisions, or judgements, was usually based upon either a religious foundation (if the head of the state held his position by some divine right), or the approval of the assembled citizens of the community. Consistency in the decisions handed down by these courts in similar cases eventually created the body of rules known as the law.

In England, the early courts and the law were imposed on the inhabitants by a number of invaders in succession. Following the Roman Conquest of England in 43 B.C., the country was subject to *lex romana* (Roman law) and its administrative machinery. In theory at least, in those areas

---

[6]*Hemmings et al. v. Stoke Poges Golf Club, Ltd. et al.*, [1920] 1 K.B. 720.

under Roman control, the law was uniform in nature and application. This lasted throughout the period of Roman occupation.

The disintegration of the Roman Empire, and the invasion of England by the Germanic tribes produced a decentralized system of government under a king which consisted of shires and counties, each with its own government, and to varying degrees, freedom from royal interference. The shires were further divided into smaller communities called hundreds, which were administrative units about the size of a township. Within these units were the boroughs, or local communities.

In the pre-Norman period, the law in each of these shires developed according to local custom or need, and it was not until after 1066 that the trend was reversed. The only laws that were common throughout the land were the small number of written laws relating to general crimes that several of the kings had pronounced as law. These laws frequently set out the penalty in monetary terms, with a part of the money to be paid to the king by the perpetrator of the crime, and the balance to be paid to the injured party or his next of kin. These laws were enforced by a relatively weak central government (called a `witenagemot`), which governed the country along with the king.

The Norman Conquest in 1066 brought with it a more centralized system of administration, and shortly thereafter, the establishment of a central judicial system. The Conquest had very little effect on English custom, but it did have a considerable effect on the administration of the country. The power of the shires was brought under the control of the king, and the right of the shire court or county court to hear cases concerning land and certain criminal cases (known as pleas of the Crown) was transferred to the king's justices.

The establishment of a central judiciary under King Henry II to hear the more serious cases was an important factor in the development of the common law in England. After 1180, justices of the royal court travelled regularly throughout the country to hear cases, and on their return to London, discussed their cases with one another or exchanged notes on their decisions. Amongst themselves they gradually developed what later became a body of law common throughout the land.

During the 12th and 13th centuries, the administration of justice became more centralized and the king's justices began keeping their own records after 1234. Early decisions were largely based on local custom, but this gradually changed as the judges based their decisions more upon the written records of the court, and less upon what was alleged to be local custom. After 1272, written records of decisions were maintained to assist the fledgling legal profession, and though sparce during the early period following 1272, they improved over the next three centuries to the point where they were useful as statements of the common law. Better case reports, and their consolidations in the years that followed, developed the body of law known as the common law of England. The discovery and subsequent settlement of English colonies in North America established the common law in Canada and the United States. Today, these principles represent in a large and flexible body of law, which is adaptable and responsive to the needs of our society.

SOURCES OF LAW

The Common Law and Equity
The common law represents an important source of law in Canada. It is sometimes referred to as "case-law" because that is

where statements of the common law may be found. Another reason is to distinguish it from the second major source of law: statute law.

In common law provinces, and in those countries with common law systems, the law (except statute law) is not found in a code, but in the recorded judgements of the courts. Judgements were not always recorded, but in 1290, during the reign of Edward I, the Year Books were commenced. These books provided *reports* of the cases, but in the early years, *reasons* for the decisions were seldom included. With the introduction of printing in England in 1477, the Year Books were improved, and printed copies became available to the legal profession. The reporting of cases in the form of law reports took place in the 16th century; from that point on, the decisions of the judges were reported without a break by various law reporters. Judicial reasoning and the principles applied by the judges were readily available by way of these reports, and the common law could be determined from them through the doctrine of *stare decisis.*

Stare decisis ("to let a decision stand" or "to stand by a previous decision") is the theory of precedent in common law. In its application the doctrine means that a judge must apply the previous decision of a similar case to the one before him if the facts of the two cases are the same, *providing* such decision is (1) from his own court; (2) from a court of equal rank; or (3) from a higher (or superior) court.

The need for certainty in the law (in the sense that it must be clear in its meaning and predictable in its application) was quickly realized by judges. The adoption of the theory of precedent provided a degree of stability to the common law without sacrificing its flexibility, although at times the courts became so reluctant to move from previous decisions that their application of the law made no sense at all to the case at hand. Fortunately, judges have been adaptable in their formulation of the law, and over the years have maintained the common law as a blend of predictable, yet flexible principles, capable of conforming to the changing needs of society. This has been due, in part, to a reluctance on the part of the judiciary to accept precedent as a hard and fast rule. The facts of any two cases are seldom precisely the same, and differences in the facts or circumstances are sufficient to permit a judge to decide that a particular obsolete precedent should not apply to the case before him if the application of such a precedent would produce an unsatisfactory result. In this fashion, the courts have gradually adapted the common law to changing times.

The adaptability of the common law has enabled it to absorb, over a long period of time, many legal principles, customs, and laws from other legal systems and sources. The law of England before the Norman Conquest was, for the most part, local in both form and application. It consisted of a mixture of early customs, a few remnants of early Roman law, and the laws and customs brought to England by the Anglo-Saxon invaders. Decisions were handed down by judges based upon local custom, which prior to the Conquest was the only precedent available. The Norman Conquest brought with it a central system for the administration of justice, and through this centralized system, the incorporation of the customs and laws from all parts of the country into the common law.

Other laws were also incorporated into the common law as the courts of England expanded their jurisdiction. The Church had jurisdiction over religion, family and marriage, morals, and matters relating to the descent of personal property of deceased persons. The law relating to these

matters was initially administered by ecclesiastic courts, but cases concerning
some of these church-administered areas
of the law gradually found their way before judges of the civil courts, and after the
Reformation (1534-1538) much of the ecclesiastic courts' jurisdiction passed to the
royal courts. In dealing with cases that had
previously fallen within the province of
the ecclesiastic courts, the judges naturally
looked at the decisions of those courts in
reaching their own decisions, and as a result, many of the rules of canon or church
law became a part of the common law.

In much the same fashion, a substantial
part of the law relating to commerce and
trade was incorporated into the common
law. Early merchants belonged to guilds,
as did the artisans. Customs of the various
trades gradually developed into a body of
rules that were similar throughout much
of Western Europe, and disputes which
arose between merchants were frequently
settled by the application of these rules.

Initially, most of the merchants sold
their wares and goods at fairs and markets, and any disputes which arose were
settled by the senior merchants, whose
decisions were final and binding. Later,
decision-making became somewhat more
formal, and the decisions more uniform.
Gradually, rules of law relating to commercial transactions began to emerge as
the decisions of the guild courts became
firmly established and consistent in their
application by the merchant guilds. These
courts had jurisdiction only over their
members, of course, and for a long period
of time, the body of law known as the law
merchant was within the exclusive domain
of the merchant guilds. Eventually, merchants who were not guild members
began to trade, and when disputes arose
they appealed to the courts of the land for
relief. The judges, in dealing with these
disputes, applied the law merchant, and
by way of their decisions the large body of
law relating to commerce gradually became a part of the common law.

Other rules of law were incorporated
into the common law by more direct
means. The law relating to land tenure,
which had its roots in feudal law, was introduced by the Normans following the
Conquest in 1066, and the courts thereafter were obliged to apply these rules in
dealing with land disputes.

Even customs or practices which have
developed over time have found their way
into the common law. The courts have
often recognized long-standing practices
in determining the rights of parties at law,
and in this fashion, have established the
custom or practice as a part of the common
law.

The last important source of law administered by the common law courts was the
body of law called *equity*. The rules of
equity are not, strictly speaking, a part of
the common law, but, rather, a body of
legal principles that take precedence over
the common law where the common law
and the rules of equity conflict. The rules
of equity developed largely because the
common law in England had become rigid
in its application by the 15th century, and
litigants often could not obtain a satisfactory remedy from the courts. To obtain the
kind of relief desired, they would frequently petition the king. The king, and
later his chancellor, heard these cases and
made in each case what was called an
equitable decision; one which was not necessarily based upon the law, but one
which the king considered to be fair. The
ideas of fairness which the king expressed
as the basis for his decisions gradually
took on the form of principles, or rules,
which he applied in other cases which
came before him, and over time, became

known as principles of equity. These principles were later followed by the chancellor, and later still by the courts of chancery. Eventually, they took on the form of rules of law. In the late 19th century, the courts of chancery and the common law courts merged, and the rules of equity became a part of the body of law which the courts could apply in any civil case that came before them. As a result, a judge may apply either the common law rules or the principles of equity to a case before him, and where the common law might be inappropriate, the equitable remedy is usually available to ensure a fair and just result. How these laws are administered is the subject-matter of the next chapter.

Statute Law

Statutes are laws which are established by the governing bodies of particular jurisdictions, and which have their roots in the latin word *statutum* which means "it is decided." Governments are vested with the power to make laws, either under the terms of a written constitution, such as that of the United States, or as a result of long-standing tradition, such as in England.

Canada's "constitution" is in the form of an English law: the *British North America Act, 1867*.[7] This particular statute, in addition to creating the governing bodies at the federal and provincial levels, also divides and assigns the legislative powers between the two levels of government.

Section 92 specifies the exclusive authority of the provinces to make laws pertaining to such matters as property and civil rights (heading 13); matters of a local or private nature in a province (heading 16); the incorporation of companies (head-

ing 11); the licensing of certain businesses and activities (heading 9); the solemnization of marriage (heading 12); and local works and activities (heading 10).

Section 91 gives the federal government exclusive jurisdiction over the regulation of trade and commerce (heading 2); criminal law (heading 27); bankruptcy and insolvency (heading 21); navigation and shipping (heading 10); bills of exchange and promissory notes (heading 18), and a wide variety of other activities totalling 31 in all.

Most important, s. 92 gives the federal government residual powers over all matters not expressly given to the provinces, and it is under this particular power that the federal government has assumed authority over relatively recent technological developments such as communications, radio, television, aeronautics, and atomic energy. While ss. 91 and 92 appear to clearly divide the authority to make laws, the nature of the wording of the two sections has raised problems. For example, would the regulation of a particular provincial commercial practice constitute regulation of trade and commerce under s. 91, or would it be property and civil rights under s. 92? More particularly, would the construction of a pipeline from an oil-well in the bed of a river be navigation and shipping, and hence, a federal matter, or would it be a local work or undertaking and within the jurisdiction of the province? These are the kinds of problems associated with the interpretation of this statute.

When a statute is properly enacted within the legislative jurisdiction of a provincial or the federal government, it will, when declared to be law, apply to all those persons within that jurisdiction. Statute law in Canada can be used to create laws to cover new activities or matters not cov-

---

[7]*British North America Act, 1867*, 30 Vict., c. 3, as amended.

ered by the common law, or it may be used to change or abolish a common law rule or right. Statutes may also be used to codify the common law by collecting together in one law the common law rules or principles relating to a specific matter.

The particular advantage of statute law over the common law is the relative ease by which the law may be changed. The common law is generally very slow to respond to changing societal needs, and follows a gradual, evolutionary pattern of change, rather than a quick response. Statute law, on the other hand (in theory at least), may be quickly changed in response to the demands of the public. The disadvantage of statute law is that it will be strictly interpreted by the courts; unless it is very carefully drafted, it may not achieve its intended purpose. Occasionally, a badly drafted statute only serves to compound the problems that it was intended to solve, and may require additional laws to respond to the problems which it created. In spite of the potential problems inherent in statute law, the general direction of the law appears to be toward more (rather than less) statute law to deal with social change.

In contrast to the rest of Canada, the Province of Quebec has codified much of the law that is normally found in the common law of other provinces. As a result, this body of law, which is known as the *Civil Code*, may be consulted in the determination of rights and duties. These same rights and duties would ordinarily be found in the common law in other jurisdictions.

This particular method of establishing the law of a jurisdiction is not a new or novel approach. It is simply an alternate method of setting out the law that has a long history. The first codification of law of major significance took place under the direction of the Roman emperor Justinian, who ordered a compilation of all of the laws of Rome dating back to the time of Cicero. The collection of the laws was an enormous task that took seven years to complete, and on completion in 534 A.D. became the famous *Corpus Juris Civilis*. This body of law formed the basis of the law in a large part of continental Europe for the next 1 200 years, and it was not until the 18th century that major revisions were made. Frederick the Great of Prussia directed the preparation of a new code during his reign but it was not adopted until 1794, some eight years after his death. Shortly thereafter, France (under Napoleon), began a codification of French law in 1804, and it was this code that influenced the codification of the law in Spain, Italy, Belgium, and by way of colonization, much of South America, the State of Louisiana, and the Province of Quebec. The 1900 codification of the law in Germany, which replaced Frederick the Great's Prussian Code, found favour as a model for many countries, the most notable being Japan, Switzerland, and Greece.

The codification of the common law in England was never seriously considered, even though it was urged by such respected English writers as Sir Francis Bacon. Nor did the idea find much favour in the United States, or the common law provinces of Canada. Codification of some parts of the common law in all three countries, however, has taken place. England codified the common law as it stood in 1882 with respect to bills of exchange and negotiable instruments, and in 1890, codified the law with respect to partnership. The common law relating to the sale of goods was codified in 1893, but after that, the process lost its impetus. Since then, no major effort has been made to codify other branches of mercantile law except to modify or settle matters of difficulty relating to particular issues.

The American Bar Association, during the late 19th century and early 20th century, proposed a number of uniform statutes relating to commercial practices in an effort to eliminate the differences that existed in state legislation, but their efforts were unsuccessful. It was not until after the Second World War that there was sufficient interest in codification to produce the United States *Uniform Commercial Code*. This Code, which relates to commercial law practices, was first drafted in 1952, and following a number of amendments, eventually became law in all states by 1975. Unfortunately, the goal of true conformity of legislation, as envisaged by the Bar Association was not realized. Not all of the states adopted the entire Code, and some altered the Code to suit their own particular needs. Substantial conformity, however, was achieved in the United States at least with respect to a number of areas of commercial law.

Proponents of codification have long argued that the advantage of this method over the common law is certainty. According to their argument, if the law is written down, it is there for all to see and know. In theory, the judge decides a dispute by reference to the appropriate part of the code, or if no specific article covers the dispute, then the decision is based upon general principles of law set out in the code. The particular difficulty with the code is that it might be interpreted differently in some cases by different judges, and unless some uniformity exists between judges in deciding similar cases, one of the important advantages of the code would be lost. To avoid this, judges in Quebec, and those countries with civil codes, do consider the decisions of other judges who have decided similar cases when they apply the law.

Administrative Law

A growing part of statute law is an area of law called administrative law. The primary focus of this body of law is directed toward the regulations made under statute law and enforced by administrative bodies. While legislation usually creates laws, or repeals old laws, it may also create agencies or administrative tribunals to regulate activities or do specific things. The activities of these tribunals and agencies are said to be administrative acts, and the body of law that relates to their activities is administrative law.

Administrative law is not a new area of the law, but rather, an area of law that has increased substantially in size and importance since World War II. In early times in England, Parliament would authorize the king and his officials to carry out such activities as the collection of taxes, the maintenance of the armed forces, and the operation of the courts. In the beginning, the king and his officials carried out these duties, but gradually a public service was established to perform these tasks. In this fashion, Parliament did not directly supervise the activity, but merely authorized it, and set out guide-lines for the officials to follow in the performance of their duties. Today, Parliament and the provincial legislatures use this method to regulate many activities which fall within their legislative jurisdiction. Examples of some of the activities under the control of regulatory agencies include the sale of securities by public companies, labour relations, employment standards, aeronautics, broadcasting, the sale and consumption of alcoholic beverages, land use, and a wide variety of commercial activities.

The process is usually quite uniform. In most cases, a statute is passed to create a tribunal to supervise an activity but the Act will only set out broad guidelines for the regulation of the activity by the body created. To enable the tribunal to carry out the particular public policy goals of the statute it is generally permitted to establish its own procedures and rules, which may either be approved by the government as an Order in Council, or by the Minister in charge of the tribunal, depending upon the importance attached to the regulations.

The regulations of administrative tribunals represent a body of subordinate legislation which governs activities subject to supervision by an agency or board. These regulations, together with the decisions of the tribunals, form a part of the body of law which is known as administrative law. The general trend of governments at all levels to exercise greater control over the activities of citizens within their respective jurisdictions has resulted in a proliferation of boards and agencies, often acting in conflict with one another. The net result of this trend has been the creation of a large and unwieldy bureaucracy at provincial and federal levels of government, and a substantial restriction of the freedom of the individual in a tangled web of regulations. In recent years, complaints from the public concerning the actions of the many boards and tribunals prompted governments to study the need for so many administrative agencies, but to date nothing has been done to reduce the size of this bureaucracy. Given the nature of the public service in Canada, and the propensity of governments at all levels to create more laws, rather than reduce their number, it is unlikely that government regulation of the individual will diminish significantly in the foreseeable future.

CLASSIFICATION OF LAWS

Statute law and the common law may be classified in two broad, general categories. The first is called *substantive law,* and includes all laws which set out the rights and duties of individuals. The second broad classification is called *procedural law.* This area of the law includes all laws which set out the procedures by which individuals may enforce their substantive law rights or duties.

By way of illustration, an old observation of the law relating to assault says that "your right to swing your arm stops just short of your neighbour's nose." Put another way, you owe a duty to your neighbour not to injure him if you swing your arm in his presence. If you should strike him through your carelessness, he has a right for redress for the injury which you caused. His right is a substantive right, and it represents a part of the substantive law. To enforce his right, he would institute legal proceedings to obtain redress for the injury, and the steps he would take would be part of the procedural law.

Substantive law may be further subdivided into two other types of law: *public law* and *private law.*

Public law deals with the law relating to the relationship between the individual and the government (or its agencies). The *Criminal Code* and the *Income Tax Act* are two examples of this kind of law at the federal level, and the various Highway Traffic Acts are an example of a similar public law at the provincial level. Under these statutes, if an individual fails to comply with the duties imposed it is the Crown that institutes proceedings to enforce the law.

Private law concerns the relationship between individuals, and includes all laws relating to the rights and duties which the parties may have, or which they may create between themselves. Much of the common law is private law, but many statutes also represent private law. The law of contract is private law; such statutes as the *Partnerships Act*[8] and the *Sale of Goods Act*[9] are examples of private law as well. Legal rights, if private law in nature, must be enforced by the injured party. For example, Anderson is digging a trench alongside a sidewalk, and is placing the excavated soil on the walkway. Brown is walking along the sidewalk, and complains to Anderson that the soil is blocking his way. Anderson is angered by Brown's complaint, and strikes him with his shovel.

In this situation, Anderson has violated s. 244 of the Canadian *Criminal Code*[10] by striking Brown with the intention of causing him injury. The *Criminal Code* is a public law, and it is the Crown that will take action against Anderson for his violation of the law.

Anderson, in this example, also owes a duty to Brown not to injure him (a private law duty), and if Anderson injures Brown, as he did in this case, Brown has a common law right in tort to recover from Anderson the loss that he has suffered as a result of Anderson's actions. Brown's right at common law is a private law matter, and Brown must take steps himself to initiate legal proceedings to enforce his right against Anderson.

In this case, both the Crown in the enforcement of the *Criminal Code*, and Brown in taking legal action against Anderson, use procedural law to enforce their rights.

Private law is sometimes referred to as civil law to distinguish private laws of a non-criminal nature from public laws (principally the *Criminal Code*). Unfortunately, this has caused some confusion in Canada, because most of the private law in the Province of Quebec has been codified, and the law there is referred to as the *Civil Code*. While both the common law and the Code deal with private law, care must be taken to note the distinction between the two bodies of law when reference is made to civil law.

[8]*Partnerships Act*, R.S.O. 1980, c. 370.
[9]*Sale of Goods Act*, R.S.O. 1980, c. 462.
[10]*Criminal Code*, R.S.C. 1970, c. C-34, s. 244, as amended.

|||||||||||||||||||||||||||||||||||||||||||||||||||||||||||||||||||||||||||||||||||||||||||||||||||||||||||||||||||||||||||||||||||||||||||||||||||||||

SUMMARY   The law is the principal means by which the State maintains social control, and the system of courts is the vehicle used for its enforcement. The first laws were not laws as such, but family behavioural rules, and later, religious and non-religious taboos. These were enforced, first, by the family elders, and later by the community. As the community became stronger, it gradually assumed more and more of the duties of law-making, and with the development of the early city states, law-making and enforcement took on an organized character. As the power of the State has increased, so too, have the areas of human endeavour that the State has brought under its control. The law which we have today has evolved over a long period of time, and now represents a very complex system which consists of the common law, statute law, and a subordinate type of law called administrative law. These laws may be classified as either substantive law or procedural law, with the former setting out rights and duties, and the latter, as the name indicates, setting out the procedure for the enforcement of the substantive law rights.

DISCUSSION QUESTIONS

1. *In answer to an examination question asking students to write a brief discussion of the origin and development of the law, a student responded: "Law according to Judeo-Christian history had its origin in the Garden of Eden. The first law was promulgated around the time of the creation of Eve. Laws have increased in direct proportion to the growth of the female population." From this rather novel opening, the student went on to explain his answer. The instructor marking the examination answer gave the student full marks. Could you formulate an answer based upon this opening statement that would justify a similar grade?*

2. *Differentiate between "rights" and "privileges."*

3. *Do you feel the law is a restricting or liberalizing entity? Relate your answer to the world's varied political systems.*

4. *Define substantive law, and explain how it differs from procedural law.*

5. *What legal need arose with the rise of the city state? What factors generated this need?*

6. *Personal vengeance has taken many forms in the face of wrongdoing, and constitutes the result of one of man's stronger emotional responses. Explain fully the limitations on personal vengeance with reference to the "negative effect" principle.*

7. *Differentiate between "common law" and "statute law."*

8. *Sections 91 and 92 of the* British North America Act, 1867 *are well known to many Canadians, but is it an Act of a British or Canadian Parliament? What matters fall under it? Under whose authority does its interpretation lie?*

9. *What is codification?*

10. *Identify remnants of canon law and the law merchant in our present common law.*

11. *Explain the differences that exist between the Province of Quebec and other provinces with respect to public and private law.*

12. *Discuss the relative merits of codification of common law.*

13. *How does equity affect the common law?*

14. *"Regulatory rules and 'subordinate legislation' frequently represent the most direct application of the law to our daily lives, and illustrate the State's control of activities that should be matters for self-regulation." Discuss the validity of this statement.*

15. *"The theory of* stare decisis *is probably the most important principle of common law, yet our personal knowledge tells us no two cases are identical. Further, many classic precedents are many years old, thus outdating them with respect to the needs of today's society. In addition to this, the inflexibility of the theory is appalling. Should we not rock this unstable foundation, or replace it?" Discuss the relative merits of this suggestion.*

CHAPTER 2

The Judicial System

A court, by definition, is a place where justice is administered.[1] It may also be used to describe the judge or judges who sit to hear disputes, since the term was originally one which referred to the king and his council when they held "court" to settle disputes between subjects. The original term for court was *curia* and the king's court was known as the *curia regis*. Over time, the king delegated the task of settling disputes and administering the

[1]Osborn, P.G., *The Concise Law Dictionary*, 4th ed. (Sweet & Maxwell Ltd., 1954: London), p. 99.

law to appointed officials, and the term gradually became restricted to mean the place where a judge or judges sit to administer justice.

THE DEVELOPMENT OF THE LAW COURTS

The legal system as we know it today evolved over a long period of time. It developed gradually as the law developed, and it was not until the State was strong enough to require resort to the courts and the rule of law that the courts assumed an important place in the social system. The Canadian and American judicial systems had their beginnings in England, and while both North American jurisdictions have since evolved in slightly different ways, they are both an outgrowth of the English court system, and consequently share the same heritage.

The earliest "courts" were not courts as such, but were meetings of people. In England, they were sometimes referred to as Communal Courts by legal historians, but they were basically meetings held to discuss a variety of matters, hence the name *gemot* or "moot" (a meeting of the people). The tunmoot, for example, was the town or township moot. Its most important function was to allocate the arable land each year, rather than deal with ordinary disputes between individuals.

Higher moots also existed. Each shire (which was the equivalent of our county) was made up of a number of "hundreds," and each of these divisions had its own hundred moot that met every four weeks to deal with matters of concern to the hundred. The moot was presided over by a hundred man and 12 others, and a part of its duty was to hear minor disputes between inhabitants.

The shire had its own moot as well. It was called the *shire-gemot* or shire moot, and in theory it was a meeting of all freemen in the shire. It dealt with matters of concern to the entire shire, and heard cases where the injured parties alleged that they could not obtain justice from the hundred moot. It would also hear cases that involved disputes between individuals living in different hundreds. The earl, shire reeve (sheriff), and bishop usually presided over the shire moot.

In addition to these three moots, there was a high court, or national assembly of all freemen in the kingdom called the *witenagemot* (meeting of the wise). In practice, only those freemen summoned by the king attended the meeting and discussed matters of national concern. This particular body, interestingly enough, elected or deposed the king in addition to its regular duties of hearing complaints between important people of different shires and disputes of national importance. It also acted as an appeal body in cases where a person complained that he could not get justice from the shire moot.

It is important to note that these courts were meetings of the people, and even though they were presided over by an individual, or group of individuals, the judgement handed down was that of the people present. The judgement was not the decision of those in charge of the proceedings.

Changes occurred, however, after the Norman Conquest. The Normans brought to England a different system of landholding and property rights. As a result of the Conquest, the land belonged to the king, and he, in turn, granted the land in large blocks to tenants, who in their turn, parcelled the land out to sub-tenants. Where at least two persons held land from a landlord, the land was called a manor. The elaborate network of land-holdings under the feudal system also altered the ownership of the land in a different and more fundamental manner: individuals held land, rather than families or communities. This change shifted the decision-making power with respect to the use of land from the community to an individual. The old Anglo-Saxon communal moots had previously dealt with disputes concerning land, but after the Conquest this jurisdiction was transferred to the lord of the manor where the land was situated, and his new manorial court decided rights and matters concerning the land. The communal moots still had jurisdiction over personal injuries and debts, but so few matters were left for them to decide that the tunmoot, and later the hundred moot, gradually faded out of existence.

With the demise of these lesser moots, a new court, called a Court of Request, was established to hear cases concerning small debts. This court, however, had no jurisdiction to hear disputes concerning land or matters of a more serious nature.

The shire moot continued, nevertheless, but took on the Norman French name. "Shire" was "conte," and *"gemot"* (or moot) was "cour," hence the new name: county court. Its jurisdiction was also changed a few years after the Conquest. Ecclesiastical disputes were transferred from the county courts to the ecclesiastic courts (which were presided over by bishops and archbishops) in 1074, and after that date all cases that came before the court were judged by canon law, rather than the ordinary customs of the shires or counties.

The *witenagemot* of the Anglo-Saxons became the *curia regis*—the king's court or council. It consisted of all of the king's tenants-in-chief, or barons as they were called, and met only occasionally. The king, however, had a smaller, permanent court which consisted of a number of officials. These officials were concerned with: (1) the collection of funds due to the king, and the payment of his debts (the exchequer), (2) the issuance of commands or orders in the king's name (the chancery), and (3) the administration of justice.

Because the king travelled about the country on frequent tours of inspection, and took his justices with him, the word court took on a special meaning. *Curia regis* became associated with the king and his justices, and the term gradually became synonymous with the Court of King's Bench, even though the name applied as well to the other bodies or assemblies associated with the king.

This particular court gradually acquired jurisdiction over civil disputes dealing with trespass to goods, and debt cases with the passage of the Statute of Gloucester in 1278. The statute in its later form was interpreted to limit the County Court's jurisdiction in monetary cases to 40 shillings, and to give the king's court all cases involving more than that sum. Inflation during that period effectively placed jurisdiction in these matters in the hands of the king's court.

Jurisdiction over land matters was gradually acquired from the manorial courts by the king's court. This was done by the use of its special writs which tended to restrict the manorial courts, and by 1267, the jurisdiction in matters concerning freehold land was completely in the hands of the king's court.

The king's court had always retained

the exclusive jurisdiction to hear pleas of the Crown, as these were breaches of the "king's peace" and for the most part criminal in nature. Thus, by the middle of the 13th century the king's court had acquired jurisdiction over most civil and criminal matters of law.

In the meantime, however, the workload of the king's court had increased to the point where it was necessary to split the court into two parts. In 1272, the two parts of the king's court were named the Court of Kings' Bench and the Court of Common Pleas. The Court of Common Pleas remained stationary, hearing ordinary civil matters or common pleas at Westminster Hall, near London, and the Court of King's Bench travelled with the king throughout the country, "on circuit" for the assizes.

Other courts were also established. Disputes that arose between the king and his subjects concerning taxation were originally dealt with by clerks in the king's financial department (the exchequer), but with the passage of time, a number of clerks were assigned the exclusive role of dealing with pleas concerning exchequer matters. During the 13th century, the king's exchequer was divided into two separate divisions, one concerned with ordinary financial matters, and the other with the hearing of disputes. This second division became the Exchequer of Pleas after 1268, and subsequently, the Court of Exchequer.

The last court to emerge was the Court of Chancery. The procedure in the common law courts did not provide relief for disputes concerning such matters as trusts, the care of infants, redemption of mortgages, or where special relief was sought, and it became a common practice to petition the king for justice in these cases. These petitions were addressed to the king's chancellor, and the chancellor would then refer the petition to the king's council, where the dispute would be heard and decided. As the number of cases increased, the king delegated much of the work to the chancellor, and by 1474 the chancellor was sitting alone to hear petitions. As the chancellor's work-load increased, vice-chancellors were appointed to hear cases, and gradually chancery became a court with jurisdiction to hear matters which the common law courts, because of their procedure or the rigidity of the common law, were unable to provide an equitable remedy. Hence, laymen and lawyers alike frequently referred to the Court of Chancery as the "Court of Equity."

The Court of the Star Chamber had a slightly different history since it represented the remnant of the king's original council after chancery became a separate court. This court, which presumably acquired its name from the name of the room in which it was held, existed for almost a century before it received official recognition as a court under the reign of Henry VII. The court was originally a court of equity, hearing matters which fell within the king's prerogative. It also heard cases concerning a variety of crimes and offences which threatened the security of the realm. The court's decisions were based upon equity and natural justice during the early period of its existence, but by the 17th century its reputation for the use of torture to obtain evidence, and a series of cruel and rather inhumane penalties in cases which were political as well as criminal in nature, gave the court a bad reputation. It was eventually abolished in 1641, and with it the last direct involvement of the old king's court in the judicial system.

Appeals from the decisions of the

courts were originally heard by the king's council or *curia regis,* but later this duty shifted to the House of Lords for all of the courts except Chancery. With the 17th century changes in the powers of the king, and with the establishment of parliament's supremacy, appeals from the Court of Chancery decisions also fell to the House of Lords. This was also the case with appeals from colonial courts in Canada and pre-revolutionary America.

Minor reform of the courts took place from time to time during the 17th century and the 18th century, but it was not until the 19th century that major reform occurred, and even then, the change was not complete until 1925, when the classical court system was merged into a High Court of Justice with a separate King's (now Queen's) Bench Division, Chancery Division, and a third division to hear specialized matters called the Probate, Divorce and Admiralty Division.

Colonial courts in British North America were organized in accordance with the English court system, but the variation which existed amongst the early settlements precluded uniformity. Royal settlements (which had a governor and council) bore the closest resemblance to the homeland after the settlement had become firmly established, but even then much variation existed. Equity and common law were usually dispensed by the same court, and informality was the norm during the early period. Appeals from the colonial courts were heard either by the governor and his council, or by the king in England.

THE UNITED STATES JUDICIAL SYSTEM

A significant change took place in court procedure as a result of the United States War of Independence. The war severed both political and legal ties with England, but the law, and much of the legal system remained in the former colonies. Pensylvannia, for example, continued to call its civil trial court the Court of Common Pleas, and the law which the court dispensed was the common law. Most states at the time of the War of Independence adopted English common law as it stood in 1776, with appropriate modifications to meet local needs and conditions. States which joined the union later, however, brought with them a different legal background. Louisiana, for example, had a French legal history, and followed the French *Civil Code* for non-criminal matters.

The United States judicial system after the War of Independence became a dual system with two sets of courts: state and federal courts.

State and Federal Courts

The Constitution of the United States established as federal jurisdiction such matters as questions of law arising out of the Constitution, any Act of Congress, and any treaty between another country and the United States. It also included admiralty and maritime cases, certain cases involving citizens of more than one state (where the sum involved exceeded $10 000), disputes between a United States citizen and a citizen residing in another country, and disputes which involve the United States as a party.

The federal court system formed to hear these cases includes essentially three general types of courts, and a number of special courts. The judges of all of these courts are appointed by the President of the United States on the advice of, and with the consent of, the senate.

The lowest of the federal courts is the

District Court. It is a Trial Court where a litigant brings an action for the first time to be heard by either a single judge, or by a panel of two or three (and occasionally more) judges, depending upon the nature of the case. These courts are called District Courts because the country, under the federal court system, is divided into districts, with each of the less populous states forming a district, and the more populous states, such as New York, containing more than one district.

Appeals from the decisions of the District Court may be made to a Federal Court of Appeals, although some matters may be appealed directly to the Supreme Court of the United States. The country is divided into 11 areas for appeal purposes, each with an Appeal Court that is usually presided over by a panel of three judges, although the number may vary. These areas are called "circuits" even though the judges no longer travel the circuit as they once did. The Courts of Appeals hear appeals from District Courts, and also review the orders of federal administrative agencies.

The final court of appeal is the United States Supreme Court, which at present, consists of nine justices. The Supreme Court is an Appellate Court for cases that have been reviewed by the federal Courts of Appeals, or occasionally the highest state Courts of Appeals. Appeal to the Supreme Court is discretionary, and the court will only hear an appeal if it concludes that the issue in dispute is of sufficient importance to warrant a hearing.

A number of other federal courts also exist. These include the United States Tax Court, the Customs Court (a court which deals with customs disputes), the Court of Claims (it hears claims against the federal government), and the Court of Customs and Patent Appeals (essentially an Appeal Court to hear appeals from the Customs Court, and decisions of the Patent and Trademark Office). A number of other specialized courts such as Military Courts and Territorial Courts form the remaining part of the federal court system.

At the state level, some variation exists, but in every state a system of Trial and Appeal Courts has been established to hear legal disputes which fall within the jurisdiction of the particular state. The names of the courts vary, as do the methods of selecting or appointing the judiciary. In some states judges are elected; in others, they are appointed by the state governor. The Trial Courts are usually divided into two classes: one to hear minor cases, such as small debt disputes, and a second to hear more serious matters. Justices of the Peace frequently preside over the first class of courts, which are sometimes called Municipal Courts, or Small Claims Courts.

The second class of Trial Court, which has jurisdiction to hear the more important cases, is usually called the County Court, District Court, or sometimes, the Superior Court. In some states, this court may hear appeals from a Small Claims Court, as well as hear the trials of more important civil matters. Some states may also have special courts to hear particular kinds of disputes, such as probate cases or criminal trials.

In addition to its Trial Courts, each state has an Appeal Court which is usually called the Supreme Court of the state. This court is normally presided over by from five to seven justices. A number of states have an Intermediate Appeal Court as well. Where an Intermediate Appeal Court exists, the right to appeal to the Supreme Court of the state is usually discretionary, with only the more important legal issues receiving a second review.

THE JUDICIAL SYSTEM IN CANADA

Historical Development of Canadian Courts

Canada did not experience the wrenching changes brought about by the War of Independence in the United States. Instead, the Canadian system of courts gradually changed as the country moved from a colonial status to that of a dominion. After 1663, the law in what is now Quebec, Ontario, Prince Edward Island, and part of Nova Scotia consisted of the Customs of Paris which had been declared the law of New France by the Conseil Superieur of France. The Seven Years' War, however, resulted in the capture by England of Louisbourg in 1758, and Quebec in 1759, and the imposition of English law in New France. France formally surrendered to England what is now Quebec, Cape Breton, and Prince Edward Island by the Treaty of Paris in 1763, and the law administered by the new civil courts established in 1764 was English law. The *Quebec Act*[2] of 1774 made a further change in the legal system by introducing a Court of King's Bench, and a significant change in the law—the criminal law in the new British Province of Quebec was declared to be English law, but the civil law was to be based upon Canadian law. Canadian law in Quebec was essentially the Customs of Paris that had been introduced in 1663, and Quebec, as a result, continued to follow this law until 1866, when a new Quebec *Civil Code* was compiled and put into effect.

When the United States War of Independence officially ended in 1783, more than 10 000 United Empire Loyalists left the United States, and moved into the western part of Quebec. The new settlers did not understand, nor did they like French civil law. Initially, in response to their demands, the western part of Quebec (which is now Ontario) was divided into four districts. Each district had a Court of General Sessions to hear minor criminal cases, a civil Court of Common Pleas, and a Prerogative Court to deal with wills and intestacy. In 1791, the *Canada Act*[3] created two separate provinces: the Province of Upper Canada (now Ontario) with its own governor, executive council and elected house of assembly; and the Province of Lower Canada.

The first Act passed by the new House of Assembly for the Province of Upper Canada was the *Property and Civil Rights Act*. This Act provided that English law (as it existed on October 15, 1792, and as amended or modified by subsequent Acts) would be the law of the province in all matters concerning property and civil rights. This Act is still in force.[4]

The following year, the courts were reorganized by the replacement of the Prerogative Courts in each district with a Surrogate Court. A Probate Court was also established to hear appeals in cases concerning wills and intestacy on a province-wide basis.

In 1794, the *Judicature Act*[5] was passed. The effect of this Act was to abolish the former Court of Common Pleas, and replace it with the Court of King's Bench. The new court had jurisdiction over both civil and criminal matters for the entire province. The judges of the new court were also different from the old (all of the new judges having been members of the Bar of either Upper Canada, England, or some other English jurisdiction). A later

---

[2]*Quebec Act*, 14 Geo. III, c. 83.

[3]*Canada Act*, 31 Geo. III, c. 31.
[4]*Property and Civil Rights Act*, R.S.O. 1980, c. 395.
[5]*Judicature Act*, 34 Geo. III, c. 2.

Act[6] provided for the appointment of judges "during the period of their good behaviour," and required an address from both the Council and the Assembly to remove a judge from office.

The Court of Chancery was established in 1837 for the Province of Upper Canada, and was composed of the chancellor (also the governor), and a vice-chancellor. All judicial powers were exercised by the vice-chancellor who handled all of the legal work. In 1849, the office of chancellor became a judicial office, and a second vice-chancellor was appointed.

The courts were again changed in 1849, this time by the creation of a Court of Common Pleas. Its jurisdiction was concurrent with that of the Court of Queen's Bench, and in 1856 the procedure of the two courts was modernized and unified. In the same year, a new Appeal Court for Upper Canada was established—the Court of Error and Appeal. This court consisted of all of the judges of the Courts of Queen's Bench, Common Pleas, and Chancery sitting together as an appeal body at Toronto. This particular court later became the Court of Appeal. The *British North America Act, 1867* did not change the composition of these courts, but simply changed the name from Upper Canada to Ontario.[7] The names of the courts in the other provinces also remained unchanged upon joining Confederation. The courts in most of the older provinces had developed along lines similar to those of Ontario, although legislation which brought about the change was passed at different times, and with some variation.

In the latter part of the 19th century,

changes that took place in the structure of the courts in England soon appeared in Canada. The many Law Reform Acts which were passed in England (1873-1925) were reflected in a number of changes in Canadian law and its judicial system. The western Prairie Provinces were influenced not only by law reform in England, but also by other Canadian provinces in the establishment of their court systems. When Ontario introduced its own law reform legislation in 1881, 1909, and 1937 which reorganized the Supreme Court into two parts (a High Court of Justice as a Trial Court, and a Court of Appeal to hear appeals), a number of other provinces followed suit.[8]

Law reform in Canada has been an evolutionary process. The general trend has been toward a streamlining of the judicial process, with a gradual reduction in formal procedure. Although much variation exists from province to province, a provincial judicial system generally consists of a Small Claims or Small Debts Court, a County or District Court, a Superior or Supreme Court and a Court of Appeal. In those provinces where a Court of Appeal does not exist the Supreme Court is empowered to hear appeals from courts of original jurisdiction. Criminal cases are usually heard by both Supreme Court and County Court Judges. In addition, each province has a Provincial or Magistrate's Court (presided over by either a Provincial Judge or Magistrate) for the purpose of hearing minor criminal matters, and cases concerning violations of non-criminal provincial statutes. In 1979, under the *Provincial Offences Act*,[9] the Province of Ontario introduced new procedures to deal with

---

[6]"An Act to Render the Judges of the Court of King's Bench in This Province Independent of the Crown," 4 Wm. IV, c. 2.

[7]*British North America Act, 1867*, 30 Vict., c. 3, as amended.

[8]See the *Judicature Act*, 9 Edw. VII, c. 5, as an example of the New Brunswick Acts of the General Assembly.

[9]*Provincial Offences Act*, R.S.O. 1980, c. 400.

non-criminal violations of provincial stat-utes, such as the *Highway Traffic Act*,[10] and the *Liquor Control Act*,[11] by the creation three pleas: guilty of the violation, guilty with an explanation, and not guilty. Only the latter plea will result in a full court hearing to determine the case. How well this attempt to alleviate court congestion will work remains to be seen.

The Structure of the Judicial System

In Canada, there are many different courts at the present, each with a different juris-diction. In this context, jurisdiction means the right or authority of a court to hear and decide a dispute. Jurisdiction may take a number of different forms. Usually the court must have the authority to deal with cases of the particular type brought before it, in addition to authority over either the parties or the property in dispute. With re-spect to the first type of jurisdiction, the authority of the court may be monetary or geographic in the sense that the court has been authorized to hear cases concerning money up to a set amount, or to hear cases concerning land within the particular county or area where the land is situated. In the case of jurisdiction over the parties to a dispute, the court must have the au-thority or power to compel their atten-dance or to impose its decision on them.

Courts of law may be placed in two rather general classifications. The first group are called *courts of original jurisdic-tion*. These are courts before which a dis-pute or case is heard for the first time by a judge, and where all the facts are pre-sented to enable the judge to render a de-cision. Courts of original jurisdiction are sometimes referred to as Trial Courts,

[10]*Highway Traffic Act*, R.S.O. 1980, c. 198, as amended.
[11]*Liquor Control Act*, R.S.O. 1980, c. 243, as amended.

where both civil and criminal cases are first heard.

Courts which fall into the second group are called *courts of appeal*. These courts, as the name implies, hear appeals from the decisions of courts of original jurisdiction. Courts of appeal are superior or "higher" courts in that their decisions may overrule or vary the decisions of the "lower" or Trial Courts. Their principal function is to review the decisions of Trial Courts where one of the parties to the action in the lower court believes that the Trial Judge made an erroneous decision. They do not normally hear evidence, but argument by counsel for the parties concerning the *decision* of the Trial Court. Usually an appeal alleges that the judge hearing the case at trial erred in the application of the law to the facts of the case. Sometimes the appeal is limited to the amount of damages awarded, or in a criminal case, to the se-verity of the penalty imposed. On occa-sion, an Appeal Court may find that the judge at trial failed to consider important evidence in reaching his decision, in which case the Appeal Court may send the case back to the lower court for a new trial.

Federal Courts

In Canada, each province has a number of courts of original jurisdiction, and at least one Appeal Court. In addition, the federal court system also exists to deal with matters that fall within the exclusive juris-diction of the federal government. The Federal Court hears disputes between pro-vincial governments and the federal gov-ernment, actions against the federal gov-ernment, admiralty, patent, trademark, copyright, taxation matters, and appeals from federal boards, tribunals, and com-missions. In some cases, the court has ex-clusive jurisdiction to hear the dispute, and in others, the jurisdiction is concurrent with that of the superior provincial courts in order that a person may sue in either the Federal Court or the appropriate provincial court. A trial decision of the Federal Court may be appealed to the Federal Court, Appeal Division, and with leave, to the Supreme Court of Canada.

At the federal level, the Supreme Court of Canada is maintained to hear important appeals from the Appeal Courts of the various provinces, as well as those from the Federal Court, Appeal Division.

There is no uniform system of courts in the provinces as each province has the authority to establish its own system, and to assign to each court a specific jurisdiction. For this reason then, a provincial court may have jurisdiction to hear both civil and criminal cases. Fortunately, however, most of the provinces have established courts somewhat similar in jurisdiction. Bearing this in mind, and the fact that variation in names and powers do exist, the following list represents what might be considered to be typical of the court systems found in a province.

Criminal Courts

Magistrate's or Provincial Court

A Magistrate's Court or Provincial Court is a court of original jurisdiction which is presided over by a provincially appointed magistrate or judge. This court generally deals with criminal matters, although many provinces have empowered the court to hear cases involving the violation of provincial statutes and municipal by-laws where some sort of penalty is imposed.

The Magistrate's Court hears all criminal cases, either as a court with jurisdiction to dispose of the matter (as in cases involving less serious offences where the court has been given absolute jurisdiction), or where the accused has the right to elect to be tried

by a Magistrate. It will also hold a *preliminary hearing* of the more serious crimes to determine if sufficient evidence exists to have the accused tried by a higher court. All provinces except Quebec have a Magistrate's Court or Provincial Court. The Quebec counterpart of the Magistrate's Court is the Court of Sessions of the Peace.

County Court

The County Court or District Court is a court with both civil and criminal jurisdiction. As the name implies, these courts are organized on a county or district basis, and have jurisdiction to hear cases which arise within their geographic area. All provinces except Quebec have courts of this kind. The County Court at "General Sessions of the Peace" hears criminal cases of a more serious nature than those which fall within the absolute jurisdiction of the Magistrate's or Provincial Court. For many of these offences, the accused may elect to be tried by the judge alone, or by a judge and jury. County Courts, however, do not have jurisdiction to hear cases involving the most serious crimes: treason, piracy, murder, or rape.

The County Court may also act as an Appeal Court to hear appeals from the decisions of the Magistrate's or Provincial Court in cases concerned with minor offences. These minor offences are known as *summary conviction offences*.

Provincial Supreme Court

Each province has a Supreme Court empowered to hear the most serious criminal cases. Justices of the court periodically travel throughout the province to hear these cases (usually at the county courthouse) at sessions of the Supreme Court called assizes. In some provinces, the court follows the English custom of presenting the judge with a pair of white

Table 1 **CRIMINAL APPEALS***

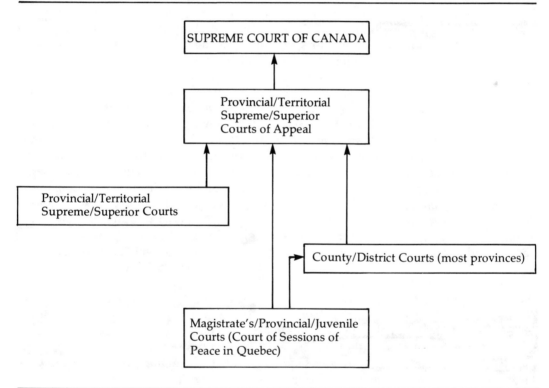

*Court names, and in some cases, appeal routes, differ for some provinces

gloves at the beginning of the session if no criminal cases are scheduled to be heard.

Juvenile Court

Juvenile offenders are subject to the *Juvenile Delinquents Act*.[12] This Act provides for special courts to hear cases involving the commission of offences by young people. While a juvenile is defined as a person under the age of 16 years, the Act also permits a province to vary the age; consequently, the age of a juvenile varies from 16 to 18 years, depending upon the province in question. Juvenile Court is closed to the general public, and is usually presided over by a Magistrate or Provincial Court Judge. The court hears offences by juveniles, and the accused, if convicted, is usually sent to a reform institution, rather than a prison. The court, however, attempts to prevent further delinquency, and will not normally commit a juvenile to an institution unless the crime committed is very serious, or previous acts of delinquency indicate that more lenient methods of behaviour modification have failed.

Family Court

Family Courts have jurisdiction to deal with domestic problems, and the enforcement of federal and provincial legislation that relates to family problems. Most of the cases in Family Court are related to non-support of family members, or family relationships that have deteriorated to the point where the actions of one or more members of a family have become a serious threat to others. Family Courts are usually presided over by a Magistrate or Provincial Court Judge in those provinces where they have been established; in

others, where separate courts do not exist, family disputes or legislation relating to family matters fall under the jurisdiction of the County or Supreme Court.

Criminal Courts of Appeal

In addition to the County Court, which in some provinces hears appeals in minor criminal cases, each province has a Court of Appeal to review the convictions of accused persons by the Juvenile Court, County Court, Supreme Court, and Magistrate's (or Provincial) Court. A panel of judges presides over the Appeal Court, and the decision of the majority of the judges hearing the appeal decides the case. The final Court of Appeal in criminal matters is the Supreme Court of Canada. It will hear appeals from the decisions of provincial Courts of Appeal; however, neither the accused nor the Crown generally have the right to appeal to the Supreme Court of Canada as a matter of right. Instead, they must obtain leave to appeal. A right to appeal, however, does exist in the case of an indictable offence if the decision of the provincial Court of Appeal on a question of law was not unanimous.

Civil Courts

Most provinces have a number of civil courts to deal with disputes which arise between individuals or between individuals and the government. Some courts have limited jurisdiction, and hear only special kinds of disputes; others hear only those appeals from inferior courts. Although most civil courts of original jurisdiction permit cases to be heard by both a judge and jury, in some courts, such as Small Claims Courts, cases are heard by a judge sitting alone. Courts of Appeal are non-jury courts.

---

[12]*Juvenile Delinquents Act*, R.S.C. 1970, c. J-3, as amended.

Table 2   **CIVIL APPEALS***

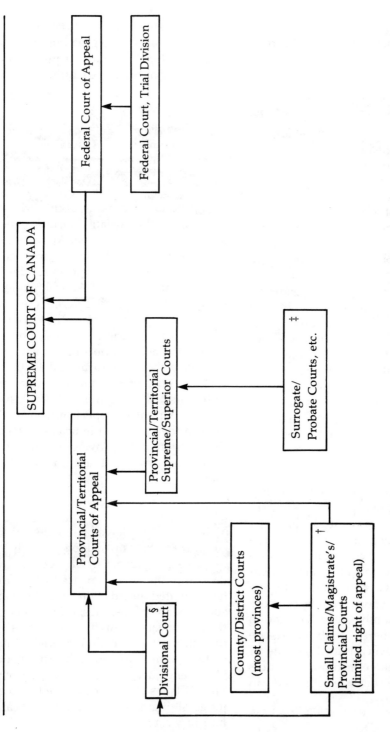

*Some provinces do not have all of the courts shown on this chart

†Appeal routes vary from province to province with respect to Small Claims Courts

‡Special courts, such as Probate or Surrogate, usually have disputes litigated in the Supreme Court of the province

§Ontario only. The Divisional Court is a unique court in that it can conduct both trials and certain types of appeals

Small Claims Court

Small Claims Courts have jurisdiction to hear cases where the amount of money involved is relatively small. In those provinces which have a Small Claims Court (Nova Scotia and Prince Edward Island, for example, do not), usually the court's jurisdiction is limited to hear only those cases where the amount of money involved is less than $1 000. Some Small Claims Courts are limited to a much smaller monetary jurisdiction.

Small Claims Courts are usually informal courts may be presided over by a County Court Judge in a number of provinces, and by a Magistrate (as a part of the Provincial Court) in others. The type of cases which the court hears are usually small debt or contract disputes, and damage cases, such as claims arising out of minor automobile accidents. Litigants in Small Claims Court frequently present their own cases, and court costs are usually low. The right to appeal a Small Claims Court decision is sometimes restricted to judgements over a specific amount, and where an appeal exists, it is usually to a single judge of the Court of Appeal of the province. *Ontario - Appeal goes to the Divisional Court*

County Court

All provinces (except Quebec) have County or District Courts to hear disputes concerning monetary amounts in excess of the jurisdiction of the Small Claims Courts. These courts are also subject to specified upper monetary limits in most provinces, although restrictions are by no means universal. Both Alberta and Newfoundland, for example, have no upper monetary limits on cases which their County Courts may hear.

County Courts are presided over by a federally appointed judge. Most cases may be heard by a judge and jury if the parties *Ontario $1001 - $15 000*

so desire. Often, appeals from the County Court are to the Court of Appeal.

Provincial Supreme Court

Each province has a Supreme Court to hear civil disputes in matters which are beyond or outside the jurisdiction of the lower courts. The provincial Supreme Court has unlimited jurisdiction in monetary matters, and is presided over at trial by a federally appointed judge.

As shown in Table 3 (over), although the Supreme Court of each province (or territory) is similar in jurisdiction, no one designation applies to all of these courts.

Cases in the Supreme Court (both jury and non-jury) may be heard by judges who travel throughout the province to the various court-houses (the assizes), or in specified cities where the court sits without a jury on a regular basis. An appeal from a decision of the Supreme Court is to the Appeal Court of the province.

In the Yukon and Northwest territories, territorial ordinances have established Trials Courts equivalent to the provincial Supreme Courts—the Territorial Court and the Supreme Court of the Northwest Territories. An unusual feature of these two courts may be found in the Rules of Procedure that apply to each. The Territorial Court of the Yukon has adopted the Rules of Procedure of the Supreme Court of British Columbia, and the Supreme Court of the Northwest Territories follows the Rules of Procedure of the Court of Queen's Bench of Alberta. *Ontario - $15 000 +*

Surrogate or Probate Court

The Surrogate Court, or Probate Court as it is called in New Brunswick and Nova Scotia, is a special court established to hear and deal with wills and the administration of the estates of deceased persons. The provinces of Newfoundland, Quebec, Brit-

Table 3

TRIAL LEVEL

Jurisdiction	*Designation of Court*
Alberta	Court of Queen's Bench of Alberta
British Columbia	Supreme Court of British Columbia
Manitoba	Court of Queen's Bench for Manitoba
New Brunswick	Supreme Court of New Brunswick, Queen's Bench Division
Newfoundland	Supreme Court of Judicature for Newfoundland, Trial Division
Northwest Territories	Supreme Court of Northwest Territories
Nova Scotia	Supreme Court of Nova Scotia, Trial Division
Ontario	Supreme Court of Ontario, High Court of Justice
Prince Edward Island	Supreme Court of Prince Edward Island
Quebec	Superior Court
Saskatchewan	Court of Queen's Bench of Saskatchewan
Yukon Territory	Territorial Court

APPEAL LEVEL

Jurisdiction	*Designation of Court*
Alberta	Court of Appeal of Alberta
British Columbia	Court of Appeal of British Columbia
Manitoba	Court of Appeal of Manitoba
New Brunswick	Supreme Court of New Brunswick, Appeal Division
Newfoundland	Supreme Court of Judicature for Newfoundland, Court of Appeal
Northwest Territories	Court of Appeal of Northwest Territories
Nova Scotia	Supreme Court of Nova Scotia, Appeal Division
Ontario	Supreme Court of Ontario, Court of Appeal
Prince Edward Island	Supreme Court of Prince Edward Island
Quebec	Court of Appeal
Saskatchewan	Court of Appeal of Saskatchewan
Yukon Territory	Court of Appeal

ish Columbia, and Prince Edward Island do not have special courts to deal with these matters, but, instead, have placed them under the jurisdiction of their Supreme Courts. In provinces that do have Surrogate or Probate Courts, the presiding judge is usually the same judge appointed as the County or District Court Judge.

Civil Courts of Appeal
Provincial Court of Appeal
Each province (or territory) has an Appeal Court although, as indicated in Table 3, no one designation applies to all of these courts.

The lines of appeal in civil cases are not always as clear-cut as those in criminal matters. Sometimes the right of appeal from an inferior court does not go directly to the Appeal Court of the province or the territory. In Ontario, for example, an appeal from a decision of the Small Claims Court (where the amount is above a certain minimum) would be appealed to a single judge of the Divisional Court, which is a part of the Supreme Court of Ontario. Supreme Court trial judgements, however, would be appealed to the provincial Court of Appeal or the Appeal Division of the provincial Supreme Court, as the case may be. County or District Court decisions in those provinces where they exist usually have an appeal route to the Court of Appeal for the province.

Supreme Court of Canada
The Supreme Court of Canada is the final and highest Appeal Court in Canada. It hears appeals from the provincial Appeal Courts, but the right to appeal is restricted. In civil cases, leave to appeal must be obtained before a case may be heard by the Supreme Court of Canada; normally the issue or legal point must be of some importance before leave will be granted.

The court also hears appeals from the Federal Court, and is the body which finally determines the constitutionality of statutes passed by both the federal and provincial governments.

THE JUDICIAL SYSTEM IN ACTION

Essentially there are three bodies which enforce the law in Canada. These are: (1) the criminal court; (2) the civil court; and (3) administrative tribunals.

As the name implies, the criminal court is concerned with the enforcement of the criminal law. A criminal court is often the same court which deals with civil law matters, or it may be a court organized to deal exclusively with law of a criminal or *quasi-criminal* nature. The Provincial Court (Criminal Division) in Ontario, or the Magistrate's Court in most other provinces, is frequently the court with jurisdiction to deal with criminal matters of a minor nature, or to act as a court where a preliminary hearing of a more serious criminal offence would be held.

In a criminal case involving a minor or less serious offence, the Crown brings the case before the court by way of the summary conviction rules of procedure. In a serious case, it will bring the case by way of indictment. In either situation, the case is first heard in the Provincial Court (Criminal Division), or in the Magistrate's Court. These courts have absolute or elective jurisdiction to dispose of the case if the matter is minor in nature. When the offence is of a more serious nature, the court will conduct a *preliminary hearing* to determine whether the Crown has sufficient evidence to warrant a full hearing of the case by a superior court.

The procedure of the Magistrate's or Provincial Court tends to be very informal.

The normal procedure at the hearing is to have the charge which the Crown has placed before the court read to the accused; the accused is then asked how he (or she) pleads. If the accused admits to the commission of the offence, a plea of "guilty" is entered, and the court will then hear evidence from the Crown to confirm the act and the circumstances surrounding it. A conviction will then be lodged against the accused, and a penalty imposed.

If a plea of "not guilty" is entered by the accused, the Crown is then obliged to proceed with its evidence to show that, in fact, the criminal act *was committed (actus reus)* by the accused, and that the accused had *intended to commit (mens rea)* the crime. Witnesses are normally called by the Crown to identify the accused as the person who committed the act and to establish this evidence. Counsel for the accused (the defence) then has the opportunity to cross-examine the witnesses.

On completion of the Crown's evidence, the defence counsel may ask the judge or magistrate to dismiss the case if the Crown has failed to prove beyond any reasonable doubt that the accused committed the crime. If the judge does not accept the defence counsel's motion, then the defence must proceed to introduce evidence to refute the Crown's case. This, too, is usually done by calling witnesses although in this instance they testify on the accused's behalf. Where defence witnesses are called, they are open to cross-examination by the Crown counsel.

Once all of the evidence has been presented to the court, both parties are entitled to sum up their respective cases, and argue any legal points which may apply to the case. The judge or magistrate then determines the accused either "not guilty" or "guilty" of the crime, and his decision with his reasons, are recorded as his judgement.

In the case of a preliminary hearing, the proceedings will normally end at the conclusion of the Crown's evidence (which will not necessarily be all of the evidence, but only that part which the Crown believes will be necessary to establish sufficient evidence to warrant a further hearing), and the case would then be referred to the court with jurisdiction to try the matter in full.

Civil cases follow a much different procedure. Before a civil case may proceed to trial the parties must exchange a number of documents called *pleadings* which set out the issues in dispute and the facts surrounding the conflict.

Civil cases may begin in a number of ways depending upon the court and the relief sought, but the usual procedure in a simple dispute is for the *plaintiff* (the injured party) to issue a *writ of summons* against the *defendant* alleging the particular injury suffered by the plaintiff, and notifying the defendant that the plaintiff intends to hold the defendant responsible for the injury set out in the *claim*. The writ of summons is usually prepared by the plaintiff's lawyer, and taken to the court's office, where the writ is issued by the court. It is then served personally on the defendant, usually by the sheriff or someone from his office.

Once the defendant receives the writ, he must notify the court's office that a defence will follow. This is done by filing a document called an *appearance*.

The next step in the proceedings is for the plaintiff to provide the defendant (and the court) with details of the claim and the facts which the plaintiff intends to prove when the case comes to trial. This document is called a *statement of claim*.

The defendant, on receipt of the statement of claim, must prepare a *statement of defence* setting out the particular defence which the defendant has to the plaintiff's claim, and if necessary, the facts which he intends to prove at trial to support the defence. The statement of defence is filed with the court and served upon the plaintiff. If the defendant also has a claim against the plaintiff, the defendant will file a pleading called a *counter-claim*, which is essentially a statement of claim. Where a counter-claim is filed, the roles of parties change, and the defendant on his counter-claim becomes the *plaintiff by counter-claim*; the plaintiff, the *defendant by counter-claim*.

On receipt of the defendant's statement of defence the plaintiff may wish to respond. In this case the response to the statement of defence will be set out in a document called a *reply* which is filed and served on the defendant. If the defendant has served the plaintiff with a counter-claim, then the plaintiff (who at this point is also the defendant by counter-claim) will usually file a *statement of defence to counter-claim*, which will set out his defence. This usually ends the exchange of documents, and the pleadings are then noted *closed*.

Occasionally, a pleading may not contain sufficient information to enable the opposing party to properly prepare a response. If this should be the case, a further document called a *demand for particulars* may be served to obtain the necessary information.

Once the pleadings have been *closed*, either party may set the action down on the list for trial by filing and serving a *notice of trial* on the other party. In some instances, where a jury may be appropriate, a *jury notice* may also be served. This indicates that the party serving the notice intends to have the case heard by a judge and jury.

To clarify points in the statement of claim and the statement of defence, the parties may also hold examinations under oath, which are called *examinations for discovery*. The *transcript* of this evidence is often used later at the trial.

At trial, the case follows a procedure that differs from that of a criminal action. In a civil matter, the counsel for the plaintiff usually begins the case with an *opening statement* which briefly sets out the issues and the facts which the plaintiff intends to prove. Witnesses are called, and evidence is presented to prove the facts in the claim. All witnesses may be subject to cross-examination by counsel.

On the completion of the plaintiff's case, counsel for the defendant may ask the judge to dismiss the plaintiff's case if the evidence fails to establish liability on the defendant's part. Again, if the judge does not agree with the defendant, the action will proceed, and the defendant must enter evidence by way of witnesses to prove that the plaintiff's claim is unfounded. Defence witnesses, like the plaintiff's witnesses, may be subject to cross-examination.

Witnesses may be of two kinds: *ordinary witnesses* who testify as to what they saw, heard, or did, and *expert witnesses*, who are experts on a particular subject, and give *opinion evidence* on matters which fall within their area of special knowledge. (A medical expert testifying as to the likelihood of a plaintiff suffering permanent physical damage as a result of an injury would be an example of this type of expert evidence.)

When all of the evidence has been entered, counsel argue the relevant points of law and sum up their respective cases for the judge. The judge will then render a decision, which with his reasons, represents his *judgement*.

If either of the parties believe that the trial judge erred in some manner (such as in his application of the law, or the admission of certain evidence), an appeal may be lodged with the appropriate Appeal Court. A *notice of appeal* must be served within a relatively short time after the trial judgement is handed down, then an *appeal book* containing all material concerning the appeal is prepared by counsel for the Appeal Court. The Appeal Court will review the case, and if it finds no errors, it will *affirm* the decision of the Trial Court and *dismiss the appeal*. On the other hand, if it should find that the Trial Court erred in reaching its decision, it may *admit the appeal* and *reverse* the decision of the Trial Court, *vary* the decision, or send the case back for a *new trial*.

THE LEGAL PROFESSION

The legal profession has a long and noble history which dates back to early Roman times. In England, attorneys were not necessary to plead cases before the Anglo-Saxon moots, as the parties to a dispute presented their own cases. By Norman times, however, a person who was old or infirm was permitted to appoint an attorney to act for him, if he agreed to be bound by the attorney's acts. This gradually changed over the next century to the point where the king's justices permitted any person to bring an action in the king's court by an attorney. The attorney, at that time, required no formal training in the law.

The first legislation regulating persons who might practise as attorneys was passed in 1402.[13] This statute required anyone who wished to practise before the courts to be first examined by the justices of the king's court, and if fit, to have their names put on a *Roll*. Only those persons whose names appeared on the Roll were entitled to practise law as attorneys. If an attorney failed to carry out his duties properly, his name could be struck from the Roll and he would be barred from appearing before the king's court ever again.

Persons who became familiar with proceedings in the chancellor's court were called solicitors because the special proceedings in the chancellor's court were begun by a petition soliciting some form of equitable relief from the court.

Attorneys and solicitors continued to be examined by the judges and the chancellor (or his senior master) for almost three centuries. By 1729, however, the examination process had become so perfunctory that complaints were made to the courts that some solicitors and attorneys were not learned in the law. To remedy this situation, legislation was passed which required both solicitors and attorneys to serve a five-year apprenticeship with a practising attorney or solicitor before taking the examination for admission to practise alone.

As early as the 14th century practitioners in England banded together in societies for the purpose of jointly purchasing and owning law manuscripts and law books, in addition to establishing premises where they could maintain their libraries and live during the time when the courts were in session. These establishments were known as *inns*. The inns were governed by senior members who, by tradi-

---

[13]"Punishment of an Attorney Found in Default," 4 Hen. IV, c. 18.

tion, dined together at a high table on a bench. Consequently, these senior members acquired the name *benchers*.

As part of their training at the inns, junior members were expected to attend after-dinner lectures and engage in "practice" moots. A *barra*, or bar similar to the bar found in the courts, was usually set up in the hall, and when an apprentice was considered to be sufficiently experienced, the benchers would allow the apprentice to plead his case from the bar. The apprentice's *call to the bar* was recognition by the profession that he had acquired the necessary skill to act as a barrister. Once the apprentice had been called to the bar he would then be permitted to plead cases in the courts (although until 1846 the Court of Common Pleas would only allow practitioners who held the degree of *serjeant* to plead before it.) The training of apprentices unfortunately declined during the late 18th and early 19th century to the point where the four Inns of Court decided (in 1852) to establish a law school to provide instruction and to conduct examinations of apprentices before the students could be called to the bar. Formal training has been required since that time for the legal profession in England.

When the *Law Society Act* was passed in Upper Canada in 1793,[14] the tradition of the Inns of Court, including the titles, was followed by the then fledgling legal profession. Similar legislation in the other colonies adopted the same traditions. The small number of lawyers in North America did not, however, permit the division of the profession (barristers and solicitors) as it existed in England, and from the beginning, lawyers in the North American colonies combined both avenues of practise into one. Formal training continued to be

patterned after the English model. For many years, formal legal training was possible in some provinces by apprenticeship and examination by the provincial bars. Over time, however, legal training gradually shifted to the universities where courses in law were offered. At first these courses were part of general university programs; later they became part of the curriculum of university law schools.

McGill University in Montreal, Quebec, established a law school in 1848, and claims to be the oldest university with a law faculty. Many other universities established law schools shortly thereafter, and by the late 19th century, law schools existed in New Brunswick, Quebec, Ontario, Nova Scotia, and Manitoba. One of the most famous, and one of the oldest, Osgoode Hall Law School, dates from 1797, but did not grant an academic law degree until the benchers of the Law Society of Upper Canada transferred the formal teaching function to degree-granting institutions (including its own school) in 1957.

Formal training of the legal profession in most common law provinces now requires a law degree as well as some form of apprenticeship to be served in the office of a practising solicitor or barrister for a specified period of time.

Legal training in the Province of Quebec requires a knowledge of the *Civil Code*, and this training is now provided by Quebec universities. The training in civil law is quite different in terms of approach and content. Even the terminology used to describe certain members of the legal profession differs from that used in the common law provinces. Much of the work normally considered a part of a solicitor's practice in other provinces is performed in Quebec by *notaries*, and the "trial work" is conducted by *avocates*.

[14]*Law Society Act,* 37 Geo. III, c. 13.

SUMMARY   The legal system is the vehicle by which the law is enforced, however, this was not always the case. The development of the legal system has been evolutionary in nature. The earliest courts were not courts as we know them today, but simply meetings of the community. Community pressure to support a decision was common until the Norman Conquest of England in 1066. After the Conquest, the gradual centralization of power began, and with it, the courts' increased authority to demand that the parties comply with their decisions. Courts established special procedures which the parties were required to follow if they wished to be heard, and these special procedures in turn gave rise to the legal profession. Modern courts in Canada and the United States still retain many of the traditions and names of the English courts, even though the kinds of cases which they hear are quite different today.

While the judicial process appears to be cumbersome and complex, much of the procedure is designed to ensure that justice is done. Safeguards in the form of rules of evidence and judicial review form an important part of the mechanism designed to eliminate arbitrary or unfair decision-making. As a result, the legal systems in Canada, the United States and the United Kingdom represent a system which is fair to all.

DISCUSSION QUESTIONS

1. Define "jurisdiction."
2. Explain the difference between a Small Claims Court and a Magistrate's Court.
3. It was once said that "a man who acts as his own lawyer has a fool for a client." Discuss the importance of professional representation in the higher courts as opposed to litigants presenting their own cases in a Small Claims Court.
4. Identify the American counterparts of the Provincial Court, the County Court, and the Supreme Court of Canada.
5. Describe the nature of the Law Reform Acts of 1873-1925 of the English Parliament.
6. Define a "court of original jurisdiction."
7. Identify the three law-making bodies in Canada, and determine which has the greatest impact on today's society.
8. State precisely the duty of the Crown in order for it to obtain a conviction in a criminal case.
9. Identify, and explain briefly the function of each document issued in a typical civil case.
10. Discuss the relative merits of the English division of the legal profession as opposed to the North American unification of such.

PART II

The Law of Torts

CHAPTER 3

Tort Concepts

TORT LAW DEFINED

The term "tort" is a legal term derived from the Latin word *tortus* meaning a "wrong." Its use in law is to describe a great many activities which result in damage to others with the exception of a breach of trust, a breach of duty which is entirely contractual in nature, or a breach of a merely equitable obligation.[1] The origin of the word being Latin, it is difficult to know if the term existed in England from the time of the Roman occupation, or if it came into English law by way of the early Norman courts' use of old French after the Conquest. In any event, the term has been used in English law for many hundreds of years to describe a wrong committed by one person against another, or against his property or reputation, either intentionally

[1]Osborn, P.G., *The Concise Law Dictionary*, 4th ed. (Sweet & Maxwell, 1954: London), p. 334.

or unintentionally. It also generally covers cases where a person causing an injury has no lawful right to do so. Unfortunately, the term is not capable of precise definition, because the area of the law which it encompasses is so broad that to determine its limits with any degree of precision would be an impossible task. We can, nevertheless, identify many of the more important areas of tort law, and examine those which have a direct bearing on ordinary personal and business activities.

THE DEVELOPMENT OF TORT LAW

Some of the earliest laws made by the community or the early judges pertained to actions which are now the subject of tort law. Indeed, most of our more familiar criminal law was once tort law, and many criminal actions today still have a concurrent tort liability attached to them. Assault causing bodily harm, for example, is an act covered by the *Criminal Code,* where the Crown would proceed against the person who committed the assault. Under tort law, the victim of the assault would also have the right to seek redress from the accused for the injury by way of civil proceedings for assault and battery.

In the past, no distinction was made between acts which were criminal, and acts which were civil in nature. Both were treated as torts. This is not so today. Because so many torts in the past have now become crimes, modern legal writers, particularly those in the United States, distinguish the two classes by referring to crimes as "public wrongs," or "wrongs against society," and the remainder of tort law as "private wrongs," or "wrongs against the individual."

Tort law and the concepts and principles associated with it have had an interesting historical development in common law countries. In early English law, torts were, for the most part, classified as felonies and non-felonies. Offences which resulted in death, serious injury to another, or were "outlaw" in nature, were open to a private prosecution of a criminal nature. This prosecution, or "appeal of felony," determined the guilt of the accused, by trial or ordeal by battle, and often the punishment to be endured. All other torts (which were non-felonious in nature) were considered to be trespasses to a person or property, and were subject to a payment to the Crown, or to the injured party. Some early 5th century Anglo-Saxon laws provided for both, for example, fines in the form of horses and livestock were sometimes divided between the chief and the victim. The particular difficulty with the early Anglo-Saxon law (if we can call it such) was the fixed penalty which attached to each type of tort. The law generally set a certain fine for a specific act, regardless of the seriousness or the extent of the injuries suffered, and it was not until after the Norman Conquest that this changed.

The appearance of the Court of King's Bench brought with it the *writ of trespass*, which allowed a person who had suffered a non-felonious injury to seek redress in the king's court. The injured party, by way of the writ, would allege that the defendant had committed a breach of the king's peace by his injury to the plaintiff, and in this manner provide the court with jurisdiction to hear the case. The allegation of a breach of the king's peace was essential with the early writs of trespass, as the court would otherwise not have authority to deal with the matter. Once the allegation had been made, however, the court would hear the dispute, and if the plaintiff had been able to prove his allegations, award the plaintiff damages for his injury as well as impose a fine on the defendant for the breach of the king's peace. The particular advantage of this method over the Anglo-Saxon system was the ability of the plaintiff to use the power of the court to enforce the judgement, a device that was not previously available. Although the writ of trespass initially covered all torts which involved a breach of the king's peace, by the end of the 13th century the forms of the writ had become very formal. Plaintiffs seeking to obtain redress were now required to bring the action within one of the specific writs recognized by the courts. The most common of these forms were trespass to the person, trespass to real property, and trespass to goods. In each of these cases, it was necessary for the plaintiff to show that the defendant had caused some injury by a direct and wilful act. The court, generally, was not interested in the extent of the damage caused by the defendant, but rather, whether the defendant had done a wilful or intentional act to injure the plaintiff.

This strict approach of the law led the Court of Chancery to expand the area of tort beyond the formal writs to include many actions which did not fit into the established writ structure. It was chancery, for example, that issued writs of trespass that did not allege a breach of the king's peace, and it was chancery that eventually allowed a plaintiff to recover from a defendant where the defendant's act which caused the injury was not wilful, but careless or thoughtless.

Eventually, actions for damages which did not fit the formal writs of trespass were heard by the court as actions for *trespass on the case*. These actions permitted the court to hear a wide variety of torts which would otherwise not fit under one of the formal writs. Actions for deceit, nuisance, and eventually negligence, were treated in this fashion.

The earliest tort cases tended to reflect the injuries which a plaintiff of that era might suffer: violent assault and battery, the seizure of one's goods, or the slander of one's name. As time passed, the scope for redress enlarged to encompass the changes that took place in society, and by the end of the 14th century, the concept of a duty of care to others had emerged. With it, one of the important ingredients of modern negligence law emerged, even though the theory of negligence liability did not emerge in its modern form until the 19th century, some 500 years later.

THE NATURE OF TORT LAW

Tort law, by and large, is an attempt by the courts to cope with the changes that take place in society, and to balance as best they can individual freedom of action with protection or compensation for the inevitable injury to others that the exercise of such freedom occasionally produces. The development of the law of torts is essentially the development of the principles and legal fictions used by the courts to effectively maintain some sort of equilibrium between these two individual desires in an ever-increasingly complex society.

Today, the scope of the law of torts has broadened to the point where it encompasses a great many areas of human endeavour, yet, for all of its applications to modern-day activity, many of the principles and concepts date back to much simpler earlier times when the courts first saw the need to remedy a wrong.

THE CONCEPT OF TORT LIABILITY

Early Concepts: Strict Liability

The basic premise upon which tort liability is founded is that individuals living in a civilized society will not (and should not) intentionally cause injury to one another or their property. This particular assumption is based upon the public policy that every person is entitled to protection of their person; if anyone should do a deliberate act which injures them or their property, then the injured party should be entitled to redress from the person causing the injury. The torts of assault and battery, and false imprisonment are notable examples of deliberate acts which injure others, and ones which the courts will recognize as actionable torts.

Initially, under tort theory, only deliberate, direct injury was open to action, and the application of the law was equally direct in its application. If a person intentionally caused injury to another, compensation according to a fixed amount (based upon a prescribed schedule) was payable.[2]

No consideration was given to the actual loss suffered by the plaintiff; the only concern of the court was that a direct injury had occurred. In effect, the early courts imposed *strict liability* in dealing with deliberate acts which caused injury to others—no inquiry was made into the circumstances surrounding the event.

Over time, the courts gradually moved away from the strict-liability approach to torts, and considered other factors as well. Some torts, however, remained subject to strict liability. Today, any person who maintains a potentially dangerous animal or thing on his land may be held strictly liable for any damage it may occasion should it escape. This may be the case even where the land-owner does everything in his power to protect others from injury, and where the escape of the dangerous animal or chattel is not due to any act or omission on his part. For example, in order to have a supply of water for the purpose of operating his mill, Rylands built a water reservoir on land which he occupied. He employed competent engineers and contractors to construct the reservoir, and when the reservoir was completed, began filling it with water. Unknown to Rylands, the land under the reservoir was a part of a coal mine which was being worked by Fletcher. Water from the reservoir found its way into the old shafts and passageways in large quantities, and flooded areas of the mine some distance away where Fletcher was working. Fletcher sued Rylands for damages. The court held in this case that Rylands was liable for the damage caused to Fletcher even though Rylands did nothing to deliberately harm Fletcher. The court, in reaching its decision, stated that anyone who accumulates anything on his land which might injure his neighbour does so at his peril, and if it should escape through no fault of his own, he should nevertheless be liable.[3]

This form of liability, which is neither based upon intent nor negligence, remains largely because the conduct, while not wrongful or improper, is so inherently dangerous or so unusual that any risk as-

[2]For example, during the late 6th and early 7th centuries, a detailed *Tariff of Compensations* was established which fixed the amount to be paid for wrongs or injuries. If an ear was lacerated, the price of the injury was 6 shillings: see Attenborough, F.L., *The Laws of The Earliest English Kings* (University Press, 1922: Cambridge, England), pp. 2-17.

[3]See *Rylands v. Fletcher* (1868), L.R. 3 H.L. 330.

sociated with it should be borne entirely by the individual wishing to proceed with it upon his property. The same principle is sometimes applied where one person controls the activity of another to such an extent that the act of one may be attributed to the other. In these cases, the courts carry the liability for the tort back to the person who (in a sense) initiated the act, and in this manner impose liability on a person not directly associated with the tortious act. At common law, an employer is considered to be vicariously liable for the torts of his employees, provided that the torts are committed by the employees in the course of the employer's business. Similarly, all partners in a partnership are vicariously liable for the torts committed by a partner in the conduct of partnership business. In a similar vein, provincial statute law has imposed a vicarious liability on the owner of a motor car, where the driver of the vehicle is negligent in its operation.

The imposition of liability on persons not directly associated with a tort reflects a departure from the tort theory that the individual who injures another should bear the loss. It also reflects a move from the former *laissez-faire* policy to a new social policy which recognizes that some satisfactory method must exist for the distribution of what is essentially a social loss amongst those best able to bear it. The modern concept of insurance is, for the most part, responsible for this shift in tort liability, and represents a further extension of this philosophy. Similar examples may be found in other statutes which deal with specific areas of tort, such as the various Workmen's Compensation Acts. These Acts essentially spread the risk of loss to workmen injured in employment-related accidents to all employers in an effort to reduce the burden that would otherwise fall on the individual or the employer.

Unintentional Torts and the Duty Not to Injure

A second important tort liability concept gradually developed to cover injuries suffered by persons who were not intentionally injured, but injured nevertheless by the actions or inactions of others. Initially, the liability for unintentional injury was established for persons with specific trades, callings, or professions where their careless conduct or performance of their professed skills injured another. The early cases were generally decided on the basis that the skilled person had failed to carry out his duties in accordance with the skills he professed he had. While these cases imposed a duty of care on persons with particular skills, the actions were not in negligence as such since the modern concept of duty and negligence did not emerge until the 19th century in tort law. What they did do, however, was to eventually shift the preoccupation of the courts *from* the defendant's deliberate action *to* both inaction and action where the intention to injure was not present. This particular shift in tort law broadened the scope for recovery to include not only deliberate acts which injure, but all acts where the cause of injury could be directly attributed to the defendant.

The enlarged area of liability was essentially a response by the courts to the changing needs of society. The early torts were related to a more violent era (where the individual's concern was for the safety of his person, and redress for violent attacks by others) but as society became more civilized the need for protection from violence lessened. The more sophisticated human endeavours associated with the advances in civilization, however, brought with them new forms of injury which required some form of control. In the light of these changes, the courts took their first steps to enlarge tort liability.

This move on the part of the courts introduced a number of new elements as well. The plaintiff, while no longer limited to cases of deliberate injury, was obliged to establish a duty on the part of the defendant not to injure, and also to satisfy the courts that the proximate cause of the injury was directly related to the breach of duty on the part of the defendant.

Proximate Cause and the Duty of Care

By the early 18th century, the courts considered the conduct of the defendant in cases where the injury to the plaintiff was unintentional. If the evidence indicated that in his actions the defendant had shown a careless disregard for others, then his conduct would be considered culpable. The plaintiff, however, was obliged to establish that the defendant's careless acts were the proximate cause of the injury. The difficulty with both of these elements of tort is obviously the question of degree. Clearly, the defendant should not be expected to answer for every careless act, nor should the cause of the injury, no matter how remote, be traceable to him, regardless of intervening factors. Both proximate cause and conduct were difficult problems for the court because both often represented difficult value judgements.

Proximate cause is perhaps the most difficult element to determine since it is very much a matter which must be decided on a case-by-case basis. Essentially, the act which the plaintiff alleges is the cause of the injury must be related in a relatively direct way to the act of the defendant without intervening events. Any break in the chain of events running from the defendant's act to the plaintiff's injury will normally defeat the plaintiff's claim that the proximate cause was the defendant's act. For example, where a person slips on a neighbour's icy sidewalk and breaks a leg, the neighbour may be liable for injury if the neighbour's failure to remove the ice was the proximate cause of the injury. However, if the injured person is being transported to a hospital to have the broken leg treated, and along the way is severely injured when the ambulance is involved in an accident with another vehicle, the neighbour's negligence cannot be said to be the proximate cause of the injuries suffered as a result of the motor vehicle accident. The intervening event of driving the person to the hospital is sufficient to break the direct link between the neighbour's action (or inaction) and the traffic accident.

The concept of a duty of care on the part of the defendant is no less easy a matter to determine. As an element of tort liability, the duty not to injure must be more than simply a moral obligation—it must be a duty which the person causing the injury owes to the injured party. This is sometimes referred to as the *right–duty relationship* in tort law. Generally, under this relationship, the duty not to injure must be owed to the party who suffers the injury; in turn, the injured party must have a legal right that has been violated by the act or omission of the other. For example, a taxi-driver owes a duty of care to his passengers, and the passengers have a right to safe transportation to their destination. A breach of the duty of care by the driver that results in an injury to the passengers would violate their right to safe transportation, and be actionable as a tort.

Much of the law relating to negligence is based upon the concept of duty of care; to this end the courts have extended their investigation of the circumstances surrounding a tort by attempting to determine the foreseeability of the defendant's actions.

The Concept of Foreseeability: The Reasonable Man

Foreseeability as an element of tort liability was a particularly difficult concept for the courts to apply due to its nebulous nature. Foreseeability was essentially a standard which had to be determined before damages for an unintentional act could flow, yet it had to be flexible enough to be applicable to a wide variety of actions. The courts eventually seized upon a mythical person, the "reasonable man," as a standard, and measured the actions of the negligent person against him. The "reasonable man" was presumed to possess normal intelligence, and exercise reasonable care in his actions toward others. This became the standard which determined the foreseeability aspect of negligence. Tort liability was (and still is) determined by asking the question: Would a reasonable man in similar circumstances have foreseen the injury to the plaintiff as a consequence of his actions? An affirmative answer would place the defendant at fault; a negative answer would render the defendant blameless.

The concept of the "reasonable man" (or reasonable person) permitted the courts to deal with a great many torts where the unintentional acts of a person caused injury to others. It also permitted the courts to establish broad guidelines for the standard of care that a person could reasonably expect to meet in the conduct of activities which had a potential for injury to others. Nevertheless, this tort concept is by no means easy to apply, as parties in tort actions frequently possess widely divergent views on whether a reasonable man would or would not foresee the result of his actions given the circumstances surrounding the case. The particular advantage of the tort concept lies in the flexibility which it gives the courts in responding to social change. In spite of the growing complexity of modern civilization, the test remains relevant as the standard can vary with the passage of time; the reasonable person acquires the degree of sophistication dictated by society itself.

Res Ipsa Loquitur

One of the particular difficulties that sometimes faces a person injured by the negligence of another is proving the negligent act. In some cases, the injured party is unaware of how the injury occurred, or what the act of the other party was that resulted in his loss. For example, a passenger on an aircraft has a right to expect a safe flight to his destination, but if the aircraft should crash on landing, and the passenger is seriously injured, can he, as a plaintiff, reasonably be expected to satisfy the courts that certain specific acts of the pilot constituted negligence? Only the pilot or the flight crew would know the circumstances that led to the crash which caused injury to the passengers. This dilemma of the injured plaintiff first came before the courts in an English case[4] in the mid-19th century, when a person standing in the street was injured by a barrel of flour that fell from the upper level of a shopkeeper's building. The person sued the shopkeeper for his injuries, but could do nothing more than relate the facts of the case available to him, and plead *res ipsa lo-*

---

[4]*Byrne v. Boadle* (1863), 2 H. & C. 722, 159 E.R. 299.

quitur (the thing speaks for itself). The court accepted this line of reasoning and ruled that since the plaintiff had established that he was injured by the defendant's barrel of flour, it was now up to the defendant to satisfy the court that he was not negligent in the handling of the barrel.

Since this decision, the rule or principle of *res ipsa loquitur* has been applied in a wide variety of negligence cases where the plaintiff has been unable to ascertain the particular circumstances surrounding the injury inflicted. For the rule to apply, however, the cause of the injury must be something which is exclusively in the care and control of the defendant at the time of the injury, and the circumstances surrounding the accident must be unusual in the sense that they constitute events that do not ordinarily occur if proper care has been taken by the defendant. If the plaintiff is in a position to satisfy the courts on these two points, the burden of proof then shifts to the defendant to show that he was not negligent; otherwise he will be held liable for his apparent actions.

Contributory Negligence and Volenti Non Fit Injuria

A final development in tort law relating to negligence occurred when the courts expanded their examination of the circumstances surrounding a tort to include the actions of the injured party. One of the earliest defences raised by a defendant in a negligence case was the argument that the injuries suffered by the plaintiff were due in some measure to his own carelessness, or to his voluntary assumption of the risk of injury by undertaking the activity which resulted in the injury. Both of these defences, if accepted by the courts, would allow the defendant to escape liability even in those cases where the defendant was, for the most part, responsible for the loss or injury suffered by the plaintiff.

The voluntary assumption of risk (*volenti non fit injuria*) and contributory negligence defences have been subject to much modification by both common law and statute law. Today, they represent only mitigating factors, rather than complete defences to claims of negligence. Initially, these two doctrines were the product of the early *laissez-faire* individualism prevalent in the 19th century, and were based upon the premise that the law should not protect those who were capable of protecting their own interests, and in particular should not protect those who were prepared to assume the risk of loss or injury on a voluntary basis.

Unfortunately, the rigid application of the law resulted in hardships for the plaintiff in cases where the plaintiff was responsible in only a very minor way for the injury or loss sustained. An attempt to mitigate the harshness of the rule appeared in the form of the doctrine of *last clear chance*. This doctrine permitted the plaintiff to succeed where it could be shown that even though the plaintiff was partly responsible for the injury, the defendant had the "last clear chance" to prevent the injury that the plaintiff suffered.

At first glance, the doctrine of last clear chance appeared to be the panacea sought after by negligent plaintiffs, but it soon became apparent that it had all the attributes of a double-edged sword. It was also used by defendants to support their claims of contributory negligence on the part of the plaintiff, and it imposed an additional obligation on the plaintiff by requiring the plaintiff to show that the defendant was not only entirely responsible for the injury, but that the defendant was the only one with the last opportunity to avoid injury. This was a particularly difficult onus on the plaintiff in automobile accident cases where the actions causing injury were often instantaneous, and the person with the last clear chance was most difficult to determine.

The unsatisfactory state of affairs which the doctrines of contributory negligence and voluntary assumption of risk had spawned were eventually remedied by statute. In 1924, the Province of Ontario passed legislation[5] which required the courts to determine the degree of responsibility of each of the parties in a tort action, and to apportion the damages accordingly. The rest of the provinces soon

followed suit with similar legislation to provide a general framework for the apportionment of loss in negligence cases in all jurisdictions.

Negligence law remains a major area of tort law, notwithstanding its relatively short history, and is an important part of the law of torts dealing with unintentional interference with individuals and property. There are, however, a number of other principles and doctrines which relate to the law of torts. The development of these particular principles and concepts may be best illustrated by an examination of the specific areas of tort law to which they generally apply. These topics will be examined in the chapters which follow.

[5]*Contributory Negligence Act, 1924,* 1924 (Ont.), c. 32.

SUMMARY   The law of torts is one of the oldest areas of law. It is concerned with injury caused by one person to another, or to their property, where the courts have determined that a duty exists not to injure. Early tort law was largely concerned with the problems of a more violent era: assault and battery, trespass to land, false imprisonment, and slander. The law, however, has developed to deal with some of the more complex wrongs of modern society by establishing a number of principles and doctrines applicable to both old and new forms of tort. Two important principles, the concept of a duty of care, and the standard of the "reasonable man," have made the law flexible in its application. In addition, the development of "foreseeability" as a test for tort liability has been an important advancement in the law. In tort cases, the courts usually attempt to compensate the injured party for the loss suffered insofar as monetary damages permit, but in cases where the injury is caused by the deliberate acts of one party the courts may award punitive damages as well.

DISCUSSION
QUESTIONS

1. *Define "tort."*
2. *Why is the distinction between a moral obligation not to injure and a duty not to injure important?*
3. *Explain a "duty of care" and the importance of this concept in the determination of liability for tort.*
4. *Do the courts still impose strict liability today? If so, provide examples.*
5. *What is meant by "proximate cause" in tort law?*
6. *What is a "reasonable man" in the eyes of the law?*

7. *In what particular ways would the reasonable man and the concept of fore-seeability be related?*

8. *Explain negligence in terms of tort law.*

9. *Explain* res ipsa loquitur.

10. *Define "vicarious liability."*

11. *Does* volenti non fit injuria *still apply in tort law?*

12. *Why was contributory negligence legislation necessary?*

13. *Tort law has been enacted to ensure that the individual who injures another bears the loss. With the aid of examples, explain why vicarious liability represents an exception to this principle.*

14. *Explain why the burden of proof shifts to the defendant when the plaintiff's claim with respect to the tort in question is* res ipsa loquitur.

15. *Describe the duty of care owed by a land-owner to a trespasser who falls into a pit. Would a "reasonable man" have foreseen this? Does trespass involve voluntary assumption of all risks by the trespasser?*

16. *Give a second title for "Tort Liability for Unintentional Injury" as it applies to professionals.*

17. *With your knowledge of intentional and unintentional torts, and the concept of negligence, define "criminal negligence."*

18. *The principle of "double jeopardy" protects an individual from being tried twice for the same crime. Outline why concurrent tort liability is not considered "double jeopardy."*

19. *Postulate a definition of "trespass" acceptable to the first Court of King's Bench.*

20. *Is the concept of the "reasonable man" a vague notion translated into a convenient defence, or is it a profound way of illustrating the defendant's responsibility in any tort? Give examples to illustrate your position.*

||||||||||||||||||||||||||||||||||||||||||||||||||||||||||||||||||||||||||||||||||||||||||||||||||||||||||||||||||||||||||||||||||||||||||

JUDICIAL DECISIONS

Negligence—Duty of Care— Foreseeability of Injury

Nova Mink Ltd. v. Trans-Canada Airlines, [1951] 2 D.L.R. 241.

On a scheduled flight, an aircraft operated by the defendant airline flew south of its usual flight path to avoid clouds and in doing so flew over a mink ranch operated by the plaintiff. The noise of the aircraft caused the female mink to devour their young, and the owner brought an action for damages against the airline.

The evidence indicated that the pilots and the airline were unaware of the location of the ranch, and had not examined an information circular which warned them not to fly low over such operations. Notwithstanding their lack of knowledge of the existence of the ranch, the building which housed the animals had "MINK RANCH" written on its roof in large letters which were clearly visible from the air.

MACDONALD, J. (after reviewing the evidence):

I come now to the vital questions:

Does the evidence establish that the defendant was under a legal duty to use care to avoid injury to the plaintiff's business as a mink ranch operator? If so, was there a breach of that duty by the defendant?

Unless both of these questions are answered in the affirmative, the plaintiff must fail in his action; for it is immaterial that the defendant's conduct caused him loss unless that conduct was wrongful as being a violation of a duty imposed upon the defendant by law.

In considering these questions it is material to keep in mind that the law of negligence has developed through the discharge by Judges and juries of their respective functions. It is the function of the Judge to determine whether there is any duty of care imposed by the law upon the defendant and if so, to define the measure of its proper performance; it is for the jury to determine, by reference to the criterion so declared, whether the defendant has failed in his legal duty. In every case, the Judge must decide the question: Is there a duty of care in this case owing by the defendant to the plaintiff and, if so, how far does that duty extend?

The common law yields the conclusion that there is such a duty only where the circumstances of time, place, and person would create in the mind of a reasonable man in those circumstances such a probability of harm resulting to other persons as to require him to take care to avert that probable result. This element of reasonable prevision of expectable harm soon came to be associated with a fictional Reasonable Man whose apprehensions of harm became the touchstone of the existence of duty, in the same way as his conduct in the face of such apprehended harm became the standard of conformity to that duty.

And so it came about that the initial question of the existence and quantum of duty, though a question of law for the Judge, is to be decided by him by reference to what the notional Reasonable Man would have foreseen in the way of danger or risk in the circumstances and what he would have done about it. In this way it was felt that the question would be decided by reference to a standard of prevision and conduct grounded in normality and practicality rather than in judicial technicality or diversity of view. Thus, in the present case, we are to determine this question by reference to our assumptions as to what the Reasonable Man would have foreseen as to the probable consequences of flying over the defendant's ranch and what he would have done in the circumstances; and to declare, accordingly, whether the defendant was under a duty of care in respect of it or not. . . .

Many attempts have been made to generalize the circumstances which create a legal duty of care. One of the most notable of these was that of Brett M.R. in *Heaven* v. *Pender* (1883), 11 Q.B.D. 503 . . . who stated the test in terms of an appearance of danger of injury arising out of circumstances of physical proximity to the person or property of another. Perhaps most influential has been that stated by Lord Atkin in *Donoghue* v. *Stevenson*, [1932] A.C. at p. 580, who based it on the foreseeable risk of injurious effects to persons who may stand in a contemplated relationship to the defendant so as to be apt to be affected by his acts at a time and place remote from their doing. What is common to both is the idea of *a relationship between parties attended by a foreseeable risk of harm.* . . .

Another influential attempt to state the circumstances which give rise to duty was that of Cardozo C. J. in *Palsgraf* v. *Long Island R. R. Co.* (1928), 248 N.Y. 339, 162 N.E. 99, who based it on relational hazards apparent to the "eye of reasonable vigilance". He held that an act is negligent in relation to others "only because the eye of vigilance perceives the risk of damage", and that even then there is a limitation as to the persons to whom the duty is owed; for "the orbit of the danger as disclosed to the eye of reasonable vigilance would be the orbit of the duty". "The risk reasonably to be perceived defines the duty to be obeyed, and risk imports relation; it is risk to another or to others within the range of apprehension." And, as he was careful to point out, the range of apprehension and the orbit of the duty are affected by the presence or absence of knowledge of any circumstance which in fact increased or diminished the apparent risk. . . .

In short, I hold that the circumstances apparent to the defendant and its servants in this case did not suggest such a probability of harm to the plaintiff's ranch as to give rise to a duty of care to avoid it by any greater distance than ordinary prudence would suggest in the case of an ordinary farm. Indeed, to say that there was such a duty would be futile; for there is no evidence upon which one could define the spatial limits of the duty. There are no data in this case upon which one could found a conclusion as to how far the Reasonable Man (or a reasonable pilot) would keep away from the ranch in order to avoid apprehended harm to the mink even if he knew of their existence and propensities. What is the hearing range or sensitivity of mink to sounds from a plane? What volume (or amplitude or pitch) of noise will frighten them? At what distance may a transit plane pass over them or near them without alarming them? How far does the speed of a plane and particular atmospheric conditions affect the audibility of plane noises from the ground?

To these and similar questions the evidence affords no answer; yet it is the postulate of Duty that it arises out of circumstances of reasonably foreseeable harm *avoidable by reasonable care.*

It would be unthinkable for a Court to hold a litigant bound to take care in respect of a condition of affairs of which the facts give no warning . . .

I hold, therefore, that in law the defendant owed no duty of care to the plaintiff in respect of the harm of which he complains . . .

Nature of Negligence— Foreseeability

Glasgow Corp. v. Muir, [1943] A.C. 448.
Mrs. Alexander, the manageress of a tea-house owned by the Glasgow Corporation granted permission to a party (which included a number of children) to use the tea-house for their picnic when a sudden rainfall forced them indoors. A large urn of tea was brought into the tea-room by two men. As they carried it through a narrow passageway where

children were milling about at a candy counter, one of the men (named McDonald) suddenly released his grip on the handle, and the hot tea spilled from the urn on a number of the children.

An action for damages against the corporation was brought on behalf of Eleanor Muir (one of the injured children).

LORD MACMILLAN:

> My Lords, the degree of care for the safety of others which the law requires human beings to observe in the conduct of their affairs varies according to the circumstances. There is no absolute standard, but it may be said generally that the degree of care required varies directly with the risk involved. Those who engage in operations inherently dangerous must take precautions which are not required of persons engaged in the ordinary routine of daily life. It is, no doubt, true that in every act which an individual performs there is present a potentiality of injury to others. All things are possible, and, indeed, it has become proverbial that the unexpected always happens, but, while the precept alterum non laedere requires us to abstain from intentionally injuring others, it does not impose liability for every injury which our conduct may occasion. In Scotland, at any rate, it has never been a maxim of the law that a man acts at his peril. Legal liability is limited to those consequences of our acts which a reasonable man of ordinary intelligence and experience so acting would have in contemplation. "The duty to take care," as I essayed to formulate it in *Bourhill* v. *Young*, "is the duty to avoid doing or omitting to do anything the doing or omitting to do which may have as its reasonable and probable consequence injury to others, and the duty is owed to those to whom injury may reasonably and probably be anticipated if the duty is not observed." This, in my opinion, expresses the law of Scotland and I apprehend that it is also the law of England. The standard of foresight of the reasonable man is, in one sense, an impersonal test. It eliminates the personal equation and is independent of the idiosyncrasies of the particular person whose conduct is in question. Some persons are by nature unduly timorous and imagine every path beset with lions. Others, of more robust temperament, fail to foresee or nonchalantly disregard even the most obvious dangers. The reasonable man is presumed to be free both from over-apprehension and from over-confidence, but there is a sense in which the standard of care of the reasonable man involves in its application a subjective element. It is still left to the judge to decide what, in the circumstances of the particular case, the reasonable man would have had in contemplation, and what, accordingly, the party sought to be made liable ought to have foreseen. Here there is room for diversity in view, as, indeed, is well illustrated in the present case. What to one judge may seem far-fetched may seem to another both natural and probable. . . .

> . . . The question, as I see it, is whether Mrs. Alexander, when she was asked to allow a tea urn to be brought into the premises under

her charge, ought to have had in mind that it would require to be carried through a narrow passage in which there were a number of children and that there would be a risk of the contents of the urn being spilt and scalding some of the children. If, as a reasonable person, she ought to have had these considerations in mind, was it her duty to require that she should be informed of the arrival of the urn, and, before allowing it to be carried through the narrow passage, to clear all the children out of it in case they might be splashed with scalding water? The urn was an ordinary medium-sized cylindrical vessel of about fifteen inches diameter and about sixteen inches in height made of light sheet metal with a fitting lid, which was closed. It had a handle at each side. Its capacity was about nine gallons, but it was only a third or a half full. It was not in itself an inherently dangerous thing and could be carried quite safely and easily by two persons exercising ordinary care. A caterer called as a witness on behalf of the pursuers, who had large experience of the use of such urns, said that he had never had a mishap with an urn while it was being carried. The urn was in charge of two responsible persons, McDonald, the church officer, and the lad, Taylor, who carried it between them. When they entered the passage way they called out to the children there congregated to keep out of the way and the children drew back to let them pass. Taylor, who held the front handle, had safely passed the children, when, for some unexplained reason, McDonald loosened hold of the other handle, the urn tilted over, and some of its contents were spilt, scalding several of the children who were standing by. The urn was not upset, but came to the ground on its base.

In my opinion, Mrs. Alexander had no reason to anticipate that such an event would happen as a consequence of granting permission for a tea urn to be carried through the passage way where the children were congregated, and, consequently, there was no duty incumbent on her to take precautions against the occurrence of such an event. I think that she was entitled to assume that the urn would be in charge of responsible persons (as it was) who would have regard for the safety of the children in the passage (as they did have regard), and that the urn would be carried with ordinary care, in which case its transit would occasion no danger to bystanders. The pursuers have left quite unexplained the actual cause of the accident. The immediate cause was not the carrying of the urn through the passage, but McDonald's losing grip of his handle. How he came to do so is entirely a matter of speculation. . . .

. . . Yet it is argued that Mrs. Alexander ought to have foreseen the possibility, nay, the reasonable probability of an occurrence the nature of which is unascertained. Suppose that McDonald let go his handle through carelessness. Was Mrs. Alexander bound to foresee this as reasonably probable and to take precautions against the possible consequences? I do not think so. The only ground on which the view of the majority of the learned judges of the First Division can be justified is that Mrs. Alexander ought to have foreseen that some accidental injury might happen to the children in the passage if she allowed an urn containing hot tea to be carried through the passage, and ought, therefore, to have cleared out the children entirely during its transit . . .

With all respect, I think that this would impose on Mrs. Alexander a degree of care higher than the law exacts.

|||||||||||||||||||||||||||||||||||||||||||||||||||||||||||||||||||||||||||||||||||||||||||||||||||||||||||||||||||||||||||||||||||||||||||||||||||||||||||||||||||||||||||||||||||

Duty of Care—Strict Liability— Dangerous Activities

Read v. J. Lyons & Co., Ltd., [1947] A.C. 156.
The defendants operated a factory for the manufacture of high explosive shells for use by the armed forces. The plaintiff was employed by the government as an inspector to examine the shells. While she was on the premises of the defendant, an explosion took place causing her injury. The explosion was not caused by the defendant's negligence. The inspector later brought an action on the basis that the defendants were strictly liable for her injuries.

LORD MACMILLAN:

The action is one of damages for personal injuries. Whatever may have been the law of England in early times I am of opinion that, as the law now stands, an allegation of negligence is in general essential to the relevancy of an action of reparation for personal injuries.

The process of evolution has been from the principle that every man acts at his peril and is liable for all the consequences of his acts to the principle that a man's freedom of action is subject only to the obligation not to infringe any duty of care which he owes to others. The emphasis formerly was on the injury sustained and the question was whether the case fell within one of the accepted classes of common law actions; the emphasis now is on the conduct of the person whose act has occasioned the injury and the question is whether it can be characterised as negligent. I do not overlook the fact that there is at least one instance in the present law in which the primitive rule survives, namely, in the case of animals *ferae naturae* or animals *mansuetae naturae* which have shown dangerous proclivities. The owner or keeper of such an animal has an absolute duty to confine or control it so that it shall not do injury to others and no proof of care on his part will absolve him from responsibility, but this is probably not so much a vestigial relic of otherwise discarded doctrine as a special rule of practical good sense. At any rate, it is too well established to be challenged. But such an exceptional case as this affords no justification for its extension by analogy . . .

The doctrine of *Rylands* v. *Fletcher*, as I understand it, derives from a conception of the mutual duties of adjoining or neighbouring landowners and its congeners are trespass and nuisance. If its foundation is to be found in the injunction *sic utere tuo ut alienum non laedas*, then it is manifest that it has nothing to do with personal injuries. The duty is to refrain from injuring not *alium* but *alienum*. The two prerequisites of the doctrine are that there must be the escape of something from one man's close to another man's close and that that which escapes must have been brought on the land from which it escapes in consequences of some non-natural use of that land, whatever precisely that may mean. Neither of these features exists in the present case. I have already pointed out that nothing escaped from the defendants' premises, and, were it necessary to decide the point, I should hesitate to hold that in these days and in an industrial community it was a non-natural use of land to build a factory on it and conduct there the manufacture of explosives. I could conceive it being said that to carry on the manufacture of explosives in a crowded urban area was evidence of negligence, but there is no such case here and I offer no opinion on the point . . .

. . . It has been necessary in the present instance to examine certain general principles advanced on behalf of the appellant because it was said that consistency required that these principles should be applied to the case in hand. Arguments based on legal consistency are apt to mislead, for the common law is a practical code adapted to deal with the manifold diversities of human life and as a great American judge has reminded us "the life of the law has not been logic; it has been experience." For myself, I am content to say that, in my opinion, no authority has been quoted from case or text-book which would justify your Lordships, logically or otherwise, in giving effect to the appellant's plea. I should, accordingly, dismiss the appeal.

|||||||||||||||||||||||||||||||||||||||||||||||||||||||||||||||||||||||||||||||||||||||||||||||||||||||||||||||||||||||||||||||||||||||||||

Negligence—Standard of Care of a Professional Person

Ostrowski et al. v. Lotto, [1971] 1 O.R. 372.
The defendant, an experienced orthopaedic surgeon, performed an operation on the plaintiff's leg. After the operation, he consulted with two skilled radiologists and another orthopaedic surgeon as to the union of the bones. When he believed the bones to be united he released the plaintiff from hospital. The bones had not properly knitted, however, and as a result, the plaintiff was required to undergo a second operation.

The plaintiff brought an action against the defendant for negligence.
AYLESWORTH, J.A. (after reviewing the evidence):

> The criteria upon which charges of negligence are decided when brought against a professedly skilled person seem to be admirably summarized by McNair, J., of the Queen's Bench Division in his charge to the jury in *Bolam v. Friern Hospital Management Committee,* [1957] 2 All E.R. 118. In dealing with the charges of negligence alleged against the surgeon in that case he told the jury at pp. 121-2:
>> "The test is the standard of the ordinary skilled man exercising and professing to have that special skill. A man need not possess the highest expert skill at the risk of being found negligent. It is well-established law that it is sufficient if he exercises the ordinary skill of an or-

dinary competent man exercising that particular art . . . Counsel for the plaintiff put it in this way, that in the case of a medical man negligence means failure to act in accordance with the standards of reasonably competent medical men at the time. That is a perfectly accurate statement, as long as it is remembered that there may be one or more perfectly proper standards; and if a medical man conforms with one of those proper standards then he is not negligent . . . I referred, before I started these observations, to a statement which is contained in a recent Scottish case, *Hunter v. Hanley* ([1955] S.L.T. 213 at p. 217), which dealt with medical matters, where the Lord President (Lord Clyde) said this:

" 'In the realm of diagnosis and treatment there is ample scope for genuine difference of opinion, and one man clearly is not negligent merely because his conclusion differs from that of other professional men, nor because he has displayed less skill or knowledge than others would have shown. The true test for establishing negligence in diagnosis or treatment on the part of a doctor is whether he has been proved to be guilty of such failure as no doctor of ordinary skill would be guilty of if acting with ordinary care.'

"If that statement of the true test is qualified by the words 'in all the circumstances', counsel for the plaintiff would not seek to say that that expression of opinion does not accord with English law. It is just a question of expression. I myself would prefer to put it this way: A doctor is not guilty of negligence if he has acted in accordance with a practice accepted as proper by a responsible body of medical men skilled in that particular art."

Adopting those criteria as I do and applying them to the case at bar, I must conclude that respondent has failed to prove appellant to have been negligent in any respect. Accordingly, I would allow the appeal with costs, if demanded, set aside the judgment below and direct that judgment go dismissing the action with costs . . .

CASE PROBLEMS FOR DISCUSSION

Case 1

Henry operated a small food-stand at an open-air market where farmers in close proximity to one another had set up makeshift stalls or tables to display their produce. To protect themselves from the hot sun, most had erected canvas or cloth canopies over their tables. The stand operated by Henry was located in the midst of the covered stalls.

For the purpose of cooking a particular delicacy which he sold, Henry had placed a tiny propane-fuelled stove on his table-top, and used it to boil a pot of oil. While he was serving a customer, a youth about 16 years old turned up the flame on the burner, and the oil immediately caught fire. In a frantic attempt to put out the fire, Henry seized the flaming pot and flung it from his food-stand. In doing so, the youth was splashed with flaming oil and was seriously burned when his clothes caught fire.

The pot of burning oil landed in a nearby farmer's stall, and set fire to the canopy which he had placed over it. The farmer kicked the flaming pot out of his stall and into a neighbouring stall where it set fire to a quantity of paper that was used for food packaging.

Before the fire was finally extinguished, three stalls had been destroyed, and both the youth and Henry hospitalized with serious burns.

Discuss the rights and liabilities of the parties involved in this incident.

Case 2

Jason was driving carefully along a street in a residential area when a large white cat jumped from behind a tree and ran in front of his vehicle. Jason, an animal lover, swerved to the left to avoid striking the cat with his automobile, and in doing so, immediately collided with an oncoming car. Both cars were damaged, and the driver of the other car was injured.

Discuss the issues that would be raised in this case if the driver of the car chose to sue Jason for his injuries and the loss he suffered. Render a decision.

Case 3

Basil, aged 14, lived in a large metropolitan city, but spent his summer vacations with his parents at a cottage in a remote wilderness area of the province. On his 14th birthday, his father presented him with a pellet rifle and provided him with instruction on the safe handling of the weapon. The father specified that the gun was only to be used at the cottage. Basil used the pellet rifle to rid the cottage area of rodents during his vacation.

On their return to the city, Basil's father stored the weapon and the supply of pellets in his workshop closet. He warned Basil that he must not touch the rifle until the next summer, but did not lock the cabinet in which the weapon was stored.

One day, when Basil was entertaining a few friends at his home, he mentioned his summer hunting activities, and at the urging of his friends, brought out the pellet gun for examination. Basil demonstrated the ease by which the magazine could be filled, and how the weapon operated. He then emptied the magazine, and allowed his friends to handle it. The gun was returned to him, and as he was replacing it in the cabinet, the weapon discharged. He was unaware that a pellet had remained in the weapon, and that he had accidently charged the gun when he handled it. The pellet struck one of his friends in the eye, and an action was brought against Basil and his parents for negligence.

Discuss the liability (if any) of Basil and his parents, and the defences (if any) which might be raised. Render a decision.

Case 4

In 1959, Anderson purchased a house lot in a suburban area of a large municipality. Brown purchased the adjoining lot. Both Anderson and Brown constructed homes on their respective lots in 1960. In 1961, Anderson planted a hedge of poplar trees on his side of the fence line which marked the boundary between the two lots. The hedge grew rapidly, and by 1970, had reached a height of 20 ft.

On several occasions in 1970, Brown noted tiny poplar shoots in the flower garden that he had established along his side of the boundary line, and he removed the tiny plants with a sharp hoe.

In 1973, small poplar shoots were growing in brown's lawn as well as in his garden, and had become a source of irritation. He complained to Anderson, who told him to take whatever steps were necessary to stop the new trees from growing on his lot.

By 1980, the trees on Anderson's lot were over 30 ft. high, and Brown's lawn and garden had become a mass of small poplar shoots that seemed to grow more vigorously with each cutting.

In June of the same year, Anderson sold his home to Carling. Carling, when informed by Brown of the problem of the encroaching trees, refused to take steps to stop the encroachment.

Brown consulted a horticulturist, and was advised that the only way the problem could be permanently resolved would be to dig out the roots that had encroached on the lot, then block further root encroachment with a concrete barrier. The estimated cost was $2 800.

Identify and discuss the legal issues raised in this case. Indicate, with reasons, the possible outcome of the case if Brown should decide to institute legal proceedings against Carling.

CHAPTER 4

Intentional Interference

INTENTIONAL INTERFERENCE WITH THE PERSON

Interference with the person in tort law includes both wilful and unintentional interference, but for ease in distinguishing between the two, we shall look at each separately. The principal forms of wilful or intentional interference are the torts of assault and battery, and false imprisonment. Both of these torts are ancient and represent breaches of the "king's peace" as well as intentional injury to the person. Today, assault and battery constitute a criminal offence under the *Criminal Code*[1] in both a serious and less serious form, a distinction which has been carried forward for this particular tort since the 13th century. Similarly, false imprisonment is an offence under the *Criminal Code* when it takes the form of kidnapping or abduction.[2] It remains a tort in those instances where persons are restrained without

[1]*Criminal Code*, R.S.C. 1970, c. C-34, ss. 244-246, as amended.
[2]*Criminal Code*, R.S.C. 1970, c. C-34, ss. 247-250.

their consent. Needless to say, the Crown is concerned with the criminal aspects of these torts, but the individual must look to the civil courts for compensation for the injury caused to the person.

Assault and Battery

Assault and battery are frequently considered to be a single tort, but in fact each term refers to a separate tort. *Assault* originally referred to a *threat of violence*, and *battery* to the *application of force* to the person. The distinction between the two torts has become blurred by the passage of time, and today, judges sometimes refer to the application of force as an assault. This evolutionary change is understandable, since an assault usually occurs before the application of force, or accompanies it. The distinction is still important, however, because not every application of force by one person on another is a battery within the meaning of the law. For example, two people passing in a dark and narrow hall may accidentally collide with one another, yet neither are injured or bruised in any way from the contact. Technically, each would have applied force to the other, but each act was not intended to cause harm, and this would distinguish the unintentional act from a battery. For the battery in this case to be actionable, it must be something more than the mere application of force. The force must be applied with the intention of causing harm; where it does not cause harm, it must be done without consent, in anger, or accompanied by a threat of injury or violence in order to constitute a tort.[3]

An assault, however, need not be accompanied by the application of force to be actionable. In an early case, a man hammered on a tavern door with a hatchet late one night, and demanded entry. When the plaintiff told him to stop, he struck at her with the hatchet but missed. He caused her no harm, but was held to have made an actionable assault.[4] In a more modern case which involved a plea of self-defence, the defendant was driving his car close to the rear of the plaintiff's vehicle. After the two cars stopped, the plaintiff got out of his car and shook his fist at the defendant. The plaintiff's actions were held to be an assault.[5]

Of course, assault and battery need not be violent. It is sufficient for it to be any situation that involves the touching of a person without consent in such a way that the recipient of such action is injured. In a number of recent cases, surgeons have been found liable for battery where they failed to inform their patients of the risks involved in operations,[6] or where they used experimental techniques without fully explaining the risks to the patients.[7]

The damages which a court may award in assault and battery cases are designed to compensate the plaintiff for the injury suffered, but in many cases, particularly where the attack on the plaintiff is vicious and unprovoked, the court may award punitive or exemplary damages as well. The principal thrust of these awards is to

[3]*Cole v. Turner* (1705), 6 Mod. 149, 87 E.R. 907.

[4]*I De S and M v. W De S* (1348), Year-Book. Liber Assisarum, folios 99, pl. 60.
[5]*Bruce v. Dyer*, [1966] 2 O.R. 705; affirmed [1970] 1 O.R. 482.
[6]*Reibl v. Hughes* (1977), 16 O.R. (2d) 306.
[7]*Zimmer et al. v. Ringrose* (1979), 89 D.L.R. (3d) 646.

deter the defendant from any similar actions in the future, and to act as a general deterrent for the public at large.

In some cases of assault and battery, a defendant may raise the defences of provocation or self-defence, but each defence is subject to particular limitations imposed by the courts. Generally, the defence of provocation will only be taken into consideration in determining the amount of punitive damages which may be awarded to the plaintiff. As a defence, it would not absolve the defendant from liability. Self-defence, on the other hand, may be a complete defence if the defendant can satisfy the court that he had a genuine fear of injury at the hands of the plaintiff, and that he only struck the plaintiff to protect himself from a threatened battery. Normally, the courts also require the defendant to establish that the amount of force used by him was reasonable and necessary under the circumstances.[8]

||||||||||||||||||||||||||||||||||||||||||||||||||||||||||||||||||||||||||

CASE 4.1
MacDonald v. Hees (1974), 46 D.L.R. (3d) 720.

COWAN, C.J.T.D.:

It is quite clear that the application of force to the person of another, without lawful justification, amounts to the wrong of battery: *Eisener v. Maxwell*, [1951] 1 D.L.R. 816, 28 M.P.R. at p. 213 [reversed [1951] 3 D.L.R. 345, 28 M.P.R. 213], Ilsley, C.J. (N.S.S.C.), at p. 823; *Salmond on the Law of Torts*, 16th ed. (1973), p. 122. In *Mann v. Balaban et al.* (1969), 8 D.L.R. (3d) 548, [1970] S.C.R. 74, Spence, J., said at p. 558:

"In an action for assault, it has been, in my view, established that it is for the plaintiff to prove that he was assaulted and that he has sustained an injury thereby. The onus is upon the plaintiff to establish those facts before the jury. Then it is upon the defendant to establish the defences, first, that the assault was justified and, secondly, that the assault even if justified was not made with any unreasonable force and on those issues the onus is on the defence."

In my opinion, the same rule applies in a case involving not assault, but battery. In *Salmond, op. cit.*, at p. 124, it is said that:

"The act of putting another person in reasonable fear or apprehension of an immediate battery by means of an act amounting to an attempt or threat to commit a battery amounts to an actionable assault."

At p. 123, it is stated that:

"Fear in the sense of alarm is not an essential ingredient of the tort of battery. Indeed, not even apprehension of the infliction of force is required; a blow from behind is a battery."

||||||||||||||||||||||||||||||||||||||||||||||||||||||||||||||||||||||||||

False Imprisonment
False imprisonment is the second type of intentional interference with the person that Canadian courts will recognize as a tort. As an actionable civil wrong, it represents any restraint or confinement of the individual by a person who has no lawful right to restrict the freedom of another. It most often arises where a shopkeeper seizes and holds a person suspected of taking goods from his shop, only to discover later that he has apprehended an innocent person. In such cases, the imprisonment need not involve the actual physical restraint of the suspect. It is sufficient if the shopkeeper makes it clear to the suspect that any attempt to leave the premises will result in the embarrassment of seizure, or pursuit accompanied by calls for help.

The law, as a matter of public policy, usually views the restraint of one individual by another with disfavour, and the defences available to the defendant are

[8]*Veinot v. Veinot* (1978), 81 D.L.R. (3d) 549.

meagre. Generally, a person may restrain another where the person apprehended is in the process of committing a crime, or where a person attempting to seize the criminal mistakenly apprehends the wrong person. In the latter case, however, the person falsely seizing the innocent person must have reasonable and probable grounds for believing that the innocent person had committed an offence, otherwise, it would be no defence to a claim of false imprisonment.[9] Peace officers, of course, may mistakenly restrain innocent persons without committing the tort of false imprisonment or false arrest, provided they had reasonable grounds for believing the person was an offender at the time of the restraint.[10]

INTENTIONAL INTERFERENCE WITH A PERSON'S REPUTATION

The law of tort which relates to the interference with a person's reputation is called *defamation*. Defamation may take the form of either libel or slander. *Slander* generally consists of false statements or gestures which injure a person's reputation. *Libel* takes the form of printed or published slander. Defamatory statements which slandered a person's good name or reputation were originally dealt with as moral matters by the old ecclesiastic courts, but with the passage of time, fell under the jurisdiction of the common law courts. Before the introduction of printing, defamation took the form of slander. This was largely a "localized" injury, but with the invention of printing, the extent of the injury changed both in terms of geographical limits and permanency. The printed word was capable of

widespread circulation, and thus spread the scandal over a larger area. In addition, it provided a permanent record of the defamation that would remain long after slanderous statements would normally be forgotten. The criminal aspects of the printed defamation (libel) originally fell within the jurisdiction of the English Court of the Star Chamber, where the person who published a libel was punished both criminally as well as civilly for the tort. When the Star Chamber court was abolished in 1641, the jurisdiction fell to the common law courts.

Generally, in a defamation action the plaintiff must establish that the defendant's statements have seriously injured his reputation; otherwise, the court will award only nominal damages. If the defendant's statements are true, the plaintiff will not succeed, as the truth of the statements will constitute a good defence to the plaintiff's claim.

Qualified and absolute privilege are also recognized by the court as defences to a claim for defamation. In certain cases, it is in the public's interest to allow defamatory statements to be made. Consequently, statements made in Parliament, before Royal Commissions, in court, and at coroner's inquests are not subject to an action for defamation by a person injured by the statements. In a recent case, it was held that in any proceeding of a *quasi-judicial* nature the defence of absolute privilege also applied.[11]

In some instances, a qualified privilege may also apply where the defendant can show that the statements were made in good faith and without malicious intent, even though the facts which he believed to be true at the time were subsequently

---

[9]*Criminal Code*, R.S.C. 1970, c. C-34, s. 449.
[10]*Criminal Code*, R.S.C. 1970, c. C-34, s. 450.

[11]*Voratovic v. Law Society of Upper Canada* (1978), 20 O.R. (2d) 255.

proven to be false. The most common example of this situation would be where A provides a letter of reference containing derogatory statements (which he believes to be true, and which he honestly believes are a fair assessment) of B. The justification for these exceptions is based upon the importance of allowing free speech on matters of public importance, and balancing this intent with the protection of the individual's reputation.[12] Some provinces now have legislation dealing with the action of libel and slander; to some extent, this legislation has modified the common law.[13]

||||||||||||||||||||||||||||||||||||||||||||||||||||||||||||||||||||||

CASE 4.2
Stopforth v. Goyer (1979), 23 O.R. (2d) 696.
JESSUP, J.A.:

[The defence of qualified privilege] is succinctly stated in 24 Hals., 3rd ed., pp. 56-7:

"100. . . . An occasion is privileged where the person who makes a communication has an interest or a duty, legal, social or moral, to make it to the person to whom it is made, and the person to whom it is so made has a corresponding interest or duty to receive it.

. . . . .

"101. . . . A reason for holding any occasion privileged is the common convenience or the welfare of society, and it is not easy to mark off with precision those occasions which are from those which are not privileged or to define what kind of social or moral duty or what measure of interest will make the occasion privileged. . . . The trend of the modern decisions is in the direction of a more liberal application or interpretation of the rule."

In my opinion the electorate, as represented by the media, has a real and *bona fide* interest in the demotion of a senior civil servant for an alleged dereliction of duty. It would want to

know if the reasons given in the House were the real and only reasons for the demotion. The appellant had a corresponding public duty and interest in satisfying that interest of the electorate. Accordingly, there being no suggestion of malice, I would hold that the alleged defamatory statements were uttered on an occasion of qualified privilege.

||||||||||||||||||||||||||||||||||||||||||||||||||||||||||||||||||||||

INTENTIONAL INTERFERENCE WITH LAND AND CHATTELS

Intentional interference with land and chattels are matters which relate to property law, but also contain an element of tort liability. The two principal classes of torts that relate to property law are trespass to land, and conversion of goods. In both of these cases (as with assault and battery, and false imprisonment), there is an element of intention associated with the act of interference.

Trespass to Land
The law relating to trespass to land represents one of the oldest actionable torts. It is the act of entering on the land of another without the express or implied consent of the person in lawful possession. It is also trespass if a person, once given permission to enter on the lands, refuses to leave when requested to do so.[14] This tort is relatively broad in its application, and includes any deliberate interference with the land as well. For example, the acts of tunnelling under another's land without permission or lawful right, erecting a wall or fence on another's land, or stringing wires or lines over another's land all constitute trespass. Involuntary entry on the lands of another, however,

[12]*Stopforth v. Goyer* (1979), 23 O.R. (2d) 696.
[13]See, for example, *Libel and Slander Act*, R.S.O. 1980, c. 237.

[14]"The Six Carpenters Case" (1610), 8 Co. Rep. 146, 77 E.R. 695.

would not constitute trespass, as the act of entry would be unintentional.[15]

Much of the law relating to trespass is well settled due to its long period of existence, but occasionally new forms of technology give rise to new claims in trespass. The invention of the airplane and radio both resulted in actions for trespass by property owners, although no such cases have apparently been reported in Canada. In any event, the control of both activities by government regulatory bodies have, for all intents and purposes, removed them from the realm of actionable trespass.

|||||||||||||||||||||||||||||||||||||||||||||||||||||||||||||||||||||||||||

CASE 4.3
Atlantic Aviation Ltd. v. Nova Scotia Light & Power Co. Ltd. (1965), 55 D.L.R. (2d) 554.

MACQUARRIE, J.:

The question of the right of the landowner in relation to the rights, if any, in air space has been the subject of both legislation and judicial decision in the United States.

Fleming on Torts, 2nd ed., refers on pp. 47-8 to the four solutions set forth by the American Courts:

"There are no English or Australian decisions which have explored the transient and harmless use of air-space over private land, but the preceding case law is not opposed to the right of flight at reasonable height which does not impair the enjoyment of subjacent soil. Indeed, such *dicta* as have adverted to the question support this view. The use of aircraft has become of such social importance that it is idle to speculate whether the courts might not inhibit it by an extravagant application of the *ad coelum* maxim; the question is rather how to adjust, with the least friction, the conflict between the competing claims of aircraft operators to reasonable scope for their activities and of land-

owners to unimpaired enjoyment of their property.

"In the United States, four solutions have been put forward. First, that it is trespass only to fly within the zone of the land-owner's 'effective possession' or such altitude up to which he might in the future make effective use of the air-space. Secondly, that there is no trespass unless the flight occurs within the zone of the land-owner's *actual* use. This view, in effect, eliminates any concept of technical trespass justifying the recovery of nominal damages, and confers protection only against actual and substantial injury to the land-owner in the enjoyment of the surface. Thirdly, that flight of aircraft is not trespass at all but that the proper remedy is in nuisance or negligence. This approach is practically identical with the second, except that it might forestall recovery for an isolated act, since nuisance ordinarily involves continuity or recurrence. Fourthly, that flight at any altitude is trespass save for a privilege of reasonable flight, analogous to the public right of navigation on navigable rivers. On this basis, an aviator is protected if he traverses the air-space of another for a legitimate purpose, in a reasonable manner and at such height so as not to interfere unreasonably with the possessor's enjoyment of the surface and the air-space above it, but he cannot enjoin the surface owner from putting up a structure, like a transmission line, which has the effect of preventing the landing of aircraft at a near-by aerodrome."

|||||||||||||||||||||||||||||||||||||||||||||||||||||||||||||||||||||||||||

Conversion and Wilful Damage to Goods

The intentional interference with the goods of another constitute the torts of conversion or trespass to goods. *Conversion* is the wrongful taking of the goods of another, or where the goods lawfully come into the possession of the person, the wilful refusal to deliver up the goods to the lawful owner. For the tort of conversion to exist, the lawful owner must be denied

---

[15]*Smith v. Stone* (1647), Style 65, 82 E.R. 533.

possession and enjoyment of the goods, and the defendant must retain the goods without colour of right. The remedy granted by the courts is usually monetary damages equal to the value of the goods.

The second form of trespass to goods involves the *wilful damage* to the goods while they are in the possession of the owner. (For example, the deliberate smashing of the windshield of a person's automobile while it is parked in a parking-lot, or the deliberate act of killing a farmer's livestock.) Both of these torts normally have a criminal element attached to them, and while a great many of these cases reach the criminal courts, the widespread use of insurance to protect against loss of goods through conversion or wilful damage has reduced the number of tort actions that might otherwise come before the courts. The two torts, nevertheless, remain as actionable wrongs.

SUMMARY   Tort law is concerned with the injury which one person causes to another, or to his property. As a result, tort law is not limited to a specific type of injury or activity. Tort law includes the *intentional injury* to another in the form of assault and battery, the *intentional restraint* of a person in the form of false imprisonment, and *injury* to a person's reputation in the form of libel and slander.

Intentional injury to a person's reputation is called defamation, and may take the form of slander (verbal defamatory statements) or libel (published statements of a defamatory nature). Both are torts, but libel is the more serious of the two due to the permanency of its nature.

Trespass to land is a form of intentional injury which involves either the unlawful entrance upon the land of another, or wilful damage to the land in some fashion (such as tunnelling under it). Trespass may also include the wilful damage to goods where the act is done deliberately. If the goods are simply retained and the owner is denied possession, the tort is conversion. Any denial of the true owner's title, or any dealing with the goods without colour of right which would deny the true owner possession also constitutes conversion.

DISCUSSION
QUESTIONS

1. Define "civil wrong."
2. Distinguish "assault" from "battery." Why is this distinction made?
3. Must assault and battery always be violent?
4. Describe the function of punitive or exemplary damages. Give two examples that would represent cases where punitive damages might be awarded.
5. Explain "false imprisonment" in the context of a tort.
6. "A peace officer's criteria for arrest is also his defence in a tort action against him for false imprisonment." Explain.
7. Distinguish between "slander" and "libel."
8. Why is libel generally more serious than slander in the eyes of the law?
9. Define and give examples of "qualified" and "absolute" privilege.
10. Explain "trespass to land."

11. *Give an example of "involuntary entry on the lands of another."*
12. *Outline a possible tort involving trespass to land with an aircraft.*
13. *Does false imprisonment always have a criminal aspect to it? Explain.*
14. *To what extent, if any, does libel differ from the publication of a slanderous statement made by a person other than the publisher?*
15. *Define "conversion" and explain how it differs from "theft."*

JUDICIAL DECISIONS
Assault—
Self-defence—
Justification

Bruce v. Dyer, [1966] 2 O.R. 705.

The defendant attempted to pass the plaintiff's car on the highway on a number of occasions, but on each attempt, the plaintiff increased his vehicle's speed to prevent the defendant from re-entering the traffic lane.

After the defendant had followed the plaintiff for some 10 miles, the plaintiff stopped his car on the paved portion of the highway, blocking the defendant's passage. The plaintiff then got out of his car and, gesturing with his fist, walked back to the defendant's car. The defendant got out of his car, and when the parties met, the defendant struck the plaintiff on the point of his chin, causing a serious fracture to his diseased jaw. The plaintiff brought an action against the defendant for damages for assault.

FERGUSON, J. (after reviewing the facts):

> The question for decision, therefore, is whether Dr. Dyer is liable in damages for the assault suffered by the plaintiff.
>
> The law concerning assault goes back to earliest times. The striking of a person against his will has been, broadly speaking, always regarded as an assault. It has been defined in the 8th American Edition of *Russell on Crime* as "An attempt or offer with force and violence to do a corporal hurt to another". So an attempted assault is itself an assault; so an attempt to strike another is an assault even though no contact has been made.
>
> Usually, when there is no actual intention to use violence there can be no assault. When there is no power to use violence to the knowledge of the plaintiff there can be no assault. There need not be in fact any actual intention or power to use violence, for it is enough if the plaintiff on reasonable grounds believes that he is in fact in danger of violence. So if a person shakes his fist at another the person so assaulted may strike back, if he, on reasonable grounds, believes that he is in danger.
>
> When the plaintiff emerged from his vehicle waving his fist, I think the defendant had reasonable grounds for believing that he was about to be attacked and that it was necessary for him to take some action to ward it off.
>
> In *Salmond on Torts*, 8th ed., p. 373, the following passage appears based on *R. v. St. George* (1840), 9 Car. & P. 483, 173 E.R. 921:
>
> > "There need be no actual intention or power to use violence, for it is enough if the plaintiff on reasonable grounds believes that he is in danger of it."

More modern cases point out that even if it later appears that no violence was intended, it is sufficient if the defendant or a reasonable man think that it is intended.

Bruce had not only emerged from his vehicle shaking his fist but in addition he blocked the defendant's passage on the road. In my opinion that blocking action on his part was an assault.

. . . . .

If the plaintiff in the case at bar had left his auto in some place where subsequently it had blocked the defendant's way, I have no doubt that the proper remedy would be an action on the case, but when, as here, he drove his car to a position on the roadway to block the defendant's vehicle, he took active steps to block the defendant and so committed an assault upon him. The defendant was then justified in defending himself from the assault thus imposed upon him: *Re Lewis* (1874), 6 P.R. (Ont.) 236, where Gwynne, J., illustrates when the action is one for assault or on the case. When a person is assaulted he may do more than ward off a blow, he may strike back: *R. v. Morse* (1910), 4 Cr. App. R. 50.

The right to strike back in self-defence proceeds from necessity. A person assaulted has a right to hit back in defence of himself, in defence of his property or in defence of his way. He has, of course, no right to use excessive force and so cannot strike back in defence of his way if there is a way around. Here, however, the evidence is that the traffic from the rear was such that it would have been a highly dangerous manoeuvre for the defendant to emerge into it, and the *Highway Traffic Act*, at all events, prohibits proceeding off the pavement and on to the shoulder for the purpose of passing. The defendant was effectively blocked for the time being at least.

The law requires that the violence of defence be not disproportionate to the severity of the assault. It is, of course, a fact that severe damage was done to the plaintiff. In my opinion, the plea of self-defence is still valid. The defendant struck one blow only. The law does not require him to measure with nicety the degree of force necessary to ward off the attack even where he inflicts serious injury. This is not a case of "beating up". The defendant was highly provoked by the plaintiff's conduct which was quite unjustified in my view. The plaintiff knew the condition of his own physical state and one would have thought that he would have, for that reason alone, refrained from such highly provocative conduct. He invited the treatment he received.

Defamation—Qualified Privilege—Reasonable Publication

Pleau v. Simpsons-Sears Ltd. (1977), 15 O.R. (2d) 436.

After the plaintiff lost his wallet and credit cards, a number of forged cheques were passed in his name. The local police requested the assistance of the defendant in the apprehension of the thief, and in response, the defendant placed a notice on all cash registers in its store. The notice advised the staff to detain anyone attempting to pass a cheque in the plaintiff's name and "call security." When the plaintiff was advised of the notice by a friend (who saw the notice), he brought an action for defamation against the defendant.

LACOURCIERE, J.A.:

I have had the privilege of reading the reasons for judgment prepared by my brother Brooke. With great respect I am unable to agree that there was any error made by the trial Judge when he ruled that the alleged defamatory statements were made on an occasion of qualified privilege.

After careful consideration of the evidence, and taking the view most favourable to the appellant's contention, I am unable to conclude that the publication of warning, allegedly defamatory, went beyond the exigencies of the occasion. The wording of the notices identified the appellant, and requested that any person presenting any cheque in his name be detained and that security be called. The wording was unfortunate, to say the least, and may have supported an innuendo that the appellant was a dishonest person. But the limited publication was clearly on an occasion of qualified privilege within the classic statement of Baron Parke in *Toogood v. Spyring* (1834), 1 C.M. & R. 181, 149 E.R. 1044. The respondent company acted at the request of the local police who asked the appellant to refrain from writing cheques during the period of investigation: it did so in the discharge of a public duty and to assist in the discovery and apprehension of a suspected forger and thief. In addition, the respondent had a private interest to warn its own cashiers, for its protection against the cashing of bad cheques.

In my view, the only question in this appeal is whether the publication complained of went beyond the exigencies of the privileged occasion so as to constitute "publicity incommensurate to the occasion" in the words of Earl Loreburn in *Adam v. Ward*, [1917] A.C. 309 at p. 321.

A similar problem of excessive publicity divided the Court of Error and Appeal in Ontario in *Tench v. Great Western R. Co.* (1873), 33 U.C.Q.B. 8, where placards describing the reasons for the dismissal for alleged dishonesty of the plaintiff, a conductor on the defendant's railway, were posted up in the company's private offices and in the circular books of the other conductors. The Court held that the communication to the employees was privileged; in a six to three division, the majority held that the mode of communication was reasonable and that there was no excess in the publication, although the placards in some of the company's private offices were visible to strangers. The minority found excess in the mode of publication, which was evidence of malice. In the leading judgment, Draper, C.J., of Appeal, said at p. 18:

"Publication so as to reach the company's numerous employees was lawful; the instructions lead to no conclusion that there was on the part of any one a desire to go beyond what was reasonable. The stationmaster's offices or the booking offices in the cases pointed out, appear to me proper places for the notice to reach those to whom it was addressed, and the caution which McGrath was directed to give the employees in regard to these placards, shews a careful intent to do no more than was necessary to convey the information to those who ought to receive it."

It is interesting to note that excessive publication was treated by Richards, C.J., in one of the minority judgments as "independent evidence of malice to go to the jury" (at p. 20), and not as an automatic forfeiture of the protection. This, with respect, is not presently the law, which is now clear that excess publication is a matter for the Judge alone. It is not until the Judge has ruled on the whole question of privilege that the question of malice can arise for the jury's consideration: see *Adam v. Ward*, at p. 321. Here the Judge has, correctly in my view, ruled that the occasion was one of qualified privilege.

The *Tench* case is helpful as an illustration of the obvious conclusion that excess of publication is a matter of degree. As pointed out by Chancellor Spragge, who was one of the dissenting three, at pp. 24-5:

"If the company had published this paper in the public journals of the day, or had caused it to be posted up in the waiting rooms of stations, there could, I apprehend, be no doubt that it would have been a circulation of the paper beyond what was warranted by the occasion; and that it would have been the duty of the Judge to tell the jury that the privilege was lost by reason of the excess in its exercise: that, to borrow the language of Erle, C.J., in *Force v. Warren*, 15 C.B.N.S. 808, the defendants 'were not acting in pursuance of either interest or duty in repeating and circulating in that way the charge contained in the paper; that the defendants were not excusable in regard to this upon either of the grounds upon which the doctrine of privileged communication rests.'

"There are degrees in the excess in which the limit rendered necessary by duty or interest may be overstepped. I have purposely put an extreme case, as a test; but there can, I apprehend, be no doubt that any excess—any excess I mean that is real and substantial—takes the case out of the privilege."

Similarly, in the case under appeal, publication of the impugned notice on a large placard exposed to public view would undoubtedly have removed the qualified privilege of the occasion. One can think of many such excesses. But this was not the case: the photographs exhibited indicate a type-written slip attached to a cash register, obviously for the private information of the cashier. The notices were of reasonable size, unlikely to attract the public's attention. It was not an uncommon practice, as appears from the evidence of the operating superintendent of the store, who testified, at p. 219, that:

"It was in the category of many of the other things, exactly similar things which come to us, a big organization with 40 stores from coast to coast and we have many more at this time, and charge plates were being stolen and credentials and it was a common thing to publish that on a register."

While the burden was on the respondent company in the first instance to establish the existence of a qualified privilege for publication, once established the burden was on the appellant as plaintiff to prove that it had been abused by excessive publication: Prosser, *Law of Torts*, 3rd ed., p. 823. I am of the opinion that the number and size of the notices and their location on the cash registers were reasonable in the circumstances and did not exceed the privilege of the occasion. While the respondent company would have no interest in publishing the notice to the public at large, it would seem to me that it adopted a reasonable and appropriate mode of publication to reach its large, changing staff of cashiers: the visibility of the notices to some members of the public at a limited number of cash registers constituted, at the most, a publication necessarily incidental to the protected publication to the staff.

By returning a general verdict in favour of the respondent, the jury, if they found the words to be defamatory, must be taken to have accepted the theory of the defence placed before them by the trial Judge, to the effect that "the type of note being posted in the location it was" eliminated any suggestion of malice. The respondent's conduct in removing the notices promptly after notification, and publishing an apology indicate its good faith throughout.

CASE PROBLEMS FOR DISCUSSION

Case 1

At his wife's request, Smith purchased a picnic basket at a hardware store in a nearby shopping mall. (The basket was not wrapped by the sales clerk at the conclusion of the transaction.) Smith carried his new basket with him to a supermarket located in the same mall, where he intended to purchase a quantity of grapefruit.

At the produce counter he could not find grapefruit on display, and inquired from the clerk if the store had any in stock. The clerk offered to check in the store-room for him. While he waited for the clerk to return, Smith picked a quantity of grapes from a display case, and ate them. A few moments later, the clerk returned to inform him that all the fruit had been sold.

As Smith left the store, he was seized by the store owner, and requested to return to the owner's office. Smith obediently followed him back inside the store. Once inside the owner's office, the owner accused Smith of theft; then, without further explanation, he telephoned the police.

When the police officer arrived, the store owner informed him that Smith was a thief, and that he had apprehended him just outside the store. Smith admitted stealing the grapes, then to his surprise, he discovered that the owner had apprehended him because he (the owner) thought Smith had stolen the picnic basket.

Both the supermarket and the hardware store sold similar baskets; even on close examination, the products appeared identical. With the aid of the sales clerk at the hardware store, Smith was able to convince the police officer that he had purchased the basket which he had in his possession.

He later decided to bring an action against the owner of the supermarket for false imprisonment.

Discuss the issues raised in this case, and determine the respective arguments of the parties. Render a decision.

Case 2

The plaintiff, a nurse, was injured in a motor vehicle accident and was taken to a local hospital. She was examined by the defendant, who could find no physical injury other than a few minor bruises. She was discharged from the hospital the next day when she admitted that she "felt fine." Within 24 hours after her release, she returned to the hospital. She complained to the defendant of painful headaches, and remained in hospital for a month. During her second stay in hospital she was examined by three neurosurgeons who could find nothing wrong with her.

On her release from the hospital, she instituted legal proceedings against the parties responsible for her automobile accident, and her solicitor requested a medical opinion from the defendant to support her case.

In response to the solicitor's request, the defendant wrote two letters which were uncomplimentary, and which suggested that the plaintiff had not suffered any real physical injury. In addition, the defendant had indicated on the plaintiff's medical records that the plaintiff was suffering from hypochondriasis.

After her discovery of the uncomplimentary letters and medical reports, the plaintiff brought an action against the defendant for libel.

Examine the arguments which might be raised in this case, and identify the defences (if any) to the plaintiff's claim. Render a decision.

Case 3

Gretel was shopping at a large shopping centre, and while walking through the crowded mall area she saw a youth pushing his way through the crowd in what appeared to be an attempt to escape from another man who was following him.

At that time, Gretel was standing near the exit to the building. When the youth finally broke through the crowd and attempted to leave the building, she stepped in front of him to block his path. The youth collided with Gretel, and the two parties fell to the floor. Both the youth and Gretel were injured as a result of the collision.

The youth, as it turned out, was hurrying through the crowd in an attempt to catch a bus, and the older man, who was following him through the crowd, was his father.

Explain this incident in terms of tort law and tort liability.

Case 4

Wilson stored his power lawn-mower in his neighbour's garage. In return for the privilege, he allowed his neighbour to use the lawn-mower to cut his own lawn.

After several years, Wilson's employment required him to take up residence in another city. At the time of his departure, he advised his neighbour that he had leased an apartment in the other city. He made no mention of his lawn-mower.

The neighbour continued to use Wilson's lawn-mower for the balance of the summer, and when Wilson did not return to retrieve his lawn-mower by late autumn, the neighbour used the machine as a trade-in on a snow-blower which he required for his own use.

The next spring, Wilson returned for his power lawn-mower. When he discovered that his neighbour had disposed of it, he brought an action against him for its value.

Discuss the rights of the parties in this case. Explain the nature of the action that Wilson could bring in the court, and render a decision.

CHAPTER 5

Unintentional Interference

UNINTENTIONAL INTERFERENCE WITH THE PERSON OR PROPERTY

Negligence

The difference between intentional and unintentional interference with the person is essentially a matter which relates to the state of mind of the person causing the interference. Intentional interference generally involves a *conscious* mental decision to act in a violent manner towards another; it may or may not involve a verbal threat of violence (or assault) before the actual battery takes place. More often than not, unintentional interference with the person is simply an *omission* on the part of the party causing the injury, or a thoughtless act which injures another. In either case, there is no *mens rea*, or deliberate decision on the part of the person causing the interference to injure the other party. Unintentional interference with the person generally falls under the broad heading of negligence, and while this distinction between negligence and assault and battery is settled today (at least with respect to assault and negligence) it was not always so. As late as 1951 the courts were still attempting to distinguish the two forms of interference.[1]

The number of ways that a person may unintentionally interfere with the person or the property of another are myriad. The negligent operation of a motor vehicle which causes injury or death to a pedestrian, the careless manufacture of a food product which poisons or injures a consumer, or the careless performance of an operation by a surgeon which disables or kills the patient are examples that come to mind. All of these cases have something in common. In each case, one party owes a duty of care not to injure the other in the performance of the act in question. Where a breach of the duty occurs, tort liability (assuming no intervening or extenuating circumstances exist) may follow. In the determination of liability, the essential ingredients are:

(1) the defendant owes the plaintiff a duty not to injure;
(2) the defendant's actions constitute a breach of that duty;
(3) the plaintiff suffers some injury as a direct result of the defendant's actions.

Unfortunately, the duty of care varies depending upon the nature of the activity. The particular duty of care may vary from slight (in the case of the occupier's duty toward a trespasser) to very high (in the case of a person handling explosives). In each case, the duty owed is a matter to be determined by the courts, and is generally subject to the test of "foreseeability," and the standard of the "reasonable man." Whether the defendant has

acted in breach of the duty (once the duty and the breach thereof have been established) is a question of fact to be decided upon from the evidence submitted in the case. Because the principles which apply in the determination of the standard for a duty of care apply to both interference with persons and their property, the more important standards for the specific activities may be discussed together, without differentiation between persons or property.

Duty of Care of Professionals

In general, the person who professes to be a professional must maintain the standard of proficiency, or exercise the degree of care in the conduct of his duties that the profession normally imposes on its members. This does not mean that the professional will not make mistakes, nor does it mean that the results of the professional's efforts will always be perfect. In many professions, the work of the professional requires much skill and judgement, often more closely resembling an "art" than an exact "science." Consequently, a successful malpractice suit against a member of a profession must measure the performance or duty of the particular practitioner with that prescribed by the profession in general, and show in the evidence that the practitioner failed to meet that standard.[2] This is not always an easy thing to do, but in many cases the professional's performance is so far below the standard set for the profession, that the determination of the duty of care and the breach thereof are not difficult.[3] For example, in the course of a ton-

---

[1]*Eisner v. Maxwell*, [1951] 3 D.L.R. 345.

[2]*Karderas v. Clow*, [1973] 1 O.R. 730.
[3]*McCormick v. Marcotte*, [1972] S.C.R. 18.

sillectomy, a surgeon used a number of sponges which did not have strings or tapes attached for easy retrieval from the child's throat. The attending nurse did not do a sponge count before and after the operation. On completion of the surgery, the anaesthetist present suggested that all of the sponges may not have been removed. The surgeon made a cursory search in the child's throat with his forceps, and when he found none, did nothing more to determine the number which were used. The child suffocated and died as a result of a sponge left in its throat.

At trial, the evidence submitted indicated that the surgeon had performed the operation carefully by using the proper techniques and suture. The evidence also indicated that it was not a common practice to use sponges with tapes attached, although some hospitals followed this practice. The surgeon's search at the end of the operation was also a normal practice.

An action in negligence was brought against the surgeon but was dismissed by the trial judge on the basis that the surgeon had followed the same practices as any other careful practitioner. On appeal, however, the court viewed the matter in a slightly different light. It concluded that the surgeon had a duty to make a thorough, rather than routine, search when a fellow professional informed him that he might not have removed all of the sponges. Because he did not employ all of the safeguards available to him, his failure to do so constituted negligence.[4]

Normally, a professional is only responsible in tort to the patient or client, but in recent cases, the courts have held some professionals liable to third parties where the professional's expertise or skill was intended to be relied upon by the third party, and the professional was aware of this fact. Accountants, in particular, have been subject to this extended tort liability, partly because they are generally aware that their statements will be relied upon by third parties, and partly because securities legislation in most jurisdictions imposes a liability on the accountant to third parties if the third party purchases securities based upon negligently prepared financial statements published in a prospectus. Liability to third parties is not unlimited, however, as the professional accountant is generally responsible only to those third parties who the accountant can reasonably expect to rely on the information provided. Liability for negligently prepared financial information is not necessarily limited to the professional accountant–third party relationship, and appears to be applicable to all persons and institutions engaged in providing financial advice.[5]

||||||||||||||||||||||||||||||||||||||||||||||||||||||||||||||||||||||||||||||||

CASE 5.1

Kangas v. Parker and Asquith, [1976] 5 W.W.R. 25.

SIROIS, J.

The medical man must possess and use that reasonable degree of learning and skill ordinarily possessed by practitioners in similar communities in similar cases and it is the duty of the specialist who holds himself out as possessing special skill and knowledge to have and exercise the degree of skill of an average

---

[4]*Chasney v. Anderson*, [1950] 4 D.L.R. 223; affirming [1949] 4 D.L.R. 71; reversing in part [1948] 4 D.L.R. 458.

[5]See, for example, *Hedley Byrne & Co. Ltd. v. Heller & Partners Ltd.*, [1964] A.C. 465; *Goad v. Canadian Imperial Bank of Commerce*, [1968] 1 O.R. 579 (bankers); *Haig v. Bamford*, [1974] 6 W.W.R. 236 (accountants); *Cari-Van Hotel ltd. v. Globe Estates Ltd.*, [1974] 6 W.W.R. 707 (real estate appraisers).

specialist in the field. Vide: *McCormick v. Marcotte*, [1972] S.C.R. 18, 20 D.L.R. (3d) 345. In *Rann v. Twitchell* (1909), 82 Vt. 79 at 84 appears the following comment:

"He is not to be judged by the result nor is he to be held liable for an error of judgment. His negligence is to be determined by reference to the pertinent facts existing at the time of his examination and treatment, of which he knew, or in the exercise of due care, should have known. It may consist in a failure to apply the proper remedy upon a correct determination of existing physical conditions, or it may precede that and result from a failure to properly inform himself of these conditions. If the latter, then it must appear that he had a reasonable opportunity for examination and that the true physical conditions were so apparent that they could have been ascertained by the exercise of the required degree of care and skill. For, if a determination of these physical facts resolves itself into a question of judgment merely, he cannot be held liable for his error."

Vide: *Wilson v. Stark* (1967), 61 W.W.R. 705, varied as to costs 62 W.W.R. 430 (Sask.); *Wilson v. Swanson*, 18 W.W.R. 49, 2 D.L.R. (2d) 193, reversed by [1956] S.C.R. 804, 5 D.L.R. (2d) 113; *Gent v. Wilson*, [1956] O.R. 257, 2 D.L.R. (2d) 160 (C.A.). Lord Hewart C.J. in *Rex v. Bateman* (1925), 41 T.L.R. 557 at 559, 19 Cr. App. R. 8, clearly and succinctly stated the desired standard of care as follows:

"If a person holds himself out as possessing special skill and knowledge and he is consulted as possessing such skill and knowledge by or on behalf of a patient, he owes a duty to the patient to use due caution in undertaking the treatment. If he accepts the responsibility and undertakes the treatment and the patient submits to his direction and treatment accordingly, he owes a duty to the patient to use diligence, care, knowledge, skill and caution in administering the treatment . . . The law requires a fair and reasonable standard of care and competence."

Occupiers' Liability

The owner or occupier of land is not subject to the ordinary rules of negligence with respect to persons entering on land or buildings for reasons which are largely historical. After the Norman Conquest of England, occupiers of land were subject to certain rules of land law which imposed specific duties according to the kind of person entering on the land. Today, the duty of care, in ascending order of importance, applies to: (1) trespassers; (2) licensees; (3) invitees.

The lowest, or least duty of care is required for trespassers. The *trespasser* entering on the occupier's land does so without permission, and consequently, at a certain risk to his person. Historically, the only obligation on the part of the occupier of land has been to avoid deliberately injuring the trespasser. Recent developments in the law, however, have imposed additional obligations on the land-owner. This is so, particularly where small children and "attractive nuisances," such as swimming-pools and dangerous premises, are concerned.[6] In a recent case, an occupier of land in Ontario was held liable for the injuries to the operator of a snowmobile after the operator had trespassed on the lands of the occupier, because the occupier allowed a particular danger to exist with the full knowledge that people used the private road, albeit as trespassers. The Supreme Court of Canada reasoned that the occupier of the land had consented by implication to the use of the land by the operators of snowmobiles. The plaintiff, by reason of the occupier's failure to take steps to prohibit his use, had become a licensee, and was entitled to a warning of any unusual or

---

[6]*City of Glasgow v. Taylor*, [1922] 1 A.C. 44.

hidden dangers.[7] The extended liability which this case imposed upon the occupier of land prompted the Ontario government to rectify the change by introducing legislation which absolves the occupier of land from liability in circumstances similar to those in this case.

The second type of person who may enter upon the lands of another is the licensee. The *licensee* normally enters on the land with either the express or implied consent of the owner, and usually for his own benefit. For example, a person requesting permission to cross the property of a land-owner in order to launch his boat on a lake would be a licensee, since the entry on the lands would be for his own benefit. The duty of the occupier of the land toward the licensee would be to protect the licensee from any concealed dangers of which the occupier had knowledge, and which were in the area where the licensee might be.

An *invitee* is owed the highest duty of care of any of the three classes of persons who enter on the lands of others. An invitee, as the name suggests, is a person who is invited to enter on the lands, usually for the benefit of the occupier. Customers of a store, and patrons of a theatre, for example, are normally classed as invitees even though a specific invitation is not given. The shopkeeper is usually considered to have offered an invitation to the public at large to enter his premises for business purposes unless he has clearly indicated otherwise. The particular duty owed the invitee is to warn or protect the invitee from any unusual dangers or hazards of which the occupier is aware or ought to be aware. The standard applied would likely be that of the

reasonable man in the event of injury to an invitee as a result of a hazard which the occupier was not aware of, but which he might have discovered had he been more diligent.

The provinces of Alberta and British Columbia have eliminated the distinction between licensees and invitees, as the United Kingdom did in 1957. The effect of this change imposes the higher standard of care on occupiers of land for both licensees and invitees; in those jurisdictions the occupier is bound to take reasonable care to protect such persons from injury.

The liability imposed on the occupier does not mean that the invitee (or licensee for that matter) is not required to act in a careful manner once warned of existing dangers. For example, if a patron of a hotel is warned by prominent signs that the floor of the hotel lobby is hazardous because it has just been waxed, a lack of care in crossing the floor which results in an injury to the patron may not entitle the patron to recover from the hotel owner. The courts normally expect the invitee to act in a reasonable and prudent manner when warned of a particular danger or hazard.

||||||||||||||||||||||||||||||||||||||||||||||||||||||||||||||||||||||||||||||||||||

CASE 5.2
Veinot v. Kerr-Addison Mines Ltd. (1974), 51 D.L.R. (3d) 533.
DICKSON, J.:

In *Herrington's* case their Lordships exhaustively considered the nature of the duty owed by occupiers to trespassers. Lord Reid applied a subjective test. He said (p. 899):

"So it appears to me that an occupier's duty to trespassers must vary according to his knowledge, ability and resources. It has often been said that trespassers must take the land as they find it. I would rather say that they must take the occupier as they find him."

[7]*Veinot v. Kerr-Addison Mines Ltd.* (1974), 51 D.L.R. (3d) 533.

and later on the same page:

"So the question whether an occupier is liable in respect of an accident to a trespasser on his land would depend on whether a conscientious humane man with his knowledge, skill and resources could reasonably have been expected to have done or refrained from doing before the accident something which would have avoided it. If he knew before the accident that there was a substantial probability that trespassers would come I think that most people would regard as culpable failure to give any thought to their safety. He might often reasonably think, weighing the seriousness of the danger and the degree of likelihood of trespassers coming against the burden he would have to incur in preventing their entry or making his premises safe, or curtailing his own activities on his land, that he could not fairly be expected to do anything. But if he could at small trouble and expense take some effective action, again I think that most people would think it inhumane and culpable not to do that. If some such principle is adopted there will no longer be any need to strive to imply a fictitious licence."

The test of common humanity was also applied by Lord Morris of Borth-y-Gest (p. 909): "In my view, while it cannot be said that the railways board owed a common duty of care to the young boy in the present case they did owe to him at least the duty of acting with common humanity towards him."

The nature of the duty of care was described by Lord Wilberforce in these words (p. 920): "Again, it must be remembered that we are concerned with trespassers, and a compromise must be reached between the demands of humanity and the necessity to avoid placing undue burdens on occupiers. What is reasonable depends on the nature and degree of the danger. It also depends on the difficulty and expense of guarding against it. The law, in this context, takes account of the means and resources of the occupier or other person in control—what is reasonable for a railway company may be very unreasonable for a farmer, or (if this is relevant) a small contractor."

and by Lord Pearson in these words (p. 922):

"It does not follow that the occupier never owes any duty to the trespasser. If the presence of the trespasser is known to or reasonably to be anticipated by the occupier, then the occupier has a duty to the trespasser, but it is a lower and less onerous duty than the one which the occupier owes to a lawful visitor. Very broadly stated, it is a duty to treat the trespasser with ordinary humanity."

Herrington's case was considered by the Court of Appeal of England in *Pannett v. McGuinness & Co. Ltd.*, [1972] 3 W.L.R. 387. The following excerpt from Lord Denning's judgment aptly expresses, in my opinion, the more salient points a Judge should have in mind when considering intrusions upon land [at pp. 390-1]:

"The long and short of it is that you have to take into account all the circumstances of the case and see then whether the occupier ought to have done more than he did. (1) You must apply your common sense. You must take into account the gravity and likelihood of the probable injury. Ultra-hazardous activities require a man to be ultra-cautious in carrying them out. The more dangerous the activity, the more he should take steps to see that no one is injured by it. (2) You must take into account also the character of the intrusion by the trespasser. A wandering child or a straying adult stands in a different position from a poacher or a burglar. You may expect a child when you may not expect a burglar. (3) You must also have regard to the nature of the place where the trespass occurs. An electrified railway line or a warehouse being demolished may require more precautions to be taken than a private house. (4) You must also take into account the knowledge which the defendant has, or ought to have, of the likelihood of trespassers being present. The more likely they are, the more precautions may have to be taken."

||||||||||||||||||||||||||||||||||||||||||||||||||||||||||||||||||||||||||||||||

Manufacturers' Liability for Defective Products

Before the Industrial Revolution, goods were normally made by craftsmen serving the local population. The Industrial Revolution permitted the mass production of goods and their distribution over a wide area, and this in turn established a remoteness from the ultimate consumer in the distribution system. Under the law of contracts, the seller of goods either expressly or impliedly warrants goods sold by him to be of merchantable quality and to be reasonably fit for the use intended. If a purchaser buys such goods by description and the goods contain a defect, the law allows the purchaser to recover his loss from the vendor. While this aspect of the law of contract will be dealt with in greater detail in subsequent chapters, it is sufficient to say at this point that the law of contracts provides a remedy to the purchaser only if the goods prove to be defective or cause some injury to the purchaser.

The limitation imposed by the law of contracts is that it does not provide a remedy for the user, or the consumer of the goods, if that person is not the purchaser. This particular shortfall of the law was eventually remedied by the law of torts in the United States. The particular case involved the sale of a motor car that contained a defect in its construction which resulted in an injury to the purchaser. The purchaser sued the manufacturer, rather than the seller of the car, and was met by the defence that the manufacturer owed a duty of care only to the immediate purchaser, i.e., the retailer. The court, however, ruled that the duty of care extended beyond the immediate purchaser to the plaintiff, who was the ultimate user of the goods.[8]

English and Canadian courts discussed the duty of care of manufacturers in a number of cases,[9] but it was not until the case of *M'Alister (or Donoghue) v. Stevenson*[10] came before the courts that the issue of responsibility of manufacturers was established. In that case, a friend of the injured plaintiff purchased a bottle of ginger-beer from a shop, and gave it to the plaintiff. The plaintiff, on consuming part of the contents, became seriously ill. The bottle of ginger-beer, unknown to the shopkeeper and the purchaser, contained a decomposed snail which had contaminated the contents. The bottle was made from an opaque glass which prevented a visual examination of the contents by a purchaser, and bore the label of the defendant manufacturer. The manufacturer denied that he owed a duty of care toward the consumer, since the consumer was not a purchaser of the product, but the court decided that the manufacturer had a duty not to injure the consumer of his product, and held the manufacturer liable for the injury suffered by the plaintiff.

In the cases that have followed the *M'Alister (or Donoghue) v. Stevenson* decision, the courts have held that the manufacturer will be liable to the ultimate consumer where it can be shown that he was negligent in the manufacture of the goods,[11] or where the goods had some danger associated with them, and that he failed to adequately warn the consumer of the danger.[12]

In the United States, the liability of the manufacturer is not limited to cases where negligence may be proven, but has been held to be strict, and accordingly, the manufacturer is liable for any injury, regardless

---

[8]*MacPherson v. Buick Motor Co.* (1916), 217 N.Y. 382.

[9]See, for example, *Heaven v. Pender* (1883), 11 Q.B.D. 503; *Le Lievre v. Gould,* [1893] 1 Q.B. 491.

[10]*M'Alister (or Donoghue) v. Stevenson,* [1932] A.C. 562.

[11]*Arendale v. Canada Bread Co. Ltd.,* [1941] O.W.N. 69; *McMorran v. Dominion Stores Ltd. et al.* (1977), 14 O.R. (2d) 559.

[12]*Austin v. 3M Canada Ltd.* (1975), 7 O.R. (2d) 200, but see also, *LEM v. Barotto Sports Ltd. et al.* (1977), 69 D.L.R. (3d) 276.

of the efforts made by him to prevent faulty products from reaching the consumer.[13]

Nuisance

The tort nuisance has been applied to a great many activities which cause injury to land-owners or occupiers, and because of its wide use it is now, to some extent, incapable of precise definition. In practice, it generally refers to any interference with a person's enjoyment of their property, and includes such forms of interference as noise, vibration, smoke, fumes, and contaminants of all sorts which may affect the use of land. Unlike some torts, nuisance is very much dependent upon the circumstances surrounding the interference, or the degree of interference, rather than the fact that the interference occurred.

The courts have long recognized that in the case of nuisance they must essentially balance the reasonable use of land by one person with the decrease in enjoyment that the reasonable use of the property produces for that person's neighbour, and in some cases, the community as a whole. To be actionable then, the interference must be such that it results in a serious decrease in the enjoyment of the property, or it causes specific damage to the land. What is a reasonable use of land is usually determined by an examination of the uses of land in the immediate vicinity. (If an individual insists on making his residence in an area of a city where heavy manufacturing activity is carried on he must expect the reasonable use of adjoining property to include the emission of noise, and perhaps odours, smoke and dust.) The remedies available to the party subjected to the nuisance would be damages, and at the court's discretion, an injunction ordering the defendant to cease the activity causing the interference. Where the nuisance is such that its restraint would be detrimental to the community as a whole, the court, in balancing the two interests, will normally place the interests of the community before those of the individual, and limit the land-owner's remedy to damages. For example, where the issuance of an injunction would have the effect of closing down a mine or smelter upon which the community depends for its very existence, the public interest would dictate that the remedy take only the form of monetary compensation.[14] On the other hand, where the interference is localized, the courts have often considered an injunction to be appropriate as well.[15]

The current concern for the environment, and the difficulty in determining the sources of pollution in a precise manner have prompted all levels of government to establish legislation for the purpose of controlling the sources of many of the more common environmental nuisances which interfere with the use and enjoyment of property. It should be borne in mind, however, that as a tort, nuisance applies to many activities which are not environmental in nature. For example, picketers unlawfully carrying picket signs at the entrances to a hotel have been declared a nuisance by the courts.[16] Similarly, while awaiting the opening of a theatre a queue of patrons who habitually blocked the entrance to an adjoining shopkeeper's premises were held to be a nuisance.[17] These are simply two of the many kinds of nuisances which the courts may

[13]See, for example, *Escola v. Coca Cola Bottling Co. of Fresno* (1944), 150 P. 2d 436.

[14]*Black v. Canada Copper Co.* (1917), 12 O.W.N. 243.
[15]*Russell Transport Ltd. v. Ontario Malleable Iron Co. Ltd.*, [1952] 4 D.L.R. 719.
[16]*Nipissing Hotel Ltd. v. Hotel & Restaurant Employees Union* (1962), 36 D.L.R. (2d) 81.
[17]*Lyons, Sons & Co. v. Gulliver*, [1914] 1 Ch. 631.

recognize as interference with the enjoyment of property.

Because nuisance generally involves a public policy decision, much of the legislation relating to property use at the municipal level is directed to this particular problem. Local zoning laws attempt to place industrial uses and residential uses of land some distance apart to permit the users maximum freedom in the respective uses of their properties, and to minimize the interference of one with the other which might take the form of nuisance. The larger problems of industrial nuisances and the environment are also the subject of increasing control by senior levels of government rather than the courts. The right of the individual to redress for interference with the enjoyment of his property, nevertheless, still remains, for many nuisances which are not subject to statutory regulation.

||||||||||||||||||||||||||||||||||||||||||||||||||||||||||||||||||||||||||||||||

CASE 5.3
Segal et al. v. Derrick Golf & Winter Club (1977), 76 D.L.R. (3d) 746.
BELZIL, J.:

The plaintiffs' major claim is for private nuisance which it seeks to have abated. A private nuisance is described as follows in 28 Hals., 3rd ed., p. 128, para. 158:

"A private nuisance is one which does not cause damage or inconvenience to the public at large but which does interfere with a person's use or enjoyment of land or with some right connected with land."

In Fleming, *Law of Torts*, 4th ed. (1971), at p. 344, private nuisance is further described as follows:

"The gist of private nuisance is interference with an occupier's interest in the beneficial use of his land. The action is thus complementary to trespass which protects his related interest in exclusive possession.

. . . . .

"The interest in the beneficial use of land, protected by the action of nuisance, is a broad and comprehensive notion. It includes not only the occupier's claim to the actual use of the soil for residential, agricultural, commercial or industrial purposes, but equally the pleasure, comfort and enjoyment which a person normally derives from occupancy of land."

That there has been interference with the plaintiffs' pleasure, comfort and enjoyment of their land is clearly established. They are unable to use and enjoy their backyard during the golfing season. Their fears for the safety of their children and for their own safety are well-founded and their home will continue to receive damage from hard-driven golf balls. Their inconvenience is serious and substantial.

As I have previously stated, this interference was entirely foreseeable from the layout of the 14th hole. The defendant as owner and operator of the golf-course has known of this interference at least since 1972, and it has permitted it to continue although it was and is within its power to prevent it by control and supervision which it has over the players using the course.

In the circumstances, the defendant as occupier of the golf-course is liable for the private nuisance to the plaintiffs. In *Sedleigh-Denfield v. O'Callaghan et al.*, [1940] A.C. 880 (H.L.(E.)), Viscount Maugham says, at p. 894:

"In my opinion an occupier of land 'continues' a nuisance if with knowledge or presumed knowledge of its existence he fails to take any reasonable means to bring it to an end though with ample time to do so."

Lord Atkin states, at pp. 896-7:

"For the purpose of ascertaining whether as here the plaintiff can establish a private nuisance I think that nuisance is sufficiently defined as a wrongful interference with another's enjoyment of his land or premises by the use of land or premises either occupied or in some cases owned by oneself. The occupier or owner is not an insurer; there must be something more than the mere harm done to the neighbour's property to make the party responsible. Deliberate act or negligence is not an essential ingredient but some degree of personal responsibility is required, which is connoted in my definition by the word 'use.' This conception is implicit in all the decisions which impose liability only where the defendant has 'caused or continued' the nuisance. We may eliminate in this case 'caused.' What is the meaning of 'continued'? In the context in which it is used 'continued' must indicate mere passive continu-

ance. If a man uses on premises something which he found there, and which itself causes a nuisance by noise, vibration, smell or fumes, he is himself in continuing to bring into existence the noise, vibration, etc., causing a nuisance. Continuing in this sense and causing are the same thing.

I find that the plaintiffs are entitled to damages for nuisance and are also entitled to an order restraining this continuing intrusion.

SUMMARY   Unintentional injury to a person, where a duty is owed not to injure, is a tort. Most torts of this nature fall under the general classification of *negligence*, which includes not only the unintentional injury to the person, but injury to property as well.

Injury to the property of another through carelessness is actionable in tort if a duty is owed not to damage the property of another. While trespass to land normally is a wilful act and an actionable tort, unintentional interference with the enjoyment of the lands of another constitutes the tort of nuisance. Land-owners, or occupiers of land, however, owe a duty not to injure persons that enter on their land, but the extent of the duty differs between trespassers, licensees, and invitees. The manufacturers of goods also owe a duty not to injure the users of their products, and are subject to a very high duty of care.

DISCUSSION QUESTIONS

1. Distinguish an "intentional tort" from an "unintentional tort."
2. Identify the essential ingredients of unintentional tort liability.
3. Does a professional owe a duty of care only to his patient or client? Under what circumstances would the duty extend beyond the relationship?
4. Explain in general terms how the law of negligence applies to the operator of a motor vehicle.
5. What standard of care would normally apply to the operator of a motor vehicle? Give examples of cases where an operator of a motor vehicle who causes damage or injury might not be liable in tort.
6. Explain the rationale behind the duty of care owed by an occupier of land to a mere trespasser.
7. Does strict liability apply in cases of negligence? Under what circumstances?
8. Describe the nature of the tort action that might arise out of a situation where striking employees block the entrance to their employer's premises.

9. *In some cases of nuisance, why are public policy and the public interest important considerations? Give examples.*

10. *How does an "invitee" differ from a "licensee" in terms of an occupier's duty towards the person?*

11. *Explain how the degree of an owner's (or occupier's) consent alters the status of a person who enters on the owner's property.*

12. *Describe briefly the normal standard of care that a professional person is expected to maintain.*

13. *Explain a manufacturer's duty of care. Does the standard vary with the nature of the product?*

14. *What is the tort "nuisance"? Are all nuisances torts? Explain.*

JUDICIAL DECISIONS

Nuisance— Basis for Tort— Remedies

Russell Transport Ltd. et al. v. Ontario Malleable Iron Co. Ltd., [1952] O.R. 621.

The plaintiffs purchased a block of vacant land near the defendant's foundry for the purpose of storing new automobiles pending delivery by the plaintiffs. The defendant's plant emitted, along with some other substances, particles of iron and iron oxide which settled on the automobiles and damaged their painted surfaces. The emissions from the defendant's plant rendered the plaintiffs' property unsuitable for the use for which it was purchased, and the plaintiffs instituted a legal action for damages and an injunction to stop the nuisance.

MCRUER, C.J.H.C. (following a detailed review of the evidence):

> The irresistible conclusion on the evidence is, and I so find, that the defendant emits from its plant particles of iron and iron oxide together with other matters which settle on the plaintiffs' lands, rendering the plaintiffs' property unfit for the purpose for which it was purchased and developed. The plaintiffs have therefore suffered and will continue to suffer material and substantial damage to their property unless the emission of injurious substances is abated.

> . . . . .

> Salmond on Torts, 10th ed. 1945, at pp. 228-31, summarizes in a comprehensive manner "Ineffectual Defences" as follows:

> 1. It is no defence that the plaintiffs themselves came to the nuisance.

> 2. It is no defence that the nuisance, although injurious to the plaintiffs, is beneficial to the public at large.

> 3. It is no defence that the place from which the nuisance proceeds is a suitable one for carrying on the operation complained of, and that no other place is available in which less mischief would result.

> 4. It is no defence that all possible care and skill are being used to prevent the operation complained of from amounting to a nuisance. Nuisance is not a branch of the law of negligence.

5. It is no defence that the act of the defendant would not amount to a nuisance unless other persons acting independently of him did the same thing at the same time.

6. He who causes a nuisance cannot avail himself of the defence that he is merely making a reasonable use of his own property. No use of property is reasonable which causes substantial discomfort to others or is a source of damage to their property.

In opening his argument Mr. Sedgwick stated that the principal defence relied on by the defendant were [*sic*] a reasonable use of its land, and prescriptive right.

It is argued that the plaintiffs established their marshalling-yard in an industrial area unsuitable for a business of that character. In the first place, the facts do not support this contention even if there were a sound basis of law for it. I shall discuss the law further in due course. When the plaintiffs acquired their lands they were surrounded on three sides by a residential area through which the Canadian Pacific Railway ran. It was unknown to them and to the defendant as well that there were any emissions from the defendant's plant that would cause injury to the finish of motor vehicles. It was not until the business had been carried on for nearly two years that either the plaintiffs or the defendant became aware of the nuisance. In fact, the defendant sold a portion of its lands to its immediate neighbour to the south to be used as a parking-lot for motor vehicles belonging to the employees of the company occupying these lands.

Any argument based on the fact that the nuisance may have existed before the plaintiffs purchased their property is completely answered by the statement of Lord Halsbury in *Fleming et al. v. Hislop et al.* (1886), 11 App. Cas. 686, where he said at p. 696: "If the Lord Justice Clerk means to convey that there was anything in the law which diminished the right of a man to complain of a nuisance because the nuisance existed before he went to it, I venture to think that neither in the law of England nor in that of Scotland, is there any foundation for any such contention. It is clear that whether the man went to the nuisance or the nuisance came to the man, the rights are the same, and I think that the law of England has been settled, certainly for more than 200 years, by a judgment of Lord Chief Justice Hide. . . ."

The last proposition that I have quoted from Salmond requires some qualification, but only a very limited one. Counsel bases his whole argument on the defence of reasonable use of the defendant's lands on a passage in the judgment of Thesiger L.J. in *Sturges v. Bridgman* (1879), 11 Ch. D. 852 at 865, where the learned lord justice, in dealing with two hypothetical cases, said:

"As regards the first, it may be answered that whether anything is a nuisance or not is a question to be determined, not merely by an abstract consideration of the thing itself, but in reference to its circumstances; what would be a nuisance in *Belgrave Square* would not necessarily be so in *Bermondsey*; and where a locality is devoted to a particular trade or manufacture carried on by the traders or manufacturers in a particular and established manner not constituting a public nuisance, Judges and juries would be justified in finding, and may be trusted to find, that the trade or manufacture so carried on in that locality is not a private or actionable wrong."

This statement of the law has been applied with caution in some cases arising out of alleged nuisances producing sensible personal discomfort, but it is not to be broadly applied nor is it to be isolated from the general body of law on the subject. It was an expression used in a case arising out of noise and vibration.

The statement of the Lord Chancellor in *St. Helen's Smelting Company v. Tipping* (1865), 11 H. L. Cas. 641 at 650, 11 E.R. 1483, is the classic authority in all cases similar to the one before me:

"My Lords, in matters of this description it appears to me that it is a very desirable thing to mark the difference between an action brought for a nuisance upon the ground the alleged nuisance produces material injury to the property, and an action brought for a nuisance on the ground that the thing alleged to be a nuisance is productive of sensible personal discomfort. With regard to the latter, namely, the personal inconvenience and interference with one's enjoyment, one's quiet, one's personal freedom, anything that discomposes or injuriously affects the senses or the nerves, whether that may or may not be denominated a nuisance, must undoubtedly depend greatly on the circumstances of the place where the thing complained of actually occurs. If a man lives in a town, it is necessary that he should subject himself to the consequences of those operations of trade which may be carried on in his immediate locality, which are actually necessary for trade and commerce, and also for the enjoyment of property, and for the benefit of the inhabitants of the town and of the public at large. If a man lives in a street where there are numerous shops, and a shop is opened next door to him, which is carried on in a fair and reasonable way, he has no ground for complaint, because to himself individually there may arise much discomfort from the trade carried on in that shop. But when an occupation is carried on by one person in the neighbourhood of another, and the result of that trade, or occupation, or business, *is a material injury to property*, then there unquestionably arises a very different consideration. I think, my Lords, that in a case of that description, the submission which is required from persons living in society to that amount of discomfort which may be necessary for the legitimate and free exercise of the trade of their neighbours, would not apply to circumstances *the immediate result of which is sensible injury to the value of the property*." (The italics are mine.)

. . . . . .

Even if on any argument a doctrine of reasonable use of the defendant's lands could be expanded to cover a case where there is substantial and material injury to the plaintiffs' property I do not think it could be applied to this case. "Reasonable" as used in the law of nuisance must be distinguished from its use elsewhere in the law of tort and especially as it is used in negligence actions. "In negligence, assuming that the duty to take care has been established, the vital question is, 'Did the defendant take reasonable care?' But in nuisance the defendant is not necessarily quit of liability even if he has taken reasonable care. It is true that the result of a long chain of decisions is that unreasonableness is a main ingredient of liability for nuisance. But here 'reasonable' means something more than merely 'taking proper care'. It signifies what is legally right between the parties, taking into account all the circumstances of the case, and some of these circumstances are often such as a man on the Clapham omnibus could not fully appreciate." (Winfield, Text-Book on the Law of Tort, 2nd ed. 1950, p. 448.) "At common law, if I am sued for a nuisance, and the nuisance is proved, it is no defence on my part to say, and to prove, that I have taken all reasonable care to prevent it." (per Lindley L.J. in *Rapier v. London Tramways Company*, [1893] 2 Ch. 588 at 599.) This is not to be interpreted to mean that taking care is never relevant to liability for nuisance. In some cases if the defendant has conducted his trade or business as a reasonable man would have done he has gone some way toward making out a defence, but only some of the way: *The Stockport Waterworks Company v. Potter et al.* (1861), 7 H. & N. 160, 158 E.R. 433.

On the other hand, if the defendant has taken no reasonable precautions to protect his neighbour from injury by reason of operations on his own property the defence of reasonable user is of little avail.

The evidence shows that in so far as the emissions from the cupola are responsible for the injury to the plaintiffs, and I think they are in large measure responsible for the injury complained of, the defendant has adopted no method of modern smoke or fume control.

. . . . .

Mr. Sedgwick sought to bring the plaintiffs' business within that class of case referred to as an exceptionally delicate trade.

In *Robinson v. Kilvert* (1889), 41 Ch. D. 88, Lopes L.J. said at p. 97: "A man who carries on an exceptionally delicate trade cannot complain because it is injured by his neighbour doing something lawful on his property, if it is something which would not injure anything but an exceptionally delicate trade."

. . . . .

Although in this case there is no admission that the defendant has violated the plaintiffs' legal right by damaging the motor vehicles stored on their property, I find as a fact that it has done so, and I cannot find that the storing of automobiles in the open air on the lots in question is a particularly delicate trade or operation. The finish of an automobile is designed to resist reasonable atmospheric contamination and it would be manifestly unjust to hold that property-owners in the vicinity of the defendant's plant have no legal right to have their automobiles protected from the emissions from the defendant's foundry simply because they do not keep them under cover.

The defence of prescriptive right remains to be dealt with. The defendant pleads that it and its predecessors in title have for a period of 40 years and more before the commencement of the action enjoyed as of right and without interruption the right to do those things which the plaintiffs claim gives them a right of action, and that their claim is therefore barred by The Limitations Act, R.S.O. 1950, c. 207. The relevant portions of ss. 34 and 35 of The Limitations Act read as follows:

"34. No claim which may lawfully be made at the common law by custom, prescription or grant, to any way or other easement, . . . to be enjoyed, or derived upon, over, or from any land . . . being the property of any person, when the way or other matter as herein last before mentioned has been actually enjoyed by any person claiming right thereto without interruption for the full period of 20 years shall be defeated or destroyed by showing only that the way or other matter was first enjoyed at any time prior to the period of 20 years, but, nevertheless the claim may be defeated in any other way by which the same is now liable to be defeated, and where the way or other matter as herein last before-mentioned has been so enjoyed for the full period of 40 years, the right thereto shall be deemed absolute and indefeasible, unless it appears that the same was enjoyed by some consent or agreement expressly given or made for the purpose by deed or writing.

"35. Each of the respective periods of years mentioned in sections 33 and 34 shall be deemed and taken to be the period next before some action wherein the claim or matter to which such period relates was or is brought into question, and no act or other matter shall be deemed an interruption within the meaning of those sections, unless the same has been submitted to or acquiesced in for one year after the person interrupted has had notice thereof, and of the person making or authorizing the same to be made."

In asserting the defence of prescription the onus rests on the defendant: *Crossley and Sons, Limited v. Lightowler* (1867), L.R. 2 Ch. 478 at 482. The defendant must show not only that it has exercised the right to deposit the substances herein complained of on the plaintiffs' lands for the prescribed period, but that the exercise of the right amounted to a nuisance actionable at the instance of the plaintiffs and their predecessors in title for the full period of 20 years: *Sturges v. Bridgman, supra; Danforth Glebe Estates Limited v. W. Harris & Co. Limited* (1919), 16 O.W.N. 41.

The latter case was a case arising out of the emission of offensive odours from the defendant's plant. After referring to *Sturges v. Bridgman*, Riddell J. said: "So long as the adjoining land remained wholly vacant, and no attempt was made to sell it, and no other damage could be shewn, the time did not begin to run. Nothing of the kind was shewn to have taken place 20 years, before this action."

. . . . . .

The evidence in support of prescriptive right consists of proof that for over 40 years the defendant's predecessors in title and the defendant carried on foundry operations on the property in question.

. . . . . .

Even if on any view of the evidence it could be considered that iron oxide and iron particles were being emitted from the defendant's plant for a period of 20 years next preceding the issue of the writ in this action, to the same extent and in the same manner as they are now being emitted, I think the defence of prescriptive right would still fail. In order to obtain a prescriptive right, the enjoyment of the right must not be secret and the servient owner must have either actual or constructive knowledge of it.

The evidence clearly shows that neither the plaintiffs' nor the defendant's officers had any knowledge that any injurious particles were being deposited on the plaintiffs' lands as emissions from the defendant's plant until late in the autumn of 1951. *Sturges v. Bridgman, supra,* has always been recognized as the leading authority for the proposition stated therein at p. 863:

". . . the laws governing the acquisition of easements by user stands thus: Consent or acquiescence of the owner of the servient tenement lies at the root of prescription, and of the fiction of a lost grant, and hence the acts or user, which go to the proof of either the one or the other, must be, in the language of the civil law, *nec vi nec clam nec precario*; for a man cannot, as a general rule, be said to consent or to acquiesce in the acquisition by his neighbour of an easement through an enjoyment of which he has no knowledge, actual or constructive, or which he contests and endeavours to interrupt, or which he temporarily licenses. It is a mere extension of the same notion, or rather it is a principle into which by strict analysis it may be resolved, to hold, that an enjoyment which a man cannot prevent raises no presumption of consent or acquiescence."

In that case a confectioner had for more than twenty years used a pestle and mortar in his back premises which abutted on the garden of a physician and the noise and vibration were not felt as a nuisance and were not complained of, but in 1873 the physician erected a consulting-room at the end of his garden, and then the noise and vibration became a nuisance to him. It was held that there being no right of action against the defendant until the plaintiff had built the consulting-room the time for prescription did not commence to run until the offensive trade became actionable.

The history of the plaintiffs' property, which I have outlined in detail, shows that for more than 20 years prior to the commencement of the action it was low-lying vacant land, formerly the site of a disused foundry. . . . Applying the principle followed in *Sturges v. Bridgman, supra* . . . I do not think it can be said that the evidence would warrant me in finding that for the whole period of 20 years prior to 1952 the plaintiffs or their predecessors in title could have maintained an action against the defendant for nuisance.

·   ·   ·   ·   ·

The plaintiffs are therefore entitled to relief against the defendant.

·   ·   ·   ·   ·

Judgment will therefore go for an injunction that the defendant, its servants and agents, be restrained from discharging or allowing to be discharged from its works in the pleadings mentioned any substance, gas or matter in such a manner or to such an extent as to occasion damage to the plaintiffs' property or the buildings thereon and/or motor vehicles or vehicles of like character that may be thereon; provided, however, that the operation of the injunction will be suspended until the 1st January 1953.

Negligence— Duty of Care— Manufacturers' Liability	**M'Alister (or Donoghue) v. Stevenson, [1932] A.C. 562.** The plaintiff and a friend entered a shop in Paisley, Scotland, where the friend purchased a bottle of ginger-beer manufactured by the defendant and gave the same to the plaintiff. The glass bottle was opaque and the contents could not be inspected before opening. The plaintiff consumed part of the bottle, then, when she emptied the remainder of the contents into her glass, she discovered the remains of a decomposed snail.

She became violently ill following the incident, and brought an action for damages against the manufacturer on the grounds of negligence.

LORD MACMILLAN:

> The law . . . concerns itself with carelessness only where there is a duty to take care and where failure in that duty has caused damage. In such circumstances carelessness assumes the legal quality of negligence and entails the consequences in law of negligence. What, then, are the circumstances which give rise to this duty to take care? In the daily contacts of social and business life human beings are thrown into, or place themselves in, an infinite variety of relations with their fellows; and the law can refer only to the standards of the reasonable man in order to determine whether any particular relation gives rise to a duty to take care as between those who stand in that relation to each other. The grounds of action may be as various and manifold as human errancy; and the conception of legal responsibility may develop in adaptation to altering social conditions and standards. The criterion of judgment must adjust and adapt itself to the changing circumstances of life. The categories of negligence are never closed. The cardinal principle of liability is that the party complained of should owe to the party complaining a duty to take care, and that the party complaining should be able to prove that he has suffered damage in consequence of a breach of that duty. Where there is room for diversity of view, it is in determining what circumstances will establish such a relationship between the parties as to give rise, on the one side, to a duty to take care, and on the other side to a right to have care taken.
>
> To descend from these generalities to the circumstances of the present case, I do not think that any reasonable man or any twelve reasonable men would hesitate to hold that, if the appellant establishes her allegations, the respondent has exhibited carelessness in the conduct of his business. For a manufacturer of aerated water to store his empty bottles in a place where snails can get access to them, and to fill his

bottles without taking any adequate precautions by inspection or otherwise to ensure that they contain no deleterious foreign matter, may reasonably be characterized as carelessness without applying too exacting a standard. But, as I have pointed out, it is not enough to prove the respondent to be careless in his process of manufacture. The question is: Does he owe a duty to take care, and to whom does he owe that duty? Now I have no hesitation in affirming that a person who for gain engages in the business of manufacturing articles of food and drink intended for consumption by members of the public in the form in which he issues them is under a duty to take care in the manufacture of these articles. That duty, in my opinion, he owes to those whom he intends to consume his products. He manufactures his commodities for human consumption; he intends and contemplates that they shall be consumed. By reason of that very fact he places himself in a relationship with all the potential consumers of his commodities, and that relationship which he assumes and desires for his own ends imposes upon him a duty to take care to avoid injuring them. He owes them a duty not to convert by his own carelessness an article which he issues to them as wholesome and innocent into an article which is dangerous to life and health. It is said that liability can only arise where a reasonable man would have foreseen and could have avoided the consequences of his act or omission. In the present case the respondent, when he manufactured his ginger-beer, had directly in contemplation that it would be consumed by members of the public. Can it be said that he could not be expected as a reasonable man to foresee that if he conducted his process of manufacture carelessly he might injure those whom he expected and desired to consume his ginger-beer? The possibility of injury so arising seems to me in no sense so remote as to excuse him from foreseeing it. Suppose that a baker, through carelessness, allows a large quantity of arsenic to be mixed with a batch of his bread, with the result that those who subsequently eat it are poisoned, could he be heard to say that he owed no duty to the consumers of his bread to take care that it was free from poison, and that, as he did not know that any poison had got into it, his only liability was for breach of warranty under his contract of sale to those who actually bought the poisoned bread from him? Observe that I have said "through carelessness," and thus excluded the case of a pure accident such as may happen where every care is taken. I cannot believe, and I do not believe, that neither in the law of England nor in the law of Scotland is there redress for such a case. The state of facts I have figured might well give rise to a criminal charge, and the civil consequence of such carelessness can scarcely be less wide than its criminal consequences. Yet the principle of the decision appealed from is that the manufacturer of food products intended by him for human consumption does not owe to the consumers whom he has in view any duty of care, not even the duty to take care that he does not poison them.

. . . . .

It must always be a question of circumstances whether the carelessness amounts to negligence, and whether the injury is not too remote from the carelessness. I can readily conceive that where a manufacturer has parted with his product and it has passed into other hands it may well be exposed to vicissitudes which may render it defective or noxious, for which the manufacturer could not in any view be held to be to blame. It may be a good general rule to regard responsibility as ceasing when control ceases. So, also, where between the manufacturer and the user there is interposed a party who has the means and opportunity of examining the manufacturer's product before he re-issues it to the actual user. But where, as in the present case, the article of consumption is so prepared as to be intended to reach the consumer in the condition in which it leaves the manufacturer, and the manufacturer takes steps to ensure this by sealing or otherwise closing the container so that the contents cannot be tampered with, I regard his control as remaining effective until the article reaches the consumer and the container is opened by him.

Duty of Care—Occupier of Land— Liability

Indermaur v. Dames (1866), L.R. 1 C.P. 274; affirmed (1867), 2 C.P.D. 311 (Exch. Ct.).

The defendant operated a sugar refinery which had a deep shaft, approximately 4 ft. square and 29 ft. deep, that was used for moving sugar. The shaft was necessary, and was used in the operation of the defendant's business. It was unfenced, and open for the purpose of ventilation and for moving the sugar into the refinery.

The employer of the plaintiff sent the plaintiff to examine a gas regulator that had been installed in the refinery, and while the plaintiff was examining the gas regulator, he accidently fell into the shaft and was injured.

WILLES, J.:

It was also argued that the plaintiff was at best in the condition of a bare licensee or guest who, it was urged, is only entitled to use the place as he finds it . . .

We think this argument fails, because the capacity in which the plaintiff was there was that of a person on lawful business, in the course of fulfilling a contract in which both the plaintiff and the defendant had an interest, and not upon bare permission. No sound distinction was suggested between the case of the servant and the case of the employer, if the latter had thought proper to go in person; nor between the case of a person engaged in doing the work for the defendant pursuant to his employment, and that of a person testing the work which he had stipulated with the defendant to be paid for if it stood the test; whereby impliedly the workman was to be allowed an onstand to apply that test, and a reasonable opportunity of doing so. Any duty to enable the workman to do the work in safety, seems equally to exist during the accessory employment of testing: and any duty to provide for the safety of the master workman, seems equally owing to the servant workman whom he may lawfully send in his place.

. . . . .

The authorities respecting guests and other bare licensees, and those respecting servants and others who consent to incur a risk, being therefore inapplicable, we are to consider what is the law as to the duty of the occupier of a building with reference to persons resorting thereto in the course of business, upon his invitation, express or implied. The common case is that of a customer in a shop: but it is obvious that this is only one of a class; for, whether the customer is actually chaffering at the time, or actually buys or not, he is, according to an undoubted course of authority and practice, entitled to the exercise of reasonable care by the occupier to prevent damage from unusual danger, of which the occupier knows or ought to know, such as a trap-door left open, unfenced, and unlighted . . . This protection does not depend upon the fact of a contract being entered into in the way of the shopkeeper's business during the stay of the customer, but upon the fact that the customer has come into the shop in pursuance of a tacit invitation given by the shopkeeper, with a view to business which concerns himself. And, if a customer were, after buying goods, to go back to the shop in order to complain of the quality, or that the change was not right, he would be just as much there upon business which concerned the shopkeeper, and as much entitled to protection during this accessory visit, though it might not be for the shopkeeper's benefit, as during the principal visit, which was. And if, instead of going himself, the customer were to send his servant, the servant would be entitled to the same consideration as the master.

The class to which the customer belongs includes persons who go not as mere volunteers, or licensees, or guests, or servants, or persons whose employment is such that danger may be considered as bargained for, but who go upon business which concerns the occupier, and upon his invitation, express or implied.

And, with respect to such a visitor at least, we consider it settled law, that he, using reasonable care on his part for his own safety, is entitled to expect that the occupier shall on his part use reasonable care to prevent damage from unusual danger, which he knows or ought to know; and that, where there is evidence of neglect, the question whether such reasonable care has been taken, by notice, lighting, guarding, or otherwise, and whether there was contributory negligence in the sufferer, must be determined . . . as matter of fact.

In the case of *Wilkinson v. Fairrie*, relied upon for the defendant, the distinction was pointed out between ordinary accidents, such as falling down stairs, which ought to be imputed to the carelessness or misfortune of the sufferer, and accidents from unusual, covert danger, such as that of falling down into a pit.

It was ably insisted for the defendant that he could only be bound to keep his place of business in the same condition as other places of business of the like kind, according to the best known mode of construction. And this argument seems conclusive to prove that there was no absolute duty to prevent danger, but only a duty to make the place as little dangerous as such a place could reasonably be, having regard to the contrivances necessarily used in carrying on the business. But we think the argument is inapplicable to the facts of this case; first, because it was not shewn, and probably could not be, that there was any usage never to fence shafts; secondly, because it was proved, that, when the shaft was not in use, a fence might be resorted to without inconvenience: and no usage could establish that what was in fact unnecessarily dangerous was in law reasonably safe, as against persons towards whom there was a duty to be careful.

Having fully considered the notes of the Lord Chief Justice, we think there was evidence for the jury that the plaintiff was in the place by the tacit invitation of the defendant, upon business in which he was concerned; that there was by reason of the shaft unusual danger, known to the defendant; and that the plaintiff sustained damage by reason of that danger, and of the neglect of the defendant and his servants to use reasonably sufficient means to avert or warn him of it: and we cannot say that the proof of contributory negligence was so clear that we ought on this ground to set aside the verdict of the jury.

||||||||||||||||||||||||||||||||||||||||||||||||||||||||||||||||||||||||||||||||||||||||||||||||||||||||||||||||||||||||||||||||||||||||||||||||||||||||||||||||||||

Negligence—
Occupiers'
Liability—
Duty

Bate v. Kileel Enterprises Ltd. (1976), 71 D.L.R. (3d) 283.

The plaintiff, a prospective patron of a beauty salon, entered the building which contained the beauty salon by way of the wrong entrance. After passing through a hallway, she pushed open a door believing it to be the entrance to the beauty salon. In doing so she fell down an unlighted stairwell, and was injured.

The plaintiff brought an action against the owner of the building.

BUGOLD, J.A. (after reviewing the evidence):

The first question then is to determine into what category the plaintiff should be placed; was she an invitee, a licensee or a trespasser on the premises in question at the time and place of the accident? The defendant contends the plaintiff was, at best, a licensee with respect to the premises at 14 Westmorland St. On the other hand, it is submitted on behalf of the plaintiff that she was an invitee.

Lord Sumner in *Mersey Docks & Harbour Board v. Procter*, [1923] A.C. 253 at p. 272, states:

"The leading distinction between an invitee and a licensee is that, in the case of the former, invitor and invitee have a common interest, while, in the latter, licensor and licensee have none."

In *Arendale v. Federal Building Corp. Ltd.* (1962), 35 D.L.R. (2d) 202, [1965] O.R. 1053 (Ont. C.A.), Roach, J.A., at p. 204, defines an invitee thus:

"The rule is firmly established that an invitee is a person who comes on
the occupier's premises with his consent on business in which the occupier and he have a common interest."

In the case of *Hillman v. MacIntosh* (1959), 17 D.L.R. (2d) 705, [1959]
S.C.R. 384, it is held that the driver of an express company who called
at a building to collect parcels from a tenant in the ordinary course of
the tenant's business was an invitee of the owner into those parts of the
building through which he had to pass. There the expressman as the
employee of the express company was in the building to transact business with the tenant. Martland, J., at p. 710 D.L.R., pp. 390-1 S.C.R.,
says:

"I think there was a common interest in that it was to the interest of the
building owner that his tenants, carrying on business on premises
leased from him, should be able to obtain the services of express company employees in connection with their commercial activities. This
being so, the relationship between the appellant and the respondent
was that of invitor and invitee."

Upon the facts of the case before us, I am of the opinion that the
plaintiff falls into the category of an invitee *quoad* the defendant with relation to the hallway at 14 Westmorland St. despite her entry to that
part of the building by mistake. Here the plaintiff came on the premises
of the defendant on business with the consent of the defendant. As to
"common interest" it was in the interest of the defendant and to its
benefit that its tenants, carrying on commercial activities on premises
leased from it, be permitted to receive customers and patrons which in
turn assisted the tenants to pay their rent to the defendant and discharge any other duty they owed to it. If the expressman in the *Hillman*
case was an invitee of the owner of the building then *a fortiori* so was
the plaintiff in the instant case.

I agree with the trial Judge that the plaintiff was an invitee of the defendant and was therefore entitled to such protection as the law affords
to invitees. The matter then resolves itself into the question whether
the defendant failed in the discharge of its duty to the plaintiff as an invitee. The duty of the defendant at its highest is as stated by Lord Hail-
sham, L.C., in *Robert Addie & Sons (Collieries), Ltd. v. Dumbreck*, [1929]
A.C. 358 at pp. 364-5:

"There are three categories in which persons visiting premises belonging to another person may fall; they may go

  "(1.) By the invitation, express or implied, of the occupier;

  "(2.) With the leave and licence of the occupier, and

  "(3.) As trespassers.

                    .   .   .   .   .

"The duty which rests upon the occupier of premises towards the
persons who come on such premises differs according to the category
into which the visitor falls. The highest duty exists towards those persons who fall into the first category, and who are present by the invitation of the occupier. Towards such persons the occupier has the duty of
taking reasonable care that the premises are safe."

This obligation of the occupier has been stated in various ways. In *Indermaur v. Dames* (1866), 35 L.J.C.P. 184, Willes, J., at p. 190, states:

"And with respect to such a visitor, at least [*i.e.*, an invitee], we consider it settled law that he, using reasonable care on his part for his own safety, is entitled to expect that the occupier shall on his part use reasonable care to prevent damage from unusual danger which he knows or ought to know, and that where there is evidence of neglect, the question whether such reasonable care had been taken by notice, lighting, guarding or otherwise, and whether there was contributory negligence in the sufferer, must be determined by a jury as matter of fact."

In whatever way the rule may be put, it seems clear that it is broken up into these elements: (a) the occupier must take reasonable care, (b) see that the premises are reasonably safe, (c) the invitee must also take reasonable care for his own safety, and (d) the question whether reasonable care was taken either by the occupier or the invitee is a question of fact varying with the circumstances of each case.

CASE PROBLEMS FOR DISCUSSION

Case 1

Hamburg, with the permission of the provincial authorities, kept a pet cougar in a large, wire-fenced run on his farm. The fence was a heavy steel mesh similar to the type of fence used to enclose commercial and government yards where public entry is prohibited. The fence was 8 ft. high, and was well maintained. The mesh was designed to prevent an adult from climbing over the fence, and the gate had a sturdy latch which could not be opened by an animal.

Unknown to Hamburg, a new family with children took possession of a neighbouring farm. A small child of the family (aged seven) wandered into Hamburg's yard while he was in town, and managed to open the cougar run. The animal escaped, and before it was re-captured, it had killed a prize calf that belonged to another neighbour.

Discuss the issues raised in this case, and explain Hamburg's liability (if any) for his neighbour's loss of a prize calf.

Case 2

Smith lived in a residential area some distance from where he worked. One morning, Smith found himself late for work because his alarm clock failed to wake him at the usual time. In his rush to leave his home, he backed his automobile from his garage after only a cursory backward glance to make certain the way was clear. He did not see a small child riding a tricycle along the sidewalk behind his car, and the two came into collision. The child was knocked from the tricycle by the impact, and was injured.

The child's mother at the front door of her home (some 75 yds. away) heard the child scream, and saw the car back over the tricycle. She ran to the scene of the accident, picked up the child, and carried him home. Smith called an ambulance, and the child was taken to the hospital where it was treated for a crushed leg.

The mother brought a legal action against Smith for damages resulting from the shock of seeing her child struck by Smith's car. An action was also brought on behalf of the child for the injuries suffered.

Discuss the validity of the claims in this case, and identify the issues and points of law that are arised by the actions of Smith. How would you decide the case?

Case 3

Thompson operated an ice-cream truck owned by Smith. During the summer months Thompson travelled throughout the residential areas of a large city selling ice-cream products. Thompson's principal customers were children, and Thompson would drive along the streets ringing a series of bells attached to his truck to signal his arrival in the area.

Alberta, a five-year-old child, and her brother were regular customers of Thompson, and on the day in question heard the bells which signalled the approach of Thompson's ice-cream truck. Martha, Alberta's mother, was talking to her husband on the telephone at the moment that the ice-cream truck arrived. In response to the cries of her two small children for money to buy ice-cream, she gave them enough money to buy an ice-cream bar each. The children ran across the street to where the truck was parked, and each ordered a different ice-cream product. Thompson served Alberta first, and then turned to serve her brother. At that instant, Alberta ran into the street with the intention of returning home, and was struck by a car driven by Donaldson.

Alberta was seriously injured as a result of the accident, and an action for damages was brought against Thompson, the operator of the ice-cream truck, Smith, the owner of the truck, and Donaldson, the owner and driver of the automobile.

Discuss the basis of the action on Alberta's behalf against the owners and drivers of the vehicles, and determine the basis of the liability of each party under the law of torts. Render a decision.

Case 4

Sampson operated a bowling-alley in a commercial area that was adjacent to a residential area. Many small children used the parking-lot near the bowling-alley as a playground, and Sampson was constantly ordering the children off the premises for fear that they might be injured by motor vehicles.

One young boy, about six years old, was a particular nuisance in that he would climb to the flat roof of the bowling-alley by way of a fence at the back of the building. Sampson ordered the child off the roof on several occasions, but to no avail. The child continued to climb on the roof at every opportunity in spite of Sampson's instructions to the contrary.

On one occasion, when Sampson was away from the premises, the child climbed to the roof, and while running about, tripped and fell to the ground. The fall seriously injured the child, and an action was brought on his behalf against Sampson.

Discuss the liability of Sampson, and his defences, if any. Render a decision.

Case 5

Holbrook grew rare and valuable flowers in a walled garden, and had recently been robbed of flowers and roots by a person or persons unknown. In an effort to discourage thieves, he set up in his garden a spring gun with a number of trip-wires designed to swivel and fire the gun in the direction where the wire was touched. Holbrook did not post a notice to warn persons that he had a gun set in his garden, as it was his intention not to warn the thief.

One afternoon some time later, a hen owned by a neighbour escaped from its pen, and flew into Holbrook's yard. Bird, a young man, saw the hen fly over the wall, and in an effort to recover it for its owner, climbed the wall and stood on top. He called two or three times to determine if anyone in the area had seen the hen, and when he received no answer, jumped down into the garden. As he did, his foot contacted a trip-wire, and the gun discharged, injuring his leg.

Bird brought an action against Holbrook for his injury.

Discuss the nature of Bird's action in this case, and discuss the arguments that may be raised by the parties. Render a decision.

Case 6

On a clear September day, Smith walked across a parking-lot adjacent to his home for the purpose of buying a newspaper at a convenience store in a shopping plaza. He purchased the newspaper and left the store, but before he had walked more than one or two paces, his foot struck a raised portion of a sidewalk slab, and he fell heavily to the concrete.

Smith was unable to work for a month as a result of his injuries, and he brought an action for damages against the tenant who operated the convenience store and the owner of the shopping plaza.

When the case came to trial, the evidence established that the maintenance of the sidewalk outside the store was the sole responsibility of the owner of the shopping plaza, but the owner had not inspected the sidewalk for some months. The sidewalk, while not in disrepair, had been slightly heaved by the previous spring frost, and presented an uneven surface upon which the patrons of the plaza were forced to walk. Many of the concrete slabs were raised from ¼" to ½", but some protruded above abutting slabs by as much as 1¾". The particular slab which caused Smith's fall protruded approximately 1⅜".

The tenant who occupied the milk store was aware of a "certain unevenness of the slabs" but did not realize that it was hazardous.

Discuss the liability (if any) of the defendants and render, with reasons, a decision.

PART III

The Law of Contract

CHAPTER 6

An Introduction to the Legal Relationship

INTRODUCTION

A contract may be defined as an agreement made between two or more persons which is enforceable at law.[1] It is not something which is tangible (although in some cases evidence of its existence may take that form)—it is a legal concept. It comes into existence, in a legal sense, when the parties have established all of the elements which make it enforceable; until they have done so, no enforceable agreement exists. This chapter, and the next eight, will examine the nature of each of these elements.

Contract law differs from the law of torts and many other areas of law in a rather remarkable way: if the parties comply with the principles laid down for the creation of an enforceable contract, they are free to create specific rights and duties of their own which the courts of law will enforce. In some respects, they create their own "law," which they are

[1]Osborn, P.G., *The Concise Law Dictionary*, 4th ed. (Sweet & Maxwell, 1954: London, England).

obliged to follow. How these concepts were developed is largely a matter of history, although as a body of law, the law of contract is not old. Its development parallels the rise of the mercantile class in England and North America, but it did not reach a position of importance until the 19th century. Blackstone, in his Commentaries, for example, devoted only 28 pages to contract law, and over 300 to the law of real property. Such was the relative importance of contract law in 1756. The next 100 years, however, saw the growth of contract law to the point where it became one of the most important areas of the common law. Today, contract law forms the basis of most commercial activity.

HISTORICAL DEVELOPMENT OF THE LAW OF CONTRACT

The law of contract is essentially an area of law relating to business transactions, and until the rise of the merchant class in England, business transactions as we know them today were not common. Under the feudal system, each manor was relatively self-sufficient, and such trade that did exist was frequently by barter, or by purchase at a local fair or market. Transactions were usually instantaneous in the sense that goods changed hands as soon as the exchange was agreed upon. Disputes that arose between merchants were promptly settled by the merchants themselves, and later by way of the rules set down by their guilds. Disputes arising out of the informal contracts or agreements that did not reach the courts most often fell within the jurisdiction of the ecclesiastic courts on the basis that a breach of a solemn promise was a moral issue to be dealt with by the church. Minor cases

(the equivalent of our breach of contract), however, were occasionally handled by manor courts, where damages were sometimes awarded for breach of the promise.

After the Norman Conquest, the common law courts enforced promises (which were not unlike our modern contracts) by way of a number of different writs. These included actions of debt, detenue, and covenant, which allowed for the recovery of rent due under a lease agreement, payment for a benefit received, such as goods sold and delivered, or money lent (debt), retention of goods (detenue), and the enforcement of a formal promise in writing (covenant). This latter document, which formed the basis for an action, probably bears the closest resemblance to a modern formal contract, but at that time the law was concerned only with the enforcement of the promise and matters surrounding the breach, rather than the formation of the agreement.

These three actions, and another action called an action of account (which was originally an action open to a land-owner to recover money or goods from persons who had collected them on his behalf) were gradually supplemented by actions for trespass and deceit in tort. The right of action in trespass established the early concept of duty in the performance of obligation under an agreement, and the tort deceit provided a remedy for the early equivalent of a breach of a warranty or guarantee. By this point, the courts provided remedies in cases where a person failed to carry out his promise in accordance with the terms of the agreement (a breach of duty, and hence, liability in trespass), and where he failed to perform entirely (a breach of a promise which he had made), he would be liable for deceit. It was not until the 17th century that the courts recognized implied promises of payment where the price was not mentioned, but understood. The 17th century also saw the development of the "bargain theory" of a contract whereby each party to the agreement derived some benefit from the agreement in return for his promise to do or give something in return. This benefit–detriment approach formed the basis of modern contract, and from that point on in time, the law developed rapidly as it responded to the changes taking place in society. The decline of the feudal system and the rise of the merchant class saw a change in the economic order which required new methods of dealing with the changing activities of the people. The development of the law of contract was essentially a response to those needs, rather than a gradual evolution of older common law.

THE ELEMENTS OF A VALID CONTRACT

The Intention to Create a Legal Relationship

The concept of a contract as a bargain or agreement struck by two parties is based upon the premise that the end result will be a meeting of the parties' minds on the terms and conditions which will form their agreement with each other. Each will normally agree to do, or perhaps refrain from doing, certain things in return for the promise of the other to do likewise. In the process of reaching this meeting of the minds, the parties must establish certain elements of the contract itself.

Negotiations relating to the agreement must, of necessity, have a beginning, and if the agreement, by definition, consists of promises made by the parties, then one of the essential elements of the agreement must be a promise. Obviously, not all promises can be taken as binding on the party making them. Some, which are frequently made with no intention of fulfilment, cannot be taken as the basis for a contract. The first requirement, then, for a valid contract, must be the formation of the *intention* on the part of the promisor to be *bound* by the promise made. This intention to create a legal relationship is an essential element of a valid contract, and is generally considered to be a presumption at law in any commercial transaction where the parties are dealing with one another at arm's length.

The intention to create a legal relationship is a presumption at law because the creation of the intention would otherwise be difficult to determine; by presuming that the party intended to be bound by the promise shifts the onus to prove otherwise, if the intention did not exist. If the intention is denied, the courts will usually use the conduct of the party at the time that the statements were made as a test, and assess such conduct and statements from the point of view of the "reasonable person."

The reason for the presumption that strangers who make promises to one another intend to bound by them is essentially an approach that permits the courts to assume that the promises are binding, unless one or both of the parties can satisfy the courts that they were not intended to be so. The law, nevertheless, recognizes certain kinds of promises or statements as ones which are normally not binding, unless established as such by the evidence. For example, promises made between members of a family would not normally be considered to be binding as an enforceable contract, and generally speaking, advertisements are not normally taken as enforceable promises which are binding on the advertiser.

The reasons for these two exceptions are obvious. Members of a family frequently make promises to one another that they would normally not make to strangers. Advertisers, on the other hand, in the presentation of their goods to the public, are permitted to describe their products with some latitude and enthusiasm, provided of course, that they do not mislead the prospective purchaser. While these two groups are not normally subject to the presumption that their promises represent an intention to create a legal relationship, they may, nevertheless, be bound by their promises if the party accepting their promises can show that the promise was, in fact, intended to be binding on the promisor.

An early example of this point was an English case[2] which involved a manufacturer of a pharmaceutical product that advertised the product as a cure for influenza. The company had promised in its advertisement that it would pay £100 to anyone who used the product according to the prescribed directions, and later contracted the illness. The advertisement also contained a statement to the effect that it intended to be bound by its promise, and that to show its good faith it had deposited £1 000 for this purpose with a particular banking institution. When a person, who had purchased and used the product according to the instructions, later fell ill with influenza and claimed the £100, the company demured on the basis that its advertisement was not an intention to create a legal relationship. The court held, however, that it had, by its words in the advertisement, clearly expressed the intention to be bound, and it accordingly could not later avoid or deny it.

The rule that can be drawn from this case is that while an advertiser is not normally bound by the claims set out in an advertisement, if a clear intention to be bound by them is expressed, then the courts will treat the promise as one made with an intention to create a legal relationship.

As a general rule, the courts view an advertisement (or for that matter, any display of goods) as a mere invitation to do business, rather than an offer to the public at large. The purpose of the advertisement or display is merely to invite offers which the seller may accept or reject. This particular point becomes important in determining when a contract is made where goods are displayed for sale in a self-serve establishment. The issue was decided in an English case where the court held that the display of goods in a self-serve shop was not an offer to the patron of the shop, but merely an invitation to the public to offer to purchase the goods. The possession of the goods by the prospective purchaser was of no consequence, as the offer to purchase and the acceptance of the offer by the seller did not take place until the seller dealt with the goods at the check-out counter. It was at this point in time that the contract was made—not before.[3]

|||||||||||||||||||||||||||||||||||||||||||||||||||||||||||||||||||||||||||||||||||||

CASE 6.1
Merritt v. Merritt, [1970] 2 All E.R. 760.
LORD DENNING, M.R.:

The first point taken on his behalf by counsel for the husband was that the agreement was not intended to create legal relations. It was, he says, a family arrangement such as

[2]*Carlill v. Carbolic Smoke Ball Co.*, [1893] 1 Q.B. 256.

[3]*Pharmaceutical Society of Great Britain v. Boots Cash Chemists (Southern) Ltd.*, [1952] 2 All E.R. 456.

was considered by the court in *Balfour v Balfour* and in *Jones v Padavatton*. So the wife could not sue on it. I do not think that those cases have any application here. The parties there were living together in amity. In such cases their domestic arrangements are ordinarily not intended to create legal relations. It is altogether different when the parties are not living in amity but are separated, or about to separate. They then bargain keenly. They do not rely on honourable understandings. They want everything cut and dried. It may safely be presumed that they intend to create legal relations.

Counsel for the husband then relied on the recent case of *Gould v Gould*, when the parties had separated, and the husband agreed to pay the wife £12 a week "so long as he could manage it". The majority of the court thought that those words introduced such an element of uncertainty that the agreement was not intended to create legal relations. But for that element of uncertainty, I am sure that the majority would have held the agreement to be binding. They did not differ from the general proposition which I stated:

"When . . . husband and wife, at arm's length, decide to separate and the husband promises to pay a sum as maintenance to the wife during the separation, the court does, as a rule, impute to them an intention to create legal relations."

In all these cases the court does not try to discover the intention by looking into the minds of the parties. It looks at the situation in which they were placed and asks itself: would reasonable people regard the agreement as intended to be binding?

||||||||||||||||||||||||||||||||||||||||||||||||||||||||||||||||||||||||||

Offer and Acceptance

The Nature of an Offer

The second element of a binding contract deals with promises made by the parties. Only a promise made with the intention of creating a legal relationship may be en-forced, but in the normal course of negotiations a person seldom makes such a promise unless some condition is attached to it. Consequently, such a promise is only tentative until the other party expresses a willingness to comply with the condition. The tentative promise made subject to a condition is therefore not binding on the offering party (the offeror) until the proposal is accepted. It is only when a valid acceptance takes place that the parties may be bound by the agreement. These two additional requirements constitute the second and third elements of a valid contract: offer and acceptance.

Communication of an Offer

If the analysis of the negotiations is carried further, an obvious observation can be made: an offer must be communicated by the offeror to the other party (the offeree) before the offer may be accepted. From this observation flows the rule for offer and acceptance: *An offer must be communicated by the offeror to the offeree before acceptance may take place.*

This rule may appear to be self-evident, but an offer is not always made directly to the offeree by the offeror. In some cases the parties may deal with each other by letter, telegraph, telex, or a variety of other means of communication, and it is important for the offeror to know when the offeree becomes aware of the offer. This is so because an offer is not valid until it is received by the offeree, and the offeror is not bound by the offer until such time as it is accepted. This means that identical offers which cross in the mail do not constitute a contract, even though there is an obvious meeting of the minds of the parties as evidenced by their offers. The essential point to make here is that no person can agree to a contract of which he is unaware. If the acceptance, for example, takes place before the offer is made, the offeror is not bound by the promise. This is particularly true in the case of offers of reward. For example, Jones returns from work one evening to discover his prize dog missing. The next morning, on his way to work, he places an advertisement in the local newspaper offering a $50 reward for the return of his lost dog. Later that morning, his neighbour, Smith, finds the dog on the street, and returns the animal to Mrs. Jones, who is home at the time. Mrs. Jones calls Mr. Jones and tells him the dog has been returned, but it is too late for Jones to remove the advertisement from the newspaper. That afternoon, Smith discovers the offer of reward in the newspaper and claims the $50 from Jones because he found and returned his lost dog.

In this case, Jones did not communicate the offer to Smith until after Smith had fully performed what was required of him under the terms of the offer of reward. Smith, therefore, cannot accept the offer, because he returned the dog without the intention of creating a contract. His act was gratuitous, and he cannot later claim the right to payment. This concept will be examined more closely with respect to another element of a contract, but for the present, it may be taken as an example of the communication rule.

If the negotiation process is examined closely, another rule for offer and acceptance can be drawn from it. A person who makes an offer frequently directs it to a specific person, rather than to the public at large. A seller of goods may wish to deal with a specific person for a variety of sound reasons. For example, a seller of a prize dog may wish to sell it only to a person who would appreciate and care for the animal, or a seller of a specific type of goods may wish to sell the goods to only those persons trained in the use of the goods if some danger is attached to their use. Hence, we have the general rule that *only the person to whom an offer is made may accept the offer.*[4] If an offer is made to the public at large, this rule naturally does not apply, for the offeror is, by either his words or conduct, implying in such an offer that the identity of the offeree is not important in the contract.

Acceptance of an Offer

While both an offer and its acceptance may be made or inferred from the words or the conduct of the parties, the words or conduct must conform to certain rules that have been established before the acceptance will be valid. These rules have been formulated by the courts over the years as a result of the many contract disputes that came before them, and at present, the major rules for acceptance are now well settled.

The first rule is simply the reverse of the rule for offers. It states that the *acceptance of the offer must be communicated to the offeror in the manner presented or contemplated by the offeror in the offer.* The acceptance must take the form of certain words or acts in accordance with the offer that will indicate to the offeror that the offeree has accepted the offer. These words or acts need not normally be precise, but they must convey the offeree's intentions to the offeror in the manner contemplated for acceptance.

For example, if a person who writes a letter to a seller of a particular product states in the letter that he wishes to purchase a given quantity of the goods, and requests that they be sent to him, the letter would contain an offer to purchase. The acceptance would take place when the seller acted in accordance with the instructions for acceptance set out in the letter. It

---

[4]*Cudney v. Lindsay* (1878), 3 App. Cas. 459.

would not be necessary for him to write a reply conveying his acceptance of the offer, because the offer contemplates acceptance by the act of sending the goods to the offeror. The acceptance would be complete when the seller did everything required of him by the terms of the letter.

This particular issue was raised in the case mentioned previously, where a pharmaceutical product was offered to the public at large as a cure and prevention for influenza. One of the arguments raised by the manufacturer was the fact that the plaintiff had not communicated her acceptance of the offer before using the product, and hence, no contract existed. The court disposed of this argument by saying that if the terms of the offer intimate a particular mode of acceptance to make the promise binding, it is sufficient for the offeree to comply with the indicated mode of acceptance, and notification to the offeror of the acceptance would then be unnecessary.[5]

In the case of an offer which requires some expression of acceptance by written or spoken words, a number of specific rules for acceptance have been set down. If acceptance is specified to be by verbal means, the acceptance would be complete when the acceptance is communicated by the offeree either by telephone, or when he meets with the offeror, and speaks the words of acceptance directly to him. With this form of acceptance there is no question about the communication of the words of acceptance. It takes place when the words are spoken.

The time of acceptance, however, is sometimes not as clear-cut with other modes of acceptance, and the courts have been called upon to decide the issues as the particular modes of acceptance came before them. In the case of an offer that stipulates acceptance by post, the rule which has been established is that the acceptance of the offer takes place when the letter of acceptance, properly addressed, and the postage paid, is placed in the postbox or post office.[6] The reasoning behind this decision is sensible. The offeree, in preparing a letter of acceptance and delivering it to the post office, has done everything possible to accept the offer when the letter moves into the custody of the postal system. The postal system, as the agent of the addressee, is responsible for delivery from that point on. If the acceptance should be lost while in the hands of the post office, the contract would still be binding, as it was formed when the letter was posted. The offeror, by not specifying that acceptance would not be complete until the letter is received, assumes the risk of loss by the post office, and any uncertainty that might accompany this specified mode of acceptance.

The courts have also held that where an offer does not specifically state that the mail should be used for acceptance, but where it is the usual or contemplated mode of acceptance, then the posting of the letter of acceptance will constitute acceptance of the offer.[7]

A somewhat similar rule also applies to the telegraph as a mode of acceptance. The acceptance is complete when the telegram of acceptance is delivered to the telegraph office for transmission to the offeror.[8] For all other modes of communication, the acceptance would not be complete until the offeror was made aware of the acceptance.

A number of other rules also apply to ac-

[5]*Carlill v. Carbolic Smoke Ball Co.*, [1893] 1 Q.B. 256 at p. 269.

[6]*Household Fire Ins. Co. v. Grant*, [1878] 4 Ex.D. 216.
[7]*Henthorn v. Fraser*, [1892] 2 Ch. 27.
[8]*Cowan v. O'Connor* (1888), 20 Q.B.D. 640.

ceptance in addition to the rules relating to the time and place. Of particular importance is the nature of the acceptance itself. When an offer is made, the only binding acceptance would be one which clearly and unconditionally accepted the offeror's promise, and complied with the accompanying condition. Anything less than this would constitute either a counter-offer, or an inquiry. If the acceptance is not unconditional, but changes the terms, then it would have the effect of rejecting the original offer, and would represent, in itself, an offer which the original offeror could then either accept or reject. For example, Smith writes a letter to Jones in which he offers to sell Jones his automobile for $3 000 cash. Jones writes a letter of reply in which he "accepts" Smith's offer, but states that he will buy the automobile on the payment of $1 000 cash and give Jones a promissory note for $2 000 to be payable $200 per month over a 10-month period.

In this example, Smith's offer is to sell his automobile for a cash payment of $3 000. Jones has expressed his willingness to purchase the automobile, but has changed the offer by altering the payment provision from $3 000 cash to $1 000 cash and a promissory note for $2 000. The change in terms represents a counter-offer for Smith (who now becomes the offeree) which he must accept or reject. The counter-offer submitted by Jones has the effect of terminating the original offer which was made by Smith; if Smith should reject the counter-offer, Jones may not accept the original offer unless Smith wishes to revive it.

The desirable approach for Jones to follow in a situation where some aspect of the offer is unacceptable to him would be to inquire if Smith would be willing to modify the terms of payment before a response is made to the offer in a definite manner.

In this fashion, he might still retain the opportunity to accept the original offer if Smith should be unwilling to modify his terms of payment.

A somewhat different matter is a rule that states that silence cannot be considered to be acceptance unless a pre-existing agreement to this effect has been established between the parties. The rationale for this rule is obvious. The offeree should not be obligated to refuse an offer, nor should he be obliged to comply with an offer made to him simply because he has failed to reject it. The only exception to this rule would be where the offeree has clearly consented to be bound by this type of arrangement.

Recent consumer protection legislation in a number of provinces has reinforced this common law rule by providing that no person shall be obliged to pay for unsolicited goods delivered to him, nor should he be liable for the goods in any way due to their loss or damage while in his possession. Neither the common law nor the legislation, however, affect a pre-existing arrangement whereby silence may constitute acceptance of a subsequent offer. This is a common characteristic of most book and record clubs, which operate on the basis that a contract will be formed and the book or record will be delivered to the offeree if the offeree fails to respond to the offeror within a specified period of time after the offer has been made. Contracts of this nature are generally binding because silence is considered acceptance due to the pre-existing agreement which governs the future contractual relationship of the parties.

Acceptance, while it must be unconditional and made in accordance with the terms of the offer, may take many forms. The normal method of accepting an offer is to state or write "I accept your offer," but acceptance may take other forms as well. For example, it may take the form of an affirmative nod of the head, and a handshake; at a auction sale, it may take the form of the auctioneer dropping his hammer, and saying the word "sold" to the person making the final offer.

Where a particular method of accepting the offer is specified, the offeree must, of course, comply with the requirements. If the offeror has stated in his offer that acceptance must only be made by telegraph, then the offeree, if he wishes to accept, must use this form of communication to make a valid acceptance. Offerors usually do not impose such rigid requirements for acceptance, but often suggest that a particular method of communication would be preferred. In these cases, if a method other than the method mentioned in the offer is selected, the acceptance would only be effective when it was received by the offeror.[9]

Offers which require the offeree to complete his part of the contract as a mode of acceptance form a special class of contracts called *unilateral agreements*. These agreements usually do not call for the communication of acceptance before the contract is to be performed, but rather, signify that the offer may be accepted by the offeree completing his part of the agreement. Once completed, the offeror would then perform his part. The danger with this mode of acceptance is obvious: if the offeror should withdraw his offer before the offeree has fully performed his acceptance, then no contract would exist, and any expense or inconvenience incurred by the offeree would not be recoverable. To remedy this situation, the courts have held that where an offeree is obliged to perform his part of the contract in order to accept the offer, then the offeror will not be permitted to withdraw the offer so long as the offeree is in the course of performing his part. This rule assumes that the offeror has not expressly reserved the right to withdraw the offer at any time during the offeree's act of acceptance. The offer of a reward for the return of a lost animal would be an example of a contract where the offer would be accepted by the act of the offeree.

|||||||||||||||||||||||||||||||||||||||||||||||||||||||||||||||||||||||||||||||||||||||||

CASE 6.2
Saint John Tug Boat Co. Ltd. v. Irving Refinery Ltd. (1964), 49 M.P.R. 284.

RITCHIE, J.:

The test of whether conduct, unaccompanied by any verbal or written undertaking, can constitute an acceptance of an offer so as to bind the acceptor to the fulfilment of the contract, is made the subject of comment in Anson on Contracts, 21st ed., p. 28, where it is said:

"The test of such a contract is an objective and not a subjective one, that is to say, the intention which the law will attribute to a man is always that which his conduct bears when reasonably construed, and not that which was present in his own mind. So if A allows B to work for him under such circumstances that no reasonable man would suppose that B meant to do the work for nothing, A will be liable to pay for it. The doing of the work is the offer; the permission to do it, or the acquiescence in its being done, constitutes the acceptance."

In this connection reference is frequently made to the following statement contained in the judgment of Lord Blackburn in *Smith v. Hughes* (1871), L.R. 6 Q.B. 597 at 607, which I adopt as a proper test under the present circumstances:

"If, whatever a man's real intention may be, he so conducts himself that a reasonable man would believe that he was assenting to the terms proposed by the other party, and that other party upon that belief enters into a contract with him, the man thus conducting him-

[9]*Henthorn v. Fraser,* [1892] 2 Ch. 27.

self would be equally bound as if he had intended to agree to the other party's terms."

The American authorities on the same subject are well summarized in Williston on Contracts, 3rd ed. Vol. I, para. 91A where it is said:

"Silence may be so deceptive that it may become necessary for one who receives beneficial services to speak in order to escape the inference of a promise to pay for them. It is immaterial in this connection whether the services are requested and the silence relates merely to an undertaking to pay for them, or whether the services are rendered without a preliminary request but with knowledge on the part of the person receiving them that they are rendered with the expectation of payment. In either case, the ordinary implication is that the services are to be paid for at their fair value, or at the offered price, if that is known to the offeree before he accepts them."

It must be appreciated that mere failure to disown responsibility to pay compensation for services rendered is not of itself always enough to bind the person who has had the benefit of those services. The circumstances must be such as to give rise to an inference that the alleged acceptor has consented to the work being done on the terms upon which it was offered before a binding contract will be implied.

As was observed by Bowen L.J., in *Falcke v. Scottish Imperial Insur. Co.* (1885), 34 Ch. D. 234 at 248:

"Liabilities are not to be forced upon people behind their backs any more than you can confer a benefit upon a man against his will."

Like the learned trial judge, however, I would adopt the following excerpt from Smith's Leading Cases, 13th ed. at p. 156 where it is said:

"But if a person knows that the consideration is being rendered for his benefit with an expectation that he will pay for it, then if he acquiesces in its being done, taking the benefit of it when done, he will be taken impliedly to have requested its being done: and that will import a promise to pay for it."

Lapse of an Offer

Until an offer is accepted, no legal rights or obligations arise. Offers are not always accepted, and even in areas where the offeree may wish to accept, events may occur or conditions may change which will prevent the formation of the agreement. The death of either party, for example, will prevent the formation of the contract, because the personal representative of the deceased normally may not complete the formalities for offer and acceptance on behalf of the deceased. (When an offeree dies before accepting an offer, the offer lapses, because his personal representative cannot accept an offer on his behalf. By the same token, acceptance cannot be communicated to a deceased offeror, as the personal representative of the offeror would not be bound by the acceptance, except under special circumstances where the offeror has bound them to the offer.)

The same rule would hold true in the case of the bankruptcy of either of the parties, or if a party should be declared insane before acceptance is made.

An offer will also lapse as a result of a direct or indirect response to the offer which does not accept the offer unconditionally and in accordance with its terms. If the offeree rejects the offer outright, it lapses, and cannot be revived except by the offeror. Similarly, any change in the offer's terms in a purported acceptance will cause the original offer to lapse, as the modified acceptance would constitute a counter-offer.

Offers may also lapse by the passage of time, or the happening of a specified event. Obviously, an offer which must be accepted within a specified period of time or by a stipulated date will lapse if acceptance is not made within the period of time or by the particular date. An offer may also lapse within a reasonable time if no time of acceptance has been specified. What constitutes a reasonable time, needless to say, will depend upon the circumstances of the transaction and its subject-matter. An offer to sell a truckload of perishable goods would have a much shorter "reasonable" time for acceptance than an offer to sell a truckload of non-perishable goods which are not subject to price or market fluctuation.

As a general rule, where an offer is made by a person in the company of another, and where no time-limit for acceptance is expressed, the offer is presumed to lapse when the other party departs without accepting the offer, unless of course, the circumstances surrounding the offer would indicate otherwise.

Revocation of an Offer
Revocation, as opposed to lapse, requires an act on the part of the offeror in order to be effective. Normally the offeror must communicate the revocation to the offeree before the offer is accepted, otherwise the notice of revocation will be ineffective. With an ordinary contract, an offeror may revoke the offer at any time, even where he has gratuitously agreed to keep the offer open for a specified period of time. If the offeree wishes to make certain that the offeror will not revoke his offer, the method generally used is called an *option*. An option is a separate promise which obliges the offeror to keep the offer open for a specified period of time, either in return for some compensation, or because the promise is made in a formal document under seal. (The effect of the seal on a document will be examined in the next chapter, as will the effect of compensation paid to an offeror in return for his promise, but for the present it is sufficient to note that *either* of these two things will have the effect of rendering the promise to keep the offer open for a specified period of time irrevocable.)

A second aspect of revocation of an offer is that it need not be communicated in any special way to be effective. The only requirement is that the notice of revocation be brought to the attention of the offeree *before* the offer is accepted. This does not mean, however, that the same rules apply to revocation as apply to acceptance where some form of communication other than direct communication is used. Because the offeree must be aware of the revocation before it is effective, the courts have held that the posting of a letter revoking an offer previously made does *not* have the effect of revoking the offer. The notice of revocation is only effective when it is finally received by the offeree.[10] The same rule would apply to a telegraph message.

The question of whether indirect notice of revocation will have the effect of revoking an offer is less clear. For example, Ambrose offers to sell his car to Burton, and promises to keep the offer open for three days. On the second day, Ambrose sells his car to Coulson. The sale of the car would clearly be evidence of Ambrose's intention to revoke the offer to sell to Burton. If a mutual friend of Burton and Coulson told Burton of the sale of the car to Coulson, would this indirect notice prevent Burton from accepting the offer? This very question arose in an English case in which an offer had been made to sell certain property, and where the offeree was given a number of days to accept. Before the time had expired, the offeror sold the property to another party, and a person not acting under the direction of the offeror informed the offeree of the sale. The offeree then accepted the offer (within

---

[10]*Byrne v. Von Tienhoven* (1880), 5 C.P.D. 344; *Henthorn v. Fraser*, [1892] 2 Ch. 27.

the time period for acceptance) and demanded conveyance of the property. The court held in this case that the offeree was informed of the sale by a reliable source, and this knowledge precluded acceptance of the offer by him.[11]

The essential point to note in cases where notice of revocation is brought to the attention of the offeree by someone other than the offeror or his agent is the reliability of the source. The offeror must, of course, prove that the offeree had notice of the revocation before the offer was accepted. The onus would be on the offeror to satisfy the courts that the reliability of the source of the knowledge was such that a reasonable person would accept the information as definite evidence that the offeror had withdrawn the offer. Cases of indirect notice, consequently, turn very much on the reliability of the source when the notice comes from some source other than the offeror or his agent. The case cited represents only an example of how a court may deal with the problem of indirect notice, rather than a statement of the common law on this issue.

||||||||||||||||||||||||||||||||||||||||||||||||||||||||||||||||||||||||||||||||||

CASE 6.3
Dickinson v. Dodds (1876), 2 Ch.D. 463.

MELLISH, L.J.:

. . . the law says—and it is a perfectly clear rule of law—that, although it is said that the offer is to be left open until Friday morning at 9 o'clock, that did not bind *Dodds*. He was not in point of law bound to hold the offer over until 9 o'clock on Friday morning. He was not so bound either in law or in equity. Well, that being so, when on the next day he made an agreement with *Allan* to sell the property to him, I am not aware of any ground on which it can be said that that contract with *Allan* was not as good and binding a contract as ever was made. Assuming *Allan* to have known (there is some dispute about it, and *Allan* does not admit that he knew of it, but I will assume that he did) that *Dodds* had made the offer to *Dickinson*, and had given him till Friday morning at 9 o'clock to accept it, still in point of law that could not prevent *Allan* from making a more favourable offer than *Dickinson*, and entering at once into a binding agreement with Dodds.

Then *Dickinson* is informed by *Berry* that the property has been sold by *Dodds* to *Allan*. *Berry* does not tell us from whom he heard it, but he says that he did hear it, that he knew it, and that he informed *Dickinson* of it. Now, stopping there, the question which arises is this—If an offer has been made for the sale of property, and before that offer is accepted, the person who has made the offer enters into a binding agreement to sell the property to somebody else, and the person to whom the offer was first made receives notice in some way that the property has been sold to another person, can he after that make a binding contract by the acceptance of the offer? I am of opinion that he cannot. The law may be right or wrong in saying that a person who has given to another a certain time within which to accept an offer is not bound by his promise to give that time; but, if he is not bound by that promise, and may still sell the property to some one else, and if it be the law that, in order to make a contract, the two minds must be in agreement at some one time, that is, at the time of the acceptance, how is it possible that when the person to whom the offer has been made knows that the person who has made the offer has sold the property to someone else, and that, in fact, he has not remained in the same mind to sell it to him, he can be at liberty to accept the offer and thereby make a binding contract? It seems to me that would be simply absurd. If a man makes an offer to sell a particular horse in his stable, and says, "I will give you until the day after tomorrow to accept the offer," and the next day goes and sells the horse to somebody else, and receives the purchase-money from him, can the person to whom the offer was originally made then come and say, "I accept," so as to make a

[11]*Dickinson v. Dodds* (1876), 2 Ch.D. 463.

binding contract, and so as to be entitled to recover damages for the non-delivery of the horse? If the rule of law is that a mere offer to sell property, which can be withdrawn at any time, and which is made dependent on the acceptance of the person to whom it is made, is a mere *nudum pactum*, how is it possible that the person to whom the offer has been made can by acceptance make a binding contract after he knows that the person who has made the offer has sold the property to some one else? It is admitted law that, if a man who makes an offer dies, the offer cannot be accepted after he is dead, and parting with the property has very much the same effect as the death of the owner, for it makes the performance of the offer impossible. I am clearly of opinion that, just as when a man who has made an offer dies before it is accepted it is impossible that it can then be accepted, so when once the person to whom the offer was made knows that the property has been sold to some one else, it is too late for him to accept the offer, and on that ground I am clearly of opinion that there was no binding contract for the sale of this property by *Dodds* to *Dickinson*.

SUMMARY The law of contract, unlike many other laws, does not set out the rights and duties of the parties. Instead, it permits the parties to establish their own rights and duties by following a series of principles and rules for the formation of a contract. A contract is essentially an agreement which is enforceable at law, and as such, must contain all of the elements of a true agreement. It must, first of all, be a "meeting of the minds of the parties," and an intention on the part of both parties to create a legal relationship must be present. There must also be an offer of a promise by one party subject to some condition, and the offer must be properly accepted by the other party. If the offer is not properly accepted, no contract will exist, and the offer may be terminated or replaced by a counter-offer. If nothing is done to accept the offer it will lapse, or the offeror may withdraw it. In either case, if validly done, no contract will exist. If an unconditional acceptance has been properly made in accordance with the terms of the offer, and before the offer lapses or is withdrawn, then the parties will be bound by the agreement they have made, and their promises will be enforced by the courts. Offer and acceptance, and an intention to create a legal relationship represent two very important elements of a contract. There are other elements which the parties must establish to have a valid contract, and they represent the subject-matter of the following chapters.

DISCUSSION QUESTIONS

1. *Explain briefly the nature of a contract.*
2. *Why is an intention to create a legal relationship important in order to have a binding contract?*
3. *Identify the three requirements which, when met, constitute a valid contract.*
4. *What is the essential feature of an offer that distinguishes it from other promises?*

5. *Identify the 17th century theory that forms the basis of the modern law of contract.*

6. *Explain the nature of the contract implied in an advertisement where a reward is offered to the finder of a lost wallet.*

7. *Why is the element of communication important with respect to a reward?*

8. *Distinguish an "advertisement" from an "offer." Under what circumstances might an advertisement constitute an offer?*

9. *"If it isn't written down, it isn't legal." Illustrate how this is a misconception by giving an example of a contract where the intention, offer, acceptance, and communication are all either indirect or not written.*

10. *Define the term "binding acceptance."*

11. *How does a conditional acceptance alter the offeror-offeree relationship? What is it called?*

12. *Explain the rationale behind the rule that states that acceptance by mail is complete when the properly addressed letter is dropped into the post-box.*

13. *Outline four factors that can lead to the lapse of an offer.*

14. *What condition is placed on revocation before it is effective?*

15. *In cases of indirect notice of revocation, what burden is placed upon the offeror by the courts?*

||||||||||||||||||||||||||||||||||||||||||||||||||||||||||||||||||||||||||||||||||||||||||||||||||||||||||||||||||||||||||||||||||||

JUDICIAL DECISIONS

Offer—
Acceptance—
Time of an Offer—
Time of Acceptance

Pharmaceutical Society of Great Britain v. Boots Cash Chemists (Southern) Ltd., [1952] 2 Q.B. 795.

The defendants operated a self-serve drug store. Some drugs which were classed as "poison" under government legislation were displayed on self-serve shelves, but the sales were recorded by a qualified pharmacist at the check-out counter. The defendant was charged with selling poisons contrary to the Act by failing to have a registered pharmacist supervise the sale of the product. The case turned on when, and where, the sale took place.

LORD GODDARD, C.J. (after reviewing the evidence):

> The question which I have to decide is whether the sale is completed before or after the intending purchaser has passed the scrutiny of the pharmacist and paid his money, or, to put it in another way, whether the offer which initiates the negotiations is an offer by the shopkeeper or an offer by the buyer.
>
> . . . . .
>
> I think that it is a well-established principle that the mere exposure of goods for sale by a shopkeeper indicates to the public that he is willing to treat but does not amount to an offer to sell. I do not think I ought to hold that that principle is completely reversed merely because there is a self-service scheme, such as this, in operation. In my opinion it comes to no more than that the customer is informed that he may himself pick up an article and bring it to the shopkeeper with a view to buying it, and if, but only if, the shopkeeper then expresses his willingness to

sell, the contract for sale is completed. In fact, the offer is an offer to buy, and there is no offer to sell; the customer brings the goods to the shopkeeper to see whether he will sell or not. In 99 cases out of a 100 he will sell and, if so, he accepts the customer's offer, but he need not do so. The very fact that the supervising pharmacist is at the place where the money has to be paid is an indication to the purchaser that the shopkeeper may not be willing to complete a contract with anybody who may bring the goods to him.

Ordinary principles of common sense and of commerce must be applied in this matter, and to hold that in the case of self-service shops the exposure of an article is an offer to sell, and that a person can accept the offer by picking up the article, would be contrary to those principles and might entail serious results. On the customer picking up the article the property would forthwith pass to him and he would be able to insist upon the shopkeeper allowing him to take it away, though in some particular cases the shopkeeper might think that very undesirable. On the other hand, if a customer had picked up an article, he would never be able to change his mind and to put it back; the shopkeeper could say, "Oh no, the property has passed and you must pay the price."

It seems to me, therefore, that the transaction is in no way different from the normal transaction in a shop in which there is no self-service scheme. I am quite satisfied it would be wrong to say that the shopkeeper is making an offer to sell every article in the shop to any person who might come in and that that person can insist on buying any article by saying "I accept your offer." I agree with the illustration put forward during the case of a person who might go into a shop where books are displayed. In most book-shops customers are invited to go in and pick up books and look at them even if they do not actually buy them. There is no contract by the shopkeeper to sell until the customer has taken the book to the shopkeeper or his assistant and said "I want to buy this book" and the shopkeeper says "Yes." That would not prevent the shopkeeper, seeing the book picked up, saying: "I am sorry I cannot let you have that book; it is the only copy I have got and I have already promised it to another customer." Therefore, in my opinion, the mere fact that a customer picks up a bottle of medicine from the shelves in this case does not amount to an acceptance of an offer to sell. It is an offer by the customer to buy and there is no sale effected until the buyer's offer to buy is accepted by the acceptance of the price. The offer, the acceptance of the price, and therefore the sale, take place under the supervision of the pharmacist.

Offer to Public at Large—Acceptance—Notice to Offeror

Carlill v. Carbolic Smoke Ball Co., [1893] 1 Q.B. 256.

The defendants were manufacturers of a medical preparation called the "carbolic smoke ball." To sell their product they inserted an advertisement in a number of newspapers which read:

100*l.* reward will be paid by the Carbolic Smoke Ball Company to any person who contracts the increasing epidemic influenza, colds, or any disease caused by taking cold, after having used the ball three times daily for two weeks according to the printed directions supplied with each ball. 1000*l.* is deposited with the Alliance Bank, Regent Street, shewing our sincerity in the matter.

During the last epidemic of influenza many thousand carbolic smoke balls were sold as preventives against this disease, and in no ascertained case was the disease contracted by those using the carbolic smoke ball.

One carbolic smoke ball will last a family several months, making it the cheapest remedy in the world at the price, 10*s.*, post free. The ball can be refilled at a cost of 5*s.* Address, Carbolic Smoke Ball Company, 27, Princes Street, Hanover Square, London.

The plaintiff purchased and used the preparation according to the instructions and was then attacked by influenza. She brought an action against the defendant for the £100 reward.

LINDLEY, L.J.:

The first observation I will make is that we are not dealing with any inference of fact. We are dealing with an express promise to pay 100*l.* in certain events. Read the advertisement how you will, and twist it about as you will, here is a distinct promise expressed in language which is perfectly unmistakable—"100*l.* reward will be paid by the Carbolic Smoke Ball Company to any person who contracts the influenza after having used the ball three times daily for two weeks according to the printed directions supplied with each ball."

We must first consider whether this was intended to be a promise at all, or whether it was a mere puff which meant nothing. Was it a mere puff? My answer to that question is No, and I base my answer upon this passage: "1000*l.* is deposited with the Alliance Bank, shewing our sincerity in the matter." Now, for what was that money deposited or that statement made except to negative the suggestion that this was a mere puff and meant nothing at all? The deposit is called in aid by the advertiser as proof of his sincerity in the matter—that is, the sincerity of his promise to pay this 100*l.* in the event which he has specified. I say this for the purpose of giving point to the observation that we are not inferring a promise; there is the promise, as plain as words can make it.

Then it is contended that it is not binding. In the first place, it is said that it is not made with anybody in particular. Now that point is common to the words of this advertisement and to the words of all other advertisements offering rewards. They are offers to anybody who performs the conditions named in the advertisement, and anybody who does perform the condition accepts the offer. In point of law this advertisement is an offer to pay 100*l.* to anybody who will perform these conditions, and the performance of the conditions is the acceptance of the offer. . . .

But then it is said, "Supposing that the performance of the conditions is an acceptance of the offer, that acceptance ought to have been notified." Unquestionably, as a general proposition, when an offer is made, it is necessary in order to make a binding contract, not only that it should be accepted, but that the acceptance should be notified. But is that so in cases of this kind? I apprehend that they are an exception to that rule, or, if not an exception, they are open to the observation that the notification of the acceptance need not precede the performance. This offer is a continuing offer. It was never revoked, and if notice of acceptance is required—which I doubt very much, for I rather think the true view is that which was expressed and explained by Lord Blackburn in the case of *Brogden* v. *Metropolitan Ry. Co.*—if notice of acceptance is required, the person who makes the offer gets the notice of acceptance contemporaneously with his notice of the performance of the condition. If he gets notice of the acceptance before his offer is revoked, that in principle is all you want. I, however, think that the true view, in a case of this kind, is that the person who makes the offer shews by his language and from the nature of the transaction that he does not expect and does not require notice of the acceptance apart from notice of the performance.

. . . . .

It appears to me, therefore, that the defendants must perform their promise . . .

||||||||||||||||||||||||||||||||||||||||||||||||||||||||||||||||||||||||||||||||||||||||||||||||||||||||||||||||||||||||||||||||||||||||||||||||||||||||||||||||||||||||

Offer and Acceptance— Intervening Negotiations— Counter-Offer Livingstone v. Evans, et al., [1925] 4 D.L.R. 769.

Evans wrote to Livingstone offering to sell him a parcel of land for $1 800. On receipt of the letter, Livingstone wired a reply: "Send lowest cash price. Will give $1600 cash. Wire." Evans then responded: "Cannot reduce price." Livingstone immediately wrote a letter accepting the offer when he received the telegram, and when Evans refused to complete the transaction, he brought an action for specific performance.

WALSH, J.:

> It is quite clear that when an offer has been rejected it is thereby ended and it cannot be afterwards accepted without the consent of him who made it. The simple question and the only one argued before me is whether the plaintiff's counter-offer was in law a rejection of the defendants' offer which freed them from it. *Hyde* v. *Wrench* (1840), 3 Beav. 334, 49 E.R. 132, a judgment of Lord Langdale, M.R., pronounced in 1840, is the authority for the contention that it was. The defendant offered to sell for £1000. The plaintiff met that with an offer to pay £950 and (to quote from the judgment at p. 337)—"he thereby rejected the offer previously made by the Defendant. I think that it was not competent for him to revive the proposal of the Defendant, by tendering an acceptance of it."

. . . . .

Hyde v. *Wrench* has stood without question for 85 years. It is adopted by the text writers as a correct exposition of the law and is generally accepted and recognized as such. I think it not too much to say that it has firmly established it as a part of the law of contracts that the making of a counter-offer is a rejection of the original offer.

The plaintiff's telegram was undoubtedly a counter-offer. True, it contained an inquiry as well but that clearly was one which called for an answer only if the counter-offer was rejected. In substance it said:—"I will give you $1600 cash. If you won't take that wire your lowest cash price." In my opinion it put an end to the defendants' liability under their offer unless it was revived by the telegram in reply to it.

The real difficulty in the case, to my mind, arises out of the defendants' telegram "cannot reduce price." If this was simply a rejection of the plaintiff's counter-offer it amounts to nothing. If, however, it was a renewal of the original offer it gave the plaintiff the right to bind the defendants to it by his subsequent acceptance of it.

With some doubt I think that it was a renewal of the original offer or at any rate an intimation to the plaintiff that he was still willing to treat on the basis of it. It was, of course, a reply to the counter-offer and to the inquiry in the plaintiff's telegram. But it was more than that. The price referred to in it was unquestionably that mentioned in his letter. His statement that he could not reduce that price strikes me as having but one meaning, namely, that he was still standing by it and, therefore, still open to accept it.

|||||||||||||||||||||||||||||||||||||||||||||||||||||||||||||||||||||||||||||||||||||||||||||||||||||||||||||||||||||||||||||||||||||||||||||||||||||

CASE PROBLEMS FOR DISCUSSION

Case 1

Jones lived in Calgary, Alberta, and owned a cottage on Vancouver Island. Percy, who lived in Victoria, British Columbia, was interested in purchasing the cottage owned by Jones. On September 10th, he wrote a letter to Jones in which he offered to purchase the cottage and lot for $25 000. Jones received the letter on September 15th, and sent Percy a telegram in which he offered to sell the cottage to him for $28 000.

Percy did not respond to the telegram immediately, but on a business trip to Calgary on September 22nd, he spoke to Jones about the cottage in an effort to determine if Jones might be willing to reduce the price. Jones replied that the price was "firm" at $28 000.

When Percy returned to Victoria, he sent a letter to Jones accepting his offer to sell the cottage at $28 000. The letter was posted at 11:40 a.m. on September 23rd, but through a delay in the mail, was not delivered to Jones in Calgary until 4:20 p.m. on September 28th.

In the meantime, when Jones had not heard from Percy by September 26th he offered to sell the cottage to Johnson, who had expressed an interest in purchasing the cottage some time before. Johnson accepted the offer, and the two parties executed a written purchase agreement in Johnson's office on the morning of September 27th.

Identify the various rights and liabilities which developed by the negotiations set out above.

Case 2

McKay operated a large farm on which he grew a variety of vegetables for commercial canners. He would also grow a smaller quantity for sale to local retailers and wholesalers as fresh produce. On August 5th, Daigle approached McKay and offered to purchase 100 bushels of tomatoes from him at a fixed price per bushel. McKay stated that the price was acceptable to him, but he was uncertain as to whether his crop would be sufficient to make up the 100 bushels. He told Daigle he could definitely supply 80 bushels, and that he would be in a position to tell Daigle by the next week if the additional 20 bushels would be available. Daigle nodded approval, and left.

A few days later, McKay discovered that crop failures in other parts of the province had pushed tomato prices substantially above the price offered by Daigle. McKay's crop, however, was abundant, and he discovered that he had 120 bushels when the crop was harvested.

At the end of the week, Daigle called to determine if McKay could supply him with 100 bushels, or only 80. McKay refused to supply Daigle with any tomatoes, and informed him that it was his intention to sell the crop elsewhere.

Discuss the negotiations between the parties, and determine the rights (if any), and liabilities (if any) of the parties. Assume that Daigle brought an action against McKay. Discuss the nature of the action, and render, with reasons, a decision.

Case 3

Armstrong wrote a letter to Bishop on May 2nd, and offered to sell him 200 tons of scrap mica at $180 per ton. Bishop received the letter on May 3rd. A few weeks later, Bishop checked the price of mica, and discovered that the market price had risen to $185 per ton. On May 22nd, Bishop wrote Armstrong accepting the offer. Armstrong did not receive Bishop's letter until May 30th. Armstrong refused to sell the mica to Bishop at $180 per ton, but expressed a willingness to sell at the current market price, which was $187 per ton.

Bishop instituted legal proceedings against Armstrong for breach of the contract which he alleged existed between them.

Discuss the rights (if any), and the liabilities (if any) of the parties, and render a decision.

Case 4

Clancy enjoyed a special variety of apple which only Ely grew in his orchard, and each year he would purchase several bushels of the fruit for winter use. As a result of Clancy's long-standing practice of purchasing several bushels, each year Ely would simply deliver the apples to Clancy's home, and leave them in his garage. Clancy would then forward payment to Ely at the going market price. The arrangement had carried on for some 20 years, when Clancy suddenly fell ill with a disease which required him to maintain a very strict diet. The diet did not include apples, but Clancy did not advise Ely, even though the two men met occasionally.

In the fall of the year, Ely delivered the usual apple supply and placed them in Clancy's garage. When Clancy discovered the apples in his garage, he moved them to his backyard, and attempted to reach Ely by telephone to have him pick up his apples. Clancy was unable to reach Ely by telephone for a number of days, and by the time he finally contacted him, the apples had deteriorated from exposure to the hot sun. Ely refused to take back the apples, and Clancy refused to pay for them.

Advise the parties of their rights in this case, and determine the probable outcome if Ely should bring an action against Clancy for the value of the goods.

CHAPTER 7

‖‖‖

Requirement of Consideration

CONSIDERATION
Nature of Consideration

The *bargain theory* of contract suggests that a contract is essentially an agreement between parties where each gets something in return for his or her promise. If this is the case, then every promise by an offeror to do something must be conditional. The promise must include a provision that the offeree, by his acceptance, will promise something to the offeror. The "something" which the promisor receives in return for his promise is called *consideration*—an essential element of every contract which is not made under seal.

Consideration can take many forms. It may be a payment of money, the performance of a particular service, a forbearance to do something by the promisee, the relinquishment of a right, the delivery of property, or a myriad of other things including a promise in return for the promise, but in every case, the consideration must be something done with respect to the promise offered by the promisor. Unless a promisor gets something in return for his promise, the promise is merely gratuitous. Generally, consideration for a promise must exist for the contract to have validity.

There are, however, certain exceptions to this rule, but they are few in number; most date back to times before the concept of modern contract was developed. It has long been a rule of English law that a gratuitous offer of a service, if accepted, must be performed with care and skill, otherwise the promisor will be liable for any loss suffered as a result of his negligence. This liability, however, would not flow from any breach of contract, but rather, from the tort committed.

A second major exception dates back to the days of the law merchant, and remains today as a part of our legislation dealing with negotiable instruments. A person may be liable on a promissory note, or other negotiable instrument, to a subsequent endorser even though no consideration exists between them. Under the same body of law, a party who endorses a bill of exchange to enable another to negotiate it may be held liable on the bill even though no consideration was given as a result of the endorsement.

A modern-day exception to the rule concerns the promise of a donation to a charitable organization. If the rule relating to consideration is strictly applied to a promise of a donation to a charity, the agreement would be unenforceable, as the promise would be gratuitous. This is because the donor would receive nothing in return for his promise. While this is the usual situation where a donation to a charity is concerned, the courts have made exceptions in some cases. If the charity can show that it undertook a specific project on the strength of the donor's pledge, then the promise may be enforced. This, of course, would only be applicable where the donor's promised donation was such that it represented a substantial part of the funds necessary for the project. For example, in a city in Manitoba, the YMCA solicited donations for the construction of a new building, and obtained a substantial pledge from one person. The amount of the pledge prompted the YMCA to commit itself in contract to erect and equip the new building. After construction was underway, the pledgor refused to honour his promise of payment, and the YMCA sued for the amount. The pledgor's defence was that the promise was unenforceable due to a lack of consideration, but the court ruled otherwise. The charity satisfied the court that it would not have begun the project without the particular pledge, and had incurred liability on the strength of the promise of funds. The court decided that this was sufficient consideration for the promised donation.[1]

If the promised donation is not significant, the courts will not enforce the gratuitous promise. In the case of *Governors of Dalhousie College v. Boutilier*,[2] the university solicited funds for the maintenance and the construction of new facilities. Mr. Boutilier promised a donation, but died before the payment was made. When his

[1]*Sargent v. Nicholson* (1915), 25 D.L.R. 638.
[2]*Governors of Dalhousie College v. Boutilier*, [1934] 3 D.L.R. 593.

estate refused to pay the pledge, the university sued to obtain the amount promised. The amount pledged, however, was small in comparison with the total funds contributed. As a result, the court refused to enforce the pledge against the estate on the basis that the university had not relied on the specified subscription of Mr. Boutilier when it undertook the repairs and new construction.

||||||||||||||||||||||||||||||||||||||||||||||||||||||||||||||||||||||

CASE 7.1
The Great Northern Railway Co. v. Witham (1873), L.R. 9 C.P. 16.

BRETT, J.:

The company advertised for tenders for the supply of stores, such as they might think fit to order, for one year. The defendant made a tender offering to supply them for that period at certain fixed prices; and the company accepted his tender. If there were no other objection, the contract between the parties would be found in the tender and the letter accepting it. This action is brought for the defendant's refusal to deliver goods ordered by the company; and the objection to the plaintiffs' right to recover is, that the contract is unilateral. I do not, however, understand what objection that is to a contract. Many contracts are obnoxious to the same complaint. If I say to another, "If you will go to York, I will give you 100*l*.," that is in a certain sense a unilateral contract. He has not promised to go to York. But, if he goes, it cannot be doubted that he will be entitled to receive the 100*l*. His going to York at my request is a sufficient consideration for my promise. So, if one says to another, "If you will give me an order for iron, or other goods, I will supply it at a given price;" if the order is given, there is a complete contract which the seller is bound to perform. There is in such a case ample consideration for the promise. So, here, the company having given the defendant an order at his request, his acceptance of the order would bind them. If any authority could have been found to sustain Mr. Seymour's

contention, I should have considered that a rule ought to be granted. But none has been cited. *Burton* v. *Great Northern Railway Co.* is not at all to the purpose. This is matter of every day's practice; and I think it would be wrong to countenance the notion that a man who tenders for the supply of goods in this way is not bound to deliver them when an order is given. I agree that this judgment does not decide the question whether the defendant might have absolved himself from the further performance of the contract by giving notice.

||||||||||||||||||||||||||||||||||||||||||||||||||||||||||||||||||||||

Seal as Consideration
A final, major exception to the requirement for consideration in a contract is a device that was used by the courts to enforce promises long before modern contract law emerged. This particular device is the use of a seal on a written contract. In the past (as early as the 13th century), a written agreement would be enforced by the court if the promisor had placed his seal on the document. The original purpose of the seal was to prove the authenticity of the agreement, leaving the promisor free to prove the document fraudulent if the seal was not present. As time passed, the document became a formal agreement which the courts would enforce if the seal was present. The general thinking of the judges of the day was that any person who affixed his seal to a document containing a promise to do something had given the matter considerable thought, and the act of affixing his seal symbolized his intention to be bound by the agreement. In a sense, the promisor, by affixing his seal to the written promise, was formalizing his intention to be bound. This particular method of establishing an agreement, and this ritual, distinguished the formal contract from the ordinary or simple contract which may or may not be in writing.

Originally, the person entering into the agreement would affix his seal (a wax impression of his family crest or coat of arms) to the document, then place a finger on the impression and express his intention to be bound by the promise. This formal act gave the document its validity. Over time, the act became less formal; today, most formal legal documents which require a seal either have the seal printed on the form, or have a small gummed wafer attached to the form by the party who prepares the document before it is signed by the promisor. The binding effect of a formal contract under seal, however, persists today. The courts will not normally look behind a contract under seal to determine if consideration exists, because the agreement derives its validity from its form (i.e., the signature plus the seal).

In spite of its ancient roots, the contract under seal is a useful form of contract today. For example, where parties wish to enforce a gratuitous promise, the expression of the promise in writing with the signature of the promisor and a seal affixed is the usual method used.

Many formal agreements still require a special form and execution under seal to be valid. For example, in those provinces where the Registry System applies to land transfers, the various Short Forms of Conveyances Acts require a conveyance of land to be in accordance with a particular form, as well as signed, sealed, and delivered to effect the transfer of the property interest to the grantee. A power of attorney must also be executed under seal to authorize an attorney to deal with a grantor's land.

Some legal entities can only execute a formal document by way of a seal. A corporation, for example, can only act through its agents to carry out its objects, and for many kinds of simple contracts it may be bound by its properly authorized agent without the use of the corporation seal. To be bound by a formal contract, however, it must have its corporate seal affixed by the agent.

‖‖‖

CASE 7.2
Sanitary Refuse Collectors Inc. v. City of Ottawa (1971), 23 D.L.R. (3d) 27.

LIEFF, J. :

The legal relationship between City and Sanitary is difficult of precise definition. The City alleges forfeiture of deposit for breach of contract. Sanitary alleges that there was merely an unenforceable agreement to enter into a contract, or, in the alternative, the City, by agreeing to Sanitary's withdrawal of its tender, voluntarily waived any right it might have had to the deposit. I feel neither theory accurately describes the position of the parties. . . .

There was no contract in the ordinary sense between the parties. The City's calling for tenders was merely an offer to negotiate, and Sanitary's tender was the submission of an offer. Rogers on *The Law of Canadian Municipal Corporations*, 2nd ed., at p. 1063, states:

"Calling for tenders is merely an offer to negotiate and an invitation for offers has no binding effect; it is optional to accept any tenders or none. Although it is customary to insert a stipulation in the notice that the municipality does not bind itself to accept the lowest or any tender, this is unnecessary. On the other hand, the conditional acceptance of a tender for the construction of certain works does not bind the tenderer without his consent and the tender can be revoked. The tender and deposit can be withdrawn at any time before acceptance which, in the case of a municipality, means any time before a binding contract is authorized by by-law and is executed under seal. If it is desired to have tenders which cannot be withdrawn at any time before acceptance, they should be under seal. In Ontario it is not sufficient that tenders be accepted by resolution; before the municipality is bound, a formal contract authorized by by-law must be entered into . . ."

See also Hudson's *Building and Engineering Contracts*, 10th ed., c. 3.

Thus, when Sanitary submitted its bid, this was an offer under seal accompanied by a deposit, and not an agreement to enter into a contract. However, the deposit referred to here is different from most deposits.

The usual type of deposit, as described in *Howe v. Smith* (1884), 27 Ch.D. 89, is a payment made by a purchaser pursuant to the execution of a contract of purchase and sale which stands as a guarantee that he will fulfil his obligations and takes on the character of part payment when he so does. The deposit in the present case is distinctly different from the norm for two reasons:

(1) There is no executed contract between the parties.

(2) The depositor will not become the party which incurs the obligation of payment should a contract be executed, rather it will be the party to receive payment.

This deposit is a guarantee *simpliciter* that if awarded the project Sanitary would execute and fulfil the contract.

The result of the tender being under seal is that it is an irrevocable offer: *Nelson Coke & Gas Co. et al. v. Pellatt* (1902), 4 O.L.R. 481; *Re Provincial Grocers Ltd., Calderwood's Case* (1905), 10 O.L.R. 705; *Manes Tailoring Co., Ltd. v. Willson* (1907), 14 O.L.R. 89, and *Re Nipissing Planing Mills, Ltd., Rankin's Case* (1909), 18 O.L.R. 80. Sanitary's letter of June 9, 1969, was an attempt to revoke the offer. I hold it to be a statement of revocation and not merely a request to withdraw. The City's reply of June 12, 1969, is a statement of its election to accept the revocation as a breach of the condition rather than futilely holding Sanitary to its offer.

In other words, the tender being under seal results in the offer having two special characteristics:

(1) It is irrevocable. Any attempt to revoke it would be legally ineffective and the offeree could treat it as open until it lapses under its own terms.

(2) Its irrevocability makes it a contract, the breach of which gives rise to a cause of action.

The offeree may elect to treat any purported revocation as it sees fit, subject to the rights of innocent third parties.

Adequacy of the Consideration

In general, the courts are not concerned about the adequacy of consideration because they are reluctant to become involved as arbiters of the price or value which a person receives for a promise. Apart from the requirement that the consideration be legal, their main concern is with the presence or absence of consideration, rather than whether the promisor received proper compensation for his or her promise. In some cases, however, the courts will look more closely at the adequacy of the consideration. If the promisor can satisfy the courts that the promise was made under unusual circumstances (such as where an error occurred which rendered the consideration totally inadequate in relation to the promise made), the courts may intervene. For example, Able writes a letter to Baker offering to sell his car to Baker for $3 500. Baker refuses the offer, but makes a counter-offer to Able to purchase the car for $3 000. Able sends a wire in return, rejecting Baker's offer to purchase in which he makes an offer sell his car for $3 200. In sending the wire, the telegraph office mistakenly shows the price as $3.20, instead of $3 200. If Baker should "snap up" the offer, he could not enforce Able's promise to sell, because the courts would reject his claim on the basis of the obvious error in the offer. Able, after offering his car for sale for $3 500, and rejecting an offer for $3 000 would not then offer to sell the car for a nominal consideration of $3.20.

If the error, however, was in Able's original letter in which he intended to sell the car for $3 500, but inadvertently offered it to Baker for $3 000, and Baker accepted the offer, he would probably be bound by the contract. In this case, the courts would have no way of determining Able's intention at the time the offer was made, and would not inquire into the adequacy of the consideration.

To be valid, consideration must also be something of value which the person receives in return for his promise. It cannot be something which the person has received before the promise is made, nor can it be something which a person is already entitled to receive by law, or under another enforceable agreement.

In the first case, if a person has already received the benefit for which he offers the promise, nothing is received in return for the promise. The consideration is essentially past consideration, which is no consideration at all, and the promise is gratuitous. The consideration offered must be something which the promisee will give, pay, do, or provide, either at the instant the promise is made (present consideration), or at a later date (future consideration).

In the second case, the consideration which the promisee agrees to provide in return for the promise must not be something which the promisee is already bound to do at law or under another agreement. In both instances it would not constitute a benefit which the promisor would receive in return for his promise, and it would not constitute valuable consideration. If a person already has a duty to do some act, provide some service, or pay something to the promisor, then the promisor receives nothing from the promisee in return for the promise, other than that which he or she is already entitled to receive. There is no consideration given in return for the promise; again, the promise would be gratuitous. For example, Smith enters into a contract with Jones to construct a house for him on his property for $50 000. Smith underestimates the cost of constructing the house, and when the house is partly finished, he refuses to proceed with the construction unless Jones agrees to pay him an additional $10 000. If Jones agrees to pay the additional amount, and Smith completes the construction, Jones is not bound by the promise if he should later decide to withhold the $10 000. Smith is already under a duty to construct the house for Jones, and Jones receives nothing in return for his promise to pay the additional amount of money to Smith.[3] His promise is gratuitous and unenforceable by Smith.

Quite apart from the aspect of lack of consideration, the enforcement of a contract of the kind illustrated in this example would be contrary to public policy. If this type of contract was enforceable, it would open the door to extortion in the sense that an unethical contractor could threaten to cease operations at a critical stage in the construction unless additional funds were made available to him to complete his part of the contract.

As noted earlier, the consideration in a contract must be legal. If Able should promise Baker $1 000 on the provision that Baker murders Charlie, and later, if Able fails to pay Baker the $1 000 when Charlie is murdered, the courts would not enforce Able's promise. Public policy dictates that the contract must be lawful in the sense that the promises do not violate any law or

[3]The courts in the United States have, on occasion, taken a slightly different approach in cases of this type. Because the contractor is free to abandon the contract at any time, and compensate the owner for any damages which he might suffer, some American courts have held that the promise to pay an additional amount constitutes a part of a new contract between the parties, as the original contract is executory and there is consideration on the part of both parties to terminate it and replace it with a new agreement. See, for example, *Pittsburgh Testing Laboratory v. Farnsworth & Chambers Co. Inc.*, 251 F 2d 77 (1958). And also see *Owens v. City of Bartlett*, 528 P 2d 1235 (1974), for a discussion of the exception as well. Most American courts, however, would probably follow the consideration rule.

public policy. For this reason, an ordinary business contract containing a clause requiring the buyer to resell goods at a fixed or minimum price would be unlawful under the *Combines Investigation Act*, and would be illegal as well as unenforceable.

||||||||||||||||||||||||||||||||||||||||||||||||||||||||||||||||||||||||||||||||

CASE 7.3
Gilbert Steel Ltd. v. University Construction Ltd. (1973), 36 D.L.R. (3d) 496.

PENNELL, J.:

The validity of the oral agreement remains to be considered. It is assailed as invalid for want of consideration to support it.

It is familiar learning that the doctrine of consideration has been criticized as anomalous and unjust. Although the Courts may have sometimes protested they have bowed to it in deference to precedent. It may have been whittled down by artificial distinctions but its hold upon the common law remains firm and real; it is embedded in the very foundation of the law of contract.

The instant case, therefore, hinges upon first principles. Long ago it was held that there is no consideration if all the plaintiff does is to perform, or promise the performance of an obligation already imposed upon him by a previous contract between himself and the defendant: *Stilk v. Myrick* (1809), 2 Camp. 317, 170 E.R. 1168. Another case may be cited, not so similar in its facts and yet pointing in the same direction: *Sharpe v. San Paulo R. Co.* (1873), 8 Ch. App. 597 at p. 608. The ancient rule to that effect is sustained in modern times *Smith v. Dawson* (1923), 53 O.L.R. 615. It controls the case at hand. The plaintiffs had contracted to deliver reinforcing steel at a fixed price. In the circumstances they could not have done less without being guilty of a wrong. The plaintiffs, therefore, did nothing more than it was their duty to do without additional reward. I think the oral agreement stands condemned for want of a consideration.

||||||||||||||||||||||||||||||||||||||||||||||||||||||||||||||||||||||||||||||||

QUANTUM MERUIT AND QUANTUM VALEBANT

Occasionally a person may request goods or services of another, and the goods will be provided or the services rendered without mention of the price for either. In effect, no mention of consideration is made. No remedy was available for the unfortunate seller or tradesman for this kind of situation until the 17th century. Prior to that date, an unpaid seller could not recover for the goods by way of an action of debt because the sum certain had not been agreed to for the debt. Nor could he recover by way of *assumpsit*, because the recipient of the goods or service had not made an express promise to pay. The law simply did not provide a remedy. By the 17th century, the courts had come to recognize this problem, and determined that by requesting the goods or the service the parties had made an agreement whereby the goods would be supplied or the service rendered in return for the implied promise of payment of a reasonable price for the goods (*quantum valebant*) or a reasonable price for the services rendered (*quantum meruit*). Because contracts of this type frequently involve the supply of goods as well as services, such as where an electrician is called to replace a faulty light switch, or where a plumber replaces a worn faucet, the term *quantum meruit* has come to be used to cover both situations.

If the parties agree upon a price for the services or goods at any time after the services have been performed or the goods supplied, the agreed price will prevail, and the contract will become an agreement for a fixed price. If the parties cannot agree upon a reasonable price, then the courts will decide what is reasonable, based upon the price of the goods or the service in the area where the contract was made.

THE DEBTOR–CREDITOR RELATIONSHIP

The debtor–creditor relationship is one which has long been recognized by the courts, although in early cases, the action taken by the unpaid creditor was one of *detinue*, claiming that a sum of money in the hands of the debtor was his. The question of consideration did not arise; instead, it was necessary for the creditor to show that the debtor was in possession of a sum of money that rightfully belonged to the creditor.

Under the law of contract, a debt paid when due ends the debtor–creditor relationship, as the debtor has fully satisfied his obligations under the contract. Similarly, the creditor has no rights under the contract once he has received payment in full. Where the law relating to consideration applies is where the debtor and creditor agree that the amount payable on the due date should be less than the full amount actually due. At first glance, it would appear that this common business practice is perfectly proper. The creditor, if he agrees to accept a lesser sum than the amount due, should be free to do so, and his promise should be binding upon him. Unfortunately, this practice runs counter to the doctrine of consideration; unless the parties bring themselves within one of the four following exceptions to this rule, the creditor's promise is simply gratuitous and unenforceable.

Under the doctrine of consideration, where a creditor agrees to accept a lesser sum than the full amount of the debt on the due date, there is no consideration for his promise to waive payment of the balance of the debt owed. To recover this amount the creditor can, if he wishes, sue for payment of the balance immediately after receiving payment of the lesser sum.

The difficulties that the application of this principle raise for the business community are many, and the courts, as a result, have attempted to lessen the impact or harshness of the law in a number of ways. The most obvious method of avoiding the problem of lack of consideration would be for the parties to include the promise to take a lesser sum in a written document which would be under seal and signed by the creditor. The formal document under seal would eliminate the problem of lack of consideration entirely. A second method would be for the creditor to accept something other than money in full satisfaction of the debt. For example, the debtor could give the creditor his automobile or stamp collection as payment in full, and the courts would not inquire into the adequacy of the consideration.[4] Payment of the lesser sum in full satisfaction of the debt before the due date would also be consideration for the creditor's promise to forgo the balance, since the payment before the time required for payment would represent a benefit received by the creditor. A final exception to the consideration rule arises where the lesser sum is accepted as payment in full by the creditor under circumstances where a third party makes the payment in settlement of the creditor's claim against the debtor. For example, Able is indebted to Baker for $1 000. Charlie, Able's father, offers Baker $900 as payment in full of his son's indebtedness. If Baker accepts Charlie's payment as settlement of the $1 000, he cannot later sue Able for the remaining $100, as it would be a fraud on the stranger (Charlie) to do so.[5]

---

[4]*Pinnels' Case* (1602), 5 Co. Rep. 17.

[5]For a discussion of this point see the dictum of Willes, J., in *Cook v. Lister* (1863), 13 C.B. (N.S.) 543 at p. 595.

The difficulties which this particular rule for consideration raise in cases where indebtedness has been gratuitously reduced have been resolved in part by legislation in some jurisdictions.[6] In all provinces west of Quebec, statute law provides that a creditor who accepts a lesser sum in full satisfaction of a debt will not be permitted to later claim the balance once the lesser sum has been paid. The eastern common law provinces, however, remain subject to the requirement of consideration, and the parties must follow one of the previously mentioned methods of establishing or avoiding consideration if the debtor is to avoid a later claim by the creditor for the balance of the debt.

The relationship between an individual creditor and debtor, however, must be distinguished from an arrangement or a *bona fide* scheme of composition between a debtor and his creditors. This differs from the isolated transaction in that the creditors agree with each other to accept less than the full amount due them. Each creditor promises the other creditors that he will forgo a portion of his claim against the debtor (and forbear from taking legal action against the debtor to collect the outstanding amount) as consideration for their promise to do likewise.

It is also important to note that an agreement between a creditor and debtor whereby the creditor agrees to accept a lesser sum when the amount owed is in dispute does not run afoul of the consideration rule. If there is a genuine dispute concerning the amount owed, and the creditor accepts a sum less than the full amount claimed, the consideration which he receives for relinquishing his right to take action for the balance is the debtor's payment of a sum which he honestly believes he does not owe the creditor.

GRATUITOUS PROMISES CAUSING INJURY TO ANOTHER: EQUITABLE OR PROMISSORY ESTOPPEL

A gratuitous promise is, by definition, a promise which the promisor has no legal obligation to perform. Occasionally, when the recipient of such a promise relies on the promise to his detriment, the following social question arises: Should the promisor, having misled the promisee, be required to compensate the promisee for his loss, when after all, it was the promisor's conduct or promise which induced the promisee to act to his detriment?

It is a settled point of law that once a fact is asserted to be true (even if it is later proved otherwise) and another person relies on it to his detriment, that statement cannot be denied by the person who made the assertion. This particular concept is known as *estoppel.* The essential characteristics of estoppel are the expression of a fact as being true, and the reliance on that statement by the other party. In the late 19th century, the doctrine of equitable estoppel was developed by the English courts as a defence to a promisor's claim against a promisee where the promisee suffered some injury by his reliance on a gratuitous promise made by the promisor.[7] The courts in the United States extended this reliance to gratuitous promises made with the intention of creating legal relationships, and which caused the pro-

---

[6]See, for example, Ontario: *Mercantile Law Amendment Act*, R.S.O. 1980, c. 265, s. 16.

[7]*Hughes v. Metropolitan Railway Co. et al.* (1877), 2 App. Cas. 439; *Birmingham v. District Land Co. v. London & North Western Railway Co.* (1888), 40 Ch. D. 268.

misee injury. The principle in American law became known as detrimental or injurious reliance, and provided a remedy for the innocent promisee who suffered as a result of his reliance on the promise of another.

The doctrine of *injurious reliance* was slow to emerge in English common law. In the case of *Central London Property Trust, Ltd. v. High Trees House, Ltd.* [8] Lord Denning applied the concept of equitable estoppel to a case where a landlord had gratuitously reduced the rent on a long-term lease because it was not possible for the tenant to lease the apartments in the building during the war years. At the end of the war, the receiver for the debenture holders claimed against the tenant for the full amount of the rent. There was clearly no consideration given for the promise to reduce the rent, but Lord Denning was of the opinion that the tenant had relied on the promise to his detriment, and that the full rent should not be payable for the entire period when the difficult conditions existed. Lord Denning's view of equitable or promissory estoppel as a defence was approved in a second case which followed closely on the heels of the *High Trees* case. [9] The doctrine has since been expanded and it is now at the point where it has been suggested that it might be used not only as a defence, but also as a cause of action. [10] In this respect it would be similar to the United States doctrine of injurious reliance. Canadian courts, however, are still reluctant to adopt the American approach as recent cases appear to limit the change. [11] As a result, its principal use may continue to be as an effective defence against a claim relating to the enforcement of contractual rights where the promisee has relied upon a gratuitous promise to his detriment. [12]

||||||||||||||||||||||||||||||||||||||||||||||||||||||||||||||||||||||||||||||||||||||||

CASE 7.4
Watson v. Canada Permanent Trust Co. (1972), 27 D.L.R. (3d) 735.

ANDERSON, J.:

The question then remains as to whether, in all the circumstances, the plaintiff was estopped from withdrawing his promise (not to withdraw his offer). . . .

Denning, L.J., who gave the judgment in *Central London Property Trust, Ltd. v. High Trees House, Ltd.*, [1947] K.B. 130, in giving his judgment in *Combe v. Combe, supra*, said in part at p. 220:

"The principle, as I understand it, is that, where one party has, by his words or conduct, made to the other a promise or assurance which was intended to affect the legal relations between them and to be acted on accordingly, then, once the other party has taken him at his word and acted on it, the one who gave the promise or assurance cannot afterwards be allowed to revert to the previous legal relations as if no such promise or assurance had been made by him, but he must accept their legal relations subject to the qualification which he himself has so introduced, even though it is not supported in point of law by any consideration but only by his word.

"Seeing that the principle never stands alone as giving a cause of action in itself, it can never do away with the necessity of consideration

---

[8]*Central London Property Trust, Ltd. v. High Trees House, Ltd.*, [1947] K.B. 130.

[9]*Ledingham v. Bermejo Estancia Co.*, [1947] 1 All E.R. 749. Equitable estoppel was also recognized as an appropriate defence in a Canadian case before the *High Trees* decision. See *Pierce v. Empey*, [1939] S.C.R. 247.

[10]*Conwest Exploration Co. Ltd. et al. v. Letain*, [1964] S.C.R. 20.

[11]*Watson v. Canada Permanent Trust Co.* (1972), 27 D.L.R. (3d) 735 at p. 743.

[12]*Owen Sound Public Library Board v. Mial Developments Ltd. et al.* (1980), 26 O.R. (2d) 459; *Bojtar v. Parker* (1980), 26 O.R. (2d) 705.

when that is an essential part of the cause of action. The doctrine of consideration is too firmly fixed to be overthrown by a sidewind."

In the same case Lord Asquith said in part at p. 225:

"The judge has decided that, while the husband's promise was unsupported by any valid consideration, yet the principle in *Central London Property Trust Ltd. v. High Trees House Ltd.*, [1947] K.B. 130, entitles the wife to succeed. It is unnecessary to express any view as to the correctness of that decision, though I certainly must not be taken to be questioning it; and I would remark, in passing, that it seems to me a complete misconception to suppose that it struck at the roots of the doctrine of consideration. But assuming, without deciding, that it is good law, I do not think, however, that it helps the plaintiff at all. What that case decides is that when a promise is given which (1.) is intended to create legal relations, (2.) is intended to be acted upon by the promisee, and (3.) is in fact so acted upon, the promisor cannot bring an action against the promisee which involves the repudiation of his promise or is inconsistent with it. It does not, as I read it, decide that a promisee can sue on the promise. On the contrary, Denning, J., expressly stated the contrary."

It will be seen that a cause of action cannot be based on promissory estoppel, but if the defendant can bring himself within the principles enunciated by the learned Judges he can prevent the plaintiff from asserting his legal rights (withdrawing his offer and suing for the return of the shares or damages).

SUMMARY   Consideration is an essential requirement for any contract not under seal. If the promise is gratuitous, the promise must be made in writing and under seal to be enforceable. Consideration must be legal, and must have some value in the eyes of the law. The courts, however, will not consider the adequacy of the consideration unless it is grossly inadequate given the circumstances surrounding the transaction. Since consideration is the price that a person receives for his promise, the consideration must move from the promisee to the promisor. In cases where the consideration is not specified, and a request is made for goods or services, the consideration will be determined by the courts at a reasonable price.

The courts have permitted the injurious reliance on the part of a party to be used as a defence in cases where a plaintiff attempts to enforce an original agreement that had been altered by a gratuitous promise. In cases involving promises of donations to charitable organizations, gratuitous promises have been enforced where the promise was such that it induced the charity to act to its detriment on the strength of the promise.

DISCUSSION QUESTIONS

1. *Define "consideration."*
2. *Explain why consideration need not be shown when a contract bears a seal.*
3. *Illustrate three exceptions to the rule that consideration must be shown to enforce a contract.*

4. *Distinguish between "present" and "future" consideration.*

5. *Give two examples, one of* quantum valebant *and one of* quantum meruit, *and explain the difference betwen them.*

6. *Something in place of consideration may be shown to result in a successful action by unpaid creditors. What is it?*

7. *Under what circumstances would a creditor's promise to accept a lesser sum later be deemed enforceable?*

8. *What differences in the debtor–creditor relationship can be found in the law east of Ontario?*

9. *Does acceptance of the lesser sum extinguish a creditor's right to sue for the balance owing on a debt? If not, describe what must take place to make this true. What are the differences in the law west of the Quebec border?*

10. *Define "promissory estoppel."*

11. *Where and under what circumstances might injurious reliance be used as a cause of action?*

|||||||||||||||||||||||||||||||||||||||||||||||||||||||||||||||||||||||||||||||||||||||||||||||||||||||||||||||||||||||||||||||||||||||||||||||||||||||||||||||||||||||||||||||||

JUDICIAL DECISIONS
Contracts—
Consideration—
Promissory
Estoppel

John Burrows Ltd. v. Subsurface Surveys Ltd. et al. (1968), 68 D.L.R. (2d) 354.

A creditor permitted the debtor to habitually make late payments of instalments on a promissory note, even though the note provided that in the event of default for more than 10 days, the creditor might, on one month's notice, accelerate the maturity date of the note. Over a period of 16 months, late payments were made and accepted by the creditor without objection. The creditor then gave notice for payment in full as provided in the note.

The debtor resisted payment on the basis that the creditor, by his silence, was estopped from demanding payment in accordance with the terms of the note.

The Trial Judge gave judgement for the creditor; the Court of Appeal reversed the decision; and the matter was appealed to the Supreme Court of Canada.

RITCHIE, J. (after reviewing the evidence and prior judgements):

It remains to be considered whether the circumstances disclosed by the evidence were such as to justify the majority of the Court of Appeal in concluding that this was a case to which the defence of equitable estoppel or estoppel by representation applied.

Since the decision of the present Lord Denning in the case of *Central London Property Trust Ltd. v. High Trees House Ltd.*, [1947] K.B. 130, there has been a great deal of discussion, both academic and judicial, on the question of whether that decision extended the doctrine of estoppel beyond the limits which had been therefore fixed, but in this Court in the case of *Conwest Exploration Co. Ltd. et al. v. Letain*, 41 D.L.R. (2d) 198 at pp. 206-7, [1964] S.C.R. 20, Judson, J., speaking for the majority of the Court, expressed the view that Lord Denning's statement had not done anything more than restate the principle expressed by Lord Cairns in *Hughes v. Metropolitan R. Co.* (1877), 2 App. Cas. 439 at p. 448, in the following terms:

". . . it is the first principle upon which all Courts of Equity proceed, that if parties who have entered into definite and distinct terms involving certain legal results—certain penalties or legal forfeiture—afterwards by their own act or with their own consent enter upon a course of negotiation which has the effect of leading one of the parties to suppose that the strict rights arising under the contract will not be enforced, or will be kept in suspense, or held in abeyance, the person who otherwise might have enforced those rights will not be allowed to enforce them where it would be inequitable having regard to the dealings which have thus taken place between the parties."

In the case of *Combe v. Combe*, [1951] 1 All E.R. 767, Lord Denning recognized the fact that some people had treated his decision in the *High Trees* case as having extended the principle stated by Lord Cairns and he was careful to restate the matter in the following terms [p. 770]:

"The principle, as I understand it, is that where one party has, by his words or conduct, made to the other a promise or assurance which was intended to affect the legal relations between them and to be acted on accordingly, then, once the other party has taken him at his word and acted on it, the one who gave the promise or assurance cannot afterwards be allowed to revert to the previous legal relations as if no such promise or assurance had been made by him, but he must accept their legal relations subject to the qualification which he himself has so introduced, even though it is not supported in point of law by any consideration, but only by his word."

It seems clear to me that this type of equitable defence can not be invoked unless there is some evidence that one of the parties entered into a course of negotiation which had the effect of leading the other to suppose that the strict rights under the contract would not be enforced, and I think that this implies that there must be evidence from which it can be inferred that the first party intended that the legal relations created by the contract would be altered as a result of the negotiations.

It is not enough to show that one party has taken advantage of indulgences granted to him by the other for if this were so in relation to commercial transactions, such as promissory notes, it would mean that the holders of such notes would be required to insist on the very letter being enforced in all cases for fear that any indulgences granted and acted upon could be translated into a waiver of their rights to enforce the contract according to its terms.

As Viscount Simonds said in *Tool Metal Mfg. Co. v. Tungsten Electric Co., Ltd.*, [1955] 2 All E.R. 657 at p. 660:

". . . the gist of the equity lies in the fact that one party has by his conduct led the other to alter his position. I lay stress on this, because I would not have it supposed, particularly in commercial transactions, that mere acts of indulgence are apt to create rights . . ."

The learned trial Judge dealt with the rule of estoppel by representation as applied to the circumstances of the present case in the following brief paragraphs [*sic*]:

"It is my opinion, however, that for such a rule to apply, the plaintiff must have known or should have known that his action or inaction was being acted upon by the defendant and that the defendant thereby changed his legal position. I do not believe that John Burrows ever gave any consideration to the fact that in accepting late payments of interest on the note, he was thereby leading Mr. Whitcomb—as an officer of the defendant corporation—into thinking that strict compliance would not be required at any time. It is a matter of regret that Mr. Burrows did not see fit to advise Mr. Whitcomb by letter or verbally of his intention to require strict adherence to the terms of the note; but be that as it may, it is my opinion that both defendants were always aware of the terms of P. 1 and knew that default in payment of interest exceeding 10 days could result in the plaintiff demanding full payment, as the plaintiff has now done."

With the greatest respect for the reasoning of the majority of the Court of Appeal, I prefer the interpretation placed on the evidence by the learned trial Judge and by Bridges, C.J.N.B., in his dissenting reasons for judgment where he said [p. 705]:

"For estoppel to apply, I think we must be satisfied that the conduct of Burrows amounted to a promise or assurance, intended to affect the legal relations of the parties to the extent that if an interest instalment became in default for 10 days the plaintiff would not claim the principal as due unless it had previously notified the defendants of its intention to do so or, if it had not so notified them, that notice would be given them the principal would be claimed if such instalment so in default were not paid. This is, I think, a great deal to infer."

I do not think that the evidence warrants the inference that the appellant entered into any negotiations with the respondents which had the effect of leading them to suppose that the appellant had agreed to disregard or hold in suspense or abeyance that part of the contract . . .

For all these reasons I would allow the appeal and restore the judgment of the learned trial Judge.

**Offer—
Acceptance—
Consideration—
Contract Not
Under Seal**

Foakes v. Beer (1884), 9 App. Cas. 605.

Mrs. Beer had successfully sued Dr. Foakes for the sum of £ 2 090 and recovered judgement. Dr. Foakes and Mrs. Beer entered into a written agreement whereby Foakes would immediately pay £ 500, and the balance over five years if Mrs. Beer would take no proceedings on the judgement. The money was paid, and after receipt of payment Mrs. Beer took action against Dr. Foakes for interest on the funds. No interest had been mentioned in the agreement.

EARL OF SELBORNE, L.E.:

. . . the question remains, whether the agreement is capable of being legally enforced. Not being under seal, it cannot be legally enforced against the respondent, unless she received consideration for it from the appellant, or unless, though without consideration, it operates by way of accord and satisfaction, so as to extinguish the claim for interest. What is the consideration? On the face of the agreement none is expressed, except a present payment of £500, on account and in part of the larger debt then due and payable by law under the judgment. The appellant did not contract to pay the future instalments of £150 each, on the times therein mentioned; much less did he give any new security, in the shape of negotiable paper, or in any other form. The promise de futuro was only that of the respondent, that if the half-yearly payments of £150 each were regularly paid, she would "take no proceedings whatever on the judgment." No doubt if the appellant had been under no antecedent obligation to pay the whole debt, his fulfilment of the condition might have imported some consideration on his part for that promise. But he was under that antecedent obligation; and payment at those deferred dates, by the forbearance and indulgence of the creditor, of the residue of the principal debt and costs, could not (in my opinion) be a consideration for the relinquishment of interest and discharge of the judgment, unless the payment of the £500, at the time of signing the agreement, was such a consideration. As to accord and satisfaction, in point of fact there could be no complete satisfaction, so long as any future instalment remained payable; and I do not see how any mere payments on account could operate in law as a satisfaction ad interim, conditionally upon other payments being afterwards duly made, unless there was a consideration sufficient to support the agreement while still unexecuted. Nor was anything, in fact, done by the respondent in this case, on the receipt of the last payment, which could be tantamount to an acquittance, if the agreement did not previously bind her.

. . . . .

The distinction between the effect of a deed under seal, and that of an agreement by parol, or by writing not under seal, may seem arbitrary, but it is established in our law; nor is it really unreasonable or practically inconvenient that the law should require particular solemnities to give to a gratuitous contract the force of a binding obligation. If the question be (as, in the actual state of the law, I think it is), whether consideration is, or is not, given in a case of this kind, by the debtor who pays down part of the debt presently due from him, for a promise by the creditor to relinquish, after certain further payments on account, the residue of the debt, I cannot say that I think consideration is given, in the sense in which I have always understood that word as used in our law.

|||||||||||||||||||||||||||||||||||||||||||||||||||||||||||||||||||||||||||||||||||||||||||||||||||||||||||||||||||||||||||||||||||||||||||||||||||||

Gratuitous Promise of Gift— Consideration— Enforceability **Governors of Dalhousie College v. Boutilier, [1934] 3 D.L.R. 593.**
Boutilier promised to donate the sum of $5 000 to the university for the general improvement of the institution. The promise of a donation was made as a result of a subscription campaign by the university. Boutilier died without making the payment and the university brought an action against his estate.

CROCKET, J.:

So far as the signed subscription itself is concerned, it is contended in behalf of the appellant that it shows upon its face a good and sufficient consideration for the deceased's promise in its statement that it was given in consideration of the subscription of others. As to this, it is first to be observed that the statement of such a consideration in the subscription paper is insufficient to support the promise if, in point of law, the subscriptions of others could not provide a valid consideration therefor. I concur in the opinion of Chisholm, C.J., that the fact that others had signed separate subscription papers for the same common object or were expected so to do does not of itself constitute a legal consideration. . . .

The doctrine of mutual promises was also put forward on the argument as a ground upon which the deceased's promise might be held to be binding. It was suggested that the statement in the subscription of the purpose for which it was made, *viz*:: "of enabling Dalhousie College to maintain and improve the efficiency of its teaching, to construct new buildings and otherwise to keep pace with the growing need of its constituency" constituted an implied request on the part of the deceased to apply the promised subscription to this object and that the acceptance by the college of his promise created a contract between them, the consideration for the promise of the deceased to pay the money being the promise of the college to apply it to the purpose stated.

I cannot think that any such construction can fairly be placed upon the subscription paper and its acceptance by the college. It certainly contains no express request to the college either "to maintain and improve the efficiency of its teaching" or "to construct new buildings and otherwise to keep pace with the growing need of its constituency," but simply states that the promise to pay the $5,000 is made for the purpose of enabling the college to do so, leaving it perfectly free to pursue what had always been its aims in whatever manner its Governors should choose. No statement is made as to the amount intended to be raised for all or any of the purposes stated. No buildings of any kind are described. The construction of new buildings is merely indicated as a means of the college keeping pace with the growing need of its constituency and apparently to be undertaken as and when the Governors should in their unfettered discretion decide the erection of any one or more buildings for any purpose was necessary or desirable.

It seems to me difficult to conceive that, had the deceased actually paid the promised money, he could have safely relied upon the mere acceptance of his own promise, couched in such vague and uncertain terms regarding its purpose as the foundation of any action against the college corporation.

So far as I can discover, there is no English or Canadian case in which it has been authoritatively decided that a reciprocal promise on the part of the promisee may be implied from the mere fact of the acceptance by the promisee of such a subscription paper from the hands of the promisor to do the thing for which the subscription is promised. There is no doubt, of course, that an express agreement by the promisee to do certain acts in return for a subscription is a sufficient consideration for the promise of the subscriber. There may, too, be circumstances proved by evidence, outside the subscription paper itself, from which such a reciprocal promise on the part of the promisee may well be implied, but I have not been able to find any English or Canadian case where it has actually been so decided in the absence of proof that the subscriber has himself either expressly requested the promisee to undertake some definite project or personally taken such a part in connection with the projected enterprise that such a request might be inferred therefrom. . . .

To hold otherwise would be to hold that a naked, voluntary promise may be converted into a binding legal contract by the subsequent action of the promisee alone without the consent, express or implied, of the promisor. There is no evidence here which in any way involves the deceased in the carrying out of the work for which the promised subscription was made other than the signing of the subscription paper itself.

||||||||||||||||||||||||||||||||||||||||||||||||||||||||||||||||||||||||||||||||||||||||||||||||||||||||||||||||||||||||||||||||||||||||||||

CASE PROBLEMS FOR DISCUSSION

Case 1

Able and Baker were good friends for many years. Able wished to make a gift to Baker of a house he owned that was subject to two mortgages held by a third party. In order to avoid the gift tax legislation in force at the time, the parties agreed that Able would convey the property to Baker and take back an interest-free mortgage equal to the difference between the two existing mortgages and the value of the property. The third mortgage would be forgiven each year in an amount equal to the permissable tax-free gift allowed each year under the *Gift Tax Act*. The gift transaction was a lawful method of disposing of the property, and Baker accepted the gift of the property. Baker moved into the house and made the payments on the first two mortgages for a number of years; then, after a difference of opinion on another matter, Able demanded payment of the third mortgage. Baker refused to pay, and Able sued Baker for the amount owed.

Discuss the respective positions of the parties to the transaction, and render a decision.

Case 2

Hansen and Brown owned cottage lots which abutted each other along a line at right angles to a lake front. Nothing marked the boundary between the two lots, and neither land-owner could recall with any degree of accuracy where the lot line actually lay. The parties had mentioned a survey of the lots on several occasions, but nothing had been done to fix the boundaries.

One summer, when both Hansen and Brown were vacationing at their respective cottages, Brown noticed a large diseased limb on a tall tree which was growing at a point approximately equidistant from each cottage. As he was concerned that the limb might fall on his cottage, Brown suggested to Hansen that he do something about the situation. To this suggestion Hansen replied: "That tree is growing on your lot, and it is up to you to cut the limb. If it should fall my way and damage the roof of my cottage, I would look to you for the repairs."

Brown decided to cut down the entire tree instead of just the diseased limb. He did so with some reluctance because the elimination of the tree would remove the only protection Hansen had from the hot afternoon sun.

Hansen did not object to the cutting of the tree at the time. Some time later, however, when a survey which he had requested revealed that the tree had been entirely on his side of the property line between the two cottage lots he brought an action against Brown for damages.

Identify the defences which might be raised by Brown, and explain how the courts might decide this case.

Case 3

On a cold evening in January, the furnace in Smith's home failed to operate properly, causing the water pipes to freeze and later burst, flooding his basement. Smith made a hurried telephone call to Brown, a plumber, when he discovered the water in his basement, and asked him if he could come over immediately and fix the leaking pipes.

Brown agreed to do so, and arrived about an hour later, only to find that Smith had discovered the leak and fixed it himself. Brown left immediately, and the next day he submitted an account to Smith for $25 for services rendered. Smith refused to pay Brown's account.

If Brown should sue Smith on the account, explain the arguments that might be raised by each of the parties, and indicate how the case might be decided.

Case 4

Simple travelled from Ontario to the east coast of Canada for his summer vacation. After his return to Ontario, he noticed small tin containers, labelled "Genuine East Coast Fog," for sale in a gift shop. Simple purchased a container for $5, and opened the can as soon as he reached his home. The can appeared to be empty, save for a few small rust spots on the interior surface.

Simple returned to the store and demanded his money back on the basis that he received no consideration for his payment of $5. The store operator told Simple the can was not meant to be opened, and refused to give him his money back. To this statement Simple responded: "How am I to know if I am getting anything for my money unless I am permitted to open the can?"

Explain the issues raised in this case, and assuming that Simple could bring an action against the seller, describe how the case might be disposed of by the judge.

Case 5

A service club in a small community decided to raise funds for the purchase of a special wheelchair which it intended to donate to a crippled child. The wheelchair was of a special design, and made only on special order. The estimated purchase price was $5 600.

Donations were solicited throughout the community, and a total of $2 100 was raised toward the purchase price. The club, unfortunately, found it difficult to solicit further donations as the $2 100 represented the contributions of nearly every family in the community.

A meeting of the club members was held to discuss ways and means of raising the further $3 500, and after some discussion, one member stood up and promised to "match dollar for dollar every additional contribution received, if the club can raise a further $1 750."

The next day, the local newspaper reported the club member's pledge, and the publicity produced a large number of donations to the fund. By the end of the week, the donations totalled $3 700 of which $1 600 had been donated that week. The club immediately placed an order for the special wheelchair, confident that the additional $150 could be raised by the club members.

A few weeks later, the club was advised that the wheelchair was ready for delivery, and the price would be $5 300 instead of the $5 600 originally quoted. The club was delighted to receive the news that the wheelchair would only cost $5 300, and immediately notified the club member who had promised to match the contributions.

When the member was advised that the $1 600 donated together with his matching pledge would be sufficient, along with funds previously collected, to pay for the wheelchair, he responded: "I promised to match dollar for dollar only if the club could raise a further $1750. Since it did not do so, I have no intention of matching the donations."

Discuss the position at law of the parties in this case, and explain how this matter might be determined if each party exercised his (or its) legal rights (if any).

Case 6

Anderson and Bacon were good friends as well as neighbours, and when Anderson was about to leave for a three-week vacation at his cottage, he asked Bacon to "keep an eye on" his house, and if anything should happen, to call him on the telephone. Bacon agreed to do so.

By the end of the second week of Anderson's vacation, Bacon noticed that Anderson's lawn and yard were in need of a "cut and trim." He spent most of his week-end mowing Anderson's lawn and weeding the garden.

When Anderson returned, he was so pleased to discover that Bacon had kept his grounds in such good order that he promised Bacon a 1967 silver dollar which he knew Bacon required for his coin collection. Bacon was delighted with Anderson's offer, and readily accepted. Anderson promised to deliver the dollar as soon as he could remove it from his safety deposit box at the bank.

A few days later, before Anderson had picked up the silver dollar from his bank, the two friends had a violent disagreement on politics, and Anderson vowed that he would never give Bacon the silver dollar.

Bacon brought an action against Anderson claiming he was entitled to the coin.

Discuss the legal issues raised in this case, and identify the particular points of law that the parties must address in their arguments. Render a decision.

CHAPTER 8

|||||||||||||||||||||||||||||||||||||||||||||||||||||||||||||||||||||||||||||||||||||||||||||||||||||||||||||||||||||||||

Legal Capacity to Contract

THE MINOR OR INFANT

Not everyone is permitted to enter into contracts which would bind them at law. Certain classes of promisors must be protected as a matter of public policy, either for reasons of their inexperience and immaturity, or their inability to appreciate the nature of their acts in making enforceable promises. The most obvious class to be protected is the group of persons of tender age called minors or infants. An infant at common law is a person under the age of 21 years, but in most provinces this has been lowered to 18 or 19 years of age by legislation.

Public policy dictates that minors should not be bound by their promises; consequently, they are not liable on most contracts that they might negotiate. The rule is not absolute, however, because in many cases, a hard and fast rule on the liability of a minor would not be in his or her best interest. For example, if a minor could not incur liability on a contract for food or clothing, the hardship would fall on the minor, rather than the party with full power to contract, as no one would be willing to supply an infant with food, shelter, or clothing on credit.[1] The law, therefore, attempts to balance the protection of the minor with the need to contract by making only those contracts for necessary items enforceable against a minor.

Enforceability and the Right to Repudiation

The enforceability of any contract for non-necessary goods will depend to some extent on whether the contract has been fully executed by the minor, or whether it has yet to be performed. If the contract made by the minor has been fully performed (and consequently, fully executed) then he may very well be bound by the agreement, unless he can show that he had been taken advantage of by the merchant, or he can return all of the goods purchased to the other party. If the contract has not been fully performed, then the agreement (if for a non-necessary item) may be voidable at his option. This rule would probably apply as well to a necessary item, if the minor has not taken delivery of the goods. For example, if a minor orders a clothing item from a mail order house, and then repudiates the contract before delivery is made, he would probably not be bound by the agreement, even though the item is a necessary.

The adult with full capacity to contract is bound in every case by the contract negotiated with an infant, since he has no obligation to do business with an infant unless he wishes to do so. If he decides to enter into a contract with a minor, then he assumes the risk (in the case of a contract for a non-necessary) that the minor might repudiate the agreement.

A minor or infant of tender age is normally under the supervision of a parent or guardian, and the need to contract in his own name is limited. The older minor, however, is in a slightly different position, with a need in some cases to enter into contracts for food, clothing, shelter, and other necessaries. For this latter group, the law provides that an infant will be bound by contracts for necessaries, and will be liable for a reasonable price for the goods received or the services supplied. The effect of this rule is to permit a merchant to provide necessaries to an infant or minor, yet limit the infant's liability to a reasonable price. This is eminently reasonable to both contracting parties: the merchant is protected because the minor is liable on the contract; the infant is protected in that the merchant may only charge the infant a reasonable price for the goods.

The unusual aspect of the law relating to minors is the criteria used by the courts to determine what is a necessary for a minor. The courts will examine the social position of the infant in deciding the question. Such an approach smacks of different standards for different minors, and has its roots in a number of older English cases,[2] but it nevertheless remains as the law today. A second requirement, which is perhaps of more concern to a modern day merchant, is the requirement that the goods supplied to the minor are actually necessary, and that the minor is not already well supplied with similar goods. Since the merchant in each case has the onus of proving these facts, some care is obviously essential on the part of merchants supplying goods of this nature to

---

[1]*Zouch d. Abbott v. Parsons* (1765), 3 Burr. 1794, 97 E.R. 1103.

[2]*Ryder v. Wombwell* (1868), L.R. 3 Ex. 90; reversed L.R. 4 Ex. 31; *Nash v. Inman*, [1908] 2 K.B. 1.

infants. The entire issue becomes rather obscure when the merchant must also distinguish between what constitutes a necessary, and what might be a luxury, bearing in mind the minor's station in life.

Contracts of employment or apprenticeship are contracts considered to be beneficial to minors, and are enforceable against them. Although some educational ventures which involve minors may not be viewed by the courts as being beneficial, many are held enforceable, even when the educational aspect is unusual. In the case of *Roberts v. Gray*,[3] an infant entered into a contract with a professional billiard player to take part in a world tour as his playing opponent. He later repudiated the contract before the tour was scheduled to take place, and the adult contracting party took action against him for breach of contract. The court held that the infant was bound by the contract because the experience of playing billiards with a professional would be valuable instruction for a minor who wished to make billiards his career.

The Effect of Repudiation

The general rule relating to executory contracts for non-necessary goods or services is that the minor or infant may repudiate the contract at any time at his option. This rule applies even when the terms of the contract are very fair to the infant. Once the contract has been repudiated, the minor is entitled to a return of any deposit paid to the adult contractor, but where the minor has purchased the goods on credit and taken delivery, he must return the goods before he may receive a return of any monies paid. Any damage to the goods which is not a direct result of the minor's deliberate act is not recoverable by the merchant: the merchant may not deduct the "wear and tear" to the goods from the funds repayable to the infant. The reasoning of the courts in establishing this rule is that the merchant should not be permitted to recover under the law of torts what he cannot recover by the law of contract.[4] However, if the minor deliberately misrepresents the use for which he intends the goods, and the goods are damaged, then the merchant may be entitled to recover the loss by way of an action for tort.[5]

The protection extended to a minor under the rules of contract may not be used by a minor to perpetrate a fraud on an unsuspecting merchant. On the other hand, an adult entering into a contract with a minor who has represented himself as having attained the age of majority will not be permitted to hold the minor to the contract. The mere fact that a minor misrepresents his age does not generally alter the fact that he cannot bind himself in a contract for non-necessaries.[6]

In contracts for non-necessary goods where the minor has falsely represented that he is of full age when, in fact, he is not, the merchant may be entitled to recover the goods on the basis of the minor's fraud. Additionally, where a minor attempts to use his incapacity to take advantage of merchants, the criminal law relating to obtaining goods under false pretenses may also be applicable. What the law attempts to do in providing protection to the minor is to impose only a limited liability toward others, based upon what is perceived as being in the best interests of the minor. The treatment of

---

[3][1913] 1 K.B. 520.

[4]*Jennings v. Rundall* (1799), 8 T.R. 335, 101 E.R. 1419; *Dickson Bros. Garage & U Drive Ltd. v. Woo* (1957), 10 D.L.R. (2d) 652; affirmed 11 D.L.R. (2d) 477.
[5]*Burnhard v. Haggis* (1863), 32 L.J.C.P. 189; *Ballett v. Mingay*, [1943] K.B. 281.
[6]*Jewell v. Brood* (1909), 20 O.L.R. 176.

minors is, in a sense, a matter of equity; where a minor has attempted to use his minority in a manner which is contrary to public policy, the courts will either provide the other contracting party with a remedy for the loss caused by the infant, or prevent the infant from avoiding liability under the contract.

Where the minor has entered into a contract of a continuing or permanent nature under which he receives benefits and incurs obligations (such as engaging in a partnership, or purchasing non-necessary goods on a long-term credit contract), the contract must be repudiated by the minor within a reasonable time after attaining the age of majority, otherwise it will become binding on him for the balance of its term.

The reverse is true for contracts for non-necessary items purchased by a minor under a contract that is *not* of a continuing nature. The infant must expressly ratify such a contract on attaining the age of majority in order to be bound by it. For example, a minor enters into a contract to purchase a sail-boat in the fall of the year. The minor gives the merchant a deposit to hold the boat until spring, and promises he will pay the balance at that time. The contract would be voidable at the infant's option, and he would be free to ignore the contract, or repudiate it any time before reaching the age of majority. If the minor wished to be bound by the transaction, he would be obliged to ratify it after attaining the age of majority.

||||||||||||||||||||||||||||||||||||||||||||||||||||||||||||||||||||||||||||||

CASE 8.1
Noble's Ltd. v. Bellefleur (1963), 37 D.L.R. (2d) 519.

McNAIR, C.J.N.B.:

While an infant may be liable in tort generally, he is not answerable for a tort committed in the course of doing an act directly connected with, or contemplated by, a contract which, as an infant, he is entitled to avoid. An infant cannot, through a change in the form of action to one *ex delicto*, be made liable for the breach of a voidable contract: *R. Leslie, Ltd. v. Sheill*, [1914] 3 K.B. 607 at p. 611 (C.A.), 83 L.J.K.B. 1145, [1914-15] All E.R. Rep. 511.

In the well-known case of *Jennings v. Rundall* (1799), 8 Term R. 335, 101 E.R. 1419, an infant who had hired a mare and injured her by excessive and improper riding was held not liable in tort for negligence. The act contemplated by the hiring was riding the mare. The fact it became excessive and improper was not sufficient to carry it beyond what was contemplated by the contract so as to render the infant liable in tort.

Dickson Bros. Garage et al. v. Woo Wai Jing et al. (1957), 11 D.L.R. (2d) 477, 23 W.W.R. 485, is a case which, in my opinion, is on all fours with that now before us. The defendant, an infant, hired an automobile and, in the course of using it for a purpose permitted by the contract of hiring, drove so negligently that he wrecked it. The plaintiff sued in contract and in tort for the resulting damage. The British Columbia Court of Appeal, applying *Jennings v. Rundall, supra*, held that, as it could not be said the infant drove the car so wantonly that what he did was outside the purview of the contract, he could not be held liable in tort for his negligence.

The plaintiff, when selling the car, clearly contemplated the defendant would drive it. The conditional sale contract provided the car was to be at the defendant's risk and placed no restriction on the manner in which it should be driven. That the plaintiff had in mind the possibility of physical damage resulting from the driving of the car is evidenced by the stipulation in the contract that the defendant would procure and maintain insurance against all physical damage risks.

The amount of the damages which the plaintiff claimed was the equivalent of the deferred balance of the purchase-price less the financing charge. The action was framed in tort, but the real purpose was to recover under the contract. As at the time of its destruction the car was being used in a manner contemplated by the parties to the conditional sale agreement, any claim against the plaintiff in tort, founded on his negligent driving, must fail.

|||||||||||||||||||||||||||||||||||||||||||||||||||||||||||||||||||||||||||||||

Statutory Protection of Minors

Statute law has modified the common law on the question of ratification to some extent. The provinces of New Brunswick, Newfoundland, Nova Scotia, Ontario, and Prince Edward Island have all passed legislation which requires the ratification to be in writing before it will be binding on the infant. British Columbia has carried the matter one step further in its protection of minors: an infant cannot ratify a contract of this nature in any fashion which would render it enforceable by the adult contracting party. This legislation also has the effect of rendering contracts for non-necessaries and debt contracts "absolutely void." This particular term, however, is open to question as to whether it will only be applied to the liability of the minor, or to both the minor and the other contracting party if the issue should be raised. If the adult contracting party fails to perform the contract, the question arises: Is the contract absolutely void, and is the infant deprived of a remedy, or would the words "absolutely void" be construed to mean void as against the minor? The question remains unresolved at the present time, but given the intent of the legislation, an interpretation that would deprive the minor of a right of action would appear to be counter to the intention of the statute.

Minors Engaged in Business

Contracts of employment, if lawful, and which contain terms which are not onerous, are generally binding on minors. Since agreements of this type are generally contracts of indefinite hiring, the minor need only give reasonable notice to terminate, and he would be free of all obligations imposed by the agreement. A minor engaging in business himself, or in a partnership, is quite a different matter, as the law generally does not support the thesis that an infant must, of necessity, engage in business activity as a principal.

The rules relating to contracts engaged in by an infant merchant are, for the most part, consistent with those for minors in general. Since it is not necessary for an infant to engage in business, any attempt to purchase business equipment, even if the equipment is necessary for the business, will probably be treated by the courts as a contract for non-necessaries. This renders the contract voidable at the option of the minor, and if he has not taken delivery of the goods, it may permit him to repudiate the contract, and obtain a refund of any deposit paid. Similarly, if he has taken delivery of goods on credit, he may return the goods and cancel his obligation. Where the goods are accidently damaged while in the minor's possession, he will not normally be liable for the damage. However, if he has sold the goods, he will be required to deliver up any monies he has received.

In the case of a sale of goods by an infant merchant, the infant merchant cannot be obliged to perform the contract if he does not wish to do so, as this type of contract is also voidable at his option. If he received a deposit or part-payment with regard to a sale of goods or services he would not be required to deliver the goods, but he would, of course, be required to return the deposit.

These general rules for contracts engaged in by infant merchants are also consistent with the general rules for the enforcement of infant contracts. Even though they tend to place hardship on adults dealing with minors, public policy, neverthe-less, dictates protection of the minor over the rights of persons of full contracting age. With freedom to contract, an adult is under no obligation to deal with an infant merchant any more than there is an obliga-tion on the adult merchant to deal with an infant customer. Since the opportunity to take advantage of the infant's inexperience in business matters exists in both cases, unfair treatment is avoided by the exten-sion of infant protection rule to the infant merchant as well.

In the case of a minor joining a partner-ship, the protection afforded the minor is again consistent with the general public policy concerning infants' contracts. A partnership agreement which involves a minor in a contract for non-necessaries is voidable by the minor, even though the adult parties remain bound. Since the con-tract is a continuing contract, the infant must repudiate it promptly on or before reaching the age of majority if he wishes to avoid liability under it.[7] If he continues to accept benefits under the contract after reaching the age of majority, he will be bound by the contract, even though he did not expressly ratify it. Ratification will be implied from his action of taking benefits under the contract.

Should the minor repudiate the partner-ship agreement, he would not be liable for any debts incurred by the partnership dur-ing his minority; it would also appear that he would not be entitled to withdraw his contribution to the partnership until the debts of the partnership have been set-tled.[8]

The Parent-Infant Relationship

Parents are not normally liable at common

[7]*Hilliard v. Dillon*, [1955] O.W.N. 621.
[8]See, for example, the *Partnerships Act*, R.S.O. 1980, c. 370, s. 44.

law for the debts incurred by their infant children. This rule, however, has been modified to some extent by family law leg-islation in some provinces. This legislation obligates parents to support a child under the age of 16 years, and renders parents jointly and severally liable with the child for any necessaries supplied to the child by merchants. The minor may, as the parents' "agent of necessity," pledge the parents' credit to obtain necessaries of life, and the parents will be bound by the minor's ac-tions. Apart from this statutory require-ment, there are a number of other circum-stances under which parents may become liable for the debts of their infant children. In some cases, a parent may have ap-pointed the child to act as his or her agent to purchase goods on credit. In these situ-ations, a true agency situation would exist in which the parent, as principal, would be liable for payment. However, if the child were to later purchase goods on credit for his own use, and the parent continued to pay the merchant, the parent would be bound to pay the debts of the infant in the future, because he implied by his conduct that he would continue to honour the debts incurred. In such cases, the parent must specifically state to the merchant that he does not intend to be bound by any subsequent purchases of his infant child if he wishes to avoid liability for future pur-chases negotiated by the minor.

DRUNKEN AND INSANE PERSONS

The courts treat drunken and insane per-sons in much the same way as infants with respect to the capacity to contract. Those persons who have been committed to a mental institution cannot normally incur any liability in contract. Persons who suffer mental impairment from time to time are subject to a number of special contract rules.

In general, a person who suffers from some mental impairment caused either as a result of some physical or mental damage, or as a result of drugs or alcohol, will be liable on any contract for necessaries negotiated him, and he will be obliged to pay a reasonable price for the goods or services. In this respect, the law makes no distinction between infants and persons suffering from some mental disability. The merchant involved would be entitled to payment even if he knew of the insane or drunken state of the purchaser. Again, this is a matter of public policy which dictates that it is in the best interests of the drunken or insane person to be entitled to obtain the necessaries of life from merchants, and to be bound by such contracts of purchase.

Contracts for non-necessary items, however, are treated in a different manner from contracts for necessaries. For this particular group of persons who lack capacity, the rules are different from those pertaining to infants. If a person is drunken or insane at the time that he enters into a contract for what might be considered a non-necessary item or service, and where his mental state is such that he is incapable of knowing or appreciating the nature of his actions, if he can establish by evidence that he was in such a condition, and the other contracting party knew he was in that condition, then the contract may be voidable by him when he becomes aware of the contract on his return to a sane or sober state.

It is important in the case of an intoxicated or insane person that the contract be repudiated as soon as it is brought to his attention after his return to sanity or sobri-

ety. If the contract is not repudiated promptly, and all of the goods returned, the opportunity to avoid liability will be lost. Similarly, any act which would imply acceptance of the contract while sane or sober would render the contract binding. For example, Able attended an auction sale while in an intoxicated state. Everyone at the sale, including the auctioneer, was aware of his condition. When a house and land came up for auction, Able bid vigorously on the property, and was the successful bidder. Later, when in a sober state, he was informed of his purchase, and he affirmed the contract. Immediately thereafter he changed his mind, and repudiated the contract on the basis that he was drunk at the time, and the auctioneer was aware of his condition.

When the case came before the court, the court held that he had had the opportunity to avoid the contract when he became sober, but instead, he affirmed it, and having done so, was bound by his acceptance. He could not later repudiate the contract.[9]

The position of both the common law and equity are in accord with respect to intoxicated and insane persons in cases where the contract is affirmed, then subsequently repudiated. The effect of the affirmation renders the contract binding, and the insane or intoxicated person would be liable for breach of contract if the agreement was later rejected. If the contract concerned goods or services, the injured party would be entitled to monetary damages for the loss suffered. In the case of a contract concerning land, the equitable remedy of specific performance would be available to force the person to complete the transaction.

[9]*Matthews v. Baxter* (1873), L.R. 8 Ex. 132.

ENEMY ALIENS

An *alien* is a person residing in Canada who is not a Canadian citizen. An alien is not restricted in the right to contract except for a few special laws in some provinces which are applicable to certain kinds of contracts.[10] An *enemy alien*, on the other hand, is a person who, in time of war, has a permanent residence or business in the country which is the declared enemy of Canada. Once hostilities are declared, all contracts between enemy aliens and residents of Canada are generally void and illegal as a matter of public policy. Nationality is not necessarily the determining factor in deciding if a person is an enemy alien. A Canadian citizen living in the enemy country and carrying on a business there would probably be classed as an enemy person with respect to any contract entered into with a resident of Canada.[11] Where the curtailment of the enemy alien's activities would not be in the public interest, the Crown will often grant the enemy alien the right to continue business operations in Canada as if he were an alien friend, but where this is done, strict controls relating to dealings with the enemy country are usually imposed. In some cases, contracts of a continuing nature that existed at the time hostilities began may be suspended if it can be shown that the suspension is in the public interest. Again, permission of the Crown would probably be required if the contract required any contact between a resident of Canada and the enemy alien.

[10]*Porter v. Freudenberg*, [1915] 1 K.B. 857; *Daimler Co. v. Continental Tyre Co.*, [1916] 2 A.C. 307.
[11]For example, in some provinces, an alien may not be permitted to engage in certain kinds of professional work, such as law, until a license to practice (which may be restricted to Canadian citizens) is obtained.

CORPORATIONS

A corporation is a creature of statute, and as such may possess only those powers which the statute may grant it. Corporations formed under Royal Charter or letters patent are generally considered to have all the powers to contract that a natural person may have—the statute which provides for incorporation may specifically give the corporation these rights as well. The legislature need not give a corporation broad powers of contract if it does not wish to do so; indeed, many special-purpose corporations do have their powers strictly controlled or limited. Many of these corporations are created under a special Act of a legislature or Parliament for specific purposes. If they should enter into a contract that is beyond their limitations the contract will be void, and their action *ultra vires*. While this may appear to be harsh treatment for an unsuspecting person who enters into a contract with a "special-Act" corporation which acts beyond the limits of its powers, everyone is deemed to know the law, and the statute creating the corporation, and its contents, including the limitations on its contractual powers, is considered to be public knowledge, and familiar to everyone.

Business corporations in most provinces are usually incorporated under legislation which gives the corporations very wide powers of contract; in many cases, all the powers of a mature natural person. This is not, however, always the case. A corporation, in its articles of incorporation, may limit its own powers for specific reasons, and depending upon the legislation under which it was incorporated, the limitation may bind third parties. A full discussion of the effect of these limitations on the capacity of a corporation to contract is reserved for Chapter 18, "Corporation Law."

LABOUR UNIONS

A labour union is an organization with powers that vary considerably from province to province. Originally, a union was an illegal organization, since its object was restraint of trade, but legislation in the 19th century changed the status of the union from an illegal to a legal status. A contract which a labour union negotiates with an employer would not normally be enforceable were it not for specific legislation governing its negotiation and enforcement. Apart from a brief period in Ontario when the courts had the authority to enforce collective agreements,[12] the courts have not normally been concerned with labour contracts. The reason for this may be found in the law itself. The legislation in most provinces, and at the federal level, provide for the interpretation and enforcement of collective agreements by binding arbitration rather than the courts. In addition, the legislation in all provinces specifically provide that a labour union certified by the Labour Relations Board has the exclusive authority to negotiate a collective agreement for the employees it represents. The capacity of a labour union in this regard is examined in detail in Chapter 20, "Labour Law."

BANKRUPT PERSONS

A person who has been declared bankrupt has a limited capacity to contract. Until he receives his discharge, a bankrupt person may not enter into any contract except for necessaries. All business contracts entered into before bankruptcy become the responsibility of the trustee in bankruptcy, and the bankrupt, on discharge, is released from the responsibility of the contracts and all related debts, except those relating to breach of trust, fraud, and certain orders of the court.

To protect persons who may not realize that they are dealing with an undischarged bankrupt, the *Bankruptcy Act*[13] requires the undischarged bankrupt to reveal the fact that he is an undischarged bankrupt before entering into any contract which involves more than $500.

[12]*Collective Bargaining Act, 1943*, 1943 (Ont.), c. 4.

[13]*Bankruptcy Act*, R.S.C. 1970, c. B-3.

|||||||||||||||||||||||||||||||||||||||||||||||||||||||||||||||||||||||||||||||||||||||||||||||||||||||||||||||||||||||||||||||

SUMMARY   Not everyone has the capacity at law to enter into a contract which the courts will enforce. Minors or infants, being persons who have not reached the age of majority, as a general rule, are not liable under any contract they may make, but in the interests of the minor, the courts will hold the minor liable in contracts "for necessaries." Necessaries generally include food, shelter, clothing, employment, and education, but do not include contracts negotiated by an infant or minor engaged in business for himself. All contracts, other than contracts for necessaries, are voidable at the infant's option.

Other persons may also lack the capacity to contract. Enemy aliens during hostilities are neither permitted to enter into, nor enforce, contracts with others. Intoxicated persons and insane persons are bound to pay a reasonable price for necessaries contracted for while in a drunken or insane state, but they will not generally be liable for other contracts if they can show that they were drunken or insance at the time of making the contract, and the other party was aware of it. They must, however, repudiate the contract promptly on becoming sane or sober. Bankrupt persons are prohibited from entering into contracts except for necessaries until they are discharged by the courts.

Corporations and labour unions, because of their nature, may be subject to certain limitations in their capacity to contract. The limitations are based, in part, on their activities, with the rights and powers in respect to their contracts or collective agreements clearly delineated by statute. Apart from the restrictions placed upon these groups, and certain limitations on a few others (such as native Indians living on reservations), the courts recognize all persons that have reached the age of majority as persons with full capacity to contract.

DISCUSSION QUESTIONS	1. *Identify the three general classes of persons protected by public policy in contract law.*

DISCUSSION QUESTIONS

1. *Identify the three general classes of persons protected by public policy in contract law.*
2. *In what type of contract may a minor incur liability?*
3. *What are the criteria used to determine when a minor may be liable for necessaries?*
4. *What unstated risk is undertaken by an adult with full capacity to contract in contracts with minors?*
5. *An adult with full capacity to contract enters into a contract for a non-necessary item with a minor. If the adult believes, without asking, that the infant is of legal age, could the adult use this as a defence if the infant later repudiates the contract? Could the adult use this as a cause of action?*
6. *In the case above, assume that the minor falsely claimed that he was of age. Discuss the status of the contract.*
7. *In what light do courts view contracts of apprenticeship or employment?*
8. *How would you interpret the British Columbia legislation which uses the phrase "absolutely void" when the adult contracting party fails to perform the contract?*
9. *In your opinion, are the laws pertaining to a minor in business closer to those for an adult in business, or closer to those for minors in general? Make reference to passages of the text.*
10. *Define "agent of necessity."*
11. *In what respect do the courts make no distinction between minors and those persons with mental disabilities?*
12. *Does the burden of proof lie with an impaired purchaser who cannot appreciate the nature of his actions or with the vendor who does not know he is in that state?*

13. *In what respect does the return to sobriety play in the repudiation of a contract for non-necessaries?*

14. *How can a contract entered into by a "special-Act" corporation be avoided?*

15. *What legal limits are placed on bankrupt persons with regard to their capacity to contract?*

||||||||||||||||||||||||||||||||||||||||||||||||||||||||||||||||||||||||||||||||||||||||||||||||||||||||||||||||||||||||||||||||||||||||||||||||||||||||||||||||||||||||||||||||||

JUDICIAL DECISIONS

Capacity to Contract—Infants —Necessaries

Nash v. Inman, [1908] 2 K.B. 1.

The defendant was an infant university student who purchased 11 fancy suits when he already had an ample supply of clothes. The plaintiff tailor brought an action for the price of the clothes when the infant refused to pay for the goods.

FLETCHER MOULTON, L.J.:

I think that the difficulty and at the same time the suggestion of hardship to the plaintiff in such a case as this disappear when one considers what is the true basis of an action against an infant for necessaries. It is usually spoken of as a case of enforcing a contract against the infant, but I agree with the view expressed by the Court in *Rhodes* v. *Rhodes*, in the parallel case of a claim for necessaries against a lunatic, that this language is somewhat unfortunate. An infant, like a lunatic, is incapable of making a contract of purchase in the strict sense of the words; but if a man satisfies the needs of the infant or lunatic by supplying to him necessaries, the law will imply an obligation to repay him for the services so rendered, and will enforce that obligation against the estate of the infant or lunatic. The consequence is that the basis of the action is hardly contract. Its real foundation is an obligation which the law imposes on the infant to make a fair payment in respect of needs satisfied. In other words the obligation arises *re* and not *consensu*. I do not mean that this nicety of legal phraseology has been adhered to. The common and convenient phrase is that an infant is liable for goods sold and delivered provided that they are necessaries, and there is no objection to that phraseology so long as its true meaning is understood. But the treatment of such actions by the Courts of Common Law has been in accordance with that principle I have referred to. That the articles were necessaries had to be alleged and proved by the plaintiff as part of his case, and the sum he recovered was based on a quantum meruit. If he claimed anything beyond this he failed, and it did not help him that he could prove that the prices were agreed prices. All this is very ancient law, and is confirmed by the provisions of s. 2 of the Sale of Goods Act, 1893—an Act which was intended to codify the existing law. That section expressly provides that the consequence of necessaries sold and delivered to an infant is that he must pay a reasonable price therefor.

The Sale of Goods Act, 1893, gives a statutory definition of what are necessaries in a legal sense, which entirely removes any doubt, if any doubt previously existed, as to what that word in legal phraseology means. [The Lord Justice read the definition.] Hence, if an action is brought by one who claims to enforce against an infant such an obligation, it is obvious that the plaintiff in order to prove his case must shew that the goods supplied come within this definition.

. . . the plaintiff has to shew, first, that the goods were suitable to the condition in life of the infant; and, secondly, that they were suitable to his actual requirements at the time—or, in other words, that the infant had not at the time an adequate supply from other sources. There is authority to shew that this was the case even before the Act of 1893. In *Johnstone* v. *Marks* this doctrine is laid down with the greatest clearness, and the ratio decidendi of that case applies equally to cases since that Act. Therefore there is no doubt whatever that in order to succeed in an action for goods sold and delivered to an infant the plaintiff must shew that they satisfy both the conditions I have mentioned. Everything which is necessary to bring them within s. 2 it is for him to prove.

Passing on from general principles, let me take the facts of the present case. In my opinion they raise no point whatever as to the duty of the judge as contrasted with the duty of the jury arising from the peculiar character of the action. We have only to follow the lines of the law consistently administered by this Court for many more years than I can think of, an example of which as applied to the case of the supply of necessaries to an infant is given by the decision of the Court of Exchequer Chamber in the case of *Ryder* v. *Wombwell*.

. . . . . .

The issue is that case was whether certain articles were suitable to the condition in life of the defendant, the infant, and the Court of Exchequer Chamber thought that no jury could reasonably find that those articles were suitable to the condition of that defendant, and therefore they said that the judge—not by reason of any peculiar rule applicable to actions of this kind, but in the discharge of his regular duties in all cases of trial by a jury—ought not to have left the question to the jury because there was no evidence on which they could reasonably find for the plaintiff. We have before us a similar case, in which the issue is not only whether the articles in question were suitable to the defendant's condition in life, but whether they were suitable to his actual requirements at the time of the sale and delivery; and how does the evidence stand? The evidence for the plaintiff shewed that one of his travellers, hearing that a freshman at Trinity College was spending money pretty liberally, called on him to get an order for clothes, and sold him within nine months goods which at cash prices came to over 120*l*., including an extravagant number of waistcoats and other articles of clothing, and that is all that the plaintiff proved. The defendant's father proved the infancy, and then proved that the defendant had an adequate supply of clothes, and stated what they were. That evidence was uncontradicted. Not only was it not contradicted by any other evidence, but there was no cross-examination tending to shake the credit of the witness, against whose character and means of knowledge nothing could be said. On that uncontradicted evidence the judge came to the conclusion, to use the language of the Court in *Ryder* v. *Wombwell*, that there was no evidence on which the jury might properly find that these goods were necessary to the actual requirements of the infant at the time of sale and delivery, and therefore, in accordance with the duty of the judge in all cases of trial by jury, he withdrew the case from the jury and directed judgment to be entered for the defendant. In my opinion he was justified by the practice of the Court in so doing, and this appeal must be dismissed.

|||||||||||||||||||||||||||||||||||||||||||||||||||||||||||||||||||||||||||||||||||||||||||||||||||||||||||||||||||||||||||||||||||||||||||||||||||||||||||||||||||

Capacity to Contract— Infants—Fraud on Part of Infant

Gregson v. Law and Barry (1913), 5 W.W.R. 1017.

An infant made a transfer of land to a person who was unaware of her infancy in return for the market value of the property. In the affidavits accompanying the deed, the infant swore that she was of full age. She later repudiated the conveyance, and brought an action for a return of the property.

MURPHY, J.:

> In this action I am forced to hold on the evidence that the plaintiff well knew when she executed the final deed to Law that, being a minor, she could not legally do so, and that, with such knowledge, she proceeded to complete and execute the same, including the making of the acknowledgment representing herself to be of full age. No hint of the true condition of things was given to Law, and I hold this was done knowingly, and that therefore the plaintiff is now coming into court to take advantage of her own fraud. Whilst, apparently, it is true to say that being an infant she could not be made liable on a contract thus brought about, it is, I think, an altogether different proposition to say the court will actually assist her to obtain advantages based entirely on her own fraudulent act.
>
> The authorities cited in argument show in fact, I consider, that infants are no more entitled than adults to gain benefits to themselves by fraud, or at any rate establish the proposition that the courts will not become active agents to bring about such a result.
>
> The action is dismissed.

|||||||||||||||||||||||||||||||||||||||||||||||||||||||||||||||||||||||||||||||||||||||||||||||||||||||||||||||||||||||||||||||||||||||||||||||||||||||||||||||||||

CASE PROBLEMS FOR DISCUSSION

Case 1

Alice, a young woman 17 years of age, saw an advertisement in a magazine which offered a 24-piece set of silver flatware for sale on the following terms: "$100 payable with order, and monthly payments of $50 each, payable over a three-year term."

The advertisement was accompanied by a coupon which set out the terms of payment, and required the purchaser to provide his or her name and address, and signature in the space provided.

Alice completed the coupon and mailed it, together with a cheque for $100, to the seller. A few weeks later, the 24-piece set of silverware arrived by post.

Alice made a number of payments according to the terms of the agreement, then decided that she did not wish to continue with the agreement. A week before her 18th birthday, she wrote to the seller and repudiated the contract, but did not offer to return the silverware because she had lost several of the teaspoons.

The seller and Alice then engaged in a protracted round of correspondence in which the seller demanded a return of the silverware and the retention of all money paid as the price of her release from the agreement. Alice refused to return the silverware, and maintained that she was entitled to a return of the payments as she was a minor at the time she entered into the agreement.

The seller, some 10 months later, brought an action against Alice for the balance of the purchase price.

Discuss the defences (if any) which Alice might raise in this case, and render a decision.

Case 2

Hamish, a university student and a football enthusiast, travelled with his university football team to watch a game played at an out-of-town university. After the game, he visited a local bar with some friends, and drank much more than he expected. He was quite drunk when he stumbled into the hotel where he had arranged accommodation, but managed to sign the hotel register and find his way to his room.

The next morning, he awoke late and discovered that he had only a few minutes to catch the bus back to the university. He raced from the hotel, and arrived at the bus stop just before the bus was ready to leave. Some time later, he discovered the key to the hotel room in his pocket, and realized that he had not paid for his room.

In a few days' time, Hamish received a statement from the hotel for $75. He thought that this rate for the room was excessive, and refused to pay the account on the basis that he was intoxicated at the time. The hotel then brought an action against him for the rental of the room.

Discuss the rights of the parties, and the issues which might be raised in this case. Render a decision.

Case 3

Sharp had operated a small wholesale grocery business for a number of years with limited success. Eventually, he found himself seriously in debt as a result of a number of unfortunate purchases of goods that spoiled before he could find a market for them, and he made a voluntary assignment in bankruptcy.

A few weeks later, while still an undischarged bankrupt, he purchased $600 worth of farm produce on credit from a farmer who was unaware of the fact that he was an undischarged bankrupt. Sharp sold part of the goods at a profit to a friend, and kept the remainder of the food for his own use.

When Sharp failed to pay the farmer, the farmer instituted legal proceedings to collect the $600.

Explain the rights of the farmer in this case, and render a decision.

Case 4

Jones entered into a rental agreement with Cross-Moto-Cycle for a one-month lease of a motorcycle by misrepresenting his age as being 20 when, in reality, he was only 17 years of age. The agreement which Jones signed prohibited the use of the motorcycle in any race or contest, and required Jones to assume responsibility for any damage to the machine while it was in his possession.

A week after Jones acquired the machine, he made arrangements to enter a motorcycle race which was to be held in a nearby city. On his way to the race, he lost control of the motorcycle on a sharp turn in the road, and the machine was badly damaged in the ensuing accident.

Jones refused to pay for the rental and the damage on the basis that he had not attained the age of majority, and was not liable on the contract.

Discuss the rights of Cross-Moto-Cycle, and comment on its success if it should take legal proceedings against Jones.

CHAPTER 9

Requirement of Legality

ENFORCEABILITY OF AN ILLEGAL AGREEMENT

Agreements which offend the public good are not enforceable. If parties enter into an agreement which has an illegal object as its subject-matter or purpose it may not only be unenforceable, but illegal as well. Under these circumstances, the parties may be liable to a penalty or fine for either making the agreement, or attempting to carry it out. However, certain contracts are only rendered void by public policy in general, or by specific statutes. In these cases, the law has simply identified certain contractual activities which it will not enforce if the parties fail to comply with the statute or the policy. In other cases, the law declares certain activities to be not only illegal, but the contract pertaining thereto void, or absolutely void. As a result of these various combinations, the absence of legaility does not always neatly classify contracts as those which are unlawful, and those which are void, since an overlap exists.

LEGALITY UNDER STATUTE LAW

An illegal contract, if considered in a narrow sense, includes any agreement to commit a crime, such as an agreement to rob, assault, abduct, murder, obtain goods under false pretenses, or commit any other act prohibited under the *Criminal Code*.[1] For example, an agreement by two parties to commit the robbery of a bank would be an illegal contract, and subject to criminal penalties as a conspiracy to commit a crime, even if the robbery was not carried out. If one party refused to go through with the agreement, the other party would not be entitled to take the matter to the courts for redress because the contract would be absolutely void and unenforceable.

Another type of agreement that would be equally illegal would be an agreement relating to the embezzlement of funds by an employee where the employee promises the shop-owner restitution in return for his promise not to report the crime to the police. The victim of the theft is often not aware that he has an obligation to report the crime, and the formation of an agreement to accept repayment of the funds in return for a promise to not report the matter is illegal, and the contract would accordingly be unenforceable.

A statute which affects certain kinds of contracts and which, in essence, is criminal law is the *Combines Investigation Act*.[2] This statute renders illegal any contract or agreement between business firms which represents an activity in restraint of competition. The Act covers a number of business practices which are contrary to the public interest, the most important being contracts or agreements which tend to fix prices, eliminate or reduce the number of competitors, allocate markets, or reduce output in such a way that competition is unduly restricted. The Act applies to contracts concerning both goods and services, and attempts to provide a balance between freedom of trade and the protection of the consumer. The formation of mergers or monopolies which would be against the public interest are also prohibited under the Act, and all contracts relating to the formation of such a new entity would also be illegal. Similarly, any agreement between existing competitors which would prevent new competition from entering the market would be prohibited by the Act, and the agreement would be illegal.

Statute law, other than criminal law, may also render certain types of contracts illegal and unenforceable. The *Lord's Day Act*,[3] for example, states that all contracts negotiated and made on a Sunday are illegal if the subject-matter of the agreement does not fall within one of the exempted activities. The Act permits the provinces to modify the provisions of the Act itself, and in many provinces this right has been further delegated to the municipalities. As a result, many municipalities permit sports and other forms of entertainment to take place on Sunday, and they permit the promoters to lawfully sell tickets to the spectators on that day.

Several provinces, notably Ontario and Manitoba, have passed legislation[4] designed to supplement the *Lord's Day Act* by

---

[1]*Criminal Code*, R.S.C. 1970, c. C-34, as amended.
[2]*Combines Investigation Act*, R.S.C. 1970, c. C-23.

[3]*Lord's Day Act*, R.S.C. 1970, c. L-13.
[4]*Retail Business Holidays Act, 1975*, R.S.O. 1980, c. 453, c. 9; *Retail Business Holiday Closing Act, 1977 (Man.)*, c. 26.

prohibiting the sale of goods and services on Sundays and certain holidays. The general thrust of the legislation is to limit retail activity on the days in question to essential and holiday-related services, rather than to allow large-scale retailing. The legislation attempts to exempt many small businesses from the prohibition, and renders all other contracts made on Sundays and holidays void and illegal by a prohibition on the sale of goods and services on the specified days.

Other statutes, such as workmen's compensation legislation, land-use planning legislation in some provinces,[5] and wagering laws[6] render any agreement made in violation of the Act void and unenforceable. The courts have long frowned upon gamblers using the courts to collect wagers, and as a matter of policy have treated wagering contracts as unenforceable except where specific legislation has made them enforceable.

One type of contract that contains an element of wager, that is not treated as being illegal or void is the contract of insurance. An insurance transaction, while it bears a superficial resemblance to a wager, is essentially an attempt to provide protection from a financial loss which the insured hopes will not occur. This is particularly true in the case of life insurance. In this sense, it is quite different from placing a wager on the outcome of a football game or a horse race, where the gambler hopes to be the winner.

[5]For example, the *Planning Act*, R.S.O. 1980, c. 379, as amended, provides that any subdivision and sale of land which violates the Act is absolutely void: see s. 29 (as amended).
[6]The *Gaming Act*, R.S.O. 1980, c. 183, s. 3, however, permits bets on cards, dice or other games to be recoverable if the amount of money involved does not exceed $40. It does not apply to other kinds of wagers.

What distinguishes the contract of insurance from a simple wager is the insurable interest of the party taking out the insurance. Since the insured is presumed to have an interest in the insured event not happening (particularly if the insurance is on his life) this type of wager assumes an air of legitimacy. The provincial legislatures have recognized this difference, and passed legislation pertaining to insurance contracts which render them valid and enforceable, provided that an insurable interest exists, or the provisions of the Act permit the particular interest to be insured. The importance of this type of agreement as a risk-spreading or risk-reducing device for business and the public in general far outweighs the wager element in the agreement. Public policy has, on this basis, generally legitimated insurance contracts by legislative enforcement.

One type of contract which the courts treat as illegal is a contract between an unlicensed tradesman, or professional, and a contracting party. If the jurisdiction in which the tradesman or professional operates requires the person to be licensed in order to perform services for the public at large, then an unlicensed tradesman or professional may not enforce a contract for payment for the services if the other party refuses to pay the account. In most provinces, the licensing of professionals is on a province-wide basis, and penalties are provided where an unlicensed person engages in a recognized professional activity. The medical, legal, dental, land surveying, architectural, and engineering professions, for example, are subject to such licensing requirements in an effort to protect the public from unqualified practitioners. The same holds true for many trades, although in some provinces, these are licensed at the local level.

Where a licence to practice is required, and the tradesman is unlicensed, it would appear to be a good defence to a claim for payment for the defendant to argue that the contract is unenforceable on the tradesman's part because he is unlicensed.[7] However, where the unlicensed tradesman supplies materials as well as services, the defence may well be limited only to the services supplied, and not to the value of the goods. In a recent case,[8] the Supreme Court of Ontario held that an unlicensed tradesman may recover for the value of the goods supplied, because the particular by-law licensing the contractor did not contain a prohibition on the sale of material by an unlicensed contractor. It should be noted, however, that the reverse does not apply. If the tradesman fails to perform the contract properly, and the injured party brings an action against him for breach of contract, the tradesman cannot claim that the contract is unenforceable because he does not possess a licence. The courts will hold him liable for the damages that the other party suffered.[9]

|||||||||||||||||||||||||||||||||||||||||||||||||||||||||||||||||||||||||

CASE 9.1

Archbolds (Freightage) Ltd. v. S. Spanglett Ltd., [1961] 1 Q.B. 374.

DEVLIN, L.J.:

The effect of illegality upon a contract may be threefold. If at the time of making the contract there is an intent to perform it in an unlawful way, the contract, although it remains alive, is unenforceable at the suit of the party having that intent; if the intent is held in common, it is

[7]*Kocotis v. D'Angelo* (1958), 13 D.L.R. (2d) 69.
[8]*Monticchio v. Torcema Construction Ltd. et al.* (1980), 26 O.R. (2d) 305.
[9]*Aconley and Aconley v. Willart Holdings Ltd.* (1964), 49 W.W.R. 46.

not enforceable at all. Another effect of illegality is to prevent a plaintiff from recovering under a contract if in order to prove his rights under it he has to rely upon his own illegal act; he may not do that even though he can show that at the time of making the contract he had no intent to break the law and that at the time of performance he did not know that what he was doing was illegal. The third effect of illegality is to avoid the contract ab initio and that arises if the making of the contract is expressly or impliedly prohibited by statute or is otherwise contrary to public policy.

|||||||||||||||||||||||||||||||||||||||||||||||||||||||||||||||||||||||||

LEGALITY AT COMMON LAW: PUBLIC POLICY

There are a number of different circumstances at common law under which a contract will not be enforceable. Historically, these are activities which were contrary to public policy, and remain so today. Contracts which are designed to obstruct justice, injure the public service, or injure the State are clearly not in the best interests of the public, and are illegal as well as unenforceable. An agreement, for example, which is designed to stifle prosecution, or influence the evidence presented in a court of law, is contrary to public policy.[10]

In a similar fashion, contracts which tend to promote litigation in a speculative manner are void, and contrary to public policy. The legal profession in most provinces is prohibited from undertaking litigation on behalf of a client in return for a percentage of the proceeds, if any; any agreement to this effect would not be enforceable. The reasoning behind this rule is that a solicitor–client relationship based

[10]*Symington v. Vancouver Breweries and Riefel*, [1931] 1 D.L.R. 935.

upon a splitting of the proceeds of litigation would tend to promote unnecessary law suits, since the client would have virtually nothing to lose by the undertaking. The lawyer, as well, having a personal interest in the outcome of the legal proceedings, may be inclined to promote an action knowing full well that it is not *bona fide*. Both attitudes represent something that would not be in the best interests of the public or the profession, hence the prohibition on contracts which would tend to abuse the legal process. Two points, however, should be noted with respect to this rule. First, it is not improper for a lawyer to assist a poor person who cannot afford legal assistance by providing legal services, even though the suit may not be successful. The important distinction is that the assistance is made available in a disinterested manner, and not for a percentage of the outcome.[11] Second, the need for legal assistance to maintain an action is now, for the most part, provided by provincial legal aid, and is available to those persons who are unable to afford legal counsel on their own. This second fact, in particular, eliminates any justification for a member of the legal profession to undertake a case on behalf of a client that may be speculative with respect to outcome, and with respect to his fees. Some states in the United States, however, do permit members of their bar to carry on litigation for clients in return for a percentage of the outcome, if any, but this is not the case in either Canada or the United Kingdom.

Contracts prejudicial to Canada in its relations with other countries would also be void on the grounds of public policy. An example of a contract of this nature would be an agreement between a resident of Canada and an enemy alien during a period when hostilities had been declared between the two countries.

Public policy also dictates that any contract which tends to interfere with or injure the public service would be void and illegal. For example, an agreement with a public official whereby the official would use his position to obtain a benefit for the other party in return for payment would be both illegal and unenforceable.

Another class of contract that would be contrary to public policy is a contract which involves the commission of a tort, or a dishonest or immoral act. In general, agreements of this nature which encourage or induce others to engage in an act of dishonesty or immoral conduct will be unenforceable.

Contracts for debts where the interest rate charged by the lender is unconscionable are contrary to public policy. Where a lender attempts to recover the exorbitant interest from a defaulting debtor, the courts will not enforce the contract according to its terms, but may set aside the interest payable, or in some cases, order the creditor to repay a portion of the excessive interest to the debtor.[12]

The law with respect to contracts of this nature is not clear as to what constitutes an unconscionably high rate, as there is often no fixed statutory limit for contracts where this issue may arise. Interest rates fall within the jurisdiction of the federal government, and while it has passed a number of laws which fix interests rates for different types of loans, the parties in many cases are free to set their own rates. To prevent the lender from hiding the actual interest rate in the form of extra

---

[11]*Harris v. Brisco* (1886), 17 Q.B.D. 504.

[12]*Morehouse v. Income Investments* (1966), 53 D.L.R. (2d) 106.

charges, consumer protection legislation now requires disclosure of true interest rates and the cost of borrowing for many kinds of consumer loan transactions. For others, the courts generally use, as a test, the rate of interest that a borrower in similar circumstances (and with a similar risk facing the lender) might obtain elsewhere.[13]

CONTRACTS IN RESTRAINT OF TRADE

Contracts in restraint of trade fall into three categories:

(1) agreements contrary to the *Combines Investigation Act* (which were briefly examined earlier in this chapter),

(2) agreements between the vendor and purchaser of a business which may contain an undue or unreasonable restriction on the right of the vendor to engage in a similar business in competition with the purchaser, and

(3) agreements between an employer and an employee which unduly or unreasonably restrict the right of the employee to compete with the employer after the employment relationship is terminated.

Of these three, the last two are subject to common law public policy rules which determine their enforceability. The general rule in this respect states that all contracts in restraint of trade are *prima facie* void and unenforceable. The courts will, however, enforce some contracts of this nature if it can be shown that the restraint is both reasonable and necessary, and does not offend the public interest.

---

[13]*Miller v. Lavoie* (1966), 60 D.L.R. (2d) 495; *Scott v. Manor Investments Ltd.*, [1961] O.W.N. 210.

Restrictive Agreements Concerning the Sale of a Business

When a vendor sells a business that has been in existence for some time, the goodwill which the vendor has developed is a part of what the purchaser acquires and pays for. Since goodwill is something that is associated with the good name of the vendor, and represents the propensity of customers to return to the same location to do business, its value will depend in no small part on the vendor's intentions when the sale is completed. If the vendor intends to set up a similar business in the immediate vicinity of the old business, the "goodwill" which the vendor has developed will probably move with him to the new location. The purchaser, in such a case, will acquire little more in the sale than a location and some goods. He will not acquire many of the vendor's old customers, and consequently, he may not value the business at more than the cost of stock and the premises. On the other hand, if the vendor is prepared to promise the purchaser that he will not establish a new business in the vicinity, nor will he engage in any business in direct competition with the purchaser until some time after his old customers have become familiar with the purchaser of his business, the goodwill of the business will have some value to both parties. The value, however, is in the enforceability of the promise of the vendor not to compete or do anything to induce the customers to move their business dealings from the purchaser after the business is sold.

The difficulty with the promise of the vendor is that it is *prima facie* void as a restraint of trade. The courts, however, recognize the mutual advantage of such a promise with respect to the sale of a business, and if the purchaser can convince the courts that the restriction is reasonable, and if he can show that the restriction does not adversely affect the public interest, then the restriction will be enforced.

The danger that exists with restrictions of this nature is the temptation on the part of the purchaser to make the restriction much broader than necessary to protect the goodwill. If care is not taken in the drafting of the restriction, it may prove to be unreasonable, and will then be struck down by the courts. If this should occur, the result will be a complete loss of protection for the purchaser, as the courts will not modify the restriction to make it enforceable. For example, Victor operates a drug store in a small town, and enters into a contract with Paul whereby Paul will purchase Victor's business if Victor will promise not to carry on the operation of a drug store within a radius of 100 miles of the existing store for a period of 30 years.

In this case, the geographical restriction would be unreasonable. The customers of the store, due to the nature of the business would be persons living within the limits of the town, and within a few miles' radius. No substantial number of customers would likely live beyond a five-mile radius. Similarly, the time limitation would be unreasonable, as a few years would probably be adequate for the purchaser to establish a relationship with the customers of the vendor. The courts, in this instance, would probably declare the restriction unenforceable; with the restriction removed, the vendor would be free to set up a similar business in the immediate area if he wished to do so.

Agreements of this nature might be severed if a part of the restriction is reasonable, and a part overly restrictive. In a classic case on this issue, a manufacturer of arms and ammunition transferred his business to a limited company. As a part of the transaction, he promised that he would not work in or carry on any other business manufacturing guns and ammunition (subject to certain exceptions), nor would he engage in any other business which might compete in any way with the purchaser's business for a period of 25 years. The restrictions applied on a worldwide basis. The court, in this case, recognized the global nature of the business and held that the restriction preventing the vendor from competing in the arms and ammunition business anywhere in the world was reasonable, and the restriction enforceable. However, it viewed the second part of the restriction (which prevented the vendor from engaging in any other business) as overly restrictive, and severed it from the contract on the basis that the two promises were separate.[14]

An unenforceable restriction may only be severed if the agreement's meaning will remain the same after the severance. This rule, the "blue pencil rule," was applied by English courts in a number of cases concerning restraint of trade where the unreasonable restriction was reduced to a reasonable covenant by the elimination of a few words.[15] This approach was rejected in later cases,[16] however, and is now limited to "blue penciling" an entire or severable unreasonable restriction, leaving the remainder of the restrictions intact. Even this practice would appear to be limited to restraint of trade restrictions contained in agreements between the vendors and purchasers of a business.[17]

[14]*Nordenfelt v. Maxim Nordenfelt Guns & Ammunition Co. Ltd.*, [1894] A.C. 535.

[15]*Goldsoll v. Goldman*, [1915] 1 Ch. 292.

[16]*Putsnam v. Taylor*, [1927] 1 K.B. 637.

[17]*Mason v. Provident Clothing Co.*, [1913] A.C. 724; *E.P. Chester Ltd. v. Mastorkis* (1968), 70 D.L.R. (2d) 133.

||||||||||||||||||||||||||||||||||||||||||||||||||||||||||||||||||||||||||

CASE 9.2
Stephens v. Gulf Oil Canada Ltd. et al. (1974), 3 O.R. (2d) 241.

HENRY, J.:

As usual in all such cases it is necessary to choose between or to reconcile, according to principle, important public policies that may be or appear to be in conflict with one another. Here, these policies are:

Freedom under the law—Freedom of a person to conduct himself as he wishes subject to any restraint imposed upon him by the law.

Freedom of commerce—The right of a person or firm to establish the business of his choice assuming that he has the capital and ability to do so, to enter a market freely, to make contracts freely with others in the advancement and operation of his business and to gain such rewards as the market will bestow on his initiative.

Free competition—The right of business to compete for supplies and customers on the basis of quality, service and price, and the right of the public at large, whether industrial consumers or end users, to a choice in the market of competing goods and services of competitive quality and at prices established by competition.

It will at once be apparent that these public policy principles are inherent in the private enterprise economy which depends for its proper working on a free competitive market. The market under this concept will determine what is produced, who produces it, who obtains the product or service and at what price.

It must be recognized, however, that the Canadian economy is not universally a free market economy; it is a mixed economy, substantial areas of which are subject to regulation by Governments or public agencies in accordance with federal or provincial statutes. In these areas may exist to a greater or lesser degree, economic or social controls which replace in whole or in part the free market operations in those areas. There, market forces as the main

influence in economic decision-making may be replaced by state agencies or officials who in accordance with valid statutes may determine questions of entry, production, distribution and price. Inroads are thus made on the three public policy principles which I have mentioned. But in the areas of the economy not so regulated, the private enterprise-competitive market system prevails. This is the fundamental mechanism whereby economic resources are allocated to their most productive uses and economic efficiency is encouraged, inefficiency penalized and waste controlled.

It will also be apparent that the public policy in relation to freedom of commerce, particularly freedom of contract, may and frequently does, come into conflict with the public policy in relation to free competition. For example, an agreement between two or more suppliers to deny supplies of an essential commodity or service to a new entrant to a market may foreclose that market to the newcomer and so destroy his right to establish or expand the business of his choice.

Such conflicts are nowadays ordinarily adjusted, if public policy requires it, by appropriate legislation. But it is also open to the common law Courts to do so by the development of jurisprudence . . .

||||||||||||||||||||||||||||||||||||||||||||||||||||||||||||||||||||||||||

Restrictive Agreements Between Employees and Employers

The law distinguishes restrictive agreements concerning the sale of a business from restrictive agreements made between an employer and an employee. In the latter case, an employer, in an attempt to protect his business practices and business secrets, may require an employee to promise not to compete with the employer upon termination of employment. The legality of this type of restriction, however, is generally subject to close scrutiny by the courts, and the criteria applied differs from that which the law has established for contracts where a sale of a business is concerned.

The justification for the different criteria is based upon the serious consequences that may flow from a restriction of the employee's chances to obtain other employment and to exercise his acquired skills or knowledge. In general, the courts are reluctant to place any impediment in the way of a person seeking employment, and as a consequence, a restrictive convenant in a contract of employment will not be enforced unless serious injury to the employer can be clearly demonstrated. This reluctance of the courts stems from the nature of the bargaining relationship at the time the agreement is negotiated between the employer and the employee. The employee is seldom in a strong bargaining position vis-à-vis the employer when the employment relationship is established, and the employment contract is often an agreement on the employer's standard form which the employee must accept or reject at the time. Public policy recognizes the unequal bargaining power of the parties by placing the economic freedom of the employee above that of the special interests of the employer.

In some cases, however, the special interests of the employer may be protected by a restrictive covenant in a contract of employment. The courts have held, for example, when an employee has access to secret production processes of the employer, he may be restrained from revealing this information to others after he leaves his employ.[18]

The same view is taken where the employee has acted on behalf of the employer in his dealings with customers, and then later uses the employer's customers lists to solicit business for a new employer.[19] The courts will not, however, prevent an employee from soliciting business from his previous employer's customers under ordinary circumstances, nor will the courts enforce a restriction that would prevent a person from exercising skills and production practices acquired while in the employment relationship after the relationship is terminated.[20]

In contrast, contracts of employment which contain restrictions on the right of employees to engage in activities or businesses in competition with their employer while the employment relationship exists are usually enforceable, provided that they do not unnecessarily encroach on the employees' personal freedom, and provided of course that they are reasonable and necessary. The usual type of clause of this nature is a "devotion to business" clause in which the employees promise to devote their time and energy to the promotion of the employer's business interests, and to refrain from engaging in any business activitiy which might conflict with it.

A second type of restriction sometimes imposed by an employer is one which requires the employee to keep confidential any information of a confidential nature concerning the employer's business which should come into his possession as a result of his employment. An employee subject to such a covenant would conceivably be liable for breach of his employment contract (and damages) if he should reveal confidential information to a competitor that results in injury or damage to the employer. Restrictions of this type are frequently framed to extend beyond the termination of the employment relationship, and if reasonable and necessary, they may be enforced by the courts.[21] The particular reasoning behind the enforcement of these clauses is not based upon restraint of trade, but rather, upon the duties of the employee in the employment relationship.

[18]*Reliable Toy & Reliable Plastics Co. Ltd. v. Collins*, [1950] 4 D.L.R. 499

[19]*Fitch v. Dewes*, [1921] 2 A.C. 158; *Western Inventory Service Ltd. v. Flatt and Island Inventory Service Ltd.* (1919), 9 B.C.L.R. 282.

[20]*Herbert Morris, Ltd. v. Saxelby*, [1916] 1 A.C. 688.

[21]*Reliable Toy & Reliable Plastics Co. Ltd. v. Collins*, [1950] 4 D.L.R. 499.

The employer has a right to expect some degree of loyalty and devotion on the employee's part in return for the compensation paid to him. Actions on the part of the employee which cause injury to the employer represent a breach of the employment relationship, rather than restraint of trade, and it is usually only when the actual employment relationship ceases that the public policy concerns of the court come into play with respect to restrictive covenants.[22]

CASE 9.3

Sherk et al. v. Horwitz, [1972] 2 O.R. 451.

DONOHUE, J.:

I find that the defendant signed the agreement, ex. 3, being well aware of the restrictive covenant therein and that he was under no duress or at any disadvantage in so doing. The agreement was supported by the mutual promises of the plaintiffs and in any event, it was under seal. Were it not for other aspects of this case, I would hold that it was binding on the defendant and the plaintiffs were entitled to the injunction which they seek.

The first other aspect of the matter which, in my view, renders the covenant unenforceable is the public interest. . . .

In my view, the public interest is the same as public policy.

In the *Harvard Law Review*, vol. 42 (1929), p. 76, Professor Winfield, then of St. John's

[22] An interesting restrictive covenant concerning pension rights may be found in the case of *Taylor v. McQuilkin et al.* (1968), 2 D.L.R. (3d) 463.

College, Cambridge, England, at p. 92, defines public policy as: " 'a principle of judicial legislation or interpretation founded on the current needs of the community.' " He goes on to say that public policy may change not only from century to century but from generation to generation and even in the same generation.

This author goes on to say at p. 97 that in ascertaining what is public policy at any time, one guide that Judges are certain to employ whenever it is available is statutory legislation *in pari materia*.

It will, therefore, be apposite to consider how statute law in the Province of Ontario affects medical care for the residents of this Province. . . .

Now the beneficial purpose of this legislation is to provide the widest medical care for the residents of the Province. Clearly this is in the public good. And I think it follows that the public are entitled to the widest choice in the selection of their medical practitioners.

In the light of this modern development, ex. 26 at the trial may have some special significance where in May, 1971, a resolution of the council of the Ontario Medical Association was passed as follows:

"RESOLVED that the Ontario Medical Association disapproves the concept of restrictive covenants in the contracts of one physician with another."

A further feature to be considered is whether a restrictive covenant between medical people tends to further limit the right of the public to deal with a profession which has a strong monopoly position. I believe that it does and I think that to widen that monopoly would be injurious to the public.

SUMMARY The legality of the subject-matter of a contract determines its validity and enforceability. Legality is generally determined on the basis of public policy or public interest; any agreement contrary to these considerations may be illegal or void. Contracts or agreements to commit a criminal offence are clearly illegal, and as such are unenforceable. So, too, are agreements between businesses which restrain competition contrary to the *Combines Investigation Act*. Agreements which violate specific laws are generally treated in this legislation as being either void or illegal. Other contracts in restraint of trade at common law may be simply unenforceable in a court of law. Some contracts, such as loan agreements which require the borrower to pay an unconscionable rate of interest, may only be enforceable in part; and others, which tend to offend the public good, such as agreements which injure the public service or obstruct justice, will not be enforceable at all. Some restraint of trade agreements which are beneficial to the parties, and which do not offend public policy may be enforced where the restrictions can be shown to be reasonable and necessary.

DISCUSSION QUESTIONS

1. *How is "legality" generally determined?*
2. *Explain the difference between "illegal" and "void" with respect to contract law.*
3. *In a case where an employee is caught stealing funds from his employer, and makes full restitution, a promise by the employer not to report the incident to the police would be illegal. Why?*
4. *Under certain circumstances collusion is named as an offence under the* Combines Investigation Act. *Give an example of an illegal contract that falls under this heading.*
5. *Explain why a contract of insurance differs from a wagering agreement when both have a somewhat similar object.*
6. *What factors compound the risk that an unlicensed contractor undertakes when he enters into contracts to perform unlicensed services?*
7. *Explain the rationale behind the rule that forbids the splitting of litigation proceeds between a solicitor and his client.*
8. *What name is generally given to contracts made with public officials where the official uses his position in return for some recompense under the contract?*
9. *Would a contract of debt with an unconscionable interest rate be deemed unenforceable if that contract was signed and made under seal?*
10. *What are the three categories of contracts that may be deemed to be made in restraint of trade?*
11. *Explain "prima facie void."*
12. *Outline the "blue pencil rule."*
13. *Under what circumstances would a restrictive covenant in the sale of a business be enforceable?*
14. *Why are the courts reluctant to enforce a restrictive covenant in a contract of employment?*
15. *Under what circumstances would a restrictive covenant in a contract of employment be enforceable?*
16. *What role does public policy play in the enforceability of a restrictive covenant in a contract of employment? In a contract of sale?*

17. Explain the purpose of "devotion to business" clauses in contracts of employment, and explain why and how they are enforceable at law.

JUDICIAL DECISIONS

Contract in Restraint of Trade— Employer and Employee— Reasonableness of Contract

Herbert Morris, Ltd. v. Saxelby, [1916] 1 A.C. 688.

The plaintiffs employed the defendant first as a draftsman and later as an engineer. The contract of employment contained a covenant whereby the defendant agreed not to compete with the plaintiff as an employee or otherwise in the same field of manufacture anywhere in the United Kingdom or Ireland.

ATKINSON, L.J.:

I think it has been generally assumed that the law upon this subject of the validity or invalidity of contracts in restraint of trade has been authoritatively determined by the decision of this House in the *Nordenfelt Case*, as it is, for the sake of brevity, commonly called, and that it is laid down in the clearest and most happily selected language in the oft-quoted passage of the judgment of Lord Macnaghten, so that it is, I think, no longer necessary to refer to the earlier authorities. The passage runs thus: "The true view at the present time, I think, is this: The public have an interest in every person's carrying on his trade freely: so has the individual. All interference with individual liberty of action in trading, and all restraints of trade of themselves, if there is nothing more, are contrary to public policy, and therefore void. That is the general rule. But there are exceptions: restraints of trade and interference with individual liberty of action may be justified by the special circumstances of a particular case. It is a sufficient justification, and indeed it is the only justification, if the restriction is reasonable—reasonable, that is, in reference to the interest of the parties concerned and reasonable in reference to the interest of the public, so framed and so guarded as to afford adequate protection to the party in whose favour it is imposed, while at the same time it is in no way injurious to the public. That, I think, is the fair result of all the authorities."

It will be observed that Lord Macnaghten uses the plural, "parties concerned," in the earlier portion of this passage, meaning, apparently, to include both the covenantor and covenantee, while in the latter portion of the passage he merely speaks of "protection" being given to the covenantee, which does not injure the public. But in the opening lines of the passage he had already said that the individual (here the covenantor), as well as the public, have an interest in freedom of trading.

If it be assumed, as I think it must be, that no person has an abstract right to be protected against competition per se in his trade or business, then the meaning of the entire passage would appear to me to be this. If the restraint affords to the person in whose favour it is imposed nothing more than reasonable protection against something which he is entitled to be protected against, then as between the parties concerned the restraint is to be held to be reasonable in reference to their respective interests, but notwithstanding this the restraint may still be held to be injurious to the public and therefore void; the onus of establishing to the satisfaction of the judge who tries the case facts and circumstances which show that the restraint is of the reasonable character above mentioned resting upon the person alleging that it is of that character, and the onus of showing that, notwithstanding that it is of that character, it is nevertheless injurious to the public and therefore void, resting, in like manner, on the party alleging the latter.

. . . . .

". . . All the cases, when they come to be examined, seem to establish this principle, that all restraints upon trade are bad as being in violation of public policy, unless they are natural, and not unreasonable for the protection of the parties in dealing legally with some subject matter of contract. The principle is this: Public policy requires that every man shall be at liberty to work for himself, and shall not be at liberty to deprive himself or the State of his labour, skill, or talent, by any contract that he enters into. On the other hand, public policy requires that when a man has by skill or by any other means obtained something which he wants to sell, he should be at liberty to sell it in the most advantageous way in the market; and in order to enable him to sell it advantageously in the market it is necessary that he should be able to preclude himself from entering into competition with the purchaser. In such a case the same public policy that enables him to do that does not restrain him from alienating that which he wants to alienate, and, therefore, enables him to enter into any stipulation however restrictive it is, provided that restriction in the judgment of the Court is not unreasonable, having regard to the subject matter of the contract."

These considerations in themselves differentiate, in my opinion, the case of the sale of goodwill from the case of master and servant or employer and employee. The vendor in the former case would in the absence of some restrictive covenant be entitled to set up in the same line of business as he sold in competition with the purchaser, though he could not solicit his own old customers. The possibility of such competition would necessarily depreciate the value of the goodwill. The covenant excluding it necessarily enhances that value, and presumably the price demanded and paid, and, therefore, all those restrictions on trading are permissible which are necessary at once to secure that the vendor shall get the highest price for what he has to sell and that the purchaser shall get all he has paid for. Restrictions on freedom of trading are in both classes of case imposed, no doubt, with the common object of protecting property. But the resemblance between them, I think, ends there.

In all cases such as this, one has to ask oneself what are the interests of the employer that are to be protected, and against what is he entitled to have them protected.

He is undoubtedly entitled to have his interest in his trade secrets protected, such as secret processes of manufacture which may be of vast value. And that protection may be secured by restraining the employee from divulging these secrets or putting them to his own use. He is also entitled not to have his old customers by solicitation or such other means enticed away from him. But freedom from all competition per se apart from both these things, however lucrative it might be to him, he is not entitled to be protected against. He must be prepared to encounter that even at the hands of a former employee.

|||||||||||||||||||||||||||||||||||||||||||||||||||||||||||||||||||||||||||||||||||||||||||||||||||||||||||||||||||||||||||||||||||||||||||||||||||||||||||||||

Contract in Restraint of Trade— Reasonableness of Covenant in Restraint of Trade Where Vendor Becomes Employee of Purchaser of Business

J. G. Collins Insurance Agencies Ltd. v. Elsley (1976), 70 D.L.R. (3d) 513.

The defendant sold an insurance business and agreed to work for the purchaser as his sales manager. At that time, the defendant signed a covenant whereby he would not compete with the plaintiff as a general insurance agent for a period of five years within a given area.

The defendant left the employ of the plaintiff and set up his own business within the five-year period and within the defined area.

EVANS, J.A. (after reviewing the evidence and the trial judgement):

The general rule is that clauses restricting the scope of a man's future business activities, whether contained in agreements of employment or of sale of a business, must be reasonable both as between the parties and with reference to the public interest. Otherwise such a clause is unenforceable as being in restraint of trade and contrary to public policy. Public policy is not a fixed and immutable standard but one which changes to remain compatible with changing economic and social conditions. The old doctrine that any restraint on trade was void as against public policy must be balanced against the principle that the honouring of contractual obligations, freely entered into by parties bargaining on equal footing, is also in the public interest. These competing principles of public policy are frequently in conflict in the commercial world and the question whether a particular non-competition agreement is void and unenforceable is one of law to be determined on a consideration of the character and nature of the business, the relationship of the parties and the relevant circumstances existing at the time the agreement was entered into.

Courts recognize that some restraints must be imposed, otherwise the purchaser of a business could not with safety buy the goodwill of the business unless the vendor could be enjoined from setting up next door in competition. A similar problem would arise in certain employer and employee situations where, because of the confidential nature of the relationship, the employee has access to customer lists, trade secrets or other matters in which the purchaser or the employer has a proprietory interest.

The modern and authoritative position is stated in the recent decision of the Privy Council in *Stenhouse Australia Ltd. v. Phillips*, [1974] 1 All E.R. 117. That appeal involved consideration of a clause in an employment contract prohibiting an employee from soliciting clients of his former employer, an insurance broker, within a defined area and for a specified time following termination of his employment. It was pointed out that the success of an insurance agency depends a great deal on its relationship with its clients which may have taken some time to develop and to build up and yet it is recognized that such relationship is a fairly tenuous connection which, because of its comparative fragility, makes the risk of solicitation of clients by a former employee more serious. These factors demonstrate the very real need of protection by way of injunctive restraint of an insurance broker's proprietory interest in its customer lists. In the above decision Lord Wilberforce at p. 122 stated:

". . . the employer's claim for protection must be based on the identification of some advantage or asset inherent in the business which can properly be regarded as, in a general sense, his property, and which it would be unjust to allow the employee to appropriate for his own purposes, even though he, the employee, may have contributed to its creation. For while it may be true that an employee is entitled—and is to be encouraged—to build up his own qualities of skill and experience, it is usually his duty to develop and improve his employer's business for the benefit of his employer. These two obligations interlock during his employment: after its termination they diverge and mark the boundary between what the employee may take with him and what he may legitimately be asked to leave behind to his employers."

Adopting the above reasons, as I do, there can be no doubt in the present case that the plaintiff had a substantial proprietory interest which he was entitled to have protected. At the time of purchase of the business, both parties recognized that goodwill represented by the customer lists had an economic value and that this business connection was a substantial asset. The defendant moved from owner-vendor to manager and ostensible owner of the business that had been his originally without any break in time or in his relationship with the customers. I am satisfied, as was the trial Judge, that the covenant against competition is not invalid as an unreasonable restraint of trade and any challenges to the covenant on that ground cannot succeed.

Turning to a consideration whether the present covenant is wider than is necessary to protect the plaintiff's proprietory right, it must be pointed out at the outset that the defendant is not precluded from carrying on his life insurance and real estate business. The plaintiff only seeks to restrain him from enticing away the plaintiff's general insurance customers. The burden of establishing the validity of the restrictive covenant is on the plaintiff and tests it has to meet have been defined by Birkenhead, L.C., in these words (*McEllistrim v. Ballymacelligott Co-operative Agricultural & Dairy Society, Ltd.*, [1919] A.C. 548 at p. 562):

"A contract which is in restraint of trade cannot be enforced unless (*a*) it is reasonable as between the parties; (*b*) it is consistent with the interests of the public."

Before submitting the present covenant to the above tests it must be made clear that there is a distinction to be drawn between a restrictive covenant in a vendor and purchaser agreement and that contained in an employment contract. Those given in the context of employment are more rigorously examined than those in sale transactions. The learned trial Judge in drawing this distinction quoted from *Attwood v. Lamont*, [1920] 3 K.B. 571 at p. 589 (C.A.), where Lord Justice Younger stated: "An employer is not entitled by a covenant taken from his employee to protect himself after the employment has ceased against his former servant's competition per se, although a purchaser of goodwill is entitled to protect himself against such competition on the part of his vendor."

In cases dealing with sale transactions, the Courts have been reluctant to interfere with restrictive covenants contained in agreements entered into by businessmen having a presumed equality of bargaining power. On the other hand, such clauses in employment agreements are carefully scrutinized and are frequently held unenforceable on the ground that they extend beyond the interest which the employer is properly entitled to protect.

The present case does not fit neatly into either a sale or an employment category as it involves both. It was argued on behalf of the appellant that the background association between the parties with respect to the purchase and sale of the defendant's business should be disregarded and that the Court should limit its consideration only to the restrictive covenant contained in the employment contract. I am not in agreement with that submission. To take such a narrow view would be to ignore the realities of the situation in which the sale and the employment contract are inextricably bound together. Their combined effect provided the defendant with an unusual opportunity over a period of 17 years to acquire an intimate knowledge of the plaintiff's customers and of their insurance needs. The additional fact that the business was carried on under their joint names and that the plaintiff took a relatively inactive part in the business meant that to the customers the defendant, for all practical purposes, was *their* agent for *their* general insurance requirements. The proof of this situation is demonstrated by ex. 10, a list of approximately 200 former customers of the plaintiff who advised that they were transferring their insurance business to the defendant. Some of those transfers involved customers whose business and goodwill the defendant had originally sold to the plaintiff. In my view these facts are all relevant in determining the reasonableness of this particular restrictive covenant.

. . . . . .

The generally accepted test as to which employees may be restrained is set out by Lord Parker in *Herbert Morris, Ltd. v. Saxelby*, [1916] 1 A.C. 688 at p. 709, as those employees who will acquire not merely knowledge of customers, but in addition, influence over them:
"A restraint is not valid unless the nature of the employment is such that customers will either learn to rely upon the skill or judgment of the servant or will deal with him directly and personally to the virtual exclusion of the master, with the result that he will probably gain their custom if he sets up business on his own account."
(Cheshire and Fifoot, *Law of Contract*, 8th ed. (1972), p. 369.)

There is no doubt that the present defendant falls into the category of a confidential employee. The defendant's name which had been sold to the plaintiff along with the goodwill of the business appeared in the new firm name under which the business was conducted. The defendant continued throughout the period of his employment to carry on his own real estate and life insurance business from an office at which sales of general insurance for the plaintiff were effected and premiums paid. He had access to customer files and because of his day-to-day supervision of the business had personal contact with the customers and was in a position to influence them. When the defendant terminated his employment he took with him two insurance salesmen and an insurance clerk formerly employed by the plaintiff. I think it fair to say that to the staff and the general public the defendant was the key man in the plaintiff's general insurance business.

I agree with the trial Judge that the plaintiff has established special circumstances which justify the non-competition clause and that it does not afford him more protection than is needed to protect and preserve his general insurance business.

Whether a particular clause is to be held invalid as being too wide in its area of restriction or because it extends for a period of time which is too lengthy must depend on the circumstances. The degree of confidentiality, the length of association, the status of the former employee in the organization and his business connections in the particular area are relevant factors. Viewed in that aspect a time period of five years is not unreasonable *inter partes* and is consonant with public policy. Normally, fire insurance policies are written for a three-year term while auto policies expire after one year and it would be extremely difficult for the plaintiff to supervise and protect himself against the activities of the defendant in switching policies within those periods. The area covered in the covenant in effect covers the present City of Niagara Falls and cannot be considered too broad as far as geographical boundaries are concerned. In fact the defendant does not seriously question the area of restriction but submits that the restriction should apply, if at all, only to those customers which the plaintiff had at the time the defendant terminated his employment. It is true that in some cases involving an employer-employee relationship a general covenant against engaging in a certain business in a given area has been held invalid on the ground that it would cover persons who had never been customers of the employer or persons who had become such only after the termination of the employment: *New Method Cleaners & Launderers Ltd. v. Hartley*, [1939] 1 D.L.R. 711, [1939] 1 W.W.R. 142, 46 Man. R. 414. However, in the present case a different standard of reasonableness must be applied. The plaintiff and the defendant were competent and successful businessmen, each of whom stood to gain by their agreement. There was no inequality of bargaining power between them. Against that background, the non-competition covenant which the plaintiff seeks to enforce in the present City of Niagara Falls for the protection of a legitimate proprietory interest in his general insurance business does not appear unreasonable and in my view is a legal and enforceable obligation and entitles the plaintiff to the injunctive relief sought.

The covenant having been breached, the plaintiff's entitlement to damages has been established.

|||||||||||||||||||||||||||||||||||||||||||||||||||||||||||||||||||||||||||||||||||||||||||||||||||||||||||||||||||||||||||||||||||||||||||||||||||||||||||||||||||||

Illegal Contract for Work and Materials— Unlicensed Contractor— Whether Licensing Affects Sale of Goods

Monticchio v. Torcema Construction Ltd. et al. (1979), 26 O.R. (2d) 305.

R.E. HOLLAND, J.:

Two applications were brought before me. The first was to amend the statement of claim and the second to determine a point of law.

The plaintiff is an unlicensed drain contractor and entered into a written contract with the defendant Torcema Construction Limited to supply work and material, the work being that of a drain contractor. The statement of claim as originally delivered, claimed for the amount owing pursuant to the contract. The amendment, which I allowed, includes a claim for the amount alleged to be owing on the basis of *quantum meruit*.

The point of law is as follows:

"Whether the fact that the plaintiff was not a licensed drain contractor as pleaded in paragraph 8 of the defendant's statement of defence, operates as a complete defence and renders the contract illegal and unenforceable."

By-law 107-78 of the Municipality of Metropolitan Toronto provides, in part, as follows:

"2. There shall be taken out by:

. . . . .

(17) every drain contractor, drain layer and person who installs septic tanks,

. . . . .

a licence from the Commission authorizing them respectively to carry on their several trades, callings, businesses, and occupations in the Metropolitan Area . . ."

Section 23(2) provides for a fine for contravention of the above subsection.

It is to be noted that the claim before me is based on a contract for services and materials and, in the alternative, on *quantum meruit*.

In *Kocotis v. D'Angelo*, [1958] O.R. 104, 13 D.L.R. (2d) 69, the Court of Appeal dealt with a claim by an unlicensed electrician for work and materials and Laidlaw, J.A., with whom Gibson, J.A., concurred, said this, at p. 110 O.R., p. 73 D.L.R.:

"It is plain to me that the object of the by-law was to protect the public against mistakes and loss that might arise from work done by unqualified electricians. It was not to secure the revenue from certificates or from licenses, because only certain qualified persons could obtain such certificates or licenses. It was plainly intended by the by-law to prohibit a maintenance electrician from undertaking the work of a master electrician or electrical contractor, and no maintenance electrician could lawfully contract for any electrical work . . . Such a contract would be illegal and could not be enforced in the Courts.''

Schroeder, J.A., dissented, and at p. 127 O.R., p. 89 D.L.R., expressed the view that if the purpose sought to be effected by the by-law was to deprive the unlicensed electrician of compensation for his services or for materials supplied, such restriction upon his common law rights should have been expressed in clear and unequivocal language. He also pointed out that the legislation being dealt with was purely municipal and did not have the force of a general law. He concluded that the only consequences of the violation of the provisions of the by-law are those which the by-law itself prescribes.

The decision in *Kocotis* was followed by Mr. Justice Lerner in *Calax Construction Inc. v. Lepofsky* (1974), 5 O.R. (2d) 259, 50 D.L.R. (3d) 69. This case involved an unlicensed building contractor and again dealt with a mechanics' lien claim. Lerner, J., concluded that the contract was illegal and unenforceable and dismissed the action. An opposite conclusion was reached in *Day & Night Heating Ltd. v. Brevick* (1962), 35 D.L.R. (2d) 436, a decision of Judge Fraser of the Westminster County Court of British Columbia.

In *Kingshott v. Brunskill*, [1953] O.W.N. 133, the plaintiff operated a fruit farm with an apple orchard. He sold upgraded apples contrary to the *Farm Products Grades and Sales Act* and Regulations passed thereunder. Roach, J.A., for the Court, pointed out at p. 135 that the main object of the statute and Regulations was the protection of the public and the penalty was imposed wholly for the protection of the public. He concluded the sale was illegal and that the plaintiff could not recover in an action for the price, notwithstanding that the purchaser of the applies graded the apples and sold them at a profit. This decision and other similar decisions have been criticized on the basis that it appears grossly disproportionate to the evil of the infraction to deprive the seller of his crop or the workman of the price of his services: see *The Law of Contracts*, S. M. Waddams (1977), pp. 352-3.

Much as I am attracted by the dissent of Schroeder, J.A., and the criticism of the doctrine, I would, of course, feel myself bound by the decision of the Court of Appeal in *Kocotis*. However, the requirement of the by-law is merely that the contractor be licensed and there is no prohibition against the sale of material. This situation was dealt with by the Divisional Court in *Horlock v. Pinerich Developments Ltd. et al.* (1978), 19 O.R. (2d) 223, 84 D.L.R. (3d) 413, a case where an unlicensed electrician supplied material and performed work. The Court concluded that there was nothing in the statute (the *Apprenticeship and Tradesmen's Qualification Act*, R.S.O. 1970, c. 24), from which an inference could be drawn that the Legislature intended to prohibit the supply of material by an unlicensed electrician.

It appears to me, therefore, that, in the present case, the action can properly be continued for materials that were allegedly supplied. So far as the work is concerned, there is a claim not only in contract but for *quantum meruit* and it may be that such a claim could succeed even though the contract is held to be void: see *Craven-Ellis v. Canons, Ltd.*, [1936] 2 K.B. 403, and a discussion of this case in 55 *L.Q. Rev.* 54 (1939).

For the above reasons, I have come to the conclusion that the fact that a plaintiff was not a licensed drain contractor does not operate as a complete defence, although that fact may well render the contract itself illegal.

Importance of License— Position of Unlicensed Person	**Kocotis v. D'Angelo (1958), 13 D.L.R. (2d) 69.**

The plaintiff, an unlicensed electrician under a municipal by-law, agreed to install electrical wiring in the defendant's building. The installation was approved by an inspector for the local Hydro-Electric Power Commission. Some payments were made to the plaintiff under the contract, but the defendant refused to pay the balance owing. The plaintiff brought an action against the defendant for the balance of the price.

LAIDLAW, J.:

It is plain to me that the object of the by-law was to protect the public against mistakes and loss that might arise from work done by unqualified electricians. It was not to secure the revenue from certificates or from licenses, because only certain qualified persons could obtain such certificates or licenses. It was plainly intended by the by-law to prohibit a maintenance electrician from undertaking the work of a master electrician or electrical contractor, and no maintenance electrician could lawfully contract for any electrical work in the City of Ottawa. It matters not whether the prohibition in the by-law was express or implied. In either case, if a maintenance electrician contracted to do the work of an electrical contractor, the contract would be contrary to the intent and purpose of By-law No. 134. Such a contract would be illegal and could not be enforced in the Courts.

I shall refer to a number of cases from many in support of my opinion:

In *Bensley v. Bignold* (1822), 5 B. & Ald. 335, 106 E.R. 1214, it was held that a printer could not recover for labour or materials used in printing any work unless he affixed his name to it, pursuant to a statute in force at the time. Bayley J. stated that the statute established regulations for public purposes. He said (pp. 340-1): "Where a provision is enacted for public purposes, I think that it makes no difference whether the thing be prohibited absolutely or only under a penalty. The public have an interest that the thing shall not be done, and the objection in this case must prevail, not for the sake of the defendant, but for that of the public."

In *Forster v. Taylor* (1834), 5 B. & Ad. 887, 110 E.R. 1019, Littledale J. at pp. 895-6 referred to *Bartlett v. Vinor* (1693), Carth. 252, 90 E.R. 750, and the opinion of Lord Holt, that " 'every contract made for or about any matter or thing which is prohibited and made unlawful by any statute, is a void contract, though the statute itself doth not mention that it shall be so, but only inflicts a penalty on the offender; because a penalty implies a prohibition, though there are no prohibitory words in the statute.' "

He referred, further, to the opinion of the Court in that case: " 'In every case where a penalty is annexed to the doing of such an act, though it be not prohibited, yet if such a thing appears upon the record to be the consideration, the agreement is void.' "

Further: " 'In every case, where the statute inflicts a penalty for doing such an act, though the act be not prohibited, yet the thing is unlawful.' "

The Court decided in *Cope* v. *Rowlands* (1836), 2 M. & W. 149, 150 E.R. 707, that: "A broker cannot maintain an action for work and labour, and commission for buying and selling stock, etc., unless duly licensed by the mayor and aldermen of the city of London, pursuant to 6 Anne, c. 16." [headnote]

The opinions expressed in that case have been quoted many times.

Parke B. stated at p. 157: "It is perfectly settled, that where the contract which the plaintiff seeks to enforce, be it express or implied, is expressly or by implication forbidden by the common or statute law, no court will lend its assistance to give it effect. It is equally clear that a contract is void if prohibited by a statute, though the statute inflicts a penalty only, because such a penalty implies a prohibition."

. . . . .

In *Re an Arbitration between Mahmoud and Ispahani*, [1921] 2 K.B. 716, an Order made under the Defence of the Realm Regulations provided that (headnote):

" 'A person shall not either on his own behalf or on behalf of any other person buy or sell or otherwise deal in . . . any of the articles specified in the schedule hereto, whether situated within or without the United Kingdom, except under and in accordance with the terms of a licence issued by or under the authority of the Food Controller.' Linseed oil was one of the articles specified in the schedule.

"During the operation of the Order the plaintiff sold to the defendant a quantity of linseed oil. The plaintiff had a licence under the Order, and before entering into the contract he asked the defendant whether he had a licence under the Order, and the defendant told the plaintiff that he had. The defendant in fact had not a licence. The licence to the plaintiff provided that sales for delivery within the United Kingdom were only to be made to persons holding a licence. The plaintiff, being induced by the misrepresentation of the defendant and in the honest belief that he had a licence entered into the contract of sale. The defendant subsequently refused to accept delivery of the linseed oil on the ground that the contract was illegal, as he (the defendant) had no licence under the Order. In a claim for damages for non-acceptance of the oil:—

"*Held* that, as the defendant had no licence, the contract of sale was prohibited by the Order and was therefore illegal, and as the prohibition was in the public interest no claim could be made under the contract."

Scrutton L.J. at pp. 728-9 referred to *Cope* v. *Rowlands* and to *Bartlett* v. *Vinor, supra*, and stated: " 'And it may be safely laid down, notwithstanding some dicta apparently to the contrary, that if the contract be rendered illegal, it can make no difference, in point of law, whether the statute which makes it so has in view the protection of the revenue, or any other object. The sole question is, whether the statute means to prohibit the contract?' If the contract is prohibited by statute, the Court is bound not to render assistance in enforcing an illegal contract."

. . . . .

My opinion is that the contract upon which the respondent bases his claim was illegal and that the Courts will not give its [*sic*] aid to enforce it.

||||||||||||||||||||||||||||||||||||||||||||||||||||||||||||||||||||||||||||||||||||||||||||||||||||||||||||||||||||||||||||||||||||||||||||||||||||||||||||||||||||||||||||||||||||||||

CASE PROBLEMS FOR DISCUSSION

Case 1

A company owned a parcel of land upon which it wished to have a commercial building constructed. An architect was engaged to design the building, and a contractor was contacted to carry out the construction. Contracts were signed with both.

Before the construction was completed, it was discovered that the building violated a municipal by-law which required certain safety features to be included in the building. Neither the architect nor the contractor were aware of the by-law at the time they entered into their respective agreements with the company.

The safety features required by the by-law could be incorporated in the building at a cost of approximately $10 000, but the contractor refused to do so unless he was paid for the work as an "extra" to the contract price. The company refused to do so, and withheld all payment to the contractor on the basis that the construction contract was illegal. The contractor then instituted legal proceedings against the company.

Explain the nature of the contractor's claim, and the defence raised by the company. Discuss the issue of responsibility in the case. Render a decision.

Case 2

The Suburban Medical Centre was founded in 1961 as a medical clinic by eight physicians and surgeons. In 1977, the clinic advertised in the medical press for an obstetrician. Harvey, a Toronto specialist, answered the advertisement. Following an interview, Harvey was employed by the clinic, and signed an employment contract that contained the following clause:

Should the employment of the Party of the Second Part by the Parties of the First Part terminate for any reason whatsoever, the Party of the

Second Part COVENANTS AND AGREES that he will not carry on the practice of medicine or surgery in any of its branches on his own account, or in association with any other person or persons, or corporation or in the employ of any such person or persons or corporation within the said City of Suburbia or within five miles of the limits thereof for a period of five years (5) thereafter.

In May of 1980, an argument arose between Harvey and one of the founders of the clinic. As a result of the argument, Harvey resigned. He immediately set up a practice in the same city. The clinic continued to operate without the services of Harvey, and later brought an action for damages and an injunction against him.

Discuss the factors the court should consider in deciding this case. Render a decision.

Case 3

The Allen Laundry, a corporation which manufactured laundry equipment and also operated a laundry in a particular city, employed Murphy in its laundry operation. Shortly after Murphy was hired, he was requested to enter into a written employment contract which contained a clause whereby he agreed, in return for the wages paid to him, that he would not engage in the laundry business anywhere in Canada for a period of three years. Murphy was employed by the corporation for six years, during which time he normally worked in the laundry operation. At the end of the sixth year, he tendered his resignation to the corporation, and a few months after he left its employ, purchased a laundry business in the same city.

Allen Laundry took legal action to enforce the agreement which Murphy had signed.

Discuss the issues raised in this case, and render a decision.

Case 4

In 1965, Herbert entered into the employ of TOPE Limited as an electrical engineer. He was employed to design electronic testing equipment, which the company manufactured. At the time he was hired, he signed a written contract of indefinite hiring as a salaried employee. The contract contained a clause whereby he agreed not to disclose any confidential company information. The contract also required him to agree not to seek employment with any competitor of the company if he left the employ of TOPE Limited.

In October, 1979, Herbert was requested to develop a dwell tachometer suitable for sale to home mechanics through a particular hardware store chain under the chain's brand name. He produced a prototype in less than a week, and attended at the president's office to discuss the development and production of the equipment.

During the course of the discussion, Herbert and the company president became involved in a heated argument over manufacturing methods. At the end of the meeting, the president suggested that Herbert might begin a search for employment elsewhere, as his job would be terminated in three months' time.

The next morning, Herbert went to the president's office once more, ostensibly to discuss the dwell tachometer. Instead, Herbert informed the president as soon as he entered the room that he no longer intended to work for the firm. He complained that the company had never given him more than a two-week vacation in any year, and that he often worked as much as 50 hours per week, with no overtime pay for the extra hours worked. In a rage, he smashed the dwell tachometer prototype on the president's desk, breaking it into a dozen small pieces. He then left the room.

The following week, Herbert accepted employment with a competitor of TOPE Limited to do a type of work similar to that which he had done at his old firm. He immediately developed a dwell tachometer similar in design to the previous model, and suggested to the management of his new employer that they consider the sale of the equipment through the same hardware chain that TOPE Limited had contemplated for its product. The competitor was successful in obtaining a large order for dwell tachometers from the hardware chain a short time later.

TOPE Limited presented its new product to the hardware chain a week after the order had been given to the competitor, and only then discovered that Herbert had designed the equipment for that firm. The hardware chain had adopted the competitor's product as its own brand, and was not interested in purchasing the product of TOPE Limited in view of its apparent similarity in design.

TOPE Limited had expected a first year's profit of $21 000 on the dwell tachometer if they obtained the contract from the hardware chain.

Discuss the nature of the legal action (if any) which TOPE Limited might take against Herbert, and indicate the defences (if any) which Herbert might raise if TOPE Limited should do so.

CHAPTER 10

The Requirements of Form and Writing

FORMAL AND SIMPLE CONTRACTS

Under the law of contract there are two general classes of contracts. A contract which derives its validity from the form which it takes is referred to as a formal contract, or, sometimes (under English law), a *covenant*. The second class of contract is the informal or simple contract, which may be implied, oral, or in writing. These two classes of contracts evolved in different ways under early English law, with the formal contract being the older of the two. It is important to bear in mind that both forms of contract were not normally matters which the early king's justices felt should fall under their jurisdiction. As a consequence, agreements in the nature of mutual promises were either under the jurisdiction of the ecclesiastic courts, or the early local, or communal, courts. A breach of an agreement, then, took on the character of a breach of a promise, which if solemnly made, was considered to be a breach of faith, and hence, a religious matter. Promises which bore no solemn or ritualistic aspect presumably fell under the jurisdiction of local or communal court for consideration. In any event, the king's courts did not concern themselves with the forerunners of modern contracts until the early 13th century, when the royal court began to expand its jurisdiction.

Disputes concerning promises came before the court by way of an action of covenant—an early writ that was originally designed to protect leases, but which was rapidly expanded to enforce a variety of promises (except debt) provided that the promise was of a formal nature. By the end of the 13th century, covenants in writing (except for debt), if under the seal of the promisor, were enforced by the king's courts on the basis that the impression of the seal was an expression of the promisor's intention to be bound by the promise made. While these early agreements were not the same as modern contracts, the use of a seal has continued to the present day.

In most provinces, many kinds of agreements must still be made under seal to be enforceable. An example of a modern formal "covenant" would be a *power of attorney*, which is a formal document frequently used to empower a person to deal with the land of another. The grant of the power must be made under the seal to be valid. Another formal "covenant" is a deed of land under the Registry System in Ontario and a number of other provinces in Eastern Canada. To be valid, the deed must be in writing, and signed, sealed, and delivered in order to convey the property interest in the land to the grantee. Apart from these, and a number of other special types of agreements

which must be in a specific form and under seal, the formal agreement has been largely replaced by the second type of agreement: the informal contract.

Informal contracts developed along a distinctly different route. In English law, the informal agreement, like the formal agreement, was initially enforced by the Church or communal courts if some formality was attached to the agreement to render it morally binding. In this respect, the actions of the parties assumed immense proportions in determining the question of enforceability. The handshake, for example, rendered a promise binding, and in this respect, the informal agreement and the early formal agreement were similar. At that time, the ceremonial aspects surrounding the agreement were important determinants of enforceability.

Apart from the early similarities and common tribunals used for the enforcement of the promises, the historical path which the two types of contracts followed differed substantially, and it was not until the 17th century, when the concept of the modern contract took shape, that the two were recognized as being basically similar. Prior to that, early contractual agreements (if they may be properly called that) were only enforceable by way of tort law *writs of trespass.*

In the early cases, the courts would enforce the duties promised by persons in particular trades or professions if they improperly carried out their duties. No action would lie, however, if they simply did nothing to fulfil their promises, because there could be no trespass if a person did nothing. This early deficiency was remedied in part by the application of the action of *deceit* (also a tort) in the early

16th century, which provided a remedy where one party had fully performed, but where the other refused to do so. If neither party had performed there was still no remedy, and it was not until the 17th century that the courts were finally prepared to enforce executory promises by way of a *writ of assumpsit*. From that point on, the theory of consideration and the modern concept of contract developed rapidly, and with them, the enforceability of the informal contract by common law, rather than the law of tort. Today, the informal or simple contract does not depend upon a prescribed form for its enforceability. Had it not been for a statute passed in 1677,[1] no simple contract would have been required to be evidenced in writing under any circumstances to be enforceable at law.

THE STATUTE OF FRAUDS

The particular statute that imposed the requirement of writing for certain informal contracts was the *Statute of Frauds*—an Act that was passed by the English Parliament, and introduced to Canada and the United States while both were colonies. The law still remains as a statute in parts of the United States, and in all common-law provinces except British Columbia, even though it has been repealed in England.[2]

The *Statute of Frauds* was originally passed following a period of political upheaval in England, and was ostensibly designed to prevent perjury and fraud with respect to leases and agreements concerning land. The statute went further than perhaps was intended at the time, and

encompassed, as well, a number of agreements which, today, are simple contacts in nature.

In most provinces, this particular section of the Act now provides:

No action shall be brought whereby to charge any executor or administrator upon any special promise to answer damages out of his own estate, or whereby to charge any person upon any special promise to answer for the debt, default or miscarriage of any other person, or to charge any person upon any agreement made upon consideration of marriage, or upon any contract or sale of lands, tenements or hereditaments, or any interest in or concerning them, or upon any agreement that is not to be performed within the space of one year from the making thereof, unless the agreement upon which the action is brought, or some memorandum or note thereof is in writing and signed by the party to be charged therewith or some person thereunto by him lawfully authorized.

The effect of the law was that none of the following could be brought in a court of law unless they were in writing and signed by the party to be charged (or his authorized agent): an agreement or contract concerning an interest in land, a special promise by an executor or administrator to settle any claim out of his own personal estate, a guarantee agreement, an agreement made in consideration of marriage,[3] and a contract that could not be performed within a year.

The law did not prohibit or render void these particular agreements if they did not comply with the statute—the law simply rendered them unenforceable by way of the courts. The agreement continued to exist, and while rights could not be exercised to enforce the agreement, it was possible to appeal to the courts in the

---

[1]"An Act for Prevention of Frauds and Perjures," 29 Car. II, c. 3.

[2]See, for example, The *Statute of Frauds*, R.S.O. 1980, c. 481, s. 4.

[3]This particular type of contract has been removed from the statute in some provinces. See, for example, the *Family Law Reform Act*, R.S.O. 1980, c. 152, s. 88.

event of breach under certain circumstances. For example, if a party had paid a deposit to the vendor in an unwritten agreement to buy land, the vendor's refusal to convey the land would entitle the prospective purchaser to treat the agreement as at an end, and recover his deposit. The courts, however, would not enforce the agreement, since it would not be evidenced in writing and signed by the vendor. The agreement was caught by the statute, but once it was repudiated the purchaser could bring an action to recover the deposit.

The justification for the statutory requirement is obvious. Each of the five particular kinds of contracts at the time were agreements which were either important enough to warrant evidence in writing to clearly establish the intention of the particular promisors to be bound by the agreement, or the nature of the agreement was such that some permanent form of evidence of the terms of the agreement would be desirable for further reference.

The application of the law to each of these contractual relationships produced a number of responses by the courts to avoid the hardships imposed by the law. Each response was an attempt to assist innocent parties who were unaware of the implications of the lack of evidence in writing on their agreements.

Contracts by Executors and Administrators

The protection which the Act provides to the executor or administrator of an estate from a claim that he promised to answer for a debt or default out of his own estate is perhaps the most justifiable reason for the statute's continued existence. An executor or administrator undertakes to collect, care for, and distribute the assets of a deceased person, and essentially to keep the assets of the deceased's estate separate from his own. However, an executor might be tempted to pay, out of his "own pocket," outstanding debts of the deceased's estate should the state of affairs of the estate render prompt payment inopportune. This temptation might stem from a concern to protect the good name of the deceased, or it might simply provide the executor with immediate relief from persistent creditors. In any event, it is important to note that an executor has no obligation to pay the debts of the estate out of his own pocket, but should he decide to do so, his intention *must be clearly indicated in writing* as the statute requires.

Assumed Liability: The Guarantee

The second legal agreement which the statute embraces is an agreement whereby a person agrees to answer for the debt, default, or tort of another. One particular type of agreement of this nature, that requires a memorandum to be in writing and bear the signature of the party to be charged, is the guarantee. This relationship always involves at least three parties: a principal debtor, a creditor, and a third party, the "guarantor." The guarantor's role in a guarantee agreement is to provide a promise of payment in the form of a contingent liability. If the principal debtor does not make payment when the debt falls due, the creditor may then look to the guarantor for payment. The guarantor is never the party who is primarily liable. His obligation to pay is always one which arises if and when the principal debtor defaults. The consideration for the guarantor's promise is usually based upon the creditor's act or promise to provide to the principal debtor goods on credit, or funds in circumstances where the creditor would not ordinarily do so.

If a principal debtor fails to make payment when required to do so, the creditor may call upon the guarantor to pay. The guarantor is then liable for payment of the principal debtor's indebtedness, and if he pays the obligation, he may demand an assignment of the debt. Once the debt is paid, the guarantor possesses the rights of the creditor, and may demand payment from the debtor if he should choose to do so.

The distinction between a guarantee and a situation where a person becomes a principal debtor by a direct promise of payment is important. If the promise to pay is not conditional upon the default of the principal debtor, but a situation where both parties become principal debtors, then the agreement need not be in writing or signed to be enforceable. By the same token, if the third party requests that the creditor release the principal debtor from the debt, and promises to assume payment of the indebtedness himself, the transaction would also be outside the statute, because the agreement would simply be an agreement to substitute principal debtors.

A guarantee agreement between parties is not a simple arrangement, because the guarantor's potential liability is of a continuous nature. Consequently, the requirement that the guarantee be reduced to writing and signed by the guarantor is not unreasonable. As with any agreement extending over a long period of time, memories become hazy, facts may be forgotten, and interpretations may change. Far from being onerous, the requirement of evidence of the agreement in writing makes good sense. As a result, the courts have not attempted to circumvent the statute with respect to guarantees to avoid injustice. One form of relief which the courts have employed in guarantee cases, however, relates to agreements made between the creditor and principal debtor subsequent to the guarantee agreement. If these two parties alter the security which the guarantor may look to in the event of default, or alter the debt agreement without the consent of the guarantor, the alteration may release the guarantor. Where the change in the agreement is detrimental to the guarantor, the courts will normally not enforce the guarantee if the principal debtor should later default.

||||||||||||||||||||||||||||||||||||||||||||||||||||||||||||||||||||||||||||

CASE 10.1

Western Dominion Investment Co., Ltd. v. MacMillan, [1925] 1 W.W.R. 852.

DYSART, J.:

Reduced to its simplest terms a guaranty is the promise of one man to pay the debt of another if that other default. In every case of guaranty there are at least two obligations, a primary and a secondary. The secondary—the guaranty—is based upon the primary, and is enforceable only if the primary default. It is so completely dependent upon the *unchanged continuance* of that primary, that if any, even the slightest, unauthorized changes are made in the primary, as, e.g., by extension of time for payment, or by reducing the chances of enforcing payment, as, e.g., by releasing any part of the securities, the secondary thereby falls to the ground. In other words, the secondary is not only collateral to, but is exactly co-extensive with, the primary, as the primary existed when the secondary came into existence. Lastly, if the secondary obligor pays the debt he is entitled, as of right, to step into the creditor's shoes.

||||||||||||||||||||||||||||||||||||||||||||||||||||||||||||||||||||||||||||

Assumed Liability: Tort

A second promise of a somewhat similar

nature to the guarantee is also covered by this particular section of the *Statute of Frauds*. Any agreement whereby a third party promises to answer for the tort of another must be in writing and be signed by the party to be charged, otherwise the promise will not be enforceable. This is not unlike the guarantee, but it applies where a third party promises to compensate a person who is injured by the tortious act of another, rather than by the person's failure to pay a debt. For example, Thompson, Jr., a young man aged 16 years, carelessly rode his bicycle on the sidewalk and collided with Varley. The collision caused injuries to Varley and placed him in the hospital. Thompson, Sr., the father of Thompson, promised to compensate Varley for his injuries, if Varley would promise not to sue Thompson, Jr. If Varley wishes to enforce the promise of Thompson, Sr., he must insist that Thompson, Sr., put his promise in writing and sign it. Otherwise it would be caught by the *Statute of Frauds*, and would be unenforceable against Thompson, Sr.

Consideration of Marriage

A further type of contract to which the statute applies is an agreement made in consideration of marriage. Of greater importance perhaps at the time that the statute was passed, than today, the Act in some provinces still requires any promise of payment of money or property settlement conditional upon, or in consideration of a marriage taking place, be evidenced in writing and signed to be enforceable. It is important to note, however, that in this section the statute does not refer to promises of marriage between individuals who intend to marry, but rather, to a promise usually made by a third party to pay a sum of money if the marriage takes place.

Contracts Concerning Interests in Land

Of the remaining two kinds of agreements subject to the statute, the requirement of writing for contracts concerning the sale or other dealing with land has given the courts the most concern. The vagueness of the wording initially gave rise to much litigation, and the courts were forced to struggle with an interpretation which would limit the application of the statute to those cases concerned specifically with the sale or other disposition of interests in land. The courts gradually excluded agreements that did not deal specifically with the land itself, in addition to agreements concerned with the repair of buildings, and contracts for "room and board." A great many other agreements that were remotely concerned with the disposition of land were also held to be outside the statute. For those cases encompassed by the statute, it was necessary to devise ways and means to prevent the law itself from being used to perpetrate a fraud on an unsuspecting party by way of an unwritten agreement.

The most important relief developed by the courts to avoid the effect of the statute was the doctrine of *part performance,* a concept which allowed the courts, on the basis of equity, to enforce an unwritten agreement concerning land. The doctrine, unfortunately, is quite limited in its application, and a party adversely affected by a failure to place the agreement in writing must be in a position to meet four criteria to successfully avoid the statute:

(1) The acts performed by the party alleging part performance must be demonstrated to be acts which refer only to the agreement and the lands in question, and to no other.

(2) It must be shown that to enforce the statute against the party who partly

performed for the lack of a written memorandum would perpetrate a fraud and a hardship on that person.

(3) The agreement must relate to an interest in land.

(4) The agreement itself must be valid and enforceable apart from the requirement of writing, and verbal evidence must be available to establish the existence of the agreement.[4]

To meet these four criteria is seldom an easy task. For example, Anderson enters into a verbal agreement with Baxter to purchase Baxter's farm for $30 000. Anderson gives Baxter $100 in cash to "bind the bargain," and takes possession of the buildings and property. He removes an old barn on the premises, and makes extensive repairs to the house. After Anderson has completed the repairs, Baxter refuses to proceed with the transaction, and raises the absence of a written agreement as a defence.

To meet the first criterion, the payment of $100 cash will not do, as it was not an act which would solely relate to this particular transaction (it could represent payment of rent). The acts of removing the old barn and repairing the house, however, might meet this requirement. A person would not normally undertake activities of this nature unless he had some interest in the land. Therefore, his acts would refer to such a contract, and to no other, under the circumstances.

The second criterion would also be met by Anderson's expenditure of time and expense in making renovations and removing the barn. These actions would represent acts which a person would only

perform in reliance on the completion of the unwritten agreement, and would constitute a detriment or loss if the agreement was not fulfilled. To allow the land-owner to refuse to complete the transaction at that point would constitute a fraud on the purchaser, and represent unjust enrichment of the vendor.

The third criterion would be met by the nature of the agreement itself: it constitutes a contract for an interest in land, and one that equity would enforce by way of an action for specific performance.

The last criterion would be one which the purchaser might be able to prove by showing the court that the agreement, apart from the requirement of writing, contained all of the essential components of a valid agreement—this might be by way of the evidence of witnesses who were present at the time of the making of the agreement, and who might be in a position to establish the terms.

||||||||||||||||||||||||||||||||||||||||||||||||||||||||||||||||||||||||||||

CASE 10.2

Brownscombe v. Public Trustee of the Province of Alberta (1969), 5 D.L.R. (3d) 673.

HALL, J.:

The facts are summarized by the learned trial Judge in the opening paragraph of his judgment as follows:

"In 1932 when Canada and the world in general were in a severe business depression, the plaintiff, whose home was in Prince George, B.C., and who was then 16 years of age, applied to the late Robert Marcel Vercamert at the latter's home, not far from Rockyford in Alberta, for work. The said Vercamert, a bachelor, somewhat severely crippled by heart trouble and able to do but little work on the farm where he lived and which he conducted, took the plaintiff into his home. On the evidence I find that plaintiff worked faithfully for his employer

---

[4]See *Rawlinson v. Ames*, [1925] 1 Ch. 96 at p. 114; *Brownscombe v. Public Trustee of the Province of Alberta* (1969), 5 D.L.R. (3d) 673.

with but little financial reward for a considerable number of years. I find that on a number of occasions when plaintiff thought of leaving Vercamert's employ he was dissuaded by the latter's promised assurance that on his demise the farm would go to plaintiff by will. In January 1961, Vercamert died intestate and this action is the result."

. . . . . .

And then he said:

"The contract relating to land is within s. 4 of the *Statute of Frauds*, and there is no memorandum in writing. Therefore, part performance is necessary for the plaintiff to succeed on his claim for specific performance. *Per* Cranworth, L.C., in *Caton v. Caton* (1866), L.R. 1 Ch. App. 137 at p. 147: Part performance will afford relief from the operation of the statute '. . . in many cases . . . when to insist upon it would be to make it the means of effecting instead of preventing fraud'. However, not all acts done in pursuance of the unenforceable contract will constitute part performance in law. They may be found to relate only to a contract of service as in *Maddison v. Alderson* (1883), 8 App. Cas. 467, and *Deglman v. Guaranty Trust Co. of Canada and Constantineau*, [1954] 3 D.L.R. 785, [1954] S.C.R. 725, except where such acts are 'unequivocally referable in their own nature to some dealing with the land which is alleged to have been the subject of the agreement sued upon . . .': *Per* Duff, J., in *McNeil v. Corbett* (1907), 39 S.C.R. 608 at p. 611, approved by the Supreme Court of Canada in *Deglman*."

. . . . . .

The issue for decision by this Court is whether the acts relied upon by the appellant over the period 1932 to 1961 are acts which are "unequivocally referable in their own nature to some dealing with the land which is alleged to have been the subject of the agreement sued on", as stated by Duff, J. (as he then was), in *McNeill v. Corbett* (1907), 39 S.C.R. 608, and approved by this Court in *Deglman v. Guaranty Trust Co. of Canada and Constantineau*, [1954] 3 D.L.R. 785, [1954] S.C.R. 725.

It is clear that not all the acts relied on as testified to by the appellant and his wife can be re-

garded as "unequivocally referable in their own nature to some dealing with the land", but in my view the building of the house on the lands in question in the years 1946 and 1947 at the suggestion of Vercamert almost, if not wholly, at the appellant's expense was, as the learned trial Judge found "unequivocally referable" to the agreement which the appellant alleged had been made and inconsistent with the ordinary relationship of employee or tenant.

||||||||||||||||||||||||||||||||||||||||||||||||||||||||||||||||||||||||||||||||||||||||||||

Long-Term Contracts

The last type of agreement to which the statute applies is an agreement which is not to be performed within the period of one year from the date it is made. The logic behind the requirement that a contract of this nature be evidenced by a written memorandum is readily apparent. Any agreement which is not to be performed within a relatively short space of time is subject to the frailties of human memory, and the risk of misinterpretation at a later date. The requirement of writing makes a great deal of sense, but it, nevertheless, by its arbitrary nature, may cause hardship as well. To overcome this drawback, the courts have limited its application to those agreements which cannot be fully performed by either party within the space of one year, and to those contracts which do not permit termination on reasonable or express notice within the one-year period. Since many contracts are written in such a way that they run for an indefinite period of time, the courts have generally treated them as if they were potential short-term agreements in order to avoid difficulty. The reasoning behind this approach is that even though the agreement might conceivably run for more than one year, it might also be terminated within the one-year period if one of the parties so desires.

As a result, contracts for an indefinite period of time, even though not in writing, are generally enforceable if termination is possible within the one-year period.

REQUIREMENTS FOR THE WRITTEN MEMORANDUM

To comply with the statute, evidence of the contract in writing need not be embodied in a formal document. It is essential, however, to include in the written document all of the terms of the contract; evidence having the effect of adding new terms to, or contradicting the written document may not be adduced later.

The first requirement is that the parties to the agreement be identified either by name or description, and that the terms of the agreement be set out in sufficient detail that the contract may be enforced. For example, an agreement may consist of an exchange of letters which identify the parties, contain the offer made, describe the property as well as the consideration paid, or to be paid, and include a letter of acceptance. The two documents taken together would constitute the written memorandum. The final requirement is that the written memorandum be signed by the party to be charged. It is important to note that *only* the party to be charged need sign the memorandum. The party who wishes to enforce the agreement need not be a signatory, since the statute requires only that it be signed by the party to be charged.[5]

Of importance, where written agreements are concerned, is the *parol evidence rule*, which limits the kind of evidence which may be introduced to prove the terms of a contract. By this rule, no evidence may be adduced by a party which would have the effect of adding new terms to the contract, or change or contradict the terms of a clear and unambiguous written agreement. Evidence may only be admitted to rectify or explain the terms agreed upon, or to prove some fact such as fraud or illegality which may affect the enforceability of the agreement.

The application of the rule is not arbitrary, however, and the courts have accepted a number of different arguments which allow parties to circumvent the effect of the rule. The argument that a *condition precedent* exists is an example. A condition precedent, as the name implies, is an event that must occur before the contract becomes operative. The parties frequently place this term in the written agreement, but they need not do so. If the condition is agreed to by the parties, or in some cases, if it can be implied, then the written agreement will remain in a state of suspension until the condition is satisfied. If the condition cannot be met, then the contract does not come into existence, and any money paid under it may usually be recovered.

For example, Allan and Brewster discuss the purchase of Brewster's car by Allan. Allan agrees to purchase the car for $3 000 if he can successfully negotiate a loan from his banker. Allan and Brewster put the agreement in writing, but do not include in the agreement the term that the purchase is conditional upon Allan obtaining a loan for the purchase. While the parol evidence rule does not permit evidence to be admitted to add to the contract, the court will admit evidence to show that the agreement would not come into effect until the condition was met. The distinction here is that the evidence relating to the condition precedent does not relate to the contract terms, but, rather, to the cir-

---

[5]*Daniels v. Trefusis,* [1914] 1 Ch. 788; *McLean v. Little,* [1943] O.R. 202.

cumstances under which the written agreement would become enforceable.

A second exception to the parol evidence rule is the application of the doctrine of *implied term*. Occasionally, in the writing of an agreement, the parties may leave out a term which is usually found in contracts of the type the parties negotiated. If the evidence can establish that the parties had intended to put the term in, and that it is a term normally included in such a contract by custom of the trade, or normal business practice, the courts may conclude that the term is an implied term, and enforce the contract as if it contained the term. Generally, the type of term that will be implied is one which the parties require in the contract in order to implement the agreement. It must be noted, however, that if the term conflicts, in any way, with the express terms of the agreement, the parol evidence rule will exclude it. Similarly, an express term may be incorporated in a written agreement by reference if the agreement is a "standard form" type of contract, and if the term is expressed before the agreement is concluded. For example, a large sign in a parking-lot which states that the owner will not be responsible for any damage to the patrons' vehicles may be binding upon the patrons even though the limitation is not expressly stated on the ticket, but referred to in small print on the back.

A third important exception to the parol evidence rule is the *collateral agreement*. A collateral agreement is a separate agreement which the parties may make that has some effect on the written agreement, but which is not referred to in it. One of the difficulties with the collateral agreement is that it usually adds to, or alters, the written agreement, and if it were allowed at all times, it would effectively circumvent the parol evidence rule. For this reason, the courts are reluctant to accept the argument that a collateral agreement exists unless the parties can demonstrate that the collateral agreement does in fact exist in every respect. The application of this criteria usually defeats the collateral agreement argument because the collateral agreement seldom contains separate consideration from that of the written agreement. In those cases, however, where a separate agreement does exist, the courts will enforce the collateral agreement even though it may conflict to some extent with the written agreement.

With all of these exceptions to the parol evidence rule, one element is common. In each case, the modifying term precedes, or is concurrent with, the formation of the written agreement. Any verbal agreement made by the parties after the written agreement is effected may alter the terms of the written agreement,[6] or cancel it.[7] The parol evidence rule will not exclude evidence of the *subsequent agreement* from the court. The reason for this distinction is that the subsequent agreement represents a new agreement made by the parties which has as its subject-matter the existing agreement.

||||||||||||||||||||||||||||||||||||||||||||||||||||||||||||||||||||||||||||||

CASE 10.3

MacLean v. Kennedy (1965), 53 D.L.R. (2d) 254.

ILSLEY, C.J.:

There are two principles of law that must be kept in mind.

. . . . .

In *Cushing v. Knight* (1912), 6 D.L.R. 820 at p. 824, 2 W.W.R. 704, 46 S.C.R. 555, Duff, J., said:

[6]*Johnson Investments v. Pagritide*, [1923] 2 D.L.R. 985.
[7]*Morris v. Baron and Co.*, [1918] A.C. 1.

"The fact that such a formal agreement was contemplated is, as Lord Cranworth said in *Ridgway v. Wharton*, 6 H.L. Cas. 238, strong evidence that the parties did not intend finally to bind themselves until that agreement should be completely constituted . . ."

In *Ridgway v. Wharton* (1857), 6 H.L.C. 238, 10 E.R. 1287, the Lord Chancellor said (p. 268): "I again protest against its being supposed, because persons wish to have a formal agreement drawn up, that therefore they cannot be bound by a previous agreement, if it is clear that such an agreement has been made; but the circumstances that the parties do intend a subsequent agreement to be made, is strong evidence to show that they did not intend the previous negotiations to amount to an agreement."

In *Von Hatzfeldt-Wildenburg v. Alexander*, [1912] 1 Ch. 284, Parker, J., said at pp. 288-9:

"It appears to be well settled by the authorities that if the documents or letters relied on as constituting a contract contemplate the execution of a further contract between the parties, it is a question of construction whether the execution of the further contract is a condition or term of the bargain or whether it is a mere expression of the desire of the parties as to the manner in which the transaction already agreed to will in fact go through.

. . . . .

The second principle of law to be kept in mind is that the material terms of the contract must not be vague, indefinite or uncertain. This principle has been variously stated.

. . . . .

If an oral agreement is vague, indefinite or uncertain, it would appear that this fact may be taken into account in deciding whether the execution of a formal agreement is a condition or term of the oral agreement. At least this would seem to follow from certain observations of Meredith, C.J., in *Stow v. Currie* (1910), 21 O.L.R. 486 at pp. 493 and 494, and of Clute, J., at p. 496. In *Stow v. Currie*, the uncertain agreement was written, not oral, but it was held that it was intended to be subject to a new and formal agreement, the terms of which were not expressed in detail, and one reason for so holding was its uncertainty in certain respects.

|||||||||||||||||||||||||||||||||||||||||||||||||||||||||||||||||||||||||||||||||||||||||

SALE OF GOODS ACT

A second important statute which contains a requirement of writing is the *Sale of Goods Act*. [8] The particular requirement of writing was originally a part of the *Statute of Frauds*, and had remained there for several hundred years. After 1893, when separate legislation concerning the sale of goods was passed in England, the requirement of writing was removed from the *Statute of Frauds* and embodied in the new Act. The provincial legislatures in Canada copied the English legislation, and varied the value of the goods to which the requirement of evidence of the agreement in writing applied. The legislation fortunately provided, as well, a number of activities on the part of the parties which would permit them to enforce the agreement even though the contract was not evidenced by a written memorandum. Because the parties normally comply with one of the exceptions where the contract of sale is not in writing, the requirement does not pose a hazard for most buyers and sellers. Of more importance today is the consumer protection legislation applicable to many kinds of contracts. This legislation often requires certain types of sales contracts to be in writing, and imposes penalties for the failure to provide consumers with a written purchase agreement disclosing information concerning the sale and any credit terms.

[8]All provinces (except Quebec) have legislation pertaining to the sale of goods patterned after the English statute. A detailed examination of this topic may be found in Chapter 22. British Columbia has since altered its *Sale of Goods Act*, R.S.B.C. 1979, c. 370, s. 8, by removing the requirement of writing. It has, however, placed the requirement of writing in another statute designed to provide consumer protection.

SUMMARY   Formal and informal contracts developed along distinctive lines, and each has a different legal history. Formal contracts generally derive their validity from the form which they take, and may be required to effect particular transactions. All formal contracts are evidenced by writing, and most are subject to the requirement that they be signed, sealed, and delivered, before they become operative.

Informal contracts may be written, oral, or in some cases, implied, although certain informal contracts (those subject to the *Statute of Frauds*) must be evidenced by a memorandum in writing setting out their terms, and must be signed by the party to be charged before they are enforceable by a court of law.

Written contracts are subject to a number of rules, principles, and doctrines which have been developed to mitigate the hardship that is sometimes imposed by the statute. A notable example of one of these special rules or doctrines is the doctrine of part performance, which may be applied in some cases where land is sold without written evidence of the transaction.

Not all of the rules, however, are designed to prevent hardship. Written agreements are also subject to the parol evidence rule, which excludes evidence of any prior or concurrent agreement which might add to, or contradict, the terms of the written agreement in question. Exceptions to this rule nevertheless exist in the form of conditions precedent, implied terms, and genuine collateral agreements. All may take either a written or oral form. Additionally, agreements made subsequent to a written agreement may alter or terminate the contract, even though the subsequent agreement is verbal in nature.

Special requirements for consumer contracts have been established by legislation in many provinces in recent years. These statutes usually require certain kinds of transactions to be in writing. While ostensibly designed to require the seller to disclose information concerning the sale to the buyer, the statutes also require the written memorandum to contain specific information, otherwise fines or penalties may be imposed upon the seller. The contract of sale and the legislation pertaining thereto are. examined at length in Chapters 22 and 23.

DISCUSSION   1. *Identify the two classifications of agreements under the law of*
QUESTIONS   *contracts.*

2. *On what basis did early ecclesiastic courts deal with breach of promise?*

3. *Historically, what action in the formation of an agreement placed the agreement within the jurisdiction of the king's courts?*

4. What circumstances surrounding the formation of an agreement formed important elements of informal "contracts"?

5. Define "writ of assumpsit."

6. Explain fully how the English Statute of Frauds has affected today's requirements of form and writing.

7. Distinguish a "guarantee" from an "indemnity."

8. Explain the third-party relationship of contingent liability.

9. Explain the rationale behind the requirement of writing for contracts not to be completed within a period of one year. Why have exceptions been made to this rule?

10. Describe fully the doctrine of part performance.

11. Define "action for specific performance."

12. Briefly outline the legal requirements for a written memorandum.

13. Describe the parol evidence rule and explain its application.

14. When parties offer to purchase a rural property, they frequently do so with the stipulation that water be found on the land and that it must pass local health regulations. Explain the nature of this stipulation.

15. Explain the "collateral agreement" and doctrine of implied term "exceptions to the parol evidence rule."

16. Why is a subsequent agreement which terminates a written agreement not subject to the requirement of writing? Under what circumstances might writing be required?

Case studies

||||||||||||||||||||||||||||||||||||||||||||||||||||||||||||||||||||||||||||||||||||||||||||||||||||||||||||||||

JUDICIAL DECISIONS

Contracts— Agreement in Writing— Implied Terms

Canada Square Corp. Ltd. et al. v. Versafood Services Ltd. et al. (1979), 25 O.R. (2d) 591.

The plaintiff and defendant corporations exchanged letters pertaining to a prospective lease agreement by the parties regarding the "top floor" of a building to be constructed. One of the letters contained the statement, "This will confirm our verbal understanding . . .," and another stated "this constitutes the general principles of our agreement." The letters did not specify a number of matters, including payment of rent and the exact description of the premises to be leased. The defendant took the position that no lease agreement existed.

CARRUTHERS, J.:

. . . I wish to outline what, in my opinion, are relevant general principles of law found in a number of authorities.

In a decision of the House of Lords, *G. Scammell & Nephew, Ltd. v. Ouston et al.*, [1941] A.C. 251, Lord Maugham said at pp. 254-5:

"The reason for these different conclusions is that laymen unassisted by persons with a legal training are not always accustomed to use words or phrases with a precise or definite meaning. In order to constitute a valid contract the parties must so express themselves that their meaning can be determined with a reasonable degree of certainty. It is plain that unless this can be done it would be impossible to hold that the contracting parties had the same intention; in other words the consensus ad idem would be a matter of mere conjecture. This general rule, however, applies somewhat differently in different cases. In commercial documents connected with dealings in a trade with which the parties are perfectly familiar the court is very willing, if satisfied that the parties thought that they made a binding contract, to imply terms and in particular terms as to the method of carrying out the contract which it would be impossible to supply in other kinds of contract . . ."

In the same decision, Lord Wright said, at pp. 268-9:

"There are in my opinion two grounds on which the court ought to hold that there was never a contract. The first is that the language used was so obscure and so incapable of any definite or precise meaning that the court is unable to attribute to the parties any particular contractual intention. The object of the court is to do justice between the parties, and the court will do its best, if satisfied that there was an ascertainable and determinate intention to contract, to give effect to that intention, looking at substance and not mere form. It will not be deterred by mere difficulties of interpretation. Difficulty is not synonymous with ambiguity so long as any definite meaning can be extracted. But the test of intention is to be found in the words used. If these words, considered however broadly and untechnically and with due regard to all the just implications, fail to evince any definite meaning on which the court can safely act, the court has no choice but to say that there is no contract. Such a position is not often found . . . It is a necessary requirement that an agreement in order to be binding must be sufficiently definite to enable the court to give it a practical meaning. Its terms must be so definite, or capable of being made definite without further agreement of the parties, that the promises and performances to be rendered by each party are reasonably certain.

. . . . .

"But as Lord Dunedin said in *May & Butcher v. The King*, [1934] 2 K.B. 17, 21*n*, reported in a note to *Foley v. Classique Coaches, Ld.*, [1934] 2 K.B. 1, 'To be a good contract there must be a concluded bargain and a concluded contract is one which settles everything that is necessary to be settled and leaves nothing to be settled by agreement between the parties. Of course it may leave something which has still to be determined but then that determination must be a determination which does not depend upon the agreement between the parties.' "

In *Kelly v. Watson* (1921), 61 S.C.R. 482 at p. 490, 57 D.L.R. 363 at p. 369, [1921] 1 W.W.R. 958, Mr. Justice Mignault said:

"Recognizing to the fullest extent that where a contract has been partly performed, the court, when asked to decree specific performance, will struggle against the difficulty ensuing from the vagueness of the contract, still it is obvious that the court cannot make a contract for the parties if the latter have not agreed on its material terms."

Versafood suggests that there is uncertainty in the description of the premises to be demised. The first paragraph of ex. 1, the agreement of October 14, 1969, reads as follows:

"This is to confirm our verbal understanding of this morning regarding the restaurant on top of the new TransAmerica Building which is to become a part of Canada Square, and is located at 2180 Yonge Street."

On p. 3 of the agreement, being part of the 14th paragraph, are these words:

"Sales in this case will include all sales from coffee wagons, take-out, dining room and space in the subway lobby, as well as space on the mezzanine floor lobby, up to a gross amount of 600 square feet in that lobby . . . In addition, if private dining room space is developed on the top floor of the TransAmerica Building . . ."

These are the only references to the area of the building to be leased by Versafood under that agreement. From reading the words alone, I would have to agree that it is not possible to know what part or portion of the "top" or "top floor" is to be leased by Versafood. In addition, it is not definite where the space in the mezzanine floor lobby is to be located once the actual amount thereof is determined. I do not believe, however, that this deficiency will prevent the agreement from being enforceable. I am entitled, in my view of the law, to admit and consider parol evidence and to examine extrinsic circumstances found in the evidence so as to arrive at "all the just implications" in order to ascertain the exact location and extent of the part of the building to be leased.

||||||||||||||||||||||||||||||||||||||||||||||||||||||||||||||||||||||||||||||||||||||||||||||||||||||||||||||||||||||||||||||||||||

**Contracts—
Requirement of
Writing—
Statute of
Frauds**

Smith v. Gold Coast & Ashanti Explorers, Ltd., [1903] 1 K.B. 285.

The plaintiff was a solicitor who was engaged under a verbal contract for a period of one year commencing December 7, 1901. The contract was made on December 6, 1901. When the agreement was repudiated by the defendants, the plaintiff sued. The defence was that the contract was unenforceable under the *Statute of Frauds*.

LORD ALVERSTONE, C.J.:

In one sense the contract may be said to be one which is not to be performed within the space of one year from the date when it was made. It depends upon whether the period of service is to exclude or include the day next after that on which the contract was entered into. It is contended for the defendants that a year's service "from" December 7, 1901, would commence on December 8—that is to say, that the year would exclude December 7, 1901, and would include December 7, 1902. If that is the contract, then it is clear, on the authority of *Britain* v. *Rossiter*, that the contract is within the statute, for it was there decided that where the service is to commence on the second day after that on which the contract is made, the contract is one which is not to be performed within a year. But if the contract in this case was for a year's service commencing on December 7, 1901—that is, on the day next after that on which the contract was made—and terminating on December 6, 1902, there is authority for holding that such a contract is not within the statute. In *Cawthorne* v. *Cordrey* it had been ruled at the trial that an agreement made on a Sunday for a year's service to commence on the Monday was not within the statute. In the course of the argument on a rule for a new trial Willes J. said: "If a builder undertakes to build a house within a year, that means a year from the next day"; and Byles J. said: "If you adopt the reasonable rule which excludes fractions of a day, taking the receipt to define the duration of the contract, there would be only three hundred and sixty-five days." These dicta are an expression of opinion in favour of the view that the statute does not apply where the service is to commence on the day next after the agreement. Then Brett L.J. in *Britain* v. *Rossiter*, referring to *Cawthorne* v. *Cordrey*, said: "There was however a dictum of Willes J., which seems to be supported by the opinion of Byles J.; these are great authorities; and that dictum seems to have been that if a contract is made on a day, say Monday, for a service for a year, to commence on the following day, say a Tuesday, the service is to be performed within 365 days from the making of the contract; but that inasmuch as the law takes no notice of part of a day, and the contract was made in the middle of the Monday, the service to be performed within 365 days after that, the law did not count that half-day of the Monday, and therefore the contract was to be performed within 365 days after it was made, and that was within a year. This view was founded upon a fiction, namely, that the law does not take notice of part of a day. I am not prepared to say that under like circumstances one might not follow that dictum, and carry it to the length of a decision. It is not necessary to say so here, because the case has not arisen." The case has now arisen for our decision, and I cannot regard that passage from Brett L.J.'s judgment as being intended to express disapproval of the dicta in *Cawthorne* v. *Cordrey*. On the contrary, I think that these cases shew that a contract for a year's service to commence on the day next after the day on which the contract was made is not an agreement which is not to be performed within the space of one year from the making thereof, within the meaning of s. 4. The contract set up by the plaintiff is, therefore, not of necessity within the statute . . .

CASE PROBLEMS FOR DISCUSSION

Case 1

Reid owned a car and travel trailer which he wished to sell. The trailer was equipped with a stove and refrigerator as built-in equipment, and Reid had added a small television set and antenna as a part of the equipment. The television set was not built into the trailer.

Calder expressed an interest in the car and trailer, and examined the equipment. Reid advised Calder that the price was $8 600 and that the television set would be $100 extra if Calder wished to buy it as well. Calder indicated that he wished to do so.

Reid prepared a written purchase agreement which itemized the car and trailer, but simply referred to the appliances as built-in equipment. The contract price was $8 600, and the agreement called for a deposit of $100. Both parties signed the agreement, and Calder gave Reid a deposit cheque in the amount of $200.

Reid changed his mind about the sale of the television set, and shortly before Calder was due to return for the car and trailer, Reid telephoned to say that he was selling only that which was specified in the written agreement.

Explain Calder's rights (if any) in this case.

Case 2

Simon, a professional engineer, entered into an agreement with Easy Exploration whereby he agreed to spend a year in Peru in search of a number of different kinds of minerals. The verbal agreement was made on September 7th, and Simon was to begin work for the company the following week on September 10th. The contract was to terminate on September 10th of the following year. Easy Exploration offered to prepare a formal agreement for Simon's signature before he departed on September 10th.

On September 9th, Easy Exploration decided to cancel its exploration program, and notified Simon that there was no need for him to sign the employment contract as his services would not be required.

Discuss Simon's rights (if any), and Easy Explorations position at law.

Case 3

Amber, a young musician, obtained a position with an orchestra, and wished to acquire a musical instrument of better quality. The conductor of the orchestra accompanied Amber to Smith's Music Supply, where Amber selected a relatively expensive violin on the conductor's recommendation. Smith agreed to accept Amber's present violin in trade, but was reluctant to extend credit to Amber for the $1 000 difference between the value of the two instruments.

To enable Amber to acquire the violin, the conductor agreed to guarantee his indebtedness if Smith would take a chattel mortgage on Amber's rather old automobile. It was also agreed that Amber would insure the violin against loss or damage, and Smith would hold a chattel mortgage on the violin as well.

A few months later, Amber was late for rehearsal as a result of engine trouble with his automobile. When he explained his problem to the conductor, the conductor suggested that he should consider finding something more reliable as transportation.

After the rehearsal, Amber arranged to sell his automobile, and purchased a motorcycle of equal value. In order to effect the transaction, Amber arranged with Smith to have the automobile released from his chattel mortgage, and a chattel mortgage placed on the motorcycle.

On his way to rehearsal the next day, Amber was involved in an accident in which both motorcycle and violin were destroyed. He was hospitalized as a result of the accident, and unable to work.

The payments to Smith fell into arrears, and in spite of repeated requests for payment, Amber failed to comply. Eventually, Smith called upon the conductor to honour his guarantee, and pay the balance of the debt owed.

At that point, the conductor discovered that Amber had not insured the violin, and that the property secured by the chattel mortgage no longer existed.

The conductor refused to make payment, and Smith took legal action against him to enforce the guarantee.

Explain the positions of the parties at law, and render a decision.

Case 4

Clement entered into a verbal agreement with Calhoun to purchase Calhoun's farm for $40 000. In the presence of his friend Saunders, Clement gave Calhoun $500 in cash "to bind the bargain." The farm adjoined the farm Clement already owned, and immediately after the deal was made, both he and Saunders proceeded to remove an old fence which separated the two farms.

A few days later, Clement plowed a large field on his "new" farm, and Saunders cut down a few trees. Later that day, he prepared a cheque in the amount of $39 500, and took it to the farmhouse where Calhoun was still living.

Calhoun met Clement at the door and said that he had changed his mind. He did not wish to move off the land, and had decided not to sell the farm.

Discuss Clement's rights (if any) in this case. Explain the possible outcome if Clement should decide to take legal action against Calhoun.

CHAPTER 11

|||||||||||||||||||||||||||||||||||||||||||||||||||||||||||||||||||||||||||||||||||||||||||||||||||||||||

Failure to create an Enforceable Contract

INTRODUCTION

In their negotiations, the parties may meet all of the essentials for the creation of a binding agreement, but they may nevertheless occasionally fail to create an enforceable contract. Offer and acceptance, capacity, consideration, legality of object, and an intention to create a legal relationship all must be present, together with the requirements of form and writing under certain circumstances. But even when these elements are present, the parties may not have an agreement which both parties may enforce, because the parties must also show that they both meant precisely the same thing in their agreement. There are essentially four situations of this general nature which could arise that might render the agreement either void or voidable.

MISTAKE

If the parties in their negotiations are mistaken as to some essential term in the agreement, they may have failed to create a contract. Mistake at law, however, does not mean the same thing to both the layman and the legal practitioner. Mistake from a legal point of view has a relatively narrow meaning, and generally refers to a situation where the parties have entered into an agreement in such a way that the contract does not express their true intentions. This may occur in cases where the parties have formed an untrue impression concerning an essential element, or where they have failed to reach a true meeting of the minds as to a fundamental term in the agreement.

Generally, mistake may take the form of a mistake of law or a mistake of fact. Both of these, nevertheless, are limited insofar as their effect on the contract is concerned, as the courts tend to limit the grounds upon which this objection may be raised. For example, if Andy offers to sell his car to Burt for $1 800, then realizes that his car is worth $1 900, the courts would probably not allow Andy to avoid the agreement on the basis of mistake. Because Andy made the offer to Burt, and then later alleged that he had made a mistake as to the value of the subject-matter, the courts would have no real way of knowing Andy's true state of mind at the time the offer was made. On the other hand, if the consideration is clearly out of line, and the mistake is obvious, the courts may not allow the other party to "snap up" the bargain.[1] Where the mistake, however, is due to the party's own negligence, the contract, under certain circumstances, may be binding.[2]

Mistake of Law

The general rule for a mistake of law is that any monies paid under such a mistake are not recoverable unless the statute in question provides relief. Most statutes which require monetary payment (such as the *Income Tax Act*) do provide for this eventuality, and consequently, no difficulty exists when a mistake is made. If the statute fails to provide relief, then the party making the payment must find other grounds which would entitle him to a return of his money if he wishes to successfully recover it. If both parties are equally at fault in their mistake, then the courts generally consider the parties to be *in pari delecto*, and do not permit the party who paid the money to recover it.[3] If both parties are not equally at fault, then the courts may consider the surrounding circumstances, and dispose of the matter in a suitable fashion.

Mistake of Fact

Mistake of fact may take many forms, and for many of these kinds of mistakes, the courts do provide relief. As a general rule, if the parties are mistaken as to the existence of the subject-matter of the contract, then the contract will be void.[4] For example, Alice offers to sell Beverley her canoe, and Beverley accepts the offer. Unknown to both Alice and Beverley, the boat-house in which Alice had stored her

[1]*Hartog v. Colin & Shields*, [1939] 3 All E.Rep. 566; *Imperial Glass Ltd. v. Consolidated Supplies Ltd.* (1960), 22 D.L.R. (2d) 759.

[2]*Timmins v. Kuzyk* (1962), 32 D.L.R. (2d) 207; *Hydro Electric Comn. of Township of Nepean v. Ontario Hydro* (1980), 27 O.R. (2d) 321.
[3]*O'Grady v. City of Toronto* (1916), 37 O.L.R. 139.
[4]*Barrow, Lane, & Ballard Ltd. v. Phillips & Co.*, [1929] 1 K.B. 574.

canoe was destroyed by fire the previous day, and Alice's canoe had burned in the fire. The subject-matter did not exist at the time that Alice and Beverley made the contract, and the contract was void due to a mistake as to the existence of the subject-matter. In essence, there was no canoe to sell at the time the parties made their agreement. The same rule might well apply if the canoe had been badly damaged in the fire, and was no longer usable as a canoe. Under the common law, the courts would not require the purchaser to accept something different from that which she had contracted to buy.

A second type of mistake of fact applies where there is a mistake as to the identity of one of the contracting parties. This is essentially an extension of the rule for offer and acceptance that states that only the person to whom an offer is made may accept the offer. With a mistake of fact of this nature the courts will generally look at the offer to determine if the identity of the person in question is an essential element of the contract. If the identity of the party is not an essential element of the agreement, then the agreement may be enforceable,[5] but if one party to the contract does not wish to be bound in an agreement with a particular contracting party, and is misled into believing that he is contracting with someone else, the contract may be voidable when the true facts are discovered.[6]

Mistake may also occur where one of the parties may be mistaken as to the true nature of a written contract, but this is a very narrow form of mistake that represents an exception to the general rule that a person will be bound by any written agreement which he signs. The important distinction here is that the circumstances surrounding the signing of the written document must be such that the person signing the document was led to believe that the document was of a completely different nature from what it actually was, and had he known what the agreement really was, he would not have signed it. This exception is subject to a number of constraints, and has a very limited application, because a person signing a written agreement is presumed to be bound by it. A failure to examine the written agreement does not usually absolve a person from any liability assumed under it. Nor is a person absolved from liability if he is aware of the nature of the agreement as a whole, but remains ignorant of a specific term within it.[7] To avoid liability, a person must be in a position to establish that the document was completely different in nature, and that he was obliged to rely on another person to explain the contents. He must also establish that he was not in a position to obtain an independent opinion or assistance before signing the written form. This particular exception, which represents a form of mistake, is a defence known as *non est factum* (it is not my doing).

Under this defence, if a person is incapable of reading or understanding the written agreement because of advanced age, infirmity, illiteracy, or other disability, and the person relies on the other contracting party to explain the nature of the document, the document will be a nullity if it proves to be something of a completely different nature. For example, if an elderly person with failing eyesight is

---

[5]*Elliyatt v. Little,* [1947] O.W.N. 123.
[6]*Said v. Butt,* [1920] 3 K.B. 497; *Boulton v. Jones,* (1857) 2 H&N 564, 157 E.R. 232. *Cundy v. Lindsay* (1878), 3 App. Cas. 459.

[7]*Sumner v. Sapkas* (1955), 17 W.W.R. 21.

induced to sign a document believing it to be a letter of reference, when in fact it is a guarantee, he will be able to avoid liability under it if he can show that he relied upon the person presenting it for his signature, and it was described to him as being a completely different document. The infirmity which made a personal examination and understanding of the document impossible must, of course, also be established to the satisfaction of the court, but once this is done, the party will not be bound by the document.[8]

The important point to note here is the true nature of the document. If the document is completely different in nature from the document which the party believed he was signing, then a plea of *non est factum* will succeed. If, however, the document is not of a different nature, but, rather, the same type of document as described, differing only in degree, then a defence of *non est factum* will be unsuccessful, because the party would have been aware of the true nature of the agreement at the time of signing, and no mistake as to the nature of the document would have existed.[9] The justification for this rule of law is obvious. Public policy dictates that a person should be bound by any agreement signed; the excuse that it was not read before signing is essentially an admission of carelessness or negligence on the part of the signor. The courts are not prepared to offer relief to those persons who are so careless in the management of their affairs that they are unwilling to take the time to read the terms and conditions which are contained in an agreement. There are, however,

persons who, as a result of advanced years, some infirmity, or simply the lack of opportunity, are unable to read the written agreement, and it is this group that the courts are prepared to assist if, through their reliance on another, they have been misled as to the true nature of the agreement that they signed. Even here, the disadvantaged persons are expected to assume some responsibility for their own protection. If the opportunity for independent advice is available, and they refuse to avail themselves of it, the courts may not permit them to avoid the contract. For example, where a person heard the contract read aloud, and then later pleaded *non est factum*, the claim was rejected, and the contract enforced.[10]

||||||||||||||||||||||||||||||||||||||||||||||||||||||||||||||||||||||||||||||||||||

CASE 11.1

Prudential Trust Co. Ltd. and Canadian Williston Minerals Ltd. v. Forseth and Forseth, [1960] S.C.R. 210.

MARTLAND, J.:

The learned trial judge gave judgment in favour of the appellants. On the main issue of *non est factum* he made certain important findings of fact as follows:

"I can find no reason for disbelieving Benson and I accept his evidence as to what in fact took place. I found him to be an honest and reliable witness. Regrettably, I cannot say the same for the plaintiffs. Apart from the obvious contradictions in their evidence, their demeanour in the box belied the story which they told. . . .

. . . . .

"I, therefore, find there was no fraudulent misrepresentation as alleged and that the plaintiff Harry Forseth executed the documents in question with full knowledge of the

---

[8]*W.T. Rawleigh Co. v. Dumoulin*, [1926] S.C.R. 551; *Commercial Credit Corp. v. Carroll Bros.* (1971), 16 D.L.R. (3d) 201.
[9]*Dorsch v. Freeholders Oil Co.*, [1965] S.C.R. 670.

[10]*Prudential Trust Co. Ltd. v. Forseth*, [1960] S.C.R. 210.

terms thereof. I find further that the documents contain the agreement entered into between Benson on behalf of his principal and the plaintiff Harry Forseth. There was no misunderstanding as to the terms of the assignment or option.''

The judgment at the trial was reversed by the Court of Appeal, which refused to accept the findings of fact made by the learned trial judge. The appellants have appealed from that judgment.

. . . . .

With respect, after reviewing carefully all of the reasons advanced in the judgment of the Court of Appeal, I am of the opinion that the circumstances of this case were not such as to warrant the exceptional course of reversing the findings of fact of the learned trial judge. On the contrary, I think there was ample evidence to justify them.

In my view the most important fact of all is the one which was not only admitted by the respondents, but was pleaded in their statement of claim; namely, that Mrs. Forseth actually read aloud the contents of the assignment to her husband. Counsel were unable to refer us to any case in which a plea of *non est factum* had been upheld where a literate person executed a document after having read it through, or after having heard its contents completely read. The fact that some of the terms may be difficult to comprehend, a matter which weighed heavily in the Court of Appeal, does not serve to establish such a plea. This goes only to the issue of a misconception as to the contents of the document and not as to its nature and character. A literate person who signs a document after reading it through, or hearing it fully read, must, I think, be presumed to know the nature of the document which he is signing.

This proposition does not conflict in any way with the judgment of this Court in *Prudential Trust Company Limited v. Cugnet*, a case which involved the same sort of documents as those in question here and in which a plea of *non est factum* was upheld. In that case the respondent had never read the assignment or

heard it read. The agent who obtained his execution of the document was not called as a witness and the learned trial judge found in fact that the respondent had relied upon misrepresentations by the agent.

My conclusion, therefore, is that the learned trial judge was right in rejecting the plea of *non est factum* and that Williston, as a *bona fide* purchaser for value, is entitled to enforce the agreement.

||||||||||||||||||||||||||||||||||||||||||||||||||||||||||||||||||||||||||||||||||||||||||||

Unilateral and Mutual Mistake

Mistake may take one of two forms insofar as the parties are concerned. The mistake may be made by only one party to the agreement, in which case, it is called *unilateral mistake*, or it may occur that both parties are unaware of the mistake, and the mistake is a *mutual mistake*. In the case of unilateral mistake, usually one of the parties is mistaken as to some element of the contract, and the other is aware of the mistake. Cases of this nature closely resemble misrepresentation when one of the parties is aware of the mistake, and either allows the mistake to exist, or actively encourages the false assumption by words or conduct. The major difficulty with this form of mistake is establishing a general rule for its application. The best that might be said here is that the courts tend to treat contracts as being unenforceable where a party makes or accepts an offer which he knows the other party thinks or understands to be materially different from that which he, himself, makes or accepts.

Mutual mistake, on the other hand, is generally the easiest to deal with, because it encompasses common forms of mistake such as mistake as to the existence of the subject-matter, or mistake as to its identity. Only the latter sometimes presents problems, and when it does so, the courts frequently decide that a mistake has occurred, and the contract is therefore unenforceable.[11] Cases of this sort tend to place a hardship on the plaintiff, because the courts, in effect, reject the plaintiff's interpretation of the contract. Nevertheless, if a reasonable interpretation is possible, it may be accepted by the court in an effort to maintain the agreement.

A special form of relief is available in the case of mistake in a written agreement which renders performance impossible. This is known as *rectification.* It is sometimes used to correct mistakes or errors that have crept into a written contract, either when a verbal agreement has been reduced to writing, or when a written agreement has been changed to a formal agreement under seal. In each of these cases, if the written agreement does not conform with the original agreement established by the parties, the courts may change the written words to meet the terms of the original agreement. The purpose of this relief is to "save" the agreement which the parties have made. It is not intended to permit alteration of an agreement at a later date to suit the wishes or interpretation of one of the parties. It is, essentially, a method of correcting typographical errors, or errors which have crept into the writing through the omission of a word, or the insertion of the wrong word in the agreement.

To obtain rectification, however, it is necessary to convince the courts through evidence that the original agreement was clear and unequivocal with regard to the term which was later changed when re-

duced to writing, and that there were no intervening negotiations or changes in the interval between the establishment of the verbal agreement, and the preparation of the written document. It would also be necessary to establish that neither party was aware of the error in the agreement at the time of signing.[12] For example, Ashley and Burton enter into an agreement by which Ashley agrees to supply a large quantity of fuel oil to Burton's office building at a fixed price. The building is known municipally as 100 Main St. When the agreement is reduced to writing, the address is set out in error as 1000 Main St., an address that does not exist.

After the contract is signed, Burton discovers that he could obtain fuel oil at a lower price elsewhere, and attempts to avoid liability on the basis that Ashley cannot perform the agreement according to its terms. In this case, Ashley may apply for rectification to have the written agreement corrected to read 100 Main St., the address that the parties had originally agreed would be the place of delivery.

||||||||||||||||||||||||||||||||||||||||||||||||||||||||||||||||||||||||||||||||||

CASE 11.2
McMaster University v. Wilchar Construction Ltd. et al., [1971] 3 O.R. 801.

THOMPSON, J.:

If the mistake is as to a term of the contract and is known to the other party, it will avoid the contract; see *Chitty on Contracts,* 23rd ed. (1968), vol. 1, p. 104, art. 211. Mistake merely as to the quality or the substance of the thing contracted for must be distinguished from mistake as to a term of the contract, for in the former case it will be an error merely as to motive which will not avoid a contract: *Chitty, op. cit.,* p. 104, art. 212.

---

[11]See *Raffles v. Wichelhaus* (1864), 2 H&C 906, 159 E.R. 375 for an example of a case of mutual mistake which the court found insoluable insofar as an interpretation of the interest was concerned.

[12]*Paget v. Marshall* (1884), 54 L.J. Ch. 575.

In the application of any particular decided authority relating to the topic of mistake as applied to contracts, one must exercise caution. Not only is it a difficult and elusive topic, but some confusion has arisen in the cases as to the distinction between the legal and equitable principles to be applied. Although the fusion of law and equity has to some extent alleviated this situation, there still is a tendency to apply the more narrow common law principles where justice could more readily be done by the discretionary use of equitable remedy. Thus, it is that the principles upon which the Courts will intervene and the circumstances in which they will do so have not been precisely settled and the decided cases are open to a number of varying interpretations and are difficult to reconcile.

The distinction between cases of common or mutual mistake and, on the other hand, unilateral mistake, must be kept in mind. In mutual or common mistake the error or mistake in order to avoid the contract at law, must have been based either upon a fundamental mistaken assumption as to the subject-matter of the contract or upon a mistake relating to a fundamental term of the contract. There, the law applies the objective test as to the validity of the contract. Its rigour in this aspect has been designed to protect innocent third parties who have acquired rights under the contract.

Normally a man is bound by an agreement to which he has expressed assent. If he exhibits all the outward signs of agreement, at law it will be held that he has agreed. The exception to this is in the case where there has been fundamental mistake or error in the sense above stated. In such case, the contract is void *ab initio*. At law, in unilateral mistake, that is when a mistake of one party relating to the contract is known to the other party, the Courts will apply the subjective test and permit evidence of the intention of the mistaken party to be adduced. In such case, even if one party knows that the other is contracting under a misapprehension, there is, generally speaking, no duty cast upon him to disclose to the other circumstances which might affect the bargain known to him alone or to disillusion that other, unless the failure to do so under the circumstances would amount to fraud. This situation, of course, must be distinguished from the case in which the mistake is known to or realized by both parties prior to the acceptance of the offer.

The law also draws a distinction between mistake simply nullifying consent and mistake negativing consent. Error or mistake which negatives consent is really not mistake technically speaking in law at all, as it prevents the formation of contract due to the lack of consensus and the parties are never *ad idem*. It is rather an illustration of the fundamental principle that there can be no contract without consensus of all parties as to the terms intended. This is but another way of saying that the offer and the acceptance must be coincident or must exactly correspond before a valid contract results.

A promiser is not bound to fulfil a promise in a sense in which the promisee knew at the time that the promiser did not intend it. In considering this question, it matters not in what way the knowledge of the meaning is brought to the mind of the promisee, whether by express words, by conduct, previous dealings or other circumstances. If by any means he knows there was no real agreement between him and the promisee, he is not entitled to insist that the promise be fulfilled in a sense to which the mind of the promiser did not assent: see *Colonial Investment Co. of Winnipeg v. Borland* (1911), 1 W.W.R. 171, 5 Alta. L.R. at p. 72; affirmed 6 D.L.R. 211, 2 W.W.R. 960, 5 Alta. L.R. 71; *Smith v. Hughes* (1871), L.R. 6 Q.B. 597.

As a general rule, equity follows the law in its attitude towards contracts which are void by reason of mistake. If the contract is void at common law, equity will also treat it as a nullity. Equity, however, will intervene in certain cases to relieve against the rigours of the common law, even though the mistake would not be operative at law. If, for lack of consensus, no contract comes into existence, there, of course, is nothing to which an equity can attach. It is only in cases where the contract is not void at law that equity may afford relief by declaring the contract voidable. It gives relief for certain types of mistakes which the common law disregards and its remedies are more flexible. Thus, equity does not require the certainty which had led to the narrow common law doctrine of fundamental mistake. It seeks rather the more broad and more elastic approach by attempting to do justice and to relieve against hardship. In equity, to admit of correction, mistake need not relate to the essential substance of the contract, and provided that there is mistake as to the promise or as to some material term of the contract, if the Court finds that there has been honest, even though inadvertent, mistake, it will afford relief in any case where it considers that it would be unfair, unjust or unconscionable not to correct it: see *Webster v. Cecil, supra; Hartog v. Colin and Shields, supra,* and *A. Roberts & Co. Ltd. et al. v. Leicestershire County Council,* [1961] 1 Ch. 555, [1961] 2 All E.R. 545.

MISREPRESENTATION

Misrepresentation is a statement or conduct which may be either innocent or fraudulent, and which induces a person to enter into a contract. Normally, a person is under no obligation to make any statement which may affect the decision of the other party to enter into the agreement. Any such statement made, however, must be true, otherwise it may constitute misrepresentation if material to the contract. Additionally, the law recognizes a small group of contractual relationships where the failure to disclose all material facts may also amount to misrepresentation. Misrepresentation does not, however, render a contract void *ab initio*. Misrepresentation, whether innocent, fraudulent, or by means of non-disclosure, will only render the agreement voidable at the option of the party misled by the misrepresentation. In every instance, it is important that the injured party cease accepting benefits under the agreement once the misrepresentation is discovered, otherwise the continued acceptance of benefits may be interpreted as a waiver of the right to rescind the contract. Exceptions have been made to this general rule by both statute law[13] and recent cases concerning fraudulent misrepresentation,[14] but the behaviour of the injured party, once the misrepresentation is discovered, is still of paramount importance.

The false statement must be a statement of fact, and not a mere expression of opinion. Whether the fact is material or not is determined on the basis of whether the innocent party to the negotiations would have entered into the agreement had he known the true fact at the time. If the innocent party did not rely on the particular fact, or if he was aware of the falsity of the statement made, then he cannot avoid the contract on the basis of misrepresentation by the other party. Rescission is only possible where the innocent or injured party relied on the false statement of fact made by the other party.

Misrepresentation seldom arises out of a term in a contract. It is generally something which takes place before the contract is entered into, and is something which induces a party to enter into the agreement. Misrepresentation must be of some material fact, and not simply a misstatement of a minor matter which does not go to the root of the contract. If the parties include the false statement as a term of the con-

---

[13]See, for example, insurance legislation in each province which does not permit the insurer to avoid liability on a policy where the insured failed to disclose a material fact many years before a claim is made on the policy.

[14]See, for example, *Siametis et al. v. Trojan Horse (Burlington) Inc. et al.* (1979), 25 O.R. (2d) 120.

tract (such as a statement as to quality or performance), then the proper action, if the statement proves to be untrue, is an action for a breach of contract, rather than misrepresentation.

Innocent Misrepresentation

Innocent misrepresentation is the misrepresentation of a material fact which the party making the statement honestly believes to be true, but which is discovered to be false after the contract has been entered into by the parties. If the statement can be shown by the injured party to be a statement of a material fact which induced him to enter into the agreement, then he may treat the contract as voidable, and bring an action for rescission. If the injured party acts promptly, the courts will normally make every effort to put the parties back in the same position that they were in before the contract was made. For example, Abrums and Baxter enter into negotiations for the purchase of a building lot which Abrums owns. Baxter asks Abrums if the land is suitable for the construction of a small apartment building, and Abrums (who had inquired from the municipality some months before and determined that the land was indeed suitable, and approved for the proposed use) answers "Yes." Unknown to Abrums, the lands had subsequently been rezoned for single-family dwellings, and the construction of apartment buildings was prohibited. Baxter, on the strength of Abrums' statement, enters into an agreement to purchase the lot. A short time later, before the deed is delivered by Abrums, Baxter discovers that the land is not zoned for multiple-family dwellings, and refuses to proceed with the contract. In this case, Baxter would be entitled to rescission of the agreement on the basis of

Abrums' innocent misrepresentation. At the time that Abrums' statement was made, the land was not zoned for the use intended by Baxter, and even though Abrums honestly believed the land to be properly zoned at the time that he made the statement, it was untrue. Since Baxter had relied on Abrums' statement, and it was material to the contract, the courts would probably provide the relief requested by Baxter, and rescind the contract. The courts would probably order Abrums to return any deposit paid by Baxter, but would not award punitive damages.[15]

||||||||||||||||||||||||||||||||||||||||||||||||||||||||||||||||||||||||||||||||||||||||||||

CASE 11.3
Newbigging v. Adam (1886), 34 Ch.D. 582.

BOWEN, L.J.:

If we turn to the question of misrepresentation, damages cannot be obtained at law for misrepresentation which is not fraudulent, and you cannot , as it seems to me, give in equity any indemnity which corresponds with damages. If the mass of authority there is upon the subject were gone through I think it would be found that there is not so much difference as is generally supposed between the view taken at common law and the view taken in equity as to misrepresentation. At common law it has always been considered that misrepresentations which strike at the root of the contract are sufficient to avoid the contract on the ground explained in *Kennedy v. Panama, New Zealand, and Australian Royal Mail Company*; but when you come to consider what is the exact relief to which a person is entitled in a case of misrepresentation it seems to me to be this, and nothing more, that he is entitled to have the contract rescinded, and is entitled accordingly to all the incidents and consequences of such rescission. It is said that the injured party is entitled to be

[15]*Derry v. Peek* (1889), 14 App. Cas. 337; *Alessio v. Jovica* (1973), 42 D.L.R. (3d) 242.

replaced in *statu quo*. It seems to me that when you are dealing with innocent misrepresentation you must understand that proposition that he is to be replaced *in statu quo* with this limitation—that he is not to be replaced in exactly the same position in all respects, otherwise he would be entitled to recover damages, but is to be replaced in his position so far as regards the rights and obligations which have been created by the contract into which he has been induced to enter.

||||||||||||||||||||||||||||||||||||||||||||||||||||||||||||||||||||||||||||||

Fraudulent Misrepresentation

Unlike innocent misrepresentation, where a party honestly believes a fact to be true when the fact is stated, fraudulent misrepresentation is a statement of fact which, when made, is *known* to be false, and is made with the *intention* of deceiving the innocent party. If a party makes a false statement recklessly, without caring if it is true or false, it may also constitute fraudulent misrepresentation. In each case, however, the statement must be of a material fact, and must be made for the purpose of inducing the other party to enter into the agreement.[16]

In the case of fraudulent misrepresentation, the innocent party must prove fraud on the part of the party making the false statement. This is because the action is based upon the tort *deceit* as well as the equitable remedy of rescission. Rescission is limited to those cases where the courts may restore the parties to the position in which they were before the contract was entered into, but this is not the case with tort. If the innocent party is able to prove fraud on the part of the party making the statement, then the courts may award punitive damages against that party committing the tort as punishment for that act.

This remedy would be available in all cases where fraud may be proven, even where it would not be possible to put the injured party back in the same position that he was in before the contract was established. As with innocent misrepresentation, the injured party must refrain from taking any benefits under the agreement once the fraud is discovered, as the continued acceptance of benefits may prevent a future action for rescission. Usually the parties must act promptly to have the agreement rescinded, because the remedy would not be available if a third party should acquire the title to any property which may have been the subject-matter of the agreement.

Insofar as the tortious aspect of the misrepresentation is concerned, prompt action by the innocent party is usually also important in order to avoid any suggestion that that party had accepted the agreement notwithstanding the fraud. Delay does not always preclude relief, however, as the courts have awarded damages under certain circumstances even after the passage of a lengthy period of time.[17]

||||||||||||||||||||||||||||||||||||||||||||||||||||||||||||||||||||||||||||||

CASE 11.4
Charpentier v. Slauenwhite (1971), 3 N.S.R. (2d) 42.

JONES, J.:

The plaintiffs contend that Mrs. Slauenwhite's statements respecting the water supply amounted to a fraudulent misrepresentation . . . representation is discussed in the Sixth Edition of Cheshire and Fifoot on the Law of Contract at p. 226. The authors state,

"A representation is a statement made by one party to the other, before or at the time of contracting, with regard to some existing fact or to some past event, which is one of the causes that induces the contract. Examples are a state-

---

[16]*Derry v. Peek* (1889), 14 App. Cas. 337.

[17]*Siametis et al. v. Trojan Horse (Burlington) Inc. et al.* (1979), 25 O.R. (2d) 120.

ment that certain cellars are dry, that premises are sanitary, or that the profits arising from a certain business have in the past amounted to so much a year."

. . . . .

The leading case on deceit is *Derry v. Peek* (1889), 14 App. Cas. 337. The law was stated by Lord Herschell at p. 374,

"First in order to sustain an action of deceit, there must be proof of fraud, and nothing short of that will suffice. Secondly, fraud is proved when it is shown that a false representation has been made, (1) knowingly, or (2) without belief in its truth, or (3) recklessly, careless whether it be true or false. Although I have treated the second and third as distinct cases, I think the third is but an instance of the second, for one who makes a statement under such circumstances can have no real belief in the truth of what he states."

||||||||||||||||||||||||||||||||||||||||||||||||||||||||||||||||||||||||||||||||

Misrepresentation by Non-Disclosure

In contrast to the general rule that a party is under no duty to disclose material facts to the other contracting party, the law does impose a duty of disclosure in certain circumstances where one party to the contract possesses information which, if undisclosed, might materially affect the position of the other party to the agreement. This duty applies to a relatively narrow range of contracts called contracts of "utmost good faith." It also applies to cases where there is an active concealment of facts, or where partial disclosure of the facts has the effect of rendering the part disclosed as false. With respect to this latter group, the courts will normally treat the act of non-disclosure, or act of partial disclosure, as a fraud, or an intention to deceive. In contracts of "utmost good faith" the failure to disclose, whether in-

nocent or deliberate, may render the resulting contract voidable.

Contracts of utmost good faith, fortunately, constitute a rather small group of contracts, of which the most important are contracts of insurance, partnership, and those where a relationship of special trust or confidence exists between the contracting parties. The courts have indicated that the class of contracts which may be identified as being of utmost good faith are not limited, but they have generally been reluctant to expand the class.[18] This is perhaps due in part to the fact that the duty of disclosure, in many cases, has been dealt with by statute, rather than the common law.[19]

Contracts of insurance, in particular, are contracts which require full disclosure on the part of the prospective insured because usually the applicant for insurance knows essentially everything about the risk which he wishes to have insured, and the insurer, very little. The reasoning behind the law under these circumstances is that an obligation rests on the insured to reveal all material facts, first, to enable the insurer to determine if he wishes to assume the risk, and second, to have some basis upon which he might fix the premium payable for the risk assumed. This is particularly important in the case of life insurance, where the insurer relies heavily on the insured's statement as to his health record in determining insurability and the premium payable. Even here, limits have been imposed on innocent non-disclosure. Most provinces have legislation for particular kinds of insurance which limit the insurer's right to avoid liability on a contract

---

[18]See, for example, *Hogar Estates Ltd. in Trust v. Shelbron Holdings Ltd. et al.* (1979) 25 O.R. (2d) 543; *Laskin v. Bache & Co. Inc.*, [1972] 1 O.R. 465.

[19]See, for example, consumer protection legislation, and recent securities legislation in most provinces.

of insurance for non-disclosure beyond a fixed period of time.

Partnership agreements, and all other contracts which represent a fiduciary relationship, are similarly subject to the rules which require full disclosure of all material facts in any dealings which the parties may have with each other. In all of these circumstances, withholding information of a material nature by one party would entitle the innocent party to avoid liability under the agreement affected by the non-disclosure.

||||||||||||||||||||||||||||||||||||||||||||||||||||||||||||||||||||||

CASE 11.5
Re Gabriel and Hamilton Tiger-Cat Football Club Ltd. (1975), 57 D.L.R. (3d) 669.

O'LEARY, J.:

. . . there is a limited class of contracts in which one of the parties is presumed to have means of knowledge which are not accessible to the other and is, therefore, bound to tell him everything which may be supposed likely to affect his judgment. They are known as contracts *uberrimae fidei*, and may be avoided on the ground of non-disclosure of material facts. Contracts of insurance of every kind are in this class. There are other contracts, though not contracts *uberrimae fidei* in the same sense, which impose a duty of full disclosure of all material facts by the parties entering into them. Contracts for family settlements and arrangements fall into this category. I am dealing here with a contract of personal service. The House of Lords in *Bell et al. v. Lever Bros. Ltd. et al.*, [1932] A.C. 161, refused to extend the duty of disclosing material facts to contracts for service. Lord Atkin, at pp. 227-8 said:

"I see nothing to differentiate this agreement from the ordinary contract of service; and I am aware of no authority which places contracts of service within the limited category I have mentioned. It seems to me clear that master and man negotiating for an agreement of service are as unfettered as in any other negotiation. Nor

can I find anything in the relation of master and servant, when established, that places agreements between them within the protected category."

Accordingly, I conclude that this contract does not fall into a class which requires full disclosure by its very nature alone.

|||||||||||||||||||||||||||||||||||||||||||||||||||||||||||||||||||||||||||

UNDUE INFLUENCE *— is a presumption, not a fact*

The law of contract assumes that the parties to a contract have freely assumed their respective duties under the agreement, but such is not always the case. Occasionally, a party may enter into an agreement under circumstances where he is so dominated by the power or influence of another that he is unable to make a free and deliberate decision to be bound by his own act. In essence, undue influence occurs where the party is so dominated by another that the decision is not his own. A contract obtained under these circumstances would be voidable, if the dominated party acts to avoid the contract as soon as he is free of the dominating influence.

Undue influence must be established before the courts will allow a contracting party to avoid the agreement. Where no special relationship exists between the parties, the party alleging undue influence must prove the existence of such influence. In certain cases, however, where a special relationship exists between the parties, a rebuttable presumption of undue influence is deemed to exist. These cases are limited to those relationships which historically have been relationships of trust or good faith, and which frequently have a confidential aspect to them. These special relationships include solicitor-client, medical doctor-patient, trustee-beneficiary, parent-child, and spiritual advisor-parishioner relationships. In all of these relationships, if undue influence is alleged, the onus shifts to the dominant party to prove that no undue influence affected the formation of the contract. The onus is usually satisfied by showing the courts that the fairness of the bargain or the price (if any) paid for the goods or service was adequate; that a full disclosure was made prior to the formation of the agreement, and that the weaker party was free to seek out the advice of others, and to seek out independent legal advice, if appropriate. If the presumption cannot be rebutted by evidence, then the contract is voidable by the weaker party, and the courts will grant rescission. Again, prompt action is necessary to obtain relief from the courts. If the weaker party fails to take steps promptly on being free of the undue influence, or ratifies the agreement either expressly or by inaction for a long period of time, the right to avoid the agreement may be lost, and the agreement will be binding.

The presumption of undue influence does not apply to the husband-wife relationship. Consequently, undue influence must be proven by the party raising the allegation. The relationship, however, is treated in a slightly different manner from one where the relationship is deemed to exist and where the presumption lies, as the courts in the case of the husband-wife relationship normally look at the degree of domination of the subordinate party by the dominant party, and the fairness or unfairness of the bargain struck between them in deciding the question of enforceability.

A frequent business situation which has given rise to an allegation of undue influence is one which is related to the requirement made by banks that a wife guarantee her husband's indebtedness. No presumption of undue influence exists in these cases, but banks often require an assurance that the wife has had independent legal advice before signing a guarantee of her husband's loan to avoid any later claim that the guarantee is unenforceable on the basis of undue influence.[20]

DURESS — use of force or threat to use it

The last basis for avoiding a contract is, fortunately, a rare occurrence, but nevertheless, grounds for rescission. If a person enters into a contract under a threat of violence, or as a result of actual violence to his person, or to one of his family (or a close relative)[21] the contract may be avoided on the basis of duress. The threat of violence, however, must be made to the person, and not simply directed toward his goods or chattels. Again, it is important that the victim of the violence take steps immediately on being free of the duress to avoid the contract, otherwise the courts are unlikely to accept duress as a basis for avoiding the agreement.

---

[20]See, for example, *Bank of Montreal v. Stuart*, [1911] A.C. 120.

[21]*Kaufman v. Gerson*, [1904] 1 K.B. 591.

SUMMARY   The parties may comply with all of the essentials for the creation of a valid contract, but if there is no true meeting of the minds, or if some mistake occurs that affects the agreement in an essential way, the contract may be either void or voidable. If a mistake should occur as to the existence of the subject-matter, the identity of a contracting party, or in some cases, the nature of the agreement, then the agreement may be unenforceable. If a party is induced to enter into a contractual relationship as a result of innocent misrepresentation of a material fact by a party, then the contract may be voidable at the option of the injured party when the misrepresentation is discovered. If the misrepresentation is made deliberately, and with the intention of deceiving the other party, then the party making the fraudulent misstatement may also be liable in tort for deceit. A contract may also be voidable if a party enters into the agreement as a result of undue influence or duress. In each case, the victim must take steps to avoid the agreement as soon as he is free of the influence or threat. In all cases where the contract is voidable, if the party continues to take benefits under the agreement, or affirms the agreement after becoming aware of the defect, misrepresentation, undue influence, or duress, the right to rescind the contract may be lost.

DISCUSSION QUESTIONS

1. *Identify an essential and frequently unstated principle that may render a contract unenforceable even though all of the usual legal elements are present.*
2. *Define "mistake" in its legal context.*
3. *Identify two forms of mistake.*
4. *Define "unilateral" and "mutual" mistake.*
5. *Where both parties have made a mistake of law, and the parties are in pari delecto, what is the normal outcome?*
6. *Where a contract is made with a lawyer acquiring the land for the purchaser "in trust," can the vendor claim mistake of identity, if and when he learns who the true purchaser is, and decides that he does not wish to be bound with that particular person in contract?*
7. *By verbal agreement, Anderson agreed to sell his land to Roberts for $75 000. Roberts then drew up a written agreement for the sale with a consideration of only $55 000.*
   (a) Could Anderson, who failed to read the agreement before signing, later claim mistake?
   (b) What would be the outcome if Anderson was illiterate and Roberts read the contract aloud, making its nature clear to Anderson, but stating the consideration as $75 000 instead of the written $55 000?

8. *In a claim for rectification, what evidence must be presented to the court if the applicant wishes to be successful?*
9. *Outline innocent and fraudulent misrepresentation.*
10. *Explain the differences likely to exist between innocent and fraudulent misrepresentation in terms of damages.*
11. *Give an example of a contract of "utmost good faith."*
12. *How does the husband-wife relationship compare to other "special" relationships?*
13. *Explain the difference between "undue influence" and "duress."*

|||||||||||||||||||||||||||||||||||||||||||||||||||||||||||||||||||||||||||||||||||||||||||||||||||||||||||||||||||||||||||||||||||||||||||||||||||||||||||||||||||||||

JUDICIAL DECISIONS

Contracts of Good Faith— Duty of Disclosure by a Partner

Hogar Estates Ltd. in Trust v. Shebron Holdings Ltd. et al. (1979), 25 O.R. (2d) 543.

The plaintiff and defendant were engaged in a joint venture agreement to develop a certain parcel of land. The principal shareholder of the defendant advised the plaintiff that the venture should be terminated as the development of the land was blocked by the local planning authority. The statement was true when made, but the defendant subsequently discovered that the land could be developed and did not disclose the new facts to the plaintiff. The joint venture was duly terminated and the lands transferred to the defendant as a part of the transaction.

The plaintiff later discovered the true facts and brought an action to have the agreement declared null and void.

CROMARTY, J.:

The underlying principle of law which applies here is found in the judgment of Fry, J., in *Davies v. London & Provincial Marine Ins. Co.* (1878), 8 Ch. D. 469, in which he said at pp. 474-5:

"In the next place, there are certain contracts which have been called contracts *uberrimae fidei* where, from their nature, the Court requires disclosure from one of the contracting parties. Of that description there are well-known instances to be found. One is a contract of partnership, which requires that one of the partners should disclose to the other all material facts. So in the case of marine insurance, the person who proposes to insure a ship or goods must make an entire disclosure of everything material to the contract. Again, in ordinary contracts the duty may arise from circumstances which occur during the negotiation. Thus, for instance, if one of the negotiating parties has made a statement which is false in fact, but which he believes to be true and which is material to the contract, and during the course of the negotiation he discovers the falsity of that statement, he is under an obligation to correct his erroneous statement; although if he had said nothing he very likely might have been entitled to hold his tongue throughout. So, again, if a statement has been made which is true at the time, but which during the course of the negotiations becomes untrue, then the person who knows that it has become untrue is under an obligation to disclose to the other the change of circumstances."

It is also stated in another way in *Brownlie v. Campbell et al.* (1880), 5 App. Cas. 925 at p. 950, in Lord Blackburn's speech which is quoted by Lord Wright, M.R., in *With v. O'Flanagan*, [1936] Ch. 575 at p. 584, as follows:

"The underlying principle is also stated again in a slightly different application by Lord Blackburn in *Brownlie v. Campbell*. I need only quote a very short passage. Lord Blackburn says: 'when a statement or representation has been made in the *bona fide* belief that it is true, and the party who has made it afterwards comes to find out that it is untrue, and discovers what he should have said, he can no longer honestly keep up that silence on the subject after that has come to his knowledge, thereby allowing the other party to go on, and still more, inducing him to go on, upon a statement which was honestly made at the time when it was made, but which he has not now retracted when he has become aware that it can be no longer honestly persevered in.' The learned Lord goes on to say that would be fraud, though nowadays the Court is more reluctant to use the word 'fraud' and would not generally use the word 'fraud' in that connection because the failure to disclose, though wrong and a breach of duty, may be due to inadvertence or a failure to realize that the duty rests upon the party who has made the representation not to leave the other party under an error when the representation has become falsified by a change of circumstances."

Lord Wright continues at p. 585:

"I have discussed the law at some little length because the cases to which I have referred show, I think, that this doctrine is not limited to a case of contracts uberrimae fidei or to any cases in which owing to confidential relationship there is a peculiar duty of disclosure; on the contrary, the passage which I read from the judgment of Fry J. shows quite clearly that he distinguishes this consequence as one which arises in cases in which if the party was silent, there would be no duty to disclose at all.

.   .   .   .   .

It seems clear that the relationship between Klaiman and Bolter was a fiduciary one which required Klaiman to make full and fair disclosure of all material facts known to him. The proper test to be applied under these circumstances is discussed in *McMaster v. Byrne*, [1952] 3 D.L.R. 337, [1952] 1 All E.R. 1362, a decision of the Privy Council which is not reported in the official reports, a case in which a solicitor entered into a transaction with a former client involving profit for himself. At p. 345 Lord Cohen said:

"As in their Lordships' view the respondent was under a duty to McMaster on March 22, 1947, it becomes necessary to consider what the measure of that duty was. It is plain that the respondent did not discharge that duty unless he communicated to McMaster all material facts within his knowledge, a description which their Lordships think would include the facts within his knowledge as to the negotiations between

Sovereign Potters Ltd. and Johnsons. It is also plain that the onus of upholding the transaction lay on the respondent."

For these reasons there will be a declaration that the purported agreement dated December 3, 1973, between Hogar Estates Limited, Shebron Holdings Limited and Sam Klaiman is null and void and of no force and effect . . .

|||||||||||||||||||||||||||||||||||||||||||||||||||||||||||||||||||||||||||||||||||||||||||||||||||||||||||||||||||||||||||||||||||||||||||||||||||||||||||||||||||||||||||||||||||||||||||

**Contracts—
Fraudulent
Misrepresentation—
Damages**

Siametis et al. v. Trojan Horse (Burlington) Inc. et al. (1979), 25 O.R. (2d) 120.

The plaintiffs purchased a restaurant business based upon fraudulent statements and information provided by the defendants. The fraud was not discovered until some months after the plaintiffs had operated the business and expended funds of their own in an attempt to make the business profitable.

The plaintiffs brought an action against the defendants for damages as well as rescission of the contract.

LERNER, J.:

It has long been recognized that where a party is found to be guilty of participating in a fraudulent scheme, he is not entitled to excuse his own illegality and fraud by establishing that the victim of the fraud in fact suffered no injury. In *Scheuerman v. Scheuerman* (1916), 52 S.C.R. 625, 28 D.L.R. 223, 10 W.W.R. 379, a husband had put property in his wife's name to delay or hinder a creditor until a certain debt for the payment of which he was being pressed had been discharged. The intention of both parties was that the property be in the wife's name to conceal the fact that the husband was the owner, thus protecting it from proceedings by the creditor who already held a judgment. This debt was subsequently satisfied so that the creditor's claim was not defeated by the fraud. The wife's refusal to convey the property to her husband subsequently was upheld by the Supreme Court of Canada. In the *Scheuerman* case Idington, J., stated at pp. 628-9 S.C.R., p. 225 D.L.R.:

"Many authorities have been cited which I have, in deference to the argument and divided opinions below, fully considered. But from none of them can I extract authority for the proposition of law that when a man has, out of the sheer necessity to prove anything upon which he can hope to rest the alleged claim of trust, to tell of an illegal purpose as the very basis of his claim, that he may yet be entitled to succeed. I find cases where the man has, accidentally as it were, or incidentally, to the relation of his story told that which he might if skilfully directed both in pleading and in giving evidence have avoided telling, yet has told enough to disclose that he was far from being always guided by the law or morality in his intentions, and still entitled to succeed because he had in fact established, by the untainted part of his story as it were, enough to entitle him to succeed without reliance upon that which was either illegal or immoral.

"This is not respondent's case, but the other kind of case I have just referred to is."

In the same judgment, Brodeur, J., stated, at p. 641 S.C.R., p. 233 D.L.R.: "The general principle is that fraud vitiates all contracts", and at pp. 642-3 S.C.R., p. 234 D.L.R.:

"The courts should never help any person who has acted with a fraudulent intent, and the same rule should apply whether a transfer is made for the purpose of defeating subsequent creditors or when it is made with the purpose of defeating existing creditors who may exercise their right upon the increased value of the property."

The plaintiff could not have discovered the fraud by examining the statements, including the Trojan Horse statement, for the first year's business. A cheat may not escape even if the fraud could be uncovered by a more sophisticated purchaser. That Siametis may have been a foolish and unwise purchaser did not absolve the deceivers: Fleming, *Law of Torts*, 4th ed. (1971), at p. 560.

Once the fraud was proved, the onus was upon the vendors to satisfy the Court that the fraudulent misrepresentation was not an inducement for execution by Siametis of the offer to purchase, ex. 2. In *Barron v. Kelly* (1918), 56 S.C.R. 455, 41 D.L.R. 590, it was stated by Anglin, J., at p. 482 S.C.R., p. 609 D.L.R.:

"Fraudulent misrepresentation in a matter *prima facie* material and likely to operate as an inducement having been shewn by the plaintiff, the onus of satisfying the court that it did not in fact so operate is certainly cast upon the defendants."

If the misrepresentation is fraudulent, the case for relief is overwhelming. The person deceived is entitled to damages and rescission: Waddams, *The Law of Contracts* (1977), p. 248. The problem here is whether Siametis is entitled to both or only to damages.

. . . . .

In *McConnel v. Wright*, [1903] 1 Ch. 546, Lord Collins, M.R., pointed out the distinction between damages for breach of contract and damages for fraud or deceit. At p. 554, he stated concerning an action for fraud:

"It is not an action for breach of contract, and, therefore, no damages in respect of prospective gains which the person contracting was entitled by his contract to expect to come in, but it is an action of tort—it is an action for a wrong done whereby the plaintiff was tricked out of certain money in his pocket; and therefore, prima facie, the highest limit of his damages is the whole extent of his loss, and that loss is measured by the money which was in his pocket and is now in the pocket of the company."

In *Doyle v. Olby (Ironmongers) Ltd. et al.*, [1969] 2 Q.B. 158 at p. 166, Lord Denning, M.R., preferred and adopted the statement of Lord Atkin in *Clark et al. v. Urquhart*, [1930] A.C. 28 at pp. 67-8, wherein Lord Atkin stated:

" 'I find it difficult to suppose that there is any difference in the measure of damages in an action of deceit depending upon the nature of the transaction into which the plaintiff is fraudulently induced to enter. Whether he buys shares or buys sugar, whether he subscribes for shares, or agrees to enter into a partnership, or in any other way alters his position to his detriment, in principle, the measure of damages should be the same, and whether estimated by a jury or a judge. I should have thought it would be based on the actual damage directly flowing from the fraudulent inducement. The formula in *McConnel v. Wright*, [1903] 1 Ch. 546, may be correct or it may be expressed in too rigid terms.' "

Lord Denning was of the opinion that Lord Collins' statement in *McConnel, supra*, was too rigid and he then went on to state, at p. 167:

"I think that Lord Collins did express himself in too rigid terms. He seems to have overlooked consequential damages. On principle the distinction seems to be this: in contract, the defendant has made a promise and broken it. The object of damages is to put the plaintiff in as good a position, as far as money can do it, as if the promise had been performed. In fraud, the defendant has been guilty of a deliberate wrong by inducing the plaintiff to act to his detriment. The object of damages is to compensate the plaintiff for all the loss he has suffered, so far, again, as money can do it. In contract, the damages are limited to what may reasonably be supposed to have been in the contemplation of the parties. In fraud, they are not so limited. The defendant is bound to make reparation for all the actual damages directly flowing from the fraudulent inducement. The person who has been defrauded is entitled to say:

" 'I would not have entered into this bargain at all but for your representation. Owing to your fraud, I have not only lost all the money I paid you, but, what is more, I have been put to a large amount of extra expense as well and suffered this or that extra damages.' "

"All such damages can be recovered: and it does not lie in the mouth of the fraudulent person to say that they could not reasonably have been foreseen. For instance, in this very case Mr. Doyle has not only lost the money which he paid for the business, which he would never have done if there had been no fraud: he put all that money in and lost it; but also he has been put to expense and loss in trying to run a business which has turned out to be a disaster for him. He is entitled to damages for all his loss, subject, of course to giving credit for any benefit that he has received. There is nothing to be taken off in mitigation: for there is nothing more that he could have done to reduce his loss. He did all that he could reasonably be expected to do."

. . . . .

The measure of damages in a case such as this was stated simply in the inimitable style of Lord Denning, *Doyle v. Olby, supra*, at p. 167, where he stated:

"The person who has been defrauded is entitled to say:

" 'I would not have entered into this bargain at all but for your representation. Owing to your fraud, I have not only lost all the money I paid you, but, what is more, I have been put to a large amount of extra expense as well and suffered this or that extra damages.' "

All such damages can be recovered and the defrauders cannot plead that the damages could not reasonably have been foreseen.

Siametis is entitled to damages for all of his loss "subject to allowances for any benefit that he has received".

CASE PROBLEMS FOR DISCUSSION

Case 1

Schuster owned two volumes of a rare edition of Chaucer's *The Canterbury Tales*. One volume was in excellent condition. The second volume was in poor shape, but nevertheless intact. Schuster sold both volumes to MacPherson.

MacPherson loaned the two volumes to a local library for a rare book display, but unknown to MacPherson only the volume in excellent condition was put on display with a collection of other rare books. The second copy was placed in a display designed to show how rare books might be repaired, but the book was placed in such a position that neither its title nor its contents could be determined.

A week after the books had been returned to their owner, Holt, a collector of rare books, telephoned MacPherson to determine if he had a copy of *The Canterbury Tales* for sale. MacPherson replied that he did, but it was "not in top shape." Holt then asked if the copy had been on display at the library, and MacPherson said, "Yes."

Holt informed MacPherson that he had seen the display of books at the library, and would be interested in purchasing the volume. A price was agreed upon, and Holt sent a cheque to MacPherson for the agreed amount.

MacPherson sent the volume which was in poor condition to Holt by courier, and on its receipt, Holt complained that the volume was not the same one which had been on display at the library. MacPherson maintained that it was, and refused to return Holt's money.

Holt brought an action against MacPherson for a return of the money which he had paid MacPherson.

Indicate the nature of Holt's claim, and express an opinion as to the outcome of the case.

Case 2

Chamberlain carried on business as a used-furniture dealer, and would occasionally purchase all of the furnishings in a person's home if the person was leaving the country, or moving a long distance.

Mrs. Lyndstrom, an elderly widow, indicated to Chamberlain that she intended to sell her home and furniture, as she was planning to move into her daughter's home to live with her. Chamberlain expressed an interest in purchasing her furniture, and an appointment was arranged for Chamberlain to examine the contents of the Lyndstrom home.

When Chamberlain arrived, Mrs. Lyndstrom took him to each room and indicated the furniture which she intended to sell. Chamberlain listed the different items by groups, such as "all chairs and table in kitchen," or "bedroom suite in front bedroom." When they reached the living-room, Mrs. Lyndstrom said, "all the furniture in here," and Chamberlain recorded, "all the furniture in living-room." Chamberlain offered $3 500 for the lot when the list was complete. Mrs. Lyndstrom agreed, and Chamberlain added to the bottom of the list: "Agreed price of all above furniture $3 500." Both signed the document.

The next day, Chamberlain arrived with a truck to pick up the furniture, and carried with him the cheque for the $3 500. As he was about to have the grand piano moved from the living-room, Mrs. Lyndstrom informed him that he was to take only the furniture, and not the piano. Chamberlain protested that the piano was included, but Mrs. Lyndstrom argued that a piano was not furniture, but a musical instrument.

Explain how this matter might be resolved.

Case 3

Corgi was the breeder of prize-winning pedigree dogs which often sold for very high prices. Reynolds, a wealthy businessman who had recently retired, decided to purchase a prize-winning dog with the intention of entering the animal in the various dog shows that were held from time to time across the country.

Reynolds knew very little about dogs, and explained to Corgi that he wished to purchase a young dog that was already a prize-winning specimen of the breed. Corgi took Reynolds to a fenced run where several young dogs were caged, and pointed to one dog which he said, in his opinion, had the greatest potential, and which had already won a prize at a local dog show. He pointed to a red ribbon pinned to the opposite wall of the kennel building, and explained that the ribbon was a first prize ribbon which the dog had won. Reynolds did not bother to examine the ribbon.

Reynolds purchased the dog for $1 000 and took it home. His neighbour later saw the dog in Reynolds' backyard, and instantly recognized it as the dog that had recently won the first prize ribbon in the children's pet show at the neighbourhood park. When he told Reynolds where he had last seen the dog, Reynolds telephoned Corgi immediately and demanded his money back.

Corgi refused to return Reynolds' money or take back the dog, and Reynolds threatened to take legal proceedings against him. Reynolds was unable to do so immediately, however, as he was called out of town on a family matter the next day. He was obliged to leave the dog with his neighbour during his absence, and he advised the neighbour to take care of the animal as if it was his own.

Reynolds was out of town for several weeks. During the time, his neighbour entered the dog in a dog show sponsored by a kennel club; the dog won first prize in its class for its breed. On Reynolds' return, the neighbour advised him of his success, and the two men decided to enter the dog in another dog show which was scheduled to be held in a nearby city.

At this second show, the dog placed only third in its class, and Reynolds was disappointed. He returned home and immediately took legal action against Corgi.

Discuss the basis of Reynolds' claim, and the defences (if any) of Corgi. Render, with reasons, a decision.

Case 4
Gordon was an avid golfer who played golf every week-end during the summer months, and practised in his backyard in the evenings on weekdays.

One evening, while practising putting in his yard, he became annoyed at his lack of success, and struck the ball a much harder blow than usual, so much so that the ball travelled over the fence, and continued through his neighbour's picture window. He immediately went to his neighbour's home and offered his apologies for shattering the glass. He declined, however, from offering to pay for the damage, and when his neighbour demanded payment, he refused.

The neighbour became angry at his refusal, and called the police. A police officer arrived on the scene almost immediately, and suggested that Gordon provide his neighbour with a written undertaking to pay for the damage. Gordon reluctantly did so, and signed the paper.

A week later, the neighbour presented Gordon with an account for replacement of the window which amounted to $425. Gordon refused to make payment, and the neighbour brought an action against him for his breach of the agreement.

Discuss the possible success of the neighbour's action, and indicate the defence (if any) which Gordon might raise. What alternate action might the neighbour have taken?

CHAPTER 12

|||||||||||||||||||||||||||||||||||||||||||||||||||||||||||||||||||||||||||||||||||||||||||||||||||||||||||||||||||||||||||||||||||||||||||||||

The Extent of Contractual Rights

PRIVITY OF CONTRACT

Once a valid contract has been negotiated, each party is entitled to performance of the agreement according to its terms. In most cases, the contract calls for performance by the parties personally, but the parties may either attempt to confer a benefit on the third party by way of contract, or attempt to impose a liability on a third party to perform a part of the agreement.

At common law, the rule relating to third-party liability is relatively clear: apart from any statutory obligation or obligation imposed by law, a person cannot incur liability under a contract to which he is not a party. By this rule, parties to an agreement may not impose a liability on another who is not a party to the contract except in those circumstances where the law imposes liability. For example, under the law of partnership, a partner (in the ordinary course of partnership business) may bind the partnership in contract with a third party. The remaining partners, although not parties to the agreement, will be liable under it, and obligated to perform. The law provides in such a case that the partner entering the contract acts as the agent of all of the partners, and negotiates the agreement on their behalf as well.

Under certain circumstances a person may acquire liability under a contract negotiated by others if he accepts land or goods which have conditions attached to them as a result of a previous contract. In this case, the person would not be a party to the contract, but nevertheless, would be subject to liability under it. This situation, however, may be distinguished from the general rule on the basis that the person receiving the goods or the property accepts them subject to the conditions negotiated by the other parties, and is fully aware of the liability imposed at the time that the goods or property are received. The acceptance of the liability along with the goods or property resembles, in a sense, a subsidiary agreement relating to the original agreement under which one of the original contracting parties retains rights in the property transferred.

For example, Alton is the owner of a large power boat, which he wishes to sell, but which is presently leased to Chambers for the summer. Burrows enters into a contract with Alton to purchase the boat, aware of the lease which runs for several months. Burrows intends to make a gift of the boat to his son, and as a part of the contract he requires delivery to his son of the ownership papers pertaining to the vessel by Alton. If Burrows' son accepts the ownership of the boat, aware of the delay in delivery, he would probably be required to respect the contract and accept the goods under the conditions imposed by the contract between Alton and his father.[1]

An important exception to the privity of contract rule concerns contracts which deal with the sale, lease, or transfer of land. In general, the purchaser of land takes the land subject to the rights of others who have acquired prior interests in the property, or rights of way over the land. The purchaser, however, is usually aware of the restrictions before the purchase is made. With the exception of some tenancies, all restrictions running with land, and all rights of third parties, must be registered against the land in most jurisdictions. Consequently, the person acquiring the land has notice of the prior agreements at the time of the transfer of title. Actual notice of an unregistered contract concerning the land may also bind the party, depending upon the jurisdiction and the legislation relating to the transfer of interests or land. Apart from this limited form of restriction or liability imposed by law, a person who is not a party to a contract may not normally incur liability under it.

The second part of the rule relating to third parties concerns the acquisition of rights by a person who is not a party to a contract, but upon whom the parties agree to confer a benefit. The principle of consideration, however, comes into play if the third party attempts to enforce the promise to which he was not a contracting party. When the principle of consideration is strictly applied, it acts as a bar to a third party claiming rights under the contract. This is so because the beneficiary gives no consideration for the promise of the benefit. Only the person who is a *party* to the agreement, and who *gives consideration* for the promise would have the right to insist on performance.

The strict enforcement of the rule had

---

[1]See, for example, *Lord Strathcona Steamship Co. v. Dominion Coal Co.*, [1926] A.C. 108.

the potential for abuse at common law whenever a party to a contract who had the right to enforce the promise was unable or unwilling to do so. To protect the third party the courts of equity provided a remedy in the form of the doctrine of *constructive trust*. Under this equitable doctrine, the contract is treated as a contract to confer a benefit on the third party, and the promisor is obliged to perform as the trustee of the benefit to be conferred on the third party beneficiary. Under the rules of trust, the trustee, as a party to the contract, has the right to sue the contracting party required to perform, but if the trustee refuses or is unable to take action, the third party beneficiary may do so by simply joining the trustee as a party defendant.

A formal contract under seal also represents an exception to the general rule concerning privity of contract. If the formal agreement is addressed to the third party, and contains covenants which benefit the third party, the delivery of the agreement to the third party would enable the third party to maintain an action against the promisor to enforce the rights granted under the agreement should the promisor fail or refuse to perform.

Since rights are frequently conferred on third parties in certain types of contracts, the legislation governing these types of contracts generally provides the third party with the statutory right to demand performance directly from the contracting party without regard for consideration or the common law rule concerning privity of contract.[2] The right of a beneficiary under a contract of life insurance is a notable example of the legislative establishment of third party rights to a benefit

under such a contract. Without statutory assistance (and assuming that a trust cannot be ascertained) the doctrine of privity of contract would apply and the beneficiary would be unable to collect from the insurance company. This is so because under the privity of contract rule a person not a party to a contract would not acquire rights under the agreement. This rule also applies to the liability of outside parties. Unless the person can be shown to be liable by way of some statutory or common law rule, a person who is not a party to a contract cannot be liable under it.

The acquisition of rights and the assumption of liabilities by third parties may, nevertheless, be expanded at common law to include parties who are closely related to the agreement and aware of the terms. In a number of cases, the courts have held that a party who receives a benefit under a contract may take advantage of implied terms within it,[3] or be subject to the liabilities which were negotiated.[4]

From a practical point of view, another route is available whereby a third party may acquire a right against another. By the law of contract, only the purchaser under a contract of sale would have a right of action if the goods purchased prove to be unfit for the use intended, but under the law of torts, if the user or consumer can establish a duty on the part of the manufacturer not to injure the consumer, and if injury ensues as a result of use by the third party, a right of action would lie against the manufacturer, even though no contractual relationship ex-

---

[2]See, for example, the *Insurance Act*, R.S.O. 1980, c. 218, ss. 164-169.

[3]*Shanklin Pier Ltd. v. Detel Products Ltd.*, [1951] 2 K.B. 854.

[4]*Pyrene Co. Ltd. v. Scindia Navigation Co. Ltd.*, [1954] 2 Q.B. 402; *Anticosti Shipping Co. v. Viateur St.-Armand*, [1959] S.C.R. 372.

isted. The availability of these alternate remedies to third parties has eased the pressure for changes in the privity of contract rule, and perhaps slowed the move toward broadening the exceptions to it. Apart from the use of the law of torts, the general trend seems to be to provide for specific cases in legislation or by alternate remedies, rather than to alter the basic concept of privity of contract.

||||||||||||||||||||||||||||||||||||||||||||||||||||||||||||||||||||||||

CASE 12.1
Shanklin, Pier Ltd. v. Detel Products Ltd., [1951] 2 K.B. 854.

McNAIR, J.:

This case raises an interesting and comparatively novel question whether or not an enforceable warranty can arise as between parties other than parties to the main contract for the sale of the article in respect of which the warranty is alleged to have been given. [His Lordship stated the facts set out above and continued:]

The defence, stated broadly, is that no warranty such as is alleged in the statement of claim was ever given and that, if given, it would give rise to no cause of action between these parties. Accordingly, the first question which I have to determine is whether any such warranty was ever given. [His Lordship reviewed the evidence about the negotiations which led to the acceptance by the plaintiffs of two coats of D.M.U. in substitution for the paint originally specified, and continued:]

In the result, I am satisfied that, if a direct contract of purchase and sale of the D.M.U. had then been made between the plaintiffs and the defendants, the correct conclusion on the facts would have been that the defendants gave to the plaintiffs the warranties substantially in the form alleged in the statement of claim. In reaching this conclusion, I adopt the principles stated by Holt, C.J., in *Crosse* v. *Gardner* and *Medina* v. *Stoughton* that an affir-

mation at the time of sale is a warranty, provided it appear on evidence to have been so intended.

Counsel for the defendants submitted that in law a warranty could give rise to no enforceable cause of action except between the same parties as the parties to the main contract in relation to which the warranty was given. In principle this submission seems to me to be unsound. If, as is elementary, the consideration for the warranty in the usual case is the entering into of the main contract in relation to which the warranty is given, I see no reason why there may not be an enforceable warranty between A and B supported by the consideration that B should cause C to enter into a contract with A or that B should do some other act for the benefit of A.

||||||||||||||||||||||||||||||||||||||||||||||||||||||||||||||||||||||||||||||||

ASSIGNMENT OF CONTRACTUAL RIGHTS
Novation
A third party may, of course, wish to acquire rights or liability under a contract by direct negotiation with the contracting parties. Should this be the case, the third party may replace one of the parties to the contract by way of a process called *novation*. This process does not conflict with the privity of contract rule because the parties, by mutual consent, agree to terminate the original contract, and establish a new agreement whereby the third party (who was outside the original agreement) becomes a contracting party in the new contract, and subject to its terms. The old agreement terminates, and the original contracting party who was replaced by the third party becomes free of any liability under the new agreement. By the same token, the original contracting party, being no longer a contracting party, is subject to the privity of contract rule.

The process of novation, as a means of transferring contractual rights to a third party, while a useful method of avoiding the privity of contract rule, is not only cumbersome in modern business practice, but inappropriate for certain kinds of transactions where the third party may only be interested in a particular aspect of the transaction. For example, Able sells goods to Brock on credit. Able may not wish to have his funds tied up in a large number of credit transactions, and may wish to have access to his money to finance his own business. Campbell is prepared to buy Brock's promise to pay from Able, but if novation is the only method of transfer of these rights, all parties would be obliged to consent. Assuming Brock is willing to surrender his rights against Able in the contract of sale, a new contract between Brock and Campbell would have to be formed in which Campbell would be obliged to give some consideration for Brock's promise to pay, or the contract would have to be under seal. Novation would clearly be an unwieldy tool for such a simple business transaction.

||||||||||||||||||||||||||||||||||||||||||||||||||||||||||||||||||||||||||

CASE 12.2

Re Abernethy-Lougheed Logging Co.; Attorney-General for British Columbia v. Salter, [1940] 1 W.W.R. 319.

SLOAN, J.A.:

First of all, what are the essential elements necessary to establish a complete novation? The answer to that is to be found in the terse and explicit language of Begbie, C.J., in *Polson v. Wulffsohn* (1890) 2 B.C.R. 39, at 43 (affirmed on appeal [see footnote p. 44]). While I can find no mention of this case in my notes of argument of counsel I think that neither the earlier nor later

cases cited contain any better definition than that of Sir Matthew Begbie. To bring about a complete novation he said

". . . three things must be established: First, the new debtor must assume the complete liability; second, the creditor must accept the new debtor as a principal debtor, and not merely as an agent or guarantor; third, the creditor must accept the new contract in full satisfaction and substitution for the old contract; one consequence of which is that the original debtor is discharged, there being no longer any contract to which he is a party, or by which he can be bound."

He added:

"All these matters are in our law capable of being established by external circumstances; by letters, receipts, and payments and the course of trade or business."

In other words, in the absence of an express agreement the intention of the parties may be inferred from external circumstances including conduct.

||||||||||||||||||||||||||||||||||||||||||||||||||||||||||||||||||||||||||

Equitable Assignments

One of the difficulties at common law which prevented the development of a simpler, more streamlined method of bringing a third party into a contractual relationship was the fact that, originally, the common law courts would only recognize rights in contracts between parties as personal rights which were not subject to transfer. These particular rights, called *choses in action* (in contrast to *choses in possession*, which are goods and things of a physical nature), however, were treated differently by the court of equity. Equity recognized the need for flexibility in the transfer of rights under contracts and business agreements, and would enforce rights that had been transferred to a third party if all of the parties could be brought before the court. If the court could be satisfied that a clear intention to assign the rights had been intended by the parties to the agreement, the contract would be enforced. While this process, too, was cumbersome, it nevertheless permitted the assignee a right to enforce it against the promisor.

Equity did not normally permit an assignee to bring an action on an assignment in his own name, but, rather, imposed a duty on the assignee to attach his name to the action. This step was normally necessary in order to have all parties before the court, and to prevent a further action in the common law courts by the assignor against the debtor at a later date. The presence of the assignor, while sometimes inconvenient, was necessary since equitable assignments need not take any particular form, and may be either oral or written. The only essential part of the assignment was that the debtor be made aware of the fact that the assignment had been made to the third party. If this was done, any other evidence surrounding the assignment, or the original agreement would be available to the court by way of evidence at trial.

Under the rules of equity, an assignment did not bind the debtor or promisor until notice had been given to him of the assignment. From that point on, the assignment was effective, and he was obliged to comply with it. The assignment, however, was subject to any rights which existed between the debtor and the assignor, for the assignee took the assignment subject to any defences to payment which existed between the original parties to the contract.

Certain contracts were recognized as unassignable in both the common law courts and the courts of equity. Any contract which required the personal service or personal performance by a party to the

contract could not be performed by a third party to the agreement. For example, if a person engaged an artist to paint his portrait, the artist who was engaged would be required to do the painting. The only procedure enabling a third party to perform would be novation, which would require all parties to consent to the change. In some circumstances the courts did permit a modified form of personal performance to take place where the contract did not specifically state that only the contracting party could perform. In these contracts, the party to the contract remains liable for the performance according to the terms of the agreement, but the actual work done, or performance, is carried out by another person under a separate agreement with the contractor. This type of performance is known as *vicarious performance*, and involves two or more contracts. The first contract is the contract between the parties in which the contractor agrees to perform certain work or services. The contractor, in turn, enters into a second contract, which may be a contract of employment with one of his employees, or it may be a contract with an independent contractor to have the actual work done. In all cases, the primary liability rests with the contractor if the work is done improperly; and the unsatisfied party to the contract would not sue the person who actually performed the work, but would sue the contractor. The contractor, in turn, would have the right under the second contract to take action against the party who actually performed the work, if the work was done negligently.

These contracts conflict neither with the privity of contract rule nor with the rules relating to novation and the assignment of contractual rights. Both contracts remain intact, and a third party does not acquire rights under either contract. The only difference is that the actual performance of the work in one contract is done by a party to the second contract.

As a general rule, most contracts for the performance of work or service may be vicariously performed if there is no clear understanding that only the parties to the contract must perform personally. Most parties to business transactions do not contemplate that the other party to the agreement will personally carry out the work, nor in many cases would the parties consider it desirable. Consequently, by customs of the trade in most business fields, the contracts may be vicariously performed. Only in the case of professionals, entertainers, and certain other specialized activities where special skills or talents are important would personal service be contemplated.

Statutory Assignments

By the middle of the 19th century, the need for a more streamlined method of transferring contractual rights, other than novation, vicarious performance, and equitable assignments, became apparent. Business frequently assigned contractual rights, but when difficulties arose, the practice of the courts of equity to require all parties to be present often proved inconvenient. This was particularly so if the assignor had made a complete assignment of his rights to the assignee, and the dispute concerned only those events which transpired after the assignment had been made. To eliminate these difficulties, the law was altered by an English statute in 1873[5] to give the assignee of a chose in ac-

tion a right to institute legal proceedings in his own name if he could satisfy four conditions:

(1) the assignment is in writing and signed by the assignor,
(2) the assignment is absolute,
(3) express notice of the assignment is given in writing to the party charged, the title of the assignee taking effect from the date of the notice, and
(4) the title of the assignee is taken subject to any equities between the original parties to the contract.[6]

Essentially, the change in the law did nothing more than permit the assignor to bring an action in his own name to enforce a contractual right that had been assigned absolutely, and provide the form in which notice of the assignment should take. In effect, however, it enormously increased the efficiency by which assignments could be made. In all other respects, the rights and duties of the parties remained much the same as those for equitable assignments which the courts of equity had enforced before the statutory change.

The statutory requirement of written notice of the assignment was a beneficial change in procedure. In the past, the notice for equitable assignments could be either written or oral, and indeed, in many cases where the debtor was illiterate, the creditor saw no need to prepare a written notice, only to be obliged to explain it to the debtor on delivery. The change, however, reflected the changes that had taken place in society and the relative rarity of illiteracy, particularly in the business community by the end of the century. It also had the added advantage of fixing the time at which the title in the assignee is estab-

---

[5]The *Supreme Court of Judicature Act*, 36 & 37 Vict., c. 66, s. 25(6). Similar legislation was passed in most common law provinces of Canada.

[6]See, for example, *Conveyancing and Law of Property Act*, R.S.O. 1980, c. 90, s. 54(1).

lished insofar as enforcement of the debt is concerned. Until the written notice is received by the debtor, any payment could properly be made to the creditor, and if the assignee was tardy in delivering the notice of the assignment, the payment of the debt to the original creditor would discharge the debtor. The assignee would then be obliged to recover the money from the assignor. Conversely, any payment made to the original creditor after notice of the assignment is received by the debtor would be at the debtor's risk, for the assignee would be entitled to payment of the full amount owing from the time the notice is given. If the debtor fails to heed the notice, he could conceivably be obliged to pay the amount over again to the assignee, if he is unable to recover it from the original creditor.

In the event that a creditor has assigned the same debt to two different assignees, by either accident or design, the assignee first giving notice to the debtor would be entitled to payment, provided that he had no notice of any prior assignment. Thus, if the first assignee delays giving notice to the debtor, and the second assignee of the same debt gives notice to the debtor without knowledge of the prior assignment, and is paid by the debtor, the debtor is discharged from any obligation to pay the first assignee.

Some risk is involved from the assignee's point of view when an assignment takes place, because the assignee takes the contract as it stands between the parties at the time of the assignment. While the assignee can usually obtain some assurance as to the amount owing on the debt, the risk that the debtor-promisor may have some defence to payment, or some set-off, is ever-present. The assignee gets the same title that the assignor had,

and if the assignor obtained his title or rights by fraud, undue influence, duress, or some other improper means, the debtor may raise this as a defence to any claim for payment. While the assignee would not be liable in tort for any deceit, the defence would allow the debtor to avoid payment, as the contract would be voidable against both the assignor and assignee. The same rule would also apply if the assignor became indebted to the debtor before the notice of the assignment was made. The debtor, in such circumstances, would be entitled to deduct the assignor's debt from the amount owing by way of set-off, and be obliged to pay the assignee only the difference between the two debts. If the assignor's obligation was greater than the amount of the debt assigned, then the assignee would be entitled to no payment at all. He would not, however, be liable to the debtor for the assignor's indebtedness.

In addition to the provision made for the assignment of ordinary contractual rights by which the parties must prepare a document in writing, and give notice, there are a number of other statutory assignments which come into effect on the death or bankruptcy of an individual. Certain other statutory rights also come into play in some cases where a person is incapable of managing his or her own affairs. Under all of these circumstances, some other person assumes all of the contractual rights and obligations of the individual, except for those which require personal performance. For example, when a person dies, all of the assets of the deceased, and all contractual rights and obligations by operation of law are assigned to the executor named in the deceased's will, or to the administrator appointed if the person should die intestate. Similarly, when a person makes a voluntary assignment in bankruptcy or is adjudged bankrupt, a trustee is appointed. The trustee acquires an assignment of all contractual rights of the bankrupt for the purpose of preservation and distribution of the assets to the creditors. The rights and duties of both the executor and trustee are governed by statute, as are the rights and duties of persons similarly appointed under other legislation to handle the affairs of incapacitated persons or corporations.[7]

[7]For example, the public trustee in the case of a person committed to a mental institution.

SUMMARY	The general common law rule with respect to contractual rights and liabilities states that no person may acquire rights or liability under a contract to which he is not a party. By novation, a party may replace another in a contract and become bound if all parties consent. The contract, however, is a new agreement and the replaced party no longer has rights or liability under the agreement. In some cases, parties may acquire rights if they are in a position to establish that a constructive trust for their benefit was created by a contract. Apart from these exceptions, the common law rule applies to all contracts, unless of course, a statute specifically provides a right to a third party.

Rights under a contract may also be performed by another under vicarious performance, unless the contract calls for personal performance. At law, rights may be assigned either by an equitable assignment, or by a statutory assignment. In each case, notice of the assignment must be given to the promisor before the assignment is effective, and even then, the assignee receives only as good a title to the right as the assignor had. Any defence which the promisor or debtor is entitled to raise to resist or avoid a payment demand by the assignor may be raised against the assignee.

Where parties are no longer capable of dealing with their own affairs, due to death, incapacity, or bankruptcy, statute laws assign their contract rights to others to manage.

DISCUSSION QUESTIONS	1. Outline "privity of contract."
	2. Define the "doctrine of constructive trust." What potential abuse led to its implementation?
	3. Explain how a contract under seal may differ from other contracts with respect to the rules for privity of contract.
	4. What two instances can collectively form an exception to the privity of contract rule?
	5. What general rule of contract law prevents a person who is not a party to a contract from enforcing rights under it? What are the exceptions to this rule?

6. *Explain and give examples of the process of* novation.
7. *Define "choses in action."*
8. *A normal practice of a building contractor is to have the work done by other specialist contractors. The process of finding plumbers, carpenters, and electricians is known as subcontracting. Explain by example how a subcontractor may perform a contract which usually requires the personal service of the building contractor.*
9. *On the basis of your answer to the preceding question, form a concise definition of "vicarious performance."*
10. *Why were the rules for equitable assignments inconvenient?*
11. *What four conditions must an assignee of a chose in action satisfy before he may institute legal proceedings in his own name?*
12. *Explain the purpose of notice in a statutory assignment.*
13. *What risk does the assignee of a contract take when he accepts an assignment?*
14. *Outline the circumstances under which a debtor might claim a "set-off."*
15. *Adams purchased fireworks and pyrotechnics for use in a Victoria Day celebration. Bailey used them as prescribed and without negligence, in the presence of Adams and others. If a defective firework injured both Adams and Bailey, Adams may sue the seller for damages as the purchaser under a contract of sale. The question is: could Bailey, who was not a party to the contract, take action against the seller?*

||||||||||||||||||||||||||||||||||||||||||||||||||||||||||||||||||||||||||||||||||||||||||||||||||||||||||||||||||||||||||||||||||||||

**JUDICIAL
DECISIONS**

**Contracts—
Third Parties—
Enforcement
of Rights**

Dunlop Pneumatic Tyre Co., Ltd. v. Selfridge & Co., Ltd., [1915] A.C. 847.

An agreement between the manufacturer and the purchaser of tires included a term that stipulated that the purchaser must resell the tires at not less than a set price. The tires were resold to a second purchaser, Dew. Dew resold the tires at less than the stipulated price. The plaintiff took action for breach of the agreement.

VISCOUNT HALDANE, L.C.:

My Lords, in the law of England certain principles are fundamental. One is that only a person who is a party to a contract can sue on it. Our law knows nothing of a jus quaesitum tertio arising by way of contract. Such a right may be conferred by way of property, as, for example, under a trust, but it cannot be conferred on a stranger to a contract as a right to enforce the contract in personam. A second principle is that if a person with whom a contract not under seal has been made is to be able to enforce it consideration must have been given by him to the promisor or to some other person at the promisor's request. These two principles are not recognized in the same fashion by the jurisprudence of certain Continental countries or of Scotland, but here they are well established. A third proposition is that a principal not named in the contract may sue upon it if the promisee really contracted as his agent. But again, in order to entitle him so to sue, he must have given consideration either personally or through the promisee, acting as his agent in giving it.

My Lords, in the case before us, I am of opinion that the consideration, the allowance of what was in reality part of the discount to which Messrs. Dew, the promisees, were entitled as between themselves and the appellants, was to be given by Messrs. Dew on their own account, and was not in substance, any more than in form, an allowance made by the appellants. The case for the appellants is that they permitted and enabled Messrs. Dew, with the knowledge and by the desire of the respondents, to sell to the latter on the terms of the contract of January 2, 1912. But it appears to me that even if this is so the answer is conclusive. Messrs. Dew sold to the respondents goods which they had a title to obtain from the appellants independently of this contract. The consideration by way of discount under the contract of January 2 was to come wholly out of Messrs. Dew's pocket, and neither directly nor indirectly out of that of the appellants. If the appellants enabled them to sell to the respondents on the terms they did, this was not done as any part of the terms of the contract sued on.

No doubt it was provided as part of these terms that the appellants should acquire certain rights, but these rights appear on the face of the contract as jura quaesita tertio, which the appellants could not enforce. Moreover, even if this difficulty can be got over by regarding the appellants as the principals of Messrs. Dew in stipulating for the rights in question, the only consideration disclosed by the contract is one given by Messrs. Dew, not as their agents, but as principals acting on their own account.

The conclusion to which I have come on the point as to consideration renders it unnecessary to decide the further question as to whether the appellants can claim that a bargain was made in this contract by Messrs. Dew as their agents; a bargain which, apart from the point as to consideration, they could therefore enforce. If it were necessary to express an opinion on this further question, a difficulty as to the position of Messrs. Dew would have to be considered. Two contracts—one by a man on his own account as principal, and another by the same man as agent—may be validly comprised in the same piece of paper. But they must be two contracts, and not one as here. I do not think that a man can treat one and the same contract as made by him in two capacities. He cannot be regarded as contracting for himself and for another uno flatu.

My Lords, the form of the contract which we have to interpret leaves the appellants in this dilemma, that, if they say that Messrs. Dew contracted on their behalf, they gave no consideration, and if they say they gave consideration in the shape of a permission to the respondents to buy, they must set up further stipulations, which are neither to be found in the contract sued upon nor are germane to it, but are really inconsistent with its structure. That contract has been reduced to writing, and it is in the writing that we must look for the whole of the terms made between the parties. These terms cannot, in my opinion consistently with the settled principles of English law, be construed as giving to the appellants any enforceable rights as against the respondents.

Third Party Beneficiary— Right to Enforce an Agreement

Smith et al. v. River Douglas Catchment Board, [1949] 2 All E.Rep. 179.

The defendant entered into a contract with the owners of land adjacent to a river under which the defendant agreed (under seal) to widen and deepen the river and maintain its banks "for all time." The land-owner later conveyed the land to the plaintiff, and the plaintiff brought an action against the defendant when it failed to maintain the river bank.

DENNING, L.J.:

This action is brought by the second plaintiffs, the tenants of the field, against the board to recover the value of the crops they have lost. The first plaintiff, the present owner, joins in the action claiming his loss of rent, but the substantial claim is by the tenants. It is my opinion that the board broke their contract. It was an implied term that they should do the work with reasonable care and skill so as to make the banks reasonably fit for the purpose of preventing flooding. The proper way of doing this, according to the experts, was to put a clay core in the banks, or to make them very much wider, but they did not do either. It may be that the board had not sufficient funds available to carry out such works, but that seems to me to be an irrelevant consideration, or, at any rate, just as irrelevant in the case of a public board as in the case of a private contractor. No private contractor who was engaged to make works for a specific purpose could excuse himself for bad results by saying that he had not sufficient money to erect proper works. It follows, therefore, that if the original landowner with whom the agreement was made had himself cultivated the fields and suffered damage by the breach he could recover from the board, but he sold the land and he has suffered no damage. The damage has been suffered partly by the first plaintiff, the man who purchased the land, but principally by the tenants, the second plaintiffs, and the question is whether the second plaintiffs can sue on the contract.

Counsel for the board says that the plaintiffs cannot sue. He says that there is no privity of contract between them and the board, and that it is a fundamental principle that no one can sue on a contract to which he is not a party. That argument can be met either by admitting the principle and saying that it does not apply to this case, or by disputing the principle itself. I make so bold as to dispute it. The principle is not nearly so fundamental as it is sometimes supposed to be. It did not become rooted in our law until the year 1861 (*Tweddle* v. *Atkinson*) and reached its full growth in 1915 (*Dunlop Pneumatic Tyre Co., Ltd.* v. *Selfridge & Co., Ltd.*). It has never been able entirely to supplant another principle whose roots go much deeper. I mean the principle that a man who makes a deliberate promise which is intended to be binding, that is to say, under seal or for good consideration, must keep his promise; and the court will hold him to it, not only at the suit of the party who gave the consideration, but also at the suit of one who was not a party to the contract, provided that it was made for his benefit and that he has a sufficient interest to entitle him to enforce it, subject always, of course, to any defences that may be open on the merits. It is on this principle, implicit if not expressed, (i) that the courts ever since 1368 have held that a covenant made with the owner of land for its benefit can be enforced against the covenantor, not only by the original party, but also by his successors in title: see *The Prior's Case* which is set out by LORD COKE in his work on LITTLETON, at p. 384*a*, and in his report of *Spencer's* case: in SMITH'S LEADING CASES, 13th ed., p. 55; (ii) that the courts of common law in the 17th and 18th centuries repeatedly enforced promises expressly made in favour of an interested person: see *Dutton* v. *Poole*, approved by LORD MANSFIELD in *Martyn* v. *Hind*; (iii) that LORD MANSFIELD held that an undisclosed principal is entitled to sue on a contract made by his agent for his benefit, even though nothing was said about agency in the contract: see *Rabone* v. *Williams*, cited in *George* v. *Clagett*; and (iv) that LORD HARDWICKE, L.C., decided that a third person is entitled to sue if there can be spelt out of the contract an intention by one of the parties to contract as trustee for him, even though nothing was said about any trust in the contract, and there was no trust fund to be administered: see *Tomlinson* v. *Gill*. Throughout the history of the principle the difficulty has been, of course, to say what is sufficient interest to entitle the third person to recover. It has sometimes been supposed that there must always be something in the nature of a "trust" for his benefit: see *Vandepitte* v. *Preferred Accident Insurance Corpn. of New York* ([1933] A.C. 79), but this is an elusive test which does not explain all the cases, and it involves the trustee being made a nominal party to the action either as plaintiff or defendant, unless that formality is dispensed with, as it was in *Les Affreteurs Réunis Société Anonyme* v. *Leopold Walford (London), Ltd.* The truth is that the principle is not so limited. It may be difficult to define what is a sufficient interest. While it does not include the maintenance of prices to the public disadvantage, it does cover the protection of the legitimate property, rights and interests of the third person, although no agency or trust for him can be inferred. It covers, therefore, rights such as the following which cannot justly be denied— the right of a seller to enforce a commercial credit issued in his favour by a bank under contract with the buyer; the right of a widow to sue for a pension which her husband's employers promised to pay her under contract with him: see *Dutton* v. *Poole* and *cf. Re Schebsman* ([1943] 2 All E.R. 779); or the right of a man's servants and guests to claim on an insurance policy, taken out by him against loss by burglary, which is expressed to cover them: *cf. Prudential Staff Union* v. *Hall* ([1947] K.B. 689, 690). In some cases the legislature itself has intervened, as, for instance, to give the driver of a motor car the right to sue on an insurance policy taken out by the owner which is expressed to cover the driver, but this does not mean that the common law would not have reached the same result by itself.

The particular application of the principle with which we are concerned here is the case of covenants made with the owner of the land to which they relate. The law on this subject was fully expounded by Mr. *Smith* in his note to *Spencer's Case* which has always been regarded as authoritative. Such covenants are clearly intended, and usually expressed, to be for the benefit of whomsoever should be the owner of the land for the time being; and at common law each successive owner has a sufficient interest to sue because he holds the same estate as the original owner. The reason which LORD COKE gave for this rule is the reason which underlies the whole of the principle now under consideration. He said in his work on LITTLETON (p. 385*a*) that it was "to give damages to the party grieved." If a successor in title were not allowed to sue it would mean that the covenantor could break his contract with impunity, for it is clear that the original owner, after he had parted with the land, could recover no more than nominal damages for any breach that occurred thereafter. It was always held, however, at common law that, in order that a successor in title should be entitled to sue, he must be of the same estate as the original owner. That alone was a sufficient interest to entitle him to enforce the contract. The covenant was supposed to be made for the benefit of the owner and his successors in title, and not for the benefit of anyone else. This limitation, however, was, as is pointed out in SMITH'S LEADING CASES, p. 75, capable of being "productive of very serious and disagreeable consequences," and it has been removed by s. 78 of the Law of Property Act, 1925, which provides that a covenant relating to any land of the covenantee shall be deemed to be made with the covenantee and his successors in title "and the person deriving title under him or them" and shall have effect as if such successors "and other persons" were expressed. The covenant of the catchment board in the present case clearly relates to the land of the covenantees. It was a covenant to do work on the land for the benefit of the land. By the statute, therefore, it is to be deemed to be made, not only with the original owner, but also with the purchasers of the land and their tenants as if they were expressed. Now, if they were expressed, it would be clear that the covenant was made for their benefit, and they clearly have sufficient interest to entitle them to enforce it because they have suffered the damage. The result is that the plaintiffs come within the principle whereby a person interested can sue on a contract expressly made for his benefit.

||||||||||||||||||||||||||||||||||||||||||||||||||||||||||||||||||||||||||||||||||||||||||||||||||||||||||||||||||||||||||||||||||||||||||||||

CASE PROBLEMS FOR DISCUSSION

Case 1

Adams was a naturalist who made a wildlife film which he hoped to use in conjunction with lectures which he gave to conservation and hiking groups throughout the country. He engaged Basso, a well-known musician in his community, to prepare the musical background for the film.

Adams paid Basso $1 000 for his work, but unknown to Adams, Basso had given the work to another musician, Smith, and paid him $500 for his efforts.

Adams used the film on one of his lecture tours, and the newspaper reviews without exception declared his film to be the highlight of his performance. Many of the reporters commented favourably about the beautiful musical background to the film.

Some months later, while on a second lecture tour, a musician in the audience recognized Smith's musical style, and mentioned to Adams how much he enjoyed listening to the musical accompaniment which the musician had provided. Adams was annoyed when he discovered that the background music had not been played by Basso, but by another. On his return home, he confronted Basso with the evidence, and Basso admitted that he had been too busy to do the musical background.

Discuss the outcome of the case if Adams should decide to take legal action against Basso.

Case 2

Personalized Performance Garage advertised "personalized service" for its customers. A large sign at the front of the garage depicted the owner of the establishment placing a checkmark in a box on a work order which read "personally inspected and repaired by a certified A-1 Mechanic."

Simple was impressed with the advertisement and the prospect of obtaining careful repair of his expensive automobile. He delivered the automobile for a minor engine adjustment, and inquired if the owner did provide personal service. In response to his question, the owner replied, "I look at every one."

Simple left the car at the garage, and returned home. About an hour later, he received a telephone call from the garage owner who informed him that he had fixed the engine, but the automobile had a leak in its radiator. Simple requested that the leak be repaired as well.

Some time later, Simple attended at the garage and was informed that the car was "ready." He paid his account, then drove away in his automobile, only to have the vehicle break down a few blocks away because the radiator had not been filled with coolant after it had been repaired.

The garage refused to repair the damage, and informed Simple that the radiator had been repaired by another repair shop which specialized in radiator repairs. It was apparently not a custom of the trade for ordinary mechanics to repair radiators in view of the special skill and equipment involved.

Discuss the rights of the parties in this case.

Case 3

Shylock operated a used-car business, and sold Fox an automobile which he indicated was in good condition and suitable for use by Fox as a taxi. In the course of discussion of the automobile, Shylock stated that, in his opinion, the vehicle was "hardly broken in" as the odometer registered only 10 000 miles.

Shylock suggested that Fox test drive the car to satisfy himself as to its condition. Fox did so, and on his return from a short drive, agreed to purchase the automobile for $5 000. Fox signed a purchase agreement whereby he would pay for the car by monthly payments over a three-year period.

On the completion of the transaction, Shylock immediately sold the purchase agreement to the Neighbourhood Finance Company for $4 500. Fox was duly notified in writing of the assignment.

A week later, the automobile broke down and when the vehicle was examined by a mechanic, Fox was informed that most of the running gear and the engine were virtually worn out. Unknown to both Shylock and Fox, the previous owner had driven the automobile 110 000 miles, and the odometer which registered only six digits (including 10ths of miles) was counting the second time over.

When Fox discovered the condition of the automobile, he refused to make payments to the finance company.

Discuss the rights of the parties in this transaction.

Case 4

White sold his snowmobile to Brown for $1 000 under an agreement whereby Brown was to pay White $100 per month over a 10-month period, commencing on March 1st of that year. Before the first payment was due, White, who owed Brown $500, assigned the agreement to Black. Notice of the assignment was given to Brown, and when he discovered that he was to make all payments under the agreement to Black, informed Black that he would not make a payment until August. He would then make only the five remaining payments under the agreement, and consider the debt fully satisfied.

Discuss the rights of Brown and Black, and the reasoning behind Brown's response to the notice.

Case 5

Riggs owned a yacht named "The Satanita" and arranged to enter her in a 50-mile race that had been arranged by a yacht club to which he belonged.

The entry form which Riggs signed contained a clause which stated that while sailing in the race he agreed to be bound by the sailing rules of the racing association, and by all the rules and by-laws of the club to which he belonged.

Some time before, the racing association had published a series of rules which were attached to the entry form. One of the rules provided: "If a yacht should by negligence damage another yacht, the yacht owner shall forfeit any prize and pay for the damage caused to the other yacht."

During the race, Riggs carelessly sailed "The Satanita" into the side of another yacht, and caused it to sink. He later refused to pay for the damage caused.

The owner of the other vessel brought an action against Riggs for the value of the lost yacht. His claim was based on the agreement attached to the entry form which provided that Riggs must pay for the damage.

Assess the plaintiff's claim, and indicate the arguments which Riggs might raise in his defence. Render a decision.

What alternate action would be open to the owner of the sunken yacht? ·

CHAPTER 13

Performance of Contractual Obligations

THE NATURE AND EXTENT OF PERFORMANCE

A contract which contains all of the essential requirements for a binding agreement, and which does not contain an element enabling a party to avoid the agreement, must be performed by the parties in accordance with its terms. Performance must always be exact and precise in order to constitute a discharge of a contractual obligation, and anything less than complete compliance with the promise would render the party in default liable for breach of the contract. For example, where a party entered into a contract to supply a quantity of canned fruit packed 30 cans to the case, and on delivery, supplied some of the goods in cases containing 24 cans, the failure to supply the goods in the correct size of case entitled the buyer to reject the goods, even though the total number of cans was correct.[1]

If the performance of the promises of the parties is complete, the contract is said to be discharged. If, however, one of the parties does not fully perform the promise made, then the agreement remains in effect until the promise is fulfilled or the agreement is discharged in some other way. Whether the performance is complete or not must be determined by comparing the promise made, in all its detail, with the actions of the promisor; if any duty or obligation has not been fully complied with performance cannot be said to be complete. Only when a promisor has carried out his promise in its entirety is he discharged under the contract, and until that time, his liability exists. The act of offering to perform the promise is called *tender of performance,* and may take one of two general forms: *tender of payment* or *tender of performance of an act.*

Tender of Payment

If a promisor simply agrees to purchase goods from a seller, performance would be made when payment is offered to the seller at the required time, and at the place fixed for delivery under the contract. The sum of money offered in payment at that time must be in accordance with the terms of the agreement; if the form of payment is not specified, then currency, which is known as *legal tender,* must be offered to the seller. Legal tender may not be refused when offered in payment providing that it is the exact amount. Unless specified in the agreement, a personal cheque, credit card, bill of exchange, or other form of payment may be rejected by the seller, and would

constitute a failure to perform by the buyer.

In the case of a debt owing, once the debtor tenders payment to the creditor in the proper amount of legal tender at the required time and place, the tender of payment is complete. If the creditor is unwilling to accept payment, the debtor need not attempt payment again. Once a proper tender of payment is made, interest ceases to run on the debt, and while the debtor is not free of his obligation to pay, he need only hold the amount of the debt until the creditor later demands payment, then pay over the money. If he should be sued by the creditor, or if the creditor attempts to seize an asset of the debtor, the debtor may prove the prior tender, and pay the money into court. The courts, in such circumstances, will normally penalize the creditor with costs as a result of his actions.

Where the contract concerns the purchase and sale of land, the purchaser, on the date fixed for closing the transaction, has an obligation to seek out the seller and offer payment of the full amount in accordance with the terms of the contract. Once this is done, any refusal to deliver up the deed to the land would probably entitle the purchaser to bring an action in court for specific performance. By this action, if the purchaser can satisfy the court that he was ready and willing to close the transaction, and was prepared to pay the required funds, he may obtain an order from the court ordering the seller to deliver up the land.

||||||||||||||||||||||||||||||||||||||||||||||||||||||||||||||||||||||||

CASE 13.1
Blanco v. Nugent, [1949] 1 W.W.R. 721.
BEAUBIEN, J.:

The question of the validity of a tender has been exhaustively dealt with by Bergman, J.A.

---

[1] *Re An Arbitration Between Moore & Co. Ltd. and Landauer & Co.,* [1921] 2 K.B. 519.

in the judgment of the Court of Appeal of this province in *Mus v. Matlashewski* [1944] 3 WWR 358, 52 Man R 247 (concurred in by McPherson, C.J.M. and Dennistoun, J.A.). At p. 385 he says:

"The tender was bad for the further reason that it was made conditional on the execution of a transfer to the plaintiff, and the defendant was justified in refusing to execute such transfer: *Hallson v. Brounstein* [1925] 3 WWR 337, 20 Sask LR 57. It is well-settled law that a tender must be unconditional (7 *Halsbury*, p. 200, sec. 279; *Jenks' Digest of English Civil Law*, p. 106, sec. 236; 38 *Cyc.*, p. 152; 62 *Corpus Juris*, p. 675, sec. 45). 'In order to support a plea of tender, there must be evidence of an offer of the specific sum, unqualified by any circumstance whatever:' *Brady v. Jones* (1823) 2 Dow & Ry KB 305. The condition here sought to be imposed—that the defendant execute a transfer to the plaintiff—is entirely unwarranted and vitiates the tender."

And at p. 387:

"The tender was bad for the further reason that Mr. McFadden did not tender the exact amount payable, but tendered a larger amount and asked for change. 'The amount tendered ought to be the precise amount that is due. If the debtor tenders a larger amount and . . . requires change it is not a good tender:' 7 *Halsbury*, p. 198, sec. 277; 62 *Corpus Juris*, p. 663, sec. 10; 38 *Cyc.*, pp. 139-140.''

||||||||||||||||||||||||||||||||||||||||||||||||||||||||||||||||||||

Tender of Performance

The seller's performance is not by tender of money but by the tender of *an act*. For the sale of goods, the seller must be prepared to deliver the goods to the buyer at the appointed time and place, and in accordance with the specifications set out in the agreement. If the buyer refuses to accept the goods when the tender is made, the seller need not tender the goods again, but may simply institute legal proceedings against the buyer for breach of the contract. If the contract concerns land, the equitable remedy of specific performance may be available to the seller. seller.

The remedy of specific performance is a discretionary remedy, and to obtain this relief, the seller must show that he was prepared to deliver the title documents for the property to the purchaser as required under the agreement, and that on the closing date he attempted to transfer the deed, but the purchaser was unwilling to accept it. Unless the purchaser had a lawful or legitimate reason to refuse the tender of performance by the seller, the courts may order the payment of the funds by the purchaser, and require him to accept the property. In this respect, the tender of performance of a seller of land differs from the seller of goods, but apart from this difference, the tender itself remains the same. The seller must do everything required in accordance with his promise if he wishes to succeed against the purchaser for breach of contract.

A contract may, of course, involve performance in the form of something other than the delivery of goods or the delivery of possession of land. It might, for example, require a party to carry out some work or service. In this case, the other contracting party must permit the party tendering performance to do the required work. Any interference with the party tendering performance of the act might entitle that party to treat the interference as a breach of contract.

|||||||||||||||||||||||||||||||||||||||||||||||||||||||||||||||||||||||||||

CASE 13.2

Canada Cycle & Motor Co. Ltd. v. Mehr (1919), 48 D.L.R. 579.

LATCHFORD, J.:

The agreement created by the defendants' acceptance of the plaintiffs' proposal is what the plaintiffs called it—a "contract." On the part of the defendants it was a contract to purchase from the plaintiffs the plaintiffs' accumulations of specified scrap produced in their works at Weston during a period of one year.

The case appears to me clearly to fall within the class referred to by Cockburn, C.J., in *Churchward v. The Queen*, (1865), L.R. 1 Q.B. 173, at p. 195: "Although a contract may appear on the face of it to bind and be obligatory only upon one party, yet there are occasions on which you must imply—although the contract may be silent—corresponding and correlative obligations on the part of the other party in whose favour alone the contract may appear to be drawn up. Where the act done by the party binding himself can only be done upon something of a corresponding character being done by the opposite party, you would there imply a corresponding obligation to do the things necessary for the completion of the contract. . . . If A covenants or engages by contract to buy an estate of B, at a given price, although that contract may be silent as to any obligation on the part of B to sell, yet as A cannot buy without B selling, the law will imply a corresponding obligation on the part of B to sell: *Pordage* v. *Cole* (1607), 1 Wm. Saund. 319 *i* (85 E.R. 449)."

||||||||||||||||||||||||||||||||||||||||||||||||||||||||||||||||||||||||||||||||||||||

DISCHARGE BY MEANS OTHER THAN PERFORMANCE

Contracts may be discharged in a number of other ways in addition to performance. The law itself, under certain circumstances, may operate to terminate a contract, or the parties themselves may agree to end the contract before it is fully performed. Often, the parties may specifically provide in the agreement itself that the contract may be terminated at any time on *notice*, or on the happening of a subsequent event. The contract may also provide that the contract does not operate unless some *condition precedent* occurs. In addition, the parties may, by mutual agreement, decide to terminate the contract and replace it with a *substituted agreement*, or simply decide before either has fully performed that the contract should be discharged.

Many other methods of discharge may also be possible. The parties could replace the existing agreement with a substituted agreement, either by a *material alteration of the terms*, or by *accord and satisfaction* (a means by which one party offers different goods in satisfaction of a promise made under the agreement, and which the buyer is prepared to accept as a substitute for the goods originally requested). Each of these, in turn, has a different effect on the obligation of the parties to perform their specific promises in the agreement.

Termination as a Right

An *option to terminate* is a method of discharging an agreement, which is usually effected by either party giving notice to the other. The option frequently has a time-limit attached to the notice, and at the expiry of the notice period, the agreement comes to an end. Agreements which contain a notice or option to terminate often provide for some means of compensating the party who has partly performed at the time the notice is given, but this is not always the case.

The right to terminate, if exercised in accordance with the specific terms of the agreement, may entitle a party to terminate the agreement without liability for any loss suffered by the other. For example, Arnold and Brown enter into a contract whereby Brown agrees to sell Arnold a new automobile. As part of the contract, Arnold reserves the right to cancel the agreement, without incurring liability, on notice to Brown at any time before Brown has the car ready for delivery. After Brown receives the automobile from the factory, but before he services it in preparation for delivery, Arnold notifies Brown of his intention to cancel the order. In this instance, Arnold would not be obliged to purchase the car—under the terms of the contract, the notice would have the effect of terminating the agreement, and Arnold would be free of any liability under it. Brown, who had assumed the risk of Arnold's cancellation, would have no rights against Arnold, but he would also no longer be liable to deliver an automobile to Arnold.

External Events

Express Terms

If a contract is discharged upon the occurrence of a particular event, the circumstance which gives rise to the termination is called a *condition subsequent*. It is not uncommon to make provision in contracts of a long-term or important nature for events which might arise to prevent the performance of the agreement by one party or both. These are sometimes referred to as *force majeure* clauses, and may either specifically or generally set out the circumstances under which the contract may be terminated. (In Roman law, the term is interpreted to mean a major force in the nature of an act of God.) *Force majeure* usually indicates an unforeseen and overpowering force affecting the ability of a party to perform the contract, although the parties may indicate in their contract that the interference need not be that serious to constitute discharge. Since the parties making the contract are free to insert whatever clauses they are prepared to mutually agree upon, either, or both of the parties, may set out a large number of

circumstances which, if any one should occur, would discharge the agreement.

Implied Terms

In certain fields, conditions subsequent are sometimes implied in contracts by the courts from customs of the trade. For example, common carriers who are normally liable for any ordinary loss or damage to goods carried, may be exempted from liability if the loss is due to an "act of God" or some other event that could not have been prevented by the carrier.[2] Partial destruction of the goods would not discharge the carrier from his obligation to deliver, however, but the carrier would not be liable for the damage caused by the act of God. If the goods are inherently dangerous and self-destruct while in the possession of the carrier, the carrier would also be absolved from any liability, and indeed, if dangerous goods were deliberately mislabelled by the shipper, the carrier might have a right of action against the shipper for any damage caused by the goods. Rather than rely on implied terms, most carriers take the added precaution of making the terms express by inserting them on their bills of lading.

Implied Terms and the Doctrine of Frustration

Where performance is rendered impossible due to circumstances not contemplated by the parties at the time the agreement was entered into, and through no fault of their own, the agreement may be said to be *frustrated* and thereby discharged. This particular doctrine has been applied to a number of different situations, the simplest being one where the agreement

---

[2]See, for example, *Nugent v. Smith* (1875), 1 C.P.D. 423.

could not be performed due to the destruction of something essential to the performance of the contract. For example, Allen, a theatre owner, enters into a contract with Black to provide the premises for a concert which Black wishes to perform. Before the date on which the concert is scheduled, the theatre burns to the ground. Allen, as a result of the fire, is unable to perform his part of the contract through no fault of his own. In this case, the courts would assume that the contract was subject to an implied term that the parties would be excused from performance if an essential part of the subject-matter should be destroyed without fault on the part of either party.[3]

Where the contract involves the sale of goods, the Sale of Goods Act in most provinces provide that the destruction of specific goods (through no fault of either the buyer or seller) before the title to the goods passes to the buyer will void the contract. This particular section of the Act represents a codification of the doctrine of implied term with respect to the sale of goods, and would apply in most cases where specific goods are destroyed before the title to the goods passes to the buyer.

The doctrine of frustration is also applicable in cases where the personal services of one of the parties is required under the terms of the agreement, but through death or illness, the party required to provide the personal service is unable to do so. For example, Albert enters into a contract with Roberts whereby Roberts agrees to perform at Albert's theatre on a particular date. On the day before the performance Roberts falls ill with a severe case of influenza, and is unable to perform. In this case, the courts would include as an implied term the continued good health of the party required to personally perform. The occurrence of the illness has the effect of discharging both of the parties from the contract.[4]

A third and somewhat different application of the doctrine may apply in cases where the event which occurs so alters the circumstances under which the agreement is to be performed that performance will be virtually impossible for a promisor. Many of these cases arose during the First and Second World Wars, where goods were diverted for war purposes. In these cases the hostilities were not contemplated by the parties, and therefore, to impose the contract after hostilities ceased would, in effect, be imposing an entirely different agreement on the parties.[5]

Although less common, the doctrine may also apply to cases where the performance of the agreement is based upon the continued existence of a particular state of affairs, and the state of affairs changes to prevent the performance of the agreement. For example, Adams enters into a contract with Bullock to erect a particular type of building on lands owned by Bullock. However, before a building permit is obtained, the zoning of the land is changed to prevent the construction of the type of building contemplated by the parties. In this case, the actions of the municipality over which the parties have no control, render performance impossible. As a result, the courts would probably find that the contract had been frustrated.

While the courts may be prepared to find that a contract has been frustrated as a result of unforeseen circumstances, they

---

[3]*Taylor v. Caldwell* (1863), 3 B. & S. 826, 122 E.R. 309.

[4]*Robinson v. Davidson* (1871), L.R. 6 Ex. 259.
[5]*Morgan v. Manser*, [1948] 1 K.B. 184.

will not relieve a party from performing simply because performance turned out to be more onerous or expensive than expected at the time the agreement was made. Nor will they provide relief in cases where the performance has been rendered impossible by the deliberate act of a promisor in an effort to avoid the agreement. For example, Baxter enters into an agreement with the local municipality whereby he agrees to spray the road allowances alongside all rural roads with a particular herbicide for the purpose of controlling the growth of weeds. He later discovers that the herbicide costs twice the price which he contemplated at the time he made the agreement, and as a result he can only perform his part of the agreement at a loss. He then sells his spraying equipment, and claims that he cannot perform the contract. Under the circumstances Baxter would be liable to the municipality for breach of contract, as the courts would not allow Baxter to avoid the contract on the basis of self-induced frustration.

When an event occurs which renders performance impossible, or changes the conditions under which the contract was to be performed to such an extent that the parties would have provided for its discharge in such circumstances, the courts will treat the agreement as frustrated and relieve both parties from any further performance after the frustrating event occurs. The frustrating event in the eyes of the courts would have the effect of bringing the contract to an end automatically. This was a reasonable conclusion for the courts to reach, but in some of the early cases the rule worked a hardship on one of the parties.

Initially, the courts let the loss fall on the parties as at the time the event occurred, and if rights had accrued to a party at the

time of the event, they could still be enforced.[6] This was later modified to provide that if the contract was wholly executory by one party, and if the other party had paid money under the agreement, but received no benefit for it, the money could be recovered on the basis that no consideration had been received for the payment.[7]

The unsatisfactory state of the common law prompted the English Parliament to pass a *Frustrated Contracts Act* in 1943.[8] This legislation permits a court to apportion the loss somewhat more equitably by providing for the recovery of deposits and/or advances, and the retention of part of the funds, to cover expenses where a party has only partly performed the contract at the time the frustrating event occurs. The legislation also permits a claim for compensation where one party, by partly performing the contract, has conferred a benefit on the other party.

Six provinces, Alberta,[9] Manitoba,[10] New Brunswick,[11] Newfoundland,[12] Ontario,[13] and Prince Edward Island,[14] subsequently passed legislation somewhat similar to the English Act, while the remainder of the provinces remain subject to the common law. This legislation, however, does not apply to an agreement for the sale of specific goods under the Sale of Goods Act where the goods have perished without fault on the part of the seller (or buyer), and before the risk passes to the

---

[6]*Chandler v. Webster*, [1904] 1 K.B. 493.
[7]*Fibrosa Spolka Akcyjna v. Fairbairn Lawson Combe Barbour, Ltd.*, [1943] A.C. 32.
[8]*Law Reform (Frustrated Contracts) Act, 1943,* 6 & 7 Geo. VI, c. 40.
[9]*Frustrated Contracts Act,* R.S.A. 1970, c. 151.
[10]*Frustrated Contracts Act,* R.S.M. 1970, c. F 190.
[11]*Frustrated Contracts Act,* R.S.N.B. 1973, c. F-24.
[12]*Frustrated Contracts Act,* R.S. Nfld. 1970, c. 144.
[13]*Frustrated Contracts Act,* R.S.O. 1980, c. 179.
[14]*Frustrated Contracts Act,* R.S.P.E.I. 1974, c. F-14.

purchaser. Nor does it apply to certain types of contracts such as insurance contracts, or those contracts which are expressly excluded by the Act.[15]

|||||||||||||||||||||||||||||||||||||||||||||||||||||||||||||||||||||||||||||||||

CASE 13.3

Cahan v. Fraser, [1951] 4 D.L.R. 112.

ROBERTSON, J.A.:

The rights of the parties fall to be determined at the moment when impossibility of further performance supervened, that is, at the moment of dissolution. See Viscount Simon L.C.'s speech in *Fibrosa Spolka Akcyjna* v. *Fairbairn Lawson Combe Barbour Ltd.*, [1943] A.C. 32 at pp. 46-7, and Lord Wright's at p. 67, and Lord Porter's at p. 83. The effect of frustration is that while the parties are relieved from any further performance under it, it remains a perfectly good contract up to that point, and everything previously done in pursuance of it must be treated as rightly done.

The same event which automatically renders performance of the consideration for the payment impossible not only terminates the contract as to the future, but terminates the right of the payee to retain the money which he has received only on the terms of the contract performance. . . .

The payment for the option in *Goulding's* case, [1927] 3 D.L.R. 820, was an "out and out" payment, that is, there was no provision for its return or for its application on the purchase-price if the option were exercised. An "out and out" payment cannot be recovered in the event of frustration—see *Fibrosa's* case pp. 43, 67-68, 74-75.

In the case at bar the sums paid were not "out and out" but were to be applied on the purchase-price; the payment was originally conditional. The condition of retaining it was eventual performance. Accordingly, when that condition failed the right to retain the money must simultaneously fail. . . .

|||||||||||||||||||||||||||||||||||||||||||||||||||||||||||||||||||||||||||||||||

[15]See, for example, the *Frustrated Contracts Act*, R.S.A. 1970, c. 151, ss. 3 and 4.

Condition Precedent

The parties may also provide in their agreement that the contract does not come into effect until certain conditions are met or events occur. These conditions, if they must occur before the contract is enforceable, are called *conditions precedent*.

Often, when a condition precedent is agreed upon, the agreement is prepared and signed; only the performance is postponed pending the fulfilment of the condition. Once fulfilled, performance is necessary to effect discharge; if the condition is not met, it then has the effect of discharging both parties from performance. It may be argued that an agreement cannot exist until the condition is satisfied, in which case the agreement only then comes into effect, but regardless of the position adopted, the condition is the determining factor with respect to the termination of the agreement or the establishment of contractual rights between the parties.

|||||||||||||||||||||||||||||||||||||||||||||||||||||||||||||||||||||||||||||||||

CASE 13.4

Turney et al. v. Zhilka, [1959] S.C.R. 578.

JUDSON, J.:

The . . . defence pleaded was that the purchaser failed to comply with the following condition of the contract:

"Providing the property can be annexed to the Village of Streetsville and a plan is approved by the Village Council for subdivision."

The date for the completion of the sale is fixed with reference to the performance of this condition—"60 days after plans are approved". Neither party to the contract undertakes to fulfil this condition, and neither party reserves a power of waiver.

.   .   .   .   .

The obligations under the contract, on both sides, depend upon a future uncertain event, the happening of which depends entirely on the will of a third party—the Village council.

This is a true condition precedent—an external condition upon which the existence of the obligation depends. Until the event occurs there is no right to performance on either side. The parties have not promised that it will occur. In the absence of such a promise there can be no breach of contract until the event does occur. The purchaser now seeks to make the vendor liable on his promise to convey in spite of the non-performance of the condition and this to suit his own convenience only. This is not a case of renunciation or relinquishment of a right but rather an attempt by one party, without the consent of the other, to write a new contract. Waiver has often been referred to as a troublesome and uncertain term in the law but it does at least presuppose the existence of a right to be relinquished.

||||||||||||||||||||||||||||||||||||||||||||||||||||||||||||||||||||||||||

Operation of Law

A contract may be discharged by the operation of law. For example, Anderson, a Canadian citizen and resident, and Black, a resident and citizen of a foreign country, enter into a partnership agreement. Shortly thereafter, hostilities break out between the two countries. The contract between Anderson and Black would be dissolved, as it would be unlawful for Anderson to have any contractual relationship with an enemy. Similarly, if Anderson and Black entered into a partnership to carry on a type of business in Canada which was subsequently declared unlawful, the agreement between Anderson and Black would be discharged.

Specific legislation also discharges certain contracting parties from contracts of indebtedness. The *Bankruptcy Act*,[16] for example, provides that an honest but unfortunate bankrupt debtor is entitled to a dis-

charge from all debts owed to his creditors when the bankruptcy process is completed. The *Bills of Exchange Act* provides that a bill of exchange which is altered in a material way without the consent of all of the parties liable on it has the effect of discharging all parties except the person who made the unauthorized alteration, and any subsequent endorsers.[17] A holder, in due course, however, would still be entitled to enforce the bill according to its original tenor if the alteration is not apparent.[18]

The law also comes into play when a person allows a lengthy period of time to pass before attempting to enforce a breach of contract. At common law, in cases where a party fails to take action until many years later, the courts will sometimes refuse to hear the case, because the undue and unnecessary delay would often render it impossible for the defendant to properly defend against the claim. Undue delay in bringing an action against a party for failure to perform at common law is known as *laches*, and under this doctrine, a court may refuse to hear a case not brought before it until many years after the right of action arose. It is important to note, however, that the doctrine only bars a right of action; it does not void the agreement. In effect, it denies a tardy plaintiff a remedy when a defendant fails to perform.

While the doctrine of laches still remains, all of the provinces have passed legislation which state the time-limits during which an action must be brought before the courts following a breach of an agreement. These statutes, which are usually called Limitations Acts[19] provide

---

[16]*Bankruptcy Act*, R.S.C. 1970, c. B-3.

[17]*Bills of Exchange Act*, R.S.C. 1970, c. B-5, s. 145(1).
[18]*Bills of Exchange Act*, R.S.C. 1970, c. B-5, s. 145(2).
[19]See, for example, *Limitations Act*, R.S.O. 1980, c. 240.

that actions not brought within the specified time-limits will be *statute-barred*, and the courts will not enforce the claim or provide a remedy. As with laches, the statutes do not render the contracts void—they simply deny the injured party a judicial remedy. The contract still exists, and if liability should be acknowledged (such as by part-payment of a debt, or part-performance) the contract and a right of action may be revived.

Merger may also discharge an agreement. For example, Abrums and Brown enter into an informal written agreement whereby Abrums agrees to sell Brown a parcel of land. If the informal written agreement is later put into a formal agreement under seal and is identical to the first except as to form, then a merger of the two takes place, and the informal agreement is discharged. The delivery of a deed on the closing of a real estate transaction normally has the same effect on an agreement of purchase and sale (relating to the same parcel of land), although there are a number of exceptions to this general rule.

Agreement

Often, the parties to an agreement may wish to voluntarily end their contractual relationship. If neither party has fully performed their duties, they may mutually agree to discharge each other by waiver. In the case of waiver, each party agrees to abandon his right to insist on performance by the other. As a result, there is consideration for the promises made by each party. However, if one of the parties has fully performed the agreement, it would be necessary to have the termination agreement in writing and under seal in order for it to be enforceable. For example, Alford and Bruce enter into an agreement whereby Bruce agrees to drive Alford to a nearby town for the payment by Alford of $10 upon arrival at their destination. Alford and Bruce may mutually agree to terminate their agreement at any time before they reach their destination, and the mutual promises will be binding, but as soon as they reach the destination, Bruce would have fully performed his part of the contract. If Bruce chose to waive his rights under the agreement after they reached their destination (after he had fully performed his part of the contract), his promise to do so would be gratuitous and he would be required to sign and seal a written promise to that effect before it would be enforceable by Alford.

The parties may also discharge an existing agreement by mutually agreeing to a change in the terms of the agreement or to a change in the parties to the agreement. Both of these changes require the consent of all parties, and have the effect of replacing the original agreement with a new contract. A substituted agreement differs from merger in several ways: In the case of merger, the terms and the parties to the agreement remain the same—only the *form* of the agreement changes. The parties are simply replacing a simple agreement with a formal one, or replacing a formal agreement with a particular type of formal agreement dealing with the same subject-matter (e.g., replacing an agreement for the sale of land under seal with a deed for the same land). On the other hand, a substituted agreement may involve a change in the *parties* to the agreement, or a change of a *material nature* in the terms of the contract. For example, Appleby, Ballard and Crawford enter into an agreement. Appleby later wishes to be free of the contract and Donaldson wishes to enter the agreement and replace Appleby. This may be accomplished only with the consent of all parties. The arrangement would be a novation situation where Appleby would be discharged from his duties under the agreement with Ballard and Crawford, and the parties would establish a new agreement between Ballard, Crawford, and Donaldson.

A material alteration of the terms of an existing agreement has the effect of discharging the existing agreement, and replacing it with a new agreement containing the material alteration. The alteration of the terms of the existing agreement must be of a significant nature before the agreement will be discharged by the change. As a general rule, the change must go to the root of the agreement before it constitutes a material alteration, as a minor alteration, or a number of minor alterations, would not normally be sufficient to create a new agreement unless the overall effect of the changes completely altered the character of the agreement. For example, if Amos places an order to purchase a truck of a standard type with a truck dealer, then later decides to have the vehicle equipped with a radio and a special brand of tires, the changes would constitute only a variation of terms of the agreement. If, however, Amos should decide to change his order after acceptance to a special-bodied truck of a different size, and with different equipment, the changes would probably be sufficient to constitute a discharge of the first agreement, and the substitution of a new one. The nature of the agreement (i.e., the purchase of a truck) would still be the same, but the subject-matter would be altered to such an extent by the changes that it would represent a new agreement.

If it is the intention of the parties to discharge an existing agreement by a substitute agreement, the substituted agreement may effect the discharge, even if it is unenforceable in itself. This situation is likely to arise where the parties enter into a written contract to comply with the *Statute of Frauds,* and then later agree to discharge the written agreement by a subsequent agreement. The statute simply requires agreements to be in writing to be enforceable, but does not require compliance with the statute to dissolve such an agreement. Consequently, if the parties, by way of a subsequent mutual agreement, agree to discharge an existing contract and replace it with a verbal agreement that is rendered unenforceable by its non-compliance with the *Statute of Frauds*, the subsequent agreement will discharge the prior agreement, but will be unenforceable with respect to the remainder of its terms.[20]

The last method of discharge is by breach of contract. This act gives rise to a right of action by the party affected by the breach, and it is the courts' disposal of the action which acts as a discharge of the agreement and its replacement with a judgement. In addition, the breach of contract by one party in certain circumstances will have the effect of discharging the injured party from any further performance under the agreement. Discharge of a contract by breach covers a wide range of activities and remedies, and is examined in detail in the next chapter.

[20]See, for example, *Morris v. Baron,* [1918] A.C. 1.

||||||||||||||||||||||||||||||||||||||||||||||||||||||||||||||||||||||||||||||||||||||||||||||||||||||||||||||||||||||||||||||||||||||

SUMMARY   The usual method of discharging a contract is by performance. To constitute a discharge, however, the performance must exactly match the performance required under the terms of the agreement, as anything short of full and complete performance will not discharge the contract. The parties may also provide in the agreement that it may be terminated at the option of one or both of the parties, or they may provide that the agreement will automatically terminate on the occurrence of a particular event.

Where events occur which were not contemplated by the parties and which render the promises of one or both of the parties impossible to perform, the courts may treat the contract as frustrated, and exempt both parties from further performance. Specific legislation in the form of a Frustrated Contracts Act (in some provinces) attempts to equitably distribute the loss where performance is rendered impossible, and in the remainder of the provinces, the common law rules apply.

Some contracts are discharged by the operation of law on the happening of particular events which are set out in the statutes, or provided for at common law. In other cases, the failure to enforce rights under a contract may result in what amounts to a discharge of the agreement by the extinguishment of the right to enforce performance.

The parties may also, by mutual agreement, decide to discharge a contract either by waiver or by the substitution of a new agreement for the existing contract.

A final method of discharge which arises out of a breach of the contract has special consequences which are dealt with in the following chapter.

||||||||||||||||||||||||||||||||||||||||||||||||||||||||||||||||||||||||||||||||||||||||||||||||||||||||||||||||||||||||||||||||||||||||||||||||||||||||||||||||||||||

DISCUSSION QUESTIONS

1. *To what degree must performance conform to the terms of the contract?*
2. *What constitutes a tender?*
3. *Explain the consequences of a failure to perform in accordance with the terms of a contract.*
4. *Define "specific performance."*
5. *Give examples of "subsequent events" that might discharge a contract.*
6. *Under what circumstances would "custom" affect the performance of a contract?*
7. *Instead of rewriting a contract, could parties simply initial amendments on the original document, and have the contract retain its legal status?*
8. *Define and illustrate a* force majeure *clause.*
9. *Illustrate, by example, the doctrine of the implied term, and outline the criteria the courts consider when deciding if the doctrine applies to a particular case.*
10. *Explain the difference between a contract that is void and one that is frustrated.*
11. *What is the difference between "frustration" and "mistake"?*
12. *If you were buying a parcel of rural land with the intention of building a*

home, what might be a condition precedent which you would attach to your offer?

✓13. *Why is a bankrupt person absolved from performance of contracts?*

14. *Distinguish a "substituted agreement" from a "merger."*

✓15. *What effect does a decision to terminate a contract have on the rights of the parties where one party has fully performed the agreement?*

||||||||||||||||||||||||||||||||||||||||||||||||||||||||||||||||||||||||||||||||||||||||||||||||||||||||||||||||||||||||||||||||||||||||||||

JUDICIAL DECISIONS

Frustration of Contract— Failure of Consideration

Fibrosa Spolka Akcyjna v. Fairbairn Lawson Combe Barbour, Ltd., [1943] A.C. 32.

The respondents agreed to sell the appellants certain machinery before the out-break of World War II. Partial payment was made, but before delivery of the goods the country was occupied by the enemy and the contract could not be performed by the respondents. The appellants demanded a return of the deposit.

LORD RUSSELL OF KILLOWEN:

My Lords, that which has been described during the argument of this case, and at other times, as "the rule in *Chandler* v. *Webster*" should, I think, rather be called the rule (to put it shortly) that in cases of frustration loss lies where it falls, or (at greater length) that where a contract is discharged by reason of supervening impossibility of performance payments previously made and legal rights previously accrued according to the terms of the contract will not be disturbed, but the parties will be excused from liability further to perform the contract. I say this because, as I read the judgment of the Master of the Rolls in *Chandler* v. *Webster*, he does not purport to be framing any new rule, or laying down any new law. He thought that the case which he was deciding was one which, on its facts, was governed by a rule already established by the authorities. . . . We must examine the rule as it exists in the law of England, and determine whether the appellants are entitled to be repaid the 1000*l.* If *Chandler* v. *Webster* was rightly decided, they would clearly not be so entitled.

It is to be observed that the doubt as to the correctness of the rule only arises in cases in which one of the parties to the contract has paid over to the other party the whole or part of the money payable by him as the consideration for what he is to receive as the consideration moving from the other party. If no such money has been paid the rule must apply, for I know no principle of English law which would enable either party to a contract which has been frustrated to receive from the other compensation for any expense, or indemnity from any liability, already incurred in performing the contract. Nor could moneys paid before frustration be recovered if the person making the payment has received some part of the consideration moving from the other party for which the payment was made. In such a case the rule would still apply.

But I am of opinion that this appeal should succeed because of another aspect of the matter. In the present case the appellants, before frustration, paid in advance a part of the price of the machines. We heard an elaborate argument as to what was the exact consideration moving from the respondents for that part of the contract which stipulated for payment of part of the price in advance. I am not aware of any justification for splitting up the consideration in this way, and assigning a consideration for each separate provision of a contract. Under the contract here in question the consideration moving from the respondents was either the delivery of the machines at Gdynia, or the promise to deliver the machines at Gdynia. I think that the delivery was the consideration, but in whichever way the consideration is viewed, it is clear that no part of the consideration for which part of the price of the machines was paid ever reached the appellants. There was a total failure of the consideration for which the money was paid. In those circumstances, why should the appellants not be entitled to recover back the money paid, as money had and received to their use, on the ground that it was paid for a consideration which has wholly failed? I can see no reason why the ordinary law, applicable in such a case, should not apply. In such a case the person who made the payment is entitled to recover the money paid. That is a right which in no way depends upon the continued existence of the frustrated contract. It arises from the fact that the impossibility of performance has caused a total failure of the consideration for which the money was paid. In his judgment in *Chandler* v. *Webster* the Master of the Rolls states that the right to recover moneys paid for a consideration which has failed only arises where the contract is "wiped out altogether," by which expression I understand him to mean is void ab initio. This is clearly a misapprehension on the part of the learned judge. The money was recoverable under the common indebitatus count, as money received for the use of the plaintiff. The right so to recover money paid for a consideration that had failed did not depend on the contract being void ab initio. There are many such cases in the books in which the contract has not been void ab initio, but the money paid for a consideration which has failed has been held recoverable. Thus, as one example, money paid as a deposit on a contract of sale which has been defeated by the fulfilment of a condition is recoverable: *Wright* v. *Newton*. It was submitted by the respondents, but without argument, that money paid for a consideration which had failed was recoverable only when the failure was due to the fault of the other party to the contract, but, on the authorities, this submission is clearly ill-founded. *Chandler* v. *Webster* was, accordingly, in my opinion, wrongly decided. The money paid was recoverable, as having been paid for a consideration which had failed. The rule that on frustration the loss lies where it falls cannot apply in respect of moneys paid in advance when the consideration moving from the payee for the payment has wholly failed, so as to deprive the payer of his right to recover moneys so paid as moneys received to his use, but, as I understand the grounds on which we are prepared to allow this appeal, the rule will (unless altered by legislation) apply in all other respects.

Vendor and Purchaser— Condition Precedent— Tender of Payment

Dacon Construction Ltd. v. Karkoulis et al., [1964] 2 O.R. 139.

EVANS, J.:

This action arises from an agreement in writing, dated April 10, 1963, in which the plaintiff, as purchaser, agreed to purchase certain lands in the City of Kingston, from the defendants.

The offer to purchase, which was prepared by the president of the plaintiff company, contained, in addition to the usual terms, two (2) conditions, only one (1) of which is of importance in this action. It is as follows:

"This offer is subject to the purchaser being able to obtain a Zone Variance on the Northern 293" more or less, from R1B to R3. The cost of the rezoning application is at the Purchaser's expense."

The offer provided that the sale was to be completed on or before September 1, 1963, and further stated that time shall be the essence of the agreement.

Immediately after acceptance of the offer, the plaintiff filed an application to rezone and was advised in September that the application was refused.

On November 6th some further negotiations apparently were carried out and the terms of the new arrangements are set out in a letter, dated November 8th, which provided for an increase in the purchase price and for an extension of the closing date to December 31, 1963. The new proposal was conditional upon the plaintiff obtaining a rezoning of a part of the lands to be purchased. This letter was signed by one of the defendants indicating his approval and is apparently accepted by counsel for the defendants as indicating an approval of all three defendants.

On December 31, 1963, the date to which closing had been extended, Mr. Sly, the president of the plaintiff company, was advised that his request for a further extension of the closing date had been refused by the defendants and he then advised his office manager in Kingston, since he was then at Sarnia, to advise the defendants that he was prepared to waive the condition in the agreement relative to rezoning and would close. This information was never communicated to the solicitor for the defendants before the time fixed for closing but was communicated, through Mr. Zakos, a real estate agent, who held a listing agreement on the property, to John Karkoulis after 5:00 p.m. on December 31st. There is some uncertainty on the evidence of Mr. Zakos as to the exact reply made by John Karkoulis, but in my opinion, the reply did not indicate other than an acceptance of the fact that Mr. Zakos was conveying a message that the plaintiff was ready to close. It cannot be considered as more than that. It definitely cannot be construed as a waiver on the part of the defendants.

Mr. Sly concedes that on December 31st, no funds were made available to his solicitors to close nor had a mortgage for the balance of the purchase price been executed. In fact, the mortgage and the balance of the cash payment amounting to $12,000 were not tendered to the solicitors for the defendants until January 21, 1964, when they were refused. The solicitors for the defendants had, on January 2, 1964, advised the plaintiff that the defendants considered the agreement to have been terminated.

The plaintiff claims:

(a) That the agreement, dated April 10, 1963, is a valid contract for the sale of the lands specified therein.

(b) For specific performance of the contract.

(c) For a reference to determine the damages suffered by the plaintiff by reason of the repudiation of the contract by the defendants.

. . . . .

The defendants submit that the defendants were entitled to consider the agreement terminated by reason of: (a) Nonfulfilment of a condition precedent in the contract; (b) failure to tender within the time limited for closing. . . .

I am of the opinion that the plaintiff's action fails and must be dismissed with costs.

Jackson v. Executors of Farwell Estate, 27 D.L.R. (2d) 275, [1961] O.R. 322, and *Turney and Turney v. Zhilka,* 18 D.L.R. (2d) 447, [1959] S.C.R. 578, would appear to be in answer to the plaintiff's contention that the condition could be waived by the plaintiff without the concurrence of the defendants.

". . . the fact that the purchaser made the conditional offer for his own benefit did not entitle him to waive it. Once accepted by the vendor, the condition became part of the agreement and was a true condition precedent on whose fulfilment the whole contract depended. It was not one to be performed by either party. [O.R. headnote in *Jackson v. Executors of Farwell Estate.*]"

As to the contention of the plaintiff's counsel that even if the condition were a condition precedent that there was a waiver on the part of the defendant, I must disagree. Waiver presupposes a right to be relinquished to a promised advantage or a promised performance, which is solely for the benefit of the party waiving and is severable from the contract. Here, there is no right to be waived. The obligations under the contract on both sides depend upon a future uncertain event the happening of which depends on a third party, in this case, the municipal corporation.

This is a true condition precedent in that it is an external condition upon which the existence of the obligation depends, and until the event occurs, there is no right of performance on either side. The parties have not promised that it will occur and in the absence of such promise, there can be no breach of contract until the event occurs. There is nothing in writing to indicate waiver on the part of the defendants, and I cannot find on the evidence that there was any oral agreement to waive the condition precedent.

I have already stated that in my opinion there was a condition precedent and further that there was no waiver of the condition precedent on the part of the defendants. Having reached the above decision, I do not believe it to be necessary to consider the question of tender at any great length. Counsel for the plaintiff referred to *Shaw v. Holmes*, [1952] 2 D.L.R. 330, [1952] O.W.N. 267. In that case there was dilatory conduct on the part of the vendor's solicitors and the purchasers had shown themselves ready, prompt, eager and desirous of carrying out the agreement. In addition, it was clear from the evidence that the failure to close on the due date was waived by the subsequent dealings between the parties and in my opinion that case does not apply to the instant case.

Counsel for the plaintiff further submitted that there was no obligation upon his client to tender the balance of the purchase moneys and the mortgage since he had not received a draft deed and statement of adjustments from the vendor's solicitors. In *Watts v. Strezos*, [1955] O.W.N. 701 the judgment of LeBel, J., is summarized in part as follows:

"The mere fact that a vendor [of land] has not prepared and submitted a draft deed for approval [within the time limited in the agreement] will not necessarily preclude him from relying on the purchaser's default; it will have that effect only if it prevents the purchaser from completing the purchase according to the terms of the agreement."

The defendants' failure to submit a draft deed in no way prevented the plaintiff from completing tender if it so desired.

Before a party to a contract in which the time is made of the essence can secure specific performance, he must show that he is ready, willing and able to carry out the agreement and that he has not been the cause of the other party's delay or default. These requirements have not been established by the plaintiff.

The significance of tender is as proof that the party tendering is ready, willing and able to complete his part of the contract and I cannot find on the evidence that the plaintiff was in a position to close. He did not tender the balance of the purchase money nor the mortgage required on his part to complete the transaction until well after the date in the contract.

In September, the plaintiff was made aware of the fact that the rezoning application was refused and on November 8th obtained the extension above referred to. The defendants had been made aware of the refusal. Subsequent to that time he took no proceedings until December 31st and I am of the opinion that the defendants were entitled to assume that the contract has been abandoned by the plaintiff. The action is accordingly dismissed with costs.

||||||||||||||||||||||||||||||||||||||||||||||||||||||||||||||||||||||||||||||||||||||||||||||||||||||||||||||||||||||||||||||||||||||

CASE
PROBLEMS
FOR
DISCUSSION

Case 1

Taylor owned and operated a large gravel truck. He entered into a contract with Road Construction Contractors to haul gravel for them at a fixed price per load for a period of six months, commencing May 1st. On April 24th, he appeared at the construction site with his truck, and when he examined the distance he would be required to haul the gravel, he realized that he had made a contract which he could only perform at a substantial loss.

He approached one of the partners of the firm with which he had contracted, and informed him that he could not perform the agreement. The partner pursuaded Taylor not to be hasty in his decision, but to wait until the next day, when he could discuss the matter with the other partners. Taylor agreed to wait, and left his truck in the contractor's garage overnight.

During the night, a fire at the garage destroyed Taylor's truck, and some of the contractor's equipment which had also been stored in the garage.

Analyze the events which occurred in this case, and discuss the legal position of both of the parties.

Case 2

Hamish, an experienced painting contractor, entered into an agreement with Mr. McPhail to paint the McPhail residence both inside and out for $1 200. Mrs. McPhail selected the colours, and Hamish proceeded with the work. During the time Hamish was painting the interior of the house, Mrs. McPhail constantly complained that he was either painting too slowly and interfering with her house cleaning, or painting too fast, and splattering paint on the wood trim. Hamish, at no time, responded to her remarks.

By the fifth day, Hamish had painted all of the house except the eavestroughs and down-spouts. As he was climbing the ladder to begin painting the eavestroughs, Mrs. McPhail appeared and warned him not to drop paint on her prize Azaleas.

At that point, Hamish turned, and without a word, climbed down from the ladder, and left the premises.

The next day, he presented his account for $1 200 to Mr. McPhail. When Mr. McPhail refused to make payment, Hamish instituted legal proceedings to collect the amount owing.

Discuss the nature of the claim, and indicate the defence (if any) which Mr. McPhail might raise. Render a decision.

Case 3

Potter owned a farm which had a rather odd-shaped land formation at its centre. Gill, a road contractor, suspected that the land formation might contain a large quantity of gravel, and entered into a purchase agreement with Potter to purchase the farm for $80 000. On the offer to purchase Potter deleted the words "or cheque" and insisted that he be paid only in cash.

Before the date fixed for Gill and Potter to exchange the deed and money, Potter heard rumors that Gill wished to buy the farm because it contained a "fortune in gravel." Potter accused Gill of trying to steal his land by offering him only a fraction of its true worth, and instructed his lawyer not to prepare the deed. In actual fact, the $80 000 was slightly more than the value of most similar farms in the area.

On the date fixed for closing, Gill arranged with the bank for $80 000 in cash, and drove to Potter's farm with the money in a brief case. At the gate, he met Potter who refused to allow him entry. Gill pointed to the brief case, and said that he had the money, and wanted the deed. Potter refused, and Gill returned to the city.

Discuss the actions of Gill and Potter in this case, and determine the rights and obligations of each, if Gill should institute legal proceedings to enforce the contract. Render a decision.

Case 4

Hansen admired a sports car which Ross owned and wished to sell. Hansen informed Ross that he would buy the automobile if he could obtain a loan from the bank to cover a part of the $7 000 asking price. Ross agreed to hold the car until Hansen could check with his bank.

Hansen discussed a loan with his bank manager. The manager stated that he would be prepared to make a $5 000 loan, but due to the nature of the purchase, he must first get approval from the regional office. He indicated that this was usually just a formality, and he did not anticipate any difficulty in obtaining approval for the loan.

Hansen then entered into a written agreement with Ross to purchase the sports car, with payment to be made in 10 days' time. Both parties signed the agreement, and Hansen paid Ross a $100 deposit. Ross retained the sports car pending payment of the balance.

A few days later, the bank manager telephoned Hansen to say that he had encountered a problem with the loan approval, and the most he could lend would be $4 000. As a result of the reduction in the loan amount, Hansen found himself $1 000 short of cash.

Advise Hansen of his position at law, and indicate how the case might be decided if Ross wished to enforce the agreement.

CHAPTER 14

Breach of Contract

THE NATURE OF BREACH OF CONTRACT

The express or implied refusal to carry out a promise made under a contract is a form of discharge. When the refusal occurs, it creates new rights for the injured party which entitles him to bring an action for the damages suffered as a result of the breach. Under certain circumstances, a breach of contract may also permit the injured party to treat the agreement as being at an end, and to be free from any further duties under it. The courts may either grant compensation for the injury suffered as a result of the non-performance, or in some cases, issue an order requiring performance according to the terms of the contract by the party who committed the breach.

Express Repudiation
Breach of contract may be either express or implied. Where a party to a contract expressly repudiates his promise to per-

form, either by his conduct or by a form of communication, his repudiation is said to be an *express* breach. For example, Armstrong and Baxter enter into a contract under which Armstrong agrees to sell Baxter a truck load of firewood. Delivery is agreed to be made at Baxter's residence on September 1st, but Armstrong does not deliver the firewood on that date. In this case, Armstrong has committed an express breach of contract by his failure to deliver the goods on the date fixed in the agreement. His breach of the agreement would give Baxter a right of action against him for damages for breach of the contract.

Repudiation of a promise before the time fixed for performance is known as *anticipatory breach*. If the repudiated promise represents an important condition in the agreement, then the repudiation of the promise would entitle the other party to treat the agreement as at an end. The injured party, however, has an alternate remedy available. He may also treat the contract as a continuing agreement, and wait until the date fixed for performance by the other party notwithstanding the express repudiation, and then bring an action for non-performance at that time. If the injured party should elect to follow the latter course, presumably with the hope that the party who repudiated the agreement might experience a change of mind, the injured party must assume the risk that the agreement may be discharged by other means. For example, Maxwell and Fuller enter into a contract for the purchase of a new car which Fuller has on display in his show-room. Maxwell is to take delivery of the car at the end of the month. Before the end of the month, Fuller advises Maxwell that he does not intend to sell the car, but plans to keep it as a display model. Maxwell does nothing to treat the contract as an end, and continues to urge Fuller to change his mind. The day before the date fixed in the agreement for delivery, the car is destroyed in a fire at Fuller's show-room. The destruction of the specific goods would release both Maxwell and Fuller from their obligations under the agreement, and as a consequence, Maxwell would lose his right of action for breach of contract.

Generally, a breach of contract which takes the form of express repudiation would entitle the injured party to a release from his promise of performance under the contract, but if the promises are such that each party must perform independently of the other, the injured party may not be entitled to treat the contract as at an end. For example, Russell and Hall, two farmers, enter into an agreement whereby Russell agrees to cut Hall's hay, and Hall agrees to harvest Russell's wheat crop for him in return. The parties agree that the value of each service is approximately equal, and if both services are performed they will cancel each other out in terms of payment. If Russell should later refuse to cut Hall's hay crop, Hall is not necessarily released from his agreement to harvest Russell's wheat crop, but he would be entitled to bring an action against Russell for damages arising out of the breach.

Similarly, if the repudiated promise has been partly fulfilled, the party injured by the repudiation may not be entitled to avoid the contract unless the repudiation goes to the very root of the agreement. If the repudiated promise is one which has been substantially performed before repudiation, the injured party is usually bound to perform the agreement in accordance with its terms, subject only to a deduction for the damages suffered as a result of the breach by the other party.

The particular rule of law which may be applied in cases where a contract has been substantially performed before the breach occurs is known as the doctrine of *substantial performance*. It is frequently employed by the courts to prevent the injured party from taking unfair advantage of the party who commits a breach after his promise has been largely fulfilled. For example, Smith enters into an agreement with Bradley to have Bradley erect a garage on his premises. Payment is to be made in full by Smith upon completion of the construction. Bradley purchases the materials and erects the garage. When the garage has been completed, save and except for the installation of some small trim boards, Bradley leaves the job to do some work on another more important project. Because the agreement had been substantially completed by Bradley before he repudiated the contract, Smith could not treat the contract as at an end. He would be required to perform his part of the agreement, but would be entitled to deduct from the contract price the cost of having the construction completed by some other contractor. The doctrine of substantial performance would prevent Smith from taking unfair advantage of Bradley, and from obtaining a benefit from Bradley's breach which would be disproportionate to the injury which he suffered as a result of the breach.

A rule somewhat similar to the doctrine of substantial performance is also applicable in cases of express repudiation where the repudiation is of a subsidiary promise, rather than an essential part of the agreement. These subsidiary promises are referred to as *warranties* where a sale of goods is concerned, and do not permit a party to avoid the agreement as a result of the repudiation or non-performance by the other party. The general thrust of this rule is similar to that of the doctrine of substantial performance. If the repudiated promise does not go to the root of the agreement, or is not a *condition* (an *essential* term) then the parties should both be required to fulfil their obligations under the agreement with appropriate compensation going to the injured party for the incomplete performance of the other. This approach is consistent with the general policy of the courts to uphold the contract whenever it is just and reasonable to do so.

||||||||||||||||||||||||||||||||||||||||||||||||||||||||||||||||||||||||||||||||||||

CASE 14.1
Bolton v. Mahadeva, [1972] 1 W.L.R. 1009.

CAIRNS, L.J.:

Perhaps the most helpful case is the most recent one of *Hoenig* v. *Isaacs* [1952] 2 All E.R. 176. That was a case where the plaintiff was an interior decorator and designer of furniture who had entered into a contract to decorate and furnish the defendant's flat for a sum of £750; and, as appears from the statement of facts at p. 177, the official referee who tried the case at first instance found that the door of a wardrobe required replacing, that a bookshelf which was too short would have to be remade, which would require alterations being made to a bookcase, and that the cost of remedying the defects was £55 18s. 2d. That is on a £750 contract. The ground on which the Court of Appeal in that case held that the plaintiff was entitled to succeed, notwithstanding that there was not complete performance of the contract, was that there was substantial performance of the contract and that the defects in the work which there existed were not sufficient to amount to a substantial degree of non-performance.

In considering whether there was substantial performance I am of opinion that it is relevant to take into account both the nature of the defects and the proportion between the cost of rectifying them and the contract price. It would be wrong to say that the contractor is only entitled to payment if the defects are so trifling as to be covered by the de minimis rule.

||||||||||||||||||||||||||||||||||||||||||||||||||||||||||||||||||||||||||||||||||||

Implied Repudiation

The most difficult form of anticipatory breach to determine is *implied repudiation* of a contract. This occurs where the repudiation must be ascertained from the actions of a party, or implied from statements made before the time fixed for performance. Where a party acts in a manner that indicates that he might not perform on the date fixed for his performance, the other party to the agreement is faced with a dilemma. To assume from the actions of a party that performance will not be forthcoming in the future is hazardous, yet to wait until the date fixed for performance may only exacerbate the problem if the performance does not take place.

The same problem exists where a party is required to perform over a period of time, or where a seller promises to deliver goods to a buyer from time to time in accordance with the terms of a contract. In each of these cases, a failure to perform in accordance with the contract initially may not permit the other party to treat the sub-standard performance as a breach. Continued failure to meet the requirements, however, may permit the injured party to be free of the agreement if the failure on the part of the other party falls so short of the performance required in

the agreement that performance of the promise as a whole becomes impossible.

Where a party infers from the circumstances that performance will be below standard in the future, or where the party decides, on the basis of incomplete information, that performance may not take place as required, to treat the contract as at an end becomes risky indeed. For example, Anderson enters into a contract with Baker to clear snow from Baker's premises during the winter months. After the first snowfall is cleared, Anderson complains bitterly about the poor contract he made with Baker.

A week later, and before the next snowfall, Baker is informed by Carter, a business acquaintance, that he has just purchased Anderson's snow removal equipment. Baker assumes that Anderson has no intention of performing the snow removal contract, and enters into a contract with Dawe for snow removal for the balance of the winter.

The next evening, a snowstorm strikes the area, and Baker discovers that both Anderson and Dawe are at his door arguing over who has the right to remove the snow. Anderson had sold his old snow removal equipment and purchased a new and larger snowblower. He had no intention of repudiating the contract.

The dilemma of Baker in this example illustrates the hazard associated with the determination of repudiation where the intention of a party must be inferred from the party's conduct. In this case, Baker's own actions placed him in a position where he himself was now in breach of the contract.

Fundamental Breach

Occasionally, where the performance by a party is so far below that required by the terms of the contract it may be treated as a *fundamental breach* of the agreement. Fundamental breach permits the party injured by the breach to be exonerated from performance even though the contract may specifically require performance by him in the face of a breach. This particular doctrine was developed by the courts in a line of English and Canadian cases which dealt with contracts containing exemption clauses. In part, the doctrine was a response by the courts to the problems that have arisen as a result of the unequal bargaining power between buyers and sellers in the marketplace. In the past, contract law was based upon the premise that the agreement was freely made between two parties with equal bargaining power, or at least equal knowledge of the terms of the agreement and their implications. The shift of marketing power in favour of sellers permitted them to insert exemption clauses in standard form contracts to protect themselves from the risks of liability for defects, price changes, and the obligation to comply with implied warranties and other terms designed to protect the buyer.

Exemption clauses usually require the buyer to perform even though the seller may avoid performance, or substitute performance of a different nature by way of the exemption clause. While the courts will normally enforce exemption clauses (except where the clauses are excluded by legislation) they construe them strictly, and against the party who inserts them in the agreement. Even so, if the breach on the part of the party who seeks to hide behind an exemption clause is so serious as to constitute non-performance of a fundamental term of the agreement, the courts may not allow that party to use the clause to avoid liability. For example, a person purchased a new truck from a seller of trucks under a contract which contained a broadly worded exemption clause. When the buyer discovered that the truck had many defects, and was so difficult to drive as to be unsuitable, the court held that the seller had delivered a truck that was totally different from that which the parties had contracted for, and the buyer was entitled to rescind the contract.[1] The court, in that particular case, decided that the buyer was entitled to a vehicle that was relatively free from defects, and reasonably fit for the use intended. The truck turned out to be wholly unsatisfactory, and the court decided that the delivery of such a vehicle by the seller constituted a repudiation of the agreement. The failure to deliver a vehicle which the parties had contracted for constituted a fundamental breach of the agreement, and notwithstanding the exemption clause, the buyer was entitled to treat the contract as at an end.

Canadian courts have frequently employed the doctrine of fundamental breach to provide relief from onerous exemption or disclaimer clauses, although its articulation has taken on many forms. In an early case it was expressed as a "failure of consideration,"[2] and a "failure to deliver what was ordered."[3] As the concept continued to develop, the term became "the foundation upon which the contract was built,"[4] and finally, the doc-

---

[1] *Cain et al. v. Bird Chevrolet-Oldsmobile Ltd. et al.* (1976), 69 D.L.R. (3d) 484.
[2] *Canada Foundry Co. Ltd. v. Edmonton Portland Cement Co.*, [1918] 3 W.W.R. 866.
[3] *Schofield v. Emerson Brantingham Implement Co.* (1918), 43 D.L.R. 509.
[4] *Arrow Transfer Co. Ltd. v. Fleetwood Logging Co. Ltd.* (1962), 30 D.L.R. (2d) 631.

trine of fundamental term or fundamental breach. The doctrine permits the buyer to ignore the exemption clause entirely when the court determines that the seller's performance was totally different from that which the parties contemplated.[5]

A problem for an injured party may arise in cases where that party continues to hold the agreement in effect after the other contracting party has failed to properly perform an important part of his promise. The effect of the delay may change a condition into a mere warranty. This has important implications for the parties to a contract due to the nature and effect of these terms. Generally, the essential terms of the contract constitute *conditions,* which if not performed may entitle the other party to treat the contract as being at an end. *Warranties,* on the other hand, are generally minor promises or terms which may be express or implied, and collateral to the object of the agreement. A breach of a warranty usually does not permit the injured party to treat the contract as being at an end; it only entitles the injured party to sue for damages. However, if a party should refuse to perform a condition or important term which would entitle the other party to avoid performance, and that party does not act at once to do so, the condition may become a mere warranty. The same holds true if the party injured by the breach of the condition continues on with the contract and accepts benefits under it, for the condition becomes a *warranty ex post facto.* In effect, the injured party's ac-

tions constitute a waiver of the right to avoid the agreement, and he will be obliged to perform with only the right to damages as compensation for the breach by the other party.[6]

||||||||||||||||||||||||||||||| |||||||||||||||||||||||||||||||||||||||||||||||||

CASE 14.2
Zender et al. v. Ball et al. (1974), 5 O.R. (2d) 747.

PENNELL, J.:

. . . ordinarily a want of title would entitle the purchaser to commence an action for rescission and the return of all moneys paid. However, the purchaser is only entitled to rescind on the neglect or refusal of his vendor to deliver a registrable conveyance on the date fixed by the contract if he has tendered or paid all his purchase money or otherwise performed his part of the contract. The purchaser cannot recover, at law, his deposit where he has constructively or expressly abandoned the contract, wrongfully repudiated, or unequivocally manifested his inability to carry out his part of the contract and the vendor is willing to complete. The deposit, under the terms of the contract, is in the nature of a guarantee or security for the performance of a contract and is not merely a part payment of the purchase price. To permit a purchaser to recover his deposit on his default, where he has abandoned or wrongfully repudiated the contract, would be to permit him to take advantage of his own wrong. Ordinarily, a demand by the purchaser for the return of his deposit from the defaulting vendor is an election to rescind and specific performance is no longer available.

|||||||||||||||||||||||||||||||||||||||||||||||||||||||||||||||||||||||||||||

REMEDIES
The Concept of Compensation for Loss
A breach of contract gives the party injured by the breach the right to sue for

---

[5]*Cain et al. v. Bird Chevrolet-Oldsmobile Ltd. et al.* (1976), 69 D.L.R. (3d) 484; *Murray v. Sperry Rand Corp. et al.* (1979), 5 B.L.R. 284.

[6]*Couchman v. Hill,* [1947] 1 K.B. 554.

compensation for the loss suffered. Loss or injury as a result of the breach must be proven, and if this is done, the courts will attempt to place the injured party in the same position as he or she would have been in had the contract been properly performed. Compensation may take the form of monetary damages, or it may, in some circumstances, include the right to have the contract promise, or a part of it, performed by the defaulting promisor. It may also take the form of *quantum meruit,* a *quasi*-contract remedy.

The usual remedy for a breach of contract is monetary damages. The reason why the courts usually award compensation in this form is that most contracts have as their object something which can be readily translated into a monetary amount in the event of non-performance. For example, Fuller offers to sell Brown six crates of apples at $5 per crate. On the date fixed for delivery, Fuller delivers the apples to Brown, but Brown refuses to take delivery. Fuller later sells the apples to Caplan, but the price by then had fallen to $4 per crate. Fuller has suffered a loss of $1 per crate, or $6 in total, as a result of Brown's breach of the contract. If Fuller should sue Brown for his breach of contract, the courts would probably award Fuller damages in the amount of $6 to place him in the same position that he would have been in had Brown carried out his part of the agreement. This basic principle of damages is sometimes referred to as the principle of *restitutio in integrum,* which originally meant a restoration to the original position, although this is not what the common law courts attempt to do. In the case of a breach of contract, they attempt to place the injured party in the same position as if the contract had been performed. *Restitutio in integrum* was originally a principle of the old courts of equity,

and was applied in cases where it was desirable to place the parties in the position they were in before the agreement had been formed. Today, the term is usually used by the courts to mean "to make the party whole," or to compensate for the loss suffered.

The Extent of Liability for Loss

While damages may be readily determined in the event of a breach of a simple contract, some contracts may be such that a breach or failure to perform may have far-reaching effects. This is particularly true where a contract may be only a part of a series of contracts between a number of different parties, and the breach of any one may adversely affect the performance of another. The manufacturer of automobiles, for example, depends heavily upon the supply of components from many subcontractors, with the manufacturer's assembly plant performing the function of merging the various parts into the finished product. The failure of any one supplier to provide critical parts could bring the entire assembly process to a standstill, and produce losses of staggering proportions. Fortunately, automobile manufacturers usually take precautions to prevent the occurrence of such a state of affairs, but the example illustrates the fact that a breach of contract may have ramifications which extend beyond the limits of the simple contract.

Since a party may generally be held liable for the consequences of his actions in the case of a breach of contract, it is necessary to determine the extent of the liability which might flow from the breach. At law, it is necessary to draw a line at some point which will end the liability of a party in the event of a breach of contract. Beyond this line, the courts will treat the damages as being too remote. In an early English case[7] which involved a contract between a milling firm and a common carrier to deliver a broken piece of machinery to the manufacturer to have a replacement made, the mill was left idle for a lengthy period of time because the carrier was tardy in the delivery of the broken mill part to the manufacturer. The miller sued the carrier for damages which resulted from the undue delay. In determining the liability of the carrier, the court formulated a principle of remoteness which identified the damages that may be recovered as those that the parties may reasonably contemplate as flowing from such a breach. The case, in effect, established two rules to apply in cases where a breach of contract occurs. The first identifies the damages which might obviously be expected to result from a breach of the particular contract as contemplated by a reasonable person. The second "rule" carries the responsibility one step further, and includes any loss which might occur from special circumstances relating to the contract which both parties might reasonably be expected to contemplate at the time the contract was made.

These two "rules" for the determination of remoteness in the case of a breach of contract were enunciated in 1854, and with very little modification were used as a basis for establishing liability for over a century. More recently, however, the two rules were rolled into a single rule which states that ". . . any damages actually caused by a breach of any kind of contract is recoverable, providing that when the contract was made such damage was reasonably foreseeable as liable to result from the breach."[8]

This particular rule would hold a person contemplating a breach liable for any damages which would reasonably have been foreseen at the time that the contract was formed, but the person would only be liable for those damages that would be related to the knowledge available to him which might indicate the likely consequences of the contemplated breach.

The Duty to Mitigate Loss

In the case of breach, the injured party is not entitled to remain inactive. The prospective plaintiff in an action for damages must take steps to mitigate the loss suffered, otherwise the courts may not compensate him for the full loss. If the party fails to take steps to reduce the loss which flows from a breach, then the defendant, if he can prove that the plaintiff failed to mitigate, may successfully reduce the liability by the amount that the plaintiff might otherwise have recovered, had it not been for his neglect. For example, Ashley enters into a contract with Bentley for the purchase of a case of strawberries. The purchase price is fixed at $10, and when Bentley delivers the case of berries, Ashley refuses to accept delivery. If Bentley immediately seeks out another buyer for the strawberries, and sells them for $5, he would be entitled to claim his actual loss of $5 from Ashley. On the other hand, if Bentley does nothing after Ashley refuses to accept delivery of the berries, and as a result, the berries become worthless, a claim against Ashley for the $10 loss suffered by Bentley may be reduced substantially if Ashley can successfully prove that Bentley did nothing to mitigate his loss.

It should also be noted that if Ashley refused to accept the berries, and Bentley sold them to Carter for $10, Bentley would still have a right to action against Ashley for breach of contract. Bentley, however,

[7]*Hadley et al. v. Baxendale et al.* (1854), 9 Exch. 341, 156 E.R. 145.

[8]*C. Czarnikow Ltd. v. Koufos,* [1966] 2 W.L.R. 1397 at p. 1415.

would only be entitled to nominal damages under the circumstances, because he suffered no actual loss.

||||||||||||||||||||||||||||||||||||||||||||||||||||||||||||||||||||||||||||||

CASE 14.3
Asamera Oil Corp. Ltd. v. Sea Oil & General Corp. et al. (1978), 89 D.L.R. (3d) 1.

ESTEY, J.:

We start of course with the fundamental principle of mitigation authoritatively stated by Viscount Haldane, L.C., in *British Westinghouse Electric & Mfg. Co., Ltd. v. Underground Electric R. Co. of London, Ltd.*, [1912] A.C. 673 at p. 689:

"The fundamental basis is thus compensation for pecuniary loss naturally flowing from the breach; but this first principle is qualified by a second, which imposes on a plaintiff the duty of taking all reasonable steps to mitigate the loss consequent on the breach, and debars him from claiming any part of the damage which is due to his neglect to take such steps. In the words of James L.J. in *Dunkirk Colliery Co. v. Lever* (1898), 9 Ch. D. 20, at p. 25, 'The person who has broken the contract is not to be exposed to additional cost by reason of the plaintiffs not doing what they ought to have done as reasonable men, and the plaintiffs not being under any obligation to do anything otherwise than in the ordinary course of business.'

"As James L.J. indicates, this second principle does not impose on the plaintiff an obligation to take any step which a reasonable and prudent man would not ordinarily take in the course of his business. But when in the course of his business he has taken action arising out of the transaction, which action has diminished his loss, the effect in actual diminution of the loss he has suffered may be taken into account even though there was no duty on him to act."

||||||||||||||||||||||||||||||||||||||||||||||||||||||||||||||||||||||||||||||

Liquidated Damages

If the parties, at the time the contract is entered into, attempt to estimate the damages that might reasonably be expected to flow from a breach of contract, and insert the estimate as a term, the courts will generally respect the agreement, provided that the estimate is a genuine attempt to estimate the loss. Usually the clause takes the form of a right in the seller to retain a deposit as liquidated damages in the event that the buyer refuses to complete the contract, but occasionally the parties may insert a clause which requires a party in default to pay a fixed sum. However, if the amount is unreasonable in relation to the damage suffered, the sum may be treated as a penalty rather than liquidated damages, and the courts will not enforce the clause. Similarly, if a party has paid a substantial portion of the purchase price at the time the contract is entered into, and the contract contains a clause which entitles the seller to retain any payments made as liquidated damages, a failure to perform by the buyer would not entitle the seller to retain the entire part-payment. The seller, instead, would only be entitled to deduct his actual loss from the partial payment, and would be obliged to return the balance to the purchaser. The reasoning of the courts behind this rule is that punitive damages will not be awarded for an ordinary breach of contract. Only in cases where the actions of a party are reprehensible will a party be penalized, and in the case of contract, the circumstances would probably be limited to those relating to contracts negotiated under fraud or duress.

||||||||||||||||||||||||||||||||||||||||||||||||||||||||||||||||||||||||||||||

CASE 14.4
Stevenson v. Colonial Homes Ltd., [1961] O.R. 407.

KELLY, J.A.:

Whether or not the appellant is entitled to the return of the $1,000, in the view I take of the case, depends upon whether the $1,000 was paid as a deposit or whether it was part payment of the purchase-price.

A useful summary of the law upon this point is to be found in the judgment of Finnemore, J., in *Gallagher v. Shilcock*, [1949] 2 K.B. 765 at pp. 768-9:

"The first question is whether the 200£ which the plaintiff buyer paid on May 17 was a deposit or merely a pre-payment of part of the purchase price. When money is paid in advance, it may be a deposit strictly so called, that is something which binds the contract and guarantees its performance; or it may be a part payment—merely money pre-paid on account of the purchase price; or, again it may be both: in the latter case, as was said by Lord Macnaghten in *Soper v. Arnold* (1889), 14 App. Cas. 429, 435: 'The deposit serves two purposes—if the purchase is carried out it goes against the purchase-money—but its primary purpose is this, it is a guarantee that the purchaser means business.' If it is a deposit, or both a deposit and prepayment, and the contract is rescinded, it is not returnable to the person who pre-paid it if the rescission was due to his default. If, on the other hand, it is part-payment only, and not a deposit in the strict sense at all, then it is recoverable even if the person who paid it is himself in default. That, I think, follows from *Howe v. Smith*, 27 Ch. D. 89, and from *Mayson v. Clouet*, [1924] A.C. 980, a case in the Privy Council. As I understand the position, in each case the question is whether the payment was in fact intended by the parties to be a deposit in the strict sense or no more than a part payment: and, in deciding this question, regard may be had to the circumstances of the case, to the actual words of the contract, and to the evidence of what was said."

As was stated by Lord Dunedin in *Mayson v. Clouet*, at p. 985: "Their Lordships think that the solution of a question of this sort must always depend on the terms of the particular contract." The contract between the appellant and the respondent should be critically examined to see if from it can be drawn the intention of the parties as to whether the $1,000 was to be a deposit or a part payment of purchase-price only.

SPECIAL REMEDIES
Specific Performance

In rare cases, where monetary damages would be an inadequate compensation for breach of contract, the courts may decree specific performance of the contract. The decree of specific performance is a discretionary remedy which has its origins in the English Court of Chancery. The remedy requires the party subject to it to perform the agreement as specified in the decree; a failure to comply with the decree would constitute contempt of court. Unlike an ordinary monetary judgement, the decree of specific performance carries with it the power of the courts to fine or imprison the wrongdoer.

Specific performance is generally available as a remedy when the contract concerns the sale of land. The unique nature of land is the reason why the courts will enforce the contract, as no two parcels of land are exactly the same. Even then, the courts expect the injured party to show that the fault rests entirely on the party in breach before the remedy will be granted. The plaintiff (the injured party) must satisfy the court that he was willing and able at all times to complete the contract, and did nothing to prompt the refusal to perform by the party in breach. To satisfy this particular onus, the plaintiff must usually make a *tender* of either the money or the title documents as required under the contract. This must be done strictly in accordance with the terms of the contract on the day, and at the time and place fixed for performance. The plaintiff must also satisfy the court that the other party refused to perform at that time. If the court is satisfied on the evidence presented that the plaintiff did everything necessary to perform, and that the other party was entirely at fault for the breach, it may issue a decree of specific performance which would require performance of the contract by the party in breach.

Specific performance may apply to either a vendor or a purchaser in a land transaction: the courts may order performance by either a defaulting seller or buyer in the contract. The remedy of specific performance may also be available in a case where the contract has a "commercial uniqueness" or has as its subject-matter a chattel which is rare and unique,[9] but for most contracts which involve the sale of goods, monetary damages would normally be the appropriate remedy. Moreover, the courts will not grant specific performance of a contract of employment or any contract which involves the performance of personal services by an individual—the principal reason for not doing so being that it will not enforce promises which it would be obliged to continually supervise.

Injunction

A remedy similar to specific performance may also be available in the case of a breach of contract where the promise which the party refuses to perform is a promise to forbear from doing something. The difference between this remedy, an *injunction*, and a decree of specific performance is that the injunction usually orders the party to *refrain* from doing something which he promised that he would not do, while a decree of specific performance usually requires the party to do a positive act.

Like a decree of specific performance, an injunction is an equitable remedy, and may be issued only at the discretion of the courts. Its use is generally limited to the enforcement of "promises to forbear" contained in contracts, although the courts are sometimes reluctant to grant the remedy

in contracts of employment if the effect of the remedy would be to compel the promisor to perform the contract to his detriment. For example, Maxwell and Dixon enter into an agreement whereby Maxwell agrees to work exclusively for Dixon for a fixed period of time, and to work for no one else during that time. If Maxwell should repudiate his promise, and work for someone else, Dixon may apply for an injunction to enforce Maxwell's promise not to work for anyone else. If the injunction should be granted, it would enforce *only the negative covenant*, and not Maxwell's promise to work exclusively for Dixon. In other words, Maxwell need not remain in the employ of Dixon, but, because of the injunction, he would not be in a position to work for anyone else. It should be noted, however, that if circumstances were such that Maxwell did not have independent means, and was obliged to work for Dixon in order to support himself, the courts may not issue an injunction, since the injunction, in effect, would constitute an order of specific performance of the entire contract. Usually contracts containing a negative promise limit the party to the acceptance of similar employment, rather than employment of any kind. By placing only a limited restriction on the employee's ability to accept other employment, the plaintiff may argue that the defendant is not restricted from other employment, but only employment of a similar nature, and therefore, he would not be restricted to working only for the plaintiff.

In other types of contracts, an injunction may be issued to enforce a negative covenant if the covenant is not contrary to public policy. It may be granted, for example, in the case of a contract for the sale of a business to enforce a covenant made by the vendor where he agrees not to compete with the purchaser within a specific

[9]*Re Wait,* [1927] 1 Ch. 606.

geographic area for a specified period of time. It may also be available to enforce a negative covenant with respect to the use of premises or equipment. For example, Dawson may enter into an agreement with Ballard to allow Ballard the use of certain premises for business purposes. In turn, Ballard promises that he will not operate the business after a certain hour in the evening. If Ballard should continue to operate the business past the stipulated hour, Dawson may be entitled to an injunction to enforce Ballard's negative covenant. It is important to note, however, that an injunction, like a decree of specific performance, is discretionary, and the courts will not issue an injunction unless it is fair and just to do so.

Quantum Meruit

In some cases, where a contract is repudiated by a party, and the contract is for services, or goods and services, the remedy of *quantum meruit* may be available as an alternative for the party injured by the repudiation. *Quantum meruit* is not a remedy which arises out of the contract, but, rather, it is a remedy based upon *quasi*-contract. In the case of *quantum meruit*, the courts will imply an agreement from a request for goods or services, and require the party who requested the service to pay a reasonable price for the benefit obtained.

Quantum meruit may be available as a remedy where the contract has only been partly performed by the injured party at the time the breach occurred. To succeed, however, the injured party must show that the other party to the contract repudiated the contract, or did some act to make performance impossible. The breach by the party cannot be of a minor term, but must be of such a serious nature that it would entitle the party injured by the breach to treat the contract as at an end. *Quantum meruit* is not normally available to the party responsible for the breach, but under the doctrine of substantial performance, the party may be entitled to recover for the value of the work done. Similarly, *quantum meruit* would not apply where a party had fully performed his part of the contract at the time the breach occurred. The appropriate remedy in that case would be an action for the price if the party in breach refused or failed to pay. *Quantum meruit* would also be inapplicable where the contract itself required complete performance as a condition before payment may be demanded.

The distinction between the two remedies is also apparent in the approach the courts may take to each. In the case of an ordinary breach of contract, the remedy of monetary damages is designed to place the injured party in the position that he would have been in had the contract been completed. This is not so with *quantum meruit*. Where a claim of *quantum meruit* is made, the courts will only be concerned with compensation to the party for work actually done, and the compensation will be the equivalent of a reasonable price of the service rendered. This may differ substantially from the price fixed in the repudiated agreement, and it is not designed to place the injured party in the same position that he would have been had the other party not broken the agreement.

SUMMARY   Breach of contract is the express or implied refusal by one party to carry out a promise made to another in a binding contract. Express or implied repudiation before the date fixed for performance is called anticipatory breach. If the refusal to perform is such that it goes to the root of the agreement, and is made before the agreement has been fully performed by the other party, the injured party may be released from any further performance, and may sue for the damages suffered. However, if the party who refused to complete the contract has substantially performed the agreement, the doctrine of substantial performance may apply, and the injured party may only obtain damages for the deficient performance.

The remedies available in the case of breach are: (1) monetary damages; (2) specific performance; (3) an injunction; and (4) the *quasi-contract* remedy of *quantum meruit*.

Specific performance and the injunction are equitable remedies which may be awarded only at the discretion of the courts, and are normally only awarded to enforce contract clauses where it is fair and just to do so. These circumstances are usually limited to contracts concerning land, commercial uniqueness and rare chattels in the case of specific performance, and to the enforcement of a negative promise in the case of an injunction. In most other cases, monetary damages are adequate compensation. As an alternative to damages, if the contract has not been fully performed by a party, the remedy of *quantum meruit* may be available. *Quantum meruit*, however, only entitles the party to a reasonable price for the service or the work done, and is not designed to put the party in the position he would have been in had the contract been performed.

||||||||||||||||||||||||||||||||||||||||||||||||||||||||||||||||||||||||||||||||||||||||||||||||||||||||||||||||||||||||||||||||||||||||||||||||||||||

DISCUSSION QUESTIONS

1. *Give examples (other than those in the text) of "express" and "implied" repudiation.*
2. *What circumstances surround an "anticipatory breach"?*
3. *Explain the doctrine of substantial performance, and give an example of its application.*
4. *Why does a repudiated subsidiary promise not qualify as grounds for non-performance by the injured party?*
5. *"When repudiation is inferred by a party's conduct, and this turns out to be an incorrect assumption, it only goes to prove that the dilemma so caused arises not from a flaw in this area of the law, but from a reliance on circumstantial evidence." Do you agree with this statement? Explain your position.*
6. *The doctrine of fundamental breach is an important concept in modern contract law. Outline its history, application, and ramifications.*
7. *Show how ex post facto, a condition becomes a warranty.*
8. *Illustrate the train of judicial thought behind the principle of restitutio in integrum.*
9. *How can "remoteness" affect one's liability for breach of contract, and how is this "remoteness" determined?*

10. *What responsibility does the plaintiff have to mitigate his loss? How might this ultimately affect damages received in an action for breach of contract?*
11. *Explain the nature and use of a decree of specific performance.*
12. *Outline the difference between an "injunction" and a "decree of specific performance."*
13. *Should a contract not be completely performed, what principle might be applied to enable a workman to be paid for the work which he had partially completed?*

|||||||||||||||||||||||||||||||||||||||||||||||||||||||||||||||||||||||||||||||||||||||||||||||||||||||||||||||||||||||||||||||||||||||||||||||||||||||||

JUDICIAL DECISIONS Breach of Contract— Quantum of Damages

Hadley et al. v. Baxendale et al. (1854), 9 Exch. 341, 156 E.R. 145.
The plaintiffs were millers who operated a steam-powered mill. The crankshaft of the engine cracked, and it was necessary to obtain a new part from the engine manufacturer. A common carrier contracted to deliver the old part to the manufacturer the next day if he received the part before noon. The old part was accordingly delivered to the carrier, but through neglect was not delivered to the engine manufacturer for some time.

The plaintiffs instituted legal proceedings against the carrier for the loss suffered as a result of the delay.

ALDERSON, B.:

Now we think the proper rule in such a case as the present is this:— Where two parties have made a contract which one of them has broken, the damages which the other party ought to receive in respect of such breach of contract should be such as may fairly and reasonably be considered either arising naturally, i.e., according to the usual course of things, from such breach of contract itself, or such as may reasonably be supposed to have been in the contemplation of both parties, at the time they made the contract, as the probable result of the breach of it. Now, if the special circumstances under which the contract was actually made were communicated by the plaintiffs to the defendants, and thus known to both parties, the damages resulting from the breach of such a contract, which they would reasonably contemplate, would be the amount of injury which would ordinarily follow from a breach of contract under these special circumstances so known and communicated. But, on the other hand, if these special circumstances were wholly unknown to the party breaking the contract, he, at the most, could only be supposed to have had in his contemplation the amount of injury which would arise generally, and in the great multitude of cases not affected by any special circumstances, from such a breach of contract. For, had the special circumstances been known, the parties might have specially provided for the breach of contract by special terms as to the damages in that case; and of this advantage it would be very unjust to deprive them. Now the above principles are those by which we think the jury ought to be guided in estimating the damages arising out of any breach of contract.

||||||||||||||||||||||||||||||||||||||||||||||||||||||||||||||||||||||||||||||||||||||||||||||||||||||||||||||||||||||||||||||||||||||||||||||||||||||||||||||||||||

Contracts—
Fundamental
Breach—
Exemption
Clause in
Printed Contract

Harbutts' "Plasticine" Ltd. v. Wayne Tank & Pump Co. Ltd., [1970] 1 Q.B. 447.

The plaintiffs entered into a contract with the defendants to have the defendants design and install a heavy wax dispenser. The printed contract contained an exemption clause which limited the defentants' liability to the value of the contract.

The equipment, when installed, failed to operate properly as a result of a negligently designed heater. When the machine was left unattended with the heat on, a fire resulted and burned the plaintiffs' plant.

In an action which followed, the Trial Court held that a fundamental breach of contract had occurred, and the exemption clause did not apply.

DENNING, M.R.:

Assuming that condition 15 does, in terms, purport to limit the liability of the defendants, the next question is whether the defendants were guilty of a fundamental breach of contract which disentitled them from relying on it. I eschew in this context the word "repudiation" because it is applied so differently in so many different contexts, as Lord Wright explained in *Heyman* v. *Darwins Ltd.* [1942] A.C. 356, 378. There was no repudiation in this case by the defendants—not, at any rate, in its proper sense of denying they are bound by the contract. The defendants have always acknowledged the contract. All that has happened is that they have broken it. If they have broken it in a way that goes to the very root of it, then it is a fundamental breach. If they have broken it in a lesser way, then the breach is not fundamental.

In considering the consequences of a fundamental breach, it is necessary to draw a distinction between a fundamental breach which still leaves the contract open to be performed, and a fundamental breach which itself brings the contract to an end.

(i) *The first group*

In cases where the contract is still open to be performed, the effect of a fundamental breach is this: it gives the innocent party, when he gets to know of it, an option either to *affirm* the contract or to disaffirm it. If he elects to *affirm* it, then it remains in being *for the future* on both sides. Each has a right to sue for damages for *past or future* breaches. If he elects to disaffirm it (namely, accepts the fundamental breach as determining the contract), then it is at an end from that moment. It does not continue into the future. All that is left is the right to sue for past breaches or for the fundamental breach, but there is no right to sue for *future* breaches.

(ii) *The second group*

In cases where the fundamental breach itself brings the contract to an end, there is no room for any option in the innocent party. The present case is typical of this group. The fire was so disastrous that it destroyed the mill itself. If the fire had been accidental, it would certainly have meant that the contract was frustrated and brought to an end by a supervening event; just as in the leading case in 1863 when the Surrey Music Hall was burnt down: see *Taylor* v. *Caldwell* (1863) 3 B. & S. 826. At the time of the fire at this mill, the cause of it was not known. It might have been no one's fault. In that case the contract would plainly have been frustrated. It would have been automatically at an end, so far as the future was concerned, with no option on either side. Does it make any difference because, after many years, the cause of the fire has been found? It has been found to be the fault of the defendants. I cannot think that this makes any difference. The contract came to an end when the mill was burnt down. It came to an end by a frustrating event, without either side having an election to continue it. It is not to be revived simply because it has been found to be the fault of one of the parties. All that happens is that the innocent party can sue the guilty party for the breach.

All that I have said thus far is so obvious that it needs no authority. But now I come to the great question. When a contract is brought to an end by a fundamental breach by one of the parties, can the guilty party rely on an exclusion or limitation clause so as to avoid or limit his liability for the breach?

I propose to take first the group of cases when the fundamental breach does not automatically bring the contract to an end, but it has to be accepted by the innocent party as doing so. Such a case was *Karsales (Harrow) Ltd.* v. *Wallis* [1956] 1 W.L.R. 936, where the hirer, on discovering the fundamental breach, at once rejected the car. In this group it is settled that once he accepts it, the innocent party can sue for the breach and the guilty party cannot rely on the exclusion or limitation clause. That clearly appears from the speeches in the House of Lords in *Suisse Atlantique Société d'Armement Maritime S.A.* v. *N.V. Rotterdamsche Kolen Centrale* [1967] 1 A.C. 361. Lord Reid said, at p. 398:

"If fundamental breach is established the next question is what effect, if any, that has on the applicability of other terms of the contract. This question has often arisen with regard to clauses excluding liability, in whole or in part, of the party in breach. I do not think there is generally much difficulty where the innocent party has elected to treat the breach as a repudiation, bring the contract to an end and sue for damages. Then the whole contract has ceased to exist including the exclusion clause, and I do not see how that clause can then be used to exclude an action for loss which will be suffered by the innocent party after it has ceased to exist, such as loss of the profit which would have accrued if the contract had run its full term."

And Lord Upjohn said, at p. 425:

"the principle upon which one party to a contract cannot rely on the clauses of exception or limitation of liability inserted for his sole protection, is . . . that if there is a fundamental breach accepted by the innocent party the contract is at an end; the guilty party cannot rely on any special terms in the contract."

When their Lordships said the contract "is at an end," they meant, of course, for the future. Such an ending disentitles the guilty party from relying on an exclusion clause in respect of the breach.

Such, then, is established as law when there is "a fundamental breach accepted by the innocent party," that is, when the innocent party has an *election* to treat the contract as at an end and does so. The position must, I think, be the same when the defendant has been guilty of such a fundamental breach that the contract is *automatically* at an end without the innocent party having an election. The innocent party is entitled to sue for damages for the breach, and the guilty party cannot rely on the exclusion or limitation clause: for the simple reason that he, by his own breach, has brought the contract to an end; with the result that he cannot rely on the clause to exempt or limit his liability for that breach.

The one question in this case is, therefore: Were the defendants guilty of a fundamental breach which brought the contract to an end? for, if so, they cannot rely on the limitation clause. It was suggested that, in order to determine whether a breach is fundamental or not, you must look at the quality of it, and not at the results. I do not accept this suggestion. It is not the breach itself which counts so much, but the event resulting from it. A serious breach may have slight consequences. A trivial breach grave ones. Take this very case. The specification of durapipe was, no doubt, a serious breach; but it would not have done much harm if it had been discovered in time and replaced by stainless steel. In that event the plasticine company could not repudiate the contract or treat it as at an end. But it did, in fact, do great harm because of the consequences. The results were so grave as to bring the contract to an end. You must, therefore, look not only at the breach but also at the results of it. Diplock L.J. made that clear in *Hongkong Fir Shipping Co. Ltd.* v. *Kawasaki Kisen Kaisha Ltd.* [1962] 2 Q.B. 26, 68, 69, when he pointed out that it is *"the event resulting from the breach* which relieved the other party of further performance of his obligations." A good instance is the recent case of *Garnham, Harris & Elton Ltd.* v. *Alfred W. Ellis (Transport) Ltd.* [1967] 1 W.L.R. 940.

So I come to the question: were the breaches by the defendants and the consequences of them so fundamental as to bring the contract to an end, and thus disentitle the defendants from relying on the limitation clause? The judge thought that they were. I agree with him. I think that the case is very like *Pollock & Co.* v. *MacCrae & Co.*, 1922 S.C.(H.L.) 192, except that, instead of "a congeries of defects" there is "a congeries of faults." The words of Lord Dunedin, at p. 200, are applicable:

"Now, when there is such a congeries of defects as to destroy the workable character of the machine, I think this amounts to a total breach of contract . . ."

which prevents the suppliers from relying on the conditions.

Before leaving this part of the case, I would just like to say what, in my opinion, is the result of the *Suisse Atlantique* case. It affirms the long line of cases in this court that when one party has been guilty of a fundamental breach of the contract, that is, a breach which goes to the very root of it, and the other side accepts it, so that the contract comes to an end—or if it comes to an end anyway by reason of the breach—then the guilty party cannot rely on an exception or limitation clause to escape from his liability for the breach.

If the innocent party, on getting to know of the breach, does not accept it, but keeps the contract in being (as in *Charterhouse Credit Co. Ltd. v. Tolly* [1963] 2 Q.B. 683), then it is a matter of construction whether the guilty party can rely on the exception or limitation clause, always remembering that it is not to be supposed that the parties intended to give a guilty party a blanket to cover up his own misconduct or indifference, or to enable him to turn a blind eye to his obligations. The courts may reject, as a matter of construction, even the widest exemption clause if it "would lead to an absurdity or because it would defeat the main object of the contract, or perhaps for other reasons. And where some limit must be read into the clause it is generally reasonable to draw the line at fundamental breaches": see Lord Reid [1967] 1 A.C. 361, 398.

So, in the name of construction, we get back to the principle that, when a company inserts in printed conditions an exception clause purporting to exempt them from all and every breach, that is not readily to be construed or considered as exempting them from liability for a fundamental breach; for the good reason that it is only intended to avail them when they are carrying out the contract in substance: and not when they are breaking it in a manner which goes to the very root of the contract.

NOTE: The English House of Lords recently overruled the above case by its decision in *Photo Production Ltd. v. Securicor Transport Ltd.*, [1980] 1 All E.R. 556. No Canadian decisions are available at the present time to indicate the direction the law might take in Canada.

|||||||||||||||||||||||||||||||||||||||||||||||||||||||||||||||||||||||||||||||||||||||||||||||||||||||||||||||||||||||||||||||||||||||||||||||||||||||||||

Case 1

CASE PROBLEMS FOR DISCUSSION

Hatfield owned a large farm on which he grew grain. His combine was inadequate in relation to the acreage of grain which he harvested annually, and as a result, on several occasions his crops had been adversely affected by rain and poor weather conditions. He reasoned that a larger machine could reduce the time spent harvesting by as much as two-thirds, and thereby reduce the chances of bad weather affecting his harvest.

At an agricultural exhibition, he examined a new self-propelled combine that was advertised as capable of harvesting grain at three times the speed of his old equipment. The machine was much larger and more powerful than his old combine, and appeared to be of the correct size for his farm.

On his return home, he contacted the local dealer for the combine, and after explaining his needs, was assured by the dealer that the size he was considering would be capable of harvesting his crop in one-third of the time taken by his older model. He placed an order for the combine, with delivery to be made in July, well before he would require the equipment.

The machine did not arrive until the beginning of the harvest, and Hatfield immediately put the machine into service. Unfortunately, the machine was out of adjustment, and Hatfield was obliged to call the dealer to put it in order. The equipment continued to break down each time Hatfield operated it at the recommended speed, and in spite of numerous attempts by the dealer to correct the problem, the equipment could not be operated at anything more than a very slow speed without a break-down. Hatfield found that notwithstanding the large size of the equipment, his harvest time was no faster. When the harvest was completed, he returned the machine, and demanded his money back.

The equipment dealer refused to return his money, and pointed to a clause in the purchase agreement which Hatfield had signed, and which read: "No warranty or condition, express or implied, shall apply to this agreement with respect to fitness for the use intended or as to performance, except those specifically stated herein."

The only reference in the agreement to the equipment stated that it was to be a "new model XVX self-propelled combine."

Advise Hatfield of his rights (if any).

Case 2

Mrs. Field listed her home for sale with a local real estate agent. The agent introduced Mr. Smith to Mrs. Field as a prospective purchaser, and after Mr. Smith had inspected the house, obtained a written offer to purchase from him. The offer provided that he would purchase the house for $60 000 if Mrs. Field could give him vacant possession of the premises on September 1st, some three weeks' hence. The offer was accompanied by a deposit in the amount of $1 000.

Mrs. Field accepted the offer in writing, then proceeded to lease an apartment under a two-year lease. She moved her furniture to the new premises immediately, and vacated her home in preparation for closing. A few days before the date fixed for delivery of the deed, Mrs. Field was informed by one of her new neighbours (who was a friend of Mr. Smith) that Mr. Smith's employer intended to transfer him to a new position in another city some distance away.

Discuss the rights and obligations (if any) of the parties in this case, and suggest a course of action which Mrs. Field might follow.

Case 3

Trebic was a skilled cabinet-maker of European extraction. Moldeva, who had emigrated to Canada from the same country, requested him to build a set of kitchen cupboards "in the old country style." The two men discussed the general appearance desired, then Trebic drew up a list of materials which he required to construct the cupboards. Moldeva obtained the necessary lumber and supplies for Trebic, then took his family on a vacation.

On his return, Moldeva found the work completed, and admired the craftsmanship and design which Trebic had exhibited in the making of the cabinets. Trebic had carefully carved the "old country designs" on the trim boards, and had skillfully constructed the drawers and cabinets using wooden dowels, rather than nails, again in accordance with "old country tradition." In the execution of his skill he had used only hand tools, and then only the tools used by old country craftsmen in the cabinet-making trade. In every detail, the cabinets were "old country style."

When Moldeva indicated that he was completely satisfied with the cabinets, Trebic submitted his account in the amount of $1 600. The sum represented 80 hours' work at $20 per hour, the normal rate charged by skilled cabinet-makers in the area.

Moldeva, who was a building contractor himself, objected to the amount of Trebic's account, and stated that carpenters in his shop could manufacture kitchen cabinets of the general size and shape of those made by Trebic in only a few days' time. He offered Trebic $400 as payment in full.

Trebic refused to accept the $400 offer, and brought an action against Moldeva on the $1 600 account.

Discuss the possible arguments of the parties, and render a decision.

Case 4

Andrews, a skilled carpenter, agreed to construct a garage for Henderson for a contract price of $800, the plans and materials to be supplied by Henderson.

Andrews constructed the garage according to the plans, and when the building had been framed, he discovered that the siding boards which Henderson had purchased were of poor grade lumber. The boards could only be made to fit with a great deal of hand labour and cutting.

Andrews complained to Henderson, and demanded that he provide siding boards which were of "construction grade" lumber. Henderson refused to do so, and an argument followed in which Andrews refused to complete the work until Henderson provided suitable materials.

At the time of the argument, the foundation, the roof, and the walls had been erected. The work which remained included the installation of the wall siding, the doors and windows, and the trim.

Discuss the rights of the parties, the nature of the claims, and defences of each. Indicate the possible outcome, if the case should come before the courts.

PART IV
Business
Relationships

CHAPTER 15

Forms of Business Organization

INTRODUCTION

Business organizations may take on many forms which represent legal relationships at law. Many of these organizations, from a conceptual point of view, are based upon the law of contract. For example, the agency and the partnership are, for the most part, special contracts, while the corporation, another special form of organization, is an entity that contracts with third parties through agents.

Apart from the form which a business itself may take, most of its activities are conducted by way of the law of contract. The organization buys and sells goods, hires employees, acquires premises, advertises its wares, reduces risk, and generally carries on its business operations through the medium of contract. The law relating to all of these activities will be examined in detail in the chapters which follow, but the important point to note is that the law of contract forms a basis for the law in each case. The special features of the law merely relate to the particular nature of the relationship that arises out of the contract in each situation.

FORMS OF BUSINESS ORGANIZATION

A business organization may be established to carry out a particular project or venture, produce a certain product or product line, or provide a service to the public or a part thereof. In the classic view, a business begins when an entrepreneur conceives a particular need in a community for a product or service, and proceeds to satisfy the need. The business is established in a small way in the beginning, then grows, if the entrepreneur has accurately assessed the market until the business, through investment and the development of new or better products or services, becomes a large business entity. This developmental sequence of a business organization, needless to say, is not the only way that large firms may develop. Large organizations are often created to carry on business activities which have been developed by larger organizations, and not infrequently, businesses which require a large amount of capital for their establishment generally begin their existence as large organizations. In these cases, the organizations do not pass through different forms of organization. Nevertheless, the classic type of business growth pattern remains as one of the most common patterns of development, and one which illustrates the number of forms of organization which a business may take during the period of its progression from a small entrepreneurial venture to a large corporate organization. The purpose of this chapter is to examine some of the more general laws that affect the nature of the firm as it passes through the various stages of development from its beginning to its final stage.

Sole Proprietorship

The sole proprietorship represents the simplest form of business organization insofar as the law is concerned. The sole proprietor, as the owner of the business, owns all of the assets, is entitled to all of the profits, and is responsible for all of the debts. The sole proprietor also makes all of the decisions in the operation of the business, and is directly responsible for its success or failure.

Sole proprietorships, especially those of a service nature, often begin as a part-time business activity carried on by an individual in addition to regular full-time employment. As the business grows, the part-time proprietor frequently converts the business into a full-time business, eventually acquires premises in which to carry on the activity, and hires employees to assist in its operation. While the legal requirements for the establishment and the conduct of this form of business organization may vary from province to province, the requirements tend to be minimal.

One of the important requirements for a sole proprietorship is the registration or the licensing of the business. Persons who offer the public services of a professional nature must generally be licensed to practice the particular skill in a province before they may carry on a professional practice. The legislation governing professions such as medicine, dentistry, law, architecture, and others is usually provincial, and must be complied with before the practice may be established. Other semi-professional, and skilled trade activities are also subject to provincial licensing or registration.

In addition to legislation relating to the *qualifications* of the sole proprietor, many business activities are subject to provincial legislation which control the *right* to carry on the activity through licensing or registration. This is usually done to protect the public from unscrupulous operators. Door-to-door businesses, carriers of goods, and persons selling real estate and securities are examples of businesses which are generally subject to this type of legislation.

Municipalities often impose their own registration or licensing of certain businesses in an effort to protect or control the activity. Skilled trades, the operation of taxi businesses, and many other service-oriented businesses frequently require municipal licenses to operate within the confines of the municipality.

In addition to acquiring a license to carry on a business or profession, a sole proprietor conducting a business activity under a name other than his or her own must, in most provinces, register the business name and provide the details of the business entity to the registrar. The purpose of this type of legislation is to enable a person who deals with such a business to determine the identity of the proprietor of the firm. If a person fails to register the business, the legislation in some provinces not only provides for a fine or penalty, but prohibits the person from taking or defending any action in a court of law which relates to the business activity until registration is effected.

In some cases, the nature of the business requires compliance with special legislation before it may be carried on. Federal and provincial laws relating to the storage and handling of products which are hazardous or potentially dangerous generally require the construction of special storage facilities for the products, and the approval of the premises by the public authority before the business may commence. Legislation of this nature is usually coupled with the licensing of the handlers of the goods to ensure compliance with the legislation at all times. Explosives, gasoline, dangerous chemicals, and drugs are subject to legislation of this type. Activities which require the maintenance of a high degree of cleanliness, such as food processing and food service, are also subject to similar methods of inspection and control in some provinces.

Apart from the licensing and registration requirements of sole proprietorships by various levels of government, the sole proprietor who carries on a business without employees has few other controls on the business activity. Local zoning by-laws may require the proprietor to locate the place of business in certain areas of the municipality; the entrepreneur may require a permit to acquire goods without payment of sales tax, and to act as a collector of the tax when goods are sold— these limitations or obligations, however, would only apply in those jurisdictions that have retail sales tax and local zoning regulations in effect.

The additional obligations imposed by the law on a small sole proprietor multiply once employees are hired to assist in the performance of business activities. Workmen's compensation legislation designed to protect employees from loss of wages if injured while employed require most employers to provide coverage for their employees under the statute. Other provincial legislation may control hours of work, working conditions, minimum wages, and benefits that must be provided for employees. In addition, the employer is obliged to comply with federal legislation concerning unemployment insurance premiums, Canada Pension Plan contributions, and income tax deductions for remittance to Revenue Canada. The record-keeping normally associated with government legislation generally requires the sole proprietor to maintain a set of account books in something more than a casual manner. While the addition of employees compounds the record-keeping obligations of the sole proprietor, it does not in any major way affect the rights of the proprietor to carry on the business as he sees fit except in two important aspects: *First*, as an employer, the proprietor must comply with all employee-related legislation, and *second*, as an employer, the proprietor becomes vicariously liable for all acts of the employees done within the scope of their employment. The supervision of employee activity accordingly becomes an important aspect of the proprietor's obligations in the conduct of his business.

Advantages and Disadvantages of a Sole Proprietorship

In spite of the many legislative and regulatory requirements, the sole proprietorship remains an attractive form of business organization, and in most instances, is subject to a minimum of government control. The particular advantages of the sole proprietorship may be briefly summarized as follows:

(1) It represents a low-cost form of organization for a business activity.
(2) It may be carried on in many cases as a part-time activity while the entrepreneur acquires capital or customers.
(3) All decision-making is in the hands of the proprietor.
(4) The proprietor is entitled to all of the profits earned by the business.

(5) The success of the business lies entirely with the proprietor.
(6) Record-keeping is generally simple for a sole proprietorship.
(7) A sole proprietor may enjoy certain tax advantages not available to employees.
(8) Information concerning the business need not be revealed to the public at large, as is the case with some corporations.

The sole proprietorship, while possessing these advantages, is not without a number of drawbacks. The more important disadvantages are the following:

(1) The capital available to the business is limited to the assets of the proprietor, and the extent of his credit. As a result, the sole proprietorship is initially limited to business activities which have relatively low capital requirements.
(2) The sole proprietor has unlimited liability for the debts of the business. The personal assets of the sole proprietor are exposed to creditor claims as well as to those of persons who may have claims as a result of the proprietor's negligence.
(3) The management skills available to the business are normally limited to those possessed by the sole proprietor. A sole proprietor can seldom afford to hire experts to assist in the operation of the business until the business reaches a size where some other form of organization should be considered.
(4) The sole proprietorship lacks the continuity that other forms of business organization possess. The death or incapacity of the proprietor either terminates the business or seriously affects its operation, a disadvantage which is

not found, for example, with the corporate form of organization.

(5) The successful sole proprietorship may possess a tax disadvantage when compared to the corporation. Sole proprietorships are taxed at progressive personal tax rates, and a sole proprietorship which generates a high income would result in a much larger tax liability for the sole proprietor than a corporation with a similar income. The special, low small business corporation tax rates generally dictate the incorporation of the successful sole proprietorship if only to avoid the progressively higher tax rates which apply to sole proprietorship income.

In spite of the many disadvantages of sole proprietorship, the freedom which it allows the individual in the operation of the business frequently makes it the most attractive form of business organization for a new small enterprise. The flexibility of the operation during the formative period is often as important as the speed by which decisions may be made, but as the business becomes larger, the need for new, and varied management skills may require a change in the form of the organization.

Partnerships

From a progressive point of view, the second phase which a small business may enter is that of the partnership. A partnership differs in a number of ways from a sole proprietorship, but it, too, is essentially a simple form of business organization. The increase in the number of proprietors to two or more provides additional management expertise in the operation of the firm, and usually additional capital as well. Lending institutions, if they are in a position to look to the assets of several proprietors, are generally more willing to extend credit in large amounts to a partnership than to a sole proprietorship. In addition, partners usually possess a greater interest in the success of the business than do employees, and the introduction of new proprietors may substantially increase the chances for growth and development of the enterprise.

Partnerships, unfortunately, have their own drawbacks. The change from a sole proprietorship to a partnership also changes the nature of the organization. A partnership agreement, setting out the rights and duties of the partners is usually necessary, and the partnership must be duly registered in the appropriate public office. Once established, the liability, although shared, increases, because each partner may bind the partnership in contracts made within the ordinary scope of partnership business, and the torts of a partner committed during the conduct of partnership business become those of the partnership as well. Because the partnership is treated as little more than a collection of individuals, the partnership does not provide the special tax advantages that apply to the corporate form of business organization. Nevertheless, a partnership made up of compatible, experienced, business-oriented persons frequently turns a successful sole proprietorship into a larger, and more successful business entity that requires a further transformation to the corporate form.

Corporations

The corporation, unlike the sole proprietorship or partnership, is a separate entity which has a legal existence of its own. If it is organized to carry on a business, it is the corporation that "owns" the business—not the people who own shares in it. It is also the corporation that earns the profit and bears the responsibility for any losses. The shareholders cannot bind the corporation in contract, nor are they directly responsible to its creditors for its debts.

The corporate form is useful because it represents a vehicle that may be used to amass the large amounts of capital necessary to set up and carry on business activities which require capital in excess of that which a partnership or sole proprietorship can acquire. Its continuous existence, and ability to bring together the necessary expertise to undertake large and complex business activities have also contributed to its widespread use as the appropriate form for all large-scale business enterprises.

Not the least of its advantages lies in the special income tax treatment granted to corporations by governments. Corporations are not taxed in accordance with the same progressive tax scales as individuals, and they generally pay a substantially lower rate of tax than sole proprietors or partnerships with large incomes. The shareholders of a corporation also receive special treatment when corporate earnings are distributed to them.

In spite of the advantages of the corporate form, the corporation also brings with it a number of disadvantages. Being a separate entity, its operation must be in accordance with the rules set down in the laws relating to corporations, and for corporations who offer their shares to the public, much of the information concerning the firm's finances must be published. Trading in the shares of the corporation also becomes public knowledge with respect to directors and holders of substantial blocks of shares. Notwithstanding these drawbacks, the corporation is essentially the only form of organization which can bring together the necessary management and productive skills for a large undertaking. The nature of these business entities, and the law relating to them may be found in the chapters which follow.

Agencies

An agency is a particular form of business organization that is subject to its own rules of law. In the strict sense, it is not a form of business organization like a partnership or corporation, although the agency business may take on either form as a method of organization. It is essentially a service relationship which operates as an extension of other organizations to carry out their business activities. It is also a relationship which may exist between individuals within an organization. The law of agency, because of its application to so many other forms of business organization, is examined in detail in the next chapter.

‖‖

SUMMARY There are essentially three main forms of organization which a business might assume. The simplest of the three is the sole proprietorship which permits a person at very low cost and with a minimum of formality to establish a business enterprise. It has a number of advantages, the most important being the freedom to manage the business and the accrual of all the profits to the sole proprietor. It has, however, certain disadvantages as well, the most notable being the unlimited liability of the proprietor for the debts of the business.

The partnership form of organization represents a somewhat more elaborate form of organization with the added advantages of increased management talent and capital, but it, too, has its disadvantages. The acts of each partner may bind the business, and the partnership form requires each partner to comply with the formalities of registration and dissolution, as well as all other duties imposed by the law on this form of organization.

The third general form of organization is the corporation, which is an entity separate from its shareholders, and which protects them by way of limited liability. Its nature at law, however, requires compliance with a great many formalities with respect to its operation, and the disclosure of much of its financial data, if it is a corporation which offers its shares to the public. The law relating to corporations and partnerships is examined in the chapters which follow Chapter 16, "Law of Agency."

||||||||||||||||||||||||||||||||||||||||||||||||||||||||||||||||||||||||||||||||||||||||||||||||||||||||||||||||||||||||||||||||||||||||||||||||||||||||||||

DISCUSSION QUESTIONS

1. Explain the term "sole proprietor."
2. What special advantages apply to the sole proprietorship form of business organization?
3. What legal matters should be considered by a sole proprietor before commencing business operations?
4. Define a "partnership."
5. What legal obligations apply to a partnership that do not apply to a sole proprietorship?
6. Define a "corporation," and explain how it differs from a "partnership."
7. What major advantages does a corporation have over other forms of business organization?
8. In what capacity is a business organization an agent of the Crown?
9. Classify the following with respect to possible forms of organization: a multi-national automobile manufacturer; a small grocery store; the law firm of Smith, Brown, and Jones; a franchised convenience store; a person carrying on a part-time printing business; a realtor; a licensed electrician.
10. What forms of business organization may an agency assume?
11. Describe the classic development model that a business may follow in its growth from the part-time activity of its founder to the stage where it becomes a large national organization.
12. In what way does the employment of persons to assist in a business operation complicate matters for the business proprietor?

JUDICIAL DECISIONS

Liability of Contractor Under Illegal Contract— Liability in Tort

Keystone Fisheries Ltd. v. Leftrook and Mid-West Truck Lines Ltd. (1959), 16 D.L.R. (2d) 680.

The plaintiff and the defendant entered into a contract to carry live frogs to a third party. The defendant carrier was not licensed to carry live frogs, although it was licensed to carry fish and other agricultural products. Through a delay on the part of the carrier, most of the frogs died en route to their destination.

The plaintiff brought an action against the defendant for the loss, but the defendant alleged there was no cause of action as the contract was illegal.

ADAMSON, C.J.M.:

The plaintiff alleges that the loss was caused by the unreasonably long time taken in making delivery and neglecting to take proper care of the shipment in transit.

The contract to transport frogs was illegal. This was not known by either the plaintiff or the defendants. The illegality arose from the fact that the defendant company operates under a Public Service Vehicle certificate issued by the Motor Carrier Board. This certificate only authorizes the "transportation of fish and unmanufactured agricultural products", and does not include frogs. Under the provisions of s. 165(1) of the *Highway Traffic Act*, R.S.M. 1954, c. 112, the contract was therefore illegal.

It was submitted to us that the contract being illegal the plaintiff had no cause of action. It is well settled law that a Court will not lend its aid to enforce an illegal agreement: *North Western Salt Co.* v. *Electrolytic Alkali Co.*, [1914] A.C. 461; *Bain* v. *Maddison*, [1930], 1 D.L.R. 63, S.C.R. 299.

The action, however, is not upon the contract or to enforce an agreement; it is for a tort based on the negligence of the defendant and its employees: "An action of tort is an action based on facts which constitute a tort, that is, which constitute and are regarded as a breach of duty on the part of the tortfeasor, where such breach arises out of a liability which is independent of any personal obligation undertaken by contract, even though there may happen to be a contract between the parties": 32 Hals., 2nd ed., p. 160, para. 227.

This has been the law for many years. In *Tattan* v. *Gt. Western R. Co.* (1860), 2 El. & El. 844, 121 E.R. 315, it was held that: "An action against a common carrier for the breach of his duty to carry safely goods delivered to him, as such, to be carried for hire, whereby the goods are lost, is an action not of contract but of tort, in substance as well as in form; the duty being imposed upon him by the custom of the realm, and being distinct from and independent of his obligation under the contract of carriage, in respect of which latter he may also be sued in an action of contract."

Cockburn C.J., and Crompton, Hill and Blackburn JJ., constituted the Court. In his reasons Crompton J. said [pp. 853-4]: "It is said, for the defendants, that the present is substantially an action of contract and not on the case. But ever since *Pozzi* v. *Shipton* (8 A. & E. 963) it has been settled law that an action against a common carrier, as such, is substantially an action of tort on the case, founded on his common law duty to carry safely, independently of the particular contract which he makes. *Marshall* v. *York, Newcastle and Berwick Railway Company* (11 C.B. 665) is a recent decision to that effect. It is, therefore, impossible for us to say that the present is an action of contract within the meaning of stat. 19 & 20 Vict. c. 108, s. 30.''

. . . . .

The numerous cases in our Courts of actions by passengers against taxicab companies and others are in tort. It would be astonishing if a taxicab company could plead as a defence in such a case that the driver's licence to drive had been suspended; that the contract was illegal and there was accordingly no cause of action.

It is clear that the defendant company having the custody and possession of this cargo had a duty to the owner, not referable to the contract, to use reasonable care to see that the goods were not injured or destroyed.

||||||||||||||||||||||||||||||||||||||||||||||||||||||||||||||||||||||||||||||||||||||||||||||||||||||||||||||||||||||||||||||||||||||||||||||||||

Sole Proprietorship— Transfer of Assets to Wife to Avoid Creditors— Validity of Conveyance

Vasey v. Kreutzweiser (1965), 8 C.B.R. 225.

The debtor, a sole proprietor of a retail establishment, transferred his house to his wife in an effort to place the property beyond the reach of his creditors. The consideration was $1 and "natural love and affection." The debtor, some years later, became bankrupt, and the trustee in bankruptcy attempted to recover the property from the debtor's wife.

BENNETT, LOCAL MASTER:

Having found that the conveyance in December 1961 was a settlement of property by Kreutzweiser within five years of his bankruptcy and that Kreutzweiser was at the time of making the settlement unable to pay all his debts without the aid of the property settled, the next question to be decided is whether Mrs. Kreutzweiser was a purchaser in good faith and for valuable consideration under s. 60(3) of The Bankruptcy Act.

On the question of whether there was valuable consideration for the conveyance from the bankrupt to his wife, the consideration recited in the conveyance is the sum of $1 and natural love and affection. The mortgage outstanding against the property was not listed as an encumbrance to be assumed by the purchaser. In her examination-in-chief at the trial, Mrs. Kreutzweiser testified that she agreed with her husband to pay the mortgage on the house (QQ. 353, 354 and 363) and that she would sell the house. On cross-examination Mrs. Kreutzweiser also stated that it was her intention to sell the house, retaining the proceeds after paying off the mortgage for her benefit or for her and her husband's joint benefit. Mr. Hanbidge estimated that the value of the property was in the neighbourhood of $18,000. According to Mrs. Kreutzweiser, the principal of the mortgage stood at about $6,700 in December 1961. On all the evidence, it seems clear that Mrs. Kreutzweiser intended at the date of the conveyance to her in December 1961 to sell the house, pay off the mortgage and retain the proceeds. . . . I conclude therefore that there was no valuable consideration for the conveyance from the bankrupt to his wife in December 1961. It is also my opinion for the same reasons that Mrs. Kreutzweiser was not a "purchaser" within the meaning of s. 60(3)(*b*) but was merely a beneficiary under a settlement.

I turn now to the question of good faith. On her examination for discovery (p. 18, Q. 127, p. 19, Q. 134), Mrs. Kreutzweiser stated she persuaded her husband to execute the conveyance so that he could not mortgage the house to pay debts at the store which Mrs. Kreutzweiser said he had done a short time before. At the trial, Mrs. Kreutzweiser gave as the sole reason for the transfer, the drinking problem of her husband and her fear that the property would be lost as a result of a claim arising out of an automobile accident caused by the negligence of her husband when he was impaired or drunk. Even if this evidence at the trial were accepted as the sole reason for the conveyance, I would find that the conveyance in December 1961 to Mrs. Kreutzweiser was not made in good faith because it was a conveyance made in contemplation of a debt arising in the future (See *The Bank of British North America v. Rattenbury* (1859), 7 Gr. 383, not a bankruptcy case but where this principle is applied). However I am satisfied that one of the substantial reasons, if not the main reason for the conveyance, was to place the house beyond the control of her husband so that it could not be mortgaged or be made available to her husband's creditors. When confronted with what she had said on her examination for discovery to the effect that she had persuaded her husband to execute the conveyance so that he could not mortgage the house to pay debts, Mrs. Kreutzweiser stated that she must have thought her answers to have been true at the time but insisted that the sole reason for the conveyance was to avoid liability resulting from a car accident caused by the bankrupt's drinking. I am satisfied that Mrs. Kreutzweiser was well aware that her husband owed substantial sums of money in December 1961 which he could not pay if he stayed in business without resorting to the residential property. I accept the evidence of Mr. Myatt that he discussed the bankrupt's financial position many times with Mrs. Kreutzweiser during the years 1958 to 1961 inclusive and that she knew that her husband was not meeting his obligations. Mrs. Kreutzweiser on cross-examination could not remember Mr. Myatt discussing the financial position of the business with her. She did not deny it but said she did not remember. Mrs. Kreutzweiser did admit that Mr. Myatt told her that her husband owed money to the accounting firm. I also accept the evidence of Mr. Lemon that Mrs. Kreutzweiser came to his office several times to discuss the state of the store account and on one occasion said words to the effect that "they did not want to lose the house." Mr. Lemon could not pin point the dates of the interviews with Mrs. Kreutzweiser but Mrs. Kreutzweiser said, "I imagine it was before the transfer of the house." It seems probable that her remark to the effect that "they did not want to lose the house" was made before the conveyance in 1961. Again Mrs. Kreutzweiser made the statement to Mr. Bradford, the landlord, that she did not know "what we are going to do" some time prior to the date of the conveyance in 1961. Mrs. Kreutzweiser then was very concerned in December 1961—she knew her husband's business was in trouble, caused partly at least by his drinking, that he owed a substantial amount of money which he could not pay from the earnings of his business and that the creditors were pressing for payment. She knew too that her husband had borrowed money previously on the house to pay store bills and I believe that the reason Mrs. Kreutzweiser gave on discovery for obtaining the conveyance, namely, to prevent such further borrowing, was one of the reasons if not the principal one behind the conveyance. I conclude therefore that the conveyance in December 1961 was not a transaction carried out in good faith but one to place the property beyond the reach of the creditors, present and future.

Having found therefore that:

(a) Kreutzweiser made a settlement upon his wife within five years of his bankruptcy;

(b) Kreutzweiser was at the time of making the settlement unable to pay all his debts without the aid of the property settled and

(c) the conveyance to Mrs. Kreutzweiser was not for valuable consideration and not a transaction in which Mrs. Kreutzweiser was acting in good faith,

I find that the said conveyance dated the 31st December 1961 from the said Reginald James Kreutzweiser to Margaret Kreutzweiser is void pursuant to the provisions of s. 60 of the Bankruptcy Act.

. . . . .

In the instant circumstances, the settlor and the person receiving the settlement both were well aware that the settlor was not meeting his obligations, in fact owed a great deal of money, that the creditors were pressing and that the conveyance was not made for any good consideration. I draw the inference from all the evidence that the debtor had the guilty intent to place the property beyond the reach of his creditors for the benefit of his wife or for their joint benefit.

|||||||||||||||||||||||||||||||||||||||||||||||||||||||||||||||||||||||||||||||||||||||||||||||||||||||||||||||||||||||||||||||||||||||||||||||||||||

CASE PROBLEMS FOR DISCUSSION

Case 1

Emily was a young woman who worked for a large Toronto publishing house until she was obliged to resign her position and return to her home town to care for her recently widowed invalid mother.

On her return home, she discovered that some printing equipment which her father had acquired a number of years before his death had not been disposed of by her mother. While the equipment was old, she determined that it was suitable for the printing of greeting cards, stationery, theatre programs, and similar items.

Emily had some experience in the operation of the equipment, and decided that a small printing business might be something which she could operate from her mother's home. Since her mother would require a great deal of care, the time she could devote to the business would be limited, but a neighbour that had some printing experience was available, on a part-time basis, to assist her in the operation of the business.

Her first printing work was for herself: the production of business cards, letterhead and invoice forms bearing the name of her new business, which she called "Emily's Print Shop."

Assume that Emily calls upon you for advice as to the legal considerations and requirements for the establishment of a small business. Advise her of the various legal requirements which she might be obliged to comply with in order to operate a printing shop, and in particular, the implications of engaging a neighbour to assist her in the conduct of her business.

Case 2

Samuels was a qualified journeyman electrician who was employed by a municipal public utilities commission on a full-time basis. On weekends and evenings, he occasionally assisted friends who were constructing their own homes by installing their electrical wiring for them. In most cases he did the installation work gratuitously, but from time to time he would be given a sum of money in appreciation of his services.

One day, while on vacation at his summer cottage, a neighbouring cottage-owner who was renovating his cottage approached Samuels and inquired if he might be interested in taking on the job of rewiring the cottage. Samuels thought about the offer, then agreed to do so, and a price was agreed upon. Samuels would do the work and supply the materials (estimated at $950) for $1 400.

A few days later, Samuels purchased the necessary materials, and proceeded to rewire the cottage. Upon completion of the job, Samuels presented his account for $1 550, which represented the cost of materials at $1 100, and his labour at $450.

Samuel's neighbour refused to pay the account, insisting that the agreed price was $1 400. Samuels' argument was that the $950 price quoted was only an estimate, and subject to change. The only firm part of his quote, he maintained, was his labour charge of $450.

The two parties continued to argue over the price for several months, and eventually Samuels instituted legal proceedings to collect the account.

Identify and discuss the legal issues which might arise in this case and which could affect Samuels' right to recover payment. If you were called upon to act as counsel for the defendant, what inquiries would you make?

Case 3

Herman and Hilda, a married couple, have an opportunity to purchase a small, commercial charter flying operation located in a remote northern area. Both are fully qualified pilots with commercial licenses.

The business consists of a base station and two single-engine float planes, along with an assortment of miscellaneous equipment necessary to conduct the operation. The business, which presently employs two persons in addition to the owner, is offered for sale at $180 000, and could be expected to yield a net return of about $50 000 per year.

If both Herman and Hilda performed the roles of pilots, a third person would be necessary to maintain the base station in their absence. A friend of the couple, who is also a qualified commercial pilot, has expressed an interest in joining the venture, but has no assets. Another friend, who has no flying experience, but does have considerable business experience and $30 000 cash to invest in a business, is interested as well. Herman and Hilda have about $90 000 between them for investment. The present owner is prepared to pursue one of the following courses of action: (1) retain a 50% financial interest in the business as a non-participant in its active operation and sell the remaining 50% interest in the business over a five-year period; or (2) sell the business outright for a 50% down payment, and receive payment of the balance over a five-year period.

What factors should Herman and Hilda consider in their decision to purchase the business, and what forms of organization might be appropriate?

CHAPTER 16

Law of Agency

THE ROLE OF AN AGENT

The law of agency is concerned with the relationship that arises when one individual either expressly or impliedly uses the services of another to carry out a specific task on his behalf. The relationship may arise through an express agreement, conduct, or necessity, but in every case the relationship involves three parties: the principal, the agent, and a third party. The purpose of the agency relationship is to enable the principal to accomplish some particular purpose, usually the formation of a contract with the third party. If the law has been properly complied with, the end result will be the accomplishment of the task without direct dealings between the principal and the third party.

Agents are generally engaged in business activities which involve the negotiation of contracts, but agents may also be used for many other purposes. For example, a lawyer may be engaged as an agent to perform certain legal services on behalf of his client, or a real estate agent may be engaged to bring a buyer and seller together but with no authority to bind his principal, the seller, in contract. Still, the most common use of an agent is to bind the principal in contract with a third party.

HISTORICAL DEVELOPMENT OF THE LAW OF AGENCY

The law of agency has its roots in the law relating to tort, contract, *quasi*-contract, and equity. Some evidence indicates that agency existed in the early medieval period, but legal historians appear to be in dispute as to its true source. Some seem to think that it may have been Roman in origin, but most believe that this is unlikely. The concept probably had roots of Germanic origin in the forerunner of their early law of uses,[1] and found its way to England along with the Germanic invaders who settled in parts of the country. By the time of the Norman Conquest, the use of an agent to act on behalf of a principal had been firmly established, and as society developed during the next three centuries, the use of agents gradually became more common. Agents were not widely used during the medieval period for the reason that it was seldom necessary for a person to engage another

to perform a service in a community that was small and mostly self-sufficient. It was only with the growth of trade and the rise of the mercantile class that the use of agents became important and widespread. As trade expanded, so too did the use of agents, and the courts were then called upon to define the rights and duties of the parties. By the end of the 14th century, the laws relating to agency coalesced. The basic rule of agency—that a principal may be liable for the acts of his agent—was established, and a number of legal principal–agent relationships were recognized by the courts.[2]

In the late 17th century, the social changes that had taken place, paralleling the decline of the feudal system and the development of commerce, redefined employment relationships. Independent contractors were established who would act on behalf of principals in a variety of different commercial activities. These new contractors were viewed by the courts as persons capable of binding their principals in business transactions.

During the 18th century many of the agency concepts took shape. The Chancery courts first treated the agency relationship as if it were a form of trust; later, the courts borrowed a number of principles from maritime law in the development of the law relating to *agency of necessity*, and the law fixing the liability of a principal for the torts of the agent. The for-

---

[1] The ancient German law of uses was similar in some respects to the law relating to trusts, where a person as trustee undertakes to carry out the settlor's wishes with respect to property entrusted to him.

[2] Masters were held liable for the acts of their apprentices during this period, and in one case, an abbott was held liable for goods purchased by a monk for use in the monastery. See F. Pollock and F.W. Maitland, *The History of English Law*, 2nd ed. (Cambridge University Press, 1898: Cambridge, England), vol. 2, p. 228.

mer became the basis for the concept of *implied authority* of an agent, and the latter, the basis for the modern principle of *vicarious liability* in contracts of employment.

During the late 18th century, and throughout the 19th century, the rapid growth of industry and commerce created the need for a common law response to the problems which rapid change had brought about. The law of contract was a part of this response, and with it, the law of agency was refined. In their respective spheres of influence, both the common law courts and equity moulded the concepts and ideas which now form the basis of modern agency law. This period saw the determination of the law relating to estoppel, the implied authority of particular mercantile agents, undisclosed principals, and the contractual nature of the relationship.

The law of agency itself was distinguished from the law of employment by means of a subtle blend of maritime and mercantile law, and tort, contract, and trust concepts, which the courts modified and merged into the present-day body of law. These rules of law which relate to agency may be divided into a number of distinct categories, each of which refer to a particular aspect of the agency relationship.

THE NATURE OF THE RELATIONSHIP

By definition, an agent is a person who is employed to act on behalf of another. If the act of an agent is done within the scope of his authority, the act will bind his principal.[3] As a great many agents are

[3]Osborn, P. G., *The Concise Law Dictionary*, 4th ed. (Sweet & Maxwell, 1954: London), p. 22.

independent business people that might be employed by a number of employers at any one time to act for each in a variety of different business transactions, the employment of an agent should not be viewed merely as the ordinary employment relationship of employer–employee.

The general rules of contract normally apply to an agency relationship. An infant, for example, may be a principal, but any contract negotiated on his behalf (except a contract for necessities) would remain voidable at his option, even if the agent was of full age. Since the agent is simply a conduit by which a contract may be effected between the principal and a third party, the capacity of the agent is to some extent unimportant. An agent must not be insane. He may still be a minor, however, and negotiate a binding agreement on behalf of a principal with full capacity to contract. The agency agreement between the principal and agent, nevertheless, is subject to the ordinary rules of contract, and may be voidable at the option of the infant, even though the other party may be bound.

Agency by Express Agreement

The principal–agent relationship may arise as a result of an express agreement, which could be either oral or in writing. The relationship may also be inferred from the actions of the principal, in which case it is sometimes called agency by conduct or estoppel. A third type of agency which may arise in certain circumstances is referred to as an agency of necessity.

Agency which arises out of an express agreement is contractual in nature, and is subject to the ordinary rules of contract with respect to its formation and performance. While it may be oral and binding under most circumstances, it must comply with the Statute of Frauds if the agreement cannot be fully performed within a year. The agreement must also comply with any special requirements for formal contracts, if the agent, as a part of his duty, is expected to execute such a document on behalf of his principal. For example, if Anderson engages Baker as his agent to sell a parcel of land for him and to execute a conveyance of the land to the purchaser, the agent must be empowered to do so by a grant of the power under seal, since the document he would be expected to sign would be under seal. The particular document under seal which would authorize the execution of the conveyance would be a *power of attorney*—a legal document which would appoint the agent as the principal's attorney for the purpose of conveying the land.

The advantage of a written agency agreement is that the terms and conditions of the agency, and in particular the duties of the principal and the agent, are set out in a document for future reference. Not every agency agreement requires this formality, since a verbal agreement is perfectly adequate in many cases. For example, if Martin requests Thomas to purchase an item for him from the local hardware store, an agency relationship would be created whereby Thomas would be authorized to act as Martin's agent in the purchase from the shopkeeper. A written agreement would not normally be required for this simple agency task.

The ordinary agency relationship extends beyond the agreement between the principal and the agent, and usually involves a second contract with a third party. The two contracts are separate, but in the case of the contract negotiated by the agent and the third party, if the agent acts within the scope of his authority, the rights and duties under the agreement become those of the principal and the third party. The agent, in effect, drops from the transaction once the agreement is executed, and has neither rights nor liabilities under it.

A point to note with respect to agency is the nature of the relationship between the principal and agent. Unlike many contractual relationships, the parties in an agency relationship must act in good faith in their dealings with each other. Under agency law, the principal has a duty to pay the agent either the fee fixed, or a reasonable fee for his services. The principal must also indemnify the agent for any reasonable expenses that he properly incurs in carrying out the agency agreement. At common law, the agent is entitled to payment immediately on the completion of his services, but it is customary for the parties to fix the time for payment at some later date, usually when the accounts have been settled.

The agent has a number of obligations toward his principal. First, he must obey all lawful instructions of the principal, and keep confidential any information given to him by his principal. Secondly, he must keep in constant contact with his principal, and inform him of any important developments which might occur as negotiations progress. This is a particularly important duty on the part of the agent, for the law holds that any notice to an agent is notice to the principal, and the principal is therefore deemed to know everything which is communicated to the agent by the third party.

If an agent possesses special skill or competence to perform the act required under the agency agreement, then the agent must maintain the standard required for that skill in the performance of his duties. The agent may be liable to the principal if he fails to maintain that standard, and if his failure results in a loss to the principal. He normally may not, except with the express permission of his principal, delegate his duties to a sub-agent, because the principal is entitled to rely on the special skills and judgement of the agent alone. While there are certain exceptions to this rule, generally, a principal is entitled to personal service by his agent.

Where an agent is authorized to receive funds or goods on behalf of the principal, the agent has a duty to account for the goods or the money. To fulfil this obligation, the agent must keep records of the money received, and keep the funds separate from his own. The usual practice of agents in this regard is to place all funds in a trust account or a special account identified as the principal's, and to remit money to the principal at regular intervals. If the agent is entitled to deduct his commission from the funds received under the terms of the agency agreement, or by custom of the trade, then the deduction is usually made at the time that the balance of the account is remitted to the principal.

The agency relationship is a relationship of the utmost good faith, and the agent is obliged to always place the principal's interest above his own. To fulfil this duty, the agent must bring to the principal's attention any information which he receives that might affect the principal, and in any activity in which he engages on behalf of his principal, he must act only in the best interest of his employer. For example, he must endeavour to obtain the best price possible for goods which he sells for the principal, or if he is engaged to purchase goods, he must seek out the lowest price he can find in the market place. In both cases, he must act in the best interests of his principal rather than in his own, and seek the most favourable price, rather than the quickest commission.

An agent has a duty only to his principal, and not to any third party with whom he negotiates. He may not act for both parties without the express consent of his principal and the third party, and if he should obtain a commission or benefit from the third party without disclosing the fact to his principal, the agent would not be entitled to claim a commission from the principal.[4] For example, Newsome enters into an agency agreement with Wilson to sell his business, and agrees to pay Wilson a commission if he is successful. Wilson, without Newsome's knowledge or permission, enters into an agreement with Bray to find Bray, a business on the payment of a commission if he is successful. Wilson negotiates the sale of Newsome's business to Bray and collects a commission from both Newsome and Bray. In this case, there would be no enforceable commission contract, as Wilson would be liable to Newsome for the return of any commission paid for his actions. Similarly, if Newsome engaged Wilson to sell a quantity of goods for him, and Wilson sold the goods to Bray as if they were his own, and at a higher price than the price reported to Newsome, Newsome would be entitled to recover the secret profit made by Wilson in the transaction.[5]

---

[4]*S. E. Lyons Ltd. v. Arthur J. Lennox Contractors Ltd.,* [1956] O.W.N. 624; *Andrews v. Ramsay,* [1903] 2 K.B. 635; *McPherson v. Watt* (1877), 3 App. Cas. 254.
[5]*Fullwood v. Hurley,* [1928] 1 K.B. 498; *Industries & General Mortgage Co. v. Lewis,* [1949] 2 All. E.R. 573.

CASE 16.1

Andrews v. Ramsay & Co., [1903] 2 K.B. 635.

LORD ALVERSTONE, C.J.:

It seems to me that this case is only an instance of an agent who has acted improperly being unable to recover his commission from his principal. It is impossible to say what the result might have been if the agent in this case had acted honestly. It is clear that the purchaser was willing to give 20*l*. more than the price which the plaintiff received, and it may well be that he would have given more than that. It is impossible to gauge in any way what the plaintiff has lost by the improper conduct of the defendants. I think, therefore, that the interest of the agents here was adverse to that of the principal. A principal is entitled to have an honest agent, and it is only the honest agent who is entitled to any commission. In my opinion, if an agent directly or indirectly colludes with the other side, and so acts in opposition to the interest of his principal, he is not entitled to any commission. That is, I think, supported both by authority and on principle; but if, as is suggested, there is no authority directly bearing on the question, I think that the sooner such an authority is made the better.

Agency by Conduct

Agency may arise in ways other than by express agreement. A person may, by his actions, convey the impression to another that he has conferred authority on a particular person to act as his agent in specific matters, in which case, an agency relationship may be created by conduct. If a person permits this state of affairs to occur, and the agent enters into a contract with a third party on his behalf, he may not be permitted to later deny it. In this instance, he may be said to have created an agency relationship by *estoppel*. The authority of the agent under these circumstances would not be real, but apparent. The binding effect of the agent's actions, however, would be real if the principal led the third party to believe that the agent had the authority to act on his behalf.[6]

Agency by estoppel arises most often from a contractual relationship wherein the principal has adopted a contract negotiated by another, and as a result has given the third party the impression that the contract was one of agency. For example, a person may engage another to make cash purchases of goods on his behalf on a number of occasions. If the same person is engaged at some later time to purchase goods on credit without the authority of the person for whom they were intended, and that person adopts the contract by paying the account, the third party seller would be led to believe that the agent had the authority to pledge the principal's credit. This would be inferred from the principal's conduct of settling the account. Unless the principal makes it clear to the seller that the agent does not have authority to pledge his credit, he may be estopped from denying the agent's authority to pledge his credit in the future.[7] His action would in effect "clothe the agent with apparent authority" to act on his behalf.

There are other instances where apparent authority may exist apart from the situation where the conduct of the principal creates the agency relationship. A wife, for example, is presumed at common law to have the authority to purchase goods and services for household use as her husband's agent.[8] This particular presump-

---

[6]*Reid and Keast v. McKenzie Co.* (1921), 61 D.L.R. 95; *Agnew v. Davis* (1911), 17 W.L.R. 570.

[7]*Reid and Keast v. McKenzie Co.* (1921), 61 D.L.R. 95; *Agnew v. Davis* (1911), 17 W.L.R. 570.

[8]*Miss Gray Ltd. v. Earl Cathgart* (1922), 38 T.L.R. 562, but see also *Family Law Reform Act, 1978,* R.S.O. 1980, c. 152, s. 64.

tion at law arises out of cohabitation as a rebuttable presumption only, rather than a right at law. The presumption may be rebutted by the husband establishing that notice was given to the shopkeepers that they were not to supply goods on credit; that the wife was provided with an adequate cash allowance to make the purchases, and forbidden to purchase on credit; that the household was already adequately supplied with such goods, or possibly that the goods were extravagant, in light of the husband's station in life and income. However, if the wife had pledged the husband's credit previously, and if the accounts had been paid by the husband without giving notice to the shopkeepers that future purchases were not to be on credit, the husband may be bound by his conduct on his wife's future credit purchases.

Agency by conduct may result in liability for the principal if the principal fails to notify third parties that the agency relationship has terminated. Until such time as the third party becomes aware of the termination of the agency relationship, he is entitled to assume that the agency continues to exist, and that the agent has authority to bind the principal. Again, the authority of the agent would only be apparent, because the termination of the agency relationship would have the effect of ending the agent's real authority. The third party may, nevertheless, hold the principal liable on a contract negotiated by the agent on the basis of the agent's apparent authority.[9]

An agent may also possess the implied authority to bind the principal in circumstances where the agency agreement expressly withholds real authority to do so from the agent. If a principal engages an agent to perform a particular service for him, and agents performing such a service customarily have the authority to engage in other forms of contract on behalf of their principals, any restriction on the agent's authority must be brought to the attention of the third party, otherwise the principal may be bound if the agent should exceed his actual authority, and negotiate a contract within what may be described as his implied authority. For example, a retailer has the implied authority to sell goods placed in his possession. If a principal sends goods to a retailer on the express agreement that they must not be sold before a particular time, a sale by the retailer before that time would be binding on the principal, as a retailer is normally clothed with the authority to sell goods in his possession without restriction as to time of the sale.

||||||||||||||||||||||||||||||||||||||||||||||||||||||||||||||||||||||||||||||||||||||||||

CASE 16.2
Reed and Keast v. McKenzie Co., Ltd., [1921] 3 W.W.R. 72.

LAMONT, J.A.:

The defendants admit that they sent [the agent] out armed with the forms of the contracts actually entered into. They admit also that he had authority to get the plaintiffs to sign these contracts, and that he had authority to sign them on behalf of the defendants, subject to this, that he must stipulate that the contracts were not to come into effect until the company had approved of the samples. He represented to the plaintiffs that he had authority to enter into these contracts on behalf of the defendants. As evidence of that authority he produced the contract forms. He did not mention, as the trial Judge has found, the limitations on his authority which had been verbally given to him, but which did not appear on the forms.

·   ·   ·   ·   ·

---

[9]*Trueman v. Loder* (1840), Vol. 11, Ad. & El. 589, 113 E.R. 539.

The arming of the agent with the defendants' contract forms and the sending him out to have these forms executed by the plaintiffs was, in my opinion, a clear holding out by the defendants that he had their authority to make the contracts. The defendants were, therefore, bound by the contract entered into by Thompson, as the plaintiffs had no notice of the limitations which had been placed upon his authority.

||||||||||||||||||||||||||||||||||||||||||||||||||||||||||||||||||||||||||||||

Agency by Operation of Law

Agency may also arise by operation of law. In certain circumstances it may be necessary for a person to act as an agent (such as in an emergency) where it is impossible to obtain authority to perform the particular acts from the property owner. With modern day communications, the circumstances under which an agency of this nature may arise are limited, nevertheless, in an emergency certain persons may at common law act as *agents of necessity* on behalf of others, and bind them in contract. For example, a shipmaster at common law is presumed to have the power to bind the shipowner in contract in the event of an emergency if it is necessary to do so to preserve the ship and its cargo, though this right would only arise if the shipmaster is unable to communicate with the owner, and if it is necessary to do so to secure the safety of the ship. The same right at law would permit the shipmaster to sell or otherwise deal with the cargo in an emergency, even though no express authorization would be given by the owner of the cargo to do so.

A wife may also be an agent of necessity at common law. If a husband fails to maintain his family as he is required to do by law, then his wife may, as an agent of necessity, pledge his credit in order to purchase necessaries. In most provinces, special legislation has been passed which sets out a husband's obligation to support his family, but in some, recent family law changes have altered the common law obligation of a husband to support his wife and family, and in so doing, may have altered the common law right of a wife to act as an agent of necessity. At the present time, the trend in support obligation appears to spread the obligation over the entire family, rather than place the full burden on the husband. As a result of the recent legislation, the question is unclear as to whether the credit of one person may be pledged by an agent of necessity when the obligation rests on other members of the family as well.[10]

The common law limits the circumstances under which a person may act as an agent of necessity. The courts have recognized a number of instances where an agency of necessity may arise, such as in a true emergency, but the relationship is generally limited to those cases where a pre-existing legal relationship exists between the principal and the agent of necessity. In one case, a railway carrying perishable goods sold the goods to avoid total loss, because a labour strike prevented the railway from making delivery. The court in that instance ruled that the railway acted as an agent of necessity, since a true emergency existed, and the owner could not be reached for authority to act.[11]

However, the court will not normally find an agency of necessity where no pre-

---

[10]For example, in some jurisdictions, self-supporting children may be responsible for the maintenance of their parents, and both spouses may be jointly responsible for the support of each other and their dependent children: *Family Law Reform Act, 1978,* R.S.O. 1980, c. 152.

[11]*Sims & Co. v. Midland Railway Co.,* [1913] 1 K.B. 103. See also *Hastings v. Village of Semans,* [1946] 3 W.W.R. 449; *Campbell v. Newbolt* (1914), 20 D.L.R. 897.

existing relationship can be shown. In an old case where a man found a dog and maintained it until its master came to retrieve it, the court would not hold that the man was an agent of necessity and entitled to compensation for the expense of caring for the animal, because no pre-existing legal relationship could be shown between the agent and the owner.[12] The rationale of the court in reaching this conclusion was that no person should be entitled to force an obligation upon another unless express or implied consent has been given.

RATIFICATION OF CONTRACTS BY A PRINCIPAL

A principal may in certain circumstances wish to take advantage of a contract which an agent negotiated on his behalf, and which the agent clearly had no authority to make. The process of acceptance of a contract of this type is called *ratification*, and if properly done, it has the effect of binding the principal in contract with the third party as of the date it was negotiated by the agent.

A principal may ratify a contract if the principal was in existence at the time the contract was made by the agent, and was identified in the agreement as the principal. This particular rule generally applies to corporations rather than to individuals, since corporations have a particular time at which they come into existence. Unless the legislation under which corporation is created permits the adoption of pre-incorporation contracts,[13] the corporation may not ratify a contract made before it was created.

In addition, the subject-matter of the contract must be something which the principal would have been capable of doing at the time the contract was made by the agent, and at the time of ratification. Again, this rule would have direct application to corporations rather than individuals. Corporations in some jurisdictions are limited to the objects for which they are incorporated, and if the subject-matter of the contract should be something which the corporation is not permitted to do, the subsequent change of the objects clause (to permit the corporation to undertake a particular activity) would still not permit the corporation to ratify the contract unless statutory authority permitted the ratification.[14]

Ratification in every case must be made within a reasonable time after the agent enters into the contract, and the principal becomes aware of its existence. Effective ratification must be of the whole agreement, and not simply of the favourable parts. The ratification, however, need not be expressly stated, as it may be implied from the conduct of the principal. The principal, for example, may accept benefits under the contract, or perform the promises made on his behalf to signify his ratification. His silence would not normally constitute acceptance, but in circumstances where his agent has exceeded his authority in negotiating the contract, a refusal to promptly repudiate the agreement on becoming aware of it may imply acceptance.

In each case, ratification of the contract by the principal dates the time of accep-

---

[12]*Binstead v. Buck* (1776), 2 Black., W. 1117, 96 E.R. 660.

[13]See, for example, *Business Corporations Act*, R.S.O. 1980, c. 54, s. 20(2), and the *Canada Business Corporations Act*, 1974-75 (Can.), c. 33, s. 14(2).

[14]*McKay v. Tudhope Anderson Co., Ltd.,* (1919), **44** D.L.R. 100.

tance back to the date on which the contract was made. It does not run from the date of ratification. As a result of this rule, the actions of the third party may be altered by the subsequent ratification of the contract by the principal. The law on this particular point is unclear at the present time, but in an English case, the court held that repudiation by the third party, before ratification, was ineffective if the principal subsequently ratified.[15] However, this decision has been questioned in Canada, and reversed in the United States. The law in the United States presently seems to state that withdrawal from the agreement by the third party, or the institution of legal proceedings against the agent for breach of warranty of authority, would prevent later ratification of the agreement by the principal.[16] The position in Canada appears to fall somewhere between the two extremes, with some case-law suggesting that the principal may not ratify if the ratification would adversely affect parties other than the third party,[17] and others following the English law.[18]

||||||||||||||||||||||||||||||||||||||||||||||||||||||||||||||||||||||||

CASE 16.3

Bolton Partners v. Lambert (1889), 41 Ch.D. 295.

COTTON, L.J.:

The rule as to ratification by a principal of acts done by an assumed agent is that the ratifica-

---

[15]*Bolton Partners v. Lambert* (1889), 41 Ch. D. 295; *Pickles and Mills v. Western Ass'ce. Co.* (1902), 40 N.S.R. 327.

[16]See, for example, *LaSalle National Bank v. Brodsky*, 51 Ill. App. 2d 260, (1964). See also American Law Institute, *Restatement of the Law Second. Agency*, 2d., American Law Institute Publishers, St. Paul, Minn., 1958, Vol. 1, p. 226, § 88.

[17]*Goodison Thresher Co. v. Doyle* (1925), 57 O.L.R. 300; *Peterson v. Dominion Tobacco Co.* (1922), 52 O.L.R. 598.

[18]*Farrell & Sons v. Poupore Lumber Co.*, [1935] 4 D.L.R. 783.

tion is thrown back to the date of the act done, and that the agent is put in the same position as if he had had authority to do the act at the time the act was done by him. Various cases have been referred to as laying down this principle, but there is no case exactly like the present one. . . . The rule as to ratification is of course subject to some exceptions. An estate once vested cannot be divested, nor can an act lawful at the time of its performance be rendered unlawful, by the application of the doctrine of ratification.

||||||||||||||||||||||||||||||||||||||||||||||||||||||||||||||||||||||||

THIRD PARTIES AND THE AGENCY RELATIONSHIP

In an ordinary agency relationship between a principal, agent, and third party, the agent (if he negotiates a contract within the scope of his authority) will bind the principal. The performance of the contract will be by the principal and the third party. The agent must clearly indicate to the third party that he is acting only as an agent, and will usually identify the principal for whom he acts. This is normally done by the agent signing the principal's name on the agreement and adding his own, together with words to indicate that his signature is that of an agent only. For example, an agent may sign as follows: "Mary Smith per Jane Doe" where Mary Smith is the principal, and Jane Doe the agent. The use of the term *per* is a short form of *per procurationem* which means "on behalf of another," or in agency law, "by his agent." It is also possible to specifically state in the agreement that a party is only acting as agent for another; that is, John Doe may sign the contract as follows: "John Doe as agent for John Smith."

Where the agent has revealed to the third party that he is acting as an agent only, and acts in accordance with his authority, the principal alone is liable to the third party. The agent has no rights and duties under the contract with respect to the third party, nor may he claim any of the benefits which flow to the principal.

If the principal does not wish to have his identity revealed, and instructs the agent to enter into an agreement without revealing his identity, the agent may proceed in either of two ways: He may enter into the agreement in his own name, without revealing that he is acting as an agent, or he may enter into the agreement as agent for an unnamed principal.

Where the agent enters into an agreement without disclosing the fact that he is an agent, the third party may assume that the agent is acting as a principal. If the agreement is reduced to writing, and if the agent in the negotiations holds himself out as a principal describing himself and signing as principal, then the agreement from the third party's point of view will be one of direct contractual relations with a principal, rather than with an agent. The agent alone in this case would be liable.[19] Under these circumstances, the third party may look to the agent for damages if the contract is not performed, because the agent under the contract would be personally responsible for performance. The agent, by the same rule of law, would be entitled to enforce the agreement against the third party if the third party should fail to perform the agreement in accordance with its terms.

A different liability would fall on the agent if the agent contracts on behalf of a fictitious or non-existent principal, and the third party discovers the non-existence of the principal. He may sue the agent for breach of warranty of authority.[20] The same right would also be available to the third party if the agent entered into the agreement on behalf of a principal for whom he did not have authority to act.[21] In each of these cases, the agent would not be liable on the contract, but would be liable to the third party for damages arising from his warranty that he had authority to act for the named principal.[22] In the first instance, where the principal was fictitious or non-existent, if the intention of the agent was to deceive the third party, his actions would amount to fraud, and an action for deceit would be available to the third party as well.

In the case of an agreement negotiated by an agent (where the agent neither describes himself as a principal or agent), if the principal should decide to come forward and reveal his identity, he may enforce the contract, but if he should do so, the third party may then bring an action against him instead of the agent if a breach should occur. The third party, however, is restricted in this regard. He may sue either the principal or the agent, but not both.[23] A particular exception to this rule does exist with respect to a contract under seal in which the agent signs as a contracting party. In this case, only the agent may enforce the agreement, and only the agent would be liable under it.[24]

If the agent enters into a contract with a third party in which he expressly describes himself as an agent, but without disclosing the identity of his principal, the agent will not be personally liable. The fact that he describes himself as an agent, and that the third party is willing to enter into a con-

[19]*Lawson v. Kenny* (1957), 9 D.L.R. (2d) 714; *Collins v. Associated Greyhound Racecourses, Ltd.,* [1930] 1 Ch. 1.

[20]*Gardiner v. Martin and Blue Water Conference Inc.,* [1953] O.W.N. 881.

[21]*Wickberg v. Shatsky* (1969), 4 D.L.R. (3d) 540.

[22]*Austin v. Real Estate Listing Exchange* (1912), 2 D.L.R. 324.

[23]*M & M Insulation Ltd. v. Brown* (1967), 60 W.W.R. 115; *Phillips v. Lawson,* (1913) 4 O.W.N. 1364.

[24]*Pielsticker and Draper Dobie & Co. v. Gray,* [1947] O.W.N. 625.

tract with him on that basis protects the agent from personal liability. However, if the agent simply does not disclose that he is acting as an agent, and enters into a contract with the third party, the third party may elect to hold either the principal (if he discovers his identity) or the agent liable. Of importance, in the case of an undisclosed principal, is the position of the principal. If the principal makes his existence known after the contract has been made by an agent who did not disclose his existence, the principal may be in a position somewhat analogous to that of an assignee of a contract: he may take the agent's place, but in doing so, he would also be obliged to accept the relationship as it stands between the agent and the third party. If the third party had contracted in the belief that the agent was in fact a principal, then any defence that the third party might have had against the agent may be raised against the principal. For example, if Smith entered into a contract with Jones without disclosing that he was acting as an agent for Brown, and if Brown should come forward after the contract is made and sue on it when Jones defaults, any defence which Jones might have against Smith could be raised against Brown. If Smith owed Jones a sum of money, Jones might legitimately claim the right to deduct Smith's debt with him from any sum owing under the contract.[25]

||||||||||||||||||||||||||||||||||||||||||||||||||||||||||||||||||||||

CASE 16.4
Phillips v. Lawson, [1913] O.W.N. 1364.

THE MASTER:

The . . . defendants' motion is supported by reference to Anson on Contracts, 12th ed., pp. 382, 383, and Smethurst v. Mitchell (1859), 1 E. & E. 622. These authorities shew that

[25]*Campbellville Gravel Supply Ltd. v. Cook Paving Co.*, [1968] 2 O.R. 679.

"where an agent acts on behalf of a principal whose existence he does not disclose, the other contracting party is entitled to elect whether he will treat principal or agent as the party with whom he dealt:" Anson, p. 383. In Smethurst's case, it was said by Hill, J. (p. 630): "All the cases establish that a vendor selling to the agent of an undisclosed principal must elect to sue the principal within a reasonable time after he discovers him." Crompton, J., at p. 631, says: "The election to sue an undisclosed principal must be made within a reasonable time after he is discovered."

It was argued by Mr. MacGregor that there was here no case for election. His view was, that the plaintiff was suing only in respect of one bargain; that he was doubtful against whom his proper remedy was to be taken. He relied on Tate v. Natural Gas and Oil Co. of Ontario (1898), 18 P.R. 82. But that case is different in its facts. There is here no uncertainty as to the party liable. Both are liable if a definite bargain was made to buy the land in question. But this is not a joint but a separate liability, and the plaintiff must declare against which one he is proceeding . . .

||||||||||||||||||||||||||||||||||||||||||||||||||||||||||||||||||||||

LIABILITY OF PRINCIPAL AND AGENT TO THIRD PARTIES IN TORT

The general rule in agency law is that a principal may be held liable for a tort committed by his agent, if the tort is committed by the agent in the ordinary course of carrying out the agency agreement. A tort which an agent might commit is sometimes based upon fraudulent misrepresentation, and constitutes the tort deceit. If a third party should be induced to enter into a contract by an agent as a result of a fraud on the part of the agent, then both principal and agent will be liable if the tort was committed in the ordinary course of the agent's employment. However, if the tort is committed outside the scope of the agent's employment, only the agent will be liable. Also, the principal will not be liable for damages for a failure to perform such an agreement, unless he adopts the contract or accepts benefits under it.

If a third party is induced to enter into a contract on the basis of a false statement which the agent innocently makes, the third party may repudiate the contract on the basis of innocent misrepresentation. Similarly, if the third party is in a position to prove that the principal knew the statement was false, but allowed the agent to innocently convey it to the third party, the principal may be liable for fraud.[26]

TERMINATION OF THE PRINCIPAL–AGENT RELATIONSHIP

In many cases, agency relationships created by express agreement also provide for termination. If the agreement specifies that either party may terminate the agency relationship by giving the other party a particular period of notice and, if such notice is given, the agency will then terminate on the expiry of the notice period. As the right to terminate may be implied in the agreement where if no specific time for termination is fixed in it, either party may give notice to end the relationship. An agency may also terminate in other ways. Agency agreements may be made for the purpose of accomplishing a particular task. When the task is complete, the agency relationship will automatically terminate. For example, Baxter may own a quantity of wood, and engage Dawe to sell it as his agent. Once the wood is sold, the task is complete, and the agency ends.

The incapacity of the principal or of the agent (by way either of death or insanity) has the effect of terminating the relationship, but the general legal incapacity of an agent or principal if the agent or principal is a minor, may not. As with infant's contracts in general, in some jurisdictions the agency contract in which one party is a minor may only be voidable at the option of the infant or minor.

The bankruptcy of the principal terminates the agency agreement, and the principal would not be bound by any agreement negotiated by the agent after the point when the bankruptcy took place. The agent is expected to be in constant touch with the principal, and therefore aware of the principal's financial state. Consequently, a contract negotiated by an agent after the principal becomes bankrupt may render the agent liable to the third party for damages for breach of warranty of authority.

In all cases where the agency relationship is for more than a specific task, it is of the utmost importance that the principal inform all third parties that had dealings with the agent that the agency has been terminated. If the principal fails to notify the third parties of the termination of the agency, the agent may still bind the principal in contract on the basis of his apparent authority. For example, for many years Joliet, as Alford's agent, purchased goods on Alford's credit from Claude. Alford terminated the agency relationship but did not notify Claude. Joliet later purchased goods from Claude on Alford's credit and sold them. Alford would be liable to Claude for the payment as Joliet had the apparent authority to purchase goods as his agent in the absence of notice to the contrary.[27]

---

[26]*Campbell Motors Ltd. v. Watson (Crescent Motors),* [1949] 2 W.W.R. 478.

[27]*Consolidated Motors Ltd. v. Wagner* (1967), 63 D.L.R. (2d) 266; *Watson v. Powell* (1921), 58 D.L.R. 615.

||||||||||||||||||||||||||||||||||||||||||||||||||||||||||||||||||||||||||||||||||||||||||||||||||||||||||||||||||||||||||||

SUMMARY The law of agency is concerned with the relationship that exists when one person either expressly or impliedly uses the services of another to carry out a specific task on his behalf. This relationship may be created by express agreement, through conduct, or by necessity. If the agent has negotiated a contract on behalf of the principal within the scope of his authority, only the principal and the third party will be bound by the contract. An infant may be an agent and still bind the principal if the principal is of full age, but for a contract negotiated on behalf of an infant, the infant principal would not be bound except for necessaries. If an agent should negotiate a contract on behalf of a principal without the authority to do so, it may be possible for the principal to ratify the agreement, and by ratification, the contract would be effective from the date it was entered into by the agent.

Ordinarily, if a contract is negotiated by an agent within the scope of his authority, only the principal will be liable on the agreement, and entitled to enforce the rights under it. However, if the agent negotiated a contract on behalf of a fictitious or non-existent principal, the agent would be liable to the third party on the basis of breach of warranty of authority. Similarly, if the agent negotiated an agreement on behalf of a principal, and had no express or apparent authority to do so, the agent, and not the principal, would be liable. In cases where the agent did not disclose the identity or existence of the principal to the third party, depending upon the circumstances, the third party may elect to hold one or the other liable. If a fraud is involved in the contract negotiated, both the principal and agent may be liable, provided that the agent acted within the scope of his employment.

Agency may be terminated on the death or insanity of either the principal or the agent, and also in the case of bankruptcy of the principal. It may automatically end on the completion of the task for which it was formed, or by notice, either as specified in the agreement, or at any time, if no notice period is required. Where an agency agreement is terminated (other than by death, insanity or bankruptcy) notice to third parties is important, otherwise the agent may still bind the principal in contract with an unsuspecting third party.

||||||||||||||||| |||||||||||||||||||||||||||||||||||||||||||||||||||||||||||||||||||||||||||||||||||||||||||||||||||||||||||

DISCUSSION 1. Define "agency."
QUESTIONS 2. What historical events led to the rise of the use of agents?
3. What is the most common use of an agent?
4. What distinguishes an "agent" from an "employee"? Is there a distinction in some cases?
5. For a relationship of agency by necessity to exist, what key factor must be present?

6. *Why are cases of agency by necessity so rarely encountered today?*

7. *How may liability of the principal arise in an agency created by conduct?*

8. *Define ratification.*

9. *"This agency business isn't fair; if the agent is terminated the principal can wiggle out of any further contracts, or take advantage of them if he benefits!" Does a fallacy exist here?*

√ 10. Define per procurationem. *What is its use?*

√ 11. *Under what circumstances would an agent acting for an unnamed principal be personally liable to the third party?*

√ 12. *What general rule of agency law applies in the case of a tort committed by an agent?*

13. *Describe the conditions under which the automatic termination of an agency agreement would take place.*

14. *An agent acting for an undisclosed principal enters into a contract under seal. Can the principal come forward and enforce the contract? Would your answer be any different if the contract was not under seal?*

JUDICIAL DECISIONS

Undisclosed Principal— Agreement Under Seal Between Agent and Third Party—Right of Principal

Pielsticker and Draper Dobie & Co. v. Gray, [1947] O.W.N. 625.

LAIDLAW, J.A.:

The appellant agreed with the respondent Pielsticker to sell to him 50,000 shares of capital stock of Bear Exploration and Radium Limited (hereinafter, for convenience, referred to as "Bear" shares) and to give him an option upon certain terms and conditions to buy 300,000 additional shares divided into lots of 50,000 shares each. It was further understood and agreed that a contract in writing should be prepared showing the parties to the transaction to be the appellant and Draper Dobie and Company. Draper Dobie and Company consented to the use of its name. A contract in that form, bearing date 7th January 1944, without mention of Pielsticker or his interest therein, was executed under seal by both parties. The appellant delivered a total of 300,000 of these shares in January and February 1944, but then refused to deliver any more. The respondents claim that the option to buy the undelivered balance of 50,000 shares was properly exercised and that the appellant is bound in law to deliver them.

Counsel for the appellant argues that the respondent Pielsticker cannot sue on the contract because it is under seal and he is not named or described therein. It is, of course, a well-known principle of law that an undisclosed principal may sue or be sued on a contract, although the contract has been made in the name of another person who was the agent of the undisclosed principal. That principle is subject to the limitation that an undisclosed principal cannot sue or be sued on the contract if to do so would be to violate a term of the written contract. . . . The principle stated is not applicable to deeds. "When a deed is executed by an agent as such but purports to be a deed of the agent and not of the principal, then the principal cannot sue or be sued upon it at law, by reason of the technical rule that those persons only can sue or be sued upon an indenture who are named or described in it as parties": Pollock on Contracts, 12th ed. 1946, p. 81, referring to *Lord Southampton et al. v. Brown* (1827), 6 B. & C. 718; *Beckham v. Drake* (1841), 9 M. & W. 79, affirmed 11 M. & W. 315; Parke B. in *Beckham v. Drake, supra*, refers to the mistake "in applying to contracts which are, point of law, parol, although reduced into writing, the doctrine which is applicable exclusively to deeds, regularly framed instruments between certain parties." He states: "Those parties only can sue or be sued upon an indenture, who are named in it as parties; but this doctrine is applicable to deeds only, and I was not aware of any opinion being entertained, before this case occurred, that the same rule extended to all written contracts."

In *Montgomerie et al. v. United Kingdom Mutual Steamship Association, Limited*, [1891] 1 Q.B. 370 at 371, Wright J. says:

"There is no doubt whatever as to the general rule as regards an agent, that where a person contracts as agent for a principal the contract is the contract of the principal, and not that of the agent; and, prima facie, at common law the only person who may sue is the principal, and the only person who can be sued is the principal. To that rule there are, of course, many exceptions . . . the principal may be excluded in several . . . cases. He may be excluded if the contract is made by a deed inter partes, to which the principal is no party. In that case, by ancient rule of common law, it does not matter whether the person made a party is or is not an agent."

In *Porter v. Pelton and Holden* (1903), 33 S.C.R. 449, Nesbitt J., at p. 455, refers to *Beckham v. Drake, supra*, and *In re International Contract Company; Pickering's claim* (1871), L.R. 6 Ch. 525. In reference to the argument that an undisclosed principal is bound by a sealed instrument signed on his behalf, and the further argument that the parties signing the instrument did so for the benefit and on behalf of the undisclosed principal, he states: "The cases for over a century establish the rule of law firmly that where partners contract under seal they are bound by the form of the instrument, and where parties so signing are merely acting as agents and are so described, only the parties signing can be bound. A principal or partner cannot be bound unless he has given authority for his signature under seal, and is designated as a party to the deed. A cestui que trust cannot either sue or be sued upon a covenant made by and in the name of a trustee on his behalf." *Porter v. Pelton and Holden, supra*, was followed in *Winnett v. Heard*, 62 O.L.R. 61, [1928] 2 D.L.R. 594.

I am bound by the authorities to which I have referred to hold that the respondent Pielsticker cannot maintain an action to enforce the contract in question.

Apparent Authority of Agent— Liability of Principal	**Freeman & Lockyer v. Buckhurst Park Properties (Mangal) Ltd. et al.,** [1964] 2 Q.B. 480. K, a director of the defendant company, engaged the plaintiffs to do certain professional work on behalf of the company. The plaintiffs completed the work and submitted an account for their fees. When the company failed to pay, legal action was instituted to collect the account. The defendants argued that the director K was not a managing director (the firm did not have one), and therefore he did not have authority to bind the company.

DIPLOCK, L.J.:

It is necessary at the outset to distinguish between an "actual" authority of an agent on the one hand, and an "apparent" or "ostensible" authority on the other. Actual authority and apparent authority are quite independent of one another. Generally they co-exist and coincide, but either may exist without the other and their respective scopes may be different. As I shall endeavour to show, it is upon the apparent authority of the agent that the contractor normally relies in the ordinary course of business when entering into contracts.

An "actual" authority is a legal relationship between principal and agent created by a consensual agreement to which they alone are parties. Its scope is to be ascertained by applying ordinary principles of construction of contracts, including any proper implications from the express words used, the usages of the trade, or the course of business between the parties. To this agreement the contractor is a stranger; he may be totally ignorant of the existence of any authority on the part of the agent. Nevertheless, if the agent does enter into a contract pursuant to the "actual" authority, it does create contractual rights and liabilities between the principal and the contractor. It may be that this rule relating to "undisclosed principals," which is peculiar to English law, can be rationalised as avoiding circuity of action, for the principal could in equity compel the agent to lend his name in an action to enforce the contract against the contractor, and would at common law be liable to indemnify the agent in respect of the performance of the obligations assumed by the agent under the contract.

An "apparent" or "ostensible" authority, on the other hand, is a legal relationship between the principal and the contractor created by a representation, made by the principal to the contractor, intended to be and in fact acted upon by the contractor, that the agent has authority to enter on behalf of the principal into a contract of a kind within the scope of the "apparent" authority, so as to render the principal liable to perform any obligations imposed upon him by such contract. To the relationship so created the agent is a stranger. He need not be (although he generally is) aware of the existence of the representation but he must not purport to make the agreement as principal himself. The representation, when acted upon by the contractor by entering into a contract with the agent, operates as an estoppel, preventing the principal from asserting that he is not bound by the contract. It is irrelevant whether the agent had actual authority to enter into the contract.

In ordinary business dealings the contractor at the time of entering into the contract can in the nature of things hardly ever rely on the "actual" authority of the agent. His information as to the authority must be derived either from the principal or from the agent or from both, for they alone know what the agent's actual authority is. All that the contractor can know is what they tell him, which may or may not be true. In the ultimate analysis he relies either upon the representation of the principal, that is, apparent authority, or upon the representation of the agent, that is, warranty of authority.

The representation which creates "apparent" authority may take a variety of forms of which the commonest is representation by conduct, that is, by permitting the agent to act in some way in the conduct of the principal's business with other persons. By so doing the principal represents to anyone who becomes aware that the agent is so acting that the agent has authority to enter on behalf of the principal into contracts with other persons of the kind which an agent so acting in the conduct of his principal's business has usually "actual" authority to enter into.

|||||||||||||||||||||||||||||||||||||||||||||||||||||||||||||||||||||||||||||||||||||||||||||||||||||||||||||||||||||||||||||||||||||||||||||||||||||||||||||||||||||||||||||||||||||||||||||||

Agency— Fiduciary Relationship— Accountability for Secret Profit by Agent

McNeel and McNeel v. Low, Low & Renfrew Realty Ltd. (1962), 35 D.L.R. (2d) 226.

A corporate real estate agent employed Low as a salesman. The appellants listed their property for sale with the agent for $78 000. The salesman found an offeror willing to purchase the property for the listed price, but the offeror could not raise sufficient funds. The salesman and the offeror then entered into an agreement to purchase the property from the appellants for $70 000 under an arrangement which allowed the salesman to make a secret profit of $8 000.

When the appellants discovered the true facts, they brought an action for recovery of the secret profit.

TYSOE, J.A.:

There are innumerable kinds of fiduciary relationships and they exist in innumerable forms. They may arise from specific contract but they may and often do arise out of acts or relationship creating a duty. In the circumstances existing here, Low was in a fiduciary position in relation to the appellants. Renfrew Realty Ltd. being a limited company, the exigencies rendered it necessary that its duties to the appellants be performed by and through the instrumentality of some person selected by it. In undertaking those duties, Low placed himself in a position of fiduciary relationship to the appellants. There rested upon him the same fiduciary obligations and responsibilities and duties to the appellants as rested upon the limited company. In this respect he was in the same position as he would have been had he himself been appointed the appellants' agent. The principles of equity do not allow him to do for himself that which the limited company could not do for itself.

In *Regal (Hastings), Ltd. v. Gulliver et al.* [1942] 1 All E.R. 378, Viscount Sankey at p. 381 said:

"In my view, the respondents were in a fiduciary position and their liability to account does not depend upon proof of *mala fides*. The general rule of equity is that no one who has duties of a fiduciary nature to perform is allowed to enter into engagements in which he has or can have a personal interest conflicting with the interests of those whom he is bound to protect."

In the same case Lord Wright at p. 392 said:

"My Lords, of the six respondents, two, Gulliver and Garton, stand on a different footing from the other four. It is in regard to the latter that the important question of principle brought into issue by the decisions of WROTTESLEY, J., and the Court of Appeal call for determination. That question can be briefly stated to be whether an agent, a director, a trustee or other person in an analogous fiduciary position, when a demand is made upon him by the person to whom he stands in the fiduciary relationship to account for profits acquired by him by reason of his fiduciary position, and by reason of the opportunity and the knowledge, or either, resulting from it, is entitled to defeat the claim upon any ground save that he made profits with the knowledge and assent of the other person. The most usual and typical case of this nature is that of principal and agent. The rule in such cases is compendiously expressed to be that an agent must account for net profits secretly (that is, without the knowledge of his principal) acquired by him in the course of his agency. The authorities show how manifold and various are the applications of the rule. It does not depend on fraud or corruption."

. . . . . .

In *Charles Baker Ltd. v. Baker & Baker*, [1954] 3 D.L.R. 432, [1954] O.R. 418, Mackay, J.A., delivering the judgment of the Court, at p. 440 D.L.R., p. 432 O.R. said:

"The onus is upon the agent to prove that the transaction was entered into after full and fair disclosure of all material circumstances and of everything known to him respecting the subject-matter of the contract which would be likely to influence the conduct of his principal. The burden of proof that the transaction was a righteous one rests upon the agent, who is bound to produce clear affirmative proof that the parties were at arm's length, that the principal had the fullest information upon all material facts, and that having this information he agreed to adopt what was done."

That these statements are correct statements of the law, there can be no doubt.

In *Dunne v. English* (1874), L.R. 18 Eq. 524, Sir G. Jessel, M.R., said at p. 533:

"It is not enough for an agent to tell the principal that he is going to have an interest in the purchase, or to have a part in the purchase. He must tell him all the material facts. He must make a full disclosure."
And at pp. 534-5:
"I will only read a few words from another well-known case, *Lowther* v. *Lowther* (13 Ves. 95, 102), in which Lord *Erskine*, then Lord Chancellor, states the doctrine as Lord *Eldon* had laid it down: 'Considering the Defendant *Bryan* as an agent, the principle upon which a Court of Equity acts in cases of this kind is very properly admitted; having been settled in many instances, particularly in the time of Lord *Eldon*; resting upon grounds connected with the clearest principles of equity and the general security of contracts, viz., that an agent to sell shall not convert himself into a purchaser, unless he can make it perfectly clear that he furnished his employer with all the knowledge which he himself possessed.' So that the older authorities and the modern authorities agree.

"Now, what is the meaning of 'knowledge which he himself possessed'—'full disclosure of all that he knows?' Is it sufficient to say that he has an interest? Is it sufficient to put a principal on inquiry? Clearly not. Upon that point I have before me the case of *Imperial Mercantile Credit Association* v. *Coleman* (L.R. 6 H.L. 189, 194). There is a passage in the argument of the counsel for the Appellants which, I think, very fairly and properly states the law: 'It is not enough to say that the directors were sufficiently informed to be put upon inquiry. They ought in such a case to have the fullest information given to them, and ought not to be driven to inquiry;' for which two cases are cited: *Fawcett* v. *Whitehouse* (1 Russ. & My. 132) and *Hichens* v. *Congreve* (1 Russ. & My. 150, n.). I take it that is a correct statement of the law."

Low was clearly in breach of his duty to the appellants.

CASE PROBLEMS FOR DISCUSSION

Case 1

A property owner listed his property for sale and provided the agent with authority to sell the property on his behalf if the terms of any offer received met the terms set out in the listing agreement. A prospective buyer inspected the property during the period of time that the property was listed for sale, but did not make an offer to purchase.

After the agency agreement had expired, the prospective buyer made an offer to purchase the property that corresponded with the terms of the listing agreement, and the agent accepted the offer on behalf of the property owner.

When the buyer discovered that the agency agreement had expired, he brought an action against the agent.

Explain the nature of the buyer's action, and indicate how the case may be decided. Could the property owner ratify the agreement? What factors would affect the ratification?

Case 2

Shylock Motors, an automobile dealer, engaged Simple as its agent to sell its automobiles in a nearby city. In November, 1980, Hyde agreed to purchase a new 1981 model through Simple, with delivery to be made in May, 1981. The order was duly placed with Shylock Motors, and a vehicle delivered to Simple in April, 1981.

Simple recognized the vehicle as a 1980 model, but urged Hyde to complete the sale in April rather than May, as the automobile was ready for delivery. Hyde did so, but a few weeks later discovered that the vehicle was a 1980 model, and not a 1981 model, as he had ordered.

Hyde brought an action against Simple for damages, then brought a second action against Shylock Motors.

Explain the nature of Hyde's claim against Simple and Shylock Motors. What problem does the second action raise? On what basis will the litigation likely be resolved?

Case 3

Smith was interested in the purchase of the shares of a manufacturing firm that was in financial difficulties due to a high debt load. He contacted Jones, a business consultant, to provide him with an assessment of the firm, and to negotiate the purchase on his behalf if his investigation indicated that the purchase of the shares represented a good investment.

Jones suggested that Brown, a consulting engineer, be engaged to assess the condition and value of the manufacturing equipment, and to provide some advice on what might be done to improve the profitability of the operation. Smith agreed, and Jones and Brown proceeded with their assessment of the firm.

During their examination, Jones and Brown realized that the firm represented a good investment if the equity to debt ratio could be altered and some manufacturing processes changed to improve efficiency. The two then established a corporation, and indicated to the present owners of the manufacturing firm (whom they had met through Smith) that they also represented a corporation that might be interested in the purchase if Smith should decide against the investment.

Jones and Brown completed their assessment of the business which in their written opinion to Smith was worth approximately $1.1 million. They submitted accounts of $3 000 and $3 500 respectively, which Smith promptly paid.

A few days later, Smith presented the owners of the manufacturing firm with an offer to purchase the shares for $1 million. The offer was promptly rejected, and before Smith could submit a new offer, the corporation that Jones and Brown had incorporated made an offer of $1.1 million for the business. The second offer was accepted, and the shares transferred to the corporation for the $1.1 million.

When Smith discovered that Jones and Brown were the principal shareholders of the corporation that had made the $1.1 million offer, he brought an action against them for damages.

Describe the nature of Smith's action, and discuss the possible arguments that might be raised by both the plaintiff and the defendants. Identify the main issues, and render a decision.

Case 4

Chesley engaged Kent to act as his agent in the sale of 3 000 live rabbits. Without disclosing the fact that he was only an agent, Kent offered the rabbits to Somerset at $1 each. Somerset agreed to purchase the lot, but at the conclusion of the discussion, reminded Kent that he owed him $500. Kent responded "when this sale is completed you will get your $500."

Kent informed Chelsey of the sale, and Chelsey delivered the rabbits to Somerset's farm where he informed him that he was delivering the rabbits in accordance with the sale that Kent had negotiated on his behalf.

Somerset agreed to take delivery, and offered his cheque in the amount of $2 500. Chelsey demanded the full $3 000, and threatened to sue Somerset if he did not pay the purchase price in full.

Advise Chelsey and Somerset in this case, and offer a possible outcome if Chelsey should carry out his intention to institute legal proceedings against Somerset.

Case 5

Johnson used Birkett as his stockbroker for most of his investments. Occasionally, when Johnson had spare funds, he would seek the advice of Birkett as to investments he should make. On one such occasion, Birkett recommended two companies as investments with potential for profit. At the time, Birkett indicated that he personally preferred stock "B" over stock "A" and intended to purchase some shares on his own account. Johnson ignored his advice, however, and purchased stock "A."

During the next few weeks, stock "A" dropped in value as a result of unexpected political upheaval in a Third World country where the company had extensive holdings. Stock "B," on the other hand, gradually increased in value during the same period until it reached a price approximately 20% above its value when Birkett recommended it as a possible investment.

Johnson discussed his investment with Birkett, and Birkett suggested he sell stock "A." Johnson did so, and requested Birkett to invest the proceeds in stock "B." Birkett cautioned Johnson that the stock had already climbed in price, and might not be as attractive an investment as it was some weeks earlier. Johnson, nevertheless, insisted that he buy the shares. Birkett then transferred some of his own shares to Johnson at the current market price, without disclosing the fact to Johnson.

The shares almost immediately declined in value for reasons unknown to both Johnson and Birkett.

A month later, Johnson discovered that the shares which he had acquired had been transferred to him by Birkett. He immediately brought an action against Birkett for the amount of his loss.

Explain the nature of the claim which Johnson might make against Birkett, and indicate how the case might be decided.

CHAPTER 17

Law of Partnership

HISTORICAL DEVELOPMENT

A partnership is a relationship which subsists between two or more persons carrying on business in common with a view to profit.[1] This definition represents a narrower delineation of the relationship than most persons might realize, as it excludes all associations and organizations which are not carried on for profit. Social clubs, charitable organizations, and amateur sports groups are not partnerships within the meaning of the law, and many business relationships are excluded as well. For example, the simple debtor–creditor relationship and the ordinary joint ownership of property do not fall within its ambit.

The partnership is an ancient form of organization, and undoubtedly one which existed long before the advent of the written word and recorded history. The first

[1] The *Partnerships Act*, R.S.O. 1980, c. 370, s. 2. All common law provinces have similar legislation relating to partnership. Quebec partnership law is found in the *Civil Code*.

associations had their roots in early trading ventures, where merchants banded together for mutual protection from thieves and vandals. The natural extension of these loose associations was for the merchants to join together in the trading itself, and to share the fortunes of the ventures. The partnership form of organization has been used by merchants for thousands of years. Reference to early partnerships are found both in biblical writings[2] and in early Roman history. These sources indicate that partnerships were frequently used for many commercial activities.

The partnership had developed by the time of the Roman Empire into a common form of business organization, and was subject to a number of different rules of law. The earliest partnerships tended to be joint ventures by merchants engaged in the purchase or sale of goods in distant places, or by merchants banding together to undertake an activity which required more capital than one merchant alone was prepared to risk or invest. These early associations were often informal, and were based upon mutual trust and confidence between the partners—two characteristics of the relationship which have remained as essential elements of the modern form of organization.

In England, the feudal system discouraged the development of all forms of organization more durable than the partnership,[3] and as a result, the partnership

became the dominant form of business organization throughout the feudal period. Even after the feudal system fell into disfavour, the partnership served the needs of the business community adequately, because large amounts of capital were seldom necessary for the type of trade and industry carried on at that time.

It was not until the discovery of distant markets and the New World in the 15th and 16th centuries that the capital requirements of the merchants demanded an alteration of the ordinary partnership organization. To meet these needs, the *société en commandite* was developed in Continental Europe. This form of organization allowed the contribution of capital by investors and a share of the profits from the venture, although no rights to actively participate in the management of the organization were attached to the investment. As a result, the investors were given limited liability for the debts of the organization. The concept in a modified version found favour in England in the 16th century in the form of the joint stock company. This organization was essentially a partnership in which the investors, as partners, delegated the authority to manage the organization to a board of management, but, unlike the European *société en commandite*, unlimited liability of the individual partners remained.

Joint stock companies were generally divided into two types: companies organized for foreign trading which operated under Royal Charters, and domestic trading companies which were essentially large partnerships characterized by delegated authority to manage. Joint stock companies which operated under Royal Charter occasionally had limited liability, but most did not. Domestic trading com-

---

[2]Ecclesiastes 4:9-10 (about 977 B.C.).
[3]The rights of the feudal lord to land were to some extent based upon the demise of tenants, and in addition, the acquisition of land by the Church was a matter of concern. Statutes controlling the holding of land by organizations that were corporate in nature were passed as early as 1279 in England.

panies on the other hand, almost without exception, were similar to the ordinary partnership insofar as the liability of the stockholders was concerned.

The joint stock company permitted the organizations to amass large amounts of capital, but the form of organization was unsatisfactory from the investors' point of view. Investors had no control over the board of management, and bad management rendered the investors vulnerable to the claims of creditors if the organization became insolvent.

A number of spectacular business failures in the 17th and 18th centuries brought the joint stock company form of organization into disrepute, but the partnership in its usual form continued as the principal form of domestic business organization until the middle of the 19th century.

Initially, the English courts had difficulty resolving disputes relating to partnerships. The common law courts presented an unsatisfactory forum for partnership cases, and as a result, the Chancery Court was most often used by litigants. The nature of the association was such that the court procedures and equitable remedies of Chancery were more suitable than those of the common law courts. In particular, two special advantages of Chancery—the opportunity for the parties to be heard, and the power of the court to order an accounting in the settlement—were often of the utmost importance to the litigants. Therefore, Chancery established many of the precedents which later determined the legal nature of the relationship and the rules relating to its operation.

In the early decisions, the partnership was identified as a relationship of utmost good faith. Within the organization, each partner was entitled to participate in its management, and each partner bore responsibility for its debts. But many issues remained confusing and contradictory in the determination of the nature of the organization. The issue of whether the partnership was an entity separate from its members, or simply the aggregation of individuals was never finally resolved until the 19th century.

By the late 18th century the courts began to examine the partnership and its activities in the light of contract law. The expansion of trade, both domestic and foreign, during this period and throughout the 19th century increased the use of partnerships as a form of business organization, until the inevitable litigation associated with such a large number of entities produced a large body of law concerning the relationship. By the latter part of the 19th century, the law had reached a stage of maturity where codification was both possible and desirable.

In 1879, Sir Frederick Pollock was requested to prepare a draft bill for the English Parliament which would codify the law of partnership. A second directive was to outline a mechanism for the formation and regulation of a form of limited liability organization similar to that of the European *société en commandite*. A third directive was to determine a system for the registration of partnerships. The bill was duly prepared, and presented, but did not come before Parliament until 10 years later. During that interval, the system for registration was dropped.

The rapid rise of the corporation was seen as a more logical development for larger organizations than the limited liability *société en commandite*. It too, was dropped from the draft bill, and the bill alone, which was eventually passed in

1890, became the codification of partnership law.

The Act was carefully drawn to reflect the common law at the time and, as a part of legislation, retained the rules of equity and common law relating to partnerships, except where the rules were inconsistent with the express provisions of the Act.[4]

Since the *Partnership Act* was passed in England, it has been adopted with some minor modifications in all of the common law provinces of Canada and in many other countries which have remained in the British Commonwealth. Partnership legislation permits the formation of partnerships for all commercial enterprises, except for a number of activities such as banking and insurance, where the corporate form (and special legislation) is necessary. By definition, a partnership must consist of at least two persons, and while some provinces restrict the number of partners to a specific maximum,[5] no limit is imposed in most.

NATURE OF A PARTNERSHIP

The essential characteristic of the partnership is that it is a relationship which subsists between persons carrying on business in common with a view to profit.

The partnership, however, must be distinguished from other relationships such as joint or part ownership of property,

profit-sharing schemes, the loan of money, and the sharing of gross receipts from a venture, as the foregoing associations in themselves do not constitute partnerships.[6] The existence of a partnership turns very much on the particular agreement made between the parties, but as a general rule, the sharing of the net profits of a business is *prima facie* evidence of the existence of a partnership.[7] In contrast, the remuneration of a servant or agent by a share of the profits of the business, would normally not give rise to a partnership,[8] nor would the receipt of a share of profits by the widow or child of a deceased partner.[9]

There must usually be something more than simply sharing gross profits before a partnership agreement exists. If the parties have each contributed capital, and have each actively participated in the management of the business, then these actions would be indicative of the existence of a partnership. Even then, if the "business" simply represents the ownership of a block of leased land or perhaps a rental building on the land, the relationship may not be a partnership. It may, instead, be co-ownership of land; that is, a relationship which closely resembles a partnership, but which is treated in a different manner at law. Co-ownership, when examined carefully and compared to a partnership, is a distinct and separate relationship. The principal differences between the two may be outlined as follows:

—A partnership is a contractual relationship. Co-ownership may arise in several ways; it may arise through success-

---

[4]The *Partnerships Act*, R.S.O. 1970, c. 339, s. 45. Reference in this chapter will be made to specific sections of the Ontario Act, but most other provincial statutes are similar.

[5]Newfoundland limits the number of partners to 10. Alberta, British Columbia, and Saskatchewan fix the number at 20, but British Columbia permits the number to go as high as 35 with special permission. All other common law provinces have no limit on the number.

[6]The *Partnerships Act*, R.S.O. 1980, c. 370, s. 3.
[7]*Ibid.*, s. 3(*a*).
[8]*Ibid.*, s. 3(*b*).
[9]*Ibid.*, s. 3(*c*).

ion, or through the inheritance of property from a deceased co-owner.

—A partnership is a relationship which is founded on mutual trust. It is a personal relationship which is not freely alienable. Co-ownership, on the other hand, may be freely alienable without the consent of the other co-owner. For example, Alexander and Bradley may jointly own a block of land, Alexander may sell his interest to Calvin without Bradley's consent, and Bradley and Calvin will then become co-owners. This is not possible in the case of partnership.

—A partner is generally an agent of all other partners in the conduct of partnership business. A co-owner is normally not an agent of other co-owners.

—A partner's share in partnership property is never real property; it is always personalty, as it is a share in the assets, which can only be determined (unless there is an agreement to the contrary) by the liquidation of all partnership property. In contrast, co-ownership may be of either personalty or realty. Two persons as co-owners, for example, may purchase an automobile, or they may purchase a parcel of land. In each instance they would be co-owners of the property, but they would not be partners in the absence of an agreement to the contrary.

—A partnership is subject to the *Partnership Act* in its operation, and dissolution is by the Act. Co-ownership may be dissolved or terminated under legislation which provides for the division or disposition of property held jointly.[10]

A partnership may, in a sense, be established from the point of view of, and for purposes of, third parties by *estoppel*. If a person holds himself out as being a partner, either by words for conduct, or permits himself to be held out as a partner of the firm, that person may be liable as a partner if a third party, on the strength of the representation, advances credit to the firm. This would apply even where the representation or holding out is not made directly to the person advancing the credit.[11] For example, if Oxford, an employee of a partnership, holds himself out as a partner, and Baker, a merchant, sells goods on credit to the partnership on the faith of Oxford's representation, Oxford will be liable to Baker as if he was a partner. The same would hold true if the partnership held out Oxford as a partner and he permitted them to do so, even though he was only an employee. By allowing the firm to hold him out as a partner, he would become liable as if he was a partner for any debts where the creditor advanced money in the belief that he was a partner.

All persons with capacity to enter into contracts have the capacity to become partners. An infant or minor may become a partner, but if he should do so, the ordinary rules of contract apply. The contract is voidable at his option, and since it is deemed to be a continuing relationship, he must repudiate the agreement either before or shortly after he attains the age of majority. If the infant fails to repudiate, then he would be bound by the agreement, and would be liable for the debts of the partnership incurred after he reached the age of majority. Where repudiation takes place before the infant reaches the age of majority, then he will not normally be liable for the debts of the partnership

---

[10]For example, in Ontario under the *Partition Act*, R.S.O. 1980, c. 369.

[11]The *Partnerships Act*, R.S.O. 1980, c. 370, s. 15(1).

unless he committed a fraud. Once repudiation takes place, the infant is not responsible for the liabilities of the partnership, but he is not entitled to his share in the profits until the liabilities have been paid.

|||||||||||||||||||||||||||||||||||||||||||||||||||||||||||||||||||

CASE 17.1
Lampert Plumbing (Danforth) Ltd. v. Agathos et al., [1972] 3 O.R. 11.

PHELAN, CO.CT.J.:

The *Partnerships Act*, R.S.O. 1970, c. 339, s. 15(1), provides as follows:

"15(1) Every person, who by words spoken or written or by conduct represents himself or who knowingly suffers himself to be represented as a partner in a particular firm, is liable as a partner to any person who has on the faith of such a representation given credit to the firm, whether the representation has or has not been made or communicated to the persons so giving credit by or with the knowledge of the apparent partner making the representation or suffering it to be made."

In *Perry v. Johnston* (1928), 34 O.W.N. 82, Riddell, J.A., in holding a member of a partnership firm liable for a partnership debt said [p. 84]: "Either [he] was a partner . . . or he represented himself as such, in which case he is liable as by estoppel."

. . . . .

It is clear from s. 15 of the *Partnerships Act* and from the authorities that the person holding himself out as a partner "is liable as a partner" to one who has relied in good faith upon the representations made. Since in my view Agathos did hold himself out as the sole proprietor of the defendant construction company to Kreizman he incurs liability to the plaintiff company as if he were in fact a partner of the construction company or its sole proprietor.

|||||||||||||||||||||||||||||||||||||||||||||||||||||||||||||||||||

LIABILITY OF A PARTNERSHIP FOR THE ACTS OF A PARTNER

The persons who form a partnership are collectively called the firm, and the business is carried on in the firm name.[12] In a partnership, every partner is the agent of the firm in the ordinary course of partnership business, and may bind the firm in contract with third parties, unless the person with whom the partner was dealing knew that the partner had no authority to do so.[13] The act which the partner performs (for example, where he enters into a contract to supply goods, or to perform some service) must be related to the ordinary course of partnership business before his act binds the other partners. If the act is not something that falls within the ordinary scope of partnership business, then only that partner would be liable.[14]

A firm may also be liable for a tort committed by a partner, if the tort is committed in the ordinary course of partnership business.[15] Examples of this might be where the partner is involved in an automobile accident while on firm business, or where the partner is negligent in carrying out a contract and, as a result, injures a third party. The firm would also be liable where a partner, within the scope of his apparent authority, receives money or property either directly from a third party, or from another partner, and while it is in the custody of the firm misappropriates it or takes it for his own use.[16]

The admission of a new partner to a firm does not automatically render the new

[12]*Ibid.*, s. 5.
[13]*Ibid.*, s. 6.
[14]*Ibid.*, and see, for example, s. 8 where credit is pledged.
[15]*Ibid.*, s. 11.
[16]*Ibid.*, s. 12.

partner liable for the existing debts of the partnership. Under the *Partnerships Act,* a new partner is not liable for any debts incurred before he becomes a partner,[17] but he may, if he so desires, agree to assume existing debts as a partner, by express agreement with the previous partners. Much the same type of judicial reasoning is applied to the case of a retiring partner. A retiring partner is not relieved of debts incurred while he was a partner,[18] but if proper notice of retirement is given to all persons who had previous dealings with the firm (and to the public at large) he would not be liable for partnership debts incurred after his retirement.

RIGHTS AND DUTIES OF PARTNERS TO ONE ANOTHER

The rights and duties of partners are normally set out in a partnership agreement, since most partners wish to arrange their own affairs and those of the partnership in a particular manner. As with most agreements, the parties, within the bounds of the law of contract and the specific laws relating to partnerships, may establish their own rights and duties with respect to each other. They are free to fix their rights and duties in the contract, and they may vary them with the consent of all partners at any time. They need not have a written agreement if they do not wish to have one, but if they do not, their rights and obligations to one another will be defined as in the Act.

Under the Act, all property and rights brought into the partnership by the partners, and any property acquired by the partnership thereafter, becomes partnership property, and must be held and used for the benefit of the partnership, or in accordance with any agreement of the partners.[19] Any land acquired by, or on behalf of, a partnership, regardless of how the title is held by the partners (or a single partner), is considered to be bought in trust for the benefit of the partnership unless it is established to be otherwise.[20] Insofar as the partners themselves are concerned, the land is not treated as real property, but as personal property, since an individual partner's interest in partnership property is only personalty.[21]

The Act provides a number of rules which, in the absence of any express or implied agreement to the contrary, determine the partner's interests with respect to each other. The rules, as they appear in the Ontario statute,[22] provide as follows:

1. All the partners are entitled to share equally in the capital and profits of the business, and must contribute equally towards the losses, whether of capital or otherwise, sustained by the firm.

2. The firm must indemnify every partner in respect of payments made and personal liabilities incurred by him,
   (a) in the ordinary and proper conduct of the business of the firm;
       or
   (b) in or about anything necessarily done for the preservation of the business or property of the firm.

3. A partner making, for the purpose of the partnership, any actual payment or advance beyond the amount of capital which he has agreed to subscribe, is entitled to interest at the rate of 5% per annum from the date of the payment or advance.

---

[17]*Ibid.,* s. 18(1).
[18]*Ibid.,* s. 18(2).

[19]*Ibid.,* ss. 21(1) and 22.
[20]*Ibid.,* ss. 21(2) and 22.
[21]*Ibid.,* s. 23.
[22]*Ibid.,* s. 24.

4. A partner is not entitled, before the ascertainment of profits, to interest on the capital subscribed by him.

5. Every partner may take part in the management of the partnership business.

6. No partner shall be entitled to remuneration for acting in the partnership business.

7. No person may be introduced as a partner without the consent of all existing partners.

8. Any difference arising as to ordinary matters connected with the partnership business may be decided by a majority of the partners, but no change may be made in the nature of the partnership business without the consent of all existing partners.

9. The partnership books are to be kept at the place of business of the partnership, or the principal place, if there is more than one, and every partner may, when he thinks fit, have access to and inspect and copy any of them.

In addition to these general rules, the Act also provides that in the absence of an express agreement to the contrary, a majority of the partners may not expel any partner from the partnership.[23] The only method that a majority may use if they wish to get rid of a partner would be to terminate the partnership, then form a new partnership without the undesirable partner. Of course, this method of expelling a partner has certain disadvantages, but it is the only procedure available to the partners if they have failed to make express provisions for the elimination of undesirable partners in an agreement.

Because a partnership is a contract of utmost good faith, the partners have a number of obligations which they must perform in the best interests of the partnership as a whole. Every partner must render a true account of any money or information received to the other partners,[24] and deliver up to the partnership any benefit which arises from personal use of partnership property.[25] For example, a partnership owns a boat which is occasionally used for partnership business. One of the partners, for personal gain, and without the consent of the other partners, uses the boat on week-ends to take parties on sightseeing cruises. Any profits earned by the partner using the partnership boat must be delivered up to the partnership, as the earnings were made with partnership property. The same rule would apply where a partner, without the consent of the other partners, uses partnership funds for an investment, then returns the money to the partnership, but retains the profits. The other partners could insist that the profits be turned over to the partnership as well.

In addition to the unauthorized use of partnership property by a partner, the obligation of good faith extends to activities which a partner might engage in that conflict with the business interests of the firm. A partner, for example, may not engage in any other business which is similar to, or competes with, the business of the partnership, without the express consent of the other partners. If a partner should engage in a competing business without consent, any profits earned in the competing business may be claimed by the partnership, and the partner may be obliged to provide an accounting for the profits.[26]

A final important matter relating to the duties of a partner to the partnership

---

[23]*Ibid.*, s. 25.

[24]*Ibid.*, s. 28.
[25]*Ibid.*, s. 29(1).
[26]*Ibid.*, s. 30.

arises where a partner may assign his share in the partnership to another, or change his interest. The assignment does not permit the assignee to step into the position of the partner in the firm. The assignee does not become a partner because of the personal nature of a partnership, but only becomes entitled to receive the share of the profits of the partner who assigned his interest. The assignee acquires no right to interfere in the management or operation of the partnership, and must be content with receipt of a share of the profits as agreed to by the partners.[27] If the assignment takes place at the dissolution of the partnership, the assignee would then receive the share of the assets to which the partner was entitled on dissolution.[28]

DISSOLUTION OF A PARTNERSHIP

The parties to a partnership agreement may provide for the term of the agreement, and the conditions under which it may be dissolved. A common clause in a partnership agreement is one which provides for a period of notice if a partner wishes to dissolve the partnership. Another common practice is to provide for the disposition of the firm name on dissolution, if some of the partners should desire to carry on the business of the partnership following its termination. Coupled with this provision, the parties may also provide a method of determining the value of the business and the partners' shares if some should wish to acquire the assets of the dissolved business.

Apart from special provisions in a partnership agreement to deal with notice of dissolution, a partnership agreement

drawn for a specific term will dissolve automatically at the end of the term.[29] If the agreement was to undertake a specific venture or task, then the partnership would dissolve on the completion of the task or venture.[30] Where the agreement is for an unspecified period of time, then the agreement may be terminated by any partner giving notice of dissolution to the remainder of the partners. Once notice is given, the date of the notice is the date of dissolution, but if no date is mentioned, then the partnership is dissolved as of the date that the notice is received.[31]

A partnership may also be dissolved in a number of other ways. The death or insolvency of a partner will dissolve the partnership, unless the parties have provided otherwise,[32] and the partners may, at their option, treat the charging of partnership assets for a separate debt as an act which dissolves the partnership.[33] A partnership will be automatically dissolved if it is organized for an unlawful purpose, or if the purpose for which it was organized subsequently becomes unlawful.[34]

In addition to these particular events which dissolve a partnership, there are instances when a partner may believe that a partnership for a fixed term should be terminated before the dates fixed for its expiry. If a partner is found to be mentally incompetent or of unsound mind,[35] or if a partner becomes permanently incapable of performing his part of the partnership business,[36] the other partner may apply to

---

[27]*Ibid.*, s. 31(1).
[28]*Ibid.*, s. 31(2).

[29]*Ibid.*, s. 32(*a*).
[30]*Ibid.*, s. 32(*b*).
[31]*Ibid.*, s. 32(*c*).
[32]*Ibid.*, s. 33(1).
[33]*Ibid.*, s. 33(2).
[34]*Ibid.*, s. 34.
[35]*Ibid.*, s. 35(*a*).
[36]*Ibid.*, s. 35(*b*).

the courts for an order dissolving the relationship. Relief is also available from the courts in cases where a partner's conduct is such that it is prejudicial to the carrying on of the business,[37] or where the partner wilfully or persistently commits a breach of the partnership agreement, or so conducts himself that it is not reasonable for the other partners to carry on the business with such a partner.[38] The courts may also dissolve a partnership if it can be shown that the business can only be carried on at a loss,[39] or where, in the opinion of the court, the circumstances were such that it would be just and equitable to dissolve the relationship.[40] This latter authority of the courts to dissolve a partnership has been included in the *Partnerships Act* to provide for unusual circumstances which may arise that are not covered by specific provisions in the Act, and which may be shown to work a hardship on the partners if they were not permitted to otherwise dissolve the agreement.

Once notice of dissolution has been given, either in accordance with the partnership agreement, or the Act, the assets of the firm must be liquidated, and the share of each partner determined. The partner's share is something which is distinct from the assets of the business, and unless otherwise specified in the agreement, cannot be ascertained until the assets are sold; however, until the share is determined and paid, the partner has an equitable lien on the assets.[41]

Unless the partnership agreement provides otherwise, the assets of the partnership must be first applied to the payment of the debts to persons who are not partners of the firm,[42] then each partner must be paid rateably what is due for advances to the firm (as distinct from capital contributed).[43] The next step in the procedure is to pay each partner rateably for capital contributed to the firm,[44] and then to divide the residue (if any) amongst the partners in the proportion in which profits are divisible.[45] Any losses are to be paid first out of profits, then out of capital, and if insufficient funds are available to cover the debts, by contributions from the partners in the proportions in which they were entitled to share profits.[46] However, the procedure where one partner is insolvent, represents an exception to this rule as a result of a case tried some years after the *Partnership Act* was passed in England. The judges in that case stated that if one partner should be insolvent, the remaining solvent partners would be obliged to satisfy the demands of the creditors, not in proportion to the manner in which they share profits, but in proportion to the ratio of their capital accounts at the time of dissolution.[47] The reasoning of the court in reaching this particular conclusion was rather obscure, but presumably was based upon the presumption that the ratio of the capital accounts represented a better indicator of the ability of the remaining partners to sustain the loss than the ratio in which profits were shared.

Once a partnership has been dissolved, it is necessary to notify all customers of the firm, and the public at large. This is particularly important if some of the partners are retiring, and the remaining partners intend to carry on the business under the old

---

[37]*Ibid.*, s. 35(c).
[38]*Ibid.*, s. 35(d).
[39]*Ibid.*, s. 35(e).
[40]*Ibid.*, s. 35(f).
[41]*Ibid.*, s. 39.

[42]*Ibid.*, s. 44(2)(a).
[43]*Ibid.*, s. 44(2)(b).
[44]*Ibid.*, s. 44(2)(c).
[45]*Ibid.*, s. 44(2)(d).
[46]*Ibid.*, s. 44(1).
[47]*Ibid.*, and see *Garner v. Murray*, [1904] 1 Ch. 57.

firm name. If notice is not given to all customers of the firm, the retiring partners may be held liable by creditors who had no notice of the change in the partnership.[48] The usual practice is to notify all old customers of the firm by letter, and notify the general public by way of a notice published in the official provincial *Gazette*. The notice in the *Gazette* is treated as notice to all new customers who had no dealings with the old firm, and even if the new customers were unaware of the published notice, the retired partner could not be held liable for the debt.[49]

If a partner should die, and the firm thereby dissolve, no notice is necessary to the public, but the deceased partner's estate would remain liable for the debts of the partnership to the date of that partner's death.

Once dissolution is under way, the business may be conducted by the partners only insofar as it is necessary to close down the operation. This right usually includes the completion of any projects under way at the time of dissolution, but does not include taking on new work. The individual partners may continue to bind the partnership, but only to wind up the affairs of the firm.[50]

After the partnership relationship has terminated, each partner is free to carry on a business similar to the business dissolved, and normally any restriction on the right to do so would be unenforceable unless it is a reasonable restriction limited to a particular term, and within a specified geographic area. Even then, all of the rules of law relating to restrictive covenants would apply.

||||||||||||||||||||||||||||||||||||||||||||||||||||||||||||||||||||||||||||||||||||||||

CASE 17.2
Clarke v. Burton, [1958] O.R. 489.

McRUER, C.J.H.C.:

The following ordinary principles of law to be applied may be stated thus:—

1. The ordinary law is that while the retirement of a partner in no way affects his rights or obligations to strangers in respect of past transactions: *Lindley, Partnership*, 11th ed., p. 369, yet if one not known to be a partner retires, the authority of his late partners to bind him ceases on his retirement although no notice of it be given: *op. cit.*, p. 287.

2. A known partner who has retired from the partnership will be liable for debts of the partnership contracted after his retirement until notice is given even though the creditor has had no dealings with the firm prior to dissolution: *Reid & Co. v. Coleman* (1890), 19 O.R. 93.

3. When an apparent partner retires, or when a partnership between several known partners is dissolved, those who dealt with the firm before the change took place are entitled to assume that no change has occurred until they have notice to the contrary: *per* Anglin, C.J.C., *Huffman v. Ross*, [1926] S.C.R. 5. In such case the onus is on the retired partner to prove direct notice or facts and circumstances from which knowledge of retirement might fairly be inferred.

4. If a creditor did not know a particular partner was a partner and that partner retired then, as from the date of his retirement, he ceases to be liable for partnership debts contracted by the firm to such person: *Tower Cabinet Co. v. Ingram*, [1949] 2 K.B. 397, see also *Eagle Shoe Co. Ltd. v. Thompson* (1956), 2 D.L.R. (2d) 755.

5. If notice can be established, no matter by what means, it is sufficient. No formality is required. . . .

||||||||||||||||||||||||||||||||||||||||||||||||||||||||||||||||||||||||||||||||

✳LIMITED PARTNERSHIP

A limited partnership is a partnership in which a partner under certain circumstances may limit his liability for partner-

---

[48]*Ibid.*, s. 36(1).
[49]*Ibid.*, s. 36(2).
[50]*Ibid.*, s. 38.

ship debts, and protect his personal estate from claims by the creditors of the partnership. The limited partnership bears a resemblance to the European *société en commandite*, which found its way into the Quebec *Civil Code* from French law, and into the laws of other provinces by way of the laws of England. All of the common law provinces except Prince Edward Island have enacted legislation for the formation of limited partnerships, and the provisions of each statute which govern the relationship are somewhat similar.

While legislation exists for the formation and operation of limited partnerships, the limited partnership is seldom used. The corporation has been found to be more suited to the needs of persons who might otherwise form a limited partnership; as a result, this type of entity is not commonly found except in family business relationships.

The legislation pertaining to limited partnerships is not uniform throughout Canada, but in general, it provides that every limited partnership must have at least one or more general partners with unlimited liability and responsibility, both jointly and severally, for the debts of the partnership.[51] In addition, the partnership may have one or more limited partners whose liability is limited to the amount of capital contributed to the firm.[52]

Only the general partners may actively transact business for the partnership and have authority to bind it in contract.[53] The name of the limited partner usually must not be a part of the firm name, and if a limited partner's name should be placed on letterhead or stationery, in most jurisdictions he would be deemed to be a general partner.[54] The limited partner may share in the profits, and may examine the partnership books, but must refrain from actively participating in the control of the business, otherwise the limited partner will be treated as a general partner, and lose the protection of limited liability.[55] The limited partner is further restricted with respect to the capital contributed. Once the limited partner has contributed a sum of money to the business, he may not withdraw it until the partnership is dissolved.[56]

To provide public notice of the capital contribution of the limited partners, and to identify the general partners in the business, information concerning the limited partnership must be filed in the appropriate public office specified in the provincial legislation. The registration of the notice is very important, as the partnership is not deemed to be formed until the partnership has been registered, or the certificate filed,[57] and a failure to file, or the making of a false statement in the documents filed, in some jurisdictions renders all limited partners general partners.

While the form of the document filed to register the limited partnership varies from province to province, the information contained generally provides the name under which the partnership operates, the nature of the business, the names of the general and limited partners, the amount of capital contributed by the limited partner, the place of business of the partnership, the date, and the term.[58] Changes in the partnership require a new filing, otherwise the limited partners may either lose their protection or the change is ineffective.

---

[54]*Ibid.*, s. 58(1).
[55]*Ibid.*, s. 63(1).
[56]*Ibid.*, s. 60 and 65.
[57]*Ibid.*, s. 55.
[58]See, for example, The *Business Names Registration Act*, R.S.M. 1970, c. B-110, ss. 4(1) and 8(1).

[51]*The Partnership Act*, R.S.M. 1970, c. P-30, s. 52.
[52]*Ibid.*, ss. 52 and 53.
[53]*Ibid.*, s. 54.

The information contained in the document is designed to provide creditors and others who may have dealings with the limited partnership with the necessary information to enable them to decide if they should do business with the firm or, alternatively, information that they might need to institute legal proceedings against the firm if it fails to pay its debts or honour its commitments.

Notwithstanding the limited use of this type of partnership, some provinces have recently revised their legislation in an effort to clarify and expand the rights and duties of limited partners.[59] How useful these changes will be and whether they stimulate interest in this form of business organization remains to be seen.

REGISTRATION OF PARTNERSHIPS

Limited partnerships are not the only business entities subject to registration requirements. Most provinces require the registration of ordinary partnerships and of sole proprietorships, if the sole proprietor is carrying on business under a name other than his own. Provincial legislation is not uniform with respect to registration, and some provinces exempt some types of partnerships from registration. For example, professions governed or regulated by provincial bodies are frequently exempt, and in at least one province, farming and fishing partnerships need not be registered. The purpose of registration is the same as for limited partnerships, that is, to provide creditors and others with information concerning the business and the persons who operate it.

Declarations generally require the partners to disclose the name of the part-

nership, the names and addresses of all partners, the date of commencement of the partnership, and the fact that all partners are of the age of majority (or if not, the date of birth of the infant partners).[60] The declaration must normally be filed in a specified public office, usually the local Registry Office (or a central registry for the province), within a particular period of time after the partnership commenced operation.[61] Changes in the partnership usually require the filing of a new declaration[62] within a similar time period.

The provinces of Nova Scotia and Ontario provide in their legislation that no partnership or member may maintain any action or other proceeding in a court of law in connection with any contract unless a declaration has been duly filed.[63] The significance of this particular section looms large in the event that an unregistered partnership wishes to defend or institute legal proceedings, as the failure to register would act as a bar to any legal action by the partnership until such time as registration is effected.

Sole proprietorships normally need not be registered in most provinces, but a sole proprietor carrying on business under a name other than his own is usually required to register in much the same manner as a partnership, since persons doing business with such a business entity would be interested in knowing the identity of the true owner.

All partners in a partnership required to register under registration legislation usually remain liable to creditors until a notice of dissolution is filed in the proper office. The declaration of dissolution acts as a public notice that a partnership has been dissolved, and if afterwards the firm is to continue on, composed of the remain-

[59]See, for example, the *Limited Partnerships Act*, R.S.O. 1980, c. 241.
[60]The *Partnerships Registration Act*, R.S.O. 1980, c. 371, s. 2, as amended.
[61]*See, for example, s. 3.*
[62]*Ibid.*, s. 4(1).
[63]*Ibid.*, s. 9 and see the *Partnership and Business Names Registration Act*, R.S.N.S. 1967, c. 225, s. 19.

ing or new partners, the old partners may
still be deemed partners until the declaration of dissolution has been filed.

SUMMARY

The partnership is an ancient form of business organization. It is a relationship of utmost good faith, and requires the partners to disclose to one another all information of importance to the firm. Partners are agents of the firm, and one partner acting within the apparent range of his authority may bind the partnership in contract with third parties. A partnership may also be liable for the torts of partners committed within the ordinary course of partnership business.

Partnership agreements are usually written contracts signed by the parties. A partnership agreement, however, need not be in writing, and need not specify the terms of the partnership, but where no terms are set out, the provisions of the *Partnerships Act* apply to determine the rights and obligations of the partners.

Partners must not use partnership assets or funds to make secret profits at the expense of the partnership, and the partners must not engage in other businesses which compete with the partnership, unless they have the express permission of all of the other partners.

A partnership may be dissolved by the completion of the specific venture for which the partnership was formed, or at the end of a specified term, or it may be terminated on notice, if no term is specified. It may also terminate on the death or insolvency of a partner, or where the purpose for which it was organized is unlawful. The court under certain circumstances has the right to dissolve a partnership. Where a partnership is dissolved, all creditors and the public at large must be notified of the dissolution by the partners if the retiring partners wish to avoid liability for future debts of the partnership.

Subject to certain exceptions, partnerships must be registered, and the limited partnership which may be established in most provinces, depends upon registration to establish the limited liability of the limited partners.

**DISCUSSION
QUESTIONS**

1. *Define "partnership."*
2. *What specific historical circumstances gave rise to the* société en commandite?
3. *Does an organization of persons not formed for profit constitute a partnership?*
4. *Although people may have a common view to profit, they may or may not be partners. What distinguishes "partnership" from "co-ownership"?*
5. *A partner is generally an agent of the firm, and binds the other partners when he enters into a contract. Under what circumstances would the other partners not be liable?*
6. *Explain why a written partnership agreement is desirable. Must all partnership agreements be in writing?*
7. *Why must land and other real property be classed as personal property with respect to partnership law?*

√ 8. What circumstances automatically dissolve a partnership?

√ 9. Distinguish between "advances to the firm" and "capital contributed."

10. Outline the process of satisfying the claims of the creditors and partners upon dissolution of the firm.

11. An "ostensible partner" is sometimes one who, by virtue of his notoriety, is associated with a firm. If a sports star endorses the products of a partnership, or otherwise lends his name, what might such a person's liability be?

12. Why must the name of a limited partner not appear in the firm name, and be clearly delineated as such on the firm's letterhead?

√ 13. Explain the purpose of registration of a partnership.

14. How is the limited liability of a partner established?

15. What is the purpose of publication of the termination of a partnership in the provincial Gazette?

JUDICIAL DECISIONS

Assignment of Partnership Interest to Third Party—Effect —Rights of Third Party and Partners

Freedman v. Lawrence et al. (1978), 18 O.R. (2d) 423.

The plaintiff was the assignee of a portion of the interest of a partner in a partnership which owned a golf club. The defendants refused to recognize the plaintiff's interest, and refused to provide the plaintiff with information as to the management and operation of the club. The plaintiff instituted legal proceedings.

STEELE, J.:

The plaintiff claims a declaration that he is an undivided one-sixth owner of the golf-club lands . . . as well as a declaration that the plaintiff and the defendants are partners with respect to the land . . .

. . . . .

It was submitted that on the authority of *Int'l Airport Industrial Park Ltd. v. Tanenbaum et al.*, [1977] 2 S.C.R. 326, 69 D.L.R. (3d) 1, 11 N.R. 248, that where a partner assigns his interest or part of his interest to another person who is not accepted in the partnership, the assignee's only right against the partnership is to receive the share of the profits and that the assignee has no interest in the partnership itself. The specific quotation from that case is set out at pp. 337-8 S.C.R., pp. 9-10 D.L.R., and I quote as follows:

"International submitted that, at the least, Fischtein had assigned to it part of his interest in the partnership agreement with Tanenbaum. This, however, does not assist the appellant. *The Partnerships Act*, R.S.O. 1970, c. 339, s. 24, rule 7, provides that, subject to an express or implied agreement between the partners, new partners may be introduced into a partnership only with the consent of each existing partner. On Mayzel's own testimony, it is clear that Tanenbaum would not have agreed to accept International as a partner, although he was willing to allow Fischtein to deal with his partnership interest as he pleased. Section 31 of the Act provides that where a partner assigns his interest or part of his interest to another person who is not accepted into the partnership, the assignee's only right against the partnership is to receive the share of profits to which the assigning partner would be entitled on the basis of the account of profits agreed to by the partners. The assignee is not entitled to interfere in the management or administration of the partnership. If, as in this case, the partnership produces no profits, the assignee has no rights against the partnership."

In applying that decision to the present case, it is important to refer to what the agreements were between the parties involved. It is obvious from the agreement in the *Int'l Airport* case that there was a partnership for a limited period of years, and I quote as follows from para. (3) of the agreement [at p. 329 S.C.R., p. 3 D.L.R.]:

"(3) In the event that a residential subdivision and/or such other commercial or industrial development as may be required is not approved by the Town of Oakville or the lands are not sold by the date of expiration of the partnership as set out herein, the Developer shall cease to have any interest in the said lands and shall not be entitled to remuneration of any kind for services rendered to or on behalf of the said partnership other than such profits as may accrue pursuant to paragraph 2 hereof."

It is obvious from this that, under the facts of that case where the lands were not sold nor had there been any approval as contemplated, the plaintiff had no further interest in the partnership and therefore had no interest in the lands. That is not what is alleged in the present case, and therefore I am of the opinion that the decision of the Court in *Int'l Airport Industrial Park Ltd. v. Tanenbaum et al.* is not applicable to the case before me.

I am of the opinion that the provisions of s. 31(2) of the *Partnerships Act* are applicable to the present case. They are as follows:

"31(2) In the case of a dissolution of the partnership, whether as respects all the partners or as respects the assigning partner, the assignee is entitled to receive the share of the partnership assets to which the assigning partner is entitled as between himself and the other partners, and, for the purpose of ascertaining that share, to an account as from the date of the dissolution."

Where it is alleged that there was a partnership between the defendants which was dissolved, it is my opinion that the assignee is entitled to receive the share of the partnership assets to which the assignor was entitled and, for the purpose of ascertaining that share, to an account as from the date of the dissolution. . . . it is my opinion that there is a possible claim by the plaintiff in the partnership assets themselves as opposed to any interest in the management or operation of the partnership or the day-to-day accounting and profits of the partnership.

|||||||||||||||||||||||||||||||||||||||||||||||||||||||||||||||||||||||||||||||||||||||||||||||||||||||||||||||||||||||||||||||||||||||||

Registration of Partnership— Liability of Retired Partner Who Failed to Register Dissolution

Clarke v. Burton, [1958] O.R. 489.

A partner retired from a partnership that had been registered in accordance with the provincial *Partnership Registration Act*. A creditor who was aware of the partner's retirement continued to do business with the remaining partners. He later attempted to hold the retired partner liable for partnership debts because the retired partner had not filed a declaration with respect to dissolution.

McRUER, C.J.H.C.:

Where customers have dealt with the firm prior to dissolution, registration of a certificate of dissolution is not enough. There must be notice. On the other hand, the law contemplates that a customer who deals with a firm for the first time after a notice of dissolution has been registered is taken to have notice, as the law contemplates that he should search before first supplying the firm with goods, but customers who supplied the firm with goods after the registration of the partnership are not required to continue to search from day to day to see if dissolution has taken place.

In *Re Merrick, Jamieson v. Trustee*, [1933] O.W.N. 295, two Merrick brothers and one Sims had registered a certificate under the Partnership Registration Act in March 1924. One Mrs. Jamieson advanced $7,500 to them. Sims retired from the partnership about the end of 1924 when the assets and liabilities of the firm were taken over by the Merrick brothers who carried on business until 1927 when a certificate of dissolution of the partnership of the two brothers was registered. No document had been registered when Sims retired. T. W. Merrick, one of the brothers, continued the business, assuming sole control and responsibility until his bankruptcy. The changes in the firm were known to and agreeable to Mrs. Jamieson and there was complete novation as far as the debt was concerned. The trustee in bankruptcy contended that Mrs. Jamieson could not rank against the estate until other creditors were paid in full, relying on s. 122 of the Bankruptcy Act and the Partnership Registration Act. He maintained that the partnership was still subsisting by reason of the failure to register a certificate of dissolution. Middleton, J.A., at page 297, said:—

"The contention as to the failure to register the certificate of dissolution is based upon an entire misconception of the purpose and meaning of the Partnership Registration Act. The effect of this Act is to impose a liability in the nature of an estoppel upon the partner who fails to record the dissolution of the partnership. Creditors may hold him liable as though he had continued to be a partner. . . . It is a very different thing to suggest that the failure to register a dissolution of partnership will operate in any way as an estoppel against the creditor."

It is to be noted that in this case Middleton, J.A., referred to the effect of the Partnership Registration Act as imposing a liability in the nature of an estoppel. It may be that what was said is *obiter* in view of the fact that the matter decided was that the failure to register a dissolution of partnership will not operate in any way as an estoppel against a creditor. However, I do not think this judgment can be interpreted that Middleton, J.A., intended to lay down any principle that creditors who had actual notice of the dissolution could nevertheless claim against a retired partner for goods supplied after the dissolution because no certificate of dissolution had been registered under the Act.

Of all the cases I think *Oakville v. Andrew* (1905), 10 O.L.R. 709, throws the most light on the problem that I have to solve. In this case a partnership in a private banking business which had existed between the defendant and one H. was dissolved, but the business continued to be carried on in the firm name and no notice of dissolution was given nor any certificate thereunder registered. After the dissolution H., who was also treasurer of the municipality, received as such, moneys belonging to the municipality out of which, and other moneys, he made certain payments for the municipality and deposited the balance in a bank where the firm kept its account, subsequently using it in the firm's business. On the death of H. the account was overdrawn and the municipality sought to hold the defendant liable on two grounds: (1) that he held himself out to be a partner or that the partnership in fact continued to exist; and (2) if the partnership was dissolved no declaration of dissolution had been filed. Moss, C.J.O., after stating that Falconbridge, C.J.K.B., had given judgment for the plaintiffs, chiefly on the ground that the defendant in consequence of his failure to file a declaration of dissolution of partnership must be deemed to be a partner, said, at p. 715:—

"It is not necessary to place a construction upon the provisions of the Act because the absence of any notice and the continued use of the defendant's name rendered him liable to be treated by all persons dealing with the firm as still a member of the firm. *The filing of a declaration was one mode of giving notice to the public,* and the defendant neglected this as well as the usual common law methods of freeing himself from future liability to persons dealing with the firm. [Emphasis added]"

The appeal was allowed on the ground that the plaintiff was not a customer and did not deal with the partnership in the transaction in question. It was contended, however, that the former partner, as treasurer of the municipality, was their agent to deal with the partnership. The learned Chief Justice said, at p. 716:—

"If he acted as the authorized agent of the plaintiff he knew at the time that the defendant was not a partner, and his knowledge should be attributed to the plaintiff."

These passages from the judgment of the learned Chief Justice appear to me to clearly indicate that in his opinion a creditor who continues to deal with the partnership with full notice of the dissolution cannot claim against a retired partner merely because a certificate of dissolution has not been registered.

If the liability imposed under the statute is in the nature of estoppel as Middleton, J.A., said in the *Merrick* case, the principles of law applicable to estoppel ought to apply. These principles can be no more clearly stated than in the language of Lord Birkenhead in *MacLaine v. Gatty*, [1921] 1 A.C. 376, at p. 386, where he said:—

"The learned counsel cited various authorities in which these doctrines have been discussed, but the rule of estoppel or bar, as I have always understood it, is capable of extremely simple statement. Where A has by his words or conduct justified B in believing that a certain state of facts exists, and B has acted upon such belief to his prejudice, A is not permitted to affirm against B that a different state of facts existed at the same time. Whether one reads the case of *Pickard v. Sears* (1837), 6

A. & E. 469, or the later classic authorities which have illustrated this topic, one will not, I think, greatly vary or extend this simple definition of the doctrine.''

If this is the doctrine of estoppel to be applied, I cannot see how one who has specific notice of the dissolution of the partnership can take advantage of an estoppel created by statute. To come to any other conclusion would, in my opinion, reduce the law to an absurdity. Take, for example, in this case, if the solicitor that the defendant consulted had written to the plaintiff and told him that the partnership was dissolved, that the defendant was no longer connected with it, and that he was commencing business for himself and the plaintiff continued to supply goods to the partnership, could any Court in good conscience give him judgment against the defendant simply because the formality of the registration of a dissolution had not been gone through, a formality that in no way affected the plaintiff? My conclusion is that there is no merit in the action and it should be dismissed on this ground alone.

Having arrived at this conclusion, it is not necessary for me to consider whether the persons involved were ''associated in partnership for trading or manufacturing . . . purposes''. The action will therefore be dismissed with costs.

||||||||||||||||||||||||||||||||||||||||||||||||||||||||||||||||||||||||||||||||||||||||||||||||||||||||||||||||||||||||||||||||||||||||||||||||||||||

Dissolution of Partnership— One Partner Insolvent— Liability of Other Partners for Deficiencies in Capital

Garner v. Murray, [1904] 1 Ch. 57.

Three persons carried on business in partnership until it was necessary to dissolve the relationship. One partner had no assets, and the deficiency which resulted in payment of creditors' claims had to be covered by the two remaining partners. The parties had contributed unequal amounts of capital, but had agreed to share profits and losses equally.

The question put before the court was: How should the deficiencies be paid?

JOYCE, J.:

The real question in this case is how, as between two partners, the ultimate deficit, which arises in the partnership assets from the default of a third partner to contribute his share of the deficiency of the assets to make good the capital, is to be borne by them. We have now in the Partnership Act, 1890, a code which defines the mode in which the assets of a firm are to be dealt with in the final settlement of the accounts after a dissolution.

Sect. 44 is plain. [His Lordship read the section, and continued:—] I do not find anything in that section to make a solvent partner liable to contribute for an insolvent partner who fails to pay his share. Sub-s. (*b*) of s. 44 proceeds on the supposition that contributions have been paid or levied. Here the effect of levying is that two partners can pay and one cannot. It is suggested on behalf of the plaintiff that each partner is to bear an equal loss. But when the Act says losses are to be borne equally it means losses sustained by the firm. It cannot mean that the individual loss sustained by each partner is to be of equal amount.

There is no rule that the ultimate personal loss of each partner, after he has performed his obligations to the firm, shall be the same as or in any given proportion to that of any other partner. I have to follow the Act, and I see no difficulty in doing so in this case. The assets must be applied in paying to each partner rateably what is due from the firm to him in respect of capital, account being taken of the equal contributions to be made by him towards the deficiency of capital.

CASE	**Case 1**
PROBLEMS	Sarah, aged 17 years, and Jane aged 19 years, had been shopping in a
FOR	large shopping mall. Jane wished to purchase a lottery ticket, but had
DISCUSSION	only $1 in her purse. She turned to Sarah, and said: "Do you have $4?

They are selling lottery tickets here." Without a word, Sarah took the money from her pocket and gave it to Jane. Jane purchased a ticket which she and Sarah agreed bore a lucky number. The next week, the ticket which Jane had purchased was the winner of $25 000.

When news of the win reached Jane, she immediately visited her friend Sarah and attempted to pay her the $4 which she said she had borrowed. Sarah, who had also heard the good news, refused to accept the $4 and demanded her share of the winnings.

If the above dispute should be brought before a court, describe the arguments that might be raised by each of the parties in support of their respective positions. Indicate how the case might be decided.

Case 2

Henry, Able, Charlie and Kim established a tree pruning business under the firm name of HACK Enterprises. Except for Henry, who was a minor, the partners had all reached the age of majority. Most of their equipment was acquired from their respective families, or by way of cash purchases at farm auction sales. The group, however, lacked funds to purchase a chain-saw which they required to cut large trees. The original capital of $400 which represented a $100 contribution from each partner, had already been used to acquire small tools, and all that remained in the firm's account was $26.

Henry, without the consent of the remaining partners, purchased a chain-saw at a local hardware store which had been placed on sale at $300. The merchant was reluctant to sell the saw to him on credit because he was under age. When Henry told the merchant that he was buying it for HACK Enterprises, the merchant agreed to make the sale, because he had seen advertisements placed by the firm in the local newspaper.

Henry gave a cheque in the firm name for $25 and signed an agreement whereby the firm would be obliged to make regular monthly payments of $25 each until the balance of the purchase price had been paid.

The firm made several payments on the saw, then ceased to do so when the partners decided to disband the partnership. Henry took the saw as his part of the partnership proceeds when the four partners divided the assets.

A month later, the hardware merchant discovered that the partnership had dissolved, and contacted Henry for payment. Henry refused to make payment, and refused to return the saw.

Discuss the issues raised in this case, and explain how the matter might be ultimately resolved if the merchant should take legal action to recover his loss.

Case 3

In 1969, Smith, who operated a business under the name "Downtown Grocery," employed Jones as a clerk in his store at a weekly salary of $75. Jones received regular salary increases in the years 1970–80, and by 1980, earned $240 per week.

Early in 1981, Jones approached Smith with a request for a further increase in his wages, but Smith refused on the basis that low business profits limited his ability to pay more than $240 per week. A lengthy discussion followed, and the two parties reached the following agreement:

Jones would receive $240 per week and in addition, would receive 20% of the net profits. He would continue to perform the duties of clerk, but would assume responsibility for the Meat Department. He would make all management decisions concerning meat purchases and pricing.

Smith would continue to handle the general management of the business. He would draw the amount of $500 per week, and would be entitled to 80% of the net profits.

Jones would be permitted to examine the business account books, and would be consulted in all major business decisions by Smith.

A few weeks after the agreement was reached, Smith discovered that Jones was purchasing groceries (for his personal use) at a competitor's store. In a rage, he barred Jones from entering the store, and told him that he would send him his severance pay by mail.

Shortly thereafter, Jones instituted legal proceedings for a declaration that he was a partner in Downtown Grocery.

Discuss the merits of the action taken by Jones, and discuss the arguments that might be raised by the parties. How would you expect the matter to be decided?

Case 4

Harold Green and Herbert Green, who were unrelated persons with the same surname, carried on parcel delivery businesses in the same city. Each operated as a sole proprietor under the name "Green Delivery," and carried on business from the same warehouse building. The two men were good friends, and frequently assisted each other by one carrying parcels for the other in deliveries to outlying parts of the city. To complicate matters further, the two proprietors would sometimes use the spare truck owned by the other when their own vehicles had breakdowns or required service. Apart from the fact that each had a different telephone number, it was impossible to distinguish between the two firms. Over time, regular customers often referred to the two firms collectively as "Green Brothers Delivery," even though the two men were not related to each other.

Smith, an antique dealer, who frequently used the delivery services of both men requested Harold Green to deliver an expensive antique chair to his country home. Harold Green, at the time of the request for pick-up, advised Smith that he would sent his truck out to pick up the chair. However, Herbert Green picked up the chair at Smith's place of business, and took it to the warehouse for delivery. That day a fire of unknown origin destroyed the warehouse and its contents. The charred remains of the chair were found in the jointly used part of the warehouse after the fire.

The chair had a value of $3 000, and each of the sole proprietors denied liability for the loss.

Advise Smith as to how he might proceed in this case.

Case 5

Williams, Oxford, Ogilvie, and Lennox carried on business in partnership for many years as wool merchants. The widespread use of synthetic materials, however, adversely affected the fortunes of the business, and eventually the partners found themselves at the point where the business could no longer be carried on at a profit. Before anything could be done to sell the business, Lennox became insolvent. It was then necessary to wind up the business in accordance with the partnership agreement.

The partnership agreement provided that the parties share losses and profits equally. On dissolution, the capital accounts of the partners were as follows:

Williams	$5 000
Oxford	3 000
Ogilvie	2 000
Lennox	—

Creditors' claims at dissolution amounted to $35 000; whereas the total assets of the firm were $25 000.

Explain the nature of the liability of the firm, and calculate the liability of each of the partners as between themselves with respect to creditor claims.

CHAPTER 18

Corporation Law

Federal & Provincial Gov't
have control over
~~corporate~~ Constitutional
Authority over corporate
law

The company decides what
which Gov't has control

Corporations are a legal
person or separate entity
- anything recognized
by our law having legal rights
& obligations
Corporations are artificial
persons

Someone has to run a corporation
on its behalf

HISTORICAL DEVELOPMENT OF THE CORPORATION

A corporation is an entity which has an existence at law which is separate from those who form it, and which is separate from those who from time to time possess shares in it, or who are responsible for its direction and control. A corporation is a creature of the State, and owes its continued existence to the legislative body responsible for its creation. One of its principal uses is as a vehicle by which large amounts of capital may be accumulated for business purposes. Throughout its history, it has represented a means by which a large number of persons could participate in business transactions which require more capital than one individual or a small group possessed, or cared to risk, in a venture.

The corporation is not a new form of business organization. Its history dates back to the time of the first city states when trade became an important activity. Since the earliest times, its creation and operation have generally remained under the control of the sovereign or state. Most of the early corporations were formed for the purpose of carrying out public or quasi-public functions, or to provide essential services or goods to the community. In Rome, for example, corporations were generally created for public purposes, and guilds were sometimes incorporated. Some business activities, such as mining, were permitted to use the corporate structure in order to accumulate the necessary capital to undertake the operation, but as a rule their use for trading purposes was limited.

In England, the corporate form was used generally for the purpose of establishing municipal bodies, churches, universities, charitable organizations, and guilds during the period prior to the Norman Conquest. The principal use, apart from the church and municipal organizations, was to grant the organization monopoly power. Such was the case with the guilds; for, once incorporated, they were given the exclusive authority to regulate both a particular trade and the persons associated with it.

The Norman Conquest and the introduction of the feudal system discouraged the use of the corporate form except for public bodies. The Crown recognized the advantages of the separate and perpetual

existence of the entity from the perspective of administrative efficiency but it jealously maintained the sole right to confer corporate status. As as result, the authority was seldom exercised. Because the creation of a corporation was a Royal prerogative, the common law courts realized that they lacked the power to interfere in any way with the creation or dissolution of the corporation, and any litigation with respect to the corporation was generally left to the king, and later, the chancery.

The early corporations had a number of characteristics in common with the modern corporation. Once the sovereign granted corporate status to a group of persons by Letters Patent (a document which created the entity), the corporation acquired the capacity to hold property and to sue and be sued as a separate person. While the persons who had an interest in the early corporation seldom had limited liability, the advantages of the corporate form more than offset any disadvantages. Because the corporation was treated as a separate entity, it could be used as a vehicle to hold property for its constituents, and its operations could only be controlled by way of an appeal to the Courts of Equity.

The corporate form was seldom used for trading organizations until the reign of Elizabeth I in England. Trade had developed by that time to the point where there were distinct advantages to the incorporation of trading corporations as monopolies to hold land, or to undertake particular trading activities. Merchants traded initially under the umbrella of these corporations on their own account, as most of the corporations were organized for the purpose of regulating the conditions under which foreign trade was to take place. It was not until the late 17th century that corporations as such began to engage in trade themselves. Unfortunately, a number of spectacular failures of trading companies shortly thereafter brought the corporate form into disfavour, and for almost a century the number of corporations created for business and trading purposes were few. Yet, some of the old corporations continued to exist, the most notable example being the Hudson's Bay Company, which was incorporated in 1670.

The expansion of trade and the Industrial Revolution in the 18th century brought about an increased need for improved inland transportation facilities. Beginning with canal building, and later, with the railroads, the need for large amounts of capital revived interest in the formation of corporations. The few corporations created, however, were created by special Acts of Parliament, rather than by Royal prerogative, but the purpose was much the same, and that was to grant a particular monopoly to the new entity. It was not until the 19th century that trading corporations in general were permitted once again to incorporate, and even then, it was only during the last half of the century that limited liability was available to the shareholders. The modern form of corporation, incorporated by simply following the procedure set out in a general statute, did not emerge until the middle of the century. Even then, its introduction was decades behind a similar change in the United States and Canada.

In the United States, the War of Independence severed ties between the colonies and England, and the Royal prerogative was replaced by special legislation for the incorporation of companies. In 1811, the State of New York passed a statute

which in form was a general incorporation Act, and which was alleged to have furnished the model for the first incorporation Act in the United Provinces of Upper and Lower Canada in 1848–49. Prior to that time, companies had been formed in Canada under special Acts of the Legislature, but the new legislation permitted the incorporation of a company by complying with the statute. The Act limited incorporation to companies for the purpose of constructing roads and bridges, but the next year (i.e., 1850), the Parliament of the United Provinces passed a new, general Act which permitted incorporation for the commercial purposes of manufacturing, mining, and other activities.

The year 1864 saw the introduction of the Letters Patent corporation under a general Act, and the new concept raised a number of difficulties respecting the rights and powers of the entity. These difficulties were not resolved until after the turn of the century. A few years later, the problems were compounded by the *British North America Act, 1867* which established the rights of both the provinces and the federal government to incorporate companies. As a result, legislation at both the federal and provincial levels was introduced to provide for the incorporation and control of corporations. The legislation, unfortunately, was not uniform, with the result that considerable variation existed from province to province. The newer provinces, as they joined Confederation, passed their own legislation, which again was subject to some variation, and consequently, no uniform legislation exists in Canada today.

NATURE OF A CORPORATION

A corporation is neither an individual nor a partnership. It is a separate legal entity in the sense that it has an existence at law, but no material existence. A corporation possesses many of the attributes of a natural person, but it is artificially created, and never dies. Its rights and duties are delineated by law, and its existence may be terminated by the State. It has a number of important characteristics which may be summarized as follows:

(a) a corporation is separate and distinct from its shareholders, and it acts not through them, but through its authorized agents;

(b) a properly authorized agent may bind the corporation in contract with third parties;

(c) the shareholders of a corporation possess limited liability for the debts of the corporation, and the creditors may look only to the assets of the corporation to satisfy their claims.

This latter characteristic particularly distinguishes the corporation from the ordinary partnership or sole proprietorship in which the parties have unlimited liability for debts incurred in the course of business.

The management of a corporation is vested in a small group of shareholders chosen by the general body of shareholders at an annual meeting held for the purpose of electing the management group. This group bears the title *directors of the corporation*, and it, in turn, selects from its number the principal officers of the corporation. These individuals are normally charged with the responsibility to bind the corporation in formal contracts with third parties.

The directors of the corporation are free to carry out the general management functions of the corporation in accordance with the corporations' objects, but their powers are limited by any restriction imposed on them in the articles of incorporation or the charter. To keep the shareholders informed of their activities, the directors are obliged to report to them on a regular basis. The shareholders normally do not participate in the management of the corporation, except where major changes in the corporation are proposed. In these cases, the shareholders usually must approve the proposal before it becomes effective.

Except for private or closely held corporations which do not offer their shares to the public, the shareholders may freely dispose of their interests in the corporation. This is permitted because the relationship is not of a personal nature. The fortunes of the corporation are not dependent upon the personal relationship between shareholders, nor are the creditors of the corporation normally concerned with the shareholders' identity, since the shareholders' liability is limited to the amount which they paid or agreed to pay for the shares which they purchased from the corporation. In general, the corporate form of business organization overcomes many of the disadvantages associated with the partnership. We can compare the differences between these two forms of organization by an examination of each under three major headings, i.e., control, liability, and transfer of interests.

Control

In a partnership, every partner is an agent of the partnership as well as a principal. All of the partners have input into how the business may be operated, and on important matters all parties must agree before a change can be made. In a large partnership, these particular rights of each partner often render decision-making awkward and time-consuming, and make general control difficult.

In a corporation, management is delegated by the shareholders to an elected group of directors. The ordinary shareholder does not possess the right to bind the corporation in contract. Only the proper officers designated by the directors may do so. The directors have the authority to make all decisions for the corporation, although the shareholders may periodically be called upon to approve major decisions at meetings held for that purpose.

Limited Liability

In an ordinary partnership, every general partner has unlimited liability for the debts incurred by the partnership. Since any partner may bind the other partners in contract by his actions, the careless act of one partner may seriously affect all. The personal estates of each partner, then, are exposed to the creditors in the event of a loss which exceeds the partnership assets.

The corporate form eliminates this particular risk for ordinary shareholders. A shareholder's loss is limited to his investment in the corporation, and his personal estate may not be reached by creditors of the corporation. The creditors of a corporation must be content with the assets of the corporation in the event of a loss, as a creditor is aware at the time (when extending credit to a corporation) that the only assets available to satisfy his claim are those possessed by the corporation.

Transfer

A partnership is a contractual relationship which is personal in nature, and based upon the good faith of the parties in their dealings with each other. The right of each partner to bind the partnership in contract, coupled with the unlimited liability of each of the partners, precludes the unfettered right of a partner to transfer his interest in the partnership to

another. The retirement of a partner raises a similar problem. Since the retiring partner's interest is not freely transferable, the remaining partners must either acquire the retiring partner's share in the partnership, or wind up the business. Neither of these solutions may be entirely satisfactory to either the retiring partner or those who remain. The death of a partner represents another disruptive event which also raises the problem of transfer of interests in the partnership. Unless special provisions are made in the partnership agreement (such as provision for the payment of a deceased partner's share by way of insurance) the retirement or death of a partner will generally have a serious effect on the relationship and the business associated with it.

The corporate form of organization differs substantially in this regard. The rights of the shareholders in a corporation do not include the right to bind the corporation in contract, nor may creditors look to the personal assets of the shareholders in determining whether or not credit should be extended to the corporation. Under these circumstances, the identity of the shareholder, to some extent, becomes unimportant, as does his personal worth. Once a corporation issues a share to a shareholder and receives payment for it, no further contribution may be demanded from the shareholder. If the shareholder should desire to transfer the share to another, it has no real effect upon the corporation save for a change in the identity of the person holding the share. For these reasons, shares may be freely transferred in a public company, thus overcoming one of the main drawbacks of the partnership.

The corporation has a number of other advantages over the partnership. These are subsequently noted.

of shares you own are in a small, private corp.
2 problems   1) Probably no market for shares
*2) There will be share transfer restrictions

Term of Operation of the Business

A partnership's existence is limited by the life of its members. If a partner should die, the partnership is dissolved, but may be reformed by the remaining parties, if the agreement so provides. A partnership may continue as long as its partners wish it to do so, but the death of a partner, or his retirement, is disruptive to the operation.

A corporation, on the other hand, theoretically has an unlimited term of operation. It never dies, even though the persons who own shares in it may do so. The death of a shareholder has no effect on the continued existence of the corporation. A corporation may be dissolved by the State, or it may voluntarily be wound up, but in each case, the act is not dependent upon the life or death of a shareholder. For example, some corporations have been in existence for many hundreds of years, the most notable being the Hudson's Bay Company that was incorporated in 1670 and remains in existence today. No partnership (at least with original unincorporated members) is likely to match this record.

Because a corporation's existence is not affected by the fortunes of the shareholders, a corporation is free to accumulate or acquire large amounts of capital, either through the issue of shares, or by the issue of bonds and debentures. These latter forms are special types of security instruments which a corporation might issue, and which can be used where large sums of money are required.

Operation of the Business Entity

A partnership is governed by the partnership agreement that establishes the rights and duties of the partners and the man-

ner in which the partnership is to operate. In the absence of an agreement (or where the agreement is silent) the partnership is governed by the *Partnerships Act,*[1] and a number of other related statutes.

In contrast, the corporation is governed by the statute under which it is incorporated (as well as a number of other statutes such as securities legislation) which sets out the conditions that apply to its operation. The rights and duties of the shareholders and directors with respect to the corporation are statutory, rather than contractual in nature, although both the corporation and partnership are subject to statute.

Separate Existence of the Corporation

At law, the partnership is in a sense indistinguishable from the partners, yet it does possess many of the attributes of a separate entity. Contracts are made in the firm name, and a partnership in most jurisdictions may be sued in the firm name, but the fact remains that the parties individually as well as collectively are responsible for its operation. The corporation has a clearly defined separate existence at law.

This particular issue was established in a case which came before the English courts in 1896.[2] The case dealt with the principal shareholder and a corporation which he had incorporated to take over his successful shoe and leather business. The principal shareholder had taken back a debenture from the corporation, and when the corporation later became insolvent, the principal shareholder claimed priority in payment of the debenture over the claims of the general creditors. In the litigation

---

[1] All provinces have legislation governing this relationship. See, for example, the *Partnerships Act*, R.S.O. 1980, c. 370.
[2] *Salomon v. A. Salomon & Co., Ltd.*, [1897] A.C. 22.

that followed, the court held that the corporation was an entity separate and distinct from its shareholders, and permitted the principal shareholder to obtain payment of the debenture from the money available, before claims of the general creditors could be satisfied.

Corporate Name

The corporation name is an asset of the business.[3] The name must not be the same as the name of any other existing corporation, and in the case of a corporation incorporated to carry on a business (other than a corporation incorporated under a special statute), the last word in the name must be a word which identifies it as a corporation. The words that may be used vary from jurisdiction to jurisdiction, but generally must be *Limited* or *Ltd.*, *Incorporated* or *Inc.*, or *Corporation* or *Corp.* The purpose of the identification word is to distinguish a corporation from a partnership, and/or sole proprietorship. Partnerships are not permitted to use any word reserved for corporation identification, or any word that might imply corporate status.

As a general rule, the corporation's name may not be one which denotes any connection with the Crown, nor may the name be obscene, too general, or such that it would cause confusion with other existing names, or the names of well known incorporated or unincorporated organizations.[4]

A corporation must clearly indicate its name and its place of business on all printed letterhead and business forms. It must formally execute documents by the use of a seal (which contains the corporation name) and which the authorized

officers of the corporation will impress upon all written documents which require the formal 'signature' of the corporation.

METHODS OF INCORPORATION

Royal Charter *King makes law or company*

The original method of incorporation was by Royal Charter. The issue of the Charter was for the purpose of creating a legal existence for the entity, to permit it to either operate as a monopoly, or to own land. The Hudson's Bay Company, for example, was granted rights to all of the land drained by the rivers flowing into Hudson's Bay. The British South Africa Company was granted a similar type of Charter with respect to large amounts of land in South Africa.

The Royal Charter was an exercise of the king's prerogative, and the issue of the Charter gave the entity all the rights at law of a natural person (subject to certain exceptions). The Charter, however, did not generally give those persons connected with the corporation limited liability if the corporation was a trading company. The Royal Charter method of incorporation has not been used to incorporate ordinary trading corporations for many years.

Letters Patent *– still used in Ont. for charitable organizations*

The Letters Patent system of incorporation is a direct development of the Royal Charter form. When the Crown ceased the issue of Royal Charters for trading corporations, a new system was developed whereby legislation was passed which set out the criteria for the issue of letters patent by a representative of the Crown.[5] The

---

[3]*Hunt's Ltd. v. Hunt* (1924), 56 O.L.R. 349.
[4]*Tussaud v. Tussaud* (1890), 44 Ch.D. 678.

[5]For example, prior to 1970, under the *Corporations Act* of Ontario, R.S.O. 1960, c. 71, the Provincial Secretary issued the Letters Patent. At the federal level, the Secretary of State issued Letters Patent prior to 1976.

application for incorporation would then be prepared and submitted in accordance with the legislation, and the Crown's representative would issue the incorporating document.

Letters Patent simply means a government document which grants a special right or privilege, and in the case of a corporation, it represents the creation of a legal entity. A corporation created by Letters Patent acquires all of the powers of a Royal Charter corporation, and has, as a result, all of the usual rights at law of a natural person.[6] The federal government, and the provinces of Manitoba, New Brunswick, Ontario, Prince Edward Island, and Quebec used the Letters Patent system for many years. However, after 1970, some of the provinces and the federal government adopted a different system, and at the present time, only Quebec, New Brunswick, and Prince Edward Island still retain the Letters Patent system.

Third parties dealing with a Letters Patent corporation may assume that the corporation has the capacity to enter into most ordinary contracts. If the officers of the corporation with apparent authority to bind the corporation enter into a contract of a type prohibited by the objects or by-laws of the corporation, the corporation would still be bound, unless the third party had actual notice of the lack of authority in the officers of the corporation.

Special Act

The third type of incorporation represents a quite different form. Parliament may use its powers to create corporations by way of special statute. These corporations are known as special-Act corporations, and instead of the broad powers possessed by a corporation incorporated under Royal Charter, the special-Act corporation has only the powers specifically granted to it by the statute. Special-Act corporations, as the name implies, are corporations incorporated for special purposes. Many are for public or quasi-public purposes, such as for the construction of public utilities, or for activities which require a certain amount of control in the public interest. Banks, telephone companies, railroads, and Crown corporations (such as the Canadian Broadcasting Corporation) are examples of corporations incorporated under special legislation. Special Act corporations as a general rule do not use the words *limited*, *incorporated*, or their abbreviations in the corporate name. For example, chartered banks use no corporate identification at all in the corporation's name.

The legislation sets out the rights and obligations of the corporation, and if the corporation should attempt to perform an act which it is not authorized to do under the statute, the act is *ultra vires* (beyond the powers of) the corporation, and a nullity. For example, in a case which involved an English corporation that was limited by special Act to borrowing £25 000, the corporation exceeded the amount, and eventually borrowed £85 000. When a secured creditor attempted to recover money loaned to the corporation, the court held that the plaintiff creditor could not enforce the security, because the corporation had no authority to issue it. In rejecting the claim, the court held that all the security issued in excess of the £25 000 authorized by statute was a nullity.[7]

---

[6]*Bonanza Creek Gold Mining Co. v. The King,* [1916] 1 A.C. 566.

[7]*Baroness Wenlock v. River Dee Co.* (1887), 36 Ch. 674 at p. 685.

general business corps.

||||||||||||||||||||||||||||||||||||||||||||||||||||||||||||||||||||||||||||

CASE 18.1

Baroness Wenlock v. River Dee Co. (1887), 36 Ch. D. 674.

KEKEWICH, J.:

. . . there is a large difference between [an ecclesiastical] corporation and a corporation such as we are dealing with here, called into existence by statute, the creature of statute for specific purposes, and armed with specific powers which must not be exceeded for the fulfilment of those particular purposes. Looking at the exercise of any alleged power on behalf of a corporation of that kind we must see whether it is either expressly given by the statute, or is necessarily implied in order to the fulfilment of its powers. If we cannot bring it within that— and a necessary implication in such a case differs not at all from expression—then the company cannot exercise the alleged power.

||||||||||||||||||||||||||||||||||||||||||||||||||||||||||||||||||||||||||||

General Act *Canadian Business Corp. Act*
Ontario Business Corp. Act

In Canada, a few of the provinces patterned their legislation after the English general-Act system, and as a result, Canadian business corporations may be incorporated under either Letters Patent (in some provinces) or two forms of general-Act incorporation. In those provinces that patterned their legislation after the English general Act, the incorporators need only comply with the preparation and filing requirements to form a corporation. Alberta, British Columbia, Newfoundland, Nova Scotia, and Saskatchewan adopted the English registration system for their incorporation Acts. The document filed in these jurisdictions is referred to as the *memorandum of association*. The memorandum contains the details of the corporation as required by the Act, and on filing, the corporation comes into existence.

The federal government, Ontario, and Manitoba used the Letters Patent system

until very recently. In 1970, Ontario introduced a general Act for the incorporation of business corporations which borrowed some of its terminology from the United States model, rather than the English one. In Ontario, the document filed is called the *articles of incorporation* and the document issued by the government is referred to as a *certificate of incorporation*. In 1975, the federal government introduced legislation for the incorporation of business corporations which was patterned after the Ontario legislation, and Manitoba shortly thereafter introduced similar legislation.

The general-Act corporation, like the special-Act corporation, is a creature of statute, and its powers are limited to those powers specifically granted under the Act. Unlike the Royal Charter and Letters Patent corporation, it does not necessarily have all the powers of a natural person, but only those powers set out in the statute and its memorandum of association. Incorporating jurisdictions in some cases have attempted to extend to a general-Act corporation the powers of a natural person. British Columbia, Manitoba, and the federal government in their corporation legislation for example, have specifically set out that a business corporation incorporated under their legislation shall have all the powers of a natural person.[8] Ontario employed different wording, which states that no act of the corporation is invalid simply because it lacks the power or capacity to do the act.[9] In the remainder of the general-Act provinces, the powers of the corporation are limited to those established by the statute and the powers set

[8]See, for example, the *Canada Business Corporations Act*, 1974-75 (Can.), c. 33, s. 15(1); the *Corporations Act*, 1976 (Man.), c. 40, s. 15(1).

[9]The *Business Corporations Act*, R.S.O. 1980, c. 54, s. 16.

out in the memorandum of association filed under the statute.

The courts treat both the statute and the memorandum of association as the body of law which delineates the powers of the corporation. Any act of a corporation incorporated by memorandum of association which is beyond or outside the powers set out in either the statute or the memorandum is considered *ultra vires* and a nullity. The harshness of the doctrine of *ultra vires*, however is generally avoided by incorporators taking special care in the drafting of their memorandum of association. By stating their objects and powers as broadly as possible in the document, problems which may develop as a result of lack of capacity are less likely to be encountered.

The limited capacity of the general-Act corporation carries with it a danger for those who deal with it. Because the statute and the memorandum of association are treated as public documents, and the public is deemed to be aware of their contents, any person dealing with a general-Act corporation is also deemed to be aware of any limitations on the power of the corporation to contract, or to do specific acts. For example, if the memorandum of association prohibits the directors of the corporation from engaging in a particular type of activity, and the directors proceed to do so, any contract negotiated in that respect would be *ultra vires* the corporation, and could not be enforced by the other contracting party. This rule would apply even though the contracting party was unaware of the limitation on the power of the corporation, and it is known as the *doctrine of constructive notice*.

To avoid the doctrine, a number of general-Act jurisdictions have included in their legislation a clause which avoids the problems raised by the doctrine, and which protect third parties from unusual limitations on the corporation, or on the powers of the directors. British Columbia, Manitoba, Ontario, and the federal government have included such clauses in their legislation.[10] The general effect of these clauses is to protect third parties from any unusual limitations on the powers of directors, or on the corporation itself, by providing that a third party contracting with the corporation is not deemed to have notice of any limitation on the rights or powers of the corporation or its officers. When this clause is coupled with the clause which provides that the corporation has the capacity of a natural person, third parties acquire protection similar to that which they would have in contracts with natural persons. However, in those general-Act provinces where the legislation does not give the corporation the broad powers of a natural person, and does not do away with the doctrine of constructive notice, the third party dealing with a corporation must use extreme care. The third party in those circumstances would be obliged to ascertain not only that the officers of the corporation had the authority to commit the corporation, but that the corporation had the power to do the particular act contemplated in the contract.

In all cases where a third party is dealing with a corporation, once the corporation is determined to have the power to enter into a particular type of contract, the third party is entitled to rely on what is known as the *indoor management rule* for the validity of the acts of the officers of the corporation. If the officers of the corporation, for example, are required to obtain the ap-

[10]See, for example, the *Canada Business Corporations Act*, 1974-75 (Can.), c. 33, s. 17.

proval of the shareholders before a contract may be effected, the third party may accept the evidence submitted by the officers that shareholder approval was obtained. The third party may rely on this evidence if it appears to be regular, and need not inquire further into the internal operation of the corporation. It would not apply, of course, where a third party is deemed to have notice of a limitation on the powers of the corporation contained in its memorandum of association, or in the statute. Its application is directed to the internal operation of the corporation, of which the third party normally would have no actual knowledge.

||||||||||||||||||||||||||||||||||||||||||||||||||||||||||||||||||||||

CASE 18.2

Biggerstaff v. Rowatt's Wharf, Ltd., [1896] 2 Ch. 93.

LINDLEY, L.J.:

What must persons look to when they deal with directors? They must see whether according to the constitution of the company the directors could have the powers which they are purporting to exercise. Here the articles enabled the directors to give to the managing director all the powers of the directors except as to drawing, accepting, or indorsing bills of exchange and promissory notes. The persons dealing with him must look to the articles, and see that the managing director might have power to do what he purports to do, and that is enough for a person dealing with him bonâ fide. It is settled by a long string of authorities that where directors give a security which according to the articles they might have power to give the person taking it is entitled to assume that they had the power.

||||||||||||||||||||||||||||||||||||||||||||||||||||||||||||||||||||||

THE INCORPORATION PROCESS

In most jurisdictions, the incorporation process begins with the preparation of an application for incorporation which sets out the name of the proposed corporation, the address of the head office and principal place of business, the names of the applicants for incorporation (usually called the incorporators), the objects of the corporation (except under the *Canada Business Corporations Act*), the share capital, any restrictions or rights attached to the shares, and any special powers or restrictions which apply to the activities of the corporation. The applicants for incorporation usually must also indicate whether the corporation will offer its shares to the public, or whether it will remain "private" in the sense that it will not make a public offering of its securities. This last matter is generally quite important from the point of view of the incorporating jurisdiction. Corporations which intend to offer their shares to the public usually must follow elaborate procedures under the jurisdiction's securities legislation or corporations act to ensure that the public is properly advised of all details of the corporation and the purpose for which the shares are offered to the public. A corporation which does not offer its shares to the public, but which may offer them to investors by private negotiation, is usually relieved of many of the special formalities imposed by the legislation to protect shareholders and the public at large. For example, the shareholders of such a corporation may, if they so desire, dispense with the formal audit of the corporation's books each year, because a small group of shareholders (as few as one in some jurisdictions) may not require the elaborate examination of the financial records of the corporation that is necessary for a public corporation. A corporation that does not offer its shares to the public may also impose restrictions on the transfer of shares in the corporation to enable the remaining shareholders to exercise some control over persons who become a part of the small group. Corporations that offer their shares to the public must not place restrictions on the transfer of their shares. A number of other differences exist between the two forms of incorporation. Suffice to say that the distinction is made to relieve the closely held corporation of many of the onerous obligations imposed on the large public corporation for the protection of its shareholders.

The complete application for incorporation must be submitted to the appropriate office in the incorporating jurisdiction, together with the fee charged for the incorporation. In the case of a jurisdiction which issues Letters Patent, the company will be incorporated when the Letters Patent are issued. In general-Act provinces, where a memorandum of association is filed, the filing date becomes the date of incorporation. In those general-Act provinces where articles of incorporation are filed, the corporation comes into existence when the *certificate of incorporation* is issued.

Following incorporation, the incorporators, as first directors, proceed in the case of Letters Patent and certificate corporations with the remaining formalities of establishing by-laws and passing resolutions. These rules for the internal operation of the corporation set out the various duties of the officers and directors, provide for banking, borrowing, the issue of shares, and perhaps for the purchase of an existing business, if the corporation was incorporated for that purpose.

If the incorporators are not the permanent directors of the corporation, they usually hold a special meeting at which time they resign as first directors, and the shareholders then elect permanent directors to hold office until the next annual meeting. The permanent directors will, amongst themselves, elect the officers of the corporation to hold the offices of presi-

dent, secretary, treasurer, etc. Once under way, the directors carry on the operation of the corporation until the annual meeting of shareholders. At the annual meeting, the directors and officers report to the shareholders for their performance since the previous meeting.

CORPORATE SECURITIES

Corporations may issue a variety of different securities to acquire capital for their operations. One of the most common forms of acquiring capital is to issue *shares* in the organization. A share is simply a fraction of the ownership of the corporation, and represents a part-ownership equal to one part of the total number of shares issued. For example, if a corporation has issued 1 000 shares, each share would represent a one-thousandth part-ownership of the corporation. Unfortunately, corporations may issue many different kinds of shares at different values, and with different rights attached to them, and to determine the actual value of the part-ownership that a share represents is sometimes difficult.

Shares may be either fixed or *par value* shares, or *no par value* shares in which case the value of the share is not fixed. Some jurisdictions have abolished par value shares,[11] since their importance as a share interest has diminished in recent years. Shares may also be classed as either *common* or *preference* shares. All corporations must have some voting common shares, as these are the usual form of shares issued to the shareholders who will elect the directors of the corporation. Corporations sometimes issue preference shares, which, as the name denotes, will have special

[11]The *Canada Business Corporations Act*, 1974-75 (Can.), c. 33, s. 24(1).

[Handwritten annotations at top of page: "Dividend – return of profits to shareholders / Debenture – a form of loan of corporation / Bonds – more secure loan/creditor – debenture – fixed rate of return / Shares → profits → dividend ↘ ownership equity"]

rights attached to them, such as the right to a fixed rate of return in the form of dividends, special voting privileges, or a priority in payment over the common shareholders in the event that the corporation should be wound up.

A corporation may also issue securities which do not represent a share of the ownership of the corporation, but a debt. The debt may be either secured by a *fixed charge* attaching to specific assets of the corporation, or a *floating charge*, which does not usually attach to any particular assets of the corporation, but simply to the assets in general. Corporate securities which represent a charge against specific assets of the corporation are generally called *mortgage bonds*. Those which are normally subordinate to mortgage bonds in priority are usually called *debentures*. The degree of security which each type represents depends to a considerable degree on the priority of the rights which it has to the corporation's various assets in the event that the corporation should default on its debts. The rights of these security holders are examined in Chapter 32 "Security for Debt," and in Chapter 33 "Bankruptcy."

DIVISION OF CORPORATE POWERS

Duties and Responsibilities of Directors

The various corporation Acts attempt to separate ownership from management insofar as it is practicable in order to clearly identify the particular rights and duties of shareholders and directors. Most rights with respect to management have been given exclusively to the directors. For example, the right to declare dividends, and

to conduct the business of the corporation, fall exclusively to the directors. Major changes in the nature of the corporation although initiated by the directions, must generally be referred to the shareholders to confirm. For example, the shareholders must be the ones to ultimately decide if the corporation is to change its objects, wind up, or alter its capital structure. The purpose of the division of powers between shareholders and the directors is essentially one of balancing the need for shareholder protection with the need for freedom to manage on the part of the directors. This balance is reflected in the rights and duties of each group.

The directors are responsible for the day-to-day operations of the corporation. Once the shareholders have elected a board of directors, they have little more to do with the management of the corporation until the next annual general meeting. The ultimate responsibility rests with the shareholders, however, as they are free to elect new and different directors at the next annual meeting if the directors fail to perform satisfactorily. Under extreme circumstances the shareholders may also take steps to terminate the appointment of directors before the next annual meeting.

The directors, once elected, have a duty to conduct the affairs of the corporation in the best interests of the corporation as a whole, rather than in the interests of any particular group of shareholders. This distinction is most important, because the directors may be held accountable at law for a breach of their duty to the corporation. Usually the shareholders' interests and the interests of the corporation are the same, but this is not always so, and where they are divergent, the directors must concern themselves with the interests of the corporation alone.

The relationship between a director and the corporation is fiduciary in nature, and requires the director to act in good faith at all times in his dealing with, and on behalf of, the corporation. At common law, the duty on the part of the director to act in good faith is augmented by a duty to use care and skill in carrying out corporation business. Some jurisdictions have imposed an additional statutory duty on directors to exercise the powers and duties of their office honestly with the care and skill of a reasonably careful and prudent person in similar circumstances.[12]

The fiduciary relationship which a director has with the corporation precludes the director from engaging in any activity which might permit the director to make a profit at the corporation's expense. For example, the director must not use the corporation's name to acquire a benefit for himself, nor must he use his position in the corporation to make a profit for himself which rightfully belongs to the corporation.

A director may, under certain circumstances, engage in a business transaction with the corporation, but considerable care is necessary, otherwise the director will be in violation of this duty as a director. As a general rule, in any transaction with the corporation, the director must immediately disclose his interest in the particular contract or property, and refrain from discussing or voting on the matter at the directors meeting.[13] Also, in some jurisdictions, shareholder approval of contracts in which a director has an interest is required.[14]

A director may not normally engage in any business transaction with a third party which might deprive the corporation of an opportunity to make a profit or acquire a particular asset. For example, if a director becomes aware of an opportunity to acquire a valuable property through his position as a director he may not acquire the property for himself if the corporation might be interested in acquiring it. To do so would be a violation of his duty of loyalty to the corporation. In an instance of this nature, the courts would apply the principle or doctrine of *corporate opportunity*, and find that the director's acquisition of the property was in trust for the corporation, and treat the corporation as the beneficial owner. If the director had already disposed of the property, the court might require him to deliver any profit made on the transaction to the corporation.

A similar situation may arise where a director trades in shares of the corporation. A director may lawfully buy and sell shares of the corporation on his own account, and retain any profit which he might make on the transaction. However, if he uses information which he acquires by virtue of his position in the corporation, and buys or sells shares using that information to the detriment of another, he may be liable for the loss which that person suffers as a direct consequence of his actions. In most jurisdictions, the legislation pertaining to corporations requires "insiders" such as the directors, officers, and persons usually holding over 10% of the shares in a public corporation to report their trading each month to a government regulatory body or official. This information is then made available to the public as a deterrent to directors who might be tempted to use inside information for their own profit.

[12]See, for example, the *Canada Business Corporations Act*, 1974-75 (Can.), c. 33, s. 117(1).

[13]The *Canada Business Corporations Act*, 1974-75 (Can.), c. 33, s. 115.

[14]The *Business Corporations Act*, R.S.O. 1980, c. 54, s. 134.

||||||||||||||||||||||||||||||||||||||||||||||||||||||||||||||||||||||||||||||||

CASE 18.3
Canadian Aero Service Ltd. v. O'Malley et al. (1973), 40 D.L.R. (3d) 371.

LASKIN, J.:

. . . the fiduciary relationship goes at least this far: a director or a senior officer like O'Malley or Zarzycki is precluded from obtaining for himself, either secretly or without the approval of the company (which would have to be properly manifested upon full disclosure of the facts), any property or business advantage either belonging to the company or for which it has been negotiating; and especially is this so where the director or officer is a participant in the negotiations on behalf of the company.

An examination of the case law in this Court and in the Courts of other like jurisdictions on the fiduciary duties of directors and senior officers shows the pervasiveness of a strict ethic in this area of the law. In my opinion, this ethic disqualifies a director or senior officer from usurping for himself or diverting to another person or company with whom or with which he is associated a maturing business opportunity which his company is actively pursuing; he is also precluded from so acting even after his resignation where the resignation may fairly be said to have been prompted or influenced by a wish to acquire for himself the opportunity sought by the company, or where it was his position with the company rather than a fresh initiative that led him to the opportunity which he later acquired.

||||||||||||||||||||||||||||||||||||||||||||||||||||||||||||||||||||||||||||||||

Personal Liability of Directors
Over the years, there has been a general trend towards holding the directors liable for different things which might take place as a result of their actions. Many of these responsibilities have been imposed on directors as a result of directors using their position or the corporation in such a way that it causes hardship to third parties, employees, or shareholders.

As a general rule, the directors may be held liable for any loss occasioned by the corporation itself, if the directors commit the corporation to an act that is clearly *ultra vires* regarding its objects' clause, or contrary to its by-laws. The corporation usually is the body which suffers a loss in such a case, and an action may be taken by the shareholders against the directors to recover the loss. They would also be liable to the company if they should sell shares at a discount contrary to the statute, or declare a dividend which impairs the capital of the corporation.

In some jurisdictions, a special liability is imposed on directors with respect to employee wages in the event of bankruptcy of the corporation. The law imposes a duty on the directors to satisfy the amounts owing to employees for unpaid wages if the corporation lacks the funds to do so. The liability for unpaid wages is in a sense, a contingent liability because it would only come into play if the assets of the corporation were insufficient to satisfy the employee wage claims.

In addition to these particular liabilities, the directors are exposed to a number of penalties and fines if they should fail to comply with the legislation concerning the filing of notices, or if they should fail to make returns to the various government agencies which monitor corporation activity.

Shareholders' Rights
The shareholders, as owners of the corporation, are entitled at regular intervals to a full disclosure by the directors of the corporation's business activities. In addition to the right to information, the shareholders have the right to elect the directors at general meetings of the shareholders, and

to approve the actions of the directors since the previous meeting. Shareholders must also approve all important matters which concern the corporation, and which usually take the form of special by-laws. Usually these special by-laws do not become effective until shareholders' approval has been received, and in this fashion, the shareholders have ultimate control over all major decisions of the directors affecting the corporation's structure or purpose.

Each year, the shareholders review the management of the directors at the annual general meeting of the corporation, and at that time elect directors for the ensuing year. All common shareholders have a right to vote at the meeting with the number of shares held determining the number of votes which a shareholder might cast.

At the general meeting, the auditor's report is discussed by the shareholders, and if necessary, the auditor may be present to explain matters of a financial nature which pertain to the audit. The shareholders also appoint an auditor for the next year at the annual meeting. The auditor's duty is to the shareholders, and not to the directors or the corporation. The auditor is responsible for the examination of the books and financial affairs of the corporation on the shareholders' behalf. In order to perform the audit the auditor has access to all financial accounts and books, but the shareholders do not. The shareholders are only entitled to the financial reports provided by the directors' and auditor's report at the year end. The shareholders, however, do have access to certain other corporation records. A shareholder may, for example, examine the minute-books of shareholders' meetings, the shareholder register, the list of directors, the incorporating documents, and the by-laws and resolutions of the corporation, but a shareholder may not examine the minute-books for directors' meetings.

Special meetings of shareholders may be convened for a variety of purposes relating to the corporation if a number of shareholders[15] believe that the meetings are necessary. The group of shareholders usually requests the directors to call the meeting, but if the directors should fail to do so within a fixed period of time, the shareholders may do so themselves, and the corporation will be obliged to reimburse them for the expenses incurred.[16] At the meeting, the shareholders may deal with the subject-matter of the requisition, and where appropriate, take action in the form of a by-law or resolution. An example of a special meeting called by shareholders might be to remove an auditor, or to object to a particular course of action which the directors have taken, and which might be reversed by a special resolution or by-law of the shareholders.

The fact that shareholders must approve all important decisions of the directors prevents the directors from engaging in certain activities which might be contrary to the interest of the majority of the shareholders. Unfortunately, it does little to protect minority shareholders if the majority of the shares are held by the directors or those who support them. Because the "majority rules" for most decisions within a corporation, a minority shareholder has only limited rights where there is a misuse of power by the majority. At common law, it is normally necessary for the complain-

---

[15]The number is usually presented as a small percentage of the total number of shares outstanding. See, for example, *Canada Business Corporations Act*, 1974-75 (Can.), c. 33, s. 137, where the percentage is set at 5%.
[16]The *Canada Business Corporations Act*, 1974-75 (Can.), c. 33, s. 137(4) and (6).

ant to show some injury has occurred as a result of the decision of the majority. This is particularly difficult in the case of a minority shareholder of a corporation, because the corporation, and not the shareholder, is usually wronged by the misuse of power or the breach of duty.[17] Where the corporation is controlled by the very majority that has committed the breach of duty, or misused its power, the corporation is not likely to take action against that particular group.

To overcome this difficulty, the common law courts have recognized a number of exceptions to the "majority rule," and have permitted minority shareholders to take action on behalf of the corporation against the majority (or the directors): where the act objected to is *ultra vires* the corporation, where the act personally affects the rights of the minority shareholders, where the corporation has failed to comply with the procedural requirements for approval of the act, or where the act of the majority constitutes a fraud on the minority shareholders. The last exception to the general rule includes cases where the majority attempt to appropriate the minority interests for themselves, or where they attempt to acquire corporate property at the expense of the corporation.

The rights of minority shareholders have also been expanded by the addition of statutory rights and remedies in some jurisdictions. Ontario has, for example, established the right of the minority shareholder(s) to institute a representative action on behalf of the corporation if the shareholder can satisfy the court that the action was brought in good faith and after a reasonable attempt had been made to have the corporation take the action itself. The particular disadvantage attached to this minority right is that the shareholder may be held liable for court costs, if the action is ultimately dismissed by the court.[18]

The Ontario Act also provides a right to a minority shareholder in a corporation, which does not offer its shares to the public, to demand that the corporation purchase his or her shares at a fair price (or if a fair price cannot be agreed upon, a price fixed by the court). This right arises where the shareholder has voted against a resolution of the shareholders to sell or otherwise dispose of most of the assets of the corporation, or where the proposal was the amalgamation with another corporation, or where the resolution was for the removal of a restriction on the transfer of shares of the corporation.[19] Once notice is given in writing, the dissenting shareholder is entitled to payment for the shares within a reasonable time, and the corporation is obliged to accept the shares.[20] The corporation, however, would not be obliged to make the purchase if the payment would render it insolvent.[21]

---

[17]This situation arose in the case of *Foss v. Harbottle* (1834), 2 Hare 461; 67 E.R. 189.

[18]The *Business Corporations Act*, R.S.O. 1980, c. 54, s. 99.
[19]*Ibid.*, s. 100(1).
[20]*Ibid.*, s. 100(2).
[21]*Ibid.*, s. 100(3).

||||||||||||||||||||||||||||||||||||||||||||||||||||||||||||||||||||||||||||||||||||||||||||||||||||||||||||||||||||||||||||||||||||||||||||||||||||||||||

SUMMARY A corporation is a legal entity which has an existence separate from its owners. The powers which the corporation may acquire varies from something close to the powers possessed by a natural person to very restricted and narrow powers, where the corporation is incorporated by a legislature under a statute for a very specific purpose.

The method of incorporation varies from province to province, and may take a number of different forms, each granting a corporation different rights and powers. In some provinces, incorporation is by the issue of letters patent, which is very similar to the Royal Charter form of incorporation, and which gives the corporation virtually all of the powers of a natural person. Other provinces provide for incorporation under a general statute, which limits the powers of the corporation to those powers acquired under the statute and contained in the memorandum of association filed under it. The federal government and several provinces use a general Act for incorporation, but use a slightly different terminology, and have given corporations incorporated under the legislation all the powers of a natural person.

Regardless of the form of incorporation, the corporate body takes on a separate existence from its incorporators, and continues in existence until it is wound up, or it surrenders its Charter.

A corporation acts through its agents, and is liable to its creditors for all corporation debts. The shareholders who own the corporation have limited liability for the debts of the corporation, their limit being the value of the shares which they purchased in the corporation.

In a corporation, the shareholders elect directors annually to manage the affairs of the corporation. The directors, once elected, have a general duty to operate or manage the business in the best interests of the corporation, and owe a duty of loyalty and good faith to the corporation in all of their dealings on its behalf. The shareholders, on the other hand, do not participate in the active day-to-day management of the business, but are entitled to information from the directors on the corporation's performance. If the shareholders disapprove of the directors' management, they may remove the directors at the annual general meeting of shareholders, and elect other directors in place of those that previously held the office.

Corporation legislation attempts, in general, to balance the powers of the directors to manage the corporation with the protection of the investment of the shareholders and, to some extent, also considers the rights of the public. It does this through the imposition of special duties and obligations on the directors, and permits the shareholders to take action either within the corporation, or through the courts, when the directors fail to comply with the duties and responsibilities imposed upon them.

DISCUSSION QUESTIONS

1. *Describe the legal concept of a "corporation." How does a corporation differ from a partnership?*

2. *For what purposes were early corporations formed?*

3. *Why did the Industrial Revolution and the concept of a corporation go hand in hand?*

4. *To what sector of business do special-Act corporations generally confine their activities.*

5. *Define "Letters Patent." How does a Letters Patent corporation differ from a corporation formed under a "general Act"?*

6. *Compare the effect of a transfer of an interest in a partnership with the transfer of interest in a corporation.*

7. *How is a corporation generally identified to distinguish it from an unincorporated body?*

8. *Describe the shareholders' relationship with the corporation with respect to liability, rights, and control.*

9. *Explain the doctrine of corporate* ultra vires, *and indicate how it differs with respect to each form of incorporation.*

10. *Describe the* indoor management rule.

11. *Distinguish between "public", "private," and "Crown" corporations. What other terminology is used to describe each?*

12. *Why is disclosure important for promoters, directors, and all other persons engaged in the sale and distribution of securities of corporations to the public?*

13. *Outline the principle of "corporate opportunity."*

14. *While the "majority rules" in most corporations, what special rights are generally available to minority shareholders?*

15. *Outline the obligation of the directors of a corporation, and state where their final responsibility rests.*

JUDICIAL DECISIONS

Nature of a Corporation— Limited Liability— Existence Separate From Shareholders

Salomon v. Salomon & Co., Ltd., [1897] A.C. 22.

A. Salomon operated a successful leather and footwear business. He incorporated a company and sold the business to the company in return for 20 000 shares and certain debentures. Members of his family each held one share to meet the requirements of the Act, which required seven shareholders. The company later became insolvent, and both the unsecured creditors and Salomon claimed the remaining assets which were allegedly secured by Salomon's debentures.

LORD HERSCHELL:

It is to be observed that both Courts treated the company as a legal entity distinct from Salomon and the then members who composed it, and therefore as a validity constituted corporation. This is, indeed, necessarily involved in the judgment which declared that the company was entitled to certain rights as against Salomon. Under these circumstances, I am at a loss to understand what is meant by saying that A. Salomon & Co., Limited, is but an "alias" for A. Salomon. It is not another name for the same person; the company is ex hypothesi a distinct legal persona. As little am I able to adopt the view that the company was the agent of Salomon to carry on his business for him. In a popular sense, a company may in every case be said to carry on business for and on behalf of its shareholders; but this certainly does not in point of law constitute the relation of principal and agent between them or render the shareholders liable to indemnify the company against the debts which it incurs. Here, it is true, Salomon owned all the shares except six, so that if the business were profitable he would be entitled, substantially, to the whole of the profits. The other shareholders, too, are said to have been "dummies," the nominees of Salomon. But when once it is conceded that they were individual members of the company distinct from Salomon, and sufficiently so to bring into existence in conjunction with him a validly constituted corporation, I am unable to see how the facts to which I have just referred can affect the legal position of the company, or give it rights as against its members which it would not otherwise possess.

The Court of Appeal based their judgment on the proposition that the formation of the company and all that followed on it were a mere scheme to enable the appellant to carry on business in the name of the company, with limited liability, contrary to the true intent and meaning of the Companies Act, 1862. The conclusion which they drew from this premiss was, that the company was a trustee and Salomon their cestui que trust. I cannot think that the conclusion follows even if the premiss be sound. It seems to me that the logical result would be that the company had not been validly constituted, and therefore had no legal existence. But, apart from this, it is necessary to examine the proposition on which the Court have rested their judgment, as its effect would be far reaching. Many industrial and banking concerns of the highest standing and credit have, in recent years, been, to use a common expression, converted into joint stock companies, and often into what are called "private" companies where the whole of the shares are held by the former partners. It appears to me that all these might be pronounced "schemes to enable" them "to carry on business in the name of the company, with limited liability," in the very sense in which those words are used in the judgment of the Court of Appeal. The profits of the concern carried on by the company will go to the persons whose business it was before the transfer, and in the same proportions as before, the only difference being that the liability of those who take the profits will no longer be unlimited. The very object of the creation of the company and the transfer to it of the business is, that whereas the liability of the partners for debts incurred was without limit, the liability of the members for the debts incurred by the company shall be limited. In no other respect is it intended that there shall be any difference: the conduct of the business and the division of the profits are intended to be the same as before. If the judgment of the Court of Appeal be pushed to its logical conclusion, all these companies must, I think, be held to be trustees for the partners who transferred the business to them, and those partners must be declared liable without limit to discharge the debts of the company. For this is the effect of the judgment as regards the respondent company. The position of the members of a company is just the same whether they are declared liable to pay the debts incurred by the company, or by way of indemnity to furnish the company with the means of paying them. I do not think the learned judges in the Court below have contemplated the application of their judgment to such cases as I have been considering; but I can see no solid distinction between those cases and the present one.

It is said that the respondent company is a "one man" company, and that in this respect it differs from such companies as those to which I have alluded. But it has often happened that a business transferred to a joint stock company has been the property of three or four persons only, and that the other subscribers of the memorandum have been clerks or other persons who possessed little or no interest in the concern. I am unable to see how it can be lawful for three or four or six persons to form a company for the purpose of employing their capital in trading, with the benefit of limited liability, and not for one person to do so, provided, in each case, the requirements of the statute have been complied with and the company has been validly constituted. How does it concern the creditor whether the capital of the company is owned by seven persons in equal shares, with the right to an equal share of the profits, or whether it is almost entirely owned by one person, who practically takes the whole of the profits? The creditor has notice that he is dealing with a company the liability of the members of which is limited, and the register of shareholders informs him how the shares are held, and that they are substantially in the hands of one person, if this be the fact. The creditors in the present case gave credit to and contracted with a limited company; the effect of the decision is to give them the benefit, as regards one of the shareholders, of unlimited liability. I have said that the liability of persons carrying on business can only be limited provided the requirements of the statute be complied with; and this leads naturally to the inquiry, What are those requirements?

The Court of Appeal has declared that the formation of the respondent company and the agreement to take over the business of the appellant were a scheme "contrary to the true intent and meaning of the Companies Act." I know of no means of ascertaining what is the intent and meaning of the Companies Act except by examining its provisions and finding what regulations it has imposed as a condition of trading with limited liability. The memorandum must state the amount of the capital of the company and the number of shares into which it is divided, and no subscriber is to take less than one share. The shares may, however, be of as small a nominal value as those who form the company please: the statute prescribes no minimum; and though there must be seven shareholders, it is enough if each of them holds one share, however small its denomination. The Legislature, therefore, clearly sanctions a scheme by which all the shares except six are owned by a single individual, and these six are of a value little more than nominal.

It was said that in the present case the six shareholders other than the appellant were mere dummies, his nominees, and held their shares in trust for him. I will assume that this was so. In my opinion, it makes no difference. The statute forbids the entry in the register of any trust; and it certainly contains no enactment that each of the seven persons subscribing the memorandum must be beneficially entitled to the share or shares for which he subscribes. The persons who subscribe the memorandum, or who have agreed to become members of the company and whose names are on the register, are alone regarded as, and in fact are, the shareholders. They are subject to all the liability which attaches to the holding of the share. They can be compelled to make any payment which the ownership of a share involves. Whether they are beneficial owners or bare trustees is a matter with which neither the company nor creditors have anything to do: it concerns only them and their cestuis que trust if they have any. If, then, in the present case all the requirements of the statute were complied with, and a company was effectually constituted, and this is the hypothesis of the judgment appealed from, what warrant is there for saying that what was done was contrary to the true intent and meaning of the Companies Act?

It may be that a company constituted like that under consideration was not in the contemplation of the Legislature at the time when the Act authorizing limited liability was passed; that if what is possible under the enactments as they stand had been foreseen a minimum sum would have been fixed as the least denomination of share permissible; and that it would have been made a condition that each of the seven persons should have a substantial interest in the company. But we have to interpret the law, not to make it; and it must be remembered that no one need trust a limited liability company unless he so please, and that before he does so he can ascertain, if he so please, what is the capital of the company and how it is held.

||||||||||||||||||||||||||||||||||||||||||||||||||||||||||||||||||||||||||||||||||||||||||||||||||||||||||||||||||||||||||||||||||||||||||||||||||||||||||||||||||||||||||

Promoters of Corporation— Duty of Disclosure of Any Secret Profit Earned

Gluckstein v. Barnes, [1900] A.C. 240.

A number of promoters acquired property, then incorporated a limited company to purchase the property from them. The promoters elected themselves as first directors of the company and then solicited applications for the purchase of shares by way of a prospectus. The prospectus did not disclose the fact that the promoters would earn a secret profit of £20,000 on the sale.

EARL OF HALSBURY, L.C.:

My Lords, in this case the simple question is whether four persons, of whom the appellant is one, can be permitted to retain the sums which they have obtained from the company of which they were directors by the fraudulent pretence that they had paid 20,000*l*. more than in truth they had paid for property which they, as a syndicate, had bought by subscription among themselves, and then sold to themselves as directors of the company. If this is an accurate account of what has been done by these four persons, of course so gross a transaction cannot be permitted to stand. That that is the real nature of it I now proceed to shew.

In the year 1892 the freehold grounds and buildings known as "Olympia" were the property of a company which in that year was being wound up. That company had issued debentures of the extent of 100,000*l.* as a first charge and a mortgage as a second charge for 10,000*l.* The four persons in question knew that the property would have to be sold, and they combined to buy it in order that they might resell it to a company to be formed by themselves. The combination, which called itself the Freehold Syndicate, but which, perhaps, the common law would have described by a less high-sounding title, proceeded to buy up so far as they could the incumbrances on the property called "Olympia." They expended 27,000*l.* in buying debentures. These, of course, were very much depreciated in value, and they gave 500*l.* for the mortgage of 10,000*l.* As soon as this transaction had been completed they, partners in it, proceeded to form a company, and it was of course necessary that the company should be willing to help, and accordingly the four persons in question were made by the articles of association the first directors.

The property was sold on February 8 by the chief clerk of North J. for 140,000*l.*, and the syndicate purchased nominally for that sum, but, by reason of the arrangement to which I have referred, that sum was less by 20,734*l.* 6*s.* 1*d.* than what they appeared to give. On March 29 they completed as directors the purchase of the property for 180,000*l.*, and they as directors paid to themselves as members of the syndicate 171,000*l.* in cash and 9000*l.* in fully paid-up shares—in all 180,000*l.*

The prospectus by which money was to be obtained from the public disclosed the supposed profit which the vendors were making of 40,000*l.*, while in truth their profit was 60,734*l.* 6*s.* 1*d.*, and it is this undisclosed profit of 20,000*l.*, and the right to retain it, which is now in question.

My Lords, I am wholly unable to understand any claim that these directors, vendors, syndicate, associates, have to retain this money. I entirely agree with the Master of the Rolls that the essence of this scheme was to form a company. It was essential that this should be done, and that they should be directors of it, who would purchase. The company should have been informed of what was being done and consulted whether they would have allowed this profit. I think the Master of the Rolls is absolutely right in saying that the duty to disclose is imposed by the plainest dictates of common honesty as well as by well-settled principles of common law.

Of the facts there cannot be the least doubt; they are proved by the agreement, now that we know the subject-matter with which that agreement is intended to deal, although the agreement would not disclose what the nature of the transaction was to those who were not acquainted with the ingenious arrangements which were prepared for the entrapping the intended victim of these arrangements.

In order to protect themselves, as they supposed, they inserted in the prospectus, qualifying the statement that they had bought the property for 140,000*l*., payable in cash, that they did not sell to the company, and did not intend to sell, any other profits made by the syndicate from interim investments.

Then it is said there is the alternative suggested upon the agreement that the syndicate might sell to a company or to some other purchaser. In the first place, I do not believe they ever intended to sell to anybody else than a company. An individual purchaser might ask inconvenient questions, and if they or any one of them had stated as an inducement to an individual purchaser that 140,000*l*. was given for the property, when in fact 20,000*l*. less had been given, it is a great error to suppose that the law is not strong enough to reach such a statement; but as I say, I do not believe it was ever intended to get an individual purchaser, even if such an intention would have had any operation. When they did afterwards sell to a company, they took very good care there should be no one who could ask questions. They were to be sellers to themselves as buyers, and it was a necessary provision to the plan that they were to be both sellers and buyers, and as buyers to get the money to pay for the purchase from the pockets of deluded shareholders.

My Lords, I decline to discuss the question of disclosure to the company. It is too absurd to suggest that a disclosure to the parties to this transaction is a disclosure to the company of which these directors were the proper guardians and trustees. They were there by the terms of the agreement to do the work of the syndicate, that is to say, to cheat the shareholders; and this, forsooth, is to be treated as a disclosure to the company, when they were really here to hoodwink the shareholders, and so far from protecting them, were to obtain from them the money, the produce of their nefarious plans.

I do not discuss either the sum sued for, or why Gluckstein alone is sued. The whole sum has been obtained by a very gross fraud, and all who were parties to it are responsible to make good what they have obtained and withheld from the shareholders.

I move your Lordships that the appeal be dismissed with costs.

CASE PROBLEMS FOR DISCUSSION

Case 1

Skyscraper Towers Ltd. was a corporation which had been incorporated for the purpose of building and operating a large office building. The corporation later acquired a large quantity of tobacco products as a result of an unauthorized contract which an employee of the corporation had made with a tobacco company. The employee, who was the manager of the purchasing department for Skyscraper Towers, was unaware of the fact that neither the objects of the corporation, nor its by-laws permitted the corporation to purchase the tobacco goods which he intended to sell to tenants of the building.

When the error was discovered and brought to the attention of the directors by a shareholder, the corporation had already taken delivery of the tobacco, but had not yet paid the invoice. In addition, it had set up a tobacco kiosk in the lobby of the building, and a clerk had sold some of the tobacco goods.

The shareholder of the corporation who brought the error to the attention of the directors wishes to stop the sale of the product in the building, and to have the purchase contract rescinded.

If the corporation is incorporated under the laws of Alberta, what action might be taken? How would your answer differ if the corporation was incorporated in Prince Edward Island? In Ontario?

Case 2

Model T Motors Ltd. was indebted to Simple Finance for a substantial sum of money. The finance company held a number of mortgages on the corporation's assets, but pressed the corporation for a blanket demand chattel mortgage as additional security. Under pressure from the finance company, one of the principal shareholders, who was also one of the signing officers of the corporation, executed a blanket chattel mortgage to the creditor. The mortgage was not made under the corporation seal, and only one of the two signatures required by the corporation's by-laws was placed on the document.

Some time later, the finance company obtained the corporate seal of Model T Motors for another purpose, and affixed it to the chattel mortgage. A few weeks later, when a payment on the loan was overdue, Simple Finance seized the assets of Model T Motors under the blanket chattel mortgage.

Advise Model T Motors of its position in this case. If the matter came before the courts how would you expect the case to be decided?

Case 3

A corporation owned a parcel of vacant land on which it stored its construction equipment. The land was not large enough for the requirements of the company, and when the adjoining land-owner expressed a desire to purchase the property from the company, the directors informally considered the offer, and agreed that they would sell the land for $50 000. No directors' meeting was held to formally deal with the matter, but the secretary-treasurer, on the basis of the informal agreement amongst the directors, contacted the offeror and advised him of the price. The price was acceptable to the purchaser, and the secretary-treasurer then drew up a written purchase agreement which he signed on behalf of the corporation in his capacity as secretary-treasurer. The purchaser also signed the document.

The directors later decided not to carry through with the sale, and the purchaser brought an action against the corporation for specific performance of the contract.

What defences might be raised by the corporation in this case? What legal principles are involved? Render a decision.

Case 4

Ritchie owned 13 shares of the Vermilion Mining Co. Three other share-holders held four shares each. The remainder of the 2 400 shares of capital stock was held by the three directors of the company. The company owned certain mining claims on which some preliminary exploration work had been done, but which required the investment of a large amount of capital in order to establish a mine. Because the company had not been in a position to proceed with the development of the properties, the company faced the prospect in the near future of forfeiture of the mining claims as a result of their forced inaction.

The directors, who were shareholders in another mining company, entered into an agreement to sell the mining claims to that company in exchange for shares in the second company. The share exchange for the mining claims would give Vermilion a 10% interest in the other company.

A meeting of shareholders was called to approve the transaction, at which time the directors declared their interest in the other mining company. The directors explained that in their opinion the transfer represented fair market value for the claims, and urged approval of the transaction. The directors voted in favour of the sale over the objections of Ritchie, who was the only dissenting shareholder.

He accused the directors of attempting to confer a benefit on a company in which they had an interest, to the detriment of the company in which they were directors. He eventually brought an action to restrain the directors from completing the sale of the mining claims to the other company.

Discuss the issues raised in this case, and render a decision.

Case 5

Cinema Ltd. owned a theatre that it wished to sell. To make the property more attractive to a prospective purchaser, the directors decided to acquire a second theatre in the same city and offer the two properties as a "package deal."

Some inquiries were made as to the purchase price of a second theatre, and a price of $100 000 was determined for the property. A subsidiary company was incorporated to acquire the second theatre, with the intention that the shares in the subsidiary would be wholly owned by Cinema Ltd. Unfortunately, the lending institutions would only advance Cinema Ltd. $60 000 on its assets. In order to effect the purchase of the second theatre, the three directors of the corporation, and a lawyer (who frequently acted for the corporation), each agreed to invest $10 000 to make up the necessary $40 000. The subsidiary corporation issued 100 000 shares valued at $1 each to the parent company and the four investors in return for the $100 000 in cash, and proceeded with the purchase of the second theatre.

Some time later, a purchaser was found for the two theatres, and a purchase agreement completed. The purchaser, however, insisted on acquiring the second theatre by way of a purchase of the shares in the subsidiary company. The share price was determined at $1.25, which netted Cinema Ltd. a profit on the sale of $15 000, and each of the others $2 500. When details of the sale were revealed to the shareholders, one shareholder demanded that the four individuals pay over their profits to the corporation. When the three directors and the lawyer refused to do so, the shareholders instituted legal proceedings to have the funds paid to the corporation.

Discuss the various legal arguments that might be raised in this case by the parties, and indicate how the case might be decided.

PART V

Special Contractual Relationships

CHAPTER 19

Employment Relationship

CONTRACT OF EMPLOYMENT

The origins of the employment relationship have their roots in antiquity, and it is impossible to know at what point the first individual voluntarily consented to do the bidding of another in return for a wage. The employment relationship of master and servant developed in early England as slavery and villeinage declined. Slavery and villeinage, unlike the master–servant relationship, was a relationship of virtual ownership, rather than of contract; under it the servient individual had few rights. In contrast, the master–servant relationship subsisted between free men. The rise of towns and guilds fostered the climate for the new form of servitude, and by the middle of the 14th century in England there were sufficient numbers of workmen and craftsmen employed to warrant legislation to fix their wages.

In 1349, following the Black Plague (which reduced the population by about one-third), the demand for workmen and servants pushed their wages to unreasonable levels (at least in the eyes of the nobility) and prompted the king to issue a proclamation known as the *Statute of Labourers*.[1] This statute attempted to regulate the wages and conditions under which workmen were employed, and required them to work for reasonable wages. Shortly thereafter, a second statute was passed by the English Parliament that was similar in form and effect.[2] Both of these laws represented early legislation designed to control the master–servant relationship, but they were not enforced with any degree of enthusiasm, due to the limiting nature of the law.

By 1494, the payment of wages in other than coin of the realm was forbidden,[3] and sporadic attempts were made from time to time thereafter to control the wages paid to workmen, and the conditions under which they were obliged to work. Most of the legislation gave local justices of the peace or magistrates the authority to set wages in the various areas where they had jurisdiction, but regulation of working conditions in a significant way did not develop until the beginning of the 19th century.

The first of the *Factory Acts*, as they were commonly called, was passed in 1802, and following it, a series of similar Acts was introduced to release workmen from many of the less pleasant aspects of the Industrial Revolution. Working conditions in plants and factories were the subject of much of the legislation, but hours of work, and the age at which persons might be employed were also covered.

The first Act which dealt specifically with the contract of employment was the *Master and Servant Act* of 1867, which was subsequently adopted in Canada by a number of provinces.[4] This statute modified the common law contract of employment by imposing limits on the length of time a written contract of employment might bind the parties, and specifying many of the terms and conditions which relate to the relationship. Legislation which protected workmen from injury arising out of work accidents in England took the form of a *Workmen's Compensation Act* in 1897, and it, too, was introduced in a number of Canadian provinces some time later.

Apart from legislation which had a direct bearing on employment, the common law, over a long period of time, had gradually established the relationship as one of contract. The courts saw the relationship as a form of "bargain," struck between the master and the servant, in which the servant (in return for a wage) agreed to submit to the direction of the master in the performance of his work. The relationship, however, was never considered to be one of pure contract in which the parties, both vested with equal bargaining power, devised an agreement to their mutual satisfaction. The law of master and servant had been around too long to abandon all of the law that had developed over many centuries, and as a result, the relationship was never treated as being strictly contractual. Masters, for example, had historically been held liable

---

[1]23 Edw. III. The statute was apparently not a true statute, as Parliament had been prorogued because of the Plague. It was, however, treated as such.
[2]25 Edw. III, c. 1.
[3]4 Edw. IV, c. 1, s. 5(13).

[4]For example, the *Master and Servant Act*, R.S.O. 1897, c. 157, and R.S.M. 1891, c. 96.

for the torts of their servants committed in the performance of the masters' business, and the breach of a master's contract by a servant at law was the master's default. Since it was first established, the relationship has been modified by case-law during the 19th and 20th centuries through the imposition of additional duties or limitations on the master. Nevertheless, the basic concept of employment as a contract has remained mainly intact.

Much of the legislation during the past century has been directed at abuses of the employment relationship by employers, rather than the alteration of the nature of the relationship itself; yet one significant change has occurred as a result of the organization of labour unions by employees. The desire on the part of the employees to band together and negotiate their conditions of employment through a bargaining agent produced the concept of collective bargaining and the collective agreement. The collective agreement, which is negotiated by an employer and a labour union (representing a unit of employees), is a special form of contract that sets out certain terms and conditions of employment and certain conditions under which work will take place. The special nature of the collective agreement is the result of labour legislation which governs its creation and enforceability. As a result, its operation does not fall under the common law courts, but instead, under the purview of an administrative tribunal. The individual contract of employment, nevertheless, remains as a contractual relationship subject to the common law and to a number of statutes related to employment.

NATURE OF THE RELATIONSHIP

The common law contract of employment involves the payment of wages or other remuneration by the employer to the employee in return for the services of the employee. As with other forms of contract, the agreement must contain the essential elements of a contract to be enforceable. The basic characteristic of the relationship, which determines whether a person is an employee or not, is generally considered to be the degree of control which one person exercises over the other. For many years, the courts considered the relationship to be one of employment where the employer had the right to direct the work to be done, and the manner in which it was to be done.[5] This basic test proved to be inclusive, however, as employment relationships in the 20th century took on a wide variety of forms, and the courts gradually came to realize that control in itself was insufficient to determine the relationship. Eventually, a more complex test was devised to meet the complex interpersonal relationships that had arisen in modern business. The test was essentially a fourfold one of which only one of the factors considered was control. The courts added to this three other factors: the ownership of tools, the chance of profit, and the risk of loss.[6]

More recently, the courts have recognized the limitations of their fourfold test, and appear to be groping their way towards an *organization test*, which examines the relationship in relation to the business itself. This later test is based upon the services of the employee, and whether they represent an integral part of the business or something which is adjunct or accessory to the normal business activities of the employer.[7] In recent cases which have come before the courts, its

[5]*Harris v. Howes and Chemical Distributors, Ltd.*, [1929] 1 W.W.R. 217.

[6]*City of Montreal v. Montreal Locomotive Works Ltd. et al.*, [1947] 1 D.L.R. 161.

[7]*Co-Operators Ins. Ass'n v. Kearney* (1964), 48 D.L.R. (2d) 1; *Armstrong v. Mac's Milk Ltd.* (1975), 7 O.R. (2d) 478; *Mayer v. J. Conrad Lavigne Ltd.* (1979), 27 O.R. (2d) 129.

principal application has been to distinguish between employees and independent contractors, not an easy task in today's complex business world.

The independent contractor has usually been distinguished from the employee on the basis that the initiative to do the work and the manner in which it is done are both under the control of the contractor. This has been generally characterized by the right of the contractor to exercise his own discretion with respect to any matter not specifically stipulated in the contract,[8] but in recent years this distinction has become blurred in situations where the contractor acts alone.

Where the contractor employs others to do the work for him, the relationship is generally that of an independent contract, rather than employment, because the independent contractor exercises the function of an employer as well.[9] It was, however, the difficulties associated with the determination of the true relationship in cases where no employees were engaged by the independent contractor, that required the courts to devise an *organization test* to identify the nature of the contract. The test examines the contractor's role in the context of the employer's business, and the relationship is determined on the basis of whether the work done is a part of the business or something outside it.

The same test might be applied to distinguish the agency relationship from that of the employer–employee. Generally, the principal has the right to direct the work that the agent is to perform, but not the manner in which it is to be done.[10] Again, this is not always so, particularly where the agent acts only for a single principal, and the principal exercises a substantial degree of control over the agent. Other characteristics of the principal–agent relationship may also apply which may distinguish a case of agency from employment in given circumstances, but the application of the *organization test* represents a useful tool to identify and distinguish the two relationships.[11]

|||||||||||||||||||||||||||||||||||||||||||||||||||||||||||||||||||||||||||||||

CASE 19.1

Montreal v. Montreal Locomotive Works Ltd. et al., [1947] 1 D.L.R. 161.

LORD WRIGHT:

In earlier cases a single test, such as the presence or absence of control, was often relied on to determine whether the case was one of master and servant, mostly in order to decide issues of tortious liability on the part of the master or superior. In the more complex conditions of modern industry, more complicated tests have often to be applied. It has been suggested that a fourfold test would in some cases be more appropriate, a complex involving (1) control; (2) ownership of the tools; (3) chance of profit; (4) risk of loss. Control in itself is not always conclusive.

|||||||||||||||||||||||||||||||||||||||||||||||||||||||||||||||||||||||||||||||

FORM OF THE CONTRACT

A contract of employment need not be in writing to be valid and binding on the parties, but a contract which is to run for a fixed term of more than one year is subject to the *Statute of Frauds*, and must be in writing to be enforceable. If the contract may be terminated on proper notice in less than one year, or if the agreement has no fixed term of duration, then it has generally been held to be a contract of indefinite hiring, and not subject to the statute.[12]

Where evidence in writing is required to render the contract enforceable, the courts are prepared to accept informal,

---

[8]*McAllister v. Bell Lumber Co. Ltd.*, [1932] 1 D.L.R. 802.
[9]*Dominion Shipbuilding & Repair Co. Ltd.; Henshaw's Claim* (1921), 51 O.L.R. 144.
[10]*Mulholland et al. v. The King*, [1952] Ex. C.R. 233.

[11]*Co-Operators Ins. Ass'n v. Kearney* (1964), 48 D.L.R. (2d) 1.
[12]*Campbell v. Business Fleets Ltd.*, [1954] O.R. 87.

rather than formal, written evidence. For example, in one case the writing requirement was satisfied by an exchange of letters between the employer and the employee, offering and accepting the employment, but without mention of wages,[13] and in another case, the entry of details of the hiring in the corporation minute-book, which had been signed by the corporation officers, was held as sufficient evidence to satisfy the statute.[14]

Employment contracts are often verbal agreements of indefinite hiring, although most employment relationships where the employee is likely to have access to secret processes or confidential information of the employer are reduced to writing and subject to a restrictive covenant. An employer may insert a restrictive covenant in an employment contract in an effort to protect his business secrets, but the ability to enforce such a restriction on the employee is limited to those situations where the restriction is reasonable and necessary to protect the employer from serious loss. Restrictive covenants usually may not restrict an employee from exercising skills learned on the job, but may limit his use of secret or confidential information if he should leave his employment.[15] Apart from these few provisions, most employment contracts tend to be informal documents.

CASE 19.2

Campbell v. Business Fleets Ltd., [1954] O.R. 87.

J. K. MACKAY, J.A.:

In the case at bar, in accordance with the

findings of the learned trial judge, the agreement was to continue in force as long as the plaintiff was satisfied with the salary and bonuses, but if not so satisfied the plaintiff could terminate the employment at any time. Therefore, the plaintiff could terminate his employment within the space of one year. Moreover, the contract (if there was no wrongdoing on the part of the plaintiff, and such wrongdoing was not suggested) was to continue for his (the plaintiff's) life which might or might not be for a period of one day, one month, one year or twenty years. It is to me manifest that this contract must have come to an end at any time the plaintiff was not satisfied with his salary and bonus or on the death of the plaintiff, which might or might not be within the year: *Glenn v. Rudd* (1902), 3 O.L.R. 422.

We are of opinion that on the above authorities the law is that the statute has no reference to cases in which the whole contract may be performed within one year, but there is no definite provision as to its duration, even although it may appear as a fact that the performance has extended beyond that time; that where the contract is such that the whole may possibly be performed within a year and there is no express stipulation to the contrary, the statute does not apply; and that the same principle has been applied to promises in terms of unlimited duration made by or to a corporation when performance of the promise is by the nature thereof limited to the life of the corporation or to the life of the individual . . . The Court is of opinion, therefore, that in the case at bar this verbal contract is without the provisions of s. 4 of The Statute of Frauds . . .

DUTIES OF THE EMPLOYER

The duties of the employer have been the subject of much of the labour legislation since the beginning of the 19th century. Laws relating to minimum wages, hours of work, and working conditions have been largely directed against employer abuses in the employment relationship, and over-

[13]*Goldie v. Cross Fertilizer Co.* (1916), 37 D.L.R. 16.
[14]*Connell v. Bay of Quinte Country Club* (1923), 24 O.W.N. 264.
[15]*Management Recruiters of Toronto Ltd. v. Bagg*, [1971] 1 O.R. 502.

ride contract terms made contrary to them. For example, each province has passed laws frequently referred to as employment standards or industrial standards laws which regulate the terms and conditions of employment, and the conditions under which work may be performed. These laws may be divided into two separate classes: those which deal with employee safety and working conditions, and those which deal with the terms of the employment contract.

The former class of laws usually deal with the physical aspect of employment, such as sanitary facilities, control of dust, fumes, and equipment which might affect employee health and safety in a plant or building. Government inspectors enforce these laws and visit an employer's premises from time to time to make certain that these work hazards are minimized.

Health and safety legislation frequently dictates that the employer must provide employees with safety equipment where hazards are associated with a particular job. The failure on the part of the employer to provide safety equipment normally entitles the employee to refuse to do the work until the equipment is made available. In addition, the legislation usually imposes stiff penalties on the employer if the employer should violate the safety requirements.

The latter class of laws, those which deal with the employment contract, generally impose minimum terms of employment on the parties, and allow them to negotiate more favourable terms (from the employee's point of view) if they wish to do so. Most of these provincial statutes establish minimum wage rates, fix maximum hours of work, set conditions under which holiday and vacation pay must be given, and impose minimum conditions for termination of the contract by the parties.

While some similarity exists in the legislation, the provinces have generally written their laws to meet their own particular employment needs. Consequently, the laws relating to working conditions, wage rates, and other aspects of employment vary somewhat from province to province.

In addition to the terms of employment imposed by statute, many duties of the employer are implied by common law. The most important of these relate to compensation. The employer must pay wages or other remuneration to the employee in return for his services, and generally must indemnify the employee for any expenditures or losses which he might incur in the normal course of his employment, if made at his employer's direction.[16] For example, if the employer requires the employee to travel to a neighbouring community to carry out some duty on behalf of the employer, the employer would normally be expected to reimburse the employee for his travel and other expenses associated with the assignment unless customs of the trade or the terms of employment provided otherwise.

Two further duties of the employer are implied in the employment relationship: the employer is obliged to provide the employee with sufficient tools to do his work where it is not the custom of the trade for the employee to provide his own, and the employer must provide the employee with sufficient information to allow the employee to calculate the remuneration due to him where he is paid on some system other than a salary or hourly rate. For example, the employer who operates a iron mine would be obliged to provide a group of employees with sufficient information to calculate the bonuses due to them for

---

[16]*Dugdale et al. v. Lovering* (1875), L.R. 10 C.P. 196.

mining over and above a stipulated minimum amount of ore, where the bonus is based upon the tonnage mined.

DUTIES OF THE EMPLOYEE

Apart from specific duties which may be set out in a contract of employment, an employee is subject to a number of implied duties which arise out of the employment relationship. As a general rule, the employee has a basic duty to obey all reasonable orders of the employer which fall within the scope of his employment,[17] and in addition, an obligation to use the property or information of the employer in a careful and reasonable manner.[18] Any confidential information which he obtains from the employer must be kept confidential during the course of his employment,[19] and afterwards.[20] The employee is also under an obligation to devote the agreed hours of his employment to the employer's business, and the employer is entitled to the profits earned by the employee during those intervals of time.[21] The employee's spare time, however, is his own.[22]

If the employee should represent to his employer that he has a special skill or professional qualification, then it is an implied term of his employment contract that he will perform his work in accordance with the standard required of his skill or profes-

sion.[23] An employee that professes to be skilled and is negligent in the performance of his task may be liable for damages suffered by his employer as a result of his negligence, provided that there are no intervening factors, or special controls exercised over the employee by the employer.[24]

||||||||||||||||||||||||||||||||||||||||||||||||||||||||||||||||||||||||||||||||||

CASE 19.3
William R. Barnes Co. Ltd. v. MacKenzie (1974), 2 O.R. (2d) 659.

EVANS, J.A.:

The principle that a dishonest agent is not entitled to a commission from his principal is well recognized as is the right of a principal to any secret profit earned by his dishonest agent. An agent stands in a fiduciary relationship with his principal with his remuneration usually attributable to separate transactions. If he is dishonest in one transaction he forfeits his commission thereon but not on other transactions faithfully performed. In the instant case the relationship is basically that of master and servant rather than principal and agent and the remedy of a master against his defaulting servant is restricted to a right of instant dismissal and to damages which flow from the default. I do not consider wages paid to be such an item of damages and disagree with that part of the judgment in *Protective Plastics Ltd. v. Hawkins* which appears to hold otherwise.

I adopt the view of the trial Judge that wages paid cannot be recovered if one allows to the plaintiff all secret profits made by the delinquent employee and also holds the employee liable for any loss sustained by the employer as a result of the employee's breach of his employment contract. The argument is that the damages awarded the employer place him in the same position as if the delinquent employee had in fact been performing his duties as a

---

[17]*Smith v. General Motor Cab Co. Ltd.*, [1911] A.C. 188.

[18]*Lord Ashburton v. Pape*, [1913] 2 Ch. 469.

[19]*Bents Brewery Co. Ltd. et al. v. Luke Hogan*, [1945] 2 All E.R. 570.

[20]*Robb v. Green*, [1895] 2 Q.B. 315.

[21]*William R. Barnes Co. Ltd. v. MacKenzie* (1974), 2 O.R. (2d) 654; *Bennett-Pacaud Co. Ltd. v. Dunlop*, [1933] 2 D.L.R. 237.

[22]*Sheppard Publishing Co. v. Harkins* (1905), 9 O.L.R. 504.

[23]*Lister v. Romford Ice & Cold Storage Co. Ltd.*, [1957] A.C. 555.

[24]*Harvey v. R.G. O'Dell Ltd. et al.*, [1958] 1 All E.R. 657.

faithful employee and that since all benefits ultimately accrue to the employer, the employee should be compensated for his time and labour in producing such benefits. The employer has already received the fruit of the employee's efforts, honest or otherwise, and cannot repudiate his obligation to pay. I recognize that in an agency situation the principal may take the benefit and refuse to pay the commission but I am not aware of any binding authority which requires me to extend that principle to a master and servant situation.

||||||||||||||||||||||||||||||||||||||||||||||||||||||||||||||||||||||||||||

TERMINATION OF THE CONTRACT OF EMPLOYMENT

The notice required to terminate a contract of employment has been the subject of legislation in most provinces. Many of these statutes provide a minimum period of notice which varies depending upon the length of service of the employee. This period of notice is generally the minimum requirement, but in some cases, it may replace the common law rule that reasonable notice of termination is required to terminate the contract.

At common law, unless the contract stipulates a specific termination date, or a period of notice for the termination of the agreement, both parties are obliged to provide reasonable notice of termination.[25] The adequacy or "reasonableness" of the notice is a matter of fact to be determined from a number of factors, including the nature of the contract, the method of payment, the type of position held by the employee, the length of service, the customs of the business, and even the age of the employee. All of these factors would be considered in the determination of what would constitute a reasonable time period.

In some of the older cases, where the employee was unskilled, and employed for only a short period of time at an hourly rate, the length of notice was often very short. The trend, however, has been away from short notice since the middle of the current century, with a one-week notice period commonly determined as the minimum for an employee, and as much as a year or more as reasonable notice for a longer-service employee or an employee engaged in a senior position in the firm.[26]

DISMISSAL AND WRONGFUL DISMISSAL

In the absence of an agreement to the contrary, an employer has the right to dismiss an employee without notice where the employee is incompetent or grossly negligent in the performance of his duties. The employer would also be entitled to do so where the employee concurs in a crime against the employer, or where the employee's actions are such that they would constitute a breach of the contract of employment. In each case, however, the onus would be on the employer to establish that he was justified in terminating the employment relationship, otherwise, the employee would be entitled to damages against the employer for wrongful dismissal.

Some provinces have attempted to clarify the matter of dismissal and termination without notice by setting out in their legislation conditions which permit an employer to terminate an employee without notice. Ontario, for example, provides in its legislation that the notice provisions do not apply to "an employee who has been

---

[25]*Havard v. Freeholders Oil Co.* (1952), 6 W.W.R. (N.S.) 413.

[26]*Campbell v. Business Fleets Ltd.*, [1954] O.R. 87; *Bardal v. The Globe & Mail Ltd.* (1960), 24 D.L.R. (2d) 140.

guilty of wilful misconduct or disobedience or wilful neglect of duty that has not been condoned by the employer."[27]

Where an employee believes that he has been wrongfully dismissed, he may bring an action against the employer for the failure to give reasonable notice of termination. If the employee should decide to pursue this course, he must in the meantime do everything which a reasonable man might be expected to do to minimize his loss. He would be expected to seek other employment immediately, and take whatever other steps that may be necessary to mitigate his loss. His actual loss would be the loss which he incurred between the time when he was terminated and the end of a reasonable notice period. For example, if Able was employed by Baker in a responsible position where reasonable notice might be determined as six months, if Baker should wrongfully dismiss Able, Able would be obliged to seek new employment immediately. If he could not find suitable employment within a six-month period, then his damages would be the lost wages and benefits which he would ordinarily have received from the employer during that period. Had he found employment during the six-month interval, his actual loss would be reduced by the income he received during the period, and that amount would be deducted from the damages to which he would be entitled as a result of the wrongful dismissal.

The purpose of damages for wrongful dismissal is to place the injured employee in relatively the same position that he would have been in had he been given proper notice of termination of the contract. The courts will normally not award punitive damages, nor will they compensate the employee for any adverse effects which the wrongful dismissal might have on the employee's reputation or stature in the business community. Judges, however, have recently awarded extra compensation where the actions of the employer were such that they caused the employee undue mental distress as a result of the termination.[28]

EMPLOYER LIABILITY TO THIRD PARTIES

The general rule with respect to third-party liability is that the employer is liable for any loss or damage suffered by a third party as a result of an employee's failure to perform a contract in accordance with its terms, or for any negligence on the part of the employee acting within the scope of his employment that causes injury or loss to the third party. This rule imposes *vicarious liability* on the employer for the acts of the employee which occur within the scope of the employee's employment.[29] For example, if Arthurs takes his automobile to Gordon's garage for repairs, and an employee, Smith, negligently performs the repairs, Arthurs would be entitled to recover from Gordon for the breach of contract. Similarly, if an employee is sent

[27]The *Employment Standards Act, 1974*, R.S.O. 1980, c. 137, s. 40(3)(c), as amended. It should be noted, however, that this section of the Act does not apply to employees in certain trades, businesses and professions: see s. 40(3)(e).

[28]See, for example, *Pilon v. Peugeot Canada Ltd.* (1981), 29 O.R. (2d) 711, where the plaintiff was awarded damages to cover the mental distress associated with termination from what he was led to believe was a life-time position with the company.
[29]See *McKee et al. v. Dumas et al.; Eddy Forest Products Ltd. et al.* (1975), 8 O.R. (2d) 229, for the difficulty in determining which employer may be vicariously liable where an employee is also under the direction of a temporary employer.

to a customer's home to repair a defective boiler, and the employee negligently damages the equipment, causing it to explode, the customer would be entitled to look to the employer for the loss on the basis of the employer's vicarious liability for the acts of his employee.

The reason for the imposition of liability on the employer for the acts of the employee has a historical perspective and justification. In the past, employees seldom possessed the financial resources to compensate third parties for any loss suffered as a result of their negligence, and the third party would be unlikely to obtain compensation, even if a judgement was obtained against the employee. However, most employers did have the financial resources to cover a loss which a third party might suffer, and in view of the fact that the employee was under the control of the employer, the courts simply carried the liability through the employee to the party primarily responsible for the employee's actions.

Employer liability is limited to those acts of the employee which fall within the ordinary scope of the employee's duties, but does not include acts of negligence which take place outside the employee's normal duties. For example, an employer sends an employee to another city to perform certain services on his behalf for a customer. After the work has been completed the employee decides to spend the evening in the city, and rents a hotel room for the night. His careless smoking sets fire to the carpet in the room, and results in a loss to the hotel. If the work had been completed in time for the employee to return, and if he had been instructed to do so, but failed to heed his employer's instructions, he would be personally liable for the loss. However, if the employer had required the

employee to use the room to display goods to prospective customers and to remain overnight in the room, the employer might be held liable for the loss suffered by the hotel if it could be established that the employee's occupancy of the room was at his employer's direction and in the course of his employment.

EMPLOYER LIABILITY FOR AN EMPLOYEE'S INJURIES

At common law, an employee injured while working for his employer was generally faced with a dilemma. If the injury occurred as a result of the negligence of another employee, it would be necessary to bring an action against the employer for that employee's negligence. The recovery of damages from the employer under such circumstances would be unlikely to enhance the employee's advancement or career with the particular employer. Nor was the prospect of bringing an action against the employer any more promising if the employee was injured by equipment or machinery which he was using. If the employee was successful, the employer would be obliged to pay for the injury, but again, the legal action would likely result in termination of the employee by reasonable notice. On the other hand, if the employer could prove negligence on the part of the employee, or if the employer could establish that the employee had voluntarily assumed the risks which resulted in the injury, the employee would not be successful in the action for damages.

In spite of a number of attempts by the courts to accommodate the injured employee, the law relating to employee on-the-job injury remained unsatisfactory, and it was not until the close of the 19th century that legislation in England remedied the situation. In 1897, the *Workmen's Compensation Act* was passed which provided compensation to workmen injured out of and in the course of their employment. In essence, the Act was an insurance scheme similar in concept to ordinary accident insurance. All employees covered by the Act were entitled to compensation without the need to take legal action to prove fault if they were injured out of and in the course of their employment. All employers subject to the legislation were required to contribute to a fund from which the compensation was paid, and the employee was not entitled to take action against his employer if he received compensation from the fund. Similar legislation was eventually passed in all provinces and territories in Canada, and in many states of the United States. The legislation has been further refined since its introduction into England at the end of the last century, and has virtually eliminated actions against employers for injuries suffered by employees.

SUMMARY The common law contract of employment is a special type of agreement which sets out the rights and duties of the employer and employee. It need not be in writing unless subject to the *Statute of Frauds*. The essential characteristic of the employment relationship is the control of the employee by the employer. Originally, the relationship was that of employment if the employer had the right to direct the work to be done, and the manner in which it was to be done, but modern forms of business organization have required the courts to look beyond the simple control aspect to other determinants, and have included consideration of the ownership of tools, the chance of profit, the risk of loss, and in some cases, the relationship of the employee's work to the overall operation of the employer.

Under the contract of employment both the employer and employee have a number of implied duties, the most important being the employer's obligation to pay wages in return for the employee's services, and the employee's obligation to obey all reasonable directions of the employer. If an employee acts in breach of his duty, the employer may be entitled to dismiss the employee, but if the dismissal is unwarranted, the employee may bring an action against the employer for wrongful dismissal. A failure to give reasonable notice of termination, where such is required, would also be grounds for wrongful dismissal, and entitle the employee to damages. The employee, however, must act promptly to mitigate his loss by seeking employment elsewhere.

An employer is vicariously liable for the acts of his employees, if the acts are done within the scope of the employee's employment. The employer, however, may have a right over and against a skilled or professional employee if the employee was negligent in the exercise of his professional skill in the performance of his duties.

DISCUSSION QUESTIONS

1. *Identify the elements that constitute the basis for an employment relationship. Why was a fourfold test necessary?*
2. *Does a "contract of service" differ from a "contract for services"?*
3. *How does the organization test distinguish an "employee" from an "independent contractor"?*
4. *In what way does a contract of indefinite hiring differ from other forms of employment?*
5. *Describe the duties of an employer to his employee.*
6. *Describe the duties of an employee to his employer.*
7. *Under what circumstances would some duties of an employee extend beyond the period of employment? What remedies are available to the employer in the event of a breach by the employee?*
8. *Explain the rationale behind the rule of law which imposes vicarious liability on an employer for the acts of his employee.*
9. *What constitutes "reasonable notice" of termination of a contract of indefinite hiring?*
10. *Under what circumstances would an employer be entitled to dismiss an employee without notice?*
11. *Where an employee is wrongfully dismissed, what obligations are imposed by the courts in order that the employee might successfully recover his loss?*
12. *How are damages for wrongful dismissal calculated by a court? What factors are considered in the calculation?*
13. *Does the Statute of Frauds apply to a contract of employment? If so, in what way?*
14. *Explain the purpose of workmen's compensation legislation. Why is it necessary?*

JUDICIAL DECISIONS

Master and Servant—Test for Employment Relationship

Mayer v. J. Conrad Lavigne Ltd. (1979), 27 O.R. (2d) 129.

The plaintiff sold television time for the defendant on a straight commission basis. He was required to attend regular sales meetings of the defendant each day, and file sales reports. Some direction of the plaintiff's activity was carried out by the sales manager, but this was generally limited to where, and to whom to sell. When the defendant failed to pay the salesman vacation pay, the salesman instituted legal proceedings.

MACKINNON, A.C.J.O.:

The law and cases were much canvassed before us, but as the determination of whether a particular individual is a servant or an independent contractor is completely dependent on the facts, it would serve no useful purpose to review them all only to distinguish them on their facts. The emphasis in the earlier authorities was on the extent of the "control" that the master had over the servant to determine whether there was, indeed, a master-and-servant relationship. The concept of this relationship has, however, been an evolving one, changing with the changes in economic views and conditions. As Lord Wright put it in the leading case of *Montreal v. Montreal Locomotive Works Ltd. et al.,* [1947] 1 D.L.R. 161 at p. 169, [1946] 3 W.W.R. 748: "In the more complex conditions of modern industry, more complicated tests have often to be applied." He postulated a fourfold test involving: (1) control, (2) ownership of the tools, (3) chance of profit, and (4) risk of loss. This test has been enlarged by the more recent "organization test" which was approved and applied by Spence, J., in *Co-operators Ins. Ass'n v. Kearney* (1964), 48 D.L.R. (2d) 1. In that case (pp. 22-3), he quoted with approval the following passage from Fleming, *The Law of Torts,* 2nd ed. (1961), at pp. 328-9:

" 'Under the pressure of novel situations, the courts have become increasingly aware of the strain on the traditional formulation [of the control test], and most recent cases display a discernible tendency to replace it by something like an "organization" test. Was the alleged servant part of his employer's organization? Was his work subject to co-ordinational control as to 'where' and 'when' rather than the 'how'? [citing Lord Denning in *Stevenson, Jordan & Harrison Ltd. v. Macdonald,* [1952] 1 T.L.R. 101, 111.]' "

Lord Denning in *Stevenson Jordan & Harrison, Ltd. v. MacDonald et al.,* [1952] 1 T.L.R. 101, referred to by Fleming, said this:
"One feature which seems to run through the instances is that, under a contract of service, a man is employed as part of the business, and his work is done as an integral part of the business; whereas, under a contract for services, his work, although done for the business, is not integrated into it but is only accessory to it."

In my view, the facts as recited satisfy whichever test is used. The appellant had and exercised the control necessary to establish a master-and-servant relationship. The "when" and "where" was within the master's control, and to a certain extent, the "how" when clients were transferred from one salesman's list to another. Because of the training, skill, and experience of the respondent, one would not expect that the appellant would control "how" the respondent sold the air-time, any more than any other skilled or professional servant would be directed how to do his work. Equally, the relationship satisfies the "organization" test. The respondent's work was a necessary and integral part of the appellant's business. It supplied the financial life-blood of the appellant, and his work was subject to the co-ordinational control of management. His work was clearly integrated into the business and not merely accessory to it. In my view, applying the common law tests, the facts establish that the respondent was a servant and employee of the appellant.

||

Wrongful Dismissal— Reasonable Notice— Considerations —Duty to Mitigate Loss

Bardal v. The Globe & Mail Ltd. (1960), 24 D.L.R. (2d) 140.

The plaintiff was employed by the defendant newspaper on a contract of indefinite hiring. He was first hired as advertising manager. Sixteen years later, by which time he had become Director of Advertising, he was terminated without notice.

The plaintiff immediately sought other employment, and some months later, found a new position which paid substantially less in salary and benefits.

An action for wrongful dismissal was instituted against his previous employer.

MCRUER, C.J.H.C.:

> In every case of wrongful dismissal the measure of damages must be considered in the light of the terms of employment and the character of the services to be rendered. In this case there was no stipulated term during which the employment was to last. Both parties undoubtedly considered that the employment was to be of a permanent character. All the evidence goes to show that the office of advertising manager is one of the most important offices in the service of the defendant. In fact, it is by means of the revenue derived under the supervision of the advertising manager that the publication of a newspaper becomes a profitable enterprise. The fact that the plaintiff was appointed to the Board of Directors of the defendant goes to demonstrate the permanent character of his employment and the importance of the office.
>
> It is not argued that there was a definite agreement that the plaintiff was employed for life but the case is put on the basis of an indefinite hiring of a permanent character which could be terminated by reasonable notice.
>
> In *Carter v. Bell & Sons*, [1936], 2 D.L.R. 438 at p. 439, O.R. 290 at p. 297, Mr. Justice Middleton concisely and with great clarity stated the law applicable to this case in this way: "In the case of master and servant there is implied in the contract of hiring an obligation to give reasonable notice of an intention to terminate the arrangement."
>
> On this branch of the case the only remaining matter to be considered is what should be implied as reasonable notice in the circumstances of the contract in question. In *Carter* v. *Bell* Middleton J.A. went on at p. 439 D.L.R., p. 297 O.R. to say: "This notice in a case of an indefinite hiring is generally 6 months, but the length of notice is always a matter for inquiry and determination, and in special circumstances may be less."
>
> The contractual obligation is to give reasonable notice and to continue the servant in his employment. If the servant is dismissed without reasonable notice he is entitled to the damages that flow from the failure to observe this contractual obligation, which damages the servant is bound in law to mitigate to the best of his ability.

In *Grundy v. Sun Printing & Publishing Ass'n* (1916), 33 T.L.R. 77, the plaintiff was an editor of a newspaper earning a salary of £20 a week. The jury awarded the plaintiff damages based on the failure to give 12 months' notice of termination of the contract. On appeal to the Court of Appeal this award was sustained. In delivering the judgment of the Court Lord Justice Swinfen Eady said at p. 78: "In cases which had come before this Court a custom has been proved that an editor was entitled to 12 months' notice, and a sub-editor to six months' notice. In the absence of evidence of custom it could not be said that the view of the jury in this case was unreasonable."

There is no evidence of custom in the case before me and I think I must determine what would be reasonable notice in all the circumstances and proper compensation for the loss the plaintiff has suffered by reason of the breach of the implied term in the contract to give him reasonable notice of its termination.

There can be no catalogue laid down as to what is reasonable notice in particular classes of cases. The reasonableness of the notice must be decided with reference to each particular case, having regard to the character of the employment, the length of service of the servant, the age of the servant and the availability of similar employment, having regard to the experience, training and qualifications of the servant.

Applying this principle to this case, we have a servant who, through a lifetime of training, was qualified to manage the advertising department of a large metropolitan newspaper. With the exception of a short period of employment as manager of a street car advertising agency, his whole training has been in the advertising department of two large daily newspapers. There are few comparable offices available in Canada and the plaintiff has in mitigation of his damages taken employment with an advertising agency, in which employment he will no doubt find useful his advertising experience, but the employment must necessarily be of a different character.

I have come to the conclusion, as the jury did in the *Sun Printing & Publishing Ass'n* case and as the Court of Appeal agreed, that 1 year's notice would have been reasonable, having regard to all the circumstances of this case.

That being true, the next question to decide is what damages have flowed from the failure of the defendant to give a year's notice and how far have those damages been mitigated by the receipt by the plaintiff of a salary from another employer.

The plaintiff's salary with the defendant was $17,750 per year. In his new employment he has been receiving $15,000 per year since July 1, 1959. He is therefore entitled to recover $3,254.15 for loss of salary from April 25th to July 1st and $2,245.20, being the difference between the salary which would have been received from July 1, 1959 to April 24, 1960, and the salary actually received in his new employment during that time.

Upon the termination of the plaintiff's employment with the defendant his pension rights were said to have been valued as an employee with 16 to 17 years' service. According to ex. 7 the pension allowed to the plaintiff was based on the defendant's contribution to his pension at 40%. If he had been continued in the service for another year, pursuant to proper notice, the defendant's contribution would have been on a higher basis. The matter of what the dollar value of the plaintiff's pension would have been had he been employed for another year is a matter for actuarial computation. This aspect of the case was not developed in argument. It is, however, quite clear that had the plaintiff been given proper notice according to the implied term of the contract he would have had another year's service with the defendant which would have increased his pension allowance. In view of the unsatisfactory condition of the evidence, I am unable to make a proper assessment of what damage the plaintiff has suffered in loss of pension by reason of his employment having been terminated a year sooner than it ought to have been terminated. If the parties cannot agree as to these damages, I would direct a reference to the Master to ascertain these damages.

Three other aspects of damage remain to be considered: the alleged loss of the Christmas bonus, participation in the profit-sharing plan and loss of director's fees. I do not think the plaintiff is entitled to recover under any of these heads. The Christmas bonus was a purely voluntary gift distributed among the employees as a matter of good will between employer and employee. I do not think this case comes within the principles applied in *Manubens v. Leon*, [1919] 1 K.B. 208. In that case Lush J. allowed a plaintiff who was a hairdresser's assistant damages for loss of tips that he might reasonably have expected to have received from his customers, if his employment had not been wrongfully terminated. It was held that it was within the contemplation of the parties at the time of the engagement that the assistant would receive gratuitous payments from his customers. I think that is quite different from the case before me where the bonus was something that came from the employer and was not within the contemplation of the parties at the time that the plaintiff entered the service.

The case for claiming damages for loss of any share in the distribution of profits is still weaker. The profit-sharing plan was not founded on contract. It was instituted by the chief shareholder of the defendant and was not applicable to all employees but only those who were selected by a committee appointed by him. There was no obligation to put anyone on the list of those who should receive benefits in this way. It would appear to me that it would have been very improbable that the committee would have distributed profits to an employee who had received notice of the termination of his contract. I therefore allow no damages under this heading.

The appointment of the plaintiff to the Board of Directors of the defendant was an appointment at the will of the shareholders of the company and they were under no obligation to continue him on the Board for any period of time. There is no foundation for a claim for loss of director's fees.

It was argued that in his new employment the plaintiff is entitled to certain stock option rights and some allowance should be made in assessing damages on this account. I do not think it has been established in evidence that any allowance should be made in mitigation of the damages by reason of these alleged benefits. In the first place, the value of the stock option rights is purely speculative. There is no evidence that any events have happened to entitle the plaintiff to stock under the agreement nor is there evidence that the stock would be worth anything if he did become entitled to it under the provisions of the agreement.

The plaintiff will therefore be entitled to judgment for $5,499.35, with a reference to the Master to ascertain the amount by which the dollar value of the plaintiff's participation in the pension plan was reduced by reason of the termination of his employment before April 24, 1960. The plaintiff will have the costs of the action.

| CASE | **Case 1** |

CASE PROBLEMS FOR DISCUSSION

Case 1

Martin was employed by Chemical-Cosmetic Distributors to sell its products in a defined territory on a commission basis. Martin was not subject to strict hours of work, but signed a devotion to business agreement with Chemical-Cosmetic Distributors whereby she agreed to devote her time to the sale of their products, subject to her right to sell other non-competing lines of goods, provided that they did not interfere with her promotion of those of Chemical-Cosmetic Distributors. Under the terms of the agreement she was required to visit each retail outlet in her territory at least once a month, and report the sales of each establishment to Chemical-Cosmetic Distributors.

One day Martin was travelling along a country road in her automobile en route to a retail customer of Chemical-Cosmetic Distributors, when a young man on a bicycle suddenly appeared in front of her car. She attempted to brake the car, but could not do so in time to avoid a collision. The young man was seriously injured as a result of the accident, and some time later, brought an action for damages against Martin and Chemical-Cosmetic Distributors. Evidence of the police officer who investigated the accident, indicated that the accident was largely the fault of Martin.

Advise Chemical-Cosmetic Distributors of their liability in this case, and indicate how the matter might be decided by the court.

Case 2

Willard had been well-known as a racing-car driver for many years. He had driven a number of different types of racing cars during his racing career, either under the sponsorship of automobile manufacturers, or as an "independent."

Following a spectacular race in which Willard had won first prize, a sports car distributor offered him a position in his organization as Director of Marketing. The offer included a starting salary of $30 000 per year, participation in a profit-sharing plan open only to senior management, a generous pension plan, and a variety of other benefits which included the use of a company-owned automobile. The position also gave him a place on the board of directors of the company.

As a part of his duties, Willard was expected to enter and drive company racing cars in a number of highly publicized race events held each year.

During his first year with the company, Willard won four of the five races which he had entered, and worked hard at all other times to boost sales for the company. As a result of his efforts, sales increased by 20%. Willard received a year-end bonus of $5 000 in addition to his salary and share of profits, and was advised by the president of the company that his salary for the next year would be raised to $40 000.

The second year of Willard's employment did not match the previous year. Willard won only two of the five races, and in spite of spending extra time promoting his employer's sports cars, sales decreased by 3%. At a year-end directors' meeting, a bitter argument occurred between Willard and the company president over the poor sales performance of the company. The president blamed the drop in sales on Willard's poor showing on the race circuit, and Willard blamed the unreliability of the new model of the car for his poor performance. The argument ended with the president dismissing Willard.

The next day, Willard received a cheque from the company to cover his salary to that date, along with a formal notice of his termination.

Prior to his dismissal, Willard had arranged for a two-week holiday in Europe, and he decided to follow through with these plans, then look for other employment on his return.

Willard searched dilligently for a similar position when he returned from his holiday, but could find nothing. Eventually, some six months after his termination, he found a position as a staff writer for a sports car magazine at an annual salary of $18 000.

Under the terms of his employment at the time of his dismissal, Willard was entitled to receive (in addition to his salary of $40 000 per year), pension contributions by the company on his behalf of $2 000 per year, director's fees of $1 000 per year, a profit-sharing plan payment of approximately $6 000, and the use of a company automobile.

He eventually brought an action for wrongful dismissal against the company and, in addition, alleged damage to his reputation as a professional driver as a result of his summary dismissal by his employer. He claimed $100 000 for damage to his reputation.

Indicate the arguments that might be raised by the parties to this action. Discuss the factors that would be taken into consideration by the court, and render a decision.

Case 3

McKenzie was a qualified and licensed driver of tractor trailers and other heavy types of trucks. He was first employed by FMP Company in 1953, and was steadily employed by the company as a truck driver until 1979. At that time he was voluntarily placed "on loan" to Timber-Hall Trucking under an agreement which provided as follows:

(1) Timber-Hall will provide and maintain trucks and equipment to haul logs from FMP Company logging sites to the FMP Mill.

(2) FMP Company will provide any qualified truck drivers required by Timber-Hall. Drivers will continue to be paid their regular wage rates and benefits by FMP Company.

(3) Timber-Hall will have the right to direct and supervise the work of the drivers, but will not have the right to discharge or discipline drivers provided by FMP Company.

Timber-Hall operated a fleet of 36 trucks used for hauling timber from various logging sites to the FMP mill. Of the drivers, 32 were employees of Timber-Hall, and four were "on loan" from FMP Company. All drivers were under supervision of Timber-Hall management at both the loading and unloading points, and the drivers were directed to specific locations by Timber-Hall supervisors.

McKenzie was directed to a particular loading area by Timber-Hall and told to deliver the load to the FMP Company mill some 60 miles away. McKenzie picked up the load of timber and set out for the FMP mill. En route, McKenzie encountered an icy road condition as he descended a long hill, and before he could bring the heavy truck under control, it careened from the road, and collided with a road-side cabin owned by McGee.

The cabin was demolished, and McGee brought an action against McKenzie, Timber-Hall, and FMP Company for damages. Both Timber-Hall and FMP Company alleged in their defence that they were not the employer of McKenzie.

Discuss the arguments which may be put forward by the defendants, and the issues raised by the case. Render a decision.

Case 4

Harkin entered into a contract of employment with the Periodical Publishing Company under the terms of which he agreed to devote his time to the advertising interests of the employer's business, and to engage in no other business in competition with the employer during the term of his employment.

Harkin assumed the position of "advertising agent" for the company, and worked in that capacity for a number of years. During that time, however, he entered into an arrangement with a business acquaintance to publish an "Elite Directory" which contained brief biographical sketches and pictures of prominent individuals who resided in the city.

The directory, which was printed by a competitor of Periodical Publishing Company, contained no advertising, but was sold at a profit by Harkin and his associate.

Some time later, Harkin's employer brought an action against him for an accounting of the profits made on the sale of the directory. The basis of the complaint (apart from the breach of the covenant) was that the directory competed with a weekly "society magazine" which the company produced.

Harkin argued that the directory was done in his spare time, and that it did not conflict with his position of advertising agent. He admitted, however, that some of the information that came to his attention was obtained from reading his employer's weekly society magazine.

Indicate the legal issues, and the arguments relating to them. Render a decision.

CHAPTER 20

Labour Law

LABOUR LAW DEFINED

Labour law is an area of law concerned with the employment relationship. By strict definition, it would include all laws which touch on employment, including the common law and statutes. In the previous chapter, the common law contract of employment, employment standards legislation, and workmen's compensation laws were mentioned, but it is worthwhile to note that many other laws have been passed at both the federal and provincial levels of government which affect the employment relationship as well.

Canada does not have a national labour policy due to the fact that employment falls for the most part within the jurisdiction of the individual provinces. Nevertheless, the federal government has jurisdiction in labour relations matters in some areas, because a number of business activities and industries such as banking, navigation and shipping, aviation, inter-provincial railways, and communications are federal matters under the *British North America Act, 1867.*[1] As a result of the split jurisdiction, all provincial governments and the federal government exercise control over the employment relationship within their respective spheres.

At the federal level, nation-wide employment-related legislation includes a contributory pension plan for most employees, and a number of employment assistance schemes in the form of national unemployment insurance, manpower training, and placement programs. In addition, the federal government has implemented employment standard's laws and collective bargaining legislation which apply to firms which operate within those defined industries and businesses that come under its jurisdiction.

The provinces generally are responsible for the establishment of labour legislation applicable to most business activities, as employment (except in those areas within the control of the federal government) is considered to be a matter of "property and civil rights" and, consequently, under the jurisdiction of the provinces.[2] As a result, all of the provinces have introduced legislation concerning many aspects of the employment relationship.

In addition to the broad definition of labour law, a second, and narrower definition is sometimes used to describe a particular type of legislation relating to collective bargaining. This body of law is concerned with most aspects of employ-ment where employees have decided to negotiate their terms and conditions of employment on a collective basis through a trade union.

COLLECTIVE BARGAINING AND THE LABOUR MOVEMENT

Little more than a century ago, collective bargaining and labour unions were still looked upon with disfavour, and their activities treated as contrary to public policy. Since that time, statute law has legitimized many of their actions, and permitted collective bargaining to take place by way of statutory authority and regulation. The process, however, was a slow, and for the most part, evolutionary one, rather than a sudden reversal of public policy. During this period of time, most of the legislation was introduced as a response to the growth and activities of the labour movement, rather than as an attempt to lead labour in a new direction. The laws have simply attempted to deal with the growth of the labour movement, and the impact of its activities, as it gradually acquired a prominent position in the conduct of economic activity in Canada.

The labour movement has a long and interesting history in both England and North America. Initially, organizations of workmen were treated as combinations in restraint of trade, and therefore contrary to public policy. This made the employee organization illegal if its purpose was to restrict trade in any way. To avoid this, many of the early unions in England were organized as *friendly societies* whose purpose was ostensibly to provide help and assistance to the less fortunate of its members. In reality, one of the purposes

[1] 30 & 31 Vict., c. 3.
[2] The matter was determined by the case of *Toronto Electric Com'rs v. Snider*, [1925] A.C. 396.

of the organization was to co-ordinate the activities of the members in their dealings with their employer in an effort to obtain higher wages and better working conditions. Because employers at the time wished to avoid dealing with their employees on a collective basis, they would seldom knowingly hire a member of one of the early unions for fear that the person would organize the remainder of the work-force. As a result, the early unions tended to be secret societies in the sense that members did not make their membership known to their employer unless a large majority of the employees were also members of the organization.

In spite of the fact that the law did not permit the early trade unions to engage in activities that were in restraint of trade, many unions did so, and did negotiate wages and conditions of employment for their members with employers. The earliest unions were generally formed by skilled craftsmen, due largely to the fact that the skilled craft groups had a common interest in protecting their work from encroachment by unskilled and semi-skilled employees, and because, as a group, they were often difficult to replace in a plant. The skilled groups were also in a better position to support such organizations because they were generally better paid than ordinary employees, and consequently, had surplus funds to maintain themselves if a strike was necessary to enforce their demands on their employers.

In North America, early unions of skilled tradesmen began to appear in the late 18th century,[3] but the trade union movement did not gain momentum until many years later when the United States and Canada began to change from an agrarian to an industrial society. By the latter part of the 19th century, the northeastern part of the United States had emerged as an industrialized area where a large part of the population was employed in mining, manufacturing, and related industrial activity. With this growth, there emerged parallel organizations of workmen. By the end of the century, most of the skilled trades had established their own trade unions, and had formed a national federation, which was known as the American Federation of Labour.[4]

The American Federation of Labour was the first truly national body of organized labour, and its formation permitted the trade union movement to develop with some degree of co-ordination and direction. The federation pressed for legislation favourable to the union movement, and expanded the organization of skilled employees in industrial plants both in the United States and Canada. The concerted effort on the part of United States-based unions to organize locals in Canada resulted in a strong and close affiliation of labour organizations in both countries with the American Federation of Labour. It also permitted the labour movement in both countries to urge the governments of the day to remove the legal restraints on unions, and to permit free collective bargaining by employees.

DEVELOPMENT OF LABOUR LEGISLATION IN CANADA

In Canada, the earliest significant legislation related to the labour movement was

---

[3]Shoe workers in Philadelphia, Pennsylvania, had formed a union as early as 1792, and workers in the ship-building trades in Halifax, Nova Scotia, had organized by the early 1800s. Printers in what is now Toronto, Ontario, had a union as early as 1832.

[4]The American Federation of Labour was formed in 1886. There were other organizations as well.

introduced at the federal level of government. In 1872 (following a similar change in the law in England), Canada amended its criminal laws to recognize trade unions as lawful entities.[5] As a result of this change, unions, and their membership were free from criminal prosecution in the conduct of their collective bargaining activities, provided that their actions were otherwise lawful in nature. The change in status permitted the union movement to expand rapidly in the industrialized areas of Canada, particularly in the skilled trades, and later, in the forestry and mining fields.

Following labour unrest in a number of sectors of industry in the early part of the 20th century, the federal government introduced legislation to assist the parties in industrial disputes.[6] The legislation limited the right to strike until an attempt had been made to resolve the dispute by way of conciliation, but the legislation was for the most part ineffective. Some years later, it was held to be *ultra vires* the powers of the federal government, except in those areas of industry where the federal government had exclusive jurisdiction under the *British North America Act, 1867*.[7] The effect of the decision was to force the provinces to provide their own collective bargaining laws. As a result, many of the more industrialized provinces introduced legislation to adopt the federal legislation as the law applicable to labour disputes in their respective jurisdictions.

Prior to 1930, the more practical problems of organized labour were generally those associated with the preservation of skilled trade crafts from encroachment by the unskilled. The organization of skilled trades into trade unions was, for the most part, an easy matter for the craft groups because of their common interests and concerns. In addition, the skilled groups generally had little difficulty gaining recognition of their unions by their employers. This was not so, however, for the unskilled employees in the mass production industries. Employers willing to recognize and bargain with a craft union which represented a small group of skilled employees in a plant frequently refused to recognize a union that had organized the unskilled workers, and the result often took the form of a disruptive *recognition strike*.

Collective bargaining legislation introduced in the United States[8] resolved this particular problem by recognizing the right of employees to organize and bargain collectively. The laws established a National Labour Relations Board to determine the right of a union to represent employees, and to require the employer to bargain with the union with respect to wages and working conditions of the employees.[9] This legislation produced a rapid organization of the mass production industries by labour unions, and the spillover of enthusiasm to Canada produced a similar interest in organization for collective bargaining purposes by Canadian employees in the mass production industries.

Canadian jurisdictions, however, lacked the legislative and administrative

---

[5] The *Trade Unions Act*, 35 Vict., c. 30; *Criminal Law Amendment Act*, 35 Vict., c. 31.

[6] The *Industrial Disputes Investigation Act*, 6-7 Edw. VII, c. 20.

[7] *Toronto Electric Com'rs v. Snider*, [1925] A.C. 396.

[8] The *National Labor Relations Act*, 49 Stat. 449 (1935) U.S.

[9] This legislation was first introduced in 1933 as a part of the *National Industrial Recovery Act*, 48 Stat. 195 (1933) U.S., and later embodied in the *National Labor Relations Act (Wagner Act)*, 49 Stat. 449 (1935) U.S.

machinery to deal with rapid unionization of the work-force, and the result was much labour unrest and disruptive recognition strikes in the years which preceded the outbreak of World War II.

The onset of hostilities in 1939 brought with it a need for uninterrupted war production, and under the *War Measures Act*,[10] Orders in Council eventually established a legislative collective bargaining framework that bore some similarity to the United States laws.[11] The new laws applied to all industries engaged in war production, and provided for recognition of trade unions and the right of employees to bargain collectively. Administrative machinery was set up to determine the rights of unions to represent employees, and a procedure was set out to assist the parties in their collective bargaining.

In 1943, Ontario introduced legislation to provide for collective bargaining by employees in those industries that were not engaged in essential war production.[12] The legislation, which did much to establish collective bargaining in the province in an orderly fashion, was administered by a labour court, rather than a labour relations board. While effective in its application, the legislation was in operation for less than a year.[13] The need for uniform legislation applicable to all industries in all provinces (as well as certain political considerations) led the Ontario government in 1944 to repeal the law, and bring itself under expanded labour legislation introduced by the federal government.

Canada, during the war years, did nothing to discourage the unionization of industry, and when the war ended, most of the major firms in the manufacturing, mining, and forestry sections of the economy were unionized. Since labour relations fell generally under the jurisdiction of the provinces, all provincial governments found it necessary to introduce collective bargaining legislation when the federal government wartime controls were removed. As with most provincial laws, each province introduced labour legislation to suit its own particular needs, and as a consequence, the law relating to collective bargaining varied from province to province. Some basic aspects of the laws, nevertheless, were similar, due in part to the fact that many of the procedural aspects of the new legislation were adaptations of the rules and regulations set down by the labour relations boards under the wartime legislation.

The general approach taken to labour relations law in each province was to remove the collective bargaining relationship from the common law and the courts (insofar as possible) and place it under the supervision of an administrative tribunal. The laws normally placed the selection of a union as a bargaining agent by employees, the negotiation of the collective agreement, and the resolution of disputes relating to negotiations (unfair practices, and bargaining in bad faith) under the jurisdiction of the tribunal. The laws also set out the rights and duties of the employer, the union, and the employees in the legislation to be administered by that body.

COLLECTIVE BARGAINING LEGISLATION

Each of the provinces and the federal gov-

---

[10]The *War Measures Act*, 5 Geo. V, c. 2 (now R.S.C. 1970, c. W-2).

[11]See, for example, Order in Council P.C. 1003 (1944) under the *War Measures Act*.

[12]The *Collective Bargaining Act*, 7 Geo. VII, c. 4.

[13]See, for example, Willes, J.A., *The Ontario Labour Court 1943-1944* (Queen's University, 1979: Kingston, Ontario).

ernment have enacted labour legislation which provides for the control of labour unions and collective bargaining in their respective jurisdictions, and each has established a labour relations board to administer the law.

Labour legislation in each jurisdiction generally assigns a number of specific duties to the respective labour relations board established under it. The boards normally have the authority to determine the right of a labour union to represent a group of employees, the nature and make-up of the employee group, the wishes of the employees to bargain collectively through a particular union, the certification of a union as a bargaining agent, and the enforcement of the rights and duties of employers, employees, and unions under the legislation. In some jurisdictions, the board is given the power to deal with strikes and lockouts as well.

The general thrust of the legislation is to replace the use of economic power by unions and employers with an orderly process for the selection of a bargaining representative for the employees, and for the negotiation of collective agreements. The use of the strike or lockout is prohibited with respect to the selection and recognition of the bargaining agent, and severely restricted in use as a part of the negotiation process. In most jurisdictions the right to strike or lockout may not be lawfully exercised until the parties have exhausted all other forms of negotiation, and compulsory conciliation or other third party assistance has failed to produce an agreement.

The Certification Process

Collective bargaining usually begins with the desire on the part of a group of em-

ployees to bargain together, rather than on an individual basis with their employer. To do this, they must first establish an organization to act on their behalf. This may be done by the employees themselves forming their own organization, or more often, by calling upon an existing labour union for assistance. Most large labour unions have trained organizers whose job consists of organizing employees into new unions or *locals* affiliated with the larger union organization. These persons will assist the group of employees in the establishment of their own *local union*. Once the organization is in existence, with its own constitution and officers, its executive and members will then attempt to interest other employees of the firm to join. When the organization believes that it has the support of a majority of the employees in the employer's plant, shop, or office, it may then approach the employer with a request to be recognized as the bargaining representative of the employees. If the employer agrees to recognize the union as the bargaining representative, he may meet with representatives of it, and negotiate a *collective agreement* which will contain the terms and conditions of employment that will apply to the group of employees represented by the union. On the other hand, if the employer refuses to recognize the union as the bargaining representative of the employees, the union is obliged to be *certified* as the bargaining representative by the labour relations board before the employer is required to bargain with it. This process is known as the *certification process*.

The process formally begins with the submission of a written application (by the labour union) to the labour relations board of the correct jurisdiction for certification as the exclusive bargaining representative of a particular group of employees. On receipt of the union's application, the labour relations board will usually require a new union to prove that it is a *bona fide* trade union which is neither supported financially (or otherwise), nor dominated in any way by the employer. Once this has been accomplished by the union, the labour relations board will then determine the unit of employees appropriate for collective bargaining purposes.

The group of employees, or the *bargaining unit*, is usually determined by the board in accordance with the legislation or regulations which sets out the kinds of employees eligible to bargain collectively. While variation exists from province to province and federally, only "employees" are entitled to bargain collectively, and within this group some professionals employed in a professional capacity, management employees, and persons employed in a confidential capacity with respect to labour relations are usually excluded. As well, the legislation does not apply to certain employee groups. Most provinces have special legislation to deal with collective bargaining by persons engaged in essential services, and in the employ of government. In some provinces, persons employed in certain activities (such as hunting and trapping) may be excluded from collective bargaining entirely.

Labour relations boards usually hold hearings to receive the representations of the employer, the union, and employees, if the parties cannot agree upon an appropriate bargaining unit. The determination of the bargaining unit, however, is a board decision, and when the decision is made, the board will then proceed with the determination of employee support for the union in the particular unit. It may do this by an examination of union membership records, and the examination of union witnesses at a hearing, but if any doubt exists, the board will usually hold a *representation vote* to determine the true wishes of the employees.[14] If a majority of the votes are cast in favour of collective bargaining through the union, then the board will certify the union as the exclusive bargaining representative of all of the employees in the bargaining unit. Certification gives the union the right to negotiate on behalf of the employees the terms of their employment, and the conditions under which their work will be performed. It also permits the union to demand that the employer meet with its representatives to negotiate the collective agreement which will contain these provisions.

The Negotiation Process

The negotiation process begins when the certified trade union gives written notice to the employer of its desire to meet with representatives of the employer to bargain for a collective agreement. On receipt of the notice, the employer must arrange a meeting with the union representatives, and bargain in good faith with a view to making a collective agreement. This does not mean that the employer is obliged to accept the demands of the union, but it does mean that the employer must meet with the union and discuss the matters put forward by it. Nor does it mean that the demands are always one-sided. Employ-

[14]Some provinces require the Labour Relations Board to hold a vote where the support of the employees falls within a certain percentage range, eg.: Ontario.

ers often introduce their own demands at the bargaining table. For example, employers generally insist upon the insertion in the collective agreement of terms which set out the rights of management to carry on specified activities without interference by the union or employees.

Where the parties reach an agreement on the terms and conditions of employment, and on the rights and duties of the employer, the union, and the employees, the agreement is put in writing and signed by the employer and representatives of the union. When approved by the employees, the agreement then governs the employment relationship during the term specified in the agreement.

Collective agreements must normally be for a term of at least one year, and either the employer or the union may give notice to bargain for a new agreement, or for changes in the old agreement, as the expiry date of the agreement approaches. The minimum term is generally dictated by the governing legislation, and usually cannot be reduced without the consent of the labour relations board. The purpose of the minimum term is to introduce an element of stability to collective bargaining by requiring the parties to live under the agreement they negotiate without stoppage of work for at least a reasonable period of time.

If the parties cannot reach agreement on the terms and conditions of employment, or the rights and duties of the employer and the union, most jurisdictions provide for third party intervention in the negotiations to assist the parties. This intervention may take the form of conciliation, mediation, or in some cases, fact-finding. The purpose of the intervention is to assist the parties by clarifying the issues in dispute and (in the case of mediation) by taking an active part in the process through offers of assistance in resolving the conflict. Only when third party intervention is exhausted are the parties permitted to strike or lockout to enforce their demands.

Strikes and Lockouts

A *strike* is considered to be a concerted refusal to work by the employees of an employer, although in some jurisdictions, any slow-down or concerted effort to restrict output may also be considered a strike.[15] A lawful strike under most labour legislation may only take place when a collective agreement is not in effect and after all required third party assistance has failed to produce a collective agreement. A strike at any other time is usually an unlawful strike, regardless of whether it is called by the union, or whether it is a spontaneous walk-out by employees (i.e., a *wildcat strike*).

A *lockout* is, in some respects, the reverse of a strike. It is the closing of a place of employment or a suspension of work by an employer and lawful when a collective agreement is not in effect and after all required third party intervention has failed to produce an agreement.

Lawful strikes and lockouts must normally be limited to the premises of the employer that has a labour dispute with his employees. Under a lawful strike, the employees may withhold their services from their employer, and if they so desire, they may set up *picket lines* at the entrances of the employer's premises to inform others of their strike. Lawful picketing is for the purpose of conveying information,[16] and any attempt by pickets to prevent persons

---

[15]See, for example, the *Labour Relations Act*, R.S.O. 1980, c. 228, s. 1(1)(o).

[16]*Criminal Code*, R.S.C. 1970, c. C-34, s. 381. See also *Smith Bros. Construction Co. Ltd. v. Jones et al.*, [1955] O.R. 362.

from entering or leaving the plant may be actionable at law. Where property is damaged or persons injured while attempting to enter or leave the employer's premises, the usual action on the part of the employer is to apply for a court order limiting the number of pickets to only a few, and in this fashion the lawful purpose of picketing is served, and the likelihood of damage or injury substantially diminished.

Striking employees are not permitted to picket the premises of strangers to the labour dispute, such as the customers of the employer, or his suppliers. These individuals are innocent bystanders to the dispute, and are entitled to protection at law if the strikers attempt to injure them in an effort to pressure the employer into a collective agreement by such tactics.[17] This form of picketing, which is known as *secondary picketing* is unlawful, except in certain cases where the customer or supplier is so closely related to the employer that he might be considered to be involved in the dispute as a part of the employer's overall operation.[18]

|||||||||||||||||||||||||||||||||||||||||||||||||||||||||||||||||||||||||||||||

CASE 20.1

Nipissing Hotel Ltd. and Farenda Co. Ltd. v. Hotel & Restaurant Employees & Bartenders International Union C.L.C., A.F. of L., C.I.O., et al. (1962), 36 D.L.R. (2d) 81.

LANDREVILLE, J.:

Either party has a definite course to follow if negotiations break down. A request for conciliation services is available to them. I repeat that any act by an employer or a union which at that stage in the negotiations is not in conformity with the "rules" set out in the Act to achieve

[17]*Hersees of Woodstock Ltd. v. Goldstein et al.* (1963), 38 D.L.R. (2d) 449.
[18]See, for example, *Canadian Pacific Ltd. v. Weatherbee et al.* (1980), 26 O.R. (2d) 776.

agreement between the parties, allows drawing an inference of bad faith as it is not pursued by legal and peaceful steps as contemplated by statute. It then becomes an attempt to circumvent the Act and the use of parading, picketing, or in any way affecting the business of the employer or the liberty of the employees is a process or substitute to foster the contract by a procedure not contemplated nor within the purview of the Act.

|||||||||||||||||||||||||||||||||||||||||||||||||||||||||||||||||||||||||||||||

Compulsory Arbitration

The strike or lockout, however, is not available to all employee groups when negotiations break down. Persons employed in essential services, such as hospitals, fire-fighting, and police work, are usually denied the right to strike, and compulsory arbitration is used to resolve the issues which they cannot settle in the bargaining process.

Where compulsory arbitration is imposed, an arbitration process replaces the right to strike or lockout, and permits work to continue without interruption. Under this system, if the employer and union cannot reach an agreement, they are generally required to have the issues in dispute decided by a representative tribunal called an *arbitration board*. The tribunal is usually made up of one representative each chosen by the employer and union, and an impartial third party chosen by the representatives (or appointed by the government) who becomes the chairman of the board. The tribunal will hold a hearing where the arguments of both sides concerning the unresolved issues may be presented. At the conclusion of the hearing the board will review the presentations and the evidence, then make a decision. The parties will be bound by the decision of the arbitration board, and the decision of the board, together with the other agreed upon terms, will become the collective agreement which will govern the employment relationship for the period of its operation.

While compulsory arbitration is normally applied to employers and employees engaged in activities where the disruption of services by a strike or lockout would be injurious to the public, some jurisdictions have provided for the use of arbitration as an optional means of settling outstanding issues in those industries and services that are not treated as essential. This method of settlement is generally available as a method which may be adopted by the parties as a part of their negotiations, or it may be employed as a means of resolving a labour dispute where the parties have been engaged in a lengthy strike or lockout.

The Collective Agreement and Its Administration

The collective agreement differs from the ordinary common law contract of employment in a number of fundamental ways. The collective agreement sets out the rights and duties not only of the employer and the employees, but of the bargaining agent as well. It is also an agreement which is sometimes negotiated under conditions which would render an ordinary common law contract voidable. The imposition of economic sanctions, or the threat of their use is treated as a legitimate tactic in the negotiation of a collective agreement, but one which would not be tolerated by the courts in the case of a common law contract.

Most jurisdictions require the parties to insert special terms in their collective agreement which will govern certain aspects of their relationship. The agreements must usually include a clause whereby the employer recognizes the union as the exclusive bargaining representative of the employees in the defined bargaining unit. This has a twofold purpose. First, it is a written acknowledgement by the employer that the union is the proper body to represent the employees. Secondly, recognition of the union as the exclusive bargaining representative prevents the employer from negotiating with any other union purporting to act on behalf of the employees while the collective agreement is in existence.

Most jurisdictions also require the parties to provide in their agreement that no strike or lockout may take place during the term of the agreement, should a dispute arise after the agreement is put into effect. Coupled with this requirement is the additional requirement that the parties provide in their agreement some mechanism to settle disputes that arise out of the collective agreement during its term of operation.

The most common method of dispute resolution is arbitration. This is generally compulsory under most collective bargaining legislation, and the law frequently sets out an arbitration process which is deemed to apply if the parties fail to include a suitable procedure in their collective agreement. As a rule, any dispute which arises out of the interpretation, application, or administration of the collective agreement, including any question as to whether a matter is arbitrable is a matter for arbitration. The procedure would also be used where a violation of the collective agreement is alleged.

Collective agreements usually provide for a series of informal meetings between the union and the employer concerning these disputes (called *grievances*) as a possible means of avoiding arbitration. The series of meetings, which involve progressively higher levels of management in both the employer and union hierarchy is referred to as a *grievance procedure*, and it is usually outlined as a series of steps in a clause in the collective agreement. If, after the grievance procedure is exhausted no settlement is reached, either the employer or the union may carry the matter further, and invoke the arbitration process.

The parties under the terms of their collective agreement may provide for the dispute to be heard by either a sole arbitrator or an arbitration board. If the procedure calls for a board, it is usually a three person board, with one member chosen by the union, and one by the employer. The third member of the board is normally selected by the two persons so nominated, and becomes the impartial chairman. If the parties cannot agree on an independent chairman, the Minister of Labour usually has the authority to select a chairman for the arbitration board.

An arbitration board (or sole arbitrator) is expected to hold a hearing where each party is given the opportunity to present their side of the dispute, and to introduce evidence or witnesses to establish the facts upon which they base their case. When all of the evidence and argument has been submitted, the arbitrator (or arbitration board) renders a decision called an *award* which is binding upon the parties.

Arbitrators and arbitration boards are usually given wide powers under the legislation to determine their own procedure at hearings, to examine witnesses under oath, and to investigate the circumstances surrounding a dispute, but they are obliged to deal with each dispute in a fair and unbiased manner. If they fail to do so, or if they exceed their jurisdiction, or make a fundamental error in their award, their award may be quashed by the courts.

While arbitration is used as a means of interpreting rights and duties of the employer and the union under the collective agreement, it may also be used by the union to enforce employee rights. Employees who are improperly treated by the employer under the terms of the collective agreement, or who believe that they have been unjustly disciplined or discharged may file grievances which the union may take to arbitration for settlement.

The rights of employees under collective bargaining to some extent differ from the rights of persons engaged in employment under the common law. The common law right of an employee to make a separate and different contract of employment with the employer is lost insofar as the collective agreement is concerned, but this is balanced by way of new collective bargaining rights. For example, employees under a collective agreement are subject to different treatment in the case of disciplinary action by the employer. An employer may suspend or discipline an employee (usually for just cause) under a collective agreement in cases where discharge is perhaps unwarranted. This represents an approach to discipline which is not found at common law. Where the right is exercised, however, the employer's actions may be subject to review by an arbitrator, as they might also be if the employee is discharged without good reason by the employer.

A difference also exists between the remedies available to an arbitrator and the remedies available to the courts in the case of discharge. In most jurisdictions, an arbitrator has the authority to substitute a suspension without compensation where discharge is too severe a penalty, or unwarranted. The arbitrator may also order the reinstatement of an employee wrongfully dismissed, with payment of compensation for time lost. The courts, on the other hand, are unwilling to order the reinstatement of an employee wrongfully dismissed, and limit the compensation of the employee to monetary damages.

THE UNION–MEMBER RELATIONSHIP

As a party to a collective agreement, and as an entity certified by a labour relations board as the exclusive bargaining agent for a group of employees, a trade union is unique. It was initially an illegal organization at common law, whose lawful existence was made possible only by legislation. In some provinces, such as Ontario and Saskatchewan, it is not a sueable entity by virtue of statute law,[19] but in others, the courts have held that trade unions have acquired a legal existence through legislation that has clothed them with special rights and powers. As a result, in some provinces their actions may be subject to legal action, except in matters directly related to collective bargaining.[20]

Apart from its special status as a bargaining agent under labour legislation, a trade union is similar to any club or fraternal organization. As an unincorporated entity, it has no existence separate from its members, and its relationship with its members is contractual in nature.[21] In concept, it consists of a group of individuals who have contracted with one another to abide by certain terms embodied in the organization's *constitution* (and which form a part of each member's contract) in order to carry out the objects or goals of the organization. The rights of each member, then, are governed by the contract, and if a member fails to abide by the contract, the remainder of the members may expel the offending member from the organization.

Most jurisdictions in their collective bargaining legislation have imposed certain limits on the rights of trade unions to refuse membership, or to expel existing members, because of the effect that membership has on an individual's ability to find employment in unionized industries. This is due to the fact that many unions have required employers to insert in their collective agreements a term whereby the employer agrees to hire only persons who are already union members (a *closed shop* clause), or a clause whereby continued employment by an employee is conditional upon union membership (a *union shop* clause). In both of these cases, a loss of union membership would either prevent an employer from hiring the person, or oblige the employer to dismiss the employee. To safeguard the rights of individuals, and to protect them from arbitrary action by labour unions, the right to refuse membership or expel an existing member must be based upon legitimate and justifiable grounds. Membership, for example, generally may not be denied on the basis of race, creed, colour, sex, nationality, place of origin, or other discriminatory factors. Nor may membership normally be denied or revoked simply because a person belongs to a rival union. Once membership is granted, it may not be withdrawn at the whim of a union officer or union executive.

Membership, for the union member, like the membership in any club or organization, involves adherence to the rules and obligations set out in the organization's constitution. If the member fails to abide

---

[19]See the *Rights of Labour Act*, R.S.O. 1980, c. 456, Saskatchewan *Trade Union Act*, R.S.S. 1978, c. T-17.

[20]*Int'l Brotherhood of Teamsters v. Therien* (1960), 22 D.L.R. (2d) 1.

[21]*Astgen v. Smith*, [1970] 1 O.R. 129.

by the terms of the contract made with the rest of the organization, the membership may take steps to end its relationship with the offending member. The explusion of the member must not, however, be made in an unfair or arbitrary way. The courts generally require that the *rules of natural justice* be followed by the organization, and the accused be given an opportunity to put before the membership his case before any decision is made. This would involve giving the accused member full details of the alleged violation, an opportunity to prepare his case, and the conduct of a hearing before the membership which would allow the accused to face his accusers and answer their charges by way of evidence and cross-examination.[22] Only then may the decision of the membership be made on the question before them.

||||||||||||||||||||||||||||||||||||||||||||||||||||||||||||||||||||||||||||||

CASE 20.2
Lee v. Showmen's Guild of Great Britain, [1952] 1 All E.R. 1175.

DENNING, L.J.:

The jurisdiction of a domestic tribunal, such as the committee of the Showmen's Guild, must be founded on a contract, express or implied. Outside the regular courts of this country, no set of men can sit in judgment on their fellows except so far as Parliament authorises it or the parties agree to it. The jurisdiction of the committee of the Showmen's Guild is contained in a written set of rules to which all the members subscribe. This set of rules contains the contract between the members and is just as much subject to the jurisdiction of these courts as any other contract.

. . . . .

Although the jurisdiction of a domestic tribunal is founded on contract, express or implied, nevertheless the parties are not free to make any contract they like. There are important lim-

itations imposed by public policy. The tribunal must, for instance, observe the principles of natural justice. They must give the man notice of the charge and a reasonable opportunity of meeting it. Any stipulation to the contrary would be invalid. They cannot stipulate for a power to condemn a man unheard. . . .

The question in the present case is: To what extent will the courts examine the decisions of domestic tribunals on points of law? This is a new question which is not to be solved by turning to the club cases. In the case of social clubs the rules usually empower the committee to expel a member who, in their opinion, has been guilty of conduct detrimental to the club, and this is a matter of opinion and nothing else. The courts have no wish to sit on appeal from their decisions on such a matter any more than from the decisions of a family conference. They have nothing to do with social rights or social duties. On any expulsion they will see that there is fair play. They will see that the man has notice of the charge and a reasonable opportunity of being heard. They will see that the committee observe the procedure laid down by the rules, but will not otherwise interfere . . . It is very different with domestic tribunals which sit in judgment on the members of a trade or profession. They wield powers as great, if not greater, than any exercised by the courts of law. They can deprive a man of his livelihood. They can ban him from the trade in which he has spent his life and which is the only trade he knows. They are usually empowered to do this for any breach of their rules, which, be it noted, are rules which they impose and which he has no real opportunity of accepting or rejecting. In theory their powers are based on contract. The man is supposed to have contracted to give them these great powers, but in practice he has no choice in the matter. If he is to engage in the trade, he has to submit to the rules promulgated by the committee. Is such a tribunal to be treated by these courts on the same footing as a social club? I say: "No." A man's right to work is just as important, if not more important, to him than his rights of property. These courts intervene every day to protect rights of property. They must also intervene to protect the right to work.

---

[22]*Evanskow v. Int'l Brotherhood of Boilermakers et al.* (1970), 9 D.L.R. (3d) 715.

SUMMARY While labour law in the broad sense refers to all law relating to the employment relationship, it is a term that is often used to refer to the area of employment law concerned with collective bargaining. Collective bargaining is concerned with the negotiation of the terms and conditions of employment by a group of employees with their employer using a trade union as their bargaining agent. Collective bargaining is conducted under legislation which sets out procedures for the selection of a barbaining agent (the certification process), the negotiation of the collective agreement (the negotiation process), and for the administration of the negotiated agreement (the administration process).

Unlike the common law contract of employment, the collective agreement is a special contract of employment which applies to unionized employees. It is not a contract brought before the courts for interpretation, but an agreement which falls within the jurisdiction of a tribunal. The law relating to the collective agreement is *administrative law*, rather than common law. Labour legislation, of which the law relating to collective bargaining is a part, represents a body of statute law which has grown substantially during the last century to meet the needs of employees in more complex industrial and commercial employment settings.

DISCUSSION QUESTIONS

1. *Define a collective agreement.*
2. *What body of law applies to a collective agreement?*
3. *Why were early trade union activities illegal?*
4. *What is the role of a trade union in collective bargaining?*
5. *Define "bargaining unit."*
6. *How does a "collective agreement" differ from a "contract of employment" at common law?*
7. *In what manner is the common law employment relationship affected by the certification of a labour union?*
8. *Why does the collective bargaining legislation of most jurisdictions provide for third party intervention when the parties fail to reach a collective agreement?*
9. *Do all employees have the right to bargain collectively? If not, why not?*
10. *Explain why employees in essential services are denied the right to strike, but allowed to bargain collectively. How are their disputes resolved if they cannot reach an agreement?*
11. *Describe the arbitration process for disputes that arise out of a collective agreement.*
12. *Explain "compulsory arbitration." How does it apply to a collective agreement?*
13. *Do arbitral remedies differ from those of the common law in the case of wrongful dismissal of an employee subject to a collective agreement? Explain.*

14. *Describe the legal nature of a union. Explain how it differs from other types of organizations.*

15. *Why is "fairness" so important in the treatment of a union member where the member is alleged to have acted in such a way that expulsion is proposed?*

|||

JUDICIAL DECISIONS

Trade Union —Nature of Organization

Astgen et al. v. Smith et al., [1970] 1 O.R. 129.

Two trade unions agreed to a merger, but the constitution of one of the unions made no provision for a merger procedure. When some of the employees objected to the merger, the question arose: Was the merger invalid because some of the members objected to it? The case turned on the legal nature of the particular union.

EVANS, J.A.:

Prior to dealing with the merger agreement I consider it desirable to determine the precise legal status of a trade union or labour union, the relationships existing among the membership *inter se* and the relationships of each member to the totality of the persons associated together. I concede at the outset that a labour union under the *Labour Relations Act*, R.S.O. 1960, c. 202, and allied legislation has a "status" conferred by such legislation which makes it somewhat different from a fraternal organization or an athletic club but apart from such statutes a labour union is essentially a club, a voluntary association which has no existence, apart from its members, recognized by law. A club is basically a group of people who have joined together for the promotion of certain objects and whose conduct in relation to one another is regulated in accordance with the constitution, by-laws, rules and regulations to which they have subscribed.

The proposition that a trade union has a special status, that it is a sort of hybrid corporation, has no foundation in law. This misconception is fostered by the "legal entity" character which labour legislation has thrust upon trade unions but is not legally supportable outside the purview of those statutes. While trade unions have historically strenuously opposed and rejected any movement toward corporate status with its attendant strictures, there has evolved a concept, which has no basis in law, that unions have a *quasi*-legal entity; that they have a peculiar status which clothes them with the advantages of corporations but shields them from the restrictions and liabilities attaching to corporate entities. This misunderstanding, and it is a fundamental one, must not be allowed to becloud the issues herein.

We are not concerned in this appeal with the pseudocorporate status bestowed on labour unions by statute; nor are we assisted by English case law in view of the fact that under various Trade Union Acts, trade unions in England may be registered and upon registration are vested with certain powers and responsibilities. Ontario has no comparable legislation and resort must be had to the common law to determine both status and capacity. Mine Mill is not a corporation, individual or partnership, and is accordingly not a legal entity; it is an unincorporated group or association of workmen who have banded together to promote certain objectives for their mutual benefit and advantage and in law nothing is recognizable other than the totality of members related one to another by contract. The objects and purposes of the association are spelled out in the memorandum of association usually referred to as the "constitution"; the by-laws or rules provide the machinery for the proper carrying out of activities intended to advance the objectives and purposes of the voluntary association. Each member of Mine Mill, upon being granted membership, subscribed to those purposes and objects and in so doing entered into a contractual relationship with every other member of Mine Mill. Rand, J., in *Orchard et al. v. Tunney*, [1957] S.C.R. 436 at p. 445, 8 D.L.R. (2d) 273 at p. 281, stated:

". . . each member commits himself to a group on a foundation of specific terms governing individual and collective action . . . and made on both sides with the intent that the rules shall bind them in their relations to each other."

I adopt also the proposition stated by Thompson, J., in *Bimson v. Johnston et al.*, [1957] O.R. 519 at p. 530, 10 D.L.R. (2d) 11 at p. 22, which was affirmed on appeal [1958] O.W.N. 217, 12 D.L.R. (2d) 379:

". . . that a contract is made by a member when he joins the union, the terms and conditions of which are provided by the union's constitution and by-laws . . . The contract is not a contract with the union or the association as such, which is devoid of the power to contract, but rather the contractual rights of a member are with all other members thereof."

The prevalence in our society of the corporate entity has led to the adoption with reference to unincorporated associations of terms strictly applicable to the incorporated corporations. Particularly is this so with respect to the term *ultra vires*. Apart from those accustomed to the strict observance of accurate terminology, *ultra vires* is applied both—to purported corporate acts beyond the statutory capacity of the corporation and—to the purported exercise by the officers and directors of an authority to bind the corporation which they do not possess.

In this jurisdiction where generally upon incorporation the incorporated body is given the status equivalent to that of a person at common law, no act otherwise legal is *ultra vires* in the sense that it is beyond the capacity of the corporation; *ultra vires* properly refers only to the exceeding of authority of the persons purporting to act on behalf of the corporation.

There is no limit to the lawful objects for the furtherance of which men may associate voluntarily, and in my view, provided it is properly authorized by every member of the association, there is no restriction upon the powers of the members to alter the objects for which they became associated or to terminate the relationship *inter se* of those associated, or to agree individually to become bound by other contractual relationships to the members of the same or some other group of associates. In this sense of the meaning of *ultra vires* I do not consider that the realization of what was contemplated by the provisions of the merger agreement would be beyond the capacity of the members of Mine Mill provided that there was unanimous approval individually or by means of some procedure which all of the members had agreed upon.

The contract of association is not between the member and some undefined entity which lacks the capacity to contract; it is a complex of contracts between each member and every other member of the union. These are individual contracts impressed with rights and obligations which cannot be destroyed in the absence of the specific consent of each person whose rights would be affected thereby.

Labour Dispute— Secondary Picketing	**Hersees of Woodstock Ltd. v. Goldstein et al. (1963), 38 D.L.R. (2d) 449.**

A clothing manufacturer was involved in a labour dispute with his employees, and a strike took place. Some time later, members of a labour organization affiliated with the striking union picketed the premises of a retailer who normally sold goods produced by the clothing manufacturer. The retailer was located in a distant city, and had no involvement in any way with the clothing manufacturer or his labour dispute. The picketing of the retailer, however, resulted in a loss of business, as customers were unwilling to enter the store while pickets were present. The retailer brought an action against the pickets for an injunction and damages. The action was first dismissed, then appealed by the plaintiff retailer.

AYLESWORTH, J.A.:

> The learned Chief Justice of the High Court rejected the submission of appellant's counsel that there was a conspiracy to bring about a breach of contract between appellant and the Deacon Company or that there was a conspiracy to injure the plaintiff in his trade. He thought, too, upon the material that the "predominant motive in the minds" of the defendants was not to injure the plaintiff as distinct from the "main object of benefiting themselves" and that there was no contract between appellant and the Deacon Company. He thought the defendants were merely exercising a common law right to peacefully communicate information by causing a placard to be carried with a simple statement of fact on it and an implied invitation to those in sympathy with organized labour to buy only goods bearing the union label. He also found that on the material before him there was nothing to substantiate the plea that the defendants were committing an actionable nuisance.

> To me the matter is not nearly so clear as it was to the learned Chief Justice of the High Court upon some of these issues raised by the ap-

pellants but I find it unnecessary to deal with them all in detail. While I am not prepared to disturb his findings negativing conspiracy and nuisance, I think with respect, and as I have already indicated, that there was a contract extant between appellant and the Deacon Company and that respondents, acting individually at least, tried to induce appellant to break it. I think further that the chief, if not only purpose of the subsequent picketing, was to force appellant's hand in this respect and thus indirectly to bring pressure to bear upon the Deacon Company.

In this day and age the power and influence of organized labour is very far indeed from negligible. "Loyalty to the picket line" is a credo influencing a large portion of any community such as the City of Woodstock with its own District Labour Council and numerous member unions; nor does the matter rest there, for doubtless to many private citizens not directly interested in the labour movement the presence of pickets before business premises is a powerful deterrent to doing business at those premises. In *Smith Bros. Construction Co. v. Jones et al.,* [1955] 4 D.L.R. 255, 113 C.C.C. 16, [1955] O.R. 363, McLennan, J., in the course of his judgment makes the following observations at p. 264 D.L.R., p. 26 C.C.C., pp. 370-1 O.R.:

"There was no evidence that the pickets did anything else than walk up and down at the site of the construction jobs, carrying the signs. There was no evidence of any violence or disturbance or persuasion of any kind other than the mere fact of their presence with the signs, and it was not suggested there was any libel. However, in my opinion, if the development of the Trade Union movement has reached the point where workers will not cross a picket-line to go to work, that is just as effective an interference with contractual relations as any other form of restraint might be. Loyalty to the rule that I have mentioned having been developed, the rule should not be abused for a wrongful purpose and where there is no justification."

McLennan, J., had already found as a fact in the case before him that the employees of more than one employer whose premises had been picketed refused out of "loyalty to the picket-line" to cross that line. In this and in several other cases in Canadian Courts judicial notice has been taken of "the rule" so far as employees are concerned. I am prepared to take judicial notice that the rule affects as well, many other members of the public who are not employees of the employer whose premises are picketed, particularly such other members of the public in a community where, as in the case at bar, there is a widespread organization of labour. It is in the light of these considerations that the nature of the picketing and its effect upon the appellant are to be gauged.

One side of the placard in question tells him who reads, that "this campaign" has the support of the force of labour in Woodstock. What campaign? To ascertain any sort of answer from the placard itself necessitates a reading of both sides thereof. The other side of the placard in large type calculated to stand out from the rest of the wording on that side, links the Deacon Company, the appellant and non-union labour. To me, and I should think to anyone seeking to do business at the appellant's premises, the inference is unmistakable—Hersees is in a dispute of some kind with organized labour; don't become involved! I think any other conclusion is simply unrealistic and I would hold on the facts of the case that appellant's apprehension of damage to its business as a result of the picketing is completely justified.

Upon this branch of the case, therefore, I summarize my conclusions as follows: appellant had a contract with the Deacon Company; respondents knew of the contract and attempted to induce appellant to break it by picketing his premises; such picketing is a "besetting" of appellant's place of business causing or likely to cause damage to appellant; not being "for the purpose only of obtaining or communicating information" the picketing is unlawful—*Criminal Code*, 1953-54 (Can.), c. 51, s. 366—and it ought to be restrained.

But even assuming that the picketing carried on by the respondents was lawful in the sense that it was merely peaceful picketing for the purpose only of communicating information, I think it should be restrained. Appellant has a right lawfully to engage in its business of retailing merchandise to the public. In the City of Woodstock where that business is being carried on, the picketing for the reasons already stated, has caused or is likely to cause damage to the appellant. Therefore, the right, if there be such a right, of the respondents to engage in secondary picketing of appellant's premises must give way to appellant's right to trade; the former, assuming it to be a legal right, is exercised for the benefit of a particular class only while the latter is a right far more fundamental and of far greater importance, in my view, as one which in its exercise affects and is for the benefit of the community at large. If the law is to serve its purpose then in civil matters just as in matters within the realm of the criminal law, the interests of the community at large must be held to transcend those of the individual or a particular group of individuals. I have been unable to find clear and unequivocal precedent for this principle in any of the numerous decisions at all relevant to the question, to be found anywhere in Canada.

CASE PROBLEMS FOR DISCUSSION

Case 1

Cleaning Company employs a number of employees in its office cleaning business, and is known as a demanding employer that is reluctant to pay more than the statutory minimum wage unless forced to do so.

Six of the 10 employees decide to organize a union, and bargain collectively with their employer in an effort to pressure it into improving working conditions and wage rates. The employees are aware that the company would not likely recognize their union once it was formed, and they decide to follow whatever procedures are necessary in order to enable them to compel the company to bargain collectively with them.

What advice would you offer the employees? How should they proceed? Explain the various steps which the employees must follow.

Case 2

Gear Manufacturing Company carries on business in a part of a factory building in an industrial park located at the outskirts of a large municipality. The remainder of the building is leased by Gear Warehousing Company, a wholly-owned subsidiary of Gear Manufacturing Company. Gear Warehousing Company is essentially the storage and marketing subsidiary of Gear Manufacturing Company, which purchases and markets all standard types of gears manufactured by the parent company, even though it is a separate entity.

The employees of Gear Manufacturing Company are represented by the Gear Makers' Union. In 1979, the union negotiated a collective agreement that expired some months ago. Collective bargaining took place before the expiry of the old agreement but Gear Manufacturing Company and the union could not agree on the terms of a new collective agreement. They requested conciliation services offered by the Ministry of Labour (which were required before a strike or lockout could take place), but the services failed to produce an agreement. Eventually, the employees went out on strike, and set up picket lines at the entrances of the plant of Gear Manufacturing Company. They also set up picket lines at the entrances to Gear Warehousing Company to prevent the shipment of goods from the warehouse.

A few days later, the employees set up a picket line at Transmission Manufacturing Company, an important customer of Gear Warehousing Company even though the company's only connection with Gear Manufacturing and Gear Warehousing was as a purchaser of Gear products. The pickets prevented Transmission Manufacturing from shipping a large truck-load of transmissions to another manufacturer, and as a result, the company suffered a loss of $2 500 by its failure to make delivery on time.

Advise Gear Warehousing Company and Transmission Manufacturing Company of their rights (if any), and suggest a course of action that they might take.

Case 3

Bonsor was a member of the Piano Players' Union. He was 55 years old, and had been a professional musician for most of his working life. He had joined the union some time before 1947, and by so doing, worked regularly at the union wage scale in the years that followed.

Regular payment of union dues was a requirement for maintenance of membership in the union, and Mr. Bonsor was a regular contributor up to a particular time, when, through oversight or neglect, he failed to pay his weekly contribution. Under the union rules, a failure to pay union dues was a cause for expulsion, and the union secretary, acting in accordance with the rules, promptly erased Bonsor's name from the membership register.

The effect of the secretary's act was catastrophic for Bonsor. Because the musicians were highly organized and employed the closed shop as a union security measure, Bonsor was unable to find employment as a musician. He appealed to the secretary for reinstatement, but was refused, and as a result, was reduced to working at a variety of unskilled jobs to earn a meagre living.

Some time later, he brought an action against the union for wrongful expulsion and damages.

Discuss the arguments that might be raised by Bonsor and the union in this case, and render a decision.

Case 4

Smith was employed as a taxi-driver by the Rapid Cab and Cartage Company, and on May 23, 1980, while driving his taxi, was involved in a serious collision with a train at a level crossing. The taxi was demolished as a result of the accident, and three passengers riding in the rear seat of the taxi were seriously injured. Smith, by some miracle, escaped injury.

An investigation of the accident revealed that Smith had been racing the train to the level crossing and had collided with the side of the engine when the train and the vehicle reached the crossing at the same instant. As a result of the investigation, Smith was charged with criminal negligence, and released on bail pending his trial.

The employees of the company worked under a collective agreement, and were represented by a truck drivers' union. The company manager and the union representatives met on May 27, 1980, to discuss Smith's accident, and at the request of the union, the company agreed to allow Smith to continue to drive until his trial.

Smith had been employed by the company for five years prior to the accident, and had an accident-free driving record until April of 1980. During April, Smith was involved in four minor accidents which were clearly his fault, and on May 9th (only two weeks before the accident on May 23rd) had crashed his vehicle into the side of the taxi garage, causing extensive damage to both the vehicle and the building. On that occasion, and the two previous occasions, he had been given verbal warnings by the supervisor that he would be dismissed if he continued to drive in a careless manner.

Smith's case came before the courts on June 10, 1980. He was convicted and given a six-month jail term. His driving privileges, however, would be reinstated on his release. Following his conviction, the union, on his behalf, arranged for a six-month leave of absence from the company, subject to the right of the company to review the matter on his return to work.

Before Smith was released from jail, several large damage claims were made against the company as a result of the accident, and the insurer expressed concern over Smith's accident frequency rate. The company manager thereupon notified the union of its intention to dismiss Smith, and advised Smith that his services would no longer be required on his release.

Upon receipt of the notice of dismissal, Smith immediately filed a grievance through the union, requesting reinstatement. The grievance was filed in accordance with the time period and procedure outlined in the collective agreement.

The collective agreement contained the following clause:

> 12.01 The company shall have the right to establish reasonable rules of conduct for all employees, and shall have the right to discipline or discharge employees for just cause, subject to right of grievance as set out in this agreement.

The company had posted the following rule on the office bulletin board in September of 1978:

> Rule 6 Any failure on the part of a driver to place the comfort and safety of passengers before his (or her) own convenience shall be cause for discipline or dismissal.

As the sole arbitrator in this case, how would you deal with this grievance? Prepare an award and give reasons for your decision.

CHAPTER 21

The Law of Bailment

NATURE OF BAILMENT

Bailment is a special arrangement between a person (a *bailor*) who owns or lawfully possesses a chattel, and another person (a *bailee*), who is given possession of the chattel for a specific purpose. By definition, bailment consists of the delivery of an article on the express or implied condition that the article will be returned to the bailor or dealt with according to the bailor's wishes as soon as the purpose for which the article was bailed is completed.[1]

A bailment then, consists of three elements:

(1) the delivery of the goods by the bailor;
(2) possession of the goods by the bailee for a specific purpose;
(3) a return of the goods to the bailor at a later time, or the disposition of the goods according to the bailor's wishes.

[1]Osborn, P.G., *The Concise Law Dictionary*, 4th ed. (Sweet & Maxwell Ltd., 1954: London), p. 45.

Under certain circumstances, a second bailment may take place, in which case the bailee becomes the *sub-bailor*, and the person who takes delivery of the goods from the sub-bailor becomes the *sub-bailee*. Sub-bailment, however, must normally only be by special agreement between the bailor and bailee, or be a custom or practice of the trade relating to the particular type of bailment. The right to make a sub-bailment is not a part of every trade activity, but the courts have held that a bailment which involves automobile repairs, the carriage of goods, or the storage of goods, are trade activities in which a sub-bailment may customarily be made by the bailee.[2]

In each case, however, the right of sub-bailment may only be made where the bailor is not relying on the special skill of the bailee to perform the work or service. If the bailee makes a sub-bailment under such circumstances, then he would do so at his own risk. If a sub-bailment is permissible, either by custom of the trade, or by express agreement, the terms of the sub-bailment must be consistent with the original bailment, otherwise it will have the effect of terminating the original bailment. The bailor will then have a right of action against the bailee if the bailee cannot recover the goods from the sub-bailee. In addition, the bailee may be liable to the bailor for any loss or damage to the goods while in the hands of the sub-bailee.

Because the essence of a bailment is the delivery of possession of a chattel by one person to another, delivery must take place before the bailor–bailee relationship may come into existence. Where the goods are physically placed in the hands of the bailee by the bailor, delivery is apparent. For example, if Smith delivers a book to Jones on the condition that it be returned at a later time, the transfer of possession creates the bailment. The element of delivery becomes less clear, however, where the bailee takes only constructive possession of the goods. For example, Zelda enters a restaurant, and places her coat on a coat-rack located beside her table. Has she created a bailment by the act of placing her coat on the rack which the proprietor has obviously placed there for that specific purpose? The basic requirement for a bailment is delivery of possession. If the coat has not been placed in the proprietor's charge, then no bailment may exist. Clearly, if the bailee is unaware of the delivery, and has not consented to it, there may be no bailment. But if the proprietor has either expressly or impliedly requested that the coat be placed upon the rack, then a bailment may have been created by the proprietor's actions. The proprietor under such circumstances may be said to have constructive possession of the goods.[3]

An important characteristic of a bailment is the retention of the title to the goods by the bailor. The bailee receives possessions only, and at no time does the title to the goods pass. The rights of the bailee, nevertheless, once delivery has taken place, are much like those of the owner. The bailee has the right to institute legal proceedings against any person who interferes with the property or his right of possession, even though he does not have the legal title to the goods. The

---

[2]*Edwards v. Newland*, [1950] 1 All E.R. 1072.

[3]*Murphy v. Hart* (1919), 46 D.L.R. 36.

bailee may also recover damages from any person who wrongfully injures the goods, but the money recovered which relates to the damage must be held for the bailor.

The third aspect of bailment is the return of the goods or chattel to the bailor, or the disposition of the goods according to the bailor's directions. The same goods must be returned to the bailor, except *fungibles*, which are interchangeable commodities, such as grain and other natural foodstuffs, fuel oil, gasoline, or similar goods which are frequently stored in large quantities in elevators or tanks. Fungibles of the same grade or quality, and in the same quantity must be returned in that case. If the bailee refuses to return the bailed goods, the bailor is entitled to bring an action against the bailee for conversion.

The law of bailment is a very old area of the law which dates back to the Middle Ages in England, and which developed as a result of the problems which persons had when they entrusted goods to others, or when their goods were at the mercy of a stranger, such as an innkeeper. As the law developed, the courts determined different standards for each of the forms of bailment which they were required to consider. As a result, the liability of a bailee for loss or damage to goods while they are in his possession varies significantly from one type of bailment to another. There are many different general bailment relationships which the courts recognize, and the liability of the bailee differs for each.

Regardless of the standard of care fixed for a bailee, if the bailor can establish that the bailee failed to return the goods, or if the goods when returned were damaged or destroyed (reasonable wear and tear excepted, if the bailee was entitled to use the goods) then the onus shifts to the bailee to satisfy the court that he maintained the standard of care fixed for the particular kind of bailment, and the loss or damage was not a result of his culpable negligence.

The reason for the placement of the onus on the bailee to show that he was not negligent, rather than the normal legal practice of requiring a plaintiff to prove the defendant negligent, is based upon the respective knowledge of the parties. While the goods are in the hands of the bailee, only the bailee is likely to know the circumstances surrounding any damage to the goods. The bailor during the period of time would unlikely have any knowledge of how the loss or damage came about, and the courts have accordingly recognized this fact. If the bailee is unable to offer any reasonable explanation for the loss, or if he is unable to show that he was not negligent, then responsibility of the loss is likely to fall on him. In this sense, the bailor's position is much like that of a person claiming *res ipsa loquitur* in an ordinary tort action: He need only prove the existence of the bailment, and the subsequent loss. The onus then shifts to the bailee to satisfy the court that he was not negligent.

Because of the obligation imposed upon bailees to maintain a relatively high standard of care in most bailment relationships, it is not uncommon for the bailee to attempt to limit his liability in the event of loss. The usual method used by bailees to limit their liability is to insert a clause which is known as an *exculpatory clause* in the bailment agreement.

An exculpatory clause (or exemption clause as it is sometimes called) if carefully drawn, and brought to the attention of the bailor before the bailment is effected, generally has the effect of binding the bailor to the terms of the limited liability (or no liability at all) as set out in the clause.[4] Recent cases, however have tended to reduce the protection offered by exemption clauses, and if the clause is so unreasonable that it amounts to a clear abuse of freedom of contract, the exemption may not be enforced.[5]

GRATUITOUS BAILMENT

A gratuitous bailment is a bailment which may be for the benefit of either the bailor or the bailee, or both, and which, as the name implies, is without monetary reward. In the case of a gratuitous bailment, the liability for loss or damage to the goods varies with the respective benefits received by the parties to the bailment, unless the parties have fixed the standard of care by agreement. If the bailment is entirely for the benefit of the bailor, such as where the bailee agrees to store the bailor's canoe or sailboat during the winter months, without charge, then the bailee's liability is minimal. The bailee in such a case is only obliged to take reasonable care of the goods by protecting them from forseeable risk of harm. The actual standard, unfortunately, appears to vary somewhat, depending upon the nature of the goods delivered. Some years ago, in an English case, the court held that the bailee, in a gratuitous bailment which was entirely for the benefit of the bailor, would only be liable for gross negligence—a degree of carelessness which

would constitute neglect in the eyes of a reasonable man.[6] More recent cases, however, have tended to require a somewhat higher standard of care in similar circumstances.[7]

Conversely, where the bailment is entirely for the benefit of the bailee, for example, where the bailor gratuitously loans the bailee his automobile, the bailee would be liable for any damage caused to the goods by his negligence, reasonable wear and tear being the only exception.

The liability for loss or damage to the goods tends to fall between the two extremes where the bailment is for the benefit of both the bailor and the bailee. For example, Adams stores his sailboat at Burley's cottage, and grants Burley permission to use the boat if he wishes to do so. If the boat should be damaged, the standard which might apply would be that of the ordinary prudent person, and how that person might take care of his own goods.[8]

BAILMENT FOR REWARD

Bailment for reward includes a number of different bailment relationships. The bailment may be for storage (or deposit) such as in the case of a warehouseman, or it may take the form of the delivery of goods to a repair shop for repairs. It may also take the form of a rental of a chattel, the carriage of goods, or the pledge of valuables or securities as collateral for a loan. It would apply as well, to the safe-keeping of goods by an innkeeper. Again, the liability of each of these particu-

[4]*Samuel Smith & Sons Ltd. v. Silverman* (1961), 29 D.L.R. (2d) 98.
[5]*Gillespie Bros. & Co. Ltd. v. Roy Bowles Transport Ltd.*, [1973] Q.B. 400; *Davidson v. Three Spruces Realty Ltd.* (1978), 79 D.L.R. (3d) 481.

[6]*Master v. London County Council*, [1947] 1 K.B. 631.
[7]*Riverdale Garage v. Barnett Bros.*, [1930] 4 D.L.R. 429; *Desjardins v. Theriault* (1970), 3 N.B.R. (2d) 260.
[8]*Roy v. Adamson* (1912), 3 D.L.R. 139; *Chaing v. Heppner* (1978), 85 D.L.R. (3d) 487.

lar bailees varies, due to the nature of the relationship that exists between each type of bailee and the bailor.

STORAGE OF GOODS

The storage of goods for reward may take on many forms, but each represents a bailment if possession and control of the goods passes into the hands of the party offering the storage facility. The bank or trust company that rents a safety deposit box to a customer, the marina that offers boat storage facilities, or the warehouse-man that offers storage space for a person's furniture are bailees for reward. So, too, are the operators of grain elevators, fuel storage facilities, and parking-lots if the parking-lot operator obtains the keys to the vehicle.

The bailee is expected to take reasonable care of the goods while they in his possession, and the standard is normally that which would be expected of a skilled storekeeper.[9]

In other words, the bailee would be expected to protect the goods from all forseeable risks. If the goods have a particular attribute which requires special storage facilities, and the warehouseman holds himself out as possessing those facilities, then the failure to properly store the goods would render the warehouseman liable for any loss. For example, if a bailee holds himself out as the operator of a cold storage warehouse, and a bailor delivers to him a quantity of frozen meat which requires the temperature of the goods to be held at some point below freezing, the failure to store the meat at that temperature would render the bailee liable for any loss if spoilage should occur.

It is important to note that the liability of a bailee for storage is not absolute. The bailee is generally only liable if he fails to meet the standard of care fixed by the courts for the nature of the business which he conducts. The bailee may be liable for the negligence of his employees if the goods are damaged through their carelessness, but the courts are unlikely to hold the bailee responsible in cases where the loss or damage could not, or would not, have been forseen by a careful and vigilant shopkeeper.[10]

Contracts for the storage of goods frequently involve what is known as a warehouse receipt, or evidence of the contract of bailment. The receipt entitles the bearer to obtain the goods from the bailee. Often the original bailor of the goods sells the goods while they are in storage and, as a part of the sale transaction, provides the purchaser with the warehouse receipt. The presentation of the receipt by the new bailor would entitle him to delivery of the goods from the bailee. The bill of lading used by carriers of goods performs a similar function when goods are shipped to a purchaser.

The bailment of a motor vehicle represents one of the most common short-term bailment relationships, but it is important to distinguish the true bailment of an automobile from the mere use or rental of space for parking. Again, the transfer of possession by the driver of the vehicle to the parking-lot operator is essential to create the bailment. If the operator of the lot accepts the keys to the automobile, and parks the vehicle, a bailment is created. The operator has possession of the bailor's property. Similarly, if the operator of the parking-lot directs the per-

---

[9]*Brabant & Co. v. King*, [1895] A.C. 632.

[10]*Bomert v. Parks* (1964), 50 D.L.R. (2d) 313.

son to place the vehicle in a certain place on the parking-lot, and requests that the keys be deposited with him, the deposit of the keys would also create a bailment. The simple act of parking a vehicle as a "favour" for the patron, however, may not create a bailment which would render the parking-lot operator liable as a bailee if the car should subsequently be damaged or stolen.[11]

If the agreement between the parking-lot operator and the patron is one of rental of a space for parking purposes, and if the patron parks his own vehicle and retains the keys, possession does not pass from the patron to the operator of the lot. The retention of the keys by the vehicle owner precludes any control over the vehicle by the parking-lot operator, and consequently, a bailment does not arise. In these cases, the courts generally view the transaction not as a bailment, but as an arrangement whereby the parking-lot operator *licenses* the use of the parking space by the vehicle driver on a contractual basis.[12]

The enforcement of exculpatory clauses arises frequently in cases concerning the bailment of vehicles, and the success of a bailee in avoiding liability by way of an exculpatory clause depends in no small measure on the steps taken to bring the limitation on the bailee's liability to the attention of the bailor either before or at the time that the bailment takes place. The simple printing of a limitation on liability on the back of the parking-lot ticket is clearly not enough;[13] the limitation must be forcefully brought to the attention of the bailor, either by direct reference to the limitation, or by placing clearly marked signs in conspicuous places where they will not fail to catch the eye of the bailor.[14]

At common law, in the absence of a specific right contained in an agreement, the ordinary bailee for storage is not entitled to retain the goods until storage charges are paid, but all provinces have passed legislation which provide for a statutory lien which may attach to the goods in the warehouse operator's possession.[15] The legislation generally provides that the warehouse operator may retain the goods until payment is made, and to sell the goods by public auction if the bailor fails to pay the storage charges. The statutes generally require special care be taken by the bailee with respect to notice and advertisement of the sale to ensure that the bailor has an opportunity to redeem the goods, and that the sale of the goods be conducted in a fair manner. The right to a lien, however, is based upon the possession of the goods by the bailee, and if the bailee voluntarily releases the goods to the bailor before payment is made, the right to claim a lien is lost.

||||||||||||||||||||||||||||||||||||||||||||||||||||||||||||||||||||||||||||||||

CASE 21.1

Bata v. City Parking Canada Ltd. (1973), 2 O.R. (2d) 446.

SCHROEDER, J.A.:

Bailment has been defined as a delivery of personal chattels in trust on a contract express

---

[11]*Palmer v. Toronto Medical Arts Buildings Ltd.* (1960), 21 D.L.R. (2d) 181; *Martin v. Town N'Country Delicatessen Ltd.* (1963), 45 W.W.R. 413.

[12]*Palmer v. Toronto Medical Arts Buildings Ltd.* (1960), 21 D.L.R. (2d) 181.

[13]*Sponner v. Starkman*, [1937] 2 D.L.R. 582.

[14]*Samuel Smith & Sons Ltd. v. Silverman* (1961), 29 D.L.R. (2d) 98.

[15]See, for example, *Warehousemen's Lien Act*, R.S.O. 1980, c. 529, s. 2; R.S.N. 1970, c. 391, s. 3; R.S.S. 1978, c. W-3, s. 3; R.S.A. 1970, c. 386, s. 3; R.S.N.B. 1973, c. W-4, s. 2.

or implied that the trust shall be duly executed and the chattels redelivered in either their original or an altered form as soon as the time or use for, or condition on which they were bailed shall have elapsed or been performed. This definition which is taken from Bacon's Abridgment was approved and adopted in *Re S. Davis & Co., Ltd.*, [1945] Ch. 402. There is a very wide divergence between the relationship of bailor and bailee and that of licensor and licensee in that the latter, in the absence of some special contractual provision, carries no obligation on the part of the licensor towards the licensee with respect to the chattel subject to the licence.

. . . . .

The respondent in the present case admitted that he was given a ticket which contained a number and also a triangular heading with the words "City Parking". The latter two words appear in large capital letters. The ticket also contained the following wording:
"Charges are for use of parking space only.
"This company assumes no responsibility whatever for loss or damage due to fire, theft, collision or otherwise, to the vehicle or its contents, however caused."

. . . . .

. . . the words which appear on the parking ticket given to the customer indicate in a very real sense the nature of the rights which the proprietor of a car may expect to enjoy under the arrangement into which he is entering. The words "charges are for use of parking space only", exclude at once any notion that the arrangement entered into is one of bailment, and if there is any doubt on that score the words "This company assumes no responsibility whatever for loss or damage due to fire, theft, collision or otherwise to the vehicle or its contents, however caused" should effectively remove any doubt in the matter.

||||||||||||||||||||||||||||||||||||||||||||||||||||||||||||||||||||||||||

BAILMENT FOR REPAIR OR SERVICE

Where chattels require repair or service, a bailment takes place if the owner delivers the goods to the repair shop and leaves them with the proprietor. The bailee is expected to protect the goods entrusted to him for repair, and even though no charge is made for the bailment separate from the repair charge, the bailment is nevertheless a bailment for reward, and the bailee is expected to take reasonable care of the goods while they are in his possession. If the goods are lost or damaged while they are in the bailee's possession, the bailee may be liable if the loss is due to his negligence. If the goods are sub-bailed to a sub-bailee in accordance with the customs of the trade, then the bailee may also be liable for loss or damage to the goods by the neglect or wilful acts of the sub-bailee. For example, Smith delivers his automobile to Baker for repairs, and Baker, by way of a sub-bailment, places the car in Carter's possession to have some specialized work done on the vehicle. If Carter negligently damages the goods while they are in his possession, Baker may be liable to Smith for the damage. However, if Baker has held himself out to be skilled in the performance of the task, and Smith contracts with Baker for personal performance, the sub-bailment would be improper, and Baker would become liable for any damage to the goods, whether caused by Carter's negligence or not. The particular reason for this additional liability for an improper bailment is that Smith, in placing the goods in Baker's possession, is accepting a particular set of circumstances or risks relating to the repair of his goods, but an unauthorized sub-bailment would be a change in the risk without his consent. To protect the bailor in such cases, the courts have simply imposed liability for any loss or damage to the goods on the bailee.

The bailee who professes to have a particular repair skill is expected to execute the repairs in accordance with the standards set for the skill, and is expected to exercise the duty of care attendant with the skill in the protection or handling of the goods while in his possession. For this service, he is entitled to compensation which may be either agreed upon at the time the goods are placed in his possession, or to a reasonable price for his services when the work is completed. If the bailor refuses to pay for the work done on the goods, at common law, the bailee has a right of lien, and may retain the goods until payment is made. If payment is not made within a reasonable time, subject to any statutory requirements which set out the rights of the bailee, he may have the goods sold (usually by public auction) to satisfy his claim for payment.[16]

Should the bailee be negligent in the repair of the goods, or not possess the particular skill which he professed to have, the bailor would be entitled to institute legal proceedings for damages to cover the loss he suffered. This claim may cover not only the value of the chattel damaged, but any other loss which would flow from the bailee's breach of the agreement to repair, if the loss was forseeable at the time the agreement was made.

||||||||||||||||||||||||||||||||||||||||||||||||||||||||||||||||||||||||||

CASE 21.2

Chaing v. Heppner et al. (1978), 85 D.L.R. (3d) 487.

McMORRAN, CO.CT.J.:

The question to be determined here is whether any responsibility for the loss of the watch rests with Heppner as a result of his accepting, for reward, the possession of the watch for repair, there being no contract with special provisions and conditions between the parties.

---

[16]Most provinces and territories have legislation covering this type of bailment: see, for example, *Mechanics' Lien Act*, R.S.Nfld. 1970, c. 267, s. 48.

. . . . .

In *Heriteau et al. v. W. D. Morris Realty Ltd.*, [1944] 1 D.L.R. 28, [1943] O.R. 724, it was held that where goods are lost or damaged while in a bailee's possession, the onus is on him to prove that it occurred through no want of ordinary care on his part.

Leck et al. v. Maestaer (1807), 1 Camp. 138, 170 E.R. 905, states that a workman for hire is not only bound to guard the thing bailed to him against ordinary hazards, but likewise to exert himself to preserve it from any unexpected danger to which it may be exposed and further, in effect, that where there is need for precaution, the defendant would be answerable for defects of this deficiency.

. . . . .

In essence, what emerges from the authorities is: that the defendant was a bailee for consideration and owed a duty to the plaintiff to exercise that care and diligence which a careful and diligent man would exercise in the custody of his own goods in the same circumstances; that there being loss of the goods bailed the onus is on the defendant (bailee) to show that he exercised a proper degree of care; that failure to observe that duty is negligence; that the unexpected and accidental destruction of the goods while in the possession of the defendant (bailee) for reward, may still render the defendant liable if during his possession of the goods he did not exercise to a reasonable extent the skill or ability which he held out as an expected duty of his calling; and that while no specific period of time may be arranged for the completion of the work to be done the defendant must perform it within a reasonable time, and if delay in the performance is caused by the defendant's negligence, he is liable.

||||||||||||||||||||||||||||||||||||||||||||||||||||||||||||||||||||||||||

HIRE OR RENTAL OF A CHATTEL

The hire of a chattel is a bailment for reward in which the bailor–owner delivers possession of a chattel for use by the bailee–hirer in return for a monetary payment. This type of bailment is usually in the form of a written agreement with the rights and duties set out, but it need not be in writing to be enforceable, unless by its terms it falls subject to the *Statute of Frauds*.

Under a bailment for the hire of a chattel the bailee is required to pay the rental fee for the use of the chattel which the parties have agreed upon, or if no fee was specified at the time the agreement was entered into, then the reasonable or customary price for the use of the goods. If the bailment is for a fixed term, the bailee is usually liable for payment for the full term, unless the bailor agrees to take back the chattel and clearly releases the bailee from any further obligation to pay. Apart from the payment of the rental fee, and except for any specific obligations imposed upon the bailee, the bailee is entitled to possession and use of the goods for the entire rental period.

The bailee at common law must not use the goods for any purpose other than the purpose for which they were intended, and must not sub-bail the goods, or allow strangers to use them, unless permission to do so is obtained from the bailor. In the event that the bailee should do any of these things without permission, he would become absolutely liable for any loss or damage to the chattels. Otherwise, the bailee will only be liable if he fails to use reasonable care in the operation or use of the goods.[17] The bailee would not be liable for ordinary "wear and tear" which may result from use of the chattel unless the agreement specifically holds him responsible, as the maintenance of the equipment in fit condition for the use intended is usually the responsibility of the bailor.

Under an agreement for the hire of a chattel, the prime responsibility of the bailor is to provide the bailee with goods that are reasonably fit for the use intended. The goods must be free from any defects which might cause damage or loss to the bailee when the equipment is put into use, and if the bailor knew or ought to have known of a defect when the goods were delivered, the bailor may be liable for the damage caused by the defective equipment. For example, Lyndsey hired a truck from Foster for the purpose of delivering crates of eggs to market. If Foster knew or ought to have known that the truck had defective brakes, and as a result of the defect, the truck swerved off the road when the brakes were applied and destroyed Lyndsey's load of eggs, Foster would be liable for Lyndsey's loss. However, if the defect was hidden, and would not be revealed by a careful inspection, Foster may not be liable.

Where the goods hired have an inherent danger or risk associated with their use, the bailor is normally under an obligation to warn the bailee of the danger, or possible dangers, associated with the use, but where the bailee is licensed or experienced in the use of the equipment, any loss or damage which may result from the use of the equipment may be assessed in part against the bailee.[18]

CARRIAGE OF GOODS

The carriage of goods may include a number of different forms of bailment. The carriage of goods involves the delivery of

---

[17]*Morris v. C.W. Martin & Sons Ltd.*, [1965] 2 All E.R. 725.

[18]*Hadley v. Droitwich Construction Co. Ltd. et al.*, [1967] 3 All E.R. 911.

goods by the bailor to the bailee for the purpose of delivery to some destination by the bailee. As with all bailments, the goods are in the possession of the bailee for a particular purpose, but the title is in someone else.

A carrier of goods is normally a carrier for reward, but this is not always the case. A carrier may be a gratuitous carrier who transports goods without reward, such as where a person agrees to deliver a parcel to the post office for a friend. With a gratuitous carrier, if the service provided is entirely for the benefit of the bailor, the bailee is only expected to use reasonable care in the carriage of the goods.

There are two classes of carriers for reward: private carriers and common carriers, and the standard of care differs for each. A private carrier is a carrier that may occasionally carry goods, but who is normally engaged in some other business activity. A private carrier is free to accept or reject goods as he sees fit, but if he should decide to act as a carrier of goods for reward, then he would have a duty to take reasonable care of the goods while they are in his possession.

The common carrier, unlike the gratuitous carrier and the private carrier, carries on the business of carriage of goods for reward, and offers to accept any goods for shipment if he has the facilities to do so. For example, a trucking company or railway company that engages in the carriage of goods would be classed as a common carrier. The rates chargeable by common carrier's are for the most part fixed by statute, and the statute generally limits the carrier's ability to escape liability in the event that the goods which he carries are lost or damaged. The common carrier is essentially an insurer of the goods, and liable for any damage to the goods except in certain circumstances.

The principal reason for the very high standard of care required of the common carrier is that the goods are entirely within the control of the carrier for the entire period of time that the bailment exists. Unlike other forms of bailment where the bailor could presumably check on the goods, once the goods are in the hands of the carrier, they are no longer open to inspection by the bailor until they reach their destination. Under the legislation pertaining to common carriers, the carrier is usually permitted by contract to limit the amount of compensation payable in the event of loss or damage to the goods, and also to avoid liability if the damage to the goods was caused by an act of God, the improper labelling or packing of the goods by the shipper, or if the nature of the goods was such that they were subject to self-destruction during ordinary handling. The carrier would also be exempt from liability if the damage was as a result of the actions of the Queen's enemies in time of war.

Most common carriers are subject to legislation which imposes certain responsibilities on their operation. These statutes usually either set out the liability of the carrier, or set out his rights and duties in the carriage of goods. In many cases, the rights and duties must be included in the contract of carriage, and these terms are frequently found in small print on the back of the contract. Since separate legislation governs railways, trucking firms, and air carriers, the specific liability tends to vary somewhat for each. The basic liability, however, remains the same.

Under a contract of carriage, the bailor also has certain responsibilities. The bailor is obliged to pay the rates fixed for the shipping of the goods, and if the bailor fails to pay, the carrier may claim or receive under the terms of the contract, the right of lien on the goods until payment is made. If the charges are not paid within a reasonable length of time, the goods normally may be sold to cover the carrier's charges. The bailor is also required to disclose the type of goods shipped, and must also take care not to ship dangerous goods by carrier unless a full disclosure of the nature of the goods is made.

A common occurrence in the carriage of goods is a change of ownership of the goods while in the hands of the carrier. The original bailor is not always the recipient at the destination when goods are shipped, and indeed, in most cases, the goods are shipped by the bailor to some other person. The contract with the carrier (sometimes called a *bill of lading*) names the person to whom the goods are consigned, and the carrier will deliver the goods to the person named as consignee. Goods shipped under a second type of contract of carriage, called an *order bill of lading*, is essentially a contract combined with a receipt and document of title, and may be endorsed by the consignee, if he so desires, to some other person. An order bill of lading must be surrendered to obtain the goods from the carrier.

PLEDGE OR PAWN OF PERSONAL PROPERTY AS SECURITY FOR DEBT

Bailment may be associated with debt transactions in the sense that personal property may be delivered to a creditor to be held as security for a loan. The particular personal property may take the form of such securities as bonds, share certificates, or life insurance policies, and these securities may be held by the creditor as collateral to the loan. Because the creditor takes possession of the securities, the transaction represents a bailment, and the credi-

tor as a bailee would be responsible for the property while in his possession. When the debt is paid, the same securities must be returned to the bailor. The delivery of securities or similar personal property to the creditor as security for a loan is called a *pledge*, and if the bailor–debtor should default on the loan, the bailee–creditor may look to the securities pledged to satisfy the debt. Any surplus, however, from the sale of the securities would belong to the debtor, and must be paid over to the debtor by the creditor.

A *pawn* is similar to a pledge, but is confined to a transaction between a debtor and a pawnbroker, and is concerned with the delivery of goods to the pawnbroker as security for a loan. Pawnbrokers are licensed in Canada, and may accept goods as security under loan agreements which entitle them to sell the goods if default on the debt occurs. While the goods are in the possession of the pawnbroker a bailment exists, and the pawnbroker must take reasonable care of the goods. As with other forms of bailment, the pawnbroker has only possession of the goods, and the bailor–debtor retains the title. The bailment, however, is made on the express condition that the goods may be sold by the creditor if default should occur, at which time the creditor may give a good title to the goods to a third party. Any surplus from the sale would belong to the debtor, and conversely, any deficiency would remain as an obligation.

INNKEEPERS

The liability of the innkeeper or hotel keeper extends back to the Middle Ages in England to a time when a traveller's goods were at the mercy of the innkeeper. The early English inns (and for that matter, many of the inns in both Canada and the United States until as late as the 19th century) provided a large single room for sleeping purposes, and only a few separate bedchambers. The guests were easy prey for thieves while they slept, and the innkeeper was seldom unaware of the pilfering, and often an accomplice in the act. To discourage theft, and to ensure that the innkeeper was not a party to the crime, the common law imposed a very high standard of care on the innkeeper with respect to goods brought on the premises by guests. At common law, the innkeeper was held to be responsible for any loss, even if it was not his fault, the only exception being where the loss was due to the guest's own negligence. The innkeeper in effect was someone who closely resembled an insurer of the goods in the event of loss, in spite of the fact that the goods were not in his possession, and even though the guest exercised some control over the goods as well.

An innkeeper, however, must be distinguished from other persons who offer accommodation to guests, as the special liability applies only to innkeepers. Persons who offer only room accommodation to travellers, or who are selective in offering room and meals (for example, a rooming-house) are not usually innkeepers by definition, and a restaurant that offers only meals and no sleeping accommodation would not be classed as an "inn." To be treated as an innkeeper, it would appear that both meals and room accommodation must be offered to the public.[19]

An innkeeper has a public duty to accept any transient person and their belongings as a guest, provided accommodation

exists, and provided also that the traveller is "fit and orderly" and has the ability to pay. An innkeeper is defined in the *Innkeepers Acts* of most provinces and territories as a person who offers accommodation and meals to the travelling public. Once the proprietor of the establishment falls within the definition, the liability under the statute also applies. Each province has legislation which sets out the rights and obligations of innkeepers, but unfortunately, the legislation is not uniform. In general, with respect to the protection of the goods and belongings of travellers, the innkeeper may in most provinces limit his liability to a fixed sum which varies from $40 to $150, where the loss or damage is not due to the negligence of, or the wilful or deliberate act of the innkeeper or his employees, or where the goods are not placed in the innkeeper's custody for safe keeping. The legislation in most provinces provides that to obtain the protection of the Act, the innkeeper must post the relevant sections in all bedrooms and public rooms in the inn.[20]

Because the innkeeper and the guest to some extent share responsibility for the protection of the guest's goods, the liability of the innkeeper is not absolute. If the innkeeper can establish that the loss of the guest's goods were due entirely to the guest's negligence, he may be able to avoid liability.[21] Full liability applies where the goods have been placed in the hands

---

[19]*King v. Barclay and Barclay's Motel* (1960), 24 D.L.R. (2d) 418.

[20]Newfoundland and Saskatchewan require only that the sections of the Act be placed in the hall and entrance: see R.S.Nfld. 1970, c. 173, s. 5, and the *Hotel Keepers Act*, R.S.S. 1978, c. H-11, s. 11. The Manitoba Act does not require the posting of a notice as the Act does not hold the innkeeper liable for loss except as set out in the statute: see the *Hotel Keepers Act*, R.S.M. 1970, c. H-150.

[21]*Loyer v. Plante*, [1960] Que. Q.B. 443; *Laing v. Allied Innkeepers Ltd*, [1970] 1 O.R. 502; *Hansen v. "Y" Motor Hotel Ltd.*, [1971] 2 W.W.R. 705.

of the innkeeper for safe keeping, and in most provinces, full liability will also apply if the innkeeper refuses to accept the goods when requested to do so by a guest.[22]

||||||||||||||||||||||||||||||||||||||||||||||||||||||||||||||||||||||||||

CASE 21.3

Hansen v. "Y" Motor Hotel Ltd., [1971] 2 W.W.R. 705.

McDERMID, J.A.:

At common law an innkeeper was responsible to his guests if any of their goods were lost or stolen while on his premises. In *Shacklock v. Ethorpe Ltd.*, [1939] 3 All E.R. 372, Lord MacMillan, whose opinion was concurred in by all of

[22]See, for example, *Innkeepers Act*, R.S.O. 1980, c. 217, s. 6; R.S.A. 1970, c. 186, s. 9.

the other Law Lords, applied the words of Lord Esher M.R. in *Robins & Co. v. Gray.*, [1895] 2 Q.B. 501 at 503, who said:

"The duties, liabilities, and rights of innkeepers with respect to goods brought to inns by guests are founded, not upon bailment, or pledge, or contract, but upon the custom of the realm with regard to innkeepers. Their rights and liabilities are dependent upon that, and that alone; they do not come under any other head of law . . . the innkeeper's liability is not that of a bailee or pledgee of goods; he is bound to keep them safely. It signifies not, so far as that obligation is concerned, if they are stolen by burglars, or by the servants of the inn, or by another guest; he is liable for not keeping them safely unless they are lost by the fault of the traveller himself. That is a tremendous liability: it is a liability fixed upon the innkeeper by the fact that he has taken the goods in . . ."

||||||||||||||||||||||||||||||||||||||||||||||||||||||||||||||||||||||||||||||||||||||||||||||||||||||||||||||||||||||||||||||||

SUMMARY A bailment is created by the delivery of possession of a chattel by the bailor (who is usually the owner) to a bailee. Bailment involves the transfer of possession, and not title, but a bailee may exercise many of the rights normally exercised by an owner while the goods are in his possession. Bailment may be either gratuitous or for reward. Liability is least for a gratuitous bailee who receives no benefit from the bailment, and highest for special forms of bailment for reward such as the common carrier of goods, where the bailee is essentially an insurer for any loss or damage. If the agreement between the parties permits a sub-bailment, the bailee may make such a bailment. The bailee may also do so in some cases where sub-bailment in the absence of an agreement to the contrary may be made by custom of the trade.

Bailment for reward may take the form of bailment for storage, for the carriage of goods, the deposit of goods for repair, the hire of a chattel, and the pledge or pawn of goods to secure a loan. The liability of the bailee in each of the bailment relationships arises if the bailee fails to take reasonable care of the goods while in his possession, but in the case of the common carrier and the innkeeper (who is similar to a bailee) a much higher standard prevails. A bailee may limit his liability by an express term in the contract. However, legislation governing such bailees as warehouse operators, carriers of goods, and innkeepers, contain specific provisions and limitations which generally govern these special relationships.

|||||||||||||||||||||||||||||||||||||||||||||||||||||||||||||||||||||||||||||||||||||||||||||||||||||||||||||||||||||||||||||||||||||||||||||||||||||||||||||||||||||||||||||||||||||||||||||||||||

DISCUSSION QUESTIONS

1. *Identify the three elements required to establish a bailment.*
2. *What rights does a bailee have with respect to goods in his possession?*
3. *Is the standard of care with respect to goods placed in the hands of a gratuitous bailee higher for a bailee who receives a benefit from the bailment than for a bailment solely for the benefit of the bailor? Why? How does the standard differ?*
4. *Discuss the liability of a bailee in the case of an unauthorized sub-bailment. Under what circumstances is a sub-bailment proper?*
5. *Give an example of a case of a "constructive bailment." What evidence is necessary to establish a constructive bailment?*
6. *What essential element generally distinguishes the "bailment of an automobile" from the "rental of parking space"?*
7. *Why is the standard of care of the common carrier virtually that of an insurer of the goods?*
8. *What defences are available to a common carrier in some instances where the bailed goods are destroyed?*
9. *To what extent does the law impose the duties of a bailee on an innkeeper? Why?*
10. *Describe a situation where an innkeeper would have (1) absolute liability; (2) limited liability; (3) no liability in the case of loss of goods which belong to a guest.*
11. *Do all bailees for reward possess a right of lien as security for payment?*
12. *Under what circumstances would an appliance repair man be a bailee?*
13. *What effect does an exemption clause in a contract for storage have on the rights of the bailor in the event of loss or damage to the goods? How are these clauses viewed by the courts?*
14. *Define (1) pledge; (2) pawn; (3) private carrier, (4) act of God.*

|||||||||||||||||||||||||||||||||||||||||||||||||||||||||||||||||||||||||||||||||||||||||||||||||||||||||||||||||||||||||||||||||||||||||||||||||||||||||||||||||||||||||||||||||||||||||||||||||||

JUDICIAL DECISIONS

Bailment— Storage for Reward—Car Parked in Parking-Lot —Signs and Ticket Excluding Liability for Loss

Samuel Smith & Sons Ltd. v. Silverman (1961), 29 D.L.R. (2d) 98.

The plaintiff parked his car in a parking-lot and left the keys with the lot attendant. He received a ticket in return for payment of the parking fee. The ticket contained a statement stating that the owner of the parking-lot was not responsible for damage to the car or its contents. Several large signs at the entrance to the lot contained the same message. When the plaintiff returned to the lot some time later, he found his car damaged.

An action was brought against the owners of the parking-lot for damages.

SCHROEDER, J.A.:

It is conceded by counsel for the appellant that this is a true case of bailment since Sussman had been requested by the parking attendant

to leave the keys in the motor car in order that it could be driven as required to a suitable place on the lot. It was therefore received into the
custody of the defendant and a contract of bailment for reward has
been made out. At the time of the delivery of the car to the defendant's
servant Sussman was given a parking ticket containing the following
terms:

> "WE ARE NOT RESPONSIBLE FOR THEFT OR DAMAGE OF CAR
> OR CONTENTS HOWEVER CAUSED."

These terms are spelled out in bold black type and in letters large
enough to dispel any suggestion of an attempt on the part of the defendant to conceal the limiting conditions from the recipient. Had the defendant looked at this ticket he could not possibly have failed to see the
terms quoted.

. . . . .

When a chattel entrusted to a custodian is lost, injured or destroyed,
the onus of proof is on the custodian to show that the injury did not
happen in consequence of his neglect to use such care and diligence as
a prudent or careful man would exercise in relation to his own property. Counsel for the appellant admits that the plaintiff having proved
that its motor car was damaged while in the care and custody of the defendant, it made out a *prima facie* case, subject to any special conditions
in the contract, limiting or relieving the appellant from his common law
liability. At the trial no attempt was made to show how or when the
loss or damage in question occurred, and apart from such conditions,
the plaintiff would be entitled to succeed. It is well settled that a custodian may limit or relieve himself from his common law liability by special conditions in the contract, but such conditions will be strictly
construed and they will not be held to exempt the bailee from responsibility for losses due to his negligence unless the words of limitation are
clear and adequate for the purpose or there is no other liability to which
they can apply: *Can. Steamship Lines v. The King*, [1952],
2 D.L.R. 786 at p. 793, A.C. 192 at pp. 207-8.

In *Olley v. Marlborough Court Ltd.*, [1949] 1 All E.R. 127, Lord Justice
Denning stated at p. 134:

"People who rely on a contract to exempt themselves from their common law liability must prove that contract strictly. Not only must the
terms of the contract be clearly proved but also the intention to create
legal relations—the intention to be legally bound—must also be clearly
proved. The best way of proving it is by a written document signed by
the party to be bound. Another way is by handing him before or at the
time of the contract, a written notice, specifying certain terms and making it clear to him that the contract is in those terms. A prominent public notice which is plain for him to see when he makes the contract
would, no doubt, have the same effect, but nothing short of one of
these three ways will suffice."

The learned trial Judge accepted the evidence of the plaintiff to the
effect that he had not parked a car on this property before. He testified
that he had not seen any signs erected on the premises, and that he had

not read the conditions set out on the parking ticket which he had been given at the time the contract was made. There was evidence given on behalf of the defendant by the defendant's manager who stated that there were four signs erected on the defendant's lot, two of them at the front near the Victoria St. entrance, and the other two on the rear parking lot. They were at a height of approximately 8 to 10 ft. from the ground, 2½ by 3 ft. in dimension, and contained the following words:

"WE ARE NOT RESPONSIBLE FOR THEFT OR DAMAGE OF CAR
OR CONTENTS HOWEVER CAUSED."

The learned Judge accepted this evidence. He found as a fact that there were signs on the lot in the four places indicated, which were lighted at the time in question, and which bore the words set out above. The point to which the Court should address itself in a case where the defendant relies upon signs of this nature is clearly stated in the judgment of Baron Alderson in the old case of *Walker et al. v. Jackson* (1842), 10 M. & W. 160, 152 E.R. 424, from which I quote at p. 173:

"The acts proved by the plaintiffs, upon which they relied to substantiate the existence of a contract, were those done with respect to persons bringing carriages. These notices were stuck up in the way for foot passengers, and it appeared that the plaintiff did not go by that way; neither was it shewn that any person with a carriage ever went by it. No reasonable probability, therefore, existed that the plaintiff, or any parties going with carriages, ever saw them."

It may well be that if the defendant were forced to rely solely upon the limiting conditions set out on the parking ticket given to the plaintiff's agent, the reasoning in *Spooner v. Starkman* and in *Appleton et al. v. Ritchie Taxi* might prevail against his defence. Here, however, notice of the limiting condition was also provided in four prominently displayed signs, two of which were placed near the entrance on Victoria St., which any reasonably attentive person should have seen.

In *Brown v. Toronto Auto Parks Ltd.*, [1955] 2 D.L.R. 525, O.W.N. 456, this Court had to consider a defence based on limiting conditions contained on signs displayed on the custodian's premises. Laidlaw, J.A., delivering the judgment of the Court there stated [p. 527 D.L.R., p. 457 O.W.N.]:

"In the instant case we are all satisfied that the signs displayed by the appellant were displayed with such prominence and in such a way that the respondent ought to have seen them and ought to have had knowledge of what was on the signs. We think that a person exercising reasonable care and diligence would have seen those signs and in particular he would have seen, first, that there was an attendant—the words were 'Attendant in charge', and that the car and contents were left at the owner's risk. But the appellant did not satisfy the learned trial Judge, nor has it satisfied this Court, that the loss sustained by the respondent did not happen in consequence of the appellant's breach of its duty to use such care and diligence as a prudent and careful man would exercise in relation to his own property. It has not discharged the onus of proof resting in law on it as a bailee for valuable consideration."

It was held that the exculpatory signs did not assist the defendant, for while the plaintiff should reasonably have seen them, the words "car and contents at owner's risk" did not suffice clearly to relieve the defendant for liability for negligence. The Court applied the strict rule of construction to which I have referred and supported the judgment for the plaintiff on that ground alone.

The words printed on the ticket and the signs in question are not susceptible of this criticism. The clear declaration that the defendant was not to be responsible for theft or damage of car or contents *however caused*, is sufficiently broad in its terms to extend to a case where the damage occurred through the negligence either of the defendant or his servants, or the negligence or carelessness of a third party whether lawfully on the premises or not.

|||||||||||||||||||||||||||||||||||||||||||||||||||||||||||||||||||||||||||||||||||||||||||||||||||||||||||||||||||||||||||||||||||||||||||||||||||||||||||||||||||||||||||

Innkeepers— Liability of Innkeeper Liability for Chattels of Guest Left in Automobile— Whether Goods *Infra Hospitum*

George v. Williams, [1956] O.R. 871.
The plaintiff drove his automobile into a parking-lot that bore a sign which indicated free parking for hotel guests. An attendant directed him to a parking place where he parked his car. He removed some of his luggage, leaving a suitcase and some clothing on the rear seat. He then locked the car, and went into the hotel where he arranged for a night's lodging. The next morning he discovered that someone had broken into his car and removed the clothing and luggage.

An action was brought against the hotel for the loss.

ROACH, J.A.:

The question raised by this appeal may be stated thus: Was the property which was stolen from the plaintiff's car within the hotel?

The goods of a guest are considered in law to be within the hotel if they are "*infra hospitium*". Those descriptive words were apparently first applied to this subject by Lord Coke in *Calye's Case*, (1584), 8 Co. Rep. 32*a*, 77 E.R. 520, but as Denning L.J. said in the recent case of *Williams v. Linnitt*, [1951] 1 K.B. 565 at 586, [1951] 1 All E.R. 278 at 291, ". . . we are left with the question: 'what is infra hospitium?' " Answering that question in that case the Court of Appeal in England held that a parking-area which was contiguous to the inn and in which a guest with a car was customarily invited to leave it, there being no evidence that any other accommodation for cars was provided by the inn and it being part of the defendant's normal business to provide accommodation for the cars of guests, was within the *hospitium* of the inn.

In the absence of evidence to the contrary, I think it should be concluded as a matter of reasonable inference that the man to whom I earlier referred as the attendant was in fact an attendant in charge of the parking-area, and clothed with authority on behalf of the management of the hotel to direct and supervise the parking of motor vehicles within that area. The sign must lead to the conclusion that the management of this hotel was catering to those of the motoring public who might be prospective guests at the hotel, and it informed those prospective guests that this area constituted accommodation for their cars. It was an open invitation to prospective guests to park their cars in that area. There is no evidence that there was any other accommodation for cars provided by the inn, and in my opinion that area must be held to have been within the *hospitium* of the defendant's hotel at least in relation to the car.

The fact that the parking-area was not contiguous to the hotel building but was separated from that building by a lane did not, in my opinion, make that area *"extra hospitium."*

. . . . .

It does not follow, because this parking-area was within the *hospitium* of the hotel in relation to the car, that it was also within that *hospitium* in relation to the chattels that were stolen. Those chattels are in a different category to the accoutrements such as knee-robes or cushions which we think of as associated with the car for its more comfortable use. We think of the stolen chattels as being associated with the person rather than with the car.

I do not think the sign posted in the parking-area should be construed as a wide-open invitation to prospective guests to leave within their cars, if parked within that area, such chattels as the whim or judgment of the owner might dictate, so as to bring that area within the *hospitium* of the hotel in relation to those chattels. We have all seen motor cars travelling along the highway loaded down with all sorts of stuff— on occasions a boat strapped on top and a rear seat packed to the ceiling with a varied assortment of household equipment. If the plaintiff's car had been thus laden, would he have a claim against this defendant for the loss by theft of the boat or household effects on the ground that in relation to them this area was within the *hospitium* of the hotel? I think not, for the reason that those chattels, although on or in the car, would ordinarily not be associated with the motor car of a traveller. For the same reason, the stolen chattels in the instant case should be held to have been *extra hospitium* of the hotel.

The common law liability of the innkeeper had its origin and the greater part of its development when the mode of travel was by horse and carriage. We were not referred to any case in which the *hospitium* of an inn was held to extend to the traveller's personal effects left by him in the carriage which brought him to the inn and which itself came within the *hospitium* of the inn. Such personal effects were not likely to be left in a carriage housed in a stable or carriage-house at the inn. That may be the reason why there is no reported case in which the guest sought to impose liability on the innkeeper for goods left in the carriage. The motor car has largely supplanted the carriage as a conveyance for the traveller. It was logical, therefore, to extend the application of the common law to this new means of transportation, but in my opinion to extend it to every chattel which the motoring traveller might willy-nilly leave in the car would be carrying it too far. The defendant as the proprietor of the hotel, although he extended the *hospitium* to the car itself, had a right to expect that the guest would bring his chattels which were not associated with the car itself, into the hotel proper, where the proprietor would have the opportunity of protecting himself against his common law liability in respect of them. I do not think it is a sufficient answer to say that the defendant could have guarded these chattels against theft by having an attendant on duty in the parking-area for that purpose every hour of the day and night. Too impose that obligation on the proprietors of hotels in every little hamlet throughout the Province in my opinion would be most unreasonable.

The plaintiff retained the key of the car and thus had control over the chattels which he left in it. He elected to leave them there plainly visible to a thief. He ran the risk of their being stolen and he must bear the loss.

CASE PROBLEMS FOR DISCUSSION

Case 1

Hart operated a restaurant and bakery shop which was located on a busy downtown street. The front portion of the premises contained the bakery shop, and the rear part of the building housed the restaurant. Patrons entering the building were required to pass through the store portion to reach the restaurant. In the store area, near the entrance to the restaurant, the owner had installed a number of coat hooks in a recess in the wall of the building. Employees of the shop and restaurant used the alcove to store their overcoats and hats.

Murphy, a stranger to the community, entered the shop for the purpose of dining, and proceeded through the shop to the restaurant area. Along the way he noticed the clothing in the alcove, and placed his overcoat and hat on one of the unused hooks. He then entered the restaurant where he ordered a meal. Some time later, when he was about to leave the restaurant, he discovered that his overcoat and hat were missing.

Hart denied responsibility for the loss, and Murphy brought an action against him for the value of the hat and coat.

Discuss the arguments that the parties might raise in this case, and identify the legal issue involved. Render a decision. Would your decision differ in any way if the coat hooks were located in the restaurant beside Murphy's table?

Case 2

Harriet, a licensed pilot, rented an aircraft from Aircraft Rental Services at a local airport. The purpose of the rental was to fly a friend to a large metropolitan city some 300 miles away, and return before nightfall. At the time that she arranged for the use of the aircraft, she assured the owner that she would leave the city in ample time to return the aircraft before dark. She paid a deposit for the use of the aircraft, and accompanied by her friend, made an uneventful flight to the distant city. Before returning home, however, she spent some time shopping, and lost track of time. Eventually, she realized that she was behind schedule, and hurried to the airport.

The weather report for the return trip was not promising, but she nevertheless decided to chance the flight. She took off at 3:45 p.m. some two hours before official nightfall on that particular January night. En route, she discovered that the weather had deteriorated, and that visibility was decreased by the combination of sundown and low cloud conditions.

At 7:05 p.m., some 20 minutes after official nightfall, she found that she could proceed no further, as the poor weather and semi-darkness made recognition of her route on the ground virtually impossible. To avoid further difficulties, she made a forced landing in a farmer's field, which resulted in extensive damage to the airplane's undercarriage.

Harriet assumed that the aircraft owner's insurance would cover the cost of the repairs, but was surprised to hear that the insurance covered only public liability, and not damage to the aircraft itself. The cost of repairs amounted to $2 165. When Harriet refused to pay for the damage, Aircraft Rental Services brought an action for damages against her for the amount of its loss.

In her defence, Harriet alleged no negligence on her part, as the landing was made in accordance with accepted forced landing procedures, and skilfully executed on her part. She argued that in any forced landing some damage to the undercarriage could be expected, and that the mere fact that damage occurred was not an indication of negligence.

The plaintiff brought out in the evidence that Harriet was licensed to fly under daylight conditions only, and did not have what was called a "night endorsement" on her license that would permit her to fly after dark. The plaintiff alleged that her act of flying after official nightfall was a violation of *Air Regulations* under the *Aeronautics Act*.

Discuss the nature of the plaintiff's claim in this case, and the various other arguments that might be raised by the parties. Indicate the issues that must be decided by the court, and render a decision.

Case 3

Brown parked his automobile in a parking-lot owned by Smith. At the request of the parking-lot attendant, he left his keys at the attendant's office, and received a numbered ticket as his receipt for the payment of the parking fee. Before leaving his keys with the attendant, he made certain that the doors of the vehicle were securely locked, as he had left a number of valuable books on the rear seat of the car.

Unknown to Brown, the attendant closed at midnight, and delivered the keys to the cars on the lot to the attendant of the parking-lot across the street which was also owned by Smith, and which remained open until 2:00 a.m.

Brown returned to the parking-lot to retreive his automobile shortly after midnight, only to discover no attendant in charge, and his vehicle missing. By chance, he noticed the attendant on duty at the lot across the street, where he reported the missing vehicle, and found the attendant in possession of his keys.

The police found Brown's automobile a few days later in another part of the city. The vehicle had been damaged, and stripped of its contents, including Brown's rare books.

Brown brought an action against Smith for his loss, but Smith denied liability on the basis that the ticket (which Brown received at the time of delivery of the keys) read: "Rental of space only. Not responsible for loss or damage to car or contents however caused." Smith also alleged that the attendant's office had a sign posted near the entrance which bore the same message.

Identify the issues in this case and prepare the arguments which Brown and Smith might use in their claim and defence respectively. Render a decision.

Case 4

The Frasers considered moving to western Canada from the City of Toronto on Mr. Fraser's retirement, and for the purpose of determining an appropriate community in which to reside, they visited a number of West Coast cities by automobile.

On their visit to one community, which appeared to be a delightful place to live, they met the owner of a warehouse business. The warehouse owner suggested that he would be prepared to receive their household goods if they wished to ship them to him, and he would hold them in storage until such time as they found a permanent residence.

On their return to Toronto, the Frasers decided to move immediately, and dispatched their household goods to the warehouseman that they had met on their visit to the city. Instead of taking up residence immediately, they planned an extensive vacation which would take them across the United States, and eventually to the particular community.

While on vacation, the household goods arrived at the warehouse, and the owner issued a warehouse receipt, which he mailed to the Frasers at the temporary address which they had given him. The warehouse receipt set out the terms and conditions of storage, one item being a condition which read: "All goods stored at owner's risk in case of fire (storage rates do not include insurance)."

On their return from their vacation, the Frasers found the warehouse receipt in their mail, but did not read the document. They proceeded to obtain a new home, but before they could retrieve their goods from the warehouse, the building was burned by an arsonist who had apparently gained entry to the building by way of an open roof-top sky-light window. The household goods which belonged to the Frasers were totally destroyed by the fire.

When the warehouseman refused to compensate the Fraser's for their loss, an action was brought claiming damages for the value of the goods.

Discuss the nature of the plaintiff's claim, and the defences which the warehouseman might raise. Render a decision.

Case 5

The spouses of a number of business executives in a small northern community belonged to a women's social club. Each year they would plan a banquet dinner at a hotel in a large city some 100 miles distant in order to combine a shopping trip with club activities that marked their year-end.

In 1980, the club arranged for their banquet and overnight room accommodations for their members at the Municipal Hotel. Most of the members arrived early for the dinner in order to check into their rooms. One member, however, arrived late, and instead of checking in at the desk, went directly to the banquet room where the dinner was about to be served. Before entering the room, she noticed a coat room adjacent to the dining-room which contained a number of coats, and hung her fur jacket on a hanger. No attendant was in charge of the coat room, although an attendant wearing a hotel porter uniform was standing near the doorway to the room.

The club member spent the evening in the banquet room, and at the end of the dinner meeting went to the coat room to retrieve her jacket. The jacket was missing.

The hotel offered her as compensation the sum of $40 which was the amount which an innkeeper was obliged to pay under the *Innkeeper's Act* of the province, and explained that as a guest in the hotel, this was the extent of its liability to her. The hotel manager pointed out that the club member was aware of the limited liability of the hotel by virtue of the notice to that effect which was posted in all hotel bedrooms.

The club member refused to accept the sum offered as payment, and brought an action against the hotel for $2 800, an amount which she alleged was the appraised value of the fur jacket.

Discuss the issues raised in this case, and indicate how the courts might deal with them. Would your answer be any different if the club member's jacket had been stolen from a locked hotel room?

CHAPTER 22

The Sale of Goods

CODIFICATION OF THE LAW

The law that relates to the sale of goods represents a direct response to the need for clear and precise rules to govern transactions which involve the exchange of money for goods. The existence of laws of this nature are indicative of the stage of development of a society. In a primitive society, where the individual members live at or near the subsistence level, no laws are necessary, because the sale of goods seldom occurs. Any surplus production of one product is usually exchanged for other necessary products, usually by barter. It is only when a genuine surplus is produced that a basis for trade is established, and even then, a number of other conditions must be present before laws are necessary to govern the exchanges.

In England during the Middle Ages, most families and communities were relatively self-sufficient, and any goods which could not be produced within the family were usually acquired by way of exchange or barter with neighbours. Surplus goods of one community were often carried to nearby communities and exchanged for goods not available locally, as the same products were seldom concurrently in surplus supply in both. The rise of towns, however, set the stage for commerce. Not only did towns provide a ready market for agricultural products, but they also produced goods required by the agricultural community and represented a convenient place where exchanges might take place.

Trade was initially by barter at the market "fairs" held in each town, and was largely local, but as the towns grew in size, foreign merchants began to appear, either with goods to sell, or with money to purchase the surplus goods of the community.

Trade was encouraged by the government during the period in which the feudal system declined, and the larger market towns (called Staple towns) became trading centres where foreign merchants were permitted to buy and sell goods. As trade increased, a merchant class developed in England, and the market fairs became permanent markets where goods were exchanged or brought and sold on an ongoing basis.

Transactions between merchants were first governed by the *law merchant*, and disputes concerning the sale of goods which arose were settled by the merchants themselves. Dealings between merchants and members of the community, however, were sometimes taken to the common law courts. Where the particular transaction involved the sale of goods, the courts would often apply the same rules which the merchants used in their own transactions, and over the years, a body of common law related to the sale of goods gradually developed.

The law, unfortunately, was far from satisfactory. The methods which a plaintiff was obliged to use to obtain relief were cumbersome, and in spite of a desire on the part of the merchants for change, the courts did not re-examine the nature of the transaction until the 18th century. At that time, the modern concept of contract emerged, and the sale of goods was treated as a contractual relationship between the buyer and seller.

During the next century, the rules of law relating to the sale of goods developed rapidly, and by the late 19th century the law had matured to the point where the business community pressed for the law's organization into a simplified and convenient statute. The government responded in 1893 with the codification of the common law in the form of a single statute entitled the *Sale of Goods Act*.[1]

MacKenzie D. Chalmers, a prominent English county court judge, at the request of the government of the day, prepared the draft bill that set out the law relating to the sale of goods as a clear and concise body of rules. Chalmers was familiar with the common law relating to the contract of sale, and as a result, the statute became one of the best drafted laws on the English statute books. Other countries were quick to recognize the advantages of having a codification of this part of the law,

---

[1] *Sale of Goods Act, 1893*, 56 & 57 Vict., c. 71.

and it was soon after adopted by the common law provinces of Canada, and a number of other jurisdictions in the British Empire.

The legal profession in the United States proposed similar legislation there, and a *Uniform Sales Act* was prepared, based upon the English *Sale of Goods Act*. The Act was adopted by many of the states, occasionally with modifications, and eventually found its way into the U.S. *Uniform Commercial Code* in a somewhat different form as Article 2. At the present time, the Code has been adopted by all states except Louisiana. This widespread adoption of the English principles and rules relating to the sale of goods reflects the clarity and simplicity of the original law which Mr. Chalmers had so carefully drawn, and it remains today in virtually unaltered form on the statute books of many jurisdictions.

NATURE OF A CONTRACT OF SALE

A contract of sale, as the name implies, is a type of contract. Consequently, the rules which relate to the formation, discharge, and impeachment of ordinary contracts also apply to the contract of sale, except where the Act has specifically modified the rules.

A contract of sale, however, is something more than an ordinary contract, because the contract not only contains the promises of the parties, but often represents evidence of a transfer of the ownership of the property to the buyer as well. It must, therefore, operate in accordance with the Act to accomplish this purpose.

Under the Act, "a contract of sale of goods is a contract whereby the seller transfers or agrees to transfer the property in goods to the buyer for a money

consideration called the price. . . ."[2] Two different contracts are contemplated by this definition. In the first instance, if the ownership is transferred immediately under the contract, it represents a *sale*. In the second, if the transfer of ownership is to take place at a future time, or subject to some condition which must be fulfilled before the transfer takes place, the transaction is an *agreement to sell*. Both the "sale" and the "agreement to sell" are referred to as a *contract of sale* under the Act where it is unnecessary to distinguish between the two. An agreement to sell may apply to goods that are in existence at the time, or it may apply to a contract where the goods are not yet in existence, such as where a farmer enters into a contract with a food processor to sell his entire crop of fruit or vegetables before they are grown.

The sale or agreement to sell must be for goods, as distinct from land, and anything attached to the land. Buildings, for example, form a part of the land, because they are attached to it, and so, too, would any right to use the land or the buildings. Transactions concerning land are not covered by the statute. The Act, as the title indicates, concerns a sale of goods, but even then, some "goods" are excluded. A sale of goods subject to the Act would include tangible things such as moveable personal property, but the term "goods" would not include money or intangible things such as shares in a corporation, bonds, negotiable instruments, or "rights" such as patents or trademarks.

The contract itself must be for the sale of goods, and in this sense is distin-

[2]*Sale of Goods Act*, R.S.O. 1980, c. 462, s. 2(1). Reference to the Act in this chapter will refer to the Ontario Act. While the name of the Act and the numbering of the sections of the other provincial statutes may vary, the rules stated usually may be found in the laws of all provinces and the territories.

guished from a contract for *work and materials*. It is sometimes difficult to differentiate between a contract for work and materials and an agreement to sell, where the goods are not yet produced. However, as a general rule, if the contract is for a product of which the cost of the materials represents only a small part of the price, and the largest part of the cost is labour, the contract may be treated as a contract for work and materials, and the *Sale of Goods Act* would not apply. For example, if a person engages another to paint a house, or if a person takes his watch to the repair shop to be cleaned and to have a minor part replaced, the contracts would probably be treated as for work and materials rather than a sale of goods. In both cases, most of the purchase price would be represented by the "work" rather than the goods themselves.

A second distinction between a contract of sale and other forms of contract is the requirement that the property in the goods be transferred for a monetary consideration. By this definition, a barter or exchange of goods where no money changed hands would not be a contract of sale within the meaning of the Act; nor would a consignment, where the title to the goods is retained by the owner, and the seller has only possession of the goods pending a sale to a prospective buyer.

No special form is required for either the sale contract or the agreement to sell. The contract may be in writing, under seal, verbal, or in some cases, implied from the conduct of the parties, but if the contract is for the sale of goods valued at more than a particular amount,[3] the agreement must be evidenced by a memorandum in writing, and signed by the party to be charged (or his agent) to be enforceable.

The requirement of writing was originally found in the *Statute of Frauds*, and later included in the English *Sale of Goods Act*. When the legislation was adopted by the Canadian provinces and territories the requirement of writing was included. Three exceptions are provided in the Act, however, which permit the parties to avoid the requirement of writing. The agreement need not be in writing if the buyer:

(1) accepts part of the goods sold;
(2) gives something "in earnest" to bind the contract; or
(3) makes a part-payment of the contract price.[4]

In each of these cases, the actions of the buyer must relate specifically to the particular contract of sale. The acceptance of part of the goods has been interpreted by the courts to mean any act which would indicate acceptance or adoption of the pre-existing contract, including the ordinary inspection of the goods. The part-payment of the contract price must be just that: a payment of money that relates specifically to the particular contract. The third requirement, the giving of something "in earnest" refers to an old custom of giving something valuable for the purpose of binding the agreement. The object might be an article, or something of value, other than a part-payment of the purchase price. This practice is seldom followed today.

Transfer of Title

A final observation with respect to the nature of the contract of sale is that it repre-

---

[3]The amount in Ontario, New Brunswick and Nova Scotia is $40. Newfoundland, and the three western provinces fixed the amount at $50, and Prince

Edward Island placed the amount at $30. British Columbia, following the English example, repealed the requirement of writing in 1958.
[4]*Sale of Goods Act*, R.S.O. 1980, c. 462, s. 5(1).

sents an agreement to transfer property in the goods to the buyer. The "property in the goods" is the right of ownership to the goods, or the *title*. The ownership of the goods normally goes with possession, but this is not always the case. A person may, for example, part with possession of goods, yet retain ownership, and it is this attribute that creates most of the difficulties with the sale of goods. The parties in their agreement may determine when the title will pass, and this may differ from the time when possession takes place. Since the risk of loss generally follows the title, in any agreement where the transfer of possession is not accompanied by a simultaneous transfer of ownership, any damage to the goods while the title is not in the person in physical possession of them can obviously raise difficulties.

Goods which are not in a deliverable state (i.e., goods that must be produced, weighed, measured, counted, sorted, or tested before they are identifiable as goods for a particular contract) unless otherwise provided, remain at the seller's risk until such time as they are "ready for delivery." Under the Act, no property in the goods is transferred to the buyer until the goods are in this state.[5] In a contract for goods which are specific or ascertained, the property in the goods may be transferred to the buyer at such time as the parties intend the transfer to take place.[6] In most cases, this intention will be determined by an examination of the contract terms, the conduct of the parties, or the circumstances under which the contract arose.[7] If the parties specify when the title passes, then the parties

themselves have decided who should bear the loss in the event that the goods should be destroyed or damaged before the transaction is completed. If they have not dealt with this matter in their agreement, or if it cannot be ascertained from their conduct (or the circumstances of the case), then the Act provides a series of rules which are deemed to apply to the contract. These rules deal with a number of different common contract situations. The first rule deals with goods that are specific (i.e., identified and agreed upon at the time the contract is made) and in a deliverable state.

Rule 1. Where there is an unconditional contract for the sale of specific goods in a deliverable state, the property in the goods passes to the buyer when the contract is made, and it is immaterial whether the time of payment or the time of delivery or both be postponed.[8]

Example. Henderson enters Nielsen's shop, and purchases a large crystal bowl which Nielsen has on display in his shop window. Henderson pays for the item, and informs Nielsen that he will pick it up the next morning.

During the night, a vandal smashes the shop window and destroys the crystal bowl. The title passed in this case when the contract was made, because the goods were specific and in a deliverable state. Henderson, if he wished, could have taken the bowl with him at the time the contract was made, but he elected not to do so. Since loss follows the title, the particular goods destroyed belonged to the buyer, and not to the seller, and it is the buyer who must bear the loss.

---

[5]*Ibid.*, s. 17; *Harns v. Clarkson*, [1931] O.W.N. 325.
[6]*Ibid.*, s. 18(1): see also *Goodwin Tanners Ltd. v. Belick and Naiman*, [1953] O.W.N. 641.
[7]*Sale of Goods Act*, R.S.O. 1980, c. 462, s. 18(2).
[8]*Ibid.*, s. 18.

The second rule is a variation of Rule 1. It is applicable to a contract where the seller must do something to the goods to put them in a deliverable state. Title in this case does not pass until the seller does whatever is necessary to put the goods in a deliverable state, and notifies the buyer that the goods are now ready for delivery. The rule states:

Rule 2. Where there is a contract for the sale of specific goods and the seller is bound to do something to the goods for the purpose of putting them in a deliverable state, the property does not pass until the thing is done and the buyer has notice thereof.[9]

Example. Leblanc entered into a contract with Ross to purchase a used car on display at Ross' car lot. The door lock on one door was inoperable, and Ross agreed to fix the lock as a term of the contract. Leblanc paid the entire purchase price to Ross. Ross repaired the lock, but before he notified Leblanc that the car was ready for delivery, the car was destroyed by a fire at Ross' garage. Leblanc would be entitled to a return of the purchase price in this case, as the title was still in Ross' name. The title would not pass until Ross notified Leblanc that the car was ready for delivery, and the risk was his until the buyer received the notice.

The third rule is again a variation of Rule 1, and applies where the contract is for the sale of specific goods in a deliverable state, but where the seller must weigh, measure, test, or do something to ascertain the price. Under this rule, the property in the goods does not pass until the act is done and the buyer notified.

Rule 3. When there is a contract for the sale of specific goods in a deliverable state, but the seller is bound to weigh, measure, test, or do some other act or thing with reference to the goods for the purpose of ascertaining the price, the property does not pass until such act or thing is done, and the buyer has been notified thereof.[10]

Example. Grange agrees to purchase a quantity of grain which Thompson has stored in a bin in his warehouse. Thompson agrees to weigh the material and inform Grange of the price. If the grain should be destroyed before Thompson notifies Grange of the weight and price, the loss would be the seller's, as the property in the goods would not pass until the buyer has notice. If, however, Thompson weighed the grain and notified Grange of the weight and price, the title would pass immediately, and if the goods were subsequently destroyed before Grange took delivery, the loss would be his, even though the goods were still in the seller's possession.

It is important to note with respect to Rule 3 that the seller must have the duty to weigh, measure, or otherwise deal with the goods. In a case where the buyer took the goods and agreed to weigh them on the way home, then notify the seller, a court held that Rule 3 did not apply to transfer the property interest. The title passed to the buyer when he took the goods.[11]

The fourth rule for the transfer of ownership in goods deals with contracts for the sale of goods ''on approval'' or with return privileges. This rule is a two-part rule which provides that the title will pass if the

---

[9]*Ibid.*, s. 19: see also *Underwood Ltd. v. Burgh Castlebrick & Cement Syndicate*, [1921] All E.R. Rep. 515.

[10]*Sale of Goods Act*, R.S.O. 1980, c. 462, s. 19.
[11]*Turley v. Bates* (1863), 2 H & C 200, 159 E.R. 83.

buyer, on receipt of the goods, does anything to signify his acceptance or approval of the goods, or the adoption of the contract. If he does nothing but retain the goods beyond a reasonable time, then the title will pass at the expiry of that period of time. The buyer must do some act that he would only have the right to do as the owner in order to fall under the first part of this rule. The sale of the goods by the buyer, for example, would constitute an act of acceptance, as it would be an act which only a person who had adopted the contract would normally do. The same rule would hold if the buyer mortgaged the goods. In that case, the title would pass to the buyer the instant that the act of acceptance took place.

Under the second part of the rule, if the buyer simply does nothing after he receives the goods, the title will pass when the time fixed for return expires, or if no time is fixed, after a reasonable time. The purpose of this second part of the rule is to ensure that a buyer cannot retain "approval" goods beyond a reasonable time. The delivery of goods is frequently a courtesy extended by the seller, and to allow the prospective purchaser to retain the goods an unnecessarily long time would only increase the chance of loss or damage to the goods while the risk is still with the seller.

Rule 4. Where goods are delivered to the buyer on approval or "on sale or return" or other similar terms, the property therein passes to the buyer:
(i) when he signifies his approval or acceptance to the seller or does any other act adopting the transaction;
(ii) if he does not signify his approval or acceptance to the seller but retains the goods without giving notice of rejection, then if a time has been fixed for

the return of the goods, on the expiration of such time, and if no time has been fixed, on the expiration of a reasonable time, and what is a reasonable time is a question of fact.

Example A. Baxter purchased a small bulldozer on approval, and a few days later pledged it as security for a loan at his bank. The machine was later damaged in a fire. In this case, the buyer, Baxter would be considered to have accepted the goods at the time he pledged the machine as security, and the resulting loss would be his.

The terms of the contract may alter the liability of the parties, however. In a case where goods were delivered "for cash or return, goods to remain the property of the seller until paid for" it was held that Rule 4 did not apply, as the seller had specifically withheld the passing of the title.[12]

Example B. A buyer ordered 140 bags of rice from a seller. The seller delivered 125, with 15 bags to follow. The buyer asked the seller to hold delivery of the remaining 15 bags. After the passing of a reasonable time, the seller asked the buyer if he was appropriating the 125 bags, but the buyer did not reply. The seller later sued the buyer for the price of the 125 bags of rice. In this case the court held that the buyer in failing to reply within a reasonable time had implied acceptance.[13]

The fifth rule applies to unascertained goods (or goods that are not as yet produced) and which would therefore be the subject-matter of an *agreement to sell* rather than a *sale*. Under this rule, as soon as the goods ordered by description are produced and in a deliverable state and are unconditionally appropriated to the con-

---

[12]*Weiner v. Gill*, [1905] 2 K.B. 172.
[13]*Pignitaro v. Gillroy*, [1919] 1 K.B. 459.

tract, either by the seller, or by the buyer (with the seller's consent), the property in the goods will pass. This rule again is in two parts which provide:

Rule 5.

(i) Where there is a contract for the sale of unascertained or future goods by description, and goods of that description in a deliverable state are unconditionally appropriated to the contract, either by the seller with the assent of the buyer, or by the buyer with the assent of the seller, the property in the goods therein passes to the buyer, and such assent may be expressed or implied, and may be given either before or after the appropriation is made.

(ii) Where, in pursuance of the contract, the seller delivers the goods to the buyer or to a carrier or other bailee (whether named by the buyer or not) for the purpose of transmission to the buyer, and does not reserve the right of disposal, he is deemed to have unconditionally appropriated the goods to the contract.[14]

Example A. A pipeline contractor ordered a quantity of special steel pipe from a manufacturer. When the pipe was produced, the contractor sent one of his trucks to the manufacturer's plant with instructions to have the pipe loaded. After the truck was loaded, it was stolen (through no fault of the manufacturer) and destroyed in an accident. The pipe, as a result of the damage suffered in the accident, was useless. Here, the goods were unconditionally appropriated to the contract and the title had passed to the contractor.

Again, the time at which the title passes is deemed to be when the buyer obtains possession of the goods either himself or through his agent, or when the seller loses physical control of the goods.

Example B. A buyer in England ordered certain dyes from a seller in Switzerland, knowing that the seller had them in stock. The seller sent the order by mail to the buyer in England, and in so doing was accused of infringement of the English patent. One of the issues in the case was: Where and when did title pass? The court held that since the buyer had given his implied assent to delivery by mail, as soon as the seller filled the order and placed it in the mail the title passed to the buyer.[15]

This decision is consistent with cases dealing with the use of common carriers to deliver the goods to the buyer as provided in the second part of the rule. Unless the seller has reserved the right of disposal, goods delivered to the carrier have essentially been disposed of by the seller. Once delivered, the seller no longer has control of the goods, and usually only the buyer may recover the goods from the carrier. Since the seller has effectively transferred control over the goods to the buyer's agent, the rule is sensible in providing for the passing of ownership from the seller to the buyer at the moment when the seller parts with possession.

The importance of withholding title by the seller, or reserving the right of disposal if goods are delivered to the buyer or a carrier have important implications in the event that the buyer should become insolvent at some point in time during the sale. The general rule is that the trustee in bankruptcy is only entitled to claim as a part of the bankrupt's estate those goods which belong to the bankrupt at the time of the

---

[14]*Sale of Goods Act*, R.S.O. 1980, c. 462, s. 19.

[15]*Badische Analin and Soda Fabrik v. Basle Chemical Works, Bind Schedler*, [1898] A.C. 200.

bankruptcy. If the seller has retained the title to the goods, he may, in many cases, be in a position to recover the goods, or stop their delivery to the bankrupt if they are in the hands of a carrier. Hence the importance, for example, of reserving the title until the goods are paid for in full by the buyer.

CONTRACTUAL DUTIES OF THE SELLER

The *Sale of Goods Act* permits the parties to include in their contract any particular terms or conditions relating to the sale that they wish, and the seller is obliged to comply with these terms. Sometimes the contract is one which is not carefully drawn in terms of the particular rights and duties of the parties, and in these cases, the Act implies certain obligations. These obligations generally are imposed upon the seller in terms of warranties and conditions with respect to the goods. Under the Act, these terms have particular meanings:

A *condition* is a fundamental or essential term of the contract, which if broken would generally entitle the innocent party, if he so elects, to treat the breach as a discharge, and be released from any further performance himself.

A *warranty* is not an essential term in the contract, but rather a term which, if broken, would not end the contract, but would entitle the injured party to take action for damages for the breach. A warranty is usually a minor term of the contract, and not one which goes to the root of the agreement.

The Act stipulates the particular terms in the contract of sale which constitute conditions, and those which, if broken, would only be warranties. For example, the time for delivery of the goods is treated as a condition, and the promise of payment a mere warranty.

As to the title of the seller, unless the contract indicates otherwise, there is an implied condition that in the case of a sale, the seller has the right to sell the goods, and in the case of an agreement to sell, that he will have the right to sell the goods at the time when the property or the title in the goods is to pass to the buyer.[16] There is also an implied warranty that the goods are free from any charge or encumbrance (such as a chattel mortgage) in favour of a third party, unless the seller has informed the buyer of the charge or encumbrance either before or at the time the agreement is made.[17] An additional implied warranty relates to the seller's title. It states that the buyer shall have quiet possession of the goods. The term "quiet possession" has nothing to do with solitude; it simply means that no person will later challenge the buyer's title to the goods by claiming a right or interest in them.[18]

Goods that are sold by description are subject to an implied condition that the goods will correspond with the description.[19] For example, if a buyer purchases goods from a catalogue, where the specifications are given, and perhaps a picture of the goods is shown, the goods ordered by the buyer must correspond with the catalogue specifications, otherwise the seller will be in breach of the contract, and the buyer will be entitled to reject the goods. If

---

[16]*Sale of Goods Act*, R.S.O. 1980, c. 462, s. 13(*a*): see also *Cehave N.V. v. Bremer*, [1975] 3 All E.R. 739; *Wickman Machine Tool Sales Ltd. v. L. Schuler A.G.*, [1972] 2 All E.R. 1173; affirmed [1973] 2 All E.R. 39.

[17]*Sale of Goods Act*, R.S.O. 1980, c. 462, s. 13(*c*).

[18]*Ibid.*, s. 13(*b*).

[19]*Ibid.*, s. 13: see also *Beale v. Taylor*, [1967] 3 All E.R. 253.

the goods are sold by description as well as by sample, then the goods must correspond to the description as well as the sample.[20]

Where goods are sold by sample alone, there is an implied condition that the bulk of the goods will correspond to the sample in quality,[21] and that the buyer will have a reasonable opportunity to examine the goods and compare them with the sample.[22] Even then, there is an implied condition that the goods will be free from any defect rendering them unmerchantable which would not be apparent on reasonable examination of the sample.[23] For example, a seller sold cloth by sample to a buyer to be resold by sample to tailors, but unknown to both the seller and buyer, the cloth dye was such that perspiration would cause the colours to run. When the defect was later discovered the tailors who manufactured the overcoats complained to the buyer, who in turn complained to the original seller. The defect was not apparent on ordinary examination of the cloth, but was in both the sample and the bulk of the cloth. When the seller refused to compensate the buyer, the buyer sued the seller for breach of contract. The court held that the examination need only be that which a reasonable man would make. There was no need to conduct elaborate chemical tests. The standard for the examination would be the same as that which a reasonable man buying an overcoat would have made of the material.[24]

---

[20]*Sale of Goods Act*, R.S.O. 1980, c. 462, s. 14.
[21]*Ibid.*, s. 16(2)(*a*). See also *Buckley v. Lever Bros. Ltd.*, [1953] O.R. 704.
[22]*Sale of Goods Act*, R.S.O. 1980, c. 462, s. 16(2)(*b*). See also *Godley v. Perry*, [1960] 1 All E.R. 36.
[23]*Grant v. Australian Knitting Mills*, [1935] All E.R. 209.
[24]*Drummond & Sons v. E. H. Van Ingen & Co.* (1887), L.R. 12 H.L. 284.

||||||||||||||||||||||||||||||||||||||||||||||||||||||||||||||||||||||||||||||||||

CASE 22.1
James Drummond & Sons v. E.H. Van Ingen & Co. (1887), L.R. 12 H.L. 284.

LORD MACNAGHTEN:

The sample speaks for itself. But it cannot be treated as saying more than such a sample would tell a merchant of the class to which the buyer belongs, using due care and diligence, and appealing to it in the ordinary way and with the knowledge possessed by merchants of that class at the time. No doubt the sample might be made to say a great deal more. Pulled to pieces and examined by unusual tests which curiosity or suspicion might suggest, it would doubtless reveal every secret of its construction. But that is not the way in which business is done in this country. Some confidence there must be between merchant and manufacturer. In matters exclusively within the province of the manufacturer the merchant relies on the manufacturer's skill, and he does so all the more readily when, as in this case, he has had the benefit of that skill before.

Now I think it is plain upon the evidence that at the date of the transaction in question merchants possessed of ordinary skill would not have thought of the existence of the particular defect which has given rise to this action, and would not have discovered its existence from the sample. It appears to me, therefore, that the sample must be treated as wholly silent in regard to this defect, and I come to the conclusion that if every scrap of information which the sample can fairly be taken to have disclosed were written out at length, and embodied in writing in the order itself, nothing would be found there which could relieve the manufacturer from the obligation implied by the transaction.

I prefer to rest my view on this broad principle. But it seems to me that the obligation of the manufacturer may be put in another way with the same result. When a manufacturer proposes to carry out the ideas of his customer, and furnishes a sample to show what he can do, surely in effect he says, "This is the sort of thing you want, the rest is my business, you may depend upon it that there is no defect in the manufacture which would prevent goods made according to that sample from answering the purpose for which they are required."

CAVEAT EMPTOR

As to quality and fitness for a particular purpose, the buyer is, to a certain extent, subject to *caveat emptor* ("let the buyer beware"). The law assumes that the buyer, when given an opportunity to examine goods, can determine the quality and the fitness for his purpose. The Act does, however, impose some minimum obligations on the seller. Where the seller is in the business of supplying a particular line of goods, and where the buyer makes the purpose for which he requires the goods known to the seller, and where he relies on the seller's skill or judgement to supply a suitable product, there is an implied condition that the goods provided shall be reasonably fit for the use intended.[25] This rule, however, would not apply in a case where the buyer requests a product by its patent or trade name, as there would then be no implied condition as to its fitness for any particular purpose.[26] This particular proviso means that any time that a purchaser orders goods by "name" rather than leaving the selection to the seller, the buyer will have no recourse against the seller if the goods fail to perform as expected, as the buyer was not relying on the seller's skill to select the proper product.

[25]*Sale of Goods Act*, R.S.O. 1980, c. 462, s. 15(*a*). See also *Canada Building Materials Ltd. v. W. B. Meadows of Canada Ltd.*, [1968] 1 O.R. 469.
[26]*Sale of Goods Act*, R.S.O. 1980, c. 462, s. 15(*a*). See also *Baldry v. Marshall*, [1925] 1 K.B. 260.

CASE 22.2
Baldry v. Marshall, [1925] 1 K.B. 260.

BANKES, L.J.:

The mere fact that an article sold is described in the contract by its trade name does not necessarily make the sale a sale under a trade name. Whether it is so or not depends upon the circumstances. I may illustrate my meaning by reference to three different cases. First, where a buyer asks a seller for an article which will fulfil some particular purpose, and in answer to that request the seller sells him an article by a well-known trade name, there I think it is clear that the proviso does not apply. Secondly, where the buyer says to the seller, "I have been recommended such and such an article"—mentioning it by its trade name—"will it suit my particular purpose?" naming the purpose, and thereupon the seller sells it without more [*sic*], there again I think the proviso has no application. But there is a third case where the buyer says to a seller, "I have been recommended so and so"—giving its trade name—"as suitable for the particular purpose for which I want it. Please sell it to me." In that case I think it is equally clear that the proviso would apply and that the implied condition of the thing's fitness for the purpose named would not arise. In my opinion the test of an article having been sold under its trade name within the meaning of the proviso is: Did the buyer specify it under its trade name in such a way as to indicate that he is satisfied, rightly or wrongly, that it will answer his purpose, and that he is not relying on the skill or judgment of the seller, however great that skill or judgment may be?

In general, where goods are bought by description from a seller who deals in such goods, there is an implied condition that the goods shall be of merchantable quality, but if the buyer has examined the goods, the implied condition would not apply to any defect in the goods which would have been revealed by the examination.[27]

The seller also has a duty to deliver goods as specified in the contract in the right quantity, at the right place, and at the right time. The time of delivery, if stipulated in the contract, is usually treated as a condition, and if the seller fails to deliver the goods on time, the buyer may be free to reject them if delivery is late.[28] If no time for delivery is specified, the goods must usually be delivered within a reasonable time.[29]

Delivery of the proper quantity is also important. If the seller should deliver less than the amount fixed in the contract, the buyer may reject the goods, as this generally is a condition of the contract, and a right of the buyer under the Act.[30] If the buyer accepts the lesser quantity, then he would be obliged to pay for them at the contract rate.[31] The delivery of a larger quantity than specified in the contract, however, does not obligate the buyer to accept the excess quantity. He may reject the excess, or may reject the entire quantity delivered, but if he should accept the entire quantity, he usually must pay for the excess quantity at the contract price per unit.[32]

||||||||||||||||||||||||||||||||||||||||||||||||||||||||||||||||

CASE 22.3
Shipton, Anderson & Co. v. Weil Brothers & Co., [1912] 1 K.B. 574.

LUSH, J.:

. . . the right to reject is founded upon the hypothesis that the seller was not ready and willing to perform, or had not performed, his part of the contract. The tender of a wrong quantity evidences an unreadiness and unwillingness, but that, in my opinion, must mean an excess or deficiency in quantity which is capable of influencing the mind of the buyer. In my opinion, this excess is not. I agree that directly the excess becomes a matter of possible discussion between reasonable parties, the seller is bound to justify what he has done under the contract; but the doctrine of de minimis cannot, I think, be excluded merely because the statute refers to the tender of a smaller or larger quantity than the contract quantity as entitling a buyer to reject.

I wish to add this. The reason why an excess in tender entitles a buyer to reject is that the seller seeks to impose a burden on the buyer which he is not entitled to impose. That burden is the payment of money not agreed to be paid. It is prima facie no burden on the buyer to have 55 lbs. more than 4,950 tons offered to him, and there is nothing to suggest that these sellers would have ever insisted, or thought of insisting, upon payment of the 4s. over the 40,000*l*. The sellers' original appropriation appeared to be within the proper quantity. The excess of 55 lbs. appears when the quantity shipped is converted from kilos into tons. If the sellers had expressly or impliedly insisted upon payment of the 4s. upon their view of the contract, the case would have been different; but nothing of that kind can be supposed to have taken place here.

||||||||||||||||||||||||||||||||||||||||||||||||||||||||||||||||||||||||||||

The place for delivery is usually specified in the contract, but if the parties have failed to do so, the seller is only obliged to have the goods available and ready for delivery at his place of business if he has one, or if not, at his place of residence. If the parties are aware that the goods are stored elsewhere, then the place where the goods are located would be the place for delivery.[33] The place of delivery is often ex-

[27]*Sale of Goods Act*, R.S.O. 1980, c. 462, s. 15(*b*).
[28]*Ibid.*, s. 27.
[29]*Ibid.*, s. 28(2).
[30]*Ibid.*, s. 29(1).
[31]*Ibid.*, s. 29(1).
[32]*Ibid.*, s. 29(2).
[33]*Ibid.*, s. 28(1).

pressly or impliedly fixed when goods are sold, and if this should be the case, or if by some custom of the trade the delivery takes place elsewhere than the seller's place, then the seller would be obliged to make delivery there.[34]

Where a contract calls for delivery by instalments, and the seller fails to make delivery in accordance with the contract, the buyer is often faced with a dilemma. If a lesser quantity is delivered, and the contract calls for separate payments for each instalment, the buyer may take delivery, if he so desires, and pay for the goods delivered. If he wishes to reject the goods, he must take care. He may not treat the failure to deliver the proper amount on a particular instalment as a basis for repudiation of the contract unless he is certain that he could satisfy the courts that the quantity delivered was significantly below the requirement set out in the contract, and that there was a high degree of probability that the deliveries would be equally deficient in the future.[35] This problem, however, is normally limited to instalment contracts requiring separate payments. If the contract does not provide for a separate payment for each instalment, the contract is generally treated as being indivisible, and the buyer is free to repudiate the whole agreement.

In contracts of sale which are not sales to a consumer, the seller may, by an express term in the contract exclude all implied conditions and warranties which are imposed under the Act. Where this is done, however, the seller must comply exactly with the terms of the contract made. For example, a buyer entered into a contract with a seller for the purchase of a new truck for his business. The purchase agree-

ment provided that "all conditions and warranties implied by law are excluded." The truck delivered by the seller was slightly used, and did not correspond to the description. The buyer in this case was entitled to reject the truck, as he did not receive what he contracted for (a *new* truck).[36] The particular thrust of most cases on exemption clauses is to limit the extent to which a seller may avoid liability. Many cases of this nature are decided on the basis of *fundamental breach*, or on the basis of strict interpretation of the seller's duties under the agreement. Additional protection is afforded to consumers in most provinces and territories by limiting or eliminating entirely the seller's right to exclude implied conditions and warranties in contracts for the sale of consumer goods.[37]

The protection of the consumer has been carried one step further in some jurisdictions. Not only is the seller prevented from excluding implied warranties and conditions from the contract in a consumer sale, but any verbal warranties or conditions expressed at the time of the sale not included in a written agreement would also be binding on the seller.[38] In addition, consumer protection legislation often provides a "cooling-off period" for certain consumer sales contracts made elsewhere than at the seller's place of business. This allows the buyer to avoid the contract by giving notice of his intention to the seller within a specified period of time after the contract is made. The most common type of contract of this nature is one in which a door-to-door salesperson sells goods to the con-

---

[34]*Ibid.*, s. 28(1).
[35]*Ibid.*, s. 30(2).

[36]*Andrews Bros. (Bournemouth) Ltd. v. Singer & Co. Ltd.*, [1934] 1 K.B. 17.
[37]*Consumer Protection Act*, R.S.O. 1980, c. 87, s. 44*a*(2), as amended by 1971 (Ont.), c. 24, s. 2(1).
[38]*Business Practices Act*, R.S.O. 1980, c. 55, s. 4.

sumer in the consumer's own home.[39] The purpose of the "cooling-off period" is to allow the buyer to examine the contract at his leisure after the seller has left, and if, after reviewing his actions, he decides that he does not wish to proceed with the contract, he may give the seller notice in writing within the specified period (usually 48 hours) and the contract will be terminated. In each case of this kind, where the legislation applies, the contract is essentially in suspension until the cooling-off period expires, and it is only then that it becomes operative.

The general trend in consumer protection legislation in recent years has been to impose greater responsibility on the seller in the sale of goods. While the rule of *caveat emptor* is still very much alive, the right of the buyer to avoid a contract has been expanded beyond the normal rights of the commercial buyer. The justification for the change is based upon the premise that the buyer and seller are no longer the equals presumed by contract law. Many sales are offered on a "take it or leave it basis," and in other instances, high pressure selling techniques or methods have placed the buyer at a particular disadvantage. The widespread use of exemption clauses has also been a factor which prompted legislation to redress the balance in negotiating power, and to ensure honesty on the part of the seller in his dealings with the buyer.

CONTRACTUAL DUTIES OF THE BUYER

Apart from the general duty on the part of the buyer to promptly examine goods sent on approval, or to compare goods delivered to a sample, the buyer has a duty to take delivery and pay for the goods as provided in the contract of sale, or in accordance with the Act. The delivery of the goods and the payment of the price are concurrent conditions in a sale unless the parties have provided otherwise.[40] For example, if the contract is silent on payment time and place, then the buyer would be obliged to pay a reasonable price at the time of the delivery of the goods.[41]

Payment is not a condition under the contract unless the parties specifically make it so. Under the Act, payment is treated as a mere warranty,[42] and as such, it would not entitle the seller to avoid performance if the buyer failed to pay at the prescribed time. The seller would, however, have the right to claim against the buyer for breach of the warranty, and recover any damages he might have suffered as a result of the buyer's default.[43]

REMEDIES OF THE BUYER
Rescission

The seller has a number of conditions and warranties imposed upon him apart from those which may be set out in the contract itself. The rights of the buyer under the contract are, for the most part, governed by the manner in which the seller fulfils the contract terms, and the manner in which he complies with the various implied warranties and conditions. If the seller's breach of the agreement is a breach of a *condition* or a breach that goes to the very root of the agreement (for example, something which the courts would treat as a fundamental breach) the buyer may be in a position to repudiate the contract, and

---

[39]*Consumer Protection Act,* R.S.O. 1980, c. 87, s. 33(1).

[40]*Sale of Goods Act,* R.S.O. 1980, c. 462, ss. 26, 27.
[41]*Ibid.,* s. 9(2).
[42]*Ibid.,* s. 47.
[43]*Ibid.,* s. 47.

reject the goods. Where he is entitled to repudiate the contract he also has the right
to refuse payment of the purchase price, or
if he has already paid the price, or a part of
it, he may recover it from the seller. The
buyer has an alternate remedy in a case
where the seller fails to delivery the goods.
He may purchase the goods elsewhere,
then sue the seller for the difference between the contract price and the price paid
in the market.[44]

Damages

In some cases, the seller may be in breach
of contract, but only of a minor term, or
one which does not go to the root of the
contract. For example, in a contract where
the seller is obliged to deliver goods according to sample by instalments at a fixed
price each, he may make one delivery
which is slightly deficient, in which case
the buyer would not be entitled to repudiate the contract as a whole, but only the
particular instalment.[45] "Microscopic"
variation in deliveries, however, would
not likely be treated as a breach of contract.[46] If the contract is not severable, and
the buyer has accepted the goods, or a part
of them, or where the contract is for specific goods, and the property in the goods
has passed to the buyer, the breach of any
condition by the seller may only be treated
as a breach of warranty. Thus, the buyer
would not be entitled to reject the goods or
repudiate the agreement unless entitled to
do so by an express or implied term in the
agreement to that effect.[47] The buyer, if he

elects to do so, may treat any breach of a
condition as a breach of warranty, in
which case the contract would continue to
be binding on the buyer, but he would be
entitled to sue the seller for damages arising out of the breach.[48]

Specific Performance

A third remedy is available to the buyer on
rare occasions. If the goods in question
have some unique or special attribute or
nature, and cannot be readily obtained
elsewhere, monetary damages may not be
adequate as a remedy if the seller refuses
to make delivery. Under such circumstances, the remedy of specific performance may be available to the buyer at the
discretion of the courts.[49] Unless the contract is for the sale of something in the
nature of a rare antique or work of art,
however, the courts are unlikely to award
the remedy, as monetary damages are normally adequate in most sales transactions.

REMEDIES OF THE SELLER
Lien
The remedies available to the seller in the
event of a breach of the contract of sale are
to some extent dependent upon the passing of the title to the buyer, and the right
of the seller to retain the goods. These
rights may be exercised either against the
buyer personally, or against the goods
themselves, depending upon the circumstances and the nature of the remedy. The
seller normally may not repudiate the contract in the event of non-payment by the
buyer, unless payment has been made a
condition in the contract. The seller, however, is not obliged under the Act to deliver the goods unless payment is made, or

[44]*Ibid.*, s. 49.
[45]*Jackson v. Rotax Motor & Cycle Co.*, [1910] 2 K.B.
937.
[46]*Shipton, Anderson & Co. v. Weil Bros. & Co.*, [1912] 1
K.B. 574.
[47]*Sale of Goods Act*, R.S.O. 1980, c. 462, s. 12(3). See
also *O'Flaherty v. McKinlay*, [1953] 2 D.L.R. 514.

[48]*Sale of Goods Act*, R.S.O. 1980, c. 462, s. 12(1).
[49]*Ibid.*, s. 50.

credit terms are granted by the seller for the purchase in question.[50] In this respect, the seller may claim a lien on the goods if the sale is a cash sale, or if the sale is a credit sale, and the period of credit has expired as, for example, where the goods are sold on a "lay-away" plan. The seller may also claim a lien on the goods if the buyer should become insolvent before the goods are delivered.[51] A seller's lien depends, of course, upon possession of the goods, and if the seller should voluntarily release the goods to the buyer, the right of lien may be lost.

Action for the Price

If the seller has delivered the goods to the buyer, and the title has passed, the seller may sue the buyer for the price of the goods.[52] An action for the price would also lie where the title has not passed but the seller delivered the goods, and where delivery was refused by the buyer. In this case, the seller has no obligation to press the goods on the buyer, but may simply sue the buyer for the price.[53] The seller must, of course, be prepared to deliver the goods if he recovers the price.

Damages

A more common remedy available to the seller is ordinary damages for non-acceptance. This remedy permits the seller to resell the goods to another, and sue the buyer for the loss incurred.[54] The damages which the seller may recover would probably be the monetary amount necessary to place the seller in the same position as he would have been in had the transaction been completed, and would either be the profit lost on the sale, or perhaps the difference between the disposal price of the goods (if he sold them privately), and the contract price.

Retention of Deposit

A feature common to many contracts is a clause which entitles the seller to retain any deposit paid as liquidated damages if the buyer should refuse to perform the contract. A deposit is not necessary in a written agreement to render it binding on the parties, but its advantage would be to circumvent the requirements of writing under the *Sale of Goods Act* if the contract is unwritten, and if it is for more than the stipulated minimum. The second advantage (from the seller's point of view) is that it represents a fund which the seller might look to in the event of a breach of the agreement by the buyer. If the agreement provides for the payment of a deposit by the buyer, and if the agreement also provides that in the event of default by the buyer, the seller might retain the deposit as liquidated damages, then if the default should occur, the seller would have in his hands funds sufficient to cover his loss. The amount of the deposit required, however, must be an honest estimate by the parties of the probable loss which the seller would suffer if the buyer should default. If it does not represent an honest estimate, in the sense that the payment is a substantial part of the purchase price rather than a deposit, the seller may not retain the part-payment, but would be obliged to return the excess over and above the actual loss flowing from the buyer's default.[55]

[50]*Ibid.*, s. 39(1). See also *Lyons (J.L.) v. May & Baker* (1922), 129 L.T. 413.
[51]*Sale of Goods Act*, R.S.O. 1980, c. 462, s. 39(1).
[52]*Ibid.*, s. 47(1).
[53]*Ibid.*, s. 47(2).
[54]*Ibid.*, s. 48.

[55]*Stevenson v. Colonial Homes Ltd.* (1961), 27 D.L.R. (2d) 698; see also *R.V. Ward Ltd. v. Bignall*, [1967] 2 All E.R. 449.

Stoppage in Transitu

An additional remedy available to the seller in cases where the seller has shipped the goods by carrier to the buyer is *stoppage in transitu*. If the seller has parted with the goods, but discovers that the buyer is insolvent, he may contact the carrier and have delivery stopped. "Insolvent" does not mean in this instance the actual bankruptcy of the buyer. It means only that the buyer is no longer meeting his debts as they fall due. A particular difficulty associated with this remedy relates to this fact. If the seller should stop delivery, and if the buyer is not insolvent, he may claim compensation from the seller for the loss caused by the wrongful stoppage of the goods. However, if the buyer should be insolvent, and the seller is successful in stopping the carrier before delivery is made, then the title will not pass to anyone who has notice of the stoppage. If the seller fails to contact the carrier in time, and the goods have been delivered to the buyer or his agent, it is too late, and the title will be in the buyer.[56] The same would hold true if the buyer had sold the goods to a *bona fide* purchaser for value and without notice of the stoppage.

Resale

The act of stopping the goods in transit does not affect the contract between the buyer and the seller. It simply represents a repossession of the goods by the seller. The seller is then entitled to retain the goods pending tender of payment of the price by the buyer. If the buyer does not tender payment, then the seller has the right to resell the goods to a second purchaser, and the second purchaser will obtain a good title to the goods.[57]

[56]*Plischke v. Allison Bros. Ltd.*, [1936] 2 All E.R. 1009.
[57]*Sale of Goods Act*, R.S.O. 1980, c. 462, s. 46(2).

SUMMARY The sale of goods represents one of the most common business and consumer transactions. The law of contract in general applies to the sale, but legislation entitled the *Sale of Goods Act* sets out the special rules which apply to this type of contract. Two forms of contract of sale are covered by the Act: the sale, and the agreement to sell. The former applies to specific goods, and the latter to goods that are not yet manufactured or not yet available for delivery. The property in the goods under a contract of sale passes when the parties stipulate that it will pass, but if no time is mentioned, then a series of rules in the Act will apply to make this determination. Risk of loss follows the title, and as a result, the time that the title passes is important. Under a contract of sale, a buyer and seller may fix the terms, but if the parties do not do so, the Act contains a number of implied conditions and warranties that will apply to the contract and to the goods. Implied conditions and warranties, among other things, require the seller to provide goods of merchantable quality at the time for delivery, in the right quantity, and at the right place, and to provide a good title to the goods delivered.

In most provinces and territories, under consumer protection legislation, consumer goods contracts may not contain exemption clauses which would eliminate implied warranties and conditions. If a seller acts in breach of a condition (which is a fundamental or major term) under certain circumstances the buyer may treat the contract as at an end, and be relieved from any further obligations to perform. A breach of a warranty, which in contrast to a condition, is only a minor term, simply entitles the buyer to sue for damages. He is not entitled to avoid the contract. The buyer may, at his option, treat the breach of a condition as a breach of a warranty if he so desires.

If a breach of contract on the part of the seller occurs, the buyer may, in the case of a breach of a condition, obtain either rescission or damages, but for a breach of a warranty, he would only be entitled to damages. In rare instances, a buyer may be granted specific performance of the contract if the subject-matter is unique.

The seller has six possible remedies if the buyer refuses delivery, or fails to pay the price. He is entitled to take action for the price, or claim a lien on the goods until payment is made if the goods are still in his possession. If the buyer rejects the goods and the seller must resell them, he may sue for his loss, or he may retain any deposit paid as liquidated damages if the contract so provides. Finally, if the seller ships the goods to the buyer, and then discovers the buyer is insolvent, he may stop delivery and hold the goods until payment is made, or resell them to a second buyer. If a resale is made, the second buyer will obtain a good title to the goods notwithstanding the prior sale to the original buyer.

DISCUSSION QUESTIONS

1. *What circumstances produced the codification of the law relating to the sale of goods?*
2. *What is the difference between a "sale" and an "agreement to sell"?*
3. *Certain characteristics make a contract for the sale of goods different from other contracts. Outline these distinctions.*
4. *Define "property in the goods." Why does this notion cause so much difficulty in the sale of goods?*
5. *How might approval be signified in the case of goods delivered with return privileges?*
6. *Which has more far-reaching consequences for the seller: the breach of a condition or the breach of a warranty? Does the difference between a condition and a warranty appear arbitrary? Why?*
7. *Define "quiet possession."*
8. *Should a good that was requested by its trade name fail to perform as expected, against whom should the buyer take action, the seller or the producer?*

9. *A seller in a non-consumer transaction may expressly exclude all conditions and warranties under the* Sale of Goods Act, *but then must comply exactly with the contract. Does this imply that he has the option to provide a product that is unsuitable for the use intended?*

10. *If a good is destroyed by an act of God during a "cooling-off period," with whom does liability lie: the buyer, the seller, or neither?*

11. *Delivery of goods and payment tend to be reciprocal acts between seller and buyer. Why is delivery a condition, and payment only a warranty?*

12. *Outline the differences between the four common remedies open to the seller. Contrast the usefulness of each of these remedies.*

13. *In the case of default of payment for goods that are consumed (i.e., firewood, or a food product) what would be the seller's most expedient remedy?*

14. *Should a seller stop goods in transit before they reach an insolvent buyer, he may recover and sell the goods. However, if goods are lost in transit, title is considered to have passed from seller to buyer at time of shipping. Is there an inconsistency here?*

JUDICIAL DECISIONS

Sale of Goods—Goods Unfit for Buyer's Purpose—Remedies of Buyer

Public Utilities Com'n for City of Waterloo v. Burroughs Business Machines Ltd. et al., [1973] 2 O.R. 472.

The treasurer of the plaintiff commission, D. J. Black, wrote a letter to the defendant for information concerning computer machines made by the defendant. Several conversations took place between Mr. Black and a Mr. Murdock of the defendant corporation, following which the defendant submitted a proposal for an equipment system that it alleged would perform a number of the billing and accounting services of the plaintiff commission.

The equipment was eventually purchased and installed, but failed to operate satisfactorily. The purchaser then brought an action for rescission of the contract.

DONOHUE, J.:

> Mr. Black testified that in his invitation letter to manufacturers of business machines he specified unit record equipment.
>
> When the Burroughs' man came to call on Waterloo Public Utilities Commission in answer to the invitation of March 1967, he told Mr. Black that Burroughs did not have unit record equipment but had something better, namely, the E4000 computer.
>
> Mr. Black also states that in discussing Burroughs' equipment there appeared to be no problem about who would programme the machine. Further, Mr. Murdoch stated that Burroughs had a lot of experience in public utilities' requirements for business machine operators. Mr. Black denies that Burroughs asked that they be allowed to put one of their men into Waterloo Public Utilities Commission in order to survey the latter's needs.

I am satisfied that the machine or system called the E4000 and its complementary units supplied to the plaintiff was incapable of doing the work which the plaintiff specified. It was not faulty programming by the plaintiff's employees which was the real cause of the trouble and error if there were such faulty work by such employees, it was part of Burroughs Company's responsibility in the matter to see to it that the programming was not faulty. As Jerry Thompson, one of Burroughs' employees, said in evidence "without a system the hardware is useless". The system was part of the package which Burroughs was selling to the plaintiff and, in my view, it was the responsibility of Burroughs to see to it that the programming was right and that the hardware would process the programmes efficiently.

If, as Burroughs Company asserts, there were faults in the programming done by the plaintiff's employees, it seems to me that evidence could have been put forward of specific instances of such faults. No such evidence was introduced. Further, computer programmes can be corrected or amended. As stated, I find against this contention on the part of Burroughs Company.

It is, I think, unnecessary for me to make findings as to the various causes of failures or breakdowns of the equipment. However, one such cause was referred to by witnesses both for the plaintiff and Burroughs Company as follows: part of the system's function was to print on a customer's bill the name and address of the customer and other data. This printing function involved such a large amount of movement in the machines that the wear and tear was excessive and brought on frequent breakdowns.

As I have already stated, the machine or machines or system supplied by Burroughs Company simply could not do the job which the plaintiff specified. Here the plaintiff was relying on the skill or judgment of Burroughs Company and there arose an implied warranty on the part of Burroughs Company that the equipment which was supplied was fit for the plaintiff's purposes.

The exclusionary clause in s. 15, para. 1 of the *Sale of Goods Act* which relates to the purchase of goods by their patented or trade name does not apply here because, first, it was not a single machine which was supplied but a combination of machines. Further, it would appear by Mr. Murdoch's own letter, ex. 28, that the machine had not even been designed at the time of the contract. Further, it appears that this machine or system was tailored to the plaintiff's requirements.

The failure to do the job amounts to a fundamental breach of warranty which entitled the plaintiff to an order for rescission of the contract which I grant. Damages arising upon a fundamental breach of contract are at large: *R. G. McLean Ltd. v. Canadian Vickers Ltd. et al.*, [1971] O.R. 207, 15 D.L.R. (3d) 15.

The rescission of the contract determines that Burroughs Company owns the equipment involved in the transaction and is, of course, at liberty to remove the same and has an obligation to do so.

|||||||||||||||||||||||||||||||||||||||||||||||||||||||||||||||||||||||||||||||||||||||||||||||||||||||||||||||||||||||||||||||||||||||||||||||||||||||||||||||||||||||||

Repudiation by Buyer—Retention of Deposit by Seller—Whether Part-Payment

Stevenson v. Colonial Homes Ltd. (1961), 27 D.L.R. (2d) 698.

Stevenson entered into an agreement to purchase a prefabricated cottage. The purchase price was $2 206, and he gave the seller $1 000 at the time of signing the agreement. The balance owing was $1 206.

At the time of delivery, Stevenson refused to accept the cottage, as the package did not include material for the ceilings of the rooms. The company then informed Stevenson that he would forfeit his deposit for his breach of the contract.

Stevenson brought an action to recover the $1 000 and at trial the action was dismissed. He then appealed.

KELLY, J.A.:

On the argument of the appeal the appellant raised two principal grounds. First, that the learned trial Judge erred in failing to find that there was material misrepresentation by the defendant through its servants or agents, and second, that the $1,000 was a part payment to the return of which the appellant was entitled upon the rescission of the contract. The respondent asked for the variation of the judgment to the extent of awarding to the respondent its costs in view of its success at trial.

At the trial there was considerable conflict in the testimony with respect to statements made by the plaintiff and the servants or agents of the defendant regarding the inclusion of ceilings in the prefabricated cottage. The learned trial Judge found that the appellant was not induced to execute the contract by reason of any statements as to the inclusion of a ceiling or material for a ceiling and that the appellant is bound by the contract which he signed. After a careful perusal of the evidence I can find no reason to disagree with the finding of the trial Judge in this respect and the appeal fails on this point.

As to the return of the sum of $1,000, it was contended by the appellant that this sum was a partial payment of the purchase-price and as such the appellant, upon the rescission of the contract was entitled to its return subject, of course, to any rights of the respondent to claim damages for the breach of contract. For the respondent it was argued first that the $1,000 payment was a deposit and as such was forfeited to the respondent when the appellant failed to complete the contract, and second, that even if the $1,000 payment were a part payment of the purchase-price the appellant having failed to complete the contract, the respondent was entitled to declare the contract rescinded and to retain as its own property all payments which had been up to that time made on account of the purchase-price.

The only authority in support of the latter proposition is to be found in the judgment of Bankes, L.J., in *Harrison v. Holland & Hannen & Cubitts Ltd.*, [1922] 1 K.B. 211 at pp. 212-3:

"This 100,000£ which the plaintiff seeks to recover was stated in the contract to be payable in advance on account of the purchase price. If nothing more had been said about it, as the contract came to an end in consequence of the purchasers' own default, neither they nor their assignee would have been able to get the money back."

This cannot be now taken as a correct statement of the law. It was pointed out in *Mayson v. Clouet*, [1924] A.C. 980 at pp. 986-7 that this remark was *obiter* and that the members of the Judicial Committee of the Privy Council, before whom the case was argued, thought the *dictum* of Bankes, L.J., to be unsound.

A proper statement of the law on this subject appears in *Benjamin on Sale*, 8th ed., p. 946: "And in ordinary circumstances, unless the contract otherwise provides, the seller, on rescission following the buyer's default, becomes liable to repay the part of the price paid." This statement was approved by Stable, J., in a judgment delivered in *Dies et al. v. British & Internat'l Mining & Finance Corp.*, [1939] 1 K.B. 724 at p. 743.

I do not consider that this case can be decided solely upon the fact that the contract was rescinded by the respondent upon the default of the appellant. Whether or not the appellant is entitled to the return of the $1,000, in the view I take of the case, depends upon whether the $1,000 was paid as a deposit or whether it was part payment of the purchase-price.

A useful summary of the law upon this point is to be found in the judgment of Finnemore, J., in *Gallagher v. Shilcock*, [1949] 2 K.B. 765 at pp. 768-9:

"The first question is whether the 200£ which the plaintiff buyer paid on May 17 was a deposit or merely a pre-payment of part of the purchase price. When money is paid in advance, it may be a deposit strictly so called, that is something which binds the contract and guarantees its performance; or it may be a part payment—merely money pre-paid on account of the purchase price; or, again it may be both: in the latter case, as was said by Lord Macnaughten in *Soper v. Arnold* (1889), 14 App. Cas. 429, 435: 'The deposit serves two purposes—if the purchase is carried out it goes against the purchase-money—but its primary purpose is this, it is a guarantee that the purchaser means business.' If it is a deposit, or both a deposit and prepayment, and the contract is rescinded, it is not returnable to the person who pre-paid it if the rescission was due to his default. If, on the other hand, it is part-payment only, and not a deposit in the strict sense at all, then it is recoverable even if the person who paid it is himself in default. That, I think, follows from *Howe v. Smith*, 27 Ch. D. 89, and from *Mayson v. Clouet*, [1924] A.C. 980, a case in the Privy Council. As I understand the position, in each case the question is whether the payment was in fact intended by the parties to be a deposit in the strict sense or no more than a part payment: and, in deciding this question, regard may be had to the circumstances of the case, to the actual words of the contract, and to the evidence of what was said."

As was stated by Lord Dunedin in *Mayson v. Clouet*, at p. 985: "Their Lordships think that the solution of a question of this sort must always depend on the terms of the particular contract." The contract between the appellant and the respondent should be critically examined to see if from it can be drawn the intention of the parties as to whether the $1,000 was to be a deposit or a part payment of purchase-price only.

. . . . .

The evidence indicates that on April 24, 1958, one O'Gorman, a salesman, brought to the office of the appellant printed forms which had been prepared by the respondent, apparently in quantities. It is to be assumed from the evidence that these forms were in blank when O'Gorman came to the appellant's office and that they were filled in during the course of his interview with the appellant. The pertinent part of the contract is contained in the lower left-hand portion of the printed form. As filled out by O'Gorman and signed by the appellant, this portion of the contract reads as follows:

"Please enter my/our order for the above cottage and additions for delivery as indicated. I/we agree to pay Colonial Homes Ltd. the sum of *$2,206.00, Twenty Two Hundred and Six $*   , Payment to be made as follows $1,000.00 as down payment with this order and the balance of funds *$1,206.00* as follows: *C.O.D.*"

The words and figures italicized were written in in handwriting the balance were printed [*sic*]. Below this appears the signature of the appellant, witnessed by O'Gorman. Immediately to the right of the foregoing on the printed form in a box headed "For Head Office Use Only", are the printed words "Order Approved", "Price Approved", "Deposit Rec'd", "Credit Approved". Although the blanks after these phrases have been filled in on ex. 6, the absence of anything following these words on ex. 2 indicates that this portion was entirely blank at the time it was signed by the appellant. It is to be noted that on the portion of the contract which was signed by the appellant, the $1,000 is described as down payment, while the word "deposit" is contained in the box which I have referred to as being to the right of the portion of the contract which was signed.

The fact that the word "deposit" was contained in the box headed "For Office Use Only" and that the blanks after the phrases in this box were not filled in at the time of the execution of the contract would, in my opinion, make it unlikely that the appellant's attention was ever directed to this portion of the contract in the box. Nor do I believe that what impression he gathered as to his obligations, when he signed agreeing to pay and paying a "down payment", can be determined from the presence of the printed word "deposit" in the box.

While, as I have said, if the $1,000 were paid as a deposit, it would not be recoverable by the appellant, no authority was quoted nor am I able to find any which hold that the use of the words "down payment" is sufficient to impose on the payment the characteristics of a deposit. Where, as in this case, the contract is in writing and has been made on a printed form, drawn for its own use and supplied by the respondent, there seems to be no room to imply any terms in it which are to give rights to the respondent which are not clearly intelligible to the ordinary laymen to whom the contract will be submitted for signature. It is one thing for a Court to be asked to place an interpretation on words which the parties have used either verbally or in correspondence in good faith and which, while understood in one sense by the seller, are to the buyer of average intelligence capable of another meaning. It is an entirely different matter when a skilled and experienced seller prepares for the use of the purchaser of his product, a document which would have been written in unambiguous language and could have contained an express statement calling to the attention of the prospective purchaser the right of forfeiture reserved by the seller with respect to any payment made on account of the purchase-price. If the seller chooses to use words of uncertain meaning when he could have removed all room for doubt by the use of more specific language, a Court should not be asked to imply terms for the benefit of the seller. If the respondent had intended to induce the appellant to enter into a contract and pay money under conditions whereby the money would have been forfeited in the event of default, it should have included the word "deposit" in its contract in place of the word "down payment" or it should have spelled out with some particularity the obligation which the appellant was undertaking by signing the contract. Having failed to do so, the Court should not be asked to interpret the contract in its favour unless the document is capable of no other meaning when read by a reasonably intelligent man.

Two passages in the judgment of Stable, J., in *Dies et al. v. British Internat'l Mining & Finance Corp.*, [1939] 1 K.B. 724, seem to be applicable to the facts of the present case. The first of these appearing at p. 742, is as follows:

"In the present case, neither by the use of the word 'deposit' or otherwise, is there anything to indicate that the payment of 100,000£ was intended or was believed by either party to be in the nature of a guarantee or earnest for the due performance of the contract. It was a part payment of the price of the goods sold and was so described."

And again at p. 743, after quoting with approval the statement from *Benjamin on Sale*, which has already been set out, the learned Judge goes on to say:

"If this passage accurately states the law as, in my judgment, it does where the language used in a contract is neutral, the general rule is that the law confers on the purchaser the right to recover his money, and that to enable the seller to keep it he must be able to point to some language in the contract from which the inference to be drawn is that the parties intended and agreed that he should."

I have no difficulty in coming to the conclusion that the $1,000 paid by the appellant on the execution of the contract was a part payment of purchase-price and that, even granting that the rescission of the contract has been brought about by the default of the appellant, the appellant is entitled to the return of his part payment, subject, of course, to the respondent's claim for damages for breach of contract.

In view of the right of the appellant to receive back the part payment, the respondent is entitled to recover on his counterclaim for damages for breach of contract. While some doubt may be raised by ex. 7 as to whether the sales commission payable by the respondent is to be calculated on the quantum of the contract price or the cash receipt, the only evidence before the Court is that tendered on behalf of the respondent in which it claims that it is liable to pay the full commission of the 13½%; based on the purchase-price of $2,298, being the amount as revised by the amending contract of May 6th, the total commission would be $310.23. In addition to this the respondent is entitled to the other items of damages for office expense, cost of reconverting material and loss of profit set out in his counterclaim, amounting in the aggregate, along with the commission, to $645.20.

I would allow the appeal and direct that the judgment below be varied by allowing the plaintiff's claim for $1,000 with costs and directing that judgment be entered for the defendant on its counterclaim in the sum of $645.20 with costs.

The success on the appeal being divided, there should be no costs of the appeal.

CASE PROBLEMS FOR DISCUSSION

Case 1

Henderson contacted a local refrigeration contractor with a view to obtaining an air-conditioner for use in the beverage-room of his hotel. He explained to the contractor that he wished to install a device that would not only cool the room, but remove tobacco smoke as well. The contractor described a number of room air-conditioners (for which he was the local distributor), and recommended a particular model which he indicated was adequate for a room the size of Henderson's beverage-room. Henderson entered into a contract for the model suggested by the contractor, and had the equipment installed.

After the equipment was put into operation, Henderson discovered that the equipment did an adequate job of cooling the room, but did not remove the smoke to any significant extent. He complained to the contractor, but the contractor was unable to alter the equipment to increase its smoke-removal capacity. When the contractor refused to exchange the air-conditioner for a larger model, Henderson refused to pay for the equipment. The contractor then brought an action against him for the amount of the purchase price.

Discuss the issues raised in this case, and indicate how a judge might decide the matter.

Case 2

Grant planned to spend his winter vacation at a ski resort in the Rockies. In preparation for the holiday, he purchased a new ski outfit from a local sports clothing merchant.

The first time that he wore his new ski outfit he noticed that his wrists had become swollen and irritated where the knitted cuffs of the jacket contacted his skin. He wore the jacket the second day, and found that after skiing for a short time, he had to return to the lodge because his wrists had again become badly irritated and had blistered.

Grant required medical treatment for the injury to his wrists, and the cause of the injury was determined to be a corrosive chemical that had been used to bleach the knitted cuffs of his jacket. The chemical was one that was normally used to bleach fabric, but from the evidence, it had not been removed from the material before the cloth was shipped to the manufacturer of the jacket. Neither the manufacturer nor the retailer were aware of the chemical in the cloth, and its existence could not be detected by ordinary inspection.

The injury to Grant's wrists ruined his holiday, and prevented his return to work for a week following his vacation.

Discuss the rights (if any) and liability (if any) of Grant, the sports clothing merchant, the manufacturer of the jacket, and the manufacturer of the cloth.

Case 3

In February, 1981, O'Flynn entered into negotiations with Emerald Isle Motors for the purchase of an automobile which had 4 000 miles registered on its odometer. The salesman referred to the automobile as a "recent model," but at no time was the model year discussed. The automobile apparently had had some use as a demonstrator, and the salesman offered the vehicle to O'Flynn at an attractive price. O'Flynn purchased the automobile, and found it to be most reliable and satisfactory.

Some six months later, a friend of O'Flynn informed him that his vehicle was not a 1981 model, but the previous year's model, which was virtually identical, except for some minor body ornamentation. O'Flynn immediately checked the vehicle serial number with the manufacturer, and discovered that it was in fact the previous year's model. He parked the vehicle in his garage and made no further use of it, even though he had driven it some 7 000 miles during the previous six months. He demanded the return of his purchase price from the seller.

When the seller refused to take back the automobile and return the purchase price, O'Flynn instructed his solicitors to institute legal proceedings for rescission of the contract.

Discuss the arguments that O'Flynn and Emerald Isle Motors might raise in this case, and render a decision.

Case 4

A wholesaler in Toronto agreed to sell 2 000 cases of walnut pieces to a buyer in Vancouver, the price to be 50¢ a pound, with delivery F.O.B. Toronto. The goods were shipped by common carrier in accordance with the buyer's instructions.

The goods were subject to moisture and freezing during transit, and the buyer, on inspection of the goods, found them unfit for his purposes. The goods were then sold by the buyer for 30¢ a pound in Vancouver, while the goods were still in the hands of the carrier. The carrier, however, in the meantime had found a buyer willing to purchase the 2 000 cases of walnuts at 40¢ a pound, but was unable to complete the sale because of the buyer's actions.

The Vancouver merchant later brought an action against the Toronto wholesaler and the carrier for his loss calculated at 20¢ a pound.

Indicate the nature of the plaintiff's claim in this action, and the defences that might be raised by the defendants. Render a decision.

Case 5

Brown, a university student, owned a small automobile which he desired to sell for $800. He placed an advertisement in the university newspaper offering the vehicle for sale, and included his telephone number for further information.

A few days later, he received a telephone call from a man who identified himself as Mr. Green. Green asked Brown a number of questions concerning the car, and then expressed a desire to examine the vehicle. A meeting was arranged for later that evening, and Brown gave Green the opportunity to test drive the automobile.

Green agreed to purchase the vehicle for $800, and offered Brown a personalized cheque bearing the name "R. Green" as payment. Brown was reluctant to accept the cheque without further identification, and suggested that the two men meet the next day at the bank to close the deal. Green explained that he would not be available for the next week or two, as he was leaving town on some business. Instead, he offered a driver's licence, and a number of credit cards bearing the name "R. Green" as evidence of his identity. He offered to leave his credit cards with Brown as security. With some hesitation and concern, Brown signed the blank motor vehicle registration, and handed Green the papers necessary to transfer the ownership. In return he received the cheque and the credit cards, which he agreed to hold until Green's return.

The next day, Brown presented the cheque at Green's bank, only to discover that the cheque had been forged. The customer of the bank whose name was "R. Green" had apparently lost his wallet some time before, and the wallet contained the cheque-book as well as the credit cards and licence.

In the mean time, the purchaser of the automobile, posing as Brown, sold the vehicle to Smith for $500 cash, and disappeared.

A few weeks later, Smith wrote a letter to Brown asking if he might have the owner's manual to the automobile, and at that point, Brown demanded the return of his vehicle. Smith refused to return the vehicle. He maintained that it was now registered in his name as a result of the transaction which, from his point of view, was a *bona fide* purchase from the person who possessed the registration documents for the automobile.

Brown brought an action against Smith for return of the automobile.

Discuss the points of law which are raised in this case, and indicate how the courts might decide the matter.

CHAPTER 23

Consumer Protection Legislation

HISTORICAL DEVELOPMENT

Laws protecting the consumer are not a new phenomenon. The State has always attempted to protect its constituents from both real and imaginary harm at the hands of unscrupulous merchants. Many of the early laws were concerned with the control of suppliers of food and clothing rather than durable goods, and reflected the particular concerns of the populace in the market-place at that time. Bakers in Paris, France, for example, were subject to inspection as early as 1260, and any bread which they produced which was of insufficient weight for sale was subject to confiscation and distribution to the poor folk in the city. How uniform weights were determined undoubtedly raised some difficulties for the bakers, but by 1439, under the reign of Charles VII, the problem was solved in part by an ordinance which required the municipal magistrates to designate a place where the weights were to be kept, and grain and flour weighed. By 1710, the consumer information movement was under way, with the bakers required to mark each loaf of bread with its weight. Again, any loaf which failed to correspond to the actual weight was confiscated, and the baker subject to a fine.[1] Similar consumer protection laws were placed on the statute books in England, and later in the colonies. They were the forerunners of present-day consumer protection legislation, and serve to remind us that consumer protection is not something unique to our modern consumer society.

Governments have seldom been reluctant to pass legislation governing the activities of parties to commercial transactions where the safety or the welfare of the citizenry were concerned, but consumer protection has been subject to varying degrees of emphasis by lawmakers throughout English history. Merchants were subject to much control during the guild period, and thereafter, during the 15th to 18th centuries to a somewhat lesser degree of control. The rise of *laissez-faire,* and the concept of a contract as a bargain struck between individuals, however, resulted in a shift to *caveat emptor* as a consumer rights philosophy.

During the 18th and early 19th centuries the "hands off" approach taken by the courts was to some extent justified. Merchandizing was still very much local in nature, and the sale of goods to consumers was, for the most part, by way of contracts between individuals with more or less equal bargaining power. This is not to say that the common law permitted deception and fraud to go unnoticed. Merchants who attempted to pass off goods that did not correspond to their description soon discovered that the courts permitted buyers to reject them, and in a similar fashion, goods that were not of merchantable quality or unfit for the use intended left the sellers open to buyer claims for damages. These common law consumer protection rules eventually were codified in the late 19th century in the *Sale of Goods Act.*[2] In addition, the courts' intolerance of fraud and deception proved to be a powerful consumer protection remedy where sellers acted improperly.

In general, the common law courts attempted to inject an element of fairness into contracts between buyers and sellers where bargaining power was relatively equal. What it did not do, however, was protect the careless buyer, as the courts saw (and to some extent still see) little reason why the law should do so.

Modern consumer protection legislation is essentially a response to changes in technology and marketing practice. The major changes in technology, manufacturing, and distribution that had their beginnings in the late 19th century brought with them fundamental changes in the sale of goods to consumers. To an increasing extent, throughout the first half of the 20th century, goods became more complex. New scientific advances spawned a vast array of durable goods for

---

[1] An interesting account of the development of the ordinances under which bakers in Paris were obliged to carry on business may be found in Montague, P., *Larousse Gastronomique,* (Crown Publishers Inc., 1961: N.Y.), pp. 78-80.

[2] The *Sale of Goods Act,* R.S.O. 1980, c. 462.

household uses, so complex that they were not easily understood and were not self-serviceable. As mechanical products became more technical, so too did the chances of breakdown and costly repairs. Concurrent with the development of new household goods was the widespread use of limited warranties and the use of exclusionary clauses to eliminate the warranty protection offered by the Sale of Goods Acts.

The change to large-scale manufacturing also removed the manufacturer from the immediate area where the consumer resided. It was no longer possible to seek out the maker for repairs, nor was it as important to the manufacturer to satisfy every consumer complaint. The retailer first provided the level of service required to satisfy consumers in order to protect his own reputation in the community, but as the high service retailers were forced to compete with the discount sellers of the late 1950s and the 1960s (who offered no after service), the situation changed. Service by retailers gradually declined, and with the decline, the frustrations of consumers mounted. When consumer complaints to manufacturers went unheeded, the consumers turned to the legislators for assistance.

Political response was not uniform throughout Canada, rather it reflected the major complaints of consumers in particular jurisdictions. In most provinces, the initial changes took the form of laws which prevented sellers from excluding the implied warranties of the *Sale of Goods Act* in contracts for the sale of consumer goods.[3] Other legislation, particularly in Western Canada, required manufacturers to provide parts and service for equip-

ment in the province, and in some provinces, to warrant that the equipment would last for a reasonable period of time in use.[4]

Concern for the safety of users of consumer products also resulted in legislation at both the federal and provincial levels in an attempt to protect consumers from products which had an element of hazard associated with their use. In addition, the 1960s and 1970s saw amendments to the *Combines Investigation Act* designed to control misleading advertising, double ticketing of consumer products, bait-and-switch selling, and a number of other questionable selling techniques.

During the same period, legislation was also introduced to deal with a number of other business practices that had developed with respect to credit reporting, credit selling, and selling door-to-door. All governments dealt with these problems, but unfortunately, not in a uniform fashion. As a result, considerable variation in consumer protection legislation exists in Canada today. The different laws, for the most part, have much the same general thrust in those jurisdictions where they have been introduced, and may be classified in terms of laws relating to product safety, laws relating to product quality and performance, laws relating to credit granting and credit reporting, and laws directed at business practices in general. Depending upon the nature of the protection required, the laws have generally taken five different approaches: (1) disclosure of information to the consumer, (2) expanded consumer rights at law, (3) minimum standards for safety, quality, and performance, (4) control of sellers and others by way of registration

---

[3]The *Consumers Protection Act*, R.S.O. 1980, c. 87.

[4]See, for example, the *Consumer Products Warranties Act*, R.S.S. 1978, c. 30.

or licensing of the activities and individuals, and (5) the outright prohibition of certain unethical practices. In many cases the legislation may employ two or more of these approaches to protect the consumer. For example, consumer credit-reporting organizations in Ontario and other jurisdictions must be licensed or registered and, in addition are subject to certain disclosure rules for consumer credit information. Since only licensed or registered organizations may carry on consumer credit-reporting activities, a failure to comply with the legislation could have as a consequence the loss of the license to carry on the activity. The various methods of control are examined in greater detail with respect to each of the different types of consumer protection legislation.

CONSUMER SAFETY

Common law remedies are available to consumers injured by defective goods where the seller or manufacturer owes a duty not to injure, but the rights arise only after injury occurs. Governments long ago were quick to realize that consumer protection from hazardous products or services, to be effective, must not only compensate for injury, but must contain an incentive for the manufacturer or seller to take care. Consequently, governments everywhere have generally controlled products injurious to the health of consumers, or imposed a duty on the manufacturer or seller of the product to warn the consumer of the hazards associated with the products' use or consumption.

In Canada, the provinces and the federal government have established legislation to control hazardous activities and products. The most notable legislation, however, has been passed at the federal level in the form of a number of statutes relating to consumer goods. These include the *Food and Drugs Act*,[5] and the *Hazardous Products Act*.[6] Some overlap exists between the two statutes with respect to false or deceptive labelling of products, but the intent of the legislation in each case is to protect the consumer from injury. Both are regulatory in part, and *quasi*-criminal in nature. The *Food and Drugs Act*, for example, does not confer a civil right of action as a result of a breach of the statute,[7] but instead, imposes strict liability and penalties under the Act where a breach occurs. A manufacturer, therefore, would be strictly liable in the case of false or deceptive labelling of a product.[8]

Both statutes are designed to enhance the public's safety. The *Food and Drugs Act* has, as a primary purpose, the control of harmful products that could cause injury or illness if improperly used or injested by consumers. Under the Act, many drugs are controlled in an effort to limit their possession and application to proper medical purposes. The legislation also safeguards the purity of food products, and regulates matters such as packaging and the advertisement of food and drug products.

The *Hazardous Products Act* takes a slightly different approach to consumer safety. As the name implies, it is concerned with hazardous products, and either prohibits the manufacture and sale of products of an extremely dangerous character, or regulates the sale of those

[5]The *Food and Drugs Act*, R.S.C. 1970, c. F-27.
[6]The *Hazardous Products Act*, R.S.C. 1970, c. H-3.
[7]See, for example, *Heimler v. Calvert Caterers Ltd.* (1974), 49 D.L.R. (3d) 36.
[8]*R. v. Westminster Foods Ltd.*, [1971] 5 W.W.R. 300.

which have the potential to cause injury. Hazardous products sold to the public are usually subject to regulation with respect to packaging, and must bear hazard warnings depending upon their particular nature. In addition to written warnings, most must depict the type of danger inherent in the product by way of warning symbols. Products which are stored under pressure, corrosive substances such as acids, and products which are highly flammable or explosive are required to have these warning symbols printed on their containers.

Some products are subject to special legislation at the federal level in an effort to protect consumers from injury. The *Motor Vehicle Safety Act*[9] provides for the establishment of safety standards for motor vehicles and vehicle parts, and for notice to consumers when unsafe parts or other defects are discovered through use or testing. Similar legislation applies to aircraft in Canada,[10] with elaborate testing procedures which must be undertaken and satisfied before the aircraft may be certified as safe to fly. The statute also governs the use and maintenance of all powered and non-powered aircraft in an effort to protect the public from injury. The Act not only deals with the safety of the product, but governs the qualifications and licensing of all persons associated with the flying or maintenance of aircraft, since safety is related not only to the maintenance of the product itself, but to the skills of those engaged in its use.

CONSUMER INFORMATION

Consumer information is closely related to both consumer safety, and consumer protection from deceptive or unfair practices. Because of this fact, much of the legislation designed to protect consumers is concerned with either the disclosure of information about the product or service, or the prohibition of false or misleading statements by sellers. Some laws, however, are designed to protect consumers by providing standards by which the consumer may make direct comparisons of products and prices. The *Weights and Measures Act*[11] is one such statute. It is designed to establish a uniform system of weights and measures throughout Canada which may be applied to all goods sold. The Act fixes the units of measure which may be lawfully used to determine the quantity of goods, and to calculate the price. The statute also provides for the testing and checking of all measuring devices used for such purposes.

A complementary statute at the federal level is the *Consumer Packaging and Labelling Act*[12] which, from a consumer protection point of view, has as its purpose the protection of the public from the labelling and packaging of products in a false or misleading manner.[13] The Act provides penalties for violation, but does not provide a civil cause of action for consumers misled by the false labelling. The right to damages for any injury suffered as a result of the misleading label, however (depending upon the circumstances), may be available at common law, or under one of the provincial statutes that provide for such a right of action.

CONSUMER PRODUCT QUALITY AND PERFORMANCE PROTECTION

The first action to protect consumers in the product performance area took the

---

[9]The *Motor Vehicle Safety Act*, R.S.C. 1970, c. 26 (1st Supp.), as amended by 1976-77, c. 19. Act in force as of January 1, 1971.
[10]The *Aeronautics Act*, R.S.C. 1970, c. A-3.

[11]The *Weights and Measures Act*, 1970-71-72 (Can.), c. 36.
[12]The *Consumer Packaging and Labelling Act*, 1970-71-72 (Can.), c. 41.
[13]*R. v. Steinbergs Ltd.* (1977), 17 O.R. (2d) 559.

form of consumer protection legislation to prohibit sellers from exempting sales of consumer goods from the implied conditions and warranties available under the *Sale of Goods Act*. While these moves helped to balance the rights of buyers with those of sellers at the point of sale, after-sale service and provision for repairs were not affected. The change also did nothing to provide persons who obtained consumer goods by way of gift with enforceable rights under the original sale agreement. Manufacturers of inferior goods continued to enjoy relative protection from consumer complaints through the rules relating to privity of contract, and for the most part, only the sellers were directly affected in actions for breach of contract. To overcome some of the difficulties faced by consumers, any redress in the balance of rights between buyers and sellers had to clearly come through new legislation directed at specific abuses in the marketplace.

A comparatively recent trend in consumer protection legislation has been towards the expansion of buyers' rights and sellers' obligations with respect to consumer goods that fail to deliver reasonable performance, or that prove to be less durable or satisfactory than manufacturer's claims indicate. New Brunswick[14] and Saskatchewan[15] have both passed legislation of this nature, and other provinces appear to be in the process of considering somewhat similar consumer protection.[16]

The Saskatchewan legislation, entitled the *Consumer Products Warranties Act*, sub- stantially alters the contractual relationship between the consumer and the seller by expanding the class of persons entitled to protection under the Act, and by imposing heavy burdens on sellers and manufacturers of consumer goods who fail to provide products capable of meeting advertised performance claims. The legislation applies to all sales of consumer goods, and in addition, many goods not normally considered to be products of a consumer nature.[17] It also covers used goods sold by "second-hand" dealers,[18] but permits dealers in used goods to exempt themselves from many of the obligations imposed on sellers under the Act if they expressly exclude the warranties at the time of the sale.[19]

The Act defines a consumer in a very broad way in order that not only the immediate purchaser of a consumer product, but also persons who subsequently acquire the goods may enforce statutory warranty rights under the Act. For example, persons who obtain consumer goods by way of gift or inheritance would be entitled to enforce a breach of a statutory warranty, even though no consideration was given to acquire the goods, and no direct contractual link existed between them and the seller. In order to achieve this end, the Act provides that a manufacturer may not claim a lack of privity of contract as a defence against a claim by an owner of goods where a breach of a warranty under the Act is alleged.[20]

The legislation sets out a number of statutory warranties that apply to all sales of consumer goods.[21] The majority of these resemble sections of the Sale of

[14]The *Consumer Product Warranty and Liability Act* (Bill 75) received final reading and Royal Assent on July 16, 1980.

[15]The *Consumer Products Warranties Act*, R.S.S. 1978, c. 30.

[16]The Province of Ontario introduced the *Consumer Products Warranties Act* in 1979 (Bill 110) but the Bill did not reach the third reading stage before the session ended.

[17]For example, certain goods used in agriculture and fishing.

[18]The *Consumer Products Warranties Act*, R.S.S. 1978, c. 30, s. 6.

[19]*Ibid.*, s. 6(2).

[20]*Ibid.*, s. 14.

[21]*Ibid.*, s. 11.

Goods legislation in most other provinces, and include a warranty that the retailer has the right to sell the goods, and that the goods are free from any liens or encumbrances. Included, as well are the usual sale of goods warranties as to fitness, etc. The legislation, however, goes beyond the usual types of warranties and includes a requirement that the goods be durable for a reasonable period of time. It also requires a warranty that spare parts and reasonable repair facilities will be available for a reasonable time after the date of the sale, if the product is one which normally may be expected to require repair.

In addition to the statutory warranties, the Act imposes the obligation on the seller to comply with any or all other warranties or promises for performance made either through advertising, writing, or statements made at the time of sale.[22] These statements or representations are treated as express warranties, and actionable in the event of breach.

The Act provides a number of different remedies, depending upon the nature of the breach, and includes exemplary damages as a remedy where the seller or manufacturer wilfully acts contrary to the statute.[23] In an effort to reduce litigation arising as a result of the Act, provision is made for mediation of disputes by officials of the Saskatchewan Department of Consumer Affairs,[24] and for binding arbitration where the parties agree to have the matter decided by an arbitrator.[25]

Consumers who wish to exercise rights under the Act are obliged to do so within a relatively short time after a breach occurs, and no action may be brought which alleges a violation of the Act unless it is commenced within two years after the alleged violation took place.[26] However, since the rights set out in the Act are in addition to any other rights which the person may have at law,[27] the time-limit may not affect the ordinary common law remedies available to the consumer.

While consumer groups have advocated similar legislation in all provinces, some concern has been expressed over the introduction of laws if they should vary from province to province. Uniform legislation has been urged upon the provinces if only to provide common consumer rights throughout the country. Whether other provinces heed this admonition remains to be seen.

CONSUMER PROTECTION RELATED TO BUSINESS PRACTICES
Itinerant Sellers

Door-to-door sellers have always presented a special problem for consumers due to the conditions under which the selling takes place. The door-to-door seller conducts business in the prospective buyer's home, and as a result, the sale is not initiated by the buyer, but rather by the seller. One of the particular difficulties with door-to-door selling is the fact that the buyer cannot leave the premises if the product is not what he needs or wants, and as a consequence, often feels uncomfortable or vulnerable. Under these circumstances, high-pressure or persuasive selling techniques may result in the buyer signing a purchase contract on impulse, or under pressure, simply to get rid of the seller.

[22]*Ibid.*, s. 8.
[23]*Ibid.*, s. 28.
[24]*Ibid.*, s. 31.
[25]*Ibid.*, s. 31.

[26]*Ibid.*, s. 30.
[27]*Ibid.*, s. 3.

While many products sold by door-to-door sellers are of high quality and sold by reputable firms, the selling practices of the less reputable eventually resulted in consumer demands to have this form of selling brought under legislative control. Most provinces, as a part of their consumer protection legislation, now require door-to-door sellers to be licensed or registered in order to conduct their selling practices, and to ensure compliance with the statute and regulations.[28] While variation exists from province to province, door-to-door sales are now usually subject to a "cooling-off" period after the purchase agreement is signed. During this period, the contract remains open to repudiation by the buyer without liability, and it is only after the cooling-off period has expired that a firm contract exists between the buyer and the seller.[29]

In addition to the imposition of a cooling-off period, the contract negotiated for the sale of goods by door-to-door sellers, if it exceeds a specified sum, must be in writing. It must also describe the goods sufficiently to identify them, provide an itemized price, and give a full statement of the terms of payment. If a warranty is provided, it must be set out in the agreement, and if the sale is a credit sale, a full disclosure of the credit arrangement, including details of any security taken on the goods, must be provided.[30]

The general thrust of consumer protection legislation of this nature is to nullify or eliminate the use of questionable selling techniques, and to provide sufficient information to the consumer to allow the consumer to review the agreement during the cooling-off period. By providing the consumer with the necessary information, and an opportunity to contemplate the transaction without the presence of the seller, the law encourages the buyer to make a rational buying decision.

Unfair Business Practices

Honest sellers, as well as consumers, suffer when questionable practices are used by unethical merchants to induce consumers to purchase goods. As a result, consumer protection legislation is frequently designed to not only protect the consumer, but to maintain fair competition between merchants in the marketplace. The Province of Ontario, for example, introduced a *Business Practices Act* in 1974[31] which sets out a list of activities deemed to be unfair practices. These activities include false, misleading, or deceptive representations to consumers as to quality, performance, special attributes, or approval that are designed to induce consumers to enter into purchases of consumer goods or services.[32] The Act also covers the negotiation of unconscionable transactions that take advantage of vulnerable consumers, or which result in one-sided agreements in favour of the seller. The kinds of transactions that are considered unconscionable include: (1) those which take advantage of physical infirmity, illiteracy, inability to understand the language, or which take advantage of the ignorance of the consumer; (2) those which have a price that grossly exceeds the value of similar goods on the market; and (3) those contracts in which the consumer has no reasonable probability of making payment of the obligation in full.[33] In addition, transactions

---

[28]For example, the *Consumer Protection Act*, R.S.O. 1980, c. 87, s. 4(1).
[29]*Ibid.*, s. 33.
[30]*Ibid.*, s. 31.

[31]The *Business Practices Act*, R.S.O. 1980, c. 55.
[32]*Ibid.*, s. 2(a).
[33]*Ibid.*, s. 2(b).

which are excessively one-sided in favour of someone other than the consumer, and those in which the conditions are so adverse to the consumer as to be inequitable, are treated in the same fashion. The same part of the Act treats misleading statements of opinion upon which the consumer is likely to rely, and the use of undue pressure to induce a consumer to enter into a transaction as unfair practices.[34]

The list of unfair practices is not limited to those set out in the Act, for the legislation provides that additional unfair practices may be prescribed by regulation. The general thrust of the law, however, is to eliminate the specified unfair practices, and the legislation provides that any person that engages in any of the enumerated practices commits a breach of the Act.[35] While fines are provided as a penalty, the most effective incentive to comply may be found in the sections of the Act which permit a consumer to rescind an agreement entered into as a result of the unfair practice, or to obtain damages where rescission is not possible.[36] The Act also provides that the courts may award exemplary or punitive damages in cases where the seller has induced the consumer to enter into an unconscionable or inequitable transaction.[37]

The director responsible for the administration of the Act has wide powers of investigation,[38] and may issue cease and desist orders to prevent repeat violations. An added penalty, where violations persist, is the right to cancel the registration of the seller if the seller is engaged in a business that requires registration or a licence to carry on the activity. Safeguards are included in the Act to prevent the arbitrary exercise of powers under the Act, and limitation periods are included. These require action on the part of the consumer within a relatively short period of time after an unfair practice occurs, if the consumer wishes to obtain the relief provided by the legislation.[39]

The Ontario *Business Practices Act* approach has been incorporated in part in the legislation of a number of other provinces, but again, the provinces have not made a concerted effort to establish uniform laws in the area of unfair business practices. At the federal level, however, certain practices have been dealt with under the anti-combines legislation which has nation-wide application.

Restrictive Trade Practices

The *Combines Investigation Act*[40] specifically prohibits false and misleading advertising with respect to both price and performance. Recent amendments to the Act also prohibit deceptive practices such as bait-and-switch selling techniques, referral selling, and the charging of the higher price where two price-stickers are attached to goods. Resale price maintenance and monopoly practices detrimental to the public interest are also prohibited. A more complete description of these consumer protection measures, and others relating to restrictive trade practices, are covered in the next chapter.

---

[34]*Ibid.*, s. 2(*b*).

[35]*Ibid.*, s. 3.

[36]*Ibid.*, s. 4(1).

[37]*Ibid.*, s. 4(2) provides for this form of penalty for unfair practices of the type found in s. 2(*b*) of the Act.

[38]*Ibid.*, ss. 10 and 11.

[39]The Act provides that steps to rescind the agreement must be taken by the consumer within six months of the date the transaction was entered into. See the *Business Practices Act*, R.S.O. 1980, c. 55, s. s.4(5), s. 4(5).

[40]The *Combines Investigation Act*, R.S.C. 1970, c. C-23, as amended by 1974-75-76, c. 76.

In most provinces, many business activities have been subject to licensing and special rules in an effort to control unfair practices that are contrary to the public interest. The sellers of securities, real estate and business brokers, mortgage brokers, motor vehicle dealers, persons dealing in hazardous products, to name a few, are groups that are often subject to laws regulating their activities and practices. By imposing a licensing requirement on the particular activity, compliance with the law becomes necessary in order to maintain the licence, and violations of the statute are accordingly minimized. As a result, most provinces provide for licensing or registration as a means of control of the particular activities in the public interest.

Collection Agencies

A particular business organization that has been singled out by most provinces for the purpose of consumer protection and control is the collection agency. Collection agencies play a useful role in the collection of debts, often from delinquent consumers, but many of their collection methods in the past aroused the ire of debtors. As a result of complaints to provincial governments, all provinces now regulate collection agencies by way of licences or registration, and their activities are subject to a considerable degree of control.[41]

In general, collection agencies are not permitted to harass or threaten the debtor in any way, nor are they permitted to use demands for payment that bear a resemblance to a summons or other official legal or court form. The legislation also prohibits the agency from attempting to collect the debt from persons not liable for the debt, such as the debtor's family, or from harassing persons other than the debtor in an effort to pressure the debtor into payment. As well, the agency is usually not permitted to communicate with the debtor's employer, except to verify employment, unless the debtor has consented to the contact. These are but a few of the limitations on collection techniques of the agencies, but they serve to indicate the attempts by the provincial legislatures to balance the legitimate rights of creditors to obtain payment with protection of the debtor from undue pressure to make payment. Again, the laws relating to this form of consumer protection lack uniformity, but in each case, the method of control of the activity remains similar. Agencies which persistently violate the Act may find that the province has revoked their licence to operate.

CREDIT GRANTING AND CREDIT REPORTING CONSUMER PROTECTION

The granting of credit by a lender or seller depends to a large extent upon the credit rating of the consumer who wishes to borrow, or the buyer who wishes to purchase goods on credit.

For many years, lenders of money and sellers of goods on credit were not obliged to disclose to the borrower or buyer more than a minimum amount of information concerning the credit extended, and even then, usually only in the form of the promissory note, mortgage, or other documents that secured or evidenced the actual loan or credit sale. In many cases, the borrower was unaware of the true cost of credit because the lender often made special charges for arranging or servicing the loan,

---

[41]The *Collection Practices Act*, 1978 (Alta.), c. 47; the *Collection Agencies Act*, R.S.O. 1980, c. 73.

and added these to the amount that the debtor was obliged to pay. The lack of information, together with the inability to fully understand the documents signed to secure the loan, left the debtor bewildered, and often at the mercy of the lender or seller.

The widespread use of consumer credit following the Second World War, along with consumer complaints, prompted a review of lending practices and credit selling by governments, and resulted in legislation which requires the lender or seller to disclose the true cost of credit to the borrower or credit buyer at the outset of the transaction. During the last two decades, virtually all provincial legislatures have established the requirement that the borrower be provided with a written statement which discloses the total dollar cost of credit, including any charges, bonuses, or amounts which the borrower must pay in addition to the interest, as well as the interest amount. The cost of the credit must also be displayed as an annual percentage rate.

The general thrust of the legislation is toward consumer credit in the form of consumer loans and credit purchases, and consequently, long-term financing such as housing or other substantial purchases which utilize a land mortgage as security are treated as exempt transactions in a number of provinces.[42]

The penalties imposed for a failure to comply with the disclosure requirements, unfortunately, vary from province to province, but generally the legislation prevents the lender from collecting the full amount of interest set out in the loan document. Some provinces prohibit the lender from claiming other than the principal amount

of the loan, one province limits the lender to an amount fixed by the courts if the lender should attempt to recover on the loan,[43] and another province limits the lender to the bank prime rate.[44]

Disclosure of a different nature which is nevertheless related to consumer credit is credit reporting. Credit reporting agencies for many years have provided an important service to lenders and credit sellers by supplying credit reports on borrowers or credit buyers. The widespread use of credit, coupled with the relatively impersonal nature of credit sales created a need for quick and accurate information about prospective debtors to enable the lender or seller to decide promptly if credit should be extended. Agencies providing this type of service keep files on persons using credit, and generally include in the file all information which might have an effect on a person's ability to pay. The information is usually stored in a computer, and through nation-wide hook-ups, credit reporting organizations are usually in a position to provide credit information on borrowers anywhere in the country on relatively short notice.

The potential for error, however, becomes greater as the amount of information on an individual increases, and concern over the uses made of the information, and its accuracy, have resulted in new laws designed to control the type and use of the collected information, and to enable the consumer to examine the information for accuracy. Once again, variation exists from province to province, but generally the laws are designed to license the consumer credit-reporting agen-

---

[42]All provinces except Alberta, British Columbia and Manitoba.

[43]*Credit and Loan Agreements Act*, R.S.A. 1970, c. 73, s. 15.

[44]The *Consumer Protection Act*, R.S.M. 1970, c. C-200, s. 25(1).

cies, and limit access to the information to those persons who have the consent of the debtor, or to persons with a legitimate right to obtain the information. The nature of the information stored or revealed is also usually subject to the proviso that it be the best reasonably obtainable, and that it be relevant. If a consumer credit-reporting agency has collected information on a person, it must permit the person to examine the file, and challenge or counter any inaccurate information by way of insertion of other information of an explanatory nature in the file. In most provinces, the agency must also provide the person with the names of all persons who received credit reports during a particular interval of time, although the specifics of this obligation vary from province to province.

Persons who intend to obtain credit reports usually obtain the prospective debtor's permission to do so, but this is not always necessary in all provinces. In many cases, the creditor need only inform the prospective debtor of his intention, and the name and address of the agency which he intends to use.[45]

Where credit is refused, or where credit charges are adjusted to reflect a poor credit rating, if the action is based upon a report received from a consumer credit-reporting agency, the creditor must generally so advise the person, and supply the name and address of the credit reporting agency. The purpose of this latter provision in the legislation is to enable the person refused credit the opportunity to determine if the report was inaccurate in any way, and take steps to correct it.

The law is enforced by way of penalties, but serious repeated violations may be dealt with by the revocation of the agency's licence to operate.

[45]See, for example, the *Consumer Reporting Act, 1973,* R.S.O. 1980, c. 89.

||||||||||||||||||||||||||||||||||||||||||||||||||||||||||||||||||||||||||||||||||||||||||||||||||||||||||||||||||||||||||

SUMMARY

Laws to protect consumers from deceptive or unfair business practices are not new. At common law, for example, a contract entered into as a result of misrepresentation, whether innocent or fraudulent, is voidable at the option of the injured party. In addition, the law of torts provides a remedy where a person is injured as a result of a breach of duty by the seller or manufacturer. The recent flood of legislation in Canada takes a different approach, and is designed to protect the consumer by regulations discouraging deception or unfair practices. The laws attempt to do this by way of penalties which may be imposed upon dishonest merchants who engage in such practices. The legislation also attempts to broaden the group of persons entitled to relief by protecting not only purchasers but the users or recipients of consumer goods as well.

The laws generally fall into a number of different classifications: those designed to protect consumers from hazardous or dangerous products, those designed to provide accurate and useful information, and to prohibit deception, and those designed to control activities associated with the actual sale of goods, such as credit and credit information services. Control is generally exercised by licencing persons engaged in the particular activities where such control is considered necessary, or by way of penalties for violation of the legislation where licensing is impractical or unworkable as a means of control.

Unfortunately, there is much overlap in the various statutes at the two levels of government, and a lack of uniformity in the approaches taken to consumer protection among the provinces themselves. As a result, in Canada, no uniform consumer protection legislation exists, and consumer rights and protection vary from province to province.

|||

DISCUSSION QUESTIONS

1. *What changes in the market-place resulted in consumer protection legislation with respect to durable goods?*
2. *How did the legislation deal with the practice of sellers providing only limited warranties?*
3. *What is the general thrust of much of the consumer protection legislation at the provincial level?*
4. *How are sellers generally "controlled" under many consumer protection laws?*
5. *Describe the unfair selling practices subject to the* Combines Investigation Act.
6. *Why does much of the legislation deal with consumer information? Give examples of the different kinds of information subject to consumer protection legislation.*
7. *Identify circumstances where* caveat emptor *still applies in spite of consumer protection legislation.*
8. *Assess the value of the Saskatchewan* Consumer Products Warranties Act. *Does it place too heavy an obligation on the seller?*
9. *What is the purpose of a "cooling-off" period in contracts negotiated between a door-to-door seller and a buyer?*
10. *Why was the control of collection agencies necessary? What practices conducted by some agencies resulted in legislation to curb their activities?*
11. *Describe the role of a credit-reporting agency in a consumer credit transaction. In what way might information supplied by a credit reporting agency be unfair to the consumer?*
12. *What protection does consumer reporting legislation provide for the consumer?*
13. *Explain the purpose of disclosure in a consumer credit transaction. What minimum information must normally be provided to the debtor?*
14. *"Consumer protection legislation has increased to the point where the seller has virtually become the insurer of his products. This appears to be the case because the standard which the courts apply is not that of the 'reasonable man,' but the 'village idiot.' " Discuss the validity of this observation.*

JUDICIAL DECISIONS

Food and Drugs Act Proscribing Sale of Contaminated Food—Civil Liability of Seller under Act—Liability at Common Law

Heimler v. Calvert Caterers Ltd. (1974), 49 D.L.R. (3d) 36.

The plaintiff attended a wedding reception, and after eating some of the food that was served, became ill. The illness was later diagnosed as typhoid fever. An investigation revealed that one of the employees of the defendant caterer was a carrier of the disease, and had handled the food on the day in question.

The plaintiff brought an action for damages against the defendant caterer.

STORTINI, CO.CT.J.:

In dealing with the issue of liability on this case three matters must be considered:

(1) Does the federal *Food and Drugs Act*, R.S.C. 1970, c. F-27, confer a cause of action on the plaintiff?

(2) Is the defendant guilty of negligence?

(3) If there is no negligence on the defendant, then apart from the *Food and Drugs Act*, is there strict liability on the part of the defendant?

Question one

Does the federal *Food and Drugs Act* confer a civil cause of action?

Section 4 reads as follows:

"4. No person shall sell an article of food that

(a) has in or upon it any poisonous or harmful substance;

(b) is unfit for human consumption;

(c) consists in whole or in part of any filthy, putrid, disgusting, rotten, decomposed or diseased animal or vegetable substance;

(d) is adulterated; or

(e) was manufactured, prepared, preserved, packaged or stored under unsanitary conditions."

The *Food and Drugs Act* is a *quasi*-criminal statute, and while such statutes are commonly used in the United States to create civil liability (see *Doherty v. S. S. Kresge Co.* (1938), 278 N.W. 437), I am not aware of any Canadian Court which has done so.

In Canada where the constitutional powers given by the *British North America Act, 1867*, are jealously guarded by both the federal and provincial Legislatures, it appears that a federal statute cannot confer a civil right of action.

In the case of *Wasney v. Jurazsky*, [1933] 1 D.L.R. 616, [1933] 1 W.W.R. 155, 41 Man. R. 46, the Manitoba Court of Appeal had this to say at p. 627:

"It is obvious that under our system of divided legislative jurisdiction sec. 119, although it can be referred to as setting up a standard of care which must be recognized in civil proceedings, gives no right of action to a person injured through its breach, and that if civil redress is sought the rights of the parties must be determined by common law rules. It hardly need be said that it is otherwise if the injury results from the violation of a duty imposed by a provincial statute for the benefit of the person injured, and that it is immaterial in such an instance whether the action brought therefor is in negligence or for breach of the enactment."

In the above case a 12-year-old boy was injured by a bullet which was sold to him by the defendant contrary to the *Criminal Code*. Although the *Code* did not confer a civil cause of action, its provisions were relevant in an ensuing negligence action, and may be used by the Court to establish a conclusive standard of care therein.

In an article by E. R. Alexander entitled "Legislation and the Standard of Care in Negligence", found in 42 *Can. Bar Rev.* 243 (1964), the author approves of the view taken in the *Wasney* case, and takes the position that the Court may look to the purpose of the enactment. If the purpose is to protect a class of persons of which the plaintiff is one, the defendant's breach of the *Criminal Code* provision should be relevant in the negligence action. The Court may also consider the nature of the class protected by the *Criminal Code* provision and the seriousness of the harm contemplated by the *Code* in determining the extent to which the negligence applies.

In my view, the provisions of the *Food and Drugs Act* fail to be treated in the same manner as the protective provisions of the *Criminal Code*.

In answer to Q. 1, above, I find that the federal *Food and Drugs Act* does not confer a civil right of action to the plaintiff because of the inherent constitutional difficulties referred to, although, as it has been suggested, the provisions of the federal statute may be relevant in establishing a standard of care in the civil action.

It is clear that provincial statutes may create civil causes of action: see *Shandloff v. City Dairy Ltd. et al.*, [1936] O.R. 579, [1936] 4 D.L.R. 712, and *Grant v. Australian Knitting Mills Ltd. et al.*, [1936] A.C. 85.

In the *Shandloff* case, a vendor was held liable for breach of the *Sale of Goods Act* because the product was not fit for the purpose intended and not of merchantable quality. The defendant had sold to the plaintiff a bottle of milk containing pieces of glass.

In the case of *Lockett v. A. & M. Charles, Ltd.*, [1938] 4 All E.R. 170, a restaurant had served food to the plaintiff who subsequently became ill. The Court found that the food was unfit for human consumption and held for the plaintiff on the basis there was a breach of an implied warranty that the food was so fit.

Question two
Is the defendant guilty of negligence?

The evidence clearly establishes that at all material times Mrs. I was a servant of the defendant and acting in the course of her employment. Under the doctrine of *respondeat superior* the defendant is vicariously liable for any negligence on her part.

The defendant is in the food catering business. The duty of care resting upon it is similar to that imposed upon a restaurant. Generally, the law of negligence requires a restaurant operator to exercise a care proportionate to the serious consequences which may result from a lack of care. He is necessarily bound to ensure that the food prepared and served by him is fit for human consumption and may be eaten without causing sickness or endangering life by reason of its condition. The standard of care is to use the same degree of care in the preparation of food as would be exercised by a reasonably prudent person skilled in the art of preparing food. It has also been said that the standard of care would be the same care as a person would use in preparing his own food.

A reasonably prudent restaurateur or caterer ought to anticipate the presence of foreign and potentially dangerous substances in his food. In this case the defendant's servants were aware of the necessity of proper washing of hands after using the toilet. A sign to this effect was posted on the premises. The foreseeable risk of harm was transmission of germs, and the remedy was as simple as it was inexpensive, *i.e.*, a careful washing of the hands.

The duty of a restaurateur or caterer is no less than the duty imposed upon a manufacturer of goods. In the *Shandloff* case, the defendant could have foreseen the possibility of the breakage of glass and that chips of glass would be inherently dangerous to consumers of the contents of the bottle. It is to be noted that the defendant in the *Shandloff* case had the most advanced equipment on the market at the time and contended, therefore, that they did everything possible to prevent glass and other objects from contaminating the milk. At p. 591 O.R., p. 720 D.L.R., Middleton, J.A., responded to the contention, as follows: "The utmost care was used but that care apparently was not sufficient. . . . Some employee did blunder."

Although the *Shandloff* case is a "manufacturer's liability" case, it is similar to the case at bar in many ways. The defendant and its servants certainly appreciated the risk concerning the non-washing or improper washing of hands. I mentioned the existence of the sign and the monthly public health inspections. The defendant and its servants, and in particular Mrs. I, may not have specifically directed their minds to the possibility of contamination of the food by typhoid germs, however, certainly they contemplated and appreciated the risk of harm of spreading germs through improper hygienic habits. Such germs are incapable of inspection by the contemplated consumer and are, therefore, all the more dangerous. A consumer can examine the product he is eating but, of course, the harmful substances are microscopic in size and preclude effective inspection by the consumer. The defendant in this case cannot be relieved of his duty to take reasonable care to ensure that harmful substances have not contaminated his food by any contention that the plaintiff had the opportunity to inspect the food prior to consumption.

The defendant's servant contaminated the food with the typhoid germs she was carrying and the plaintiff contracted typhoid fever as a result of consuming the food. This contamination resulted from the failure of the servant to wash her hands, or cleanse her hands by washing her hands with warm water and soap, after using the toilet on March 19, 1971.

The servant in question testifies that she always washes her hands. However, the contamination did occur, and based on Dr. Hoskings criteria for contamination set out above, it can be reasonably inferred that on this particular occasion she failed to cleanse her hands and in the words of Middleton, J.A., in the *Shandloff* case, "Some employee did blunder."

The washing and cleansing of one's hands in the food preparation industry is one of basic importance and certainly is stressed by public health officials and the industry alike. The patron of a restaurant or the guest at a wedding reception has the right to expect that all reasonable health precautionary measures are carried out and that the food served to him will be of high quality, well prepared, and free from any contaminating germs.

Therefore, the answer to Q. 2 is "yes".

Question three—strict liability

In view of my finding of negligence it is not necessary for me to adjudicate on the issue of strict liability. I have, however, examined some leading United States cases on this issue, as follows: *Greenman v. Yuba Power Products Inc.* (1962), 377 P. 2d 897; *Levy v. Horn & Hardart Baking Co.* (1931), 157 A. 369; *Meshbesher v. Channellene Oil & Mfg. Co.* (1909), 119 N.W. 428; *Doherty v. S. S. Kresge Co.* (1938), 278 N.W. 437; *Kenower v. Hotels Statler Co. Inc.* (1942), 124 F. 2d 658; *Community Blood Bank Inc. v. Russell* (1967), 196 So. 2d 115.

The American Law Institute, *Restatement of the Law, Second, Torts 2d* (1965), vol. 2, §402A, p. 351, comment 9, defines a defective product as one which is "in a condition not contemplated by the ultimate consumer, which will be unreasonably dangerous to him".

It appears that in the past 10 years a majority of the Courts in the United States have imposed strict liability on the servers of food: see Prosser, *Handbook of the Law of Torts*, 4th ed. (1971), at pp. 638, 653.

In summary, there is no doubt in my mind that the defendant in this case would be held strictly liable in the United States. The Canadian jurisprudence has not yet developed to this extent and the law still proceeds on the basis of negligence, using the doctrine of *res ipsa loquitur* to assist the plaintiff in overcoming evidentiary burdens. The breach of the *Food and Drugs Act* because of the constitutional dichotomy of powers does not confer a civil cause of action upon the plaintiff, although the breach of the statute is important in determining the standard of care.

Having found negligence on the part of the defendant, there will accordingly be judgment for the plaintiff against the defendant for $3,283.33 and costs.

Misleading Label on Product— R. v. Westminster Foods Ltd., [1971] 5 W.W.R. 300.

The defendant made a false statement on the label of its margarine product.

Violation of Food and Drugs Act

GILES, PROV.CT.J.:

I want briefly to comment on the governing legislation. The Food and Drugs Act sections and Regulations pertinent to the charge are, in my view, unquestionably prohibitive and mandatory in character. The word "shall" is used throughout. As an example, s. 5(1) of the Food and Drugs Act contains the following statement:

"(1) No person *shall* label . . . any food in a manner that is false, misleading or deceptive . . . regarding its character . . . composition, merit . . ."

Subsection (2) of s. 5 states:

"(2) An article of food that is not labelled or packaged as required by the regulations, or is labelled or packaged contrary to the regulations, *shall be deemed* to be labelled or packaged contrary to subsection (1)."

Section 25 states as follows:

"25. Every person who violates any of the provisions of this Act or the regulations is guilty of an offence . . ."

Regulation B-09020 also states:

"No person *shall* . . . on a label of a food make any statement regarding . . . fatty acid or cholesterol content of the food except as provided in Section B-09021." (The italics are mine.)

And further, the requirement in Reg. B-09021 that the percentage be based as indicated in subs. (b) of the Regulation implies a prohibition that the percentage not be calculated in any other manner.

All pertinent sections of the Food and Drugs Act and Regulations thereunder were gazetted and in force prior to the date of the offence. Judicial notice must be taken of them, in my view, and no further notice is required to those who may be affected by them.

Therefore, those who act knowingly or otherwise in violation of the said sections and Regulations do so at their peril and, in so acting, commit an offence.

The principal defence is lack of knowledge and the absence of mens rea.

From time to time the Director of the Food and Drugs Act has sent out trade information letters but is under no obligation to do so. The defendant company received some, if not all, of these letters. I would be inclined to think that correspondence and delivered literature were sufficient to bring to the attention of the defendant the "acceptable method" of testing its products; however, I make no finding on this point as I am able to decide this case without doing so.

With reference to the question of mens rea, I refer to *Regina v. Allied Towers Merchants Ltd.*, [1965] 2 O.R. 628, [1966] 1 C.C.C. 220, 46 C.P.R. 239. This is a decision of the Ontario High Court. I am reading from the headnote [C.C.C.] which briefly summarized the proposition set out therein:

"The offence of making a materially misleading misrepresentation to the public for the purpose of promoting the sale of an article contrary to s. 33C(1) [rep. & sub. 1960, c. 45, s. 13] of the *Combines Investigation Act*, R.S.C. 1952, c. 134, is one of strict liability and does not require *mens rea*, and if a misrepresentation is in fact materially misleading, the Crown does not have to prove that the accused knew it to be so. In this type of case, the Legislature intends that the maker of the representation should take the risk and that the public should be protected . . ."

In the *Allied Towers* case the prohibition had to be found by necessary implication. A fortiori, in the case at bar, where all the applicable legislation is clearly prohibitive and imposes a strict liability, I am unable to accept the defence contention, therefore, that mens rea is a necessary ingredient of this offence.

I therefore find that the defendant, Westminster Foods Ltd., did label its products in violation of Reg. B-09021, thereby committing an offence under the Food and Drugs Act, and in so doing, caused the said labels to be misleading regarding the character, composition, and merit of the food products in question.

I therefore find the defendant company guilty on Counts 1 and 2 of the information as charged.

Product Labelling— Error in Operation of Labelling Machine— Company Employing Elaborate Training Scheme to Avoid Error— Liability

R. v. Steinberg's Ltd. (1977), 17 O.R. (2d) 559.

HARRIS, PROV.CT.J.:

The basic allegations of the Crown are easily ascertained from the charges as set forth in the two informations, which read as follows:

"(1) On or about the 4th day of August, 1976, at the Municipality of Metropolitan Toronto in the Judicial District of York, unlawfully did being a dealer, sell a prepackaged product to which was applied a label containing a false and misleading representation relating to the said product, to wit: a prepackaged product containing a portion of Bottom Round to which was applied a label describing the contents as being "SIRLOIN TIP" contrary to Section 7, subsection (1) of the Consumer Packaging and Labelling Act, Statute of Canada 1970-71-72, Chapter 41, thereby committing an offence under Section 20, subsection (1)(a) of the said Act.

"(2) On or about the 9th day of September, 1976, at the Municipality of Metropolitan Toronto in the Judicial District of York, unlawfully did being a dealer, sell a prepackaged product to which was applied a label containing a false and misleading representation relating to the said product, to wit: a prepackaged product containing a Shoulder Steak to which was applied a label describing the contents as being "BEEF SIRLOIN", contrary to Section 7, subsection (1) of the Consumer Packaging and Labelling Act, Statute of Canada 1970-71-72, Chapter 41 thereby committing an offence under Section 10, subsection (1)(a) of the said Act."

. . . . .

The relevant sections of the *Consumer Packaging and Labelling Act* (enacted 1971 and proclaimed March 1, 1974) are as follows:

. . . . .

"7(1) No dealer shall apply to any prepackaged product or sell, import into Canada or advertise any prepackaged product that has applied to it a label that contains any false or misleading representation relating to or that may reasonably be regarded as relating to that product.

"(2) For the purposes of this section "false or misleading representation" includes

(a) any representation in which expressions, words, figures, depictions or symbols are used, arranged or shown in a manner that may reasonably be regarded as qualifying the declared net quantity of prepackaged product or as likely to deceive a consumer as to the net quantity of a prepackaged product;

(b) any expression, word, figure, depiction or symbol that implies or may reasonably be regarded as implying that a prepackaged product contains any matter not contained in it or does not contain any matter in fact contained in it; and

(c) any description or illustration of the type, quality, performance, function, origin or method of manufacture or production of a prepackaged product that may reasonably be regarded as likely to deceive a consumer as to the matter so described or illustrated.

· · · · ·

LABELS

"10. Each label containing a declaration of net quantity of the prepackaged product to which it is applied shall

(a) be applied to the prepackaged product in such form and manner as may be prescribed; and

(b) in such form and manner and in such circumstances as may be prescribed show

(i) the identity and principal place of business of the person by or for whom the prepackaged product was manufactured or produced for resale,

(ii) the identity of the prepackaged product in terms of its common or generic name or in terms of its function, and

(iii) such information respecting the nature, quality, age, size, material content, composition, geographic origin, performance, use or method of manufacture or production of the prepackaged product as may be prescribed.

· · · · ·

"21(1) In any prosecution for an offence under this Act it is sufficient proof of the offence to establish that it was committed by an employee or agent of the accused whether or not the employee or agent is identified or has been prosecuted for the offence, unless the accused establishes that the offence was committed without his knowledge or consent and that he exercised all due diligence to prevent its commission."

After hearing the evidence adduced on behalf of the accused, I am satisfied beyond a reasonable doubt that the accused has established that each offence was committed without its knowledge or consent, and that the accused exercised all due diligence to prevent its commission.

It will be sufficient to detail the facts and evidence in one of the cases—it was agreed by counsel that the facts in the other were substantially similar. The packager employed by the accused had been packaging "top sirloin" and had been printing labels with the price and name thereof to be affixed to the package. When she was about to package "bottom round" she changed the price setting on the label printing machine (in fact, the price for bottom round, being a lower price than for top sirloin), but inadvertently forgot to change the printing "slug" which contained the name of the cut.

Defence evidence established the following precautions by the accused corporation, designed to avoid what in fact happened here: an elaborate scheme of employee training and education as to governmental regulations and requirements, and compliance therewith—this included manuals, oral expositions, direct discussions with affected personnel both as individuals and at group meetings; an on the job site inspection scheme, designed to accustom every employee concerned with the marketing of meat to inspect the meat counter at regular and irregular intervals—even directors and senior "head office" personnel of the company were instructed as to this, as of course were store managers, meat managers and meat packers. In my opinion, the accused company, having devised and put into operation this scheme (above outlined by me only in the barest of detail) exercised thereby all due diligence to prevent the occurrences which took place in the cases at bar. To require the steps taken by the company to absolutely prevent these occurrences under any circumstances whatsoever would go beyond "due" diligence, and would make the company a virtual "insurer" against any error. I do not think that was the intention of the legislation; the words "all due diligence" import an area of precaution sufficient to prevent the foreseeable, but not the unforeseen, the unexpected, the unknown, or the unintended. It is clear to me on the evidence that what the meat packers did and what followed therefrom (the putting out for sale and the actual sale of the offending prepackaged products) was without either the knowledge or consent of the accused. I respectfully disagree with the Crown's contention that no diligence, due or otherwise, could protect the accused. The saving "unless" clause at the end of s. 21(1) indicates to me that this is not an absolute liability offence.

Section 21(1) does raise one different problem in my mind. My inclination was that the section did not deal with possible defences, but rather with modes of proof—that is, if the "unless" clause was established by the accused, the Crown could not rely only on proof of the commission of the offence by an employee or agent of the accused. Since both Crown counsel and counsel for the accused appeared to agree that the "unless" clause, if established, was a complete defence, I do not pursue this matter further at this time. In any event, the Crown offered no other proof of the commission of the offence.

I am, therefore, of the opinion that the Crown has failed to prove the charges against the accused beyond a reasonable doubt. . . .

‖‖

CASE PROBLEMS FOR DISCUSSION

Case 1

Green was employed by an aircraft maintenance and repair company to repair and modify aircraft airframes and interiors. Green possessed the necessary Department of Transport licences to perform the type of work for which he was engaged. Since much of the work involved metal repair and refinishing, a certain amount of the work consisted of grinding and polishing, using power grinders and finishers.

While engaged in the grinding of a metal seat bracket in a large jet aircraft, Green decided to change grinding wheels on his power grinder in order to speed up the shaping of the part. He replaced the fine grit wheel on his grinder with a coarse grit wheel that bore the following warning on the package: "DO NOT USE AT MACHINE SPEEDS IN EXCESS OF 6 000 RPM."

Brown, a fellow employee, picked up the grinder after Green had completed the grinding work on the seat bracket, and began the grinding of a part of the wing assembly. He set the machine speed first at 5 000 rpm, but later increased the speed to 9 000 rpm, a common grinding speed. No sooner had the speed increased when the grinding wheel disintegrated, causing injury to Brown and a nearby worker.

What consumer protection issues are raised by this incident? What rights (if any) would Brown have at law?

Case 2

Hamlish admired a used car which Honest Harry had on display at his car-lot. Hamlish took the car for a test drive, and found the vehicle to be ideal for his purposes. When he inquired about the previous owner, the salesman told him that it was his understanding that the last owner was an elderly school teacher, who usually used the automobile only on week-ends. The odometer on the automobile indicated that the vehicle had been driven only 30 000 miles.

Hamlish purchased the automobile, but discovered a few months later that the vehicle had been used as a taxi before it was purchased by the school teacher. The automobile in effect had been driven 100 000 miles further than the odometer indicated, as it registered only five digits before returning to zero—the true distance that the vehicle had been driven was 130 000 miles.

The automobile had given Hamlish no trouble during the time he had owned it, and he had driven the vehicle over 3 000 miles. He was annoyed, however, that the machine had had so much use, even though it still had a "like-new" appearance.

Hamlish brought an action for rescission of the contract when Honest Harry refused to take back the automobile and return the purchase price.

Discuss the argument that each party might raise in this case. Render a decision.

Case 3

Harvey purchased two pounds of ground meat from Alice's Meat Market. The package was labelled "ground lean beef" and had been located in a freezer under a sign which advertised "Special sale: $1.99 for 2 lbs."

Harvey's friend, who was a meat inspector at a local packing house, dropped by for a visit while he was preparing to barbeque patties made from the ground meat. His friend examined the meat and advised Harvey that in his opinion the meat was not ground lean beef, but ordinary "hamburg" that contained close to 40% fat.

Harvey checked with Alice's Meat Market, and was told that a clerk had mislabelled the meat as ground lean beef, and that the meat was actually hamburg. The special sale, however, was for hamburg at two pounds for $1.99.

Discuss the issues raised in this case, and the legal position of Harvey and of Alice's Meat Market.

Case 4

Carter carried on a part-time business of lending money to his friends to enable them to purchase consumer goods. He would also lend money to strangers who had been directed to him by his friends. The loans were generally for a short term, and written up in a casual way. Usually the document set out the name of the party and referred only to the principal amount borrowed and the lump-sum interest amount payable on the due date.

On March 1st, John Doe approached Carter in order to borrow $800 for the purchase of a stereo system. Carter loaned him the money, and had him sign a document which read as follows:

March 1, 19__.

I promise to pay S. Carter on the first day of each month the sum of $200 until the total amount of $1 000 has been paid.

$800   principal
$200   interest
$1 000

Value received
"J. Doe"

A few weeks later, Doe advised Carter that he had no intention of paying him the money, as the paper he signed was worthless, and the debt unenforceable.

Advise Carter and Doe. What issues (if any) might arise if Carter should decide to institute legal proceedings against Doe?

Case 5

John Smith lived at 221 Pine Ave. in a large city. He had no debts, and had never previously purchased goods on credit. He did, however, wish to purchase a particular power boat, and entered into negotiations with the owner of a marina to obtain the boat on credit. He consented to the marina owner making a credit check before the transaction was completed, and was dismayed when the marina owner refused to proceed with the transaction because he was a "poor credit risk."

The credit reporting agency apparently had provided a credit report on a John Smith who some months before had resided at 212 Pine St. in the same city, and who had defaulted on a number of substantial consumer debts. John Smith knew nothing of the other John Smith, nor had he resided at 212 Pine St.

What avenues are open to John Smith in this case to rectify the situation?

Case 6

Mary Dwight purchased a vacuum cleaner from a salesman who represented himself as a sales agent for Speedy Vacuum Cleaners. The salesman gave a demonstration of the vacuum in Mary's living room, and the machine appeared to do an excellent job of cleaning dust and dirt from her carpets. At the conclusion of the demonstration, the salesman produced a form contract which called for a deposit of $50, and monthly payments of $50 each until the full purchase price of $400 was paid. Mary paid the $50 deposit, and signed the contract. Later that day, the salesman delivered the new vacuum to her residence. On his departure, he stated that he was certain that Mary would find the vacuum satisfactory, as the particular model was "the finest model which the company had produced."

The machine did operate in a satisfactory manner for some seven months, then one day while Mary was using the vacuum to clean her automobile, she noticed a wisp of black smoke seeping from a seam in the casing. She immediately unplugged the machine and threw it in the swimming-pool.

A few minutes later she retrieved the machine from the pool, and returned it to the Speedy Vacuum Cleaner store. The repair man examined the machine, and explained to her that the smoke had been caused by the melting of a small electrical part in the machine. He offered to replace the part free of charge even though the six-month written warranty had expired, but refused to provide free replacement for several other electrical parts that had been damaged by the machine's immersion in the swimming-pool. The cost of repairs amounted to $80, and Mary paid the account. At the end of the month, however, she refused to make the final $50 payment under the purchase agreement, because she felt that the company should cover at least a part of the cost of the repairs to the machine.

Eventually, the company brought an action against her for the $50 owing under the purchase agreement.

Discuss the defences (if any) that Mary might raise in this case, and indicate the possible outcome.

CHAPTER 24

Restrictive Trade Practices

INTRODUCTION

The law relating to restrictive trade practices is based upon the premise that the forces of competition and the free market should regulate industry, rather than governments or dominant members of the business community. As a consequence, both the common law and restrictive trade practices legislation have as their main thrust the preservation or protection of competition. Only those activities which tend to restrict or interfere with competition are controlled by the law, and industry is left to regulate itself by the market forces which are created by the free enterprise system.

Restrictive trade practices were originally governed by the common law, and all restraints of trade that were considered unreasonable or contrary to the public interest were actionable at law. The common law, unfortunately, was not adequate to ensure that the forces of competition remained free from manipulation by those in industry who possessed substantial economic power, and protection of competition (in the form of legislation) was necessary.

Presently, some restrictive trade practices remain subject to the common law, but most of the control of anti-competition activity is now found in the *Combines Investigation Act*.[1] The law, in general, prohibits combinations or conspiracies that prevent or lessen competition unduly, mergers or monopolies which are likely to operate to the detriment of the public, and a number of unfair trade practices such as resale price maintenance, price discrimination, discriminatory promotional allowances, false advertising, and bid-rigging. Recent amendments to the Act have dealt with services as well as products, and have introduced a number of "reviewable activities."

The current law represents an attempt by government to eliminate those forces which interfere with free competition and thereby minimize the need for direct government regulation of activities in the market-place. The regulation of business or trade is not new, however; governments have always, since the beginning of trade and commerce, maintained some degree of control over business activity, either directly through regulation or, indirectly, through the creation of an environment which allows other controls to regulate the activity. The general thrust of anti-combines legislation falls into the lat-

ter category, and, therefore, represents a means of control of industry and trade by way of prohibition of only those activities which interfere unduly with free enterprise.

This philosophical approach was not always taken towards trade and commerce. The history of the law respecting business activity was, until comparatively recent times, largely one of close control and regulation either by governments or organizations that were virtual monopolies. Early trade and commerce in England was subject to a great deal of legislative control by guilds, which were usually established under Royal Charter. The guilds controlled entry to the various trades or crafts, and generally set the prices for work done and goods sold. In most cases, the members of the guild enjoyed monopoly rights to the trade, and any person who wished to engage in a particular trade or business was obliged to belong to the guild which pertained to that craft.

Regulation of business activity also took the form of direct legislative control. The Great Plague that swept through Europe and England in the mid-14th century prompted the government of the day to pass legislation controlling workers' wages, and the prices which they might charge for their services or goods. Similar statutes designed to control or prohibit a wide range of business activities were not uncommon. Changes, however, came about with the development of trade and the gradual growth of commerce; the most significant change took place at the beginning of the industrial period in England when the country adopted the philosophy of *laissez-faire*. Adam Smith's

---

[1]The *Combines Investigation Act* R.S.C. 1970, c. C-23, as amended by 1974-75-76, c. 76.

views of competition and its benefits were embraced by the courts and the populace, and restraint of trade at common law became *prima facie* void, unless circumstances could justify some "reasonable restraint." In general, the law as a matter of public policy prohibited any unjustified interference with a person's right to trade, and all conspiracies to wilfully injure persons in their business became actionable at law.

Early unions of workers were treated as combinations or conspiracies in restraint of trade, and remained so until the latter part of the 19th century. However, actionable conspiracies at common law were not confined to workers regarding their dealings with their employers because the courts disapproved of most conspiracies and combinations which restrained or interfered with trade. A general rule gradually developed which held that any conspiracy which was not designed to further the interests of a trade, but to deliberately injure a party engaged in the trade would be actionable at common law. Any conspiracy to induce a person to break a contract relating to trade would also be actionable.

While it was not unlawful at common law for an owner of a business to purchase a competitor's business, and lessen competition accordingly, the development of large trusts and businesses which had acquired monopoly powers did alarm the legislatures in the United States and Canada in the late 19th century. In both of these countries, the adverse effects on the public of large-scale business acquisitions

by investment trusts, and the vertical integration of business activities which gave particular firms virtual monopolistic power over the supply of goods and services, prompted legislative action. The response by the governments took the form of the *Sherman Act*[2] in the United States, and a statute in Canada which prohibited any combination or conspiracy which had the effect of limiting competition unduly in a trade or manufacture.[3]

The new Canadian legislation was essentially criminal law in nature, and made the conspiracy or combination an offence punishable on conviction. The statute became the foundation of restrictive trade practices legislation, and still remains today as the core of the present Act. When the *Criminal Code* of Canada was enacted in 1892,[4] the restrictive trade practice legislation was incorporated in it as a part of the criminal law.

The protection of the public was further extended in 1897 by an amendment to the *Customs Tariff Act*[5] which permitted the investigation of combinations which unduly enhanced the prices of goods at the expense of the general public, and allowed for an adjustment of tariff rates where the practice was confirmed.

In 1910, legislation was enacted which provided for the investigation of combinations in restraint of trade by a commission, and for the imposition of penalties

[2]The *Sherman Act*, 26 Stat. 209, as amended 15 U.S.C. §§1 and 2.
[3]"An Act for the Prevention and Suppression of Combinations Formed in Restraint of Trade," 1889 (Can.), c. 41.
[4]The *Criminal Code*, 55-56 Vict., c. 29.
[5]The *Customs Tariff*, 60-61 Vict., c. 16.

where the Act was contravened.[6] The Act was revised in 1923 to provide for a different form of organization and inquiry, and to provide for substantial fines or imprisonment in the event of a conviction for a violation of the Act. Both of these statutes dealt with the investigative machinery for the anti-combines law embodied in the *Criminal Code*, and it was not until some time later that the restrictive trade practices themselves were broadened.

Apart from the deterrent effect, the anti-combines law of 1889 had little impact on Canadian business activity, since the country was still largely rural at the time of its introduction. The rapid industrialization which took place in Quebec and Ontario during the 20th century, however, gave rise to the formation of large numbers of manufacturers seeking trade advantages for their products and, by 1935, restrictive trade practices had reached the stage where action was necessary on the part of Parliament to protect the public interest.

The 1935 amendments to the *Criminal Code* prohibited price discrimination, and the practice of predatory pricing, which was frequently employed for the purpose of destroying competitors. The rigidity of the prohibition on price discrimination proved to work a hardship on sellers in areas where it was in the legitimate public interest to allow them to meet competition, and some modification of the law in this respect became apparent by 1951. The modifications were embodied in a number of amendments to the *Combines Investigation Act* during 1951-52. The practice of resale price maintenance was prohibited,

and price discrimination was modified to reduce the rigidity of the 1935 changes to the *Criminal Code*. The modifications permitted the seller to engage in limited price discrimination, provided that the discrimination did not constitute a regular practice. The change gave sellers the freedom to meet competition in particular areas, or to do so for legitimate business reasons, provided that it did not become a practice.

A further change in the law took place a few years later. The awkwardness of the legislation pertaining to restrictive trade practices, part being lodged in the *Criminal Code*, and part in the *Combines Act*, prompted the government to consolidate the law in a single statute, and in 1960 a consolidated Act was passed. The statute, entitled the *Combines Investigation Act*[7] incorporated the provisions of the *Criminal Code* in the new legislation, and added a number of additional trade practices to the prohibited list.

The 1960 amendments included misleading price advertising and discriminatory promotional allowances as restrictive trade practices, and modified a number of the provisions with respect to combinations and existing practices. Following these amendments, no major changes were made in the law until 1976, when the Act was subjected to a thorough review, and a number of major revisions made. The changes represented an attempt by Parliament to preserve and encourage free competition and was the first of a two-part overhaul of the law relating to restrictive trade practices. The Act, as it stands in its 1976 form, represents the present law in Canada with respect to restrictive trade practices.

---

[6]The *Combines Investigation Act*, 1910 (Can.), 9-10, Edw. VII, c. 9.

[7]"An Act to Amend the Combines Investigation Act and the Criminal Code," 1960 (Can.), c. 45.

NATURE OF THE LEGISLATION

The *Combines Investigation Act* is an Act of Parliament, and, as such, applies throughout Canada. Apart from certain non-criminal activities which may be "reviewed," the legislation is essentially criminal law in nature. In the past, the Act was challenged in the courts as *ultra vires* the federal government, but with success only when the government attempted to stray from the criminal law approach to the control of business activity. The law, at least with respect to those practices designated as criminal offences, would appear to be a valid exercise of the powers of the federal government under s. 91 of the *British North America Act, 1867*.[8]

The fact that the law is criminal in nature limits its enforcement to those cases where the Crown is in a position to prove beyond any reasonable doubt that an offence has occurred. The criminal law standards of proof apply, but since the accused is frequently in possession of much of the necessary evidence which the Crown would require to prove a violation of the Act, the legislation provides the Director of Investigation with very wide powers of search or seizure, and the right to compel parties to provide information. In this respect the combines legislation differs from the ordinary criminal law.

Responsibility for the administration of the Act falls under the Ministry of Consumer and Corporate Affairs, although the Attorney-General of Canada is expected to institute any criminal proceedings which might arise out of an alleged violation of the statute. The regulatory organization within the ministry consists of a Director of Investigation, and a Restrictive Trade Practices Commission.

The Director of Investigation, as the title implies, is primarily responsible for the investigation of any complaint that a violation of the Act has taken place. A complaint from a private individual to the director often results in an investigation, but the Act provides that the director must investigate any complaint or allegation of a violation of the Act which is brought to his attention in the form of an application for inquiry requested by six residents of Canada.[9]

The Act permits the director or his agents to enter on the premises of any person that the director believes may have evidence related to the inquiry, but he must first obtain either a search warrant or a certificate from the Restrictive Trade Practices Commission to authorize the search and seizure of evidence.[10] He cannot, however, use his search and seizure powers simply to engage in a "fishing expedition" for possible evidence of violation. He must only do so in accordance with an inquiry pursuant to a complaint of an alleged violation. The director's powers extend beyond the mere right to search; the certificate empowers the director to interrogate corporate officers, or require them to furnish affidavit evidence relating to the inquiry.[11]

If at any time during the inquiry the director decides that further investigation is unwarranted, he may discontinue the inquiry.[12] If, however, he finds evidence of a violation of the Act, he may either deliver the evidence to the Attorney-General of Canada for consideration, (and for such further action as the Attorney-General may wish to take), or he may make a re-

---

[8]*British North American Act*, 1867, 30 Vict., c. 3, s. 91.

[9]The *Combines Investigation Act*, R.S.C. 1970, c. C-23, as amended by 1974-75-76, c. 76, ss. 7 and 8.
[10]*Ibid.*, s. 10 (3).
[11]Ibid., s. 12.
[12]*Ibid.*, s. 14.

port to the Restrictive Trade Practices Commission.

The Restrictive Trade Practices Commission on receipt of the director's report may investigate the matter further by way of a hearing. At the hearing evidence may be called, and the parties alleged to have violated the Act have an opportunity to be heard.[13] The commission then prepares a report to the Minister in which it reviews the evidence, and sets out any effect which the trade practice examined may have had on the public interest. The report usually contains recommendations as to remedies to correct the situation.[14] Reports of the commission are normally released to the public within 30 days after submission to the Minister, but if the Minister believes that the public interest would be better served by withholding publication, he need not release the report.[15]

Reports of the commission are generally designed to correct trade practices which contain an element of restraint, or which have the potential for injury to the public interest, but which do not warrant the institution of criminal proceedings. In these cases, the recommendations of the commission usually set out the procedure that the investigated corporation or business should follow to avoid further charges of restraint of trade. For example, when an investigation was made by the commission into the manufacture and distribution of ammunition in Canada on a complaint that it was a near monopoly industry, the commission recommended that the manufacturer provide wider distribution of its products and thereby provide greater competition at the retail level.[16] The man-

ufacturer did so, and competition was restored in the market place.

The Restrictive Trade Practices Commission now has the right to review certain business activities as a result of recent amendments to the Act. Reviewable activities include exclusive dealing, "tied" selling, consignment selling, and the refusal to supply goods.[17] In each of these situations, the director must first make an inquiry, then, if the circumstances warrant, recommend that a hearing be held into the practice. Again, a full opportunity to be heard must be given to any person affected. In addition to the right to be heard, the Act also entitles such persons to cross-examine other witnesses. However, unlike an inquiry into an ordinary restrictive trade practice, the commission does not make recommendations. In the case of a reviewable practice, if the results of the hearing dictate some action on the part of the commission, it may make an order prohibiting the practice engaged in by the party, or establish procedures which the party must follow to restore competition. Under the Act, a failure to obey the order would constitute a criminal offence.[18]

||||||||||||||||||||||||||||||||||||||||||||||||||||||||||||||||||||||||||||||||||||||||||||||

CASE 24.1

R. v. British Columbia Sugar Refining Co. Ltd. and B.C. Sugar Refinery Ltd. (1960), 32 W.W.R. 577.

WILLIAMS, C.J.Q.B.:

As this is a criminal prosecution there are certain principles that I must apply to its consideration. They are: (1) The onus is on the crown throughout to prove its case and every essential part of it by relevant and admissible evidence beyond a reasonable doubt; (2) This onus never shifts; (3) There is no onus on the accused to prove their innocence; (4) To the ex-

[13]*Ibid.*, s. 18.
[14]*Ibid.*, s. 19.
[15]*Ibid.*, s. 19(5).
[16]Report of Restrictive Trade Practices Commission, 1959, No. 1 Concerning the Manufacture, Distribution and Sale of Ammunition in Canada.

[17]The *Combines Investigation Act*, R.S.C. 1970, c. C-23 as amended by 1974-75-76, c. 76, s. 31.
[18]*Ibid.*, s. 46.1.

tent that the guilt of the accused depends on circumstantial evidence, that evidence must be consistent with the guilt of the accused and inconsistent with any other rational conclusion; (5) In the construction of a penal statute, such as the *Combines Act*, if there are two or more reasonable interpretations possible, the interpretation most favourable to the accused must be adopted.

||||||||||||||||||||||||||||||||||||||||||||||||||||||||||||||||||||||||||||||||||

RESTRICTIVE TRADE PRACTICES

The *Combines Investigation Act* applies to both goods and services, and only those services or goods that fall under the control of a public regulatory body would appear to be exempt from the legislation. Any seller or supplier whose services or goods are sold at prices reviewed or determined by a government body or commission, even if the seller is in a monopoly position, would not be subject to prosecution under the *Combines Investigation Act* for any marketing activity carried on under the direct control of the regulatory body. The Act, of course, would still apply to activities of the organization which fall outside the direct control of the regulatory body, and to any action designed to prevent the regulatory body from protecting the public interest.[19]

Offences under the Act may be divided into three separate categories:
(1) offences related to the nature of the business organization itself;
(2) offences which arise out of dealings between a firm and its competitors;
(3) offences which arise out of dealings between a firm and its customers.

MERGERS AND MONOPOLIES

The first category of offences is related to the nature of the firm, if the firm should become dominant in a particular field of business or industry. This may arise in one of two ways: a firm may gradually eliminate all competition by aggressive business activity, or it may merge with other competitors to assume a dominant position. Neither of these methods of growth or dominance is in itself unlawful, but under the *Combines Investigation Act*, any merger or monopoly which is likely to lessen competition to the detriment of the public or contrary to the public interest[20] would constitute a violation of the Act. The rationale behind this prohibition is that mergers or monopolies which substantially control the market have the potential for abuse, in that the price-reducing effects of free competition no longer apply to their product or service. While it is difficult to pin-point when a merger becomes contrary to the public interest, or may have the effect of lessening competition to the detriment of the public, any merger which gives a single organization in excess of half the market for a particular product might very well come under scrutiny by the director. If the merger is found to be in violation of the Act, the courts have the power to order the merger dissolved.[21]

The courts have generally been reluctant to convict in the case of mergers and monopolies, because of the many factors that must be considered in the determination of what constitutes a lessening of competition "unduly." Apart from one case, in which a monopoly firm was so blatant in its conduct of restrictive trade practices that competition was clearly lessened "unduly" and the public interest adversely affected,[22] the Crown has had little success in the enforcement of the merger and mo-

---

[19]See, for example, *R. v. Can. Breweries Ltd.*, [1960] O.R. 601.

[20]The *Combines Investigation Act*, R.S.C. 1970, c. C-23 as amended by 1974-75-76, c. 76, ss. 2 and 33.
[21]*Ibid.*, s. 30.
[22]*Ibid.*, *R. v. Eddy Match Co. Ltd.* (1952), 13 C.R. 217; affirmed by (1954) 18 C.R. 357.

nopoly sections of the Act. Some of the reasons put forward by the courts in dismissing the Crown's cases have been the control or regulation of prices by a public body,[23] the potential for competition from large firms in other areas of the country,[24] and the fact that substitutes for the product are available.[25]

|||||||||||||||||||||||||||||||||||||||||||||||||||||||||||||||||||||||||||||||||||

CASE 24.2
R. v. Elliott (1905), 9 O.L.R. 648.

OSLER, J.A.:

The right of competition is the right of every one, and Parliament has now shewn that its intention is to prevent oppressive and unreasonable restrictions upon the exercise of this right; that whatever may hitherto have been its full extent, it is no longer to be exercised by some to the injury of others. In other words, competition is not to be prevented or lessened *unduly*, that is to say, in an undue manner or degree, wrongly, improperly, excessively, inordinately, which it may well be in one or more of these senses of the word, if by the combination of a few the right of the many is practically interfered with by restricting it to the members of the combination.

|||||||||||||||||||||||||||||||||||||||||||||||||||||||||||||||||||||||||||||||||||

CONSPIRACIES OR COMBINATIONS IN RESTRAINT OF TRADE

The earliest legislation pertaining to restraint of trade in Canada, and, indeed, the general thrust of the present legislation, has been the prohibition of conspiracies and combinations which unduly lessen competition. The relative serious-

ness of offences relating to these activities may be underscored by reference to the penalties imposed for contravention of this part of the Act: A breach of any of the sections related to combinations and conspiracies carries with it a fine of up to one million dollars, or imprisonment for up to five years.[26]

The "conspiracy and combination" section of the Act[27] provides that

32. . . . everyone who conspires, combines, agrees or arranges with another person:

(a) to limit unduly the facilities for transporting, producing, manufacturing, supplying, storing or dealing in any product,

(b) to prevent, limit or lessen, unduly, the manufacture or production of a product, or to enhance unreasonably the price thereof,

(c) to prevent, or lessen, unduly, competition in the production, manufacture, purchase, barter, sale, storage, rental, transportation or supply of a product, or in the price of insurance upon persons or property, or

(d) to otherwise restrain or injure competition unduly

is guilty of an indictable offence and is liable to imprisonment for five years or a fine of one million dollars or to both.

The obligation on the Crown to prove a violation of the Act is alleviated to some extent by a requirement in the legislation which provides that it is not necessary to prove that the combination, conspiracy, or agreement would be likely to eliminate completely or virtually eliminate competition in the market to which it relates, or that it was the object of the parties to eliminate completely or virtually, competition in that market.[28] However, the Act would

[23]*R. v. Can. Breweries Ltd.*, [1960] O.R. 601.

[24]*R. v. British Columbia Sugar Refining Co. Ltd. et al.* (1960), 32 W.W.R. (N.S.) 577.

[25]*R. v. K. C. Irving Ltd.* (1974), 7 N.B.R. (2d) 360; affirmed [1978] 1 S.C.R. 408.

[26]The *Combines Investigation Act*, R.S.C. 1970, c. C-23 as amended by 1974-75-76 (Can.), c. 76, s. 32(1).

[27]*Ibid.*, s. 32.

[28]*Ibid.*, s. 32(1.1).

not apply if the combination or agreement between the parties relates only to one of the following activities, such as:[29]

(a) the exchange of statistics,
(b) the defining of product standards,
(c) the exchange of credit information,
(d) the definition of terminology used in a trade, industry or profession,
(e) cooperation in research and development,
(f) the restriction of advertising or promotion, other than a discriminatory restriction directed against a member of the mass media,
(g) the sizes or shapes of the containers in which an article is packaged,
(h) the adoption of the metric system of weights and measures, or
(i) measures to protect the environment.

If the arrangement or agreement to carry out any of these activities restricts, or is likely to restrict any person from entering the business, trade, or profession, or has the effect of lessening, or is likely to lessen competition with respect to prices, markets or customers, channels or methods of distribution, or the quantity or quality of production, then the parties would still be subject to conviction under the Act.[30]

The Act in general only applies to conspiracies, combinations, or agreements in restraint of trade on a domestic basis, and if the activity relates wholly to the export of products from Canada, the restraint of trade restrictions would not apply,[31] unless (1) the agreement or arrangement has resulted, or is likely to result in a reduction or limitation of the volume of exports of a product; (2) has restrained or injured, or is likely to restrain or injure the export business of any domestic competitor who is not a part to the conspiracy, combination, or arrangement; (3) has restricted or is likely to restrict any person from entering the export business; or (4) has lessened or is likely to lessen competition unduly in relation to a product in the domestic market.[32]

In the case of services, a further exception is made. The courts are not to convict an accused if the conspiracy, combination, agreement, or arrangement relates only to the standards of competence and integrity reasonably necessary for the protection of the public in either the practice of the trade or profession, or in the collection and dissemination of information relating to such services.[33]

The Act also exempts affiliated corporations from the conspiracy provisions and, as a consequence, if a wholly owned subsidiary of another corporation enters into an agreement with that corporation that would otherwise be a conspiracy, it would not be subject to charges under this part of the Act.[34] However, if the parent corporation is a foreign corporation, and requires the Canadian subsidiary to enter into an agreement with another firm outside Canada that would constitute a violation of the conspiracy provisions of the Act if made in Canada, any director or officer of the Canadian corporation may be liable, even if unaware of the agreement.[35]

The practice of "bid-rigging," which represents any agreement or arrangement among two or more persons where all but one undertakes not to submit a bid in response to a call for bids or tenders (and where the person calling for bids is unaware of the arrangement) is prohibited under the Act.[36] The practice was made an

---

[29]*Ibid.*, s. 32(2).
[30]*Ibid.*, s. 32(3).
[31]*Ibid.*, s. 32(4).

[32]*Ibid.*, s. 32(5).
[33]*Ibid.*, s. 32(6).
[34]*Ibid.*, s. 32(7).
[35]*Ibid.*, s. 32.1(1).
[36]*Ibid.*, s. 32.2.

offence under the Act in 1976 in an effort to encourage greater competition by the elimination of secret arrangements. The offence differs to some extent from other restrictive trade practices in that it would not be necessary for the Crown to prove that the bid-rigging represents an undue restraint of trade. An important point to note with respect to this activity, however, is the fact that a bidding arrangement is only an offence if the fact is not revealed to the person calling for the bids, either before or at the time the bid is made. The purpose for this exemption is to allow parties to undertake projects jointly, provided that the nature of the arrangement is revealed beforehand to the other party.

Another new prohibition under the legislation was included in the Act as a result of the extension of the law to services generally. The Act now prohibits conspiracies relating to professional sports where the conspiracy is intended to limit unreasonably the opportunities for any person to participate as a player or competitor in a professional sport, or to impose unreasonable terms on persons who so participate. It also applies to any attempt to limit unreasonably the opportunity for any person to negotiate with, and (if an agreement is reached) to play for the team or club of his choice in a professional league.[37]

This provision in the legislation applies only to professional sport, and requires the courts to take into consideration the international aspects of the activity, and the unique relationship that exists between teams or clubs which compete in the same league.[38] Nevertheless, the law has necessitated a change in a number of activities associated with professional sport, the

most notable being the practice of tying a player to a club by way of a special reserve clause.

||||||||||||||||||||||||||||||||||||||||||||||||||||||||||||||||||||||||||||||||||||||||||

CASE 24.3
R. v. Canadian General Electric Co. Ltd. et al. (1976), 75 D.L.R. (3d) 664.

PENNELL, J.:

The conspiracy section of the Act was passed for the protection of the specific public interest in competition. Therefore, the Court is only concerned to determine whether or not the prevention or lessening of competition agreed to will be undue without regard to the public injury or public benefit from any other standpoint. But different considerations apply on the charge of a monopoly offence.

I am of opinion that the concept of public interest as used in the monopoly provisions of the Act embraces the proven benefits derived from the operation of the business by the accused.

I am of opinion that the concept of public interest as used in the Act also embraces the principles of a free competitive system. The Court thus has the obligation to weigh the proven benefits against the proven evils to determine if detriment has resulted. To avoid becoming lost in a maze of single instances, there must be a sifting and scrutinizing of the whole of the evidence. Whether the acts of those who control the market may be considered detrimental is a question of fact for the Court to determine. Their acts must be considered in relation to the market and industry of which they are a part. In this connection, I acquiesce to the accused's submission that the public interest includes a fair return to the accused and the agents for their capital investment and labour.

||||||||||||||||||||||||||||||||||||||||||||||||||||||||||||||||||||||||||||||||||||||||||

OFFENCES RELATING TO DISTRIBUTION AND SALE OF PRODUCTS

Offences relating to distribution are generally designed to prevent sellers from

---

[37]*Ibid.*, s. 32.3(1).
[38]*Ibid.*, s. 32.3(2) and (3).

granting special concessions to large buyers, and conversely, to prevent large buyers from insisting upon special concessions from sellers. Special concessions, usually in the form of lower prices or special allowances would grant one buyer a particular competitive advantage over other buyers, and carry with it the potential for a restriction on competition. The Act, consequently, has identified a number of distribution activities which affect competition, and which the Act prohibits.

A seller, for example, must not make a practice of discriminating between competing purchasers with respect to the price of goods sold.[39] It is important to note with price discrimination that this activity only constitutes an offence where the seller makes a practice of price discrimination between competing firms, where the goods sold are of the same quality, in the same quantity, and are sold at approximately the same time.[40] Isolated sales to meet competition, or sales between affiliated firms would probably not constitute offences under the Act.[41]

In a similar fashion, a seller is prohibited from granting buyers special rebates, promotional allowances, or grants for the advertising or promotion of goods unless the allowance or amount is made on a proportional basis.[42] Once again, the purchasers must be in competition with one another, and the seller must not discriminate. Under the Act, an allowance would be treated as proportional if it is based upon the value of sales to each competing purchaser, or, if it is in the form of services, in accordance with the kinds of services that purchasers at each level of distribution would ordinarily be able to perform.[43]

A seller must not engage in a policy of selling products in any area of Canada at prices lower than those elsewhere if the sales would have the effect of substantially lessening or eliminating competition in that area,[44] or if the policy of low prices is established for the purpose of lessening or eliminating competition.[45] In both of these cases, the Act is not attempting to prohibit lower prices, but rather to make it an offence if a seller uses lower prices to eliminate or lessen competition either on a regional or broader basis. The practice of selling goods at a low price normally would not offend the Act, but if the price is unreasonably low for the purpose of lessening or destroying competition, then the practice would probably be in contravention of the Act.

The underlying thought behind each of these prohibitions is that a seller must treat all competing buyers of his products in a fair and impartial manner, and that the selling of products must be done without some unlawful motive such as the elimination of competition. A seller is not obliged to treat non-competing buyers in the same fashion, however, and a seller may establish separate prices and discounts for each type of non-competing buyer.

A quite different sales activity is also covered by a section of the Act which prohibits the seller from controlling the prices at which his goods may be sold by others. A seller is prohibited from attempting, either directly or indirectly, by any threat or promise, or any other inducement, to influence the price upwards of his products, or from discouraging price reductions by the purchasers of his products for

---

[39]*Ibid.*, s. 34(1)(*a*).
[40]*Ibid.*, s. 32(2).
[41]*Ibid.*, s. 32(7).
[42]*Ibid.*, s. 35.

[43]*Ibid.*, s. 35(3).
[44]*Ibid.*, s. 34(1)(*b*).
[45]*Ibid.*, s. 34(1)(*c*).

resale.[46] The offence is not limited to cases where a seller attempts to fix the price at which his product may be sold, but also applies to any attempt to enhance the price, or influence the price upwards. The practice by sellers of providing a "suggested retail price" for advertising, or for price lists, or other material, would probably violate the Act unless the seller clearly indicates that the buyer is under no obligation to resell the goods at the suggested price, and that the goods may be resold at a lower price.[47]

A seller may not refuse to supply goods to a buyer in an attempt to prevent the buyer from reselling the goods to others who maintain a policy of selling the goods at lower prices, but a seller would have the right to refuse to supply goods if the buyers makes a practice of selling the goods as "loss leaders", and not for the purpose of profit.[48] The same would be the case if the goods required certain services, and the person was not making a practice of providing the level of service that a purchaser would normally expect.[49]

Recent amendments to the Act also prohibit a number of schemes used by sellers to promote sales that tend to discourage competition. These include a prohibition of "referral selling,"[50] a practice whereby a customer receives a rebate or commission on each additional customer which he obtains for the seller, and a prohibition of "pyramid selling," a practice which involves the payment of fees or commissions not based upon the sale of a product, but upon the recruitment or sales of others.[51] In the latter case, where a province has legislation governing or controlling the activity, the practice is not subject to the *Combines Investigation Act.*[52]

REVIEWABLE ACTIVITIES

In addition to prohibited activities relating to the sale of goods and services, the Restrictive Trade Practices Commission may review a number of different selling methods at the request of the director. At the present time, only a refusal to supply goods, consignment selling, exclusive dealing, "tied" selling, and market restriction are reviewable selling activities, but the commission may also review foreign directives to Canadian subsidiaries, and foreign arrangements in restraint of trade which affect Canadian business.[53] A review which confirms that the activity has taken place, and that the activity is carried on for a purpose specified in the Act, may be ordered stopped, or a remedy set out in the legislation for that particular activity may be applied. For example, the commission may order a major supplier to cease exclusive dealing arrangements if the arrangement is likely to: impede entry into or expansion of a firm in the market; impede the introduction of a product into the market; impede an expansion of sales of a product in the market, or have any other exclusionary effect in the market,[54] with the result that competition is or is likely to be lessened substantially. The commission is also permitted, in the case of exclusive dealing, to include in the order any other requirement necessary to overcome the effects of the exclusive dealing, or to include

---

[46]*Ibid.,* s. 38.
[47]*Ibid.,* s. 38(3).
[48]*Ibid.,* s. 38(8) and (9).
[49]*Ibid.,* s. 38(9)(*d*).
[50]*Ibid.,* s. 36.4.
[51]*Ibid.,* s. 36.3.

[52]*Ibid.,* s. 36.3(4).
[53]*Ibid.,* s. 31.
[54]*Ibid.,* s. 31.4(2).

any other requirement which might be necessary to restore or stimulate competition.[55]

OFFENCES RELATING TO PROMOTION AND ADVERTISING OF PRODUCTS

Misleading or false advertising, and a number of other promotional activities are subject to the *Combines Investigation Act.* The Act makes any representation to the public that is false or misleading in any material respect,[56] or any materially misleading representation to the public concerning the price at which a product or like products have been, are, or will be sold, an offence under the Act.[57] The Act, with respect to false or misleading advertising, is broadly written to include cases where the information may be technically correct but where the impression given would mislead the public in some material way.[58] The Act also puts the onus on the advertiser to prove that any claims or promises made in the form of a warranty or guarantee of performance are valid and are substantiated in accordance with recognized testing procedures. While every article or service need not meet the claim, the percentage of articles that do must be high. Where claims are made as a result of recognized tests, the percentage of articles that meet the test has been suggested to be not less than 95%.[59]

Where a testimonial of a user is included in an advertisement to establish the performance of a product, or to attest to its useable life, it is essential that the performance test was made, and that the person making the testimonial approve the content of the report and grant permission to publish it prior to its use by the advertiser.[60]

Sales above the advertised price constitute an offence under the *Combines Investigation Act*, and a seller who advertises a product at a particular price in a geographic area would be expected to sell the goods to all persons in that general area at the advertised price. The Act, however, recognizes that errors do occur in the advertisement of goods, and provides that where a false or misleading advertisement is made with respect to the price at which goods are offered for sale, prompt action by the advertiser to correct the error by placing another advertisement advising the public of the error would exempt the advertiser from prosecution under the Act.[61]

A practice somewhat related to misleading price advertising is the "double ticketing" of goods for sale. This sometimes occurs in self-serve establishments. To discourage the practice, the Act provides that the seller must sell the goods at the lowest of the marked prices, otherwise, the sale would constitute an offence.[62]

The Act also discourages the rather dubious selling technique of bait-and-switch, whereby the seller advertises goods at a bargain price for the purpose of attracting customers to the establishment when he does not have an adequate supply of the low-priced goods to sell. The practice is now an offence under the Act[63] unless the

---

[55]*Ibid.*
[56]*Ibid.*, s. 36(1)(*a*).
[57]*Ibid.*, s. 36(1)(*d*).
[58]*Ibid.*, s. 36(4).
[59]Canada, Department of Consumer and Corporate Affairs: Misleading Advertising Bulletin, 1976.

[60]The *Combines Investigation Act*, R.S.C. 1970, c. C-23 as amended by 1974-75-76 (Can.), c. 76, s. 36(1).
[61]*Ibid.*, s. 37.1(3).
[62]*Ibid.*, s. 36.2.
[63]*Ibid.*, s. 37(2).

seller can establish that he took steps to obtain an adequate supply of the product, but was unable to obtain such a quantity by reason of events beyond his control, or that he obtained what he believed to be a reasonable supply, but did not anticipate the heavy demand, and when his supply was exhausted, he undertook to supply the goods (or similar goods) at the same bargain price within a reasonable time to all persons who requested the product.[64]

Under the Act, a final promotion-related activity that should be noted is the use of promotional contests by sellers to increase the sales of a product. All promotional contests must make an adequate and fair disclosure of the number and approximate value of the prizes, the area or areas to which they relate, and any fact within the knowledge of the advertiser that might materially affect the chances of winning. The selection of participants or the distribution of prizes must also be made on the basis of skill, or on a random basis within the area where the prizes are to be awarded.[65] If the promoter fails to comply with the requirements set out in the Act, the failure constitutes an offence punishable by a fine or imprisonment.

CIVIL ACTIONS UNDER THE COMBINES INVESTIGATION ACT

Apart from the right to maintain a common law civil action for restraint of trade activities not covered by the legslation, the *Combines Investigation Act* provides that a civil action may be maintained by a party injured as a result of an alleged breach of the *Combines Investigation Act* by another. The party alleging the breach may claim damages suffered as a result of the breach of the Act, but the amount that may be recovered is limited to the actual loss.[66] In this sense, Canadian legislation differs from that of the United States, where triple damages may be recovered in restrictive trade practice cases.

The burden of proof which is imposed upon the private plaintiff in the civil action would not be the criminal burden of "beyond any reasonable doubt," but the lesser civil law burden based upon a balance of probability. The civil plaintiff, however, would be entitled to use the record of any criminal proceedings against the defendant as evidence in the civil action, provided that the action is commenced within two years of the final disposition of the criminal case.[67]

However, a number of recent judgements by the Supreme Court of Canada and the courts in several provinces have cast doubt on the validity of this part of the *Combines Investigation Act*.[68] In each of these cases the courts have ruled that the right of the federal government to establish a civil cause of action is *ultra vires* its powers under the *British North America Act, 1867*. As a result, the civil action provided in the Act would now appear to be in doubt.

---

[64]*Ibid.*, s. 37(3).
[65]*Ibid.*, s. 37.2.
[66]*Ibid.*, s. 31.1(1).
[67]*Ibid.*, s. 31.1(4).
[68]*Seiko Time Canada Ltd. v. Consumers Distributing Co.*

SUMMARY The purpose of restrictive trade practice legislation is to maintain free competition. The law is designed to permit the forces of competition to regulate trade and industry rather than government or dominant members of an industry.

The general thrust of the law is to prohibit mergers and monopolies which are contrary to the public interest, and to ban any combination or conspiracy which might unduly lessen competition. The law also prohibits certain activities (on the sellers' part) designed to drive the prices of goods and services upward, as well as to prevent price discrimination, along with certain other practices which might restrict competition.

The *Combines Investigation Act* is, for the most part, criminal in nature, but recent amendments to that Act have established a number of "reviewable" activities, plus the right of civil action for persons injured as a result of a breach of the Act. However, the right of the federal government to establish the latter has been rejected by the courts.

The legislation has worked reasonably well in controlling selling practices which are contrary to the public interest, but has failed to deal adequately with mergers and monopolies. The particular problem with the merger-monopoly parts of the legislation is related to the criminal nature of the law, and the burden of proof which it imposes upon the Crown. Proposals for change in this area of the law in the form of "Stage Two" amendments to the Act are presently (in 1980) under review by Parliament, and may be introduced in future.

DISCUSSION QUESTIONS

1. *Describe the general intent of restrictive trade practices legislation.*
2. *Why is a monopoly as defined in the* Combines Investigation Act *unlawful?*
3. *Outline a possible "discriminatory promotional allowance."*
4. *What standard of proof is required in order for a conviction to be made under the* Combines Investigation Act?
5. *Distinguish an ordinary merger from a merger which violates restrictive trade practices legislation.*
6. *Describe activities that constitute prohibited trade practices.*
7. *Why does a retailer who engages in a practice of loss-leader selling of a particular product lose the right to insist that the manufacturer supply him with that product?*
8. *What is a "reviewable" practice? Why is it not a "prohibited" practice?*

9. *How is an inquiry under the combines legislation launched?*

10. *Why does the granting of a patent not constitute a restrictive trade practice under the current legislation?*

11. *Identify circumstances under which two or more firms may engage in co-ordinated or combined activity which would not constitute a violation of the* Combines Investigation Act. *Why do these activities constitute exceptions to the general rule?*

12. *Why must a seller treat all buyers fairly and impartially? Is this an absolute rule, or is provision made for exceptional circumstances?*

13. *Why is the* Combines Investigation Act *broadly written with respect to misleading and false advertising?*

14. *The phrase "while supply lasts" in advertising can be considered as a seller's hedge against infringement of the* Combines Investigation Act. *Why is this necessary?*

15. *"Skill-testing questions" in promotional contests are often absurdly simple. This being the case, why are they necessary at all?*

16. *Define "bid-rigging."*

17. *In what ways do unfair business practices as defined in consumer protection legislation differ from "unfair" practices under restrictive trade practices legislation?*

|||||||||||||||||||||||||||||||||||||||||||||||||||||||||||||||||||||||||||||||||||||||||||||||||||||||||||||||||||||||||||||||||||||||||||||||||||||||||

JUDICIAL DECISIONS

Formation of Combine in Restraint of Trade—Prices Controlled by Public Bodies—Protection of Public

R. v. Can. Breweries Ltd., [1960] O.R. 601.

During a 23-year period the accused corporation acquired by way of merger 23 other breweries, and by 1958, controlled over 60% of beer sales in Canada. The merger was alleged to be a violation of the *Combines Investigation Act.*

MCRUER, C.J.H.C.:

The theory of the Crown as stated by Crown counsel, may be put in this way: In 1930 the accused embarked on a financial scheme or venture to merge companies in the brewing industry in such a manner as to eliminate all substantial competition, and to obtain for the accused an increasing measure of control and dominance over the policies of the industry, with the object of obtaining maximum profits on the operation. Counsel does not complain about the maximum profits in the industry, nor the size of a particular firm, if these result from the normal interplay of competitive forces, but in this case it is contended that the position obtained by the accused was a result of the artificial consolidation of various companies in the industry.

It is contended that the effect of the merger was to change the market structure of the industry and that this change, considered with the relative size of competitors, the difficulty of entry of new competition, the pattern of new acquisitions and a history of anti-competitive practices in the industry, destroyed or was likely to destroy the competitive process.

Crown counsel particularly emphasized evidence directed to show the elimination of rival producers by purchase, the prevention of new entry into the industry, and the dictation of agreements and trade practices in the industry, which facilitated agreements said to be illegal, and trade practices said to be illegal. To this may be added that it was contended that the accused, by the adoption of a policy whereby huge sums of money were spent in advertising and sales promotion, greatly increased the difficulties of new competition entering the market.

The particulars of the charge which were delivered pursuant to the order of the Court, read in part as follows

"The alleged merger, trust or monopoly has operated to the detriment or against the interest of consumers by:—(a) Carrying out a deliberate plan for the acquisition, closing, selling or dismantling of a great number of breweries; (b) Infringing the vested right of the members of the public in the continuance of free competition; (c) Reducing competition by cost-increasing practices of a promotional and advertising nature; (d) Arrangements or agreements with competitors as to prices, market quotas and trade practices; (e) The use of power, obtained by the means herein stated, to dictate the pricing and other policies or practices of the brewing industry and to influence conditions in the brewing industry and in the distribution of beer; (f) Narrowing the range of choice of brands and varieties; (g) High sale prices; (h) Using brand names that cause confusion with local trade names; (i) Creating barriers to the entry of new competition in the brewing industry."

These allegations are substantially repeated with some variations with respect to producers and others and although they are clarified and enlarged in further particulars delivered, they contain the substance of the formal allegations made against the accused.

. . . . .

In coming to a conclusion in this case I have to remind myself that the onus is on the Crown from the beginning to the end of the case to prove the accused guilty beyond a reasonable doubt. That onus never shifts and extends to every element that must be established to support the charge. In addition, the rule with respect to circumstantial evidence has some application: Where the guilt of the accused depends on circumstantial evidence the circumstances beyond a reasonable doubt, must be consistent with the guilt of the accused and, beyond a reasonable doubt, they must be inconsistent with any other rational conclusion.

There is one other principle of the criminal law to be applied: Where on the construction of a penal statute, there are two reasonable constructions open, one more favourable to the accused than the other, the one most favourable to the accused must be adopted. In other words, the Act I have to construe is a penal statute and it must be construed strictly against the Crown.

There are two main elements in the offence here charged to which these principles have special application: (1) Proof of the merger; (2) proof of the detriment or likely detriment to the interest of the public.

No question arises about the proof of the merger.

. . . . .

On behalf of the defence it is argued that the operation of the merger must be considered in the light of the provincial control that is exercised over the sale of beer in all Provinces. Defence counsel stated the theory of the defence in this way: The essence of the defence is that the merger did not prevent or lessen competition unduly having regard to the restrictions on competition validly imposed by government authorities, and also having regard to the vigorous competition from powerful and experienced competitors in those aspects of competition that were unrestricted.

In considering this argument one's mind must be directed to the constitutional field in which parliament and the legislatures are respectively permitted to legislate.

It requires no exhaustive analysis of the constitutional authorities to state that each Province has jurisdiction to regulate and control the sale of liquor within its boundaries and to fix the prices at which, and the conditions under which liquor may be sold. *Re Bd. Commerce Act 1919*, [1922] 1 A.C. 191, makes it clear that such jurisdiction does not lie within the powers of parliament except in time of emergency.

. . . . .

In all the Provinces the sale of beer is under direct government control. The extent to which control is exercised varies from Province to Province, but every provincial legislature has by statute assumed some definite control over the market.

. . . . .

The allegation in the particulars with respect to brands produced by the accused received little attention in the argument presented at the conclusion of the case. It cannot be questioned that the merger has brought about a reduction in the number of brands of beer on the market. There is no evidence to support the conclusion that this has detrimentally affected the public interest. Different witnesses called by the Crown testified to the effect that there was a sufficient diversity of brands of beer on the market to meet all the public needs.

The allegation that the merger has operated to the detriment of the public by maintaining high scale prices can be disposed of in this way. It was agreed by all counsel that I was not concerned with the question of whether the prices were high or low in relation to the cost of production and all other economic factors that enter into the pricing of products. Under the authorities, this is not a matter for the consideration of the Courts, even where the merger operates in a free market. *A fortiori*, where the prices are set by the board, the consideration of the price structure is entirely its responsibility. Apparently this is the reason why no evidence was offered in support of the allegation in the particulars that the prices of beer were too high.

. . . . .

In the indictment as drawn it would be wrong to isolate the activities of the accused in each Province for the purpose of deciding whether a breach of the statute has been committed. It is true that on the one hand, the activities of the accused in one area that has economic isolation with regard to the products involved might well bring it within the prohibition of the statute, but on the other hand, although it may not be proved that in any one area taken alone it has operated to the detriment or against the interest of the public, it may be that its operations throughout Canada taken as a whole come within the prohibitions of the statute.

It is therefore necessary to consider the operations of the accused in each of the respective Provinces, as well as its operations on a national scale. However, I may make this observation, that as far as the merchandising of beer is concerned, with the exception of Ontario and Quebec, the Provinces are largely separated by economic laws based on the cost of transportation.

. . . . .

Viewing the operations of the accused as they are carried on in the respective Provinces and on a national scale, it cannot be said that the merger has given it a monopoly in the beer market either in any one Province or in Canada as a whole.

In the last analysis, the object of the Act is to protect the public interest against the enhancement of prices that will likely flow from combines as defined in the Act. It matters not whether they arise out of agreements, mergers, trusts or monopolies. I think the Canadian cases on the subject bear me out in this statement, and it is consistent with what Lord Parker said in *A.-G. Aus. v. Adelaide SS. Co.*, [1913] A.C. 781, at p. 796

"The chief evil thought to be entailed by a monopoly whether in its strict or popular sense, was the rise in prices which such monopoly might entail."

When a provincial legislature has conferred on a commission or board the power to regulate an industry and fix prices, and the power has been exercised, the Court must assume that the power is exercised in the public interest. In such cases, in order to succeed in a prosecution laid under the Act with respect to the operation of a combine, I think it must be shown that the combine has operated, or is likely to operate, so as to hinder or prevent the provincial body from effectively exercising the powers given to it to protect the public interest. If the evidence shows that by reason of a merger the accused is given a substantial monopoly in the market, this onus, in my opinion, would be discharged.

There may, however, be areas of competition in the market that are not affected by the exercise of the powers conferred on the provincial body in which restraints on competition may render the operations of the combine illegal. In this case the only areas of competition that can be of any benefit to the consumer that are left open to the accused and its competitors, are in the matter of quality, taste, services and packaging. The evidence shows that in these limited areas, competition between the accused and others in the industry is without restraint.

I now come back to apply the language of Cartwright, J., in the *Howard Smith* case to the facts of this case, and ask myself the question: Has it been proved beyond a reasonable doubt that the merger has conferred on the accused the power to carry on its activities without competition, or substantially without competition? I think the irresistible answer is no.

I ask myself this further question: Has it been proved beyond a reasonable doubt that the merger has conferred on the accused the power to control the market so that the provincial authority in the exercise of its duty in fixing prices cannot protect the public interest? To this question I think the irresistible answer is no.

That being true, the verdict I render is not guilty.

Misleading Advertisement— Untrue Statement of Fact— Standard Used

R. v. Kraft Foods Ltd. (1972), 36 D.L.R. (3d) 376.

VALLERAND, J.:

The Crown charges Kraft Foods Limited with having infringed s. 37 of the *Combines Investigation Act*, R.S.C. 1970, c. C-23, which reads as follows:

"37(1) Every one who publishes or causes to be published an advertisement containing a statement that purports to be a statement of fact but that is untrue, deceptive or misleading or is intentionally so worded or arranged that it is deceptive or misleading, is guilty of an indictable offence and is liable to imprisonment for five years, if the advertisement is published.

(a) to promote, directly or indirectly, the sale or disposal of property or any interest therein, or

(b) to promote a business or commercial interest."

The essential facts are as follows:

Early in 1970 accused launched an advertising competition titled "Explore Canada '70", offering persons who entered, with or without proof of purchase, 15 prizes consisting of an air ticket to a destination of their choosing in Canada, a rented car at their disposal, $1,000 spending money, and finally, a set of luggage. This competition was supported by an extensive publicity campaign which spotlighted accused's products as well as the prizes. Posters and entry forms were placed in prominent positions at all retail food outlets. Colourful three-page advertisements were published in three issues of the French and English versions of the "Chatelaine" magazine, and the "Reader's Digest" and "Sélections du Reader's Digest" magazines, publications with national distribution; finally, the competition was promoted in commercials over a national television network, on popular programmes such as the "Ed Sullivan Show" and "Singalong Jubilee".

This advertising proclaimed in large lettering: "15 big chances to win!"—"15 premiers-prix—15 chances!" The rules of the competition, in smaller print, provided (except in the issues of "Reader's Digest", which objected) that each week names would be drawn from all the entry forms received and that prizes would be awarded on a regional basis.

According to the evidence the 15 prizes were distributed as follows, three each for Quebec and Ontario, two for British Columbia and the Yukon, and one for each of the remaining Provinces. The entry forms received were divided and placed in a bin, one for each Province, and the winning entry was drawn from this bin when the drawing was for the prize assigned to residents of a particular Province. One or more drawings took place each Monday starting January 12, 1970, from the entries received on the preceding Friday. Thus, the drawing for the prize assigned to Alberta residents was held on Monday, January 12, 1970, from the entries received on the preceding Friday, January 9th, while the drawing of the three prizes assigned to residents of Quebec was held on January 12th, February 23rd and March 9th respectively. The competition, which had started early in January, concluded in early April, when the last drawing (for Ontario) was held from entries received on or before March 20th.

The prosecution objects to the phrase "15 big chances to win!", displayed at the top of the advertisement and read in conjunction with regulation 4 of the competition, which provided that each week names would be drawn from all the entry forms received. It maintains that the leading phrase in the advertisement suggests that each competitor has "15 chances to win", *i.e.*, that each competitor is capable of winning one of 15 prizes. However, the Crown points out, because of the regional distribution each competitor does not have a chance at 15 prizes, a competitor in Quebec is only trying for one of three prizes, a competitor in New Brunswick for one prize, etc.

To this accused answers that the words "15 big chances to win!" have no meaning by themselves, and the consumer must of necessity seek their explanation in the regulations of the competition. According to this argument, the advertisement must be read as a whole, and on this it cites: *Federal Trade Com'n v. Sterling Drug, Inc.* (1963), 317 F. 2d 669. As regulation 4 provides that prizes will be assigned by region, it is argued that on reading the actual wording it immediately becomes clear that no competitor had 15 chances of winning, but simply that a total of 15 prizes were to be awarded.

There is some basis for this reasoning. Particularly if "15 chances to win" is taken as having no objective meaning, the likelihood of winning a competition of chance is calculated by a fractional formula in which the numerator is the number of prizes and the denominator the number of competitors. A win from a 100 entries is much more attractive than 15 chances in 300,000. The prosecution cited *R. v. Imperial Tobacco Products Ltd.* (1971), 4 C.C.C. (2d) 423, 22 D.L.R. (3d) 51, 3 C.P.R. (2d) 178, where the Alberta Supreme Court, Appellate Division, considering an advertisement that each pack of a certain brand of cigarettes contained $5 whereas in fact it only contained an entry form for a competition in which the prizes were of that amount, held in convicting the defendant that: "In my opinion once the statement is shown to be untrue that is sufficient."

In that case the advertisement complained of declared ''$5 in every pack of new Casino''. This was an exact, complete statement, the meaning of which was not open to question. In the case at bar, however, as we have seen, the statement ''15 big chances to win!'' does not by itself have any meaning.

On this point therefore, the Court might perhaps give the defendant the benefit of the doubt, to which it is entitled. However, the question becomes purely theoretical when the second allegation of the prosecution is taken into account. In fact, as we have seen, the competition lasted for a period of more than 13 weeks; drawings were held weekly for prizes awarded on a regional basis, with the result that as soon as the prize or prizes assigned to a region (or Province) had been awarded, subsequent competitors in that region were taking part in a competition which had terminated so far as they were concerned. Exhibit P-11 indicates that the only prizes assigned to residents of Alberta and those of New Brunswick were awarded at the first drawing on January 12th. On January 9th the residents of those Provinces were eliminated from the competition. In the second week, those in Nova Scotia were eliminated; the same fate overtook those in Saskatchewan on January 23rd, in Prince Edward Island on January 30th, in Manitoba on February 6th and in Newfoundland on February 13th.

Indeed, by February 13th all residents in Canada were eliminated except those in British Columbia, Ontario and Quebec. In spite of this, the competition continued until the end of March, soliciting the participation of all Canadians, without anyone thinking it necessary to point out that for some people there was no longer any chance of winning.

Further, when the competition was first advertised on national television, on the ''Singalong Jubilee'' on January 16th and the ''Ed Sullivan Show'' on January 18th, all potential competitors in Alberta, New Brunswick and Nova Scotia had already been absolutely eliminated. We are thus left with some striking figures. Of the 26,896 competitors in Alberta, only 504 participated in the drawing for prizes assigned to residents of that Province, as the over 26,000 other competitors had sent in their entries, at defendant's invitation, after the competition had concluded so far as they were concerned. In New Brunswick, 115 out of 7,733 participated in the drawing; in Nova Scotia, 584 out of 13,282, and so on. A nation-wide summary of the figures shows that of 271,072 competitors, only 150,088 participated in the various drawings, as 120,984 were no longer eligible when they entered at the invitation of Kraft Foods Limited.

It is true that regulation 4 of the competition, providing for weekly drawings and the awarding of prizes on a regional basis, could be construed as a warning. However, it was a warning which only a keen eye and a suspicious mind would have been likely to detect. And even so, the type of media chosen, the name of the sponsor and the size of the campaign did not hint at underlying circumstances as exceptional as those above stated.

Moreover, in the case of *R. v. Imperial Tobacco Products Ltd.* previously cited, the Court of appeal held [C.C.C. headnote]:

"The standard to be used . . . is that of the public, which includes the ignorant, the unthinking and the credulous and not the standards of the skeptical who have learned by bitter experience to beware of commercial advertisements."

The Court accordingly concludes that accused "caused to be published an advertisement containing a statement that purports to be a statement of fact but that is untrue, deceptive or misleading . . ."

There is no need for an elaborate analysis to conclude that accused published this advertisement "to promote, directly or indirectly, the sale or disposal of property or any interest therein, or to promote a business or commercial interest". It would be hard to see any other reason for the advertising campaign. It is true that, in accordance with the law, it was not necessary to produce proof of purchase in order to enter. Nevertheless, about 80% of the 271,000 competitors did so, and defendant kept a record in this regard, a record accompanied by comments on the success of the campaign, which leave no room for doubt. If we add to this the fact that the competition brought the name and the products of defendant to the attention of a considerable number of non-competing consumers, it can be concluded without much difficulty that the purpose of the competition was to promote the commercial interests of accused.

There remains the question of *mens rea*. It was suggested that it is for the Crown to establish that accused was aware of the purport of its actions when it committed them. The weight of the authorities cited, in particular the case of *Imperial Tobacco Products Ltd.*, is to the effect that proof of commission of the offence is sufficient, without any necessity of showing intent. In any case, there is no necessity to decide this matter here, as the evidence shows accused was fully aware of what it was doing, if only because it was put on its guard by the "Reader's Digest" magazine, which requested a correction of the advertisement which it was to publish, a correction which could not but draw attention to the significant anomalies of the competition, if this was necessary.

Accordingly the Court finds accused guilty of the charge laid against it.

||||||||||||||||||||||||||||||||||||||||||||||||||||||||||||||||||||||||||||||||||||||||||||||||||||||||||||||||||||||||||||||||||||||||||||||||||||||||||||||||||||||||||

CASE
PROBLEMS
FOR
DISCUSSION

Case 1

Prior to 1927, widgets were manufactured in Canada by three companies: World Widgets Ltd., Canadian Widgets Ltd., and E.M.C. Widgets Ltd. In 1927, the three firms merged to form the World Widget Co. Ltd., a new firm incorporated that year. As a result of the merger, World Widget Co. Ltd. became the only producer of widgets in Canada.

In January, 1928, the company issued new price lists for its products to jobbers and distributors. The new lists raised the case price from $18 (the price before the merger) to $21.91.

In March, 1928, Columbia Widgets Ltd. was incorporated in New Brunswick, and started widget production in October of that year. The price of its product (per case) to jobbers was $19.75.

In October of the same year, World Widget Co. Ltd. introduced its product under a new brand name at a very low price to jobbers in those areas where Columbia widgets were sold. World Widget also granted confidential prices or special rebates to large jobbers and distributors that agreed to handle only the World Widget product.

In 1932, Columbia Widgets Ltd. closed its doors, and sold its assets to D. Widget, an American firm controlled by World Widget. A few weeks later, the Commonwealth Widget Company Ltd. was established by D. Widget on the site occupied previously by Columbia Widgets. Prices established by the new company were in line with those published by World Widget.

In 1931, Canada Widget Ltd., a competitor, was formed by a group of Quebec businessmen, and a plant to manufacture widgets was established in Quebec. World Widget gradually acquired control of this new firm by the acquisition of shares through its subsidiary, Widget Holdings Ltd. Prices of widgets sold by Canada Widget Ltd. were brought in line with World Widget prices following the acquisition of Canada Widget Ltd. by Widget Holdings Ltd.

In 1936, Federal Widget Ltd. was organized, and a plant established in Quebec. Following the establishment of this company, World Widget offered its regular product under another brand at a lower price in all areas where Federal widgets were sold. World Widget also established special prices and rebates on a confidential basis with jobbers prepared to carry World Widgets exclusively.

World Widget maintained the selling price of its product sold in those areas where no competition existed, and entered into agreements with distributors whereby the distributor would receive a special rebate if he would certify from time to time in writing that all widgets sold by him were sold above specified minimum prices.

In addition to these practices, World Widget established an elaborate network of "contacts" within the Federal Widget firm, and with individuals in the firm's channel of distribution. Information sent to World Widget gave World Widget a complete picture of the operation of Federal Widget. World Widget was aware of the quantities of goods received or shipped by the firm, the destination of shipments, the names of the recipients, and the selling prices of the goods shipped. Documentation of the internal operation of Federal Widget was so complete that World Widget was in possession of the Federal Christmas bonus list, and aware of the Christmas presents to be given by Federal to its employees and customers before the presentations were made.

Federal Widget found competition with World Widget difficult, and eventually came under the control of Widget Holdings Ltd. through the acquisition of shares of Federal Widgets by Widget Holdings Ltd.

In British Columbia, the Western Widget Company, a new competitor, was established in 1940. Western Widget was interested in the widget market west of Ontario, and instituted an active campaign to enter this market.

World Widget, once aware of its new competition, flooded the western market with its product, using special brands and special discounts to distributors to encourage the exclusive handling and sale of World widgets.

Western Widget tried in vain to offset the activities of World Widget with its own discounts, but failed. In 1949, Western Widget, was purchased by World Widget for $210 000.

World Widget continued aggressive marketing activity until complaints triggered an investigation of its past practices. The investigation confirmed the previous actions of the company and revealed the following information:

(1) On each "take-over" (purchase of assets or shares) World Widget Co. Ltd. or Widget Holdings Ltd. would obtain an agreement from the vendor company and its officers whereby the company and its officers would agree not to engage in the widget business in Canada, either directly or indirectly, for a specified period of time (usually 20 years).

(2) World Widget Co. Ltd. restricted the distribution of its special brand-name widgets to areas where competition existed. These products were priced lower than regular widgets bearing the World Widget name, and were offered to distributors at prices that gave the distributor a larger margin. World Widget also entered into agreements with distributors that required the distributor to offer the special brand name products to retailers at reduced prices.

Assuming that a widget is an essential consumer and industrial product of standard design, difficult to differentiate, and with a very limited useful product life (purchased frequently), discuss the legality of the activities carried on by the firm. Identify any difficulties that might arise with respect to interpretation and enforcement of the law.

Case 2

In an effort to increase sales, the marketing manager of the World Widget Co. Ltd. introduced a co-operative advertising campaign whereby it agreed to pay 50% of the widget advertising expense of any retailer selling World Widget products, provided that the retailer agreed to advertise widgets at the "suggested retail price." No assistance would be given to the retailer if he did not include the price of the product in his advertisement. The 50% payment would be based upon the dollar cost of the advertising, and would be open to all who sold the company product, regardless of sales volume.

The memorandum to retailers advised all retailers taking part in the campaign that they were free to sell the product at any price they wished to establish. The memorandum also stated that retailers were free to advertise at their own expense, if they wished to advertise widgets at a price different from the suggested retail price. The proclaimed purpose of the advertising campaign, according to the marketing manager, was to promote the product on a national basis, and not to advertise the product as a special sale item.

Assess the activities of the company in the light of current trade practices legislation.

Case 3

Retailers from time to time advertised widgets at extremely low prices as an advertising gimmick to attract customers to their stores, much to the annoyance of the marketing manager of World Widget Co. Ltd. To clarify its position on "loss leaders," the company decided to issue a price list and a memorandum to discourage the use of its product in this fashion. The new price list read as follows:

Standard Model	Distributor Net Price	Regular Dealer Price	Minimum Profitable Resale Price	Fair Retail Value
(case lot)	$21.07	$24.47	$29.95	$34.95

All widget distributors were advised by the company that the sale of widgets at prices lower than fair retail value would be investigated, and any sale at a price lower than the minimum profitable resale price might be considered a loss leader sale. The company indicated that it would "assess such a sale as it related to the marketing of World Widget Co. Ltd. products."

The memorandum further stated that it was the opinion of the company that a person "loss leads" widgets when he sells the product at a gross margin less than his average cost of doing business plus a reasonable profit.

In the months that followed the issue of the memorandum, the World Widget Marketing Manager noted that two retailers continued to sell widgets at very low prices. One of the retailers, a large retail chain, regularly advertised and sold widgets at a unit price that would amount to $21 a case. Since the retailer was a purchaser at the distributor price of $21.07, the product was sold at slightly less than actual cost.

The marketing manager stopped shipments to the retailer on the completion of his investigation, and advised the customer that no further shipments would be made until World Widget had some assurance that the retailer would not "loss lead" widgets. The retailer eventually agreed to notify all branch managers that widgets should be sold at the regular price, and loss leader selling would be discontinued. A copy of the memorandum was sent to World Widget, and on its receipt, shipments of widgets to the retailer resumed.

The other retailer, who purchased widgets at $24.47 a case, sold widgets at a price equivalent to $24.90 a case. World Widget considered this to be "loss leader" selling, and refused to make further shipments until the retailer agreed to stop selling widgets as "loss leaders." The retailer eventually agreed to stop selling widgets in this manner, and further agreed to sell the product at a price not less than the "minimum profitable resale price." Shipments of widgets were resumed when this agreement was reached.

Assess the actions of the marketing manager in this case.

Case 4

In an attempt to diversify its product line, World Widget Co. Ltd. purchased all right, title, and interest in an automobile "jet ignition unit with transistors" from a Miami, Florida, inventor. The unit consisted of a small metal container, two transistors, a small spring, and a blob of tar. The designer of the unit claimed that the device would give "better automobile gas mileage, easier starting, and better performance." In support of his claim, he provided 625 testimonial letters from users of the product who reported gas mileage improvement ranging from 10% to 30%.

World Widget engineers were skeptical of the performance claims made for the jet ignition unit, but their concern was brushed aside by the general manager when he discovered that the selling price represented a 100% mark-up over cost.

During 1980, the "jet ignition unit with transistors" had been advertised in Canada by the previous manufacturer through several metropolitan television stations, and World Widget arranged for continued television advertising for 1981. The advertising indicated that the product would increase automobile gas mileage by up to 30% and would improve engine performance. It was sold under a money-back guarantee if the product was returned to the manufacturer within 30 days of purchase.

In January, 1981, a motorist purchased a unit, and when it was installed in his car, the engine would not start. He reported his experience to a government agency which then tested the motorist's unit in a number of its own vehicles. The tests indicated that the unit had no noticeable effect on engine performance or fuel consumption. The agency informed World Widget of its findings.

In the same month, another motorist wrote the company the following letter: "I purchased one of your jet ignition units recently, and I am very pleased with the change in performance of my automobile. Starting is much easier, and gasoline mileage has improved 10%. Two of my friends purchased ignition units and have obtained similar results. I heartily recommend your product."

The company received no complaints concerning its product from purchasers, and no user requested a return of the purchase price under the money-back guarantee.

Should the company continue to market the product?

Case 5

Retail Furs carried on business as a furrier in a large metropolitan city. The general manager attributed much of the Company's sales volume to the use of extensive advertising and frequent "sales." As a general practice, the store held four sales a year: a Summer (off-season) Sale, a Fall Sale, a New Year's Sale, and a Spring Sale. In addition, the general manager would occasionally hold a special sale if sales volume was below expectations for the year. Each sale normally lasted for a month, although occasionally, extensions were made to clear models that proved to be "poor sellers."

During the past year, the company held five sales, and each featured a standard type of mink jacket at 50% off the regular retail price. On the last day of the final sale for the year, a customer entered the store and wished to purchase one of the advertised jackets. The regular price was stated as $2 000, and the sale price $1 000. The customer, however, argued that the regular price was really $1 000, and the sale price should be $500, because the jacket had been selling for $1 000 for at least five of the previous 12 months.

The general manager denied that $1 000 was the regular price, and refused to sell the jacket for $500.

An investigation into the ordinary selling prices of similar jackets in the area found that prices ranged from $995 to $2 300, depending upon the quality of the fur pelts, the cut, and the style.

Discuss the issues raised in this case.

CHAPTER 25

Insurance Law

HISTORICAL DEVELOPMENT

The reduction of risk, and in particular the risk of loss from unforseen dangers, has been a quest of mankind since the beginning of time. Originally, risk was reduced by members of a family banding together to protect one another and their possessions, but as society developed, the community tended to act as an expanded family when misfortune struck one of its members. The loss of a limb, or the destruction of a dwelling often triggered a community response to aid the unfortunate individual.

Protection from the financial loss that frequently accompanied a misfortune was recognized by the early guilds in England and Continental Europe during the Middle Ages. The benefits of protection from loss due to injury was not, however, the primary reason why craftsmen and merchants joined guilds, but it did represent an attractive advantage of membership.

The principal reason for belonging to a guild was the right to lawfully practice a craft or vocation, but attendant with this was the "insurance" that the guild generally provided for those members who, through some accident or misfortune, could no longer practice their skill. The benefits afforded by the guilds were for the most part determined by the resources of each individual guild, and were usually limited to compensation for loss or injury to the person. Some guilds, nevertheless, did provide compensation to the unfortunate workman who had his tools stolen or his goods destroyed, but in every case the benefits were paid on a benevolent, rather than contractual basis.

In spite of the variation in protection offered by the guilds, they did provide a form of insurance against loss. Because insurance, from a conceptual point of view, is simply a means of transferring a loss suffered by one person to a larger group who might conceivably suffer the same type of loss, this was essentially what the guild members did. Originally the members of the group made a common pledge to compensate one another in the event of loss, but later, the individuals in the group contributed sums of money to form a pool or fund from which a loss incurred by a member would be paid. As the fund was gradually reduced by the payment of compensation for losses, additional levies were made on the group members to replenish the fund. Eventually, nearly all guilds used this method as a basis for their insurance. It should be noted, however, that insurance schemes were not restricted to the guilds alone. Some early merchants operated indemnity funds as well, and charged fees in return for a promise to indemnify a fund member in the event of loss.

Some forms of insurance in the late medieval period did bear a certain resemblance to the modern concept of insurance. The practice of spreading the risk of loss for maritime adventures among a number of individuals was apparently carried on in the early Middle Ages, and by the 12th century, merchants in the Lombard area of what is now Italy insured against some of the perils of navigation. Italian merchants that visited England to trade brought the custom with them, and by the 14th century, a form of maritime insurance was available to cover loss at sea. Disputes between the parties were normally settled by the merchants themselves in accordance with the customs that had developed to deal with these early forms of insurance.

At that time, friendly societies were also established, which had, as one of their main objectives, the provision of accident and sickness benefits for its members. Additionally, some societies provided a form of life insurance, in the sense that they paid a death benefit in the event that a member died, but the insurance arrangement was different from modern life insurance. The first society which provided life insurance similar to modern insurance was not formed until shortly after the beginning of the 18th century.

Fire insurance was available by the 17th century, and its popularity rose after the Great Fire of London in 1666. It was initially looked upon with some suspicion (due to its particular nature) but gradually, fire insurance found favour as a means of reducing the risk of loss. It was not until the middle of the 19th century that it was finally recognized as an important form of contract.

Throughout the early stages of development of the concept of insurance, the law did little to encourage the practice of reducing risk. The early merchants settled their own insurance disputes using their own law, or custom, but the members of the guilds and friendly societies had to be content with a common law, and with a court system that was unsuited to the enforcement of insurance agreements. It was not until the middle of the 18th century that widespread use of insurance prompted the courts to examine the nature of insurance, and make the common law responsive to the legal problems associated with insurance, and the enforcement of claims. By this time, the courts began to view the insurance relationship as one of contract, and treated it as such in their application of the law. The relatively favourable climate that existed thereafter permitted the creation of many types of insurance based upon this concept. A general body of law soon developed, based in part on the customs of the merchants, and in part on the law of contract.

FORMS OF INSURANCE

There are many different kinds of insurance available to the business executive today. Nearly every conceivable form of risk may be insured, the only exception being certain activities which might encourage carelessness if insured, and deliberate acts which may cause injury or loss.

Modern insurance is based upon statistical calculation of the likelihood of a particular loss occurring. As a result of accurate record-keeping over a long period of time, insurers can determine the frequency of occurrence of different types of losses, and by these records they may establish the amount of money they require from each insured in order to maintain a fund sufficiently large at all times to cover losses as they occur. Because some of these funds are invested by the insurer, the income earned is included in the fund as well to cover the insurer's expenses, profits, and to reduce the amount that the insured must pay for the insurance coverage.

Life insurance differs, to some extent, from other forms of insurance, in that the insurer will eventually be obliged to pay the face value of all policies of insurance in force at the time of death of the insured person. Statistical data on the probable life-span of individuals, called *actuarial tables*, are used to determine the likelihood of loss due to the premature death of policy holders, and to determine the premium required to cover this unexpected event. The tables are also used to calculate the expected pay-out of the value of the policy, if the policy holder dies at the end of a normal life-span.

Some life insurance policies may be used for investment purposes, as well as for protection of the beneficiaries in the case of the unexpected death of the insured. For life insurance of this type, the premiums include not only an amount to cover the cost of coverage for an unexpected loss of life, but also an amount to provide the insured a sum of money at the end of a specified period of time.

Fire Insurance

This type of insurance is designed to indemnify a person with an interest in property for any loss which might occur as a result of fire. Normally, any person with an interest in the property may protect that interest by fire coverage. The owner of the property, and any secured creditors, or tenants (to the extent of their interest) may obtain this form of protection. Fire coverage is not limited to buildings only, as chattels contained in a building may also be insured. Fire policy protection is normally extended to damage caused as a result of the fire, as in the case of smoke and water damage. Insurance policies usually only indemnify the insured against loss from "hostile" fires, i.e., a fire that is not in its proper place. In contrast, a fire in a fireplace, for example, would be classed as a "friendly" fire, rather than a "hostile" one, as it is a fire deliberately set in its proper place. Insurers distinguish between the two types of fires, because a friendly fire is usually not insured. If a friendly fire becomes a hostile fire, the resultant loss is usually covered by fire insurance, unless the actions of the insured with respect to the fire were such that the fire may be classed as arson, or as a deliberate attempt to destroy the insured premises by that fire.

Life Insurance

As the name indicates, life insurance is insurance on the life of a person, be it one's personal life, or that of another person, in which one has an insurable interest. Life insurance, in its simplest form, is payable on the death of a particular person and, unlike other forms of insurance, is based upon an event which will eventually occur. The only uncertainty attached to life insurance is the timing of the death that will render the policy payable. It differs from other forms of insurance in that the person upon whose life the insurance is placed does not receive the proceeds of the insurance, although they may be made payable to the deceased's estate if no specific beneficiary is named in the policy.

Life insurance policies usually include an *application* for the insurance, in which the insured sets out all the information required by the insurer to determine if the risk should be accepted, and if so, the premium payable for assuming the risk. The application is usually incorporated in the policy, and becomes a part of the contract. Fraudulent statements by the applicant generally permit the insurer to avoid payment under the policy when the fraud is discovered.

Under provincial legislation, a life insurance policy may take on a variety of different forms, from simple term insurance to special purpose policies. The legislation generally does not determine the specific kinds of policies which a life insurer may issue but, rather, the terms that must be contained in the policy respecting such matters as lapse, renewal, time for payment of proceeds, and the proof of death of the insured. The legislation also covers other aspects of life insurance, such as life insurers themselves, and the operation of their businesses. As with most insurers, life insurers are required to follow strict rules regarding the investment of their funds, in order to make sure that the company remains solvent, and that it is in a position to pay all claims under the policies.

Sickness and Accident Insurance

Insurance for sickness and accident represents a type of insurance which protects against or reduces the loss which a policy holder might incur through sickness or accident. The amounts payable usually vary, but upper limits on sickness benefits are normally set at an amount less than a person's normal income, and is payable on presentation of proof of the illness. Accident benefits which cover loss of limb, eyesight, or other permanent injuries are generally fixed in the policy at specific dollar amounts. As with other forms of insurance (other than life), this type of insurance is designed to provide indemnity for the loss incurred.

Liability and Negligence Insurance

Liability and Negligence insurance are designed to indemnify persons for liability for losses due to negligence in the performance of their work, profession, actions, or premises. The policy, by nature, covers specific losses such as those that may arise from negligence in the operation of a motor vehicle, the operation of a business establishment, or even a residence. These policies are designed to compensate for losses due to the torts of the individual, rather than for direct losses which an individual might suffer through no fault of his own. Of the many forms of negligence or liability insurance, automobile insurance has become so important, and its use so widespread, that it is treated separately under insurance legislation in most provinces. A standard policy form has also been devised as a result of interprovincial co-operation by those provinces that do not maintain their own compulsory government administered automobile insurance scheme.

Apart from automobile insurance, liability insurance is normally used to protect against claims of loss arising out of the use of premises (i.e., occupier's liability), manufacturer's product liability, professional negligence, and third party liability for the acts of servants or agents.

Special Types of Insurance

In addition to these general forms of insurance coverage, insurance is also available for many specialized purposes. For example, insurance policies may be obtained to protect an employer from an employee's dishonesty, for theft or loss of goods, for business interruption, for ships and cargo, and for a variety of other business activities. All of these have one characteristic in common, i.e., they are designed to indemnify the insured in the event of a loss, or in a claim for compensation.

THE NATURE OF THE INSURANCE CONTRACT

The contract of insurance, as the name implies, is a contractual relationship to which the general rules of contract, and a number of special rules apply. It is treated by the courts as a contract *uberrimae fidei* (a contract of utmost good faith). It is also a relationship which has been the subject of much control through legislation. Each province has legislation governing the contract of insurance in its various forms and, with the exception of the Province of Quebec, the legislation has tended to become uniform for most types of insurance. A number of provinces have special legislation which provides for provincially-controlled automobile insurance, or for "no-fault" insurance for automobile accident cases; for the remainder, the general legislation and the common law rules apply. Changes in standard-form policies are effected by *riders* or *endorsements* that represent changes or additions to the standard terms and coverage on the policy.

The contract of insurance is a special type of contract called a *policy* which is made between an *insurer* and an *insured*; whereby the insurer promises to indemnify the insured for any loss which may flow from the occurrence of any event described in the agreement. In return for this promise, the insured pays, or agrees to pay, a sum of money called a *premium*.

The contract of insurance bears a resemblance to a simple wagering agreement, in that the insurer must pay out a sum of money on the occurrence of a particular event. The resemblance, however, is only superficial because there are substantial differences between the two types of agreements—the most important difference being the interests of the parties. In the case of a simple wager, the basis of the agreement is generally the occurrence of an event which will not result in a loss to either party (except for the amount of the wager which each party has pledged). In contrast to this, under an insurance policy, the insured receives nothing until he suffers some loss, and even then, he will only receive a sum which will theoretically place him in the same position that he was in before the loss occurred. The exception here is life insurance, where the insured must die to collect, but even here, payment is not made unless the insured suffers the loss.

The loss which the insured suffers must relate to what is known as an *insurable interest*. This interest must be present in every insurance contract, and may be defined as anything in which the insured has a financial interest which on the occurrence of some event might result in a loss to him. An insurable interest may arise from ownership or part-ownership of a chattel or real property, or a security interest in either of them, or it may be one's own life, the life of one's spouse or child, or the life of a debtor or anyone in whom a person may have a pecuniary interest (for example, a partner or a key employee). It may also arise out of a person's profession, or activity to protect income, or assets. Most insurers, however, will not insure a person against the wilful acts which they commit against themselves, or their insured interests. For example, a person may not obtain fire coverage on his home, then deliberately burn the premises to collect the insurance proceeds. Nor would an insurer normally be obliged to pay out life insurance on the life of an insured who committed suicide, but under insurance legislation in some jurisdictions, the beneficiaries may be entitled to the insurance proceeds in the case of a suicide where the policy has been in effect for some time.[1]

In general, an insurable interest is anything which stands to benefit the person by its continued existence in its present form, and which, if changed, would represent a loss. The insurable interest, however, must exist both at the time the contract of insurance is made, and when the event occurs which results in a loss.[1a] For example, if Arthurs places a policy of insurance on a house which he owns, then later sells the house to Bond for cash, and the house is subsequently destroyed by fire, Arthurs would not be permitted to collect the insured value of the house. By selling the house he divested himself of the interest he had in the property, and he no longer had an insurable interest in the property at the time of the loss. Nor would Bond be entitled to recover under the policy, because he was not a party to the insurance contract.[2]

In addition to the requirement that the insured possess an insurable interest, the contract of insurance, being a contract of utmost good faith, requires full disclosure on the part of the applicant for the insurance of all material facts which might affect the decision of the insurer to accept the

[1]Ontario, for example, provides that payment shall be made if the policy has been in force for more than two years.
[1a]except for life insurance
[2]*Rowe v. Fidelity Phoenix*, [1944] O.W.N. 389, 600.

risk and determine the appropriate premium. With respect to disclosure, the courts have reasoned that the insurer knows nothing, and the applicant everything, hence, the obligation on the part of the applicant to disclose all material facts.

The right of the insurer to be apprised of all material facts is important. The insurer is undertaking a risk which is frequently determined from the information supplied by the applicant and, consequently, honesty on the part of the applicant is essential. If the applicant fails to disclose material facts, then the insurer may later refuse to compensate the insured if a loss occurs. For example, if the true owner of a motor vehicle arranges with a friend to have the vehicle registered in her name for the purpose of obtaining insurance, the insurance protection may not extend to the true owner if the true owner was driving the vehicle at the time of an accident which involved him, and for which he was responsible.[3]

At common law, the non-disclosure or misrepresentation of a material fact would entitle the insurer to later avoid liability when the non-disclosure or misrepresentation was discovered. This has been altered, to some extent, by statute in various provinces, but for the most part the rule still holds. The exception which the legislation makes, relates generally to innocent misrepresentation or innocent non-disclosure, but where the non-disclosure or the misrepresentation amounts to fraud, then the common law rule still holds.

The legislative modification of the common law position has, as its justification, the unfairness of an insurer refusing payment of a loss where the insured without intention to deceive failed to disclose a

fact, or stated an untruth as something which he honestly believed to be true. In these cases, the common law requirements for a contract of utmost good faith have been modified to require the insurer to carry out the policy terms if the policy has been in effect for a considerable period of time before the loss occurs (usually several years).

A contract of insurance differs from an ordinary contract in a number of other ways as well. It tends to be an ongoing relationship, which usually requires the insured to advise the insurer of any substantial changes in the risk covered by the policy. Fire insurance policies usually require the insured to notify the insurer if the insured premises will be left unoccupied for more than a specified period of time, and insured business people are expected to notify the insurer if the risks associated with the conduct of their business changes substantially. For example, if a manufacturer of children's toys suddenly changes his product line to include the manufacture of fireworks or some other dangerous product, he would be obliged to notify the insurer that a new, higher risk activity will take place on the premises.[4]

|||||||||||||||||||||||||||||||||||||||||||||||||||||||||||||||||||||||||||||||||

CASE 25.1

Mutual Life Ins. Co., N.Y. v. Ontario Metal Products Co., [1925] 1 D.L.R. 583.

LORD SALVESEN:

The main difference of judicial opinion centres round the question what is the test of materiality? Mignault, J., [1924] 1 D.L.R., at p. 145, thought that the test is not what the insurers would have done but for the misrepresentation or concealment but "what any reasonable man would have considered material to tell them when the questions were put to the insured".

---

[3]*Minister of Transport et al. v. London & Midland General Ins. Co.*, [1971] 3 O.R. 147.

[4]*Poapst v. Madill et al.*, [1973] 2 O.R. 80.

Their Lordships are unable to assent to this definition. It is the insurers who propound the questions stated in the application form, and the materiality or otherwise of a misrepresentation or concealment must be considered in relation to their acceptance of the risk. On the other hand, it was argued that the test of materiality is to be determined by reference to the questions; that the Insurance Company had by putting the question shown that it was important for them to know whether the proposer had been in the hands of a medical man within 5 years of his application, and, if so, to have had the opportunity of interviewing such medical man before accepting the risk. The question was therefore, they contended, a material one, and the failure to answer it truthfully avoids the contract. Now if this were the true test to be applied there would be no appreciable difference between a policy of insurance subject to s. 156 of the Ontario Insurance Act, and one in the form hitherto usual in the United Kingdom. All of the questions may be presumed to be of importance to the insurer who causes them to be put, and any inaccuracy, however unimportant in the answers, would, in this view, avoid the policy. Suppose, for example, that the insured had consulted a doctor for a headache or a cold on a single occasion and had concealed or forgotten the fact, could such a concealment be regarded as material to the contract? Faced with a difficulty of this kind, the appellants' counsel frankly conceded that materiality must always be a question of degree, and therefore to be determined by the Court, and suggested that the test was whether, if the fact concealed had been disclosed, the insurers would have acted differently, either by declining the risk at the proposed premium or at least by delaying consideration of its acceptance until they had consulted Dr. Fierheller. If the former proposition were established in the sense that a reasonable insurer would have so acted, materiality would, their Lordships think, be established, but not in the latter if the difference of action would have been delay and delay alone. In their view it is a question of fact in each case whether if the matters concealed or misrepre-

sented had been truly disclosed, they would, on a fair consideration of the evidence, have influenced a reasonable insurer to decline the risk or to have stipulated for a higher premium.

THE CONCEPT OF INDEMNITY FOR LOSS

The particular feature which distinguishes the contract of insurance from a wager is the fact that it is a contract of indemnity. With the exception of life insurance, and to some extent, accident insurance, all contracts of insurance prevent the insured from making a profit from a loss. A number of special insurance concepts ensure that the insured will only be placed in the position that he was in before the event occurred that caused the loss. For some forms of loss, which concern third parties, no special protection is needed for the insurer. For example, if Smith should injure Jones by his negligence, Smith's insurer will compensate Jones for his loss, or pay any judgement which Jones might obtain against Smith for his carelessness. Only the injured party will be compensated, and then only for the actual loss suffered.

With respect to chattels or property owned by the insured, three special rights of the insurer apply in the event of loss in order to prevent the insured from receiving more than the actual loss sustained. If the property is not completely destroyed, the insurer has the option to repair the chattel, or pay the insured the full value of the property at the time of loss. If the insurer pays the insured the value of the chattel, then the insurer is entitled to the property. This particular right is known as *salvage*, and it gives the insurer the right under the policy to demand a transfer of the title to the damaged goods. For example, McKay owns an automobile insured by the Car Insurance Company. The automobile is involved in an accident, and is damaged. If the Car Insurance Company compensates McKay for the value of the automobile, then McKay must deliver up the damaged automobile to the insurer in return for payment. The insurance company may then dispose of the wreck to reduce the loss which it has suffered through the payment of McKay's claim.

The same principle would apply in the case of goods stolen from the insured. If the insurer pays the insured the value of the stolen goods, and if the goods are subsequently recovered, the goods will belong to the insurer, and not the insured. By the terms of the policy of indemnity, the goods become the goods of the insurer on the payment of the claim. In a sense, the contract bears some resemblance to a purchase of the goods by the insurer.

A second form of protection for the insurer is the doctrine of *subrogation.* Subrogation concerns the right of the insurer to recover from another person that which the insured recovers from the insurer. The doctrine of subrogation arises where the insured is injured or suffers some loss due to the actionable negligence or deliberate act of another party. For example, if an insured automobile is damaged by the negligence of another driver, the owner would have a right of action against the other driver for the damage caused by the other driver's negligence. If the insurer compensates the owner for the damage to his automobile then, by the doctrine of subrogation, the insurer is entitled to benefit from the owner's right of action against the negligent party.

Contracts of insurance may contain a subrogation clause which specifically provides that the insured cedes his right to proceed against the party causing the injury to the insurer, or it may require the insured to proceed against the wrongdoer on behalf of the insurer, if the insurer pays the insured for the loss which the insured suffered.

The doctrine of subrogation represents an important insurance concept. Without the right of subrogation, the insured would be entitled to payment twice: once from the insurer under the contract of insurance, and a second amount in the form of damages which he might obtain by taking legal action against the negligent party for the injury suffered. The right of subrogation precludes double payment to the insured, and places the liability for the loss upon the person responsible for it. Subrogation has an additional beneficial side-effect; the right of the insurer to recover its losses from the negligent party substantially reduces the premiums which the insured must pay for insurance coverage.

A third factor which limits the insured's compensation to the actual amount of the loss is the right of *contribution* between insurers. Persons sometimes have more than one policy of insurance covering the same loss, but if the policies contain a clause which entitles the insurer to contribution, then each insurer will only be required to pay a portion of the loss. For example, if an insured has insurance coverage with three different insurers against a specific loss, and he suffers a loss of $1 000 he will not be permitted to collect $1 000 from each of the insurers. He will only be entitled to collect a total of $1 000 from the three (i.e., $333.33 each). Each insurer would only be required to pay his share of the loss suffered by the insured.

In some cases, if the policy so provides, the insured may become an insurer for a part of the loss if he fails to adequately insure his risks. With some risks, the likelihood of a total loss may sometimes be small, and to prevent the insured from placing only a small amount of insurance to cover the risk, the insurer may, in the policy of insurance, require the insured to become a co-insurer in the event of a partial loss. Generally, a minimum amount of insurance will be specified in the policy, and if the insured fails to maintain at least that amount, then he becomes a co-insurer for the amount of his deficiency. For example, if the policy contains an 80% co-insurance clause, then the insured must maintain insurance for at least that amount of the value of the property (or if the insurance is burglary insurance, not less than a stated sum). The formula applied in the event of a partial loss would be:

$$\frac{\text{actual amount of insurance carried}}{\text{minimum coverage required}} \times \text{loss}$$

= insurer's contribution

Thus, if the property is worth $100 000, and the insurance coverage is $60 000, a loss of $10 000 would be calculated as follows if the policy contains an 80% co-insurance clause (80% of $100 000 = $80 000 minimum coverage required).

$$\text{insurer's contribution} = \frac{\$60\ 000}{\$80\ 000} \times \$10\ 000 = \$7\ 500$$

In this example, the insurer would only be obliged to pay $7 500 of the $10 000 loss. The insured, because he failed to maintain a minimum of 80% coverage would be required to absorb the remainder of the loss himself as a co-insurer. If the loss, however, had exceeded $80 000, then the full amount of the insurance would be payable by the insurer. Co-insurance only applies where the insured suffers a partial loss of less than the required amount of insurance coverage.

THE PARTIES ASSOCIATED WITH INSURANCE CONTRACTS

Apart from the insurer and the insured, a number of other parties may be involved in either the negotiation of the contract of insurance, or the processing of claims under it. Most insurance is negotiated through *agents* or employees of the insurer, and these persons have varying degrees of authority to bind the insurer in contract. The agents are generally agents of the insurer, and liable to the insurer for their actions. However, in cases where the insured has relied on the statements of the agent that the policy written by the agent covers the risks which the insured wished to have insured, and this later proves not to be the case, the insured may have a cause of action against the agent if a loss should occur.[5]

||||||||||||||||||||||||||||||||||||||||||||||||||||||||||||||||||||||||||||||||||||||||||||||||

CASE 25.2
Fine's Flowers Ltd. et. al v. General Accident Assurance Co. of Canada et al. (1977), 81 D.L.R. (3d) 139.

WILSON, J.A.:

The agent's duty, counsel submits, is "to exercise a reasonable degree of skill and care to obtain policies in the terms bargained for and to service those policies as circumstances might require".

I take no issue with counsel's statement of the scope of the insurance agent's duty except to add that the agent also has a duty to advise his principal if he is unable to obtain the policies bargained for so that his principal may take such further steps to protect himself as he deems desirable. The operative words, however, in counsel's definition of the scope of the

[5]*Fine's Flowers Ltd. et al. v. General Accident Assurance of Canada et al.* (1974), 49 D.L.R. (3d) 641.

agent's duty, are "policies in the terms bargained for".

In many instances, an insurance agent will be asked to obtain a specific type of coverage and his duty in those circumstances will be to use a reasonable degree of skill and care in doing so or, if he is unable to do so, "to inform the principal promptly in order to prevent him from suffering loss through relying upon the successful completion of the transaction by the agent": Ivamy, *General Principles of Insurance Law*, 2nd ed. (1970), at p. 464.

But there are other cases, and in my view this is one of them, in which the client gives no such specific instructions but rather relies upon his agent to see that he is protected and, if the agent agrees to do business with him on those terms, then he cannot afterwards, when an uninsured loss arises, shrug off the responsibility he has assumed. If this requires him to inform himself about his client's business in order to assess the foreseeable risks and insure his client against them, then this he must do. It goes without saying that an agent who does not have the requisite skills to understand the nature of his client's business and assess the risks that should be insured against should not be offering this kind of service. As Mr. Justice Haines said in *Lahey v. Hartford Fire Ins. Co.*, [1968] 1 O.R. 727 at p. 729, 67 D.L.R. (2d) 506 at p. 508; varied [1969] 2 O.R. 883, 7 D.L.R. (3d) 315:

"The solution lies in the intelligent insurance agent who inspects the risks when he insures them, knows what his insurer is providing, discovers the areas that may give rise to dispute and either arranges for the coverage or makes certain the purchaser is aware of the exclusion."

I do not think this is too high a standard to impose upon an agent who knows that his client is relying upon him to see that he is protected against all foreseeable, insurable risks.

Brokers may also place insurance with insurers, and may act either for the insured or the insurer. Persons with complex insurance needs may use a broker to determine the various kinds of insurance which they require. The broker will determine the risks, then arrange for the appropriate coverage by seeking out insurers who will insure the risks for the client.

Insurance adjusters are persons employed by an insurer to investigate the report of loss by an insured, and to determine the extent of the loss incurred. Insurance adjusters report their findings to the insurer, and on the basis of the investigation, the insurer frequently settles insurance claims. When, as a result of the adjuster's investigation, the issue of liability is unclear, the insurer may carry the matter on to the courts for a decision before making payment for the loss.

||||||||||||||||||||||||||||||||||||||||||||||||||||||||||||||||||||||||||||||||||||||||||||||||||||||||||||||||||||||||||||||||||||||||||||||||||||||||||||||||||||||||||||||||||||||||||

SUMMARY   With the exception of life insurance, the contract of insurance is a special type of contract designed to indemnify an insured if he should suffer a loss insured against in the insurance policy. A contract of insurance differs from a wagering agreement in that it is only designed to indemnify the insured for the actual loss sustained. It differs also in that the insured must have an insurable interest in the property or activity before the loss becomes payable. The contract of insurance is a contract of utmost good faith, and the full disclosure of all material facts must be made to the insurer if the insured wishes to hold the insurer bound by the policy. Life insurance differs from other forms of insurance in that it is not payable to the person on whose life it is placed.

Because insurance (except life and accident insurance) is designed only to indemnify the insured for losses suffered, the insurer is entitled to the rights of salvage, subrogation, and contribution to limit the loss which he suffers as an insurer. Where an insured underinsures, some policies also make the insured a co-insurer for partial losses.

DISCUSSION QUESTIONS

1. What differentiates "insurance" from "wagering"?
2. Explain the difference between "life insurance" and other forms of insurance.
3. What prevents an unscrupulous individual from taking out life insurance policies on sick or elderly people?
4. Distinguish between a "friendly" and a "hostile" fire.
5. Would fire insurance normally cover smoke damage caused when an unfortunate householder lit a fire in a chimney clogged by a bird's nest?
6. Why is insurance a contract uberrimae fidei?
7. Why does indemnity insurance seldom cover the deliberate acts of an insured which cause damage?
8. The luxury liner Titanic sank at sea in 1912, and allegedly contained a large quantity of gold bars and valuables. If someone should raise the ship today, would that person be entitled to the ship and its contents, or would the ship and gold go to its 1912 insurer?
9. Outline the doctrine of "subrogation" and its application.
10. The right of contribution would allow three insurance companies to pay one-third of a specific loss, but the insured must pay the premium of each company as if he was insuring the full loss. Is this fair? Is it wise to have more than one policy to cover a specific loss?
11. When the loss exceeds coverage of a policy which contains a co-insurance clause, would the insurer's contribution be total or fractional?
12. How does the doctrine of subrogation affect the total premiums charged by insurers for liability insurance?
13. What mathematical principles allow insurance to be both profitable for the insurer and equitable for the insured?
14. A farmer insured his barn against fire loss for $4 000 even though its value was $10 000. The insurance policy contained an 80% co-insurance clause. Some time later, a fire caused 2 000 damage to the barn. Calculate the loss payable by the insurer.

JUDICIAL DECISIONS	**Swinimer et al. v. Corkum; Prudential Assurance Co. Ltd., Third Party (1978), 89 D.L.R. (3d) 245.**

Motor Vehicle Insurance Policy Renewal— Failure to Inform Insurer of Change Material to Risk— Enforceability of Policy Against Insurer

In 1967, the insured took out an automobile insurance policy in which he stated that his driver's license had not been suspended during the previous three years. Each year he received a renewal statement which provided that the insurance would be renewed on the basis of the statements of the insured in the original application, subject to any amendments. The insured continued to renew the insurance without reading the renewal statements. The insured's license was cancelled for a period of time in 1973, and in his renewals he did not disclose this fact. Several years later, the insured was involved in an automobile accident, and the insurer took the position that the policy was not enforceable.

MACINTOSH, J.:

Was Corkum in breach of stat. con. 1 [enacted 1966, c. 79, s. 7] of the automobile insurance part of the *Insurance Act*?

Statutory condition 1 reads as follows:

"1(1) *Material Change in Risk*—The insured named in this contract shall promptly notify the insurer, or its local agent, in writing, of any change in the risk material to the contract and within his knowledge.

"(2) Without restricting the generality of the foregoing the words "change in the risk material to the contract" include:

    (a) any change in the insurable interest of the insured named in this contract in the automobile by sale, assignment or otherwise, except through change of title by succession, death or proceedings under the Bankruptcy Act (Canada);

and with respect to insurance against loss of or damage to the automobile;

    (b) any mortgage, lien or encumbrance affecting the automobile after the application for this contract;

    (c) any other insurance of the same interest, whether valid or not, covering loss or damage insured by this contract or any portion thereof."

This statutory condition imposes a duty on the insured to notify his insurer of "any change in the risk material to the contract".

In order to show that the change of risk material to the contract it must be shown that the facts which were not disclosed would have influenced a reasonable insurer to decline the risk or to have stipulated from a higher premium.

This question was dealt with by Cromarty, J., of the Ontario High Court, in *Poapst v. Madill et al.* (1973), 33 D.L.R. (3d) 36, [1973] 2 O.R. 80, wherein he was considering whether or not a change of the use of trucks from limited local use to long haul use by an insured constituted a change to the risk. His Lordship stated at pp. 41-2:

"I therefore hold that by making long-haul runs to Florida, as he did, there was a change in the operation of the vehicle material to the risk known to the insurer when the policy, ex. 1, and the alteration endorsement made part thereof, were issued by the defendant Lloyd's.

"This problem is discussed in several cases.

"*Henwood v. Prudential Ins. Co. of America*, [1967] S.C.R. 720, 64 D.L.R. (2d) 715. This case dealt with an application for life insurance in which the applicant failed to disclose that she had undergone an emotional disturbance some time prior to making the application.

"*Per* Ritchie, J., at p. 724 S.C.R., p. 718 D.L.R.:

" 'There is, in my view, no doubt that the question of materiality is one of fact and, as the learned trial judge has pointed out, no evidence was called on behalf of the appellant to contradict the categorical statement made by the respondent's own doctor to the effect that if true information had been available to the respondent, the premium rate for the policy would have been a very high one.'

"and at pp. 727-8 S.C.R., p. 722, D.L.R.:

" 'If the matters here concealed had been truly disclosed they would undoubtedly have influenced the respondent company in stipulating for a higher premium and as there is no evidence to suggest that this was unreasonable or that other insurance companies would have followed a different course, I am satisfied that, on the evidence before us, it has been shown affirmatively that untrue answers respecting the medical advisers consulted by the insured were material to the risk. This is enough to avoid the policy.'

"The same problem with respect to a life policy was considered in *Mutual Life Ins. Co. of New York v. Ontario Metal Products Co. Ltd.*, [1925] 1 D.L.R. 583, [1925] A.C. 344, [1925] 1 W.L.R. 362, where the headnote [A.C.] is as follows:

" 'When statements made by an insured person upon his application for a policy of life insurance are not made the basis of the contract but are to be treated merely as representations, an inaccurate statement is material so as to vitiate the policy if the matters concealed or misrepresented, had they been truly disclosed, would have influenced a reasonable insurer to decline the risk, or to have stipulated for a higher premium; it is not sufficient that they would merely have caused delay in issuing the policy while further inquiries were being made.'

"An automobile policy was considered in *Johnston v. British Canadian Ins. Co.*, [1932] S.C.R. 680 at p. 687, [1932] 4 D.L.R. 281 at p. 287, where Lamont, J., said:

" 'Every fact is material which would, if known, reasonably affect the minds of prudent and experienced insurers in deciding whether they will accept the contract, or in fixing the amount of premium to be charged in case they accept it.' "

H. Mullane is an assistant branch manager of Prudential and responsible for the underwriting of this company in the Atlantic area. He testified that had Prudential knowledge of the suspension of Corkum his file would have then been automatically reviewed and if renewed would be at an increase in premium of 100%. He further stated that this was the practice of other insurance companies. There was no evidence to the contrary.

Corkum's suspension of his driving privileges for the reasons abovementioned was a "change in the risk material to the contract". His failure to notify the insurer of such change placed him in breach of stat. con. 1, thereby releasing Prudential from liability under its policy with Corkum.

||||||||||||||||||||||||||||||||||||||||||||||||||||||||||||||||||||||||||||||||||||||||||||||||||||||||||||||||||||||||||||||||||||||||||||||||||||

Insurance— Rights of Insurer to Subrogation Where Insured Not Compensated in Full for Loss

Lawton v. Dartmouth Moving & Storage Ltd. (1975), 64 D.L.R. (3d) 326.

The plaintiffs delivered to the defendant certain articles of furniture for storage. The goods were subsequently damaged by fire, and each of the plaintiffs claimed for the damage under their own fire insurance policies. The insurer compensated the plaintiffs for a part of the loss suffered by them, and brought an action in their names against the defendant for the loss.

The question to be decided was: Could an insurer claim subrogation where he did not compensate the insured for the full amount of the loss sustained?

DUBINSKY, J.:

> Mr. Oliver, in his well-prepared brief, dealt with the subject of subrogation and has cited a number of cases. I shall refer to merely one of these, *Traders General Ins. Co. v. Noel* (1956), 8 D.L.R. (2d) 341, [1956-60] I.L.R. 293. In that case, at pp. 347-8, McNair, C.J.N.B., quoted with approval the words of Brett, L.J., in *Castellain v. Preston et al.* (1883), 11 Q.B.D. 380 at p. 388:
>
> " 'In order to apply the doctrine of subrogation, it seems to me that the full and absolute meaning of the word must be used, that is to say, the insurer must be placed in the position of the assured. Now it seems to me that in order to carry out the fundamental rule of insurance law, this doctrine of subrogation must be carried to the extent which I am now about to endeavour to express, namely, that as between the underwriter and the assured the underwriter is entitled to the advantage of every right of the assured, whether such right consists in contract, fulfilled or unfulfilled, or in remedy for tort capable of being insisted on or already insisted on, or in any other right, whether by way of condition or otherwise, legal or equitable, which can be, or has been exercised or has accrued, and whether such right could or could not be enforced by the insurer in the name of the assured by the exercise or acquiring of which right or condition the loss against which the assured is insured, can be, or has been diminished.' "
>
> Mr. Oliver also quoted from *MacGillivray on Insurance Law*, 5th ed. (1961), and here again, I shall make only one brief reference to his quotations from that learned author. In para. 1930, MacGillivray states:

"Where the owner of goods is insured the insurers are subrogated to his remedy against carriers, warehousemen and other bailees responsible for the safety of the goods. . . . The insurers who have paid the owner are entitled to recover the whole loss from the carrier or wharfinger who is liable to the owner . . ."

It goes without saying that I readily subscribe to the above citations and others mentioned in Mr. Oliver's submission. However, in *Sheridan v. Tynes* (1971), 19 D.L.R. (3d) 277, 4 N.S.R. (2d) 143, wherein I dealt at some length with subrogation, I pointed out that the doctrine does not apply where the insurer has not idemnified the insured in full. As to this principle, 22 Hals., 3rd ed., p. 163, para. 312, states:

"(3) It is only on payment of the whole of the loss sustained by the assured, whether total or partial, that the insurer is entitled to be subrogated to his rights of action, so that if the amount insured is less than the amount of such loss, the insurers, though they have paid the amount insured, will not be subrogated to those rights. Therefore the assured remains *dominus litis* in an action brought by him against the person primarily liable, and will be entitled to compromise the action without the assent of the insurers, provided always that he acts bona fide, without any intention to sacrifice their interests."

Turning again to *Traders General Ins. Co. v. Noel, supra,* cited by Mr. Oliver, it will be noted that McNair, C.J.N.B., at p. 347, also quoted with approval, as had done Hodgins, J.A., in *Globe & Rutgers Fire Ins. Co. v. Truedell,* [1927] 2 D.L.R. 659 at p. 660, 60 O.L.R. 227, another passage from the opinion of Brett, L.J., in *Castellain v. Preston et al., supra,* at p. 386:

" 'In order to give my opinion upon this case, I feel obliged to revert to the very foundation of every rule which has been promulgated and acted on by the Courts with regard to insurance law. The very foundation, in my opinion, of every rule which has been applied to insurance law is this, namely, that the contract of insurance contained in a marine or fire policy is a contract of indemnity, and of indemnity only, and that this contract means that the assured, in case of a loss against which the policy has been made, shall be fully indemnified, but shall never be more than fully indemnified. That is the fundamental principle of insurance, and if ever a proposition is brought forward which is at variance with it, that is to say, which either will prevent the assured from obtaining a full indemnity, or which will give to the assured more than a full indemnity, that proposition must certainly be wrong.' "

In the *Globe & Rutgers v. Truedell* case, *supra,* Ferguson, J.A., approved of *National Fire Ins. Co. et al. v. McLaren* (1886), 12 O.R. 682, where Boyd, C., said at p. 687:

"The doctrine of subrogation is a creature of equity not founded on contract, but arising out of the relations of the parties. In cases of insurance where a third party is liable to make good the loss, the right of subrogation depends upon and is regulated by the broad underlying principle of securing *full* indemnity to the insured, on the one hand,

and on the other of holding him accountable as trustee for any advantage he may obtain over and above compensation for his loss. Being an equitable right, it partakes of all the ordinary incidents of such rights, one of which is that in administering relief the Court will regard not so much the form as the substance of the transaction. The primary consideration is to see that the insured gets *full compensation* for the property destroyed and the expenses incurred in making good his loss. The next thing is to see that he holds any surplus for the benefit of the insurance company."
(My italics.)

At p. 688, Boyd, C., went on to say:

"It is laid down in *Kyner v. Kyner*, 6 Watts (Penn.) 221, that there can be no such thing as subrogation to the right of a party whose claim is not wholly satisfied. The Court it is said cannot interfere with his security while part of his debt remains unpaid. Many other cases to the like effect are to be found in *Sheldon* on Subrogation, sec. 127. This principle appears to have guided the decision of the Court of Appeal in *Commercial Union Assurance Co. v. Lister*, L.R. 9 Ch. 483. I find it is stated in Mr. Bunyon's book on Fire Insurance, 3rd ed. p. 128, that the right to subrogation does not arise until full payment, satisfaction or indemnity is provided for."

If each of the insured herein was not indemnified in full, it would appear that the insurer's right to proceed by way of subrogation is questionable. What, it may be asked, is the effect of s. 128(1) of the *Insurance Act*, R.S.N.S. 1967, c. 148? That section reads as follows:

"128(1) The insurer, upon making *any* payment or assuming liability therefor under a contract of fire insurance, shall be subrogated to *all* rights of recovery of the insured against any person, and *may* bring action in the name of the insured to enforce such rights."
(The italics are mine.)

In *Sheridan v. Tynes, supra*, when referring to the almost identical s. 100M(1), I said the following at pp. 287-8:

"The Legislature could not have intended to mean that the insurer on making *any* payment, would be entitled to *all* rights of recovery irrespective of whether the insured was completely indemnified or not. Further, the provision says that the insurer *may* bring an action and not that he *shall* do so. It would seem to me that what was meant was that action may be taken by the insurer, should the insurer deem it proper so to do. The insurer can do that, however, only if the insured has been fully compensated—at least, so it now appears to me, and therefore I have some doubts as to whether the first action was legally taken."

From the evidence given by the two assured, I am satisfied and have concluded as a fact that neither one was indemnified in full. Although s. 128(1) of the *Insurance Act* would seem to give the insurer in each instance certain rights, I am of the same view with regard to statutory subrogation as I expressed in *Sheridan v. Tynes, supra*. I would therefore question the insurers' right to proceed herein.

||||||||||||||||||||||||||||||||||||||||||||||||||||||||||||||||||||||||||||||||||||||||||||||||||||||||||||||||||||||||||||||||||||||

Right to Proceeds of Insurance— Husband Murdered Wife Then Committed Suicide— Whether Wife's Property Passes to Husband's Estate

Re Gore, [1972] 1 O.R. 550.

The husband had insurance on his life which named his wife as beneficiary. The husband later murdered his wife and his two children, then committed suicide. The court was obliged to decide whether the next-of-kin of the husband as well as the next-of-kin of the wife were entitled to the insurance proceeds.

OSLER, J.:

At the time of her death Ruth Ann Gore was survived by her husband Joseph Hector Gore and by the two children already mentioned. It is well established that upon grounds of public policy a wrongdoer is prevented from benefiting personally by his act and hence, Joseph Hector Gore cannot share in the estate as on an intestacy. The persons entitled, therefore, were the only children, Christine Louise Gore and Laurie Ann Gore. At the time of the death of Christine Louise Gore the same principle prevents her father from sharing in her estate and hence her entire estate passed to her surviving sister Laurie Ann Gore.

Upon the death of Laurie Ann Gore, her father was disentitled and under the *Devolution of Estates Act*, R.S.O. 1960, c. 106 [now R.S.O. 1970, c. 129], her estate would go to her next of kin in equal degree. These would normally comprise the three surviving grandparents, Mabel Roberts, maternal grandmother, Hector Gore, Sr., paternal grandfather and Bertha Gore, paternal grandmother of Laurie Ann Gore.

It was argued by counsel for Mabel Roberts that she was the only person entitled as next of kin of Laurie Ann Gore, his submission being that the heirs or next of kin of a person disqualified from inheriting because of his own wrongful act were likewise disentitled and could not be permitted to benefit. While it appears that there may be some support for that submission in what was said by Ritchie, J., in *Nordstrom v. Baumann*, [1962] S.C.R. 147 at p. 156, 31 D.L.R. (2d) 255 at p. 262, 37 W.W.R. 16, that dictum was unnecessary to the decision in that case. In any event, the claims of Hector Gore, Sr., and Bertha Gore under the *Devolution of Estates Act* are direct claims upon the estate of their granddaughter arising because of their relationship and not claims exercised through the estate of Joseph Hector Gore, the father. I am therefore of the opinion that the estate of Laurie Ann Gore must be divided between all three grandparents in the manner I have indicated.

||||||||||||||||||||||||||||||||||||||||||||||||||||||||||||||||||||||||||||||||||||||||||||||||||||||||||||||||||||||||||||||||||||||

CASE PROBLEMS FOR DISCUSSION

Case 1

Speedy Goliath had a poor driving record, and found that insurers were reluctant to insure his automobile. Part of the reason for his high accident rate was the fact that he enjoyed using his automobile in race rally contests and, by ignoring the driving rules in the races, frequently became involved in minor accidents. When he purchased a new sports car, he decided that he might obtain a lower insurance rate if the ownership of the vehicle was placed in his friend's name. His friend consented to the arrangement, and insurance coverage on the vehicle was arranged.

A short time later, while Speedy was driving his friend to work, he carelessly backed up, and collided with a parked car.

The owner of the parked car demanded damages in the amount of $1 000 for Speedy's carelessness, but the insurer refused to make payment.

The owner of the damaged vehicle brought an action against Speedy as the driver of the automobile, and his friend as its owner. He obtained a judgement against them for $1 000.

Discuss the position of Speedy, his friend, and the insurer in this case.

Case 2

Hepburn lived 25 miles from the town in which he worked. The town was a northern lumbering community surrounded by forest.

A particularly dry summer increased the forest fire hazard; already a number of forest fires were burning in the general area. None of the fires were large, or out of control, and all were some distance from the town.

A small forest fire was burning several miles from where Hepburn lived. One morning, before leaving for work he noticed that the wind was high, and he became concerned that the fire might get out of control and move in the direction of his home. He warned his wife to call him by telephone at work if the fire reports indicated that the fire was spreading in their direction.

Later that afternoon, his wife called to tell him that the high winds were moving the fire towards their home, but the fire was still some miles away. On receipt of the news, Hepburn called a local agent for a fire insurance company, and asked for fire coverage. The agent asked him a number of questions concerning the type of construction of his home, its location, and the fire protection facilities in the area. Hepburn provided accurate information in answer to the questions.

As a final question, the agent asked, "Are there any fires in your area at the present time?" To this question, Hepburn replied, "There are forest fires everywhere at this time of year." The agent laughed at his response, and told him that he could consider himself covered from that moment. That evening, Hepburn mailed the agent a cheque for the amount of the premium.

Because high winds prevented the fire-fighters from containing the burn, the fire moved closer to Hepburn's home. Eventually, the fire swept through the area where his home was located, and the building was totally destroyed.

Hepburn claimed for the fire loss, but the insurer refused to pay the claim.

Discuss the defences that the insurer might raise, and the position of Hepburn. Indicate how this case might be decided if it came before the courts.

Case 3

Benton carried on a successful restaurant business in a large city. The restaurant had an excellent reputation, and this was for the most part due to the skill of Benton's gourmet chef, Simmons.

Benton realized that his business would be adversely affected if he should lose Simmons through accident or injury, so he arranged for a life insurance policy in the amount of $100 000 on Simmons' life, and named himself as the beneficiary. The annual premium in the amount of $500 was paid by Benton.

Some months later, at the end of a busy day, Benton and Simmons became involved in a violent argument, and Simmons left the restaurant saying, "Don't expect me to work tomorrow. I quit. I'll be in to pick up my personal belongings at 8:00 a.m."

On his way home from the restaurant, Simmons was involved in a serious automobile accident, and was killed. Benton claimed the $100 000 under the life insurance policy.

Should the insurer pay the claim? What defences might it raise to resist the demand for payment?

Case 4

Hector and Keech carried on a fishing business together as a partnership. Each partner's life was insured for $200 000 under an insurance policy which named the other partner as beneficiary.

One afternoon while the two partners were in their boat and fishing close to the shore, a sudden storm came up, and Hector started the engine, to run the boat back to harbour. Keech wished to remain, and insisted that they ride out the storm. The two men exchanged words, and then both struggled for the controls of the boat. In the process, Hector was pushed overboard and into the water. Before Keech could turn the boat around, Hector had disappeared beneath the surface of the choppy water.

Keech was charged with criminal negligence causing the death of Hector, and was convicted. Because of the circumstances surrounding the death, he was given only a light prison sentence.

On his release, he claimed the $200 000 under the insurance policy on Hector's life in which he was named beneficiary.

Should Keech be entitled to the insurance proceeds?

Case 5

Rosa Rugrosa carried on business as a florist. She operated a large greenhouse in which she grew most of her flowers during the cold winter months. To protect her business, she contacted her insurance agent for insurance coverage against loss or damage by fire, and for theft of stock. Because the building was largely glass and steel, she placed its value at $25 000, when in fact its actual value was approximately twice that amount.

A few month's later, on a cold winter night, vandals broke into her greenhouse, smashed some of the panes of glass by throwing potted plants against the sides of the building, and pulled the furnace flue pipe from the chimney. Smoke from the furnace filled the greenhouse, damaging most of the flowers and other plants. The vandals took with them equipment valued at $1 000.

Rosa claimed the following amounts from her insurer:

damage to building by vandals	$ 3 000
smoke damage to plants, etc.	10 000
equipment stolen	1 000
	$14 000

The insurer agreed to compensate Rosa for the stolen equipment in the amount of $1 000, and to cover the $3 000 damage to the building. The insurer, however, pointed to the 80% co-insurance clause in the fire insurance policy, and argued that it was only responsible for a part of the loss of the plants, as the damage was caused by fire.

A few days later, the vandals were apprehended by the police, and admitted causing the damage. Unfortunately, they had sold the equipment, and had spent the money before they were caught. The vandals had no personal assets.

Discuss the rights and obligations of the parties in this situation, and explain how the loss would be borne.

CHAPTER 26

||||||||||||||||||||||||||||||||||||||||||||||||||||||||||||||||||||||||||||||||||||||||||||||||||||||||||||||||||||||||||||||||||||

The Law of Negotiable Instruments

HISTORICAL DEVELOPMENT OF THE LAW

A negotiable instrument is a written document which passes a good title to the rights contained in the document from a transferor to a transferee if the transferee takes the instrument in good faith and for value, without notice of any defect in the transferor's title.[1] The law relating to this unique instrument has its roots in early mercantile customs that date back, and perhaps beyond, the time of the Roman Empire. The law developed from the practices of merchants in their dealings

[1]Osborn, P.G., *The Concise Law Dictionary*, 4th ed. Sweet & Maxwell Ltd., London: 1954, p. 230.

with each other, and from the decisions made to settle their disputes, first by their own guild members, and later by the courts.

Negotiable instruments, for the most part, are written promises or orders to pay sums of money to the holders of the instruments, and are represented in today's business world by cheques, promissory notes, and bills of exchange. The widespread use of these documents is due to the convenience and the reduced risk which has attached to them since early times. Along with some of the more recently developed credit instruments, they represent what may be loosely described as "money substitutes." Their original use was by merchants who travelled long distances to sell or trade goods, and who were anxious to avoid the hazards of carrying quantities of gold on sea voyages over waters infested with pirates, or over roads frequented by highwaymen and robbers.

Negotiable instruments were first used in international transactions between merchants. During the Middle Ages, if a European merchant who sold his goods at the various "fairs" held throughout Europe was reluctant to carry on his person the gold he received for his goods, he would arrange with a merchant in the fair town who had a business connection with a merchant in his own town to provide a note or order authorizing the payment to him (on presentation) of the amount set out in the document. In return for the note, the foreign merchant would pay over his gold to the local merchant, and carry the note with him until he returned home. There, he would present the note for payment to the merchant named in the document, and receive from him the

required amount of gold. These notes over time became known as bills of exchange.

Bills of exchange were used extensively in the trading cities of Northern Italy, first by the Florentines, and later by the Venetians. Their use gradually spread to France, and then to England. As trade grew, so too did the use of negotiable instruments, and the number of merchants who carried on the business of exchanging money for these documents. During the 13th and 14th centuries merchants continued to expand their business relationships with others in the large trading cities of Europe, and by the reign of Edward I in England, active trading between English and European merchants, using bills of exchange had been established.

The king, at that time, was particularly anxious to accommodate foreign merchants, and designated certain towns as "staple towns" where foreign trade might be carried on. Disputes that arose between merchants at the fairs held in these towns were settled by a system of courts, with the local courts or "fair" courts dealing with disputes between domestic merchants, and staple courts dealing with disputes which involved foreign traders. The *Statute of the Staple*[2] passed some years later, gave legal sanction to the informal judicial procedure of the latter type of courts. The designation of certain towns as places where the more important trade might take place tended to concentrate mercantile activity in these specific centres, and permitted the rise in number of merchants who dealt in negotiable instruments.

By the middle of the 14th century the

[2]27 Edw. III st. 2, c. 9.

Court of Admiralty assumed jurisdiction for the maritime part of the law merchant, and during the next 200 years exercised an increasing degree of control over the commercial aspects of the law merchant, and with it, negotiable instruments. During this period, however, the common law courts also heard cases concerning disputes between merchants. The decline of the guild system permitted the rise of merchants who were not guild members, and these merchants frequently took their cases to the common law courts as well as to the admiralty courts. By the late 16th century, the common law courts succeeded in confining the Court of Admiralty to the maritime aspects of the law merchant, and assumed jurisdiction over what might be designated as the commercial law parts of the law. The rules of the mercantile courts relating to negotiable instruments, as a result, gradually became a part of the common law, and the customs of the merchants in their dealings with one another on these instruments acquired a legality which they did not previously possess.

The law developed gradually after the common law courts acquired jurisdiction. Initially, only foreign bills and foreign traders used these instruments of exchange, and the early cases were largely confined to their disputes. Later, however, their use spread to merchants within the country, and the courts applied the same rules to determine their enforceability. Eventually, non-traders began to use negotiable instruments in transactions with one another, and again, these transactions were made subject to the same rules.

By the late 19th century, the law relating to negotiable instruments was relatively well settled, but found only in a myriad of court decisions, many being at slight variance with one another on the same point of law. To simplify and render certain the law, the English Parliament passed the *Bills of Exchange Act* in 1882.[3] The Act was drafted by Mackenzie D. Chalmers, a noted authority on negotiable instruments, and the passage of the statute by Parliament represented the first codification of this branch of the English common law.[4] The Parliament of Canada passed a statute in 1890 which was essentially the English statute of 1882 with a few minor modifications.[5]

The *Bills of Exchange Act* sets out the general rules of law that relate to bills of exchange, cheques, and promissory notes. Since the legislation is a federal statute, it applies throughout Canada. Very few changes have been made in the Act since its introduction in 1890, and its provisions are very similar to the laws relating to these instruments in both the United Kingdom and the United States.

Today, the important features of bills of exchange are the particular features which made them so attractive to merchants centuries ago. In particular, a bill of exchange reduces the risk involved in transporting money from one place to another. Merchants no longer carry gold coin from place to place, but its modern counter-part, legal tender of the Bank of Canada, would be required if some of the more convenient forms of negotiable instruments were not available for use in its place. In a sense, it is a convenient substitute for money.

A second advantage of a negotiable in-

---

[3]*Bills of Exchange Act*, 45 & 46 Vict., c. 61.
[4]Falconbridge, J.D., *Banking and Bills of Exchange*, 6th ed. (Canada Law Book Company Limited, 1956: Toronto), p. 402.
[5]*Bills of Exchange Act*, 1890 (53 Vict.), c. 33, now R.S.C. 1970, c. B-5 as amended.

strument is that it may be used to create credit. A great deal of modern commercial activity is based upon credit buying, and without the ease attached to the creation of credit by way of a bill of exchange, credit buying would not be as widespread as it is today. For example, Lincoln wishes to purchase goods from Timmins but will not be in a position to pay for the goods for several months. If it is agreeable to Timmins, Lincoln may give Timmins a promissory note payable in 60 days. Lincoln will receive the goods, but must be prepared to honour the note later when Timmins presents it for payment.

A third advantage of a bill of exchange is its negotiability, a particular attribute which permits it to be more readily transferred than most contractual obligations.

In addition, in some circumstances a transferee of a bill of exchange may acquire a greater right to payment than the transferor of the bill. In this respect the transferee of a bill encounters less risk in taking an assignment of the instrument than the assignee of an ordinary contract. Recent consumer protection amendments, however, have altered this particular attribute of a bill of exchange if it is issued in connection with a consumer purchase. The change is designed to prevent consumer abuse through the use of bills of exchange by unscrupulous businesses, but apart from this limitation, it remains as a method of reducing risk in an ordinary business transaction.

The Bills of Exchange Act deals at length with three general types of negotiable instruments: the promissory note, the cheque, and the bill of exchange. A cheque, however, is essentially a special type of bill of exchange, and as a result, much of what might be said in general about a bill of exchange would apply to a cheque as well. A promissory note, on the other hand, differs in form and use from both the cheque and the bill of exchange.

Each of these instruments have particular features which lend themselves to specific commercial uses, and because they developed as a separate branch of the common law, much of the legal terminology associated with the instruments differs from that used in the law of contract. For example, a contract at common law is assigned by an assignor to an assignee, usually by a separate contract. A negotiable instrument on the other hand, is negotiated by an *endorser* to an *endorsee* on the document itself. The endorser and endorsee are roughly the equivalent of the assignor and the assignee of a contract. The endorser is a person who holds a negotiable instrument and transfers it to another by signing his name on the back, and delivering it to the endorsee. The endorsement, together with delivery, gives the endorsee the right to the instrument. For example, Jones is indebted to Brown, and gives Brown a cheque for the amount of the debt. Brown is named as the payee on the cheque (i.e., he is named as the person entitled to payment). If Brown is indebted to Smith he may endorse the cheque by signing his name on the back and delivering it to Smith. On delivery, Smith becomes the endorsee and the holder of the cheque. If Brown endorsed the cheque by signing only his name on the back, the cheque then becomes a *bearer* cheque, and Smith becomes the "bearer," since he is in physical possession of the instrument. The same terminology would apply if the cheque had been made payable to "bearer" instead of to Brown, since the person in possession of a cheque made payable to bearer is also called by that name.

The person in possession of a negotiable instrument is sometimes called a *holder*, but to be a holder, the party must be either a bearer, payee, or endorsee. In addition to an ordinary holder, a person who paid something in return for the instrument is referred to as a *holder for value* to distinguish such a holder from one who received the instrument as a gift. Since every party whose signature appears on a bill or note is presumed to have acquired the instrument for value, unless it can be established to the contrary, a holder of the instrument is usually considered to be a holder for value.[6]

A third type of holder is one who obtains special rights under a negotiable instrument. If a holder takes an instrument which is complete and regular on its face, before it is overdue, without any knowledge that it has been previously dishonoured and, if he took the bill in good faith and for value and, at the time, had no notice of any defect in the title of the person who negotiated it, he would be a *holder in due course*.[7] The particular advantage of being a holder in due course of a negotiable instrument is the greater certainty of payment; many of the defences that may be raised against an ordinary holder claiming payment are not available against a holder in due course. The particular advantages of being this type of holder are examined in greater detail in the part of this chapter that deals with defences available to the parties to a negotiable instrument.

BILLS OF EXCHANGE

The modern bill of exchange bears a close resemblance to the early negotiable instruments of this type used by merchants, and until recently, was used extensively in business transactions. Its use, however, has declined since the middle of this century as a result of the greater use of cheques and other forms of payment by merchants and the general public.

Under the *Bills of Exchange Act*, a bill of exchange must be an unconditional order in writing, addressed by one person to another, signed by the person giving it, and requiring the person to whom it is addressed to pay either on demand, or at a fixed or determinable future time, a sum certain in money to, or to the order of a specified person or to a bearer.[8] The Act is very specific that the document alleged to be a bill of exchange meet these requirements. If the document fails to comply, or if it includes some other thing that a person must do in addition to the payment of money (except as provided in the Act) then the document will not be a bill of exchange.[9]

Because a bill of exchange is not used by ordinary businesses or individuals nearly as often as cheques or promissory notes, the following sample is included on page 537.

The bill of exchange in the example shown is a document in writing. It is partly printed, partly handwritten, and partly typewritten. Each of these methods of writing is permissible, but it is essential that all of the important terms be evidenced in writing.

The bill is an unconditional order as indicated by the words: "pay to the order of . . .", and it is addressed by one person to another ("To A. Jones, 100 University Avenue South, Kingston, Ontario). It is signed by the person giving it (B. Smith), and it requires the person to whom it is ad-

[6]*Bills of Exchange Act*, R.S.C. 1970, c. B-5, s. 58(1).
[7]*Ibid.*, s. 56(1).
[8]*Ibid.*, s. 17(1).
[9]*Ibid.*, s. 17(2).

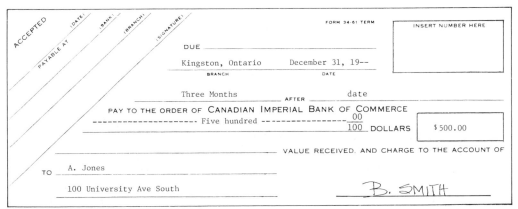

Source: Canadian Imperial Bank of Commerce.

dressed to pay (in this case, at a fixed or determinable future time—"three months after date"). The bill is drawn for a sum certain in money ($500.00) and it is payable to the order of a specified person (in this case a bank—". . . pay to the order of the Canadian Imperial Bank of Commerce, Kingston Branch").

The person who prepares the bill is called the *drawer* (B. Smith) and the *drawee* (A. Jones) is the person to whom it is addressed. In this case the *payee* is the Canadian Imperial Bank of Commerce, but the payee could also be the drawer if the drawer wished to receive the money personally, or negotiate the bill to someone else.

Once the bill is drawn, it is sent to the drawee for *acceptance*. The drawee "accepts" the bill by writing his acceptance of the bill across its face or in a corner of the bill set aside for acceptance. In this example, A. Jones would write "accepted" along with the date and where payable, then sign his name on the face of the bill. He must deliver the signed bill before acceptance is completed.[10] The drawee (who becomes the *acceptor* if he accepts the bill) is under no obligation to accept a bill

drawn on him, but if he does so, he in effect promises to pay the bill when it falls due, and may be sued for payment if he defaults. If the drawee does not accept the bill, he is said to have *dishonoured* the bill by non-acceptance. Before the date for payment a bill may be negotiated to other persons, known as *holders*. A holder usually negotiates a bill by *endorsement*. This is the act of placing one's signature on the back of the note, then delivering it to the new holder. The act of endorsement in effect represents an implied promise to compensate the holder or subsequent endorsers in the event that the bill is dishonoured, provided that the necessary procedures in the event of default are followed.

In this example, the bill is payable at a particular time that may be calculated from the information given, but the bill may also be made payable on *demand* or *at sight*. If the bill is payable "on demand" or "on presentation" or if it does not set out a time for payment, it is considered to be a *demand bill*, and will be payable without acceptance by the drawee, unless it is payable other than at the drawee's place of residence or place of business.[11] A *cheque*

[10]*Ibid.*, s. 17(2); s. 39.
[11]*Ibid.*, s. 75(2).

is an example of a demand bill which is always drawn on a bank. In Canada, three days' grace is added to the payment date except in the case of a demand bill which, like a cheque, is payable immediately on presentation. A *sight* bill, which is similar to a time bill, states that it is payable "at sight" or at a specific number of days after "sight." Sight means "acceptance," and since three days' grace would be added in the case of a sight bill, the payment date in effect becomes three days after the date it is presented for acceptance. The bill may specify that the three days' grace will not apply, in which case it becomes payable on presentation.

It should be noted that a bill of exchange will not be invalid if it is not dated, has no place fixed for payment, no mention of consideration, [12] or if there is a discrepancy between words and figures, [13] but if the bill is not dated, it must state when it is due, or it must contain the information necessary to calculate the due date. Under certain circumstances, the date may be added later if the bill is undated. [14]

The payee named in the illustration is a bank, but any person except the drawee may be named, or it may simply be made payable to the *bearer*. If the bill should be made payable to a fictitious person (such as Santa Claus or the Easter Bunny), the bill is still valid, and becomes a bill payable to the bearer. [15]

LIABILITY OF THE PARTIES TO A BILL OF EXCHANGE

Acceptance of a bill of exchange by the drawee renders the drawee liable to pay the bill at the time and place fixed for payment, or in the case of a demand bill, within a reasonable time after its issue. [16] The bill must also be presented for payment by the holder or his authorized representative at a reasonable hour on a business day [17] at the place specified in the bill, but if no place is specified, then it may be presented at the drawee's address. When payment is made, the drawee is entitled to a return of the bill from the holder in order that it might be cancelled or destroyed.

If payment is refused, then the holder must act quickly if he wishes to hold the drawer and any other endorsers liable on the bill. If the bill is dishonoured by non-payment, the holder has a right of recourse against the drawer, acceptor, and endorsers, [18] but in order to hold the parties liable, he must give them an opportunity to pay the bill by giving each of them (except the acceptor) notice of the dishonour. [19] To be valid, the notice must be given not later than the juridical or business day next following the dishonour of the bill. [20] The notice may be either in writing or by personal communication (such as telephone, or other verbal means) but it must identify the bill, and indicate that it has been dishonoured by non-payment. [21] The drawer or any endorser who does not receive notice of the dishonour is discharged from any liability on the bill, [22] unless the holder is excused from giving immediate notice as a result of circumstances beyond his control. [23] As soon as the cause

[12]*Ibid.*, s. 27.
[13]*Ibid.*, s. 28.
[14]*Ibid.*, s. 30.
[15]*Ibid.*, s. 21(5).

[16]*Ibid.*, s. 86(1)(*b*).
[17]*Ibid.*, s. 78 for the time for presentation for acceptance. The time for payment would probably be somewhat similar.
[18]*Ibid.*, s. 95(2).
[19]*Ibid.*, s. 98.
[20]*Ibid.*, s. 97.
[21]*Ibid.*, s. 98(1)(*d*).
[22]*Ibid.*, s. 96(1).
[23]*Ibid.*, s. 105(1).

for the delay ends, however, notice must promptly be given.[24] As a result, it is in the interests of all parties to make certain that the person from whom they acquired the bill receives notice, hence all endorsers will generally give notice to prior endorsers to preserve their own rights. Endorsers who receive notice have the same length of time as the holder to give notice of the dishonour to those liable to them,[25] but it is common practice to give notice to all parties liable as well. Notice of dishonour may also be dispensed with to certain parties under certain circumstances,[26] such as to the drawer where the drawer has countermanded payment,[27] or to an endorser where the endorser is the person to whom the bill is presented for payment.[28] If the bill is a foreign bill, a special procedure must be followed in the event of non-payment. A formal procedure called *protest* is used for notice, and the protest must generally be made on the same day that the dishonour occurs.[29]

CHEQUES

A cheque is a form of bill of exchange which, as noted previously, is a bill payable on demand, where the drawee is always a bank. The bank, however, is a special type of drawee in the case of a cheque because it does not become liable to a holder in the same way that an ordinary drawee does when a bill is presented for payment. A bank need only honour the cheque when it is presented in proper form, and sufficient funds of the drawer

are on hand at the bank to cover the cheque. If the drawer has insufficient funds on deposit to permit the bank to make payment, it may refuse to honour the cheque, and the holder will be obliged look to the drawer (or other endorsers) for payment. The only circumstances under which the bank might be liable would be if the cheque was properly drawn, and the drawer had sufficient funds on deposit to cover payment. Even then, it would be liable to the drawer rather than to the holder.

Cheques are sometimes presented to the bank for *certification*. This procedure alters the position of the bank with respect to the holder, in that the bank, on the presentation of the cheque, will withdraw the amount of the cheque from the drawer's account, and place the funds in an account of the bank set aside for the purpose of payment. Once the funds have been removed, the bank is in much the same position as a person accepting a bill of exchange drawn upon him. If the cheque should be certified at the request of the drawer, it may still be countermanded by the drawer before it is presented for payment. The bank usually requires the drawer to return the cheque if he has not delivered it to the payee, or if he has done so, to require the drawer to provide the bank with security in the event that the payee has already cashed the cheque.

Certification at the request of the holder places the bank in a different position. If the cheque is presented to the bank by the holder, the holder at that time would be entitled to payment. If the holder requests certification of the cheque instead, and the bank complies, the bank would become liable, and the drawer would be discharged from all liability. Since the drawer would in effect have made payment of the funds, he would no longer be in a position to stop

[24]*Ibid.*, s. 105(2).
[25]*Ibid.*, s. 101.
[26]*Ibid.*, ss. 107 and 108.
[27]*Ibid.*, s. 107(*e*).
[28]*Ibid.*, s. 108.
[29]See, generally, *Bills of Exchange Act*, R.S.C. 1970, c. B-5, s. 112 *et seq.*

payment.[30] The bank however, would be obliged to pay the cheque when presented for payment at a later time.

A cheque, like a bill of exchange, is not legal tender, and if offered as payment to a creditor, represents only conditional payment of the debt. If the cheque should be dishonoured, the debt remains, and the creditor then may take action for payment on either the debt itself, or the dishonoured cheque. A creditor or seller need not accept payment by way of a cheque, but if he should decide to do so, and the cheque is honoured, the debt will be extinguished, and the drawer will have evidence of payment in the form of the creditor's endorsement on the back of the cheque. For this reason, a debtor giving a cheque in full or part payment of a debt will often identify the purpose of the payment on the back of the cheque. The creditor's signature will then indicate that payment of the amount of the cheque had been received with respect to that specific account.

A cheque, being payable on demand, must be presented for payment within a reasonable time after its issue. This may vary depending upon the nature of the instrument, the customs of the trade, and the banks in the particular instance,[31] but the fact remains that cheques should be promptly cashed on receipt; otherwise, circumstances could affect payment.[32]

Unless the cheque is made payable to bearer, it is negotiated by endorsement in the same manner as any other bill of exchange. The endorsement may be *in blank*, in which case the endorser would only sign his name on the back. The cheque then could be passed from one person to another without further endorsement in the same fashion as a bearer instrument. If, however, the endorser wishes to restrict the endorsement to one person only, the endorsement might, for example, take the form: "Pay to J. Brown only" followed by the endorser's signature below. This type of endorsement is called a *restrictive endorsement*, and would prevent any further endorsement. Only J. Brown would be permitted to present the cheque to the bank for payment. A person may also use a restrictive type of endorsement to prevent the theft and cashing of a cheque. By writing the words "for deposit only to the account of . . ." followed by the person's name, the cheque may not be cashed. It may only be deposited to that person's bank account. A third general type of endorsement is called a *special endorsement*. A special endorsement requires the person named in the endorsement to endorse the cheque before it may be negotiated to anyone. A special endorsement would read: "pay to the order of J. Brown" followed by the endorser's signature.

Other forms of endorsement exist as well. A person may endorse a cheque for the purpose of identifying the person or the signature of the person negotiating a cheque. In this case, the party would not incur liability on the cheque, since the endorsement would be for identification purposes only. A typical endorsement of this nature might read "J. Brown is hereby identified" followed by the signature of the person making the identification.

An endorsement may be qualified, which would limit the liability of the endorser (provided that the other party should be willing to accept such an endorsement) if dishonour should later occur. This type of endorsement is usually

---

[30]*Commercial Automation Ltd. v. Banque Provinciale du Canada* (1962), 39 D.L.R. (2d) 316.

[31]*Bills of Exchange Act*, R.S.C. 1970, c. B-5, s. 16(2). Most banks consider a 'reasonable time' to be less than six months.

[32]For example, the customer might die, in which case the duty of the bank to pay the cheque would have terminated. See *Bills of Exchange Act*, s. 167(b).

called an *endorsement without recourse.* It might read: "Without recourse" followed by the signature, or it might limit the time for recourse: "Without recourse unless presented within 10 days." The unwillingness of subsequent endorsers to accept this type of endorsement has limited its use, since subsequent endorsers must look to prior endorsers for payment in the event of non-payment by the drawer of the cheque.

An endorser, under the *Bills of Exchange Act,* by signing the back of a cheque or bill of exchange impliedly contracts that he will compensate the holder or any other subsequent endorser in the event that the cheque is not honoured when presented for payment, provided that the necessary proceedings are followed by the holder on dishonour.[33] Endorsement also precludes the endorser from denying to a holder in due course the regularity in all respects of the drawer's signature, and that of all previous endorsements.[34] In addition, an endorser is precluded from denying to his immediate or subsequent endorsers that the bill was a valid bill at the time of his endorsement, and that he had a good title to it.[35]

||||||||||||||||||||||||||||||||||||||||||||||||||||||||||||||||||||||||

CASE 26.1
Ontario Woodsworth Memorial Foundation v. Grozbord et al.; Stone, Royal Bank of Canada and Bank of Nova Scotia, Third Parties (1964), 48 D.L.R. (2d) 385.

GRANT, J.:

The legal effect of certification of cheques is dealt with by Falconbridge in *Banking and Bills of Exchange,* 6th ed. (1956), at pp. 874-9. The learned author there draws a distinction between certification at the instance of the holder of the cheque and certification at the instance of

[33]*Bills of Exchange Act,* R.S.C. 1970, c. B-5, s. 133.
[34]*Ibid.,* s. 133.
[35]*Ibid.,* s. 133.

the drawer. If a cheque is certified or marked by the drawee bank at the request of the payee or other holder, the amount of the cheque being charged by the bank to the account of the drawer, and if the holder does not then and there require payment, the drawer is discharged from all liability either on the cheque or on the original consideration for which it was given. On the other hand, in the case of a cheque which is certified by the drawer before delivery, no presentment at the time of the certification is made by the holder who alone is entitled to present the cheque for payment, and therefore he cannot be said (as he can in the first case) to have elected to accept the bank's undertaking to pay in place of actual payment. The holder or payee is still entitled to present for payment and if he so desires to receive the money.

The reason why the drawer of the cheque is discharged in the first place but not in the second is stated to be as follows: The drawer's contract is that upon due presentment the cheque will be paid if the holder so desires. The holder's whole right is to present the cheque and to receive the money. The holder has no right as between himself and the drawer to present the cheque for any purpose except payment and if, when he presents the cheque and ascertains the bank is prepared to pay it, he elects not to draw the money at once, he thereby accepts the bank's undertaking to pay in place of payment. The drawer's whole obligation is performed and he is therefore discharged from liability on the cheque. The conditional payment by the giving and taking of the cheque becomes complete and the condition is fulfilled at that time.

||||||||||||||||||||||||||||||||||||||||||||||||||||||||||||||||||||||||

PROMISSORY NOTES

A promissory note differs from a bill of exchange or a cheque in that it is, as its name implies, a promise to pay, rather than an order. It differs also in its form and acceptance, as well. By definition, a promissory note is an unconditional promise in writing, signed by the maker of the note, to pay to, or to the order of, a specific person or bearer on demand, or at a fixed or determinable time, a sum certain in money.[36]

From this definition, several differences between a promissory note and a bill of exchange are readily apparent. A note does not contain an order to pay, nor does it have a drawee that must accept the instrument. Instead, a note is a promise to pay, which is signed by the party who makes the promise. A simple promissory note might appear as follows on page 543.

To be negotiable, the note must meet the essentials of negotiability as set down in the *Bills of Exchange Act*, and outlined in the definition. It is important to note that the time for payment be clearly determined if the instrument is other than a demand note, and also that the promise to pay is unconditional, and for a sum certain in money. It cannot, for example, be payable "if I should win a particular lottery," nor can it be payable in merchandise or goods, as neither of these stipulations would meet the definition of time or payment.

A promissory note, then, is signed by the maker, and contains a promise to pay a sum certain in money on certain terms. The note is incomplete until it has been signed and delivered to the payee or bearer,[37] but once this act has been accomplished, the maker of the note (with legal capacity) becomes liable to pay the note according to its terms to the holder.

Like a bill of exchange or cheque, a promissory note that is payable on demand must be presented for payment within a reasonable time; otherwise, any endorser of the note may be discharged. But, if the note with the consent of the en- dorser is used as collateral or continuing security, then it need not be presented for payment as long as it is held for that purpose.[38]

The place of payment of a promissory note is normally set out in the body of the note, and if so, presentation for payment must take place there if the holder of the note wishes to hold any endorser liable. If no place is specified, then usually the maker's known place of business or residence would constitute the place for payment.

The time for payment is also important if the holder wishes to hold endorsers liable. As with bills of exchange, three days' grace would be added in the calculation of the time for payment for all promissory notes except those payable on demand.

Endorsers of promissory notes are in much the same position as endorsers of bills of exchange. The maker of a promissory note, by signing it, engages that he will pay the note according to its original terms, and is precluded from denying to a holder in due course the existence of the payee and his capacity to endorse at the time.[39] If a promissory note is dishonoured when properly presented for payment at the date on which payment is due, the holder is obliged to immediately give notice of the dishonour to all endorsers if he wishes to hold them liable on the note. The *Bills of Exchange Act* provides for notice to the endorsers of a promissory note along the same procedural lines as set out for bills of exchange, the important difference being that the maker is deemed to correspond with the acceptor of a bill, and the first endorser of the note deemed to correspond to the drawer of an accepted bill of exchange.[40]

---

[36]*Ibid.*, s. 176(1).
[37]*Ibid.*, s. 178.

[38]*Ibid.*, s. 181.
[39]*Ibid.*, s. 185.
[40]*Ibid.*, s. 186.

```
                                                              ( i AM '2 D  A \

                                          BRANCH              c A I t
                          ON DEMAND AFTER DATE      WE    PROMISE TO PAY TO
            CANADIAN IMPERIAL BANK OF COMMERCE OR ORDER,

                                                                    DOLLARS

      AT THE   CANADIAN IMPERIAL BANK OF COMMERCE   HERE, WITH INTEREST, PAYABLE  MONTHLY, AT THE

      RATE OF           PER CENT, PER ANNUM, AS WELL AFTER AS BEFORE MATURITY, UNTIL PAID  MINIMUM CHARGE $ 5.00

      VALUE  RECEIVED.
```

PROMISSORY NOTE

Promissory notes, unlike bills of exchange or cheques, frequently provide for instalment payments. An instalment note is often used as a means of payment for relatively expensive consumer goods such as household appliances, automobiles, and boats. The seller may often take a security interest in the goods as collateral security to the promissory note, or may simply provide in the note that title not pass until payment is made in full. The advantage of using the promissory note for this purpose is that the note initially facilitates the sale by the seller to the buyer. The buyer need not pay the full price at the time of purchase, but may spread the cost of the purchase over a period of time. The advantage to the seller of the promissory note is that it is a negotiable instrument, and he may negotiate it to a bank or other financial institution, and receive his money immediately. This method permits the seller to avoid having large amounts of his own money tied up in credit transactions. Promissory notes of this nature normally provide for the payment of interest by the maker, and consequently the financial institution that receives the note collects the interest as its compensation for its investment.

A promissory note that provides for instalment payments usually provides that each instalment payment is a separate note for payment purposes, but if default should occur the whole of the balance immediately becomes due and payable. The reason for this special clause is that in its absence, the holder would only be entitled to institute legal proceedings to recover overdue payments as they occurred. This clause, which is known as an *acceleration clause*, permits the holder to sue for the entire balance of the note if default should occur on any one instalment payment.

DEFENCES TO CLAIMS FOR PAYMENT OF BILLS OF EXCHANGE

The holder of a bill of exchange, whether it be a cheque, bill of exchange, or promissory note, is entitled to present the document for payment. If an instrument has two or more endorsers, each endorsement is deemed to have been made in the order in which it appears on the instrument unless an endorser can prove that the contrary is the case.[41] In the event of default, prior endorsers must indemnify subsequent endorsers. Liability to some extent follows the order of signing or endorsement, with the last person to receive the bill or note normally entitled to payment if the bill or note is properly presented for payment.

Not every holder may successfully receive payment when the instrument is

[41]*Ibid.;* s. 65.

presented, for instruments may be made from time to time under circumstances or contain defects which would entitle a party to the instrument to resist payment. Because a negotiable instrument is similar in many respects to a contract, the courts have applied many of the rules of contract to negotiable instruments, but in spite of this the rights of the holder differ substantially from those of an ordinary promisee in a contractual setting.

One of the advantages which a holder of a bill of exchange may have over an assignee of contractual rights is a right which is particular to bills of exchange in general. For reasons which are largely historical, and which arose out of the early merchants' need for certainty in payment, a holder of a bill of exchange may, under certain circumstances, obtain a better right to payment of a bill than an ordinary assignee of contractual rights would acquire.

An ordinary assignee of contractual rights takes the rights of the assignor, subject to any defects which may exist in the assignor's title. If the contract was obtained as a result of some fraud or undue influence, or if the promisor had a right of set-off against the assignor, the assignee's right to payment from the promisor might be thwarted by such a defence. With a negotiable instrument, this is not always so. If a negotiable instrument, such as a bill of exchange, cheque, or promissory note is negotiated to a party for value and without notice of any defect in the instrument or the title of the prior holder, the holder who took the instrument under these circumstances may enforce the instrument against all prior parties in spite of any fraud, duress, undue influence or set-off that may have existed between the original parties. The only case where such a holder (called a *holder in due course*) would be un-

successful would be where the prior parties could establish that the instrument was essentially a nullity due to some defect such as forgery, or the minority of the maker.

The defences that may be raised on a negotiable instrument vary with the relationship which exists between the parties. Defences to an attempt to enforce a negotiable instrument may be divided into three separate classes, each good against a particular type of holder, if the defence can be proven.

||||||||||||||||||||||||||||||||||||||||||||||||||||||||||||||||||||||||||||||||||||

CASE 26.2
Federal Discount Corp. Ltd. v. St. Pierre and St. Pierre (1962), 32 D.L.R. (2d) 86.

KELLY, J.A.:

The rights which accrue to a holder in due course of a bill of exchange are unique and distinguishable from the rights of an assignee of a contract which does not fall within the description of a bill of exchange. The assignee of a contract, unlike the holder in due course of a bill of exchange, takes subject to all the equities between the original parties, which have arisen prior to the date of notice of the assignment to the party sought to be charged.

The special privileges enjoyed by a holder in due course of a bill of exchange are quite foreign to the common law and have their origin in the law merchant.

There is little difficulty in appreciating how trade between merchants required that he who put into circulation his engagement to pay a specified sum at a designated time and place knowing that it was the custom of merchants to regard such paper much as we do our paper currency, should be held to the letter of his obligation and be prevented from setting up defences which might derogate from the apparently absolute nature of his obligation.

At first the customs prevailing amongst merchants as to bills of exchange extended only to merchant strangers trafficking with English merchants; later they were extended to inland bills between merchants trafficking with one another within England; then to all persons trafficking and finally to all persons trafficking or not.

Thus in time the particular conditions which were recognized as prevailing amongst merchants became engrafted onto the law generally applicable and came to be looked on as arising from the document itself rather than from the character of the parties dealing with the document. It is significant, however, that the transition did not affect the legal position as to one another of immediate parties and that as between any two immediate parties, maker and payee, or endorser and endorsee, none of the extraordinary conditions otherwise attaching to the bill, serve to affect adversely the rights and obligations existing between them as contracting parties. The document itself becomes irreproachable and affords special protection to its holder only, when at some stage of its passage from payee or acceptor to holder, there has been a *bona fide* transaction of trade with respect to it wherein the transferee took for value and without any notice of circumstances which might give rise to a defence on the part of the maker. Unless the ultimate holder or some earlier holder has acquired the instrument in the course of such a transaction the earlier tainting circumstances survive and the holder seeking to enforce payment of it must, on the merits, meet any defence which would have been available to the maker. Thus it appears that the peculiar immunity which the holding of a bill of exchange brings to the holder in due course arises not from the original nature of the document itself but from the quality which had been imparted to it by at least some one transfer of it.

||||||||||||||||||||||||||||||||||||||||||||||||||||||||||||||||||||||||||||||||

Real Defences

Of the three classes of defences, the most effective are called *real defences*. Real defences are defences which go to the root of the instrument, and are good against all holders, including a holder in due course. These defences include the following:

Forgery

If the signature of a maker, drawer, or endorser is forged on a negotiable instrument, the holder may not enforce payment against any party through the forged signature unless the party claiming that it is forged is precluded from raising it as a defence by his conduct or negligence.[42] For example, White prepares a bearer cheque and forges Black's name as drawer, then negotiates it to Brown in return for goods sold to him by Brown. If Brown takes the cheque without knowledge of White's forgery of Black's signature, and presents it for payment, Black may raise the forgery of his signature as a defence to payment even though the holder Brown was innocent of the forgery. Brown's only right in this case would be to look to White for compensation.

Incapacity of a Minor

A minor cannot incur liability on a negotiable instrument, hence, it is a real defence against any holder, including a holder in due course.[43] If the party is insane, the same defence may apply in some circumstances, as the capacity to incur liability in the case of a negotiable instrument is co-extensive with the party's capacity to contract.[44]

Lack of Delivery of an Incomplete Instrument

If a drawer or maker signs a negotiable instrument, but does not deliver it, the lack of delivery may be a real defence if another party should complete the instrument, and either negotiate it, or present it for

---

[42]*Ibid.*, s. 49(1). Note that an agent without express or apparent authority to sign a negotiable instrument would render the instrument void insofar as the principal is concerned.

[43]*Ibid.*, s. 47(1).

[44]*Ibid.*, s. 47(1).

payment. Both elements must be present, however, as the lack of delivery alone does not constitute a real defence. For example, Smith signs a promissory note but does not fill in the amount, and it is stolen by Brown. If Brown fills in the amount and any other blanks, then negotiates it to Green, Smith may raise as a real defence the lack of delivery of an incomplete instrument. This defence would be good against all parties, even a holder in due course.[45]

Material Alteration of the Instrument

Under certain circumstances a person may be able to raise as a real defence the material alteration of the instrument. This defence is limited to the changes made, however, and does not affect the enforcement of the instrument according to its original tenor. For example, if Martin draws a cheque payable to Baker for $100 and Baker alters the amount to $1 100 and negotiates the cheque to Doe, Doe may only be entitled to enforce the cheque for its original amount. The material alteration may be raised as a real defence by Martin unless he was negligent by drawing the cheque in such a way that Baker could easily alter it.[46]

Fraud as to the Nature of the Instrument

Fraud as a real defence to payment is limited to those cases where *non est factum* may be raised as a defence. Fraud is normally not a real defence because a person signing a negotiable instrument owes a duty of care to all others who may receive the instrument, but if the fraud is such that the person signing the instrument is unable to ascertain the true nature of the instrument as a result of infirmity, advanced age, or partial illiteracy, and is induced to sign the instrument honestly believing it to be something else, then fraud may be raised as a real defence.[47]

Cancellation of the Instrument

Cancellation of an instrument, if the cancellation is apparent on the face of the instrument, would be a defence against a claim for payment by a holder.[48] If, however, payment should be made before the due date, and the cancellation is not noted on the instrument, the careless handling of the instrument may allow it to fall into the hands of another who may negotiate it to a holder for value. Under these circumstances, the holder may be able to require payment by the maker or drawer of the instrument a second time, and the defence of cancellation would not hold.

Defect of Title Defences

Real defences are good against all holders including a holder in due course, but there are a number of other defences which are related to the title of a person which may be good against every holder except a holder in due course. A title may be defective where it is obtained by fraud, duress, or undue influence, or where the instrument is negotiated to another by way of a breach of trust, or a promise not to negotiate the instrument after maturity. It may also arise where the consideration for the instrument is illegal, or where there is a total failure of consideration.[49] While fraud may be a real defence in cases where it is serious enough to constitute *non est*

---

[45]Falconbridge, J.D., *The Law of Negotiable Instruments in Canada*, Ryerson Press, 1923: Toronto, p. 149.

[46]See *Bills of Exchange Act*, R.S.C. 1970, c. B-5, ss. 145(1), 146 for examples of material alteration, but see *Will v. Bank of Montreal*, [1931] 3 D.L.R. 526, for negligence on the part of the drawer.

[47]See, for example, *Foster v. MacKinnon* (1869), L.R. 4 C.P. 704.

[48]*Bills of Exchange Act*, R.S.C. 1970, c. B-5, s. 143.

[49]*Ibid.*, s. 56(2).

factum; it may be a defect of title defence as well, if the fraud is insufficient to constitute a real defence. For example, where a person is induced to sign a promissory note on the strength of false representations made by the payee, the defence of fraud may be raised by the maker as against the payee, but it would not apply if the payee negotiated the note to a holder in due course. Duress and undue influence, as in the case of ordinary contract law, would be a good defence against a payee, or any other party to the instrument except a holder in due course.

A defect of title defence may also be available where a person charged with the responsibility for filling in the blanks on a negotiable instrument fills them in improperly, or releases an instrument to a holder when instructed not to do so. Similarly, if a maker or drawer prepares and signs a bill or note, and it is stolen in completed form, the absence of delivery would constitute a defect of title defence good against a holder, but not against a holder in due course.

Personal Defences

A third type of defence is a defence that is effective only as against an immediate party, and not as against a remote party. The principal personal defence is *set-off*, which entitles a party to raise as a defence the indebtedness of the party claiming payment. For example, White owes Black $1 000, and gives Black a note for that amount due in 30 days' time. In the interval, Black becomes indebted to White for $500. If, on the due date Black claims payment of the $1 000 note, White may set-off Black's indebtedness of $500, and pay only the remaining balance to Black.

A number of other personal defences also exist. The absence of consideration may be a defence which a drawer or maker

may raise against a party who obtains the negotiable instrument, but this may only be raised as a defence where the person holding the instrument has not given consideration for it, and no prior holder did so. If any prior holder gave consideration for the negotiable instrument, then the maker or drawer may not raise absence of consideration as a defence, because a holder, even though he personally did not give consideration, may enforce the instrument on the basis that he acquired all the rights of the prior holder.

Release or payment before maturity are also considered to be personal defences where a release had been given, or payment had been made before maturity, but in each of these cases, the defences would only apply against the party who gave the release or who received the payment. The defence would not apply as against subsequent holders who had no notice of the release or payment.

CONSUMER PROTECTION AND NEGOTIABLE INSTRUMENTS

In 1970, the *Bills of Exchange Act* was amended to provide for two new types of negotiable instruments called *consumer bills* and *consumer notes*. These instruments are ordinary bills of exchange or notes that arise out of a consumer purchase. According to the Act, a consumer purchase is defined as one which is a purchase of goods or services other than a cash purchase from a person in the business of selling or providing consumer goods and services. It does not include the purchase of goods by merchants for resale, nor does it include the purchase of goods for business or professional use.[50]

[50]*Ibid.*, s. 188.

The need for special legislation to govern negotiable instruments which arise from consumer purchases was recognized by the federal government in the 1960s. During that period, credit buying expanded rapidly, and companies that financed retail purchases frequently arranged with sellers to provide financing to consumers who purchased their goods. In those situations, the seller would agree to sell the goods on credit and, as a part of the sale, have the purchaser sign a promissory note to finance the purchase. The note would either be made payable directly to the finance company, or the seller would later sell the note to the finance company. In the latter case, the finance company would claim to be the holder in due course of the promissory note, and in the event that the goods were defective or misrepresented by the seller, the purchaser could not withhold payment of the note to pressure the seller to correct the situation. Because the finance company was a remote party, and could enforce payment regardless of any breach of the contract of sale by the seller, the purchaser's only remedy was to take action against the seller (if he could be found).

Often, if the finance company took action against the purchaser, the courts would attempt to tie the seller and the finance company together in an effort to assist the hapless purchaser,[51] but in many cases, it could not do so. In the end, only legislation appeared to be the solution and, in response to consumer demand, remedial legislation was introduced at the provincial and federal levels. The change at the federal level was reflected in the *Bills of Exchange Act* by identifying the particular negotiable instruments as consumer bills and consumer notes.

A *consumer bill* is a bill of exchange, including a cheque, which is issued in respect to a consumer purchase in which the purchaser or anyone signing to accommodate him is liable as a party, but it does not include a cheque that is dated the day of issue (or prior thereto), or a cheque that is post dated not more than 30 days.[52]

A *consumer note* is a promissory note which is issued in respect of a consumer purchase on which the purchaser or anyone signing to accommodate him is liable as a party.[53]

Both of these instruments are deemed to arise out of a consumer purchase if the funds secured by the note are obtained from a lender who is not dealing at arm's length with the seller.[54] In other words, if the seller directed the purchaser to a particular lending institution, or arranged the loan from the lending institution to enable the purchaser to make the purchase, the note or bill signed by the purchaser would still be treated as arising out of a consumer purchase.

Under the Act, every bill or note arising out of a consumer purchase must be marked with the words "consumer purchase" before or at the time that it is signed, and a consumer bill or note which is not so marked is void except in the hands of a holder in due course who had no notice of the fact that the bill arose out of a consumer purchase.[55]

The Act provides penalties for violation, in addition to rendering the note void as against the purchaser. The principal thrust, however, is to eliminate collusion between sellers and lenders to avoid consumer protection legislation. The *Bills of Exchange Act* provides that the holder of a negotiable instrument arising out of a con-

---

[51]See, for example, *Federal Discount Corp. Ltd. v. St. Pierre and St. Pierre* (1962), 32 D.L.R. (2d) 86.

[52]*Bills of Exchange Act*, R.S.C. 1970, c. B-5, s. 189(1).
[53]*Ibid.*, s. 189(2).
[54]*Ibid.*, s. 189(3).
[55]*Ibid.*, s. 190.

sumer purchase is subject to any defences by the consumer which might be raised against the seller of the goods if the goods prove to be defective or unsatisfactory.[56] This new amendment to the *Bills of Exchange Act* also facilitates the operation of the provincial consumer protection laws by requiring the seller (or lender) in a consumer purchase to so identify the negotiable instrument.

[56]*Ibid.*, s. 191.

SUMMARY

Negotiable instruments in the form of bills of exchange, cheques, and promissory notes are governed by the *Bills of Exchange Act*. Each of these instruments developed to meet the particular needs of merchants. Their operation was first governed by the law merchant; later, this body of law was absorbed into the common law. As a result, the law distinguished the negotiable instrument from an ordinary contract, particularly with respect to transfer. To be negotiable, an instrument must possess the *essentials for negotiability*. The instrument must be an unconditional order or promise in writing, signed by the maker or drawer, requiring the maker or the person to whom it is addressed to pay to a specific person or bearer, on demand, or at some fixed or determinable future time, a sum certain in money.

If an instrument meets the requirements for negotiability, it may be negotiated by the holder to another person by way of delivery (if a bearer instrument) or by endorsement and delivery. The endorsement of a negotiable instrument renders the person making the endorsement liable to the holder in the event that it is dishonoured by the maker, drawer, or acceptor. A holder acquires greater rights under a negotiable instrument than an ordinary assignee of a contractual right. This is particularly true if the person who holds the instrument is a holder in due course. A holder in due course generally is entitled to claim payment even though a defect of title may exist between prior holders. The only defences good against a holder in due course are defences which may be called real defences (forgery, incapacity of a minor, and others which render the instrument a nullity). Under the Act, special instruments called consumer bills and notes must be so marked to distinguish them from other negotiable instruments. These particular instruments arise out of consumer purchases, and by marking them as such, limit the right of a holder to claim the rights of a holder in due course in the event that payment is resisted by the maker or drawer for a breach of the contract of sale from which the instrument arose.

DISCUSSION QUESTIONS

1. Explain "negotiability."
2. What are the "essentials of negotiability"?
3. Define "endorser," "endorsee," "bearer," "holder," "holder for value," and "holder in due course."

4. *How do the rights of a holder in due course differ from those of an ordinary holder?*

5. *Define a "bill of exchange." What criteria must a document satisfy in order to meet this definition?*

6. *How does a "cheque" differ from an ordinary "bill of exchange"?*

7. *Explain the procedure for the acceptance of a bill of exchange.*

8. *Is a "sight bill" payable on the exact date set out in the bill? If not, why not? How does this differ in the case of a "demand bill"?*

9. *In what ways do "promissory notes" differ from "bills of exchange"?*

10. *Describe the procedure that a holder of a bill of exchange must follow if the bill is dishonoured by non-payment.*

11. *Explain the difference at law with respect to the drawer's liability on a cheque that is certified: (1) at the request of the drawer, and (2) at the request of a holder.*

12. *What is the effect of an "endorsement in blank" on the negotiation of a cheque? How does this differ from a "restrictive endorsement"?*

13. *Why are endorsee's reluctant to accept a cheque that is endorsed "without recourse"?*

14. *Explain the purpose of an "acceleration clause" in a promissory note which provides for payment by instalments.*

15. *Explain the nature of a "real defence," and give three examples of defences of this type.*

16. *How does a real defence differ from a "defect of title defence"?*

17. *What is a "personal defence"? Is it effective against a holder in due course?*

18. *How does consumer protection legislation affect the law relating to negotiable instruments?*

JUDICIAL DECISIONS **Negotiable Instrument Tendered as Payment of a Pre-Existing Debt—Whether Consideration For Instrument— Effect On Pre-Existing Debt**	**Currie et al v. Misa (1875), L.R. 10 Exch. 153; affirmed (1876) L.R. 1 H.L. 554** The defendant drew a cheque in the amount of £1999 3s. payable to Lizardi & Co. or bearer, to cover a pre-existing debt. The cheque was delivered to Lizardi's bankers for collection. At that time the defendant objected to payment of the cheque on the basis that no consideration was given for the instrument. LUSH, J.: The argument before us, however, was addressed almost entirely to the broader question, namely, whether an existing debt formed of itself a sufficient consideration for a negotiable security payable on demand, so as to constitute the creditor to whom it was paid a holder for value. As this is a question of great and general importance, and as our opinion upon it is in favour of the plaintiffs, we do not think it necessary to say more with reference to the special circumstance adverted to, than that we are not prepared to dissent from the view taken upon this question

by the Court below.

It will, of course, be understood that our judgment is based upon what was admitted in the argument, namely, that the cheque was received by the plaintiffs bonâ fide, and without notice of any infirmity of title on the part of Lizardi. We, therefore, for the purpose of the argument, regard the so-called "bill" as merely an authority to the defendant to pay the amount to Lizardi's bankers, instead of paying it to him, and treat the transaction as if the cheque had been paid to Lizardi, and he had paid it to the plaintiffs, not in order that he might draw upon it, but that it should be applied pro tanto in discharge of his overdrawn account.

It was not disputed on the argument, nor could it be, that if instead of a cheque the security had been a bill or note payable at a subsequent date, however short, the plaintiffs' title would have been unimpeachable. This has been established by many authorities, both in this country and in the American Courts. It has been supposed to rest on the ground that the taking of a negotiable security payable at a future day implied an agreement by the creditor to suspend his remedies during that period, and that this constituted the true consideration which, it is alleged, the law requires in order to entitle the creditor to the absolute benefit of the security. The counsel for the defendant accordingly contended that where the security is a cheque payable on demand, inasmuch as this consideration is wanting, the holder gains no independent title of his own, and has no better right to the security than the debtor himself had.

We should be sorry if we were obliged to uphold a distinction so refined and technical, and one which we believe to be utterly at variance with the general understanding of mercantile men. And upon consideration we are of opinion that it has no foundation either in principle or upon authority.

Passing by for the present the consideration of what is the true ground on which the delivery or indorsement of a bill or note payable at a future date is held to give a valid title to a creditor in respect of a preexisting debt, and assuming that it is the implied agreement to suspend, it does not follow that the legal element of consideration is entirely absent where the security is payable immediately. The giving time is only one of many kinds of what the law calls consideration. A valuable consideration, in the sense of the law, may consist either in some right, interest, profit, or benefit accruing to the one party, or some forbearance, detriment, loss, or responsibility, given, suffered, or undertaken by the other: Com. Dig. Action on the Case, Assumpsit, B. 1-15.

The holder of a cheque may either cash it immediately, or he may hold it over for a reasonable time. If he cashes it immediately he is safe. The maker of the cheque cannot afterwards repudiate, and claim back the proceeds any more than he could claim back gold or bank notes if the payment had been made in that way instead of by cheque. This was decided in *Watson v. Russell*, with which we entirely agree. In very many—perhaps in the great majority of cases—cheques are not presented till the following day, especially where they are crossed, and this usage is so far recognised by law that the drawer cannot complain of its not having been presented before, even though the banker stop payment in the interval. The loss in such a case falls on the drawer of the cheque, and not on the holder.

It cannot, we think, be said that a creditor who takes a cheque on account of a debt due to him, and pays it into his banker that it might be presented in the usual course instead of getting it cashed immediately, does not alter his position, and may not be greatly prejudiced if his title could then be questioned, or that the debtor does not, or may not, gain a benefit by the holding over. If this subject were worth pursuing it would not, we think, be difficult to shew that there is no sound distinction between the two kinds of securities of which we have been treating. In the course of the argument it was put to the learned counsel for the defendant whether a debtor who gave his own cheque in payment of a pre-existing debt could defend an action upon it on the ground that the creditor was not a holder for value, and Mr. Watkin Williams admitted that his argument must go to that extent, and yet it has always been the practice to sue in such a case on the cheque as well as on the original debt, and no such defence has, as far as we are aware, ever been attempted to be set up, certainly not successfully.

But it is useless to dilate on this point, for, in truth, the title of a creditor to a bill given on account of a pre-existing debt, and payable at a future day, does not rest upon the implied agreement to suspend his remedies. The true reason is that given by the Court of Common Pleas in *Belshaw* v. *Bush* as the foundation of the judgment in that case, namely, that a negotiable security given for such a purpose is a conditional payment of the debt, the condition being that the debt revives if the security is not realized. This is precisely the effect which both parties intended the security to have, and the doctrine is as applicable to one species of negotiable security as to another; to a cheque payable on demand, as to a running bill or a promissory note payable to order or bearer, whether it be the note of a country bank which circulates as money, or the note of the debtor, or of any other person. The security is offered to the creditor, and taken by him as money's worth, and justice requires that it should be as truly his property as the money which it represents would have been his had the payment been made in gold or a Bank of England note. And, on the other hand, until it has proved unproductive, the creditor ought not to be allowed to treat it as a nullity, and to sue the debtor as if he had given no security. The books are not without authorities in favour of this view, although the point has not, as far as we are aware, been directly decided. Story lays it down in his work on Promissory Notes, s. 186, that a pre-existing debt is equally available as a consideration as is a present advance or value given for the note, without suggesting any distinction between a note payable after date and one payable on demand; and the cases of *Poirier* v. *Morris*, *Watson* v. *Russell*, before cited, *Whistler* v. *Forster*, and others, contain clear expressions of opinion the same way.

On the part of the defendant the case of *Crofts* v. *Beal* was strongly relied on, where it was held that a promissory note given by a surety for

payment on demand without any new consideration was nudum pactum. It is sufficient to say of that case that the note was payable to the
plaintiff, and not to order or bearer, and was not therefore a negotiable
security. *De la Chaumette* v. *Bank of England* appears at first sight to be
more in point, but there, although it appeared as between the plaintiff
and O., by whom the bank note in question was remitted, that the state
of account was in favour of the plaintiff, it is not really so, for the note
had not been remitted in payment, but merely for collection as agent,
and the Court held that under these circumstances the plaintiff had no
better title than O. For these reasons we are of opinion that a creditor to
whom a negotiable security is given on account of a pre-existing debt
holds it by an indefeasible title, whether it be one payable at a future
time or on demand, and that, therefore, the judgment of the Court
below ought to be affirmed.

||||||||||||||||||||||||||||||||||||||||||||||||||||||||||||||||||||||||||||||||||||||||||||||||||||||||||||||||||||||||||||||||||||||||||||||||||||||||||||||

**Development of
Law Relating to
Negotiable
Instruments**

Goodwin v. Robarts et al. (1875), L.R. 10 Exch. 337.
The case before the Exchequer Court concerned the issue of scrip by a
London agent of a foreign government. The court decision, however,
traced the development of the law relating to negotiable instruments as
a prelude to its finding in the case. That part of the judgement was
stated in the following manner:

COCKBURN, C.J.:

Having given the fullest consideration to this argument, we are of
opinion that it cannot prevail. It is founded on the view that the law
merchant thus referred to is fixed and stereotyped, and incapable of
being expanded and enlarged so as to meet the wants and requirements
of trade in the varying circumstances of commerce. It is true that the
law merchant is sometimes spoken of as a fixed body of law, forming
part of the common law, and as it were coeval with it. But as a matter of
legal history, this view is altogether incorrect. The law merchant thus
spoken of with reference to bills of exchange and other negotiable securities, though forming part of the general body of the lex mercatoria,
is of comparatively recent origin. It is neither more nor less than the
usages of merchants and traders in the different departments of trade,
ratified by the decisions of Courts of law, which, upon such usages
being proved before them, have adopted them as settled law with a
view to the interests of trade and the public convenience, the Court
proceeding herein on the well-known principle of law that, with reference to transactions in the different departments of trade, Courts of
law, in giving effect to the contracts and dealings of the parties, will
assume that the latter have dealt with one another on the footing of any
custom or usage prevailing generally in the particular department. By
this process, what before was usage only, unsanctioned by legal decision, has become engrafted upon, or incorporated into, the common
law, and may thus be said to form part of it. "When a general usage has

been judicially ascertained and established," says Lord Campbell, in *Brandao* v. *Barnett*, "it becomes a part of the law merchant, which Courts of justice are bound to know and recognise."

Bills of exchange are known to be of comparatively modern origin, having been first brought into use, so far as is at present known, by the Florentines in the twelfth, and by the Venetians about the thirteenth, century. The use of them gradually found its way into France, and, still later and but slowly, into England. We find it stated in a law tract, by Mr. Macleod, entitled "Specimen of a Digest of the Law of Bills of Exchange," printed, we believe, as a report to the government, but which, from its research and ability, deserves to be produced in a form calculated to insure a wider circulation, that Richard Malynes, a London merchant, who published a work called the Lex Mercatoria, in 1622, and who gives a full account of these bills as used by the merchants of Amsterdam, Hamburg, and other places, expressly states that such bills were not used in England. There is reason to think, however, that this is a mistake. Mr. Macleod shews that promissory notes, payable to bearer, or to a man and his assigns, were known in the time of Edward IV. Indeed, as early as the statute of 3 Rich. 2, c. 3, bills of exchange are referred to as a means of conveying money out of the realm, though not as a process in use among English merchants. But the fact that a London merchant writing expressly on the law merchant was unaware of the use of bills of exchange in this country, shews that that use at the time he wrote must have been limited. According to Professor Story, who herein is, no doubt, perfectly right, "the introduction and use of bills of exchange in England," as indeed it was everywhere else, "seems to have been founded on the mere practice of merchants, and gradually to have acquired the force of a custom." With the development of English commerce the use of these most convenient instruments of commercial traffic would of course increase, yet, according to Mr. Chitty, the earliest case on the subject to be found in the English books is that of *Martin* v. *Boure*, in the first James I. Up to this time the practice of making these bills negotiable by indorsement had been unknown, and the earlier bills are found to be made payable to a man and his assigns, though in some instances to bearer. But about this period, that is to say, at the close of the sixteenth or the commencement of the seventeenth century, the practice of making bills payable to order, and transferring them by indorsement, took its rise. Hartmann, in a very learned work on Bills of Exchange, recently published in Germany, states that the first known mention of the indorsement of these instruments occurs in the Neapolitan Pragmatica of 1607. Savary, cited by Mons. Nouguier, in his work "Des lettres de change," had assigned to it a later date, namely 1620. From its obvious convenience this practice speedily came into general use, and, as part of the general custom of merchants, received the sanction of our Courts. At first the use of bills of exchange seems to have been confined to foreign bills between English and foreign merchants. It was afterwards extended to domestic bills between traders, and finally to bills of all persons, whether traders or not: see Chitty on Bills, 8th ed., p. 13.

In the meantime, promissory notes had also come into use, differing herein from bills of exchange that they were not drawn upon a third party, but contained a simple promise to pay by the maker, resting, therefore, upon the security of the maker alone. They were at first made payable to bearer, but when the practice of making bills of exchange payable to order, and making them transferable by indorsement, had once become established, the practice of making promissory notes payable to order, and of transferring them by indorsement, as had been done with bills of exchange, speedily prevailed. And for some time the courts of law acted upon the usage with reference to promissory notes, as well as with reference to bills of exchange.

In 1680, in the case of *Shelden* v. *Hentley*, an action was brought on a note under seal by which the defendant promised to pay *to bearer* 100*l*, and it was objected that the note was void because not made payable to a specific person. But it was said by the Court, "Traditio facit chartam loqui, and by the delivery he (the maker) expounds the person before meant; as when a merchant promises to pay to *the bearer* of the note, anyone that brings the note shall be paid." Jones, J., said that "it was the custom of merchants that made that good." In *Bromwich* v. *Lloyd*, the plaintiff declared upon the custom of merchants in London, on a note for money payable on demand, and recovered; and Treby, C.J., said that "bills of exchange were originally between foreigners and merchants trading with the English; afterwards, when such bills came to be more frequent, then they were allowed between merchants trading in England, and afterwards between any traders whatsoever, and now between any persons, whether trading or not; and, therefore, the plaintiff need not allege any custom, for now those bills were of that general use that upon an indebitatus assumpsit they may be given in evidence upon the trial." To which Powell, J., added, "On indebitatus assumpsit for money received to the use of the plaintiff the bill may be left to the jury to determine whether it was given for value received."

In *Williams* v. *Williams*, where the plaintiff brought his action as indorsee against the payee and indorser of a promissory note, declaring on the custom of merchants, it was objected on error, that the note having been made in London, the custom, if any, should have been laid as the custom of London. It was answered "that this custom of merchants was part of the common law, and the Court would take notice of it ex officio; and, therefore, it was needless to set forth the custom specially in the declaration, but it was sufficient to say that such a person secundum usum et consuetudinem mercatorum, drew the bill." And the plaintiff had judgment.

Thus far the practice of merchants, traders, and others, of treating promissory notes, whether payable to order or bearer, on the same footing as bills of exchange had received the sanction of the Courts, but Holt having become Chief Justice, a somewhat unseemly conflict arose between him and the merchants as to the negotiability of promissory notes, whether payable to order or to bearer, the Chief Justice taking what must now be admitted to have been a narrow-minded view of the matter, setting his face strongly against the negotiability of these instruments, contrary, as we are told by authority, to the opinion of Westminster Hall, and in a series of successive cases, persisting in holding them not to be negotiable by indorsement or delivery. The inconvenience to trade arising therefrom led to the passing of the statute of 3 & 4 Anne, c. 9, whereby promissory notes were made capable of being assigned by indorsement, or made payable to bearer, and such assignment was thus rendered valid beyond dispute or difficulty.

It is obvious from the preamble of the statute, which merely recites that "*it had been held* that such notes were not within the custom of Merchants," that these decisions were not acceptable to the profession or the country. Nor can there be much doubt that by the usage prevalent amongst merchants, these notes had been treated as securities negotiable by the customary method of assignment as much as bills of exchange properly so called. The Statute of Anne may indeed, practically speaking, be looked upon as a declaratory statute, confirming the decisions prior to the time of Lord Holt.

We now arrive at an epoch when a new form of security for money, namely, goldsmiths' or bankers' notes, came into general use. Holding them to be part of the currency of the country, as cash, Lord Mansfield and the Court of King's Bench had no difficulty in holding, in *Miller* v. *Race*, that the property in such a note passes, like that in cash, by delivery, and that a party taking it bonâ fide, and for value, is consequently entitled to hold it against a former owner from whom it has been stolen.

In like manner it was held, in *Collins* v. *Martin*, that where bills indorsed in blank had been deposited with a banker, to be received when due, and the latter had pledged them with another banker as security for a loan, the owner could not bring trover to recover them from the holder.

Both these decisions of course proceeded on the ground that the property in the bank-note payable to bearer passed by delivery, that in the bill of exchange by indorsement in blank, provided the acquisition had been made bonâ fide.

A similar question arose in *Wookey* v. *Pole*, in respect of an exchequer bill, notoriously a security of modern growth. These securities being made in favour of blank or order, contained this clause, "If the blank is not filled up the bill will be paid to bearer." Such an exchequer bill, having been placed, without the blank being filled up, in the hands of the plaintiffs' agent, had been deposited by him with the defendants, on a bonâ fide advance of money. It was held by three judges of the Queen's Bench, Bayley, J., dissentiente, that an exchequer bill was a negotiable security, and judgment was therefore given for the defendants. The judgment of Holroyd, J., goes fully into the subject, pointing out the distinction between money and instruments which are the representatives of money, and other forms of property. "The Courts," he says, "have considered these instruments, either promises or orders for the payment of money, or instruments entitling the holder to a sum of money, as being appendages to money, and following the nature of their principal." After referring to the authorities, he proceeds: "These authorities shew, that not only money itself may pass, and the right to it may arise, by currency alone, but further, that these mercantile instruments, which entitle the bearer of them to money, may also pass, and the right to them may arise, in like manner, by currency or delivery. These decisions proceed upon the nature of the property (i.e. money), to which such instruments give the right, and which is in itself current, and the effect of the instruments, which either give to their holders, merely as such, a right to receive the money, or specify them as the persons entitled to receive it.''

Another very remarkable instance of the efficacy of usage is to be found in much more recent times. It is notorious that, with the exception of the Bank of England, the system of banking has recently undergone an entire change. Instead of the banker issuing his own notes in return for the money of the customer deposited with him, he gives credit in account to the depositor, and leaves it to the latter to draw upon him, to bearer or order, by what is now called a cheque. Upon this state of things the general course of dealing between bankers and their customers has attached incidents previously unknown, and these by the decisions of the Courts have become fixed law. Thus, while an ordinary drawee, although in possession of funds of the drawer, is not bound to accept, unless by his own agreement or consent, the banker, if he has funds, is bound to pay on presentation of a cheque on demand. Even admission of funds is not sufficient to bind an ordinary drawee, while it is sufficient with a banker; and money deposited with a banker is not only money lent, but the banker is bound to repay it when called for by the draft of the customer (see *Pott* v. *Clegg.*) Besides this, a custom has grown up among bankers themselves of marking cheques as good for the purposes of clearance, by which they become bound to one another.

Though not immediately to the present purpose, bills of lading may also be referred to as an instance of how general mercantile usage may give effect to a writing which without it would not have had that effect at common law. It is from mercantile usage, as proved in evidence, and ratified by judicial decision in the great case of *Lickbarrow* v. *Mason*, that the efficacy of bills of lading to pass the property in goods is derived.

It thus appears that all these instruments which are said to have derived their negotiability from the law merchant had their origin, and that at no very remote period, in mercantile usage, and were adopted into the law by our Courts as being in conformity with the usages of trade; of which, if it were needed, a further confirmation might be found in the fact that, according to the old form of declaring on bills of exchange, the declaration always was founded on the custom of merchants.

Usage, adopted by the Courts, having been thus the origin of the whole of the so-called law merchant as to negotiable securities, what is there to prevent our acting upon the principle acted upon by our predecessors, and followed in the precedents they have left to us? Why is it to be said that a new usage which has sprung up under altered circumstances, is to be less admissible than the usages of past times? Why is the door to be now shut to the admission and adoption of usage in a matter altogether of cognate character, as though the law had been finally stereotyped and settled by some positive and peremptory enactment? It is true that this scrip purports, on the face of it, to be a security not for money, but for the delivery of a bond; nevertheless we think that substantially and in effect it is a security for money, which, till the bond shall be delivered, stands in the place of that document, which, when delivered, will be beyond doubt the representative of the sum it is intended to secure. Suppose the possible case that the borrowing government, after receiving one or two instalments, were to determine to proceed no further with its loan, and to pay back to the lenders the amount they had already advanced; the scrip with its receipts would be the security to the holders for the amount. The usage of the money market has solved the question whether scrip should be considered security for, and the representative of, money, by treating it as such.

The universality of a usage voluntarily adopted between buyers and sellers is conclusive proof of its being in accordance with public convenience; and there can be no doubt that by holding this species of security to be incapable of being transferred by delivery, and as requiring some more cumbrous method of assignment, we should materially hamper the transactions of the money market with respect to it, and cause great public inconvenience. No doubt there is an evil arising from the facility of transfer by delivery, namely, that it occasionally gives rise to the theft or misappropriation of the security, to the loss of the true owner. But this is an evil common to the whole body of negotiable securities. It is one which may be in a great degree prevented by prudence and care. It is one which is counterbalanced by the general convenience arising from facility of transfer, or the usage would never have become general to make scrip available to bearer, and to treat it as transferable by delivery. It is obvious that no injustice is done to one who has been fraudulently dispossessed of scrip through his own misplaced confidence, in holding that the property in it has passed to a bonâ fide holder for value, seeing that he himself must have known that it purported on the face of it to be available to bearer, and must be presumed to have been aware of the usage prevalent with respect to it in the market in which he purchased it.

Lastly, it is to be observed that the tendency of the Courts, except only in the time of Lord Holt, has been to give effect to mercantile usage in respect to securities for money, and that where legal difficulties have arisen, the legislature has been prompt to give the necessary remedy, as in the case of promissory notes and of the East India bonds.

||||||||||||||||||||||||||||||||||||||||||||||||||||||||||||||||||||||||||||||||||||||||||||||||||||||||||||||||||||||||||||||||||||||||||||||||||||||||||||||

CASE PROBLEMS FOR DISCUSSION

Case 1

Hanley sold Roberts a quantity of goods on 30 days' credit. As agreed, he drew a bill of exchange on Roberts naming himself as payee. The bill was payable in 30 days' time. Roberts accepted the bill and returned it to Hanley. Hanley endorsed the bill to Smith to cover his indebtedness to him. Smith endorsed the bill in blank to Brown as a gift. Brown delivered the bill without endorsing it to Jones, whom he owed a sum of money. Jones, in turn, endorsed the bill and sold it to Doe.

Doe presented the bill for payment, and it was dishonoured.

Advise Doe of his rights. Explain the liability (if any) of each of the parties.

Case 2

Ascot was in the process of negotiating the purchase of a valuable oil painting from a local art gallery. As a result of a number of telephone calls to the gallery owner, he eventually convinced the owner to sell the painting to him for $1 000. He prepared a cheque in the amount of the purchase price and signed it, but because he was uncertain as to the exact spelling of the gallery owner's name, he left that part of the cheque blank. He placed the signed cheque in his office desk drawer, with the intention of making a telephone call to the gallery later in the day for the information necessary to complete it.

Ascot determined the owner's name while at lunch, but when he returned to the office, he discovered that the cheque had been stolen.

Hines, a fellow employee of Ascot, had taken the cheque, filled in the cheque payable "to bearer," and used it to purchase items at a store where Ascot frequently shopped. The store owner accepted Ascot's cheque without question, as he was familiar with his signature, and later presented it to Ascot's bank for payment.

Within minutes after the bank had paid the cheque, Ascot telephoned to have the bank stop payment.

Advise the parties of their respective rights (if any) and liability (if any).

Case 3

James Baker found a wallet containing a cheque-book and a few other documents which identified the owner as one John Baker.

Using the name of John Baker, James Baker answered an advertisement which offered a small sail boat for sale. The price of the boat was $700. James Baker showed the owner John Baker's identification papers, and using one of the personalized cheques, gave the owner of the boat a cheque for the full amount. He signed the cheque "J. Baker."

The boat owner, an infant, endorsed the cheque over to a local merchant as a part of the purchase price for a larger boat. When the merchant presented the cheque for payment, the bank refused to honour it on the basis that the signature was not that of John Baker.

Advise the merchant of his legal position.

Case 4

Casey purchased a small pick-up truck from Shady Sam's Used Car Lot. The vehicle was licensed as a commercial vehicle, but Casey intended to use it primarily as transportation to and from his employment at a local manufacturing plant. Apart from this type of driving, he expected to use it occasionally in his part-time work as a fishing guide.

As a part of the purchase price, he signed a promissory note to Shady Sam for $3 000 which called for payments of principal and interest of $100 per month over a three year term. Shady Sam immediately sold the note to Easy Payment Finance Co. for $2 700. A few days later, Casey was notified by letter to make all payments on the note to Easy Payment Finance Co.

Before the first payment was due, Casey discovered that the truck was in need of extensive repairs, and returned it to Shady Sam. Shady Sam refused to take back the truck and return Casey's money. Casey then refused to make payments on the promissory note.

Some months later, Easy Payment Finance Co. brought an action against Casey for the amount owing on the note.

On what basis would Easy Payment Finance Co. claim payment? What defences might be available to Casey? Render a decision.

PART VI
Real Property Law

CHAPTER 27

Interests in Land

HISTORICAL INTRODUCTION

Real property is a term used to describe land and everything permanently attached to it. At common law, the term *real property* includes buildings constructed on the land, the minerals or anything below the surface, and the airspace above. It may, in some instances, include chattels attached to the land in such a way that they have become *fixtures*, but as a general rule, the term does not include ordinary moveable property. Chattels are *personal property*, and the distinction between real and personal property at law is significant, because the law relating to each form of property evolved in a distinctly different fashion.

The law which relates to land or real property is not unique to North America. It has its origins in the laws of England, which date back to the introduction of the feudal system. Much of the terminology used today in land law, and the basic concept of Crown ownership of all land was developed during that time in England. Before then, the system of land holding was very different. In many parts of England, land was held by families, rather than individuals, and no definite system existed which provided for the ownership or transfer of real property. Apart from some form of acknowledgement of ownership, an elaborate system of land law was unnecessary, for land did not change hands with the frequency that it does today. Land was the most important source of wealth at the time, and something which each family jealously guarded. Not all land, of course, was in the hands of families. Some individuals held land, and the Church was in possession of substantial parcels of land which it acquired as gifts from wealthy parishioners. Some land was also in the possession of communities, and there is some evidence to indicate that the community leaders in accordance with local custom divided this land among the inhabitants of the community each year for agricultural use.

The conquest of England by the Normans in 1066 radically altered the system of land holding in the country. The king proclaimed himself the owner of all of the land, and introduced the feudal system.

The *feudal system* was based upon Crown ownership of all land, and its primary purpose was directed at the maintenance of a strong military force to protect the country from invasion and insurrection. Because land represented the principal source of wealth and power, the Crown used this source to support a strong army. The method used by the king was to grant *estates in land* (or *fiefs*) to persons prepared to swear allegiance to the Crown, and who were willing to provide their services and the services of a number of other armed men for a particular number of days each year in defence of the country. The promise of military service was referred to as *knight service*, and the services required of the knight generally varied with the size of the estate in land granted by the Crown. In order for the knight to fulfil his commitment of armed men, he in turn granted lesser estates to lesser nobles in return for similar pledges of service, and so on down to the persons who actually worked the land. The process of granting lesser estates was known as *subinfeudation*. As a result, the feudal system was, to some extent, a political organization, based upon a system of grants of estates in land to persons in a form of hierarchy, with the Crown at the top, and a number of levels below in which each level possessed certain rights and privileges. In turn, the person at each level was required to provide certain gifts or services to the person immediately above in the hierarchy.

The feudal system was essentially a system under which land was held so long as the holder of the land complied with the promise to provide the necessary armed men or services in support of the Crown. If the holder of the land failed to comply, then the land would revert (or *escheat*) to the Crown. Since land was essentially the only source of wealth at the time, the holder of the land was generally ever mindful of the importance of providing the promised support. Not all grants, however, were made in return for military service; some grants of land were made in return for services such as the supply of agricultural produce, weapons, or administrative functions. Grants of estates in land were also made to the Church or religious orders, but these were discouraged by the Crown because they were incompatible with the feudal system. In all cases where the land was granted, the Crown retained ownership, and could recover the land from the person in possession. This was seldom done by the Crown, however, and the various estates in land gradually took on a degree of permanency, which closely resembled ownership, for all but the lowest forms of land holding.

The estates carried with them a *tenure* or right to hold the land which was either free or unfree. Estates which were *freehold* had fixed services attached to them. The type of service, the time, and the place were determined in the grant of the estate. For example, knight service was a form of freehold tenure in which the holder was usually obliged to provide the king with the services of a fully armed knight for 40 days each year, or make an equivalent payment of money. Knight service usually had additional services attached to it which were generally fixed, the only exception being the requirement that he make an additional payment of money for his lord's ransom if his lord was captured in battle.

A person who held land in return for providing a particular service, or the requirement that he must supply agricultural produce, frequently held land freehold, but for some, this type of tenancy was *unfree*, in which case, the holder had few rights. The holder of a freehold estate in land was said to be *seised of the estate* and, if ejected from it by another, could apply to the royal courts for an order to have the land returned. A person who held land by unfree or *copyhold* tenure was essentially a serf who worked the land, and had no right to apply to the royal court if he should be forced off the property. His only recourse was to the manor court presided over by his lord. Over time, however, this changed, and copyhold tenants were given the right to bring their cases before the royal courts.

While freehold estates could take on a number of different forms, the highest estate in land was one which permitted the holder to pass the estate along to his heirs by way of inheritance. This was important at the time, because it meant that the wealth represented by the land could be passed to succeeding generations as long as there were heirs. This form of estate was known as an estate of *fee simple*, the term *fee* being a derivative of the latin word *feodum* meaning fief or estate. Except for persons holding land directly from the Crown, the holder of an estate in *fee simple* was free to sell the estate if he so desired, or to devise it to another by way of a will or testamentary disposition.

As the feudal system declined in England, the practice of providing the Crown with personal services or particular quantities of produce declined with it. Instead, the services were generally satisfied by a monetary payment, which the Crown used to acquire the necessary services or goods. The development of trade, and the gradual increase in importance of the production and sale of goods provided alternative methods of acquiring wealth, and as these methods became more widespread, the value of land as a source of wealth and power declined. By the 17th century, the personal service aspects of the feudal system had all but disappeared, and in 1660, Parliament passed a statute which eliminated the last vestiges of personal servitude feudal rights.[1] What remained however, was the system of land holding based upon Crown ownership of all land, and the holding of land by individuals in the form of estates based upon the estate in *fee simple.*[2]

ESTATES IN LAND
Fee Simple

In Canada, all land is still owned by the Crown, and estates of land in *fee simple* are granted by *Crown patent* to individuals.[3] The patent sets out the conditions subject to which the grant is made, and it is not uncommon to find that the Crown in the right of the province has reserved either the right to all minerals, or the rights to certain precious metals in the grant of the land. For example, in the past, the province of Ontario and some of the provinces in eastern Canada frequently reserved all gold, silver, and precious metals. It also reserved all of the white pine trees standing on the property during the period when the British navy and merchant marine used these particular trees as material for the masts of their sailing ships. More recently, the Crown has followed the practice of reserving not only the mineral rights, but all timber standing on the property. The purchasers of the land generally purchase the timber rights separately, but the rights still represent a reservation of the Crown in the patent. In western Canada, a Crown res-

ervation of mineral rights is a common feature found in the patent of new lands.

Land which is granted by Crown patent seldom reverts to the Crown, because it is freely alienable by way of sale, will, or inheritance. As long as the land may be disposed of in one of these three ways, it does not escheat to the Crown. If a person, however, fails to dispose of the property during his lifetime and dies without heirs, or dies without a will devising the property to some person, the land will revert to the Crown.[4] In addition, the Crown may re-acquire the land for public purposes by way of *expropriation*. Expropriation differs from an escheat of the lands to the Crown, because it constitues a forceful taking of the property, for which the Crown must compensate the person in possession when land is expropriated. The taking usually must be justified as being for some public purpose, but it nevertheless represents the Crown exercising its right of ownership. Apart from expropriation, the land, once granted by Crown patent, remains in the hands of the public, unless it should, by some accident, escheat to the Crown through the failure of the owner to provide for its disposition upon his death.

If a person grants land during his lifetime, the grant is by way of a formal document called a *deed*. The grant is embodied in the document in such a way that the execution of the deed by the *grantor* under seal, and the delivery of the document to the *grantee* passes the title to the land to the recipient. The receipt of the deed *vests* the title in the grantee, and the grantee, as the new freehold tenant, is entitled to exercise all the rights of "owner" with respect to the land. The

---

[1] *Statute of Tenures*, 12 Car. II, c. 24.

[2] Some of the lesser forms of land tenures remained until the 20th century, however, see *Law of Property Act*, 1922, 12 & 13, Geo. 5, c. 16.

[3] In Ontario, for example, all property in the province was granted freehold after 1791. See The *Canada Act*, 1791, 31 Geo. III, c. 31.

[4] See, for example, the *Escheats Act*, R.S.O. 1980, c. 142.

owner of the land, for example, may use the land as he sees fit, subject only to the common law of nuisance and statutory enactments that restrict the use of property. For example, the owner may farm the land, cut down trees, construct buildings on the land, and use it for any purpose. The owner may also grant lesser estates in the land.

Life Estate

The highest estate in land that the person in possession of the *fee simple* might grant (apart from the fee itself) is a *life estate*. A life estate is a freehold estate which may be held by a person other than the owner of the *fee simple* for a particular lifetime (usually his own). This form of grant is frequently made within a family where the person who possesses the *fee simple* may wish to pass the property to younger members of the family, yet retain the use of the land during his lifetime. In this case, he would prepare a deed in which he would grant the *fee simple* to the younger member of the family, but retain for himself a life estate in the land. The effect of the conveyance would be that possession of the land would remain with the grantor during his lifetime, and on his death, possession would pass to the grantee. For example, Andrews owns a parcel of land in fee simple, and conveys the *fee simple* to Brown, reserving a life estate to himself. Brown would be the grantee of the fee, subject to the life estate of Andrews. The interest in land which Brown receives in the conveyance would be the *remainder* or *reversion* interest. On Andrews' death the life estate would end, and Brown would then possess the *fee simple*, and the right to enter on and use the land.

The owner of the land *in fee simple* may grant many successive life estates in a par-

ticular parcel of land if he should so desire. For example, Axleson might grant a parcel of land to Baker for life, then to Chapman for life, then to Dawson for life, and the remainder to Emmons. In this case, Baker would be entitled to the land during his lifetime, and then it would pass to Chapman for his lifetime, and then on to Dawson for his lifetime. On Dawson's death, the remainderman Emmons would acquire the land in fee simple.

A life tenant while in possession of a life estate is expected to use the land in a reasonable manner and to not commit *waste*. He is under no obligation to maintain any buildings in a good state of repair, but he cannot tear down buildings, nor is he permitted to deliberately destroy the property. Normally, a life tenant is not entitled to destroy trees planted to shelter the property from the wind, nor would he be entitled to destroy trees planted for ornamental purposes. He may, however, clear land for cultivation of crops, or cut trees to obtain the wood for heating purposes. Where land is transferred to a life tenant subject to a mortgage, the life tenant is normally only obliged to pay the interest on the mortgage, and the obligation to pay the principal amount rests with the remainderman. A life tenant is also usually obliged to pay land taxes, but not local improvement taxes charged to the land. Since the remainderman reaps the benefits of the local improvements, the charge is his responsibility, although the usual practice might be for the life tenant to pay the local improvement levy and recover it from the remainderman.

Life estates are not without certain drawbacks or disadvantages. The existence of a life estate frequently renders the property unsaleable. A prospective purchaser of the reversion is unlikely to be willing to wait until the life tenant dies to gain possession, and unless both the life tenant and the remainderman are willing to convey their respective interests in the land, the purchaser would probably not be interested in acquiring the property. The same would hold true for a sale of the life estate. A purchaser of a life estate only acquires the property for the remainder of the life tenant's lifetime, and the uncertainty attached to the tenure would not prompt a purchaser to pay a high price for such an estate. More important than the sale of the property, however, is the fact that the life tenant cannot alter the property during his lifetime, nor may the remainderman, as he has no right to the property until after the life tenant dies. As a result, the life estate is seldom used, except to convey interests in land within families.

Leasehold Estate

A leasehold estate differs from a life estate or an estate *in fee simple*. It represents a grant of the right to possession of a parcel of land for a period of time in return for the payment of rent to the land-owner. A leasehold estate, while an ancient form of tenancy, is contractual in nature, and given for a fixed term. The law has always treated leasehold interests as being distinctly different from freehold interests in land, and the body of law applicable to these interests in land remains separate from that which concerned leases. Since a lease is contractual in nature, the parties may insert in the agreement any rights or obligations they may wish, provided that they do not violate any law or regulation affecting leasehold interests in the jurisdiction where the land is located.[5]

A leasehold interest grants the tenant exclusive possession of the property for the term of the lease, provided that the tenant complies with the terms of the lease agreement. Specific legislation in each jurisdiction governs leasehold estates, and these are examined in greater detail in Chapter 30.

INTERESTS IN LAND
Easements

Persons other than the owner of land in *fee simple* may acquire a right or interest in land either by an express grant from the owner, by statute, by implication, or by prescriptive right. The interests are usually acquired for the better use and enjoyment of a particular parcel of land called the *dominant tenement*, and represent an interest in a second parcel called the *servient tenement*.

Interests in the lands of another may be acquired for a wide variety of reasons. For example, a person may wish to travel across the lands of another in order to gain access to a body of water that is not adjacent to the person's own land, or a person may wish to drain water from his own land across the lands of another to a catch-basin. A person may also wish to place something such as a telephone line or gas pipeline on or under the lands of another for particular purposes. These rights are known as *easements*.

An easement may be granted by the owner of the *fee simple* of a servient tenement to the owner of the dominant tenement by an express grant. This is often done where the owner wishes to obtain a permanent right which will run with the land and be binding on all future owners of the servient tenement. Similar rights

parties. See, for example, The *Landlord and Tenant Act*, R.S.O. 1980, c. 232.

may also be acquired by the owners of dominant tenements by way of expropriation rights granted under statute, where the legislation enables the owners to obtain rights of way across lands for public purposes, such as for a hydro powerline, or a pipeline.

Easements may also be implied by law. These easements are sometimes referred to as *easements or rights of way of necessity*. They usually arise where the grantor of a parcel of land has failed to grant access to the property sold. For example, if Adams buys a block of land from Baxter which is surrounded by land retained by Baxter, Adams would have no means of access to the land without trespassing on the land of Baxter. In such a case, the courts will imply a right of way for access to the land sold on the basis that a right of access was intended by the parties at the time that the agreement was made.

The same rule would also apply where a grantor sells a parcel of land, then realizes afterwards that the land retained is land-locked and without a right of access. In each situation, however, the land must be truly land-locked, and if some other means of access exists, no matter how inconvenient it might be, then a right of way of necessity will not be implied.

An easement may also arise as a result of long, open, and uninterrupted use of a right of way over the lands of another. This type of easement is known as a *prescriptive right of easement*, and it may be acquired in most provinces.[6] A prescriptive right of this nature arises where the person claiming the easement uses the property openly and continuously as if by right, usually for a period of 20 years. The use, however, must be visible and apparent to

all who might see it. The use by night, without the knowledge of anyone, would not create an easement by prescription, as the use must be open and notorious, and adverse to the owner's rights.

The exercise of the right in the face of the owner's title is an important component of the acquisition of the prescriptive right of easement. The use must be with the knowledge of the owner of the property, or under circumstances where the owner would normally be aware of the use. If the owner fails to stop the use by the exercise of his rights as owner during the 20-year period, the law assumes that the true owner is prepared to permit the use by the person claiming the prescriptive right. Any exercise of the right of the true owner to exclude the trespasser would have the effect of breaking the time period, provided that the user acknowledges the rights of the true owner, and refrains from using the easement for a period of time.

Restrictive Covenants

A *restrictive covenant* is a means by which an owner of property may continue to exercise some control over its use after the property has been conveyed to another. The covenant which creates the obligation is usually embodied in the conveyance to the party who acquires the land, and normally takes the form of a promise or agreement not to use the property in a particular way. For example, a person owns two building lots. He constructs a dwelling-house on one lot, and decides to sell the remaining lot. He is concerned that the prospective purchaser might use the land for the construction of a multiple-family dwelling, and to avoid this, includes a term in the agreement of sale that the lands purchased may only be used for a single-family dwelling. If the purchaser agrees to the restriction, the vendor may

---

[6]All except Quebec, Alberta, and Saskatchewan, and lands under the Land Titles System in other provinces.

include in the deed a covenant to be executed by the purchaser that the purchaser will not use the land for the construction of anything other than a single-family dwelling. Then, if the purchaser should attempt to construct a multiple-family dwelling on the property, the vendor may take legal action to have the restriction enforced.

Restrictive covenants may be used for a number of other purposes as well. They may be used to prevent the cutting of trees on property sold, control the uses of the land, require the purchaser to obtain approval of the vendor for any building constructed on the property, control the keeping of animals, or a variety of other limitations. Any covenant which attempts to prevent the purchase or use of land by any person of a particular race, creed, colour, nationality, or religion would be void as against public policy, but generally, any lawful restriction, if reasonable, and for the benefit of the adjacent property owner, may be enforced by the courts if it is described in terms which would permit the issue of an injunction.

Restrictive covenants are used for the better enjoyment and the benefit of the adjacent property owner, usually to maintain the value of the properties, or to maintain the particular character of the area. The widespread use of zoning and planning by municipalities has eliminated the use of restrictive covenants to a considerable degree, but in many areas they are still used for special purposes where a land-owner may wish to control the use of adjacent land in a particular manner.

Mineral Rights

The right to the minerals below the surface of land is possessed by the owners of the land *in fee simple* in most of the older provinces of Canada, as it was a practice of the Crown in the past to include in the Crown patent a grant of the right to the minerals (except perhaps for gold and silver) along with the surface rights. More recent Crown patents in all provinces usually reserve the mineral rights to the Crown unless the patentee acquires the mineral rights at the time of issue by way of an express purchase. A person who acquires the mineral rights in the lands of another acquires an interest in land known as a *profit à prendre* which must be in writing, since it is a contract concerning land. In addition, the conveyance of the interest must be in deed form to be enforceable. Unless the owner of the mineral rights owns the surface rights as well, the mining of the minerals carries with it certain obligations to the owner of the surface rights. Since the extraction of minerals normally requires some disturbance of the surface, the owner of the mineral rights must compensate the owner of the surface rights for the interference with his property.

The documents that provide for the removal of the minerals and for the surface use by the persons with rights to the minerals are frequently referred to as "leases," but they are much more than ordinary leases even though they relate to the occupancy of a portion of the surface area. It should be noted, however, that the right to remove water from the lands of another is not the same as the right to remove oil, gas, or other minerals. The right to remove water is generally considered to be an easement, rather than a *profit à prendre*.

Possessory Interests in Land

Title to land may be acquired through the possession of land under certain circumstances. In provinces where the Land Titles System does not apply, the exclusive possession of land for a long period of time which is in open, notorious, visible, uninterrupted, and undisputed defiance of the true owner's title, will have the effect of creating a possessory title in the occupier of the land. The possessory title will be good against everyone, including the true owner, if he fails to regain his possession of the property by way of legal action within a stipulated period of time. In provinces where a possessory title may be acquired, the time period varies from 10 to 20 years, and if the owner fails to take action within that period, the title in the occupier becomes indefeasible.

The period of possession must be continuous and undisputed, but it need not be by the same occupant. For example, one occupant may be in exclusive possession for a part of the time, and may convey possession to another occupant for the remainder of the time period. As long as the period of possession is continuous the time period will run. Any break in the chain of possession, such as where the true owner regains possession for a period of time, will affect the right of the occupant, and the time period will begin again only when the possession adverse to the true owner commences for a second time.

Adverse possession requires the occupant in possession to do the acts normally required of an owner of the land. For example, the occupant would be expected to use the land, pay taxes, maintain fences, and generally treat it as his own. This must be done openly, and with the knowledge of the person with title to the land.

A tenant may acquire a possessory title to leased property if he continues to possess the land for the statutory period of time after the lease has expired, provided that no act or acknowledgement of the lessor's title is made during the period. The tenant, during the period of possession following the expiry of the lease, would be obliged to pay taxes, and all other assessments usually imposed on the owner of the land, in addition to maintaining possession of the property to the exclusion of the owner for the statutory period. Any acknowledgement (such as the payment of rent), would terminate the possession time, and cause it to begin again from that point. Continuous possession is the essential requirement for the acquisition of a possessory title, and unless continuous, open, and undisturbed possession can be proven, a possessory title may not be acquired.

||||||||||||||||||||||||||||||||||||||||||||||||||||||||||||||||||||||||||||||||

CASE 27.1
Re St. Clair Beach Estates Ltd. v. MacDonald et al. (1974), 50 D.L.R. (3d) 650.

PENNELL, J.:

To understand what the law on the matter is, I must refer to the *Limitations Act*. Section 4 of that Act provides:

"4. No person shall make an entry or distress, or bring an action to recover any land or rent, but within ten years next after the time at which the right to make such entry or distress, or to bring such action, first accrued to some person through whom he claims, or if the right did not accrue to any person through whom he claims, then within ten years next after the time at which the right to make such entry or distress, or to bring such action, first accrued to the person making or bringing it."

. . . . .

It is plain on its face that the *Limitations Act* is a defence.

The Courts have been generous in elucidating the nature of the burden upon a party seeking to establish title by possession. From a long stream of cases I select, first, that of *Pflug and Pflug v. Collins*, [1952] O.R. 519, [1952] 3 D.L.R. 681; affirmed [1953] O.W.N. 140, [1953] 1 D.L.R. 841. In that case, at p. 527 O.R., p. 689 D.L.R., Wells, J. (as he then was), made it clear that to succeed the appellants must show:

(1) Actual possession for the statutory period by themselves and those through whom they claim;

(2) that such possession was with the intention of excluding from possession the owners or persons entitled to possession; and

(3) discontinuance of possession for the statutory period by the owners and all others, if any, entitled to possession.

If they fail in any one of these respects, their claim must be dismissed.

||||||||||||||||||||||||||||||||||||||||||||||||||||||||||||||||||||||||||||||

Encroachments

An encroachment is also a possessory right to the property of another that may be acquired by the passage of time. It most often takes the form of a roof "overhang," where a building has been constructed too close to the property line, or where the building has actually been constructed partly on the lands of a neighbour. If the true owner of the land on which the encroachment is made permits it to exist for a long period of time, the right to demand the removal of the encroachment may be lost. In the case of a building constructed partly on the lands of another, after undisturbed possession for a period of 10 to 20 years (according to the province) the right to object to the encroachment is lost. Encroachments are normally rights in property that may be acquired only in those areas of Canada where land is recorded under the Registry System.

FIXTURES

Fixtures are chattels which are permanently or constructively attached to real property. Real property includes land, and all things attached to it in some permanent fashion. A building constructed on a parcel of land becomes a part of the land insofar as ownership is concerned. Some ob-

jects, however, are not normally a part of the land, but are sometimes affixed to it, and the question arises: Did they become a part of the real property, or are they still chattels which may be removed? In the early cases, the rule developed to determine if a chattel had become a fixture, and a part of the land, was based upon the use and enjoyment of the particular item. Generally, it was thought that any chattel that was attached to the land to improve the land (or building), even if only slightly attached, became a part of the realty, but anything attached for the better use of the chattel did not.[7]

This test over the years has resulted in an unusually confusing series of cases which have failed to provide a clear rule as to what may constitute a fixture. For example, carpet in a hotel was held to be a fixture,[8] but a mobile home on a concrete foundation, and attached to a septic tank and drainage field was held not to be a part of the land.[9] As a result of these and similar cases, what constitutes a fixture turns very much on the particular facts of the case. The degree of annexation to the land is generally important, as is the ability of the person in possession to remove the chattel without causing serious damage to either the chattel or the building. The particular use of the chattel is also important, since some obviously have little value except as a part of the land. Made-to-measure storm-windows, designed for a particular house, for example, would normally be constructively attached to the property as fixtures, as they would be

---

[7]*Haggert v. Town of Brampton et al.* (1897), 28 S.C.R. 174; *Stack v. T. Eaton Co. et al.* (1902), 4 O.L.R. 335; *Re Davis,* [1954] O.W.N. 187.

[8]*La Salle Recreations Ltd. v. Canadian Camdex Investments Ltd.* (1969), 4 D.L.R. (3d) 549.

[9]*Lichty et al. v. Voigt et al.* (1977), 80 D.L.R. (3d) 757.

used specifically for the better use of the particular building, and in themselves, as chattels, would have very little value. The same would hold true for fences and trees planted on the land.

Where chattels are brought on the property and affixed by a tenant, the chattels are treated differently by the courts. Fixtures which are firmly affixed to the land or building become a part of the property, and may not be removed, but items which are classed as *trade fixtures* may generally be removed by the tenant. Trade fixtures include chattels such as display cabinets, shelving, signs, mirrors, equipment, and machinery. These normally may be removed at the termination of the lease, provided that the tenant does so promptly, and repairs any damage caused by their removal. Prompt removal, however, is important. Trade fixtures left on the premises for a long period of time may eventually become a part of the realty, and the tenant may not later claim them.

|||||||||||||||||||||||||||||||||||||||||||||||||||||||||||||||||||||||||||||||

CASE 27.2
Stack v. T. Eaton Co. et al. (1902), 4 O.L.R. 335.

MEREDITH, C.J.:

I take it to be settled law:—

(1) That articles not otherwise attached to the land than by their own weight are not to be considered as part of the land, unless the circumstances are such as shew that they were intended to be part of the land.

(2) That articles affixed to the land even slightly are to be considered part of the land unless the circumstances are such as to shew that they were intended to continue chattels.

(3) That the circumstances necessary to be shewn to alter the *primâ facie* character of the articles are circumstances which shew the degree of annexation and object of such annexation, which are patent to all to see.

(4) That the intention of the person affixing the article to the soil is material only so far as it can be presumed from the degree and object of the annexation.

(5) That, even in the case of tenants' fixtures put in for the purposes of trade, they form part of the freehold, with the right, however, to the tenant, as between him and his landlord, to bring them back to the state of chattels again by severing them from the soil, and that they pass by a conveyance of the land as part of it, subject to this right of the tenant.

|||||||||||||||||||||||||||||||||||||||||||||||||||||||||||||||||||||||||||||||

TITLE TO LAND

Estates in land may be held by either an individual, or a number of persons. Where a number of persons hold title to property, the interests of each need not be equal, depending upon the nature of the conveyance.

Where land is conveyed to persons in *joint tenancy*, the interests of the grantees are always equal. Joint tenancy interests in land are identical in time, interest, and possession with respect to all joint tenants. A joint tenant acquires an undivided interest in the entire property conveyed. A joint tenancy must also arise out of the same instrument, such as a deed or will, and possession must arise at the same time. For example, two parties may be granted land as joint tenants in a deed, or devised land under a will as joint tenants, but they cannot become joint tenants through inheritance in the sense that a person inherits the share of a joint tenant on his death. Joint tenancy interests vest in the surviving joint tenants on the death of a joint tenant, and consequently a joint tenancy interest may not be devised by will to another to create a new joint tenancy. A joint tenancy may be terminated by the sale of the interest of a joint tenant to another party.

A second type of tenancy is a *tenancy-in-common* which differs from a joint tenancy in that the right of survivorship does not attach to the interests of the tenants; nor do the interests necessarily need to be equal. For example, two individuals might receive a grant of land as tenants-in-common. The grant may be of equal interests, in which each would acquire an undivided one-half interest in the land. The grantor however, could convey unequal interests in the property to each person, in which case the interests would be unequal, but in the whole of the land. In the example above, one might receive an undivided three-quarters interest, and the other might receive an undivided one-quarter interest in the whole. It should also be noted in the case of a tenancy-in-common that a part of the tenancy may be inherited, or may be devised by will. Since the right of survivorship does not exist, when a tenant-in-common dies, the interest of the tenant passes by way of the tenant's will or by way of intestacy to the devisee or heirs at law, and does not vest in the surviving tenant-in-common.

If the tenants wish to divide the property, and they cannot agree upon the division, the division may be made by the courts, or under the *Partition Act* in those provinces with partition legislation.[10] The tenancy may also be dissolved by the acquisition by one tenant of the interest of the other tenant (or tenants), as the union of the interest in one person will convert the tenancy-in-common into a single *fee simple* interest.

||||||||||||||||||||||||||||||||||||||||||||||||||||||||||||||||||

CASE 27.3
Williams v. Hensman (1861), 1 J. & H. 546, 70 E.R. 862.

VICE CHANCELLOR SIR W. PAGE WOOD:

A joint-tenancy may be severed in three

ways: in the first place, an act of any one of the persons interested operating upon his own share may create a severance as to that share. The right of each joint-tenant is a right by survivorship only in the event of no severance having taken place of the share which is claimed under the *jus accrescendi*. Each one is at liberty to dispose of his own interest in such manner as to sever it from the joint fund—losing, of course, at the same time, his own right of survivorship. Secondly, a joint-tenancy may be severed by mutual agreement. And, in the third place, there may be a severance by any course of dealing sufficient to intimate that the interests of all were mutually treated as constituting a tenancy in common. When the severance depends on an inference of this kind without any express act of severance, it will not suffice to rely on an intention, with respect to the particular share, declared only behind the backs of the other persons interested.

||||||||||||||||||||||||||||||||||||||||||||||||||||||||||||||||||

REGISTRATION OF PROPERTY INTERESTS

In the past, it was necessary for the individual land-owner to closely guard all documents related to the title of land which he possessed in order to prove his right to the property. The list of title documents began with the Crown patent, and extended down through a chain of deeds from one owner to another to the deed granting the land to the present owner. If the list of deeds contained no flaws or breaks in the chain of owners, the present owner was said to have a "good title" to the land. If for some reason the title documents were destroyed through fire, or were stolen, the land-owner faced a dilemma. His legal right to the land in the form of a chain of title was gone, and a prospective purchaser was obliged to rely on his word (and perhaps the word of his neighbours) that he in fact had title to the lands which he wished to sell.

[10]For example, Ontario and British Columbia.

The difficulties attached to this system of establishing land ownership eventually gave way to a system of land registration in which all of the land in a county or district was identified, and a public record office established to act as the recorder and custodian of all documents pertaining to the individual parcels of land. A prospective purchaser could then simply attend at the public record office, and satisfy himself that the vendor had a good title to the property which he intended to sell.

Surprisingly, the widespread use of the public record office approach for the custody of documents pertaining to land, and the recording of the instruments in land registers took place in North America, rather than in England. In 1862 a Land Registry Office was established in London, but for many years, the registration of title documents was voluntary. Registry offices were established in other areas of England as well, but it was not until comparatively recent times that compulsory registration was extended to all areas of England. In this respect, Canada and the United States were many years ahead of the country in which their system of land tenure developed.

In Canada, the registration system did not develop immediately, but evolved gradually, with the public office first acting as custodian of the title documents, then providing for the registration of documents. Over the years, this was refined further to the point where, in some provinces of Canada, the province itself certifies the title of the owner of the land.

The purpose of the public registration system and the certification of titles is designed to reduce to an absolute minimum the chance of fraud in land transactions, and to eliminate the need for safeguarding title documents by the individual. All provinces have a system for the registration of interests in land, and have public record offices where a person may examine the title to property in the area. All interests in property require registration to protect the interests, otherwise any person who does not have actual notice of the interest of another in the land may acquire an interest in the land in priority over the interest of the holder of an unregistered instrument or deed. All unregistered interests in land would therefore be void as against a person who registers a deed to the property, and who had no actual notice of the outstanding interest.

Two distinct systems of registration of land interests exist in Canada. In the eastern provinces, and in parts of Ontario and Manitoba, the *Registry System* is used for land registration. In the western provinces, and parts of Manitoba and Ontario, the *Land Titles* or *"Torrens" System* is used.

The Registry System is the older of two systems of land registration. Under the Registry System, a register is maintained for each particular township lot or parcel of land on a registered plan of subdivision. All interests in land which affect the particular parcel or lot are recorded in the register which pertains to the lot, and may be examined by the general public. Any person may present for registration an instrument which purports to be an interest in the land, and it will be registered against the land described in the document. For this reason, the prospective purchaser or investor must take care to ascertain that the person who professes to be the owner of the land has, in fact, a good title.

Under the Registry System, to determine the right of the person to the property, it is necessary to make a search of the title at the Registry Office to ascertain that a good "chain of title" exists. This means that the present owner's title must be traced back in time through the registered deeds of each registrant to make certain that each person who transferred the title to the property was in fact the owner of the land in *fee simple* at the time of transfer.

In Ontario, it is necessary to establish a good chain of title for a 40-year period before the title of the present owner may be said to be "clear." Each document registered against the land must be carefully examined to make certain that it has been properly drawn and executed, and that no outstanding interests in the land exist which are in conflict with the present registered owner's title. Under the Registry System, the onus is on the prospective purchaser or investor to determine that the registered owner's title is good, and consequently, the services of a lawyer are usually necessary to make this determination. If a person fails to examine the title, and later discovers that the person who gave the conveyance did not have title to the property, or that the property was subject to a mortgage or lien at the time of the purchase, the purchaser has only the interest (if any) of the vendor in the land. The only recourse of the purchaser under the circumstances would be against the vendor (if he can be found) for damages.

The Land Titles System differs from the Registry System in a number of important aspects. Under the Land Titles System, the title of the present registered owner is confirmed and warranted by the province to be as it is represented in the land register. It is not necessary for a person to make a search of the title to the property to establish a good chain of title, as this task has al-ready been performed by the Land Registrar, and the title of the last registered owner as shown in the register for the particular parcel of land is certified as being correct. To avoid confusion, instruments pertaining to land under the Land Titles System are given different names. A *deed*, for example, is called a *transfer*, and a *mortgage* is referred to as a *charge*. The legal nature and the differences between these latter two instruments are dealt with in Chapter 29, *The Law of Mortgages*. As well, a number of other differences exist between the two systems; one of the more notable differences being, that in land titles jurisdictions, an interest in land may not normally be acquired by adverse possession.

The advantage of the Land Titles System over the older Registry System is the certainty of title under the newer system. If, for some reason, the title is not as depicted in the Land Title Register, the party who suffered a loss as a result of the error is entitled to compensation from the province for the loss.

In an effort to streamline the Registry System in Ontario, a proposal of the provincial government called *Polaris* is currently under consideration. This project, if adopted, would improve the system by simplifying the methods of registration, certify the title to lands on plans of subdivision, and generally provide greater ease and certainty in the examination of the title to land in the province. The project of modernization, which would include the extensive use of computerized information, storage, and indexing, if adopted, would be phased in over a 15-year period.

SUMMARY   Real property includes land and everything attached to it in a permanent manner. The Crown owns all land, but has conveyed estates in land by way of Crown patents. The highest estate in land is an estate in *fee simple*, and when a person states that he owns land, the estate to which he refers is ownership in *fee simple*. A life estate is another estate in land which is limited to a particular lifetime, and afterwards reverts to the grantor or the person in possession of the remainder or reversion.

An individual may possess land either alone, or jointly. This may be either by a joint tenancy or tenancy-in-common. In both cases, the interests are in the entire property, but in the case of the tenancy-in-common the interests may be unequal.

Interests in land, other than estates, exist as well. A person may acquire an easement or right of way over the land of another, or a person may exercise control over land granted to another by way of a restrictive covenant in the conveyance. Restrictive covenants are generally used to protect adjacent property by controlling the use which the grantee may make of the property.

Land or interests in land may be acquired in some parts of Canada by way of adverse possession. This usually requires the open and undisputed adverse possession of the land or right for a lengthy period of time, but once the right has been established, the lawful owner can do nothing to eliminate it.

All instruments concerning land must be registered in order that the public may have notice of the interest in land and the identity of the rightful owner. Each province maintains public registry offices where the interests in land are recorded, either under the Registry System or the Land Titles System. The Registry System is used in most of Canada east of Saskatchewan, and the Land Titles System is found in western Canada and parts of Manitoba and Ontario. Persons must satisfy themselves as to the title to lands under the Registry System, but under the Land Titles System, the province certifies the title to be correct as shown in the land register for the particular parcel. Under both systems, an unregistered conveyance or interest in land is void as against a person who has registered his interest without actual notice of the unregistered instrument.

DISCUSSION QUESTIONS

1. *Explain the nature of land ownership in Canada.*
2. *What is the nature of a freehold estate?*
3. *Define* fee simple.
4. *Under what circumstances does land escheat to the Crown?*
5. *How is a life estate created? What are the rights of a life tenant?*
6. *Distinguish a "leasehold estate" from a "life estate."*
7. *In what way does an easement differ from other interests in land?*
8. *How is a prescriptive right of easement created?*

9. *Explain the purpose of a restrictive covenant. List three common uses of this concept.*

10. *Under what circumstances might adverse possession arise?*

11. *What is a fixture? How is a fixture distinguished from an ordinary chattel?*

12. *Distinguish a "joint tenancy" from a "tenancy-in-common."*

13. *Why is a registration system for interests in land necessary? What purpose does it serve?*

14. *How is a chain of title established? Why is a "good chain of title" important to a purchaser?*

15. *Identify and explain the two principal systems of land registration used in Canada.*

16. *What special advantages attach to the Land Titles System?*

|||

JUDICIAL DECISIONS

Interests in Land—Test for Fixtures

Credit Valley Cable TV/FM Ltd. v. Peel Condominium Corp. #95 et al. (1980), 27 O.R. (2d) 433.

The plaintiff entered into an agreement to supply community television antenna and cable services to the unit owners of a condominium. The agreement provided that the cable was to remain the property of the plaintiff. The cable was installed in conduits provided in the building. The defendant later entered into an agreement with another company for the same services using a different antenna, but hooked up to the cable installed by the plaintiff. The plaintiff sued the defendant for trespass to its cable by the second system. The issue was whether the cable had become a fixture, or remained a chattel owned by the plaintiff.

GRANGE, J.:

The test for fixtures was set out in the judgment of Meredith, C.J.C.P., in the divisional court in *Stack v. T. Eaton Co. et al.* (1902), 4 O.L.R. 335. He formulated, at p. 338, five rules as follows:

"(1) That articles not otherwise attached to the land than by their own weight are not to be considered as part of the land, unless the circumstances are such as shew that they were intended to be part of the land.

"(2) That articles affixed to the land even slightly are to be considered part of the land unless the circumstances are such as to shew that they were intended to continue chattels.

"(3) That the circumstances necessary to be shewn to alter the *primâ facie* character of the articles are circumstances which shew the degree of annexation and object of such annexation, which are patent to all to see.

"(4) That the intention of the person affixing the article to the soil is material only so far as it can be presumed from the degree and object of the annexation.

"(5) That, even in the case of tenants' fixtures put in for the purposes of trade, they form part of the freehold, with the right, however, to the tenant, as between him and his landlord, to bring them back to the state of chattels again by severing them from the soil, and that they pass by a conveyance of the land as part of it, subject to this right of the tenant."

The last rule is, of course, not relevant to the case at bar. Rule (2) certainly applies at least to much of the equipment making it necessary to examine the circumstances to find out whether the articles were intended to be continued as chattels. Under rule (3) the only relevant circumstances are those which show the degree of annexation and object of such annexation "which are patent for all to see". Finally, under rule (4) the subjective intention of the affixer (which I suggest was manifestly to retain the articles as chattels) is immaterial.

Under the third rule in *Stack v. Eaton*, I must consider the degree of annexation. While it is clear that there was some affixing of the articles to the building, I think it is equally clear and more important that both equipment and cable could be readily removed with a minimum of injury to the building. Indeed that was precisely what Bertoni found to have been done by All-View to much of the equipment when he gained access to the building in early June. The removal of the cable might well cause damage to the cable but there is no evidence that the removal would cause any damage whatever to the building. The presence or absence of likelihood of damage in removal is an important factor in the determination of whether or not the article has become a fixture—see *Liscombe Falls Gold Mining Co. et al. v. James R. Bishop et al.* (1905), 35 S.C.R. 539. In my view there is not evidence of potential damage upon removal sufficient to affect the matter materially. As was said by Lord Macnaghten in *Leigh et al. v. Taylor et al.*, [1902] A.C. 157 at p. 162:

"The mode of annexation is only one of the circumstances of the case and not always the most important—and its relative importance is probably not what it was in ruder or simpler times."

What is important to me is the resolution of the intention question. It has been said more than once that the determination is based upon the facts of the particular case—see, for example, *Bing Kee et al. v. Yick Chong* (1910), 43 S.C.R. 334, *per* Davies, J., at p. 337, and Milvain, J., in *Re Burtex Industries Ltd. (in Bankruptcy); Elleker v. Farmers & Merchants Trust Co. Ltd. et al.* (1964), 47 W.W.R. 96 at p. 101, as follows:

"I have reached the conclusion that great confusion is created by courts which slavishly follow cases rather than principles. As I understand the law it is a question of intent as to whether chattels become part of the realty, and such intent is to be found in the circumstances of each case as a finding of fact."

The test (or as Milvain, J., would have it—the principle) that has been accepted is that found in *Haggert v. Town of Brampton et al.* (1897), 28 S.C.R. 174, quoted by Spence, J., in *Re Davis*, [1954] O.W.N. 187 at p. 190:

"If the object of the affixing of chattels is to improve the freehold, then, even if the chattels are only slightly affixed to the realty, they may well become part of the realty. If, on the other hand, the object of the affixation of the chattels is the better enjoyment of the chattels, then the affixation does not make them part of the realty."

It is not an easy test to follow. In a sense every chattel affixed to a building could be said to improve the building or else it would not be affixed. The test has led to some apparently conflicting results—see *La Salle Recreations Ltd. v. Canadian Camdex Investments Ltd.* (1969), 4 D.L.R. (3d) 549, 68 W.W.R. 339 (carpeting in a hotel held to be a fixture); *Lichty et al. v. Voigt et al.* (1977), 17 O.R. (2d) 552, 80 D.L.R. (3d) 757 (a mobile home cemented to the ground complete with septic tank and field bed held not to be a fixture). In any event, I think that applying the test here one must inevitably find the cable and equipment remained a chattel. Its installation in no way improved the building; all it did was make it possible for Terra to provide its subscribers with cable television. Its presence did not make the service cheaper; indeed the cost of service is prescribed by federal Regulation. In my view the situation is governed by such cases as *Re Davis, supra* (bowling alleys); *General Steel Wares Ltd. v. Ford & Ottawa Gas*, [1965] 2 O.R. 81, 49 D.L.R. (2d) 673 (gas dryers). In both cases although one might assume the articles were well affixed they were held to be chattels affixed for purposes of carrying on bowling or gas-drying and not for the benefit of the building.

The plaintiff alleges that Peel and All-View were engaged in a conspiracy to interfere with the plaintiff's contractual and economic relations with its subscribers. There is no direct evidence to support the allegation but I am asked to infer the conspiracy and the interference from the loss of custom. I am not prepared to do so. I suspect that the loss of business is a direct result of subscriber resentment at the frustration of their desire expressed in a vote of 106 to 8 to change to an MATV system; if so it is hardly actionable against the defendants.

The prayer for relief asks for an injunction prohibiting interference with the plaintiff's system, an injunction requiring the defendants to cease to operate an MATV system, a declaration that the agreement of April 22nd is in full force and effect and further asks damages for breach of contract, loss of goodwill, conspiracy and interference. As I see the matter, it is simply a trespass action by All-View with the encouragement and participation of Peel lasting for about seven days and terminating upon the granting of the interlocutory injunction. I have found that the system is the property of the plaintiff but I do not see why Peel should be required by injunction to respect the continued presence of the system in the building. The plaintiff is required to provide cable television to any subscriber who seeks it and obviously some of the subscribers do. It is a right, however, of the subscriber and not of the plaintiff; and the problem is one for resolution between the subscribers and the Condominium Corporation. It is no part of my judgment, but I should think Peel would hesitate to require the removal of the system until the consent of all subscribers had been obtained. While

I would terminate the injunction, I do not, of course, mean that the plaintiff thereby forfeits the system.

The plaintiff will be entitled to a declaration that it is the owner of the cable system installed pursuant to the agreement of April 22, 1974, and to damages against both defendants for trespass to that system in the amount of $1,000.

|||||||||||||||||||||||||||||||||||||||||||||||||||||||||||||||||||||||||||||||||||||||||||||||||||||||||||||||||||||||||||||||||||||||||||||||||||

Interests in Land—Adverse Possession— Life Estates

Re O'Reilly (No. 2) (1980), 28 O.R. (2d) 481.

A testator died leaving a will in which he devised his farm and all stock and implements to his wife for life, and on her death, to his nine children as remaindermen.

The testor's widow and three of the children remained on the farm from the testator's date of death (March 18, 1945) until May 11, 1957, when the widow died. The three children continued to reside on the farm and carry on a farming operation as owners of the property.

In 1978, one of the children, who had left the farm prior to 1945, claimed an interest in the farm as one of the remaindermen named in the will. The children who had remained on the farm claimed a possessory title to the property, and argued that the interests of the other children had been extinguished.

RUTHERFORD, J.:

As s. 43 of the *Limitations Act* has no application to the facts of this case, the operative sections of the Act are ss. 4 and 7 which provide as follows:

"4. No person shall make an entry or distress, or bring an action to recover any land or rent, but within ten years next after the time at which the right to make such entry or distress, or to bring such action, first accrued to some person through whom he claims, or if the right did not accrue to any person through whom he claims, then within ten years next after the time at which the right to make such entry or distress, or to bring such action, first accrued to the person making or bringing it."

. . . . .

The next matter to be considered is whether the plaintiffs have acquired a possessory title, so-called. The plaintiffs, to establish their claim to a possessory title, must prove:
(1) actual possession for the statutory period by themselves and those through whom they claim;
(2) the intention to possess the property to the exclusion of all others; and
(3) discontinuance of possession for the statutory period by the owners and all others, if any, entitled to possession.

With regard to the possession of the plaintiffs and the dispossession of the owners, I find as follows:

(1) Rupert, Lorne and Isabella O'Reilly entered into possession of the O'Reilly farm in May, 1957, on the death of their mother, the life tenant;

(2) that Rupert, Lorne and Isabella O'Reilly remained in possession of the property until Rupert's death in 1964, and thereafter to the present the plaintiffs have remained in possession of the property;

(3) that from 1957 to 1962, the plaintiffs and their brother Rupert carried on a beef and dairy products farming business on the property;

(4) that in 1962, they conducted an auction of much of the farm stock and equipment, and retained all proceeds for their own use;

(5) that from 1957 to the present, the plaintiffs have attended to the payment of all municipal taxes on the property;

(6) that during the period of their possession, the plaintiffs have suitably maintained the farm buildings and structures;

(7) that the plaintiffs have not accounted to anyone for any of the profits or income generated by the farming business;

(8) that from time to time during the period 1962 or 1964 to the present, the plaintiffs rented portions of the farm to neighbouring farmers, the plaintiffs acting as lessors in their own right, and that the plaintiffs have retained for their own use all rent moneys received;

(9) that from time to time during the period of their possession, the plaintiffs paid insurance premiums with respect to the farm;

(10) that the plaintiffs completed construction of the farmhouse on the property;

(11) that the plaintiffs have held themselves out as the owners of the property during the period of their possession;

(12) that the owners received no income, benefit or enjoyment from the property during the period of the plaintiffs' possession.

Based on the above, I find as a fact that the plaintiffs were in actual possession of the farm during the period from 1957 to 1978, and that the owners were correspondingly dispossessed during the same period.

. . . . .

It now remains to consider whether the plaintiff had the *animus possidendi* required to establish a possessory title. The intention to exclude all other persons, including the true owner, may be presumed from a long period of undisturbed possession: see *Re Gibbins and Gibbins* (1977), 18 O.R. (2d) 45 at p. 48, 1 R.F.L. (2d) 352 [affirmed 22 O.R. (2d) 116, 92 D.L.R. (3d) 285]; *Re Strong and Colby et al.* (1978), 20 O.R. (2d) 356 at p. 359, 87 D.L.R. (3d) 589 at p. 592. In the instant case, I find the plaintiffs' undisturbed possession of the farm for a period in excess of 20 years to be more than sufficient to raise a presumption of the requisite *animus possidendi*, a presumption the defendant has failed to rebut.

Quite apart from this presumption, the plaintiffs' conduct over the 20-year period is of itself sufficient to establish the existence of the requisite intention. Their acts of possession are consistent with their claim to ownership and are inconsistent with the claim of any other person, including the true owner. The plaintiffs' mistaken belief that they were the true owners does not prevent the characterization of their acts as being acts of possession sufficient to establish a possessory title: Anger and Honsberger, *Canadian Law of Real Property*, p. 791; *cf. Kosman et al. v. Lapointe* (1977), 1 R.P.R. 119. Such a belief in conjunction with acts of possession may support a claim of adverse possession: *McGugan et al. v. Turner et al.*, [1948] O.R. 216 at p. 221, [1948] 2 D.L.R. 338 at p. 342; *Smaglinski et al. v. Daly et al.*, [1970] 2 O.R. 275 at p. 282, 10 D.L.R. (3d) 507 at p. 514 [varied [1971] 3 O.R. 238, 20 D.L.R. (3d) 65]. The acts of possession in the instant case, when taken with the belief of ownership, albeit mistaken, establish the requisite possession by the tiffs.

Based on this and my other findings, the plaintiffs have established all the elements necessary to extinguish the title of the true owners. There will be a declaration that the titles of those beneficially entitled to the farm property of James O'Reilly, deceased, have been extinguished by virtue of the *Limitations Act*, ss. 4 and 15.

My judgment, in addition to being based on ss. 4 and 15 may be based on another footing, namely, s. 2 of the Act which provides as follows:

"2. Nothing in this Act interferes with any rule of equity in refusing relief on the ground of acquiescence, or otherwise, to any person whose right to bring an action is not barred by virtue of this Act."

. . . . . .

In the event that the interests of the beneficiaries are not extinguished under the *Limitations Act* by virtue of the running of the limitation period, I find this an appropriate case to exercise this Court's equitable jurisdiction under s. 2 of the Act. Failure to do so would result in a manifest injustice to the plaintiffs. The unreasonable delay in seeking a grant of letters of administration and the failure of the beneficiaries to enforce their rights as against the plaintiffs induced the plaintiffs to occupy the farm as their own with all the rights and obligations attendant on ownership. At this late date, the defendant cannot be heard to claim the farm as being property belonging to the estate nor can the beneficiaries be heard to claim their interests. I find that by reason of laches and acquiescence, the defendant and the beneficiaries are estopped or otherwise barred from claiming their interests in the farm property of James O'Reilly, deceased.

||||||||||||||||||||||||||||||||||||||||||||||||||||||||||||||||||||||||||||||||||||||||||||||||||||||||||||||||||||||||||||||||||||||||||||||||||||||||||||||||||||||||

CASE PROBLEMS FOR DISCUSSION

Case 1

Samuels, an elderly widower conveyed his farm land to his son Peter for life, then to his grandson Paul in *fee simple*. In the deed, he reserved to himself the right to continue to live on the farm, and to receive 50% of the income from the farm during the rest of his lifetime.

Peter operated the farm with the assistance of both Samuels and Paul for a number of years, during which time he paid his father 50% of the farm income. Eventually, Peter decided to seek employment in industry, and took a job in a nearby manufacturing plant. At that point he decided to cease farming. A short time later, the barn was accidentally destroyed by fire, and the farm machinery destroyed.

Samuels, Peter, and Paul each claimed to be entitled to the proceeds of the fire insurance on the barn and the farm machinery.

Discuss the rights (if any) of each of the parties to the insurance funds in this dispute.

Case 2

Smith owned a large farm in eastern Ontario. Part of the farm, which consisted of a woodlot, fronted on an unimproved township road. In 1954, Crockett, a middle-aged bachelor, with Smith's permission, constructed a small log cabin in the woodlot for use as a fishing and hunting camp. For several years Crockett occupied the cabin on week-ends, while fishing in the area in the summer months, and, for a few weeks in the fall of each year during the hunting season.

During the summer of 1957, Crockett took a month's vacation and spent the time at the cabin. He planted a small vegetable garden, and constructed a fence around both cabin and garden to keep animals away from his flowers and vegetables. During the hunting season of the same year he cut down a number of small trees and extended the fenced-in area to a parcel of land 75 ft. by 100 ft., and built a gate in the fence where it faced the roadway.

Smith noticed the fence and gate shortly after it was constructed, and asked Crockett why it was necessary. Crockett replied that the animals in the area were damaging the flowers that he had planted around the cabin, and he felt that the fence would probably keep them out.

The next year, Crockett decided to accept early retirement at the firm where he was employed, and spent the period from May 1st to November 30th at the cabin. He planted a vegetable garden, fished, and helped Smith with the planting of his crops, and his fall harvest. At the end of November, he left his belongings in the cabin, and spent the winter in a warmer climate.

He returned to the cabin the next April, only to be met by the local tax assessor who asked him his name, and if the cabin was his. He replied in the affirmative, and some time later, received a municipal tax bill issued in his name. He paid the municipal taxes for that year (1959).

Crockett continued to live in the cabin, spending only the coldest of the winter months away from the premises. He paid the taxes on the land and building each year. In 1970, he moved the fences to include an area 100 ft. by 150 ft. in order to enclose a larger vegetable garden. Smith did not object to the new location of the fence, but warned Crockett not to cut down two large hickory nut trees in the enclosed area. Crockett agreed to leave the trees standing.

In the summer of 1979, during a thunderstorm, lighting struck and damaged one of the large hickory trees. Without consulting Smith, Crockett cut down the damaged tree.

Several months later, Smith noticed that the tree was missing, and in a rage, ordered Crockett from the property. Crockett refused to leave, claiming he was the owner of the parcel of land.

Discuss the rights of the parties, and evaluate the arguments and evidence that each might raise if the matter should be brought before the courts to determine the rights of the parties in the land. Render a decision.

Case 3

Barron owned a parcel of land fronting on a large lake. The lake was approximately 1 200 ft. from a road which represented one of the boundaries of the property. In 1952, Barron sold to Bulkley a parcel of land with a frontage of 600 ft. on the lake and a depth of 400 ft. Included in the deed was a 20-ft.-wide access right of way which was described as follows: ". . . a free and uninterrupted right of way for the grantee, his heirs, assigns, and their agents, servants, workmen, and their animals and vehicles, provided that they maintain at their own expense a gate at each end of the said way."

The right of way was not specifically described in the deed, but an existing roadway some eight feet wide was used by Bulkley from 1952 until 1973 as a means to reach his property. Throughout the period he maintained the gates which existed at each end of the roadway. In 1973, Bulkley widened the road to 12 ft., and improved the surface by placing a few truck loads of gravel in low, marshy spots to permit the use of the road from early spring until late fall. The same year he allowed two of his friends to bring in their camping trailers and park them on his land for the summer.

Bulkley's two friends brought in their trailers again for the summer of 1975. In the summer of 1976, two other trailer owners rented space on Bulkley's property for the summer, and brought in their large trailers, bringing the total number of trailers to four. That summer Bulkley improved the roadway to the property by surfacing the entire distance (some 800 ft.) with gravel.

The next year, Bulkley rented trailer space to several others in addition to the four trailer owners of the previous year. He placed a small sign on the gate at the road side which read "Bulkley's Beach." The sign attracted a few holiday travellers, and Bulkley rented each of them trailer space, which they used for a few days before they moved on to other camp grounds. By the end of the summer of 1977, Bulkley discovered that he had earned over a hundred dollars from vacationers, and he made plans for the opening of a trailer park the next year.

In the spring of 1978 he widened the roadway to 18 ft., gravelled and rolled the roadway, then advertised his "beach" in a number of vacation magazines. The advertising attracted large numbers of tourists with trailers, and Bulkley's Beach became a busy tourist establishment.

When Barron, whose home was located near the roadway to the beach realized that Bulkley had established a full-fledged trailer camp on his property, he objected to the use of the right of way for commercial purposes. He brought an action for an injunction on the basis that the right of way was intended only as a private right of access, and not intended for use as a right of way by members of the public. He also claimed that the dust raised by the heavy use of the right of way by vehicles interferred with the enjoyment of his property on which the roadway was located.

Discuss the arguments of the parties in this dispute, and render a decision.

Case 4

Baxter owned a large block of forest land which surrounded a small lake. The lake was fed by a small stream that crossed the property, and another that drained the lake into a larger body of water some miles away.

Wilson purchased from Baxter a small parcel of land fronting on the lake with the intention of eventually constructing a cottage on the lot. On the payment of the purchase price he received a deed to the land from Baxter, and without examining it, placed it in his safety deposit box.

Wilson used the property as a camp site for several years. Because the lake was several hundred yards from the road, each time he visited the lake he would leave his automobile parked at the roadside, and carry his camping equipment through the woods to his property.

Five years after he purchased the land from Baxter, he decided to build a cottage on his lot. No road access was available to the land, but Wilson assumed that the pathway which led to his property was his access route, and he began cutting trees to widen the path in order that a truck carrying his building materials could reach his lot. No sooner had he cut the first tree, when Baxter appeared and ordered him to stop cutting. When Wilson refused, Baxter ordered him to leave the property.

Wilson protested that he was entitled to clear the trees from the access road route to his land, but Baxter replied that he had sold him only the lot, and not a roadway. According to Baxter, Wilson had water access by way of the stream if he wished to enter or leave his property; the surrounding land belonged to him.

Wilson had travelled the stream with his canoe on a number of occasions, and while it was possible to gain access to his lot in that fashion, it would not be possible to transport the heavy building materials into the property using a canoe, and the stream was too shallow to allow the use of any larger water craft. Rather than continue his argument with Baxter, Wilson decided to examine his deed to determine if Baxter was correct in his position on the access route. Wilson returned home, and read the description of the property contained in the conveyance. It described the lot only, and made no mention of a roadway to the property. According to the deed, Baxter owned all of the land surrounding Wilson's property, and his only access appeared to be by way of the small stream to the lake.

Examine the rights of the two parties in this case. If either party should decide to take legal action to enforce his rights, explain the nature of the action, and indicate the probable outcome.

CHAPTER 28

Condominium Law

INTRODUCTION

Condominium is a term used to describe a particular form of ownership of real property where the property is held in part by exclusive ownership, and in part by co-ownership. The term is usually applied to a multiple-unit dwelling or commercial building in which the occupant of each unit owns the unit exclusively, and also possesses ownership rights as a co-owner of the common use areas of the remainder of the building and the surrounding land. In concept, it differs from other forms of property ownership in that it represents two separate interests within the bounds of the same parcel: The right to exclusive possession and control over an individual unit of the condominium, and co-ownership rights over those parts of the property which are not exclusively owned units. For example, in a condominium constructed as a multiple-unit residential building similar in design to an apartment building, each dwelling-unit would be exclusively owned by the occupant. In addition, the unit owner would be a co-owner of the surrounding land and common areas of the building, and would have the right to use them in common with all other unit owners.

Modern condominium legislation usually provides that the land and building (excluding the individual units) be operated and maintained by a corporation which the owners of the individual units control and manage, but this was not always the case; until comparatively recent times, the corporation was not used for such a purpose. In its earliest form, the forerunner of the modern condominium was simply exclusive ownership of a part of a building, and a part ownership of the common elements, or a right to use them.

HISTORICAL DEVELOPMENT

The condominium as a method of property ownership was conceived long before the development of the feudal system. Legal historians have suggested that a condominium type of ownership of multiple-unit buildings existed as long ago as 500 B.C. in the Middle East, and as early as the 12th century in parts of Western Europe.[1] The condominium concept was essentially a response to the high cost or scarcity of land for dwelling construction in some of the ancient walled cities. When no space was available for the construction of separate family dwellings, each on its own parcel of land, the logical next step was to construct multiple-family dwellings, sometimes as multi-storied buildings. Separate ownership of each unit was a frequent development following construction of a multiple dwelling

[1]See, for example, Ferrer, A., and Stecher, K., *Law of Condominium*, Equity Publishing Corp., Orford, N.H., 1967, vol. 1, pp. 15-23.

unit structure where the tenants desired the security of tenure associated with the ownership of property.

While the concept has ancient roots, it is essentially an urban phenomenon. Its use spread from the walled cities of Babylon to Greece, Italy, and on to the cities of Germany and France. By the 16th century, the condominium had found acceptance in Continental Europe, but not in England. Even though the system of land tenure in England did not prevent the possession of interests in land in condominium fashion, the concept failed to gain popularity there until very recent times. Instead, as a response to the crowded conditions of some English cities, the long term lease and "flat" ownership were favoured over the condominium.

In North America, the low cost of land, and perhaps the general desire of the population for land ownership and a separate dwelling, discouraged interest in the concept even in the larger urban centres. Until World War II, the availability of inexpensive urban and suburban land made the need for condominiums a matter of low priority. The growth of urban centres following World War II, however, had an upward pressure on land prices in the cities, and by the decade of the 1960s, rapidly rising prices for residential property prompted property developers to consider other forms of residential ownership in an effort to provide something in addition to the 'apartment' as an alternative to expensive single-family dwellings. As a result of the sudden interest in this relatively new form of property ownership, legislation was introduced in most of the states in the United States, and in many of the provinces in Canada. The legislation enabled the condominium to grow in popularity, and at the present time, it represents a rapidly expanding segment of all new residential construction in urban areas.

CONDOMINIUM LEGISLATION

The common law in England and North America has long recognized the right of property ownership in either a horizontal or vertical plane, and of rights to property above and below ground. In England, the ownership of apartments or flats has long been the equivalent of condominium ownership, and the rights of the property owners over time have become clearly defined by the law. Under the common law, the sale of a part of a building situated above the ground represents a sale of "air rights" or space, but nevertheless, the sale of a recognized property right. The particular difficulty with the common law in this regard, however, is that the establishment of the necessary rights and obligations associated with the "strata title" are extremely complex. For example, to sell the second storey of a three-storey building would require the parties to define with some degree of accuracy the right of access by the owner of the second storey, the right of the owner of the remainder of the building to support of the third storey, the right to services, maintenance, and many other considerations.

While the condominium unit in the case of a multi-storey building is similar to an "air right" in property, the owner of the unit usually obtains part ownership of the common areas of the entire building, and the land on which it stands, as a tenant in common. Originally, this took the form of co-ownership, and the owners were obliged to jointly maintain the condominium, but by the 20th century, the corporation appeared as a more appropriate vehicle to manage and maintain the common

elements of the property, and to regulate the unit owners' exercise of their rights over those parts of the condominium. Modern condominium legislation in North America, as a result, has generally taken this route, although not universally. In Canada, all of the provinces except Nova Scotia[2] provide for a corporation without share capital to come into existence when the condominium is created, while in the United States, the corporate form is used in some jurisdictions, and an association or uncorporated body in others.

NATURE OF A CONDOMINIUM

A condominium is essentially a property on which some type of multiple-occupancy building is erected. It may resemble a row-housing development, in which the units are connected horizontally on the land, or it may be a multi-storey building in which the occupancy units are connected horizontally and stacked vertically. It might also be erected for residential, commercial, or industrial use. In any event, regardless of its shape or purpose, it is characterized by individual ownership of units, and some form of co-ownership of the non-unit remainder. A third element which distinguishes the condominium from other forms of ownership is the use of some type of administrative structure to manage the property.

Unfortunately, the documentation required for the creation of a condominium varies from province to province. In some provinces, the condominium comes into

---

[2]Nova Scotia provides for the creation of a "society" under its *Societies Act* which performs essentially the same function: see *Condominium Property Act*, 1968 (N.S.), c. 4, s. 11(1).

existence on the filing or registration of a *Description* and *declaration* (drawn in accordance with the legislation) at the Land Registry or Land Titles office. In other provinces additional formalities are sometimes required. British Columbia, for example[3] (where a condominium interest is referred to as a *strata title*) also requires the filing of a prospectus with the Superintendent of Insurance. In all cases, however, the creation of the condominium requires not only the intention to have the property used as a condominium, but the preparation of accurate surveyor's drawings of the overall project and the individual units in sufficient detail to allow the property interests to be identified and dealt with under the land registration system of the particular province. These documents are usually referred to as the *description.*

The document which embodies the details of the condominium is referred to by various names depending upon the jurisdiction. In Ontario, for example, it is called a *declaration*, in British Columbia, a *strata plan*, and in Alberta, a *condominium plan*. In each case, the document sets out the interests of the unit owners and provides the general outline for the management and operation of the condominium as a whole. It provides also for the creation of a corporation or society to manage the property for the use and enjoyment of the unit owners. The registration of this documentation in the Land Registry or Land Titles office automatically establishes the condominum.

A condominium frequently has its beginning as a project of a land developer. A parcel of land is acquired, then a building that is specifically designed as a condominium is erected on the land. The property is divided into units (sometimes called *apartments*), that are generally laid out so that exclusive ownership is confined to the area enclosed by the exterior walls of the unit. Usually the limits of the unit are described as being to the *planes of the centre line of all walls, ceilings, and floors* which enclose the space, although this need not always be the case. The developer is free to define it by the planes of the inside surfaces, or any combination of the two, if he so desires.[4] Sometimes the exclusive use area may include other parts of the building as well. In many buildings with underground parking or storage facilities, these are sometimes designated as exclusive use areas, and included in the description of the unit. This permits the unit owner to have the exclusive ownership of a parking space or storage locker on the premises, but it has the disadvantage that the management organization loses control over the areas in question. Whatever the extent of the units, or exclusive use areas may be, they must be so designated in the description.

The balance of the property, excluding the units (and exclusive use areas, if included) is the part of the property known as the *common elements* or *common use area*. All of the unit owners hold this part of the land jointly as tenants-in-common. Included in this part of the property are usually the exterior walls of the building, all hallways, stairwells and stairs, entrance areas, the building basement, heating plant, land, and facilities installed for use by all of the unit owners. In some cases, it also includes a unit set aside for

---

[3]*Real Estate Act*, R.S.B.C. 1979, c. 356, ss. 50-59.

[4]Saskatchewan assumes the planes of the centre-lines unless the boundaries are otherwise defined: see The *Condominium Property Act*, R.S.S. 1978, c. C-26, s. 7(2).

use by the building supervisor or manager. All of these areas, however, must be so set out in the description as common elements.

In a condominium, the co-ownership rights to the common elements are tied to the ownership of the individual units. If the interest of a person in the unit is transferred to another, the interest in the common elements also will pass, as it is not possible to sever the two by way of a deed. The interest of the individual unit owner in the common element is usually related to the value of the unit owned in relation to the other units, the relative sizes of the units, or in accordance with a formula that the developer might use to establish the interest of each unit. Only two provinces[5] impose restrictions on the methods that may be used to calculate this value and, as a result, the methods used may vary from province to province and, indeed, from condominium to condominium.

One of the simplest methods of determining the interest of the unit owner in the common elements is to divide the total cost of the condominium by the value of each unit. For example, if the cost of the condominium is $2 000 000 and the value of a particular unit $50 000 the interest of the unit owner in the common elements would be 4%. While this is an oversimplification of the method used, the percentage fixed as the interest of the unit owner would be the amount that the unit owner would receive from the proceeds of a sale should the property be sold on the termination of its use as a condominium.

The maintenance of the common elements is related to the exclusive-use

units, usually by a calculation of the maintenance cost, and an apportionment of the cost to each unit on the basis of unit size or value. Included in this cost is usually the municipal property tax, insurance, property maintenance such as cleaning, snow removal, yard maintenance, elevators, building security, and the operating costs of special facilities for recreation and entertainment. While the cost or charge apportioned to each unit may be the same percentage amount as for the interest of the unit owner in the common elements, this need not necessarily be the case. Sometimes, for example, the cost allocation to unit owners located on the ground floor may recognize the fact that some above ground floor services are not utilized by them, and their contribution to the operating expenses is correspondingly reduced.

||||||||||||||||||||||||||||||||||||||||||||||||||||||||||||||||||||||||||||||||||||||||||||||

CASE 28.1

Frontenac Condominium Corp. No. 1 v. Joe Macciocchi & Sons Ltd. (1974), 3 O.R. (2d) 331.

CROMARTY, J.:

A condominium project has two basic parts, the first being the individually-owned suites, usually referred to as the units, and the second, all the rest of the building, the land, and any auxiliary features simply defined in the Act, s. 1(1)(*e*), as "all the property except the units". These are owned by the unit owners as tenants in common and are usually referred to as the common elements.

Subsidiary to these two basic elements are other essential features:

1. A system of government, including an effective method of making each owner pay his share of the common expenses.
2. A method of transferring, leasing or mortgaging the units and the owner's interest in the common elements or restricting the same.

---

[5] Quebec and British Columbia. See, for example, the *Condominium Act*, R.S.B.C. 1979, c. 61, s. 128.

3. A method of taxing the unit and the owner's interest in the common elements.
4. Devising means of handling the destruction of the whole or part of the project, winding-up, sale, obsolescence or additions to the common elements.

To bring the Act into force, a declaration and description must be registered:

"2(6) Upon registration of a declaration and description, the land and the interests appurtenant to the land described in the description are governed by this Act."

Certain things must be provided for the declaration. Those of concern in this action are:

"3(1) A declaration shall not be registered unless it is executed by the owner or owners of the land and interests appurtenant to the land described in the description and unless it contains,

(*a*) a statement of intention that the land and interests appurtenant to the land described in the description be governed by this Act;

(*c*) a statement, expressed in percentages, of the proportions of the common interests;

(*d*) a statement, expressed in percentages allocated to the units, of the proportions in which the owners are to contribute to the common expenses . . ."

Certain other things may be provided for:

"3(2) In addition to the matters mentioned in subsection 1, a declaration may contain,

(*a*) a specification of common expenses;

(*c*) provisions respecting the occupation and use of the units and common elements;

(*g*) a specification of the majority required to make by-laws of the corporation;

(*h*) provisions regulating the assessment and collection of contributions towards the common expenses;

(*o*) any other matters concerning the property.

(3) The declaration may be amended only with the consent of all owners and all persons having registered encumbrances against the units and common interests.

"4(1) A description shall contain,

(*c*) a specification of the boundaries of each unit by reference to the buildings;"

The declaration prepared and filed by the defendant and which created the plaintiff contains, among other things:

"(a) a statement of intention

(b) a statement that the proportions of the common interests shall be as set out in a schedule which lists percentages opposite unit numbers.

(c) that each owner shall contribute to the common expenses in the proportions shown in the schedule.

(d) that common expenses, without limiting the definition of the Act, shall be realty taxes on the whole property until units are taxed separately, payment of any employees needed for the proper operation and maintenance of the property and payments under any management contract between the plaintiff and a manager.

(e) a requirement that units be used for single family residences only.

(f) a provision that by-laws may be made by a vote of members who own sixty-six and two thirds per cent of the common elements, *inter alia*,

1. governing the management of the property
2. governing the use of the units
3. governing the use of common elements
4. regulating the maintenance of the units and the common elements
5. regulating the assessment and collection of contributions towards the common expenses"

It should be observed that the provisions of the Act take precedence. If the declaration does not comply with the Act, the Act prevails. Similarly the declaration prevails over the by-laws (s. 10(2)), and the by-laws prevail over the common element rules, if any (s. 11(2)).

Management

In all Canadian provinces, the general management of the condominium is in the hands of a board of directors or executive of a *condominium corporation* (or *society* in the case of Nova Scotia). The corporation is a corporation without share capital, but each unit owner has a say in its operation. This is done by way of a right to discuss matters and vote at general meetings held for the purpose of making major decisions affecting the condominium. It is also reflected through the election of members to the board of directors. The day-to-day management and operation of the condominium, however, is left with the board of directors.

Apart from the general duty to "manage," and to maintain the common elements of the condominium in a good state of repair, the corporation has the following specific obligations:

(1) to protect the premises from damage by way of insurance.
(2) to collect common element expenses from the unit owners in accordance with the percentage liability of each unit.
(3) to enforce any rules established for the use and enjoyment of the common areas, and the condominium as a whole.

In addition to the rights granted to the corporation under provincial condominium legislation, the rights and duties of the corporation are governed by *by-laws*. The by-laws of the corporation delineate its powers and constitute the "rules" for its operation. Some provinces have specified that the buildings be regulated by by-laws, and have set out the procedures for their implementation, amendment, and enforcement. Other provinces have simply provided that by-laws may be passed by the corporation without specifying details as to their nature, or implementation, other than in general terms.

Use of Common Elements

The *by-laws* and the *rules* govern the use which the unit owners may make of their individual units and of the common elements. For example, by-laws may prohibit alteration of the structure of the unit, restrict the occupancy to one family, prohibit commercial use, prohibit the keeping of animals, prohibit the erection of awnings or shades on the outside of windows, or prohibit the playing of musical instruments on the premises if they constitute a nuisance or disturbance to neighbouring units. Common element rules generally govern behaviour of unit owners and their guests in the common areas, or in the use of facilities such as swimming-pools.

Most provinces have vested in the corporation the right of lien[6] against a condominium unit for unpaid expenses, and the right to enforce the lien in the event of non-payment. Provision is normally made in the legislation for the foreclosure or sale of the unit in a manner similar to that for mortgages or charges. The reason for the vesting in the corporation of this particular right is the importance of the contribution of each unit owner of his share of the common expenses. A failure on the part of one unit owner to pay, shifts the burden of the expense to the remaining unit owners. To allow default to continue would not only burden the remaining unit owners, but would create a serious problem for the owners as a whole if any number refused to honour their obligation.

In most other respects the corporations are not unlike other non-profit corpora-

[6]All provinces except Saskatchewan: The *Condominium Property Act*, R.S.S. 1978, c. C-26, s. 22(2).

tions. The officers of the corporation carry out their duties in accordance with the by-laws and the legislation for the general benefit of the property owners, and for the better use and enjoyment of the common elements. The right to vote for the election of directors provides a means whereby the unit owners might remove unsatisfactory directors and replace them with others more to the liking of the majority. As with most corporations, it remains in existence until the condominium is terminated, at which time it is dissolved, and any assets which it might hold are then transferred to the unit owners.

CASE 28.2

Frontenac Condominium Corp. No. 1 v. Joe Macciocchi & Sons Ltd. (1974), 3 O.R. (2d) 331.

CROMARTY, J.:

Because of some of the defences put forward it is necessary to determine the nature of the condominium corporation.

It is quite unlike the usual share capital corporation or a corporation without share capital incorporated under either the *Business Corporations Act*, R.S.O. 1970, c. 53, or the *Corporations Act*, R.S.O. 1970, c. 89.

Section 9(1) creates a corporation upon the registration of a declaration and description.

Section 9(3) immediately brings out the above distinction by providing that the *Corporations Act*, the *Corporations Information Act*, R.S.O. 1970, c. 90, and the provisions respecting mortmain of the *Mortmain and Charitable Uses Act*, R.S.O. 1970, c. 280, do not apply to the corporation.

Some assistance in determining the nature of the corporation created under s. 9(1) may be found in the *Interpretation Act*, R.S.O. 1970, c. 225, which provides in part:

"26. In every Act, unless the contrary intention appears, words making any association or number of persons a corporation or body politic and corporate,

(*a*) vest in the corporation power to sue and be sued, to contract and be contracted with by its corporate name, to have a common seal, to alter or change the seal at its pleasure, to have perpetual succession, to acquire and hold personal property or movables for the purpose for which the corporation is constituted, and to alienate the same at pleasure;

(*b*) vest in a majority of the members of the corporation the power to bind the others by their acts; and

(*c*) exempt individual members of the corporation for personal liability for its debts, obligations or acts if they do not contravene the provisions of the Act incorporating them."

However, cl. (*b*) above has its applicability cut down by the *Condominium Act, 1967*, which requires unanimity of the owners, or members of the corporation, in some matters and, it appears, a two-thirds vote in others, and under s. 17 an 80% vote in favour of certain other acts.

Clause (*c*) above does not apply to a condominium corporation because of s. 9(17) which provides:

"9(17) A judgment for the payment of money against the corporation is also a judgment against each owner at the time the cause of action arose for a portion of the judgment determined by the proportions specified in the declaration for sharing the common expenses."

Section 9(16) provides that the corporation's assets are owned, not by the corporation, but by the unit owners.

"9(16) The members of the corporation share the assets of the corporation in the same proportions as the proportions of their common interests in accordance with this Act, the declaration and the by-laws."

There is no limited liability protection for the owners as this is normally understood. If a judgment is bad against the corporation each unit owner is responsible for a percentage of the judgment which is the same as his percentage for sharing the common expenses. If, however, the percentage of the judgment exceeds the value of his unit and its appurtenant portion of the common elements, the owner will nevertheless be responsible to pay an amount greater than the value of his share in the property.

Conversely, if an action is brought with respect to the common elements and a judgment is obtained this judgment belongs to the members.

"9(18) Any action with respect to the common elements may be brought by the corporation and a judgment for the payment of money in favour of the corporation in such an action is an asset of the corporation."

The result is that the corporation as such owns nothing, except in the sense of a conduit, because s. 9(16) has said the members share the assets.

The corporation is directed to repair the units and the common elements after damage and to maintain the common elements (s. 16(2) and (3)).

||||||||||||||||||||||||||||||||||||||||||||||||||||||||||||||||||||||||

Termination of a Condominium

A condominium, once created, need not remain one forever. The unit owners may decide to terminate the condominium if the character of the building has changed or deteriorated over time, or if the property no longer serves its intended purpose. It cannot, however, be terminated by a simple majority vote of the unit owners, as provincial legislation usually requires either the unanimous consent of all unit owners (and encumbrancers) or a very high percentage (usually 80%) to signify approval. A few provinces leave the matter in the hands of the courts to decide.

A sale of the condominium is essentially the sale of a number of individual units and interests, and as a general rule, after all expenses related to the condominium have been paid, the funds available for each property owner are distributed in accordance with the proportional ownership

of the common elements, unless the sale agreement provides otherwise. Where less than unanimous consent of all unit owners is required to approve a sale (for example, 80%), dissenting owners are protected in some jurisdictions (such as Manitoba and Ontario) by a provision for arbitral determination of the fair market value of the particular interests at the time of the sale, and the payment of that amount to the dissenters. The remaining property owners would be expected to make up any deficiency in the event that the value determined by the arbitrator exceeded the sale price of the units.[7]

FUTURE OF THE CONDOMINIUM

Although it did not find favour in North America until very recently, the condominium, as a concept, is not a new or radical form of property ownership. Changes in society, however, have attracted many to this particular form of ownership, not only for residential, but for business purposes as well. The high cost of land was the initial attraction, but the general trend to smaller families, the desire to live close to work, and to have recreational facilities available in the same building has prompted many individuals and small families to opt for this form of residential accommodation over apartment living, particularly since it provides security of tenure by ownership of the unit, and some degree of control over management of the building and grounds.

The concept also has a number of attractions to business organizations. Not only does it provide the commercial unit owner with the right to use the unit as he pleases (within limits) but it frequently reduces

[7]See, for example, Ontario, the *Condominium Act, 1978*, R.S.O. 1980, c. 84.

business costs by way of shared expenses for the maintenance and operation of the common elements. Only recently have business organizations recognized the significant advantages of the condominium as a means of housing their operations, and its current uses may consequently be expanded to include a greater variety of commercial operations, in addition to its present application to office structures, shopping centres, parking garages, and light industrial complexes. If the cost of urban land and maintenance costs continue to rise, many more business organizations will undoubtedly be attracted to this form of housing for their facilities.

SUMMARY A condominium is a multiple unit building in which each unit is subject to exclusive ownership and possession, and the remainder of the building and surrounding land is held by the unit owners in co-ownership as tenants-in-common. Condominiums may be for residential, commercial, or industrial use, and the units need not have ground contact to be subject to ownership. Units of a high-rise condominium may be held in the same manner as ground floor units. The interests in the property of a condominium are tied together in such a way that the ownership of a unit carries with it an inseparable co-ownership interest in the common elements as well. The percentage interest in the common elements is usually calculated in such a way that it reflects the value of the particular unit to which it is tied, relative to all other units in the condominium.

A condominium comes into existence when the owner or developer registers in the Land Registry or Land Titles office the required description and declaration which describe and set out the details of the nature of the condominium, the rights of the unit owners, and the rules governing its operation. Once established, a corporation or society manages the common elements, and protects the interests of the unit owners. It handles the payment of expenses related to the maintenance of the common areas, and collects the charges from the co-owners. It also enforces all by-laws and rules established for the better enjoyment of the condominium.

When all, or a substantial majority of the unit owners and encumbrancers (depending upon the province) desire to terminate the condominium, they may do so, provided that they comply with the procedure for termination set out in the condominium legislation for that province.

DISCUSSION QUESTIONS

1. *Explain the legal nature of a condominium.*
2. *Why was it necessary to develop the concept of a condominium in the first place?*
3. *Why did the condominium concept not find favour in North America until*

after 1950?

4. *Can an interest in property exist which does not include the land beneath it?*

5. *How is a condominium created?*

6. *Define a "common element" or "common use area."*

7. *Explain how the unit owner's interest in the common elements is usually determined.*

8. *What is the purpose of a condominium corporation? What are its rights and duties?*

9. *Why is a right of* lien *necessary in cases where a unit owner fails to pay his portion of the common element expenses?*

10. *What procedure must unit owners follow in order to terminate a condominium? Why is unanimous consent, or the vote of a very large percentage of the unit owners in favour of the termination necessary before it may be done?*

11. *How are dissenting unit owners' rights protected in some provinces where the majority vote to terminate the condominium?*

12. *What special advantage(s) does the condominium offer to the unit owner over the apartment dweller? What disadvantages?*

||||||||||||||||||||||||||||||||||||||||||||||||||||||||||||||||||||||||||||||||||||||||||||||||||||||||||||||||||||||||||||||||||||||||||||||||||||||||

JUDICIAL DECISIONS

Condominium— Declaration— Reasonableness of Provision

Re Peel Condominium Corp. No. 11 and Caroe et al. (1974), 48 D.L.R. (3d) 503.

The owners of a number of condominium units leased the units to tenants contrary to the declaration which provided that the units could only be occupied by the owners and their respective families. The corporation attempted to enforce the declaration by way of court action for an order directing the tenants to vacate the building, and for an order restraining the unit owners from renting the units.

When the unit owners resisted, the matter came to trial.

GALLIGAN, J.:

> This is an application by the corporation pursuant to s. 23(1) of the *Condominium Act*, R.S.O. 1970, c. 77, for an order directing the respondents to perform a duty imposed by the declaration, which has been duly registered relating to the subject condominium located in the City of Mississauga. The circumstances are simple, and the point of law is a novel one, which so far as I know, has not been the subject of judicial determination. The respondent Caroe is the owner of unit No. 27 and has rented it to the respondent Delongte, who resides in it with his, the tenant's family. The respondent Ereneos is the owner of unit No. 42, and has rented it to the respondent Saunders, who resides in it with his, the tenant's family. The respondent Hamade is the owner of unit No. 74 and has rented it to the respondent Woodward, who resides in it with his, the tenant's family. The legal issue is simply whether the owner of a unit in this condominium is entitled to rent that unit to a

third person so that such person, as a tenant, may occupy the unit with his family. The main relief sought by the applicant on this motion is an order directing the respondent tenants to vacate the units occupied by them, and restraining the respondent owners from renting the units.

The contention of the applicant is that a fair interpretation of s. 9(a)(1) of the declaration, by necessary implication, prohibits the renting of a unit by the owner because the unit may only be occupied by the owner, his family and guests. The relevant provision of the declaration reads as follows:

"9(a) (1). Each unit shall be occupied only as a one-family residence by the owner of the unit(s), his family and guests. For the purpose of these restrictions, "one-family residence" means a building occupied or intended to be occupied as a residence by one family alone and containing one kitchen, provided that no roomers or boarders are allowed. A "boarder" for the purpose of these restrictions is a person to whom room and board are regularly supplied for consideration and a "roomer" is a person to whom room is regularly supplied for consideration."

If the declaration is given the meaning which the applicant contends it ought to be given, then as a practical matter there would be a substantial restriction imposed upon the very nature of the ownership that rests in the owner. One of the fundamental incidents of ownership is the right to alienate the property that one owns. With respect to real property the right to freely alienate dates to 1290, when the Imperial Statute of *Quia Emptores*, 18 Edw. I, was enacted. The provisions of that statute were made part of the law of Ontario in 1897 [R.S.O. 1897, c. 330]. (See Anger and Honsberger, *Canadian Law of Real Property* (1959), p. 21.)

Earl Jowitt, in the Dictionary of English Law, at p. 1284, considered the nature of ownership in the following terms:

"Ownership is essentially indefinite in its nature, but in its most absolute form, it involves the right to possess and use or enjoy the thing, the right to its produce and accessions, and the right to destroy, encumber, or *alienate it*;"

(The emphasis is mine.)

One of the important forms which alienation of one's property takes is leasing or renting of the property. As was said by Pearson, J., in *Re Rosher* (1884), 26 Ch.D. 801 at p. 818: "There are various modes of alienation besides sale; a persons may lease, or he may mortgage, or he may settle." The right to lease one's property is therefore one of the important ingredients of absolute ownership.

A declaration under the *Condominium Act* is a creature of that statute and is therefore prescribed by it. In my view, a declaration may only restrict rights and impose duties if the statute authorizes it to do so. Section 3 of the *Condominium Act* provides for the contents of a declaration. The only part of that section which I think is relevant to the issue before me is s. 3(2)(c), which reads as follows:

"3(2) In addition to the matters mentioned in subsection 1, a declaration may contain,

(c) provisions respecting the occupation and use of the units and common elements;"

It is necessary to consider whether that section authorizes a declaration to impose a serious restriction upon the fundamental and long established right of an owner to alienate his real property. Statutes which themselves encroach upon the rights of a subject are subject to strict construction. I think it also appropriate to strictly construe a statutory provision which may permit the encroachment on or restriction of the rights of the individual. The tenet of interpretation has been admirably expressed in *Re Stronach* (1928), 61 O.L.R. 636 at p. 641, [1928] 3 D.L.R. 216 at pp. 219-20, 49 C.C.C. 336, as follows:

" 'Statutes which encroach on the rights of the subject, whether as regards person or property, are similarly subject to a strict construction in the sense before explained. It is a recognised rule that they should be interpreted, if possible, so as to respect such rights. It is presumed, where the objects of the Act do not obviously imply such an intention, that the Legislature does not desire to confiscate the property, or to encroach upon the right of persons; and it is therefore expected that if such be its intention, it will manifest it plainly, if not in express words, at least by clear implication, and beyond reasonable doubt:' " [Maxwell on the *Interpretation of Statutes*, 6th ed., p. 501.]

Considering s. 3(2)(c) of the *Condominium Act* in that light, it is obvious that the intention of the Legislature was to authorize a declaration to make certain reasonable restrictions on the occupation and use of the units. That section would obviously authorize the declaration to provide for single family occupancy, to prohibit the use of a unit as a business premises and the like.

What I cannot see in that section is any clear indication of legislative intention to restrict that fundamental right of an owner to alienate his property. I do not think that the Legislature had any intention to restrict the owner's right of alienation and had it intended to prohibit an owner from renting his property I would have expected it to have said so in clear, unambiguous language. It is my opinion that the definition of "owner" contained in s. 1(1)(l) of the Act clearly indicates that the Legislature did not have any intention of permitting the restriction of the right of the owner to rent a unit. That section defines "owner" as follows:

"(l) "owner" means the owner or owners of the freehold estate or estates in a unit and common interest, but does not include a mortgagee unless in possession;"

It immediately becomes clear that the term "owner" by statute includes a mortgagee in possession. I think in enacting this legislation the Legislature of Ontario would have known that most mortgagees, particularly those financing substantial multi-unit dwelling complexes are large corporations. It is of course impossible for such an owner to occupy a unit with its family and guests. I certainly do not think it was the intention of the Legislature to require that a corporate mortgagee in possession of a unit would be required to let its unit stand vacant. It is my opinion that the Legislature of Ontario in enacting s. 3(2)(c) of the *Condominium Act* had no intention to permit a declaration to restrict the right of an owner of a unit to alienate his property to such an extent that he could not rent it for residential use. In my opinion, there is nothing in the *Condominium Act* which permits a declaration to prevent an owner from renting his unit. Accordingly, if the provisions of the declaration can be interpreted as suggested by the applicant, it is my opinion that such provision of the declaration is not authorized by the Act, and is invalid, and may not be enforced by an application under s. 23 of the Act.

Accordingly, the application must be dismissed.

Condominium— By-Laws— Validity

Re York Condominium Corp. No. 42 and Melanson (1975), 59 D.L.R. (3d) 524.

A condominium passed a by-law prohibiting the keeping of animals on the property. An owner of a unit owned a dog and objected when the solicitor for the condominium directed him by letter to remove his dog from the premises.

At trial, the judge ordered the unit owner to remove the animal from his unit within 90 days. He appealed the judgement of the court.

HOWLAND, J.A.:

On August 19, 1971, By-law Number Two was enacted by the Corporation. It included the following provision:

"The following rules and regulations shall be observed by the owners and the term owner shall include the owner or any other person occupying the unit with the owner's approval: . . .

14. No animal shall be allowed upon or kept in or about the property."

Paragraph 14 is hereafter referred to as the "prohibitive paragraph".

By-law Number Two was duly registered and became effective on September 9, 1971. Both By-law Number One and By-law Number Two were enacted by Delzotto Enterprises Limited as the owner of all the units and the sole member of the Corporation.

Melanson is the owner of one of the units. By letter dated August 6, 1974, from the solicitors for the Corporation, Melanson was directed to remove his dog from the condominium complex on or before August 23, 1974. An application was then made by the Corporation to enforce compliance with By-law Number Two.

The issue in this appeal is whether the Corporation has exceeded its statutory powers in enacting the prohibitive paragraph, or if it did have the power, is the prohibitive paragraph enforceable? As the Corporation is a statutory creation, the relevant rights and duties of an owner and of the Corporation must be found in the Act. The following provisions are relevant:

"2(6) Upon registration of a declaration and description, the land and the interests appurtenant to the land described in the description are governed by this Act.

"6(2) Subject to this Act, the declaration and the by-laws, each owner is entitled to exclusive ownership and use of his unit.

"7(4) Subject to this Act, the declaration and the by-laws, each owner may make reasonable use of the common elements.

"9(12) The corporation has a duty to effect compliance by the owners with this Act, the declaration and the by-laws.

"12(1) Each owner is bound by and shall comply with this Act, the declaration and the by-laws.

. . . . .

"(3) The corporation . . . has a right to the compliance by the owners with this Act, the declaration and the by-laws."

In creating a condominium corporation, a developer has to consider carefully what restrictions it is going to impose on the user of the units and common elements because such restrictions will affect the character of the condominium and the marketability of its units. The prohibitive paragraph could have been included in the declaration pursuant to s. 3(2) of the Act, just as the declaration provided that each unit should be used only as a single-family residence. However, the objection to so doing is that under s. 3(3) of the Act the declaration may be amended only with the consent of all owners and all persons having registered encumbrances against the units and common interests. In the case of a restriction such as the prohibitive paragraph this could be a formidable task.

Here the prohibitive paragraph was embodied in a by-law. This provides greater flexibility. Since no higher percentage was specified in the declaration, under s. 10(1) of the Act the making of such by-laws only required the vote of members owning 66⅔% of the common elements. If the prohibitive paragraph in question falls within the Corporation's power to make by-laws, the fact that it is described in By-law Number Two as a rule or regulation does not, in my opinion, affect its validity as a by-law. It is true that the prohibitive paragraph, whilst embodied in By-law Number Two, is referred to as a rule or regulation. In pursuance of s. 11(1) of the Act, By-law Number One authorized the owners, by a vote of members owning 51% of the common elements, to make rules, but such power was limited to rules respecting the use of the common elements. By-law Number Two draws a distinction between the units, the common elements and the property. The by-law does not contain a provision that the word "property" shall have the same meaning in the by-law as in the definition of property in s. 1(1)(*n*) of the Act, *i.e.*: "the land and interests appurtenant to the land described in the description". In my view, however, this is the only proper interpretation to be given to the word in the prohibitive paragraph. Consequently, the attempt to impose restrictions respecting the units would go beyond the powers of the members under By-law Number One to make rules.

Under s. 10(1) the Corporation has power to make by-laws:

"(b) governing the use of units or any of them for the purpose of preventing unreasonable interference with the use and enjoyment of the common elements and other units;

(c) governing the use of the common elements;"

Under s. 10(2) such by-laws shall be reasonable and consistent with the Act and the declaration.

In order to fall within the Corporation's power to make by-laws under s. 10 of the Act, four matters have to be considered:

(i) are the words "governing the use" in s. 10(1)(b) and (c) of the Act broad enough to include the making of a by-law regulating the allowing of animals upon or the keeping of animals in or about the property?

(ii) are the words "no animal" in the prohibitive paragraph so broad as to be beyond the powers of the Corporation under s. 10(1)(b) of the Act?

(iii) is the prohibitive paragraph reasonable and consistent with the Act and the declaration as required by s. 10(2) of the Act?

(iv) is the word "animal" in the prohibitive paragraph so broad that even if the Corporation had power to enact the prohibitive paragraph it is incapable of enforcement?

"Govern" is defined in The Shorter Oxford English Dictionary, 3rd ed., vol. I, at p. 816, to mean: "To rule with authority . . . to regulate the affairs of (a body of men)."

A careful distinction has to be drawn between the power to regulate or govern and the power to prohibit. In *City of Toronto v. Virgo*, [1896] A.C. 88, the Judicial Committee of the Privy Council had to consider whether under a power to pass by-laws "for . . . regulating and governing hawkers or petty chapmen, and other persons carrying on petty trades", the Council might prohibit hawkers from plying their trade at all in a substantial and important part of the city. Lord Davey stated, at pp. 93-4:

"No doubt the regulation and governance of a trade may involve the imposition of restrictions on its exercise both as to time and to a certain extent as to place where such restrictions are in the opinion of the public authority necessary to prevent a nuisance or for the maintenance of order. But their Lordships think there is marked distinction to be drawn between the prohibition or prevention of a trade and the regulation or governance of it, and indeed a power to regulate and govern seems to imply the continued existence of that which is to be regulated or governed.

. . . . .

"Several cases in the English and Canadian reports were referred to in illustration of the respondent's argument. . . . through all these cases the general principle may be traced, that a municipal power of regulation or of making by-laws for good government, without express words of prohibition, does not authorize the making it unlawful to carry on a lawful trade in a lawful manner."

In *Re Karry and City of Chatham* (1910), 21 O.L.R. 566, the Court of Appeal had to consider whether a by-law of the City of Chatham, stipulating the hours when eating houses should be closed, was a "regulation" authorized by the *Municipal Act* which provided that the Council could pass by-laws "for limiting the number of and regulating such houses". Magee, J.A., pointed out at p. 573: "The partial prohibition, it has thus long been recognised, may well come within the powers of regulation."

In *Re R. v. Napier*, [1941] O.R. 30, [1941] 1 D.L.R. 528, 75 C.C.C. 191, the statute authorized the passing of by-laws "For licensing, regulating and governing bill posters . . .". A by-law had been passed prohibiting the distributing of bills by leaving them in or on parked motor-cars or by handing them to persons on the street. Hogg, J., concluded at p. 34 O.R., pp. 531-2 D.L.R., that:

". . . the prevention of such activities in connection with this trade or calling is not of such a degree that it can be said to be practically a prohibition of the entire business or trade of bill distributors. There is still left to them the large field, which seems to constitute the greater part— or at least as great a part—of this business, namely, of leaving bills at the residences and other buildings in the municipality."

Here the power of the Corporation is to make by-laws "governing the use of units" and "governing the use of the common elements". In this appeal, the prohibitive paragraph as to allowing animals upon or keeping them in or about the units or common elements, is only a partial prohibition of the use of the units or the common elements. It would properly fall within the power to regulate the use of the units and common elements. In my view the word "governing" in s. 10(1)(*b*) is broad enough to include the restriction respecting animals in the prohibitive paragraph. It would be quite different if the power is s. 10(1)(*b*) and (*c*) of the Act had been to make by-laws governing the allowing or keeping of animals on the units or the common elements. In that event the prohibitive clause would have been *ultra vires* of the Corporation as it would have been a prohibition rather than a regulation.

It should be pointed out that the power to make by-laws under s. 10(1)(*b*) and under s. 10(1)(*c*) is with respect to "the use" of units and the common elements, whereas s. 3(2)(*c*) stipulates that the declaration may contain provisions respecting "the occupation and use" of the units and common elements.

As Lord Radcliffe pointed out in *Arbuckle Smith & Co., Ltd. v. Greenock Corp.*, [1960] 1 All E.R. 568 at p. 574:

" 'Use' is not a word of precise meaning, but in general it conveys the idea of enjoyment derived by the user from the corpus of the object enjoyed."

Robertson, C.J.O., in *R. v. Lou Hay Hung*, [1946] O.R. 187, stated at pp. 191-2:

"The words 'occupy' and 'occupant' have a variety of shades of meaning. No doubt, we commonly speak of the 'occupants' of a dwelling-house, meaning thereby all persons who, at the time, live there. We use the word in even a wider sense when we speak of the 'occupants' of premises, meaning thereby all the persons who happen to be within them at the particular time. Primarily, however, 'to occupy' means 'to take possession' . . ."

Possession is a primary element but occupation includes something more. As Lord Denning explained in *Newcastle City Council v. Royal Newcastle Hospital*, [1959] A.C. 248 at p. 255: "Occupation is matter of fact and only exists where there is sufficient measure of control to prevent strangers from interfering . . .".

Under s. 3(2)(c) of the Act, the right to include a provision in the declaration respecting occupation of the units would embrace such matters as restricting the use to single-family residences. On the other hand, the right to restrict the keeping of animals in such units as incidental to such single-family use would seem properly to fall within the power to make by-laws governing the use of units.

It will also be noted that the power to make by-laws is more restrictive under s. 10(1)(b) of the Act than it is under s. 10(1)(c). Under s. 10(1)(b) the power can only be exercised "for the purpose of preventing unreasonable interference with the use and enjoyment of the common elements and other units". This brings me to a consideration of the second question, whether the words "no animals" in the prohibitive paragraph are so broad as to be *ultra vires* of the Corporation.

The word "animal" is very comprehensive. The definition in The Shorter Oxford English Dictionary, 3rd ed., at p. 68, includes: "1. A living being, endowed with sensation and voluntary motion, but in the lowest forms distinguishable from vegetable forms . . . 2. One of the lower animals; a brute or beast, as distinguished from man." Black's Law Dictionary, 4th ed., defines "animal" as "Any animate being which is endowed with the power of voluntary motion. An animate being, not human." In The Shorter Oxford English Dictionary, *supra*, at p. 181, it is noted that the word "bird" is defined as "any feathered vertebrate animal" and at p. 705, that "fish" is defined as "In pop. language, any animal living exclusively in the water . . . In scientific language any vertebrate animal provided with gills throughout life, and cold-blooded; the limbs, if present, being modified into fins."

The words "no animal" in the prohibitive paragraph are wide enough to include not only cats and dogs but such animals as hamsters, canaries and goldfish. Can it be said that the broad prohibition against *any* animal being allowed upon or kept in or about the units is for the purpose of preventing unreasonable interference with the use and enjoyment of the common elements and other units? In my opinion it cannot. I am unable to conclude that goldfish, for example, would cause such unreasonable interference. Section 6(2) of the Act makes it clear that subject to the Act, the declaration, and the by-laws, each owner is entitled to exclusive ownership and use of his unit. One of the incidents of such ownership is the right to keep pets. The declaration does not contain any prohibition against the keeping of animals in the units. It is appreciated that it is important in a condominium development, particularly a condominium apartment building, to prevent the owner of a unit from unreasonably interfering with the use and enjoyment by others of their units and of the common elements. As Driver, Assoc. J., stated in *Sterling Village Condominium, Inc. v. Breitenbach* (1971), Fla., 251 So.2d 685 at p. 688:

"Every man may justly consider his home his castle and himself as the king thereof; nonetheless his sovereign fiat to use his property as he pleases must yield, at least in degree, where ownership is in common or cooperation with others. The benefits of condominium living and ownership demand no less."

The owners of 66⅔% or more of the common elements may wish to pass a by-law to protect themselves against unreasonable interference by way of vicious, malodorous, dirty or noisy animals, or pollution of the common elements. However, the prohibitive paragraph in question goes far beyond the limited powers in s. 10(1)(*b*) to govern the use of units and would have the effect of prohibiting animals in or about the units which could not be the cause of unreasonable interference.

In my view, the prohibitive paragraph in question, in so far as it governs the use of units, is beyond the powers of the Corporation.

It should be observed that the powers of the Corporation under s. 10(1)(*c*) are to govern the use of the common elements and there is no limitation on the exercise of this power as in the case of s. 10(1)(*b*). It would seem that under s. 10(1)(*c*) the Corporation could prohibit animals generally from being allowed upon the common elements.

If access to the units can only be obtained by passing through the common elements, then even if the portion of the prohibitive paragraph governing the use of the units were invalid, the owner of a unit might be prohibited from bringing animals into the units. The question arises whether the portion of the prohibitive paragraph which regulates the use of the units is severable from the portion which regulates the use of the common elements, or whether the entire prohibitive paragraph is *ultra vires* of the Corporation.

As Craies points out in his text on *Statute Law*, 6th ed. (1963), at p. 335, there is some difference of judicial opinion as to whether a by-law is severable or divisible. In *Strickland v. Hayes*, [1896] 1 Q.B. 290 at p. 292, Lindley, L.J., stated:

"There is plenty of authority for saying that if a by-law can be divided, one part may be rejected as bad while the rest may be held to be good."

On the question of severability, decisions respecting the exercise of the jurisdiction of the Supreme Court to quash a municipal by-law in whole or in part under s. 283(1) of the *Municipal Act*, R.S.O. 1970, c. 284, are of assistance. In *Re Morrison and City of Kingston*, [1938] O.R. 21 at p. 27, [1937] 4 D.L.R. 740 at p. 745, 69 C.C.C. 251, Middleton, J.A., said:

"It is not, I think, competent to the Court to quash part of a by-law, unless it is clearly severable from the provisions that remain."

This statement was approved by the Court of Appeal in *Re Musty's Service Stations Ltd. and Ottawa*, [1959] O.R. 342, 22 D.L.R. (2d) 311, 124

C.C.C. 85, where Aylesworth, J.A., in delivering the judgment of the Court, concluded that the invalid provisions of the by-law were integral and indispensable parts of the by-law and were not severable from the rest of the by-law.

In so far as the prohibitive paragraph itself is concerned, in view of the fact that the prohibition is made applicable to the property which includes both the units and the common elements, I do not think it is possible to sever the portion of the paragraph which deals with the units from the portion which deals with the common elements even if s. 10(1)(c) was wide enough to permit the restriction so far as the common elements were concerned.

Having reached this conclusion it is not necessary to consider the third question which arises as a result of s. 10(2) of the Act which provides:

"10(2) The by-laws shall be reasonable and consistent with this Act and the declaration."

Nor is it necessary to consider the fourth question, that the word "animal" in the prohibitive paragraph is so broad that even if the Corporation had power to enact the prohibitive paragraph it is incapable of enforcement.

Paragraph 14 of By-law Number Two is, in my view, beyond the powers of the Corporation in its entirety. It is not necessary to express any view as to the validity of the remaining provisions of By-law Number Two as para. 14 is severable from the remaining provisions of the by-law.

AUTHOR'S NOTE: For a judicial decision where the judge reached the opposite conclusion on the right of the condominium unit owner to keep an animal on the premises see *Re Peel Condominium Corp. No. 78 and Harthen et al.* (1978), 20 O.R. (2d) 225.

CASE PROBLEMS FOR DISCUSSION

Case 1

Wagner, an orchestra conductor, was the owner of a unit in a high-rise condominium which contained 210 units. The condominium corporation maintained a music room in the general recreational area of the building for use by unit owners and their guests. On Wednesday evenings, Wagner would invite the members of the orchestra to the condominium, where they would practice for several hours in the music room.

Wagner's practice sessions were carried on for a number of months before several of the unit owners complained of the noise. Wagner ignored the complaints, and eventually, a complaint was lodged with the manager employed by the corporation. The manager wrote a letter to Wagner in which he pointed out that the music room facilities were maintained for the use and enjoyment of the unit owners. He also included in the letter a copy of one of the by-laws related to the use of the common elements which read in part: "Unit owners shall not cause noise to be made or anything done which may annoy or interfere with any other owner."

Wagner's response to the letter was that he had no intention of ceasing his practice sessions. He pointed out that users of the swimming-pool in the adjacent room made substantially more noise than his orchestra and, in any event, the room was specifically designed as a place where "noise" should be made.

When the corporation threatened legal action to restrain Wagner, he countered with a threat to have the swimming-pool area closed under the same by-law.

If the dispute should come before a court, how should the matter be decided?

Case 2

McTavish purchased a ground floor unit in a large condominium which maintained all recreational and other facilities on the same floor where his unit was situated. After he had moved into the unit, he discovered that he was obliged to pay the same monthly common element expenses as the tenants on the upper floors, who used the elevators.

At the next meeting of unit owners, he proposed that the common element expenses be adjusted to reflect the fact that he and a dozen other unit owners did not use the elevators in the building. His proposal was rejected.

Undaunted by his defeat, McTavish deducted what he calculated would be his share of the cost of maintenance of the elevators (75¢) from his common element expenses for the next month, and sent his cheque in the lesser amount to the corporation.

Advise the corporation in this case. What principles are involved?

Case 3

A condominium which consisted of 204 units had included in its declaration a provision which prohibited all owners from keeping dogs, cats, reptiles, or rodents in their units or in the common elements.

Lupus owned a large wolfhound, and kept it in his unit. He exercised the dog each evening on the grounds of the condominium. He was unaware of the stipulation in the declaration which prohibited the keeping of dogs in the building, and had been informed by the real estate agent at the time of purchase that pets would be permitted. He also had a copy of the *proposed* declaration for the condominium that had been given to him by the developer which did not prohibit the keeping of pets.

Unknown to Lupus, the developer had revised the declaration before he registered the documents which created the condominium, and the revised declaration contained the prohibition with respect to the keeping of dogs, cats, reptiles, and rodents. Lupus purchased the unit without knowledge of the change.

A short time after he had purchased his unit, Lupus was notified that he must remove his pet from the property.

In response, he raised two arguments:

(1) He was misled by the real estate agent and the developer in that the proposed declaration which contained no restriction on pets was changed immediately before it was registered, and the change constituted a manifest error that should be corrected to read in accordance with the proposed declaration.

(2) The particular proviso which prohibits pets is *ultra vires* the corporation as it is not a provision "respecting the occupation and use," but rather, a proviso which attempts to "regulate the conduct of the owner," and hence, is void, as it is not permitted under the *Condominium Act*. In support of this position, Lupus cited the case of *Re York Condominium Corp. No. 42 and Melanson* in which the court held that a by-law prohibiting the keeping of pets on the property was inoperative.

The condominium corporation responded that there was no error in the declaration. It argued that the declaration was changed before it was registered to include the prohibition, and it was not done in error, but as a deliberate act which was subsequently supported by those who purchased units aware of the prohibition contained therein.

In response to the argument raised by Lupus that the provision attempted to regulate the conduct of the unit owner, the corporation argued that it was designed only to regulate occupation and use, something that was within its powers.

Assess the arguments raised by the parties. Is the *York Condominium* case, as set out in the Judicial Decisions, applicable? If the dispute should be taken before the courts, how might the case be decided?

CHAPTER 29

The Law of Mortgages

INTRODUCTION

A *mortgage* is a very old method of securing payment of indebtedness. In its simplest form, it involves the transfer of the debtor's title or interest in property to the creditor on the condition that the title or interest will be reconveyed to the debtor when the debt is paid. The mortgage is the formal agreement made between the parties, under which the debtor is referred to as the *mortgagor*, and the creditor, the *mortgagee*. The written agreement effects the transfer of the mortgagor's interest or title to the mortgagee, and contains the terms of the debt and the conditions under which the property interest will be returned to the mortgagor.

From a conceptual point of view, a modern mortgage has a number of distinct characteristics:

(1) It transfers the title of the mortgagor's property to the mortgagee.
(2) The mortgagor retains possession of the property until the debt is paid or default occurs.
(3) The document which transfers the title also contains a proviso which entitles the mortgagor to a reconveyance of the title to the property when the debt is paid.
(4) The document imposes certain obligations on the mortgagor to protect and maintain the property while the debt remains unpaid.
(5) The document also contains terms which permit the mortgagee to take steps to terminate the mortgagor's rights and interest in the property if the mortgagor defaults in payment.

Under the Land Titles System, a land or real property "mortgage" is called a *charge*. While similar to the mortgage in purpose, it does not transfer the title of the property to the creditor, but merely, as the name states, charges the land with payment of the debt. The obligations imposed on the debtor or chargor are much the same as those imposed on the mortgagor, and if default occurs, the creditor in most provinces may take steps to acquire the title and possession of the land, or have the land sold to satisfy the debt.

Under the Land Titles System, a mortgage in the ordinary sense of the word does not exist, as a charge does not involve the transfer of the title to the property to the mortgagee. Consequently, the remedies available to the mortgagee, and the procedure which must be followed to realize on the debt in some provinces may differ from the procedure in provinces under the Registry System. At the present time, the charge under the Land Titles System may be found in parts of Ontario, Manitoba, and in Saskatchewan, Alberta, British Columbia, the Yukon, and the Northwest Territories. The Registry System and the mortgage are used in parts of Ontario, Manitoba, and the provinces lying to the east of the Province of Quebec. Unfortunately, with both systems, substantial provincial and territorial variation exists, and the legislation of each jurisdiction must be consulted for the law applicable to the particular securities in question.

The mortgage is not found in the Province of Quebec. Instead, an instrument somewhat similar to the charge, which is called a *hypothec*, is used to secure debt. This particular instrument gives the creditor a security interest in the lands of the debtor, and permits the debt to be satisfied by way of a sale of the land if the debtor defaults in payment.

Land is not the only form of property which may be used as security for debt. The mortgage may also be used to establish a security interest in personal property as well. Chattels such as automobiles, boats, aircraft, furniture, and equipment of all kinds are frequently used as security for indebtedness, in which case, the security instrument is called a *chattel mortgage*. Because of the many varied and specialized uses of this form of mortgage, it is treated separately along with a number of other forms of security for debt in Chapter 32.

HISTORICAL DEVELOPMENT

The fact that land has a value, and represents a source of wealth is the principal reason why the mortgage has acquired widespread acceptance as a security instrument. When land is used for agricultural or silvacultural purposes, it provides income in the form of produce or timber, and where buildings are situated on the land, the buildings may be leased to provide income in the form of rents. Even in a raw state, land has value based upon the potential uses which may be made of it.

Land was particularly important as a source of wealth in the past. Until the Industrial Revolution, it represented one of the most important forms that wealth might take, and, as such, was naturally considered by creditors and debtors alike as something that might be conveniently pledged as security for the payment of a debt. As a result, some legal mechanism for the pledge of land as security was considered soon after individual rights to property emerged in Western Europe and England.

A form of mortgage was recognized as a means of securing debt long before the establishment of the feudal system in England. The nature of the instrument, however, was probably based upon Roman law, as the system of land-holding at that time was fundamentally different from the system introduced in England after the Norman Conquest. The use of this form of mortgage was modified substantially by the introduction of the feudal system, for it was the feudal system, and the creation of the different estates in land, that made possible the transfer of title to land, and it was at that point that the mortgage had its true beginning.

The modern form of mortgage nevertheless differs substantially from its ancient predecessors, although the concept has changed very little. The first mortgages were conceived as a means of securing debt by way of a transfer of an interest in land, and this is essentially what a mortgage does today. The older forms of mortgages, however, were subject to different formalities in execution and effect.

Since the mortgage involved a change in title, the legal nature of the transaction had to comply with procedural requirements of the law. One of the difficulties was to ensure recognition of the transaction by the appropriate courts, in the event that some dispute arose. Because the king's courts initially would not deal with ordinary debt agreements, the transaction had to involve some interest in property before the dispute could be brought before the courts. As a result, several forms of security for debt, involving the transfer of an interest in property, were developed.

By the 12th century, the transaction generally took on one of the two forms, i.e., a *vivum vadium*, or *live-gage* (pledge) in which the rents from the land would be applied to the reduction of the debt owing, or it would be in the form of a *mortuum vadium* or *dead (mort)-gage*, in which the rents would be taken by the creditor, but would not be applied to the reduction of the debt. In both cases, the mortgagee (in theory at least) moved into possession of the property, and the debtor moved out. The mortgagee, however, did not obtain an absolute title to the property due to the nature of the security agreement, and in the event of default, it was necessary for the mortgagee to obtain a judgement from the courts before the mortgagor's rights in the property were finally extinguished.[1]

One of the procedural problems associated with the early transactions that had

[1]See Holdsworth, W.S., *A History of English Law*, 3rd ed. (Methuen & Co. Ltd., 1923: London, England), vol. 2, p. 194.

to be overcome was the position of the mortgagee in relation to the land. In order to have a right to possession, it was necessary to incorporate in the document the transfer of some interest in land to the mortgagee that would be recognized by the courts. This was important because the king's courts would only provide a remedy for interference with the mortgagee's possession if the mortgagee had an interest in the land that could be the subject of a real action. The fee, as a result, was usually transferred to the mortgagee, although in some cases, a demise for a term of years was used instead.

Of the two forms of security, the *live-gage* or live pledge provided the debtor with the greatest benefit, as the rents from the land were applied to the payment of the debt, and assuming that the land yielded some reasonable return, the debt would eventually be paid. The *mort-gage* or *dead-pledge* on the other hand, had the opposite effect. All rents and profits from the land went to the mortgagee as the party in possession of the property, and were not applied in reduction of the mortgage debt. The debt remained. Since the debtor has probably relinquished his principal source of income and wealth to the mortgagee, repayment of the debt was undoubtedly difficult indeed. Hence, the term "dead pledge" or *mort gage*, meaning that the land was "dead" or "profitless" during the term of the transaction.[2]

A century later, the use of land as security for debt was modified slightly to provide for more clearly defined transactions. The *live-gage* gradually took on the form of a debt-lease transaction in which the debtor leased the land to the creditor for a term of years at a nominal amount, during which time the income from the land was paid to the creditor and applied in reduction of the debt. The *mort gage* normally took one of two forms: either the debtor conveyed the land to the creditor on the condition that the deed would be void if the debt was paid within a specified period of time, or the land was conveyed on the basis that if the debt was not paid by a particular date, the creditor would be entitled to the *fee* absolutely.[3]

These forms of security for debt persisted until the latter part of the 15th century, by which time the most common form of security instrument was one in which a conveyance of the *fee simple* was made to the mortgagee on the condition that if the debt was paid by a specific date, the conveyance would be void.[4] At this point, the term mortgage took on a new meaning: the pledge was dead, insofar as the debtor was concerned, if he failed to tender payment of the mortgage on the due date.[5]

At common law, the agreement made between the mortgagor and mortgagee was strictly enforced. For the usual type of mortgage, the title passed to the mortgagee, subject to a condition subsequent that allowed the mortgagor to acquire the title back upon payment of the debt on the due date. From the point of view of the common law courts, a failure to pay on the due date would extinguish the rights of the mortgagor, and thereafter the right to recover the property was forever lost. The debt, however, remained, and (unless the agreement provided

---

[2]See Holdsworth, W.S., *A History of English Law*, 3rd ed. (Methuen & Co. Ltd., 1923: London, England), vol. 3, p. 128, footnote 5. The meaning was attached to the word mortgage by Glanvil (circa 1187).

[3]Holdsworth, vol. 3, pp. 128-130.
[4]Holdsworth, vol. 5, (1st ed.) p. 330.
[5]Holdsworth, vol. 3, p. 128, footnote 5.

otherwise) the mortgagor was still liable to the mortgagee for payment of the money owing.[6]

The strict approach to the agreement that the common law courts followed, and the inevitable hardships which it placed on unfortunate mortgagors, led many to seek relief from forfeiture in the Court of Chancery, where equitable relief might be had. This was done because, during the 16th century, the attitude of the Court of Chancery had changed with respect to mortgage actions. At the beginning of that century, the general rule was that the mortgagor must pay the mortgage debt by the date fixed for payment, otherwise a decree of foreclosure would be issued.[7] Later, the Court of Chancery was prepared to provide relief for the mortgagor who failed to make payment on the due date, if the mortgagor could satisfy the court that the failure to make payment on time was due to some unforeseen circumstance or delay. Eventually, the court was prepared to provide relief regardless of the mortgagor's reason for the delay, so long as the mortgagor offered payment to the mortgagee within a reasonable time after the due date.[8] By this time—towards the end of the century—the court recognized the fact that the true nature of the contract was that of debt, rather than that of a transfer of land. Thereafter, it treated the transaction as a form of contract in which the land was simply held as security, and in which it was viewed as something that could be used to satisfy the debt if payment was not made by the debtor.[9]

The establishment of an *equitable right to redeem* in the mortgagor by the court also affected the mortgagee's rights. Having taken the position that a mortgagor had the right to redeem the property within a reasonable time after the contractual right was lost, the court unwittingly placed the mortgagee in a position of uncertainty with respect to the property. This in turn prompted mortgagees to seek relief from the same court, and in response to petitions from mortgagees for recognition of their titles to mortgaged lands, the court engaged in a practice of granting *decrees of foreclosure*, which confirmed the mortgagee's absolute title, and precluded the mortgagor from later demanding the right to redeem.[10]

Over time, a change also took place with respect to possession of the land by mortgagee. The inconvenience of the mortgagor losing possession during the term of the mortgage was gradually replaced by an agreement which allowed the mortgagor to remain in possession of the property, provided that the mortgage terms were complied with, and the mortgagor was not in default in payment. This change permitted the mortgagor to retain what was often the source of income necessary to pay the debt, and reflected the true nature of the transaction: the use of the property as security for a debt.

The concept of a mortgage was further refined by the courts as a security instrument (rather than a transfer of title), by requiring the mortgagee to look first to the property mortgaged for payment of the debt. This relieved the mortgagor of the double disaster of not only losing the land, but remaining liable for the debt as well, and introduced the final element of fair-

---

[6]See, for example, comments by Lord Haldane in *Kreglinger v. New Patagonia Meat & Cold Storage Co., Ltd.*, [1914] A.C. 25 at p. 35.
[7]Holdsworth, vol. 3, p. 129.
[8]See Holdsworth, vol. 5, (1st ed.) pp. 330-331.
[9]*Holdsworth*, vol. 5, p. 331.

[10]The right is described in *Cummins v. Fletcher* (1880), 14 Ch. D. 699.

ness in the transaction. Thereafter, the mortgage as a form of security for debt changed little in its basic form and effect until the late 19th century.

In Canada and the United States, the mortgage arrived with the first settlers in the colonies, and developed along basically similar lines to those in England until the late 19th century, and the introduction of the Land Titles (or Torrens) System of land registration. The adoption of this system by many of the United States and some of the provinces of Canada further changed the form of the mortgage to that of a charge on the land, rather than a transfer of title to the property. The late 19th and early 20th century also saw the introduction of legislation, relating to mortgages and charges, which clarified and modified the rights of the parties. As a result, the modern law of mortgages has become a blend of historic legal concepts, common law rules, equitable principles, and statute law.

THE NATURE OF MORTGAGES

The most common form that a mortgage may take is that of a *first mortgage* or *legal mortgage*. Only the first mortgage of a parcel of land may be the legal mortgage, since it represents a transfer of the title of the property to the mortgagee. Where the mortgagor holds an estate *in fee simple*, the mortgagee acquires the *fee*, leaving the mortgagor with possession of the property, and the right to redeem the title in accordance with the terms of the instrument.

Assuming that a willing mortgagee may be found, a mortgagor may also pledge the same property as security for debt by a *second mortgage* or *equitable mortgage*. A second mortgage differs from a first or legal mort-

gage in the sense that the mortgagor does not have a title to transfer to the mortgagee as security. The mortgagor has only an *equity of redemption*, or the right to redeem the first mortgage. It is this right that the mortgagor mortgages, hence the name *equitable mortgage*. In essence, it is the equitable right of the mortgagor that the mortgage attaches as security, a right made possible because the Court of Chancery over time treated the right of redemption as an estate in land,[11] and hence, open to mortgage.

A second mortgagee, therefore, obviously assumes substantially greater risks with respect to the property than does the first mortgagee. The second mortgagee must be ever vigilant, and prepared for default on the part of the mortgagor, for default on the first mortgage would entitle the first mortgagee to take steps to foreclose the interests of not only the mortgagor, but the second mortgagee as well. The second mortgagee must, as a result, be in a position to make payment of the first mortgage if the mortgagor should fail to do so. This greater risk associated with second mortgages explains the reluctance on the part of some lenders to advance funds under this type of mortgage, and the reason why lenders, when they do agree to make such a loan, charge a higher rate of interest.

Mortgages subsequent to a second mortgage are also possible, as the mortgagor does not entirely extinguish his equity of redemption by way of the second mortgage. A mortgagor may, for example, arrange a third mortgage on the same property, which would be essentially a

---

[11]See *Kreglinger v. New Patagonia, supra,* footnote 6. Comments by Lord Parker at pp. 47-48. See also *Casborne v. Scarfe* (1737), 1 Atk. 603 at p. 605, 26 E.R. 377 (Lord Hardwicke).

mortgage of his right to redeem the prior mortgages. Again, the risk associated with a third mortgage would be correspondingly higher than that associated with the second mortgage, as the third mortgagee must make certain that the mortgagor maintains the first and second mortgages in good standing at all times. The third mortgagee must also be prepared to put the prior mortgages in good standing or pay them out if the mortgagor should default.

The number of equitable mortgages which might conceivably be placed on a single parcel of land is generally limited to the mortgagor's *equity* in the property. For example, if a person owns a building lot *in fee simple* with an appraised market value of $50 000, it might be encumbered up to its market value by any number of mortgages. Lenders rarely lend funds on the security of land which would exceed the value of the property, unless some other security is also provided for the loan, and many are unwilling to lend up to the market value in the event that the property value might decline. It is not uncommon for lending institutions to limit the amount of a mortgage loan to 75% of the appraised value of the property, unless some other guarantee of payment is also associated with the loan.

Where property is used as security for more than one mortgage, the mortgagor must, of course, maintain each mortgage in good standing at all times, otherwise the default on one mortgage would trigger foreclosure proceedings on that particular mortgage and produce a parallel reaction among all other mortgagees holding mortgages subsequent to it.

CASE 29.1

Kreglinger v. New Patagonia Meat & Cold Storage Co., Ltd., [1914] A.C. 25.

LORD PARKER OF WADDINGTON:

Taking the simple case of a mortgage by way of conveyance with a proviso for reconveyance on payment of a sum of money upon a specified date, two events might happen. The mortgagor might pay the money on the specified date, in which case equity would specifically perform the contract for reconveyance. On the other hand, the mortgagor might fail to pay the money on the date specified for that purpose. In this case the property conveyed became at law an absolute interest in the mortgagee. Equity, however, did not treat time as of the essence of the transaction, and hence on failure to exercise what may be called the contractual right to redeem there arose an equity to redeem, notwithstanding the specified date had passed. Till this date had passed there was no equity to redeem, and a bill either to redeem or foreclose would have been demurrable. The equity to redeem, which arises on failure to exercise the contractual right of redemption, must be carefully distinguished from the equitable estate, which, from the first, remains in the mortgagor, and is sometimes referred to as an equity of redemption.

PRIORITIES BETWEEN MORTGAGEES

Where a mortgagor encumbers a parcel of land with more than one mortgage, the priority of the mortgagees becomes important. Since, in theory, only the mortgage first in time constitutes a legal mortgage (and all subsequent mortgages are merely mortgages of the mortgagor's equity) it is essential that some system be used to establish the order of the instruments, and the rights of the parties.

In all provinces, the order of priority is established for the most part by the time of registration of the mortgage documents in the appropriate land registry office.[12] Assuming that a *bona fide* mortgagee has no actual notice of a prior unregistered mortgage, the act of registration of a valid mortgage in the registry office would entitle a mortgagee to the first or legal mortgage with respect to the property. It should be noted, however, that a mortgagee must undertake a search of the title to the property at the land registry office in order to determine the actual status of the mortgage, since the registration of a document, such as a mortgage, is deemed to be notice to the public of its existence.[13] Any prior mortgage of the same property, if registered, would take priority. Consequently, a mortgagee as a rule does not accept only the word of the mortgagor that the land is unencumbered, but makes a search of the title at the land registry office as well. This is done in advance of the registration to determine the status of the mortgage before funds are advanced under it.

RIGHTS AND DUTIES OF THE PARTIES

Under mortgage law, a mortgagor is entitled to remain in possession of the mortgaged property during the term of the mortgage, provided that he complies with the terms and conditions set out in the mortgage. (If the mortgagor defaults in any material way, the mortgage usually provides that the mortgagee is entitled to take action for possession or payment.) A mortgagor also has the right to demand a reconveyance of the title to the property,

or a *discharge* of the mortgage when the mortgage debt has been paid in full. In contrast to these rights, a mortgagor has a number of duties which arise out of the mortgage itself.

A mortgage, apart from being an instrument which conveys an interest in land, is contractual in nature, and contains a number of promises or *covenants* which the mortgagor agrees to comply with during the life of the mortgage. While the parties are free to insert any reasonable covenants they may desire in the mortgage, the instrument normally contains four important covenants on the part of the mortgagor. These are:

(1) A covenant to pay the mortgage in accordance with its terms;

(2) A covenant to pay taxes or other municipal assessments;

(3) A covenant to insure the premises, if the property is other than vacant land; and

(4) A covenant not to commit *waste,* and to repair the property if any damage should occur.

Covenant of Payment

Both the mortgagor and the mortgagee are vitally interested in the payment of the debt. The mortgagee from the point of view of receiving back the principal and interest earned on the loan, and the mortgagor, to obtain a reconveyance of the title to the property. Mortgage payment terms are negotiated by the parties, and may take many forms, but the most common arrangement calls for the repayment of the principal together with interest in equal monthly payments over the term of the mortgage. The particular advantage of this form of repayment over provisions which provide for quarterly, half-yearly, annual, or "interest only" payments during the life

---

[12]See, for example, the *Registry Act,* R.S.O. 1980, c. 445, s. 69.

[13]See, for example, the *Registry Act,* R.S.O. 1980, c. 445, s. 73.

of the agreement is that any default on the part of the mortgagor will be quickly noticed by the mortgagee, and steps may then be taken to remedy the situation. Mortgages which call for periodic payments generally contain an *acceleration clause* that is triggered by default of payment of a single instalment, thereby rendering the whole of the outstanding balance due and payable immediately. This permits the mortgagee to demand payment of the full amount, and failing payment by the mortgagor, the default would entitle the mortgagee to take steps to realize the debt from the property by way of foreclosure or sale proceedings.

A mortgagee seldom demands payment in full simply because a mortgagor fails to make a monthly payment on the due date, but a failure to make a number of payments would probably result in action taken by the mortgagee on the basis of the mortgagor's breach of the covenant to pay.

Payment of Taxes

Under most tax legislation, taxes on real property levied by municipalities (or in some cases by the province), provide that the claim of the municipality for unpaid taxes becomes a claim against the property in priority over all other encumbrances. To ensure that the municipality does not obtain a prior claim against the property, mortgages usually contain a covenant on the part of the mortgagor to pay all such taxes levied when due. Again, if the mortgagor fails to pay the taxes, he is treated as being in default under the mortgage for breach of the covenant concerning taxes, and the mortgagee may then take action under the mortgage.

In the recent past and, to some extent, today, mortgagees (especially lending institutions) inserted a clause in their mortgages which required the mortgagor to make payments to the mortgagee over the course of the year (usually on a monthly basis) of sufficient funds to pay the municipal taxes on the property, and the mortgagee would then use the funds to pay the taxes when levied by the municipality. In this fashion the mortgagee was in a position to maintain the mortgage free of any claims for taxes. As an alternative, mortgagees that do not collect tax payments and pay the taxes directly may still require the mortgagor to submit the paid municipal tax bill each year for examination in order to substantiate payment and to ensure that no claims for taxes may take priority over their mortgages.

Insurance

The obligation of the part of the mortgagor to insure only applies where a building or structure is erected on the mortgaged land. The purpose of the covenant to insure is obvious: much of the value of the property is due to the existence of the building or structure, and its loss, through damage by fire or other causes, in most cases would substantially lessen the security for the mortgagor's indebtedness.

Careful mortgagees generally arrange their own insurance on the mortgaged premises in order to satisfy themselves that the insurance is adequate, and that it covers their interest in the event that loss or damage should later occur. Other mortgagees simply rely on the mortgagor to maintain the required insurance. The liability for the payment of the premium, however, remains with the mortgagor even though the insurance covers both the mortgagor and mortgagee. In the event of a loss, the proceeds of the insurance would be payable first to satisfy the principal and interest owing to the mortgagee, and the balance, if any, would then be payable to the mortgagor. The land, of course, would remain intact, and if the insurance proceeds paid the mortgage in full, the mortgagor would be entitled to a discharge of the mortgage, and a return of the title to the property.

Waste

Closely associated with insurance, but of a different nature, is the mortgagor's covenant not to commit *waste*. Waste is a legal term to describe any act which would reduce the value of the property. It would include, in the case of a mortgage, an act by a mortgagor to reduce the security available to the mortgagee. For example, a mortgagor that demolishes a building on the mortgaged property would be committing waste, because the building would represent part of the value of the property. Similarly, a mortgagor that strips and sells the top soil from the land would commit waste if the act was done without the consent of the mortgagee.

The covenant by the mortgagor not to commit waste is essentially a term which preserves the property intact during the time while the mortgage is in existence. It is inserted in the agreement to protect the mortgagee by requiring the mortgagor to maintain the property value, and a violation of the covenant by the mortgagor would entitle the mortgagee to take action under the terms of the mortgage. Waste, however, does not include ordinary deterioration of property as a result of lack of repair, and to cover this, mortgages may also include a term which obliges the mortgagor to maintain the property in a good state of repair while the mortgage is in effect.

SPECIAL CLAUSES

Not every term in a mortgage imposes an obligation on the mortgagor. Frequently the parties will agree that the mortgage should contain the privilege of prepayment, and the parties will insert in the mortgage a provision whereby the mortgagor, while not in default, may pay the whole or any part of the principal amount owing at any time without notice or without the payment of a bonus to the mortgagee. This is often a valuable privilege for the mortgagor, as the mortgagee is not required to accept payment of the mortgage money owing except in accordance with the terms of the mortgage.[14]

A mortgagor may also have the privilege of obtaining discharges of parts of the mortgaged land on the part payment of stipulated amounts of principal, if such a right is inserted in the mortgage. The particular advantage of this clause only arises where the mortgagor intends to sell parts of the mortgage land, either to pay the mortgage, or as a part of a development scheme for the property.

DISCHARGE OF MORTGAGE

If the mortgagor complies with the terms and conditions set out in the mortgage, and makes payment of the principal and interest owing as required and when due, the mortgagor is entitled to a discharge of

---

[14]See the *Interest Act*, R.S.C. 1970, c. I-18, s. 10. A mortgagee, however, in a long-term mortgage is obliged to accept payment in full if a non-corporate mortgagor tenders full payment and an additional three months' interest at any time after the mortgage has been in effect for five years.

the mortgage. Mortgage legislation, in provinces where the Registry System is in effect, generally provides that a mortgagee may release all right, title, and interest in the property subject to the mortgage by providing the mortgagor with a *discharge of mortgage*. This particular instrument, when properly executed and delivered to the mortgagor, along with the registered duplicate original copy of the mortgage, constitutes a receipt for payment, and when registered, acts as a statutory reconveyance of the title to the mortgagor. The document, in effect, releases all claims which the mortgagee may have in the land under the mortgage, and acknowledges payment of the debt. In provinces where the Land Titles System is used, the discharge of mortgage is replaced by a *cessation of charge*, which has a somewhat different effect: it acts as an acknowledgement of payment of the debt, and removes the charge from the title to the property when it is registered in the Land Titles office where the land is situate. On receipt of the cessation of charge, the office amends the title to the parcel of land to reflect the change, and to show the title free of the particular charge.

ASSIGNMENT OF MORTGAGE

A mortgagee may assign a mortgage at any time after the mortgage is executed by the mortgagor. A mortgage, however, is unlike an ordinary debt in that it represents an interest in land, and consequently, it must be made under seal and in a form which complies with the legislation pertaining to mortgages in the particular jurisdiction where the land is situated. This is due to the fact that the assignment must

not only assign the debt, but also transfer the assignor's interest in the property. Consent to the assignment by the mortgagor is not required, but actual notice of the assignment to the mortgagor is essential if the assignee wishes to protect the right to demand payment of the balance owing on the mortgage from the mortgagor.

As with the assignment of any contract debt, if notice of the assignment is not given to the mortgagor, the mortgagor may quite properly continue to make payments to the original mortgagee (the assignor). All other rules relating to the assignment of debts normally apply to a mortgage assignment. The mortgage, for example, is assigned as it stands between the mortgagor and the mortgagee at the time of the assignment, and any defence which the mortgagor might raise to resist a demand for payment by the assignor would also be effective as against the assignee. The assignee must, therefore, be certain to promptly give the mortgagor notice of the assignment following the assignment, and determine the status of the mortgage between the mortgagor and mortgagee immediately. In most cases, an assignee will determine this from the mortgagor prior to the assignment.

SALE OF MORTGAGED PROPERTY

A mortgagor is free to sell or otherwise dispose of the equity of redemption in mortgaged land at any time during the term of the mortgage, unless the mortgage provides otherwise.[15] The disposition of

---

[15]Occasionally, a mortgagee may insert a term in the mortgage that requires the mortgage to be paid in full if the mortgagor should desire to sell the property.

the property, however, does not relieve the mortgagor of the covenants made in the mortgage, and in the event that the purchaser should default on the mortgage at some later time, the mortgagee may, if he so desires, look to the original mortgagor for payment in accordance with the original covenant to pay. It should be noted, however, that this particular rule of law only applies to the original mortgagor, and not to a purchaser who subsequently sells the property subject to the mortgage before default occurs.

For example, Smith gives Jones a mortgage on a parcel of land which he held *in fee simple.* Smith later sells his equity in the land to Brown. If Brown defaults in payment of the mortgage, Jones may either claim payment from Smith under his covenant to pay the mortgage, or he may take steps to have the debt paid by way of foreclosure or sale of the property. If the mortgagee pursues the latter course, Brown would lose his interest in the land. However, if Brown does not default, but sells his equity in the land to Doe, and Doe allows the mortgage to go into default, Jones does not have a claim against Brown, but only against Smith on the covenant, or Doe, who is in possession of the land.

Mortgagees frequently require the purchaser of the mortgagor's equity to sign an agreement to assume the mortgage and all its covenants in order to increase the security for payment. A purchaser who covenants to pay the mortgage in accordance with its terms becomes liable on the covenants as a result, and is placed in much the same position as the original mortgagor with respect to payment.

DEFAULT, FORECLOSURE AND SALE

If the mortgagor defaults in the payment of principal or interest under the terms of a mortgage, or causes a breach of a covenant (such as the commission of waste), the mortgagee may at his option call for the immediate payment of the full amount owing by way of the acceleration clause in the mortgage. The demand for payment in full, however, does not necessarily mean that the mortgagor has no choice but to find the full amount required to pay the mortgage. In most provinces, the legislation pertaining to mortgages permits the mortgagor to pay the arrears, or correct the breach of covenant along with the payment of all related expenses, and thereby put the mortgage in good standing once again.[16]

Where financial difficulties prevent the mortgagor from correcting the default, the mortgagee is usually obliged to take action in order to recover the debt secured by the property. In this respect, the mortgagee has a number of options open. The most common courses of action which the mortgagee may follow are:

(1) sale of the property under the power of sale contained in the mortgage;
(2) foreclosure;
(3) judicial sale;
(4) possession of the property.

Sale Under Power of Sale

Mortgages drawn in accordance with most

[16]See, for example, the *Mortgages Act,* R.S.O. 1980, c. 296, ss. 21 and 22. See also *Township of Scarborough v. Greater Toronto Investment Corp. Ltd.,* [1956] O.R. 823.

provincial statutory forms generally contain a clause which permits the mortgagee to sell or lease the property subject to the mortgage if the mortgagor's default in payment persists for a period of time.[17] To exercise the power of sale under the mortgage, the mortgagee must give notice to the mortgagor and to any subsequent encumbrancers, then allow a specified period of time to elapse before the property may be sold. The purpose of the notice and the delay is to provide the mortgagor and any subsequent encumbrancers with an opportunity to put the mortgage in good standing once again, or to pay the full sum owing to the mortgagee.

If the mortgagor is unable to place the mortgage in good standing, the mortgagee is free to proceed with the sale, and to use the proceeds first in the satisfaction of the mortgage debt, and the remainder in the payment of subsequent encumbrances and any execution creditors. Any surplus after payment to the creditors belongs to the mortgagor. Should the mortgagor be in possession prior to the sale, the mortgagee would be obliged to bring an action for possession in order to render the property saleable. If the mortgagee is successful in this action, the courts will render a judgement for possession, which in turn would enable the mortgagee to obtain *a writ of possession*. The writ of possession is a direction to the sheriff of the county where the land is situated, authorizing him to obtain possession of the property for the mortgagee.

---

[17]In Ontario, for example, the usual clause provides that the mortgagee may begin the exercise of the power of sale when default exceeds 15 days. See also the *Mortgages Act*, R.S.O. 1980, c. 296.

Since the mortgagor is entitled to the surplus in a sale under a power of sale (and also liable for any deficiency), the mortgagee is under an obligation to conduct the sale in good faith, and to take steps to ensure that a reasonable price is obtained for the property. The mortgagee, however, is not obliged to go to great lengths to obtain the best price possible.[18]

|||||||||||||||||||||||||||||||||||||||||||||||||||||||||||||||||||||||||||||||

CASE 29.2
Farrar v. Farrars, Ltd. (1888), 40 Ch. D. 395.

LINDLEY, L.J.:

A mortgagee with a power of sale, though often called a trustee is in a very different position from a trustee for sale. A mortgagee is under obligations to the mortgagor, but he has rights of his own which he is entitled to exercise adversely to the mortgagor. A trustee for sale has no business to place himself in such a position as to give rise to a conflict of interest and duty. But every mortgage confers upon the mortgagee the right to realize his security and to find a purchaser if he can, and if in exercise of his power he acts *bonâ fide* and takes reasonable precautions to obtain a proper price, the mortgagor has no redress, even although more might have been obtained for the property if the sale had been postponed. . . .

|||||||||||||||||||||||||||||||||||||||||||||||||||||||||||||||||||||||||||||||

Foreclosure

An alternative to sale under the power of sale contained in the mortgage is an action for *foreclosure*. This type of action, if successful, results in the issue by the courts of a *final order of foreclosure* which extinguishes all rights of the mortgagor (and

---

[18]*Farrar v. Farrars, Ltd.*, (1889), 40 Ch. D. 395.

any subsequent encumbrancer) in the property. An action for foreclosure, however, gives the mortgagor and any subsequent encumbrancers the right to redeem, and the courts will provide a period of time (usually six months) to enable any party who makes such a request the opportunity to do so. If the party fails to redeem the property within the time provided, or if no request for an opportunity to redeem is made, the mortgagee may then proceed with the action, and eventually obtain a judgement and *final order of foreclosure*. In spite of its name, the final order of foreclosure is not necessarily final in every sense of the word, as the mortgagor may, under certain circumstances, apply to have it set aside after its issue, if he should find himself in a position to redeem and the mortgagee has not disposed of the property.

||||||||||||||||||||||||||||||||||||||||||||||||||||||||||||||||||||

CASE 29.3
Cummins v. Fletcher (1880), 14 Ch. D. 699.

JAMES, L.J.:

At law, independently of a legal estate, when the power of redemption given by original contract is gone, then a person comes into equity to have assistance from the Courts of Equity and asks to redeem upon what are called equitable considerations, and then the Court of Equity says: "This is the price upon which we give you the relief you seek, namely, on your paying all that is due." Then the converse of that, where a mortgagee comes with a bill of foreclosure, is no extension of that; because a bill of foreclosure (it is an action now) never gave and never was intended to give the mortgagee any active remedy. A bill of foreclosure in substance was this: "You have a right to redeem, and you may exercise that right at any time within twenty years, according to the usual practice of the Court, but I do not want to be kept in a state of uncertainty as to whether I am or am not to be redeemed, and therefore, if you want to re-deem me, redeem me now;" and the mortgagee has a right to say, "Redeem me upon those terms upon which you would be entitled to redeem if you filed your redemption suit." That is all. If you do not redeem, your equity of redemption is gone; the only result therefore of a bill for foreclosure is to deprive a man of his opportunity of filing a bill of redemption at some future time. . . .

||||||||||||||||||||||||||||||||||||||||||||||||||||||||||||||||||||

Sale

As an alternate method of obtaining payment of the mortgage, the mortgagee may apply to the courts for possession, payment, and sale of the property. Under this procedure, the property would be sold, and the proceeds distributed first in the payment of the mortgage, then in payment of the claims of subsequent encumbrancers, and finally, the payment of any surplus to the mortgagor. The sale under this procedure differs substantially from a sale under the power of sale, but the most common procedure is to have the property sold by tender or public auction, usually subject to a reserve bid. The method of sale does vary, however, since in most provinces the courts generally have wide latitude in this respect.

A sale may also be requested by the mortgagor where foreclosure action is instituted by the mortgagee. In this case, the mortgagor is usually expected to pay a sum of money to the courts to defray a part of the expenses involved in the sale. This is normally required at the time that the request for a sale is made. Once the request is received, however, the foreclosure action becomes a sale action, and the action then proceeds in the same manner as if a sale had been requested originally by the mortgagee. The advantage to the mortgagor of a sale is that the proceeds of the sale will also be applied to the payment of the claims of subsequent encumbrancers, and not just to the claim of the first mortgagee. In this manner, the mortgagor is released from all or part of the claims of the subsequent encumbrancers rather than only the claim of the first mortgagee.

Possession

When default occurs, the mortgagee has a right to possession of the mortgaged premises. If the premises are leased units, the mortgagee may displace the lessor, and collect any rents which are payable by the tenants.

The rents collected, however, must be applied to the payment of the mortgage, and the mortgagor is entitled to an accounting of any monies collected. If the mortgagor has vacated the mortgaged property, the mortgagee may move into possession, but usually this is not the case, and the mortgagee must normally apply to the courts for an order for possession. This is generally done when the mortgagee institutes legal proceedings on default by the mortgagor. The usual relief requested by the mortgagee is either foreclosure, payment, and possession, or sale, payment, and possession.

|||||||||||||||||||||||||||||||||||||||||||||||||||||||||||||||||||||||||||||||||||||||||||||||||||||||||||||||||||||||||||||||||||||||||||||||||||||||||||||||||||||||||||

SUMMARY   A mortgage is an instrument which utilizes land as security for debt. In most provinces, the mortgagee acquires an interest in the land by way of the mortgage, either in the form of a transfer of the title to the property as security (such as in eastern Canada, and parts of Ontario and Manitoba under the Registry System) or in the form of a charge on the land in those provinces under the Land Titles System. Quebec law provides for a somewhat similar instrument (called a *hypothec*) which is in the nature of a lien on the land.

A mortgage, in addition to conveying an interest in the land, contains the details of the debt, and the provisions for its repayment. In the instrument, the mortgagor covenants to protect the property by payment of taxes and insurance, and promises not to diminish the mortgagee's security by waste or non-repair. If the mortgagor defaults in payment, or fails to comply with the covenants in the mortgage, the mortgagee may institute legal proceedings to have the mortgagor's interest in the property foreclosed or sold. Foreclosure is not available in some provinces, but in all provinces, if the mortgagor fails to pay the debt after default, the property may be sold, and the proceeds used to satisfy the indebtedness.

Where more than one mortgage is registered against a parcel of land, the mortgagees are entitled to payment in full in the order of their priority. This is usually determined by the time of registration of each instrument under the land registry system in the province. If a surplus is available after the claims of all mortgagees and other creditors with claims against the land are satisfied, the sum goes to the mortgagor.

Where no default occurs during the term of a mortgage, and the indebtedness is paid by the mortgagor, the mortgagee must provide the mortgagor with a discharge of the mortgage. This acts as a statutory re-conveyance of the title and receipt for payment for a mortgage under the Registry System, or a release of the claim against the property in the case of a cessation of charge under the Land Titles System. In both instances, the discharge given to the mortgagor extinguishes the debt, and releases the property as security from the mortgagee's claim against it.

Because mortgage law developed in a different fashion in each province, the nature of mortgage instruments and the rights of the parties vary substantially from province to province. The basic concept of land as security for debt, however, is common to all provincial systems.

DISCUSSION QUESTIONS

1. *Explain the legal nature of a "mortgage."*
2. *Distinguish a "mortgage" from a "charge" or "hypothec."*
3. *In what ways did older forms of mortgages differ from the modern mortgage?*
4. *Explain the difference between the* live-gage *and* mort-gage.
5. *What is the nature of an "equity of redemption"?*
6. *Distinguish a "legal" mortgage from an "equitable" mortgage.*
7. *How are mortgage priorities determined?*
8. *Describe the usual covenants that may be found in a mortgage. Why are they important?*
9. *Why is an "acceleration clause" necessary from a mortgagee's point of view? What is its effect?*
10. *In what way does an assignment of mortgage differ from the assignment of an ordinary contract debt?*
11. *Why is the delivery of notice of an assignment to the mortgagor important?*
12. *If a mortgagor sells his interest in mortgaged lands to a purchaser, what is the nature of the relationship between the purchaser and the mortgagee? Between the mortgagor and the mortgagee?*
13. *Indicate the rights of the mortgagee when the mortgagor defaults on the mortgage. How are these rights enforced?*
14. *Distinguish a "sale under a power of sale contained in a mortgage" from a "sale action."*
15. *What rights are available to the mortgagor after the mortgagee has commenced a foreclosure action?*
16. *From the mortgagor's point of view, under what circumstances would a sale of the mortgaged property be preferable to foreclosure?*
17. *Explain the effect of a "discharge of mortgage." How does it differ from a "cessation of charge"?*
18. *Distinguish a "partial discharge" of mortgage from a "discharge" of mortgage. What is the principal purpose and use of a partial discharge?*

JUDICIAL
DECISIONS

Remedies of
Mortgagee—
Right of
Mortgagee
to Claim
Deficiency
when Property
Sold After
Foreclosure

Bank of Nova Scotia v. Dorval et al. (1979), 25 O.R. (2d) 579.

The defendants gave the plaintiff several promissory notes, and a collateral mortgage to secure their indebtedness. They later defaulted on the debt, and the plaintiff foreclosed on the mortgage. After foreclosure, the plaintiff sold the property, but the sale did not provide sufficient funds to satisfy the amount owing. The plaintiff then sued the defendants for the balance of the debt.

The trial judge gave the plaintiff judgement for the balance owing. The defendants then appealed the decision.

THORSON, J.A.:

The issue on this appeal brought by Suzanne Dorval from the above judgment is whether the Bank is precluded from suing on the promissory notes for the deficiency, by reason of its sale of the realty after obtaining the final order of foreclosure. The appellant contends that it is. The respondent Bank contends that the learned Weekly Court Judge correctly appreciated the right of the Bank, and the requirement upon it, to realize on the "collateral security" (*i.e.*, the mortgage) before seeking to realize upon what it termed the "primary security" (*i.e.*, the promissory notes) for the deficiency. In the Bank's submission, the principles of law which apply to foreclosure proceedings where the mortgage foreclosed upon represents the primary security taken to secure the loan, cannot apply to this case where the mortgage foreclosed upon represents "security collateral to and further securing the primary security represented by the promissory notes".

The arguments advanced by counsel on this appeal raise two basic principles of mortgage law. The first of these is that an action on the covenant in a mortgage may only be pursued as long as the mortgagee is able to reconvey the property. This principle was recently reiterated by Laskin, J., speaking for the majority of the Supreme Court of Canada in *Rushton v. Industrial Development Bank*, [1973] S.C.R. 552 at p. 562, 34 D.L.R. (3d) 582 at p. 589, as follows:

"I test the matter under well-recognized principles of mortgage law, applicable in Ontario, under which there has always been close regard for the rights of the mortgagor. Where a mortgagee forecloses upon mortgaged land, taking title, and then sells the land as its own, it cannot sue for the balance owing on the mortgage unless it is in a position to return the land: see *Davidson v. Sharp* (1920), 60 S.C.R. 72 at p. 82. The situation would be different if the mortgagee had exercised a power of sale under its mortgage or if it had sought a judicial sale in the foreclosure proceedings, thus obliging itself to give an accounting. Where, however, it proceeds to foreclosure only, a subsequent suit on the covenant for payment of the mortgage debt reopens the foreclosure and entitles the mortgagor to have the foreclosed property available to him as a condition of his liability. If it is not so available, the mortgagee is precluded from turning the matter into an accounting proceeding to enable it to sue for the debt when it cannot return the mortgaged land."

In an earlier case, *Mutual Life Ass'ce Co. of Canada v. Douglas* (1918), 57 S.C.R. 243, 44 D.L.R. 115, the Supreme Court of Canada stated this principle even more broadly, as one precluding not only an action on the covenant but also any action to realize upon property held as collateral security to the mortgage. Idington, J., commented, in *obiter*, at p. 253 S.C.R., p. 122 D.L.R.:

"It was settled that he, seeking to impose his common law right of suing upon a covenant for the debt, must be ready to reopen the foreclosure and ready to restore that property which had become his as absolutely as the English language could express it and further that if he had sold and conveyed away the property he had so acquired he should be restrained from proceeding to enforce that common law right whether by suing upon the covenant or in way of asserting a proprietory right over any property he had held by way of collateral security to his mortgage."

The second principle raised is that if a mortgagee holds collateral security for the payment of the mortgage debt, he should realize the security before seeking to foreclose under the mortgage because, if he obtains foreclosure first, "he deprives himself of the benefit of the security in the sense that the foreclosure will be reopened if he subsequently realizes the security": *Falconbridge on Mortgages*, 4th ed. (1977), p. 509. Falconbridge cites as authority the case of *Dyson v. Morris* (1842), 1 Hare. 413 at p. 423, 66 E.R. 1094, in which it was said:

"Again, in the case of a mortgagee, whose security was composed both of land and stock, or personal chattels, or a policy simply assigned as a security, I should probably experience little difficulty as to the decree to which the mortgagee would be entitled. In the case of securities so constituted the course usually recommended out of Court to a mortgagee is, first, to realize his collateral securities, and then to proceed to foreclose the mortgage for so much of his debt as the collateral securities may not satisfy. . . . [I]t is only by first realizing his collateral securities, and afterwards proceeding to foreclose the mortgage, that a mortgagee can get a valid decree of foreclosure without foregoing the benefit of the collateral securities, which he cannot, as a matter or course, be required to do."

In my view the *rationale* behind both rules is the same; the sale of mortgaged property after final foreclosure, unlike a sale under a power of sale or judicial sale, is not conducted under the auspices of the Court or in a manner prescribed by the mortgage or by statute. Thus, there can be no assurance that the mortgagee has obtained the full value of the property. The mortgagor has no right to question the amount realized, nor the manner in which it was realized, and if the property was sold for more than the mortgage debt the mortgagor has no right to the surplus. It would, therefore, be inequitable to allow the mortgagee to claim for any deficiency either on the covenant or on other securities, since the mortgagee, having disposed of the property without any accounting having been taken, has placed it beyond any possibility of restoration to the mortgagor and is thus no longer in a position to pursue an accounting to establish whatever debt might remain. See Marriot and Dunn, *Practice in Mortgage Actions in Ontario*, 3rd ed. (1971), at p. 16, and *DeWitt v. Simms*, [1924] 1 D.L.R. 592 at pp. 596-7, 56 N.S.R. 515 at p. 523 (N.S.S.C.), where the following statement was made, in *obiter*:

"Where the mortgagee simply forecloses the equity of redemption and then, being clothed with the equitable as well as the legal estate, sells the property, there is no assurance that he has obtained its full value and there is good reason for saying that he should not have recourse to any other securities for his debt unless he can surrender the pledge and that if he still retains the property his recourse to other securities opens up the foreclosure giving the mortgagor the right to redeem."

In my view, this is all that is imported by two cases relied on by counsel for the Bank, namely, *Miller et al. v. Budreau et al.*, [1954] O.W.N. 274 [affirmed *ibid.*, p. 560] and *Greenberg v. Rapoport*, [1970] 2 O.R. 349, 10 D.L.R. (3d) 737. These cases do not, as contended by counsel for the Bank, stand for the proposition that the holder of both primary and collateral security must, as a matter of law, realize upon the collateral security first; rather, they support a more general proposition that where security is pledged for a debt and the lender has put it beyond his power to restore the pledge, he must be taken to have elected to accept the amount realized in satisfaction of the debt and to have foregone recourse to any other security *for that same debt*, whether that other security be characterized as secondary, additional, primary or collateral.

In *Miller et al. v. Budreau et al.*, *supra*, a loan was made on a promissory note wherein the borrowers agreed to furnish, as collateral security, both a chattel mortgage and land mortgage. Subsequently, a chattel mortgage was given and a seizure was made thereunder. The lenders brought an action seeking a declaration that they were entitled to a mortgage on the lands and that such mortgage was in arrears and subject to foreclosure, since the mortgage had been promised but not actually given. It was held that the simple fact of the seizure under the chattel mortgage did not constitute a bar to the granting of the declaration. The act of seizing was not equivalent to an election to proceed only under the chattel mortgage by way of realization and an abandonment of the right to call for the security under the land mortgage, since the step toward one type of realization did not exclude the right to assert another type of realization. However, Gale, J., concluded at p. 276 that:

". . . if the plaintiffs had appropriated the goods to their own use, which would of course include disposal or realization of the goods, they could not thereafter have the declaration here sought."

Gale, J., relied on *McDonald v. Grundy* (1904), 8 O.L.R. 113, where the *rationale* for the above proposition was stated to be, as discussed above, that where the lender is unable to restore the pledges he must be found to have taken them for the debt and cannot thereafter enforce the debt itself.

The second of the cases relied on by counsel for the Bank, *Greenberg v. Rapoport, supra,* is, in my view, likewise more supportive of the appelant's position. The facts of that case, simply stated, were that the mortgagee under a chattel mortgage and collateral land mortgage seized the chattels upon default of payment under the chattel mortgage, leased them to a third person with consequent deterioration and depreciation of their value and ultimately sold them at a low price. In an application by the mortgagor for a declaration that the land mortgage given as collateral security be considered satisfied, the Court found that the mortgagee, in dealing with the chattels as he did, must be taken to have appropriated the goods to his own use so as to make himself their owner. The consequence of so doing, said Lieff, J., at p. 354 O.R., p. 742 D.L.R., is that:

". . . the mortgage debt becomes extinguished and the right to pursue the original mortgagor either on his covenant to pay or under the terms of the collateral security is lost."

Counsel for the bank contends that this holding supports the proposition advanced by him that:

"Where the holder of primary and secondary or additional security realizes against the primary security, he disentitles himself from realizing against the security given as further collateral to that primary security, and accordingly must at law realize upon the collateral security first."

In my opinion, however, the issue turns not on which security was realized first but on whether the mortgagee has put it beyond his power to restore the property pledged as security. This was apparently the view of Lieff, J., who, in holding that the realty mortgage must be considered satisfied, stated the proposition thus at p. 354 O.R., p. 742 D.L.R.:

"[W]here collateral security is held and the prime security has been sold, so that the mortgagor can no longer redeem because the mortgagee has put it beyond his own power to restore the prime security, therefore, in divesting himself of the prime security the rights of the mortgagee under the collateral security are extinguished."

If the Bank in the present case had sued first on the "primary security" (the promissory note) for payment, it would not, as I see it, have thereby disentitled itself from subsequently realizing upon the collateral security (although this is the proposition that counsel for the Bank would have us accept). This is so because:

1. The action on the note would be analogous to an action on the covenant in the mortgage for payment, and it is clear law that a judgment on the covenant does not preclude the mortgagee from later enforcing his security upon the property in respect of the balance remaining due.

2. Such an action would not offend the basic principle that where a lender realizes upon security pledged for a debt and so puts it beyond his power to restore it, he must be taken to have accepted the property in satisfaction of the debt and may not thereafter assert a claim for any deficiency.

Indeed, on the facts of this case, it is not really helpful to speak of the "primary security" as distinct from the "collateral security" herein, or to attempt to apply cases which refer to that distinction to these facts. The promissory notes are more appropriately characterized, if they need be characterized at all, as the primary *obligation*, since they are not given as "security" in the ordinary sense. Strictly speaking, if there is a "primary security" in this case it is probably the realty, since it is the property pledged to secure the performance of the obligation evidenced by the notes. Thus the respondent Bank's contention that the "authorities cited [by the appellant] reflect upon the position of the holder of the primary security and the consequence of foreclosure upon that security" is not a valid basis for distinction. This, however, does not detract from the correctness of the characterization of the mortgage itself as a "collateral security" as that expression was defined by this Court in *Royal Bank of Canada v. Slack*, [1958] O.R. 262 at p. 273, 11 D.L.R. (2d) 737 at p. 746:

"Collateral security is any property which is assigned or pledged to secure the performance of an obligation and as additional thereto, and which upon the performance of the obligation is to be surrendered or discharged."

However the promissory notes and the mortgage are characterized, I conclude that the issue in this appeal must be tested by recourse to "the well-recognized principles of mortgage law, applicable in Ontario" to which reference was made in the *Rushton* case, *supra*. An early illustration of the application of those principles in this Province is furnished by *Allison v. McDonald* (1894), 23 S.C.R. 635, in which the Supreme Court of Canada dealt with a fact situation bearing some substantial similarity to that of this case. There, two partners had borrowed money on the security of their joint promissory note and a realty mortgage. Subsequently, the lender gave one of the partners a discharge of the mortgage, but without receiving payment of his debt, and later brought an action against the other partner on the promissory note. The Supreme Court of Canada affirmed the decision of the Ontario Court of Appeal where [at p. 638] it was held that:

"[T]he mortgage and promissory note having been given for the same debt, the appellant could not recover upon the note after having released the mortgage inasmuch as . . . the respondent . . . on payment of the note, would have been entitled to a transfer of the mortgage which the appellant had, by discharging that security, put it out of his power to give him."

The Chief Justice of Canada at pp. 639-40 set out the rule and its *rationale* in so clear a manner that it merits quotation here at some length:

"The judgment of the Court of Appeal proceeds upon the point taken up in the first branch of the Chancellor's judgment, namely, that the appellant could not call upon the respondent to pay the mortgage debt without being prepared upon payment to re-convey to him the lands mortgaged to secure the debt which he had incapacitated himself from doing. . . .

"So completely is the principle upon which they have decided the case supported by authority that it would, under the old system of procedure when law and equity were administered separately, have been

of course to enjoin an action to recover on a promissory note brought under such circumstances as are disclosed by the evidence in this record. The rule is elementary and so well established that it is almost superfluous to quote authorities in support of it. *The principle is the plain and just one that he who gives a pledge in security for a debt is, upon payment, entitled to a return of that which he has given in security, from whence it follows that if the creditor is unable to return the pledge he will not be allowed to exact the debt. . . . Even if the mortgagee had obtained an absolute foreclosure by which he had made the mortgaged estate his own, and had then sold it for its fair value but for less than the mortgage debt, he could not sue the mortgagor on his bond, covenant, note or other collateral personal security for the unsatisfied residue, and that for the same reason, that he could not give him back the estate.''*
(Emphasis added.)

Much more recently, the Alberta Court of Appeal, in *Clayborn Investments Ltd. v. Wiegert* (1977), 77 D.L.R. (3d) 170, 3 Alta. L.R. (2d) 295, dealt with a fact situation even more closely resembling that of this case, but which turned on certain legislation peculiar to Alberta. There the Court was concerned with the effect of the *Judicature Act*, R.S.A. 1970, c. 193, s. 34(17)(*a*), and the *Land Titles Act*, R.S.A. 1970, c. 198, s. 109(1), on the common law of mortgages. *Allison v. McDonald, supra,* and *Rushton v. Industrial Development Bank, supra,* were referred to as stating the applicable common law. Mr. Justice Clement said, at p. 173:

"At common law, in the absence of statutory modification, *where the promissory note and the mortgage are given for the same debt and there are no circumstances to distinguish the obligation of payment under the note from that under the mortgage*, then a sale of the mortgaged premises by the mortgagee after foreclosure . . . will prevent a claim on the note for the deficiency since the mortgagee could not then reconvey the security."
(Emphasis added.)

The Court then went on to deal with the case before it on the basis of the statutory provisions in question, after Morrow, J.A., noted with reference to the *Land Titles Act* provisions that they were "almost declaratory of the common law".

For the foregoing reasons I conclude that the Bank in this case is precluded from suing on the promissory notes for the deficiency, having proceeded in the way that it did with respect to the realty that was the subject of its collateral security.

I would therefore allow the appeal and set aside the judgment of the Weekly Court Judge, on the ground that the Bank has no cause by action against the appellant Suzanne Dorval.

CASE	Case 1
PROBLEMS	Hambly was the owner of a block of land *in fee simple*. He arranged a
FOR	mortgage of the property with Blake for $50 000, and the mortgage was
DISCUSSION	duly registered in the appropriate Land Registry Office. Hambly used

the funds for the renovation of an existing building on the premises, but discovered that he had insufficient funds to complete the changes he wished to make.

A few months later, he borrowed the sum of $10 000 from his friend Clark, and gave a second mortgage on the property as security. Clark did not register the mortgage; instead, he placed it in his safety deposit box, with the intention of registering it at some later date.

When the renovations to the building were completed, Hambly decided to install a swimming-pool on the grounds, and borrowed $5 000 from Simple Finance Co. to pay the pool contractor for the installation. Simple Finance, as security for its loan to Hambly, took a mortgage on the property. The mortgage was registered the same day that the funds were given to Hambly.

Shortly, thereafter, Hambly arranged a party to celebrate the completion of the swimming-pool, and invited his many friends to attend. At the party, Clark mentioned to Anderson, another friend of Hambly, that he held a mortgage on Hambly's property, and that he would like to dispose of it in order to have the funds available for another more attractive investment.

Anderson expressed an interest in the purchase of the mortgage, and after some discussion, agreed to give Clark $9 000 for it. The next day, Anderson paid Clark the $9 000 for the mortgage (on which the full $10 000 principal was owing) and received an assignment of the mortgage. When Anderson realized that the mortgage itself had not been registered, he had the documents registered immediately. Unfortunately, he failed to notice the mortgage to Simple Finance in his examination of the title to the property.

Hambly was killed in an automobile accident a few days before he was scheduled to make his first payments on the mortgages. His only asset was his interest in the property, and Blake instituted foreclosure proceedings when the first payment required under the mortgage became overdue. An appraisal of the property indicated that it had a market value of approximately $60 000.

Discuss the position of the parties in this case, and indicate their rights in the foreclosure action. Comment on the possible outcome of the case.

Case 2

Parker owned a single-family dwelling that had been constructed on a building lot in a suburban area. To obtain the necessary funds to complete the purchase, Parker had entered into a mortgage with Green Mortgage Co. for the principal amount of $35 000, repayable in monthly installments of $600 each.

Some time later, when the mortgage amount had been paid down to $33 000, Parker sold his equity in the property to Baker for $55 000.

Baker continued to make payments on the mortgage while he occupied the house, but two years after he purchased the property, he was transferred to another city by his employer. He sold the property at that time to Brown, who assumed the mortgage and paid Baker $60 000 for the property. The mortgage had a principal balance outstanding of $31 500 at the date that the property was sold.

Brown, unfortunately, found himself over-extended financially soon after he had purchased the property, and was forced to let the monthly mortgage payments fall into arrears in order to pay more pressing debts. In spite of repeated requests for payment by the mortgage company, Brown refused to do so. Eventually, Green Co. was obliged to take action. Instead of foreclosure, however, it brought an action against Parker for payment.

Discuss the possible reasons why the mortgage company decided to take action against Parker, rather than institute foreclosure proceedings. On what basis could it do so? Discuss the rights and obligations of the parties in the light of this action by the mortgagee.

Case 3

Agricola sold his farm to Tennant for $100 000. Tennant arranged for a purchase money mortgage from the Agricultural Loan Company for $60 000, and Agricola agreed to take back a mortgage in the amount of $20 000 in order that Tennant could acquire the property. On the date fixed for closing, Agricola gave Tennant the deed to the property, and received a cheque from Tennant in the amount of $20 000. He also received a cheque from the loan company for $60 000 when the company registered its mortgage immediately after the registration of the deed to Tennant. Agricola then registered his mortgage. At the time, Agricola transferred the fire insurance policy (which covered the buildings) to Tennant. The policy transfer named Tennant as the new owner, subject to the interest of Agricola as mortgagee. Through an oversight, Agricultural Loan Company was not named as an insured on the policy.

Some time later, Tennant defaulted on the mortgage to Agricola, and it was necessary for Agricola to foreclose on the mortgage. Agricola continued to make the mortgage payments each month to Agricultural Loan Company, and allowed Tennant to remain on the property to work the farm on a crop-sharing basis.

Not long after Agricola had foreclosed on his mortgage and taken back the property, a serious fire destroyed a large barn on the premises which had a value of $50 000. The insurer noted that the fire insurance policy listed Tennant as the owner of the property, and Agricola as the mortgagee. However, before the insurance company made payment, all three parties, Agricola, Tennant, and the Agricultural Loan Company claimed the insurance proceeds.

Discuss the nature of the rights that each party might raise, and discuss the possible outcome.

Case 4

"Aunt Maud," as she was affectionately known to the college students who were boarders in her rooming-house, was quite elderly and could only read with difficulty. Her home was large, and in close proximity to the college. As such, it was a valuable piece of residential property.

Her nephew, Herman, had on numerous occasions urged her to retire, and had suggested that she sell the property. For many years she refused to consider the idea, but as a result of Herman's insistence, she eventually agreed that she would list the property with a local real estate agent to see what the market might be. A few days later, Herman appeared at her home with some papers which he said were the forms that he had obtained from the real estate agent for the listing of her property. In reality, the forms were mortgage forms, which Herman represented as "only a formality, to let the real estate agent have authority to show the house to prospective buyers." Aunt Maud signed the forms, believing them to be copies of the real estate listing agreement.

Herman later registered the mortgage (which was drawn for $50 000), and assigned it to a finance company for $40 000. He intended to use a part of the money to make the payments on the mortgage himself; the balance, he planned to use for a trip to Monte Carlo where he expected to make a fortune by employing a new system for placing bets at the gambling tables in a casino.

Herman's scheme failed, however, and he returned to Canada penniless. He soon spent the funds he had originally set aside to make a few payments on the mortgage, and again found himself without funds. The mortgage, as a result, went into default, and the finance company instituted foreclosure proceedings against the property. At that point Aunt Maud suddenly became aware of the mortgage.

Indicate the action which Aunt Maud might take in this case, and discuss the position of the finance company. What might be the outcome of its foreclosure proceedings?

CHAPTER 30

Leasehold Interests

THE LEASEHOLD INTEREST

A leasehold interest in land arises when a person who owns an estate in land grants, by way of either an express or implied contract, possession of the land to another for a fixed period of time. The owner of the estate in land holds the lordship over the particular parcel of land, and is known as the *landlord* or *lessor*. The person granted possession of the property is called the *tenant* or *lessee*, and the contract between the landlord and tenant, a *lease* or *tenancy*.

The contract is, in a sense, more than an ordinary contract, because it amounts to a conveyance of a part of the landlord's interest in the land to the tenant for the term of the lease. The lease creates a *privity of estate* between the landlord and tenant, since each have an interest in the same land. In addition, the contract itself creates a *privity of contract* between the parties. If the landlord and tenant retain their interest for the entire period of the tenancy, privity of estate and privity of contract would remain between them, but if either party should assign his interest in the land, the privity of estate ceases to exist when the new party acquires the interest in the land. The contract between the landlord and tenant remains, however, and the original tenant may continue to be bound by the covenants in the contract if it is expressly set out, even though he has parted with his interest in the land.

Privity of estate in itself creates certain rights in the landlord and in the tenant. For example, where a lease is assigned to a new tenant, by virtue of the privity of estate which exists between the landlord and tenant, the new tenant would be obliged to pay the rent, and also perform all covenants which run with the land.

The creation of a tenancy gives rise to two concurrent interests in land: the *leasehold*, and the *reversion*. The tenant acquires the exclusive possession of the land under the tenancy, and the landlord retains the reversion or the title to the property until the lease terminates. At the expiration of the term of the lease, the two interests (possession and title) merge, and the landlord's original estate becomes whole once again. In the interval, however, the tenant has exclusive possession of the property, and unless an agreement is made to the contrary, he may exclude everyone from the land, including the landlord.

A leasehold interest is an interest in land, and consequently, anything which is attached to the land becomes a part of the leasehold interest during the currency of the lease. For example, if a person leases a parcel of land that has a dwelling-house built upon it, the house becomes the possession of the tenant for the time, and any rents or benefits which the house produces would belong to the tenant, unless the parties had agreed that the rents would be used or applied in a different manner.

HISTORICAL DEVELOPMENT

A lease is a very old method of acquiring an interest in land. Long before the modern concept of contract was developed, the leasehold interest was recognized, and the rights and duties attached to it defined. Many changes have naturally taken place over the years which have altered the relationship of landlord and tenant, but the basic concept has remained the same.

Leases existed in Europe and England long before the feudal system of land tenure was adopted, and the leasehold interest was never (in England at least) a feudal tenure. It was always an interest in land which was based upon an agreement between the parties, and seldom considered to be something permanent in nature. Leases were not uncommon in England prior to 1290, but the use of the device was limited until the government took steps to prohibit *subinfeudation* of land by the statute of *Quia Emptores*.[1] After that date, the leasehold became more popular because the lesser lords were prohibited from the creation of further manors by the grant of lesser estates.

---

[1]18 Edw. I, c. 1 (Statute of Westminster III).

When the further subdivision of estates became impossible, the lesser lords turned to leases as a means of creating interests in land which would, in turn, provide them with benefits. The leasehold interest, while it lacked the permanency of a tenured estate in land, did have certain advantages. Since it was for a fixed term, the land would eventually return to the landlord, and thus the wealth associated with the land remained with the lord. In the meantime, the land produced revenue in the form of rents, or a share of the produce. It also provided the landlord with some protection against inflation (particularly after the mid-14th century), because the rents could be renegotiated at the end of the term of the lease. The advantage to the tenant under a lease, apart from the right to possession of the land, was the fact that the land did not carry with it the burdens or restrictions of feudal duties that accompanied grants of feudal estates.

Leases at that time, however, had one serious drawback. If the tenant was ejected from the property by the landlord or some other person, the tenant was not in the position of a person with a freehold estate, and could not bring his case before the royal courts to recover the land. The only remedy available to the dispossessed tenant was an action for damages for the loss which he suffered. Conditions, however, improved for tenants by the end of the 15th century under the reign of Henry VII, when the *action for ejectment* was expanded to permit a tenant who was wrongfully ejected from the land to bring an action in the king's court to recover possession.[2] Leases soon became commonplace with the protection which the action for ejectment provided.

The law relating to tenancies was further clarified during the 16th century by legislation which provided that all of the covenants and conditions in the lease which "touched and concerned" the land, passed with the reversion, if the landlord should grant the interest to another.[3] This legislation permitted the new landlord to acquire all rights under the lease which "touched and concerned" the land, in addition to the covenants which normally followed the reversion, and which included the payment of rent.

A second statute, passed some years later, gave the landlord the right to distrain against the goods of the tenant if rent was not paid.[4] *Distress* (or the right to distrain) generally permitted the landlord to seize and hold the tenant's goods until payment was made, but some goods, such as growing crops and produce, were exempt from distress at common law. The common law, however, was gradually altered with respect to many goods by a series of statutes beginning in 1689. These statutes rendered harvested crops subject to distress, and in particular permitted the landlord to follow goods which had been fraudulently and secretly removed from the premises by the tenant.[6]

A significant change in leases took place in 1677 with the passing of the *Statute of Frauds*. The statute affected leases as well as other interests in land, and required all leases to be in writing and made under seal unless the term was for a period of less than three years.[7] Under

---

[2]Under Henry VII, *De Ejectco Firmae*—the action for ejectment was established (in 1499) as a right whereby a displaced tenant could recover land.

[3]The *Grantees of Reversions Act* (1540), 32 Hen. VIII, c. 34.
[4]*An Act For The Impounding of Distress* (1554), 1 & 2 Phil. & Mar., c. 12.
[5]The *Distress Act* (1689), 2 Will. & Mar., c. 5.
[6]The *Distress for Rent Act* (1737), 11 Geo. II, c. 19.

the Act, a lease for more than three years which had not been made in writing was void.[8] The requirements imposed by this statute have continued to the present time in most common law provinces of Canada, and remain in England in the form of another statute, the *Law of Property Act*.[9]

Statutes in England were frequently enacted to deal with various aspects of the lease, and to define or establish rights of the landlord and tenant. This practice continued until the early part of the 20th century. At that point, an attempt was made to collect the common law and statute law into two statutes, namely, the *Law of Property Act*[10] and the *Landlord and Tenant Act*.[11] These Acts, as a result, incorporated much of the common law and its statutory alteration as it existed at that time.

In Canada, the law relating to the landlord and tenant relationship followed the English law, but, due to the availability of much low-cost land, was less concerned with agricultural leases. The Canadian legislation, as a consequence, has tended to be more streamlined, with the emphasis on leases of land for business or residential purposes, rather than agriculture. As in England, much of the law relating to landlord and tenant has been incorporated into provincial statutes which set out the nature of the relationship, and the rights and duties of the parties.[12]

CREATION OF A TENANCY

A lease is a contract made between a landlord and a tenant which gives the tenant exclusive possession of the property for a specific period or *term*. A lease is distinct from a *licence* in that a lessee is entitled to exclusive possession of the property, whereas a licence grants the licensee the right to use the property in common with others, but does not create an interest in land. For example, a property owner may permit certain persons to use property from time to time for the purpose of hunting, but the permission to do so would not create an interest in land. It would only give the licensee the right to lawfully enter on the property for the particular purpose set out in the licence. A lease, on the other hand, would give the tenant exclusive possession of the property, and an interest in land. The extensive use of licences for various purposes has, unfortunately, made the distinction between a lease and a licence unclear with regard to the question of when rights granted under a licence become an interest in land. The courts generally look at the intention of the parties in order to distinguish between the two, since possession alone is no longer a deciding factor.[13]

|||||||||||||||||||||||||||||||||||||||||||||||||||||||||||||||||||||||||||||||||||

CASE 30.1

Re British American Oil Co. Ltd. and DePass (1959), 21 D.L.R. (2d) 110.

SCHROEDER, J.A.:

Wherever the relationship of landlord and tenant exists there is present the element of permission or consent on the part of the landlord, and subordination to the landlord's title

---

[7]The *Statute of Frauds*. See, for example, R.S.O. 1980, c. 481, s. 3.

[8]*Ibid.*, s. 1(2).

[9]The *Law of Property Act*, 1925, 15 & 16 Geo. V, c. 20.

[10]The *Law of Property Act*, 1925, 15 & 16 Geo. V, c. 20.

[11]The *Landlord and Tenant Act*, 17 & 18 Geo. V, c. 36. This was a form of consolidation of a series of acts by the same name which dealt with the landlord-tenant relationship.

[12]See, for example, the *Landlord and Tenant Act*, R.S.O. 1980, c. 232; R.S.M. 1970, c. L-70.

[13]*Errington v. Errington*, [1952] 1 All E.R. 149; *Lippman v. Yick*, [1953] 3 D.L.R. 527.

and rights on the part of the tenant. There must be a reversion in the landlord, the creation of an estate in the tenant, and a transfer of possession and control of the premises to the tenant. The reservation of rent to the landlord is usual but not in all cases essential, and whether the rent reserved is payable in money or through some other medium has no particular significance. It will be observed, therefore, that the transmission of an estate to the tenant is an essential characteristic of the relationship of landlord and tenant. No estate in the land passes to a licensee and this, on the authorities, is the principal distinguishing trait between the two relationships. An agreement which confers exclusive possession of the premises as against all the world, including the owner, is a lease, while if it merely confers a privilege to occupy under the owner, it is a licence. It is often difficult to determine whether a particular agreement is to be regarded as a lease or a licence. Broadly speaking, however, the general concept of a licence is that it is a mere permission to occupy the land of another for some particular purpose.

||||||||||||||||||||||||||||||||||||||||||||||||||||||||||||||||||||||||||||||||

A lease is contractual in nature, and may be either an express agreement (verbal or written), or it may be implied from the conduct of the parties. The terms of the lease may set out the specific rights and duties of the parties, in which case (provided that they are lawful), they will be binding on the lessor and lessee, and delineate the tenancy. If specific terms are not set out, then the rights of the parties and their duties may be determined by statute or the common law. The nature of the relationship being contractual, the law of contract, as modified by the common law and statutes relating to leasehold interests, will apply. A lease then, must normally meet the requirements for a valid contract to be enforceable. It must contain an offer and acceptance, consideration (in the form of rent and premises), and legality of object. The parties must also have capacity to contract, and the intention to create a legal relationship.

Where the *Statute of Frauds* (or similar legislation pertaining to leases) applies to lease agreements, it requires any lease for a term of more than three years to be made in writing and under seal, otherwise it is void.[14] Leases for a term of less than three years need not be in writing, provided that the tenant goes into possession.

An infant may enter into a lease as a tenant, but unless the accommodation is necessary, the lease would be voidable at the infant's option. The infant, however, must repudiate the lease promptly on attaining majority, as the contract of lease is an agreement of a continuing nature, and to continue to acknowledge the relationship may render the lease binding.[15]

A lease by a drunken or insane person is generally held to be binding unless the person in that state at the time of the execution of the lease is in a position to prove that he was drunken or insane, and that the other party knew of his condition.[16] This rule is simply the application of the ordinary contract rule with respect to agreements made by persons incapable of appreciating the nature of their acts, but it is generally necessary to show as well that the person of sound mind took unfair advantage of the person with the disability in cases where the leased premises would be treated as a necessary. As with the ordinary law of contract, leases must be repudiated promptly by drunken or insane per-

---

[14]For example, the *Statute of Frauds*, R.S.O. 1980 c. 481, ss. 1-3.
[15]*Sturgeon v. Starr* (1911), 17 W.L.R. 402.
[16]See, for example, *Hunt v. Texaco Exploration Co.*, [1955] 3 D.L.R. 555.

sons on their return to sanity or sobriety.[17]

Legislation in a number of provinces has distinguished between residential and other tenancies in the determination of the rights and duties of the parties to a lease, and to some extent the legislation has changed the nature of the lease itself. The general thrust of the new legislation with respect to residential tenancies has been to provide greater security of tenure for the tenant, and put additional obligations on the landlord to maintain safe premises for the tenant. The particular rights and obligations generally apply to all residential tenancies, and the parties usually may not contract out of the statutory requirements. Commercial and other tenancies are subject to the ordinary common law rules for landlord and tenant, and to the general provisions of the legislation pertaining to the tenancy relationship. Many of the rules relating to the relationship are the same, but the special provisions concerning residential tenancies have substantially altered the rights of the parties.

A characteristic of a lease is that it is a grant of exclusive possession for a term certain. The lease itself must stipulate when the lease will begin, and when it will end. If it is for a term that begins at some future time, it is said to be an *agreement for a lease* rather than a lease, and with the exception of Ontario, it must be in writing to be enforceable. In Ontario, the requirement of writing would only appear to apply if the agreement to lease relates to a period of more than three years.[18] In addition to the requirement of writing for long-term leases, leases which run for more

than three years must be registered in most provinces if the tenant wishes to retain priority over subsequent purchasers or mortgagees.[19]

Where the lease does not specify a definite term, the tenancy may be a *periodic tenancy*, in which the lease period may be *yearly, monthly,* or *weekly*. A periodic tenancy automatically renews at the end of each period, and continues until either the landlord or the tenant gives the other *notice to quit*. The type of periodic tenancy is usually determined from the agreement of the parties, but in the absence of evidence to the contrary, the tenancy is usually related to the rent payment interval. For example, unless otherwise indicated, if the rent is paid monthly, the tenancy is generally considered to be a monthly tenancy. A periodic tenancy may also arise on the expiration of a lease for a term certain. If the tenant continues to occupy the premises, and the landlord accepts the rent, the lease will become a periodic tenancy which will continue until either party gives notice to terminate.

A tenancy for a term certain may also give rise to another form of tenancy which is not a tenancy in the true sense, but an occupancy of the property only. If a tenant at the end of the term remains in possession after notice to quit has been given, and the notice period expired, then the occupancy of the premises is known as a *tenancy at sufferance*. Under this form of occupancy, no rent is payable, since a tenancy does not exist, but if the landlord so desires, he may demand compensation for

---

[17]*Seeley v. Charlton* (1881), 21 N.B.R. 119.

[18]The *Statute of Frauds*, R.S.O. 1980, c. 481, s. 3; *Manchester v. Dixie Cup Co. (Canada) Ltd.*, [1952] 1 D.L.R. 19.

[19]In Ontario, a lease for more than seven years must be registered to preserve priority under the Registry System. Under the Land Titles System, notice of a lease must be registered if drawn for a term of more than three years. A copy of the lease is usually deposited with the notice. See the *Land Titles Act*, R.S.O. 1980, c. 230, s. 115(4).

the overholding tenant's possession of the property.

A form of tenancy may also be established by a land-owner who permits another to enter on his premises and occupy them where no express lease is made, and where the purpose of the occupancy is usually related to another transaction. This tenancy is known as a *tenancy at will*, and no rent is payable. The occupier remains on the premises at the pleasure of the landlord, and the landlord may at any time order the occupier from the property. It frequently arises where a property owner permits a purchaser to occupy the land pending the completion of some aspect of the sale.

A special form of tenancy arises where a tenant enters into a lease with another for a term which is less than the tenancy which he holds. A lease of a leasehold interest of this nature is called a *sub-tenancy* (or under-tenancy), and the tenant in the sub-tenancy, a *sub-tenant*. The lease creating the sub-tenancy is called a *sub-lease*, and may contain terms and obligations which differ substantially from those of the lease under which the tenant-in-chief is bound. A sub-tenancy, nevertheless, must be consistent with the term of the original tenancy in the sense that it is for a lesser term. To have a sub-tenancy, the tenant-in-chief must possess a *reversion* which would entitle him to regain possession before the expiry of his lease with the landlord. For example, a tenant may lease premises for a term of five years, then immediately enter into a lease with a sub-tenant to sub-let the premises for a period of three years. The tenant-in-chief would be liable to the landlord under the original lease, and the sub-tenant would be liable to the tenant under the sub-lease. Each would be obliged to perform their particular obligations to their respective

"landlords." On the termination of the sub-lease, the tenant-in-chief would regain possession of the premises, and in turn, would deliver up possession to the landlord on the expiry of the original lease.

RIGHTS AND DUTIES OF THE LANDLORD AND TENANT

The landlord and tenant usually specify their rights and duties in the lease agreement, which they agree will be binding upon them for the duration of the lease. Most written leases set out these rights and duties in the form of promises or *covenants* which apply to the tenancy, but where the lease is merely verbal, the common law and the statutes pertaining to landlord and tenant in most provinces will incorporate in the verbal lease a number of implied terms to form the basis for the tenancy. As previously indicated, residential tenancies in a number of provinces are now subject to special rights and obligations which have been imposed on landlords and tenants, and which distinguish residential tenancies from the ordinary landlord-tenant relationship. Some of the more important differences are noted under the following topics which deal with the general rights and duties of the parties to a lease.

Rent

The covenant which comes to mind first when a lease is suggested is the covenant to pay rent. Rent is usually paid in the form of legal tender, or a cheque of a money amount, but rent is not restricted to money only. Rent may take the form of goods in the case of an agricultural lease where the landlord is to receive a share of the crop grown on the land,[20] or it may be in the form of services, such as where a person living in an apartment building agrees to provide cleaning or janitorial services in return for an apartment in the building.[21] In rare circumstances, such as a tenancy at will, no rent may be payable at all.

The method expressed for the payment of rent may indicate the nature of the tenancy, if the parties have not expressly agreed on the term. For example, the rent may be expressed as a lump sum for the entire lease period, or it may be expressed as an annual amount. In the former example, the payment method would indicate a lease for the term, and in the latter (if no agreement to the contrary) an annual lease. If the parties agree to a periodic tenancy with the rent payable monthly, a monthly tenancy will generally be inferred, and if the rent is payable weekly it usually indicates a weekly tenancy. Tenancies for longer terms than a month often specify a total rent amount or lump-sum payment, then break the amount down into monthly rent payments, but in this type of lease agreement the requirement for monthly payments would not change the term of the lease to a monthly tenancy.

At common law, the time for payment of rent may be either express or implied from the agreement of the parties, or it may be determined by custom. If the rent is to be paid in advance, the parties must generally agree to the advance payment either expressly, or by their conduct.[22] In the case of residential tenancies, the landlord may demand rent in advance, but in some provinces the practice of demanding the equivalent of several months' rent as a

"security" or "damage" deposit has been prohibited. Instead, the landlord may retain an amount equal to the last month's rent under the lease as a deposit, but must pay interest on the sum for the period of time that the funds are in his possession.[23]

As a general rule, if no place for the payment of rent is specified, the tenant must seek out the landlord on the day on which the rent is due, and make payment as required under the lease.[24] If, however, the landlord is in the habit of collecting the rent at the leased premises, the tenant is not in default so long as he is ready and willing to make payment on demand.[25]

The covenant to pay rent affects both the landlord and the tenant. During the term of the tenancy, unless the lease provides otherwise, the rent is fixed, and may not be raised by the landlord. The tenant at common law is generally liable for the payment of rent for the entire term in cases where the land is leased, even if some of the buildings on the land may be destroyed by an act of God, or through no fault of the tenant. Where residential tenancies are concerned, some provinces have included in their legislation that the *doctrine of frustration* applies where the property is seriously damaged or destroyed by fire. In these jurisdictions, the lease may be terminated.[26] In other provinces, the doctrine of frustration would not apply, but the courts have suggested that in apartment buildings and other multi-storied buildings, where the landlord is responsible for parts of the building, if there

---

[20]*Kozak v. Misiura*, [1928] 1 W.W.R. 1.
[21]*Robertson v. Millan* (1951), 3 W.W.R. (N.S.) 248.
[22]*Brunner v. Pollock*, [1941] 4 D.L.R. 107.

[23]See, for example, Ontario, the *Landlord and Tenant Act*, R.S.O. 1980, c. 232, ss. 84 and 85.
[24]*Chemarno v. Pollock*, [1949] 1 D.L.R. 606.
[25]*Browne v. White*, [1947] 2 D.L.R. 309.
[26]See, for example, Ontario, the *Landlord and Tenant Act*, R.S.O. 1980, c. 232, s. 88.

is destruction of a part of the building, the rent would cease until repairs were completed, or if the landlord did not repair, then the lease would be terminated.[27] Some attempts have been made to clarify the law in this area, but only residential tenancies in some provinces would appear to be fully protected, and then only where the premises are totally destroyed.[28] No great pressure for legislative reform has taken place in this regard, probably because most commercial leases specifically provide for this, as do most formal leases for residential tenancies. The only leases that might not cover this eventuality would be short-term leases, and monthly, or weekly periodic tenancies. In each of these situations, only a small amount of money would be in issue if the premises should be destroyed, and the question of the tenant's continued liability for rent would unlikely be a matter which would come before the courts.

Quiet Possession

In return for the payment of rent, the tenant is entitled to possession of the premises undisturbed by any person claiming a right to the property through or under the landlord. This entitlement is in the form of an express or implied covenant by the landlord that the tenant will have *quiet possession* of the leased premises. In the case of a leasehold, the landlord covenants that he has a right to the property that is such that he is entitled to make the lease. He also promises that he will not enter on the premises or interfere with the tenant's possession, except as authorized by law. The covenant extends as well to any activities of the landlord that would be action-

able in nuisance. For example, if the landlord uses neighbouring premises in the same building in such a way that it interferes with the tenants use and enjoyment, the tenant may have a right of action against the landlord for breach of the covenant.

||||||||||||||||||||||||||||||||||||||||||||||||||||||||||||||||||||||||||||||||||||

CASE 30.2
Christin v. Dey (1922), 52 O.L.R. 308.

HODGINS, J.A.:

The extent of the covenant in a lease for quiet enjoyment has been considered in many cases. In 1795, in *Ludwell* v. *Newman*, 6 T.R. 458, the Court held that quiet enjoyment meant "a legal entry and enjoyment without the permission of any other person, which could not have taken place here on account of the prior lease granted to Rogers" (by the defendant). The most important of these cases, according to Mr. Justice Bray in *Williams* v. *Gabriel*, [1906] 1 K.B. 155, is that of *Harrison Ainslie & Co.* v. *Muncaster*, [1891] 2 Q.B. 680, where, at p. 684, Lord Esher says: "The interruption contemplated by the covenant need not necessarily be an interference with the title, but may extend to an interference with the enjoyment."

In *Sanderson* v. *Mayor of Berwick-upon-Tweed* (1884), 13 Q.B.D. 547, at p. 551, Fry, L.J., lays it down that a breach of such a covenant occurs where the "ordinary and lawful enjoyment of the demised land is substantially interfered with by the acts of the lessor, or those lawfully claiming under him."

||||||||||||||||||||||||||||||||||||||||||||||||||||||||||||||||||||||||||||||||||||

Repairs

The obligation to repair is usually set out in the lease, because at common law neither the landlord nor the tenant would be liable to make repairs, unless the lease specifically required one or the other to do so. Where neither party is obliged to make repairs, the landlord has an obligation to warn the tenant at the time the tenancy is

---

[27]*Dunkelman v. Lister*, [1927] 4 D.L.R. 612.
[28]See, for example, Ontario Law Reform Commission, *Report on Landlord and Tenant Law*, 1976, pp. 209-211.

made of any dangers which exist as a result of the non-repair of the premises. However, if the tenant causes any subsequent damage to the property, he must repair it, and he must not deliberately commit waste (such as the demolition of buildings, or the cutting of shade or ornamental trees).[29]

If the premises are leased as furnished, the property must be fit for habitation at the beginning of the tenancy, but at common law, the landlord is under no obligation to maintain the property in that state. Landlord and tenant legislation in many provinces has altered the common law rule, however, and landlords are normally required to maintain the safety of the premises. This is particularly true where provinces have imposed an obligation to repair on the landlord with respect to residential tenancies.[30] The landlord's obligation, even under recent legislation, does not extend to damage caused to the premises by the tenant's deliberate or negligent acts, but only to ordinary wear and tear, or structural defects. Even then, the landlord would only be obliged to repair those defects brought to his attention by the tenant.

Sub-Let and Assignment of Leasehold Interests

Most leases provide for the tenant's right to assign or sub-let leased premises, and unless the lease contains an express prohibition, a tenant may assign or sub-let if he wishes. At common law, the tenant is entitled to assign a lease, as the assignment does not affect the tenant's liability under the lease agreement. The tenant is still liable under the express covenants in the lease. The normal practice for leases is to include a right to assign the lease with the consent of the landlord, and to provide further that the landlord may not unreasonably withhold his consent. A number of provinces have included this change in their landlord and tenant legislation, and where special legislation with respect to residential tenancies is in force, the right to assign or sub-let with the landlord's consent is usually expressly provided.[31]

Taxes and Insurance

Most leases also provide for the payment of municipal taxes and insurance by the tenant, but unless the lease so provides, there is no obligation on the tenant to be concerned with either of these expenses. In the absence of an express covenant to pay taxes, the landlord is usually obliged to cover the cost, but if the tenant pays the taxes, depending upon the province, he may deduct the expenses from the rent payable. Municipal charges assessed for property improvements such as sewer and water lines, sidewalks, or road paving, however, are improvements to the lands, and generally a responsibility of the landlord, regardless of any obligation on the tenant in the lease to pay ordinary municipal taxes.

Insurance may be an obligation on the tenant by an express term in the lease, but apart from an express requirement, there is no obligation on the tenant to insure the premises. Most tenants, if careful and prudent, would at least insure their own chattels, and provide for liability insurance in the event of an injury to a guest on the premises. Landlords similarly insure their buildings to protect themselves from loss

---

[29]*McPherson v. Giles* (1919), 45 O.L.R. 441.
[30]See, for example, Ontario, the *Landlord and Tenant Act*, R.S.O. 1980, c. 232, s. 96(1).

[31]The *Landlord and Tenant Act*, R.S.O. 1980, c. 232, s. 91.

or damage through the negligence of the tenant in possession.

Fixtures

A tenant may bring chattels on leased premises during the currency of a lease, and unless the chattels become a part of the realty, the tenant may remove them on departure. If the chattels have become attached to the realty in the form of improvements to the building, such as walls, plumbing fixtures, or similar permanently attached chattels, they may not be removed on the expiry of the lease. Some fixtures, called *trade fixtures*, may be removed by the tenant, provided that any minor damage to the premises which occurs during removal is repaired. The nature of a fixture is dealt with in some depth in Chapter 27, and it is sufficient to note with respect to the tenant's fixtures, that goods which are normally considered trade fixtures, may be removed, if the tenant does so either on, or immediately after, vacating the premises.

RIGHTS OF A LANDLORD FOR BREACH OF THE LEASE

The rights of a landlord in the event of a breach of the lease depend to some extent on the nature of the breach committed by the tenant. The most common breach by a tenant is the breach of the covenant to pay rent. If the tenant fails to pay rent, the landlord has three remedies available. The first remedy is the right to institute legal proceedings to collect the rent owing. This is known as an *action on the covenant*. The landlord may also *distrain* against the goods of tenants until the rent is paid, or if the rent is not paid, have the goods of the tenant sold to cover the rent owing. The right of distress is very similar to a claim

for lien in the sense that the landlord may seize the chattels of the tenant (subject to certain exceptions) and hold them as security for payment of the rent owing. If it is necessary to sell the goods to cover the arrears of rent, and the proceeds are insufficient to pay the arrears, the landlord may then take action on the covenant against the tenant for any difference in the amount.[32] In some jurisdictions,[33] the right to distrain against the goods of the tenant is no longer applicable to residential tenancies.

A third right which may be exercised by the landlord in the event of non-payment of rent is the right of *re-entry*. Under landlord and tenant legislation, in a number of provinces, the landlord's right to re-enter arises when rent is in arrears for a period of time. On the expiry of the time, the landlord may repossess the premises. The exercise of the right of re-entry has the effect of terminating the tenancy, since the tenant no longer has possession. It should be noted, however, that the right of re-entry in a sense is an alternative to the right of distress, and a landlord may not distrain against the goods, and re-enter at the same time. The act of re-entry terminates the tenancy, and with it the right of distress, consequently, the landlord must distrain first, then later re-enter or choose between the two remedies.

If the tenant's breach is of a covenant or term other than the covenant to pay rent, the landlord may give notice to the tenant to correct the breach (if possible) within a reasonable time, and if the tenant fails to do so, the landlord may take action to regain the premises. The legislation in most provinces provides that the courts may re-

---

[32]*Naylor v. Woods*, [1950] 1 D.L.R. 649.
[33]See, for example, Ontario: the *Landlord and Tenant Act*, R.S.O. 1980, c. 232, s. 86(1).

lieve against forfeiture, and if the matter comes before the courts, the courts may order the tenant to correct the breach, or pay damages to the landlord for the breach of the covenant. A court may also issue an injunction to restrain any further breach by the tenant.[34] A landlord may also have the tenant evicted by court order if the court believes that such an order should be issued. In the case of residential tenancies (in some provinces) the right of re-entry for breach of a covenant is restricted, and the landlord may only regain possession by way of an order of the court. For example, in Ontario, in the case of a residential tenancy, the landlord must not only notify the tenant of a breach (other than non-payment of rent) but give the tenant seven days to correct the matter. If the tenant fails to do so, the landlord may then apply to the courts for an order to have the tenant evicted. The grounds upon which the landlord may evict the tenant at the present time are limited to undue damage, overcrowding the premises, disturbing or interfering with the enjoyment of the premises by the landlord or other tenants, and interfering with the safety or the rights of other tenants.[35]

||||||||||||||||||||||||||||||||||||||||||||||||||||||||||||||||||||||

CASE 30.3
Fuda et al. v. D'Angelo et al. (1974), 2 O.R. (2d) 605.

DONNELLY, J.:

When the defendants made default, four courses were open to the landlords:
(a) they had the right to do nothing to alter the relationship of landlord and tenant and insist on performance of the terms of the lease and sue for rent or damages on the basis that the lease continued in force;

(b) they could elect to terminate the lease retaining the right to sue for rent accrued or for damages to the date of termination;
(c) they could advise the tenants they proposed to relet the premises on the tenants' account and enter into possession on that basis, and
(d) they could elect to terminate the lease but with notice to the defaulting tenants that damages would be claimed on the basis of a present recovery of damages for losing the benefit of the lease for the unexpired term. One element of such damage would be the present value of the unpaid future rent for the unexpired period of the lease less the actual value of the premises for that period: *Highway Properties Ltd. v. Kelly, Douglas & Co. Ltd.*, [1971] S.C.R. 562, 17 D.L.R. (3d) 710, [1972] 2 W.W.R. 28.

||||||||||||||||||||||||||||||||||||||||||||||||||||||||||||||||||||||

RIGHTS OF A TENANT FOR BREACH OF THE LEASE

A tenant is entitled to enforce all covenants made for the tenant's benefit in the lease, and if the landlord fails to comply with the covenants, the tenant may avail himself of three possible remedies. A tenant may bring an action for damages against the landlord if the landlord's actions constitute a breach of the lease. For example, if a landlord wrongfully evicts a tenant from farm property, the tenant may be entitled to damages as compensation for summer fallow work done, crops planted, and the estimated future profits for the term of the lease.[36]

If the interference does not constitute eviction from the premises, the tenant may obtain relief from the courts in the form of an injunction to restrain the landlord from

[34]See, for example, the *Landlord and Tenant Act*, R.S.O. 1980, c. 232, ss. 19(2) and 20.
[35]The *Residential Tenancies Act, 1979*, R.S.O. 1980, c. 452.

[36]*Haack v. Martin*, [1927] 3 D.L.R. 19.

interfering with his or her possession and enjoyment of the property. This remedy might, for example, be brought where the landlord conducts an operation on premises adjacent to the tenant's land which creates a nuisance.

A third remedy is also available to a tenant where the landlord's breach of the lease is such that the interference with the tenant's possession amounts to eviction: the tenant may seek to terminate the lease. For example, in the case of a residential tenancy, the landlord's refusal to repair the building and maintain it in a safe condition would constitute a breach which would entitle the tenant to apply to the courts to have the lease terminated.[37]

TERMINATION

A lease may be terminated in a number of different ways. A lease for a fixed term will terminate when the term ends, or when the landlord and tenant agree to terminate the lease before the date on which it is to expire. Where the parties agree to terminate the lease, the agreement is called a *surrender*, and if the lease is made in writing and under seal, the surrender normally must take the same form.[38] A lease may also terminate if the parties agree to replace the existing lease with a new lease, or if the tenant, at the landlord's request, voluntarily gives up possession to a new tenant, and the new tenant takes possession of the premises.[39]

In the case of a periodic tenancy, a lease may be terminated by the giving of proper *notice to quit*. It should be noted, however, that recent legislation in a number of provinces has limited the right of a landlord to obtain possession on the expiry of a lease, or to give effective notice to quit in the case of residential tenancies. Generally, such legislation limits the landlord's rights to enforce the termination (apart from non-payment for rent) to those cases where the tenant has damaged the premises, or where the landlord requires possession for his own use, or to change the nature of the property. In some provinces, the landlord is obliged to obtain possession through the courts even under these circumstances, if the tenant refuses to deliver up possession.

The breach of a covenant may also give the landlord the right to treat the lease as being at an end. For example, if the tenant is in arrears of payment of rent, the landlord may, by complying with the statute, move into possession of the property and terminate the tenancy.

If the tenant abandons the property during the currency of the lease, the lease is not terminated, but any act of the landlord which would indicate that he has accepted the abandonment as a surrender on the part of the tenant, would constitute termination. For example, if the landlord moved into the premises abandoned by the tenant, or if the landlord leased the premises to another tenant without notice to the original tenant that the premises were relet on his account,[40] the lease would be treated as at an end.

[37]The *Landlord and Tenant Act*, R.S.O. 1980, c. 232, s. 96.
[38]By virtue of the requirements of the *Statute of Frauds* in most provinces. See, for example, Ontario: R.S.O. 1980, c. 481, s. 2.
[39]*Wallis v. Hands*, [1893] 2 Ch. 75.

[40]*Green v. Tress*, [1927] 2 D.L.R. 180.

SUMMARY   The landlord and tenant relationship is a contractual relationship which gives rise to two concurrent interests in land: exclusive possession of the land by the tenant, and a reversion in the landlord. A leasehold is an interest in land for a term, and at the end of the term, possession reverts to the landlord. During the term of the lease, however, the tenant is entitled to exclusive possession, and the tenant may then exercise many of the rights which are possessed by a land-owner.

A lease being contractual in nature may contain express terms which delineate the relationship, and the rights and duties of the parties, but where the lease is silent, some terms may be implied by law. The most common terms or covenants are the covenants to pay rent, repair, quiet enjoyment, pay taxes, and the right to assign or sub-let. Leases for more than three years must be in writing, and be under seal to be enforceable. In addition, the lease or a notice of lease must normally be registered to protect the tenant's interest as against subsequent mortgagees or purchasers without notice.

A failure to perform the covenants in a lease by either party may give rise to an action for damages or injunction, or perhaps permit the injured party to terminate the relationship. The particular rights of the parties, and in particular those of the landlord, have been altered in some provinces by legislation to protect tenants under leases of residential property. These changes have granted tenants greater security of tenure, and have imposed a number of statutory duties on landlords to maintain residential premises in a good state of repair. In most cases, these new laws permit the landlord to repossess residential property only through court order, if the tenant refuses to deliver up possession.

Apart from termination arising out of a breach of the lease, a lease may be terminated automatically at the end of its term, by surrender, abandonment, or by notice to quit in the case of a periodic tenancy. Again, residential tenancies in some provinces may only be terminated for limited reasons, and with the permission of the courts.

DISCUSSION QUESTIONS

1. Describe the legal nature of a "leasehold interest."
2. What is the significance of a "reversion"?
3. Distinguish a "lease" from a "licence." Under what circumstances might a tenant also be a licensee?
4. What is meant by a tenant's right to "quiet enjoyment"?
5. On what basis is the "term" of a lease established?
6. How does "privity of estate" differ from "privity of contract" in the case of a lease? In what way does each affect the rights and duties of a tenant and the assignee of a leasehold estate after the assignee acquires the estate?
7. Explain the difference between a "sub-tenancy" and an assignment of a leasehold interest. What special rights does a sub-tenancy create in the sub-lessor?

8. *In what general way does a residential tenancy differ from a commercial tenancy under the landlord and tenant laws of most provinces?*

9. *Describe the remedies available to a landlord in the event that the tenant fails to pay the agreed rent under a lease.*

10. *Indicate the usual covenants that may be found in most ordinary leases.*

11. *Describe the remedies available to a tenant if the landlord fails to abide by the terms of the lease.*

12. *A carefully drawn commercial lease will usually give the lessor the right to "distrain" for arrears of rent. What does this right mean?*

13. *Distinguish a "tenancy at sufferance" from a "tenancy at will." In what way do they differ from a "periodic tenancy"?*

14. *What procedure must be followed in order to terminate a periodic tenancy? How has this been altered in the case of a residential tenancy in some provinces?*

15. *"Surrender" is a method of bringing a leasehold interest to an end. In what way does it differ from other forms of termination?*

JUDICIAL DECISIONS

Rights of Landlord and Tenant— Rescission of Lease for Innocent Misrepresentation

Klein v. Savon Fabrics Ltd., [1962] O.W.N. 199.

A landlord and tenant entered into a tenancy agreement which provided for a rental payment of $130 per month, with the lease being terminable on one month's notice. The tenant moved into possession, but moved out shortly thereafter when it was discovered that the tenant's goods stored on the premises could not be insured.

The landlord afterwards commenced an action for one month's rent in lieu of notice, and the costs of cleaning the premises.

At trial, the plaintiff's action was dismissed. The case was then appealed by the plaintiff to the Court of Appeal.

SCHROEDER, J.A.:

It was important for the Judge to determine, first, the nature of the tenancy which was brought into being. It is unquestionably true that in the instrument setting out the terms of the lease the parties carried informality very far. It was nevertheless the duty of the Court to endeavour to place a reasonable and a proper construction upon the agreement which the parties had reduced to writing. It is well settled that a demise of property at a monthly or weekly rental affords a presumption of a monthly or weekly tenancy: *Huffell v. Armistead* (1835), 7 C. & P. 56. In *Semi-Ready v. Tew* (1909), 19 O.L.R. 227, Boyd, C., stated, at p. 230.

"In the absence of other controlling circumstances implying a different intention, the payment of monthly rent is deemed to indicate a monthly tenancy."

That proposition is so well settled that it requires no further elaboration. The agreement, on a fair and reasonable construction thereof, does not create a lease for a definite period of one month as contended, but evidences a renting for an indefinite period at a monthly rent of $130. The conclusion is inescapable that the parties intended to create and did enter into a monthly tenancy. If there were any doubt upon that point it would be dispelled by the terms of cl. 2. Clearly, therefore, the plaintiff has established that a monthly tenancy was created, and under the Landlord & Tenant Act, R.S.O. 1960, c. 206, s. 27, a month's notice to quit was required. Such notice not having been given the plaintiff is entitled to succeed and should have judgment against the defendant for the sum of $138 as claimed.

It was argued on behalf of the defendant that the document in question did not set out all terms of the lease and that it was entered into upon a condition that the defendant's goods stored on the premises would be insurable, in that Klein, had falsely and fraudulently represented to the defendant in the course of negotiations that the defendant's goods would be insurable while stored in this building. We are concerned here not with an executory contract, but with an executed contract. The lease, such as it was, was duly executed, the rent for the first month was paid, and possession of the premises had been taken by the defendant. In these circumstances it was not open to the defendant to make a claim for rescission of the written lease unless the alleged condition or warranty was expressed therein, or there was *error in substantialibus*, or fraud. The problem presented for solution must be approached from the standpoint that the contract between the parties has been executed. That being so, no action can be maintained for damages or compensation arising from errors as to quantity or quality of the thing sold or leased except in particular cases not material here, nor unless the sale or leasing has been induced by a fraudulent, as distinguished from an innocent, misrepresentation. The governing authority on that point in Canada is *Redican v. Nesbitt*, [1924] S.C.R. 135, which was followed in *Shortt v. MacLennan*, [1957] O.W.N. 1, and *Dalladas v. Tennikat*, [1958] O.W.N. 169.

In *Angel v. Jay*, [1911] 1 K.B. 666, it was held that a Court of equity would not grant rescission of an executed lease on the ground of an innocent misrepresentation. Darling, J., stated, at p. 671

"On the contrary, one of the cases cited, *Legge v. Croker* (1811), 1 Ball & B. 506, was a case of a lease, and it was there held that a lease deliberately executed cannot be set aside for a misrepresentation which is not wilful. This doctrine has not been confined to cases of conveyances, whether of freeholds or leaseholds; in *Seddon v. North Eastern Salt Co.*, [1905] 1 Ch. 326, it was applied in the case of a sale of shares in a company, and I have come to the conclusion that, there being here an executed contract and no suggestion of fraud, the County Court Judge was wrong in ordering rescission of this lease. That might have been done if the contract had not been executed; but here there had been completion, the plaintiff had gone into possession under the lease, and nothing remained to be done. That being so, on the authority of the cases cited for the appellant, we must come to the conclusion that the County Court Judge was wrong."

The trial Judge made an express finding that the representation alleged had been made, but he also found that it was not false and misleading. Thus, if it was a misrepresentation at all it was an innocent one. On a consideration of the evidence as a whole it is plain that what is alleged by the defendant by way of defence cannot even be regarded as an innocent misrepresentation, since it was not a representation of a fact but a mere expression of opinion which proved to be unfounded. So viewed, it neither affords ground for rescission of the lease nor support for the defendant's counterclaim.

The appeal will be allowed, the judgment at trial set aside, and there will be substituted therefor a judgment in favour of the plaintiffs for $138 and costs with a counsel fee at trial fixed at $25. The defendant's counterclaim will be dismissed with costs. The plaintiffs shall have the costs of the appeal fixed at $25 together with the taxable disbursements.

Requirements for Agreement to Lease— Whether an Exchange of Letters Constitute A Binding Agreement

Re Pattenick and Adams Furniture Co. Ltd., [1970] 2 O.R. 539.
The solicitors for the landlord wrote a letter to the tenant before the expiry of an existing lease, in which it was stated that the landlord would be prepared to renew the lease at a higher rent with several changes in the wording and of the rights of the parties. The tenant accepted the new rent proposed, and stated that the changes in the wording of the lease could be "agreed [to] without any difficulty."

The landlord then received an offer to lease from a third party for a substantially higher rent, and wished the tenant to exercise its right of first refusal. The tenant replied that it had already established a binding lease with the landlord at a lower rental rate by the exchange of the letters. When the matter could not be resolved, the landlord applied to the court for a declaration as to whether the tenant was a party to a lease, or an overholding tenant.

WELLS, C.J.H.C.:

This is a motion brought by one Oscar Pattenick, the owner of certain property in the Town of Parry Sound known there as 63 James St. The motion is for a declaration as to whether or not the tenant Adams Furniture Company Limited was in possession of the property as an overholding tenant without a lease or whether it was holding as one of the parties to an agreement to lease. . . .

Adams Furniture Co. Ltd. had been the tenant under a lease which commenced on July 1, 1964, and which expired on June 30, 1969. This lease was executed under seal by the lessor and the photostatic copies of the document filed before me did not indicate, while it had been signed by Adams Furniture Co. Ltd., whether the corporate seal of the company was attached or not, but this is not, I think, an issue in this matter. During the currency of the lease in the year 1965, Adams Furniture Co. Ltd. drew Mr. Pattenick's attention to the fact that they had been refused access to the rear of the premises by the owner of the adjoining land. Mr. Pattenick had undertaken to provide his tenants with a right of way over this land for the purpose of access. Nothing apparently was done about this and the parties went on paying and receiving rent. Subsequently, on March 18, 1969, Mr. J. D. Norman, acting as a solicitor for Mr. Pattenick, wrote to Adams Furniture Co. Ltd. at their offices, 4205 Cote de Liesse Rd., Montreal 9, Quebec. This letter is of some importance and I will set it out in full:

"NORMAN AND LIPSON
  Barristers & Solicitors
Jack David Norman   3101 Bathurst Street
Barry David Lipson   Toronto 19, Ontario
Samuel Lavine   Telephone: 789-5306
Joel E. Shaw   March 18, 1969.
Harvey I. Joseph

Adams Furniture Co. Limited,
4205 Cote de Liesse Road,
Montreal 9, Quebec.
        Re: Oscar Pattenick, 63 James Street, Parry Sound
Dear Sirs:

We act for Mr. Pattenick who has asked us to send you this letter.

Mr. Pattenick advises us that your lease of the above premises expires May 31st next. If you are not interested in re-renting the property for a further term commencing June 1, 1969, Mr. Pattenick would like to deal with other prospective tenants and he advises us that he has already had serious inquiries from prospective tenants.

Mr. Pattenick would be prepared to give you a new lease for a further term of five years at a rental of $450.00 per month plus tax increases with the same base tax year as in your existing lease and otherwise on the same terms and conditions as in the existing lease, save and except as follows:

(a) Change in wording in the first right of refusal clause.

(b) The right-of-way for access to the rear of the premises is to be by way of a grant of whatever right, title and interest Mr. Pattenick has to this right-of-way without any warranty.

Please be good enough to advise before the end of March whether you are interested in re-renting this property on the above terms. If we do not hear from you by the end of the month, Mr. Pattenick will solicit an offer to lease and will submit it to you in accordance with the first right of refusal provision in the existing lease.

                              Yours truly,
                              'J. D. Norman'
JDN/vj   J. D. Norman"

On March 20, 1969, Mr. W. G. Scott who is the secretary-treasurer of Adams Furniture Co. Ltd. acknowledged receipt of the letter and replied to it as follows:

"Central Offices
5375 Cote de Liesse Road
Montreal 378, P.Q.
20 March 1969

J. D. Norman, Esq.,
Norman & Lipson,
3101 Bathurst Street,
Toronto 19, Ont.

Dear Mr. Norman: OSCAR PATTENICK—PARRY SOUND

We acknowledge and thank you for your letter of 18 March in which you advise that Mr. Oscar Pattenick is willing to enter into an extension of our lease for the premises at 63 James Street, Parry Sound, for a term of five years at a rental of $450 per month plus a tax escalator clause.

We are ready to accept the rental figure of $450 per month and believe that the changes in the wording with respect to right of refusal clause and right-of-way access can be agreed without any difficulty.

Would you forward a draft lease to the attention of the undersigned.

Yours truly,
ADAMS FURNITURE CO. LIMITED
'W. G. Scott'
W. G. Scott Secretary-Treasurer."

At the time the lease was entered into it is apparent that Adams Furniture Co. Ltd. had what is known as a right of first refusal. The paragraph covering it which appears at the end of the lease is as follows:

"It is hereby agreed that the lessee shall have the right of first refusal in the event a better bona fide offer of rental is offered to the lessor at the time of expiration of this lease."

Nothing else occurred until April 14, 1969, when Norman & Lipson, the solicitors for Mr. Pattenick, wrote by registered mail special delivery, to Adams Furniture Co. Ltd. as follows:

"REGISTERED MAIL
SPECIAL DELIVERY

3101 Bathurst Street
Toronto 19, Ontario,
April 14, 1969.

Adams Furniture Co. Limited,
4205 Cote de Liesse Road,
Montreal 9, Quebec.

Re: Oscar Pattenick,
63 James St., Parry Sound.

Dear Sirs:

Shortly after we sent you our letter of March 18, Mr. Pattenick was advised by Kent Drugs Limited that it would be submitting an Offer to Lease, a true copy of which is enclosed herewith. Your existing Lease gives you "the right of first refusal in the event a better bona fide offer of rental is offered to the lessor at the time of expiration of this lease.''

Please advise whether you wish to exercise this right of first refusal with respect to the Offer of Kent Drugs Ltd.

Your existing Lease does not specify a time limit for the exercise of your first right of refusal. Mr. Pattenick suggests that ten days is a reasonable time limit and will therefore require a reply from you by April 25th next.

> Yours very truly,
> 'J. D. Norman'
> J. D. Norman''

Attached to this letter was a copy of an offer to lease signed by Kent Drugs Limited which provided for a rent of $625 a month which was considerably larger than the $400 a month which was provided for in the lease to which I have already alluded made in June 1964. Attached to this letter was also a copy of a draft lease between Pattenick and Kent Drugs Ltd. which ran for a period of five years from June 1, 1969, and ending on May 31, 1974. On receipt of this letter on April 18th Mr. Scott, secretary-treasurer of the respondent company, wrote to Mr. Norman as follows:

REGISTERED

> "Central Offices
> 5375 Cote de Liesse Road
> Montreal 378, P.Q.
> 18 April 1969

> J. D. Norman, Esq.,
> Norman and Lipson
> 3101 Bathurst Street
> Toronto 19, Ont.

> Dear Mr. Norman: OSCAR PATTENICK—PARRY SOUND

> We are somewhat at a loss to understand your letter of 14 April with respect to the renewal of our lease for premises in Parry Sound.

> We thought your letter of 18 March clearly confirmed the offer made by Mr. Pattenick to us and we believed that our letter to you of 20 March quite clearly accepted this offer.

> Yours truly,
> ADAMS FURNITURE CO. LIMITED
> 'W. G. Scott'
> W. G. Scott
> Secretary-Treasurer''

. . . . .

It is therefore apparent that the position of the parties is that as far as Adams Furniture Co. Ltd. is concerned they accepted the offer made to them to renew the lease between themselves and Mr. Pattenick in accordance with Mr. Norman's letter of March 18th, which he wrote as Mr. Pattenick's solicitor and which was acknowledged by Mr. Scott of the respondent company on March 20, 1969.

The issue between the parties therefore is whether the exchange of letters of March 18 and 20, 1969, constituted a binding agreement to lease the premises. In other words, was the letter of March 18, 1969, an offer to lease and the letter of March 20th an acceptance of that offer. The form of the letter of March 18th is of some importance. It is styled "Re Oscar Pattenick and 63 James Street, Parry Sound". The writer, who is a solicitor, stated that he and his partners acted for Mr. Pattenick who had asked that this letter be sent. He pointed out that, if they were not interested in renewing the lease of the property, Mr. Pattenick was anxious to get other tenants. Then, specifically, it is stated that "Mr. Pattenick would be prepared to give you a new lease for a further term of five years at a rental of $450.00 per month plus tax increases with the same base tax year as in your existing lease and otherwise on the same terms and conditions as in the existing lease, save and except as follows:" and there were two conditions—one was in the change of wording in the first right of refusal clause which would obviously be necessary and the other was with respect to the right of way for access to the rear of the premises which was apparently a matter in dispute between Mr. Pattenick and the adjoining landowner and was to be given by way of grant subject to whatever right, title and interest Mr. Pattenick had to the right of way without any warranty as to its sufficiency. A time limit for the acceptance of this offer was set being before the end of March. To this letter Adams Furniture Co. Ltd., through its secretary-treasurer, replied as follows:

"We are ready to accept the rental figure of $450. per month and believe that the changes in the wording with respect to right of refusal clause and right-of-way access can be agreed without any difficulty." and they asked for the submission of a draft lease.

All these facts which have been agreed on were submitted to the Court with a request that the Court rule on the same. The question is whether the letter of March 20th was an acceptance of the offer made in the letter of March 18th.

There have been many cases dealing with this problem under a variety of circumstances. One of these cases is the case of *Crossley v. Maycock* (1874), L.R. 18 Eq. 180, heard in 1874 before Sir George Jessel, M.R., and it is to be noted that Mr. Fry with Mr. Jolliffe appeared for the applicants. The matter was brought on as a suit by the vendors of land for specific performance of what was alleged to be a contract. Sir George Jessel, M.R. dealt with the matter in a short judgment as follows at pp. 181-2:

"The only question in this case is, what is the true construction of the letter of the Plaintiffs of the 27th of October, 1873. The Defendants had written to the Plaintiffs, offering to purchase the land in question, to which the Plaintiffs replied as follows:—

" 'We are in receipt of your note offering £2 per yard for the plot of land, which offer we accept, and now hand you two copies of conditions of sale, which we have signed; we will thank you to sign same, and return one of the copies to us.'

"The principle which governs these cases is plain. If there is a simple acceptance of an offer to purchase, accompanied by a statement that the acceptor desires that the arrangement should be put into so more formal terms, the mere reference to such a proposal will not prevent the Court from enforcing the final agreement so arrived at. But if the agreement is made subject to certain conditions then specified or to be specified by the party making it, or by his solicitor, then, until those conditions are accepted, there is no final agreement such as the Court will enforce.

"Here the allegation is that the agreement was subject to certain conditions of sale, which were very special, and such as no purchaser would be bound to accept under an open contract. I am of opinion that the acceptance was only conditional, and that there was no final contract."

Subsequently a similar problem, this time concerning a lease, was dealt with in the case of *Bonnewell v. Jenkins* (1878), L.R. 8 Ch. D. 70. It is interesting to note that by this time Mr. Fry had become a Judge of the Chancery Division of the High Court. The pertinent facts may be briefly stated. The plaintiff had written an agent of the defendant as follows [headnote]:

" 'In reference to Mr. *Jenkins'* premises in *Fleet Street*, I have gone into the matter, and, considering that the rent was very considerably raised last year when the lease was granted, I think £800 for the lease, fixtures, fittings, &c., excluding goodwill, is about the price I should be willing to give. Possession to be given me within fourteen days from date, and all outgoings paid by vendors up to Lady Day next. This offer is made subject to the conditions of the lease being modified to my solicitor's satisfaction, which I am informed can be done. Kindly let me hear from you as soon as possible.' "

At p. 71, Fry, J., as he then was, dealing with these facts said:

"It is said that the statement, 'We are instructed to accept your offer of £800 for these premises,' is an acceptance only of one of several terms contained in the letter of the 26th of February. Now, in my view, the true role for construing an instrument is to consider what the writer must have conceived that the reader would understand from it. What, then, in this case, would Mr. *Bousfield* conceive that Mr. *Bonnewell* would understand to be the effect of his letter? After having enumerated all the terms which constituted his proposal, he speaks of the whole as constituting one offer, because he says, 'This offer is made subject to,' &c. Mr. *Bonnewell's* conception, therefore, was that he had made one offer, and one offer only, and when Mr. *Bousfield* replies that he is 'instructed to accept your offer of £800 for these premises,' I think he is referring to the offer made in that letter of the 26th of February, describing it by reference to its most material term, namely, the amount of money to be paid for the premises. I think, therefore, that he intended, and must be deemed to have intended, to accept in an unqualified manner the offer contained in the letter of the 26th of February. No doubt that is followed by this statement: 'We have asked Mr. *Jenkins'* solicitor to prepare contract.' Now if the matter were not covered by decision, it is very probable that I should feel myself drawn to the conclusion that wherever there is a reference to a future contract the letters themselves do not constitute a contract, and for this very obvious reason, that a reference to a contract as a future thing seems to negative the notion of the existence of a contract as a present thing. But it is too late for that argument to be used before me successfully, when a long series of cases has established this proposition, that the mere reference to a future contract is not enough to negative the existence of a present one; and that principle has been very clearly expressed by the present Master of the Rolls in the case of *Crossley v. Maycock*, Law Rep. 18 Eq. 180, which, as far as I know, is the last case upon the subject. His Lordship there says: 'The principle which governs these cases is plain. If there is a simple acceptance of an offer to purchase, accompanied by a statement that the acceptor desires that the arrangement should be put into some more formal terms, the mere reference to such a proposal will not prevent the Court from enforcing the final agreement so arrived at. But if the agreement is made subject to certain conditions then specified or to be specified by the party making it, or by his solicitor, then until those conditions are accepted there is no final agreement such as the Court will enforce.' "

Taking the letters which passed between the parties prior to the lessor's announcement that he wanted to rent it to someone else or let the lessees have it for the larger rental, *i.e.*, Mr. Norman's letter, the solicitor for Mr. Pattenick, to Adams Furniture Co. Ltd. of March 18, 1969, and the letter from Mr. Scott as an officer of the respondent company, Adams Furniture Co. Ltd., it is to be observed that the offer included a new lease for a further term of five years at a rental of $450 per month plus tax increases with the same base tax year as the existing lease and likewise on the same terms and conditions as in the existing lease save (a) a change in the wording of the first right of refusal clause and (b) the right of way access to the rear of the premises in which it was proposed to include whatever interest or title Mr. Pattenick had without any warranty. In reply, Adams Furniture Co. Ltd., through Mr. Scott, confirmed the extension of the lease at the named premises, *i.e.*, 63 James St., Parry Sound, for a term of five years at a rental of $450 a month plus tax escalator clause which had been in the prior lease and it was intimated that Adams Furniture Co. Ltd. was willing to accept the rental figure of $450 and it was agreed that the right of refusal clause and right of way access could be agreed without any difficulty and it was asked that a draft lease be forwarded. In my opinion the matter of the right of way and a change in right of refusal clauses were not conditions predating a new lease but matters about which the lessee was not taking exception.

E. K. Williams, *Canadian Law of Landlord and Tenant*, 3rd ed., p. 68, sets out the requirements of a valid agreement for lease as follows:

"Article 13. To be valid, an agreement for a lease must show (1) the parties, (2) a description of the premises to be demised, (3) the commencement, and (4) duration of the term, (5) the rent, if any, and (6) all the material terms of the contract not being matters incident to the relation of landlord and tenant, including any covenants or conditions, exceptions or reservations."

The only matters which were not covered were the matter of right of first refusal which was certainly not objected to and the matter of the right of way. Previous correspondence between the parties which has been placed in the material before me consists of a letter from Adams Furniture Co. Ltd. to Mr. Pattenick pointing out that he had agreed to transfer a right of way to them and he was asked to make it available. Mr. Pattenick replied to this saying that the next-door neighbour, Ying, objected to Adams Furniture Co. Ltd. parking their truck on his property. The landlord pointed out that the front door was wide enough to move the largest pieces of furniture in and out and it was on this note that the matter was allowed to stand from 1965 until the offer for renewal on March 18, 1969. It was obviously a very minor point in the dealings between the parties and, in my opinion, the two letters when read together comply with the requirements of a valid lease as set out in Williams.

Under these circumstances, because of the view I take, I give judgment for the respondent and there will in consequence be a declaration that there is a valid agreement of lease between Oscar Pattenick and Adams Furniture Co. Ltd. for the premises in question situate at 63 James St., Parry Sound, Ontario, and that the appellant Pattenick be ordered to furnish a draft of lease to the applicant pursuant to the letter of acceptance of March 20, 1969, signed over the signature of the secretary-treasurer of the respondent company, W. G. Scott, and addressed to Mr. J. D. Norman, the agent and solicitor for Oscar Pattenick.

CASE PROBLEMS FOR DISCUSSION

Case 1

The Washa-Matic Company carries on business as the owner of coin-operated washing-machines, and entered into an agreement with "108 Suite Apartments" to provide washing-machines for use by tenants of the apartment building.

The agreement was entitled "lease agreement," and provided that the landlord "demise and lease the laundry room on the ground floor of the building to the tenant for a monthly rental equal to $1 per machine installed." The agreement was drawn for a five-year term, and provided for free access to the room by all tenants. The agreement also allowed employees of Washa-Matic the right of access to the premises "at all reasonable times" to repair or service the machines.

Some time after the machines were installed, the owner of the building sold the premises to a new owner, and the new owner requested Washa-Matic to remove the washing-machines. Washa-Matic refused, and argued that it was the lessee of the laundry room under the lease agreement.

The new owner removed the washing-machines owned by Washa-Matic, and installed new equipment. Washa-Matic Company then brought an action against 108 Suite Apartments for damages for breach of the lease, and for lost profits.

Discuss the legal issues raised in this case, and render a decision.

Case 2

The Youngs leased an apartment suite from Broughton Rd. Apartments for a one-year term, commencing July 1st. The Youngs were particularly attracted by the location of the apartment building, since it was a long, low building of Tudor design, and was surrounded by rather spacious grounds. The grounds were important to them because they required a place where their two-year-old child might have a safe place to play.

A few weeks after the tenants moved into their apartment, the owner of the building decided to remove the roof of the building, and replace it with new roofing boards and shingles. The noise of the construction work, which was carried on from approximately 8:00 a.m. to 4:00 p.m., interfered with the normal sleeping hours of Mr. Young, who worked a second shift as a night security guard at a nearby industrial plant. It also interfered with their child's customary afternoon nap.

In addition to the noise of the construction, the Youngs discovered that another tenant in the building owned a large pet snake, which was permitted to roam at will over the lawns of the property.

The Youngs protested to the landlord that the noise of the roof repairs interfered with Mr. Youngs' sleep, and the presence of the snake made the use of the grounds impossible, since they both feared the reptile, even though it was of a harmless species.

When the landlord refused to limit the construction, and failed to control the snake, the Youngs moved from the apartment. They had been in possession for less than two weeks. The landlord then brought an action to recover apartment rent and other expenses which were alleged to be owing as a result of the breach of the lease by the tenants.

Discuss the arguments which the defendants might raise in this action, and determine the issues which the court must deal with before a judgement might be given. Render a decision.

Case 3

Bingham leased a small shop from Wright under a tenancy agreement which provided for a three-year term at a monthly rental of $300 per month. The lease did not contain an option to renew, but following the expiry of the lease on October 31, 1976, Bingham continued to pay the monthly rental of $300 to Wright.

The term of the tenancy was never discussed between the parties, nor was the lease arrangement discussed until June, 1980, when Wright gave Bingham a written notice which read: "I have sold the property in which you presently occupy space, and the purchaser will require vacant possession on December 31, 1980. This letter gives you written notice to vacate in six months' time."

In response, Bingham wrote Wright, and advised him that he was in possession under a lease which did not expire until October 31, 1981, and that the notice given did not apply to his present tenancy.

Wright gave Bingham a second written notice on October 25, 1980, demanding vacant possession of the premises by November 30, 1980.

When Bingham refused to vacate the shop, Wright brought an action for a writ of possession.

Outline the arguments that might be raised by the parties in this case, and render a decision.

Case 4

Quinn leased a small retail shop from Chaplin for the purpose of establishing a fruit and vegetable market. The lease was drawn for a three-year term, commencing May 1, 1980, and provided for a total rental of $18 000, payable $500 per month. The first and last month's rent were due on May 1st. Quinn paid the two months' rent, and moved into possession.

A month later, and a few days' after the rent for the month was due, Chaplin discovered that Quinn had sold the business to Rizzoto. The sale was contrary to the terms of the lease, which permitted assignment of the lease only on consent. Chaplin immediately went to the shop, and when Rizzoto arrived, Chaplin told him that he was not willing to have anyone but Quinn operate a shop on the premises. Chaplin advised Rizzoto that Quinn was in breach of the lease by assigning it without his consent, and suggested that Rizzoto seek out Quinn to get his money back.

Chaplin then contacted a licensed bailiff, and gave him authority to collect the rent owing. The sheriff went to the store and made an inventory of the stock and ʟquipment which he valued at $5 000 and $6 000 respectively. He then changed the locks on the door, and posted a notice on the premises which informed the public that the landlord had taken possession for non-payment of rent. The next day, he notified Quinn and Rizzoto that he had distrained the chattels in the shop on behalf of the landlord. He advised the two parties that they had five days to redeem the chattels by payment of the arrears of rent, otherwise the chattels would be sold. Quinn and Rizzoto made no attempt to pay the rent.

The bailiff later attempted to sell the business, but was unsuccessful, and eventually his services were terminated by Chaplin.

Chaplin did not attempt to rent the premises, and retained the stock and equipment. In December, 1980, he brought an action against Quinn for damages for breach of the lease.

Discuss the particular issues that are raised by this case, and indicate the arguments that the parties might present with respect to each. Render a decision.

CHAPTER 31

Real Estate Transactions

INTRODUCTION

The purchase of real property, whether it involves a house and lot, cottage property, or business premises, has, in recent years, become a complex transaction for which the advice and services of a member of the legal profession is not only desirable, but virtually a necessity. In one sense, the transaction has now turned full circle. In the past, the transfer of property was characterized by much formality and ritual, and required the services of a person not only literate, but knowledgeable of the process of transfer. Over the years, the process has remained so in England, but in North America, by the 19th century and early 20th century, the transaction had acquired a large degree of informality, particularly in rural areas. During this period of time, in many localities, deeds were drawn by persons with only a limited knowledge of the formalities required to transfer title. Often the transaction consisted of little more than the preparation and delivery of a deed to the property, with no thought given to the examination of the vendor's title to the property, or the accuracy of the boundaries of the land transferred.

The informality of real estate transactions during this period may be easily explained. In rural North America, land was relatively inexpensive, and where a sale of property did occur, the parties were generally familiar with the land and its past owners. All dealings with the property were frequently common knowledge to the community at large, and the boundaries of the lands were usually settled and known. It was also a simpler age, when government planning and interference with the use of property was virtually non-existent. By the middle of the 20th century, however, the introduction of planning legislation and land use control gradually increased the complexity of real estate transactions to the point where, today, expert assistance is usually essential to properly carry out the necessary searches, clearances, and formalities required to effect the transfer of a good title to a purchaser.

In England, much formality has always been associated with the transfer of an interest in property, due in part to the value of land, and in part to the importance attached to its ownership. It should be noted, however, that during the Middle Ages, land ownership, and land occupation were two distinctly different matters. Most of the agricultural land was occupied by persons who farmed the land under *unfree tenure*, usually as *villeins*. These were persons who were virtually tied to the land, with few rights, and recourse only to the early manor courts to settle their disputes. The lord of the manor held the legal estate in land, either under some form of crown grant, or *in fee simple*. The procedure relating to the

transfer of this latter estate was the forerunner of the modern real estate transaction.

The sale of freehold land in England was originally characterized by a formal ceremony, without a written conveyance. The ceremony known as *livery of seisin* could take one of two forms: *livery in law* or *livery in deed*. Livery in law simply involved the owner of the freehold, in the presence of witnesses, pointing to the land and stating to the intended recipient that it was his intention to give him the particular property for himself and his heirs. The transfer would be complete when the party would enter into possession of the land.[1]

Livery in deed followed a slightly different pattern, which required an act (or deed) on the part of the owner of the land. The event was usually ceremonial and symbolic, with the owner, in the presence of witnesses, delivering to the intended recipient some element of property associated with the land itself, as well as providing vacant possession of the property for the new owner. The element of property was usually a branch or twig taken from a tree on the property, a ring or hasp from the door of a building, or some other item which could be placed in the hands of the recipient. Even a rock or lump of earth was sometimes delivered to symbolize the transfer of the property. This act was always accompanied by the expression of the owner's intent to transfer the property to the new party, and the subsequent departure of the owner from the land, leaving the new party in exclusive possession. The proce-

[1]Osborn, P.G., *The Concise Law Dictionary* 4th ed. Sweet & Maxwell Ltd., London, 1954, p. 206.

dure was essentially the act of the person seised of possession of the land delivering possession to another.[2]

While the delivery of the twig or lump of earth was symbolic, and an expression of the vendor's intention to transfer the property, the presence of the witnesses, and the subsequent departure by the vendor were essential to the transfer of the interest to the purchaser. The witnesses were important because they would be available later to confirm that the transfer of the property had taken place, and the departure of the vendor (as attested to by the witnesses) was necessary to establish the purchaser in exclusive possession of the land. The departure of the grantor completed the livery of seisin.

Gradually, documentary evidence of the transaction also became a part of the ceremony, first in the form of a written record of the ceremony itself, and secondly, as a written statement of the transaction in which the *grantor* described the property and the *grantee* to whom the property was delivered, accompanied by the expression of the intention to transfer and deliver up the land. The written document gradually assumed a greater significance in the ceremony, and eventually became an important part of the transfer itself.

After the Norman Conquest, the use of written evidence of livery of seisin became more common. The form of the written document took on a number of identifiable characteristics, and two distinct forms. One form was patterned after the original royal grants or writs, and the other was patterned after a form of indenture, which referred to the parties, outlined the transfer of the property, and set out the grantor's intentions to be bound by the transaction. Modern deeds stemmed from a blending of these two forms, and slowly evolved as a result of early conveyancers' use of standardized language to describe the livery of seisin in the documents.

Eventually, the written document became not only evidence of the intention of the grantor to deliver the interest in the land to the grantee, but also the embodiment of the ceremonial aspects of delivery. The transition period, however, was long, and it was not until late in the 16th century that the document itself superseded the livery of seisin in the form of symbolic delivery of vacant possession in a ceremonial transfer. As the forms of the conveyancers became more standardized, so too, did the ceremonial aspects associated with the execution of the conveyance. The earlier practice of holding the livery of seisin in the presence of witnesses gradually became translated into the execution of the documents in the presence of witnesses, with the witnesses ascribing their names to the document in order to attest to the execution of the conveyance in their presence.

The execution of the document under seal has a long history in connection with the transfer of land. After the Norman Conquest, the practice of affixing a seal as a means of execution became a common method used by grantors to evidence their intention to be bound by the covenants in the conveyance. Literate persons would sign their names as well.

For many years, the written document was used as a symbolic element in the ceremony by a practice which required the grantor in the presence of the wit-

---

[2]The significance of the ceremonial aspects associated with the transfer of property are described in Holdsworth, W.S., *A History of English Law*, 3rd ed., vol. 3, Methuen & Co. Ltd., London, 1923, pp. 222-225.

nesses to sign, seal, and deliver the deed to the grantee at the property site. Gradually, this too, changed, as the written document assumed greater importance, and the ceremonial aspects became a mere formality. Eventually, the written document became the essential element of the transfer of the title to property, but not to the total exclusion of the ceremonial component. A deed, even today, in those provinces which call for registration under the Registry System, must be "signed, sealed, and delivered" to transfer the title to the property. The role of witnesses (although not absolutely essential at common law) remains, since the execution of the document by the grantor must be in the presence of a witness, and the witness must, by a sworn affidavit, attest to the fact to enable the grantee to register the deed.[3] It should be noted, however, that under the Land Titles System, the conveyance need not be under seal, but the document must be executed in the presence of a witness.[4] The formality of delivery to the grantee also remains as an essential act before the interest in the land passes.[5] The modern real estate transaction, therefore, is concluded by a ceremony which includes some remnants of the ancient livery of seisin, in spite of continuing efforts to streamline the process.

MODERN REAL ESTATE TRANSACTIONS

The purchase and sale of real property takes place with much greater frequency at present than it did in the past. Until very recently, property (and in particular agricultural lands) often remained in the hands of families for many generations, but with the mobility that developed in the 20th century as a result of technological advances, this is not so today. Current employment and business practices often require persons to move regularly, and as a result, residential properties may change hands every few years. This change in life-style has created a need for the services of a large number of persons with expertise in the negotiation and completion of land transactions. Some of these experts, such as land surveyors and members of the legal profession, have long been associated with this type of activity, but more recently others, such as real estate agents, property appraisers and, in some cases, public accountants, now play an important role in the purchase and sale of property.

The Role of the Real Estate Agent

The complexity of the modern real estate transaction virtually obliges the vendor and purchaser to obtain the services of professionals in order to transfer the property interest. For example, some services, such as those of the real estate agent, are often essential to initiate the transaction. Most property owners rarely have the time to search for a prospective purchaser if they should desire to sell their property, and consequently, the successful sale is often dependent upon the efforts of persons whose expertise lies in the area of seeking out interested buyers, and bringing such parties into a contractual relationship with the property owner.

---

[3]This is requested by statute in most provinces. See, for example, the *Registry Act*, R.S.O. 1980, c. 445, s. 25.
[4]See, for example, the *Land Titles Act*, R.S.O. 1980, c. 230, ss. 88 and 89.
[5]It should be noted, however, that under the Land

Title System registration of the transfer is necessary to vest the title in the grantee: see the *Land Titles Act*, R.S.O. 1980, c. 230, ss. 90 and 91.

This, in essence, is the role of the real estate agent.

A real estate agent (or "broker," as he is sometimes called) is a particular type of agent who (except in special circumstances) normally acts for the vendor of the property. The relationship between the property owner and the real estate agent is usually established by a contract between the two which is called a *listing agreement*. Under the terms of this agreement, the agent agrees to seek out prospective buyers for the owner, and bring the two parties together in contract. In return for this service, the property owner usually agrees to pay the agent a *commission* (based upon a percentage of the sale price, or a fixed sum) for his services if a sale is negotiated.

The services which a real estate agent is expected to provide under a typical listing agreement are as follows:

(1) inspect and value the property or, where an expert opinion as to the value is required, arrange to have an evaluation made by a professional appraiser;

(2) actively seek out prospective purchasers of the property by way of advertisement (paid for at the agent's expense) by personal contact, and in some cases, by way of notification to other agents of the availability of the property for sale;

(3) arrange to have prospective purchasers inspect the property, and advise the purchasers of the vendor's terms of sale;

(4) prepare a written offer to purchase for execution by the prospective purchaser, and to deliver it to the owner for consideration;

(5) in extremely rare cases, execute the purchase agreement on behalf of the owner under a grant of express authority (a power of attorney); and

(6) hold all deposits paid by the prospective purchaser in trust pending the completion or termination of the transaction, and either pay the funds over to the vendor on completion of the sale, or return the money to the prospective purchaser, if the offer is rejected by the vendor.

It is important to note that the real estate agent, under a listing agreement, is expected to act at all times in the best interests of the vendor who has engaged him to sell the property. The rules of law pertaining to agency (subject to a few minor exceptions) generally apply to the relationship. The agent is not a "middleman" who is used simply to bring the parties together, but the agent of the vendor.[6] For example, a real estate agent must never act for both parties in a transaction without the express consent of both (a rare situation) and, while engaged by the owner of the property as his principal, must never attempt to obtain a benefit for the purchaser which would be to the vendor's detriment. If the agent should attempt to obtain a benefit for the purchaser which is detrimental to the agent's principal, the agent would not only be liable for the amount of the loss, but would also not be entitled to claim a commission from the vendor on the sale. This would arise from the fact that he would be in breach of his duty to his client.[7]

Assuming that the real estate agent brings together a willing vendor and pur-

---

[6]See, for example, *D'Atri v. Chilcott* (1975), 55 D.L.R. (3d) 30; *Len Pugh Real Estate Ltd. v. Ronvic Construction Co. Ltd.* (1973), 41 D.L.R. (3d) 48.

[7]*Len Pugh Real Estate Ltd. v. Ronvic Construction Co. Ltd.* (1973), 41 D.L.R. (3d) 48.

chaser, his duties are generally completed when the written offer, which he draws, and which the purchaser signs, is accepted by the vendor. At that time, the parties are bound in contract for the purchase and sale of the property that is the subject-matter of the agreement. The contract, however, only establishes the contractual relationship, and does not effect a transfer of the title to the purchaser, as the parties must both carry out a number of duties under the agreement before the title documents change hands. In addition, the offer to purchase usually provides the purchaser with a period of time in which he may make a number of searches and determinations to satisfy himself that the title to the property is in order.

||||||||||||||||||||||||||||||||||||||||||||||||||||||||||||||||||||||

CASE 31.1

D'Atri v. Chilcott (1975), 55 D.L.R. (3d) 30.

GALLIGAN, J.:

I think therefore that it is clear from the authorities that the following principles are applicable to this case:

1. That the relationship between a real estate agent and the person who has retained him to sell his property is a fiduciary and confidential one;
2. that there is a duty upon such an agent to make full disclosure of all facts within the knowledge of the agent which might affect the value of the property;
3. that not only must the price paid be adequate but the transaction must be a righteous one and the price obtained must be as advantageous to the principal as any other price that the agent could, by the exercise of diligence on his principal's behalf, have obtained from a third person, and
4. that the onus is upon the agent to prove that those duties have been fully complied with.

||||||||||||||||||||||||||||||||||||||||||||||||||||||||||||||||||||||

Appraisal

Property value is generally determined by the real estate agent at the time that the vendor enters into a listing agreement. The valuation of a residential property is usually well within the expertise of the ordinary real estate agent, but in the case of a commercial or industrial property, the services of a professional property appraiser are usually obtained in order to fix a value for sale purposes. Appraisers are frequently engaged by purchasers as well, especially for commercial or industrial purchases. The appraisal, from the purchaser's point of view, is important for two reasons:

(1) The appraisal provides the purchaser with an expert opinion as to the value of the property, and provides some guidance in the negotiation of a price.
(2) The appraisal will provide the purchaser with a general estimate of the amount of financing that might be obtained from a lending institution to assist in the financing of the purchase, since most lending institutions will fix their mortgage principal amount as a percentage of the appraised value of the property.

Unlike the real estate agent, a property appraiser charges a fixed fee for appraisal services. This service usually consists of an examination of the property, and the formulation of an opinion as to its market value based upon a number of factors, the most important being the condition of the building, the value of the land, the zoning of the property, the present rate of return (in the form of rents, etc.), the potential for development, and the known market value of similar properties. The ultimate value placed on the given property depends a great deal upon the expertise of the appraiser, but the report is particularly useful for the purchaser in the determination of the purchase price to include in the offer.

Offer to Purchase

The offer to purchase is only an offer until such time as the vendor accepts it. At that point, the agreement becomes a binding contract. Nevertheless, the usual offer to purchase generally contains a number of provisions that, if unsatisfied by the vendor, render the agreement null and void at the option of the purchaser. For example, a standard form of an offer to purchase usually provides that the purchaser will have a period of time following the acceptance of the offer by the vendor in which to examine the title to the property at his own expense. If any valid objection to the vendor's title is raised within that time that the vendor is unable or unwilling to correct, the agreement will then become null and void, and any deposit paid by the purchaser must be refunded. The right to rescind the agreement may also be available to the purchaser. This may arise, for example, where the purchaser discovers that the vendor does not have title to all the lands which he has agreed to sell. This latter discrepancy is frequently determined by way of a survey of the property, and a comparison of the surveyor's description of the property with the description of the land contained in the vendor's deed.

Other provisions in the offer to purchase that the purchaser is given time to confirm usually relate to the zoning of the property, the existence of special rights attached to the land, the suitability of the building or land for a specific purpose or use, and the confirmation of the ownership of chattels and fixtures sold with the property.

Most properties are unique, and the circumstances which surround the negotiation of the purchase agreement consequently reflect the particular concerns of each of the parties. Thus, as a general rule, the purchase agreement for each transaction is as unique as the property itself. For this reason, both the purchaser and the vendor normally seek the services and advice of experts other than the real estate agent before the agreement is executed. As a result, real estate contracts frequently include additional clauses, conditions, and assurances which must be satisfied before the transaction may be finalized, and the title transferred. Examples of these clauses include *conditions precedent* with respect to financing, the sale of some other property owned by the purchaser; tests made to determine the quality and quantity of water supply (if in a rural area); the acquisition of special licences for the use of the property in a particular fashion; the right to sever the property from a larger parcel under planning legislation; the successful application for a change in the zoning of the lands, or the issue of a building permit to erect a particular type of structure on the lot.

All of the conditions and terms of the agreement must be complied with in a real estate transaction, and the failure on the part of either party to fully perform the agreement would entitle the injured party to bring to terminate the agreement, or bring an action for either specific performance, or for damages. To satisfy themselves that the terms of the agreement are complied with, and to carry out their own duties and responsibilities, most parties to real estate transactions engage the services of legal experts, either before the offer is signed, or during the course of the transaction.

Survey

While an appraisal of the property is frequently obtained by a prospective pur-

Chapter 31 Real Estate Transactions 667

chaser before the purchase agreement is entered into, a survey is not usually obtained until after the parties have signed the contract. The reason for this procedural difference is due to the nature of the transaction. Most purchase agreements provide that the vendor must have a good title to the lands described in the agreement, and a survey is used to determine if the vendor's land as described in his deed actually coincides with the boundaries and area of land which the vendor claims to possess.

Surveys are prepared by persons trained and licensed to perform the service pursuant to provincial legislation. Statutes govern not only the procedure for the conduct and preparation of surveys, but the licensing of persons who may perform the work. One statute usually governs the technical aspects of survey work, and another, the training and licensing of the profession.

The importance of obtaining a survey (from the purchaser's point of view) is that it will uncover any encroachments on the vendor's property by adjoining property owners, and any easements or rights of way which might affect the land. It will also establish the accuracy of the boundaries of the property as described in the deed. This will not only be determined by the surveyor from the vendor's title, but by "ground reference," because the surveyor generally marks the boundaries of the property by driving steel bars or pins into the ground at each of the corners of the parcel of land. In this fashion, the legal description of the property is translated into ground area for the purchaser to examine.

If the survey reveals a boundary discrepancy, the vendor is usually obliged to have the discrepancy corrected in order that the purchaser will receive the amount of land described in the purchase agree-ment. If the discrepancy is significant, and the vendor cannot correct the title, the purchaser may agree to take the property, but with some *abatement* of the purchase price to compensate for the deficiency. However, if the difference should be substantial, the purchaser would be in a position to avoid the transaction. In this regard, the survey is used by the purchaser's solicitor to assess the vendor's title to the property, and to determine the vendor's right to the property described in the agreement.

||||||||||||||||||||||||||||||||||||||||||||||||||||||||||||||||||||||||||||||||

CASE 31.2
Wilson Lumber Co. v. Simpson (1910), 22 O.L.R. 452.

MEREDITH, C.J.:

The defendant acted in good faith in describing the lot as having a depth of 110 feet more or less, and he was led into that error from the lot having been assessed and described in the assessment notices which he received as of that depth.

The plaintiffs claim that they are entitled to specific performance, with compensation for the deficiency in depth of the lot, which they say should be fixed at $1,500; and the defendant is willing to carry out the agreement, but disputes the right to compensation.

I was not referred to nor have I found any reported English or Canadian case in which, where, as in this case, in the description of the land which was the subject of the contract its depth was stated to be greater than its actual depth, but that statement was qualified by the words "more or less," it was held that the purchaser was entitled to enforce the contract and to claim a reduction of the purchase-price sufficient to compensate him for the deficiency.

. . . . .

In the earlier patents from the Crown it was usual to add to the description by number of the lot granted a statement that it contained by admeasurement a stated number of acres more or less, and in numberless conveyances and contracts of sale lots have been similarly described, and, so far as I am aware, it has never been supposed that the statement as to quantity amounted to a representation entitling the purchaser, in the case of a contract of sale, to compensation for any deficiency, if the lot contained less land than the stated quantity.

Similarly, I should be of opinion that where, in addition to the description of such a lot, there was added a statement as to the length of its boundary lines, qualified by the words "more or less," the seller would not be bound to make compensation if these lines were not of the stated length.

In saying this, I must not be understood as including a case where the sale is by the acre or by the foot, or where the contract is based upon the supposition that the lot contains the stated area or has the stated frontage or depth, and the fact that it has not is known to the vendor.

The Role of the Legal Profession

The class of lawyers who engage in the practice of law which concerns land transactions have historically been solicitors. Both the vendor and the purchaser usually require the services of a solicitor to perform the many searches and duties associated with the transfer of the title in a sale of land. The services vary substantially depending upon whether they are for the vendor or the purchaser, and whether the transaction is one which involves the sale of residential or commercial property.

In the case of a sale of residential property, the purchaser's solicitor (depending upon the province where the land is situate) will usually be called upon to make the following searches:

(1) A search of the title to the property at the land registry office in the county or district where the land is located. If the land is under the Registry System, then the solicitor is obliged to prepare an abstract of the title to the property

in order to establish a good chain of title for a lengthy period of time.[8] This search would involve an examination of all deeds, mortgages, discharges of mortgage, and other documents registered against the title to the property to determine that the vendor's title, when traced back, represents a right in the vendor to convey a good title to the purchaser which would be free of any claims adverse to the vendor's interest in the land.

Under the Land Titles System, the solicitor's search is much easier, as the province certifies the title of the vendor as being as it stands on the register. Any charges, liens, or other instruments which might affect the title of the vendor would be recited, and the solicitor might then ascertain their status, and call on the vendor's solicitor to take steps to have the encumbrances or interests cleared from the title before it is transferred to the purchaser.

On the completion of the search (under both systems) the purchaser's solicitor, notifies the vendor's solicitor of any problems concerning the title by way of a *letter of requisitions*, which requires the vendor to clear the rights or encumbrances from the title before the closing date. The vendor's solicitor on receipt of the letter must make every effort to satisfy requisitions that represent valid objections to the vendor's title, and if the objection cannot be satisfied, the purchaser under the terms of the contract is usually free to reject the property, and the agreement becomes null and void.

---

[8] In Ontario, for example, under the Registry System, the chain of title must cover a 40-year period: see the *Registry Act*, R.S.O. 1980, c. 445, s. 111.

(2) The purchaser's solicitor also undertakes a series of searches at the local municipal office to determine:

(a) if the municipal taxes on the property have been paid, and that no arrears of taxes exist,

(b) the zoning of the property is appropriate for the existing or intended use of the property,

(c) the property conforms to the municipal building and safety standards, and that no work orders are outstanding against the property,

(d) in the case of land under development, that any obligations which the builder–developer may have under any sub-division or development agreement have been fully satisfied, or funds deposited with the municipality to cover the completion of the work,

(e) where services (such as electric power) are provided by the municipality, a careful solicitor will also inquire to determine if the payment for these services are in arrears. For this, and other municipal searches, the solicitor will obtain a certificate, or some other written confirmation, as to the status of the property.

(3) In some provinces, where the vendor is a corporation, or where one of the vendor's predecessors in title was a corporation, a search for liens for unpaid corporation taxes is required, and the solicitor will contact the appropriate government office to obtain this information. If a lien for the unpaid tax is claimed by the province, the purchaser's solicitor will require the payment of the taxes before the transaction is closed in order to clear the lien from the property. This is not a univer-

sal requirement, however, as in some provinces, the lien does not attach to the land unless a notice of the lien is registered against the title to the property in the appropriate land registry office.

(4) Where a province has a new housing warranty scheme in effect, a solicitor will make a search to determine if the builder is registered under the scheme, and that the particular dwelling-unit is enrolled under the program. Not all provinces provide this form of consumer protection, but where the transaction concerns the sale of a new housing unit, and such a scheme is in operation, the solicitor for the purchaser would be anxious to ensure that the property was properly covered by the building warranty under the program.

(5) A search for any claims or encumbrances against chattels or fixtures sold with the property would be made by the purchaser's solicitor in the appropriate government office. Depending upon the province, this might be maintained in the local land registry office, the county or district court office, or in a central registry for the entire province. A certificate is usually obtained by the solicitor which would indicate any creditor claims against the goods in question.

(6) The purchaser's solicitor would also make a search for any judgments or writs of execution in the hands of the sheriff of the county or district which might attach to the lands of the vendor. Again, a certificate would be obtained by the solicitor from the sheriff if no writs of execution were in his hands. Because a writ of execution can attach to the property under the Regis-

try System as soon as it is filed with the sheriff, it is essential that this particular search be made as close to the time of transfer of the property as possible. As a result, the purchaser's solicitor normally makes a search for executions immediately prior to the registration of the conveyance of the property to the purchaser.

Under the Land Titles System, the execution does not affect the land until it is placed in the hands of the Land Titles office, but careful solicitors nevertheless make the search to avoid the problems that might be created by the delivery of an execution at or before the closing.

In addition to the many searches which the purchaser's solicitor makes (some of which are outlined above) the solicitor attends to a number of other duties associated with the transaction itself. Insurance coverage for the property is obtained for the purchaser; the status of any mortgage or charge to be assumed by the purchaser is determined; draft copies of the conveyance and other title documents are checked; a mortgage back to the vendor (if a part of the transaction) is prepared; and the funds are obtained for the closing of the transaction.

While the purchaser's solicitor is busy with the many searches and preparations for the closing, the vendor's solicitor usually prepares[9] draft copies of the *deed* or *transfer*, and a *statement of adjustments* (setting out the financial details of the transaction), and sends them to the purchaser's solicitor for approval. The vendor's solicitor is obliged to answer any requisitions which the purchaser's solicitor

may raise concerning the title to the property, and attempt to correct them in order that the vendor may pass a good title to the purchaser. If the transaction involves the assumption of an existing mortgage by the purchaser, the vendor's solicitor must obtain a *mortgage statement* from the mortgagee to certify the status of the mortgage at the time that it is assumed by the purchaser. The vendor's solicitor must also collect in all title documents, surveys, tax bills, keys, proof of ownership of chattels to be transferred, and other documents pertaining to the sale for delivery to the purchaser on closing. The solicitor must also prepare a *bill of sale* for any chattels to be sold as a part of the transaction. This document, along with the *deed* or *transfer*, must then be properly executed by the vendor in the presence of a witness in preparation for delivery on the date fixed for the closing of the transaction.

The Closing of the Transaction

The actual closing of the real estate transaction today lacks much of the ceremony associated with a transfer of property in the past. The transaction is usually completed by the solicitors for the vendor and the purchaser on the appointed day at the land registry office. There, the purchaser's solicitor examines the deed and other documents of title, makes a last minute *sub-search* of the title to the property to make certain no changes have taken place in the register since his previous search, obtains a sheriff's certificate, and makes a final check for encumbrances or claims against any chattels to be transferred. If the final searches reveal that all is in order, the two solicitors are then ready to exchange the documents and complete the closing. The vendor's solicitor usually delivers to the purchaser's solicitor the deed or transfer, and a bill of sale for chattels (if

---

[9]This is not a universal practice, however, as the practice varies. It is not uncommon to have draft documents prepared by the purchaser's solicitor.

any), along with copies of old title documents and the keys. He receives in return, the purchase monies and any mortgage or charge which the purchaser has given back to the vendor. The purchaser's solicitor attends to the registration of the title documents, following which, the vendor's solicitor registers the mortgage or charge, if any. The delivery and registration of the documents completes the transaction, and the title at that point is registered in the purchaser's name.

Vacant possession of the property is normally a part of the transaction, and the delivery of the keys to the premises is symbolic only of the delivery of possession to the purchaser. In most cases, the vendor and purchaser arrange between themselves the time when the vendor will vacate the premises, and when the new purchaser will move into possession. This is usually on the same day that the transaction closes.

Following the closing of the transaction in the land registry office, the solicitors attend to the many final tasks associated with the change of ownership. These tasks usually take the form of providing notice of the change of ownership to municipal tax offices, assessment offices, mortgagees, public utilities, insurers, and any tenants. When these duties have been completed, the solicitors make final reports to their respective clients.

Where a purchase and sale agreement involves the sale of a commercial building or a business, the transaction is considerably more complicated, for the purchaser has contracted for not only the purchase of land and a building, but stock-in-trade, trade fixtures, goodwill, and other assets of the business. Such a sale frequently involves the transfer or acquisition of special licences, as well as compliance with legislation governing the sale of business assets "in bulk." The solicitor's work under the circumstances includes additional duties and responsibilities on behalf of their clients in order to effect the transfer of ownership of the business in accordance with this special legislation. The legislation concerning the sale of business assets is the subject-matter of a part of the next chapter.

SUMMARY The transfer of the title to real property was effected originally by way of ceremony and the expression of intent. This took the form of *livery of seisin*. Over time, the embodiment of the grantor's intentions in a written document gradually replaced the ceremony, and today, the preparation of a *deed* or *transfer* which has been signed and sealed by the grantor in the presence of a witness, and delivered to the grantee, effects the transfer of the interest in the land between the parties. The registration of the deed (or transfer) in the proper land registry office completes the transaction in terms of public notice, and in the case of a transfer under the Land Titles System, places the grantee's name on the register as the person which the province certifies as the registered owner of the particular parcel of land.

Real estate agents assist the owner of land by providing a service which brings together the owner and prospective purchasers in an effort to establish a purchase and sale agreement. Where property is listed with a real estate agent, the agent must act in the best interests of the principal at all times. The general rules of agency normally apply to the relationship between the principal and the agent.

In any sale of real property, it is essential that the lands described in a deed or transfer correspond with the land actually occupied by the title holder. To determine this relationship, a survey is used to identify the land and to ascertain if any discrepancy exists between the two. Surveys are prepared by persons trained and licensed under provincial legislation, and surveys must be prepared in accordance with statutory requirements as well.

Land ownership is presently subject to a great many controls and regulations which, if ignored, can adversely affect the owner. For this reason, the parties to real estate transactions usually engage the services of members of the legal profession to assist in the completion of the transfer of title to the purchaser. In addition to the preparation of the formal documents associated with the transaction, the lawyers involved (called solicitors) perform the many services necessary to carry out the terms of the contract. On the purchaser's part, this usually involves a number of searches in addition to an examination of the title to the property, in order that the title passed to the purchaser will be good and marketable in the future. The ceremonial aspects of the transfer (insofar as they exist) are mainly performed by the solicitors at the land registry office.

DISCUSSION QUESTIONS

1. *Explain the purpose of livery of seisin in early real estate transactions.*
2. *Why was it important in the past to provide vacant possession of the property? Is it equally as important today?*
3. *Describe the role of the witness in an ancient transfer of property. Does the witness perform the same role at the present time?*
4. *Explain the function of a real estate agent in a modern land transaction.*
5. *What is an "exclusive listing agreement"?*
6. *Describe the duties of a real estate agent to his or her principal. In what way does it differ from that of an ordinary agent?*
7. *Distinguish an "appraiser" from a real estate "agent".*
8. *Explain the purpose of a survey.*
9. *In what way is a survey used by a purchaser of property?*
10. *How does a purchaser determine the vendor's title to a property? What constitutes a good and marketable title?*
11. *How does a title search under the Land Titles System differ from a title search under the Registry System?*
12. *Describe the various searches that a purchaser (or the purchaser's solicitor) must make in order to be satisfied that the land transferred will be free from encumbrances or other claims.*

13. *Explain the purpose of a letter of requisitions.*
14. *What is meant by the term "writ of execution"? How does it affect real property?*
15. *What significance attaches to the process whereby a deed is "signed, sealed, and delivered" to the purchaser?*
16. *What steps must a purchaser take to ensure that no writs of execution attach to the land to be sold?*
17. *Describe the procedure that solicitors refer to as "the closing."*
18. *Why is the registration of a deed or transfer important? How does it affect the title to real property?*

JUDICIAL DECISIONS

Real Estate Agent With Interest in Purchaser— Notice of Interest to Vendor— Fiduciary Relationship

George W. Rayfield Realty Ltd. et al. v. Kuhn et al. (1980), 30 O.R. (2d) 271.

The real estate agent acting for a vendor had a personal interest in the corporation which offered to purchase the parcel of land owned by the vendor. The agent gave written notice of his financial interest in the purchase to the vendor before the purchase agreement was made. The agent later brought an action for a commission on the sale.

GALLIGAN, J.:

I turn now to consider the problems arising from the fiduciary responsibility which Woods had to the defendants and the provisions of s. 42 of the *Real Estate and Business Brokers Act*. Since there was no licensing agreement, only s-s. (1) of that section is applicable. That statutory provision reads as follows:

"42(1) No broker or salesman shall purchase, lease, exchange or otherwise acquire for himself or make an offer to purchase, lease, exchange or otherwise acquire for himself, either directly or indirectly, any interest in real estate for the purpose of resale, unless he first delivers to the vendor a written statement that he is a broker or salesman, as the case may be, and the vendor has acknowledged in writing that he has received the statement."

As I mentioned earlier, Woods, the salesman for Cathcart, was a principal in Bambi at the time the offer resulting in the agreement exs. 1 and 7 was made. He remained a principal in Bambi throughout the whole time that that company had contractual arrangements with the defendants. In my opinion s. 42(1) applies to him and applies to Cathcart.

I find as a fact that on September 12, 1973, Woods delivered to Kuhn the following notice:

"Please be advised that Mr. David Woods has a financial interest in Bambi Developments Limited and is purchasing the above property for the purpose of developing and/or resale. Mr. David Woods is a real estate agent and will be receiving part of the commission from the above sale."

I find as a fact that Kuhn signed an acknowledgement on September 12, 1973, that he received that notice on that day. I do not accept Kuhn's evidence that he signed it months later. Mr. Kuhn is an experienced real estate developer. He had been in that business for almost 20 years at the time this transaction developed. I think it is utterly preposterous for him to expect anybody to believe that he would sign a document such as this, months after the event. I accept that the date September 12, 1973, was probably written in by Woods, but I am quite satisfied that Kuhn would not have signed such a document in blank and I accept that that date was in there at the time he signed it.

I am not persuaded, on the reasonable balance of probability that any notice required by s. 42 was given to Petrullo at or prior to the time he executed exs. 1 and 7. Mr. Warne argued that there is no pleading of that section as a defence, nor is there any pleading about breach of fiduciary responsibility on the part of Woods as a defence. In my opinion, compliance with s. 42 is a statutory condition precedent to any right of action for commission, and it is part of a plaintiff's case to prove compliance with that section. In my opinion, there is no need for a defendant to plead it.

Likewise, in my opinion, the requirement of conforming with the obligations resting on a person in a fiduciary capacity is so important that it, too, is part of a plaintiff's case and it is not necessary for a defendant to plead breach of fiduciary responsibility, when an agent is bringing an action against his principal for a commission.

In my view, the simple failure on the part of the plaintiff Cathcart to comply with the provisions of s. 42 of the *Real Estate and Business Brokers Act* in so far as Petrullo is concerned disentitles Cathcart to any commission against Petrullo. Cathcart's claim against Petrullo must be dismissed.

It remains to be considered whether notice given to Kuhn is sufficient compliance with s. 42 and sufficient performance of Woods' fiduciary responsibility to the defendants to entitle Cathcart to claim commission against Kuhn. I think the decision of the Court of Appeal in *Christie et al. v. McCann*, [1972] 3 O.R. 125, 27 D.L.R. (3d) 544, is relevant to this case. That case involved what was then s. 49 of the *Real Estate and Business Brokers Act*. Section 49 is not exactly the same as s. 42(1). In that case the Court of Appeal held that an acknowledgement, which was substantially similar to the notice in this case, was held to comply neither with s. 49, nor to fulfil the obligations of an agent to disclose material matters to his principal.

It may be that the notice in this case does amount to technical compliance with the provisions of s. 42(1) of the Act as it now exists. However, in my opinion, it does in no way amount to compliance with or fulfilment of the high fiduciary responsibility that a real estate agent owes to his principal. The conflict between a purchaser's interest and that of a vendor is so great that, in my opinion, there must be the most complete disclosure by a real estate agent purchasing from his principal before it can be said that he has fulfilled his fiduciary responsibility to his principal.

In such a case, it is my opinion that the agent must give his principal the fullest disclosure of his knowledge of the real estate market in the area where the subject lands were situate. For example, if an agent had information that a property might even possibly be sold to some other purchaser at a higher price than that offered by the agent then that information must be brought to the attention of the principal so that the profit would be that of the principal rather than of the agent. I do not know whether, at the material time, Woods had any such knowledge, but whatever his knowledge was of the market at that time and in that place and any other factor that might affect the value of the property at the time ought to have been brought to the attention of his principals so that they could judge whether the price offered by Bambi was the most advantageous one possible.

A real estate agent dealing with his own client may not simply enter the market-place. The agent is in a position of great trust and he owes great trust to his principal. In my view, the simple disclosure that he was an agent, discloses the most abysmal ignorance of, or misconception of the very fundamental duties arising from the fiduciary relationship of a real estate agent to his principal. In my opinion, this agent was simply greedy. He wanted to purchase the property and he wanted to get a commission from the vendor as well.

In my view, it would be under the most extraordinary circumstances that an agent would be entitled to purchase from his principal and as well obtain a commission from him. In my opinion the notice given in this case is not worth the paper it is written on. It is far from amounting to a fulfilment of the duties arising from the fiduciary relationship that existed between them. In my opinion, Woods has disentitled Cathcart to any commission from anyone. Cathcart's action is dismissed.

||||||||||||||||||||||||||||||||||||||||||||||||||||||||||||||||||||||||||||||||||||||||||||||||||||||||||||||||||||||||||||||||||||||||||||||||||

Purchase and Sale of Land—Place Where Contract Made—Duty of Vendor to Provide Conveyance

Simson and MacFarlane v. Young (1918), 56 S.C.R. 388.

The vendor of a property located in Calgary, Alberta, resided in Ireland. Through an agent in Calgary, she entered into an agreement to sell the property to the purchasers, who resided in Calgary. Under the terms of the agreement, about one-half of the purchase money was paid to the vendor's agent, and the balance was to be paid some time later. On the closing date, the purchasers tendered the balance of the purchase money, but the vendor's agent was unable to produce a conveyance for the property.

After a number of futile attempts to contact the vendor in Ireland, the purchasers decided to take action to rescind the contract, and to recover the money paid to her under the agreement. The vendor, in turn, demanded specific performance of the contract. The question of where the contract was to be performed was an issue which came before the court. The question was dealt with on the appeal to the Supreme Court of Canada.

ANGLIN, J.:

Even if, upon a construction of the contract most favourable to her, the vendor, had she been present in Calgary personally or by agent, might have been entitled to defer having the transfer prepared until actual payment or tender of the balance of the purchase money, and, by delivering it on the same or the following day or even within a day or two thereafter, might have met the requirement that delivery of it should be made "immediately" upon payment, the agreement certainly did not contemplate that the purchasers should, after paying their purchase money, be obliged to wait for their transfer until it could be obtained from Ireland, remaining for a month or longer without title and with a right of action against a "foreigner" as their only security.

In my opinion the place of performance of this contract, no other being stipulated in it, was at Calgary. The ordinary rule of English law that a promisor is bound to seek his promisee, if ever applicable to a case where there are mutual obligations to be fulfilled concurrently, only governs

"where no place of performance is specified either expressly or by implication from the nature and terms of the contract and the surrounding circumstances.—7 Halsbury, Nos. 857-8."

Here all these circumstances as well as the nature and the terms of the contract furnish unmistakable indicia that the intention of the parties was that performance should take place at Calgary. The contract was entered into there. *Weyand v. Park Terrace Co.* In making it the vendor acted through an agent resident there. It concerned land there. The transfer was to be delivered immediately upon payment of the balance of the purchase money. Title would pass to the purchasers only on the registration of the transfer in the Registry Office there. (6 Edw. VII, ch. 24, sec. 41.) Mr. Justice Stuart, who spoke for the Appellate Division, seemed inclined to the opinion that the purchasers were entitled to have the actual delivery of the transfer and payment of their purchase money take place contemporaneously in the Registry Office itself, citing Hogg on "Ownership and Incumbrance of Registered Land" at page 187. In view of the provisions of the "Land Titles Act" already adverted to, not a little may be said for that view (see Williams on Vendor and Purchaser (2nd ed.) 1186)—but it is unnecessary to determine the point in the present case.

Yet, although of the opinion that

"the purchasers were not bound to go to Ireland and pay her (the vendor) the money there"

and that

"the Land Titles Office at Calgary was the only place where they could safely part with their money,"

that learned judge thought they were

"bound to communicate with her and notify her that they were ready and that if she did not produce title within a reasonable time the agreement would be repudiated."

In the first place the presence of the vendor in person or by authorized agent at Calgary being necessary for the fulfilment of the purchasers' duty to pay or tender their purchase money (if to do so should be regarded as a condition of the vendor's obligation to put herself in readiness to transfer the land), its performance would be excused by her absence. Comyn's Digest, "Condition," L. 5. The giving notice of intention to rescind if completion should be delayed beyond a named reasonable time having likewise been made impracticable by the act of the vendor's agent in stating a wrong address in the agreement (the only information the purchasers had) and her subsequent neglect to rectify that error, she cannot insist on that condition of the right of rescission, ordinarily applicable where time is not of the essence originally or has ceased to be so. A notice addressed to her at Belfast would rescission, ordinarily applicable where time is not of the essence originally or has ceased to be so. A notice addressed to her at Belfast would in fact have been futile, as is proved by the return of letters sent to that address. Although the purchasers did not know that it would have been so, the vendor cannot complain because they did not attempt to give her a notice there. *Lex neminem cogit ad vana seu inutilia.* The giving of notice of intention to rescind having been thus rendered impossible through the fault of the vendor, the purchasers were not bound to wait indefinitely for her to fulfil her contract.

Having regard to all the circumstances, the nature of the contract, its terms, the failure of the vendor to put herself in readiness to carry out her obligation, the fact that time was originally of the essence and probably remained so, and if not, that notice of intention to rescind unless the contract should be completed within reasonable time could not be given owing to fault ascribable to the vendor, that her delay both before and after she became aware of the purchasers' readiness to complete was gross and inexcusable, and that if obliged to take and pay for the property now the purchasers would be subjected to great hardship—I am, with respect, of the opinion that this is not a case for specific performance and that the right to rescission has been established. No doubt the granting of rescission does not ensue as of course because the relief of specific performance is denied; *Gough v. Bench*. The circumstances sometimes make it proper to leave the parties to their common law remedies. But if, as seems probable, time continued to be of the essence of the contract, the plaintiffs' right to rescission is unquestionable. If, on the other hand, time ceased to be of the essence of the contract, having regard to the circumstances, I think the purchasers are entitled to be placed in the same position as if they had duly given notice of intention to rescind should the vendor fail to deliver a transfer within a named reasonable time. Since they have paid a substantial sum on account of purchase money, recovery of which they would otherwise be obliged to seek by way of damages, and are themselves free from blame, equity and an application of the maxim *ut sit finis litium*, alike require that rescission and the return of the money paid on account of the purchase price and for taxes should be decreed.

The circumstances, however, are not such as warrant a judgment for damages beyond the return of the money paid with interest. Indeed with rescission the plaintiffs are probably better off than they would have been had the defendant carried out her contract.

The judgment of the learned trial judge should be restored and the appellants should have their costs in this court and in the Appellate Division.

Case 1

Brown was the registered owner of several adjoining parcels of vacant land which he had purchased in 1969, some 12 years ago. During that period of time the property had appreciated substantially in value.

In 1980, Brown was approached by a real estate agent who suggested that the property might be of interest to a number of developers that had recently begun construction in the immediate area. After some discussion, Brown entered into a listing agreement with the agent, and the agent agreed to seek out prospective purchasers for the property. $200 000 was established by Brown as the selling price he would accept for the land.

For several months, the agent attempted to find a buyer for the property, but without success. When the developers in the area were not interested in the property, the agent returned to Brown, and suggested that a corporation in which he had an interest might be willing to purchase the land. To this suggestion Brown replied that it did not matter to him who the purchaser was, so long as it was prepared to pay his price for the land.

A week later, the agent returned with an offer to purchase from the corporation in which he had an interest. The offer price was $200 000, and was described by the agent as "a clean deal—all cash." The offer was prepared on a standard real estate offer–to–purchase form, and contained a clause which read: "Any severance or impost fee plus any expenses for water and sewer connections to be included in the purchase price." Brown queried the clause, and the agent explained that it meant that the cost of obtaining permission to use the three parcels of land as separate building lots, and the hook-up costs of water and sewer lines to them would be deducted from the purchase price. He added that this "usually did not cost much."

At the agent's urging, Brown signed the offer. Some weeks later, Brown discovered to his sorrow that the severance fees and the water and sewer connections would cost close to 10% of the sale price. The municipality required the payment of 5% of the value of the property as a part of the severance fee, and the water and sewer connections accounted for the remainder. When Brown refused to proceed with the transaction, the purchaser instituted legal proceedings for specific performance, and Brown, on the advice of his solicitor, settled the action. As a result, he received only $180 000 for the property, from which the real estate agent demanded a selling commission of 5% based upon the $200 000 selling price.

Brown refused to pay the agent, and demanded that the agent compensate him for the $20 000 loss which he suffered. Eventually, the agent brought an action against Brown for the commission which he claimed was due and owing. Brown, in turn, filed a counterclaim for payment of the $20 000 loss which he had suffered.

Discuss the arguments that might be raised by the parties in this case, and render a decision.

Case 2

Abernathy was the registered owner of a building lot in a residential area of a large city. He entered into an agreement of purchase and sale with Jones, who wished to build a house on the land.

Following the execution of the agreement, Jones engaged a land surveyor to prepare a survey of the property. When the survey was completed, it disclosed that the building lot had a frontage of only 59 ft. The agreement of sale stated that the lot had "frontage of approximately 60 ft., and a depth of 125 ft. more or less." Abernathy's deed described the lot as being "60′ × 125′."

The discrepancy between the two measurements was apparently due to the fact that the owner of the adjacent lot had erected a fence which encroached on Abernathy's property. The fence had been erected some 15 years before, and was taken by the surveyor as the property line.

Determine the rights of the parties in this case, and indicate how the problem might be decided if Jones should refuse to proceed with the agreement.

Case 3

In December of 1980, Fanshawe agreed to purchase a house and lot from Bradley for a purchase price of $58 000. The property was in an area under the Registry System, and Fanshawe determined from the registry office that Bradley had what appeared to be a good title to the land. Unfortunately, he had failed to notice a mortgage which had been registered against the property to secure the indebtedness of Williams, Bradley's predecessor in title. The mortgage had been assumed by Bradley as a part of his purchase from Williams, but that fact had not been revealed to Fanshawe at time that the offer was drawn.

The offer to purchase that Fanshawe had accepted contained the following clause that read in part: "The purchaser shall have 10 days to examine the title at his own expense . . . Save as to any valid objections made to the vendor's title within that time, the purchaser shall be conclusively deemed to have accepted the title of the vendor."

Without knowledge of the existing mortgage, Fanshawe proceeded to pay over to Bradley the $58 000, and received a deed to the property. He registered the deed on January 6, 1981. Some time later, Fanshawe was contacted by the mortgagee and advised that the sum of $3 500 remained due and owing on the mortgage, and as the new owner of the property, the mortgagee would look to him for payment.

To compound Fanshawe's problems, a finance company that had obtained a judgment for $2 000 against Bradley in October of 1979 had filed a writ of execution with the sheriff of the county where the property was located. Fanshawe had not searched in the sheriff's office at the time of closing of the transaction, and was surprised to discover that the finance company now claimed that the execution had attached to the land which he had purchased.

Advise Fanshawe of his legal position in this case. What are the rights of the mortgagee and the execution creditor? What action could they take against Fanshawe or the property?

Case 4

Samuel Reynolds was the registered owner of a 300-acre farm. In July, 1971, he retired from farming, and gave his son Jacob a deed to the farm property. Jacob did not register the deed, but instead placed it in a safety deposit box which both he and his father rented at a bank.

Samuel Reynolds died in 1980. His will, dated May 3, 1968, devised the farm to his daughter, Ruth, who was living on the farm at the time, and who maintained the house for her father. The will also named Ruth as the sole executrix of his estate. When the contents of the will were revealed, Jacob announced to Ruth that their father had given him a deed to the farm some years before, and that he was the owner of the property.

No further discussion of the farm took place between the brother and sister, but after the debts of the estate were settled, Ruth had a deed to the farm prepared and executed in her capacity as the executrix of her father's estate, and delivered it to the registry office. The deed conveyed the farm property to her in her personal capacity.

Some months later, Jacob entered into an agreement of purchase and sale for the farm with Smith. Smith made a search at the registry office and discovered that the title to the property was not registered in the name of Jacob, but in the name of his sister, Ruth. Smith refused to proceed with the transaction.

Discuss the rights of the parties in this case, and indicate with reasons, the identity of the lawful owner of the property. If Jacob should show his deed to Smith, and insist that he has title to the property, what argument might Smith raise to counter Jacob's claim?

PART VII

The Creditor-Debtor Relationship

CHAPTER 32

Security for Debt

INTRODUCTION

The extension of credit or the loan of money by a lender on the strength of the borrower's unsupported promise to repay carries with it considerable risk, and a blind faith in the integrity of the borrower. Because debtors may not always be as good as their word, even in early times, creditors looked beyond the assurances of the debtors to their assets in order to ensure payment.

One of the earliest methods of securing payment of a debt was the mortgage transaction in which an interest in the debtor's lands would be transferred to the creditor on the condition that it would be returned when the debt was paid. In this arrangement, the creditor could retain the property in satisfaction of the debt if the debtor failed to pay. Apart from the use of land, chattels were also used by debtors to secure the payment of debts, either by the physical transfer of possession of the chattels to the creditor as security, or by the grant of an interest in the property by way of a transfer of title. Of these two methods, the transfer of physical possession of the goods to the creditor was probably the oldest, and one of the first to fall subject to statutory control in England.[1] This was not unusual, however, as the loan of money subject to the payment of interest, and the use of goods as security for debt were generally discouraged by the Church for many years. This general attitude was reflected in the numerous laws against usury.[2]

Before the mid-19th century, the granting of a security interest in chattels was viewed with suspicion by the courts, as it represented a means whereby a particular creditor would obtain a preference at the expense of the remaining creditors if the debtor should become insolvent. This was particularly true where the transfer of the title to the chattel permitted the debtor to remain in possession of the goods. In those instances, the transaction was subject to a rebuttable presumption that the transfer was made for the purpose of defrauding other creditors, and unless the debtor could provide an acceptable explanation for the transfer, it was subject to impeachment.[3]

A gradual change in attitude took place in the 19th century, however, as the expansion of commerce created a greater demand for credit, and for new means to protect the interests of creditors. During this period, the courts came to recognize the different interests of the debtor and creditor in chattels, and of the need to utilize goods as security for debt. This change in attitude was reflected in the repeal of the usury laws in England,[4] and the development of a variety of legal instruments designed to create security interests in chattels as well as real property.

In England, the *chattel mortgage* was the first security instrument to receive statutory recognition and general acceptance (apart from the *pledge or pawn*, which involved a physical transfer of the security to the creditor). Closely following the chattel mortgage was the *hire–purchase agreement*. Unlike the chattel mortgage, which was similar in purpose and effect to the land mortgage, the hire–purchase agreement represented a means of facilitating the sale of goods on credit. While the chattel mortgage could also be used for this purpose, the hire–purchase agreement provided a much simpler procedure for the seller to follow in the event of default by the buyer.

The *assignment of book debts* to a creditor (or creditors) was also used during this period to secure debts, but it was generally a less attractive method from the merchant's point of view. The particular disadvantage which accompanied the assignment was the fact that notice of the assignment was given to the customers of the particular merchant debtor, something which the merchant did not always wish to reveal.

Where goods were sold to a buyer, but delivery was to be made at a later date, the *bill of sale* relating to the transaction

---

[1]*An Act against Brokers* (1604), 1 Jac. I, c. 21.
[2]See, for example, "Usury Shall Not Run Against Any Within Age," 20 Hen. III, c. 5, and "An Act Appointing Who Shall Punish Usury," 15 Edw. III, Stat. 1, c. 5.
[3]*Twynes Case* (1601), 3 Co. Rep. 80b, 76 E.R. 809.

[4]*Usury Laws Repeal Act*, 17 & 18 Vict., c. 90.

was made subject to statute and the requirement of registration, in an effort to protect the rights of the buyer of the goods and the unsuspecting subsequent buyer or creditor of the seller.[5]

The 19th century also brought with it the rise of the commercial corporation, first for the purpose of constructing canals and railways, and later, as a vehicle to launch large commercial enterprises. Initially, these corporate bodies were limited to *mortgage bonds* as a means of securing debt, but as the particular nature of the organization and its assets became better understood by creditors, the *floating charge* was developed to provide a security interest in the chattels and goods of the corporation that were constantly changing through acquisition and sale.[6]

During this same period, economic activity of a rapidly growing business community in Canada produced a demand for additional means of securing credit, and a parallel desire by creditors for means whereby the payment of the debts might be secured. The various security instruments used in England were quickly adopted by Canadian debtors and creditors, occasionally in modified form. The hire–purchase agreement, in particular, found favour in a slightly modified form, known as the *conditional sale agreement*. In addition, new security instruments were developed to facilitate the expansion of business and the sale of goods on credit. Chartered banks in Canada were permitted under the *Bank Act*[7] to acquire a security interest in the present and future goods of a debtor in priority over subsequent creditors by following a simple fil-

ing procedure set out in the legislation. Laws were also passed to give workmen, suppliers, and building contractors security interests in land by way of *mechanics' lien* legislation, and shortly after the turn of the present century, creditor protection in the form of a *Bulk Sales Act* was introduced to protect the interests of unsecured trade creditors, where a sale in bulk was made of business assets.

The late 19th century and early 20th century saw much of the law relating to older forms of security for debt codified and made subject to registration procedures, in order to protect buyers of goods and subsequent creditors of the debtor. While the inevitable provincial variation developed with the codification of the various laws concerning the different forms of security, most statutes in the common law provinces provided for the registration of either the security instrument or a notice thereof, in order to protect the creditor's interest and priority. The statutes also established procedures that were to be followed by the creditor in the event of default, in order to realize on the security.

The rapid growth of commerce during the present century, and the tremendous expansion of consumer credit, coupled with the mobility of the population, particularly after 1950, eventually created a need for more modern legislation to deal with security interests. The registration and notice protection afforded by most of the statutes, while adequate for a relatively stationary population, proved to be totally inadequate where secured goods moved frequently within a jurisdiction, and from one jurisdiction to another.

The provinces of Ontario and Manitoba were the first to recognize the fact that the security registration and notice require-

---

[5]*Bills of Sale Act*, 17 & 18 Vict., c. 36.
[6]*Gardner v. London, Chatham, and Dover Rwy.* (1867), 2 Ch. App. 201.
[7]*The Bank Act, 1890*, 53 Vict., c. 31, s. 74 (Can.)

ments, and indeed many of the security instruments themselves were outmoded with regard to the needs of creditors and debtors in a credit-oriented, mobile society. In Ontario, a draft *Personal Property Security Act*, modelled after the United States' *Uniform Commercial Code*, Article 9, was prepared in 1964, and eventually passed by the Legislature in June, 1967.[8] The Act required the establishment of a province-wide registration system for chattel security interests using a single, computer-based registry. The development of the new system and its implementation required almost six years, with a further three years necessary to complete the change-over from a document file to a notice file system. The new Act finally came into force on April 1, 1976. Manitoba, with the benefit of the Ontario experience, introduced somewhat similar legislation in 1973[9] that was proclaimed in force in 1978. More recently, the province of Saskatchewan introduced its own legislation[10] based upon the United States' *Uniform Commercial Code*, rather than the Ontario and Manitoba legislation. As a result, the modernization of the law in Canada appears once again to show signs of jurisdictional preferences, rather than uniformity. At the present time, the laws with respect to security for debt vary quite substantially—with the provinces of Ontario, Manitoba, and Saskatchewan each with a modified version of the United States' *Uniform Commercial Code*, Article 9, in place, and the remaining common law provinces and the territories continuing with the older forms of legisla-

tion. The province of Quebec also has provision for the recognition and protection of security interests in chattels under its *Civil Code*. It is against this back-drop of confusion that creditors must attempt to protect their interests.

FORMS OF SECURITY FOR DEBT

Apart from the mortgage of real property (which is examined in Chapter 29), there are a number of methods which may be used by the parties to credit transactions in order to provide security for the debt. The most common forms of security with respect to chattels are the chattel mortgage, conditional sale agreement, and bill of sale. These may be used in appropriate forms for commercial and consumer credit transactions. In addition, a creditor of a commerical firm may take an assignment of book debts to secure the indebtedness of the merchant, and a chartered bank, under the *Bank Act*, may acquire a security interest in the inventory of wholesalers, retailers, manufacturers, and other producers of goods. Corporations may pledge their real property and chattel assets as security by way of bonds and debentures (including a floating charge). Each of these instruments create or provide a security interest in the property that a creditor might enforce to satisfy the debt in the event that the debtor should default in payment.

Other special forms of security are available to certain types of creditors, or to creditors in certain circumstances. These include the right of lien available to workmen, suppliers, and contractors in the construction industry, and the statutory protection of unsecured trade creditors of a business where the merchant makes a sale in bulk. All of these forms of

---

[8]The *Personal Property Security Act, 1967* (Ont.), c. 73, now R.S.O. 1980, c. 375.
[9]The *Personal Property Security Act*, 1973 (Man.), c. 5.
[10]The *Personal Property Security Act*, 1979-80 (Sask.), c. P-6. Proclaimed in force May 1, 1981.

security are subject to legislation in each province or territory, and although variation exists with respect to each under the different statutes, the nature of the particular security is usually similar in purpose and effect.

Chattel Mortgage

Before the development and judicial recognition of the validity of the chattel mortgage, the most common method of using chattels as security for debt was for the creditor to take physical possession of the goods until payment was made. This early form of security involved the transfer of possession, but not title, to the creditor, with an arrangement whereby the creditor might keep the goods or dispose of them if the debtor should default. While this form of security for debt has been subject to statutory regulation since as early as 1604 in England, and remains so today, the obvious drawback of this method is that the debtor is deprived of the use of the goods, and the creditor is obliged to care for and protect the goods while they are in his possession. To overcome the disadvantages of this form of security, the chattel mortgage was devised, which permitted the debtor to retain the goods, but granted the creditor title until the debt was paid.

In concept, the chattel mortgage is essentially the same as the real property mortgage after which it was designed. The familiarity of business persons with land mortgages in the past, led to the development and use of a similar mortgage on chattels, and this form of security for debt became one of the earliest types of chattel security available where the debtor retained possession. Statutory recognition of this security device took place in the mid-19th century, at which time the chattel security interests as well as the chattel mortgage procedures on default were codified.

Under a *chattel mortgage*, the debtor transfers his entire interest in the property to the creditor, subject to his right to possession while not in default, and the right to redeem. In Canada, chattel mortgages are subject to legislation in all of the common law provinces and territories. In Ontario, Manitoba, and Saskatchewan, where *Personal Property Security Acts* are in force, the rights of the parties are governed by these statutes; in all of the other jurisdictions, each has its own legislation pertaining to this form of security interest. Though provincial variation exists, the nature of the instrument is similar in each province and territory, and the mortgage form itself is largely standardized.

Under a chattel mortgage, the title to the property is transferred to the chattel mortgagee, and the mortgagor retains possession. The mortgage sets out the *covenants* of the mortgagor, the most important being the covenant to pay the debt, and the covenant to insure the goods for the protection of the mortgagee. The mortgage also sets out the rights of the parties in the event of default.

If the mortgagor fails to pay the debt as provided in the chattel mortgage, the mortgagee normally has the right to take possession of the mortgaged goods, and either sell the goods by public or private sale, or proceed with *foreclosure*.[11] In most jurisdictions, the mortgagee, after taking possession of the goods, must give the mortgagor an opportunity to redeem the goods before the sale or foreclosure may take place. If the goods are sold, any surplus after payment of the debt and the costs of the sale, belongs to the mortgagor, but if the proceeds of the sale are insufficient to cover the debt, the mortgagor remains liable for any deficiency.

The mortgagee's right to foreclosure in

---

[11]*Rennick v. Bender*, [1924] 1 D.L.R. 739.

the case of a chattel mortgage is much like that of a mortgagee under a land mortgage, but the procedure is less formal.[12] The mortgagor is entitled to an opportunity to redeem under the foreclosure procedure, but if the mortgagor fails to redeem, the mortgagee then obtains foreclosure, which vests the ownership of the property absolutely in the mortgagee. Foreclosure is seldom used by mortgagees, not only because the procedure is more involved than sale proceedings, but also because the mortgagee is generally interested in receiving payment of the debt rather than acquiring the chattel.

The use of a chattel mortgage as a means of securing debt required the provinces to put in place a number of procedures to protect the creditor and other interested parties. Since a chattel mortgagor retains possession of goods, and has the equity of redemption, it was necessary to provide third parties with notice of the mortgagee's interest in the goods.

To make this information available to the public at large, all jurisdictions have established either a central registry for the province, or regional registries, (usually at the County Court Office) where a chattel mortgagee might register the mortgage. The registration must be made within a short time after the mortgage is executed, and the registration has the effect of giving public notice of the creditor's security interest. The failure to register renders the chattel mortgage void as against any person who purchases the goods for value and without notice of the mortgage, or as against any subsequent encumbrancer who has no actual notice of the prior chattel mortgage. It does not, however, affect the validity of the mortgage as between the mortgagor and the mortgagee.

Unlike the real property mortgagor, who is usually free to sell or dispose of the mortgaged property without the consent of the mortgagee, the chattel mortgagor may not sell the mortgaged chattels without consent. If a mortgagor should sell the goods without the mortgagee's consent, and the chattel mortgage had been properly registered to provide notice to the buyer, the buyer of the goods takes them subject to the mortgage. For this reason, a person who purchases goods from other than a merchant should make certain that the goods are free from encumbrances, and that the seller is the lawful owner before the purchase is effected. This may be done by way of a search in the appropriate public office where registers of chattel mortgages and other security interests in chattels are maintained.

A chattel mortgage may be assigned by a chattel mortgagee if the mortgagee so desires, and this may be effected without the consent of the mortgagor. The formalities associated with assignments must, however, be complied with, and the mortgagor must be properly notified of the assignment to the assignee. The assignment of a chattel mortgage in this regard is much like the assignment of a real property mortgage.

Registration requirements usually call for the renewal of the registration from time to time, if the mortgage is to run for a long period of time. If a chattel mortgagee fails to renew the registration as required under the statute, the effect is similar to a failure to register initially, and a subsequent mortgagee could obtain priority over the initial mortgagee, or a *bona fide* purchaser without notice could obtain a good title to the goods in spite of the outstanding mortgage interest. The fact that the registration of a chattel mortgage expires after a specific time interval has limited the use of discharges of chattel mort-

---

[12]*Carlisle v. Tait* (1882), 7 O.A.R. 10. See also, *Warner v. Doran* (1931), 2 M.P.R. 574.

gages, but where a chattel mortgagor has paid the mortgage debt in full, a chattel mortgagee is obliged to provide the mortgagor with a discharge of the mortgage, if the mortgagor so desires, and the discharge may be registered in the office where the chattel mortgage was registered.

|||||||||||||||||||||||||||||||||||||||||||||||||||||||||||||||||||||||||||||

CASE 32.1
Bozsik v. Kaufmann (1963), 45 W.W.R. 316.

WOODS, J.A.:

. . . it is clear that one who purchases from a trader in the ordinary course of business *bona fide* and without notice, takes, at common law, free from chattel mortgages placed on the goods by the trader. . . . The requirements of registration in *The Bills of Sale Act, 1957*, would not alter this result as they provide that unless registration is effected the mortgage shall be void as against creditors. This in no way enhances the common-law rights of the mortgagee. It simply makes retention of such rights in the mortgagee contingent upon registration.

|||||||||||||||||||||||||||||||||||||||||||||||||||||||||||||||||||||||||||||

Conditional Sale Agreement

The conditional sale agreement differs from a chattel mortgage in that it is a security interest which arises out of a sale rather than a conventional debt transaction. The conditional sale agreement had its beginnings in the English hire–purchase agreement. The hire–purchase agreement was devised in the early 19th century[13] to permit a prospective purchaser of goods to acquire possession of the goods immediately under a lease agreement, with an option to purchase the

goods at a later date. If the option was exercised, the payments made under the hire agreement were applied to the purchase price, and the title to the goods then passed to the buyer. The first use of this type of agreement as a credit selling device was claimed by an English piano-maker in 1846, but it was the adoption of the hire–purchase agreement by the Singer Manufacturing Company for the purpose of selling sewing machines to the general public that publicized the use of this unique method of securing debt. It was adopted not long after by sellers of coal wagons, carriages, furniture, and most other durable goods.

The conditional sale agreement differs from the hire–purchase agreement in one important aspect: Under the hire–purchase agreement, the "hirer" has the *option to purchase* the goods, and it is only when the option is exercised that the title passes to the hirer, who at that point, becomes the buyer. The conditional sale agreement contains no such option. Instead, the instalment payments are applied to the purchase price from the outset, but the title does not pass to the buyer until the final payment under the agreement has been made. Under the early conditional sale agreements, if the buyer defaulted on an instalment payment, the seller was free to treat the payments as rent for the use of the goods, and recover the goods from the purchaser, since the title had never passed. The passage of legislation governing the use and application of conditional sale agreements altered the rights of the parties, and imposed certain duties on sellers, but in terms of the historical development of the concept, the legislation was relatively late in emerging. In England, legislation concerning the hire purchase did not appear until 1938, and in the provinces of Canada the relationship

[13]See, for example, *Hickenbotham v. Groves* (1826) 2 C. & P. 492, 172 E.R. 223 where reference is made to hotel furniture purchased under a hire–purchase agreement.

was not subject to statutory regulation until the 20th century when the use of this device for the purpose of selling automobiles and household appliances necessitated some form of statutory regulation. As has been the case with most matters within the jurisdiction of the provinces, each province established legislation for its own perceived needs, and consequently, the law relating to conditional sale agreements is not uniform throughout the country. More recently, some provinces have introduced new legislation of an all-encompassing nature with respect to personal property security, and have repealed their legislation which dealt specifically with conditional sale agreements.

In those provinces that have legislation governing conditional sale agreements[14] the legislation provides that the agreement must be in writing, and signed by the parties. The agreement need not be in any special form, but must set out a description of the property, and the terms and conditions relating to the sale. Since a conditional sale agreement is by definition a sale in which the goods are paid for over time, consumer protection legislatio.., which, for example, requires the true interest rate and the cost of credit to be revealed, must be complied with in the preparation of the sale agreement. As with chattel mortgages, the conditional buyer has possession of the goods, but not the title, and to protect the creditor against subsequent creditors' claims, or against a sale of the property to an unsuspecting purchaser, the conditional sale agreement must normally be registered in a public record office (usually the County Court Office) in order that the public be made aware of the seller's title to the property.

The legislation, with certain exceptions, provides that a failure to register the agreement renders the transaction void as against a *bona fide* purchaser for value of the goods without notice of the seller's interest, or as against a subsequent encumbrancer without notice of the prior claim. The failure to register the agreement, however, does not render it void as between the buyer and the seller. It should also be noted that some provinces have exempted the conditional seller from the requirement of registration for certain kinds of goods where the seller's name is affixed to the goods, and in some cases, provided special registration procedures for conditional sale agreements for specific chattels such as automobiles and farm machinery.

Registration of a conditional sale agreement must usually be made within a relatively short period of time after the sale is made, failing which, the seller must usually obtain a judge's order to permit registration. The time interval for registration varies from province to province and ranges from 20 to 30 days, with the latter being the most common. Once registered, the conditional sale agreement is usually protected for a period of three years.[15] If the goods are moved to another county, or to another province or territory, the registration of the conditional sale agreement would also be necessary in the new location in order to provide continued protection for the seller's interest and rights.

The registration of a conditional sale agreement between a manufacturer (or wholesaler) and a retailer would not, however, be effective against a purchaser of the goods from the retailer. A retailer who sells goods in the ordinary course of busi-

---

[14]All provinces except Ontario, Manitoba, Quebec, and Saskatchewan. The territories also have legislation for conditional sale agreements.

[15]The time-period in Nova Scotia is five years. See The *Conditional Sales Act*, R.S.N.S. 1967, c. 48 s. 11(1).

ness would give a good title to the goods to the purchaser, because the retailer had purchased the goods from the manufacturer for the purpose of resale. This particular rule makes good sense from the purchaser's point of view. Where a purchaser makes a purchase of goods from a retailer who deals in the goods, the purchaser should not be obliged to look behind the transaction to make certain that the retailer has good title. Instead, the law provides that the retailer gives a good title if the sale is in the ordinary course of business, and if the goods had been acquired for resale. An exception to this rule exists, however, with used goods, as a seller, even though a retailer, may not give a good title to used goods if the goods acquired were subject to the conditional sale made between a retailer and the person who had sold the used goods to a second retailer. For example, a manufacturer of snowmobiles sells a snowmobile to a retailer of snowmobiles under a conditional sale agreement that was subsequently registered. A purchaser of the snowmobile would acquire a good title to the snowmobile, even though the conditional sale agreement existed between the manufacturer and the retailer. This is the case, because the retailer had purchased the goods for resale. If we assume further that the sale by the retailer to the purchaser was by a registered conditional sale agreement, and the purchaser then traded the used snowmobile to another retailer for a different type of machine, the sale by the second retailer to a subsequent purchaser would not be protected. The purchaser of the used snowmobile would not get a good title to the machine, as the title would still be in the first retailer, who was the conditional seller. The reason why the second sale falls within the exception is that the sale by the

first retailer of the snowmobile was an "end sale" and not for the purpose of resale, hence the title would not pass from the conditional purchaser to the second retailer. The second retailer, as a result, could not pass a good title to a purchaser of the used machine.

A conditional seller may assign to a third party the title to goods covered by a conditional sale agreement. The rules applicable to the assignment of ordinary contracts also apply to conditional sale agreements. A common practice of merchants who sell goods by way of conditional sale agreements is to arrange with a financial institution (usually a finance company) to purchase the agreements once signed by the buyers, and to collect the money owing. The merchant with this type of arrangement assigns the agreements to the financial institution that would then register the agreements, give notice to the conditional buyers of the assignment, and collect the instalments as they fall due. As with all contracts, the assignee takes the agreement as it stands between the conditional buyer and the seller, and any defence which the buyer might have against the seller could also be raised against the assignee.

Apart from the protection of the seller's interest in the goods, conditional sale agreement legislation is generally designed to provide the buyer with relief against sellers who place onerous terms in the agreement itself. This usually takes the form of providing the buyer with time to redeem after default, since sellers frequently provide in their conditional sale agreements that they are entitled to repossess and sell the goods immediately on default.

Except in those provinces with consumer protection legislation that prohibits repossession where a substantial portion of the purchase price has been paid,[16] or where the goods are exempt from repossession,[17] the seller is generally free to repossess the goods when default occurs. Again, this is subject to qualification, as some provinces require that a "notice of intention to repossess" be first given, or a judge's order be obtained before the goods may be taken, but in no case may force be used to acquire possession of the goods. Once acquired however, the seller may then proceed with the sale of the chattels to recover the amount owing on the debt. To provide relief from a seller's right of immediate sale, and to introduce an element of fairness in the relationship, a buyer in default is given a period of time to find the funds necessary to complete the payment. Most provinces in their statutes require the seller who repossesses goods on default to hold the goods for a period of time before selling them. The time interval varies depending upon the province and method of repossession,[18] and ranges from 14 to 30 days, with 20 days being the most common time period for the buyer to redeem the goods.

A seller who repossesses goods with the intention of resale must comply strictly with the resale procedure requirements of the statute. For example, depending upon the particular province, the seller must provide written notice to the buyer of his intention to sell the goods. The notice must contain a detailed description of the goods, the amount owing and required in order for the buyer to redeem, and the time period in which the buyer has to make payment. In order to conduct a valid sale, the seller must carefully comply with the notice requirements, then wait the full statutory period before proceeding with the sale.

If the buyer fails to pay the balance owing within the prescribed time period, the seller may then proceed with the sale, and the proceeds obtained would be applied to the outstanding indebtedness. In some provinces, the seller may look to the buyer for any deficiency if the proceeds of the sale fail to pay the balance owing in full, but this right is only available when the seller has expressly established the right in the conditional sale agreement. Any surplus which the conditional seller may receive as a result of the sale, however, must be turned over to the buyer. All of the common law provinces and territories except Saskatchewan, provide an alternate remedy to the conditional seller in the event of default by permitting the seller to take legal action on the contract to recover the amount owing.

Bills of Sale

A bill of sale is a contract in which the title to goods passes to the buyer, but it is important from the buyer's point of view that certain formalities be followed where goods are purchased, and possession of the goods remains with the seller. Under these circumstances, if the buyer wishes to protect his interest in the goods, the bill of sale must be registered in accordance with the requirements of the provincial legislation relating to this type of transaction.

---

[16]New Brunswick, Nova Scotia, and Ontario, for example, prohibit repossession after two-thirds of the purchase price has been paid unless a court order is obtained. Manitoba fixes the amount at 75% of the selling price.

[17]Saskatchewan, for example restricts the right to repossess certain goods such as agricultural implements and certain household goods. See The *Exemptions Act*, R.S.S. 1978, c. E-14, s. 2.

[18]Alberta provides that the Sheriff must repossess and hold the goods for 14 days: see the *Seizures Act*, R.S.A. 1970, c. 338, s. 28.

The territories and all provinces except Quebec have legislation which requires a buyer of goods who takes title but not immediate possession to register the bill of sale in a designated public registry office (usually the County Court Office) within a specified time after the bill of sale is executed. The time for registration varies from province to province, and ranges from 5 days to 30 days.[19] Most statutes require that the bill of sale be accompanied by affidavit evidence of the buyer to the effect that the sale was a *bona fide* sale, and not for the purpose of defeating the claims of the seller's creditors. In addition, most provinces require affidavit proof that the seller signed the bill of sale, and some provinces impose special requirements on the parties where the bill of sale concerns the sale of an automobile.

The purpose of the legislation requiring the registration of the bill of sale is two-fold: First, it protects the interest or title of the buyer in the goods in the event that the seller should attempt to sell the goods a second time to another, unsuspecting buyer. Second, the registration provides public notice that the title has passed to the buyer, and creditors of the seller will be made aware that the ownership of the goods in the hands of the seller lies elsewhere. The affidavit of *bona fides* attached to the bill of sale is designed to discourage sellers from transferring the ownership of goods in their possession to a third party by way of a bill of sale to defeat their creditors. The fact that the document is registered in a public record office represents notice to the public at large of the transaction which has taken place.

Registration is generally effective for three years,[20] and a failure to register would permit an innocent third party who purchases the goods from the seller to obtain a good title to the goods, leaving the unregistered owner with only a right of action against the seller.

Assignment of Book Debts

The assignment of book debts is a method whereby a creditor of a merchant might take an assignment of the accounts receivable of the merchant and collect the debt to him from customers indebted to the merchant. The assignment is similar in many respects to the ordinary assignment of a contract in the sense that the debtors must be notified to make payment to the assignee, if the assignee should decide to have the debts paid directly to him. Because merchants are not enthusiastic at the thought that their customers will be notified by the creditor to make payments of their accounts directly to the creditor, the creditor and the merchant frequently agree that the general assignment of book debts will not be acted upon by the creditor while the merchant is not in default under the debt payment arrangement between them.

The assignment of book debts is subject to registration requirements under provincial legislation, in order that the creditor might preserve his claim to the book debts as security.[21] British Columbia, for example, requires an assignment of book debts to be registered within 21 days of the date upon which the assignment was exe-

---

[19]British Columbia requires registration within 21 days from the date of execution: see the *Bills of Sale Act*, 1961 (B.C.), c. 6, s. 10(a).

[20]Registration in Prince Edward Island is effective for five years. See the *Bills of Sale Act*, R.S.P.E.I. 1974, c. B-3, s. 11(2).

[21]This is provided under personal property security legislation in some provinces. See, for example, Ontario, the *Personal Property Security Act*, R.S.O. 1980, c. 375, s. 47(3) as amended by 1973, c. 102.

cuted.[22] Most other provinces have similar registration provisions. Registration is usually in the same public office where chattel mortgages and conditional sale agreement registers are maintained. Ontario, Manitoba, and Saskatchewan provide for registration of the security interest in a province-wide central registry under their personal property security legislation.[23] The mere fact that the assignment has been registered, however, does not give the creditor under a general assignment priority over a subsequent creditor who obtained an assignment of a specific debt, and gave notice to the debtor of the merchant to make payment of the debt to him.[24] A particular advantage of the properly executed and registered assignment of book debts, however, is that the assignee will acquire a secured claim to the book debts over the trustee in bankruptcy should the merchant become insolvent.

Personal Property Security Legislation

At the present time, three provinces[25] have modernized their legislation concerning the use of chattels and other personal property as security for debt, by the introduction of personal property security legislation. In addition, a number of other provinces and territories are in the process of introducing similar legislation.

The province of Ontario was the first Canadian province to implement the new system, which is based upon the United States' *Uniform Commercial Code*, Article 9.

In concept, the Act represents a complete overhaul of the older systems of registration of security interests and the elimination of a number of conflicting rules with respect to creditor's rights. The general thrust of the new legislation is to simplify transactions associated with securing debts, and to provide a simple system for the registration of all personal property security interests. The Act recognizes the fact that all of the older security devices had a common purpose: to provide the creditor with a security interest in personal property. To simplify the process of establishing the security interest, it abolishes the registration requirements of the older security devices, and replaces them with a single registration procedure for the *security interest*. This interest would represent, for example, the rights of the mortgagee under a chattel mortgage, or the rights of a conditional seller under a conditional sale agreement. The property to which this security interest attaches is called the *collateral*, which may be almost any type of personal property.

Under the Act, the proper registration of the security agreement *perfects* the security interest in the creditor. The registration establishes the creditor's priority right to the security interest in the personal property, and if it should be necessary for the creditor to take steps to realize on the collateral, the act of taking possession of the property (for example, under a conditional sale agreement) would be perfecting the creditor's interest in the collateral.

The Ontario statute establishes a procedure whereby security interests are registered at county registry offices in Ontario, and the information then transmitted to a central, computer-based storage system. This enables any person to make a search to determine if a security interest is claimed in personal property located any-

---

[22]The *Book Accounts Assignment Act*, R.S.B.C. 1979, c. 32, s. 6.

[23]See, for example, Ontario, the *Personal Property Security Act*, R.S.O. 1980, c. 375.

[24]*Snyder's Ltd. v. Furniture Finance Corp. Ltd.* (1930), 66 O.L.R. 79.

[25]Ontario, Manitoba and Saskatchewan.

where in the province. A failure to register, as required under the Act, would allow a subsequent purchaser to obtain a good title to the goods, or a subsequent creditor to obtain a security interest in the goods in priority over the unregistered security interest.

If a debtor defaults under a security agreement, depending upon the nature and provisions of the security agreement, the creditor may repossess the collateral and dispose of it by public or private sale in accordance with the procedure set out in the statute, and in the case of consumer goods the creditor must normally proceed with the sale within 90 days of repossession where the debtor has paid at least 60% of the amount owing. If the sale provides a surplus after all expenses have been paid, the balance must be paid over to the debtor. The right to redeem however, unless otherwise provided in writing is available to the debtor until the collateral is sold by the creditor, or until the creditor signifies in writing his intention to retain the goods in full satisfaction of the debt.

Secured Loans under the Bank Act, s. 178

In addition to ordinary secured loans which a bank may make under the *Bank Act*,[26] the legislation gives a bank the right to lend money to wholesalers, retailers, shippers, and dealers in "products of agriculture, products of the forest, products of the quarry and mine, products of the sea, lakes and rivers or goods, wares and merchandise, manufactured or otherwise" on the security of such goods or products, and to lend money to manufacturers on their goods and inventories. The Act also makes special provision for such loans to farmers, fishermen, and forestry producers on their equipment and goods as well as their crops and products.[27]

The Act provides that the borrower must sign a particular bank form and deliver it to the bank in order to vest in the bank a first and preferential lien on the goods or equipment similar to that which the bank might have acquired if it had obtained a warehouse receipt or bill of lading for the particular goods.[28] The bank usually extends the security interest to include after-acquired goods of a similar nature. To perfect its security interest, the bank need only register with the Bank of Canada a *notice of intention* to take the goods as security for the loan at any time within the three years prior to the date on which the security is given.[29] The registration is designed to give the bank priority over subsequent creditors and persons who acquire the goods (except for *bona fide* purchasers of the goods) or equipment, and over the trustee in bankruptcy in the event that the debtor should become insolvent, but the priority is not absolute. The failure to register the notice of intention as required under the Act would render the transaction void as against subsequent purchasers and mortgagees in good faith and for value.

The obvious advantage of the procedure under the *Bank Act* is the ease by which the security interest is established, and the broad reach of the claim to after-acquired goods. Its use, however, is limited only to those lenders set out in the legislation, and although this type of loan is available to a large group in terms of the commercial or business community, it represents only a

---

[26]The *Banks and Banking Law Revision Act*, 29 Eliz. II, c. 40. In force December 1, 1980.

[27]*Ibid.*, s. 178(1). This part of the new Act represents a revision of the s. 88 provisions of the previous Act.
[28]*Ibid.*, s. 178(2).
[29]*Ibid.*, s. 178(4).

small number, when compared to the consumer–borrower group who are not eligible for loans under this particular section of the Act.

Bonds, Debentures and Floating Charges

Corporations may use a variety of different methods of acquiring capital using the assets of the corporation as security for the debt. A corporation may, for example, mortgage its fixed assets, or it may pledge as security its chattels under a chattel mortgage. In addition to these various methods, a corporation has open to it the opportunity to raise funds by way of the issue of bonds and debentures.

Bonds and *debentures* are instruments issued by corporations which represent a pledge of the assets of the corporation or its earning power as security for debt. The two terms are used interchangeably to refer to debt obligations of the corporation, since no precise legal definition exists for either of these terms. Nevertheless, the term *bond* is generally used to refer to a debt that is secured by way of a mortgage, charge, or hypothec on the assets of the corporation. Such bonds are sometimes referred to as *mortgage bonds*.

The term *debenture* is frequently used with reference to debt that is unsecured or secured to the extent that it takes priority over unsecured creditors, but subsequent to secured debt such as first mortgage bonds. The practice however, of issuing bonds which secure debt by way of a mortgage on the fixed assets and chattels, and a *floating charge* on all other assets, leaves subordinate security holders with very little security in the event that the corporation becomes insolvent. As a result, holders of subordinate obligations are sometimes in much the same position as ordinary unsecured creditors.

Where the security is given to a single creditor, such as a bank or other financial institution, a single instrument is prepared and executed, but where the amount of capital desired through the issue of the bonds or debentures is substantial, and the terms of the debt obligation lengthy, the common practice is to prepare a *trust indenture* which embodies all of the terms and conditions of the indebtedness, and then issue shorter, less detailed debentures which incorporate the terms of the trust indenture by reference. These are then sold to the public as a means of acquiring capital for the corporation, and the purchasers of the securities become creditors of the corporation.

The practice of including a *floating charge* in the debt instrument provides the bond or debenture holders with added security. A floating charge is an equitable charge which does not affect the assets of the corporation or its operation so long as the terms and conditions of the security instrument are complied with, but in the event that some breach of the terms of the debt instrument occurs, the charge ceases to "float," and crystalizes. At that point it becomes a fixed charge, and attaches to the particular security covered by it. For example, finished goods of a manufacturer may be covered by a floating charge, and while the charge remains as an equitable charge, the corporation is free to sell or dispose of the goods, as it has the title and the right to do so. Default, however, will crystalize the charge, and it will immediately attach to the remaining goods in possession of the corporation. The goods will then become a part of the security which the holders of the debt obligation may look to for the purpose of satisfying their claims.

Legislation in each province requires corporations which issue securities or which pledge their assets by different forms of debt obligations to file the particulars of the bond or debenture and a true copy of the debt instrument with the Minister responsible for the administration of the Act.[30] The failure to do so within the prescribed time (usually 30 days) renders the bonds or debentures void as against any subsequent purchasers or encumbrancers for value and without notice of the prior debt obligations.

|||||||||||||||||||||||||||||||||||||||||||||||||||||||||||||||||||||||||

CASE 32.2
Evans v. Rival Granite Quarries, Ltd., [1910] 2 K.B. 979.

BUCKLEY, L.J.:

A floating security is not a future security; it is a present security, which presently affects all the assets of the company expressed to be included in it. On the other hand, it is not a specific security; the holder cannot affirm that the assets are specifically mortgaged to him. The assets are mortgaged in such a way that the mortgagor can deal with them without the concurrence of the mortgagee. A floating security is not a specific mortgage of the assets, plus a licence to the mortgagor to dispose of them in the course of his business, but is a floating mortgage applying to every item comprised in the security, but not specifically affecting any item until some event occurs or some act on the part of the mortgagee is done which causes it to crystallize into a fixed security. Mr. Shearman argued that it was competent to the mortgagee to intervene at any moment and to say that he withdrew the licence as regards any particular item. That is not in my opinion the nature of the security; it is a mortgage presently affecting all the items expressed to be included in it, but not specifically affecting any item till the happening of the event which causes the security to crystallize as

regards all the items. This crystallization may be brought about in various ways. A receiver may be appointed, or the company may go into liquidation and a liquidator be appointed, or any event may happen which is defined as bringing to an end the licence to the company to carry on business. There is no case in which it has been affirmed that a mortgagee of this description may at any moment forbid the company to sell a particular piece of property or may take it himself and keep it, and leave the licence to carry on the business subsisting as regards everything else. This would be inconsistent with the real bargain between the parties, which is that the mortgagee gives authority to the company to use all its property until the licence to carry on business comes to an end.

|||||||||||||||||||||||||||||||||||||||||||||||||||||||||||||||||||||||||

STATUTORY PROTECTION OF CREDITOR SECURITY

In addition to the secured rights that a creditor might obtain by taking a security interest in the property of the debtor, most provinces have provided the creditors of certain debtors with special statutory rights in cases where the actions of the debtor could seriously affect the rights of the creditors to payment. The first of these statutes is the *Bulk Sales Act*, and the second, the *Mechanics' Lien Act*. Both are designed to protect the rights of creditors in transactions in which the creditor may not be a party, and both provide the creditor with rights which were not originally available at common law.

Bulk Sales Act

Statutes pertaining to sales "in bulk" refer to the sale of all or large quantities of stock by a merchant in a transaction that is not in the ordinary course of business, or the sale of assets and equipment of the business it-

---

[30]In Ontario, for example, the filing must be made with the Minister of Consumer and Commercial Relations under the *Corporation Securities Registration Act*, R.S.O. 1980, c. 94, s. 56.

self to a purchaser. The purpose of the legislation is to protect the creditors of a merchant by requiring the merchant to comply with the procedure set down in the Act for all sales not in the ordinary course of business.

Canadian bulk sales legislation had its origins in the laws of the United States, rather than the laws of England. The first bulk sales statute was enacted in Ontario in 1917,[31] and most other provinces have since followed the Ontario example. At the present time, all provinces and the territories have bulk sales legislation in place, although provincial variation exists, in spite of attempts to draft uniform legislation.

Under the statutes of most provinces, a prospective buyer of the goods or assets of a business is obliged to follow the procedure set out in the Act, otherwise the sale may be declared void, and the buyer perhaps unable to recover the purchase price from the seller. The procedure set down for bulk sales generally permits the prospective buyer to make only a small deposit or down-payment on the goods or equipment, and withhold the balance until the seller in bulk either provides an affidavit to the effect that all creditors have been paid, or that arrangements have been made to pay the creditors in full from the proceeds of the sale. In the latter case, unless the creditors waive their rights in writing, the prospective buyer is obliged to have the proceeds paid to a trustee, who will arrange for the payment of the creditors.[32]

In some provinces a statement of indebtedness must also be provided to the prospective buyer, showing the amounts owing to each creditor of the seller. If the creditors claims do not exceed a stipulated amount (in Ontario, unsecured and secured creditor claims must be each less than $2 500[33] the buyer may then pay over the balance. In some provinces, it is also possible to obtain an order from the court to complete a sale in bulk if the court can be convinced that the transaction is in the best interests of the creditors.[34]

If the buyer fails to comply with the Act, an unpaid creditor may within a stipulated time, which ranges from 60 days in Saskatchewan[35] to 6 months in most other provinces,[36] attack the sale in bulk and have it declared void. The effect of such a declaration would be to make the goods purchased by the buyer available to satisfy the creditor's claims, and leave the buyer in the position where his only recourse is against the seller who may, under the circumstances, be difficult to find.

Mechanics' Lien Act

A *mechanics' lien* is a statutory right of a workman or contractor to claim a security interest in property to ensure payment for labour or materials applied to land or a chattel. A mechanics' lien is a creature of statute, and hence, is not a right available to a party except as provided under the legislation responsible for its creation and application. The lien takes two forms: a lien against real property, and a lien against chattels. Each is distinct and separate in the manner in which it is claimed and enforced, and consequently some provinces have established separate legislation to govern the two distinct types of liens. Other provinces, however, have in-

---

[31]The *Bulk Sales Act, 1917* (Ont.), 7 Geo V, c. 33.
[32]See, for example, Ontario, the *Bulk Sales Act*, R.S.O. 1980, c. 52, s. 9.
[33]The *Bulk Sales Act*, R.S.O. 1980, c. 52, s. 8.
[34]See, for example, Ontario, the *Bulk Sales Act*, R.S.O. 1980, c. 52, s. 3.
[35]The *Bulk Sales Act*, R.S.S. 1978, c. B-9, s. 39.
[36]See, for example, Ontario, the *Bulk Sales Act*, R.S.O. 1980, c. 52, s. 19.

corporated both in the same statute, but distinguished the procedure applicable to each.[37]

A mechanics' lien, like a sale in bulk, is subject to legislation which found its way into the common law provinces of Canada by way of the United States. The right of lien under the circumstances provided in mechanics' lien statutes is not of common law origin, but rather, has its roots in Roman law, and later, in the civil codes of European countries. As a result, the province of Quebec was the first Canadian province to possess legislation similar to the *Mechanics' Lien Acts* that were eventually enacted by the common law provinces. Manitoba and Ontario were the first common law provinces to adopt mechanics' lien legislation,[38] and the other provinces, over time, followed suit. At present, all provinces and territories in Canada have legislation which provide workmen with a right of lien against land, and although the legislation is not uniform, the general thrust and application of the law is similar everywhere.

A right of lien to protect the labour and materials of workmen and contractors was found to be necessary in the latter part of the 19th century, when the vulnerability of persons engaged in the construction industry became evident. The construction of buildings, regardless of size, usually requires large quantities of materials and the special skills of many craftsmen and professionals. At the time, these parties were tied together by a series of contracts under which each was required to invest labour or materials in a property in which they had no security interest to protect their in-

vestment. If the owner sold the property, and failed to pay the contractor, the contractors only recourse was legal action for breach of contract against the owner. Subcontractors were equally vulnerable. If the principal contractor became insolvent during the course of construction, the subcontractors and workmen had no recourse against the owner of the property for payment because their contract was with the principal contractor. In order to protect all parties who expended labour and materials on property, the *Mechanics' Lien Acts* were passed to give each workman or contractor a right to claim a lien against the property as security for payment, regardless of the relationship between the party and the property owner.

Under the mechanics' lien statutes of all provinces, the term "owner" is broadly defined to include not only the person who holds property *in fee simple*, but persons with lesser legal or equitable interests in property, and may include a mortgagee, or a tenant who enters into a construction contract. The broad definition of the term owner is compatible with the intent of the Act: to prevent the person entitled to the real property from obtaining the benefit of the labour and materials expended upon the land without providing compensation for the benefit received.

The class of persons entitled to claim a lien is equally as broad in most jurisdictions. It includes wage earners, subcontractors, material suppliers, suppliers of rental equipment used for construction purposes (in some provinces), the principal or prime contractor and, under certain circumstances, the architect.[39]

In addition to providing the right of lien to persons who expend labour and materi-

---

[37]The legislation in Ontario, for example, covers both types of liens in the same statute: see the *Mechanics' Lien Act*, R.S.O. 1980, c. 267, s. 48.

[38]The *Mechanics' Lien Act of 1873* 36 Vict., c. 27 (Ont.); the *Mechanics' Lien Act* 36 Vict., c. 31 (Man.) (1873).

[39]*Re Computime Canada Ltd.* (1971), 18 D.L.R. (3d) 127.

als to enhance the value of real property, the legislation also provides a simplified procedure for the enforcement of lien rights. Low cost and general compliance with formalities are emphasized in the enforcement procedure, but certain aspects, such as the time-limits set out in the Act are rigidly enforced.

The right to claim a lien arises when the first work is done on the property by the claimant, or when the material supplier delivers the first supplies to the building site. Thereafter, the workman, subcontractor, or material supplier may claim a lien at any time during the performance of the contract, and until a stipulated time after the work has been substantially performed. The time-limit following the date on which the last work was done (or material supplied) varies from province to province, and ranges from 30 days to 60 days, depending upon the nature of the work and the province. For example, in British Columbia, the time for registration of a lien is 31 days from the date on which the last work was done, but in the case of a mine or quarry, the time-limit is extended to 60 days.[40] In Ontario, the time-limit is 37 days.[41] In order to preserve the right to a lien, a *lien claim* must be registered in the land Registry Office in the jurisdiction where the land is situated, and notice of the lien claim given to the owner of the property.[42] In some provinces, however, a lien claimant's rights may be protected if another claimant has instituted lien proceedings, and filed a *certificate of action* within the time limits appropriate to protect the unregistered claimant. The registration of a lien gives the lien claimant priority over subsequent encumbrancers and subsequent mortgagees of the lands.

Following the registration of a lien claim, a lien action must be commenced within a relatively short period of time based upon the date when the last work was done, materials supplied, or lien filed (depending upon the province). An informal legal procedure then follows to determine the rights of the lien claimants, and the liability of the contractor and "owners" of the property. Lien claimants are treated equally in a lien action and, with the exception of wage earners who are entitled to all or a part of their wage claims in priority over other lien claimants, all are entitled to a share *pro rata* in the funds or property available.

In order to avoid disputes that may arise between the contractor and subcontractors, or others, the owner may avoid liability for payment of lien claims by complying with the *holdback* provisions of the Act. These sections require the owner to withhold a certain percentage of the monies payable to the contractor (15% in the case of Ontario)[43] for a period of time following the completion of the contract (37 days in the case of Ontario).[44] The holdback replaces the land for lien purposes, and if claims for lien should be filed within the period that the "owner" is obliged to holdback the funds, the owner may pay the lien claims (or pay the money into court if the claims exceed the holdback) and obtain a *discharge of the lien* or a *vacating order* to clear the liens from the title of the property. The failure of an owner to hold back the required funds would oblige the owner to pay the amount necessary to clear the liens (up to the amount of the required

[40]*Builders Lien Act,* R.S.B.C. 1979, c. 40, s. 22(1).
[41]The *Mechanics' Lien Act,* R.S.O. 1980, c. 261, s. 21.
[42]*Ibid.,* ss. 16, 21 and 22.

[43]The *Mechanics' Lien Act,* R.S.O. 1980, c. 261, s. 11(1).
[44]*Ibid.*

holdback) in order to free the property from lien claims. If the "owner" should be insolvent or unable to pay the holdback, the lien claimants may proceed with the lien action, and have the property sold by the court to satisfy their claims.

Some provinces, notably British Columbia, Manitoba, New Brunswick, Ontario, and Saskatchewan, provide additional protection to subcontractors and wage earners by declaring in their legislation that all sums received by the contractor from the "owner" constitute trust funds for the benefit of the subcontractors, work-

men, and material suppliers. These funds must be used first for the payment of the suppliers of labour and materials before the contractor is entitled to the surplus. A failure to distribute the funds in this fashion would constitute a breach of trust on the part of the contractor.

The trust provision of the various lien acts has been the subject of much litigation in order to establish the rights of creditors and other parties to the funds, but the provision, nevertheless, remains as an added security for the payment of those who depend upon the contractor for payment for their goods or services.

SUMMARY

The desire of creditors to reduce risk in debt transactions is reflected in the development of the large and varied assortment of debt instruments available to the business community today. With the exception of the land mortgage, and the pledge of goods as security for debt, most of these instruments have been developed within the past few centuries. The chattel mortgage was one of the first security instruments to be developed and recognized as a means of securing debt against chattels by way of a transfer of the title to the creditor. The conditional sale agreement was used in a somewhat similar fashion, but the seller simply retained the title, and gave the conditional buyer possession. When the price was paid, title passed to the buyer. Both of these instruments were used to facilitate purchases of goods.

Corporations are permitted to use a number of different methods of raising capital on the security of their assets. These take the form of bonds and debentures, which may represent charges on specific assets by way of mortgage, or they may be simply unsecured debentures, or debentures secured by way of a floating charge.

The need for business to finance purchases of goods resulted in the development of other security interests. The assignment of book debts permitted creditors to obtain security for debt on loans to merchants and, under the *Bank Act*, banks were entitled to make loans to wholesalers, manufacturers, lumber businesses, farmers, and fishermen on a security interest in inventories, equipment, crops and machinery. In addition to these forms of creditor security, statutory protection for unsecured creditors also developed in the form of legislation designed to establish creditors' rights to payment when a sale of the assets of a business was made in bulk, or where subcontractors, workmen, and material suppliers increased the value of property by their labour and materials. In the former case, unsecured creditors in a bulk sale were given the right to have a sale declared void if they were not paid, and in the latter case, mechanics' lien legislation established a statutory right of lien against the property to secure payment of the claims of subcontractors and workmen.

Apart from legislation designed to establish special rights for unsecured creditors and persons in the construction industry, all security interests are designed to protect creditors' claims to the debtor's assets in the event of default. Because of the many confusing procedures and security instruments associated with these interests, attempts have been made by some provinces to streamline and simplify the procedures. These statutes, which are commonly referred to as *Personal Property Security Acts*, are already in place in Ontario, Manitoba, and Saskatchewan.

||||||||||||||||||||||||||||||||||||||||||||||||||||||||||||||||||||||||||||||||||||||||||||||||||||||||||||||||||||||||||||||||||||||||||||||||||||||||||||||||||||||||||||||||||||||||||||

DISCUSSION QUESTIONS

1. *Distinguish a "chattel mortgage" from a "pledge" or "pawn" of a chattel.*
2. *What rights are available to a chattel mortgagee in the event that the mortgagor should default in payment?*
3. *Why were early chattel mortgages viewed with suspicion by the courts?*
4. *Distinguish a "chattel mortgage" from a "conditional sale agreement." Is a conditional sale agreement identical to a "hire–purchase agreement"? If not, why not?*
5. *Why is registration necessary in the case of chattel mortgages and conditional sale agreements? How does a failure to register affect the rights of the chattel mortgagee or conditional seller?*
6. *Explain the purpose of the* Personal Property Security Acts *that several of the provinces have enacted. In what way do they affect chattel mortgages and conditional sale agreements?*
7. *What is the purpose and effect of an "assignment of book debts"?*
8. *Under what circumstances must a "bill of sale" be registered?*
9. *Apart from mortgages of land and chattel mortgages, what other types of securities might be given to creditors of a corporation to secure repayment of the corporation's borrowing of funds?*
10. *Explain the nature of a "floating charge." Why is this particular type of security interest frequently included in the bonds and debentures of a corporation?*
11. *Describe the nature of the security which a chartered bank might take for funds advanced under s. 178 of the* Banks and Banking Law Revision Act. *What procedure must the bank follow to secure the loan?*
12. *"The Bulk Sales Act is designed to preserve the assets of a business for unsecured creditors, but the Act does not affect transactions made in the ordi-*

nary course of business by the merchant." Why is this so? What is the purpose of the Act?

13. *Identify the purpose and intent of the* Mechanics' Lien Act. *What special rights does the legislation give persons who supply goods or materials in the construction of buildings on land?*

14. *How does a mechanics' lien arise? How is it enforced?*

15. *Why is a "holdback" of a portion of the contract price by the "owner" necessary when the contractor demands payment of the contract price on the completion of construction?*

16. *What is a "trust fund" under the* Mechanics' Lien Act? *How does this device protect workmen and subcontractors?*

JUDICIAL
DECISIONS

Assignment of
Book Debts—
Conditional
Sale
Agreements
—Priority
of Creditors

Snyder's Ltd. v. Furniture Finance Corp. Ltd. (1930), 66 O.L.R. 79.
The plaintiff manufactured furniture and sold the goods to Fagel, a retailer. To secure the indebtedness, the plaintiff took an assignment of existing and future book debts from the retailer, and registered the assignment pursuant to the *Assignment of Book Debts Act*. Some time later, the retailer entered into an arrangement with the defendant to sell goods under conditional sale agreements, and assign the agreements to it.

When the plaintiff discovered the arrangement between the retailer and the defendant, it brought an action against the defendant claiming that it was entitled to the payment of all funds under the conditional sale agreements.

At trial, the action was dismissed, and the plaintiff appealed to the Court of Appeal.

ORDE, J.A.:

> The plaintiff is claiming by virtue of a general assignment to it by one Fagel of "all debts, accounts, claims, moneys, and choses in action which now are or which may at any time hereafter be due or owing to or owned by the undersigned (i.e. Fagel), and also all contracts, bills, notes, and other documents now held or owned or which may be hereafter taken, held, or owned by the undersigned, or any one on behalf of the undersigned, in respect of the said debts, accounts, claims, moneys, and choses in action, or any part thereof." This assignment was taken "as a general and continuing collateral security for payment of all existing and future indebtedness and liability" of Fagel to the plaintiff.

> This assignment was duly registered as required by the Assignment of Book Debts Act, which is now R.S.O. 1927, ch. 166, and some stress was laid upon this registration as if it in some way placed the plaintiff in a position superior to that of the defendant. This is, of course, not the effect of the Act. The Act does not either expressly or impliedly confer any greater right upon an assignee of a chose in action than he had before. All it does is to make a general assignment of book-debts void, as

against creditors and subsequent purchasers or mortgagees in good faith and for value, unless registered. By registration the plaintiff here has preserved whatever rights it acquired by virtue of the assignment and no more. In other words, its rights are to be determined exactly as if the Act had never been passed.

What are those rights? The assignment as such transferred to the plaintiff no rights in the choses in action which were recognised at common law. Its efficacy was and still is based solely upon principles of equity, with the additional statutory right given to the assignee to bring action in his own name, instead of that of the assignor, against the debtor, upon giving notice to the latter: Conveyancing and Law of Property Act, R.S.O. 1927, ch. 137, sec. 49. The assignee takes subject to all the equities. He cannot acquire higher rights against the debtor than those of the assignor himself, and his rights may be defeated or impaired by the intervention of some other assignee who, by giving notice to the debtor of his assignment, or for some other reason, acquires a superior equitable title.

Let us see how these principles are applicable to the present transaction. Fagel is a dealer in furniture. If he were to make an absolute sale of some article to a customer upon credit, the resulting debt would clearly come within the assignment to the plaintiff. If, in spite of that assignment, Fagel were to assign the debt to some other person, and that other were to give notice thereof to the debtor, the equity of the second assignee would be superior to that of the plaintiff.

The alleged debts or choses in action in this present case are not of that simple character. Fagel, as the owner of the furniture he was dealing in, was free to sell it upon any terms he chose, either by a simple sale for cash or upon credit, or by means of more complicated contracts, such as conditional sales, whereby the title to the goods remained in him and the purchaser could get no title until payment in full. Still retaining the title in the goods, there was nothing to prevent him from transferring that title with the purchaser's obligations in respect thereof to the defendant, either for cash, or in discharge of previous advances made to him, or upon credit. Had he sold or transferred the conditional sale contracts for cash or in satisfaction of previous advances, the plaintiff could have no greater rights than if the plaintiff had sold direct to the customer for cash, and had retained the cash or used it to discharge his indebtedness to the defendant. If the sale or transfer to the defendant were upon credit, so that the defendant took over all the benefits and assumed all the obligations of Fagel under the conditional sale contract, then there would be, of course, a simple book-debt or chose in action owing by the defendant to Fagel, which the plaintiff, after giving due notice in compliance with the statute, could enforce against the defendant.

That is not what the plaintiff seeks in this action. The whole cause of action set up by the statement of claim and the prayer for relief are founded upon the supposed right by virtue of the assignment to compel the defendant to account to the plaintiff in respect of any debts to Fagel which were assigned by him to the defendant, and for all moneys received by the defendant in respect thereof. It is not alleged or attempted to be proved that the plaintiff ever attempted to place its equity upon a higher footing than that of the defendant by giving notice to Fagel's debtors. Having regard to the nature of the debts themselves and the terms of the conditional sales agreements by which they were incurred, how effective any such notice would have been may be open to question, for it is clear that an assignee of money payable under a contract takes the assignment subject to the conditions of the contract: *Government of Newfoundland* v. *Newfoundland Railway Co.* (1888), 13 App. Cas. 199; *Tooth* v. *Hallett* (1869), L.R. 4 Ch. 242. See also the judgment of this Court in *Interior Trust Co.* v. *Essex Border Utilities Commission* (1928), 62 O.L.R. 551.

Had the plaintiff claimed to recover moneys due by the defendant to Fagel in respect of their dealings with each other—and, as I have said, the general assignment by Fagel to the plaintiff embraced all such choses in action—different considerations would have arisen and the evidence would have been directed to that issue.

It is to be observed that the form of conditional sale contract used by Fagel contains an express provision that the contract may be assigned to the defendant company. This right reserved by Fagel as a term of the contract was an equity to which the plaintiff's assignment was subject, upon the principle exemplified by the cases I have just mentioned. When Fagel exercised that right, there was in fact, as a result of the very bargain between himself and his customer, the purchaser, a complete novation whereby the purchaser became indebted to the defendant, and there was nothing left upon which the plaintiff's assignment could operate, so far as any debt due by the purchaser to Fagel was concerned. Having regard to the nature of each contract, to the provision therein just mentioned, and to the fact that Fagel specifically assigned and transferred to the defendant for value all his interest therein and in the moneys payable thereunder, and also in the goods conditionally sold thereby, the defendant became absolutely entitled as against the plaintiff to the moneys payable by the customer; and, if there were any equities arising out of the transaction at all, the equity of the defendant was higher than that of the plaintiff. There was no evidence that the defendant had any notice of the existence of the plaintiff's assignment, which might perhaps have affected the defendant's equities, and there is nothing in the Assignment of Book Debts Act to make mere registration notice to the world at large.

For these reasons, I think the plaintiff fails and its appeal must be dismissed.

||||||||||||||||||||||||||||||||||||||||||||||||||||||||||||||||||||||||||||||||||||||||||||||||||||||||||||||||||||||||||||||||||||||||||||||||||||||||||||||

Mechanics' Liens—Owner's Holdback— Claimant's　**Hill et al. Ltd. v. Pozzetti and Davis, [1936] O.W.N. 632.**

The plaintiff, a material supplier, claimed a mechanics' lien for materials supplied to the owner and contractor for the construction of a house. The required holdback by the owner was 20% of the contract price

Right to Full Amount of Claim After Notice Given

(under the Act as it stood at the time) and the owner held back that amount. The supplier argued that the lien should cover the full amount owing to the supplier as a result of its notice to the owner. The trial judge decided in favour of the plaintiff. The defendants then appealed.

LATCHFORD, C.J.:

. . . delivering the written judgment of the Court, said that the judgment appealed from declared that under The Mechanics' Lien Act, R.S.O. 1927, ch. 173, the plaintiff was entitled to a lien upon certain described land owned by the defendant Pozzetti for $1,913.81, debt and interest, with costs amounting to $312.68, or, in all, $2,226.69.

Then the judgment directs that if the amount of the debt should be paid into Court before a date, now long past, the lien of the plaintiff should be discharged, and the money so paid into Court paid out in satisfaction of the claim of the plaintiff.

In case of default the judgment ordered that the lands be sold and the purchase money paid into Court to the credit of this action. The judgment further orders that the purchase money be applied in and towards payment of the plaintiffs' claim with subsequent interest and costs as computed by the Master of the Court at Cochrane. If the purchase money should be insufficient to pay the plaintiff's claim in full, the defendants, Pozzetti and Davis, were to pay to the plaintiff the amount remaining due forthwith after the same should be ascertained by the plaintiff.

Pozzetti's notice of appeal sets forth that the judgment should be varied in that it should be entered against Pozzetti for the sum of $759.36 only and without costs, on the following stated grounds:

(1) that the judgment so far as it found Pozzetti indebted to the plaintiff for anything in excess of $759.36 was against the evidence and the weight thereof,

(2) that tender of the $759.36 was made to the plaintiff before action brought; and

(3) that the defendant Pozzetti is still ready to pay the same amount, when the action should be dismissed as against Pozzetti without costs.

It is then alleged that the plaintiff failed to establish any binding agreement by Pozzetti to pay any moneys to the plaintiff, and that the appellant complied with the provisions of section 11 of The Mechanics' Lien Act, and thereby absolved himself from any liability to the plaintiff beyond the said sum of $759.36.

What seems to be the most material ground alleged by the appellant is that the plaintiff failed to establish an agreement on the part of Pozzetti to pay any moneys to the plaintiff for materials supplied to Davis. Whether such an agreement was made or not was a question of fact, found against the appellant upon evidence directly contradictory.

Against the evidence of Pozzetti the learned trial Judge credited Burnes, the manager of the plaintiff company, corroborated as it was to some extent by the witnesses Calverly and Connolly. The circumstances fully warranted the conclusion on this point reached by the learned trial Judge.

Pozzetti had given a contract to Davis for the erection of a particular house on the former's property in the Town of Timmins. The amount payable to Davis on completion of the building was to be $4,183. Pozzetti was a man of substance, while Davis had no financial standing, as Burnes was well aware. The plaintiff was a company dealing in lumber and other building materials. On July 9, 1935, Davis ordered certain lumber from the plaintiff to be used in the construction of the Pozzetti house. On the same day Burnes addressed a letter to Pozzetti stating on behalf of the plaintiff that it was furnishing "some building material to P. L. Davis for the construction of your residence . . . and we would ask you to see that this material is paid for before settling with Davis in full; otherwise we will have to protect ourselves in the usual manner."

The price of the material supplied on the 9th, 10th, and 11th of July was not very great, but during the next two weeks additional material to the value of about $600 was delivered to Davis, bringing the total amount then owing to the plaintiff to about 20 per cent. of the contract price, required by section 11 of the Act to be held by the owner for thirty days after the completion or abandonment of the work. As Pozzetti did not reply to the plaintiff's letter Burnes refused to supply Davis with more materials unless a definite undertaking was given by Pozzetti that he would become personally responsible for the whole amount.

The appellant, undoubtedly, had the interview deposed to by Burnes, and gave, as was found against him, the undertaking to pay for all material delivered to Davis. Ultimately materials to the value of $1,898.91 were supplied to the contractor for use in the construction of Pozzetti's house.

After receiving from Pozzetti about $3,000, and having some additional sums paid for him by the owner, Davis abandoned the contract. It cost the owner, according to his evidence, about $300 to finish the building.

It does not seem to be disputed that what the appellant paid Davis and paid on his account amounted to $3,166.33, leaving in the owner's hands the difference between that sum and the contract price, or $1,016.37, a sum sufficient to pay about 40 per cent. of the outstanding claims of the plaintiff and other material men and mechanics. Pozzetti, through his solicitor, offered to pay to the plaintiff that percentage of its claim or $759.50, "if accepted as in full payment of the $1,898.91." The plaintiff refused to accept the amount so tendered, and proceeded to enforce a lien which had been duly filed and registered against the appellant's property pursuant to the provisions of the Act. The lien was for the whole sum due to the plaintiff, and the judgment appealed against decides, as already mentioned, that the lien is enforceable against the land on which the house was constructed.

In determining that a lien for all that was claimed, with costs, could be enforced for such sums, the judgment was erroneous, and the appeal should be in part allowed.

Twenty per cent. of the contract price and much in excess of that percentage had been held by Pozzetti. His liability was not enlarged by the letter of July 9th, but rests on his agreement made for good consideration that he would pay the respondent for what it furnished to Davis. The amount of the lien is strictly limited by the Statute and can properly affect the land of the plaintiff no more heavily than the statute permits. The lien against Pozzetti's property should be limited to that amount.

||||||||||||||||||||||||||||||||||||||||||||||||||||||||||||||||||||||||||||||||||||||||||||||||||||||||||||||||||||||||||||||||||||||||||||||||||||

CASE PROBLEMS FOR DISCUSSION

Case 1

Hazel purchased a sewing machine from the Easy-So Company under a conditional sale agreement which required her to make 36 equal monthly payments of $15 each in order to fully pay for the machine. Easy-So Company assigned the conditional sale agreement to Easy Finance immediately after the agreement was signed by Hazel. Easy Finance registered the agreement in accordance with the provincial legislation pertaining to security instruments of this type, and notified Hazel of the assignment.

Hazel used the machine for several months, during which time she found that the machine required constant adjustment by the seller. Eventually, Hazel came to realize that the sewing machine was unsuitable for her purpose, and she arranged with Easy-So to take back the machine as a trade-in on a different type of sewing machine which the dealer also sold. Hazel paid the cost difference of $100, and took the new machine home.

Without advising Easy Finance of the change in the transaction, Easy-So Company sold the trade-in model to Henrietta for $350 cash.

Some time later, Hazel defaulted in her payments to Easy Finance, and the finance company repossessed her sewing machine. When the finance company indicated that it intended to sell the machine to satisfy the debt, Hazel demanded the return of the machine on the basis that it was not the sewing machine described in the conditional sale agreement. When Easy Finance confirmed the error, it traced the machine covered by the conditional sale agreement to Henrietta, then seized the proper sewing machine.

Both Hazel and Henrietta brought a legal action against Easy Finance for a return of their respective sewing machines. Advise all parties of their legal position in this case, and indicate the possible outcome. What is the legal position of Easy-So Company?

CASE 2

Casey, a resident of the United States, visited Canada with his sail boat, and while in Canada sold the boat to his friend Donald, who resided in Toronto, Ontario. The friend purchased the sail boat for $10 000. Some time later, Donald purchased a power boat from a dealer, and used the sail boat as a trade-in to cover part of the purchase price. The dealer made a search for security interests under the provincial *Personal Property Security Act,* and found no claims against the sail boat. The boat dealer sold the sail boat some time later to Morgan under a conditional sale agreement, and registered the security interest. Morgan later sold the sail boat to Kidd for $8 000, and moved to the province of Alberta.

Kidd did not make a search for creditor claims at the time of the purchase, and had paid over the money unaware of the boat dealer's registered security interest in the property.

The conditional sale agreement went into default when Morgan neglected to make a payment to the boat dealer, but before the dealer could find the boat, Customs and Excise claimed that the sail boat had been illegally brought into Canada, and the property in the goods as a result had vested in the Crown.

Discuss the rights of the parties, including the Crown, in this case.

CASE 3

Smith carried on business as a wholesaler, and operated a fleet of delivery trucks to supply his customers. He found the cost of maintaining the delivery equipment excessive, and decided to sell his fleet of trucks. He arranged to have all delivery work handled by a local cartage company, and advertised for a buyer for his delivery equipment.

Eventually, he found a buyer willing to purchase the trucks for $80 000 and the sale was immediately completed.

Some months later, a creditor of Smith discovered that he no longer possessed a fleet of trucks, and complained that the trucks should not have been sold without his permission, even though he was only an unsecured creditor to whom Smith owed $6 000 on a trade account.

What are the rights of the parties in this case? What steps should Smith have taken to avoid creditor complaints?

CASE 4

Baxter owned a block of land which fronted on a large lake, and on May 1st, entered into a contract with Cottage Construction Company to have a custom-designed cottage constructed on the site. Cottage Construction Company fixed the contract price at $50 000, payable $10 000 on the signing of the agreement, and the balance on the completion of the contract. Baxter signed the contract, and urged the building contractor to begin construction immediately. On May 1st, he gave the contractor a cheque in the amount of $10 000.

Cottage Construction Company entered into the following subcontracts for the construction work:

(a) $3 000 contract with Able Excavation to excavate and prepare the foundation. Work to be completed on June 1st.

(b) $15 000 contract with Larch Lumber Company for materials, the last to be delivered by July 1st.

(c) $10 000 contract with Ace Framing Contractors to provide labour only to erect and close in the cottage by July 20th.

(d) $5 000 contract with Roofing Specialty Company to install and shingle the building roof by July 20th.

(e) $5 000 contract with Volta Electrical for wiring and electric heating equipment, the work to be completed by August 1st.

Cottage Construction Company agreed in its contract to have the cottage completed and ready for occupancy by August 6th. Work progressed on schedule, and each subcontractor completed the subcontract on the agreed finish date. By August 1st, the cottage was almost ready for occupancy; only the door trim and eavestroughing remained unfinished.

On August 1st, the proprietor of Cottage Construction Company approached Baxter and asked him if he might receive the balance of the contract price, as he wished to use the funds to pay his subcontractors. Baxter gave him a cheque for the remaining $40 000, confident that the contract would be completed.

On August 2nd, a dispute arose between Cottage Construction and Ace Framing Contractors over the terms of the contract between them, and Cottage Construction refused to make payment. Ace Framing Contractors registered a mechanics' lien against the cottage lot later the same day. All of the other subcontractors immediately became aware of the lien claim, and registered liens on August 3rd.

The next day, Cottage Construction Company was found to be insolvent without having paid the subcontractors.

Discuss the legal rights (if any) and liability (if any) of the various subcontractors, Baxter, and Cottage Construction Company. Indicate the probable outcome of the case.

CHAPTER 33

Bankruptcy and Insolvency

HISTORICAL INTRODUCTION

The debt transaction carries with it a risk that the loan or debt will not be repaid, either as a result of some misfortune that falls upon the debtor, or as a result of the debtor's deliberate refusal to make payment. The secured transaction is essentially an attempt by a creditor to ensure repayment, regardless of the circumstances which might affect the debtor's ability to repay the debt in the future. Secured transactions, in terms of time, are relatively recent phenomena. Most early security transactions required the creditor to take physical possession of the debtor's property, either by moving into possession of the mortgagor's land, in the case of a mortgage, or taking actual possession of goods pledged as security for debt. The more common forms of security such as chattel mortgages, conditional sale agreements, and mechanics' liens did not receive judicial or statutory (in the case of mechanics' liens) recognition until the 19th century. Before that time, and indeed until well into the 20th century, trade debt transactions were for the most part unsecured, as were most concerning personal debt. The extension of credit was generally based upon the promise of repayment by the borrower or credit buyer. As a result, the reputation of the debtor was the major criterion in the creditor's decision to lend money or extend credit. Nevertheless, debtors with the best of intentions sometimes encountered financial difficulties due to unforeseen illness or injury, loss of employment, or a decline in business, and found themselves unable to pay their debts. To compound the problems of creditors, persons who deliberately set out to defraud creditors seemed to be ever present.

In past times, debtors who found themselves in the position where they were unable to pay their debts often were obliged to place themselves and their families at the mercy of their creditors. Under early Roman law, a debtor was generally brought before the judges, and if the debt was proved, could be taken by creditor and placed in chains for 60 days pending payment of the debt. If the debtor's relatives and friends were unable to make payment, the creditor had the right to put the debtor to death if he so desired, or he could sell the debtor into foreign slavery.

Much later, Roman law recognized the distinction between the honest but unfortunate debtor, and the debtor who obtained credit by fraud or deception, and established separate remedies for the creditor in each case. The debtor who could establish that his inability to repay the debt was due to matters beyond his control could avoid execution by delivering up his assets to his creditors. The dis-

honest debtor, on the other hand, was not granted this privilege.

The term, "bankruptcy," did not appear until the Middle Ages, and was of Italian origin. With the rise of trade and the general increase in commercial activity, many small businesses developed, and invariably some tradesmen or artisans encountered financial difficulties. The solution adopted by creditors during that period was to attend at the place of business of the debtor, and break up his work-bench. The term bankruptcy was derived from the Italian *bankarupta* which literally translated means "broken bench."

While the *bankarupta* process of the early Italian creditors was no doubt an effective method of demonstrating their displeasure with the debtor's default, it did little to satisfy their financial loss. The Roman law, however, still applied, and the debtor's assets (other than his work bench) presumably remained open to seizure by the creditors to satisfy their debts.

The law in England took a different approach with respect to the early Lombardy merchants who travelled to England (from what is now Italy) to sell their wares. If a Lombard merchant left England without paying his debts, the entire company of Lombard merchants was obliged to answer for it. This statutory protection[1] afforded to English creditors, was one of the first laws introduced to deal with insolvency and fraud by traders.

The expansion of trade carried with it an expansion of credit, and the inevitable problem of default by debtors (either by

---

[1]"The Debt of a Lombard Unpaid Shall Be Satisfied By His Company," 25 Edw. III, Stat. 5, c. 23.

accident or design) to the sorrow of their creditors. The common law at the time did not address itself to the problems of trade creditors, and provided only a rather complex procedure which a creditor was obliged to follow in order to attach the property of a debtor. For this reason, creditors were, for all practical purposes, left with the rules of the law merchant (such as they were) in their dealings with debtors, and it was not until the 16th century that the government recognized the unsatisfactory state of affairs that developed when a debtor became insolvent.

The first statute to deal with the problem of debtor default was passed in 1542,[2] and provided a means whereby all of the debtor's property, both real and personal, was delivered up and liquidated. The proceeds were then distributed ratably to the creditors. The statute was designed, however, for more than simply the distribution of the debtor's assets, for its principal thrust was the determination and punishment of any fraud on the part of the insolvent debtor. The legislation was subsequently amended (in 1571) to limit the right to "bankruptcy" to persons engaged in trade.[3] The ordinary debtor, as a result, was subject to imprisonment until friends or relatives satisfied the creditor's claims.

The bankruptcy laws were modified again in the late 17th and early 18th century with the passage of statutes which permitted an insolvent merchant to surrender himself to the court for examination, and to deliver all of his property to his creditors.[4] If he complied with the statute, he would be granted a discharge from his debts, but if he had committed any fraud, or attempted to conceal assets, the penalty was severe: The laws provided that the merchant be hanged.

Bankruptcy legislation during the 19th century was provided for the non-trader as well as the merchant–debtor. The law was first modified to provide that a person imprisoned for debt could be released if he surrendered all of his assets to his creditors under the supervision of the court. Later, both insolvent trade debtors and ordinary debtors were brought under new bankruptcy legislation passed in 1861 which established special procedures, and a Court of Bankruptcy.[5] In 1869, a new *Bankruptcy Act* was passed which abolished imprisonment for debt (except in the case of a person with assets who wilfully refused to pay his debts), and established a different procedure for the distribution of the assets of the debtor amongst the creditors. The new Act provided for a system of creditor control over the liquidation and distribution of the debtor's assets. Under the Act, a trustee was appointed, who administered the debtor's estate under the supervision of a committee of creditors appointed by the general body of creditors. Difficulties with the procedure, however, prompted the government in 1883 to change the law again, and a modified system was introduced which provided for a joint system of control by the creditors and court officials.[6]

Bankruptcy law in England with minor modifications was accepted by the financial community and debtors alike. It was

[2]"An Act Against Such Persons As Do Make Bankrupt," 34 & 35 Hen. VIII, c. 4.
[3]"An Act Touching Orders For Bankrupts," 13 Eliz. I, c. 7.
[4]"An Act For The Further Description Of Bankrupts, etc.," 21 Jac. I, c. 19. This Act was extended by "An

Act to Prevent Frauds Frequently Committed By Bankrupts," 4 Anne, c. 17.
[5]The *Bankruptcy Act, 1861*, 24 & 25 Vict., c. 134.
[6]The *Bankruptcy Act, 1883*, 46 & 47 Vict., c. 52.

not, however, used as a model for Canadian legislation to the same degree as other English statutes adopted later in the century. Instead, Canada introduced its own insolvency legislation in 1869,[7] then some years later repealed the Act,[8] leaving the problems of insolvency and debt with the provinces until 1919, when it once again occupied the field.[9]

The *Bankruptcy Act* of 1919 provided for the liquidation of the debtor's assets, and the release of the honest debtor, with no protection for the debtor in cases of fraud or wilful wastage of assets. Over the next 30 years, the Act proceeded through a series of amendments, with greater official supervision of the liquidation and disposition process added by each change. These changes were made by borrowing in part, some of the provisions of the English Act of 1883. By 1949, however, an overhaul of the legislation was necessary in order to clarify and simplify the procedures and the application of the Act. The revisions became the *Bankruptcy Act, 1949*,[10] and apart from a major amendment in 1966,[11] and a number of minor alterations over the years, the Act constitutes the principal bankruptcy and insolvency legislation in Canada at the present time.

BANKRUPTCY LEGISLATION IN CANADA
Purpose and Intent

The present bankruptcy legislation has a threefold purpose. It is designed first of all to provide an honest but unfortunate debtor with a release from his debts if he delivers up his assets to his creditors in accordance with the Act. The second general thrust of the legislation is to eliminate certain preferences, and provide a predictable and fair distribution of the assets of the debtor amongst the unsecured creditors in accordance with the priorities set out in the statute. A third purpose of the law is to uncover and punish debtors who attempt to defraud creditors by various means. The legislation, being federal law, has the added benefit of providing a uniform system for dealing with bankruptcy throughout Canada.

||||||||||||||||||||||||||||||||||||||||||||||||||||||||||||||||||||||||||||||||||

CASE 33.1
Re Buell, [1955] O.W.N. 421.

SMILY J.:

I think it is a fair statement to say that originally bankruptcy and insolvency legislation was designed to enable the assets of an honest debtor to be equitably distributed among his creditors, and to enable him to have a livelihood, in business or otherwise, which he might have difficulty in doing unless he was freed of the burden of his debts, and, with respect to a debtor who was not engaged in business but who had been imprisoned for non-payment of his debts, that he might be released from imprisonment. Bankruptcy laws are now of wider application and provide for the right of persons who are not engaged in business to make assignments of their property to trustees for distribution amongst their creditors and for discharge from further liability with respect to their debts, subject, of course, to certain rules and conditions. But, as has been said, The Bankruptcy Act should not be regarded as a clearing-house for the liquidation of debts solely, irrespective of the circumstances in which they were incurred. As to the position of the debtor, if it is a case of a person being so

---

[7]*The Insolvent Act of 1869*, 32-33 Vict., c. 16 (Can.).
[8]"An Act to repeal the Acts Respecting Insolvency Now In Force in Canada," 43 Vict., c. 1 (Can.).
[9]The *Bankruptcy Act*, 9-10 Geo. V, c. 36 (Can.) (1919).
[10]The *Bankruptcy Act, 1949*, 13 Geo. VI, c. 7 (Can.).
[11]"An Act to Amend the Bankruptcy Act," 14-15 Eliz. II, c. 32 (Can.) (1966).

weighed down by his debts as to be incapable of properly earning a living or of performing the ordinary duties of citizenship, including the support of a wife and family, that is one thing; but where the only object to be served is the comfort and convenience of the debtor and his being freed from the necessity for using his earning-capacity or any property he may acquire or be able to acquire in the future for the discharge or partial discharge of his debts, it is quite another.

||||||||||||||||||||||||||||||||||||||||||||||||||||||||||||||||||||||||||||

Application

The *Bankruptcy Act* is administered by a Superintendent of Bankruptcy who appoints and exercises supervision over all trustees who administer bankrupt estates under the Act. In 1966, the Superintendent was given additional powers to investigate suspected violations of the Act, particularly in the case of complaints concerning fraud.

The Act designates a particular court, usually the highest trial court in each province or territory, as the court to deal with bankruptcy matters in that jurisdiction.[12]

Bankruptcy falls within the jurisdiction of the federal government under the *British North America Act, 1867*, and as a consequence, the law applies to all parts of the country. The *Bankruptcy Act* is not, however, the only statute which pertains to bankruptcy and insolvency, nor does it apply to all persons and corporations. Proceedings under the *Winding Up Act*[13] are available to creditors of a corporation, and the *Companies' Creditors Arrangement Act*[14] is available to the bondholders of a corporation, if the corporation is in financial difficulties. Farmers also have special legislation applicable to them in the case of insolvency in the form of the *Farmers' Creditors Arrangement Act*.[15]

In addition to these special statutes, the *Bankruptcy Act* does not apply to certain persons, or to corporations of special kinds. For example, the Act at the present time does not apply to farmers or fishermen, or any wage-earner or commission salesman whose income is less than $2 500 per annum, although these persons may make a voluntary assignment in bankruptcy. Nor does the Act apply to any chartered bank, trust or loan company, insurance company, or railway, as special provision is made in the legislation governing each of these if they should become insolvent. The *Bankruptcy Act*, however, does apply to most other corporations, and takes precedence over the *Winding Up Act* in its application.

Acts of Bankruptcy

The failure on the part of a debtor to pay a creditor does not automatically render the debtor bankrupt, nor does it establish that the debtor is insolvent. A debtor may have good reason not to pay a particular creditor, or circumstances may prevent the debtor from doing so. For example, a debtor may, through oversight, fail to have sufficient funds available when a debt falls due, but nevertheless possess assets worth many times the value of the indebtedness. Under such circumstances, the debtor's problem would be one of liquidity, rather than *bankruptcy*.

---

[12]For example, in Newfoundland, the court is the Trial Division of the Supreme Court; in Alberta it is the Court of Queen's Bench, and in Ontario, it is the Supreme Court of Ontario: *Bankruptcy Act* R.S.C. 1970, c.B-3, as amended by 1978-79, c. 11, s. 10(1).

[13]*Winding Up Act*, R.S.C. 1970, c. W-10.

[14]*Companies' Creditors Arrangement Act*, R.S.C. 1970, c. C-25.

[15]*Farmers' Creditors Arrangement Act*, R.S.C. 1970, c. F-5.

Under bankruptcy law, a distinction is made between insolvency and bankruptcy, even though the former may be a part of the latter. Insolvency is essentially the inability of an individual or corporation to pay debts as they fall due, and frequently represents a financial condition which precedes bankruptcy. Bankruptcy on the other hand, is a legal condition which arises when a person has debts exceeding $1 000, and has committed one of the 10 acts of bankruptcy set out in the Act within six months prior to a creditor filing a petition in bankruptcy against the debtor. The particular activities which the Act defines as *acts of bankruptcy* are as follows:[16]

24(1) A debtor commits an act of bankruptcy in each of the following cases:

(a) if in Canada or elsewhere he makes an assignment of his property to a trustee for the benefit of his creditors generally, whether it is an assignment authorized by this Act or not;

(b) if in Canada or elsewhere he makes a fraudulent conveyance, gift, delivery, or transfer of his property or of any part thereof;

(c) if in Canada or elsewhere he makes any conveyance or transfer of his property or any part thereof, or creates any charge thereon, that would under this Act be void as a fraudulent preference;

(d) if with intent to defeat or delay his creditors he does any of the following things, namely, departs out of Canada, or, being out of Canada, remains out of Canada, or departs from his dwelling-house or otherwise absents himself;

(e) if he permits any execution or other process issued against him under which any of his property is seized, levied upon or taken in execution to remain unsatisfied until within four days from the time fixed by the sheriff for the sale thereof or for fourteen days after such seizure, levy or taking in execution, or if the property has been sold by the sheriff, or if the execution or other process has been held by him for fourteen days after written demand for payment without seizure, levy or taking in execution or satisfaction by payment, or if it is returned endorsed to the effect that the sheriff can find no property whereon to levy or to seize or take, but where interpleader proceedings have been instituted in regard to the property seized the time elapsing between the date at which such proceedings were instituted and the date at which such proceedings are finally disposed of, settled or abandoned shall not be taken into account in calculating any such period of fourteen days;

(f) if he exhibits to any meeting of his creditors any statement of his assets and liabilities that shows that he is insolvent, or presents or causes to be presented to any such meeting a written admission of his inability to pay his debts;

(g) if he assigns, removes, secretes or disposes of or attempts or is about to assign, remove, secrete or dispose of any of his property with intent to defraud, defeat or delay his creditors or any of them;

(h) if he gives notice to any of his creditors that he has suspended or that he is about to suspend payment of his debts;

(i) if he defaults in any proposal made under this Act;

(j) if he ceases to meet his liabilities generally as they become due.

Bankruptcy Proceedings

There are essentially three routes that a debtor in financial difficulties may follow to resolve his financial problems. He may make a proposal to his creditors, make a voluntary assignment in bankruptcy, or permit his creditors to petition for a receiving order. Of the three methods, only the first two may be undertaken by the debtor as voluntary acts, the third being an involuntary procedure from the debtor's point of view.

---

[16]*Bankruptcy Act*, R.S.C. 1970, c. B-3, s. 24(1).

The *Bankruptcy Act* provides that an insolvent person may make a *proposal* to his creditors through a licensed trustee for the purpose of resolving his financial problems.[17] The trustee will arrange a meeting with the creditors and discuss the proposal, and if a majority of the creditors (who must also hold three-quarters of the value of the claims) accept the proposal, the trustee will then have the proposal approved by the court. The approval by the court has the effect of binding the parties to the terms of the proposal, and compliance with the proposal by the debtor will preclude any creditor from taking independent proceedings against him. The successful performance of the agreement by the debtor would have the same force and effect as if the debtor had paid his debts in full. A proposal may be made at any time, but if it is made after bankruptcy proceedings have begun, it operates to annul the proceedings, and revest the property in the debtor, or any person designated by the court.

An insolvent person may make a voluntary assignment[18] in bankruptcy as an alternative to a proposal. A voluntary assignment differs from creditor instituted proceedings only at the outset. Under a voluntary assignment, the debtor files with the official receiver an assignment of his property for the general benefit of his creditors, with the assignee's name left blank.[19] The official receiver then selects a trustee to accept the debtor's property and to proceed with the bankruptcy. Once this is done, the *Bankruptcy Act* procedure comes into play, and the administration of the bankrupt's estate begins.

The third method of instituting proceedings under the Act is through the action of a creditor. Where a debtor, as defined in the Act, has debts owing to one or more creditors in excess of $1 000, and has committed an act of bankruptcy, a creditor may at any time within the six months after the act of bankruptcy occurred, file a *petition* for a *receiving order* with the registrar in bankruptcy of the provincial or territorial court designated under the *Bankruptcy Act* to hear such matters.[20] If the debtor does not object to the petition (or consents) a receiving order is issued by the registrar which determines the debtor to be bankrupt, and which permits the appointment of a licensed trustee to administer the estate of the bankrupt. If the debtor objects, the matter is heard by a judge, and the debtor may then present evidence to satisfy the court that he is not bankrupt. If the debtor is successful, then the judge will dismiss the petition; if not, the receiving order is issued.

Provision is made under the Act for the appointment of an *interim receiver* if it should be necessary to preserve the assets or the business of the debtor pending the hearing of the petition by the court. The interim receiver usually becomes the trustee who administers the debtor's estate if the receiving order is later issued by the court.

Following the issue of the receiving order, the appointed trustee has a duty to call together the creditors of the bankrupt, at which time the trustee's appointment is affirmed, or a new trustee appointed. He then reports the assets of the debtor, and determines the amount of the creditors' claims. The debtor must be present at the first meeting of creditors, at which time

---

[17]*Ibid.*, s. 32.
[18]*Ibid.*, s. 31.
[19]*Ibid.*, s. 24(1)(*a*). An assignment for the general benefit of creditors constitutes an act of bankruptcy.

[20]*Ibid.*, s. 25(1).

the creditors are free to examine the debtor as to the state of his affairs, and the reasons for his insolvency. At the first meeting, the creditors also appoint *inspectors* (not exceeding five) who assume responsibility for the supervision of the trustee on behalf of the rest of the creditors. The inspectors usually meet with the trustee following the first meeting of creditors and instruct the trustee on all matters concerning the liquidation of the bankrupt debtor's estate. The trustee, even though an officer of the court, and subject to its direction, must act in accordance with their instructions, as they must authorize all important decisions concerning the realization of the assets, provided that their decisions are consistent with the Act.

The trustee usually collects all assets of the bankrupt and converts them to cash. Assets which are subject to security interests such as land mortgages, chattel mortgages, or conditional sale agreements (to name a few) must be made available to the secured creditor, and if the goods are sold, any surplus goes to the trustee to be included in the estate for distribution to the creditors. If the proceeds from the disposition of the particular security are insufficient to satisfy a secured creditor's claim, the secured creditor is entitled to claim the unpaid balance as an unsecured creditor. The assets not subject to secured creditors' claims, and any surplus remaining from the disposition of assets subject to security interests, when liquidated, are distributed by the trustee in accordance with the priorities set out in the Act. The legislation provides that certain *preferred* creditors be paid before the unsecured general creditors in the following order:[21]

107(1) Subject to the rights of secured creditors, the proceeds realized from the property of

[21]*Ibid.*, s. 107(1).

a bankrupt shall be applied in priority of payment as follows:

(*a*) in the case of a deceased bankrupt, the reasonable funeral and testamentary expenses incurred by the legal personal representative of the deceased bankrupt;

(*b*) the costs of administration, in the following order,

  (i) the expenses and fees of the trustee,

  (ii) legal costs;

(*c*) the levy payable under section 118;

(*d*) wages, salaries, commissions or compensation of any clerk, servant, travelling salesman, labourer or workman for services rendered during three months next preceding the bankruptcy to the extent of five hundred dollars in each case; together with in the case of a travelling salesman, disbursements properly incurred by him in and about the bankrupt's business, to the extent of an additional three hundred dollars in each case, during the same period; and for the purposes of this paragraph commissions payable when goods are shipped, delivered or paid for, if shipped, delivered or paid for within the three-month period, shall be deemed to have been earned therein;

(*e*) municipal taxes assessed or levied against the bankrupt within two years next preceding his bankruptcy and that do not constitute a preferential lien or charge against the real property of the bankrupt, but not exceeding the value of the interest of the bankrupt in the property in respect of which the taxes were imposed as declared by the trustee;

(*f*) the landlord for arrears of rent for a period of three months next preceding the bankruptcy and accelerated rent for a period not exceeding three months following the bankruptcy if entitled thereto under the lease, but the total amount so payable shall not exceed the realization from the property on the premises under lease, and any payment made on account of accelerated rent shall be credited against the amount payable by the trustee for occupation rent;

(*g*) the fees and costs referred to in subsection 50(2) but only to the extent of the realization from the property exigible thereunder;

(*h*) all indebtedness of the bankrupt under any Workmen's Compensation Act, under any Unemployment Insurance Act, under any provision of the *Income Tax Act* or the *Income War Tax Act* creating an obligation to pay to Her Majesty amounts that have been deducted or withheld, *pari passu*;

(*i*) claims resulting from injuries to employees of the bankrupt to which the provisions of any Workmen's Compensation Act do not apply, but only to the extent of moneys received from persons or companies guaranteeing the bankrupt against damages resulting from such injuries;

(*j*) claims of the Crown not previously mentioned in this section, in right of Canada or of any province, *pari passu* notwithstanding any statutory preference to the contrary.

The unsecured creditors, being at the bottom of the list share *pro rata* in any balance remaining. This amount is usually calculated in terms of "cents on the dollar." For example, if, after the payment of secured and preferred creditors in a bankruptcy, the sum of $4 000 remains, and unsecured creditors' claims amount to $10 000, the creditors' individual claims would be paid at the rate of forty cents for each dollar of debt owing to the creditor.

Discharge

Until a bankrupt is *discharged* by the court, he is not released from his debts. In effect, any earnings or other income received by the debtor before his discharge may be applied to the payment of the creditors if the court so orders. Apart from this, the bankrupt must not engage in any business without disclosing that he is an undischarged bankrupt, and he must not purchase goods on credit except for necessities (and then only for amounts under $500 unless he discloses that he is an undischarged bankrupt).

Bankruptcy also places certain limitations on the activities of the bankrupt until a discharge is obtained. The debtor may not become a director of any limited liability corporation, nor may the debtor accept an appointment to the Senate (a matter unlikely to be of concern to most bankrupts in any event).

The trustee will generally arrange for the discharge of the bankrupt shortly after bankruptcy proceedings are under way. In most cases, if the bankrupt was an honest but unfortunate debtor who had done nothing to defraud the creditors, and who had complied with the Act and his duties and obligations under it during the course of the proceedings, a discharge will normally be granted on application by the trustee. This usually occurs from three to six months after proceedings were instituted, but normally not later than 12 months. The debtor may, however, make an application for discharge on his own behalf and at his own expense if the trustee does not do so, but the debtor is not likely to succeed unless he can satisfy the court that the creditors have received at least 50¢ on the dollar as payment of their debts, and that no fraud existed. Whether the bankruptcy was the debtor's first, and whether he carried out his duties under the Act are also factors considered by the court in reaching a decision. Even then, the court has wide powers to impose conditions on the bankrupt, the conditions to some extent being governed by the circumstances which led to the bankruptcy, and the debtor's conduct thereafter.

A discharge releases the bankrupt from all debts and obligations except those arising from the debtor's wrong doing, and those associated with the debtor's marital obligations. All fines and penalties imposed by law, and any obligation which arose out of the fraud of the debtor or a breach of trust would remain, as would any personal obligation arising out of a maintenance or alimony agreement or order.[22] Any debts incurred for necessaries would not be released, if the court so ordered.

A corporation, unlike an individual, is not entitled to a discharge unless all of the creditors' claims are paid in full.[23]

Summary Proceedings

The 1949 *Bankruptcy Act* provides a simplified procedure for the administration of small estates where the assets of the bankrupt debtor are $500 or less. This procedure was frequently used by non-trader bankrupt debtors as a means of making a fresh start, as the procedure provided for a prompt discharge. However, a more recent procedure, introduced in 1972 by the federal Department of Consumer and Corporate Affairs, permits a debtor to pay the sum of $50 as a partial payment of the cost of administration, and have the bankruptcy proceedings conducted by a federally-appointed public servant. Under this procedure, the assets of the debtor are sold, and the proceeds are distributed, first to pay the costs of administration of the bankruptcy (the standard trustee fee, etc.), and the balance, if any, is then allocated to the creditors in accordance with the provisions of the Act.

Bankruptcy Offences

The *Bankruptcy Act* is not only designed to provide an orderly procedure for the distribution of a debtor's assets to his creditors, but it is designed to identity and punish debtors who attempt to take advantage of their creditors by means of fraud or other improper means. The legislation therefore addresses the problem by establishing a series of offences punishable under the Act by way of fine or imprisonment, as well as by the withholding of discharge from the bankrupt.

Under the Act, the superintendent has wide powers to investigate fraudulent practices and allegations of violation of the Act by bankrupt debtors. The principal offences under the legislation include any action whereby:[24]

169. Any bankrupt who

(a) fails, without reasonable cause to do any of the things required of him . . .

(b) makes any fraudulent disposition of his property before or after bankruptcy;

(c) refuses or neglects to answer fully and truthfully all proper questions put to him at any examination held pursuant to this Act;

(d) makes a false entry or knowingly makes a material omission in a statement or accounting;

(e) after or within twelve months next preceding his bankruptcy conceals, destroys, mutilates, falsifies, makes an omission in or disposes of or is privy to the concealment, destruction, mutilation, falsification, omission from or disposition of a book or document affecting or relating to his property or affairs unless he proves that he had no intent to conceal the state of his affairs;

(f) after or within twelve months next preceding his bankruptcy obtains any credit or any property by false representations made by him or made by some other person to his knowledge;

(g) after or within twelve months next preceding his bankruptcy fraudulently conceals or removes any property of a value of fifty dollars or more or any debt due to or from him; or

(h) after or within twelve months next preceding his bankruptcy pawns, pledges or disposes of any property which he has obtained on credit and has not paid for, unless in the case of a trader such pawning, pledging or disposing is in the ordinary way of trade and

---

[22]*Ibid.*, s. 148(1).
[23]*Ibid.*, s. 139(4).

[24]*Ibid.*, 169.

unless in any case he proves that he had no intent to defraud;

is guilty of an offence and is liable on summary conviction to imprisonment for a term not exceeding one year or on conviction under indictment to imprisonment for a term not exceeding three years, and the provisions of the *Criminal Code* authorizing the imposition of a fine in addition to or in lieu of imprisonment do not apply.

As a general rule investigations are conducted by an official receiver under the direction of the Superintendent of Bankruptcy. These investigations are usually to determine the cause of the bankruptcy, but in a case where fraud or a criminal act is suspected, the investigation may extend to those matters as well.[25] If the court suspects that the debtor might attempt to leave Canada with assets to avoid paying his debts, or to take other similar action to avoid his creditors, the court has the power to order the debtor's arrest.[26]

PROPOSALS FOR REFORM

The 1966 amendments to the *Bankruptcy Act*[27] extended the powers of the Superintendent of Bankruptcy in an effort to deal with fraudulent bankruptcies and a number of other deficiencies which had become apparent since the previous major overhaul of the legislation in 1949. The need for a full review of the law, however, was obviously necessary, and in the same year, the Minister of Justice who was responsible, at the time, for the administration of the Act, appointed a Committee to examine the legislation.

The Committee examined the bankruptcy systems of not only Canada, but those of a number of European countries, and the laws of the United States and Australia. It submitted a report in 1970 which suggested that a new and comprehensive Act be passed to replace the existing legislation relating to bankruptcy and insolvency.[28] The proposals included special procedures for small debtors who required only time to pay their creditors in full, and a simple procedure for small debtors who were prepared to make a proposal to their creditors. It was suggested that both procedures be tied into an assistance program designed to teach the debtors the fundamentals of proper financial management in an effort to reduce the likelihood of a repetition of their financial difficulties. For both small debtor "procedures," the Committee proposed restrictions on the rights of secured creditors to realize on their security.

For large bankruptcies, the Committee suggested that the present system of "acts of bankruptcy" be abolished, and that a presumption that the debtor had ceased to pay his debts generally should be the only criterion. As with the small debtor insolvencies, the Committee proposed restrictions on the rights of secured creditors, and a revised system of creditor priorities which would eliminate preferences given to the Crown, municipal taxes, funeral expenses, and a landlord's right to accelerated rent. The protection of wage earner's priority (at an increased amount), trustees' fees, and other expenses associated with the bankruptcy were to be retained.

To streamline the process, the Committee proposed greater government involvement in the administration of estates, and that greater investigative powers be placed in the hands of the Superintendent. Credi-

[25]*Ibid.*, s. 132.
[26]*Ibid.*, s. 138(1).
[27]"An Act to Amend the Bankruptcy Act," 14-15 Eliz. II, c. 32 (Can.) (1966).

[28]*Report Of the Study Committee On Bankruptcy And Insolvency*, (The Queen's Printer, 1970: Canada).

tor control would be replaced by a shared system of control, with the power vested in the administrative official. The proposals also suggested that the new legislation should provide greater powers to the administrators of the legislation to deal with crime and the protection of the credit system.

Following the report of the committee, a number of draft bills were introduced, but all, through inherent weakness or circum-

stance, failed to receive passage. The most recent bill, Bill C-12, a much modified version of the committee's original draft, received a first reading in 1980, and appears to be stalled at that stage at the present time (April, 1981). It remains to be seen whether the current economic problems, with their obvious effect on business, will create the necessary pressure on government to move the new bill through Parliament and into law.

SUMMARY Bankruptcy legislation is a federal statute, and in its present form is an attempt to provide an honest but unfortunate debtor with an opportunity to start afresh and free of debts. The procedure requires the debtor to deliver up his property to a receiver or court-appointed trustee for the purpose of distribution to the creditors in accordance with certain specified priorities. The Act also deals with fraudulent and improper actions by debtors who attempt to defraud their creditors. Penalties are provided in the statute for persons found guilty of these bankruptcy offences.

Before persons may be subject to bankruptcy proceedings, they must first commit an act of bankruptcy. The commission of any one of the acts by a debtor would entitle a creditor (or creditors) owed at least $1 000 by the debtor, to petition for a receiving order at any time within six months after the commission of the act of bankruptcy. If the debtor fails to convince the court that he is not bankrupt, the receiving order is issued, and a trustee establishes control of the debtor's assets for liquidation and distribution to the creditors. Inspectors, appointed by the creditors, supervise the trustee until the estate has been fully distributed. The debtor, if he has acted without fault, is entitled to a discharge of all debts except such debts as fines, court maintenance orders for support or alimony, and funds acquired by fraudulent means or by breach of trust. of trust.

A voluntary procedure, and two summary procedures are available to debtors, in addition to the creditor-initiated process. Recent proposals for change in the legislation, however, if implemented, would make fundamental changes in the present rights of creditors, and the procedure for the administration of bankrupt estates.

DISCUSSION QUESTIONS

1. Distinguish "insolvency" from "bankruptcy." Why is this distinction made?

2. *Trace the changes in the attitude of the public towards bankruptcy from the 14th century to the present time.*

3. *What constitutes an "act of bankruptcy"?*

4. *Explain the role of the Superintendent of Bankruptcy under the present legislation.*

5. *What routes are open to a bankrupt merchant when he realizes that he can no longer carry on his business except by incurring further losses?*

6. *In what way does a "proposal" differ from an "assignment"?*

7. *Under what circumstances may a creditor institute bankruptcy proceedings against a debtor? Describe the procedure which follows when a creditor institutes bankruptcy proceedings.*

8. *Describe the role of "inspectors" in a bankruptcy.*

9. *What obligations are imposed on a bankrupt until he is discharged by the court?*

10. *Does a discharge relieve the bankrupt debtor of all debts and financial obligations? If not, what obligations remain?*

11. *Outline the priorities of unsecured creditors with respect to payment in a bankruptcy. How does a bankruptcy affect secured creditors?*

12. *What constitutes an "offence" under the Bankruptcy Act?*

13. *Why did Parliament consider it necessary to grant the Superintendent of Bankruptcy wide powers of investigation in bankruptcy matters?*

14. *What remedies are available to the court where a fraudulent transaction is discovered?*

JUDICIAL DECISIONS

Bankruptcy—Actions of Debtor Considered—Conditional Discharge

Re Palach and Palach, [1955] O.W.N. 278.

The debtor, as a result of an automobile accident incurred a substantial debt, and made an assignment in bankruptcy. It was alleged that the only reason for the assignment was to free himself of the single debt. The application for discharge was opposed by the creditor.

SMILY, J.:

As counsel for the Minister of Highways has intimated, there are, no doubt, many situations of this kind, where there are judgments against people of little or no means, which would make it difficult for them to pay the judgments, although in many cases they could probably make some payments on account, but that situation can be unsatisfactory. In *In re Shackleton; Ex parte Shackleton* (1889), 6 Morr. 304 at 307-8, Cave J. said on a similar application, or at least when settling the question of imposing a condition on a debtor before granting discharge:

"In deciding that question the Court ought to have regard to public morality and to the interests of the public generally, and unless the Court finds a man in receipt of income derived from his earnings or otherwise which is more than sufficient to keep his family in enjoyment of the ordinary necessities of life according to their station, or unless it is satisfied that he is likely to succeed to property, it is not a wise thing to grant an order subject to a condition affecting after-acquired property. The Court ought to be careful to see it does not by a condition of that sort do away with the motive which a man has for exertion to work in his calling which is a good thing for the public interest generally. If such a burden is put on a man that he can have no hope of bettering his position he will not make the effort, and few men are more easily discouraged than that class of men who become bankrupt."

Whether or not what he said would apply entirely to conditions at the present time, I think there is something to it, and it is worthy of consideration. On the other hand, as I have said in *Re Parker Buell* (unreported), The Bankruptcy Act R.S.C. 1952, c. 14, should not be regarded solely as a clearing-house for the liquidation of debts, irrespective of the circumstances in which they were incurred.

As to the position of the debtor, if it is a case of a person being so weighed down by debts as to become unable to earn a living or perform the ordinary duties of citizenship, including the support of a wife and family, that is one thing, but where the only object to be served is the comfort and convenience of the debtor and his being freed from the necessity of using his own capacity or any property he may acquire or may be able to acquire in future for the discharge or partial discharge of his debts it is quite another. In *Re Parker Buell, supra*, it appeared that there was the possibility of the debtor's inheriting property from his mother, but that might not take place until some time in the distant future.

As I say, the matter has given me considerable concern because of the number of cases that no doubt exist, since there might be a tendency of debtors to consider that they were entitled to obtain a discharge of a judgment against them for damages in motor car cases, or in other cases, as a matter of course, simply by going through bankruptcy proceedings *pro forma*, which would not be a satisfactory condition of affairs. Such debtors would not feel that there was any necessity for them to make the effort to make some payment on the judgment, but on the other hand a situation may arise from time to time where a debtor is prevented by such a judgment from properly earning his living or if not prevented, then, in the spirit of the case to which I have referred, discouraged from working to earn his living and provide for his family and from performing the ordinary duties of citizenship, and matters of that nature, such as supporting a wife and family.

I think that every such case must be dealt with on its own merits, and cannot be taken as a general pattern other than what I have enunciated in my previous judgments—that The Bankruptcy Act must not be considered to be a clearing-house solely for the liquidation of debts.

There was another case in England, *In re Bullen; Ex parte Arnaud* (1888), 5 Morr. 243, that dealt with the making of an order for a conditional discharge or a discharge providing for a judgment being entered against the bankrupt, and there Bowen L.J. said during the argument, at p. 245: "With regard to this point I will just say, may not the line be whether there is reasonable probability of the creditor getting more by the debtor going into bankruptcy?" And Lindley L.J. said at p. 247: "There is no evidence at all that the man will ever have any after-acquired property and under those circumstances, I think *prima facie* one ought not to tie a man up by such a judgment as that under section 28, sub-section 6." That section in the English Act provides for making an order of discharge subject to the debtor consenting to a judgment against him.

Now in this case material has been filed to indicate that this debtor at the present time is making a relatively small weekly wage amounting to $21.60. He has a wife and three children. It would seem obvious that with that wage he would not be able to provide properly for his wife and children and have anything left over to pay on this judgment. He may have a larger wage in the spring, but it is not very encouraging for a man, an ordinary labourer, to have to liquidate or try to liquidate a judgment of such an amount by payments from what money he can spare from his wages after providing properly for his wife and children. He has an opportunity to go into farming. I think farming in this country is a very desirable and essential occupation. It is well known that there is a tendency for persons to leave the farm and come to the city for work, and the occupation of farming is not too popular. I think that it could almost be said that anything that would encourage the taking up of farming is desirable, and it may be that if this debtor is able to carry out this plan he will be successful in it and able to make proper provision for his wife and family and also possibly to do something toward this obligation, which is undoubtedly an obligation.

I have in mind that this might be an appropriate case in which to make an order on condition, but the condition must be such as not to discourage this debtor from carrying out the condition and from performing useful labour and looking after the duties of citizenship, to use the words previously referred to, including the proper provision for his wife and family. I, therefore, propose to make an order of discharge on condition that the debtor will consent to a judgment for $1,000 in favour of this judgment creditor, and that execution is not to issue or other proceedings to be taken under the judgment without leave of the Court.

||||||||||||||||||||||||||||||||||||||||||||||||||||||||||||||||||||||||||||||||||||||||||||||||||||||||||||||||||||||||||||||||||||||||||||||||||||||||||||||||

Bankruptcy—Fraudulent Preferences—Payment to Creditor Aware of Insolvency

Briscoe v. Molsons Bank (1922), 69 D.L.R. 675.

A bank that was aware of the insolvency of a customer accepted payments on account and took securities as payment even though the securities could not be cashed until after the bankruptcy. The payments to the bank were alleged to be a fraudulent preference given to one creditor.

At trial, the judge found that a fraudulent preference had been made.

MEREDITH, C.J.C.P.:

The question involved in this issue is: whether certain payments, or any of them, made by the bankrupt to the defendants in the issue, are "fraudulent and void as against the trustee" in bankruptcy of the bankrupt's estate.

Section 31 of the Bankruptcy Act provides, among other things, that every payment made by any insolvent person in favour of any creditor with a view to giving such creditor a preference over other creditors, or which has the effect of giving such creditor a preference over the other creditors, shall, if the person paying the same make an authorised assignment within three months after the date of paying, if made with such view as aforesaid, be deemed fraudulent and void as against the trustee. The enactment then goes on to provide for the case of payment, etc., which has the effect of giving such a preference, creating a *prima facie* presumption only that such payment, etc., was made, etc., with a view to giving the creditor a preference over other creditors.

All that seems plain enough, but Parliament did not deem it sufficient and added another section—32—in which, subject to some provisions of the Act not applicable to this case, it is provided that nothing in the Act shall invalidate any payment by the bankrupt to any of his creditors provided that certain conditions are complied with, one of which is: that the payment "is in good faith" and takes place before the date of the receiving order or authorised assignment; and the other is: that the person (other than the debtor) to whom the payment is made has not at the time of the payment notice of any available act of bankruptcy committed by the bankrupt or assignor.

This somewhat roundabout way of expression does not at all dim the meaning of the enactment in its effect upon this case: there are just two questions involved in it, either of which, being answered in the plaintiff's favour, concludes the case against the defendants upon the main point involved in it.

The questions are: (1) Were the payments in question payments made in good faith before the date of the assignment to the plaintiff? and (2) Had the defendants, at the times of payment, notice of any available act of bankruptcy committed by the bankrupt?

As I deem that the second question must be answered in favour of the defendants, I shall consider it first.

At the time of all these transactions, an available act of bankruptcy was: "an act of bankruptcy available for a bankruptcy petition at the date of the presentation of a petition on which a receiving order is made:" sec. 2(*h*) of the Act. How can that be applicable to this case, which is one of an authorised assignment only? The amendment to the Act in this respect was made after all these transactions: The Bankruptcy Act Amendment Act, 1921, 11 & 12 Geo. V, ch. 17, sec. 3.

The act of bankruptcy alleged relates to a writ of execution in a sheriff's hands; I do not consider whether or not an act of bankruptcy has been proved in respect of it, because that is unnecessary: as I am unable to find that the defendants had notice of it. It is strange that they did not, if in very truth they had not; but I am unable, in view of the positive denial of their manager in the witness-box, to find that they had, whichever way the onus of proof may lie.

But, on the whole evidence, I cannot but find in favour of the plaintiff on the first question.

However it might seem under sec. 31 alone, it is tolerably plain—though not nearly as plain as it might and should have been made—that both parties must be implicated in the want of good faith which invalidates a transaction.

It is not needful either to consider what "good faith" is, because the facts of this case prove the want of it, whatever reasonable, definite meaning may be given to the words "good faith."

The payments in question with two exceptions were by the bankrupt, when in a hopeless state of insolvency, for the one purpose of preferring his creditors, the defendants, so that his guarantors to them might be relieved from their obligations, under their guaranties held by the defendants, as much as possible; and the defendants, when the moneys were paid to them, knew that.

The bankrupt was so insolvent that the trustee's estimation is that his estate shall pay only about 10 cents in the dollar; for about a writ of execution lay in the sheriff's hands against him in full force and virtue, binding all his property; and all the payments in question were made within a few days of his voluntary assignment in bankruptcy; indeed it is contended and is literally a fact that some were paid after it.

The defendants' manager knew that judgment had been entered up against his debtor in the sum of over $4,000 at the suit of a competing bank; he learned then that his customer had gone to and was dealing with the other bank without having informed him and without his knowledge; he knew that that judgment had been reported by the mercantile agencies; and that thereby the debtor's credit should be ruined, and that his creditors should come down upon him "like a thousand of bricks;" and he had had a conversation with the debtor's bookkeeper, who had gone to see him with a view to "all getting together to pull Hanning out of the hole," and he knew that she on finding how much the indebtedness to the bank was, had given up the effort "to pull Hanning out of the hole," as hopeless. On that occasion they discussed the Standard Bank affair, and the defendants' manager seemed to know all about it. He was of course complaisant, knowing that the defendants were fully secured and that all payments really should enure to the debtor's relative, connection, and friend, and who were his guarantors to the defendants.

Therefore, generally, the plaintiff succeeds; but there are some minor points yet to be considered; some actual present consideration was given for some parts of the payments in question; the plaintiff cannot recover the whole payments, the value so given must be deducted: sec. 32(1)(d). This affects two items.

For the plaintiff it was contended: that the four payments credited to the bankrupt in the defendants' books on and after the date of the assignment should go to the plaintiff under any circumstances, not having been made before the date of the assignment: sec. 32(1)(i).

These amounts were the proceeds of sales by the defendants of Victory bonds given to them by the bankrupt before the date of the assignment, the proceeds of which were not received and credited until after that date. But I find that the bonds were intended to be treated as cash, and the fact that they had to be sold before the exact amount of the payment could be known and credited did not, under or for the purposes of the Act, prevent the transaction being then and now treated as a "payment" at the time when the bonds were delivered as and for that purpose. It, however, is further evidence of the intention to feather the nest of the guarantors with all kinds of material that could be made available for that purpose.

The parties can, no doubt, readily calculate and agree upon the amount that the plaintiff should recover from the defendants, and should do so; but, if they will not, the local registrar should ascertain and state it in the presence of or after notice to the parties; and in that case the matter is to be mentioned to me again, otherwise it need not.

The guarantors of the defendants are parties to the issue and joined with the defendants in resisting the plaintiff's claim and so are bound by this judgment; but no other judgment or order affecting them can rightly be made here; it is nothing like a case for indemnity or contribution; the defendants can recover against them only on their guaranties, and any such action is quite foreign to these bankruptcy proceedings.

The bank appealed this decision and the Ontario Supreme Court, Appellate Division (at p. 678 D.L.R.) dealt with the matter as follows:

MULOCK, C.J.EX.:

This appeal must fail, because the learned trial Judge found that there was a lack of good faith on the part of the bank. It was successfully contended at the trial by the trustee in bankruptcy that there was a fraudulent preference, and that the bank knew that the payment to it was illegal, because it had notice. There is sufficient evidence to support the view taken by the learned Judge at the trial.

||||||||||||||||||||||||||||||||||||||||||||||||||||||||||||||||||||||||||||||||||||||||||||||||||||||||||||||||||||||||||||||||||||||||||||||||||||||||||||||||||||

CASE PROBLEMS FOR DISCUSSION

Case 1

Simple purchased a small business from a well established proprietor for $100 000. To finance the transaction, he borrowed $80 000 by way of a mortgage on the premises, and prevailed upon the proprietor to accept a chattel mortgage on the equipment for the balance. He then arranged with the trade suppliers to sell him his inventory on credit.

The business was a high volume, low mark-up type of business, and a large amount of money passed through Simple's hands each day, even though the portion which represented his profit was small. During the first few months of operation, he purchased a new, expensive automobile, refurnished his apartment, and took a quick four-day holiday to Las Vegas where he lost several thousand dollars at the gambling tables.

When his suppliers began pressing him for payment of their accounts, he managed to pacify them by staggering payments in such a way that each received the payment of some accounts, but their total indebtedness remained about the same. He accomplished this in part by seeking out other suppliers and persuading them to supply him with goods on credit.

A few months later, it became apparent to Simple's creditors that he was in financial difficulty, and several creditors threatened to institute bankruptcy proceedings. To forestall any action on their part, Simple paid their accounts in full. The threats of the creditors brought his desperate financial position forcefully to his attention, however, and he promptly transferred $10 000 to his wife, and placed a further $10 000 in a bank account which he opened in another city.

A few days later, Simple purchased two, one-way airline tickets for a flight to Brazil that was scheduled for the next week. Before the departure date, a creditor to whom Simple owed a trade account in excess of $5 000 became aware of his plans, and instituted bankruptcy proceedings against him.

Discuss the actions of Simple, and indicate how the provisions of the *Bankruptcy Act* would apply. What steps may be taken to protect the creditors in this case?

Case 2

Able carried on business as a service station operator. In addition to repairing automobiles, he maintained a franchise for the sale of a line of new automobiles. He also sold gasoline and the usual lines of goods for the servicing of vehicles. Business was poor, however, and Able made a voluntary assignment in bankruptcy in which he listed as assets:

land and building	$50 000
new automobiles (3)	24 000
gasoline & oil	3 000
parts, supplies, and equipment	3 000
accounts receivable	2 000
bank	100
personal assets (furniture, etc.)	1 900
	$84 000

His creditors' claims were as follows:

1st mortgage	$40 000
2nd mortgage	7 000
Conditional sale agreements on automobiles	22 000
due and owing to fuel supplier	5 000
due and owing to other trade creditors	18 000
municipal taxes owing	1 000
personal debts (unsecured)	10 000
	$103 000

When the trustee attended at Able's place of business he discovered that (1) the new cars had been taken by the manufacturer, (2) the fuel tanks had been emptied by the fuel supplier, and (3) Baker, an employee of Able's was on the premises and in the process of removing an expensive set of tools which he maintained had been given to him by Able in lieu of wages for his previous week's work.

Discuss the steps that the trustee might take as a result of his discoveries.

Case 3

The Acme Company carried on business, for many years, as a manufacturer of consumer products. In 1975, it embarked on an ambitious program of expansion which involved the acquisition of a new plant and equipment. Financing was carried out by way of real property mortgages, chattel mortgages, and conditional sale agreements, with very few internally-generated funds being used for the expansion.

The general decline in demand for its product line as a result of the energy crisis and poor economic climate placed the company in a serious financial situation by 1980, and as a result of a failure to pay a trade account to one creditor, bankruptcy proceedings were instituted.

The trustee disposed of the assets of the company and drew up a list of creditors entitled to share in the proceeds. His preliminary calculations were as follows:

Sales of assets, etc.

Sale of land and buildings	$350 000
Sale of production equipment	35 000
Sale of trucks & automobiles	25 000
Sale of inventory of finished goods, etc.	30 000
Accounts receivable	45 000
Cash	3 000
	$488 000

Expenses and Creditor claims

1st mortgage on land and buildings	$290 000
2nd mortgage on land and buildings	45 000
3rd mortgage on land and buildings	40 000
1st chattel mortgage on trucks & automobiles	22 000
2nd chattel mortgage on trucks & automobiles	40 000
Bank claim under s. 88 (now 178) of Bank Act	25 000
unsecured trade creditors	60 000
unpaid wages (12 employees @ $250 each)	3 000
unpaid commissions to salesmen 1 @ 1,500	1 500
Bankruptcy expenses, fees & levy	39 000
unpaid municipal taxes	9 000
Production equipment conditional sale agreement	10 000
	$584 500

Calculate the distribution of the funds to the various creditors and calculate the cents per dollar amount which the unsecured trade creditors would receive.

PART VIII
Special Legal Rights

CHAPTER 34

Patents, Trade Marks, and Copyright

INTRODUCTION

Patents, trade marks, and copyright are essentially claims to the ownership of certain types of industrial and intellectual property. A *patent* is a right to a new invention; a *trade mark* is a mark used to identify a person's product or service, and a *copyright* is a claim of ownership and the right to copy a literary or artistic work. Bridging trade marks and copyright is a fourth form of protection, known as an *industrial design*, which is simply the right to produce in quantity some artistic work such as a piece of furniture, or article of a unique design.

The authority to pass legislation concerning these rights falls under the exclusive jurisdiction of the federal government by virtue of the *British North America Act, 1867*[1] and statutes have been passed concerning each of these rights which apply uniformly throughout Canada. In addition, Canada has signed a number of international "conventions" which provide procedures by which the owner of a patent, trade mark, or copyright work may obtain protection for the work in the various convention countries.

From a public policy point of view the purpose and intent of each statute is somewhat different, but each statute attempts to balance the right of public access to, and the use of ideas and information, with the need to foster new ideas and new literary and artistic works. As a result, the legislation incorporates special benefits or rights to promote the particular activities, along with appropriate safeguards to protect the public interest.

Patent legislation is designed to encourage new inventions and the improvement of old ones by granting the inventor monopoly rights (subject to certain reservations) for a period of time. Copyright laws are also designed to encourage literary and artistic endeavour by vesting in the author or creator of the artistic work the ownership and the exclusive right to reproduce the work over a lengthy period of time. Registered design legislation has a similar thrust. Trade mark legislation, on the other hand, has a slightly different purpose and intent. It is designed to protect the marks or names which persons use to distinguish their goods or services from those of others, and to prevent unauthorized persons from using them.

[1]The *British North America Act, 1867*, 30 Vict., c. 3, s. 91. Patents fall under s. 91(22); copyright under s. 91(23); trade marks would presumably fall under s. 91(2) or (29) since they are not specifically covered in s. 91.

Originally, the rights associated with intellectual and industrial property were not subject to legislation; inventors, authors and artists had very little or no protection for their creative efforts. The general need for protection, however, did not arise until the invention of printing, and the Industrial Revolution in England. These two changes created an economic environment in which the creators of industrial and intellectual property were in a position to profit from their creativity. The changes also created an opportunity for others to reap the rewards of an inventor's or author's endeavours without providing the creators with compensation for their loss. The common law proved unequal to the task of establishing and enforcing ownership rights to inventions and creative works of a literary or artistic nature, and it was eventually necessary for the English Parliament to deal with each specific property right by way of legislation.

PATENTS
Historical Development of Patent Law

Early patents in England were essentially monopoly rights granted by the Crown under Letters Patent. These rights were granted to individuals or guilds which gave them exclusive rights to deal in the particular commodity, or the right to control a particular craft or skill. Most of these grants were made ostensibly for the purpose of fostering the trade or the skill, but in many cases, they were simply privileges bestowed upon a subject by the Crown for the general enrichment of the individual. Over time, however, pressure on the government to limit the grant of monopolies to those in the public interest culminated in a number of statutes which established the right of English merchants to practice their trades or conduct their business without interference by those claiming monopoly rights.[2] Nevertheless, the grants of monopolies continued, for the most part by way of exclusive rights to import goods, or to encourage the production of new goods or services.

The issue of monopoly rights to encourage the production of new products was justified on the basis of public policy generally, since England lacked the special skills and equipment necessary to produce the many kinds of goods available on the Continent, especially cloth and metal wares. To encourage English and foreign entrepreneurs to bring in artisans with the necessary skills to produce similar goods in England, monopoly rights were frequently granted, the justification being that the new skills would be learned by native craftsmen, and the country as a whole would benefit. This policy was pursued with a vengeance, particularly under Elizabeth I, when the express intention of the government was to make the country as independent as possible in the production of goods.

Most of the early "patents" stipulated that the holder of the patent must provide a quality product in sufficient supply to satisfy the market. The patentee, as a consequence, was obliged to establish production facilities, and train his workmen in order to comply with the stipulations in the patent. The incentive to do so, in many cases, was a proviso in the patent to the effect that a failure to comply with the conditions set out in the document would result in a revocation of the grant.

In spite of the lofty public policy goals expressed by the Crown, abuses of the right did occur, and were the cause of much public discontent. Initially, the only route for complaint was to the Crown or the government, as the matter was generally considered to be outside the purview of the common law.[3] Eventually, however, the increase in commercial activity produced the inevitable conflict between merchants which resulted in a case which fell within the ambit of the common law courts. This occurred at the beginning of the 17th century, in a dispute which involved a grant of a monopoly right to import playing cards into England.[4] The case discussed the right of the monopolist to interfere with the complainant's right to trade, but more importantly, it established the common law rule that monopolies granted only for the private gain of the monopolist were unlawful.

Some time later, a second case came before the courts which concerned a grant of a monopoly to an inventor of a new cloth process.[5] In that case, the court held that a person who discovers something new and useful, and who takes the risks of producing it, should have exclusive rights to it for a period of time, and the Crown should grant a monopoly to so reward the inventor.

The right to a patent, once recognized at common law as a lawful exercise of Crown prerogative, was affirmed by a declaratory statute in 1624.[6] The Act declared all grants of monopolies null and void except those which were granted for new and useful inventions. The latter could be granted a monopoly for a fixed

---

[2]See, for example, the *Statute of Cloths*, 25 Edw. III, Stat. 4, c. 2.

[3]The court which frequently dealt with these matters was the Court of Star Chamber.
[4]*Darcy v. Allin* (1602), 11 Co. Rep. 84b, 74 E.R. 1131.
[5]The *Clothworkers of Ipswich* case (1615), Godb. 252, 78 E.R. 147.
[6]*An Act concerning Monopolies and Dispensations, etc.*, 21 Jac. I, c. 3.

term of 14 years (or less), provided that it was in the public interest to do so.[7] In the years that followed, the general spirit of the statute was recognized in the grants of patents, and apart from an occasional lapse into old habits by the succeeding monarchs, the statute remained as the basis for the issue of patent rights until the mid-19th century.[8] The Act was revised at that time, and later in 1883, when the issue of patents was placed entirely in the hands of the Patent Office.[9]

The province of Lower Canada introduced legislation in 1823 relating to patents by the statutory recognition of the right of inventors to the exclusive making, use, and selling of their new inventions, provided that they were British subjects and residents of the province.[10] The province of Upper Canada established similar legislation three years later.[11] In 1869, two years after Confederation, the first federal law was introduced which took a different approach to patent rights. This was due, in part, to events which occurred in the United States and, in part, to the fact that patents in England at the time were still issued under the Great Seal of the Crown.

As a result of the severance of its ties with England by the Revolutionary War, the United States had introduced its own patent law in 1790.[12] The statute blended the right of the individual to the fruits of his labours with the right of the state to permit free trade for the benefit of the public. The product of this blend was essentially a bargain struck between the state and the inventor, whereby the inventor, by revealing the secrets of his invention, would obtain monopoly rights to its use and manufacture for a fixed period of time. When the time period expired, the invention became public property.

Canada adopted the procedure outlined in the United States' law, but retained the common law for the interpretation and expression of patent rights. In this sense, it incorporated English case-law as authoritative for the exercise of the patent rights. The Canadian Act[13] was subsequently amended on a number of occasions, the most important being the introduction of a compulsory license requirement in 1903,[14] and the complete revision of the Act in 1923 to set out the rights and duties of the patentee, and to prevent abuse of the system.[15] These amendments were based upon the 1919 English *Patents and Designs Act*,[16] with the result that the Canadian law became a unique blend of both English and United States' laws. Since that time, the statute has been subject to numerous amendments that were designed to change the rights of the patentees, or protect the public interest. The law is presently under review.

The Patent Act

The present patent legislation is available to inventors of any "new and useful art, process, machine, manufacture, or com-

---

[7]*Ibid.*, s. 6.
[8]The *Patent Law Amendment Act, 1825*, 15 & 16 Vict., c. 83.
[9]*Patents, Designs and Trade Marks Act, 1883*, 46 & 47 Vict., c. 57.
[10]"An Act to Encourage the Progress of Useful Arts In This Province," 4 Geo. IV, c. 25 (Lower Canada).
[11]"An Act to Encourage the Progress of Useful Arts Within the Province," 7 Geo. IV, c. 5. (Upper Canada).
[12]The *Patent Act, 1790*, 1 Stat. at L. 109 (U.S.).

[13]The *Patent Act of 1869*, 32-33 Vict., c. 11 (Can.).
[14]"An Act to Amend the Patent Act, 1903," 3 Edw. VII, c. 46 (Can.).
[15]The *Patent Act*, 13-14 Geo. V, c.23, (Can.).
[16]*Patent Act*, R.S.C. 1970, c. P-4, s. 2.

position of matter, or any new or useful improvement of the same."[17] To "invent," however, means to produce something new and different: something which did not exist before.[18] What is created must be more than that which a skilled workman could produce, in the sense that it must be something more than mere mechanical skill which is the subject-matter of the patent.[19] It must also be new in terms of time as well, as any invention which has been worked for more than two years, or described in detail in a publication more than two years before the date of application for the patent is not patentable, as it is deemed to be in the public domain. In general, it is not possible to patent something which is only a vague idea or abstract theory, nor is it possible to patent a very slight improvement in an existing invention.[20] It should also be noted that any invention which has an unlawful purpose is not subject to patent protection. For example, a new "5-in-one burglary tool" would not be granted a patent, no matter how handy or useful it might be for a burglar.

IIIIIIIIIIIIIIIIIIIIIIIIIIIIIIIIIIIIIIIIIIIIIIIIIIIIIIIIIIIIIIIIIIIIIIIIIIII

CASE 34.1

Barter v. Smith (1877), 3 Ex.C.R. 455.

TACHÉ, D.M.A.:

It is universally admitted in practice, and it is certainly undeniable in principle, that the granting of letters-patent to inventors is not the creation of an unjust or undesirable monopoly, nor the concession of a privilege by mere gratu-

itous favor; but a contract between the State and the discoverer.

In England, where letters-patent for inventions are still, in a way, treated as the granting of a privilege, more in words however than in fact, they, from the beginning, have been clearly distinguished from the gratuitous concession of exclusive favors, and therefore were specially exempted from the operation of the statute of monopolies.

Invention being recognized as a property, and a contract having intervened between society and the proprietor for a settlement of rights between them, it follows that unless very serious reasons, deduced from the liberal interpretation of the terms of the contract, interpose, the patentee's rights ought to be held as things which are not to be trifled with, as things sacred in fact, confided to the guardianship and to the honor of the State and of the courts.

As it is the duty of society not to destroy, on insufficient grounds, a contract thus entered upon, so it is the interest of the public to encourage and protect inventors in the enjoyment of their rights legitimately, and sometimes painfully and dearly, acquired. The patentee is not to be looked upon as having interests in direct opposition to the public interest, an enemy of all in fact.

IIIIIIIIIIIIIIIIIIIIIIIIIIIIIIIIIIIIIIIIIIIIIIIIIIIIIIIIIIIIIIIIIIIIIIIIIIIIIIIIIIIIIIIIIII

Patent Procedure

An application for a patent may be made by the inventor or his agent[21] at the Patent Office. The first inventor is entitled to the patent, but prompt application for a patent is important, as foreign inventors, as well as Canadians, may apply for patent protection for their inventions, and it is always possible that someone elsewhere in the world may develop essentially the same device or process.

[17]*Ibid.*, s. 2.
[18]*Ibid.*, ss. 2 and 28.
[19]*Can. Raybestos Co. Ltd. v. Brake Service Corp. Ltd.*, [1927] 3 D.L.R. 1069.
[20]*Lightning Fastener Co. v. Colonial Fastener Co.*, [1932] Ex. C.R. 89, reversed on appeal, [1937]1 D.L.R. 21.

[21]Patent agents (or attorneys) are registered with the Patent Office under the *Patent Act*, R.S.C. 1970, c. P-4.

The usual practice in a patent application is for the inventor to engage the services of a *patent attorney* (or *patent agent* as they are called in Canada) to assist in the preparation of the documentation and in the processing of the patent. Patent agents are members of the legal profession who specialize in patent work, and in addition to training in the law, most agents usually have a specialized professional background. Patent agents frequently possess professional engineering degrees, or advanced training in another field of science, and are skilled in the assessment of inventions in terms of their being new and useful.

The patent agent will generally make a *search* at the Patent Office for any similar patents before proceeding with an application on behalf of the inventor. This search is a useful first step in the patent process, because any patents which have already been issued which cover a part of the invention (or possibly all of it) would indicate that the invention may not be patentable at all, or subject to patent for only those parts which are new. The same would hold true if the search revealed that the same invention had been patented some time ago, and the invention was now in the public domain.

If the search reveals that the invention is in fact something new, and open to patent, the next step is that the inventor make an application for patent protection for the invention. This is done by the preparation of a *petition* for the patent, which the inventor must submit, along with detailed *specifications* of the invention, a part of which must be a *claims statement* that indicates what is new and useful about the invention. A *drawing* of the invention is usually required if the invention is something of the nature of a machine, product, etc., that has a shape or parts which must be assembled. To complete the application, the inventor must submit the patent filing fee, and a short *abstract* of the disclosure written in simple language, capable of being understood by the ordinary technician. Each of these documents is important from the applicant's point of view, and must be carefully prepared.

The most important document is the *specifications* and *claims statement* which describes the invention in detail, and sets out what is new and useful about the discovery. It must contain a description of all important parts of the invention in sufficient detail to enable a skilled workman to construct the patented product from the information given when the patent protection expires. If the inventor intentionally leaves out important parts of the invention in order to prevent others from producing it, the patent may be void. Hence, accuracy is important to obtain patent protection.

The *claims statement* is equally as important, as it sets out the various uses of the invention and what is new in the product or process that would entitle the inventor to a patent. The claim must also be accurate, as too broad a claim could cause difficulties for the inventor later if the invention should fail to live up to its "claims."

The *abstract* which accompanies the application is simply a brief synopsis of the detailed submission to enable a person searching later to determine the general nature of the invention and its intended uses. It is written in non-technical language, and seldom exceeds a few hundred words in length.

Once the material filed is in order, the staff of the Patent Office proceed with a detailed examination of the material and the Patent Office records to determine if the invention infringes on any other patent. If the patent staff determine that the invention is indeed new and different, then a patent is issued to the inventor. The search and issue occasionally takes a lengthy period of time. For example, a patent for the manufacture of a type of plastic dinnerware was applied for in 1935, but the patent was not issued until 1956, some 21 years later. Delay in issue, however, is seldom a serious matter, as most manufacturers of the product for which the patent has been applied for may institute a special process for rapid examination and issue of the patent if some other manufacturer should produce the product without the inventor's consent. The prompt issue of the patent under these circumstances would place the other manufacturer in the position of infringing on the patent, and liable to the inventor for damages once the patent is issued. As a result, few manufacturers would likely trouble themselves to tool up for the manufacture of goods knowing that a patent has been applied for. The making of goods "patent pending" or "patent applied for" has no other purpose than to notify others that the application has been made for the patent. It has no special significance at law, as the rights of the inventor only arise on the issue of the patent.

The issue of a patent provides the inventor with exclusive right to the invention and its manufacture and distribution for a period of 17 years from the date of its issue.[22] To enable others to know how long the patentee's rights run, the article or product must be marked with the date of issue of the patent. If the product cannot be so marked, then a label must be attached containing the information.[23]

Foreign Patent Protection

During the 19th century, patent protection was the subject of discussion at a number

of meetings held by industrialized countries in an effort to devise a system whereby inventors might obtain patent protection for their inventions in countries other than that of their place of residence. Eventually, at the meeting in Paris, France, in 1883, agreement was reached whereby an inventor who had applied for patent protection in his own country, could make an appropriate application in any other country that was a party to the agreement within 12 months after the original application, and the application in the foreign country would have the same filing date as that of the first filing. This permitted any inventor residing in a country which belonged to the *Union Convention of Paris, 1883* to obtain a uniform filing date in all countries where patent protection was applied for. For example, if an inventor applied for a patent in Canada on February 1st, and applied for a patent on the same invention in the United Kingdom on August 1st, the effect of the convention would be that the inventor's application in the United Kingdom would be back-dated to the date of the original filing in Canada (i.e., February 1st). This would give the application a prior filing date to any application for a patent for the same invention made after February 1st, and before August 1st, by another inventor.

Compulsory Licences

One of the obligations of a patentee is that he must work the invention to satisfy public demand for the new product or process. This is essentially a public duty which the patentee must perform in return for the grant of monopoly rights to his discovery. Most inventors are usually only to happy to perform this duty, either by the production of the product themselves, or by *licensing* others to manufacture the product

---

[22]*Patent Act*, R.S.C. 1970, c. P-4, c. 48.
[23]*Ibid.*, s. 24.

in return for a *royalty* payment. If the patentee so desires, he might also *assign* the patent rights to another, in which case the obligation to work the patent would shift to the assignee.

The Act provides that for certain inventions, a *compulsory licence* may be in order for the general benefit of the public. Compulsory licensing, for example, may arise where the working of the patent is dependent upon the right to produce a part covered by an earlier patent. If such a licence is required to work the later patent (usually an improvement on some part of the original patent), the patentee of the improvement may apply to the Commissioner of Patents for the issue of a compulsory licence.

If a patentee fails to work a patent to meet public demand for the invention, or if the price for the product is unreasonably high, any interested party may apply to manufacture the invention under licence at any time after the patent has been in effect for three years. If the patentee cannot refute the claim that he cannot supply the demand for the invention, a licence may be issued to the applicant on whatever terms would appear reasonable in the circumstances. This usually means the issue of a licence to manufacture on a royalty basis, but depending upon the circumstances, a failure or refusal to work a patent in the face of demonstrated public demand for the invention could also result in a revocation of the patent.

Infringement

The issue of a patent is essentially a grant of a monopoly to the patentee for a 17-year period, during which time the patentee, subject to certain public interest limitations, has the exclusive right to deal with the invention. The production of a product or use of the process covered by the patent by any person not authorized to use it would constitute *infringement*, and entitle the patentee to take legal action against the unauthorized producer, user or seller. Infringement is very broad in its application, and includes not only unauthorized production of the invention but the importation of the product, or any other working of the patent without the consent or payment of royalties to the patentee.

To succeed against the unauthorized producer or importer of the invention, the patentee (assignee or licensee) must prove that infringement has taken place, since damages do not automatically flow from the production of an invention which is subject to a patent. For example, a defence against a claim for infringement might be that the patent is invalid, or that the patent had expired before the goods were produced. A patentee may also be faced with the defence of *estoppel* if the validity of the patent was successfully attacked by another person prior to the patentee's claim of infringement, or if the patentee had allowed the infringement to take place with his tacit approval for some time before claiming infringement. Infringement cases tend to be very complex, and infringement itself very much a question of fact, consequently, the defences can be many and varied.

TRADE MARKS
Historical Development of the Law

A trade mark is a mark which may be used by a producer or merchant to distinguish his goods or services from those of others. It may take the form of either a *trade mark* or a *trade name*, but the purpose of the mark or name is the same: to identify the goods or services of the owner of the mark.

The use of trade marks to distinguish or identify the wares of a producer or seller would appear to be a practice with a long history. Early craftsmen such as the brickmakers of early Babylon, and the water pipe manufacturers of ancient Rome marked their wares with their distinctive symbols or signatures. Later, members of some of the early guilds established their own special marks for the goods which they produced.

In England, one of the first recorded cases dealing with trade mark infringement concerned an action in which a manufacturer of cloth claimed damages for deceit from another who had passed off his goods by marking the cloth with the plaintiff's mark.[24] The court found in favour of the plaintiff, but some doubt exists as to whether the plaintiff was in fact the cloth manufacturer or a purchaser of the cloth who was deceived by the improper use of the mark. At common law, if the plaintiff was the purchaser, the action was an ordinary action of deceit, but if the plaintiff was the manufacturer, the case would be common law recognition of the right of action for infringement. The matter remained confused for over two centuries following the initial case, however, and it was not until the early 19th century that the right of action for infringement was clarified. The law, nevertheless, continued to progress. Damages were awarded in an infringement case at common law in 1824,[25] and some years later, an injunction was issued by the Chancery Court in another similar action.[26] By the middle of the century, the rights of persons to protect their marks through legal action was well established at both common law and Equity, but the procedure was unsatisfactory. Expensive litigation was the only means of protection and, after a lengthy court action, the successful plaintiff often found that his victory was a hollow one, as the defendant was frequently a person of few means, and incapable of paying the judgement.

The need for legislation to establish ownership of trade marks was recognized by 1875, and the *Trade Marks Registration Act*[27] was introduced to remedy the situation. The Act provided that by registration, the owner of a trade mark would establish the *prima facie* right to use the mark exclusively, and that after five years, the right became absolute, so long as the owner used the mark in business. The Act set out the various requirements for registration, and a general outline of the type of marks that were registrable. During the next eight years the Act was subject to a certain amount of amendment, and eventually was replaced by the *Patents, Design and Trade Marks Act, 1883.*[28]

The Act of 1883, in turn, was subject to much amendment and revision, particularly in 1905, when the law was for all intents and purposes rewritten.[29] The Act of 1905 finally provided a definition of the term "trade mark," and expanded the categories of registrable marks. Further revisions were made in 1919 and 1937, and the law was finally repealed and replaced by a new statute in 1938.[30]

Trade marks legislation in Canada followed a similar pattern of development,

---

[24]*Southern v. How* (1618), Popham 143, 79 E.R. 1243.
[25]*Sykes v. Sykes* (1824), 3 B. & C. 541, 107 E.R. 834.
[26]*Millington v. Fox* (1838), 3 My. & Cr. 338, 40 E.R. 956.

[27]*Trade Marks Registration Act, 1875,* 38 & 39 Vict., c. 91.
[28]*Patents, Design and Trade Marks Act, 1883,* 46 & 47 Vict., c. 57.
[29]*Trade Marks Act, 1905,* 5 Edw. VII, c. 15.
[30]*Trade Marks Act, 1938,* 1 & 2 Geo. VI, c. 22.
[31]*The Trade Mark and Design Act of 1868,* 31 Vict., c. 55 (Can.) (1868).

with the first statute introduced in 1868.[31] The Act provided for the registration of marks under a procedure which gave the registered user the right to exclusive use of the mark. An unusual feature of the Act was the sharing of the fine for infringement on a 50–50 basis between the Crown and the party injured by the infringement. The Act, along with legislation pertaining to patents and copyright at the time was placed under the administration of the Department of Agriculture.[32]

Trade marks legislation passed through a number of amendments and changes during the latter part of the 19th century, with a complete revision of the Act in 1879[33] which repealed and replaced the prior legislation except for those Acts dealing with the marking of timber,[34] and the law dealing with the fraudulent marking of merchandise.[35] While not following the English legislation in detail, the law in Canada underwent a number of changes to expand the nature of the protection available to users of marks by including *certification marks* (marks used to identify goods or services produced or performed under controlled conditions, or of a certain quality), the importation of trade marked goods, the licensing of users of trade marks by the "owner," and a revision of the penalties for unfair practices and infringement. The last major revision of the Act was in 1953, but more recently, the legislation has been subject to study and proposed revision.[36]

Trade Marks Act

The present *Trade Marks Act*[37] is a federal statute which governs the use of all trade marks and trade names in use in Canada. The Act defines a *trade mark* as any mark "used by a person for the purpose of distinguishing or so as to distinguish wares or services manufactured, sold, leased, hired or performed by him from those manufactured, sold, leased, hired or performed by others."[38] The Act also provides for the registration of trade marks, and maintains a *register* of marks at the Trade Marks Office. Protection under the Act is provided by a registration process and any mark which is not descriptive, not in use by another prior user, not confusing with existing marks, and not contrary to the public interest, may be registered.

At the present time, there are a number of different types of marks which may be registered under the Act:

(1) *Service marks*, which are marks that are used by service industries such as banks, air lines, and trucking companies, where the principal business is that of providing a service to the public. The mark, however, may also be applied to any product which the user might sell, such as an airline which sells flight bags or toy models of its aircraft.

(2) *Certification marks*, which are marks used to distinguish goods or services of a certain quality which, in the case of goods, are produced under certain working conditions, or in the case of services, performed by a certain class of persons, or goods or services produced in a particular area. Most certification marks are used for franchise operations where the owner of the

---

[31]31 Vict., c. 53 (1868) (Can.).
[33]The *Trade Mark and Design Act of 1879*, 42 Vict., c. 22 (Can.).
[34]"An Act Respecting the Marking of Timber," 33 Vict., c. 36 (Can.).
[35]"The Trade Mark Offences Act, 1872," 35 Vict., c. 32 (Can.).
[36]See, for example, *Working Paper on Trade Marks Law Revision* (Ministry of Consumer and Corporate Affairs, 1974).

[37]*Trade Marks Act*, R.S.C. 1970, c. T-10.
[38]*Trade Marks Act*, R.S.C. 1970, c. T-10, s. 2.

mark does not produce the goods or perform the services directly, but merely sets and enforces the standard for the goods or services to which the mark is applied. Certification marks are essentially "quality marks."

(3) *Distinctive guise*, a distinctive or distinguishing guise is a trade mark which takes the form of a particular shape to distinguish it from the products of others. Distinguishing guises are generally in the form of the package, or the shape of the product itself, and may be protected by the Act. Utilitarian features of the guise, however, may not be protected. For example, a moulded, or built-in handgrip on a bottle or box.

(4) *Trade name*, a trade name is generally a name coined or chosen to describe a business. It must not be a name which might be confused with any other name, but as a rule, a person is not prohibited from using his or her own name, simply because it is the same as that of a well-known establishment.

|||||||||||||||||||||||||||||||||||||||||||||||||||||||||||||||||||||||||||||

CASE 34.2

Singer Mfg. Co. v. Loog (1880), 18 Ch. D. 395.
JAMES, L.J.:

Upon the question of law which is involved, there is, to my mind, no dispute whatever. I have often endeavoured to express what I am going to express now (and probably I have said it in the same words, because it is very difficult to find other words in which to express it)— that is, that no man is entitled to represent his goods as being the goods of another man; and no man is permitted to use any mark, sign or symbol, device or other means, whereby, without making a direct false representation himself to a purchaser who purchases from him, he enables such purchaser to tell a lie or to make a false representation to somebody else who is the ultimate customer. That being, as it appears to me, a comprehensive statement of what the law is upon the question of trade-mark or trade designation, I am of opinion that there is no such thing as a monopoly or a property in the nature of a copyright, or in the nature of a patent, in the use of any name. Whatever name is used to designate goods, anybody may use that name to designate goods; always subject to this, that he must not, as I said, make directly, or through the medium of another person, a false representation that his goods are the goods of another person. That I take to be the law.

|||||||||||||||||||||||||||||||||||||||||||||||||||||||||||||||||||||||||||||

Registration Requirements

A trade mark must be *distinctive* and *used* in order to be registrable under the Act, but special provision is made for *proposed marks* which may be cleared as suitable trade marks, then later registered, once they are put in use. The Act does not permit all marks to be registered which are distinctive and used, as certain marks are prohibited by the statute. Prohibited marks are usually associated with royalty, governments, or internationally known agencies, and may not be used without their consent. A mark must also be such that it cannot be associated with any famous or well-known living person (or a person who has died within the previous 30 years), and it cannot be an offensive symbol. The "distinctive" requirement is often the most difficult to meet, as the mark must be such that it cannot be confused with the mark of another.

Marks that are searched in the register and found to be acceptable are advertised in the *Trade Marks Journal* to advise the public of the intended registration of the mark. If no objections arise as a result of the public notice, the mark may then be registered, and if its distinctiveness is not challenged within the next five years, it becomes incontestable unless it can be shown that the applicant knew of other users prior to the application for registration. A mark that should not have been registered in the first place would, of course, be open to challenge as well. An example of the latter objection would be a mark that was later discovered to be an offensive symbol.

Enforcement

A person who has registered a trade mark is entitled to protect the mark by taking legal action to prevent the use of the mark by another. The usual remedy is an injunction, but where unauthorized goods or services were sold under the registered mark, an accounting for the lost profits due to the use of the mark may be had. The forgery of a trade mark, or the passing off of goods as being the goods of another is also a criminal offence,[39] and criminal penalties may be imposed if criminal proceedings are taken against the unlawful user of the trade mark.

If the trade mark is no longer used, or has lost its distinctiveness because the product has become so successful that the name has become *generic*, the user may no longer claim exclusive rights to the use of the name. The trade mark "Linoleum," for example, became the generic word through public use of the term to mean all floor coverings of that type, and the word lost its distinctiveness with respect to its user's product. The name "Aspirin" suffered the same fate in the United States, but to date it is a registered trade name in Canada. Users of well-known trade marks, as a result, are careful to guard their trade marks and names to prevent the word from being used by the news

media as a generic term for all products of a similar type.

Foreign Trade Marks

As with patents, Canada is a member of an international convention concerning trade marks which permits a user of a trade mark in a foreign country to apply for registration there, and if an application is also made in Canada within six months thereafter, the application in Canada will be dated as of the date of application in the foreign country. Special filing requirements, however, are imposed upon the foreign trade mark applicant.

COPYRIGHT
Historical Development of the Law

Copyright is a term which means what it says: it is the "right to copy." The law pertaining to copyright is concerned with the control of the right to copy, and recognizes the right of the original creator of any writing or artistic work to control the reproduction of the work. Included in the type of work which copyright covers is all writing in the form of books, articles, and poems, and written work of every description, including musical compositions (both music and lyrics) and dramatic works. The right also covers all forms of artistic work in the nature of sculpture, paintings, maps, engravings, sketches, drawings, photographs, and motion pictures. Because reproduction in the case of music and dramatic works involves, in many cases, the recording of the music or work on a phonograph record, tape, or film, the right extends to the right to record the work by electronic or mechanical means. The same holds true for the reproduction of any literary or other work photocopied or stored in a computer retrieval system. Subject to certain exceptions, the law pro-

---

[39]*Criminal Code*, R.S.C. 1970, c. C-34, ss. 364-369.

tects the original author's right to control all reproduction of his work.

At common law, the right of the author of a literary or artistic work was not entirely clear. This was due in part to the fact that reproduction of a literary or artistic work prior to the invention of printing was a laborious undertaking, and it was not a matter likely to be of much concern before the courts. After the invention of the printing press, written work acquired a special commercial value, and the question of ownership of written work and the right to reproduce it became important (at least from the author's point of view). The establishment of a printing press and the printing of the first book in England in 1477 by William Caxton, in a sense, created the need for a law which would determine the right of an author to control the reproduction of his work.

At common law, the right of an author to control unpublished work was generally settled: the author was entitled to do as he wished with the material, because it was his, and his alone.[40] The right to control the copy of the work once published, however, was another matter. On this point, the law was unclear, so much so that many legal authorities believed that the right did not exist once the work was published, as publication was in a sense, placing the work in the public domain.

In 1709, the first statute was passed to establish the rights of authors in their published works.[41] The Act gave authors of published material the exclusive right to control the printing of their work for a period of 14 years (21 years in the case of works already published). The law was later amended (in 1801) to give the author of unpublished works the sole ownership of the material. This was done to incorporate the common law with respect to unpublished works in the statute.[42] The rights of authors were enlarged a dozen years later by a new statute which gave authors (or their assigns) copyright for 28 years, or for the rest of the author's natural life.

A series of statutes followed the foregoing basic acts, and extended copyright to musical and dramatic works, and later, to photographs and other products of the advancing technology of the 19th and early 20th centuries. By 1909, copyright in England was covered by a number of different statutes, and rationalization was clearly in order. To clear away the confusion, a new Act was introduced in 1911 to clarify and consolidate the law.[43]

The new legislation protected the rights of the author or artist for the creator's lifetime and 50 years after death in not only literary works but in a wide variety of other works of a musical, dramatic, or artistic nature that might be reproduced in printed form, by performance, or on record, film, or other means of reproduction. The Act included provisions for the licensing of the published work, and protection of the public by way of a limitation on the author's rights which permitted "fair dealing" and limited use for particular purposes. As with previous statutes, the legislation extended the protection to authors anywhere in the British Empire and its Dominions, including Canada.

The law pertaining to copyright in Canada (apart from the laws of England) had

---

[40]*Jefferys v. Boosey* (1854), 4 H.L. Cas. 815, 10 E.R. 681.

[41]"An Act for the Encouragement of Learning by Vesting Copies of Printed books in the Authors and Purchasers of Such Copies," 8 Anne, c. 19.

[42]"An Act for the Further Encouragement of Learning, etc.," 41 Geo. III, c. 107.

[43]Copyright Act, 1911, 1 & 2 Geo. V, c. 46.

its beginnings in a statute of Lower Canada,[44] which recognized an author's rights in all literary work. The law, however, related only to what is now the province of Quebec. The remainder of Canada was subject to the English law, beginning with the Act of 1709. The passage of the *British North America Act, 1867*, however, transferred the legislative authority to the federal government, and the first copyright Act was passed the following year.[45] The Act established the copyright in work in the author, and placed the administration of the Act under the Department of Agriculture. A broader and more elaborate Act was passed in 1875,[46] but it did not deal with dramatic or musical performances, as these were subject to the English *Dramatic Copyright Act*[47] and the *Copyright Act, 1842*[48] which had been made applicable to Canada. Copyright law in Canada continued to concern itself only with the authors of literary work (including music and dramatic writing) but did not include *performing rights* until the *Copyright Act* of 1921[49] was passed. The new law incorporated performing rights into the Canadian legislation, and has remained as our copyright law until the present time with few amendments.[50]

The 1921 Act, which came into force in 1924, covered virtually all literary and artistic endeavour, and provided for a Registrar of Copyrights, and a Copyright Office. The Act provided for the registration of copyrights, and set out an elaborate list of material that was subject to copyright. It also included penalties for the infringement of copyright.

The Copyright Act

The present legislation[51] provides that the sole right to publish or reproduce an original work of a literary or artistic nature is in the original author of the work. The protection of the right extends for the life of the author and for 50 years after his death. Work not published during the author's lifetime is subject to copyright for a period of 50 years, and in the case of recorded works, runs for a period of 50 years from the date the recording is cut or first made. Registration of the copyright is not essential in order to claim copyright, but registration is public notice of the copyright, and becomes proof of ownership of the work if the author should be required to bring an action for damages against a person who copies the work without permission.

It is important to note that the author is the first owner of the work, and entitled to claim copyright in it, unless the author was employed by another for the purpose of producing the work, painting, photograph, etc., providing that the parties did not agree to the contrary. However, only the arrangement of the words, or the expression of the idea is subject to copyright; the idea, or the subject-matter of the work is not subject to protection. For example, two authors might each write an article for a magazine dealing with energy conservation, and each article may contain the same ideas or suggestions. Each would be entitled to claim copyright in the arrangement of the words, but the ideas contained in the articles, although identical, would not be subject to a claim of copyright by

---

[44]"An Act to Protect Copy Rights," 2 Will. IV, c. 53 (Lower Canada).
[45]The *Copyright Act of 1868*, 31 Vict., c. 54 (Can.).
[46]The *Copyright Act of 1875*, 38 Vict., c. 88 (Can.).
[47]*Dramatic Copyright Act, 1833*, 3 & 4 Will. IV, c. 15.
[48]*An Act to Amend The Law of Copyright, 1842* 5 & 6 Vict., c. 45.
[49]The *Copyright Act, 1921* 11 & 12 Geo. V, c. 24.
[50]*Ibid.*, s. 25.

[51]*Copyright Act*, R.S.C. 1970, c. C-30.

either of the writers. Protection of copyright usually takes the form of registration of the work and the marking of material by the symbol © followed by words to indicate the date of first publication, and the name of the author. Canada has been a member of the *Universal Copyright Convention* since 1962,[52] and the marking of the published material is notice to all persons in those countries a part of the Convention that copyright is claimed in the marked work. The enforcement or protection of the copyright, however, is the responsibility of the owner.

An author or artist is entitled to assign a copyright either in whole or in part to another, but to be valid, the assignment must be in writing. Assignments of copyright are normally registered as well, to give public notice of the assignment. The Act also provides for the issue of licences to print published works in Canada where a demand exists and the author has failed to supply the market. Where a licence is issued, the publisher is expected to pay a royalty to the author as compensation. If a work is printed or copied without either the permission of the author, or a licence, the reproduction of the work may constitute infringement, and expose the unauthorized publisher to penalties under the Act and/or an action for infringement by the holder of the copyright.

Infringement consists of unauthorized copying of the protected work except for "fair dealing" with the work by others for the purpose of private study, research, criticism, review, or newspaper summary. Certain other exceptions exist as well, such as the reading in public of short excerpts from a copyright work, the performance of a musical by a church, school, or charitable body (if the work is performed for educational or charitable purposes by unpaid performers) and a number of other uses of the material.[53] In the case of infringement, the copyright owner is usually entitled to an injunction and an accounting, as well as damages.

Legislative Reform

The copyright laws in Canada, except for a few minor changes, are essentially statements of the law and the establishment of rights in a society as it existed in 1920. The Act does not adequately address itself to the major changes in information processing or technology that have occurred in the past 60 years. Consequently, efforts have been made to determine the effect of such technological changes as the photocopier and computer-based information retrieval systems in the reproduction of printed and other material, and to revise the law to deal with them. Since 1957, copyright law has been the subject of a number of major studies[54] and, as a result of recommendations for modernization, the law is presently under review. Any new legislation will undoubtedly be more complex and far reaching, in order to protect the rights of authors and artists at a time when the processing of information is undergoing major change.

REGISTERED DESIGNS

Registered design legislation applies to certain artistic works produced by an industrial process where more than 50

---

[52]Canada is also a member of the Berne Copyright Convention which provides an author with protection in member countries.

[53]See, for example, *Copyright Act*, R.S.C. 1970, c. C-30, ss. 17, 18 and 19.

[54]*Royal Commission Report on Copyright* (Ottawa, 1957); *Copyright in Canada: Proposals for a Revision of the Law* (Consumer and Corporate Affairs, 1977: Ottawa).

copies are made. A registered design is normally a design which would be the subject-matter of copyright if it was not for the fact that it is reproduced by an industrial process. For example, new furniture designs, where more than 50 copies are made, would require registration under the *Industrial Designs Act*[55] in order to be protected. Not all products must be registered, as the Act does not apply to a variety of "artistic" products produced by industrial processes. For example, printed paper hangings, machine-made lace, and some carpets and textiles are excepted.

Registration gives the owner of the design exclusive rights to produce the design for a period of five years, renewable for a further term of five years. The design, however, must be original, and not something which is likely to be taken for the design of another. In this respect, the requirements for registration are similar to those for a patent, but the investigative process is not nearly so exhaustive. The design must also be registered within 12 months of its first publication in Canada in order to acquire protection.

Once the design is registered, the owner of the design is obliged to notify the public of the rights claimed in the design by marking the goods (or by printing a label) with the words "Rd." The date, and the design owner's name should also appear.

The ownership of the design, as with patents or copyright may be assigned, or rights to manufacture may be granted under licence. Any unauthorized manufacture, however, would entitle the owner of the design to take legal action for infringement.

[55]*Industrial Design Act*, R.S.C. 1970, c. I-8.

||||||||||||||||||||||||||||||||||||||||||||||||||||||||||||||||||||||||||||||||||||||||||||||||||||||||||||||||||||||||||||||||||||||||||||||||||||||||||||||

SUMMARY   The protection of rights to intellectual and industrial property are covered by a number of federal statutes. Each Act recognizes and protects a special property right, and confirms ownership rights in it. A patent, which is the exclusive right of ownership granted to a first inventor of a new and useful product, lasts for 17 years, during which time the holder of the patent (subject to certain exceptions related to the public interest) is granted monopoly rights in the invention. Patents, in some cases, are subject to compulsory licensing requirements and may also be revoked if they are not "worked" to meet public demand. Once a patent is issued, unauthorized production constitutes infringement, and would entitle the patentee or those claiming rights through him to bring an action for damages against the unauthorized producer.

Trade marks are rights to the exclusive use of marks which distinguish the wares or services of one person from the wares or services of another. Under the *Trade Marks Act* distinctive marks used to identify a person's product or service may be protected by registration. Registration permits the user of the name or mark to prevent others from using the mark without express permission. The unauthorized marking of goods by a person for the purpose of passing them off as being those of the authorized owner of the trade mark, constitutes the criminal offence of "passing off." It would also leave that person open to an action for damages and an injunction by the owner of the mark.

Copyright is the "right to copy" original literary or artistic work. Copyright legislation recognizes the author or composer of the work as the owner of the copyright, and the person entitled to benefit from any publication of the material. The statute provides the exclusive right in the owner for the owner's lifetime plus 50 years, but in the case of some types of copyright material, the right is limited to only 50 years. A copyright may be assigned, or licences may be granted for copyright work, but any unauthorized publication or performance of the work (subject to certain exceptions) constitutes infringement, and would entitle the owner of the copyright to receive the profits on the unauthorized publication, damages, and an injunction, depending upon the circumstances.

A registered design is somewhat similar to copyright in the sense that it is an artistic work that is reproduced by an industrial process. Registration of the design protects the owner from unauthorized reproduction of the same design by others. A registered design is protected for five years from the date of registration, but the registration may be renewed for a further five years.

Legislation concerning industrial and intellectual property is presently under review for the purpose of revising it, so that it may take into consideration the changes in technology that have occurred in the period following World War II.

‖‖‖

DISCUSSION QUESTIONS

1. Why did the Crown originally grant monopolies by way of Letters Patent for certain products? Would the same reasons hold today?
2. In essence, what is a "patent"?
3. Who may apply for a patent? How is it obtained?
4. Why must care be used in the preparation of a "specifications and claims" document?
5. How is the public interest protected in the grant of a patent?
6. What does the phrase "patent pending" mean? Does it have any legal significance?
7. Describe the manner in which patent rights are enforced.
8. Explain the procedure used by a Canadian resident to obtain patent rights in a foreign country.
9. Define a "trade mark." How does it differ from a "trade name"?
10. What protection existed at common law for trade marks?
11. Identify the additional protection given to trade marks under trade marks legislation.
12. How does a "certification mark" differ from a "service mark"?
13. Describe a "distinguishing guise." What characteristics must it possess?

14. *Explain the term "copyright." Is it a common law right?*
15. *Why was legislation necessary to protect authors and other creators of artistic works?*
16. *How does a copyright arise? What must an author do to protect the right?*
17. *What constitutes "fair dealing" with published work that is subject to copyright?*
18. *How does a "copyright" differ from a "registered design"?*
19. *Describe the procedure used to obtain protection for a design that should be registered.*
20. *What protection is offered the owner of a design that has been registered under the* Industrial Design Act?

|||||||||||||||||||||||||||||||||||||||||||||||||||||||||||||||||||||||||||||||||||||||||||||||||||||||||||||||||||||||||||||||||||||||||||||||||||||||||||||||||||||||||||

JUDICIAL DECISIONS

Trade Mark— Test for Determining Confusion with Other Names

Coca-Cola Co. of Canada Ltd. v. Pepsi-Cola Co. of Canada Ltd., [1942] 2 D.L.R. 657.

The plaintiff sued the defendant for infringement of its registered trade mark because its name was written in a script similar to that of the plaintiff's; it was a hyphenated word using the same word "cola," and applied to a similar soft drink product. The defendant argued that the words were not confusing to the public.

LORD RUSSELL OF KILLOWEN:

The plaintiff's mark consists of the words Coca and Cola joined by a hyphen and written, not in block letters, but in a script form with flourishes. It was applied to beverages and syrups, and was used for that purpose in Canada from the year 1900 (or perhaps earlier) by a company formed in the State of Georgia and called the Coca-Cola Company. It was registered by that company under the *Trade Mark and Design Act* of Canada on November 11, 1905. The mark was assigned in the year 1922 by the Georgia company to a company formed in the State of Delaware, and called also the Coca-Cola Company. The Canadian business of the last mentioned company was acquired in the following year by the plaintiff, and an assignment by the Delaware company of the mark to the plaintiff was registered on March 7, 1930. The plaintiff then renewed the registration of the mark for a period of 25 years from November 11, 1930. There is no doubt that the plaintiff has carried on and is carrying on in Canada under its registered mark a large business in the manufacture and sale of a non-alcoholic beverage known as Coca-Cola. The scale of its trade is sufficiently indicated by the fact that in the year 1936 it owned some 20 bottling plants, and in addition had contracts with some 80 independent bottlers.

The defendant was incorporated on May 29, 1934, and began to sell in Canada a non-alcoholic beverage called Pepsi-Cola, under a mark consisting of the words Pepsi and Cola joined by a hyphen and written in a script form with flourishes. Whether the defendant had acquired the goodwill of any business, and whether the defendant was properly on the register in respect of a mark which differs slightly from the mark actually in use by the defendant, were matters much discussed by plaintiff's counsel. These matters however seem to be irrelevant to the only question which their Lordships have to decide *viz.*, whether the mark which the defendant uses, infringes the plaintiff's registered mark. The respective rights of the parties are now governed by the *Unfair Competition Act*, 1932 (Can.), c. 38 to which more detailed reference must be made.

By s. 3(*c*) of that Act it is provided that no person shall knowingly adopt for use in Canada in connection with any wares any trade mark which is similar to any trade mark which is in use in Canada by any other person and which is registered pursuant to the provisions of that Act as a trade mark for the same or similar wares. There is no dispute that the mark which the defendant uses is subject to the above prohibition if it is "similar" to the plaintiff's registered mark. The other requirements as to "knowingly" and similarity of wares are admittedly fulfilled.

The word "similar" in relation to trade marks is defined by the Act (unless the context otherwise requires) thus:

"2(*k*) 'Similar,' in relation to trade marks . . . describes marks . . . so resembling each other or so clearly suggesting the idea conveyed by each other that the contemporaneous use of both in the same area in association with wares of the same kind would be likely to cause dealers in and/or users of such wares to infer that the same person assumed responsibility for their character or quality, for the conditions under which or the class of persons by whom they were produced, or for their place of origin."

The contemporaneous use of both marks in the same area in association with wares of the same kind is not in dispute. The actual question for decision in the present case may, therefore, in the light of the above definition be stated thus:—Does the mark used by the defendant so resemble the plaintiff's registered mark or so clearly suggest the idea conveyed by it, that its use is likely to cause dealers in or users of non-alcoholic beverages to infer that the plaintiff assumed responsibility for the character or quality or place of origin of Pepsi-Cola?

The President of the Exchequer Court answered the question in the affirmative; the Supreme Court answered it in the negative. Their Lordships are in agreement with the Supreme Court.

The case appears to them to be one which is free from complications, and which raises neither new matter of principle nor novel question of trade mark law. The only peculiar feature of the case is the dearth of evidence, attributable doubtless to the procedure adopted by the plaintiff at the trial. The only matters proved before the plaintiff's case was closed were (1) the plaintiff's registered mark and (2) the user by the defendant of the mark alleged to be an infringement. No evidence of (to put it shortly) confusion either actual or probable was adduced. It was contended that a statement by a witness called by the defendant (one Charles Guth) was proof of actual confusion. Guth was general manager of a United States company which owns the capital stock of the defendant. He was also President of a New York company called Loft Incorporated which owned a large number of candy stores in New York at which Coca-Cola was sold. Subsequently the sale of Coca-Cola was discontinued, and Pepsi-Cola was sold at the stores. A passing off action was brought by the Delaware Coca-Cola Co. against Loft Incorporated [(1933), 167 Atl. 900]. The Judge of the Court of Chancery, Delaware, dismissed the action holding that Loft Incorporated was not responsible for the acts of its agents of which evidence had been given. In the course of his cross-examination in the Exchequer Court Guth was asked "Then you have no quarrel with the Chancellor's decision as to the facts expressed in his opinion?" and he answered "None at all." It was argued that this answer proved the fact found in the judgment of the Chancellor *viz.* (as quoted by the President of the Exchequer Court [[1938] 4 D.L.R. at p. 167] from a report of the case) that " 'the uncontradicted evidence shows that substitutions were made by employees of the defendants of a product other than Coca-Cola for that beverage when calls for the same were made.' "

The learned President [p. 169] relied on this judgment as "very formidable support to the plaintiff's contention, that . . . there is a likelihood of confusion"; but in their Lordships' opinion he was not entitled to refer to or rely upon a judgment given in proceedings to which neither the plaintiff nor the defendant was a party, as proving the facts stated therein. Those facts are in no way proved thereby, nor are they in any way proved by the answer of Guth which has been quoted above. Guth could not of his own knowledge either quarrel or agree with the Chancellor's decision as to what it was that had happened in the numerous stores, and was described by the word "substitutions". There was accordingly no evidence before the Exchequer Court of confusion actual or probable.

In these circumstances the question for determination must be answered by the Court, unaided by outside evidence, after a comparison of the defendant's mark as used with the plaintiff's registered mark, not placing them side by side, but by asking itself whether, having due regard to relevant surrounding circumstances, the defendant's mark as used is similar (as defined by the Act) to the plaintiff's registered mark as it would be remembered by persons possessed of an average memory with its usual imperfections.

In the present case two circumstances exist which are of importance in this connection. The first is the information which is afforded by dictionaries in relation to the word "Cola". While questions may sometimes arise as to the extent to which a Court may inform itself by reference to dictionaries there can, their Lordships think, be no doubt that dictionaries may properly be referred to in order to ascertain not only the meaning of a word, but also the use to which the thing (if it be a thing) denoted by the word is commonly put. A reference to dictionaries shows that Cola or Kola is a tree whose seed or nut is "largely used for chewing as a condiment and digestive" (Murray), a nut of which "the extract is used as a tonic drink" (Webster), and which is "imported into the United States for use in medical preparations and summer drinks" (Encyclopaedia Americana). Cola would therefore appear to be a word which might appropriately be used in association with beverages and in particular with that class of non-alcoholic beverages colloquially known by the description of "soft drinks". That in fact the word "Cola" or "Kola" has been so used in Canada is established by the second of the two circumstances before referred to.

The defendant put in evidence a series of 22 trade marks registered in Canada from time to time during a period of 29 years, *viz.*, from 1902 to 1930, in connection with beverages. They include the mark of the plaintiff and the registered mark of the defendant. The other 20 marks consist of two or more words or a compound word, but always containing the word "Cola" or "Kola". The following are a few samples of the bulk:—"Kola Tonic Wine" "La-Kola", "Cola-Claret", "Rose-Cola", "Orange Kola", "O'Keefe's Cola", "Royal Cola". Their Lordships agree with the Supreme Court in attributing weight to these registrations as showing that the word Cola (appropriate for the purpose as appears above) had been adopted in Canada as an item in the naming of different beverages.

The proper comparison must be made with that fact in mind.

Numerous cases were cited in the Courts of Canada and before the Board in which the question of infringement of various marks has been considered and decided; but except when some general principle is laid down, little assistance is derived from authorities in which the question of infringement is discussed in relation to other marks and other circumstances.

The plaintiff claimed that by virtue of s. 23(5)(*b*) of the *Unfair Competition Act* 1932 its registered mark was both a word mark and a design mark; and their Lordships treat it accordingly.

If it be viewed simply as a word mark consisting of "Coca" and "Cola" joined by a hyphen, and the fact be borne in mind that Cola is a word in common use in Canada in naming beverages, it is plain that the distinctive feature in this hyphenated word, is the first word "Coca" and not "Cola". "Coca" rather than "Cola" is what would remain in the average memory. It is difficult, indeed impossible, to imagine that the mark Pepsi-Cola as used by the defendant, in which the distinctive feature is, for the same reason the first word "Pepsi" and not "Cola", would lead anyone to confuse it with the registered mark of the plaintiff. If it be viewed as a design mark the same result follows. The only resemblance lies in the fact that both contain the word "Cola", and neither is written in block letters, but in script with flourishes. But the letters and flourishes in fact differ very considerably, notwithstanding the tendency of words written in script with flourishes to bear a general resemblance to each other. There is no need to specify the differences in detail; it is sufficient to say that in their Lordships' opinion, the mark used by the defendant, viewed as a pattern or picture, would not lead a person with an average recollection of the plaintiff's registered mark to confuse it with the pattern or picture represented by that mark.

||||||||||||||||||||||||||||||||||||||||||||||||||||||||||||||||||||||||||||||||||||||||||||||||||||||||||||||||||||||||||||||||||||||||||||

Use of Industrial Design to Protect Method of Construction —Improper Use

Kaufman Rubber Co., Ltd. v. Miner Rubber Co., Ltd., [1926] 1 D.L.R. 505.

The plaintiff held two registered designs for overshoes and claimed infringement of the designs by the defendant. One design illustrated an ordinary overshoe with two straps with buckles, and two straps with dome fasteners. The other design was of an overshoe with three straps with dome fasteners and one strap with a buckle. The designs were described as a "novel configuration of overshoes or galoshes."

MACLEAN, J.:

Part II of the Trade Mark and Design Act relates to industrial designs and the registration of the same. No definition of industrial designs is contained in the Act, and there has been no litigation in our Courts upon the point so far as I know, and consequently no assistance is available from judicial decisions, in determining what constitutes an industrial design, under the statute.

A review of some sections of the statute should however furnish some light, as to what was intended to be the principal characteristics of an industrial design, and what are the necessary elements to be found in a design to sustain its registration.

Section 24 requires that the design be one not in use by any other person than the proprietor, at the time of his adoption thereof. Section 27(3) would indicate that originality of the design was necessary. Then s. 31 is to the effect that no person shall without the licence of the registered proprietor, apply a design, to the ornamentation of any article of manufacture or other article, to which an industrial design may be attached or applied, or to sell or use any article to which such design may be applied. Section 34 provides that the name of the proprietor of a design shall appear upon the article to which his design applies. Section 36 is the penalty clause for violation of this part of the Act, and s-s. (*a*) states, that any person applying a design to the ornamenting of any article of manufacture or other article, without licence, is subject to a money penalty.

The sections of the statute to which I have just referred, would therefore seem to indicate that "industrial designs" is there intended to mean some design or mark, which is to be attached to a manufactured article. The use of the word "ornamenting," in 2 different sections of the Act, would clearly indicate that a design might be adapted to purposes of ornamentation. In dealing with designs, the Legislature had I think primarily before it, the idea of shape or ornamentation involving artistic considerations. Clearly a design cannot be an article of manufacture, but something to be applied to an article of manufacture, or other article to which an industrial design may be applied, and capable of existence outside the article itself nor do I think that the registration of a design would afford any protection for any mechanical principle or contrivance, process or method of manufacture, or principle of construction. Then there must be something original in a registered design, and it must be substantially novel or original, having regard to the nature and character of the subject-matter to which it is applied.

A design to be registrable must therefore be some conception or suggestion as to shape, pattern or ornament applied to any article, and is judged solely by the eye, and does not include any mode or principle of construction. What would constitute a registrable design, is I think admirably and comprehensively expressed in *Pugh* v. *Riley*, [1912] 1 Ch. 613, at pp. 619-20, by Parker, J., and is I think quite applicable to the provisions of our statute. There he said:—"A design, to be registrable under the Act, must be some conception or suggestion as to shape, configuration, pattern, or ornament. It must be capable of being applied to an article in such a way that the article to which it has been applied will shew to the eye the particular shape, configuration, pattern, or ornament the conception or suggestion of which constitutes the design. In general any application for registration must be accompanied by a representation of the design—that is, something in the nature of a drawing or tracing by means of which the conception or suggestion constituting the design may be imparted to others. In fact, persons looking at the drawing ought to be able to form a mental picture of the shape, configuration, pattern, or ornament of the article to which the design has been applied. A conception or suggestion as to a mode or principle of construction though in some sense a design, is not registrable under the Act. Inasmuch, however, as the mode or principle of construction of an article may affect its shape or configuration, the conception of such a mode or principle of construction may well lead to a conception as to the shape or configuration of the completed article, and a conception so arrived at may, if it be sufficiently definite, be registered under the Act. The difficulty arises where the conception thus arrived at is not a definite conception as to shape or configuration, but a conception only as to some general characteristic of shape or configuration necessitated by the mode or principle of construction, the definite shape or configuration being, consistently with such mode or principle of construction, capable of variation within wide limits. To allow the registration of a conception of such general characteristics of shape or configuration might well be equivalent to allowing the registration of a conception relating to the mode or principle of construction."

· · · · ·

In the case before me, the design covers the shape or configuration of the whole overshoe, together with the buckles and straps, the means of fastening. That this is a registrable design within the contemplation of the statute, is not I think to be seriously considered. To hold that it is so registrable would be as said by Bowen, L.J., in *Le May* v. *Welch* (1884), 28 Ch. D. 24, at p. 34, "to paralyse industry, and to make the *Patents, Designs, and Trade-marks Act* a trap to catch honest traders." The registrations, are but an attempt to protect a mode of construction. There is nothing original or novel in the configuration of an overshoe as shown by the plaintiff's designs, or any part of them. The form or configuration of the overshoe, and the fastenings, whether with buckles or dome fasteners or both are old and disclose no originality. The addition of straps with buckles or straps with dome fasteners, whether concealed or exposed, or the substitution of the one for the other, or the variation in the respective number of each, merely represent a change in the mode of construction of the article. Such variations are mere trade variants, and do not represent invention, originality or novelty. The introduction or substitution of ordinary trade variants in a design, is not only insufficient to make that design new or original, but it does not even contribute to give it a new or original character.

For the reasons which I have above given, I am of the opinion that the registered designs in question, are not proper subject-matters for registration within the spirit and intendment of the Trade Mark and Design Act, and in any event neither of them possess the originality or novelty necessary to warrant registration. If it were necessary to dispose of this matter upon other grounds, I might say that the evidence does not establish, that the idea of applying the dome fasteners with a strap, beneath the flap of the overshoe which is admittedly the only original suggestion in the configuration of the overshoe, originated not with the plaintiff, but with Beddoe, who does not claim any invention for it, or the authorship of it. Then again, the statute and the rules require a description of the design, to accompany the drawing upon the application for registration. This was not done, the only description being the mere statement that the design, consists of the novel configuration of an overshoe which is no description at all. If the plaintiff's case is rested upon the contention that the design was intended to cover only a part of the configuration of the overshoe and its fastenings, then the registration is void by virtue of the absence of a description. If it was intended to comprehend the whole of the overshoe and all its parts, then the registration is also void for want of description.

The plaintiff's action therefore fails. There will be judgment directing that the 2 industrial designs, mentioned in the pleadings, be expunged from the register of industrial designs. The judgment will also contain an order allowing the defendant his costs of the action.

CASE PROBLEMS FOR DISCUSSION

Case 1

Holdsworth produced a beautiful drawing of a French Provincial love–seat at the request of Classical Furniture Manufacturing Company. Classical Furniture paid Holdsworth $500 for the drawing, and used it as the design for its love-seat in a current furniture collection. Six months after it acquired the drawing, and several months after it produced its first production models of the love-seat, the Company applied for registration of the design.

Shortly after Classical Furniture registered its design for the love-seat, it discovered that Antique Furniture Co. had a similar love-seat on display in its collection at a furniture exhibit. Classical Furniture immediately accused Antique Furniture of copying its design.

As a defence, Antique Furniture argued that the design was not original. It also came out in the course of discussion that it had acquired its own design by purchasing it from a designer by the name of Holdsworth.

If Classical Furniture should institute legal proceedings against Antique Furniture, what arguments might the parties raise on their own behalf? What is the position of Holdsworth, and what are his rights (if any) or liability (if any)? Speculate as to the outcome of the action.

Case 2

The Cod Oil Drug Company produced a concentrated vitamin product which it sold in capsule form to its customers. To identify its products, it produced its capsules with three broad red bands, the first bearing the letter "C," the second, an "O," and the third a "D." Each letter was printed in white against the red background to identify the company, and its product which was derived from cod liver oil. The centre red band, bearing the letter "O" also acted as a seal which held the two parts of the capsule together. The Cod Oil Drug Company applied for a patent on the method of sealing the two parts of the capsule together, and for registration of the three bands with the letters imprinted as a trade mark for its product.

In the course of its application for a trade mark, Cod Oil Drug Company was faced with an objection to its use of the trade mark by Careful Drug Company, a competitor that produced its product in capsule form bearing two blue bands, one on each part of the capsule, the first bearing a white "C" and the second, a white "D" against the blue bands. A thin blue band was used to join the capsule together, but it bore no letter. The design had been used by Careful Drug for many years before Cod Oil Drug developed the marking of its capsules.

On what basis would Careful Drug argue that the trade mark should not issue? What might Cod Oil Drug argue in response? How successful would the patent application likely be?

Case 3

Denton, an electronics engineer worked at the development of a miniature hearing aid in his spare time, and after much experimentation, was successful in developing what he wanted. He was a member of a local service club which frequently assisted persons with hearing problems and, for a special meeting of the club, he was invited to give the members a short lecture on hearing aids and a demonstration of how his device operated. At the meeting, he described how the device was constructed, and demonstrated its effectiveness even though it was still in the experimental stage. The meeting was later reported in the local newspaper along with some general information on Denton's presentation at the meeting. Another member of the club, who was also an electronics engineer, wrote a brief note on Denton's presentation, and submitted it to a scientific journal that subsequently printed the note in its "New Developments Section."

Several years later, Denton finally perfected his hearing device, and applied for a patent. He then set up facilities for its production, marking each unit produced with the words "patent pending." The product sold well in all parts of the country except British Columbia, and when Denton investigated the market in that area, he discovered that a west coast manufacturer was producing hearing aid units which incorporated the particular design which he had developed. His competitor had been selling the similar models for almost a year before Denton had gone into production. Unknown to Denton, the manufacturer had apparently developed his own hearing aid model from information which he had read in the scientific journal report of Denton's presentation to his service club.

Denton had the Patent Office expedite his patent application, and on its issue he instituted legal proceedings against the west coast manufacturer for infringement.

Discuss the arguments which might be raised by the parties in this case, and render a decision.

Case 4

Brown, a part-time news writer for a local newspaper, attended an air show at a local airport, and while he watched two aircraft performing synchronized aerobatics, he noticed that the wings of the two aircraft were exceptionally close to each other. He photographed the aircraft at the instant that the two aircraft collided, and took a second photograph of the pilots as they parachuted to the ground. He wrote a brief resume of the accident, and submitted the two pictures and the written material to the local newspaper for publication. The pictures and the report were published in the next edition of the newspaper, in which he received credit for the pictures and the story in a "by-line." He was paid his regular rate for the written material, and $50 for each picture. Brown later submitted the same pictures and story to an aviation magazine, and the material was subsequently published. Brown was paid $300 for the pictures and story by the magazine.

When the newspaper discovered the magazine article it instituted legal proceedings against the magazine and Brown for copyright infringement, claiming that the copyright belonged to it.

Discuss the arguments that might be raised by the parties, and indicate how the case might be decided.

GLOSSARY

The following list contains brief definitions of many of the legal terms used in the text. For a full and complete definition of each term, reference should be made to the appropriate chapter of the text, or to a legal dictionary.

Action: legal proceedings instituted in a court of law.

Act: a law enacted by a legislature.

ab initio: "from the beginning."

adverse possession: a possessory title to land under the Registry System acquired by continuous, open, and notorious possession of land inconsistent with the title of the true owner for a period of time (usually 10—20 years).

agent: a person who is appointed to act for another, usually in contract matters.

arbitration: A process for the settlement of disputes whereby an impartial third party or board hears the dispute, then makes a decision which is binding on the parties. Most commonly used to determine grievances arising out of a collective agreement, or in contract disputes.

assault: a threat of violence or injury to a person.

attorney: a lawyer.

bailee: the person who takes possession of a chattel in a bailment.

bailor: the owner of a chattel who delivers possession of the chattel to another in a bailment.

bailment: the transfer of a chattel by the owner to another for some purpose, with the chattel to be later returned or dealt with in accordance with the owner's instructions.

bargaining unit: a group of employees of an employer represented by a trade union recognized or certified as their exclusive bargaining representative.

barrister-at-law: a lawyer who acts for clients in litigation or criminal court proceedings.

battery: the unlawful touching or striking of another.

bid-rigging: a practice whereby contractors in response to a call for bids or tenders agree amongst themselves as to the price or who should bid or submit a tender. A Restrictive Trade Practice unless the person calling for the bids is advised of the arrangement.

bill of exchange: an instrument in writing, signed by the drawer and addressed to the drawee, ordering the drawee to pay a sum certain in money to the payee named therein (or bearer) at some fixed or determinable future time, or on demand.

bond: a debt security issued by a corporation in which assets of the corporation are usually pledged as security for payment.

bulk sale: a sale of the stock or assets of a merchant other than in the ordinary course of business.

common law: the law as found in the recorded judgements of the courts.

canon law: the law developed by the church courts to deal with matters which fell within their jurisdiction.

capacity: the ability at law to enter into an enforceable contract.

certification process: a process under labour legislation whereby a trade union acquires bargaining rights and is designated as the exclusive bargaining representative of a unit of employees.

charge: a secured claim similar to a mortgage registered against real property under the Land Titles System.

chattel: moveable property.

chattel mortgage: a mortgage in which the title to a chattel owned by the debtor is transferred to the creditor as security for the payment of a debt.

cheque: a bill of exchange which is drawn on a banking institution, and payable on demand.

co-insurance: a clause which may be inserted in an insurance policy which renders the insured an insurer for a part of the loss if the insured fails to maintain insurance coverage of not less than a specified minimum amount or percentage of the value of the property.

collective agreement: an agreement in writing made between an employer and a union certified or recognized as the bargaining representative of a bargaining unit of employees which contains the terms and conditions under which work is to be performed and which sets out the rights and duties of the employer, the employees, and the union.

condition precedent: a condition which must be satisfied before a contract or agreement becomes effective.

condition subsequent: a condition which alters the rights or duties of the parties to a contract, or which may have the effect of terminating the contract if it should occur.

conditional sale agreement: an agreement for the sale of a chattel in which the seller grants possession of the goods, but withholds title until payment for the goods is made in full.

condominium: a form of ownership of real property, usually including a building, in which certain units are owned in fee simple, and the common elements are owned by the various unit owners as tenants-in-common.

consideration: that which is received in return for a promise given.

conspiracy: an agreement between two or more persons to carry out an unlawful act.

contract: an agreement made by two or more parties which consists of an exchange of promises or acts, and may be either written or oral.

copyright: the right of ownership of an original literary or artistic work and the control over the right to copy it.

corporation: a legal entity created by the state.

damages: a money payment awarded by the court as compensation for injury suffered as a result of a breach of duty or breach of contract by a defendant.

debenture: a debt security issued by a corporation which may or may not have assets of the corporation pledged as security for payment.

director: under corporation law, a person elected by the shareholders of a corporation to manage its affairs.

doctrine of constructive notice: the deemed notice to the public of some fact or information as a result of registration or filing of the information in a public record office.

dominant tenement: a parcel of land to which a right-of-way or easement attaches for its better use.

double ticketing: a practice of attaching several different price tickets to goods. Under the Combines Investigation Act, only the lowest price may be charged for the goods.

dower: the right of a widow to hold for her lifetime one-third of the real property owned by her husband at the time of his death.

duress: the threat of injury or imprisonment for the purpose of requiring another to enter into a contract or carry out some act.

easement: a right to use the property of another, usually for a particular purpose.

endorsement: the signing of one's name on the back of a negotiable instrument for the purpose of negotiating it to another.

equitable mortgage: a mortgage subsequent to the first or legal mortgage. A mortgage of the mortgagor's equity.

equity of redemption: the equitable right of a mortgagor to acquire the title to the mortgaged property by payment of the debt secured by the mortgage.

execution: the post-judgement stage in a legal action whereby the judgement is enforced against the defendant.

expropriation: the forceful taking of real property by the Crown (or its agents) or by a corporation which has been granted expropriation rights (such as a municipality).

fee simple: an estate in land that represents the greatest interest in land which a person may possess, and which may be conveyed or passed by will to another, or which, on an intestacy, would devolve to the person's heirs.

fiduciary interest: an interest in property held in trust for the benefit of another.

fiduciary relationship: a relationship of utmost good faith in which a person in dealing with property must act in the best interests of the person for whom he acts, rather than in his own personal interest.

fixture: a chattel which is constructively or permanently attached to land.

floating charge: a debt security issued by a corporation in which assets of the corporation such as stock-in-trade are pledged as security. Until such time as default occurs, the corporation is free to dispose of the assets.

fraudulent misrepresentation: a false statement of fact made by a person who knows, or should know, that it is false, and made with the intention of deceiving another.

frustrated contract: a contract under which performance by a party is rendered impossible due to an unexpected or unforseen change in circumstances affecting the agreement.

fundamental breach: a breach of the contract which goes to the root of the agreement.

grievance: an alleged violation of a collective agreement.

hypothec: an instrument used to secure debt in the province of Quebec which creates a security interest in land somewhat similar to a lien.

implied term: a standard or usual term which the courts will include in a contract on the assumption that the parties had intended the term to be included, but through some oversight had failed to include it.

indenture: a written document between two or more parties which was originally prepared in duplicate on a single page, and divided in such a way that the parts could be fitted together to prove its authenticity.

infant: a person who has not reached the age of majority.

infringement: the unlawful interference with the legal rights of another.

injunction: an equitable remedy of the court which orders the person or persons named therein to refrain from doing certain acts.

insurable interest: an interest in property or in another person's life which would result in a loss to the person if the property should be damaged or destroyed, or the other person's life ended.

invitee: a person who enters upon the lands of another by invitation, usually for the benefit of the person in possession of the land.

judgement: a decision of the court.

law merchant: the customs or rules established by merchants to resolve disputes that arose between them, and that were later applied by common law judges in cases which came before their courts.

legal mortgage: a first mortgage of real property whereby the owner of lands in fee simple transfers the title of the property pledged as security to the creditor on the condition that the title will be reconveyed when the debt is paid.

lessee: a tenant.

lessor: a landlord.

licence: a right granted to someone to do something or use property in a particular way.

life estate: an estate in land in which the right to possession is based upon a person's lifetime.

loss leader selling: a practice of selling goods not for profit but to advertise or to attract customers to a place of business.

master: an employer.

mechanics' lien: a lien exerciseable by a workman, contractor, or material supplier against property upon which the work or materials were expended.

misrepresentation: a statement of fact (or in some cases, conduct) which conveys the wrong or false impression to another.

mistake: a state of affairs where a party (or both parties) have formed an erroneous opinion as to the identity or existence of the subject matter, or of some other important term.

mortgage: an agreement made between a debtor and a creditor in which the title to property of the debtor is transferred to the creditor as security for payment of the debt.

negotiable instrument: an instrument in writing which when transferred in good faith and for value without notice of defects passes a good title to the instrument to the transferee.

novation: the substitution of parties to an agreement or the replacement of one agreement by another agreement.

offer: a promise subject to a condition.

officer: a person elected or appointed by the directors of a corporation to fill a particular office (such as president, secretary, treasurer, etc.).

partnership: a legal relationship between two or more persons for the purpose of carrying on a business with a view to profit.

patent: the exclusive right granted to the first inventor of something new and different to produce the invention for a period of 17 years in return for the disclosure of the invention to the public.

pawn: the transfer of possession (but not ownership) of chattels by a debtor to a creditor who is licensed to take and hold goods as security for payment of debt.

pledge: the transfer of securities by a debtor to a creditor as security for the payment of a debt.

power of attorney: a legal document signed under seal in which a person appoints another to act as his or her attorney to carry out the contractual or legal acts specified in the document.

predatory pricing: the practice of pricing goods at a very low price for the purpose of destroying competition. An offence under the Combines Investigation Act.

principal: a person on whose behalf an agent acts.

promissory note: a promise in writing, signed by the maker, to pay a sum certain in money to the person named therein, or bearer, at some fixed or determinable future time, or on demand.

quantum meruit: "as much as he has earned." A quasi-contractual remedy which permits a person to recover a reasonable price for services and/or materials requested where no price is established when the request is made.

real property: land and anything permanently attached to it.

referral selling: a practice whereby a customer receives a rebate or discount on a purchase by a referring other customers to the seller. A prohibited practice under the Combines Investigation Act.

remainderman: a person who is entitled to real property subject to a prior interest (e.g., a life estate), and who acquires the fee when the prior estate terminates.

res ipsa loquitur: "the thing speaks for itself."

respondeat superior: the liability or responsibility imputed to one person for the actions of another who acts under the direction of that person.

right-of-way: a right to pass over the land of another, usually to gain access to property.

salvage: under insurance law, the right of an insurer to the damaged, lost, or stolen property of the insured if the insurer compensates the insured for the value of the property damaged, lost, or stolen.

servant: an employee.

servient tenement: a parcel of land subject to a right-of-way or easement.

share certificate: a certificate issued by a corporation which is evidence of a person's share ownership in the corporation.

shareholder: a person who holds a share interest in a corporation; a part owner of the corporation.

solicitor: a lawyer whose practice consists of the preparation of legal documents, wills, etc., and other forms of non-litigious legal work.

specific performance: an equitable remedy of the court which may be granted for breach of contract where money damages would be inadequate, and which requires the defendant to carry out the agreement according to its terms.

stare decisis: "to stand by previous decisions." The practice of a court to adhere to precedent in deciding the same issue as in a previous case.

subrogation: the substitution of parties whereby the party substituted acquires the rights at law of the other party, usually by way of a contractual arrangement.

tort: a civil wrong.

trade mark: a mark to distinguish the goods or services of one person from the goods or services of others.

trespass: a tort which may consist of the seizure or the injury of a person, the entry on the lands of another without permission, or the seizure or damage of goods of another without consent.

trust: an agreement or arrangement whereby a party called a trustee holds property for the benefit of another, (called a beneficiary, or cestui que trust).

uberrimae fidei: "utmost good faith." A term applied to certain contractual relationships in which full disclosure is required on the part of both parties to the agreement.

ultra vires: beyond the legal authority or power of a legislative or corporate body to do an act.

undue influence: a state of affairs whereby a person is so influenced by another that the person's judgement is not his own.

vicarious liability: the liability at law of one person for the acts of another.

volenti non fit injuria: the voluntary assumption of risk of injury.

REFERENCE LIST

The following texts and writing may be used to provide additional information on the various topics covered in the text.

GENERAL REFERENCE

Burke, John, *Osborn's Concise Law Dictionary* (6th ed.), London: Sweet & Maxwell Ltd., 1976.

Holdsworth, Sir William S., *A History of English Law* (several editions; multiple volumes) London: Methuen; Sweet & Maxwell Ltd.

James, S. Philip, *Introduction to English Law* (10th ed.), London: Butterworths, Ltd., 1979.

Maitland, Frederick W.: Pollock, Sir Frederick, *The History of English Law,* (2nd ed. re-issued) London: Cambridge University Press, 1968.

AGENCY

Bowstead, William., *Bowstead On Agency,* (14th ed. F. M. Reynolds and B. J. Davenport), London: Sweet & Maxwell Ltd., 1976.

Fridman, Gerald H. L., *The Law of Agency* (4th ed.), London: Butterworth's Ltd. 1976.

BAILMENT

Beal, Edward, *The Law of Bailments,* London: Butterworth's Ltd., 1900 (with notes to Canadian Cases by A. C. Forster Boulton).

BANKRUPTCY

Houlden, Lloyd W., Morawetz, C. H., *Bankruptcy Law of Canada,* Toronto: The Carswell Company, 1979, (looseleaf update series).

CONDOMINIUMS

Rosenberg, Alvin B., *Condominium in Canada,* Toronto: Canada Law Book Co., 1969 (update series).

CONSUMER PROTECTION

O'Grady, M. J. (Editor), *Consumers' Rights,* Toronto: The Law Society of Upper Canada, 1976.

CONTRACTS

Anson, Sir William R., *Anson's Law of Contract* (25th ed. A. G. Guest), Oxford: Clarendon Press, 1979.

Cheshire, G. C.; Fifoot, C. H. S.; and Furmston, M. P., *The Law of Contract* (8th ed.), London: Butterworth's Ltd., 1972.

Waddams, Stephen M., *The Law of Contracts,* Toronto: Canada Law Book Co., 1977.

EMPLOYMENT AND COLLECTIVE BARGAINING

Carrothers, A. W. R., *Collective Bargaining Law in Canada,* Toronto: Butterworth's Ltd., 1965.

Christie, I. M., *Employment Law in Canada,* Toronto, Butterworth's Ltd., 1980.

MORTGAGES

Falconbridge, John D., *Falconbridge on Mortgages* (4th ed. W. B. Rayner and R. H. McLaren), Agincourt: Canada Law Book Co., 1977.

NEGOTIABLE INSTRUMENTS

Falconbridge, John D., *Falconbridge on Banking and Bills of Exchange* (7th ed. A. W. Rogers), Toronto: Canada Law Book Company, 1969.

PARTNERSHIP	Lindley, N., *Lindley on The Law of Partnership* (14th ed. E. Scammell and R. C. I. Anson Banks), London: Sweet & Maxwell Ltd., 1979.
PATENTS, TRADE MARKS, COPYRIGHT	Fox, Harold G., *The Canadian Law of Copyright and Industrial Designs* (2nd ed.), Toronto: The Carswell Co., 1967.
	Fox, Harold G., *The Canadian Law and Practice Relating to Letters Patent for Inventors* (4th ed.), Toronto: The Carswell Co., 1969.
	Fox, Harold G., *The Canadian Law of Trade Marks and Unfair Competition* (3rd ed.), Toronto: The Carswell Co., 1972.
REAL PROPERTY	Megarry, Sir Robert E.; Wade, H. W. R., *The Law of Real Property* (4th ed.), London: Stevens & Sons Ltd., 1975.
SALE OF GOODS	Fridman, Gerald H. L., *Sale of Goods in Canada* (2nd ed.), Toronto: The Carswell Company, 1979.
SECURITY FOR DEBT	Macklem, Douglas N., Bristow, David I., *Mechanics' Liens in Canada* (4th ed.), Toronto: The Carswell Company, 1978.
	MacLaren, Richard H., *Secured Transactions in Personal Property in Canada*, Toronto: The Carswell Company, 1979, (update series).
TORTS	Fleming, John G., *The Law of Torts* (5th ed.), Sydney, Aus.: The Law Book Company, 1977.
	Linden, Allen M., *Canadian Tort Law*, Toronto: Butterworths, Ltd., 1977.

INDEX